The Homeowner's Complete Manual of Repair & Improvement

A DO-IT-YOURSELF BIBLE

Edited by Allen D. Bragdon

Technical Consultants:
> Monte Burch
> Doug Day
> Joseph Foley
> Dutch Meyers

ARCO PUBLISHING, INC.
New York

The technical consultants for this volume:

MONTE BURCH — former Associate Editor of *Workbench* magazine and author of over 30 books and numerous how-to articles

DOUG DAY — son of longtime do-it-yourself writer Richard Day, his own articles have been published in *Popular Science* and *How-To* magazine

JOSEPH H. FOLEY — a Senior Publications Engineer for Sperry Rand Corporation, with over 30 years' experience writing on complex technical subjects for the layperson

DUTCH MEYERS — past President of the National Association of Home & Workshop Writers

Published by Arco Publishing, Inc.
215 Park Avenue South, New York, N.Y. 10003
Copyright © 1983, 1977 by Allen D. Bragdon Publishers, Inc.
All rights reserved. No part of this book may be reproduced
without written permission from the publisher.

Library of Congress Cataloging in Publication Data
Bragdon, Allen D.
    The homeowner's complete manual of repair and improvement.

The first edition of this work was distributed under
the title *Petersen's Home Repair & Maintenance
Guide.*

    Includes index.
    1. Dwellings—Maintenance and repair. I. Title.
TH4817.B68   1983   643'.7   82-18184
ISBN 0-668-05737-8 cloth edition
ISBN 0-668-05749-1 paper edition

Printed in the United States of America

Table of Contents

INTRODUCTION 4

I. INTERIOR REPAIRS & DECORATION
- Detailed contents 11
1. Tools 12
2. Repairing walls 18
3. Hanging things on the wall 26
4. Building new walls and
   improving old ones 30
5. New ceilings 46
6. Painting 52
7. Wallpapering .62
8. Repairing floors 72
9. New floors 82
10. Projects for a child's room 94

II. WINDOWS, DOORS, SECURITY & INSULATION
- Detailed contents 98
1. Openers 100
2. The tools 102
3. Windows 106
4. Doors 132
5. Insulation 146
6. Security 164
7. Pest control .186
8. Project: Skylight 190

III. FURNITURE CARE & REFINISHING
- Detailed contents 195
1. Furniture repair 196
2. Surface prep 222
3. Brushes 230
4. First coats 232
5. Finishes 240
6. Specialty finishes 256
7. Care 268
8. Wood 282
9. Project: Picnic table 286

IV. ELECTRICAL FIXTURES, WIRING & APPLIANCES
- Detailed contents 291
1. Basics 292
2. Techniques .308
3. Simple repairs 320
4. New wiring 334
5. Switches 342
6. Ceiling fixtures 350
7. Fluorescents 358
8. Track lighting 370
9. Surface wiring 372
10. Troubleshooting appliances 374
11. Project: Outdoor lighting 382

V. PLUMBING & HEATING
- Detailed contents 387
1. Basics 388
2. Faucets 400
3. Sinks and baths 408
4. Toilets 414
5. Problem solving 420
6. Piping 428
7. Appliance repair 442
8. Private systems 450
9. Heating 458
10. Projects 474
11. Glossary 478

VI. EXTERIOR MAINTENANCE & IMPROVEMENTS
- Detailed contents 483
1. The proud house 484
2. The tools 486
3. Roof repairs .488
4. Siding 510
5. Exterior painting 518
6. Insulation 528
7. Foundations and masonry 534
8. Fences 558
9. Improvement projects 562

Credits 566
Acknowledgements 567
INDEX 568

INTRODUCTION

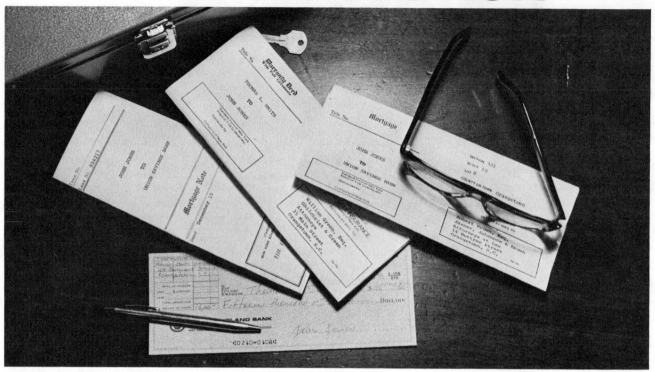

Your home is probably the most valuable possession you will ever own. Even if it's in relatively good shape, it needs care and attention. You can protect your investment and save a lot of money if you know how to diagnose its ills and keep it in good health. In fact, think of yourself as a general practitioner and your house as a patient under your care.

This section describes the internal anatomy of a house and tells how to give it a physical checkup. Especially if you are looking for a house to buy, you should know the state of its health. As with people, it is possible to predict what to look for as it ages and to correct potential problems before they become serious.

Very few houses are in perfect condition but, fortunately, most ills are curable. In some cases a little medicine or a minor operation will take care of the problem. If your house needs surgery, you need to know whether you are capable of performing it, or whether you should turn the job over to a specialist. As in the operating room, a great deal is at stake. You won't want to make any mistakes. So, like a good doctor of internal medicine, you'll need to know anatomy, diagnostic skills, and the preferred method of treatment. That's what this book is about: how to spot trouble on the inside of your house; how to trace the cause; how to select and use the proper tools and materials; and, step by step, how to repair whatever is wrong quickly, economically, and permanently.

Anatomy of a house

A house is a rather complicated thing. A pioneer's log cabin didn't take much more maintenance than slapping some mud between the chinks once in a while. A modern home is a maze of wires, pipes, wood, and wallboard. It isn't, thankfully, as complex as the human body—far from it. But it does, nonetheless, take some knowledge of what's inside before you can make an intelligent inspection of a house or tackle any of the problems that might crop up. Before you take down a wall, for example, you have to know whether it is bearing or nonbearing. You can remove a nonbearing partition as safely as dieting off a few pounds. Disturbing a bearing wall, however, is like breaking a leg bone.

The typical North American home begins with a foundation. The foundation can be a poured concrete basement, a concrete slab, or perhaps only a few cement blocks set on the ground, as in some vacation homes. But the home must rest on some solid surface which prevents it from settling unevenly or shifting as a result of heavy rains, frosts and winds.

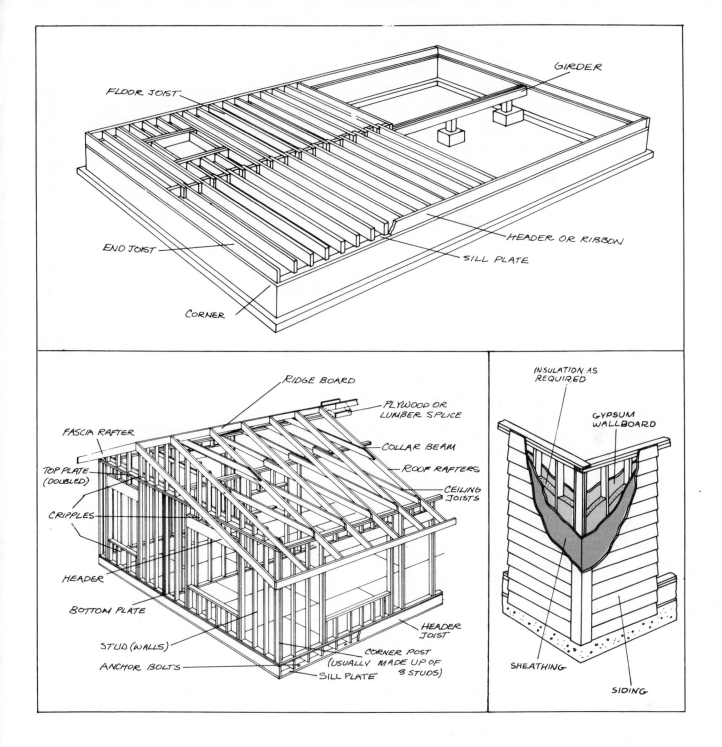

The frame or "skeleton" of the home is put up next. The frame begins with wooden bottom sills or plates resting on the foundation. Homes with basements will usually have a main girder or beam (of wood or steel) set into the foundation, its top level with the sill plates. Across the sills and beam rest joists, wood 2x8s or 2x10s, nailed every 16 inches.

The first floor is nailed to the joists, as is the outside framing, consisting of upright 2x4s called studs. The ceiling (or second-story floor) is supported by more joists set onto the top plate of the walls below. The rafters, made of the same material, are attached to the top set of joists and plates. In areas where snow is not a problem, there is no need for a pitched roof, so homes in the South and Southwest may not have rafters as such.

The "skin" of the house is attached to the framing. The outside of the home may be made of wood, brick, aluminum, or some other material. Sheathing, usually consisting of large plywood sheets, is nailed to the framing before the outside material is attached. Somewhere between the outside and inside walls, there is also insulating material made of mineral wool or a similar product. Some old homes do not have insulation between the outer sheathing and interior walls, or in the spaces between the studs and ceiling joists. Though you can have it "blown" in later, an uninsulated home has a big drawback in our modern world of ever-increasing energy costs.

Before any interior work is done (and usually before the final siding is installed), the home is roofed in. Plywood is nailed to the rafters, then thick black building paper, and finally roof shingles. After the house is reasonably waterproofed, the electricians and plumbers do their preliminary work. Wiring is strung between studs and joists; heating pipes or ducts are put in; plumbing pipes and central air-conditioning ducts, if any, are installed. All of these are placed between the framing so as to be out of sight and harm's way.

The electrician attaches "boxes" to the framing, and the plumber or sheet-metal worker installs the ducts or piping behind the walls so that the interior work can be done next. (Pockets will be left in the walls by carpenters and plasterers so that electrical and plumbing fixtures can be installed after the walls are up.)

On the inside, the studs are now covered with gypsum wallboard. You may find real plaster in some older or expensive new homes. Plaster is applied by hand over a substance called lath. Lath can consist of thin strips of wood or perforated metal nailed to the studs.

Floors in most homes are laid over an underlayer consisting of large plywood sheets nailed to the joists. Older homes may have wood boards instead. In better homes, hardwood flooring is nailed to the underlayer. Sometimes, carpeting is placed directly on the subfloor, a mark of a cheaper home (even though hardwood floors may seem wasted under carpeting). The walls are painted or papered, floors are sanded and given several coats of varnish or sealer. Cupboards, stairways, tiling, and trim are finished.

Your inspection tour

Whether you are taking a fresh look at your home with an eye to improvement, or a first look at a house you are thinking of buying, take the time to examine fine details. It's not difficult to size up a house, but some of the important things to look for are far from obvious. These are the points building inspectors check—they charge $75 or more for a two-hour examination, and competent ones are worth every cent of it.

When buying a newer home, you'll want to make sure the various craftsmen who built it have done a proper job. But the older the home, the more your inspection should be concerned with abuse, damage, decay, wear and tear, and the ravages of weather and time.

The neighborhood. First, forget about the house itself and look around. Buying the most expensive house in the neighborhood is a poor investment. You cannot, of course, go through every house on the block, but you can give the neighborhood a critical once-over. Are there signs of blight, such as peeling house paint, missing shingles, overgrown lawns, or sagging porches? Are there several mailboxes on larger homes, indicating they have been converted to apartments or boarding houses? You don't want to have a nice house in a rotting neighborhood. It's unpleasant, and bad for resale.

Exterior. Give your own prospective home the same critical eye outside, too. Examine the condition of roofing, siding, walkways, and drainage. Outside inspection is especially important for condominiums and apartments, where exterior maintenance is the responsibility of the landlord or a management group. (You will probably not be able to fix up the outside, even if you want to.)

The basement. Once inside the home, begin your inspection tour in the basement—unless of course the home is built on a concrete slab. A basement can tell you a lot. Check foundation walls for cracks in poured concrete, or disintegrating mortar in concrete block. Look carefully at the basement floor. Are there cracks or flaked-off areas? Is it wet or damp? Or perhaps it was recently mopped up. Are there high-water marks on the walls? An abnormally clean area without any dust is a suspicious sign. A sump pump is another clue that there are drainage problems, which may or may not have been cured.

A most important structural feature is the beam that carries the weight of the floor joists in the center. Homes with a small first floor may not have a beam. Larger homes may have several. Where there is a beam, look for obvious signs of sagging, settlement, or warping. You may be able to fix a sagging beam, but it isn't easy. A warped or shrunken beam may have to be replaced, a very difficult and expensive job. In any case, be wary of a home with this type of problem. Check joists for the same type of problem, particularly if there is no center beam. Look for adequate bridging, which means small

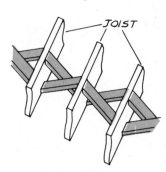

CROSS BRIDGING

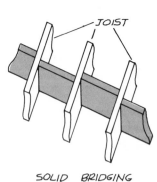

SOLID BRIDGING

pieces of wood between the joists every 5 to 8 feet. Cross bridging is better than solid bridging because it is more stable.

Check out the wooden sills on top of the foundation. Look for rot here, insect damage and cracks. Poke the wood with an awl to make sure it is solid. Check for light between the wood, a sign of poor caulking.

Look the heating unit over for signs of old age, leaks, sticking valves, boiler cracks, or other abnormalities. See if there are valves on pipes to turn off outside faucets. In colder climates, these will help prevent freezing. If there are no valves, see if the pipes are insulated. You may want to have a professional inspector check the heating plant, including the hot water tank, especially if it looks old or suspicious. (But beware of someone from a company that also sells heating equipment. Some are notorious for recommending unneeded changes.) Check the entrance panel for adequate electrical power, usually 100 amps.

Main floor. When you get upstairs, continue with your beam-and-joist inspection by placing a level on the floor, both front-to-back and side-to-side. Try it at various spots, concentrating along the beam and at other vital intersections. (You should remember their approximate locations from your basement tour.) Also, see if doors close properly. It may be that a sagging beam or joist has thrown the door frame out of whack. While you're at it, see if the doors shut tightly and latch correctly. Outside doors, in particular, should be carefully checked for weather-sealing and resistance to forced entry.

Windows. Open all windows. Do they operate easily? Are latches all in place and working properly? Check weatherstripping here, too.

Are there screens and storms for all the doors and windows, and are they marked so you can tell where they all fit?

Walls and ceilings. Sagging and warping in walls and ceilings can be an indication of a serious structural problem. How's the paint or wallcovering? This is one thing you can fix easily, but you will want to account for your anticipated redecorating when you bargain over the price of the home. Loose tiles can be replaced, and cracks between bathtub and walls are common, but all of it will mean more work for you. Lean on the walls, and press up on the ceilings. They shouldn't move.

Look for cracks in the walls and ceiling, especially over door frames. Look behind pictures. They often hide flaws. Serious cracking, plus other evidence such as crooked door frames, uneven floors or similar structural damage, may well mean that the house has a critically ill founda-

tion, or that it is sinking. Minor settlement damage, such as small cracks, can be anticipated in recently-built homes, but anything more than that is a bad danger signal.

A fairly common problem with gypsum drywall is nail pops, when nails holding the wallboard bulge out or protrude. This often happens because the framing lumber had too high a moisture content at the time of installation. When it dries out, the wood shrinks and nails loosen up. Correction is not difficult, but it's annoying and time-consuming. An associated problem is looseness in seam tape, the material used to bridge the gap between individual drywall sheets. You may also find loose or poorly fitting metal corner bead used to reinforce outside corners, or gaps where the wallboard was cut incorrectly around electrical or other outlets. These are all repairable, but they take work and expertise.

Small cracks sometimes occur when a new house settles normally.

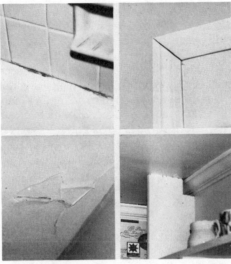

A good indication of the quality of workmanship is in the trim, or woodwork. Look for open joints, hammer marks, warps, rough nailing, and so on. One excellent clue is the way the moldings are fitted together. Take a close look at the miter joints, where two pieces of molding are cut at a 45-degree angle and joined at corners. If these are tight-fitting, the carpenters did their job properly.

Floors. As you walk over the floors, notice if they squeak or seem springy. (This is an especially common problem with exposed wooden porches.) If the floor joists are adequate, and the subfloor was laid properly, neither should happen. You can fix an incorrectly laid subfloor, but too-small joists are a serious defect. Check the flooring where it is exposed. (When it is covered by carpeting, try a closet or other hidden area or pull up a loose piece of carpeting.) Push your thumbnail into the wood. This should have no effect on hardwood, but will dent softwood slightly. Check for signs of exposed nails. Standard

Start at the top

In trying to figure out what work is needed and how to accomplish it, I've sometimes been up against unusual problems—as you will be—that how-to books have left out for one reason or another. The hunt for additional reliable information can be long and frustrating. After chasing a lot of wild geese and bum steers, I discovered that my good old Uncle Sam can be pretty useful after all. Here's how: Look in the white pages of your phone book under "U.S. Government" for "Agriculture, Department of," where you will find the number of your local "Home Economics Division." Tell them your problem. Nine times out of ten, they'll know what to do.

Practical Pete

flooring is installed in such a way that nails should not be visible.

If the weather is cold and dry, you may see spaces between the floorboards. As long as they are not too wide, they will close up by themselves in the summer.

Check stairways for loose cover materials and squeaks. Are there sturdy railings on both sides?

Built-ins. One problem that seems to be more common in newer homes, even fairly expensive ones, is cabinetry. Kitchen drawers are given a nice-looking front but are poorly constructed inside. The glides which keep the drawers sliding in and out properly give way quickly. Drawers sag, fall out, or stick. So be sure to open all drawers in cabinetry or built-ins and check their operation.

Paneling. Paneling is extremely popular in family rooms and other parts of the house. Once it is up, it's hard to tell whether it is cheap or expensive. But look at it carefully, especially where chairs rub against it. Poorly finished woods will be chipped and show evidence of wear. The veneer may be worn completely off, exposing the plywood behind it. (All paneling, no matter what its cost, is veneered, which means that a thin cover layer is glued to several other "plies" of cheaper wood behind it.)

Plumbing and electrical. Last, but certainly not least, take a studied look at the plumbing fixtures and electrical appliances that will be sold with the house. Flush all the toilets, try the faucets, see if the shower works, and fill up the tub a little to see if the water stays in and drains out properly. Look inside the toilet tank to see if the parts are corroded or bent out of shape. While in bathrooms, check for gaps or mildew on tiles, or rust stains from leaky faucets—sure signs of neglect. Try all appliances to see if they work properly. Inspect the electrical cords for wear, and try lighting fixtures, switches, and outlets. Examine any exposed wiring to make sure that the insulation is in good condition.

Housepower is a vital concern, since the use of electrical appliances is steadily increasing. If you have a lot of wattage-hungry appliances, particularly those that throw off heat or are used for cooking,

you'll need at least 100-amp service. (Check out the electrical service panel that contains the fuses or circuit breakers.) If you use a lot of power tools, 150 or 200 amps may be needed. There should be three wires entering the house to provide the 240 volts needed by electrical ranges and dryers. The bare minimum for a small house is 60 amps. Older, larger houses, where 60 amps was once standard, may need additional power, a costly improvement to make.

In addition to adequate power, there should be enough outlets. The kitchen should have several outlets on each wall; and other rooms should have them no more than 12 feet apart. Exterior outlets are a great convenience, especially for patios. A dead giveaway for inadequacy is the use of extension cords or "pigtails" at outlets to increase the number of plug-ins. This is not only inconvenient, it can be very hazardous.

When you complete your inspection tour, categorize the existing problems according to the list on the next page. The degree of difficulty in repairing the defects may vary according to your likes and talents, and is only a general guide. Similarly, the expense involved can vary widely depending on the area, the season, etc., but you will get general ideas as to the amount of time, effort, and expense needed to put the house in shape. With that, you can make a more intelligent decision as to whether the house is worth the price or not. (If you've already bought the house, it's too late, but the table will guide you in gauging and planning any necessary repair projects.)

Seeking professional help. While we have given general guidelines here, no book can answer specific questions about a specific house. Are the joists, for example, adequate in size? Does a stain on the wall mean there is a leak in the roof? It's pretty hard to tell sometimes. A contractor will be of some help, but he has a vested interest in doing the work. Professional home engineering or consulting firms that charge for inspecting homes do not do any of the work themselves, so their opinion should be unbiased. They can also be of help in telling you how to fix the problem yourself. The consultant's fee is well worth it, in our opinion. If nothing else, you may avoid an expensive cure from a zealous contractor.

Guidelines in this book. You are the best judge of whether you can or can't do a repair job yourself. Most of the how-to projects in this book start off with a "What it takes" section that gives you an idea of the approximate amount of time the job

Should you tackle it?

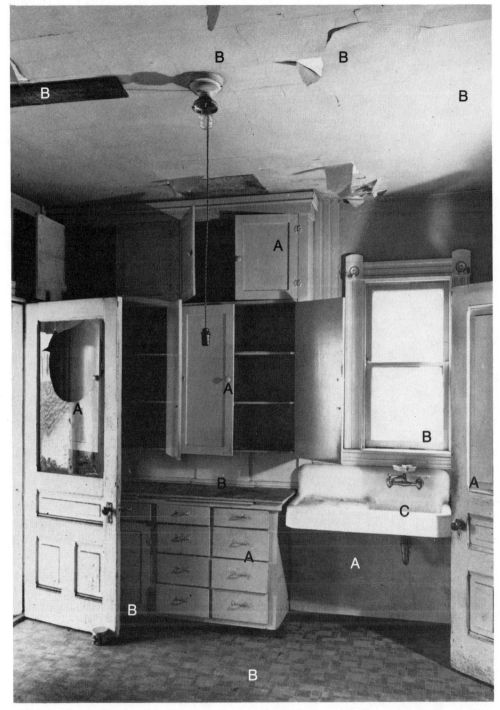

This forlorn-looking kitchen, far from being a total loss, can actually be put right with a minimum of professional help. The letters refer to the degree-of-difficulty categories listed at right.

To do or not to do

A: Easy

- Minor wall and ceiling damage
- Painting
- Wallcoverings (most)
- Minor floor damage
- Surface paneling damage
- Elementary plumbing—washer replacement, toilet repairs, clogged drains, similar tasks
- Elementary electric—replacing fuses, outlets and switches
- Hanging things on most walls

B: Medium

- Patching gypsum wallboard (walls) and small ceiling holes
- Replacing ceiling tile
- Replacing damaged paneling
- Installing new floors, any type
- Major repairs in hardwood or resilient flooring
- Removing squeaks from floors and stairs
- Installing new wiring, outlets or similar work (but always with no power to the area)
- Installing and repairing ceramic tile anywhere
- Framing
- More complex wallcoverings of all types
- Attaching things to concrete and masonry
- Repairing, replacing drywall tape or corner bead

C: Difficult

- Structural damage—foundations, main beams
- Major repairs to bearing walls
- Behind-the-wall plumbing
- Electrical work involving the entrance panel or any other work that must be done with the "juice" on
- Untrimmed wallpaper
- Major ceiling repair such as replacing gypsum board
- Plastering

is likely to take, what tools and materials will be required, and, when appropriate, the advance planning needed.

As a general rule, the jobs in this book are well within the grasp of every homeowner. Some take a little more time, a little more study, a little more patience, or a lot more money. Most, though, are simple and relatively inexpensive. If you can't drive a nail or saw a board, we'll show you how to do that, too. We'll also warn you about difficult areas before the going gets tough.

The list above groups typical interior homeowner jobs by degree of difficulty. If you're just a beginner, stick to group A. Those who have had a little experience can probably handle anything in group B. Only the truly handy should tackle group C. These jobs are the province of the professionals. They're like a heart transplant, doctor.

INTERIOR REPAIRS & DECORATION

1. TOOLS   12

2. REPAIRING WALLS   18
Patching materials   19
Patching plaster walls   19
Small flaws   19
Big flaws   20

Special solutions for special
   problems   21
Patching wallboard   22
Screen method   22
Triangular patch method   22
Replacing a damaged section   23

Correcting common defects   24
Repairing wood panels   25
Repairing ceramic tile   25
Replacing a broken tile   25
Replacing old caulking   25

3. HANGING THINGS
ON THE WALL   26
Choosing a fastener for any wall   26
How to install standard fasteners   28

4. BUILDING NEW WALLS AND
IMPROVING OLD ONES   30
Framing a wall   32
Layout and assembly   33
Framing doors and other openings   34
Framing basement walls   35

Framing attic walls   35
Insulation   35
Installing gypsum wallboard   36
Cutting wallboard   36
Cutting pockets in wallboard   38
Taping joints   38

Finishing corners   39
Putting up paneling   41
Working with moldings   42
Applying ceramic tile   43
Other wall materials   45

5. NEW CEILINGS   46
Installing wallboard overhead   46
Ceiling repairs   47

Tile ceilings   48
Ceiling tile layout   48
Furring   49

Installing ceiling tile   49
Suspended ceilings   50
Modern installation methods   50

6. PAINTING   52
Choosing the right kind of paint   52
Which paint for which surface?   53
Picking colors   53
Color selector chart   54

Painting tools   54
Estimating time   55
How much paint?   55
Preparation   56
A systematic approach   57

Brushwork   58
Roller work   59
Special problems   60
Finishes   60
Cleanup   61

7. WALLPAPERING   62
Choosing the right covering   62
Estimating quantity   63
Wallpaper repairs   63
Papering a room   64

Wallpapering tools   64
Preparing walls for papering   65
Choosing the starting point   65
Hanging wallpaper   66
Ceilings   69

Papering a switch plate   70
Double cutting   71
Prepasted papers   71

8. REPAIRING FLOORS   72
Routine maintenance   72
Wood floors   72
Resilient flooring   73
Removing spots and stains   74
Repairing wood floors   74
Surface flaws   74
Separated floorboards   74

Squeaky floors   75
Replacing a damaged floorboard
   section   76
Fixing damaged resilient flooring   77
Floor-sanding schedule   78
Refinishing wood flooring   78
Sanding   78
Staining   79

Fillers   79
Sealers   79
For a final finish   80
Varnish   80
Shellac   80
Wax   80
Moldings and other trim   81
Removing a threshold   81

9. NEW FLOORS   82
Installing new flooring   82
Preparing the subfloor   82
Underlayment   82
Attic subfloors   83
Flooring types at a glance   83
Laying floor tile   84
How to calculate   84
Installation   84
Installing border tiles   85

Estimating floor covering needs   86
Sheet vinyl   86
Installation   86
Seams   87
Installing hardwood flooring   88
Strip flooring   88
Plank flooring   88
Block flooring   88
Application   88
Nailing   89

Estimating hardwood flooring   89
Installing a ceramic tile floor   90
Replacing floor tiles   90
A new bathroom with tile   91
Installing wall-to-wall
   shag carpet tiles   92
Installing wall-to-wall carpet roll   93
To figure carpet roll length   93
Floor preparation   93

10. PROJECTS   94
Supergraphics   94
Easy-to-build furniture   95

1.TOOLS

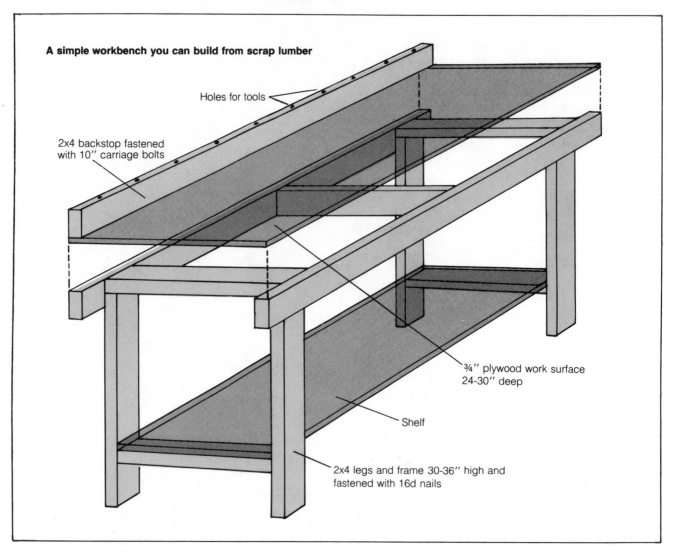

A simple workbench you can build from scrap lumber

Holes for tools

2x4 backstop fastened
with 10″ carriage bolts

¾″ plywood work surface
24-30″ deep

Shelf

2x4 legs and frame 30-36″ high and
fastened with 16d nails

Where home craftsmanship begins

Well, you've passed house anatomy; now on to the stethoscopes, thermometers, and scalpels of the home internist. Though most of the tools pictured throughout this chapter are familiar to all, it's surprising how often they are used incorrectly or ineffectively. For example, you may have noticed that many people hold a hammer near the center of the handle and whack at a nail with a straight up-and-down motion. Well, that's a very slow—and often sloppy—way of driving a nail, not to speak of the waste of energy. Beginning on page 13 we'll tell you the proper way to wield a hammer and all the other tools you're likely to be using.

Storage. The first point to consider, however, is tool storage. It's very important. When you first start out,

you may have little more than a hammer and a screwdriver. If you're like most people, you'll keep these in the kitchen junk drawer. After a while, you'll find your tools multiplying along with bits of string, rubber bands, extension cords, and the other odds and ends of the good life. At some point, trying to find a pair of pliers in all that mess becomes aggravating and even hazardous.

Early in the game, work out a plan for a mini-workship—or a full-size one, if you have the space. Start off with at least a tool box, providing space for assorted nails and screws. A tool box has the advantage of being portable and provides neat, rust-resistant storage. You can begin with a cheap, small one, but if you anticipate a good deal of work, invest in a

larger box, and reserve a separate corner of the basement for yourself.

Workshop. The home shop will ideally have a workbench, where you can function in peace and quiet, while sparing the family from dust and noise. A wise workbench builder will run a 2x4 across the back of the bench, not only to prevent tools from falling behind the bench, but also to fill with holes for such hard-to-store items as screwdrivers, drill bits, and chisels. A tempered hardboard work surface resists banging and other abuse. A vise is also a handy item.

But the bench itself can wait till later. More essential to your tool area is a sheet of perforated hardboard for hanging tools. Most lumber and hardware stores sell kits for attaching the hardboard, along with an assortment of accessories for mounting the various tools.

Buying tools. Important: don't skimp. The small amount of money you save on bargain-basement and supermarket tools will cost you much more in valuable time, replacements, and general aggravation. Some of these tools are downright dangerous. Cheap metal can chip and injure the user. But a good hammer, for example, is precisely tooled, properly weighted, and has maximum strength so that it will drive a nail straight, true, and fast. A cheap hammer will slip off the nail, drive it crookedly, and require more strokes. Often, the head is poorly attached and might even fly off at a crucial moment causing injury or damage. It just isn't worth it. The same applies to all tools.

When you shop, look for tools that are stamped with the manufacturer's name or symbol.

Hammers. There are many kinds of hammers: ball-peen hammers (for metalwork), tack hammers (for upholstery), and sledge hammers (for heavy jobs), to name a few. What most folks mean by a hammer, though, is a claw, or nail hammer. A

curved claw is designed for pulling nails; a straight claw for prying boards apart in construction work. The best choice for light home repair work is a curved claw hammer that weighs 16 ounces. The head is either firmly attached to the handle with a solid wedge and glue, or forged in a single piece with the handle (which is then covered with rubber, plastic, or leather for a firm grip).

To use a hammer correctly, grip it at or near the end, and swing it from the shoulder. It may seem unnatural

at first—you may even miss the nail entirely—but keep trying (on some scrap wood) until you get the swing

of it. It's well worth the practice. An experienced carpenter can drive large spikes this way with only a few blows.

Hammer safety
- Make sure the head fits tightly on the handle.
- Don't use a hammer handle as a pry bar. The handle may split, causing bad cuts or pinches.
- Don't try to repair a split or cracked handle. Replace it.
- Don't strike a hardened steel surface with a steel hammer. It may shatter dangerously.

Screwdrivers. One screwdriver is not really enough. To start with, you should have the most common variety, with a flat-tipped, wedged-shaped blade ¼ inch wide and about 6 inches long. This model fits most but not all screws. On large screws, the blade will be too small and could slip dangerously; on small screws, it may not fit the slot at the top and could damage the screw or the surrounding surface. So, eventually, get a smaller screwdriver with a narrow blade, and another with an extra-large one (about 8 inches long).

Although used more for automotive and machine work, a Phillips-head or criss-cross screwdriver will also come in handy around the house. It has an X-shaped end that is

used for cross-slotted screws. These screws permit a better grip and are your best bet for tough jobs, such as mounting shelf standards on walls.

A good screwdriver will have a sturdy, tempered-steel blade and a smooth fluted handle, generally of plastic and gently rounded at the end. The tip is usually polished.

Once the screw is started, a screwdriver is simple to use. But many people try to use a screwdriver without starting a hole first. This may work in soft wood but is impossible in hard wood. Use an awl, a nail, or a tool specially designed for starting screws. Many oldtimers start the screw by banging it in with a hammer, but this often results in damaged and hard-to-work screw slots.

It also helps to hold the blade and screw head together with one hand in

the beginning. This is not always possible, however, and screwdrivers are available that have metal clips next to the blade for holding the screw head to the blade. Get one of these if you have a problem. Whichever kind you use, it is essential to press firmly against the screw to hold the blade in place.

When the wood is very hard, it is wise to predrill the entire hole. Special drill bits are available for this purpose. It also helps to have two hands on the screwdriver once the screw is started, one turning the handle, and the other flat against the end to apply more pressure.

It is of course easy to remove screws once you get them started. The trouble, again, is getting them started. Screws are driven in clockwise and removed counterclockwise. If a screw won't budge, give it a quick twist in both directions. For larger, stubborn screws, a screwdriver tip in a hand drill provides extra leverage, both in driving and in removing the screws.

Screwdriver safety
- Never place any part of your body in front of the screwdriver blade.
- Don't hold a workpiece in your hand while using a screwdriver. Hold the work in a vise or clamp.
- Don't try to turn a screwdriver with a pair of pliers.
- Never use a screwdriver to check an electrical circuit.

Pliers. There are numerous types of pliers, most of them used by specialists such as electricians and electronics workers. The one homeowners use are called slip-joint pliers. They are useful for numerous hold-

ing tasks, and are often the wrong tool for the job. Pliers are not really designed for tightening and loosening nuts. Wrenches are. Yet this is a common household use, and will do as long as you don't have the right wrench around.

Use slip-joint pliers for grasping, turning, bending, or pulling bolts, wires, broken glass, sharp, or small objects. The term slip-joint is used because the tool has two grooves in which the center fastener can lodge. In one slot, the pliers grip small objects, with the forward jaws tight and parallel. When the pin is in the other slot, the concave jaws can go around larger objects.

When shopping for pliers, choose a pair that has been drop-forged, with either a polished surface or a bluish-black sheen. The center pin should be solidly fastened so you can't remove it. The outer parallel jaws should have fine gooves or gripping contours, the inner ones sharp, rugged teeth. Handles should be scored or tooled so that you can grip them firmly.

Hand saws. Saws, too, come in a wide variety of sizes and types. Purchase an 8- or 10-point crosscut saw for all-around work. The point size designates the number of teeth per

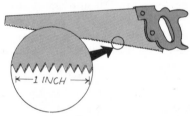

inch. More teeth mean finer but slower cutting. Crosscut means that the teeth are beveled slightly in alternating directions for cutting across the grain. Since framing and trim lumber are sold with lengthwise grain, most cutting you do will be across the grain.

Choose a crosscut saw with a blade of springy tempered steel, 24 to 26 inches in length, securely fastened to an interchangeable handle in at least four places.

The opposite of a crosscut saw is a ripsaw, although the two look very much alike. A ripsaw has squarish chisel-like teeth that cut best with the grain. Most homeowners have little need for a ripsaw. If they do much work calling for ripping, they usually go to a power saw.

A hacksaw has a removable blade and is used for cutting metals and some plastics. It consists of a

U-shaped frame into which the fine-toothed saw blades are inserted. Attach the blade first to the hook on the front end, then to the pin on the handle end, and tighten the wing nut to draw the blade taut. The frame adjusts to accept 8- to 12-inch blades.

Hacksaw safety
Any blade that is held under tension can snap dangerously in two if misused. To prevent this:
- Don't twist the blade.
- Don't press down too hard as you cut. (Let the blade do the work.)
- Don't use a dull or rusty blade.
- Keep the blade taut in the frame.
- Make sure the workpiece can't slip. (Use a vise or clamps.)

Another handy saw is the coping saw. It is similar in design to a hacksaw, but the blades are much thinner and have somewhat larger teeth. The blades are attached the

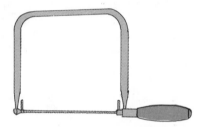

same way, except that the handle itself is turned for tightening. Because coping saw blades can be turned at various angles, they can be used for making rounded cuts.

Keyhole and compass saws are almost identical, with the keyhole blade being thinner and finer. Both

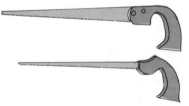

are tempered to a point and are used for making small cuts when only one side of the workpiece is accessible. You will need at least one of these for cutting pockets in paneling, gypsum wallboard, and similar material which is already nailed up. A good investment is the nested saw, consisting of one handle with interchangeable keyhole, compass, and metal-cutting blades.

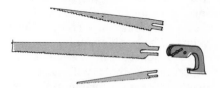

In using any saw, notice how the teeth cut. A crosscut saw, for example, has teeth set to cut on both the forward and return stroke, so be sure to use it that way. A ripsaw, hacksaw, or coping blade generally cuts in one direction only (usually forward), and trying to make it cut on the opposite stroke is only a waste of time and effort. Check the direction of the teeth, and try the saw on scrap lumber if you aren't sure.

When sawing a board, make sure the work surface is steady and level. For this, a pair of sawhorses is a good investment (or make them yourself). A sawhorse can be assembled in minutes from a pair of standard brackets, a few nails, and five scraps of 2x4.

Watch for binding when cutting large boards. The piece that is being cut off shouldn't be supported, because both pieces would fall toward the center. On the other hand, if you allow a heavy piece to fall off by itself, the wood will crack on the underside and part will break off. Best is to have someone hold the cut-off part as you finish the cut.

When sawing metal or other hard materials, score a line with a sharp instrument so that the saw will have a little bit of a start. Otherwise, the saw will slip all over the surface. Tapered saws, such as compass and keyhole, need a drilled hole or holes to start with.

When buying a saw, look for a tempered steel or chrome-nickel blade. Handles should be removable and of hardwood or high-impact plastic. Better-quality saws have tapered teeth.

Measuring instruments. Take your pick of two professional measuring devices. A 6-foot folding rule with extension is our favorite. Made of wood, it folds on brass plates and fits easily into your back pocket. The readings are large and easy to see, with

How to saw a board

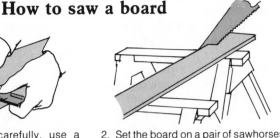

1. After measuring carefully, use a pencil and a square to mark your line across the top edge of the board.

2. Set the board on a pair of sawhorses, keeping the pencil line on the outside. Allow a couple of inches clearance for the saw.

3. Start the cut near the handle of the saw, with a few short, backward strokes at the far edge of the board.

4. Once a groove is started, saw toward yourself, maintaining a 45° cutting angle.

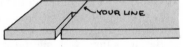

5. For an accurate cut, saw outside of your line, as shown.

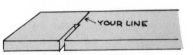

6. Don't saw on the line, because the kerf (the width of the cut) will cause the board to be too short.

---

red markings every 16 inches (the standard spacing for framing). The extension is an extra 6-inch section that slides out and allows you to take inside measurements of enclosed areas such as closets or drawers.

Some people prefer a steel tape, which is flexible enough to wind up inside a small case, yet rigid enough to stay in place when extended. A small hook on the end allows you to hold it against a long workpiece and measure by yourself. The case is

usually 2 inches long, so you can measure interiors accurately by adding the 2 inches to your reading. Some models have a friction lock to

hold the tape open, and a power return to retract it quickly.

Utility knife. An inexpensive tool with a multitude of uses, the utility knife combines a razor blade with a grip handle. Ideal for cutting gypsum wallboard, wallcoverings, thin wood, carpeting, rope, and string, it is also handy for opening cartons.

A good utility knife has a handle shaped to fit your palm, and has space for extra blades. Look for one that has a retractable blade which allows you to keep it in your pocket safely. The retracting device also lets you adjust the blade tip to the thickness of whatever it is you're cutting.

Knife safety
• The duller the blade, the greater the danger.
• Cut away from your body.
• Retract the blade after each use.

Putty and joint knives. These aren't really knives. Generally they have flexible blades and are used for applying and smoothing soft materials such as putty, spackling compound,

and wood fillers. Those with stiffer blades can also be used as scrapers. A putty knife has a 1½-to-3-inch blade and is used for filling cracks and

small holes with spackling compound or other filler. It is also used for puttying window glass and pressing grout between tiles.

Joint knives are 5 or 6 inches wide, with a flexible blade for applying

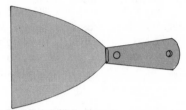

spackle or joint compound to plaster or gypsum drywall. The wide blade bridges the beveled edges of the wallboard sections and produces a smooth, undetectable joint. A similar knife, but having a stiff blade, makes a good scraper for paint, glue, wallpaper, or old furniture finishes.

Better-quality putty and joint knives have a blade that extends all the way into the handle and is attached by two rivets. The blade should be of hardened, tempered steel with a blunt end and no sharp edges.

Chisels. Although people whack at it with hammers all the time, the typical tang chisel (with the blade extended into the plastic or wood handle) is designed for hand use

only. We won't tell you not to hit it, because just about everyone does, but it will last longer if you don't.

It's nice to have a full wood chisel set, with widths ranging from ¼ inch to an inch, but it's a little expensive to start with, and you won't use all of them unless you do a lot of woodworking. A ½-inch-wide chisel is handy to have when you need to pare something down, knock out a piece of 2x4, and similar tasks.

There are many kinds of chisels, but the only other one you'll have much use for is a cold chisel. Made of hardened, tempered alloy steel, it is used for hitting steel, concrete, stone, and other hard materials. It is struck with a heavy hammer.

Spirit level. A level tells you if a surface is on a true horizontal or vertical plane. It's called a spirit level because there are little vials in the center and the ends that are partially filled with spirits—alcohol or

chloroform. The partial filling results in a bubble, which seeks the highest level in the vials because they are slightly curved. Plastic vials are better than glass ones.

Each vial is precisely aligned so that, when the edges of the tool are placed against a surface, the bubble will rest in the center (between two lines) only if that surface is perfectly level or plumb. The vials in the

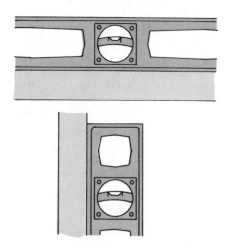

center (one for each edge) indicate level, and the vials at each end indicate plumb. The frame is made of aluminum, magnesium, or hardwood.

There are several types of levels, some of which are specialized for use by masons or other tradesmen. A carpenter's level with two vials in the center and one at each end, is about 2 feet long and is best for all-around use. If you buy a wooden level, it should have brass plates securely bound to hardwood, and these are expensive. A magnesium or aluminum level should do as well for home use. Select a model with replaceable vials in case one breaks.

Also handy is a torpedo level, a smaller level which is useful in tight places. It has a top-reading vial so that you can place it on a low or deep surface and tell whether it's level without bending down to look at it. A good torpedo level, with magnesium body, 45-degree vial, and a

magnetic plate costs half the price of a carpenter's level.

Wrenches. There are probably more different types of wrenches than any other tool. There are open-end and box wrenches, some with a combination of each, and some with half-boxes. (A box wrench completely encloses the nut.) There are ratchet wrenches that are turned like a crank, pipe wrenches, chain wrenches, and lots of others.

It is a wise idea to pick up a few wrenches as you go along, particularly if they are on sale. But to begin with, get an adjustable wrench. These, too, come in various sizes, but one about 8 inches long, with jaw capacity up to an inch, is a good

household item. This wrench has one permanent jaw, and another which can be moved away from or toward the permanent jaw by means of a knob on the head.

Look for a drop-forged, alloy steel wrench with a chrome-polished or blueblack sheen. The jaws should be exactly parallel and not loose. Some have a locking feature that holds the adjustable jaw in a constant position as long as you need it.

Turn an adjustable or open-end wrench so that the permanent jaw is

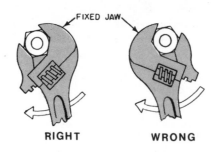

on the side from which you're applying the pressure. Never strike a wrench with a hammer.

Wrench safety
● Use a wrench that fits the nut. Keep wrenches clean and free of oil so they can't slip.
● Don't attempt to increase leverage by placing a pipe over the handle.

Power drills. Power equipment will speed up most jobs, but it is fairly expensive, and except for a power drill, the beginner should start with hand equipment until he finds the need for a particular power tool.

An electric drill is an exception because public acceptance and mass-production techniques have actually lowered the price of electric drills over the years. This tool is so

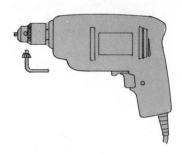

cheap, so easy and safe to use, and can be adapted for so many uses that it makes sense to get one as soon as the need for it arises.

An electric drill can make holes in wood, metal, plastics, masonry, or almost any other material—with the proper bit. In addition, accessories adapt it for sanding, buffing, grinding, driving screws, stirring paint, and a multitude of other chores.

In shopping, you should know that the larger the chuck size, the greater the torque, but the top rpms will be lower. The chuck is the adjustable front section that holds the drill bit, and the size refers to the maximum size drill shank it can hold. For many years, the ¼-inch drill was standard, but manufacturers have brought the ⅜-inch drill within the range of most homeowners.

Speed and amperage are other considerations. Higher-speed drills can drill a hole faster; high-amp drills have more power. Most manufacturers offer variable speed drills, whose speed can be controlled by trigger pressure. When drilling through wood and softer objects, high speeds make faster work, but low speeds are necessary to drill harder surfaces, particularly concrete. A variable-speed drill, in our opinion, is worth the slight extra cost.

A double-insulated drill offers a valuable safety feature to prevent electric shock if you have to work in the rain. A device that locks at the desired speed is also good to have. Some drills can be reversed. Cordless drills are now available, which are fine for outdoor or other work away from a power source, but are generally inferior for indoor use. When buying, determine what accessories are available. Look for a drill with good balance.

Hand drills. If you don't want an electric drill, there are several other options available. Hand drills come in both the cranking and the push varieties. Get one with a bit-storage handle, because bits are easy to lose. A cranking-type drill is large and bulky; a push drill is smaller, lighter, and costs about a third as much.

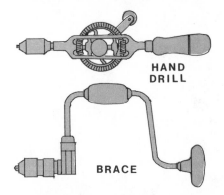

HAND DRILL

BRACE

For drilling large holes, and particularly for using large screws, a brace may come in very handy. (It's generally called a bit-and-brace, but the bits are bought separately.) This tool can apply a lot of hand pressure and is often used in fine woodworking. The reason most people don't buy one is that they cost more than many electric drills.

Other tools. This completes a basic tool supply. There are literally hundreds of specialized tools which you may want to buy for specific tasks. You can acquire them, however, as the need arises:

As your skills increase and you take on more work around the house—especially if you begin making improvements as well as routine repairs—you will find that power tools will make your work go better and faster. Briefly, here are some of the ones you should consider next.

Saber saw—for fast cutting of curved and straight lines in wood and other materials.

Circular saw—for production cutting of straight lines in wood.

Electric sander—for smooth, speedy sanding of wood, paint, or anything else removable by regular sandpaper and a sanding block.

Common nails and wood screws

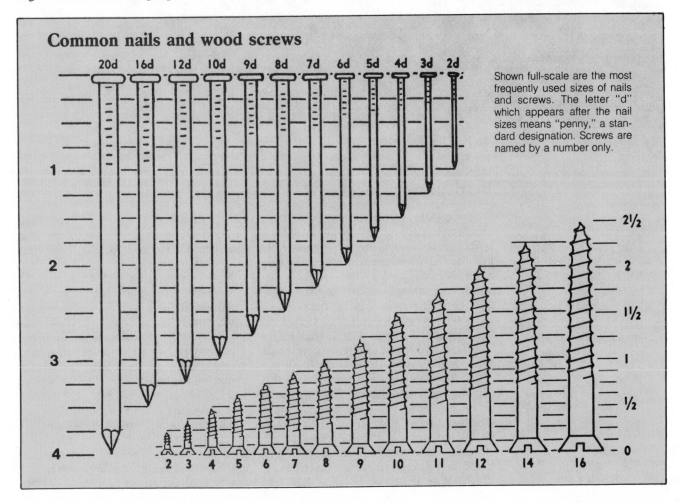

Shown full-scale are the most frequently used sizes of nails and screws. The letter "d" which appears after the nail sizes means "penny," a standard designation. Screws are named by a number only.

2.REPAIRING WALLS

Befriend your local wall

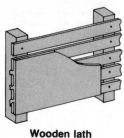

Perforated metal lath

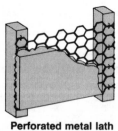

Wooden lath

Without walls and the space they enclose, needless to say our everyday life would fall apart at the seams. In fact, those four familiar walls that shape a room affect us more than we suppose and perhaps deserve more attention than they get. Yet, interior wall repairs can be done effectively without great expense or skill. Fixing up walls is a good way to start being handy around the house because you will get a significant result for a small effort.

Hand-plastered walls were once the principal type used in homes, but mass-produced wallboard products are now much preferred because of their lower installation costs. In the finest new homes old-time plaster may still be used, but it is found now mainly in homes built before World War II. If your home has real plaster walls, treasure them and keep them in good shape, because there is nothing like them for strength, sound absorption, and insulating qualities.

Modern plastering is done with perforated metal lath, which is attached to the framing and then covered with the plaster. Older homes had wooden lath, which consists of thin, undressed strips of wood. These strips, about ¾-inch wide, were nailed horizontally to studs, with gaps of about ¼ inch in between. The wet plaster was forced between and behind the lath to lock the entire mass together.

Though plaster withstands abuse much better than wallboard, it too can be damaged by a heavy blow, and it is subject to crackling and crumbling from settlement, climatic conditions, or age.

Patching materials

In repairing plaster and wallboard, you'll have three trusty allies. Spackling compound, joint cement, and patching plaster have much in common, and you'll often be able to do a given job with any one of them, though each has its own virtue.

Spackling compound consists mainly of gypsum powder and is available either in dry form for mixing or in cans already premixed and ready to use. The dry powder is cheaper, but for small jobs the premix is easier to work with. Use spackling compound to repair small cracks, holes, and bulges in plaster.

Joint cement, smoother and thinner than spackling compound, is used for closing seams between wallboard sections. It can be neatly feathered out (spread to a very thin, blending edge) to fill any gap without leaving telltale borders. Both spackling and joint compound can be sanded, painted, and papered over without show-ing any traces of the previous defects. **Patching plaster** is similar to spackling compound but contains fibers which make it effective in filling large gaps. It is highly cohesive and doesn't shrink, but feathering it out is tricky work.

Many gypsum products, including some forms of spackling compound and joint cement, contain asbestos fibers. As you may be aware, the incidence of lung cancer is 16 times higher among asbestos workers than the general population. This may be a result of prolonged exposure, but the families of asbestos workers have been known to suffer from the disease, presumably merely because the fibers were brought into the house. Need we say more? Avoid any wallboard patching product that contains asbestos. Most are now being made without asbestos, but some asbestos compounds are still on the market. Read labels carefully.

Patching plaster walls

Small flaws

To fix up cracks and small holes, you will have to clean the areas to be repaired, fill the cracks and holes with spackling compound, allow the work to dry, sand away excess material to produce an even finish, and touch up the repaired areas so they blend back in with the rest of the room. When overall repairs are slight, a can of prepared mix should take care of them nicely. Reseal the container tightly.

1. Remove loose particles of plaster by running a thin blade along the edges of the crack. Then make sure the crack is free of dirt and debris.

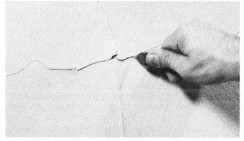

2. Enlarge hairline cracks with the point of a beer-can opener so the spackling compound will have a small furrow to cling to.

3. Take a dab of spackling compound on the tip of a flexible putty knife and work it into the hole or crack. When the crack is filled, wipe off the blade and run it over the repaired area to smooth and level it with the surrounding surface.

4. When the spackling compound has dried, sand away any excess with medium-grade (80-grit) abrasive paper on a sanding block. Restore the repaired area, as necessary, to blend back into the room decor (see page 21).

What it takes

Approximate time: Up to a minute for each minor flaw; more for gaping holes. An average room under ordinary conditions needs less than an hour's work every couple of years. The job is usually done in preparation for painting.

Tools and materials: Putty knife, joint knife, medium-grade (80-grit) sandpaper, and spackling compound.

Planning hints: Since it's not always possible to repaint an entire room or wall every time the plaster gets chipped, start now to keep a list in your paint storage area of the brand, color, and location of all paint you use around the house. Any time you paint, save a few ounces in a tightly sealed, labeled jar so you can patch and cover your tracks at will.
Large holes will require two or three applications of spackle with at least an hour's drying time in between coats. (Shining a hot lamp on the repaired area can reduce drying time.)

Big flaws

To repair larger holes, you will have to clean the damaged areas, undercut the sides of the holes, and moisten, patch, repatch, and sand the repair. Large repair jobs are often best followed by redecorating, or at least redoing the entire wall where the damage occurred. When repairs are extensive, buying powdered spackle or patching plaster and mixing it yourself will save you money.

1. Clean large holes of loose debris and remove weak plaster from the surrounding area.

2. Use a beer-can opener to undercut the sides of the damaged area so the spackling compound will have a ledge to grip.

3. Moisten the hole with a sponge so the old plaster doesn't rob the new compound of its moisture content.

4. Mix the powdered spackling compound or patching plaster to the consistency of thick cream, and fill in the hole with a wide-bladed taping knife.

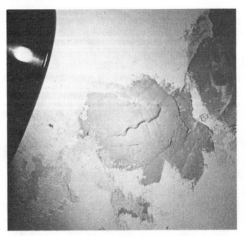

5. Allow the spackle to dry, or help it to dry by warming it with a lightbulb. As it dries, it will probably sag a little and shrink, so you will most likely have to respackle it at least once more.

6. When the hole is entirely filled and the spackle is completely hard and dry, sand the repaired area flush with the rest of the wall. Before redecorating, dust the wall with a tack cloth.

Droopy spackle?

If you've ever tried spackling a really large hole, you may have found as I did that, short of replastering, it's a virtually hopeless job. The stuff just won't stay where you put it. But I discovered I could save time and spackling compound by first nailing or gluing a thin scrap of wallboard into the hole. Gouge up the papered surface of the scrap to really roughen it, and wet it thoroughly before you apply the spackling compound to finish filling the hole.

Special solutions for special problems

For most plaster walls, the repair techniques shown on the preceding pages will solve all problems. However a few situations require special treatment.

Extensive damage. When a wall is full of cracks and holes, the repairs will go better and faster if you use a plasterer's trowel.

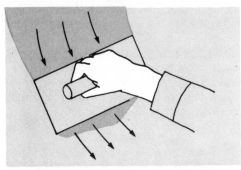

Its long edge, several times wider than the blade of a putty knife or joint knife, will quickly create a level surface on the largest possible area.

Glossy surfaces. To restore a repaired plaster wall to its original glossy surface, run a damp sponge ahead of your knife or

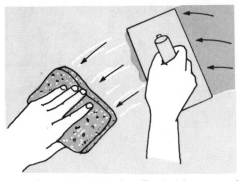

trowel as you spread a final thin coat of spackling compound.

Textured plasters. To match a gritty surface, mix some sand in with the final coat of patch (be sure to use a separate container so you don't spoil the rest of the spackle), or else add sand to the paint you use for touching up the repair.

A stucco finish can be imitated by swirl-

ing or wiggling a paintbrush in the moist spackle as it begins to set. Or, for a stippled effect, jab lightly with the brush.

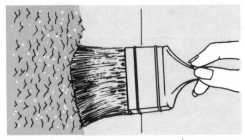

Plaster bulges. Bulges in a wall are usually caused when old plaster has crumbled and broken away from the lath. They may, however, be due to structural damage in the wall itself. To determine the cause, pull or break away the bulging plaster with a screw driver or stiff knife. If it comes

away easily, the plaster simply needs replacement as described on the opposite page. But if you find that the lath has broken or deteriorated, then you can easily nail new lath to the surrounding framing and apply new plaster with a large trowel. If neither seems to be the problem, there may be a structural defect, in which case an entire new wall (or worse) may be in order. It's time to call in the experts, at least to determine the cause.

Blending in. If the patched area is small, or not in a particularly noticeable part of the room, a coat of primer and some matching paint will bring it back up to par. Failing that, try painting a single wall. A slight color change at the corners of the room will likely be unnoticeable. However, if you can't come close enough to the required hue, pick a markedly different shade of the original color to produce a two-tone look, or use an entirely different but complementary color. Painted graphic devices, whether in the form of geometric patterns or freehand designs, can often be used to hide a patch, and they will add interest to a room at the same time.

Patching wallboard

Approximate time: For minor dents, minutes. For gaping holes, up to an hour, plus drying time.

Tools and materials: Besides the items required for patching plaster walls (page 19), you'll need either a scrap of wire mesh, a pair of shears, and string, or else a scrap of wallboard, a keyhole saw, and drywall patching tape. Use a utility knife and metal-edged ruler for measuring and cutting a patch. Plastic clips (see opposite page) are available to simplify the fitting job.

Minor cracks and dents in gypsum wallboard are repaired the same way as plaster walls. If the damage is slight and the board itself is still intact, the surface can be leveled off with spackling compound as described on the preceding pages. But be sure to remove frayed paper before you spackle.

Although wallboard goes up much more easily than plaster, it is harder to repair when it gets broken. And since it isn't as sturdy as plastered lath, this happens all too often.

There are several ways to patch a large hole in wallboard, but you cannot do it simply by pressing spackling compound into the hole, for there isn't anything back there to hold the spackle in place.

One method makes use of a scrap of wire mesh, held in place with string, to provide the necessary backing. Another method calls for cutting a triangular wallboard patch with beveled edges that grip the existing wall. A third method makes use of plastic clips to hold a patch of any desired shape in place while it is being spackled.

Screen method

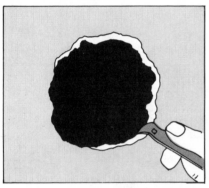 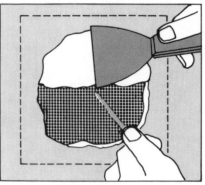 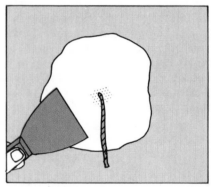

1. Clean away loose gypsum and paper from the hole. Leave the edges of the exposed gypsum jagged for better gripping.

2. Use metal shears or an old pair of scissors to cut a piece of wire mesh about 2 inches larger, all around, than the hole. Attach a piece of string to the center of the mesh, slip the mesh through the hole, and hold it in place behind the wallboard with the help of the string.

3. Fill the hole roughly with spackle while pulling the string gently toward you. Leave a small depression at the base of the string. Let the spackle set for a few minutes before letting go of the string. After a few hours, snip the string and gently apply the finish coat of spackle.

Triangular patch method

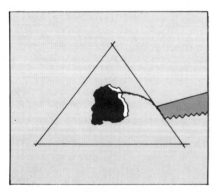 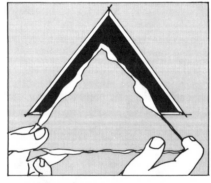 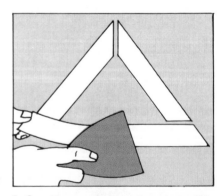

1. Cut a piece of wallboard into a triangular shape, making it large enough to cover the hole and some of the surrounding wall. Bevel the edges of the patch so the back is smaller than the front. Hold the patch over the hole, and trace the outline of the triangle onto the wall, clearing the hole on all sides. Cut the marked triangle from the wall with a keyhole saw, beveling the edges to match the bevel of the patch.

2. Spread spackling compound generously along the edges of the hole and of the patch. Fit the patch carefully into the hole with light pressure. The matching bevels will prevent the patch from falling through the hole, unless you press too hard.

3. Spackle over the patch and use thin drywall patching tape to strengthen the bond. Spackle again over the tape and sand the whole area level after it dries.

You can simplify the job of fitting a patch to a hole by using a set of specially designed plastic clips. The clips are available separately for larger holes, but you're more likely to find them in a patching kit, which contains all necessary tools in disposable plastic form. Included in the kit is a small amount of spackling compound and a 4-by-4-inch patch, which is just the right size for covering gaps left by electrical outlets or holes made by banging doorknobs, two common jobs.

1. Hold the precut patch over the hole and draw a line around it. Cut out the scribed area with a keyhole saw, just outside the line, carefully removing any pieces of frayed paper.

2. Mount the clips on opposite sides of the hole as shown. There are break-off tabs to adjust for ⅜-, ½-, and ⅝-inch wallboard thicknesses.

3. Dip the patch in water on all four sides (don't immerse it completely) and place it over the clips. Apply spackling compound into the joints and feather them out to camouflage the patch. When dry, sand the excess spackle and the front of the clips away.

Replacing a damaged section

When a large section of wallboard is damaged, it is often best to replace the problem area entirely. There is usually no need to remove the whole panel, but cut completely around the damaged area with a keyhole saw; then extend the cuts horizontally until you reach the center of the studs on either side. Make your cuts carefully so you don't damage concealed wiring or plumbing, and work with a utility knife in the vicinity of studs so you don't saw the lumber. Then use the claw of a hammer to clean away old nails and gypsum residue.

If the damage is close to the wooden cross plates at the top or bottom of the wall, you may as well extend the repair to meet them. (Remove any moldings that cover the top or bottom.) But where you saw a panel horizontally, use a level and a straightedge to ensure a square cut. Then cut a piece of 2x4 or 2x3 lumber to support the new horizontal joint from behind. Nail the lumber to the studs on either side by toenailing (driving the nails at an angle). Center the new lumber on the edge of the cut wallboard. When the framing is up, cut a new piece of wallboard to fit the opening in the wall and fasten it to the

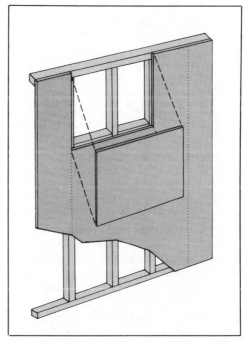

studs and the horizontal lumber with wallboard nails. (Detailed instructions for cutting and nailing wallboard are given on page 36.) Spackle and tape the edges as shown opposite.

What it takes

Approximate time: One to two hours, plus drying time, per average replacement/repair. Ceilings take longer.

Tools and materials: Keyhole saw, utility knife, metal straightedge, claw hammer, level, 2x4 or 2x3 horizontal support lumber, 8- or 10-penny common nails for attaching supports, replacement wallboard, wallboard nails, spackling compound, joint knife or trowel, thin drywall patching tape, and medium-grade (80-grit) sandpaper.

Planning hints: Use this method only if all the patch methods fail. If you can conveniently extend the repair as far as the ceiling or floor, you'll save yourself some work, because the fitting of the replacement piece won't have to be so accurate (one edge will be covered by a molding) and you'll have to install only one horizontal support.

Correcting common defects

Nail pops. A frequent problem even for professional plasterers is the working loose of nails used to hold wallboard to its backing. The most common cause of nail pops is unseasoned wood, but they can also be caused by poor workmanship. In any case, the cure for nail pops is simple, although it may be time-consuming when there are a lot of them. Drive the offending nails back into the wall with a hammer and nailset. (Pulling the nails out is preferable but rarely possible without doing further damage to the wallboard.) Then hammer new nails 1½ to 2 inches above or below the original nails. It's a little-known fact that pairing nails will discourage pops from developing in the first place.

The best nails to use in wallboard work are the ones with annular rings. The

threadlike rings on their shaft make for good gripping and give the appearance of screws. When popping is a persistent problem, use drywall screws. Their self-

drilling point, special threads, and bugle-shaped head eliminate tearing and help compress the gypsum. They are driven with a Phillips-head screwdriver. Drive either fastener until its head rests slightly below the wallboard surface. This is known as dimpling. When nailing or screwing in wallboard, press the panel against the framing with one hand or your shoulder as soon as the fastener hits solid wood. After the new fasteners are in place, go over the damaged areas with spackling compound, filling in the old nail holes and the dimples from the new nail heads.

Damaged tape and corner bead. The edges of wallboard are beveled so they can be taped, filled with joint compound, and tooled into an even, seamless surface. But sometimes the joints become a bit unhinged, and the tape gets loose. The best way to fix this is to pull out the old tape and install a completely new joint. If the tape is loose enough, simply grab a corner and pull it out. Otherwise, dig into the seam with a beer-can opener or knife blade until you get a handle on the tape. Pull out all remnants of the old tape; then scrape or sand away all the old joint cement. Finish as if you were taping a new wall (page 38).

Corner bead is usually applied at outside corners to protect them from damage; it consists of perforated or other thin metal

What it takes

Approximate time: A few minutes per nail pop; up to an hour per taped joint or corner bead, not counting drying time.

Tools and materials: For nail pops, a nailset, hammer, and drywall nails or screws; for taped joints, drywall tape; for corner bead, the nail-pop tools plus a replacement strip if necessary; for all, a joint knife or wide trowel, spackling compound or joint cement, and medium-grade (80-grit) sandpaper.

Planning hints: All these jobs are essentially do-overs and repairs of the basic procedures for installing wallboard. To avoid further inconvenience, begin by familiarizing yourself with the fundamentals of installing wallboard on pages 36-39.

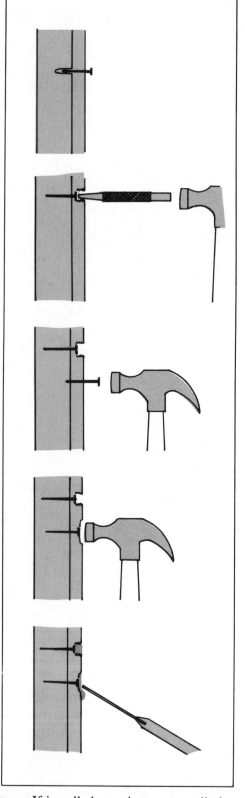

tape. If it pulls loose, it can generally be refastened with the same type of nails as used for regular wallboard. (Occasionally, if corner bead is badly bent out of shape, you will do well to replace it with a new piece.) Joint cement is then applied to smooth out the edges. Follow the instructions for new corner bead (page 39).

Repairing wood panels

Wood paneling isn't likely to take as severe a beating as unprotected wallboard. For one thing, the wood is stronger and harder; for another, the paneling is often mounted on top of wallboard, which then serves to buffer it from behind. The problems that arise with wood paneling are rather more like those of wood furnishings. The most common one is the scarring of the finish due to wear and tear caused by the room furniture, although similar damage is often caused by the same little monsters that ruin gypsum wallboard.

Minor damage to paneling, such as scrapes and gouges, can be disguised by the use of wax crayon of a matching (or almost matching) color. You can borrow the typical wood colors from the little one's crayon box. Iodine also helps for dark woods and mercurochrome for reddish tints. Large scratches and gouges can be made less noticeable by filling with wood putty (*not wood dough*), colored to match with oil stains or other pigment.

When paneling is severely damaged, which is rare, you will probably have to replace at least one entire panel. Remove baseboards and molding carefully with a screwdriver. Take care not to damage adjacent paneling when prying out the damaged panel. Installation instructions appear on page 41.

To protect paneling from future damage, give it a coat or two of wax, as you would fine furniture. A liquid wax is usually sufficient, but valuable woods are better served with hard paste wax, buffed to a warm glow. Wax buildup can be easily removed with turpentine or mineral spirits, followed by several applications of new wax. Before applying new wax, give all the panels a new coat of varnish if needed. One rarely thinks of it at the time, but it's a good idea, when putting up new paneling, to buy and save an extra sheet for future replacement.

Heavy on the mayo

When my grandmother absent-mindedly hung her umbrella up to dry on our new wood paneling, you would have wept to see the white mark it left on the wall. Nothing I tried could remove the spot. She didn't bat an eyelash, though. "Don't worry, sonny," she said. "Spread lots of mayonnaise on it right away, and it will be good as new in the morning." Convinced that she had lost the last of her marbles, I nevertheless obeyed rather than offend her. Came the dawn and (it's hard to believe) she was right. (Remember to wipe off the mayo in the morning.)

Practical Pete

Repairing ceramic tile

Replacing a broken tile

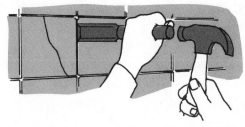

1. Replace badly cracked or loosened tiles, especially where water can get behind and do further damage, by prying out or cutting around the broken tile with an old chisel or a screwdriver. Be careful not to damage neighboring tiles.

2. Stubborn tiles should be broken up. Start a hole in the center of the tile with a center punch. Drill a hole through it with a carbide-tipped bit, revolving at slow speed. Pry out the pieces. Scrape away old adhesive and grout. Apply new adhesive to the back of the good tile and hold it in place with masking tape until it sets. Re-grout around the edges (see pages 43-44).

Replacing old caulking

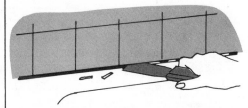

1. Dig out broken or discolored caulking from the gap where the bottom of the tiled wall meets the top of the tub or shower basin.

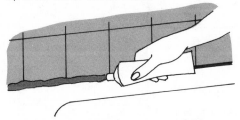

2. Use flexible caulking, the silicone rubber type, *not* tile grout. Squeeze out a continuous bead along the joint, directly out of the tube.

3. Smoothing it out is the problem. Various manufacturers recommend different methods, but a long stroke with a *wet* finger works the best.

What it takes

Approximate time: Up to an hour for minor repairs on wood paneling and ceramic tile.

Tools and materials: Your basic tool kit will suffice. Items vary with the job and are noted in the instructions.

Stopgaps and copouts

Tile covers: If you're not up to replacing a ceramic tile at the moment, you may find a new product known as vinyl tile offers an agreeable compromise. They have a self-stick backing making them easy to apply, but they tend to peel at the edges after a while.

If you can't find a solid colored replacement tile to match (though even ceramic tile colors are now standardized), pick out a tile with a picture or decoration on it that you like.

3.HANGING THINGS

Once upon a time, anyone who wanted to hang something on a wall simply drove in a nail or hook, and that was that. But walls and the things that hang on them have changed. And modern industry, with its genius for improving our life (and picking up a few bucks), has more gadgets out for hanging things than you can possibly use.

The chart below will help you to sort out the various fastener types and determine what you really need for any given job. To use it, find the box in the top row that

Choosing a fastener for any wall

Fastener ▼	Wall material ▶	Glass	Gypsum wallboard	Hard materials (brick, concrete, cinderblock, marble, stone)	
Adhesive fasteners 		Good	Good	Not recommended	
Alloyed drive anchors 		Not recommended	Not recommended	Excellent	
Anchor nails 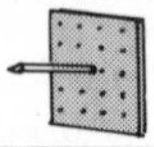		Not recommended	Not recommended	Good for light duty	
Concrete nails 		Not recommended	Not recommended	Excellent	
Double-stick tapes 		Good for light duty	Good for light duty	Not recommended	
Drive anchors 		Not recommended	Not recommended	Excellent	
Fiber anchors 		Good	Not recommended	Good	
Hollow-door anchors (jack nuts) 		Not recommended	Not recommended	Not recommended	
Lead anchors 		Not recommended	Not recommended	Good	
Nail-ins 		Good for light duty	Good for light duty	Good for light duty	
Picture hooks 		Not recommended	Good for light duty	Not recommended	
Pin fasteners 		Not recommended	Not recommended	Good for light duty	
Plastic expansion anchors 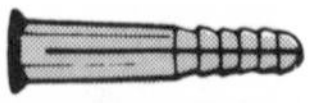		Good	Good	Good	
Screw expansion anchors (mollies) 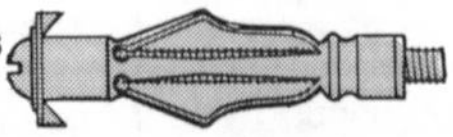		Not recommended	Good	Not recommended	
Steel expansion anchors 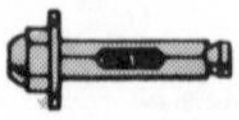		Not recommended	Not recommended	Excellent	
Toggle anchors (plastic) 		Excellent	Good	Good	
Toggle bolts (gravity & split wing) 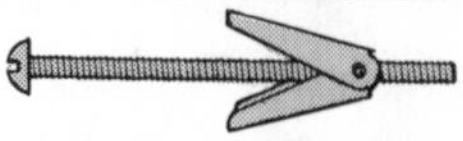		Good	Excellent	Good	
Zinc-shielded lag bolts 		Not recommended	Not recommended	Excellent	

ON THE WALL

describes the wall material you wish to fasten into. Then scan the vertical column beneath it for advice on the various fasteners named and pictured at the left of the chart. Of those recommended, pick the fastener that best corresponds to the object you wish to hang on your wall.

The proper use of many fasteners is self-evident, but you'll find instructions for the trickier ones on pages that follow. (Nails and screws are discussed on page 17, along with the tools for fastening them.)

	Metal	Plaster	Stucco, terrazzo, terra cotta	Tile (ceramic)	Wood
	Excellent	Good	Not recommended	Good	Not recommended
	Good up to 3/32″ thickness	Not recommended	Good for terrazzo only	Good	Good
	Not recommended	Not recommended	Not recommended	Not recommended	Not recommended
	Not recommended	Not recommended	Not recommended	Not recommended	Not recommended
	Good for light duty	Good for light duty	Not recommended	Good for light duty	Good for light duty
	Not recommended	Not recommended	Not recommended	Not recommended	Not recommended
	Not recommended	Good for light duty	Good	Good; best for solid walls	Not recommended
	Not recommended	Not recommended	Not recommended	Not recommended	Best for doors
	Not recommended	Not recommended	Good	Good	Not recommended
	Not recommended	Good for light duty	Good for light duty	Good for light duty	Not recommended
	Not recommended	Good for light duty	Good for light duty	Not recommended	Good for light duty
	Not recommended	Not recommended	Good for light duty on terrazzo only	Not recommended	Good for light duty on hardwood only
	Not recommended	Good	Good	Good	Not recommended
	Not recommended	Excellent	Good	Not recommended	Excellent on wood thickness of ⅝″ to 2″
	Not recommended	Not recommended	Good for terrazzo only	Not recommended	Not recommended
	Good	Good	Good	Good	Good
	Good for thin metal	Excellent	Good for hollow walls	Good for hollow walls	Not recommended
	Not recommended	Not recommended	Good for terrazzo only	Not recommended	Not recommended

How to install standard fasteners

Pin fasteners

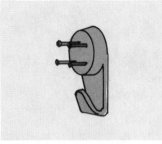 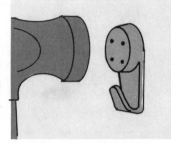 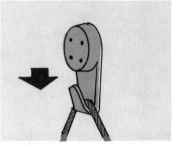

1. Select the right model. This relatively new product consists of a nylon head with tiny steel brads embedded in it. The head comes with a variety of attachments: hooks, loops, clips, snaps, and the like.

2. Hammer the pins sharply through the plastic and into the wall. Use pin fasteners only on a wall that is hard enough to give a good foothold: brick, cinderblock, plaster, hardwood, but not gypsum wallboard or softwood.

3. Suspend objects carefully from the attachment. So long as the stress is entirely vertical, the fastener's holding power will be surprisingly great; a strong outward stress, however, will eventually cause it to pull out.

Screw expansion anchors
(Molly bolts, collapsible anchors, hollow-wall anchors)

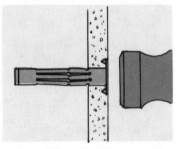 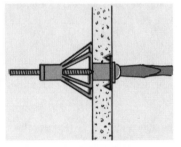 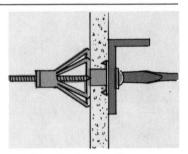

1. After drilling a hole the same size as, or slightly larger than, the anchor, insert the anchor—without the bolt—into the hole, and tap lightly until the prongs under the collar grip the wall surface securely.

2. Drive the bolt into the hole until the anchor's folding wings are drawn back to grip the inside of the wall. Don't overtighten. Then remove the bolt—the anchor will stay in place.

3. Slip the bolt through the fixture you intend to hang, and again drive the bolt into the anchor until the fixture is tight against the wall.

Hollow-door anchors
(Jack nuts)

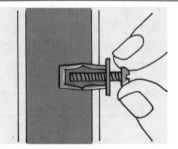 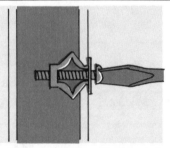 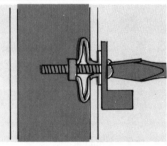

1. Insert the anchor into the hole in a hollow-core door. Jack nuts are similar to Molly bolts but are used for very thin materials.

2. Tighten the bolt, until pressure is felt, to draw the anchor back against the inside of the door. Be sure the bolt is short enough to nest in the anchor without striking the opposite panel.

3. Remove the bolt, pass it through the fixture, and drive it back into the anchor.

Anchor nails
(For masonry walls)

 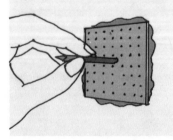 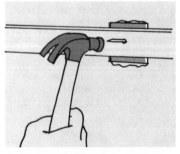

1. Apply bonding cement liberally to the back of the perforated metal plate which is fastened to the head of the anchor nail.

2. Press the plate into place on a masonry wall with a sliding, twisting motion to compress the adhesive; then remove the plate briefly from the wall, and press it back into place. Allow to dry.

3. Tap a furring strip, or any other desired fixture, all the way onto the anchor nail, and clinch the nail (bend the point over) to secure the fixture.

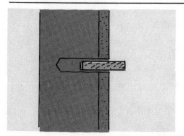

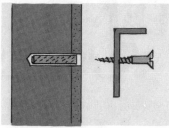

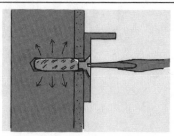

1. Insert the anchor into a hole in the wall (predrilled to fit or slightly over-size). The anchor may be of plastic, fiber, or soft metal.

2. Place a screw through the fixture you intend to mount. The screw may or may not be provided with the anchor, but most anchors will work with any kind of screw.

3. Drive the screw, with fixture at-tached, into the anchor. The screw expands the plug as it is drawn tight, squeezing the anchor against the sides of the hole.

**Toggle
bolts**
(Split-wing or
gravity)

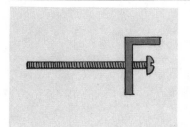

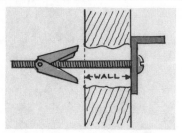

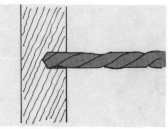

1. Slip the fixture onto the bare bolt.

2. Screw the toggle a short way onto the bolt. The span between the fixture and the flattened toggle arms must be greater than the thickness of the wall.

3. Drill a hole in the wall through which the toggle can pass when the arms are collapsed.

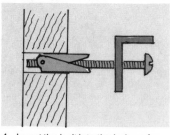

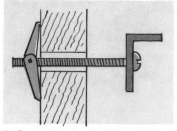

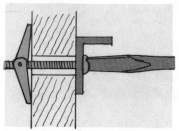

4. Insert the bolt into the hole as far as necessary for the toggle to snap open on the other side of the wall.

5. Pull the bolt back so the toggle grips the back of the wall.

6. Tighten the bolt until the fixture is firmly seated.

**Toggle
anchors**
(Combination
toggle bolt and
expansion anchor)

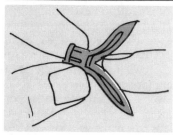

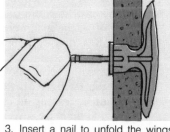

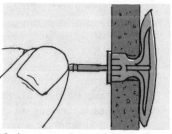

1. Redouble the anchor's flexible arms by tucking the wing tip back beneath the head.

2. Pinch the wings together to insert the anchor into a predrilled hole in the wall. Press the head against the wall so the ridges on the collar dig in.

3. Insert a nail to unfold the wings behind the wall (in the case of a hollow wall or door).

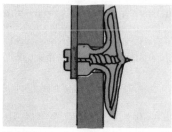

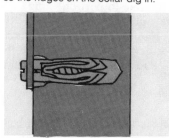

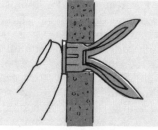

4A. Drive a sheet metal screw, with the fixture attached, into the wall. On a hollow door the toggle anchor acts like a toggle bolt.

4B. In a solid wall the device acts like an expansion anchor, because the toggle wings can only expand to fill the cavity.

4C. In a thick, hollow wall, as of gyp-sumboard, the wings open partially. In this case they both cling to the hole and press the back of the wall.

4. BUILDING NEW WALLS

Before

Make or break a room

To anyone who is new at home renovation, wall construction may seem like a formidable task. To be sure, a fair amount of know-how and dexterity are needed. But of all the major changes that can be made in a house, interior wall additions and improvements are by far the simplest. In fact, anyone who can handle basic hand tools will have little trouble building a wall or upgrading an existing wall.

There are several ways a new wall can benefit your home. You may have a large bedroom, for example, which could be divided into two smaller ones for a growing family. Or, perhaps you'd like to portion off a section of a large dining or living room for a den, family room, or library. The most usual areas for new walls, however, are the basement and attic, where you can add new living space without expensive structural additions. (These rooms will also require new ceilings.)

How you build a wall depends on where it is. First, we'll give you the basics for building partitions in the main rooms of the house, then we'll show the differences for basement and attic walls. The one aspect we won't get into, because you shouldn't either, is tearing down an existing wall. If it's a bearing wall, it *mustn't* be torn down. If not, it's still a job that calls for professional expertise, and there can be a lot of problems, such as in-wall plumbing, wiring, and heating ducts. In addition, it's difficult to do the job without damaging adjacent ceilings and floors, and even if you get past all the pitfalls, you'll still have to conceal the scars that are left.

Planning hints

Your first task is to decide what type of finishing material you will use. Are you going to use plain gypsum wallboard, wood paneling, ceramic tile, or some other material? Most materials work best with a wallboard backing. Consider where the doors, if any, will be located, and whether there will be pass-throughs or any other type of opening. Draw up a plan showing where the wall will be, and where you

AND IMPROVING OLD ONES

After

expect it to butt the other walls.

But before you settle on a final plan, check the locations of existing studs and joists in the wall(s) and ceiling that will meet with the proposed addition. If it is at all possible, plan to position the new wall so it adjoins these solid structural members. If the new wall will run across the ceiling joists, there will be no problem, for it will be tied to many joists along its length. But if the wall runs parallel with the joists, plan to build it directly beneath any one of them; and in any case, try to align the new wall with existing wall studs. (All these compromises will usually mean changing the plan by less than 8 inches in one direction or the other.) Joists and studs can usually be found by tapping a wall or ceiling lightly in straight lines with a hammer. Wherever the low-pitched hollow sound of the hammer sharpens into a solid sound, you have found a stud or a joist. Determine which way the board runs, and mark its center with a line on the wall. Almost certainly, a joist will run from one end of the room to the other, and its companions will be found on either side

at 16-inch intervals. Studs in walls will usually run from floor to ceiling and will be found to meet with the joists at the ceiling line. If you have trouble locating studs and joists, buy a stud-finder, an inexpensive magnetic device which locates these members for you by homing in on the nails that are invariably found in them.

Since the type of wall you'll be building will be nonbearing, 2x3 lumber should be sturdy enough. If you have a cathedral or other high ceiling, however, you may have to resort to 2x4s for greater stability. And, if you're building beneath a beam in the basement, 2x4s or even wider lumber may be needed to enclose the full width of the beam and its supporting columns while keeping an even surface.

Normal stud spacing is 16 inches "o.c." (on center). But for nonbearing walls, 24-inch spacing is all you really need, and it will save you time and money. But check local building codes and the manufacturer's recommendations on the finishing material you choose. It may be that codes or the materials require 16-inch centers or 2x4 lumber.

Building codes

Most of the work discussed in this section can be accomplished without worrying about building codes. The one area where you might run into potential violations is in framing walls. However, most building codes have little or nothing to say about nonbearing walls, and this is the kind you're most likely to be building. It's wise to check the local code, just in case, but you needn't anticipate any problems.

On the other hand, if you are planning to incorporate electrical or plumbing fixtures into your wall, then there will definitely be regulations to comply with, and you may even be required to apply for a permit and submit to inspections at various stages.

Framing a wall

What it takes

Approximate time: Four to eight hours for an average wall.

Tools and materials: Claw hammer, crosscut or circular saw, spirit level or plumb line, folding or metal rule, framing square, 2x3 or 2x4 lumber, 16d and 8d common nails.

If there are existing studs and joists to nail into, of if there are solid materials such as thick wood paneling or brick, no wall preparation is required. But when there is no solid material to nail into, you have to provide it. Remove all wallcovering down to the framing on either side of the wall where the partition is to be butted. Since the existing wallcovering will have to be replaced, you must provide a nailing surface for it as well as for the new wall. The best way to do this is to nail two studs together and fit them into the existing wall frame at the point where the new wall is to tie into it. If you plan to construct the new wall with 2x4 lumber (first illustration at left), you will have to insert spacer blocks at least ½-inch thick between the new studs, since the combined thickness of the two 2x4s will be only 3 inches, ½ inch less than the face of the 2x4 that will be nailed to them (see box below). But if you plan to frame the new wall with 2x3 lumber (second illustration at left), spacers will not be necessary because the face of a 2x3 measures only 2½ inches, providing plenty of room to receive the nails that will fasten the new wall to it. An alternate method is to use a 1x6 or 2x6 nailing board, held in place from behind by three or four short lengths of 2x4 nailed between existing studs (third illustration at left).

If you *must* put the partition between two parallel joists (and this should be avoided if at all possible), you will have to remove all the ceiling material on either side of the new wall location as far as the adjacent joists. In this case, put nailing

blocks between the joists at approximately 2-foot intervals, placing them 1½ inches above the joist bottoms. Nail a 2x6 into the blocks to serve as a nailing surface both for the replaced ceiling material and for the top plate of the new wall.

There are several ways to frame an inside partition. One way is to build it stud-by-stud. Another is to construct the frame on the floor and lift it into place when it is finished (see photograph above). This method can be tricky, however, because if the ceiling material is already in place, the new wall will catch on the ceiling as you try to raise it to the upright position.

To avoid this problem, you can build the wall slightly smaller than its finished height and raise it into position with the help of shims underneath. For a stronger wall, make the top-to-bottom measurements of the framing 1½ inches less than required, and then have a helper slip another 2x4 underneath the wall while you hold up the frame.

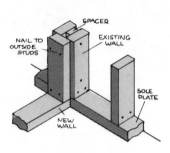

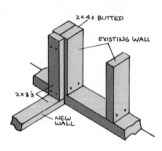

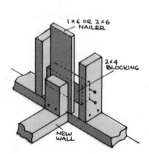

Lumber inflation

It's a curious fact that the names of the standard lumber sizes have nothing in common with what you get when you order them. One might expect a piece of 2x4 stock, for example, to measure 2 inches by 4 inches. Not so!—and you must be careful about this in framing walls or doing any other precision carpentry. (When fractions matter, measure all wood before using it.) Indeed, lumber sizes have been shrinking alarmingly over the past few years. A standard 2x4, now measuring only 1½ by 3½ inches, contains 34% less wood than its name says it should. Part, but not all, of this loss can be blamed on the finishing machinery that smooths the lumber. But in recent memory a 2x4 measured 1¾ x 3¾; then it was 1⅝ x 3⅝, and so on. The ripoff has now reached as high as 44% on some sizes. The following table shows nominal sizes of standard lumber, actual dimensions, and percentage of loss.

Nominal	Actual	Loss
1x1	¾″x¾″	44%
1x2	¾″x1½″	44%
1x4	¾″x3½″	34%
1x6	¾″x5½″	31%
1x8	¾″x7¼″	32%
1x10	¾″x9¼″	31%
1x12	¾″x11¼″	30%
2x2	1½″x1½″	44%
2x3	1½″x2½″	38%
2x4	1½″x3½″	34%
2x6	1½″x5½″	31%
2x8	1½″x7¼″	32%
2x10	1½″x9¼″	31%
2x12	1½″x11¼″	30%

Stud spacing on sole plate and top plate: 16″ o.c.

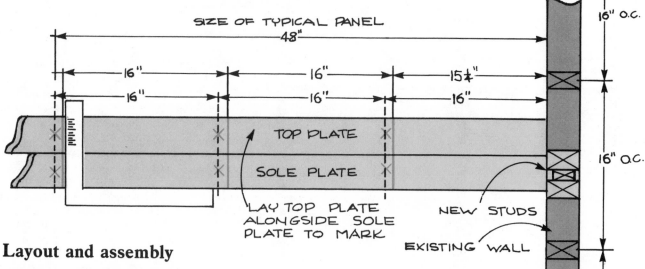

Layout and assembly

Select two long straight pieces of lumber for the top plate and bottom (sole) plate. Cut them to the desired size—the full length of the proposed wall; then lay them on the floor side-by-side with the ends even, as shown above. Mark an "X" on one end of each plate where the corner stud is to go. The center of the next stud should be located exactly 16 (or 24) inches from the *outside edge* of the first stud. Therefore, the near edge of the second stud will be 15¼ (or 23¼) inches from the outside edge of the corner stud. Measure this distance; then hold one end of the framing square flush with the edge of the plate and make a right-angle mark at its other end across both plates. (The two legs of a framing square measure 16 and 24 inches, and were designed expressly for this purpose.)

Determine the locations for the remaining studs by holding the square along the plates and making new marks every 16 (or 24) inches. Each time you make a line, mark an "X" ahead of it to show on which side of the line the stud should be nailed. If you are planning to include a door or other opening in the new wall, refer now to the instructions on page 34.

Cut studs to size, measuring from floor to ceiling and deducting a total of 3 inches for the two plates plus any space required for shims or a second sole plate. When building your wall on the ground, nail two 16-penny nails through each plate into the end of each stud. When building in place, use 8-penny nails and "toenail" (nail diagonally) through the stud into the plate. Hold the stud with your foot or free hand to keep it from slipping while you drive nails into each side (below, left). Or start the stud about ¼ inch from the line in the direction from which you're nailing. The hammering will force the stud about ¼ inch to the other side of the line, and it will be easy to drive it back on target from that side with the second nail. After each stud is secured at top and bottom, use a plumb line or spirit level to make sure it is perfectly vertical (below); if an adjustment is necessary, make it by hammering the stud in the direction it needs to go.

While toenailing into a sole plate, block the stud with your foot to keep it in place as you hammer.

Use a level or plumb bob to check the lie of each stud as soon as you have secured it to the plates.

Toenailing

Framing doors and other openings

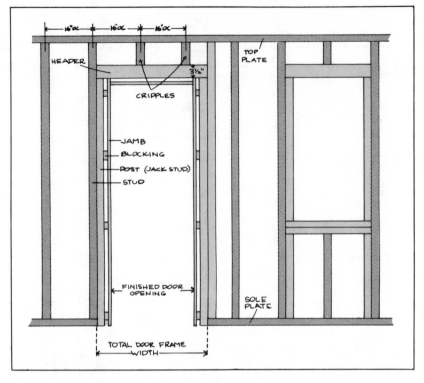

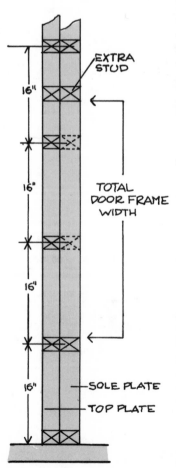

plate that lies within the door frame area (and, of course, you can forget about putting up the studs you may have previously marked in the opening). After assembling the sole plate sections, studs, and top plate, as described on page 33, cut two lengths of the framing wood you've been using (2x4 or 2x3), making them 1 inch longer than the height of the proposed door. Nail these boards, known as jack studs or door posts, to the door frame studs, as illustrated at left. Notice that the door posts are the only framing members that extend to the bottom of the sole plate, but unlike the others they don't reach the top plate. Instead, they must support a header or lintel, which is simply the top of the door frame. For stability, the lintel should consist of at least two boards joined back-to-back and fastened on edge to the tops of the posts. If the posts are of 2x4 lumber, the lintel can be formed of two 2x4s separated by a spacer of ½-inch plywood. The total width (1½″ + ½″ + 1½″) must equal the 3½-inch depth of the posts. If the posts are of 2x3 lumber—2½ inches deep—make the lintel from a 2x4 and a 1x4 with a ¼-inch spacer in

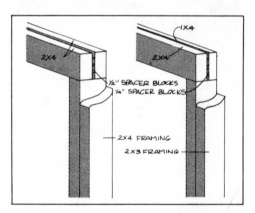

between (1½″ + ¼″ +¾″). After securing the lintel to the post with 16-penny nails, insert short studs, known as cripples, from the top of the lintel to the top plate, on the same 16- or 24-inch centers as the rest of the framing. You are now ready to fit a prehung door into the opening, following the manufacturer's instructions.

Pass-throughs, windows, and other openings are framed in the same way, except that a double 2x3 or 2x4 is needed on the bottom for a sill. Jack studs support the sill, additional jack studs support the header, and cripple studs are nailed on top of the header as well as below the sill (illustration, top left).

Try to plan doorways and other openings so they fall in places that require the least cutting and fitting of wall materials. There is a temptation to select a pair of studs (spaced one stud apart on 16-inch centers) as the uprights of the door frame, since the 30½-inch span of two stud intervals seems to be about the right size for a door. But by the time additional framing is added, the actual doorway will shrink to 25½ inches, and that's pretty skimpy, except perhaps for a closet door. A standard doorway should be about 30 inches wide. So chances are your frame opening will have to be more than two stud intervals wide. Start by selecting the finished door width you want and adding 5 inches to that (3 inches for posts and 2 for jambs). This figure is your total door frame width, as shown in the illustration above. Then, after you have marked the locations of all the wall studs (page 33), select any convenient stud to serve as one of the door frame members, and measure the total door frame width from that point along the plates. At the end of the measured span, mark the location for an extra stud to serve as the second door frame member (see illustration at left).

Next, whether you are working with the wall frame in place or preassembling it on the floor, cut away the part of the sole

Framing basement walls

While basic framing is the same no matter where the wall is, there are some differences for basements. For one thing, you cannot trust basement floors to be level. Unless your spirit level shows the contrary, it is better to attach the top and sole plates separately, using a plumb bob or spirit level with a straightedge to make sure they are on the same plane. Measure and cut the studs individually, then toenail them to the plates at top and bottom.

Obstructions are another problem. Meter boxes, plumbing, and other objects frequently get in the way. The best way to work around them is to make the ceiling as low as possible. Suspended ceilings (page 50) are ideal here and require no framing. If your ceiling is too low already, box the obstructions in with 2x2 lumber. There is

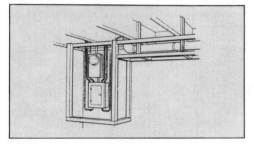

no general procedure for doing this, because no two basements are alike. Start with wall or ceiling framing and box out the obstructions with lumber until they

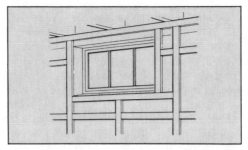

are completely framed in. (Don't close off things like meters, valves, or anything else you may need access to. If they are located in a boxed-in area, provide access with little doors.)

Framing over masonry walls can be done by fastening furring strips (1x2s or 1x3s) either horizontally or vertically, depending on the material. Use nails or one of the fasteners shown in the table on pages 26-27 to attach the furring.

Use furring also to frame around basement windows. If there is enough clearance to allow the windows to open, you can extend the finished material into the window niche (illustration, above).

Before attaching anything to basement walls or floors, make sure that all problems with dampness have been discovered and cured. For extra insurance against damp walls, staple a layer of polyethylene to masonry walls before you attach the furring or framing.

Framing attic walls

Most attic rooms have sloping ceilings following the roof line. When constructing a partition under the rafters, it is best to nail down the sole plate first, and then fasten short (dwarf) studs alongside each rafter. Rafters will usually be spaced 16 inches apart, except perhaps, in very old houses. Dwarf studs are used to create the low (knee) walls seen in finished attics.

To form a knee wall fasten studs at each end, using a level to make sure they are plumb. Then snap a chalk line between the tops of the two studs across the bottoms of all the rafters. This allows you to properly line up each short stud. Check your work with a long straightedge after each stud is installed to ensure a straight wall line.

The attic should also have collar beams already installed overhead, holding the rafters together and usually spaced on every third set of rafters (see illustration

below). If these are level (as they should be), they can serve as ceiling joists for the room. Simply install similar beams (2x4s will do) between the rafters where they are missing. Again, a line and straightedge will ensure your keeping them level.

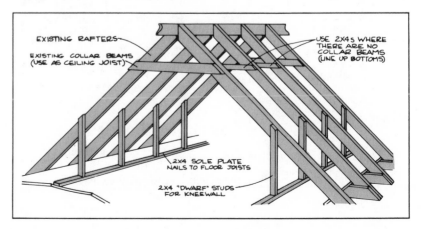

EXISTING RAFTERS

EXISTING COLLAR BEAMS (USE AS CEILING JOIST)

USE 2X4S WHERE THERE ARE NO COLLAR BEAMS (LINE UP BOTTOMS)

2X4 SOLE PLATE NAILS TO FLOOR JOISTS

2X4 "DWARF" STUDS FOR KNEEWALL

Insulation

Now that your wall is nicely framed, install all necessary electrical, plumbing, and heating connections. The next question is whether or not you need insulation. In the type of walls being built here, the answer is normally not. Interior partitions are usually heated on both sides, and the only time insulation is of any benefit is when you want to keep the heat (or air-conditioning) where it is and the elements out.

The attic is the one outstanding exception to this. In most cases, there will be insulation between the joists which are below your new attic floor. If flooring is already in place, just leave the insulation where it is. It will do neither good nor harm there, and it isn't worth the bother of digging it out. When the insulation is exposed, you can take it out and reuse it if it is still in good shape.

In any case, you will decidedly need insulation in the walls and ceiling of your new attic room. Even if you don't plan on heating it, the insulation will keep it cooler in summer. Insulation should be placed between all the studs and joists of the new space (except for any partitions between rooms). In these days of high energy costs, always buy the insulating material with the highest efficiency rating you can afford.

Basements do not usually need insulation. The thick masonry walls, plus the earth on the other side, provide plenty of insulation of their own. But if you live in an area with extremely cold winters and particularly if your house is heated electrically, you may wish to add insulation to the outside walls. In that event, use regular 2x4 framing instead of furring.

In mild-winter areas, basement rooms do not ordinarily require heat. Colder regions should have some form of heat, and it is wise to insulate any partitions between living and storage areas.

Installing gypsum wallboard

What it takes

Approximate time: Four to six hours per average wall.

Tools and materials: You'll definitely need wallboard panels (4x8 or 4x10 are recommended), drywall nails or screws, a hammer, a utility knife, a long straightedge, and a ruler. You may also need a keyhole saw and a spirit level. If you are using wallboard merely as a backing for other material, you can dispense with the following, which are needed only for finish work: joint cement, joint tape, joint knife, steel trowel, medium-grade (80-grit) sandpaper, and possibly metal corner-bead (for outside corners).

Planning hints: Low cost and good appearance make wallboard, in our opinion, an outstanding bargain among wall materials. To select the most economical way to cover your walls, and to determine the size and number of sheets you'll need, make an accurate map of your walls and draw on it the outline of panels in various configurations. Add 15% to the bare minimum order to allow for cutting and breakage. In addition you'll need 1 pound of nails, 1 gallon of joint cement, and 70 feet of joint tape for every 200 square feet of wall area. It's best to have at least one helper with you.

Stop pops

Nail pops are often a problem in humid climates or where moist wood had been used for framing. But you can banish them once and for all, as I did, by doubling nails. Instead of driving a single nail every 7 inches like the books say, drive a pair of nails an inch or 2 apart every 8 inches. This will increase your nailing time (unless you can hammer two-handed). But think of it as a small insurance policy against a big refinishing job (page 24).

Practical Pete

Now for the most enjoyable part of wall-building. Chances are you've already chosen a finishing material, but if you haven't gone wall-shopping lately, you may be in for a pleasant surprise. You'll find an endless array of paneling—both natural wood and prefinished hardboard in various forms. There'll be accurately simulated wood grains and masonry, some with special effects, fiberglass panels, plastic laminates, mirror tiles, pegboard, imitation brick, and a host of other fascinating finishing materials.

Almost any wall material you choose, except for solid wood and some thick paneling, will require a backing of gypsum wallboard. And if what you want is a plain wall (for painting or wallpapering), wallboard is *all* you'll need. Installing wallboard involves some of the techniques discussed in chapter 2, but there's more to it when you're putting it up from scratch.

Gypsum wallboard comes in panels of many sizes, the most common being 4x8, 4x10, 4x12, and 4x16 feet. The larger the sheets you use, the less work you'll have in finishing them—a significant bonus because finishing is the most arduous part of the task. But larger sheets are also heavier, more difficult to maneuver, and therefore more fragile. Most homeowners prefer the 4x8 or 4x10 panels.

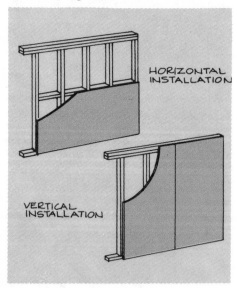

Before you buy, figure out whether you will be installing the panels horizontally or vertically. Horizontal application is usually more economical, but it depends on the wall, how many openings there are, and so forth. An extra advantage of mounting the panels horizontally is that you'll be taping the joints all on one level, without having to stretch or bend. But you'll have to pay for this convenience by installing backing blocks between the wall studs for nailing the edge of the panel to the frame (below left). In short, one way is about as good as the other.

Attach wallboard to the framing with the annular nails or screws pictured on page 24. Have an assistant hold the panel in place—or if you're working alone, apply it vertically and shim it up from the floor—while you fasten the top corners as close as possible to the ceiling or to a panel already in place above.

Be sure the vertical edges of the panel are centered on studs. (Panel spans of 4, 8, 12, and 16 feet can be made to begin and end precisely on stud centers, regardless of whether the wall was framed at 16- or 24-inch intervals. Only a 10-foot panel, mounted horizontally, is limited to the use of 24-inch stud intervals.) Once the top corners are secured, check to see that the panel is square with the ceiling line and studs; then fasten the lower corners. Drive nails or screws at 7-inch intervals around the perimeter (about ⅜ inch in from the edge) and along the studs. Dimple the nails, as described on page 24.

Cutting wallboard

Even if you were clever enough to buy panel lengths to fit your ceiling height or room width (and to cover near misses with moldings or tape), eventually you must meet up with a window, door, wall outlet, or other obstruction that calls for cutting. The best technique for straight cuts (score-fold-slit) is shown on opposite page. Few obstacles allow such a simple solution. Because wallboard panels are recessed

along the edges to camouflage joint tape, any time a beveled edge is removed and the resulting unbeveled edge is used at a seam, the taping job will become more difficult. So don't lop off a factory edge if you can help it; instead, try to work around obstructions by cutting the panels into square-edged L, C, or even O-shapes (right). Such cuts are more difficult but will save you work in the end. To form an L-shaped piece, measure the obstruction carefully and draw the outline of the cut on the face of the panel. Use a utility knife or saw blade to cut the shorter line all the way through the panel, extending a fraction of an inch past the end of the longer line (right). Then score-fold-split the longer line as you would a simple cut. For a C- or O-shape, cut all but the longest line all the way through the panel; then score-fold-slit the remaining cut (below). Slip the panel into place around the obstruction, and nail it up as usual (below right).

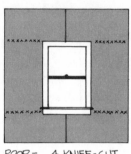

POOR— 4 KNIFE-CUT JOINTS

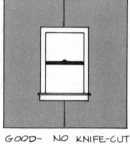

GOOD— NO KNIFE-CUT JOINTS

SAW

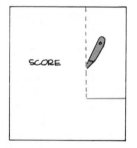

SCORE

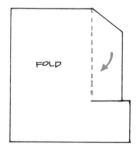

FOLD

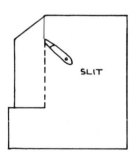

SLIT

Cutting indentations in wallboard is a snap. Saw all but the longest edge; then score, fold, slit.

Having completed the cutout, slip the panel into place, check alignment, and nail it to the framing.

NEW WALLS 37

Cutting pockets in wallboard

Cramped for work space?
A 4x8 sheet of wallboard can be pretty unwieldy in narrow halls and small rooms. And I've broken at least one panel, and gouged a few others, by trying to carry them full-size around tight corners. You can save yourself a lot of trouble by setting up a couple of sawhorses outdoors and cutting your pieces there to exact size before carrying them into the house. (Keep an eye on the weather, though. Moisture can ruin gypsum products.)

Practical Pete

Probably more blunders are made on cutouts, or "pockets," for wall switches, light fixtures, and the like, than on all other wallboarding operations combined. Our advice here is to heed the old saw "measure twice, cut once"; in fact measure twice, *twice:* first take the distance from the ceiling (or next-higher panel) to the top of the obstruction, then the height of the obstruction; then the distance to the adjacent panel or room corner, and finally the width of the obstruction. In the illustration at right, these distances are marked A, B, C, and D, respectively. Before marking the panel for cutting, remind yourself which corner will go where. Here, the notation "TL" stands for Top Left, the common point of reference for the four measurements. On the face of the panel, measure and mark the vertical distances from the top along both side edges, and the horizontal distances

from the left side along the top and bottom edges. Use a straightedge to connect the marks with long intersecting lines; the little rectangle formed where the lines cross will mark the cutout pocket.

Drill holes in two diagonally opposite corners of the rectangle. To be sure of adequate clearance, drill slightly outside the pencil rectangle. Use a keyhole saw to cut out the opening.

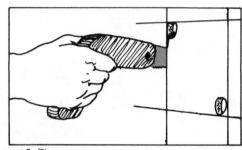

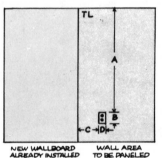

NEW WALLBOARD
ALREADY INSTALLED

WALL AREA
TO BE PANELED

PRECUTTING POCKET
ON NEW PANEL

Taping joints

Wallboard joints can be finished so cleverly that it is impossible to tell where they are on the wall. But most of us aren't that clever. You may let out a few expletives the first few times, but be patient and keep at it. You'll get it—eventually.

First fill in the area between the panels, covering the nails on both sides and slightly beyond. About 3 inches is right. The compound should be applied quite thickly, but not so thick that it forms a bump. While the compound is still wet, take the wallboard tape and center it over the joint, unrolling it from the top down, or side to side. Press the tape into the seam with your joint knife, held at about a 45-degree angle. Since the tape is perforated, some joint compound will ooze through, making a better bond.

Let the compound dry. Meanwhile, you

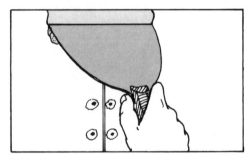

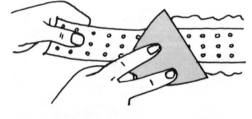

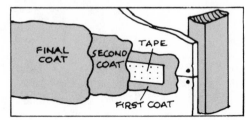

FINAL COAT   SECOND COAT   TAPE

FIRST COAT

can use the same material to cover the nailheads between joints. After the first coat hardens, go back and apply a second coat of joint compound, feathering it out to the width of your knife. This time try to

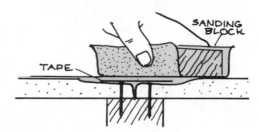

give the surface a finished look. When dry again, go over it a third time, feathering out even further until you get a perfectly uniform surface. A wide trowel will speed the work at this stage. The experts recommend a 12-14-inch seam, but 8-10 inches is adequate in most cases.

While the last coat is drying, go over the other nailheads again, filling in where the compound has shrunk or where you missed last time. Return to the joint after it has dried and sand it and the other nailheads down lightly with medium-grit abrasive paper and a sanding block.

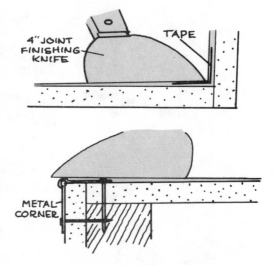

Finishing corners

Inside wallboard corners are finished like regular joints, except that the tape is creased down the center and attached to both walls (right). Metal edging, called "bead" is used for outside corners. Nail through the holes into the wood framing behind the wallboard (lower right). Give it a coat of joint compound, feathering out slightly; then another coat, etc.

None of the above is necessary if the wallboard is simply a backing for paneling or other permanent material. You will have to cover the joints for wallpaper, but you don't have to be quite so fussy if you don't want to. Some materials, like vinyl-covered wallboard, have built-in flaps, which are simply cemented over the next panel.

Stopgaps and copouts:
You can save yourself the muss and fuss of taping and spackling, while at the same time giving your room an Elizabethan-cottage look. After hanging and painting the raw wallboard, fasten strips of lattice or molding over the seams and nailheads, driving them directly into the wall studs. (Of course, you must mount the wallboard vertically.) Stain or paint the strips the same color as the baseboard and ceiling trim. It's fast work and won't cost much more than a standard finish.

Putting up paneling

The most popular types of paneling are tongue-and-groove-jointed natural wood, hardwood veneer plywood, and woodgrain hardboard. Natural wood can be purchased unfinished or prefinished, while hardboard and some veneers come with a plastic coating for wipe-clean maintenance, which is especially desirable where young children will be making extensive use of the room. In addition to the familiar wood grains (ranging from "barn siding" to such exotics as pecky cypress), panels may be finished to resemble marble, mosaic, or natural wood flake. Some are embossed to imitate burlap, basketweave, wicker, leather, and other materials. There are even plain panels with a synthetic finish in many solid colors. Paneling can be quite inexpensive, but the difference in price among the various types may run to thirtyfold or more, so shop carefully and compare costs.

Most paneling comes in 4-by-8-foot sheets, although 4-by-7-foot sheets are available in some types, while others come in tongue-and-groove-jointed lumber or 16-inch-wide planks. If your room is much higher than 8 feet, you may be able to make up the difference with an oversize baseboard and ceiling molding. Or you can install more paneling to fill the gap, but leave a painted 1- or 2-inch horizontal shadow line between the top of the lower and the bottom of the upper paneling pieces, rather than butting them tightly. (Molding can go over this later, if desired.) Still another possibility is to install a narrow display shelf to hide the open joint.

Where no backing is required, the panels are fastened directly to the studs or furring strips. A few types require special clips, but most are simply nailed or glued in place. Gluing is generally recommended for best results, but finishing nails driven into the grooves in the panel are good too.

Cut panels with a crosscut hand saw or, preferably, a table saw (face up), or a portable circular or saber saw (face down). Allow about an inch for clearance when cutting panels to height; this will be concealed by molding later on.

Starting at one corner of the room, use a caulking gun to apply panel adhesive on the full face of each stud or furring strip to be covered by the first panel. Set the panel in place with small wedges beneath, but don't apply pressure yet. Use a spirit level or plumb bob to make sure that the outside edge of the panel is perfectly plumb. If it isn't, you'll have problems with each succeeding panel. So it is best to pull the panel slightly away from the top or bottom corner to plumb it; any gaps will be covered later by the adjacent panel or by corner molding. At the same time, make sure the outer edge of the panel falls over the middle of a stud or furring strip. If it doesn't, take down the panel and trim it to fit along the edge.

When you are satisfied with the positioning of the first panel, drive a few nails along the top edge to hold it in place. Then pull the panel bottom away from the wall, and keep it from making contact with the adhesive by inserting a piece of scrap wood. The nails at the top will keep it from sliding out of position. Allow the adhesive to dry for about 10 minutes; then remove the block and press the panel into place. Using a scrap piece of 2x4 with some cloth underneath to avoid damaging the paneling, whack along the studs with a hammer to make sure that there is tight contact. Drive a few nails in along the bottom of the paneling for the same reason. (These nails will be covered later by a molding.)

Once the corner piece is in place, the rest of the panels go up quickly. Apply the adhesive, butt the new panel against the last one, and proceed as above. Some paneling manufacturers recommend a 1/32-inch gap between. When you get to the last panel, measure the distance between the preceding panel and the adjacent wall at both bottom and top. (Walls are rarely exactly plumb.) Cut to this exact shape, less ¼ inch. Don't worry about slight gaps when cutting at corners. Molding covers a mul-

What it takes

Approximate time: Three to four hours for an average wall.

Tools and materials: Paneling of your choice with matching or stock moldings, matching nails or finishing nails as recommended, black spray paint, claw hammer, crosscut saw (or, preferably, a power saw), spirit level or plumb bob, electric drill, framing or try square, coping saw and miter box with backsaw for moldings, nailset, caulking gun and adhesive cartridges if you plan to glue the panels in place, and finishing materials as recommended by the manufacturer.

Planning hints: Paneling comes in various thicknesses, and the thinner types should be installed over some sort of backing (an existing wall or new gypsumboard) for strength and rigidity. To be safe, follow the manufacturer's recommendation on this point.

Panels should be allowed to acclimate to the room for at least 48 hours before installation. Separate the panels during this period, and stand them on their long edges.

To determine how many pieces of 4x8 paneling you need, measure the perimeter of the room, divide by four and add one more panel for waste. Deduct panels as follows:
Each standard window - ¼ panel
Each standard door - ⅓ panel
Average fireplace - ½ panel

If your total includes a fraction of a panel, buy the additional panel, plus the extra one recommended. If you finish the job with a whole extra panel, you can probably return it. But it's better to save it in case patching is necessary later. As styles change, it's hard to duplicate paneling years later.

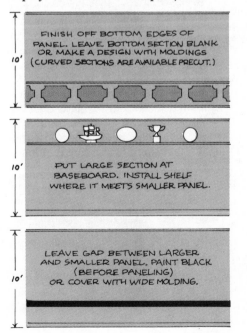

FINISH OFF BOTTOM EDGES OF PANEL. LEAVE BOTTOM SECTION BLANK OR MAKE A DESIGN WITH MOLDINGS (CURVED SECTIONS ARE AVAILABLE PRECUT.)

10'

PUT LARGE SECTION AT BASEBOARD. INSTALL SHELF WHERE IT MEETS SMALLER PANEL.

10'

LEAVE GAP BETWEEN LARGER AND SMALLER PANEL. PAINT BLACK (BEFORE PANELING) OR COVER WITH WIDE MOLDING.

10'

But it's not enough to butt
No matter how careful I was to butt one panel tightly against another, here and there minute but painfully visible white cracks showed between the panels. Later, when I looked at my brother-in-law's paneling and couldn't see any cracks, I asked him how the heck he did it. "Oh, the spaces are there, all right," he said, "but I camouflaged them by first spraying black paint on the backerboard."

Practical Pete

titude of sins. Electrical outlets and other obstructions are dealt with in nearly the same way as for wallboard. Drill holes at the corners of the pocket cut and connect them with a keyhole saw.

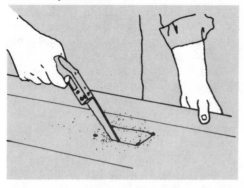

To fasten paneling to a backerboard, apply the adhesive to either the front of the backing or the back of the paneling. Apply a bead along the edges, and make a zig-zag pattern or squiggly "X" down the middle. The other steps are the same as for application to framing.

Paneling is generally thought of as large 4x8 sheets, but the term also applies to strips of lumber or plastic. To install this type of paneling, attach furring strips to the framing or right over existing walls. For vertical installation, mount furring horizontally; for horizontal installation, mount it vertically; for diagonal installation, mount it either way. The lumber strips are then nailed into the furring, but the plastic strips come with their own invisible attachment clips. Lumber should be completely stained and coated with varnish or other finishing materials before being nailed up. Much of this type of lumber comes

tongue-and-grooved for blind-nailing through each tongue. Nailheads which show, at edges and corners, can be set and filled with wood putty, or covered by moldings or baseboards.

Working with moldings

Moldings are used to cover up defects or simply to trim off a wall. Matched moldings are available for most prefinished paneling; some even include nails with heads colored to match. If you use regular finishing nails, set them below the surface of the molding and fill the holes with matching wood putty. Colored nailheads need no special treatment.

Install moldings at the ceiling line and baseboard (but only after the ceiling and floor have been finished). Where the moldings meet at corners, you can either miter them (cut them both at 45-degree angles like a picture frame) or cope them (cut one molding to fit the curve of the other). This decision will depend partly on the type of molding you choose. Whether you miter or cope, you'll need a wooden or, preferably, a metal miter

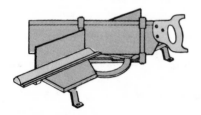

box. With your box, you should also have a good backsaw. Properly used, the backsaw and miter box can give you cuts so accurate that two 45-degree molding ends should meet in a perfect right angle.

To miter or cope a molding, start by setting it upright in the miter box in the position it is to hold on the wall. Press the molding end against the backplate, and trim it at a 45-degree

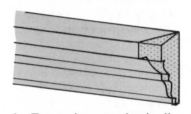

angle. For a miter cut, that is all you do, but for a coped joint, saw away the wedge-shaped excess along the mitered line so the angle from front to

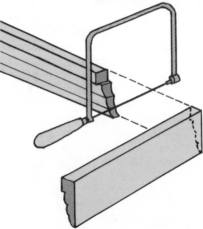

back of the molding is again 90 degrees. The resulting curve should fit nicely against the face of the adjoining piece of molding.

The simpler the molding, the likelier it is to lend itself to a miter cut; the fancier and more complex its curves, the more apt it is to require coping. But the general rule that says "miter outside corners and cope inside corners" will lead you to a good result most of the time.

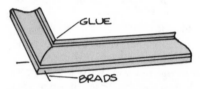

TIPS: For a tight miter joint use brads and glue. When fastening a molding to an irregular wall, nail at the gaps to pull any potential belly tight against the wall. Whenever possible, hide your nails in the recesses of patterned moldings. To cover a long stretch that requires more than one piece of molding, miter the joining edges at a matching angle (45 degrees is fine) instead of a square butt joint.

Some paneling requires special moldings which must be applied before the paneling is put up. (The panel simply slides into the molding.) For this reason, be sure to pick out moldings at the same time you purchase the paneling.

Applying ceramic tile

Tiling would be simple if all walls were built perfectly plumb and level, but in this imperfect world you can expect every corner to be at least slightly tilted from a perfect right angle. Since this is so, you cannot start to tile where logic would dictate: in a corner. Instead begin by locating the lowest spot where you expect to tile. If you are doing a complete wall, find the low point on the wall and start there. If you are working above a tub, use a level to find out the low point at the top of the tub. Place one tile on top of the low point and make a mark along its top edge. If you are using a ceramic

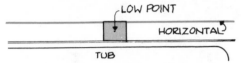

cove base, put a regular tile on top of a cove tile before marking. With the level and a straightedge draw a horizontal line level with the mark. Next, take a scrap of lumber about 3 or 4 feet long with straight edges and lay out some tiles along it, butted as they would be when installed. Make marks at each joint. Measure and mark the center

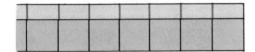

of the wall, and align one of the marks on the stick with this mark in order to gauge how wide the end tile would be. If it is

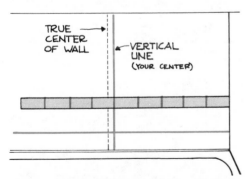

narrower than half a tile width, move the center mark half a tile width to the left or right. Draw a vertical starting line from the center mark, using the level and the straightedge as a guide.

Beginning at the intersection of the horizontal and vertical lines, cover an area of about 10 to 20 square feet with tile adhesive, applied with a notched trowel. Be careful to leave just enough space so you can see the lines. Apply each tile with a slight twisting motion, but do not slide it into

place. Give it a final tap to insure good adhesion. Work along one line, and then build up in step fashion. Once you get the

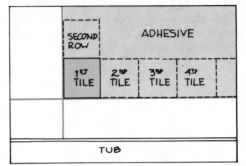

first few tiles installed correctly, the others should fall into place without much difficulty. Continue until the section is filled, then go on to the next in the same way.

Install all the whole field tile first, then proceed to the edge tiles. The easiest way to cut ceramic tiles is with a special tile cutter. The dealer will probably rent or lend you one. The cutter both scores and breaks the tile, but be careful not to press too hard when scoring, or the tile will break where you don't want it to. You can also cut tile by scoring with a glass cutter and straightedge, then snapping it over a wire hanger or similar rounded object.

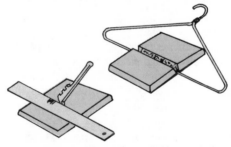

Fitting tile around obstructions can be a problem. If a pipe or fixture falls at the edge of a tile, that section can be nibbled off with a tile nipper or a pair of pliers. Always take small bites, or the tile will break. When the obstruction is near the center of the tile, cut through the middle carefully and nibble at

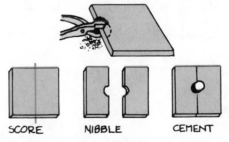

it from the cut line. Then fit the two pieces over the obstruction and cement them in place. The line will be barely noticeable.

What it takes

Approximate time: Eight to 12 hours for a typical tub area.

Tools and materials: Ceramic wall tile in single units or pre-grouted sheets, specialized tile if needed (see below), adhesive, grout or silicone rubber cartridge with caulking gun, spirit level, folding or steel rule, electric drill, tile cutter or glasscutter and coat-hanger, tile nippers or pliers, rod-saw blade in hacksaw frame, notched trowel, center punch, and sponge or squeegee.

Planning hints: Ceramic tile is only as good as the wall behind it and the care of its application. If you are putting up a new wall, get special water-resistant wallboard for tiling around bathtubs and showers. If you are tiling over an existing wall, make sure that the surface is sound, clean, dry, and free of grease and old wallpaper. Regular tile can be used for inside corners and at the base, but you may need outside corners, cove tiles, or other specialized pieces.

Estimating ceramic tile quantities is a bit tricky. One way to do it is to give your dealer the dimensions of your room (a scale plan is best) and let him do the work. The size and shape of some tiles make it very difficult to guess accurately. If you are using the standard 4¼-by-4¼-inch tiles, however, you can get a pretty fair estimate by the following method:
1. Study your plan and figure out how many specialized tiles (top edging, cove base, corner, etc.) you will need. Write down the number and deduct the space they take on the plan.
2. Using the accompanying table, determine how many tiles will be needed on each dimension. If, for example, your wall is 9 feet, 9 inches long, take the next highest dimension (10 feet) and, referring to the table, you need 29 tiles for that direction. If the other dimension is 8 ft., you need 23 tiles for that. Multiply 29 x 23 to get 667 tiles. Deduct the area covered by windows, doors, etc., and throw in an extra 15-20 tiles for waste and breakage.

Linear feet	Tiles needed
8	23
9	26
10	29
11	32
12	34
13	37
14	40
15	43

TIP: Though the above is the classic way of cutting odd shapes in tile, we find the carbide rod saw easier. This is a round blade fitted into an ordinary hacksaw frame. It saws an accurate line quite quickly. To saw around an obstruction near the center, tap with a center punch, then drill through with a carbide bit at low speed. Push the rod saw blade through the hole, then attach it to the hacksaw frame and cut in any direction.

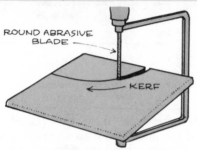

ROUND ABRASIVE BLADE

KERF

Another shortcut is to use prepared sheets of pregrouted tile, usually nine to a

sheet. Installation and grouting time is shortened considerably. At least one company makes even larger sheets in a package especially designed for use as a tub surround. Investigate these kits and compare the extra costs with the value of your time. Read manufacturer's instructions carefully, since many of these kits use silicone rubber or other materials instead of the regular grout discussed below.

Most tile requires grout between the individual tiles. Unless otherwise specified by the manufacturer, use grout powder and mix with water to a spackle-like consistency. There are quite a few different types. Insist on a grout which is waterproof, and stain- and mildew-resistant. Others are tinted to match or contrast with the tile.

Ordinarily, the grout is applied to the entire surface of the tile with a damp rag, squeegee, or sponge. Rub it into all the cracks and corners; then smooth it out with the end of a toothbrush or your finger.

When the grout dries, usually in about half an hour, wipe the tile surface clean with a damp rag and polish with a dry cloth.

Silicone rubber is also used for grouting in many of the multi-tile kits. Apply it with either a caulking gun or a tube made for this purpose. (This is the same material that is usually used for repairs around the top of the tub.)

This rambling, old-time bathroom, completely refinished in tile, invites comparison with the most lavish, modernistic layouts.

Other wall materials

There are several other wall materials you might want to consider. We mention them briefly here, not because they are less worthy of your consideration, but because there are no additional problems involved in their installation. Most are attached over existing walls or new gypsumboard. Some come with their own adhesive.

Imitation masonry. You can create the look of real brick or stone inside the home in several ways. There are panels finished to look like masonry, there are individual units simulated to look like brick that are set into a mastic, and there are multiple units that are attached with nails and screws. The joints are then filled with an authentic-looking "mortar."

Plastics. Both laminated plastics and plasticized hardboard can be used for walls. Use contact cement for the laminated plastics and cut them to shape with a saber saw. A slip sheet must be placed between the panel and the wall, since the adhesive bonds on contact. When the panel is in exactly the right position, pull out the slip sheet (heavy brown paper) a little at a time. Let the top edge bond first, check for true alignment, and slowly pull out the rest of the sheet.

Plasticized hardboard calls for its own special cement, and does not require a slip sheet. This material is especially useful in showers and baths, or other areas where watertightness or easy cleanup is a factor.

Translucent plastics. These are sold by various brand names and are made of various materials, notably acrylics. They are ideal for room dividers or other areas where light can shine through. Numerous colors and textures are available.

Perforated hardboard. This handy paneling is a mainstay in workshops for hanging tools. Assorted hooks and fasteners are inserted in the holes. But it is also made in fancier colors and textures than the natural brown, and can be a definite asset in kitchens, offices, kids' study rooms, and other places where things get lost if they aren't hung up. Perforated hardboard is offset from the wall, so purchase a kit with the appropriate attachments.

Mirror tiles. These come in large squares, either plain or decorative. They are especially useful in smaller rooms, where they can be used to give the illusion of spaciousness (a favorite trick of model-home decorators). They are applied with adhesives as directed by the manufacturer.

Cork. This has become a very expensive item, but it's great for accents and makes an attractive bulletin board. It is available in thick squares or in thin rolls and is applied with a special adhesive.

Tudor-style panels of stucco and timber might even have fooled a Shakespeare.

Panels simulating quarry stone trick the eye but are warm to the touch.

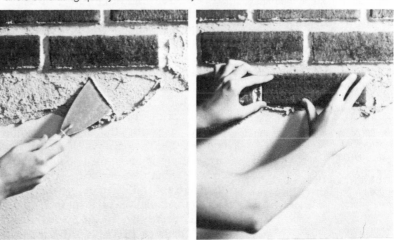

Fake brick veneer is pressed into place in a bed of adhesive that looks like mortar.

5. NEW CEILINGS

For improving existing ceilings or putting up new ones, three or four common options are open to you. If you prefer a painted ceiling, gypsum wallboard is your best bet. It's not an easy job though, and tile ceilings and suspended ceilings are available to simplify your task. With a bit more expense, ceilings can even be paneled in wood or other materials. Less common options include false beams, a stucco finish, wallpaper, ornate Byzantine designs in wood moldings, or even a mural.

Installing wallboard overhead

Though it's relatively easy to install wallboard on a vertical wall (pages 36-37), the weight of the material makes it much harder to put up on a ceiling. If you aren't sure you have the stamina, our advice is to call in a professional wallboard contractor, or else to lower your sights and plan on a tile or suspended ceiling. But if you're willing and able, the result will be worth the effort.

To put up wallboard on the ceiling you'll need to review the basic installation and finishing techniques presented earlier. Only a few things will be different: Instead of setting nails at 7-inch intervals, you'll have to halve that distance or else substitute drywall screws for the nails. Use only the 4-by-8-foot panels; the larger sizes would be too heavy. You can fasten the panels to the ceiling joists either lengthwise or crosswise, but the lengthwise arrangement gives you about 15% more backing to nail into, providing extra insurance against gradual weakening. If you are covering an existing ceiling with wallboard, use contact cement in addition to the standard fasten-

ers. You can avoid taping corners where the ceiling meets the walls by putting up moldings instead.

Begin work in a corner of the ceiling; that way the two adjoining walls will help hold the panel in place. Subsequent panels can be butted against panels already installed. If you have helpers, ask them to lift the panel into place while you insert the deadmen (see Planning hints, at left). Be sure the ladders or scaffolds do not interfere with the placement of the deadmen. The tops of the deadmen should run across the width of the panel about 2 feet in from each end. (If you are working alone, Hercules, be sure to place the deadmen within reach of your ladder before you lift the panel. Raise the panel overhead like a weightlifter, climb the ladder, and set the panel in position. Then climb a step higher so you can press the panel against the joists with one arm and the top of your head. Now reach for a deadman with your free arm. After wedging the first deadman near one end of the panel, reach for the other and insert it opposite. Whew.) Then drive a nail or screw into all four corners of the panel. Draw or snap light guidelines on the panel, if necessary, to help you gauge where the joists are, and drive nails or screws at the mentioned intervals into all the joists. Remove the deadmen only after you have driven at least two dozen nails or half as many screws.

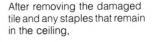

Stopgaps and copouts:

Ceiling repairs

Plaster and wallboard. Ceilings need repair less often than walls, since they are out of the way of the usual flying missiles. When they are damaged, they are generally fixed up the same way walls are (pages 18-24). Minor cracks and gouges are done exactly the same way. But patches are difficult, because they must be held securely, or gravity will take its toll. Use drywall screws rather than nails.

The mesh method of repairing large holes is of dubious value because the spackling compound tends to fall right out. The triangular-patch method may work, but the bevel in this case must run in the opposite direction so the patch will not fall through. To keep the patch up there, use thin tape, and spackle over it. The plastic clips mentioned on page 23 will work for small patches but are not recommended for big patching operations.

When a piece of ceiling wallboard starts to come loose, or cracks appear along the seams, you have a much more difficult problem than the same situation on a wall. It could be dangerous, for one thing. Gypsumboard is heavy, and could cause serious damage or injury if it falls. We recommend a professional inspection of this type of problem, and probably professional repair. The usual cause of such damage is water leaking from somewhere, often the bath upstairs.

If only a portion of the board seems loose, however, it is worth a try at fixing it yourself. Since the problem will be at the seams, drive in a few drywall nails or screws on both sides of the crack. Cover with thin tape especially made for this purpose, spackle over it, and sand to a level surface.

Ceiling tile has a rather delicate surface, which is quite easily scuffed. Any flying missile can dent or gouge it. Fortunately, there is a quick and simple repair for this type of damage: white shoe polish (assuming, as is usually the case, that the ceiling is white). Just dab on the polish and it will be scarcely noticeable.

Badly damaged ceiling tile can be replaced by cutting it out with a utility knife,

then installing a new tile. Since this type of tile is tongued and grooved on all four sides, you will have to cut off at least one tongue from the surrounding tiles, and you will have to remove the tongues from the replacement tile, or it won't fit in. Pull out all old staples or scrape off the old adhesive before making the replacement.

If the tile was cemented to existing wallboard originally, the new piece can be attached with adhesive in the same way (see page 48). The more usual method of stapling to furring (page 49) can't be used because the tongues are gone. (You cut them off, remember?) The only way to hold up the new tile is to nail through the face with small finishing nails. You can probably buy small white paneling nails for an invisible job, or set ordinary nails and cover them with spackling compound. Acoustical tiles with small holes can be nailed through the openings for an unnoticeable repair.

After removing the damaged tile and any staples that remain in the ceiling,

cut away the tongues from the replacement tile,

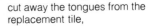

slip it into the opening, and nail at all four corners.

Suspended ceilings have their own problems and solutions. Since they are made of different materials, the old shoe-polish trick won't be effective. These panels are easily replaced, however. Simply push up on them, tip slightly, and slide them out. Replace with a matching panel. Here, if the new panel looks too clean, the other panels can be taken down one at a time and scrubbed with detergent.

Tile ceilings

What it takes

Approximate time: Furring will take 4-6 hours for an average ceiling, stapling tiles will also take 4-6 hours; for gluing subtract furring time but add about an hour to stapling time.

Tools and materials: Tiles, claw hammer, folding or metal rule, utility knife, chalk line, and framing or try square; crosscut saw, 1x3 wood strips, and 8-penny nails if you plan to install furring; either a staple gun and staples or else tile adhesive and a putty knife.

Planning hints: You must choose between staples and glue. In general, staples are easier, cleaner, and faster to work with, but they require a solid backing. If you can conveniently attach tiles directly to a wooden ceiling, joists, or furring strips, don't mess with the glue.

Since a tile ceiling is usually made of square-foot tiles, the number of tiles needed is the same as the square footage of the ceiling, plus 10% for waste. Since furring strips are nailed every foot, you will need as many lineal feet of furring as the square footage of the room, plus three extra lengths for edge tile and waste.

Look for the two-tongued tile
If you ever have to take down a tile ceiling from a solid backing, don't just start anywhere. It will take forever if you have to pry the tiles loose one at a time. Begin instead by removing *corner* tiles until you locate the one that has two tongues sticking out into the room. There can be only one such tile. Work your way out from that corner in two directions, and the tiles will fall away like dead leaves. (I realized this only after I was three quarters of the way through the job).

Practical Pete

For refurbishing old ceilings, or for new attics or basement rooms, the do-it-yourselfer's choice usually narrows down to either ceiling tile or a suspended-grid system. (Though wood and plastic paneling are also used for dramatic effect, they can be tiresome in large doses.) Tiles are best for covering existing ceilings in above-ground living areas; suspended systems are usually preferred for high ceilings or basements where there are a lot of obstructions overhead. Lowering the headroom has the additional advantage of saving on fuel.

Tiles are stapled or glued over an existing ceiling or to furring strips nailed to the ceiling joists. Suspended panels hang from the joists on wires or clips, and are easily removed for servicing of pipes and wiring overhead. Both tiles and suspended panels can be installed so that the joints become decorative elements in the ceiling. Both are also available in types that conceal the joints so that the finished ceiling looks like a one-piece installation. And, perhaps most important for a family-room situation, both are available as acoustical elements that work to keep the noise level down.

The denser the composition of the tile or suspended panel, the better it will keep sound from spreading to other areas. The sound absorbency of acoustical tile is indicated by its noise reduction coefficient rating, or NRC. The rating number is simply the percentage of sound striking the surface of the tile that will be absorbed. A spread of 10 or more NRC points (for example, a 0.50 tile compared to a 0.60 tile) indicates a definite edge for the higher-rated (0.60) product. A narrower gap is more difficult for the ear to detect.

Ceiling tile layout

Most ceiling tiles for use with furring strips are 12 inches square, although 12x24-, 16x16-, and 16x32-inch tiles are also available. The tiles are stapled to 1x3 furring strips, laid across the joists.

Start the tiles in a corner of the room. Like wall tiles, a ceiling has a better appearance if border tiles are the same width on opposite sides of the room, and are as large as possible. Unlike other tiles, ceiling tiles can't be laid out for a "dry run." To determine border tile width for the long walls of your family room, measure one of the short walls. If it is not an exact number of feet, add 12 inches (assuming you are using 12 inch tiles) to the inches left over; then divide the number of inches by two.

This is the width of the border tiles for the long walls.

Example: short wall = 10'8"
extra inches: 8"
plus 12"
divided by 2)20"
border tile: 10"

Border tiles for the short walls are figured by the same procedure.

Example: long wall = 18'4"
extra inches: 4"
plus 12"
divided by 2)16"
border tile: 8"

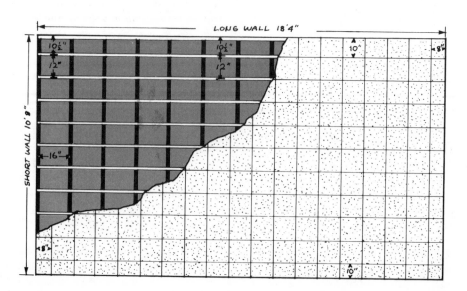

Furring

Furring strips are nailed across the joists. The first two strips must be carefully placed so that the border tiles are properly aligned. Nail the first strip flush against the wall at right angles to the joists, driving one or two 8-penny nails into each joist. The second furring strip is placed parallel to the first at a distance determined by the border tile width from the wall. For example, add ½ inch for the stapling flange to the 10-inch border tile width of our example. The center of the second furring strip should be 10½ inches from the wall (not from the first furring strip). With the second strip nailed in place, work across the ceiling, nailing each succeeding strip 12 inches from center to center. When you reach the opposite wall, the next-to-last strip should automatically be in the right position (unless your measurements somehow went awry). The final strip is placed flush against the wall, just as the first one. With all strips nailed up, make sure they are level by checking them with a long straightedge. Correct any unevenness by driving thin wood shims between strips and joists.

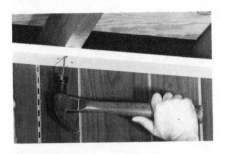

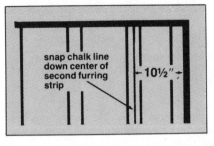

Installing ceiling tile

The first tile is the most crucial one. Snap a chalk line down the center of the full length of the second furring strip. In our example, this would be 10½ inches from the wall—the width of the border tile plus flange. Snap a second chalk line across the furring strips. Again using the example above, the short-wall border tiles measure 8 inches; add ½ inch for the tongue. The second chalk line should be 8½ inches from the wall. This line must be at an exact right angle to the first line; check it with a square before snapping the line.

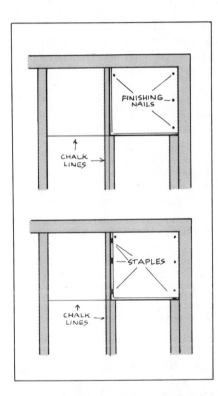

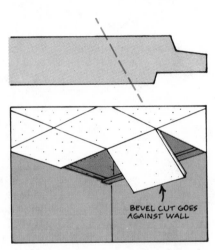

tight fit. Fasten by stapling into the remaining tongue and nailing the other end. Use all nails for the final tile; dab heads with white paint.

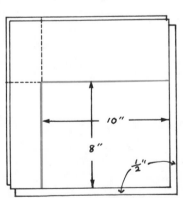

Now comes the easy part. Measure and cut each border tile individually. Remove the groove edges and leave the tongues for stapling; include the tongue in your measurement. Cut the tiles face up with a sharp utility knife.

The first tile is the corner tile. Align its tongue edges with both guidelines, nail along the edges, and staple it in place through the tongues.

The second tile runs along the border parallel to the furring strips. Slide it into the first tile; it should fit snugly, but do not force the tiles tightly together. Align the tongue with the guideline and staple only. The third tile runs along the border *across* the furring strips. Slide it into the first, align it with the mark, and staple. Work your way outward across the ceiling, installing tiles in "step" fashion. When you reach the opposite wall, cut each border tile individually, beveling the cut as shown for a

Obstructions are cut around in the same general manner as for ceramic tile (pages 43-44). It's much easier here, though, because the material is soft and cuts readily with the utility knife. Lights and other accessories can be installed directly to the framing, or to furring if they aren't too heavy (check codes on this).

Suspended ceilings

Approximate time: Six to eight hours for an average room.

Tools and materials: Claw hammer, level, pliers, utility knife, folding or metal rule, hacksaw, center punch, chalk line, framing square, and the ceiling panels of your choice, with installation hardware as required (this usually means hanging wire, clips, or straps, molding strips, main runners, cross runners, and 6-penny common nails or screw eyes.)

Planning hints: To estimate materials for a suspended ceiling, first determine the system and size of the panels. Then make a layout on graph paper. The main runners run on the long dimension, one on each side of the panel. Cross tees go the other way, again on each side of the panel. Edge molding is the same as the perimeter of your room, plus a few inches.

The big advantage of a suspended ceiling system is that it can be installed at whatever height is necessary to conceal pipes, ducts, and anything else that clutters a basement or other room. The disadvantage is that many rooms—particularly basements, where such ceilings are most useful—just do not have enough headroom to sacrifice what is necessary for such an installation. To work properly, a suspended ceiling must be at least 3 inches below the joists, ducts, pipes and other obstructions. (Some systems can be installed directly to the joists, but then they are no longer truly suspended ceilings.)

If you have enough overhead room, a suspended ceiling is fast and easy to install. The system will give you a ceiling line unbroken by protrusions of boxed-in ducts and pipes; yet it still allows easy access to these utilities for servicing (you simply lift out the ceiling panel below them). You can also provide recessed lighting with fluorescent fixtures installed above plastic translucent panels in selected areas of the room—or in the whole ceiling if you wish. Colored panels are very effective over the bar. (All-translucent ceilings are a bit overpowering except in very small rooms.) To prevent "hot spots," use fixtures especially designed for these ceilings. Otherwise, provide reflectors above the fluorescent tubes with adequate space as recommended by the manufacturer.

Suspended ceiling panels are available in a wide variety of patterns and sizes—2x2-foot and 2x4-foot panels are the most common for systems where the gridwork is exposed. Hidden-grid types use 1-foot squares, 1x4-foot panels, or long, narrow planks. The suspension systems also vary,

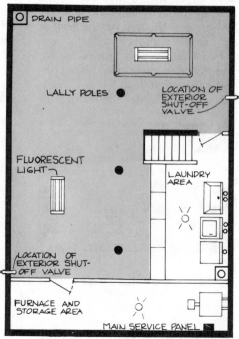

depending on the manufacturer. Specific instruction will accompany the system you purchase, though the work generally proceeds as in the following illustrated sequence. But before you begin work, make an accurate sketch of the ceiling, noting the locations of pipes, heating ducts, lights, and the like. This will help you plan the installation, and will also be an aid later on when you need access to these utilities for servicing. Determine what type of lighting fixtures you want to install (if any) and where they will be located. These are best installed before you do the ceiling. Avoid too-short border panels by adjusting the main runners to yield approximately even tiles. Use the example on page 48, adjusting for the size of your panels.

Modern installation methods

1. Determine the exact height you would like the ceiling to be, and mark this location on a wall. It must be 3+ inches below joists.

2. Snap chalk lines at the same height on all the walls of the room. Double-check on each line to make sure it is even with the others and on the level.

3. Fasten wall moldings (usually L-shaped metal fittings) to each wall so their lower edge barely covers the chalk lines. The moldings should be nailed or screwed to every stud.

4. On the walls that run parallel to the ceiling joists, mark the centers for the main supporting runners, which will run perpendicular to the joists at intervals that correspond to the length of your panels and room. Remember to keep the two end panels the same size.

5. Snap chalk lines across the bottoms of the joists to connect the marks made on opposite walls in the previous step.

6. Drive common nails or screw eyes into one side of the joists at each chalk mark.

7. Suspend wires from the nails or screw eyes in the joists. Flex the wires loosely at the approximate height of the new ceiling.

8. Suspend the main runners from the wires by means of the holes in their vertical section. Rest the ends of the runners on the wall molding at each end.

9. If the main runners are not long enough to span the room, join them end-to-end with linkage clips provided by the manufacturer.

10. Insert the ends of the cross runners into slots in the main runners (machined at the proper interval by the manufacturer).

11. Slip full-size panels into place by tilting them to pass up through the frame opening and lowering them to rest on the runners.

12. Cut edge panels to size with a utility knife and straightedge.

13. Carefully measure the location and size of obstructions.

14. Cut the panel in two, and gradually whittle away from both halves just enough material to enclose the obstruction. In the process, test for fit several times until you get it just right.

15. When the cut sections are installed, the break is virtually invisible.

6. PAINTING

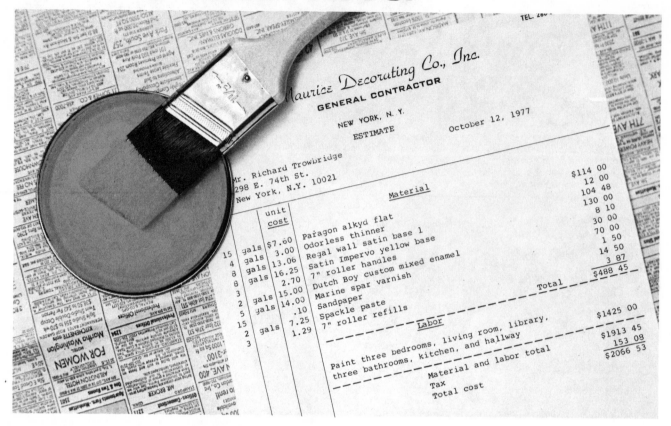

Maurice Decorating Co., Inc.
GENERAL CONTRACTOR
NEW YORK, N.Y.
ESTIMATE
October 12, 1977

Mr. Richard Trowbridge
298 E. 74th St.
New York, N.Y. 10021

Material

		unit cost		
15	gals	$7.60	Paragon alkyd flat	$114 00
4	gals	3.00	Odorless thinner	12 00
8	gals	13.06	Regal wall satin base 1	104 48
8	gals	16.25	Satin Impervo yellow base	130 00
		2.70	7" roller handles	8 10
3	gals	15.00	Dutch Boy custom mixed enamel	30 00
2	gals	14.00	Marine spar varnish	70 00
5		.10	Sandpaper	1 50
15	gals	7.25	Spackle paste	14 50
2		1.29	7" roller refills	3 87
			Total	$488 45

Labor

Paint three bedrooms, living room, library,
three bathrooms, kitchen, and hallway $1425 00

Material and labor total $1913 45
Tax   153 08
Total cost $2066 53

Choosing the right kind of paint

What it takes

Approximate time: Very much a part of every painting job is preparation and cleanup. Under typical conditions (wall surfaces more or less intact, brushwork done with reasonable care, etc.), the total preparation and cleanup time should equal about half of the actual painting time. In the case of badly deteriorated walls, or sloppy workmanship, nonpainting time can even exceed painting time. Typical (nonprofessional) rates of speed are given on page 55.

Tools and materials: Detailed on this and the next three pages.

Nearly everyone has painted at least a room at one time or another. There's nothing very complicated about it, and there are many different ways of arriving at a decent result. More than technique, the job requires forethought, and lots of care and patience. It is hard to believe that whole books have been devoted to painting. Surely a book is not what's needed, but the selected suggestions in this short chapter are worth taking note of, for they can make the difference between just getting by and doing really fine work.

One of the first and most crucial points to consider is what kind of paint you will use. In most cases, you can save yourself a lot of time and trouble by simply buying the best latex paint you can find. There really isn't a better choice. Latex is nearly *odorless*, is *quick drying* and *simple to clean* up because it is *water soluble*. However, check the table on the opposite page for a summary of your other options, especially if you will be painting an unusual surface. At the same time, consider what type of finish you want. A high-gloss finish offers the best *resistance to moisture and wear*, and is therefore a good choice for *kitchens* and *bathrooms*. Semigloss paints are *less obtrusive* and nearly as *durable*, so they are good for *baseboards, doors,*

window trim, and other *woodwork*. For walls that are not subject to heavy wear, flat paints are preferable because they are most *restful* to the eye.

Besides latex paint, you may want to use alkyd paint for extra *durability*, oil base paint for the best results on *bare wood*, *fast-drying* rubber-base paint for *moisture-proofing masonry*, slow-drying cement paint to *resurface worn masonry*, costly urethane or deck paints for an *impervious* coating on *high-stress* areas, *dripless* paint for ceilings, *fire-retardant* paint for such areas as *garages* and *basements*, polyurethane varnish for an exceptionally *durable* finish on *floors*, and stains to *enhance wood grain* and change its tone or coloration.

Before painting *raw or porous surfaces*, it is best to cover them with a coat of *primer* paint. You'll have to apply at least two coats on a job like this anyway, and using a primer may actually save you a coat. Primer paint is *less costly* than regular paint and provides a *good gripping surface* for subsequent coats.

In buying paint, don't skimp on price. Painting is one of the least expensive jobs you can do and, with many substandard discount brands available, penny-wise is definitely pound-foolish.

Which paint for which surface?

Type of surface: ▼ \ Type of coating: ▶	Latex paint	Alkyd paint – Flat or primer	Alkyd paint – Glossy	Oil-base paint	Rubber-base paint	Cement paint	Urethane paint	Deck paint	Sand or textured paint	Fire-retardant paint	Dripless paint	Polyurethane varnish
Previous coating												
Latex paint —Flat or primer	✓	✓	✓	✓	✓			✓	✓	✓	✓	✓
—Glossy	✓	✓	✓	✓				✓	✓	✓	✓	
Alkyd or oil-base paint —Flat or primer		✓	✓	✓				✓		✓	✓	
—Glossy		✓	✓	✓				✓		✓	✓	
Polyurethane varnish		✓	✓	✓			✓	✓				✓
Wallpaper	✓	✓										
Raw surfaces												
Wood, plywood	✓	✓	✓	✓			✓	✓			✓	✓
Hardboard	✓	✓	✓	✓			✓	✓	✓	✓	✓	✓
Plaster	✓				✓				✓	✓		
Gypsumboard	✓								✓	✓		
Concrete, cinderblock	✓				✓	✓	✓	✓	✓	✓		
Brick	✓	✓			✓	✓		✓	✓	✓		✓
Stucco	✓	✓			✓				✓	✓		
Ceramic tile, glass							✓					
Steel, iron		✓	✓	✓								
Aluminum	✓	✓	✓	✓				✓				✓

Picking colors

Color is a highly individual and tricky thing. What appears beautiful to one person looks horrible to another. Colors like avocado and heliotrope are here today and gone tomorrow, so no one can or should tell you exactly what colors to use. But an important rule of thumb is to select your colors from the swatches in a sample book and then *order the next lighter shade.* Paint always looks darker on a wall.

There are a few basics about the psychology of color which you should also know. The best way to approach this is the color wheel. The colors on the left of the wheel, yellow through red, are warm or "happy." The greens and blues on the right side of the wheel are cool, creating a feeling of quiet and rest. When trying to create a mood in a certain room, the color wheel will give you an idea as to what colors to choose.

When combining colors in a room, the relationship between the various colors is important. The diagram at right illustrates the various forms of color harmony. Of these, the simplest and most useful are:

Four ways to pick colors that go well together

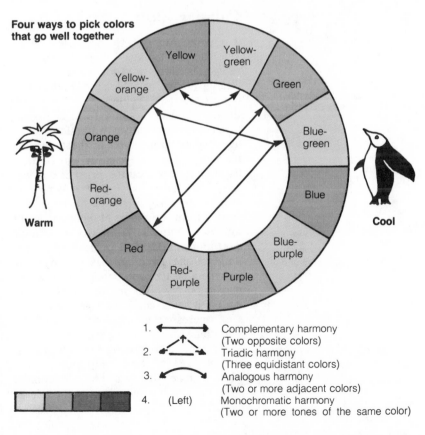

1. Complementary harmony (Two opposite colors)
2. Triadic harmony (Three equidistant colors)
3. Analogous harmony (Two or more adjacent colors)
4. (Left) Monochromatic harmony (Two or more tones of the same color)

- Consider the effect of each color. Red, for example, is a stimulating hue, but overwhelming in large doses. Too much red seems to make a room smaller. Green is tranquil, blue is soothing, yellow is cheerful with a sense of spaciousness in lighter tints.
- Mix warm and cool colors to avoid a room that is too "cold" or "hot." Warm colors should be emphasized in a room without windows.
- Proportion of color is very important. This doesn't mean giving each shade "equal time," but rather the opposite. One color should dominate, with complementary colors in various sized doses.
- Use color to camouflage room defects. Light colors make a small room look larger. On long, narrow rooms, use different colors, applying a warm color such as yellow or a deep shade of a cool one, like green, on the end walls. Make radiators or other obstructions fade by painting them the same color as the room. To highlight desirable features, use contrasting, vivid colors.

Complementary harmony—using two colors from opposite sides of the wheel. This produces contrast and liveliness.

Triadic harmony—a basic color scheme for balance, using three points equidistant from each other on the wheel.

Analogous harmony—for a feeling of softness and delicacy, use two, three or four adjacent colors on the wheel.

Monochromatic harmony—an excellent and underutilized decorating technique. This one is not on the color wheel because it involves the same color. The difference is in the intensities. Tints and shades are created by adding white or black to the original hue. The result is a sophisticated, subdued contrast of tones.

For some decorating ideas, use the color selector chart below. Find your favorite color in the column at left. Then read across the page for your basic color options and some suggestions for harmony and accent.

Color selector chart

Basic colors	Variations	Harmonizing colors	Accent colors
RED	Crimson Pink	Gray, white, and pink; steel gray and yellow Violet and blue; lime green and beige	Lime green, white Black, dark green
BLUE	Dark blue Light blue	Gray and turquoise; yellow and copper Violet and burgundy; yellow and turquoise	Crimson, white Chartreuse, black
YELLOW	Pale cream Canary yellow	Rose and crimson; brown and peach Turquoise and blue; green and white	Green, turquoise Copper, black
GREEN	Dark green Lime green	Crimson and white; beige and yellow Gray and copper; turquoise and dark green	Chartreuse, crimson Black, crimson
ORANGE	Peach Copper	Green and white; gray and yellow Beige and yellow; blue and gray	Crimson, turquoise Turquoise, black
PURPLE	Violet Burgundy	Blue and gray; yellow and turquoise Pink and gray-beige; green and chartreuse	Red, white Yellow, crimson
BLUE-GREEN	Pale blue-green Turquoise	Green and white; peach and yellow Blue and gray; copper and beige	Copper, crimson Yellow, dark brown
GRAY	Pale gray Steel gray	Yellow and lime green; blue and burgundy Peach and white; yellow and copper	Red, chartreuse Black, deep blue
BROWN	Beige Dark brown	Yellow and copper; dusty pink and olive green Light blue and yellow; cream and crimson	Turquoise, crimson Copper, chartreuse

Painting tools

The photographs on the opposite page divide painting tools and materials into two categories: those used for preparation and cleanup (above) and those used in the painting process itself (below). You'll be seeing them all in use throughout this chapter.

Whether you cover your floors with newspapers, drop cloths, or sheet plastic (a bit slippery), the newspaper will come in handy later for cleaning brushes and rollers, and plastic is a good material for draping any furniture that is too large to be carried from the room. Moving across the top row, a church key (not so easy to find in our flip-top era) is ideal for cleaning out and undercutting cracks in plaster—any similarly pointed tool will do—while wide and narrow putty knives are for patching walls with spackling compound (in can). The sandpaper in the next row is used for smoothing patched areas, and the tack cloth to its right for removing sanding dust. A roll of masking tape simplifies edging, while a single-edge razor blade in a holder and a metal straightedge reduce the fine art of window touch-up to an exact science.

The second photograph begins with a reminder: don't forget your hat (required equipment, in our opinion) and gloves (optional). A paint roller, at center, and roller cover, above it, are your best bet for flat, open areas. You'll be dipping them in the paint tray to their left and attaching the extension poles, below, to the roller handle when you need to reach the tops of walls and ceilings. For detail work, you'll want an assortment of brushes. The widest one is for areas such as corners and door panels that can't be reached with a roller; the narrower ones, with slanted bristle tips, are called sash brushes and are for edging and window trim. When you paint with a brush, you'll find a partially filled plastic bucket easier to maneuver than a heavy paint can; a stirrer (any long, thin scrap of wood) is a must. The triangular metal plate is an optional convenience for shielding rugs and floors when you are edging base trim, but the moist sponge below it should always be within reach for absorbing unexpected, but predictable, drips and spills. Not shown, but useful, is a stepladder.

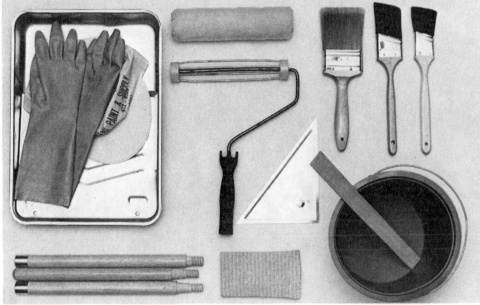

How much paint?

To calculate the total area of a rectangular room's four walls, add the length of the room to the width, multiply by 2, and multiply again by the height. Then subtract 15 for each average window and 20 for each average door.

Example:

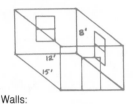

Walls:
15 ft. + 12 ft. = 27 ft.
27 ft. x 2 = 54 ft.
54 ft. x 8 ft. = 432 sq. ft.
432 - 20 - 15 - 15 = 382 sq. ft.
Ceiling:
15 ft. x 12 ft. = 180 sq. ft.

Irregularly shaped rooms can be broken down mentally into rectangles and right triangles. Calculate the area of any rectangle by multiplying two adjacent sides, and of any right triangle by multiplying the two short legs and dividing by 2.

Example:

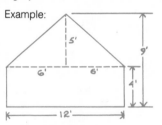

Picture this gable wall in three sections, as shown in dashed lines.
12 ft. x 4 ft. = 48 sq. ft. (rectangle)
5 ft. x 6 ft. ÷ 2 = 15 sq. ft. (each triangle)
48 + 15 + 15 = 78 sq. ft. (total area)

If you plan to do the trim with different paint, calculate its area part by part. (You'll rarely need more than a quart of trim paint for any room.)

Generally, on smooth, finished walls, a gallon of paint will cover about 400 square feet on the first coat and 450 on the second. For porous or unfinished walls, subtract 50 square feet from each of these figures. Most paints come in both gallons and quarts, and many dealers accept unopened returns, so it pays to buy your last gallon in quarts.

Estimating time

Average paint speeds (add half again as much time for preparation and cleanup on most jobs).

Painting task	Sq. ft. per hour
New plaster, wallboard, or stucco walls	
Primer/sealer	70
Each additional coat	90
New plaster, wallboard, or stucco ceilings	
Primer/sealer	60
Each additional coat	80
Previously painted plaster or wallboard walls	
First coat	100
Each additional coat	120

Painting task	Sq. ft. per hour
Previously painted plaster or wallboard ceilings	
First coat	80
Each additional coat	100
Wood floors (paint, varnish, stain)	
Primer/sealer	200
Next coat	140
Each additional coat	160
Wood trim (paint, varnish, stain)	
Primer/sealer	150
Next coat	80
Each additional coat	100
Enamel paints	50
Masonry	
First coat	60
Each additional coat	80

Preparation

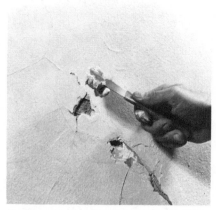

1. Remove peeling or flaking paint chips with a stiff, narrow-bladed putty knife. All paint that comes off fairly easily must be removed, but don't look for extra work by probing into otherwise solid areas. (Raised edges need only be sanded down to blend in with areas that have been stripped.)

2. After clearing away loose plaster with a church key, fill cracks and holes with spackling compound, applied with a putty knife of appropriate blade width. (See page 20.)

3. Sand repaired areas down to a smooth surface with fine-grit paper and a sanding block to prevent oversanding.

4. Use a tack cloth to remove the dust that was produced by sanding.

5. Often overlooked, but quite important, is the clearing away of cobwebs, dust, and other loose particles that could foul the paint. Use a dust mop for ceilings.

6. If you are planning a two-tone job, or a flat/semigloss contrast, mask border areas so you won't have to paint a neat line twice. But don't mask new paint; the tape will cause it to peel away in places.

7. Remove any fixtures and furniture that can be easily disassembled and carried away. Protect any that are left with sheet plastic. This saves time and, perhaps, anguish too.

8. Protecting the floor is not enough. Newspaper and drop cloths have a way of shifting around, so tape them to the edge of the floor or bottom of the baseboard.

9. Forestall the inevitable messy drips by taping the bottom of each paint can to a paper plate before breaking the seal.

Before you open that can

Misadventures with paint happen all too frequently. (Painting yourself into a corner isn't all that can go wrong.) Before starting, pause for a moment to review your plan of attack, and run through these tips to help you stay out of trouble; many of them are far from obvious.

- Don't use natural-bristle brushes with water-base (latex) paints.
- Don't use nylon-bristle brushes with varnish, enamels, or shellac.
- Don't use latex paint over oil-base paint unless the surface is primed or sanded first.
- Allow new plaster to age for at least three months before you paint it. If this is inconvenient or impossible, you can prime it with water-base paint or primer. Then seal the surface with a flat oil-based paint (except in the kitchen and bathroom, where rubber-base paint is best).
- Prime new wallboard with water-base primer only.
- Prime any newly spackled or wood-filled areas in advance.
- Never paint a radiator or pipes while they are hot. They will peel.
- If you are working in a poorly lit room (at night, or on a cloudy day), focus a lamp or spotlight on your work area to ensure that you don't miss any spots.
- Before painting bare wood, sand it lightly and wipe it down with turpentine. Prime knotholes with shellac so they won't bleed through. Fill nail holes with wood filler. Then coat the entire surface with primer. Plan on two or more additional coats of paint.
- Don't use a ladder in front of a closed, unlocked door. Either lock the door or leave it open. And don't leave paint cans on ladders.
- Keep all paints out of reach of children and pets.
- When using oil-base and alkyd paints, be especially attentive to heat and fire hazards. Fumes are toxic, so ventilate the room well.

If painting drives you to drink . . .

Plan on taking a break—and getting some fresh air, for sure—every hour or two. Have some coffee or a cold drink, but if you are using oil-base or alkyd paint, don't take any alcoholic beverages. The paint fumes become doubly poisonous, even deadly, after you've had a few drinks. And don't be fooled by those odorless paints; the fumes are still there even though you can't smell them. I know. (To get the paint off the cat, my wife wiped its fur down with cooking oil—*not* turpentine.)

Practical Pete

A systematic approach

Avoiding smears and drips will be your biggest challenge. For this, our very best advice is "take it easy." Overzealous painters are their own worst enemy. When haste or anxiety creeps into your work, slow down; check your last brush stroke or roller swath for evenness of coverage before going on to the next. If you have eager young helpers, watch them closely for signs of carelessness. A conservative, deliberate approach is more important than any "technique."

In general, paint a room from top to bottom, but leave doors and windows for last. Do brushwork first, then rollerwork. The illustration below shows the sequence for painting the parts of a room: 1. paint 2-inch brush strips around the edges of the ceiling; 2. do the same, down the corners where the walls meet; 3. the same around doors and windows; 4. roll the ceiling; 5. roll the walls; 6. paint 2-inch brush strips above baseboards; 7. switch to semigloss (if that's your pleasure) and brush-paint the baseboards, window trim, and door trim; 8. finish off the doors and windows (see page 60 for details).

Brushwork

1. After prying the can open with a screwdriver, make five or six nail holes in the recess of the rim so paint cannot accumulate there and drip down the sides of the can.

2. Mix paint thoroughly with any convenient, clean stirrer. Then use your paintbrush to remove excess paint from the stirrer so it won't make a mess.

3. Pour a small quantity of paint into a bucket, and dip the brush into the paint to a depth of no more than one third the length of the bristles.

4. You're ready to paint, but one last caution: wipe up drips and spills with a moist sponge (or dry cloth for oil paint) as soon as they occur. Otherwise you might step in them and track paint onto unprotected floors in other areas of the house.

5. Paint the ceiling corners first in a single continuous swath 2 inches wide. If your ceiling will be a different color from the walls, keep a neat line at the corner. If you're righthanded, move from left to right. Be sure of even coverage.

6. Paint the room corners next in the same way. Cover these from bottom to top so the brush itself prevents drips.

7. When you paint the baseboard, pull the drop cloth or newspaper back a few inches, and use a stiff paint shield to help you make a neat, clean line as close as possible to the floor. Be especially careful here not to overload your brush.

8. Keep looking back over newly painted areas to nip paint-runs in the bud. These will most likely occur on fancy moldings and at the corners of door panels. Simply spread them out with your brush.

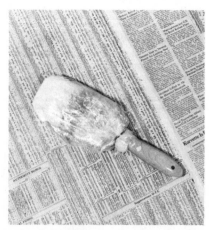

9. If you take a break for more than 15 minutes, seal your brush in a plastic lunch bag so the air can't cause the paint to cake.

Roller work

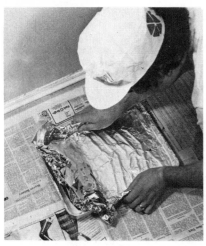

1. Wrap a sheet of aluminum foil tightly around the inside of the roller tray. This will save you a messy cleanup job later. (When you finish painting, simply roll up the foil and throw it away.)

2. Pour a small quantity of paint into the tray. Use just enough to fill the flat area. Leave the sloping, ribbed section of the tray free for rolling out excess paint.

3. Dip the roller in the paint just deep enough to cover about one quarter of its surface. Then spread the paint on the rest of the roller by running it up and down the sloping part of the tray.

4. When the roller is covered with paint, but not dripping wet, raise it to the wall or ceiling and spread the paint before it has a chance to drip. Use an extension pole for reaching ceilings and the tops of walls.

5. On walls, spread the paint in the form of a large M. Roll the first stroke from bottom to top so the paint has less of a chance to drip.

6. Complete the M within a 4-foot-square area. Press firmly but not so hard that the roller skids or paint spatters.

7. Then fill in the remainder of the square by spreading the paint that is already on the wall. Now you can press a little harder.

8. Begin another M directly below or beside the first one, and so on. Feather lightly into the previously painted area so there is no trace of overlap.

Brush or roller?

When in doubt, follow this rule: don't use a paintbrush if a roller will do the job. A roller covers open areas about three times faster than a brush can. The only times you'll really need a brush are for corners, moldings, intricate trim, and other areas where a roller can't maneuver freely. However, it does not pay to use a roller that measures less than 7 or 8 inches across. The spate of fancy mini-rollers now sold in paint stores can't stand up to a single, ordinary paintbrush.

Special problems

Doors. Paint panels, if any, first; then work from top to bottom, covering horizontal sections before vertical ones. The top and bottom edges need only be painted once—when the door is first installed—to seal the wood. Paint the latch edge the color of the room the door opens into, and the hinge edge the color of the room it opens away from. Leave hinges and other hardware unpainted unless someone else has gotten to them first. When painting the door frame, let the inside edge of the doorstop be the color dividing line.

Double-hung windows. Raise the inner sash and lower the outer sash almost as far as they will go. Paint *only* the areas shown in color at left. Do horizontal parts before vertical parts (see photo sequence below). Then return the sashes to their usual position, again leaving them slightly ajar at top and bottom. Paint the remaining areas of the sashes that are visible from the room, except for the bottom edge of the upper sash. This, and the outsides of the sashes, will be covered when you paint the exterior of your house. When the sashes are dry, move them up and down to make sure they don't stick. Then lower both sashes and paint the wooden parts of the upper jambs. Allow to dry, raise both sashes, and paint the rest of the jambs. Spray metal runners with silicone.

1. To form a neat edge and minimize window cleanup, use an angular sash brush for mullions (the strips between panes), and apply paint 1/16 inch onto the glass to form an airtight seal.

2. Straighten irregular edges by placing a straightedge against the mullion and scoring the paint with a utility knife.

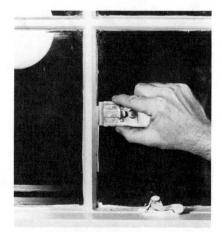

3. Use a window scraper (retractable razor blade) to lift the uneven paint from the glass. Slide the blade under the paint, and stop when you reach the score line.

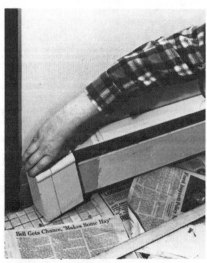

Baseboard radiators. Do these last. Remove end caps and interior swivel strips. (Note the poor job that resulted when this was not done in the past.) The front kickplates may be left on, as they are just as easy to paint in place.

After sanding away any paint that may have dripped from above and turning the radiators off, double-coat the metal with semigloss paint. Wait until the paint is completely dry before using the radiators.

Finishes

Varnish. Dip the bristles of your brush halfway into the varnish to load them thoroughly. Make long smooth brushstrokes. Don't backtrack, or the surface will bubble. Start each new stroke at the edge of the previously coated area. Sand lightly between coats. For an extra hard finish, you'll need three or more coats. Allow to dry before overcoating.

Shellac. Spread like paint. Brush marks disappear as the shellac dries. Don't use shellac over paint or other coatings because it will dissolve them. Check the date on the can; shellac begins to lose its stickiness after two months.

Stain. For best results, apply stain only to raw wood; then varnish. Spread stain lightly with a rag; then remove excess immediately. You can always darken it, but you won't be able to lighten it. Oil-base stains are best. Water-base types raise the wood grain and require sanding. Alcohol stains tend to have a streaky look.

Cleanup

1. After pouring leftover paint from the bucket or roller pan back into the can, sponge away any drips that may have formed around the rim and the outside of the container.

2. When you hammer the lid back onto the paint can, cover it first with a rag to prevent splashes. Before storing any paint, label it to remind yourself which areas of the house you painted with it.

3. Before cleaning rollers, press out all the paint you can on newspapers. Then slip the roller cover off the roller arm.

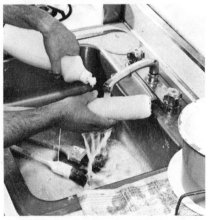

4. Washing out a roller in cold, clear water takes ten minutes or more. Use hot, soapy water and you'll cut the time by three quarters. Don't wring the delicate nap. Squeeze gently and rinse until the water runs clear. These instructions, of course, apply only to water-base paints. For oil and alkyd types, see the box at lower right.

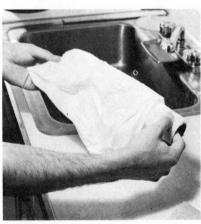

5. Store clean roller covers in an airtight plastic bag. It's best to set them on end so the nap is not damaged during storage.

6. Remove excess paint from brushes on newspaper. Then wash in hot, soapy water. Paint often accumulates in the heel of the brush. It doesn't matter if a little residue remains there, but don't give up until the visible part of the bristles is clean.

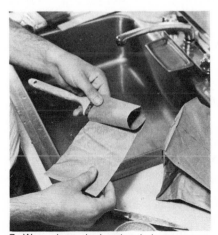

7. Wrap clean, dry brushes in brown wrapping paper or strips of a paper bag.

8. Tape the protective covering and suspend brushes from a string by the holes in the handles. Never prop a brush on its bristles; bent out of shape, it's useless.

Solvent-thinned paints

The cleanup for oil and alkyd paints is similar to the sequence shown for water-base paints. But save the soap and water for the final rinse only. First, scrub trays and buckets with paper towels dampened in turpentine or mineral spirits (see label on can). Clean brushes and rollers by dipping them repeatedly in a container full of solvent (coffee can or roller tray) and blotting up the dissolved paint with plenty of paper towels or newspaper. Change the solvent the first time only when its color grows quite dark, but use small amounts of clean solvent as you near the end of the job.

7. WALLPAPERING

Choosing the right covering

But how will it look in MY living room?

If you find book samples hard to visualize on your walls, keep these principles in mind as you leaf through the wallpaper catalogs:

- Light colors make a room look bigger, dark colors smaller.
- Strong vertical designs or stripes make a low ceiling appear higher; strong horizontals make a narrow room or hallway appear wider.
- Small patterns may be a good deal less striking on your walls than they are in the sample book.
- Large patterns are good for large rectangular rooms but will create a broken-up look in rooms with many doors, windows, or other unpapered areas.
- A high-gloss vinyl or foil paper can produce one heck of a glare in direct sunlight.

Wallcoverings, like just about everything else, have undergone tremendous change in recent years. Today, when it comes to wallpaper, there's a lot more than just paper to consider. New materials such as vinyls, foils, fabrics, cork, burlap, flocked papers, grass-cloth—you name it—are now manufactured by the roll to be pasted on the wall just like the more traditional papers.

The new materials often have greater strength than the old. This makes them easier to hang and more resistant to scuffs and tears. The extra strength also explains why more paperhanging is done by do-it-yourselfers than ever before. In addition, many of the new papers are washable, and some are resistant to steam, inviting use in kitchens and bathrooms. Most are relatively easy to strip, which means that redecoration in future will pose less of a problem than it has in the past. Pretrimming at the factory, a nearly universal practice, saves you work. Prepasting, a built-in feature which is becoming more popular, eliminates the need for a cumbersome worktable and leaves you with only the work of moistening and hanging.

With all these new options available, modern wallpaper is probably the least standardized commodity in the world of housewares. The basic unit is what is called the "single roll," and a roll usually measures 36 square feet. But a roll can be anywhere from 18 to 54 inches wide. If you have a choice, pick a narrower width, as you'll find it easier to work with.

Dealers are usually willing to give you samples and will even lend out their massive catalogs for a few days so you can shop at home and get an idea of how the paper will look on your walls. Hold your samples up to furniture, drapes, carpets, woodwork, and any other design elements in your room. Do this in daylight and again at night. You'll be surprised at the difference in different lighting.

For heavy-stress areas like hallways, children's rooms, bathrooms, or the kitchen, select a highly durable material such as washable vinyl or a fabric-backed covering (which may require special paste). Most of these papers are recommended also for bright rooms, since they resist fading in sunlight. If you don't require extreme durability, you can still get a measure of extra protection—for less money—by using regular pulp wallpaper that has been coated with a soil-resistant plastic film.

People who are all thumbs (or lazy, or intimidated) can simplify their job by selecting a pattern that is easy to match from roll to roll. Solids, weaves, tweeds, textures, certain kinds of stripes, and non-matching prints will make life easy for them, though, frankly these are rarely the more elegant patterns. Think twice before you choose a heavyweight paper; it can be hard to work with, especially if you are not blessed with a helper. Foil papers are great, but they tend to bring out the slightest imperfections in the wall surface, so use them only on smooth walls. If you work with flocked paper, be sure not to get paste on the side that shows—it won't wash off.

Estimating quantity

You've selected your pattern. The next question is how much to order. Your dealer will speak in terms of "single rolls," but some papers come in double or triple rolls. Leave that problem to him and just figure out how many single rolls you want. This is easy. A single roll contains about 36 square feet but covers only about 30 square feet after waste from match and trim is deducted. For a more-or-less rectangular room, you can figure out how many single rolls you need with the six-step formula presented in the box below.

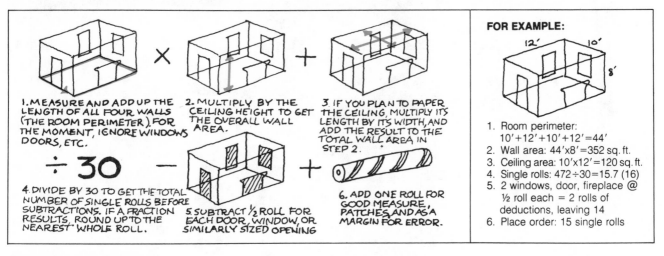

1. MEASURE AND ADD UP THE LENGTH OF ALL FOUR WALLS (THE ROOM PERIMETER). FOR THE MOMENT, IGNORE WINDOWS DOORS, ETC.

2. MULTIPLY BY THE CEILING HEIGHT TO GET THE OVERALL WALL AREA.

3. IF YOU PLAN TO PAPER THE CEILING, MULTIPLY ITS LENGTH BY ITS WIDTH, AND ADD THE RESULT TO THE TOTAL WALL AREA IN STEP 2.

÷ 30

4. DIVIDE BY 30 TO GET THE TOTAL NUMBER OF SINGLE ROLLS BEFORE SUBTRACTIONS. IF A FRACTION RESULTS, ROUND UP TO THE NEAREST WHOLE ROLL.

5. SUBTRACT ½ ROLL FOR EACH DOOR, WINDOW, OR SIMILARLY SIZED OPENING

6. ADD ONE ROLL FOR GOOD MEASURE, PATCHES AND AS A MARGIN FOR ERROR.

FOR EXAMPLE:

1. Room perimeter: 10'+12'+10'+12'=44'
2. Wall area: 44'x8'=352 sq. ft.
3. Ceiling area: 10'x12'=120 sq. ft.
4. Single rolls: 472÷30=15.7 (16)
5. 2 windows, door, fireplace @ ½ roll each = 2 rolls of deductions, leaving 14
6. Place order: 15 single rolls

Stopgaps and copouts:

Wallpaper repairs

You don't always have to invest the time and money to repaper an entire room just because you have a few spots that are torn or marred. Here are a few tricks for repairing minor flaws and blemishes:

Patches. Cut a patch somewhat larger than the torn area, making sure that the patch contains all of the pattern area you will need to replace. Align the patch with masking tape so it exactly matches the pattern.

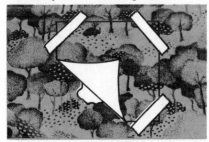

Using a sharp knife, cut through both the patch and the paper on the wall in a neat rectangle.

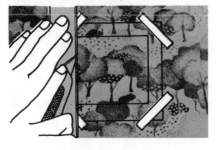

Remove the patch, and peel away the paper inside your knife cut. The patch will fit the hole exactly.

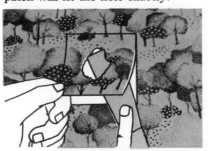

Paste it in place, following the instructions below.

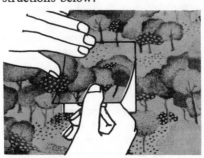

Loose edges and tears. Simply apply glue to the underside of the paper and press it back into place. Use white glue for vinyl wallpaper; for regular paper use white glue or library paste. Use a putty knife or artist's brush to spread the adhesive under the paper. Do not use so much glue that it soaks through the paper and leaves a stain. A thin, even layer the thickness of newspaper is about right. Sponge off any excess glue with water, taking care not to wet the paper enough to loosen the glue behind the wet spot.

If you have the peeling sort of tear that gets larger and larger, lift it up and apply glue to the underside; then press the paper back into place so the edges of the tear match as closely as possible. Dab away excess glue.

Blisters or bubbles. Slit a cross in the paper with a razor blade or knife, following a pattern line, and dampen the paper with a sponge. Gently lift each corner in turn without creasing the paper, and brush glue onto the underlying wall.

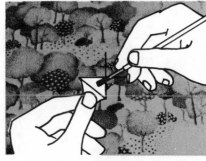

After a few minutes, sponge off any excess glue before it dries. If the edges overlap, they will shrink to fit when the paper dries completely.

Papering a room

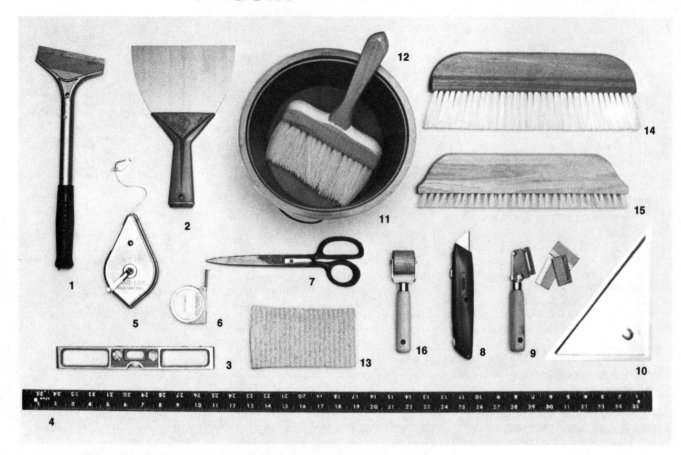

Wallpapering tools

The tools you may need for papering a room are shown above and described below. This is not to say you must use all these tools in every case. You can often get by with fewer tools, less costly substitutes, or makeshift items already on hand.

- A paper stripper (1) is handy for breaking the surface of old wallpaper.
- A flexible wall scraper (2) finishes the job of removing the old covering—with the help of a few sprinkles of water if the going gets tough. The scraper also doubles as a spackling knife, if the walls must be patched (pages 19-23) before new wallpaper can be applied.
- A level (3) and long straightedge (4) can accomplish the same result as a plumb bob (5), but with slightly more work. The straightedge can also be used to guide long, straight cuts, but for taking measurements it is not quite as convenient as a retractable steel tape (6).
- Use scissors (7) or a utility knife (8) for cutting paper from rolls, and a trimming knife with single-edge razor blades (9) for trimming at baseboards and moldings. A trimming guide (10) is useful for

these finishing cuts, as it combines the functions of straightedge and flattener in one tool.

- A plastic paste bucket (11) and a paste brush (12) are for mixing and applying the adhesive, while a clean, moist sponge (13) is for wiping away excess adhesive after each strip is hung. With prepasted paper, you won't need a pasting brush or bucket. A water tray will suffice.
- A long-bristled smoothing brush (14) is used for applying most coverings, but its stiffer, short-bristled cousin (15) works best on vinyl coverings. On prepasted paper, use a moist sponge.
- A seam roller (16) is used to give a final smoothing along the edges of the moist paper. But it can be replaced by a sponge on prepasted paper.

In addition to the items shown, you will need wall size for preparing the walls before papering; a work surface (a large folding table is best, but you could work on a clean floor if you don't mind bending); a stepladder or a reliable chair to stand on; and, for prepasted coverings, a water tray (or you could use your bathtub).

Preparing walls for papering

You can sometimes hang wallpaper directly over the old covering, but only if it is still adhering tightly to the wall in all areas. If it is loose in a few spots, you may be able to get away with removing those parts and sanding the torn edges to even off the resulting irregularity. (Vinyl paper is an exception; it should never be hung over old paper.) If a large area is loose or there are more than two layers already on the wall, it is best to remove it all.

Soak off old wallpaper with a mixture of water and commercial wallpaper remover, or else you can strip it off with a wallpaper steamer. You can rent this equipment at most wallpaper stores, but it's only necessary for the most stubborn paper. Either way, when the paper has soaked long enough to become soft, scrape it off the wall with a wide-bladed putty knife. Be careful not to gouge the wall with the knife.

Before papering new plaster walls, allow them to cure up to three months and then coat them with a commercial preparation known as wall size. In fact, it's a good idea to size all walls, new or old, before papering. The purpose of size is to promote adhesion. It comes in powder form. Add water to form a thin paste; then brush on.

After sizing new plaster walls, and sometimes old ones, you may notice pink, red, or purple patches beginning to form on them. These are important clues that the wall is too rich in alkalis for wallpaper to adhere to it, and so it must first be neutralized chemically. Wearing rubber gloves, apply a 10 percent solution of acetic acid with a soft cloth until the color fades.

Choosing the starting point

Since the patterns on adjacent strips of wallpaper should match perfectly, it is important to consider carefully where you will hang your first strip. Of course, with very small or random patterns, you won't have a matching problem, so any convenient door, window, or room corner might make a good starting point. But for wallpaper that has a recognizable repeat design, stop and think before you hang.

Your aim should be to achieve perfect symmetry on the most prominent wall in the room, and let the rest of the job take care of itself from there. Only if the area to be papered will completely surround a room (without any break from ceiling to floor such as a bookcase, fireplace, etc.) will you have to choose a stopping point as well.

For good appearance and for ease of application, you'll want to avoid using strips less than 8 inches wide. To do this, take these four easy steps with a ruler and pencil before hanging any paper:
1. Measure the width of your wallpaper roll in inches.
2. Measure the length of your most important wall in inches.
3. Divide the wall length in half.
4. Divide the result in step 3 by the wallpaper width, and note the *remainder* in the division arithmetic. If it is 8 or less, it means you'll have to center the middle strip of paper on the wall in order to avoid narrow end strips; if it is greater than 8, it means you should plan to butt two strips at the center point of the wall.

EXAMPLES:
1. Roll width = 24".
2. Wall length = 12'2", or 146".
3. One-half wall length = 73".
4. After division, remainder is 1.
Therefore: Center middle strip.

1. Roll width = 20".
2. Wall length = 15'6", or 186".
3. One-half wall length = 93".
4. After division, remainder is 13.
Therefore: Butt two strips at center.

The same method can be used to avoid narrow strips between windows and doors or above a fireplace.

In rooms where you intend to paper four walls continuously, it's best to pick an inconspicuous spot in advance as the place where the pattern will mismatch. Examples of such places might be a dimly lighted alcove, the narrow wall strip above a door or window, or—as a last resort—a room corner partly hidden by furniture.

A dimly lit alcove and the narrow wall above a door are good places to solve the mismatch problem.

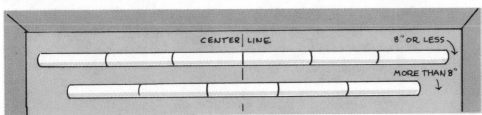

The wallpaper arrangement at the top will produce a noticeable flaw: strips at the ends less than 8 inches wide. The lower arrangement improves on this situation, leaving wider end strips.

Hanging wallpaper

1. Establish a true vertical guideline for hanging the first sheet of wallpaper. Don't trust room corners; they're probably out of plumb. Suspend a chalked plumb bob from a high point on the wall. When the bob comes to rest, pull it taut against the baseboard and snap the line at the center. The mark it leaves is a true vertical.

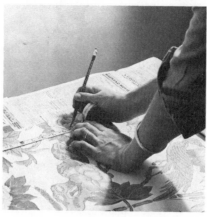

2. Measure the ceiling-to-baseboard height of the wall along the plumb line and mark off this distance, plus 4 or 5 inches, on the first strip of wallpaper.

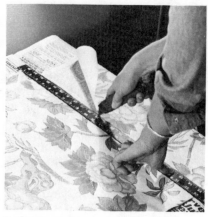

3. Cut the wallpaper into enough strips of this length to cover the first wall. Important: Make sure the patterns will match before cutting more than the first strip. If not, increase the length of subsequent strips until a neat match becomes possible within the wall area. Stack the strips on the pasting table, pattern side down.

4. Mix wallpaper paste according to the recipe given on the package. Mix powdered pastes slowly so they don't lump up.

5. To make sure the powder is completely dissolved and to produce a rich, creamy texture, use your electric mixer, but be sure to wash it off immediately.

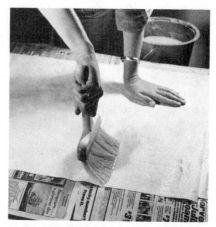

6. Brush a coat of paste onto the first strip, starting at the top. If there is no imprint on the back to tell you which end is up, check the pattern by turning the strip over. Leave an inch or two unpasted at top and bottom.

7. After pasting the entire strip, double over about one-sixth of its total length so the pasted side is touching itself. Don't crease.

8. From the other end, double over about one-half of the remaining length, almost but not quite to the point that the top edge touches the bottom edge.

9. Drape the doubled paper over your left arm as shown (assuming you are right-handed), and carry it to the wall. The top of the paper should be in position to be installed at the ceiling line.

10. Unfurl the top section by grasping the unpasted area at the end, and press it lightly into place at the top of the wall. Allow the unpasted edge to extend beyond the top of the wall. Ordinarily (but not in the example photographed) it will turn the corner at the ceiling line.

11. Use the smoothing brush to make the paper stick to the wall and drive out air pockets. Work from the top down and from the center to the sides in even strokes.

12. When the top of the strip adheres by itself, reach behind it to unroll the bottom section, guide it into place, and press it against the wall with the smoothing brush.

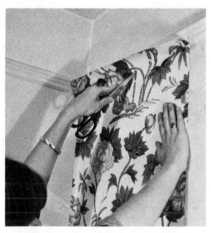

13. Use the tip of a scissors to crease and score the top edge of the paper.

14. Give the strip a final pressing with the smoothing brush.

15. If you turn a corner, arrange it so the paper extends about an inch beyond. Brush this section vigorously to keep it from unsticking. The stiff bristles of the smoothing brush will force the paper into the corner.

16. Trim off the top along the score line you made in step 13. You can also lift the strip away, cut along the score line, and return it to its original postion.

17. Use the trimming knife to remove excess paper at the baseboard and other places where pulling the paper away would be awkward or difficult.

18. Bring subsequent strips into alignment by positioning them on the wall (without brushing) a fraction of an inch away, then sliding them gently into place.

19. After the paper has been up for 10 or 15 minutes, press the seams firmly with a seam roller. Most wallpaper flaws that develop over time are due to carelessly rolled seams.

20. The areas where wallpaper meets door and window frames are tricky. Precutting to fit is the riskiest way to deal with these obstacles. Instead, put up a whole strip of wallpaper and brush it into place as far as the point where the wall meets the obstacle.

21. At the top, or bottom, of the door or window frame, cut the wallpaper diagonally to permit separation into two sections: one to extend vertically along the side of the frame, the other horizontally above, or below, it.

22. Brush the horizontal section into place and trim the abutting edge to fit neatly above or below the obstruction.

23. Trim the vertical edge next. A triangular cutting guide and trimming knife make this an easy operation. Follow the corner formed where the wall meets the frame.

24. Where protrusions are more complex, as in the case of this jutting windowsill, brush the paper as close to the obstacle as possible without risking a tear.

25. Then make horizontal cuts above and below the obstacle, to the end of but not beyond the obstacle.

26. After brushing any completed sections into place (here, the part below the sill), make whatever additional cuts are necessary to get an exact fit. In the photograph, a horizontal slit is being made between the two sections of sill, one of which protrudes farther than the other.

27. Make final cuts only after you have been able to brush the paper into place against the obstacle. The loose vertical section alongside the window frame can now be easily trimmed as in step 23.

Ceilings

1. Hanging paper on the ceiling presents a few extra problems, but none that are insurmountable. Begin by snapping a horizontal chalk line. If the ceiling is not perfectly rectangular—which few are—your line will have to be a compromise: make it as parallel as possible to the two long walls and as perpendicular as possible to the short walls.

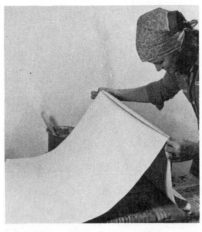

2. Instead of rolling the pasted paper back over itself, fold it, without creasing it, into a zigzagging pattern, with each section about 2 feet long. Pasted side will face pasted side, and pattern side will face pattern side in this arrangement. (The total length of the strip should be 2 inches longer than the ceiling.)

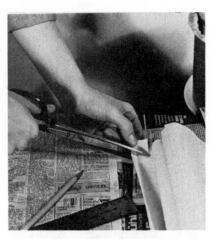

3. To facilitate placing the first strip in a corner, with a 1-inch overlap down two adjacent walls, cut a 1-inch square away from the corner at which you will begin hanging.

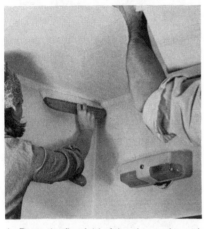

4. Press the first fold of the zigzagging strip into the corner of the ceiling and open out a few more sections, while an assistant supports the remainder of the strip. Brush the paper into place with a 1-inch overhang on the walls.

5. After unfolding the rest of the strip, brush the entire piece firmly onto the ceiling.

6. Give the corners an extra brushing to make sure they cling.

7. When the sheet is in place, peel down the uncut corner and trim away a 1-inch square to help the fit. Then press the trimmed edges into place again.

8. After 10 or 15 minutes, go over the entire strip with a clean, dry paint roller. Exert firm pressure to promote a good bond.

9. Cut away the overlapping strips on all three walls, using a trimming knife and triangular shield.

Papering a switch plate

1. You'll have to remove switch plates and other fixtures before wallpapering, whether you plan to cover them with paper or not. Turn off the current at the circuit breaker or fuse box first. Then, remove screws and pry the fixtures away from the wall.

2. With the current still off, hang paper and make X-shaped slits over the open fixtures. The moisture in the paste, and the knife blade poking into the electrical apparatus, would be hazards if the current were on.

3. Cut a rectangular scrap of wallpaper about twice the size of the switch plate and match it to the pattern surrounding the open area vacated by the fixture.

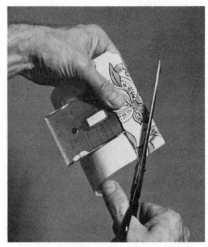

4. Install the switch plate temporarily via the screw holes and, still maintaining the pattern match, use your thumbnail to crease the patch along the edges of the switch plate.

5. Remove the switch plate and fold the patch over it along one of the crease lines.

6. Cut two corners diagonally off the patch so the scissor just misses the corners of the switch plate. Be sure the adjacent sides of the switch plate are still aligned with the creases in the patch.

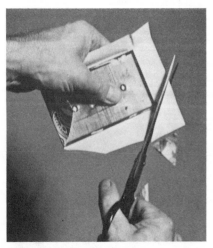

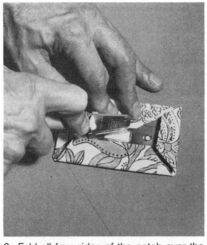

7. Before folding the opposite end of the patch over the switch plate, make diagonal cuts at the two remaining corners.

8. Fold all four sides of the patch over the switch plate and, from behind, trim away any paper that covers the toggle hole.

9. Screw the switch plate into place on the wall. After the paste has dried for a few hours, turn the current back on.

Double cutting

There are times when matching a pattern may be difficult. For example, you're running out of paper and you decide to use a few of the large scraps that have been accumulating rather than buy a fresh roll for behind the refrigerator; but the edges, no longer factory-trimmed, don't match up properly. Here's what to do:

1. Hang the wallpaper as usual, but position the adjacent sheets so one overlaps the other by a few inches, with the pattern properly matched along the rough-cut edge. While the paste is still moist, make a vertical cut within the overlap area, using a straightedge and trimming knife.

2. Lift the top sheet back from the point of the cut and peel away the two long, thin scraps that remain on the wall and on the edge of the bottom sheet.

TIP: If your paper has a repeating pictorial design, you can cut up your scraps and paste the images on wastebaskets, cribs, dressers, or anywhere else that strikes your fancy, to echo the designs that appear on the wall.

TIP: Brighten up an old door by papering the panels. Try the same on kitchen cabinets, telephones, even mirror frames.

3. Press the top sheet back in place. It will butt neatly now with its neighbor in a perfect pattern match. After a few minutes, roll the seam.

4. Use the same technique to butt untrimmed vinyl, but make a *freehand* cut through both strips. Then pull the scraps away and smooth the seam.

Prepasted papers

If you opt for prepasted paper, you *must* follow the manufacturer's recommended soaking time exactly, or the paper may not adhere properly. A water tray is a great convenience for this, though if you're doing a bathroom you could use the tub.

1. Fill the tray halfway with water *at room temperature* and place it at the foot of each wall section you are about to paper. Cut a strip to length and roll it up loosely from bottom to top with the pasted backing on the outside of the roll. Place the rolled paper in the water for the recommended soaking time (usually a minute or less) and pull the strip up into place on the wall.

2. With prepasted paper, you won't need a smoothing brush or a seam roller. A moist sponge does the job of both, while it sops up excess water once the paper is hung. All other techniques are identical to those used for traditional wallpaper.

Don't kick the bucket.
If you use a water tray, watch out. Many of the commercial ones are made of flimsy plastic and can be kicked over without any effort at all. Of course this is most likely to happen at the worst possible time: while you're giving all your attention to getting a wallpaper strip onto the wall.

Even worse, when two people carry a tray of water from the ends, the center can easily buckle, giving both of them a bath.

If you get fed up with prepasted paper in the middle of the job, you can always switch to the good old paste-brush method without switching paper.
Practical Pete

8. REPAIRING FLOORS

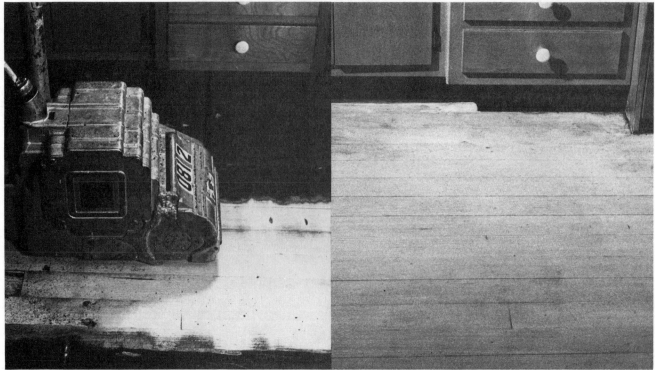

Before

After

Nothing else in your house takes a beating the way your floors do. For this reason, floors must be made of tough materials and be well protected from abuse. The tough materials are usually supplied by the builder or landlord; protection is up to you.

If you stop to think of what happens to floors, you can understand why they need such care. People walk on them, drag things across them, jump on them. Furniture legs dig into them. Kids run sharp and scratchy toys over them. Everyone spills things on them, even puts cigarettes out on them. Dampness expands them; winter dryness shrinks them. Sharp objects are dropped on them, glass is broken on them,

and do-it-yourselfers use them as a work surface—often inflicting the greatest damage of all!

Oddly enough, the floors seem to take it. Hardwood floors in ancient homes have existed through generations of such mistreatment. They may have been refinished many times, but each time they have been given a bright, new life.

There are three main materials used for floor surfaces: wood (usually hardwood, but occasionally softwoods are used), resilient flooring (tile, vinyl sheeting, etc.), and carpeting. (For carpet care, see page 93.) Ceramic tile and slate are often used in specialized areas.

Routine maintenance

Wood floors. All wood floors should have been given a good finish to begin with (see page 78). If the finish is in good shape, the floor merely needs to be waxed at regular intervals, every four months to a year, depending on the amount of wear.

Before waxing, clean the floor thoroughly with a wax-base cleaner. A damp cloth can be used sparingly, but don't ever flood any type of wood with water. Water raises wood grain—and worse—if allowed to stand. And never use waxes or cleaners, unless they are specifically designed for use on wood.

Floor-cleaning wax both cleans and waxes in one coat, but be sure that all gross materials such as chewing gum, rubbed-in food particles, and other foreign bodies are scraped off first. Then scour the affected area with fine (3/0) steel wool.

Both liquid and paste waxes are available for floors. Paste wax is preferred for most woods, but floors are generally just too big for practical use of paste wax. The "buffing" type of liquid wax is better for floors. It can be applied with cloth or a long-handled applicator and buffed after 15 to 30 minutes of standing time. A soft cloth or lamb's-wool buffing attachment on an electric drill can be used for buffing, but it pays

to rent a floor-buffing machine from time to time. (Some of these machines are equipped to apply the wax as well.) Several thin coats of wax should be applied the first time; then use one coat at the suggested intervals thereafter. Never apply any wax thickly because it only gums up and makes buffing more difficult. Allow ample drying time between coats.

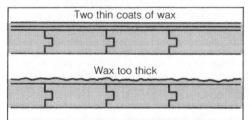

Two thin coats of wax

Wax too thick

When wax builds up to the point that it can no longer be buffed, or when dirt has become embedded in it, the old wax should be removed with turpentine, naphtha, or mineral spirits. Start over again with two or three thin coats of wax, buffing in between.

Floors should be swept daily to prevent dirt from becoming ground in. An occasional polishing with a soft cloth or electric polisher will help keep the surface smooth and dirt resistant.

Resilient flooring. Linoleum was hailed as a great advance in flooring, and it graced many a home during the years of the First World War and for decades thereafter. In 1974, after being produced for 114 years, the last linoleum plant shut down, the "wonder" product having been replaced by the more durable vinyl, vinyl asbestos, asphalt, and "no-wax" resilient floorcoverings. (Many people still call sheet flooring "linoleum," but this is a misnomer.)

Routine care of resilient flooring includes daily sweeping to remove dirt before it has a chance to cling. Spills should be sponged up immediately. An occasional mopping will remove dirt accumulation, but don't flood the floor. Water won't damage this type of floor like it will wood, but it can dull the finish.

A thorough cleaning is necessary only two or three times a year. More frequent cleanings will do more harm than good. Use a mild cleaner that contains no harmful solvents, harsh alkalis, or abrasives. Then rinse the floor lightly with warm water, and dry it with a clean mop. Try to avoid direct sunlight on any flooring, but especially on resilient flooring. It will cause fading.

Some newer flooring products claim not to need wax, and they certainly need it far less often than the usual floorcoverings. But be skeptical. Eventually they may need waxing, too. When any resilient flooring begins to look dull, try buffing first to see if the sheen returns. If not, apply a water-based liquid wax. Don't use paste wax or other waxes containing petroleum solvents. Spread the wax with an applicator thinly and evenly, using long, straight strokes in one direction only. Wait 30 minutes before walking on the floor and two hours before applying another coat. Buff with a floor-polishing machine after the second coat dries. Use a soft fiber brush, not steel wool pads. If you buff by hand, use a clean cloth and bear down hard. Remove any built-up wax with the solvent recommended by the wax manufacturer.

Floor-care tips

- Use floor protectors on legs of furniture to minimize scratches and indentations. The wider they are, the better.
- When moving heavy furniture or appliances, slip scrap carpeting face-down under each leg to avoid floor damage.
- Place mats or throw rugs at entrance ways to keep soil from being tracked inside. Indoors, don't use a rug that has synthetic foam backing. It can cause discoloration.
- Follow the routine maintenance procedures on these pages to prolong the life of your floor.
- To determine whether a brand-name floor wax is designed for use on wood or resilient flooring, look for these key phrases:

  For wood, not resilient. "Caution, combustible mixture." "Do not use on asphalt or rubber."

  For resilient, not wood. "Keep from freezing." "Do not shake." "For asphalt, rubber. . . ."

Probably the most popular of the many floor designs produced in linoleum's heyday—the 1930s—is shown at left. A modern counterpart, at right, is resilient flooring. Curiously, both designs mimic ceramic tile.

What it takes

Approximate time: Minutes.

Tools and materials: Among the items you may need, depending on the kind of stain you are trying to remove, are a cigar, 3/0 steel wool, any light oil, furniture cleaner, dry-cleaning fluid, acetone, wax cleaner, concentrated floor cleaner, mild household cleanser, paper toweling, and a rag.

I got the point later.
The first time I repaired a squeaky floorboard, I figured I would need a good, strong screw to draw all that wood down, so I picked the biggest one I could find. It worked fine, and I was quite pleased with myself until a few days later, when I stubbed my unsuspecting toe on the protruding screw tip. Now I follow the rule: combined thickness of subfloor and floorboard minus ¼ inch equals maximum screw length. When in doubt, I start with a 1-inch screw, then try 1⅛, and so on, until the board is pulled back into place.

Practical Pete

What it takes

Approximate time: Minutes for touchups; up to an hour for most squeaks.

Tools and materials: Minor surface flaws and separated floorboards may require a putty stick or sawdust, stain, and clear glue; larger flaws will call for stick shellac plus an alcohol burner to melt it, a putty knife or spatula to spread it, sandpaper to smooth it, and a small quantity of the original floor finish to camouflage the repair; warped or squeaky boards can be fixed with a wood shim, or a few screws and a screwdriver, or a power drill, hammer, nails, and a nail set.

You may be able to patch small flaws with a child's crayon, if you can find a color that approximates the wood tone.

Removing spots and stains

A floor that is kept in good shape and waxed as recommended should present few problems with spotting and staining. The whole point is in regular maintenance of the floor

The special coatings on no-wax floors should repel almost anything without staining. When problems do occur, here are some ways of curing them:

Wood flooring

White stains and spotting, especially from wet glasses, are one of the most common defects found on wood floors. Water and alcohol cause white rings or "hazing." The old furniture-refinisher's trick of rubbing in cigar ash with a little old-fashioned spittle is as good a way as any. (Plain water doesn't seem to work as well.) If that doesn't solve the problem, rub the whitened area with fine (3/0) steel wool and a little oil. Any light oil will do—lemon, mineral, corn, vegetable, or whatever.

Resilient flooring

Scuff marks are a common problem with this type of flooring. Rubbing with wax cleaner should get rid of them. Use concentrated floor cleaners with steel wool if this doesn't work. The same treatment can remove most other stains and spots. As a last resort, dust lightly with a mild house-

Surface grease can be removed by a cleaner-conditioner made for furniture. Deep grease spots and animal stains are eliminated by a dry-cleaning fluid like the one you use for clothes. Acetone will get rid of stains caused by vegetable oils. Apply these products very cautiously and away from flames. Dose them on liberally, but avoid spilling them over onto unstained surfaces. When the spot is gone, wipe dry with paper toweling. Remember always to read the manufacturer's instructions.

hold cleanser; then reapply floor cleaner with steel wool. Don't use steel wool on embossed floors, though. Regular scouring powder on a damp cloth will have the same effect without rubbing down the raised areas. Always wipe off cleansers thoroughly, rinse, and rewax.

Repairing wood floors

Surface flaws

Wood is wood, and fixing up defects in wood flooring is very much like fixing up surface damage in furniture. However, what looks like a deep scratch in flooring may only be in the wax or the finish. Usually, scratches can be rubbed out with wax or left alone until the entire floor needs rewaxing. But if you're sure a scratch extends into the wood itself, there are several ways to disguise the defect.

One easy way is to use a matching wax putty stick to fill in, just as you would on paneling. A child's crayon will also work, if you can find the right shade. But large cracks or gouges will require a more permanent repair. Heat stick shellac over a colorless flame in an alcohol burner and apply it to the crack with a heated knife or spatula. Fill in a trifle higher than the surrounding surface; then scrape off the excess carefully when it hardens. Sand with fine abrasive paper and touch up with the same finishing material used for the rest of the floor. Always rewax after any repair.

Separated floorboards

Though they are often caused by the excessive dryness of artificial winter heat, if separated floorboards don't go back into place by summer, the cause is probably green (unseasoned) wood or poor workmanship. Although the methods mentioned opposite will generally work here too—depending on the width of the crack —it is better to mix some wood putty with a stain of the same color and fill the crack with that. To get the right color, keep adding stain slowly and mixing well until it looks right. You may have to mix a few stains to get the right shade, but oak stain usually works well by itself on oak flooring.

When you are satisfied with the match, work it into the joint with a putty knife, carefully wiping off any excess from the surrounding floorboards. Smooth the surface with a finger. If there is any shrinkage after drying, apply a second coat to bring it up to the level of the floor. Sand down any bulges that may appear.

High spots caused by buckled boards can

be nailed down. If a board is badly warped, however, the nails won't hold. In that case, leave it be until the floor needs refinishing. But if the warp is unsightly or bad enough to be a hazard underfoot, it won't wait. If there are any surface nails, drive them in deeply with a nail set; then clean out the cracks with a wire brush. Set a plane to medium height and go over the high area, starting from any exposed ends and working with the grain. Keep planing until the board is flush. Go over the board with a fine cut on the plane, then give the planed-down area a sanding with fine paper. Stain the abraded wood if necessary, use a wood filler on oak, and touch up with finish to hide the repair. Be careful; work slowly.

Squeaky floors

To silence squeaks, the source of the problem must first be pinpointed. This is not too difficult if the joints are exposed below, but you'll need a helper. Have the helper walk around on the floor while you study the subfloor from below. If a spot on the flooring moves up and down as the person walks above, hammer in a wedge (wood shingles are good for this) between the subfloor and the joist. When the problem isn't near a joist, it is usually the finish flooring that is loose, not the subfloor. Screw through the subfloor into the finish flooring, but make sure you determine the thickness of the flooring first, and use screws that won't protrude through the surface. If in doubt, a 1-inch screw is usually right.

Where the joists below are covered by a ceiling, or when wedging doesn't do the trick, repairs must be made from above. It is possible that some of the floor nails have loosened, and that pounding them down again will stop the squeaks. To correct this, use a block of wood and a hammer to pound down on the flooring again. Spread newspapers or some covering over the boards to prevent damage. Keep moving the block around and pounding on it until you've covered the suspected squeak area.

If that doesn't work, you will have to drive in nails to act as wedges from above. Pre-drill holes at an approximate 75-degree angle, about 6 inches apart. Try to hit a joist if you can find one. Place special flooring nails into the holes. Drive the nails partway, stopping when the heads are about 1/4 inch above the surface. Walk over the area to see if the squeak has stopped. If not, do the same over a wider area, until successful.

Once the cure is effected, countersink the nails about 1/8 inch below the floor surface with a nail set, then fill with wood putty stained as described above. Sand and touch up with finishing material.

Squeaky stairs

Pinpointing the source of noise in staircases also requires a helper. Have your helper slowly shift his full weight to each step with as much weight as possible on the front edge over the riser. Most squeaks are caused by movement between the tread and riser. Look and listen carefully to find the source of the noise. Once the point of movement is found, the procedure for stopping the noise is similar to that previously described for floorboard problems. Most stair treads are oak. To prevent splitting, drill a pilot hole before using nails or screws.

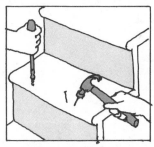

A temporary fix can sometimes be made by squirting a nonstaining silicone lubricant between the tread and riser. A better solution is to use nails or screws as shown.

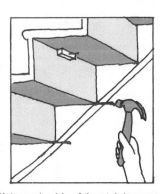

If the underside of the stair is accessible, secure a wood block as shown. Apply wood glue to the block and secure it with nails or screws.

Four ways to squelch squeaks

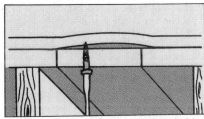

(1.) Drill pilot hole from below and drive screw through subfloor partway into finish flooring.

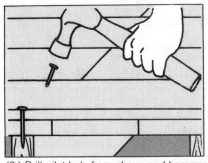

(2.) Drill pilot hole from above and hammer nails into joists below. Joists can usually be located by taking measurements from a chimney or stairwell. Trial-and-error leaves more holes to patch.

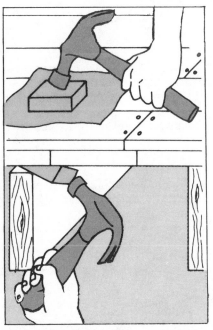

(3.) Drive a wedge into the gap between the subfloor and the joist, and/or (4.) reset old nails by pounding a wood block over newspaper-protected floorboards.

Replacing a damaged floorboard section

What it takes

Approximate time: An hour or two per board; three hours or more for larger sections, depending on extent of damage.

Tools and materials: Wide chisel, electric drill, screwdriver, claw hammer, miter box, backsaw, nail set, framing or try square, circular saw (optional), scrap or new flooring as needed, flooring nails, white glue, and wood-finishing products to camouflage repair.

I almost had a fit . . .

Trying to cut a replacement floorboard to size, I had more near-misses than I'd care to admit. Some were a hair too long to force into the hole. Others were too short to fill it without a gap. But I finally hit on a foolproof method: First I cut a length of flooring 1/32 inch oversize. Then I set my adjustable miter box at a 10-degree angle, placed the board on edge, and beveled off the lower part of one end. After carefully removing the tongue, I glued the board and the hole. Then, voila, the bevel cut made it easy to drive the board snugly into the hole—and the glue even doubled as a lubricant in the home stretch.

Practical Pete

When hardwood floorboards are damaged beyond repair, the offending areas should be removed. Draw lines with a framing square at the ends of the damaged section.

Remember that these boards are tongued and grooved, and are not easy to take up without damaging adjacent flooring. Any way you can get them out of there with that in mind is all right, but the easiest way is to drill wide holes just beyond the damaged area at both ends. Overlap the holes slightly to make a continuous open line. Don't drill so deep that you damage the subfloor. Then take the widest chisel you have and split the damaged board lengthwise down the center. With the chisel or a screwdriver,

pry out both halves of the damaged section of board. Square off the ends of the opening with your chisel on an exact right angle and remove the resulting fragments. Pull out any nails that remain, as well as the tongue of the removed board, which will probably still be lodged in the adjacent groove. Remove the tongue carefully.

Take a new piece of matching flooring and lay it alongside the opening. Mark the

board at each end and cut it perfectly square in a miter box. Test the fit of the new piece in the opening. Remove the bottom half of the groove so that the board will lay in correctly. Coat all the adjacent board edges and subfloor, as well as the new piece of board, with clear glue. Set the board into place, slipping the tongue into the adjacent groove first, then pressing down until flat. Drive two nails into each end, predrilling, setting, and finishing neatly. Use more nails in the center if the piece is very long.

The same procedures apply to plank flooring, except that these boards are usually screwed in and countersunk with a wood plug covering the screw head. Use a same-size drill bit to remove the plug. Clean out the slot of the screw head and remove the screw, trying not to strip the head.

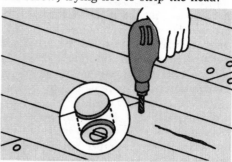

If many boards of either type are to be removed, a circular saw can be used to cut them out. Set the blade for a cut ⅜ inch deep, and saw around the perimeter of the damaged area. Start the cut at least ¼ inch in from the side edge of the board to avoid hitting nails. Begin the cut at the center of

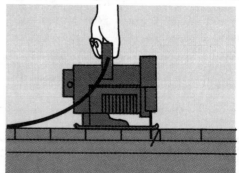

the damaged area and work toward the ends. Finish the cut with your chisel. In an extensive repair job, all boards can be nailed as in a new flooring operation (see page 88) except for the last one, which is then inserted as described above. It is of course best to stagger the locations of the board ends in a nonrepeating pattern. This will help give you the kind of strong, level floor that is so important for comfort and longevity—and it will look neater.

Fixing damaged resilient flooring

When floor tile is damaged, it is easy to replace, provided you had the foresight to save a few tiles for this purpose. If not, buy extras from the dealer and hope they match well. When all else fails, "steal" one from an inconspicuous spot such as in a closet or under an appliance.

The fastest way to remove the damaged tile is with a blowtorch. An iron is slower

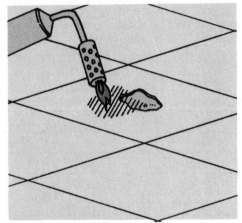

but safer. Either way, heat the tile until the adhesive melts underneath. The iron should be at a medium setting. Place aluminum foil between the iron and the tile. When the tile loosens, pry it out from any edge with a putty knife or similar tool. If the tile surface is soft, you can cut an X through it with a utility knife and pull out the pieces without heating.

To install a new tile, spread fresh tile adhesive on the open subfloor with a notched trowel. Set, don't slide, the new

tile in place and go over it with a rolling pin. Weight it down until the adhesive dries.

Tiles with curled-up edges can be reset by heating the damaged section, lifting the edge, scraping off the old adhesive, and regluing with new floor tile adhesive. Weight, as for a new tile.

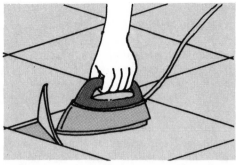

Resilient sheet flooring is a little more difficult to fix. First you have to locate the piece of scrap flooring you so cleverly saved for such an occasion. Arrange it over the damaged area so the pattern matches. Cut a

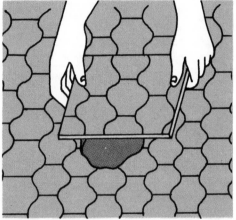

square piece with your utility knife and a straightedge. Tape the piece down firmly and cut a smaller square through the top piece deeply enough to score the flooring below. Keep your knife vertical. Remove the top piece and finish cutting through the score lines into the subfloor. Remove the damaged section as if it were a tile, unless

the flooring wasn't glued down before, in which case it will just lift out. Replace the damaged section with the new piece as for tile. This method should produce a perfect pattern match and a perfect fit. However, the barely visible trace of the patch outline probably will remain.

What it takes

Approximate time: Fifteen minutes to a half hour for tile; double for sheet flooring.

Tools and materials: You will not need all of the listed items. But a utility knife, putty knife, blowtorch or household iron, aluminum foil, notched trowel, rolling pin, scrap tile or sheet flooring, flooring adhesive, masking tape, and clear lacquer may be needed, depending on the nature of the repair.

Stopgaps and copouts
Scratches and gouges in resilient flooring can be disguised, if they are not too severe, by first scraping off some floor-covering material from a matching scrap or inconspicuous section, and mixing the fragments with clear lacquer to form a paste. Apply to the defect and level off with a putty knife.

Refinishing wood flooring

What it takes

Approximate time: Depends on size of job and difficulties that may be encountered; but consider your time in days. Three small rooms might take a full weekend.

Tools and materials: Hammer, screwdriver, pry bar, nail set, wide wood chisel, spade, hand scraper, rented belt sander, rented disc sander, sanding block, sandpaper in various grades (see chart), brushes, rags, filler, stain, sealer, turpentine.

After many years of wear, waxing may no longer be enough to restore the beauty of hardwood floors. Or, you may want to replace wall-to-wall carpeting with an area rug, or leave the floor bare, but have found the hardwood to be in deplorable condition after you take up the old carpeting (which is probably why the wall-to-wall was laid).

In any case, the floors here will have to be refinished, a time-consuming and dusty job, but one the homeowner can do if he wishes. It is both the nastiest and most satisfying project in our experience. Those who are short of time and patience may prefer to hire professional floor finishers.

No matter what type of wood your floors are made of, the technique never varies. It's basically the same job the building contractor did after he installed the floor the first time. But he did the sanding for a different reason, to level off the new boards and provide a smooth surface for the finish. You will be sanding to remove stains, scratches, and ground-in dirt.

Floor-sanding schedule

Floor type	Condition	First cut	Second cut	Third cut
Hardwood (Oak, maple, beech, birch, etc.)	Bad	Very coarse (#3) 24 grit	Med. coarse (#1½) 40 grit	Fine (#2/0) 100 grit
	Fair	Coarse (#2) 36 grit	Med. (#1) 50 grit	Fine (#2/0) 100 grit
	Good	Med. coarse (#1½) 40 grit	Med. (#1) 50 grit	Fine (#2/0) 100 grit
Softwood (Pine, fir, etc.)	Bad	Coarse (#2) 36 grit	Med. (#1) 50 grit	Fine (#2/0) 100 grit
	Fair	Med. coarse (#1½) 40 grit	Med. (#1) 50 grit	Fine (#2/0) 100 grit
	Good	Med. (#1) 50 grit	Fine (#2/0) 100 grit	(None)

Sanding

You should rent two professional sanding machines, one a large drum sander for the bulk of the job, the other a smaller disc sander for corners or other less accessible areas. Hand scrapers and sandpaper are used in areas too confined for even the disc sander to operate efficiently.

For really lustrous finishes, the experts recommend at least four sandings, although most homeowners rightly feel that they can get away with less. In no case should you give the floor fewer than two sandings. Three is better.

Start with 36-grit (#2) abrasive paper and graduate down to 50 grit (#1) and 100 grit (#2/0) for the last sanding. (For softwoods, see the chart above.) Sand with the grain wherever possible, and change the belts often to prevent clogging. Yet another sanding with 120-grit (#3/0) paper will produce a truly fine surface. It is recommended that the final traverse be done by hand, though it's hard to imagine the average handy-person doing an entire house on hands and knees after just going through several machine sandings. Still, if you want a showcase floor in a small room you might want to try it.

1. Prepare to sand floors by clearing the room of all furnishings, even those that do not rest on the floor, and seal off other living areas from the thick dust which the machines will produce. Remove radiator covers, shoe moldings and any other obstacles along the floor perimeter.

2. Use a nail set or another nail to drive protruding nail heads below the surface of the floor. They are often hard to spot in advance. Metal will tear the high-speed sanding belts. Later, if you see sparks fly from beneath the sanding drum, stop immediately and look for a nail head you may have missed earlier.

3. With the current off, mount the sander belt on the machine by inserting its two prefolded ends into the slanting groove on the drum; then tighten the belt by turning the knobs on either side in opposite directions, using the special wrenches that come with the machine. (Some machines have only a single knob and a matching key.) You will have·to change belts many times in the course of sanding a room.

4. Plug in the machine and sand as much of the room as you can conveniently reach, working in the direction of the grain. One slow pass forward followed by one faster pass backward over the same boards is usually sufficient for each paper grade. Then move to left or right, overlapping the last floorboard or two, to begin the next pass. Be sure to disengage the drum from the floor whenever the machine is at a standstill.

5. When you've gone as far as you can go on any given paper grade with the belt sander, change to the disc sander to reach the edges of the room. The edger has its pitfalls. For one thing, it tends to pull to one side and you must keep it moving or it will leave circular scars on the wood. Don't postpone edging until you've gone through a number of paper grades on the belt sander. Use the same grit on both machines simultaneously.

6. Finally, hand-scrape and hand-sand any areas, especially corners, that you were not able to reach with either machine. This is a laborious but necessary task. When the floors are as good as new, vacuum all remaining dust, and you are ready to apply a stain, if desired.

Fillers

It is important to realize that finishing shows up every crevice and hole in wood that has not been filled. Fillers are packaged as liquid or as paste. The latter needs to be thinned with turpentine or benzene. Since turpentine dries more slowly than benzene, it allows more working time.

The best way to apply filler is to brush first across the grain, and then along it. Cover about two square feet at a time. After about 10 or 15 minutes, when the filler will turn gray or dull, wipe across the grain with burlap or a rough towel. This action forces the filler into the pores of the wood. After most of it has been wiped off, wipe along the grain lightly, using a rag. It is important that you follow the manufacturer's instructions in regard to timing. If you wipe too soon, you'll pull out the filler, and if you wait too long, then it won't come off at all.

Staining

Most flooring looks fine as it is, but if you prefer a darker or colored shade, then apply stain after the sanding dust has been picked up with a damp cloth.

Remember, when choosing a stain, that the final finish coats usually make the end result a bit darker. Experiment with your stain on scrap wood first.

Wiping stains are the easiest to use. Spread the stain with a brush or a rag, then wipe with a clean cloth after it starts to set. But do not let it actually set. Cover a small area at a time. The stain imparts a slightly darker shade the longer it stands, and so let it set in each area the same length of time. Be sure to check the instructions on the can.

Sealers

Because a sealer fills wood pores, thus reducing absorbency, it keeps the number of finish coats to a minimum. For example, if an oil stain has been used, the sealer will keep it from bleeding into the finish coats. The best sealer for this purpose is shellac. Shellac can be mixed with 5 to 10 percent denatured alcohol. But shellac will deteriorate on the shelf in about 4 to 6 months. And old shellac won't dry. Shellac also can become hard and brittle.

There are sealers that you can thin with lacquer thinner and can then paint or spray on right from the can. And there are also ready-mixed stains on the market that combine sealer with stain. This is great, for it eliminates the sealing step; so long as you find a stain with the color you want.

In general, apply floor sealers across the grain first, using a clean string or sponge mop, or a long-handled applicator equipped with a lamb's-wool pad. The sealer is usually smoothed out along the grain, and the excess is wiped off with clean cloths or a squeegee. Two coats are generally advisable on floors. For best results, the dry surface should be buffed afterwards, then waxed as described on page 80.

Think!

Some machines have a lever by which you can gradually lower the spinning belt onto the floor; others need to be tilted back on their rear wheels before you activate the drum. The point is: Never let the sander work in one spot for any length of time. It must always be in motion across the floor or raised off the floor, if you don't want to produce unsightly valleys and ridges.

Too, the action of the drum produces a strong forward pull. Be ready to be yanked forward as soon as you lower the drum onto the floor. On forward passes, you'll need to restrain the beast; on return passes, you'll need to tug it back with a good deal of force. You don't have to turn yourself around—just walk the machine forwards and backwards, disengaging the drum when you change direction.

For greater efficiency, empty the dust bag as soon as it reaches half of its capacity. Turn off the machine and check the level of dust with your hand from time to time.

Keep an eagle eye out for the long electrical cord. If you rent a sander, you'll probably notice many areas where the cord has been patched with electrical tape. If you're not careful, it will surely find its way under the drum. Sling it over your shoulder and keep the excess line far from your immediate work area.

For a final finish

All wood floors need a final finish. The finish protects the wood and enhances its beauty. If you have put sealer on the wood, it will provide an excellent base for varnish.

My varnish had more bubbles than champagne

I couldn't figure why my new finish had all those bubbles in it. I was stirring it well, putting it down carefully, and taking my time. Then a friend reminded me that you shouldn't stir or shake varnish. And sure enough it's written right there in the instructions!

Practical Pete

Tip: Rags soaked in sealer can ignite spontaneously, so they must be stored where they will not cause a fire. A good method is to put them in a bucket of water. Another is to get rid of them by burning them.

Varnish

Floor varnishes come in high, medium, or low gloss. High-gloss varnish will resist wear more than the others. Which you use is really a matter of preference, but to avoid frequent refinishing jobs, don't ignore the kind of service you expect of the floor.

It is questionable whether the urethanes and polyurethanes are really varnishes. They are referred to as synthetics, but they are applied in the same way as varnish, and are often thought of as plastic varnishes.

All varnishes, the urethanes in particular, provide a hard, durable surface that resists most spots and stains. In addition, they impart a glossy glow to the wood.

Like most finishes, varnish works well only when it is applied properly. There are a few rules of thumb you should keep in mind. First, varnish should not be stirred or shaken, as this will create bubbles that will mar the surface. Second, apply the varnish with a brush. Use long, even strokes running with the grain. After several strokes, brush quickly over the varnish, this time going against the grain of the wood. To finish, lightly run a dry brush over the varnish, again going in the direction of the grain.

At least two coats of varnish are necessary—usually three. Since varnish dries fairly slowly, be sure to follow the manufacturer's instructions as to adequate drying time between coats.

When you apply varnish, be sure that the brush you use is totally free of dust and that there is no dust on the floor. Also try to keep the room free of dust while the varnish dries. Many types of varnish take several hours to dry; some are faster than others, but in any case, it is essential that dust not fall onto the wet varnish.

Sometimes air bubbles form in a varnish finish. These are caused by the brush bristles, and you can bypass the problem by avoiding excessive brushing. If bubbles form while you apply the varnish, run the brush back over the marred area, using light, feathering strokes. (This must be done before the varnish sets.)

If you use varnish on bare wood, you will have to thin it. Use one part turpentine to four parts varnish for the first coat. You can brush this in as a sealer. After the varnish has dried thoroughly, sand it lightly. Then apply flow coats of straight varnish, sanding each coat lightly before applying the next and wiping the surface clean after each sanding step.

It is a good idea to practice varnish application on scrap wood. If you put on too much varnish, the drying time will take that much longer; if you apply too little, bare spots will appear—and you will be faced with the problem of blending areas to achieve a uniform appearance. Flow the varnish along the wood grain, from the wet toward the dry area. Work slowly and carefully, stroking out any air bubbles.

Or, if you prefer, you can put a coat of wax over the sealer. In either case you must be sure to work carefully, paying extra attention to keeping the work free of dirt.

Shellac

Generally speaking, shellac is easy to work with. As noted earlier, it has a limited shelf life. After four or six months it will deteriorate. It is important to find out the age of the stock when you make your purchase.

Shellac is cut with denatured alcohol to the desired consistency. The trick is in knowing the right proportions. These vary a good bit, and so the best thing is to ask your paint dealer. Remember that the thinner the coat, the smoother the work. It is better to build up a finish with many thin coats than to use a few thick ones.

Put the shellac down freely, keeping the surface wet. Work toward the wet edge. Each stroke will blend with the previous one, so you don't need to worry about lapping. Keep brushing toward the wet edge. Keep the brush soft between coats by placing it in denatured alcohol.

Wax

You can protect your floor, whether you have used varnish, shellac, or sealer as a finish, by waxing it. (Do not apply wax to bare wood because it penetrates the wood and is therefore difficult to remove.) Wax alone is not a durable finish, but it will stand up to wear, and as long as it remains, it will protect the finish.

Moldings and other trim

When you redo floors or walls, you should remove the baseboard molding, both to protect it and to make your work easier. Baseboard molding usually consists of two different pieces—the baseboard itself and a shoe molding. The baseboard is nailed through the wall into the studs, and the shoe is nailed to the baseboard. As a rule, vinyl cove molding is used with resilient flooring, but you may have to deal with wood molding.

It shouldn't be necessary to remove the shoe molding; in most cases, it will come off with the baseboard. See where the pieces are joined on long walls, however, and remove the shoe first if its sections are joined in different places than those of the baseboard. Pry base trim loose with care.

Unless the baseboard moldings are damaged, you can put them back again when you are finished with your floor. Drive new 8-penny finishing nails in new holes, recessing them. Fill both the old and new holes with wood putty or its equivalent.

To replace just a damaged portion, cut new moldings that match the damaged section. You will need a miter box for this, as these sections will be either coped or mitered (see page 42).

Vinyl cove moldings are easily removed with a putty knife or screwdriver. The old adhesive isn't easy to get off, and so be persistent. Apply new molding with the adhesive specified by the manufacturer.

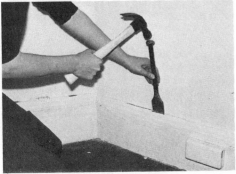

1. Use a pry bar or a thin, wide chisel and hammer to remove baseboard. Pry the board out carefully from the wall because you will want to put it back again undamaged.

2. After you have separated some of the baseboard from the wall, insert wooden wedges so that it will not crack as you progress along the wall.

Removing a threshold

Just as you have to take off the baseboard molding to refinish your floor, you may have to remove one or more door thresholds.

It is a simple procedure provided you exercise care and patience. First, swing the door wide open. If you find that you need more clearance, remove the door. You may have to remove the doorstops from the jamb if the saddle extends under it.

Use a pry bar to remove the stops; you can use the same tool, or the claws of a hammer, to lift up the saddle. Should it happen that the saddle is old and worn, you may wish to replace it. In that case, it will be an easy matter to take it up with a backsaw and wood chisel. Since you'll be discarding the saddle, it doesn't matter if this piece gets damaged.

1. You can use a chisel or pry bar to take out the door stops, and the same tool or the claws of a hammer to remove the saddle.

2. In this case, the homeowner decided to put down a new saddle. As a rule, saddles are made of hardwood and, to avoid splitting, it will be necessary to drill pilot holes for the nails. Do not drill the full length of the nail.

3. Drive finishing nails into the predrilled holes. Sink the heads with a nail set. Fill new, as well as old holes with wood putty. Use the same finish as for the floor.

9.NEW FLOORS

Installing new flooring

Unless it was poorly constructed to begin with, a floor as such doesn't wear out. The finish flooring, however, is a different matter. Linoleum has a rather short life span, as do some of the other less expensive resilient floor coverings. Hardwood, as discussed in the previous chapter, will last almost forever if it is treated well, but even the best resilient floors start to give after a number of years.

If you need to replace a floor covering—or simply want a new look—check the available materials, talk to your building-supply dealer, and figure your time and cost.

Preparing the subfloor

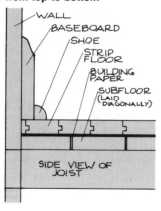

**How it looks
from top to bottom**

WALL
BASEBOARD
SHOE
STRIP FLOOR
BUILDING PAPER
SUBFLOOR (LAID DIAGONALLY)

SIDE VIEW OF JOIST

Resilient tiles or sheet flooring can be laid over most flooring, as long as it is clean, solid, level, and dry. Wood flooring can be applied over other wood (except previously applied hardwood). It can also be installed over concrete with the use of screeds—2x4-inch blocks of wood that raise the flooring above the concrete and provide a nailing surface. Any other type of floor covering (resilient, ceramic, and so on) must be removed before wood flooring is installed.

You can install resilient flooring directly over concrete, but not over hardwood floor. For that, you need to provide an underlayment grade of hardboard or plywood, as described below. If a subfloor exists, level it, if necessary, by planing high spots and filling in low spots. Remove any previously applied resilient flooring if it is starting to wrinkle or buckle. Scrape off or smooth the old adhesive. If you're working over old flooring, remove all wax. Set or pull out any nails or staples, to make a smooth base.

If you install hardwood flooring over wood, be sure that the subfloor is clean and free of protrusions. Fill all gaps, and plane down high spots. Remove all adhesives. If you are installing the wood over concrete, apply a coat of sealer made especially for concrete. Where dampness could be a problem, lay down polyethylene sheet plastic between the adhesive and the screeds. Severe dampness will call for two layers of 1 x 4-inch screeds, with plastic between them—or some other type of flooring material instead.

For screeds, use 2x4s that are 18 to 24 inches long, and set them into thick mastic spread over the floor. Stagger the blocks and overlap them by 4 to 6 inches, as shown at left. Space them so that their centers are 12 inches apart (on 12-inch centers), to provide a solid nailing surface. Run the screeds at right angles to the finish flooring.

Underlayment

Sometimes conventional subflooring might be slightly uneven, and so it is not a good surface on which to lay such materials as vinyl, linoleum, asphalt, and rubber. It is necessary, therefore, to provide an underlayment of plywood or hardboard. For this, use 4x8-foot panels, laying them in staggered fashion, so that no more than three panels meet at any one point. Nail or staple the underlayment to the subfloor at 4-inch intervals. You can rent a special nailing tool to speed up the process.

Attic subfloors

If there is no subfloor already installed, which is frequently the case in attics, you should provide one. To install a subfloor for resilient flooring, use ⅝-inch-thick plywood, spaced as for underlayment and installed so all edges rest on joists. As an extra precaution against dampness or roof leakage, use exterior-grade fir plywood.

To provide an attic subfloor for hardwood, use ½-inch-thick plywood or 1-inch-thick boards, no more than 6 inches wide. The boards should *not* be tongue and groove, although much old subflooring was. Use square-edged boards, spacing them ¼ inch apart to allow for expansion. Face-nail at every joist with two 10-penny nails. This type of subfloor should be laid diagonally; but you can install it perpendicular to the joists. Subflooring boards must always end over joists, unless you use end-matched tongue-and-groove boards. If you do, stagger the joints so that no two successive boards join in the same space. If you use plywood subflooring, nail it to each joist at 6-inch intervals with 8-penny nails. Put building paper down between the subfloor and finish floor, overlapping the sheets by 4 inches.

Flooring types at a glance

Type of flooring	Advantages	Limitations	Suitable wax and cleaner	Comments
ASPHALT TILE	Excellent durability; resists damage from alkalis.	Shows scratches easily; low resiliency; poor grease resistance; softened by spirit solvents.	Use only a water-based wax; alkaline or non-alkaline cleaners are safe.	Formerly inexpensive; not any more.
CERAMIC TILE	Excellent durability; resists grease stains very well if glazed; not affected by alkalis.	No resiliency; unglazed tile easily stained by grease; spaces between tiles are difficult to clean.	Use a sealer on unglazed tile and mortar between glazed or unglazed tiles.	Expensive.
CONCRETE	Excellent durability; not damaged by alkalis.	No resiliency; gives off dust and becomes stained by grease unless well sealed.	Use a sealer specified for concrete.	Not very good inside.
CORK TILE	Good durability; highest resiliency.	Sharp objects will gouge it; water and grease will penetrate it unless well sealed.	Use only solvent-based wax and solvent-based cleaner. Apply wood sealer when needed.	Expensive; widely unavailable.
HARDWOODS	Excellent durability; not damaged by solvents.	Moderate resiliency; damaged by water, alkalis, and grease unless well sealed.	Use only solvent-based wax and solvent-based cleaner. Apply wood sealer when needed.	Time-consuming installation.
LINOLEUM (no longer available)				
RUBBER TILE	Excellent durability; high resiliency.	Damaged by grease and spirit solvents.	Use only water-based wax and water-based cleaners.	Declining popularity.
SLATE (flag stone)	Excellent durability; not damaged by alkalis.	No resiliency; becomes stained by grease and solvents unless well sealed.	Use a sealer specified for stone floors.	Difficult installation.
TERRAZZO marble chips in cement	Excellent durability.	Has no resiliency; is damaged by alkalis; becomes stained by grease unless well sealed.	Use either water-based wax or solvent-based wax; but use only a non-alkaline cleaner. Apply a sealer for stone floors when needed.	Professional installation only.
VINYL solid, with or without backing	Excellent durability; high resiliency like rubber; high resistance to damage by alkalis, grease, and spirit solvents.	None.	Use either water-based wax or solvent-based wax; either alkaline or non-alkaline cleaners are safe.	Most popular.
VINYL-ASBESTOS	Excellent durability; high resistance to damage by alkalis and grease.	Needs wax to cover scratches; moderate resiliency.	Use either water-based wax or solvent-based wax, and either alkaline or non-alkaline cleaners.	Good over concrete in basements.

Laying floor tile

Of the available floor materials, tile is the most popular. One reason is its ease of installation. If you make a mistake, you just throw away the piece and use a new tile. On the other hand, a mistake with sheet flooring might mean you'd have to discard the entire section.'

Most tile installations are routine. Kitchens, baths, and other utility-room floors are usually covered with the same tiles throughout. There are a great many attractive types available. Don't overlook the possibility of a more intricate design, however, especially in basement or attic rooms, foyers, or decorative areas. You can use two or more colors, for example; make striped, zigzag, or other patterns, or install a contrasting border.

Whatever special effect you decide to use, and the possibilities are seemingly limitless, work it out on paper beforehand. Follow your plan carefully during installation to avoid errors that would be difficult to correct afterwards.

How to calculate

Floor tiles come in various sizes. If you select the 12x12-inch size, you'll find it simple to figure how many you will need; the number of tiles will be the same as the square footage of the room, plus a few spares to allow for cutting around the edges and possible damage during installation.

But if the tiles are the more common 9x9-inch variety, it takes a bit more math. A 9x9-tile is 9/16 of a square foot; this means that there are 16 9x9-tiles to a square yard.

A 12x15-foot floor is 180 square feet, or 20 square yards (divided by 9). For a floor this size, you would need 320 9x9-inch tiles, plus spares.

Another way to estimate requirements is to measure the length and width of the room, convert the total to inches, divide each dimension by 9, and multiply the resulting figures. For additional information—and at-a-glance estimates—see the chart on page 86.

Installation

Tiles are installed from the center of the room outward. Measure to find the center point of each end wall, disregarding any offsets, bays, alcoves, or other irregularities. Stretch a carpenter's chalk line between the two center points, having a helper hold one end of the line or securing it under a brick or other heavy object. Make sure the line is level and tight. With your free hand pull the line away from the floor and let it snap back. It will leave a line of chalk on the floor. Do the same with the two side walls. Your lines should intersect at right angles in the center of the room. Check with a square, and make any necessary adjustments.

Lay a row of loose tiles along the chalk line, from the center point to one side wall; lay another row along the line to one end wall. Measure the distance between the side wall and the last full tile. If this space is less than half the width of one tile, snap a new

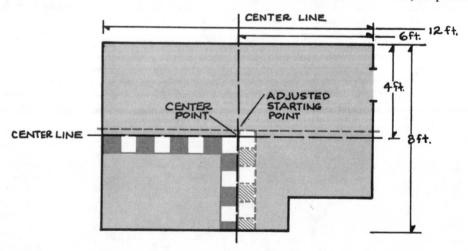

Lay a row of loose tiles along the chalk line from the center point to one side wall, and another along the line to one end wall. Measure the distance between the side wall and the last full tile. If it is less than half a tile wide, snap a new chalk line parallel to the original line, allowing the width of a half tile between the lines. Use this as your guide. Do the same for the end wall.

chalk line parallel to, and a half-tile width from, the original line, as shown opposite. Use this as your guide. It will save a lot of cutting and fitting, plus the peculiar look of very narrow tiles. Repeat the procedure for the end wall.

Some tiles come with an adhesive backing. All you do is peel off the protective paper and press the tile in place. With tiles requiring adhesive, work one quarter of the floor at a time. Use a paint brush, roller, or notched trowel to evenly spread the adhesive up to the chalk lines.

Do not spread too much adhesive; it will bleed through the joints between tiles. Allow the adhesive to set until it is tacky to the touch before you start tiling. Setting time will vary with the type of adhesive used; follow the manufacturer's directions.

Press the first tile into place where the adjusted chalk lines cross in the center of the room. Work outward from there, butting each tile tightly and neatly against the adjoining tile or tiles. Do not slide the tiles into position. That causes the adhesive to ooze up between the tiles.

Work along one end of the chalk line and lay three or four tiles; then fill out until you reach the other line bordering the room quarter. Continue in this manner until the quarter is completed, except for border tiles that must be fitted. Remove any adhesive on the tile surface with a damp cloth or fine steel wool. Do the second quarter of the room in the same way, and continue in this manner until the room is completed.

Installing border tiles

You may want to remove the moldings at this point, so you can use them to cover discrepancies in the tile-to-wall fit. If so, follow the procedure on page 81 for removing and reinstalling them. To fit the border tiles, follow the measuring procedure shown opposite. Then cut the tile carefully along the marked line. A pair of scissors does the job on most tile. For precise cuts use your utility knife and a straightedge, or rent a tile cutter. (If you are using asphalt tile, score it with a sharp awl or knife and snap it off. Or, you can heat the tile over a lamp or in an oven and cut it with a scissors or knife.) Once the tile is cut, press it in place against the wall, and butt it tightly against the last full tile. You can also get an exact fit with the moldings in place by using a compass or dividers between the wood and the marked tile. To fit tile around pipes or other protrusions, make a paper pattern; then trace the outline on the tile.

I wanted a floor, not a washboard!

My new tile floor looked like some kind of washboard, it was so buckled. Why? Because I had neglected to take out all the old nails and staples from the floor beneath it before putting down the new tiles.

Practical Pete

Tiles are installed from the center of the room outward. Measure to find the center point of each wall, and run a chalk line from center point to center point.

Some tiles come with adhesive backing. All you do is peel off the protective paper and press the tile into place.

If you have tiles that need adhesive, work on one quarter of the room at a time. You can use a brush, trowel with notches, or a roller to spread the adhesive evenly. Don't cover your chalk lines.

Fit the tiles along two adjacent chalk lines, then work back towards the walls.

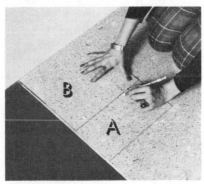

To fit border tiles, place a loose tile flush on top of the full tile closest to the wall (A). Place another loose tile (B) on top of this. Butt it against the wall; then mark the tile beneath, using the edge of the top tile as a guide.

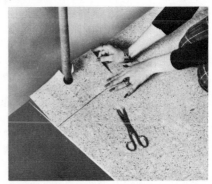

To fit tile around a protrusion, make a paper pattern, trace it on the tile, and cut the tile along the outline.

Tiles are sold by the carton. As a rule, there are 80 9x9-inch tiles per carton, and 45 12x12-inch tiles. Use this chart to figure out how many cartons you will need. Note that no matter what the size of the tile, the carton holds the same number of square feet.

Estimating floor-tiling needs

9"x9"			12"x12"		
No. of Cartons	Pieces	Sq. Ft.	No. of Cartons	Pieces	Sq. Ft.
1	80	45	1	45	45
2	160	90	2	90	90
3	240	135	3	135	135
4	320	180	4	180	180
5	400	225	5	225	225
6	480	270	6	270	270
7	560	315	7	315	315
8	640	360	8	360	360
9	720	405	9	405	405
10	800	450	10	450	450
15	1200	675	15	675	675
20	1600	900	20	900	900
25	2000	1125	25	1125	1125
30	2400	1350	30	1350	1350
35	2800	1575	35	1575	1575
40	3200	1800	40	1800	1800
45	3600	2025	45	2025	2025
50	4000	2250	50	2250	2250

Sheet vinyl

Sheet flooring used to be the bane of do-it-yourselfers, but no more. Today, new materials and methods make installing sheet goods almost as easy as putting down tiles.

Installation

First of all, remove any moldings by gently prying them away from the wall. Remove rubber or vinyl cove-base by working one corner loose and pulling it away as you break the adhesive bond with a scraping tool. Remove any nails, staples, or any other unnecessary protrusions. Finally, go over the floor thoroughly with a vacuum cleaner, and make sure that no dirt or grit remains to prevent a clean bond.

It is a very good idea to make a sketch of the room, showing counters, bays, alcoves, or other features that will affect the shape and size of the flooring. Lay the pattern face up on the vinyl, and transfer the measurements. Then cut it 3 inches larger all around. Roll up the material with the pattern showing, and tie it with a string.

When you install the flooring, allow at least ⅛ inch between the edge of the material and each wall to allow for expansion and contraction of the subfloor. (The maximum gap allowable is slightly less than the thickness of the molding you will use to cover it.)

Start at the longest and most regular wall of the room. Butt the sheet vinyl against this wall and unroll it across the room,

allowing the excess material to curve up the other three walls. If the first edge is straight with the wall, adjust the sheet to allow the proper gap for clearance. If not, straighten the edge and then adjust the flooring. In some cases, where the wall is badly bowed or crooked, you may have to bring the material up the starting wall and curve-cut it to fit.

At each of the other walls, bend the material into the joint where the wall and floor meet, and carefully cut it with a utility knife to allow the proper clearance. At doorways, the clearance can be slightly less than ⅛ inch. When the fit is right, staple the edges down. In places where the staples will show, use adhesive, following the manufacturer's recommendation as to what type.

Next, replace the moldings. If they are made of wood, allow for vertical clearance between floor and molding. This lets the walls and subfloor move without affecting the vinyl flooring. Wooden moldings should be renailed to the baseboard (not the floor). First, insert scraps of the flooring between the molding and the floor. Nail the molding in place, remove the scraps, and you will have the proper clearance. With rubber or vinyl cove-base, you need not worry about clearance.

To finish the job, install a metal saddle at doorways, fastening it to the subfloor, but not through the new sheet vinyl.

What it takes

Approximate time: About a day per room.

Tools and materials: Utility knife, folding or metal rule, tools for removing and replacing baseboard (hammer, pry bar, wood wedges), notched trowel, staple gun, staples, scissors, framing square, medium-grade sandpaper for seams (if any), sheet flooring, adhesive.

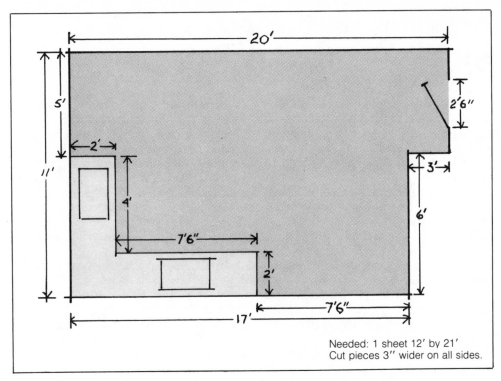

20'

5'

2'6"

2'

11'

4'

3'

7'6"

6'

2'

17'

7'6"

Needed: 1 sheet 12' by 21'
Cut pieces 3" wider on all sides.

Sketch your room and show the floor plan to your hardware dealer when you buy your flooring.

Sheet flooring is sold by the yard and comes in 6- to 12-foot-wide rolls. To figure what you need, draw a floor plan, and determine where any seams would be (you may have none). Cut the pattern and move the pieces around to avoid needless cutting and waste. Then measure the dimensions of each piece. Take the measurements to your floor dealer.

Seams

In most rooms, you can install sheet vinyl in one piece. But when the short wall is over 12 feet long (the usual maximum width of the material), you'll have to seam the material. This is not particularly difficult. To match the pattern across the seam, lap one piece of material over the other along the seam edge. Do your rough cutting, being sure to allow enough extra material in width and length to match the pattern.

Bring the material into the room and overlap it to match the pattern. After the pattern is matched, weight the flooring down or tape it in place so it will not shift. Then cut the material to fit at the three walls as before, allowing proper clearance. Using a sharp utility knife—and a metal straightedge as a guide—cut through both the pieces of vinyl in the overlapped area. Follow a natural line in the pattern when

possible. Keep the knife vertical, don't let it lean to the right or left. Remove the cutoff pieces, top and bottom.

If the underfloor has been waxed, roll back both pieces of vinyl where they meet and sand the area lightly. Then put the sheets back in place and proceed as follows: Flip back one piece of sheet vinyl at the seam. Draw a pencil line on the floor along the edge of the second piece. Flip back the second piece, and spread a 6-inch band of adhesive under the seam area, centering it on the pencil line. Spread the adhesive with a finely notched trowel (11 notches to the inch, 1/32 inch deep). Lay the sheet vinyl into the wet adhesive, and go over it with a damp cloth, using enough pressure to ensure good contact with the adhesive. Remove the excess adhesive with a damp rag before it dries.

Sometimes the simplest way requires some thought

I took the trouble to measure carefully and cut full-size paper patterns for each section of floor covering; even double-checked by laying them all out on the floor before starting to cut the covering material from them.

Then, sure enough, I went and laid one pattern upside down onto the material by mistake so, obviously, the piece didn't fit when I had cut it out. All I would have had to do was to write "UP" on every pattern when I had them all laid out on the floor correctly. It's enough to make a strong man cry.

Practical Pete

Bend the flooring material into the joint where wall and floor meet, and carefully cut it with a utility knife, using a framing square to hold your line straight. Remember to allow for proper clearance.

When you are sure that the fit is right, staple the edges. In places where the staples will show, use the adhesive recommended by the manufacturer.

Installing hardwood strip flooring

Types of wood flooring

What it takes

Approximate time: Two to three days; with finishing, another two or three days.

Tools and materials: Hammer, folding or metal rule, screwdriver, electric drill and bits, chalk line and chalk, miter box, pry bar, backsaw, rented nailer and fasteners, nail set, nails, flooring, 15-pound building paper, finishing materials, wood putty, sandpaper.

In general, wood flooring is thought of as hardwood; oak in particular. Yet, wood flooring may actually be either hardwood or softwood. The hardwoods include oak, maple, birch, and beech; the softwoods, fir and pine.

There are three types of wood flooring: strip, plank, and parquet or block flooring. Each varies in length, width and thickness. **Strip flooring** is long and thin. Lengths vary; thicknesses are 3/8, 1/2, and 25/32 inch; widths range from 1½ to 3¼ inches. There is an undercut, in the form of a wide groove, on the bottom of each piece. This allows it to lie flat and stable even though the subfloor may have slight unevenness.

Plank flooring is wider than strip flooring. Modern plank flooring is often bored and plugged at ends to simulate older types. At one time, wooden pegs were used to fasten down such planks instead of nails.

Block flooring is available in rectangular or square units, often in parquet. It is customarily made from three or four short strips of flooring glued together or joined with splines.

The safest way to estimate the amount of flooring you will need for a given room is to figure the square footage and ask your lumber dealer.

Certain types of wood flooring should be delivered several days before you plan to install it so the wood can adjust to the moisture content of the room. Other types have a specific installation moisture content, and must be put down immediately after the bundles are opened. Check this important point with your dealer.

Application

To lay hardwood strip flooring, first put down a layer of 15-pound building paper. This is vital when you work over concrete. Run lengths of building paper parallel to the short walls of the room. This places it at right angles to the strip flooring, which should be laid parallel to the long walls of the room.

In a fairly narrow room, tongue-and-groove strip flooring is started ½ inch from the wall, and with the groove side to the wall. Before you install it, though, saw off the groove. Then place the strip exactly parallel to the wall, and face-nail it to the subfloor and joists with finishing nails. Countersink the nails. You can determine where the joists are by checking the floor from the basement, or by sounding the floor with a hammer.

If you are working in a wide room, install the flooring from the middle out. Carefully measure from each wall to the room's center. Snap a chalk line that is parallel to and equidistant from both walls. Put down

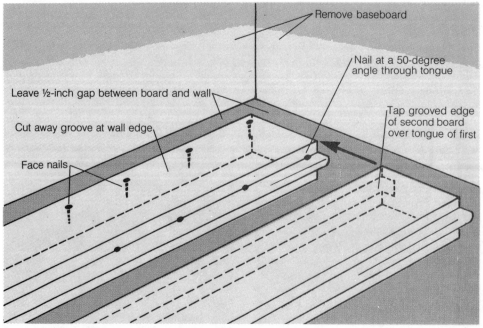

To install tongue-and-groove flooring, face-nail the first board in place as described above. Drive flooring nails through the tongue edge of the board. Recess the nails, then tap the grooved side of the adjoining board over the tongue of the first board, as shown.

a long strip of flooring along this line and face-nail it in place. Countersink the finishing nails. Fill face-nail holes with wood putty after the floor is complete.

Whether you start at the wall or in the center of the room, your next step is to lay out some strips in such a manner that no two consecutive end joints fall within 6 inches of each other. At the same time, you can choose the pieces so the wood grain and color match. It's a good idea to snap chalk lines about every 4 feet from end to end to be sure you're working in a straight line.

Lay out all the boards for a run of about four strips, rather than going back and forth to the woodpile for a new strip each time. Use boards in the random lengths in which they are shipped, and cut them only when necessary—when you reach the end walls, for example.

Nailing

Your dealer, or a tool shop, should have an automatic nailer that you can rent. This tool is almost indispensable for fast, accurate installation. Use recommended fasteners.

If you can't get ahold of an automatic nailer, use special flooring nails, and drive them into the groove between the tongue and the board at approximately a 50-degree angle. Hardwood isn't always necessarily hard, but oak is tough, and maple even more so. If you have trouble nailing into it, drill pilot holes with an electric drill. This will save you work in the long run. Use great care in nailing if the wood is prefinished. To avoid damaging the tongues, let the nail heads project a little. Recess them with a nail set before you cover the tongue with the adjoining grooved board.

When, at the end of your nailing, you reach the side wall, you will find it difficult to nail the next-to-last board in place without damaging the wall—and impossible to nail the last one. The second-last strip is left unnailed (it won't go anywhere), and the last one is face-nailed. Use a pry bar to pull the last board tight with the others while you nail it down. Finally, the borders of the room will be covered by molding.

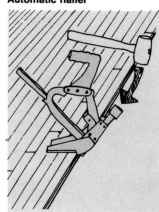

I was hitting the nail on the head—but so what!
Did you ever see so many bent nails? (A couple of floor boards got hacked into by my hammer as well.) So, after talking to my hardware dealer, I rented a nailer; and now it's a breeze. In those places where the nailer can't reach, I predrill the holes, and nail with my hammer. *Practical Pete*

Automatic nailer

Estimating hardwood flooring

To find out how many board feet of strip flooring you will need to cover a given area, find the square footage of the area, and multiply as below for size of flooring you'll be using:

Size Flooring		Multiplication Factor
$^{25}/_{32}''$ x 1½''	x	155%
$^{25}/_{32}''$ x 2''	x	142½%
$^{25}/_{32}''$ x 2¼''	x	138⅓%
$^{25}/_{32}''$ x 3¼''	x	129%
⅜'' x 1½''	x	138⅓%
⅜'' x 2''	x	130%
½'' x 1½''	x	138⅓%
½'' x 2''	x	130%

It should be evident from the unusual percentages that these figures are pretty exact. Always allow 5% extra for waste.

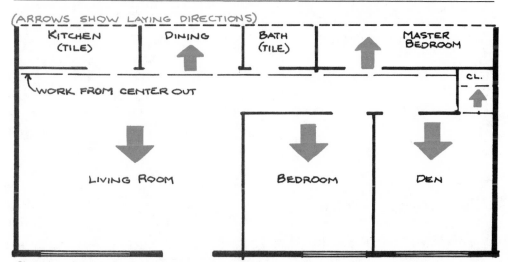

(ARROWS SHOW LAYING DIRECTIONS)

KITCHEN (TILE) — DINING — BATH (TILE) — MASTER BEDROOM — CL.

WORK FROM CENTER OUT

LIVING ROOM — BEDROOM — DEN

Sketching a floor plan is the best way to study a major flooring project. It will give you a clearer picture of your probable needs and procedures. Above is a suggested way of laying strip flooring throughout several adjoining rooms of a house.

TIP: Plane tongue-and-groove boards on the grooved edge, not the tongue.

Installing a ceramic tile floor

You can use ceramic tile for an attractive floor that should last even longer than hardwood and require less maintenance. Mosaic tile is generally used for floors, although there are larger floor tiles available, and they are just as easy to install.

Installation

Tile floors are installed in the same way as ceramic walls (page 43), with a few exceptions. Mosaic tile comes attached to sheets with mesh backing. You can remove individual tiles from the backing when necessary to get around obstructions, or you can simply cut out a section with scissors.

When you install floor tiles, you may need to use spacers. These range in size from ⅛ inch to ¼ inch, and are placed on all sides of the tile joints until the tile has set. Use those recommended by the tile dealer. A faster, easier system is to use pregrouted

tiles. For regular floor tiles, another time-saver is an adhesive sheet that is gummed on both sides, and sticks to both the old floor and new tiles (shown above.)

Replacing floor tiles

Ceramic floor tile seldom gets damaged because it is so hard; yet it does come loose on occasion. Most repairs amount to simply resetting the loosened tile with waterproof adhesive, which is available at just about any paint or hardware store. If, on the other hand, a tile does get damaged and you want to replace it, remove the tile, clean the area beneath it, apply adhesive, and fit a new tile in place. It is important that the old adhesive is thoroughly removed from the opening before the new tile is installed. Brush and vacuum first for the best results. The least particle of dirt, if not cleaned out, could cause a problem. You want to ensure a smooth and level bond.

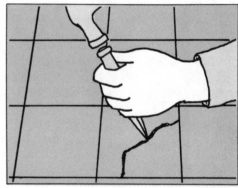

1. If a tile is loose, you can score around its edges to remove the old adhesive. If it is cracked or broken, break it out with a hammer and cold chisel as shown.

2. Apply the adhesive to the back of the new tile with a putty knife. Allow a ½-inch border between the adhesive and the tile edges.

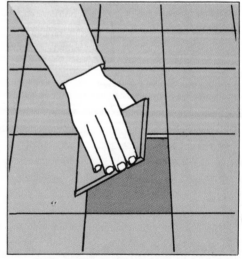

3. Hold the tile by the edges to insert it in the clean space. Make sure it is flush with the adjacent tiles.

A new bathroom with tile

The rather drab bathroom shown here needed refurbishing, but the homeowners didn't want an expensive remodeling job, with new fixtures, new windows, and so forth. They decided on one fairly costly item—ceramic tile; but they saved a good bit of money by doing the job themselves.

New decorative tile was added to the tub area, while the floor and walls were covered with sheets of pregrouted tile. This type of tile is easy to use. It is supplied in sections and backed by a sheet. When necessary for fit, the sheets are scribed with a glass cutter, and then pressed down over a metal rod. The entire sheet, trimmed or not, is set down at one time in adhesive that has already been spread. Lines between the sheets are filled with silicone rubber. How the job is done is shown below. The result—helped along with shutters on the windows, wallpaper, new shower curtains, and a few accessories—is shown at bottom.

What it takes

Approximate time: Eight to 10 hours for an average bathroom floor.

Tools and materials: Ceramic tile, adhesive, silicone-rubber cartridge and caulking gun, level, folding or steel rule, straightedge, glass cutter, metal rod, putty knife.

1. This is how the bathroom looked in the "before" stages. In remodeling, the essential thing is to see just which area needs the weight of your effort. Here, of course, it was the floor.

2. When it is necessary to cut the sheets to size, scribe them with a glass cutter, using a wood ruler as a straightedge. It is essential that the straightedge does not move once you place it on your cutting line.

3. Next, press the tile sheet over a metal rod so that it breaks along the scribed line. Be careful that you don't press too hard, or too abruptly, or the break might not be true.

4. Carefully spread the area with adhesive, then set the whole sheet down at one time. Check the manufacturer's instructions for the correct amount of adhesive.

5. Fill the lines between the sheets with silicone rubber, wiping up the excess. Be sure to check that you maintain an even floor as you go along.

6. Presto! A new bathroom appears. The new floor is its chief addition; but there are extras, such as the new window treatment and wallpaper.

Installing wall-to-wall shag carpet tiles

What it takes:

Approximate time: Depends on the size of the room; you should be able to carpet an average room within a day.

Tools and materials: Chalk line, chalk, carpenter's square, sharp knife or scissors for cutting squares, metal door trim or reducer strips; hammer, nails, shoe molding (optional).

One of the simplest ways to lay carpet is with carpet tiles. These come in 12x12-inch squares and are a snap to install. Each tile has a self-stick back, so there's no need for adhesive. Just peel the paper backing away, position the tile where you want it, and press. The tiles can be put on any of the following surfaces if they are dry: all resilient floorings, waxed or not; sealed wood that is varnished or lacquered; painted surfaces; terrazzo; ceramic tile; slate; and marble. It can also be used on concrete at any grade level, as long as it isn't continually powdery or wet.

How to install

First, measure the room to find its center point. Snap chalk lines to locate the center, following the procedure on page 84. Use a carpenter's square to make certain the lines form right angles.

Lay a row of loose squares along the chalk lines in one quarter of the room. Do this in the shape of an L. Check for fit, then install the tiles by peeling off the protective paper on the back of each one and pressing it in place. (Note: After you have removed the paper, you will see an arrow on the back of each tile. This indicates the direction of the carpet pile. Be sure you place all the squares with the arrows pointing in the same direction.)

Working quarter by quarter, and following the above procedure, carpet the entire room except for the borders.

Fit the squares along the perimeter of the room last, following the procedure shown at lower right.

To fit carpet around an irregular area, a pipe for instance, just make a paper pattern of the space you need to allow for or fill. Trace the pattern on the square; then shape it carefully with a sharp knife or scissors.

On edges that will be exposed, such as in doorways, use metal door trim or reducer strips (available at hardware stores). Nail shoe molding to the baseboard over the carpet edges—and you will end up with a really fine job.

1. Divide the room into quarters by locating the center of each wall. Connect these points by snapping chalk lines between opposite walls, across the center of the room. With a carpenter's square, make certain you have a 90-degree angle.

TIP: To remove a damaged tile, wet a clean cloth and place it on the tile. With an electric iron set at 300-350° F, press down on the wet cloth to steam the tile loose.

TIP: Sometimes a few drops of water lightly sprinkled on the back of a preglued tile will help it stick better. Do not rub.

2. As you peel the backing paper from the tiles, you will see directional arrows. Lay the squares, beginning at the center of the room, with all arrows pointing in the same direction. Press down on the carpet tile firmly. Cover the floor quarter by quarter leaving the border area for last.

3. In order to cut and fit carpet tiles next to walls, place a loose tile, with the paper side up, on top of the last full square in any row. Make certain that the arrows point in the same direction. Now place a square (pile side up) on top of the first square. Slide the top square against the wall. Using the edge of the top square as a guide, mark the square beneath it with a felt-tipped pen or soft pencil. Cut the first square along the line, and drop it into place.

4. When it is necessary to fit the carpet around pipes or other irregularities in the room, make a pattern from a 12x12-inch piece of paper. Trace the pattern on the back of a carpet square. (Make sure that the arrows are in the right direction.) Cut with a sharp scissors and fit it into place.

5. This view of the almost-completed carpet shows how it will look. This type of installation provides a professional look without messy adhesives and cleanup problems. It's all neat and accurate.

Installing wall-to-wall shag carpet roll

Wall-to-wall carpeting, long in the domain of the professional, can be a do-it-yourself job. Basically, all you need do is roll the carpet out on the floor, trim it to fit the room, and apply double-faced carpet tape at seams to hold adjacent pieces together. It's easy. There is no involved calculation, and no messy cleanup to worry about.

To figure carpet roll length

Multiply the room length by its width (in feet). Divide by 9 to get the approximate number of square yards required. Realize that this is a rough estimate; the roll comes in 12-foot widths, and you may have to pay a little extra for waste, depending on the dimensions of the room. Consider allowing for a little extra so that a small section may be used as a scatter rug or runner at the entrance to a room during bad weather or in an area where wear and tear are the greatest.

Floor preparation

Make sure that the surface of the floor is thoroughly clean. It should also be warm; about 70°F. It must *not* be below 55°F. If the floor is rough, cold, dusty, oily, or wet, the pressure-sensitive tape used for seams will not stick to it.

Remove all furniture and other movable objects from the room. (If you are working in sections, you can put the furniture on one side of the room, put down carpet, move the furniture over, and complete the room.) Try to plan before you start so that you don't have to move heavy furniture more than is really necessary.

For all carpets, with the exception of shag, remove the molding or the baseboard before installation. When the installation is completed, replace the molding. Molding helps secure the edges of the carpet and also gives it a professional look.

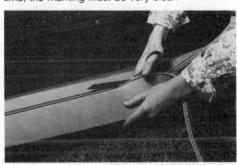

1. First run a piece of heavy chalk around the perimeter of the room. Hold it so it marks both the baseboard or wall surface and the floor at the same time; the marking must be very clear.

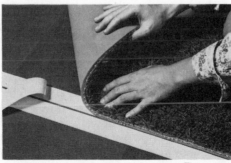

2. Roll the carpet onto the floor. Let the excess run up the walls. Press the carpet firmly into each floor-wall joint. This transfers the chalk lines to the carpet backing. Using heavy shears, cut the carpet along the line for a perfect fit at room edges.

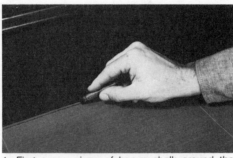

3. Joining adjacent pieces is a snap. The precut factory edges guarantee straight seams. Simply use double-faced tape, as shown. (Note: The carpet should be taped only at the seams and at doorways.) The tape must not wrinkle.

What it takes

Approximate time: Allow a full afternoon, for an average-size room.

Tools and materials: Heavy shears, thick chalk, hammer, nails, and pry bar (if you need to remove and replace molding), roll of carpet, and double-faced tape.

10. PROJECTS FOR A CHILD'S ROOM

Supergraphics

What it takes

Approximate time: Depends on the size of the supergraphic, but calculate your time in days for large work; for a smaller work, perhaps half a day.

Tools and materials: Pencil, kneaded eraser, a piece of string that will not stretch, yardstick, level (with two bubbles), plumb line, plumb bob, chalk, masking tape, vinyl or latex varnish, roller, interior wall paint, polymer matte medium, colored felt-tipped markers, 4x6-inch mohair-faced paint pads, two artists' brushes, aluminum-foil trays, old newspapers or dropcloth.

There are a lot of things you can do to liven up a child's room. With a bit of paint, carpentry, and ingenuity, you can create a whole new world for the young. The following projects are simple, easy, and fun.

A great way to start in a young person's room is with a supergraphic—a big design painted on a ceiling, or other large surface. It can be used for decoration (instead of wallpaper, which costs more), to frame a

Drawing, masking, painting

If you want to create a circle, decide on the visual center of the design. (This, and the following, also applies to painting a rainbow). The center is the area to which the eye will be drawn.

Make a compass by tying a string to a pencil. Holding the string in the center of the circle with one thumb, pull it taut, and draw the circle (or half-circle if it is to be a rainbow). For this operation, the circumference must be within your reach. If you want a larger circle, attach the string to the center with tape, and you can draw a circle as large as the wall permits. Use a ladder to reach the high points.

To draw a straight horizontal line, place a carpenter's level against the wall and a yardstick on top of it. The yardstick will reach further than the level, and it will be as true. You can do the same for vertical lines

window or piece of furniture, to define an area, to make a ceiling look higher, or the reverse, to make it seem lower.

It is a good idea to experiment on scrap material before you work on a wall. Draw your design to scale. You can improvise later as you work on the actual wall.

Before you paint the supergraphic on the wall, give it a new coat of interior wall paint, and let it dry completely.

if the level has two-way bubbles.

If you wish to draw a longer horizontal line, use a carpenter's plumb line. If the ceiling, or the floor, is level, measure from it to get the two end points of the line. Chalk the plumb line and tape it to one of the marks. Hold the line over the other mark. Make sure the line is level; then stretch with your free hand, pulling it away from the wall. Let the line snap back. It will leave a long line of chalk that should be straight. You can make vertical lines this way, too, if you use a plumb bob.

Lightly pencil your design on the wall. Then apply masking tape along any straight edges you plan to paint. (Curves are painted freehand.) Be certain you apply the tape just outside the chalk and pencil lines. Then press it down, and seal the edges by brushing clear polymer matte medium over the tape. This prevents paint from slipping under it. Now you are ready to paint.

Spread newspapers or a dropcloth for protection, and arrange your equipment—latex paint, paint pads, shallow aluminum-foil trays, artists' brushes, a damp rag or two—so all are easily within your reach. Decide in what order you will paint the colors. Then work as follows: Paint interrupted lines and top lines first; leave bottom and continuous lines till last. Pour your first paint into one of the shallow trays. Dampen a mohair-faced paint pad a little, and see which way the nap runs; feel it with your hand. Dip the pad in the paint, and wipe off the excess on the edge of the tray. Always paint *with* the nap of the pad.

Apply paint in the areas edged with tape. When you end a stripe, for instance when another color stripe intersects it, tape across the stripe that is to be ended. Seal it, and paint onto the tape so that you avoid having to paint into a point. For untaped curves, just follow the arc with the natural swing of your wrist or arm.

Wait until the paint is dry to the touch, and then peel the tape off slowly, and erase the pencil lines.

If the graphic is to be in an area that will suffer a lot of wear and tear (as it very likely will be in a child's room) you can apply a top coat of latex or vinyl varnish. It will be necessary to dilute the varnish with water. Apply with a roller when the paint is dry.

Easy-to-build furniture

With the rising cost of everything, it's a nice thought that, with proper cutting, you can make two pieces of furniture from a standard 4x8-foot piece of plywood. If you follow the cutting pattern given in the accompanying diagram, you'll end up with ten pieces of wood. Depending on how you assemble them, you can make bookshelves plus a desk, a table plus a love seat, a doll's bed plus a nursery bed—or any other combination of two that your child's room calls for. Examples are shown opposite.

How to build it

Follow the diagram shown below to mark and cut the ten pieces of wood. When you measure, remember to allow for the thickness of the saw blade (about 1/16 inch).

Assembly is a relatively simple matter. The large end pieces are slotted, and the interlocking crosspieces have ¾-inch tongues that are glued into the slots. Use a router to make the slots (up to ⅝-inch deep), or cut out the slots entirely with a keyhole saw, and fit the tongues flush. All slots are either 1½ inches from an edge or centered on the board. Carefully round and sand the edges. Apply wood filler to all edges, sand once again, and glue the parts together at all contact points. While the glue is drying, predrill holes at the points indicated in the diagram, drive screws, and finish with a coat of primer followed by at least two coats of quality enamel.

What it takes

Approximate time: Half a day per piece.

Tools and materials: Hammer; screwdriver; router and bits (optional); keyhole saw; drill and bits; one 4x8-foot sheet of ¾-inch-thick, exterior-grade plywood; wood filler; sandpaper; paint; paintbrush; 24 2-inch No. 8 round-head wood screws.

End piece variations

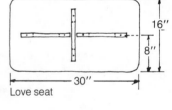

Love seat

Bookcase

Desk

Table

Cutting diagram

Details

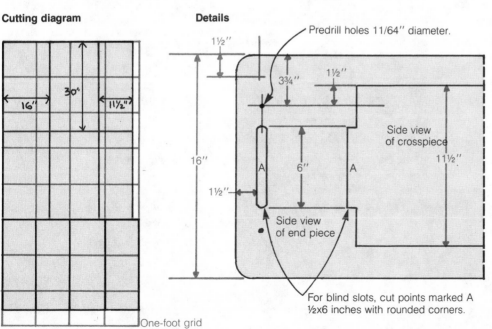

One-foot grid

Predrill holes 11/64″ diameter.

Side view of crosspiece

Side view of end piece

For blind slots, cut points marked A ½x6 inches with rounded corners.

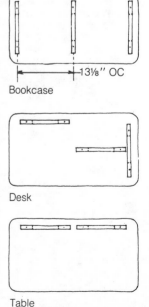

WINDOWS, DOORS, SECURITY & INSULATION

Section Two

1. OPENERS 100
   Your maintenance calendar 101

2. THE TOOLS 102
   Selection and use 102
   Measuring and leveling 103
   Cutting tools 104
   Drilling and fastening tools ... 105
   Smoothing and filling tools 105

3. WINDOWS 106
   Replacing panes 106
   Wood sash windows 107
   Metal casement windows 108
   Metal sliding and storm windows 108
   Glass cutting 108
   Sash repairs and hardware 110
   Unsticking a window 110
   Securing a loose window sash ... 111
   Crank handles and hardware 111
   Replacing double-hung windows .. 112
   Window channels 113
   Replacing sash cord 114
   Closing in a window or doorway . 115
   Special window treatments 116
   How to make a window box 116
   Make your own frosted glass 116
   How to create your own stained
       glass or door panels 117
   Screens—installing, replacing,
       maintenance 118
   Taking care of those screens ... 118
   Replacing aluminum storm
       screening 119
   What about fiberglass? 121
   Replacing a wood-frame screen .. 122
   Installing screen wire on old
       wooden screens 122
   How to bow a screen frame 123
   Installing storm windows 124
   Do-it-yourself storm windows ... 125
   Maintaining wood sash storm
       windows 125
   Painting professionally 126
   Preparing surfaces 126
   Painting sequence 126
   Painting windows and screens ... 127
   Painting doors 127
   What goes with the window 128
   Installing drapery hardware 128
   Installing and maintaining
       window shades 130
   Venetian blinds—repair and
       maintenance 131

4. DOORS 132
   The door that binds or is loose 132
   Cutting a new doorway 134
   Hanging a new door 135
   Mortising a hinge 136
   Installing a mail slot 137
   Installing a drip cap 137
   Installing a kick plate 137
   Replacing a threshold 138
   Installing a prehung door unit . 139
   Installing a sliding patio door 140
   A new storm door is an easy job 142
   Maintaining a garage door 143
   Safety glazing storm doors 144
   Safety glazing shower doors 145

5. INSULATION 146
   Where to check for heat loss ... 146
   Types of insulation (chart) 147
   The vapor barrier 148
   Insulating an unfinished attic . 149
   Insulating around openings 150
   Windows and doors 150
   Removing trim 150
   Insulating the basement 151
   Weather stripping 152
   Caulking seams 154
   Where should you caulk? 154
   How to caulk 155
   Humidity and temperature control 156
   Humidifiers 156
   Dehumidifiers 156
   The mildew problem 157
   When moisture accumulates 158
   An attic fan 158
   Air conditioners 160
   Mounting a room unit 160
   Maintenance 161
   Installing a window unit 161
   Installing a unit through the wall 161
   Soundproofing your home 162
   Acoustical ceiling tiles 163

6. SECURITY 164
   Protecting your home 164
   How a burglar operates 164
   How the burglar enters 165
   Preventing burglary 165
   About watchdogs 165
   Doors and windows: first line of
       defense 166
   Doors 166
   Windows 167
   Lock options 168
   Buying a lock 168
   Primary locks 169
   Secondary locks 169
   How to replace a broken or
       worn-out lock 170
   Changing a bored lock 170
   Replacing an old lock with
       a deadbolt 172
   Installing a mortise lock 174
   Putting up a chain lock 175
   A handy one-way viewer 175
   Installing a rim lock 176
   The lock case 176
   The strike plate 176
   Lock maintenance 177
   Broken key 177
   Stuck lock 177
   Stuck bolt 177
   Frozen lock 177
   Key control 177
   Changing locks 177
   Automatic garage-door opener ... 177
   Lighting for security 178
   Outdoor illumination 178
   Indoor lighting 178
   Burglar alarms 179
   Installing your alarm system ... 179
   Window burglar alarm 180
   Where to place protection 180
   Playing it safe 181
   Outwitting the burglar 181
   Foil and wire devices 181
   Fire precautions 182
   Knowing and eliminating causes
       of fire 182
   Fire equipment 182
   Lightning protection 184
   Storm warnings 185
   Tornadoes 185
   Hurricanes 185

7. PEST CONTROL 186
   Insecticides 187
   The six least welcome visitors . 187
   Termite control 188
   What to look for 188
   Preventive measures 188
   Creating a termite barrier 189
   Soil injection 189
   Rodent control 189

8. PROJECT 190

1. OPENERS

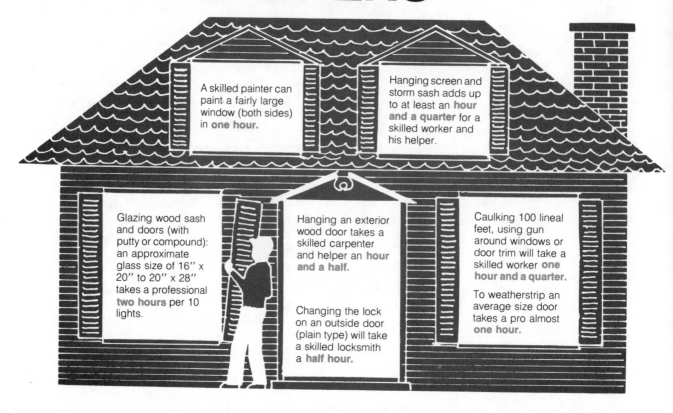

A skilled painter can paint a fairly large window (both sides) in **one hour.**

Hanging screen and storm sash adds up to at least an **hour and a quarter** for a skilled worker and his helper.

Glazing wood sash and doors (with putty or compound): an approximate glass size of 16" x 20" to 20" x 28" takes a professional **two hours** per 10 lights.

Hanging an exterior wood door takes a skilled carpenter and helper an **hour and a half.**

Changing the lock on an outside door (plain type) will take a skilled locksmith a **half hour.**

Caulking 100 lineal feet, using gun around windows or door trim will take a skilled worker **one hour and a quarter.**

To weatherstrip an average size door takes a pro almost **one hour.**

Above are a few of the jobs you will be doing around your house, along with the estimated time it takes skilled workers to do them, including travel and set-up time. Estimate the labor cost of a project by finding out the local pay rate for professionals and applying it to the above time estimate.

A house without doors and windows is about as useful as a solid sieve. Your house is 40-70 percent holes and it is the holes that make a house work. They let in what you want in, and keep out what you want out.

Taking care of those holes is essential to the appearance and well-being of any house—to keep it snugly insulated, to save on fuel and electric bills, and to be free of pests and secure from criminal entry.

Maintenance and repairs, even new window and door installations, are not difficult or dangerous because they seldom involve the structural strength of the house. So you don't need a lot of experience or technical knowledge to do them yourself. If you do have to call a professional carpenter to do these jobs, he must bill you at the same hourly rate for replacing a broken window pane, say, as he would for building a new garage. His bill could even be higher because, while these small jobs don't take much time in themselves, he must include his travel time to and from your house as well as his general overhead.

Partly for this reason it is sometimes difficult to persuade a carpenter to come and fix something *when* you need it. Although it may take you twice as long to replace a broken window pane or install a deadbolt lock, the alternative may be many days of drafts or insecurity before a profes-

sional can get to it. So try it for yourself.

This section of your manual has been written, illustrated—and organized—to show exactly how to do each of the jobs that is necessary to maintain, repair, and install things in those crucial holes in your house. All you need to know about how to handle each project is covered here—even if you have no experience in carpentry or other manual skills and are not familiar with the tools and terminology. This section is built for beginners, with even the simplest steps included. It is organized into specific projects each with its own list of tools, recommended materials, planning hints and step-by-step illustrated instructions in ordinary language. Just look up the job you need to do in the table of contents or index, turn to that page—it's all right there in one spot. You will even find an estimate of roughly how much time you should set aside to do the job.

The drawing of the house, above, shows some typical jobs you could do yourself, along with the number of hours a carpenter or handyman would take. Multiply that time by the hourly rate carpenters and handymen charge in your area (don't forget to include overhead and travel time). The result will show how much you could save by doing the job in your leisure time—not to mention the satisfaction.

Your maintenance calendar

Your maintenance check can of course continue all through the year. The calendar is simply a reminder of certain specifics. For instance, storm and screen windows and doors are always checked as the season changes. And the best time to inspect your furnace is *before* the cold weather arrives. But you can always keep an eye out for broken panes or insulation leaks, squeaking door hinges or termites.

It's useful to read the literature on new products for there are often stopgaps and new wrinkles that you can call upon which will save you time, trouble, and money.

	Northern	Temperate	Dry-hot	Wet-humid
January	Keep a close watch on heating equipment, such as your furnace, and radiators if you have them. Check temperature control systems. (Page 156)	Inspect furnace operation; see if fan motor is in need of oil. Change filters. Check temperature control systems. (Page 156)	Check all window screens. Repair or replace those in poor condition. (Page 118)	Check for windows that are loose, or tight; and for screens that may be torn or loose in their frames. (Pages 110, 118)
February	Recaulk any drafty areas you can find. Check around outside doors and windows. Change weather stripping if necessary. (Page 152)	Maintain a monthly checkup on heat outlets. Also check humidifiers. (Page 156)	Start a pest control program. Check for termites especially. (Page 186)	Take a look at dehumidifiers. See that they operate at highest efficiency and are in the best locations in your house. (Page 156)
March	Check all window glass for cracks or leakage due to loose or broken putty or compound. It's also spring cleaning time, a good moment to check drapery and shades. (Pages 106, 128-131)	Make sure everyone in household knows local tornado precautions. Oil and adjust door and window hardware. (Pages 110, 185)	Make sure that all airconditioning equipment, including wiring is in good condition. Be sure that your electrical circuit is not carrying too heavy a load. (Page 160)	Inspect for pests. It's a good idea to keep up with the literature on pest control. Keep in touch with your hardware dealer on this. (Page 186)
April	A good time to check for leaks. Inspect paint on inside of windows. And check airconditioning, etc. (Pages 126-127, 160)	Check for evidence of termites. Look in basement and in crawl space, but also in other parts of the house. (Page 188)	Clean out vents, removing old bird and wasp nests. Cover any open vents with wire screening. (Page 159)	A good time to paint doors and windows, and of course to do any reglazing that might be needed. (Pages 106-107, 126-127)
May	Check for termites in basement, especially crawl spaces. (Page 188)	Check your storm windows and repair or replace any that may need it. (Pages 124-125)	Make it a point to inform all members of your family on local tornado precautions. (Page 185)	Patio and other sliding doors will require attention, especially checking tracks and hardware. (Pages 140-141)
June	Replace, repair, paint (if necessary) storm doors and windows, and screens. Check fit on all of these. (Pages 118-125, 142, 144)	A good moment to start any major carpentry that may require cutting through an outside wall (such as for a new door or window). (Pages 112, 134)	Replace any broken or cracked glass panes. See if any windows need to be reglazed. (Page 106)	Take a look at how well your garage doors are operating. Also check cellar door and windows for leakage, as well as security. (Pages 143, 164)
July	A good time to inspect the operation of all sliding doors and windows, as well as garage and other exterior doors. This includes a check on weather stripping. (Pages 140, 152)	See that all locks are working properly, and oil them lightly. (Pages 168-177)	Are humidifiers working properly? And are they in the most advantageous areas? (Page 156)	Clean and oil all locks and make sure they are working properly. Consider the possibility of changing locks, especially if you have given out a number of keys over a period of time. (Page 164)
August	Take a look at insulation and also check and, if necessary, clean any exhaust fans. (Page 146)	Start your pest control program by cleaning any nests out of openings such as vents or fan ducts. Keep to your program. (Page 186)	If you have any plans to cut a new window or door, now is a good time to do it. (Pages 112, 134)	Make sure vents are clear and in good condition. (Page 158)
September	Oil furnace motors. Clean what parts you can. Check temperature control systems. (Page 156)	Add insulation where needed. Check weather stripping. (Page 152)	Check all locks and catches on doors and windows. Clean, if necessary, oil them. (Page 164)	Check again for termites. Familiarize yourself with ways of preventing their entry; don't wait until they are already present. (Page 188)
October	Recaulk any areas that need it. Check your fuel bills carefully and prepare a record for the coming months. (Page 154)	Recaulk where you find it necessary. Clean or replace furnace filters. Make sure that storms are in good condition. (Page 154)	Clean window and door frames, storms, screens. (Pages 118, 124)	Make sure the whole family knows local hurricane precautions. (Page 185)
November	Now is a good time to check your attic insulation; also inspect all vents. (Page 149)	Adjust and maintain all window sash, drapery hardware, venetian blinds. (Pages 110, 128)	Paint windows, storms, screens as needed. (Pages 126-127)	Replace or repair window sash as needed. But be sure before you actually replace; maybe repair is all that's necessary. (Pages 112-114)
December	A time for inside carpentry, such as repairing interior doors. Check how these doors hang, and inspect all hardware on them. (Page 132)	Build any outdoor projects you might wish to install later such as window boxes or maybe a bird feeder. (Page 116)	Take a good look at drapery hardware, blinds, and all hinges. (Pages 128-131, 132)	Recaulk any areas that need it. Check insulation, weather stripping. (Pages 152-155)

2.THE TOOLS

Basic tools for measuring and cutting:

1. Tin snips
2. Crosscut hand saw
3. Wood chisel
4. Hacksaw
5. 24" Carpenter's level
6. 6' Wood extension (zigzag) rule with metal slide extension
7. 16', ¾"-wide metal tape measure with locking button
8. Metal "rafter" square with standard 24" and 16" legs

Basic tools for drilling, fastening, smoothing, and filling:

9. Electric drill with ¼" chuck, variable speed, and reversing switch
10. Chuck key
11. Twist metal bits
12. Circle cutter
13. Screwdriver bit
14. Spade bit
15. 16-oz. curved-claw hammer
16. Caulking gun and correct type of caulking compound
17. Ratcheted push drill with screwdriver bits and hole drilling attachment
18. Brace and bits
19. Putty knife
20. Slip-joint pliers
21. Phillips-head screwdriver
22. Small and large slot screwdrivers
23. 8" Smoothing plane

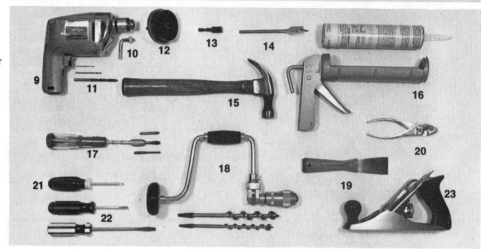

Selection and use

When you can lay your hand on the tool you need, if it is sharp and operating smoothly, you can greatly reduce the frustration factor potentially lurking in even simple jobs. This section is a guide to the selection and use of the tools you will need to maintain, repair and do light installation work on the doors and windows in your house, as well as most other light carpentry jobs.

Generally, a professional carpenter carries fewer different tools to a job than an inexperienced beginner thinks he might need to do the same job. The pro knows exactly which ones he is likely to need, his experience lets him do more jobs with a basic tool and he doesn't need mistake-preventing attachments.

Compare your own inventory of tools with the ones shown here. If yours are dull, have them sharpened. When you plan to tackle a job, check the "What it takes" section that appears in this book at the head of each job entry to see what tools and materials will be needed. Especially if you need to invest in a variety of tools or expensive ones, try looking in the classified want ads for used tools. But don't hesitate to pay for quality. Poorly made or designed tools don't hold an edge, are inconvenient to operate, and, under stress, handles break or metal parts give way. Try out a new tool where you buy it to be sure you know how to operate it; see that all its parts and advertised features work; make sure it is not so heavy and awkward to hold that it will be needlessly tiring to work with over a long stretch.

The following descriptions of the most useful tools to have in your house (shown in the photographs opposite) are grouped by their use into categories that parallel the four steps involved in most carpentry projects: measuring, cutting, fastening (including drilling) and smoothing. Painting and decorating tools are not included since they vary so much with the job.

Measuring tools

A tape measure is used for curved surfaces on long distances especially when you can hook one end over the edge of a board. A 16-foot long metal tape, ¾-inch wide, and with a locking device to hold it open at any length, will hold up well and handle all kinds of jobs. A 12-foot tape, ½-inch wide, is a slightly less expensive alternative. Metric measure alongside the inches printed on the tape will become an increasing advantage in coming years.

A folding (zigzag) rule may not be quite as accurate as a metal tape measure, but it extends 6 feet and is stiff enough to measure across horizontal openings. Get one with a 6-inch metal extension that slides out of the first section so you can take an inside measurement in one operation.

Squares are like two rulers joined at their ends to make an accurate 90° angle. They are used to measure right angles, especially for marking a cutting line across a board at an exact right angle to the sides of the board.

A steel square sometimes called a rafter or framing square, is shaped like an L with the body 24″ long and the tongue 16″ long. These are the standard distances between the studs in, respectively, the interior and exterior walls of a house. It is handy as a straightedge for drawing cutting lines as well as measuring an accurate right angle. You can lay out a 45° angle with it by drawing a line from a number on the body to the same number on the tongue where a parallel line (or other side of the board) crosses it.

A combination square (optional) is more compact. The body is usually 12 inches long, and the tongue, which slides along it and hooks over the edge of a board, usually has a level bubble set in it. It can be used to check an inside or outside right angle, measure depth, and draw a 45-degree angle as well as a right angle cutting line.

A carpenter's level is two or three feet long and has at least two, usually removable, vials in it full of liquid. A bubble floats in the exact center of the vial when the horizontal (window sill) or vertical (door jamb) surface you hold the level against is itself level.

Measuring and leveling

The metal extension that slides out of the first section of a folding rule allows you to measure across hard-to-reach inside dimensions in one operation.

Remember that you must add the width of the case to the reading on the tape when you use a steel tape to measure an inside dimension. Note the lock button on the case.

If the framing around a door or window is not level, both vertically and horizontally, the opening will not be perfectly square and the door or window won't fit.

When one leg of a try square hooks over and lies flat along the edge of a board, the other leg makes an exact right angle across it so the cut end will be square.

It wasn't exactly my fault
Even when I measured carefully and cut the board along the waste side of the line, the dang piece *still* wouldn't fit the way it should. Why? Because the ends of a board are not always sawn exactly at right angles to the sides, even when you buy new ones from the yard. So I learned to always put a square against the end I'm measuring from and, if it was cut off at an angle, to trim it square before I measure.

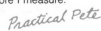

Practical Pete

Cutting tools

A hand crosscut saw has 8 points (7 teeth) to the inch filed like alternately beveled knife points so they cut and crumble away a strip through the wood, called the kerf, as the cut progresses. A crosscut saw is designed to cut *across* the grain (grain runs parallel to the natural lines in the wood). A rip saw's teeth are shaped like a row of chisels to cut parallel with the grain. A crosscut saw can also manage comfortably for short ripping.

Grip the handle with your pointer finger and thumb extended on either side to help hold the blade perpendicular to the surface of the board.

Start a crosscut saw at right angles to the board and pull upward in short strokes. Change the angle to 45 degrees and push, pull in long easy strokes almost the full length of the blade. Twist the handle to one side if the saw cut begins to wander away from the line.

The saw will bind partway through unless the board hangs free on one side of the cut, but support that end a little before you get near the end of the cut or it will break off.

Hacksaw cuts metal with a removable blade set into an expandable frame that can also tip the blade at right angles to the frame. A general-purpose blade has 18 or 24 teeth to the inch—32 for very thin metals. Install the blade so the teeth point toward the front of the frame away from the handle, and screw it tight so it is stretched rigid in the frame. Press hard on the downstroke; otherwise the blade won't bite into the metal. Work at about 50 strokes per minute; less for very hard metals.

Tin snips are useful for cutting thin metal flashing around windows and wire screens.

Chisels must be kept razor sharp and free of nicks. The two most useful sizes for general use, such as cutting insets for hinges and lock plates in doors and door jambs, are ¼- and ¾-inch wide. Good-quality ones have the metal tang running right through the length of the handle to the butt, so you can safely tap it with a hammer without splitting the handle. Lay the flat side next to the wood, tip it up at a very slight angle and push it with the heel of your hand to sliver away a slice in the same direction the grain runs.

Sawing

1. Start a cut with a crosscut hand saw held almost at right angles to the edge of the board. Rest your thumb against the blade to hold it next to the cutting line and pull upward to start the cut.

2. When the notch is deep enough to hold the blade in it, change the angle to 45 degrees and push and pull through the full length of the blade. Don't bear down on the wood; a sharp saw will cut straighter with its own weight.

Planing

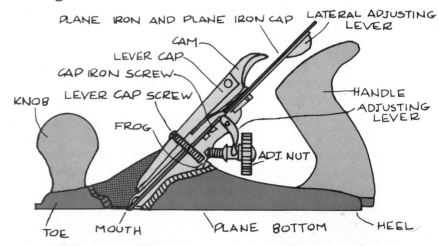

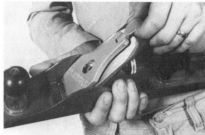

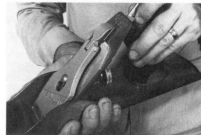

1. To take the plane apart, lift the cam so that the lever cap can be slipped out of the large hole under the screw. Note that the iron and blade underneath is inserted bevel side down.

2. The lateral adjusting lever moves left and right to tip the cutting edge of the blade horizontally in the open throat across the bottom of the plane.

3. Turn the round, serrated adjusting nut so it moves out toward the handle in order to push the blade out further in the throat so it makes a deeper cut.

4. Hold the plane flat and firmly on the surface of the board with two hands (one hand on knob). Turn it at a slight angle, across the grain during the forward cutting stroke so the blade cuts the fibers of the wood with a shearing action.

Drilling/fastening tools

A portable electric drill is so convenient, powers so many useful accessories, and is now so inexpensive that it has become a basic household tool. You can handle most household projects with one that has a ¼-inch chuck (the maximum diameter of the shanks on the bits and accessories that will fit it), spins at 2000 to 2500 top rpms, and has a trigger that controls the speed (slow speeds are for driving screws and drilling metal or concrete). Other useful features are a switch to reverse the direction of spin (for removing screws and clearing the bit from a tight hole), a double-insulated housing, and a two-pronged plug.

Tips for safe, effective use of an electric drill: Unplug it when changing accessories. (One way to remember is to fasten the chuck key to the plug end of the cord.) Center punch an indentation in the work, especially metal, so the bit won't slip as you start the hole. If it slows down, reduce pressure; if it stalls, try reverse, or remove the bit, but don't keep clicking it on and off. Go easy at the end of the hole (so you don't stall the bit or splinter the wood) and keep the bit turning as you remove it to clean the hole. Use a lubricant when drilling metals except brass or cast iron (bacon grease will do); use kerosene with aluminum. Don't leave a locking switch on when you unplug the drill. A long, too-thin extension cord may slow the rpms and damage the motor sooner or later. It's unlikely, but if you hit a live wire when drilling into a wall, don't touch any of the metal parts on the drill.

The bits and accessories for electric drills that are most useful for the jobs in your home include a set of twist metal bits for wood, especially the smaller sizes for predrilling screw holes. Use a spade bit for drilling wide (¼″ holes and up). A hole saw (sometimes called a circle-cutter) looks like a saw blade bent into a circle. It is used for cutting very large holes. Most standard lock sets need a 1⅜-inch diameter hole, for example. Use high-speed twist drill bits for metal or, better still, carbide-tipped bits which can also handle brick or cement. A screwdriver bit with a spring-loaded housing keeps the blade from slipping off the screw.

A ratcheted push drill, sometimes called a "Yankee" drill is used for pre-drilling screw holes and driving or removing screws. It leaves one hand free to hold the screw while the other hand pushes the drill and the ratchet rotates the blade. Bits store in the handle. Get a small and a large screwdriver bit for slot screws and at least one Phillips-head bit (the kind for screws with deep crosses in the head instead of a slot).

A brace and bits. Though an electric drill with spade bits and a push drill for small work can do most of the necessary boring jobs, a brace delivers tremendous turning power for removing screws that are paint stuck or corroded.

Screwdrivers should have blades that closely fit the exact length and width of the slot in the different size screws you will be using, so you will need more than one. If the blade extends out beyond the slot it will chew up the wood; if it is too short it may bend or strip the screw head. A tip-off of good quality is that the blade is shaped so the flat sides are nearly parallel, not gradually tapered down to the tip. Under pressure, the blade is less likely to ride up and strip the slot of the screw. The three most used sizes will be ⅛-, ¼-, and ⅜-inch blades. Add at least one Phillips-head screwdriver because many metal windows and lock-and-hinge sets use them.

A 16- or 20-ounce hammer (with a curved claw for pulling nails) is the correct weight for adults using it for general household repairs. A 16-ounce hammer will be easier for someone of slight build to control. The striking face of the hammer's head should be very slightly rounded so it won't dent the wood when the nail drives flush. Wood or fiberglass handles tend to absorb the impact more than steel and may be somewhat easier on the wrist and elbow if you have to drive a lot of nails. The head should be drop forged—cast iron may chip—and it should be absolutely solid on the handle. If it is even a little bit loose, the head can fly off and turn into a lethal weapon.

Slip-joint pliers are the standard gripping tool. An 8-inch size with serrated jaws and a wire cutter next to the pivot is the most versatile. Don't use them to turn tough nuts if you don't want to bark your knuckles. Pliers are not wrenches.

Smoothing/filling tools

Jack planes come in lengths of 11½ to 15 inches and they are surprisingly expensive. An 8-inch smoothing plane with a 1¾-inch wide blade will do typical light repair and maintenance jobs such as trimming down the edges of doors or window sash or removing a light layer of paint on a window sill. A dull or incorrectly set blade turns this tool into a frustrating, even destructive monster. Practice with it on scrap, moving it along, not into the lay of the grain. Hold it flat on the wood but turned at a slight angle so the blade shears the fibers rather than attacks them head on.

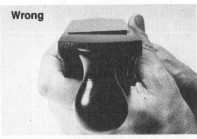

If the edge of the blade is not exactly parallel to the flat surface of the plane's bottom it will cut irregular grooves in the wood. Adjust it by moving the lateral adjusting lever to the left or right.

A putty knife with a flexible blade 1¼ inches wide is the right tool for smoothing glazing compound around window panes, breaking paint seals on stuck windows, filling holes in wood, smoothing spackle into cracks and scraping flaking paint (wear safety glasses to keep flying paint chips out of your eyes).

A caulking gun holds replaceable tubes of caulking compound and squeezes it out of the nozzle on the tube. They cost very little but be sure that the metal head and plunger are solidly attached; cheap ones tend to break off when you first put pressure on them. Before you buy a tube of compound for caulking around exterior window frames to eliminate drafts, read the label carefully to be sure it is made for that purpose and is the color you want.

3. WINDOWS

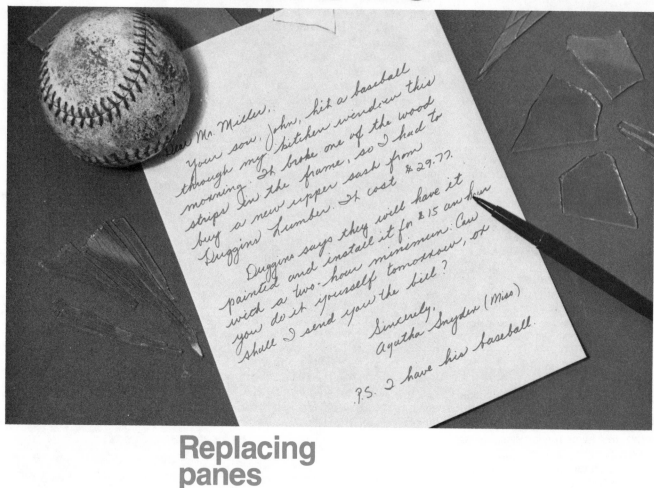

Dear Mr. Miller,

Your son, John, hit a baseball through my kitchen window this morning. It broke one of the wood strips in the frame, so I had to buy a new upper sash from Duggins Lumber. It cost $29.77.

Duggins says they will have it painted and install it for $15 an hour with a two-hour minimum. Can you do it yourself tomorrow, or shall I send you the bill?

Sincerely,
Agatha Snyder (Miss)

P.S. I have his baseball.

Replacing panes

What it takes

Approximate time: About 30 minutes per average-size glass pane.

Tools: A sharp chisel, but one you don't use for fine work. Hammer, screwdriver, putty knife, ruler, heavy work gloves, goggles, wire brush. A felt-tip pen and a glass cutter—if you plan to cut the glass yourself, rather than have it cut at the store. A glazier's point driver is worth the investment if you are going to install more than just a few panes. It works like a staple gun to drive the metal glazier's points into the wood frame to hold the glass in place.

Materials: Glazing compound, light oil, linseed oil, rust preventive paint.

Obviously, a broken pane of glass must be replaced right away, not only because broken glass is dangerous and unsightly, but because it lets all that expensively heated or cooled air escape. Cracked and loose window panes also let the outside air in.

Check the windows of your house from the outside. Even if your home is fairly new you may discover a crack or two that you didn't notice before, or places where the glazing compound has dried out and is cracked or has fallen out. By doing the reglazing yourself you can save money and even time.

Wear heavy work gloves as you carefully remove all broken glass from the frame. If you find it necessary to pry or tap the glass and dried putty loose, wear safety goggles. Gather up and dispose of any glass slivers immediately. Paint inside the glass channel of the frame (after it is thoroughly clean) with a thin coat of primer or linseed oil to feed the wood.

It is easier to work when the window is lying flat, so if you are working with a wooden sash window and can take it out easily, do so.

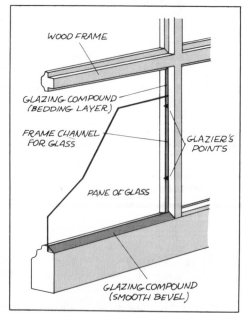

1. Remove broken glass from wood frame. 2. Clean old putty and points out of channels. 3. Smear thin layer of compound along channels. 4. Press pane down carefully but firmly so it is well seated. 5. Fix pane into channels with new glazier's points. 6. Fill each channel in turn with compound and smooth with putty knife.

Labels in diagram: WOOD FRAME, GLAZING COMPOUND (BEDDING LAYER), FRAME CHANNEL FOR GLASS, GLAZIER'S POINTS, PANE OF GLASS, GLAZING COMPOUND (SMOOTH BEVEL)

Wood sash windows

1. An old chisel with a fairly sharp edge is the best tool for removing old glazing compound. You have to clean the glass channel right down to the wood, and the old bedding putty can be hard to get off with just a putty knife or a screwdriver. You must be careful not to cut into the wood frame.

2. Pry out the metal glazier's points. Sand the glass channel smooth and use a whisk broom or vacuum cleaner to pick up the sawdust, bits of glass, and other debris. Paint the channel to match the frame. After the paint has dried, put down a thin layer of glazing compound along the channel.

Don't flip your lid.
I finally learned to put the lid back on my new can of glazier's compound right away and *tight* to keep out air. Tapping the lid back down all around with a hammer is all it takes (if I had had enough sense not to bend the lid when I pried it off the can). This stuff is a nice, gooey white putty when it's new, but it dries rock-hard in about a week when it is opened to air.

Practical Pete

3. Place the glass firmly into the frame opening, pressing down against the squeezed-up layer of glazing compound. Push the metal glazier's points into the side of the channel, tight against the glass. Space them about 6 inches apart. If you don't have a glazier's point gun (a *very* handy tool), position the point with your fingers, lay the flat tip of a screwdriver on the top of the point and push or gently tap it halfway down.

4. After first making sure that the glazing compound is thoroughly mixed (no oil on top), use a putty knife to dig out a glob about the size of a golf ball. Work it between your hands until it has a good consistency, and then roll it into a ball. Twist this into a long rope a little thicker than a pencil. Lay it along the channel next to the glass and press it down gently with your fingers so it fills the angle between the channel and the glass.

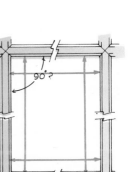

5. Place a clean putty knife, polished smooth with steel wool, against the compound so the edge of the blade is angled and lying on the wooden edge of the frame and one corner of the blade is riding on the glass. Pull the putty knife toward yourself in one long, smooth stroke, from one end of the frame side to the other. This should push the compound down into the joint and leave a smooth beveled surface. This technique requires practice.

6. If the compound pulls out or doesn't fill the joint, just take it all out, roll up another rope and start again. When you have made the joint as smooth as you can, use the blade of the knife to remove excess compound from the frame and the window glass. The compound should take a week to dry hard enough to paint.

Measure the opening of the frame inside the channels. Old frames, especially, may not be exactly square, so you can check by measuring the length of the channel on all four sides. Cut the new glass 1/16 inch smaller all around than the frame, to allow for bedding compound and irregularities. For an extra-tight seal, spread a very thin layer of glazing compound along the channel before inserting the glass.

Metal casement windows

The procedure for replacing these panes is the same as for wood sash windows (page 11), except that the glass pane is held in the frame by metal spring clips instead of glazier's points. These clips hook under a lip along the metal channel, or their tips fit into holes in the channel.

After you remove the old glass, wire-brush away any rust that may be in the channel. Wipe it clean and spray lightly with rust-preventive paint.

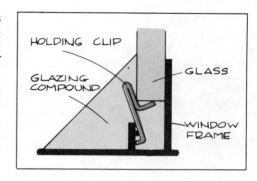

Metal sliding and storm windows

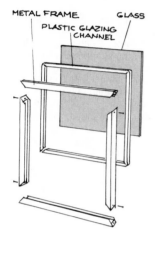

No glazing compound is required. The frames of metal sliding windows are taken apart by removing screws at the ends of the top and bottom rails, or pins at the corners. The glass is held by a plastic bead or a channel that runs around the edge.

The pane in a metal storm window is held tightly in its frame by a removable plastic gasket which you must pull out. The ends usually meet at one of the corners. When you have put in the new pane, press the gasket back in place with your fingers. Start at the corner where the ends meet and work around the frame carefully.

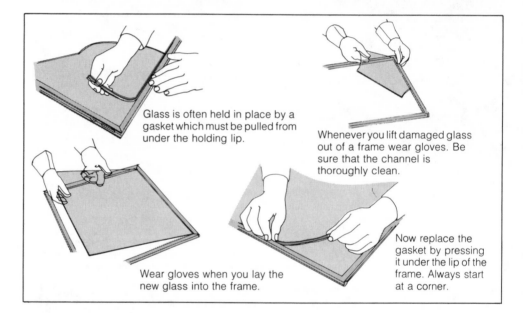

Glass is often held in place by a gasket which must be pulled from under the holding lip.

Whenever you lift damaged glass out of a frame wear gloves. Be sure that the channel is thoroughly clean.

Wear gloves when you lay the new glass into the frame.

Now replace the gasket by pressing it under the lip of the frame. Always start at a corner.

Glass cutting

Especially if you live in a house that has irregularly shaped windows, as many do, you will save time and money by doing your own glasscutting.

One of the most important things to know about cutting glass is that you must have a flat, clean surface to work on. A table top, workbench, anything will do, as long as there are no globs of paint, bits of wood or other debris that might crack or scratch the glass while you are working on it. If you can find a table with a smooth square edge, so much the better.

It is very important that you work with clean glass. If it is not clean your cut will not be smooth. Any sort of grit or even dust on the surface can impede the accurate movement of your glass cutting wheel, causing it to skip. It's wise to brush some machine oil along your cutting line.

A word of caution about handling glass in general. Work slowly and, especially if you are handling broken or cracked glass, use gloves. Whenever you do the actual cutting be sure that you are facing your work as though the cut you will be making is directly in front of you.

A pro scores the glass and snaps it off along the line in two lightning moves. The glass is more likely to break evenly if the glass molecules are still in movement from the scoring stroke. So snap it right away, but move carefully until you have had a lot of experience.

1. With the glass lying flat on the work surface, measure and mark it for the first cut. The best marker is a felt-tipped pen. Do not use a grease pencil; it will clog the cutting wheel and cause the cutter to skip.

2. With the cut marked, position a straightedge (one of the best straightedges is a shop T-square) held firmly in place with one hand so that it doesn't move as you make the cut. Lubricate the wheel of the glass cutter with machine oil.

3. Position the cutter with the cutting wheel down on the glass. Hold the cutter handle straight up and tightly against the straightedge. Grasp the cutter and push down firmly, but not so hard that you break the glass. Now make a smooth stroke along the straightedge from one edge of the glass to the other. Do not repeat the scoring stroke. This is important for you will only chip the glass and may cause it to fracture or break out when you intentionally break it along the scored line.

4. After you have scored the glass, snap or break it off along the scored line. Most experts simply position the glass with the scored line just over the edge of the table. They hold the glass on the table with one hand and with their other hand give the piece to be removed a quick downward snap. Most of the time this works, but not always. Try this technique on some pieces of scrap glass until you perfect it.

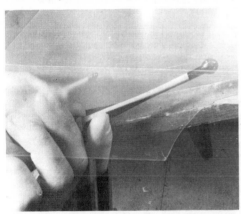

5. A safer method is to position the glass on the table so the scored line protrudes about an inch, then using the heavy ball on the end of the cutter, gently tap on the underside of the glass, following the line exactly. As you do this you will notice the crack starting along the line. Sometimes it will shoot along the line for several inches. Gently tapping on the underside causes the crack to follow the score, and the piece of glass will simply fall off on its own. Finally, you can smooth the edge of the glass with a fine wet-dry sandpaper.

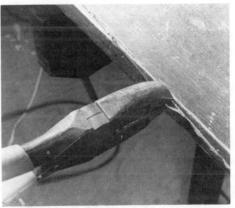

6. In some instances you may have a piece of glass that will break out of the line, for instance where a skip in the score occurs, or the glass piece to be removed may be extremely narrow. Because the small piece isn't large enough to fall by its own weight, tapping on the underside may not cause the glass to fracture. In this case you will have to break it off. Using wide-jawed pliers, grasp the glass piece and quickly snap downward. Make sure that the jaws of the pliers don't extend over the scored line.

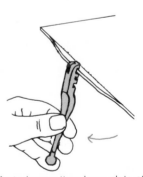

Most glass cutters have slots at one end, and these can be used to break off those small sections. However, pliers work best in most cases.

Sash repairs and hardware

Unsticking a window

What it takes

Approximate time: Minutes.

Tools: Hammer, wide chisel, small pry bar, screwdriver (Phillips or regular slot head for removing storm window if necessary), plane, wide putty knife.

Materials: Sandpaper, soap, candle, or paraffin, lightweight oil or silicone spray.

Louis Cyr, who in an earlier day was billed as "The strongest man in the world," still failed what was considered the acid test for any man of muscle; he was unable to raise and lower every window in a regulation-length Pullman train. You may appreciate this the more when you come up against that window in your house which has stuck fast and will not budge.

There are a number of reasons why a window will stick. Paint or dirt may have gotten into the channels or onto the edges of the various stop moldings. Humidity may have caused expansion or swelling of wood parts. Or, the weather stripping may

1. Place edge of small pry bar under one corner, or down rail of window, and tap in place. Being careful not to gouge the wood, gently pry window open—but work at corners only. If possible use a piece of cloth, heavy cardboard or wood shim between the bar and the window.

2. But you may have to move the stops. This is a simple operation with hammer and chisel; but again, be careful not to gouge. When you nail the stops back into their new position be sure they are in alignment with the window itself, permitting free, but not too loose, passage.

fit too tightly. This can easily be loosened. But the most common reason for jamming is dried paint.

As a rule this disaster occurs when the window is in the down position and the inside or lower sash will not come up. At this point some homeowners resort to physical assault by delivering a series of karate chops to the sash in the hope of loosening it. But this can result in loosening the glazing around the window, or you may knock out a pane of glass and cut yourself in the process.

First of all check to see that the window is not locked. Work the blade of a wide putty knife between the window sash and the parting strip. Use a hammer to tap the handle of the knife if necessary. Check the tracks above. If paint is too thick in the track, remove it with a chisel or sandpaper. Lubricate the track with a candle or a bar of soap or paraffin; use lubricating oil or silicone spray if it is metal. If the window is still fast, try prying it open with a pry bar, gently, and preferably from the outside.

Is it still stuck? Then tap around the sash with your hammer and a block of wood. You might loosen the window through vibration. The block of wood is necessary so you won't dig hammer tracks into the sash. Finally, you can tap the frame with the hammer and wood block, edging the frame away from the window.

If the window is badly swollen you may have to loosen or remove and reset the stops. If you do remove the window you may find that planing or sanding will do the trick. But be careful not to remove too much wood or the window will rattle.

3. If your window has metal channels, you can spray with lightweight oil to prevent sticking. For wood you can rub in paraffin or soap. But remove excess carefully as you go.

TIP: When painting a window position the sashes an inch or two from the top and bottom. When you have finished painting, and before the paint sets, move the window up and down. In this way the seal will not form and you will have avoided a stuck window.

Securing a loose window sash

Of the inconveniences we suffer due to malfunctioning windows, the loose sash is high on the list. Loose window sashes are often caused by poorly working old-fashioned sash weights. Or the sash weights may be gone completely—the rope supporting them having disintegrated through age or rot—and you end up the victim of an inside sash that will not stay up in place.

There was a time when this created a not-small dilemma, for it meant taking out the entire window; professional work which could be costly and time consuming. We now have an almost instant-answer through the application of *sash holders*. These marvels are available at any building supply, and you can fix them to a window in no time at all, at the same time saving yourself some money.

Push the lower or inside sash all the way up. With prongs toward the inside, spring the metal supports and push them until they are covered by the sash. At a stroke, you have probably saved enough energy to read a short novel.

Push lower or inside sash all the way up. Holding the metal supports with the prongs toward the inside, spring them a bit and push all the way up into the window channel until they're covered by the sash. Do both sides in this manner. Now simply lower the window to embed the prongs in the wood and secure the sash holders in place.

What it takes

Approximate time: 10 minutes per window.

Tools and materials: Sash holders, available at any building supplier.

Crank handles and other hardware

The casement window—except for broken panes of glass—seldom needs repair beyond tightening a loose hinge now and then, and cleaning and lubrication of the operator crank and arm.

You may have difficulty in opening and closing the window, and the thing to do then is to inspect the gear mechanism. This is concealed, and in order to get at it you must remove the screws from the crank assembly. If the gears are worn it may be necessary to replace the whole assembly. If old and hardened grease is causing the problem, wash it out with solvent and then lubricate.

The operator arm should slide easily in its tracks as you open and close the window. But there may be rust or hardened grease that has accumulated, or the arm could be bent. Remove the operator arm and straighten it, clean out debris and apply fresh grease when you reassemble.

What it takes

Approximate time: A few minutes.

Tools and materials: Screwdriver, household oil or silicone spray.

1. The first step is to lightly lubricate all moving parts of any hardware with a lightweight household oil. At the same time check to see that the piece of hardware is properly secured, neither loose nor too tight.

2. It should be a simple operation to remove any bent or broken crank handle by loosening the holding screw and sliding the handle off the shaft. If the handle has rusted, or the screw slot is stripped, you may have to take it off with a hacksaw; but this is rare. The chances are that oil or silicone spray will help any sticking.

Replacing double-hung sash windows

What it takes

Approximate time: About 2 hours for each window.

Tools and materials: Hammer, chisel, caulking gun, screwdriver, paint brush, tin snips, hand plane, level, and replacement window units.

Some "Golden Rule"!
My daddy *told* me. "Pete," he said, "measure twice, cut once." But I measured our old window casement once, very carefully, and ordered the new sash window to fit it. It had to be specially made and cost $54. It didn't fit. I had read the markings on the tape measure wrong. The feet are printed on the top half—continuous inches on the bottom half. I read the closest foot mark "2 feet," looked down and read the total inches "25¼ inches," added them together and ordered a 49¼-inch window—two feet too wide! Look at your tape measure; you'll see what I mean.

Practical Pete

TIP: It's much easier to prime, paint, or stain units before installing them permanently in place.

TIP: Save the old units; they make great cold frame covers.

TIP: Sash weights make good boat anchors for drift-fishing, weights for holding down tarps, or pulley counterweights to keep a bird feeder high out of reach until you want to lower it to fill it again.

As windows age, not only do the sash cords deteriorate, but the sashes themselves often rot through in so many places that they can't be caulked enough. In this case they should be replaced altogether.

The question at this point is whether or not you need a whole new frame. Will the new window fit into the old frame? Consider, first of all, how your house is covered. If it's brick veneer, stucco, solid masonry, or cement, you'll more than likely *only* be able to put in the exact same size of new window. These wall materials are difficult to remove in order to allow for a larger window. In fact, it's easier to put in a smaller one by building a new framework inside the old.

At the same time, if your house is built with wood shingle, or clapboard or asbestos siding it's not hard to remove pieces of the siding and then put in a new frame. But for the present, let's consider an exact replacement of the old window. This will be an easy job. All you have to do is buy a new window to match the original. The important thing is to make absolutely sure that your measurements are correct when you order your new unit from your local building supply dealer.

1. Remove the old window stops with a large chisel; these hold the window sashes in place.

2. With the old stops removed, cut the sash weights and allow them to drop down inside the wall. If you are reframing, or redoing the entire wall, then you can remove the window trim and also remove the sash weights.

3. Using a hammer and chisel, remove the sash weight pulleys. Chisel out any other stops holding the window sashes in place and remove them.

4. Try the two metal strips which you will have purchased from your window dealer. Probably they'll be just a bit long. Take a pair of tin snips and clip off their bottom ends to get an exact fit.

5. Now position the two side strips over the window units. Remember that the top window is the outside one, while the bottom window (the one with the slanted edge) is the inside. The slanted edge is positioned down. The units must fit down over the top of the spring-loaded T-bars in the metal guides.

6. Press the window units down until the top of the upper unit is flush with the metal guide strip; then gently push the entire assembly in place. If the units are a bit wide, remove them and look for any old paint lumps that may be keeping them from fitting securely. Scrape and chisel away any obstructions that may be in your way. If the units are still a bit wide, remove them from the strips and plane their edges, using a hand plane. The point is that the units should fit snugly, but not bind.

7. With the units positioned in place, put a carpenter's level against their outside edges and make sure the units are plumb. If they are not plumb, the units will not only not seal properly, but will be difficult to operate, so check very carefully.

8. With the units properly positioned, drive a couple of flat-head brads through the top and bottom of each strip and into the window casing. Replace both inside and outside stops, caulking the edge of the metal strips on the outside before installation of the outside stops.

1. First step is to take off the old window stops on the inside. These are what hold the window sash in place. Use a chisel with a wide blade and a hammer to pry them loose.

2. Now, with the old stops gone, cut the sash weights and let them fall down inside the wall. You don't need them. At the same time, if you are redoing the entire wall, or if you're reframing, then you can just take out all the window trim and save the sash weights.

3. Remove the sash weight pulleys. Best implements for this action will be hammer and chisel. Also chisel out any other stops that are holding the window sashes in place and remove them.

5. Now you're ready to put in the unit. You'll most likely have to do some juggling. The thing is to make everything level, a fit which will be snug but at the same time will allow the windows to open and close smoothly.

4. Check the two metal strips. If they are long, and chances are they will be, cut the extra off with tin snips. Try to get as near perfect a fit as you can.

The spring-lift alternative: You can recognize this type of sash window by the tube that runs from the top of the window casing channel. A spring mechanism in the tube allows the window to be raised or lowered easily.

The tube type is the most popular. Inside it is a spring attached to a twisted rod which keeps the spring tight so the sash will remain stationary. The tension allows the sash to move up or down with little pressure. Adjust the spring tension after a little use.

The spring type is a steel trap design where one looped end is fastened to the window sash and the other to the casing. This type is not adjustable.

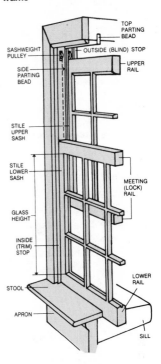

TOP PARTING BEAD

OUTSIDE (BLIND) STOP

SASHWEIGHT PULLEY

UPPER RAIL

SIDE PARTING BEAD

STILE UPPER SASH

STILE LOWER SASH

MEETING (LOCK) RAIL

GLASS HEIGHT

INSIDE (TRIM) STOP

LOWER RAIL

STOOL

APRON

SILL

Window channels

Maybe the answer to that loose or tight window lies simply in replacing the channels. Measure the vertical distance occupied by glass on one sash from inside the meeting rail (lock) to inside the upper or lower rail. Double the measurement; add 6 inches. (On Boston windows add 5.)

Remove all stops; take out the window.

Try-fit the channels in the window opening. Trim with tin snips if necessary.

Now try-fit the windows in the channels, then position them in the opening.

When the channel units fit, remove and paint the old windows, fit them back into place and tack the channels at top and bottom with brads.

What it takes

Approximate time: 15-20 minutes.

Tools and materials: Tin snips, hammer, chisel, and replacement channels.

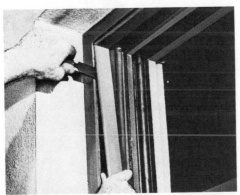

1. After carefully measuring your window, take out the stops. Remove the window and place it to one side. Then try fitting the window channels in the opening. If they need to be cut use your tin snips.

2. Try-fit the window in the channels; then position it in the opening. When the window-channel units fit properly, remove and paint the old window; then fit it back into place. Finally, tack the channels in place at top and bottom with small brads.

Replacing sash cord

What it takes

Approximate time: Under an hour.

Tools and materials: Hammer, screwdriver, single-edge razor blade, putty knife (wide blade), replacement cord.

Parts of a sash cord window

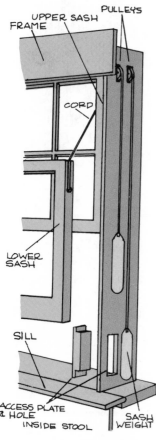

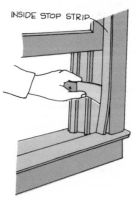

INSIDE STOP STRIP

The double-hung sash window has been used in houses for centuries. It is called double-hung because the upper, or outside sash (the frame holding the glass that moves up and down) and the inside or lower sash are both "hung" movably inside the window's frame.

Some double-hung sash windows are aluminum, but most are wood. The older style sash windows operate with ropes, weights, and pulleys which are concealed in the construction. The ropes are attached to the sash; they pass along the same tracks in which the window frame moves, up to a pulley which is at the top of the track. The rope passes over the pulley, fitting in the groove, and is tied to the hidden sash weight which acts as a counterbalance permitting the window to stay at the height to which it has been raised or lowered. It is marvelously simple.

But the rope can become frayed and will eventually break, and the weight will fall inside the frame. The consequence is that the window will no longer do what you want it to do—stay where you put it.

But it's a simple problem to cope with. Here's what to do:

1. Remove the inside stop strip from the side where the broken cord is. If you have to break the paint seal to get the strip out without breaking it, slice the seal with a sharp single-edge razor blade. Then, with a putty knife blade (not a pry bar) pry the stop strip out.

2. Now pull the sash away from the frame.

3. Untie the knot and remove the rope from the sash frame.

4. Do the same on the other side, and remove that rope. But wait—knot this rope so that it will not disappear into the wall, thus requiring removal of the frame.

5. Set aside the entire sash and look for the access plate located in the lower part of the track. It may have been painted over, in which case you will have to find it by tapping with a hammer or the handle of a screwdriver. You can then cut around its outline with a razor blade, and finally unscrew it from its place. Take the weight out. Note: Older windows do not have access plates. If you find yourself in this predicament you will have to take out the whole window frame to get at the sash weight and broken cord.

6. Untie the old cord. The two broken pieces can be used to measure your new cord. Tie a small weight onto the new cord, small enough so that it will feed in over the pulley. Now feed in the new cord. When the cord has come down to the level of the access plate opening, pull it through.

7. Now take the small weight off and tie on the regular window weight and put it back into the access hole.

8. Take the cord which is opposite to the one you have worked with and tie it to the sash; then put the sash back in the track.

9. Tie the new cord to the sash and hold the sash against the parting strip as you raise it to the top.

10. Check the weight at the access opening. It ought to be about 3 inches above the sill as you hold the sash at the top. If it isn't, adjust the rope. When the weight is correct, put back the access plate and the stop strip. The same procedure is followed if the broken cord is in the upper sash, only you must remove the lower window and parting strip before taking out the upper sash. That's all there is to it.

But while you're at it, you could just as easily replace it with a sash chain and so avoid a broken cord in the future.

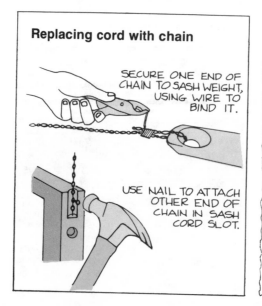

Replacing cord with chain

SECURE ONE END OF CHAIN TO SASH WEIGHT, USING WIRE TO BIND IT.

USE NAIL TO ATTACH OTHER END OF CHAIN IN SASH CORD SLOT.

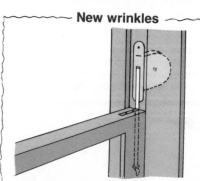

New wrinkles

Sash balances are sold in easily installed kits to replace sash weights, cords, and pulleys. The hardware fits into the hole left in the frame after you remove the old pulley. It has a spring-loaded tape inside a revolving drum—like a steel measuring tape. The tape hooks onto the bottom of an L-shaped bracket, screwed to the top corner of the sash, and rides inside the old sash cord groove.

Closing in a window or doorway

There was a time when buildings were taxed according to their number of windows. And so, enterprising landlords, chagrined over this invasion into their source of revenue, hit upon the clever idea of closing some of those taxable windows. That is to say, they bricked them in. And one can today see on certain buildings those places where the newer brick is of a different color and so reveals the outline of what had once been a window.

You may wish to close in a window for other reasons. Perhaps you've just had it with that particular window; its vagaries of behavior, the way it allows the light to strike your eyes, its seemingly unfixable draughts. Or it could be a doorway; the principle is the same. You may be remodeling your garage, for instance. In any case, the operation requires little in the way of tools or expense; nor does it take much in time or expertise.

What it takes

Approximate time: It shouldn't take more than a couple of hours.

Tools: Hammer, chisel with wide blade and/or a pry bar, sharp knife, saw, square, ruler.

1. After removing the outside trim, pry away the inside window stop, using either a small pry bar or large chisel. The inside stop is recessed into the frame and takes a bit of work to get out.

2. When you have lifted out the window sash remove all inside trim.

3. Now drive the frame out from the inside. Carefully discard the frame, making sure there are no old nails sticking up for somebody to step on.

4. Fasten a 2x4 stud in place and now you are ready to cover the wall. But remember that the stud is essential for support.

Special window treatments

What it takes

Approximate time: One to two hours.

Tools and materials: Hammer, handsaw, coping or saber saw, screwdriver, lumber, sandpaper, galvanized nails, screws, stain or paint.

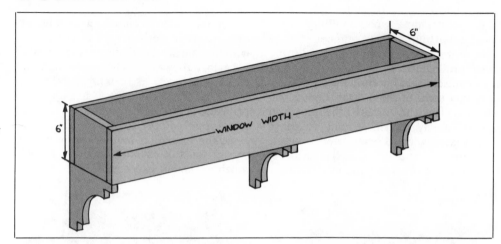

How to make a window box

One of the great things about windows is that you can look out of them. This may sound obvious, yet the fact is that the view is important. You could be looking at the side of another building, or at someone shaving, or you could be looking at a lovely lawn, a lake; or if these are not available you could look at your own garden—your window box.

Indeed, window box gardening is one of the easiest and most enjoyable ways of having flowers around your home. For one thing this form of gardening requires less weeding and other hard garden chores. The important thing is to make sure your windows are low enough to allow you easily to water and otherwise care for the plants once they are in the boxes.

Here's what to do. Purchase the boards you will need already ripped from 1x12s at your local building supply dealer.

Using galvanized rustproof nails, nail

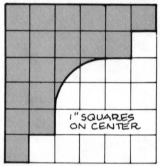

the sides and ends together. Nail the bottom in place and cut the three supports using a saber saw or coping saw.

Sand thoroughly and fasten the supports to the bottom of the box with screws.

Sand the remainder of the work thoroughly and stain or paint to suit your taste.

To fasten your new garden to your house, drive screws through the top of the backboard into the house wall studs; and follow with screws through the bottom of the supports.

Make your own frosted glass

What it takes

Approximate time: One hour.

Tools and materials: Silicon carbide powder, block of wood, epoxy cement.

Frosted glass may be just the ticket for you if you want a door or window which will allow you the benefit of light coming in, but will also give privacy.

But why not make your own frosted glass? You can do it easily enough right on the kitchen table. All you need is a block of wood, a piece of glass glued to the block with epoxy cement, and a bit of silicon carbide powder. Here's what to do:

Glue the glass to the block. Mix up a bit of silicon carbide powder with water so that you have a kind of thick soup.

Now use the carbide soup as an abrasive between the two pieces of glass to grind down the glass surface. As it loses its cutting power, add grit and water. Rinse.

How to create your own stained glass window or door panels

For centuries the stained glass window lay within the province of religion and royalty. It appeared principally in church windows, depicting religious figures or scenes.

Today it is possible to create your own stained glass windows without undergoing the exigencies of long-term apprenticeship; nor is it required that you spend a fortune.

Leaded glass is the traditional method of joining pieces of stained or clear glass between lead channels called lead "came." The leading outlines the glass pieces and is an integral part of the design. The places where the strips of came join one another are soldered on both sides to hold the construction together.

Make an exact, full-sized drawing (called a "cartoon") of the finished design on a sheet of craft paper. Number each section and note the color of the glass you will use.

Place another sheet of craft paper underneath the cartoon, interleaved with carbon paper. Tape it down and retrace.

Cut the carbon pattern into individual template patterns for cutting each piece of glass. These must be 1/16 inch smaller, all around, than the pattern to allow for the thickness of the lead came that will separate adjacent pieces of glass in the finished design. Use special pattern scissors, or instead, tape single-edge razor blades to each side of a piece of cardboard as a cutting guide.

Position the templates on the pieces of glass and fasten the backs of the templates to the glass with coils of masking tape.

Use a metal-edged ruler and glass cutter to score the straightedge pieces, and immediately snap them apart with your fingers. If they don't break, tap the back of the glass along the scored line with the ball on the glass cutter handle, and try again. Do not retrace your score. Tip: It's a good idea to keep your glass cutter in a cup of kerosene between cuts to lubricate it.

Make a right-angle wood frame with strips of wood. Use a carpenter's square to be sure you nail them onto your work surface at an exact 90-degree angle.

Cut the U-channel and H-channel lead came to the necessary lengths. The H-channel will join the glass pieces inside the design, the U-channel will frame the outer edges.

Begin assembling the glass pieces and the lead came. Insert a ¼-inch wood dowel in the other side of the channel to carefully push the lead came against each piece of glass, so the edge of the glass fits snugly all the way into the channel. Hold the assembled pieces in position as you go by temporarily tacking small nails or push pins into the work after each new piece is added.

When the design is completed, place more boards along the other two sides to complete the frame. Tap them to fit tightly, then nail them in place. Use oleic acid as the flux (applied with a small brush) and a spool of solid 60/40 wire solder. Keep a small sponge in a dish of water to clean and cool the soldering iron. Always return the iron to its stand when it is not in use. Be sure the tip of the iron is clean and properly tinned.

Start in one corner and brush each joint with a generous amount of flux.

Put solder on the heated iron until a small bead forms; roll this bead onto a joint. Do not touch the lead with the soldering iron, as it can melt the lead came and ruin your work. Pause until the solder starts to set; then quickly roll the bead of solder with the tip of the iron to cover the joint.

It's a good idea to brush the tip of the heated iron on the wet sponge to cool it before rolling the solder over the joint. This will help prevent melting the lead came.

After all the joints are soldered, remove panel, turn it, and solder the other side.

Leaded glass using lead "came" of various widths is soldered only where the edges meet.

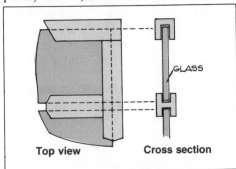

Top view　　　**Cross section**

GLASS

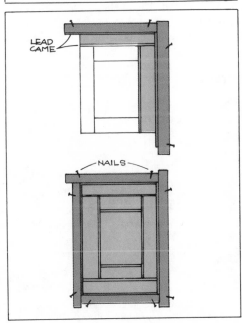

LEAD CAME

NAILS

Nail two strips to your work surface at right angles. With temporary nails hold the pieces firmly together as you go along. Finally, enclose the finished design with two more strips.

What it takes

Approximate time: About four hours for project shown; working time varies widely, depending on size and number of pieces.

Tools and materials: Heavy craft paper, lead pencil, carbon paper, masking tape, and scissors (or two single-edge razor blades and a piece of cardboard) for making the pattern and templates; pieces of colored glass, metal straightedge, glass cutter, and small cup of kerosene for cutting the glass; strips of scrap wood, carpenter's square, hammer, and 6-penny finishing nails for making an assembly frame; U- and H-channel lead came, craft knife with replaceable blades, and ¼-inch wood dowel for assembling the glass pieces; and oleic acid flux, small brush, spool of 60/40 wire solder, and small sponge in dish of water for soldering the pieces together.

Screens—installing, replacing, maintenance

What it takes

Approximate time: About 10 minutes.

Tools and Materials: Toothpick, tin snips, household cement, screening scraps.

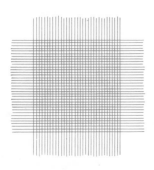

To repair a large hole, make a patch out of scrap screening.

The modern screen, unlike its ancestor of not so long ago, will last for years. If it has a fine enough mesh it will keep even the very small insects out of the house.

Today, screening is made of rustproof materials such as bronze, copper, plastic, and aluminum, and there is also a fiberglass screen and one of anodized aluminum that has a baked-enamel finish. In addition, there is a louver type of either aluminum or brass.

But even with these improvements holes will appear. It is important to repair them before they get out of hand and you have to replace the whole screen.

You can patch a small hole in a metal screen with a quick-drying waterproof glue (for plastic use acetone-type glue).

For a large hole first make a patch by cutting a piece from scrap screening which is larger than the hole in your screen. Bend the free wire ends of the patch and push them through the mesh around the hole. Then bend the ends back so that the patch holds. Plastic ends should be cemented.

Or you can mend small holes by weaving or darning strands from screening scraps; or even use wire.

Maintenance of screens is important, and this includes keeping them clean.

Keep wood frames painted. This isn't just for appearance but to keep away moisture which would cause the wood to swell and even rot. Aluminum frames can suffer from oxidation. Clean them and then coat with wax.

If joints become loose on wood frames,

reglue them or reinforce them with corner plates, mending plates, T plates, corrugated or chevron-type fasteners, wood screws, or glued-in dowels. At the same time, it's sensible to inspect the hangers now and again—both the brackets on the house itself and the hooks on the screen.

After you have cleaned both sides of the screen (you can use the round brush attachment on a vacuum), apply a thinned screen enamel, varnish, or paint to both sides with a brush or a piece of carpet.

Taking care of those screens

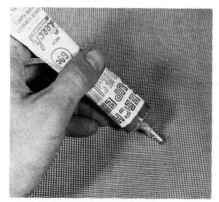

1. Fiberglass is the easiest to repair. If there is nothing more than a pinhole in the screen, use a touch of household cement to fill. Make sure the cement doesn't run down the screen and cause an unsightly appearance. You may wish to lay the screen down.

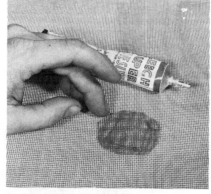

2. A larger tear or gouge can be repaired by merely cutting a tiny patch of fiberglass screening to match and gluing it in place. Again, use household cement and make sure you blot the cement carefully, to remove any excess that might run down.

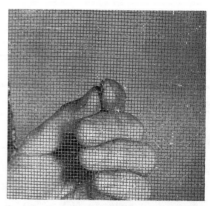

3. A tiny hole in an aluminum screen can be patched by pushing the wire back in place with a sliver of wood such as a toothpick.

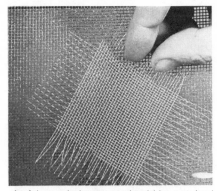

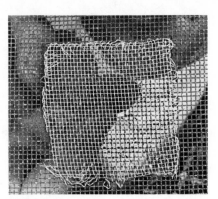

4. A larger hole or tear should be patched with a piece of aluminum screening laced to the hole.

5. Cut a patch about 2 inches larger all around than the hole. Remove a few outside cross threads, fold down the sides and push the threads through the wire, pushing the patch up against the damaged portion.

6. From the opposite side bend the protruding wires down flat against the screen and clip off any extra wires that stick out.

Replacing aluminum storm screening

One of the most put-off, but easy-to-do jobs is replacing damaged storm window screens. The screens are normally made of either fiberglass or aluminum, and you can purchase the material either way, plus the required screen retainer strips.

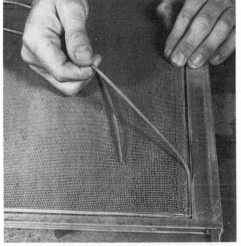

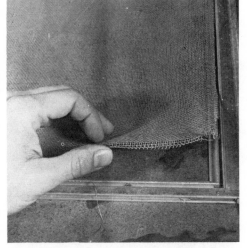

What it takes

Approximate time: An hour.

Tools: Screen installation tool (special purpose), hammer, tin snips, utility knife, replacement screening material.

1. Place the aluminum screen on a flat work surface such as a table. Using the end of a screwdriver, pry up the retaining strip and remove it entirely.

2. Carefully pull out the old screening. But be careful whenever you handle wire screening. It can cut; it can scratch.

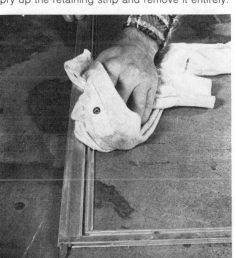

3. With a soft cloth wipe the screen retainer channel in order to remove any debris or bits of old screening, or dust.

4. After carefully measuring the screen opening, cut a piece of screening material ½-inch larger all around than the opening. Use the tin snips.

5. Lay the screening material in place and mark the exact corners of the screen. Now cut a ½-inch diagonal for each corner. This allows the material to be fitted down in the screen retainer slot without warping or buckling.

6. Using the convex roller on a screen retainer installation tool, gently roll the screen down in place. It's best to use short, light strokes, while holding the screen carefully to prevent buckling.

Leaving out the leftover can be a mistake.
After making sure the frame was perfectly square, I measured and cut my new aluminum screening to the exact size. Only I should have cut it ½ inch larger all around in order for the leftover screening to fit down into the retainer groove.

Practical Pete

7. Choose a spline or screen retainer strip of the right size, and starting at one corner, force it and the surrounding screen down in the retainer groove. Push firmly now but with short strokes.

8. Use your finger to gently crease the screen on the inside edges of the retainer strips.

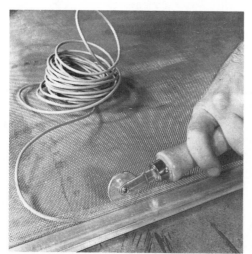

9. And again lightly push the screen on the next side down into the groove. Follow with the retainer strip, seating it firmly in the corner before starting around the next side.

10. After installing all sides, use a utility knife to cut away excess screening on the outside edge of the retainer strips.

What about fiberglass?

A man's home is his castle; but it is also a signal of his genius for improvisation. And high on the list of man's improvisations is that of fiberglass, a product of such present ubiquity that the word itself has acquired the status of place in the language.

Fiberglass is particularly useful when it comes to screening. It is easy to maintain, and moreover, it is attractive. The old screen door and window with their sagging, rusty wire are history.

Fiberglass screening, furthermore, offers the appealing feature of ease in repair. For instance, it is not necessary when replacing fiberglass screening on windows and doors to remove the panel itself. This is a sure bonus if you happen to be limited for time and space.

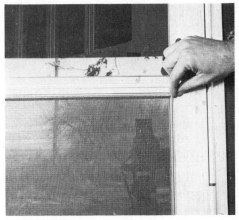

1. With fiberglass screening you can make your replacement on doors or windows without removing the panel, although it is easier to work with the panel on a flat surface.

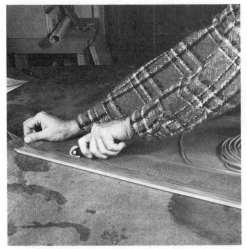

2. To replace with fiberglass screening: again, measure and cut screening material ½ inch larger all around than the screen retainer opening. Starting at one corner, gently push both the screen and retainer down in the channel at the same time, using concave side of a screen-retainer roller tool.

3. As you reach the corner, merely turn the tool and start down the next side. You won't have the problem of buckling as you would have with aluminum screening, so no need to cut away the corner.

4. The last step is to cut excess screening material away from the outside edge of the retaining strip. You can use a utility knife.

Some handy tips

- Aluminum oxide is a good cleaner for aluminum screens.

- Have a few weights to hold down corners of the screening while you're working with it, so that it won't roll up on top of your work area.

- Any time you handle screening it's a good idea to wear gloves. For those who like to work without gloves, the suggestion is that you exercise special caution against cuts and scratches.

- One of the best ways to work with screening—or for that matter, any material—is to be thoroughly prepared with a clean and orderly work surface before you start. Plan, prepare, and then you can produce.

Replacing a wood-frame screen

What it takes

Approximate time: An hour.

Tools and materials: Piece of replacement screening, hammer, two C-clamps, wide wood chisel, staple gun, small pieces of wood or cloth to go between C-clamps and screen.

TIP: Know that old screen wire can cut your hands, so be extra careful when removing it. Also make sure you don't pop any of the tacks off and lose them in an area where you might step on them or run over them with a bicycle.

TIP: Dispose of old screen wire and tacks in a tight cardboard box that you can leave for the garbage collector.

TIP: For this type of work—prying out nails, removing molding—use an old chisel, but keep the tool for that purpose. Never use one of your new, freshly sharpened chisels for such work.

There does come the time when you find you must replace a screen on a window or door. The hole is too large to patch, or repeated blows from a variety of objects have caused the screen to take on a sag which is not only unsightly but has caused an opening or tear at the edge of the molding. Or, if it's a galvanized metal screen it may have started to rust.

Using a large wood chisel, remove the screen molding that is covering the edge of the old screen wire. Be careful not to damage the molding.

Gently pull the old screen wire up, pulling out the tacks as you go. You may have to loosen some of the tacks with the chisel before removing the screen. In this event, slip the chisel under the screen wire next to the tack and pry up both wire and tack. With the old wire removed, cut a new section of screen, larger than the frame.

Now it is necessary to bow or arch the frame in order to get the screen taut. Place two 2x4s on sawhorses or a flat surface, and place the screen on it; then put a 1-inch strip under each end of the frame. Use C-clamps to draw down the center edges of the frame. This bows it. If you don't have C-clamps you can use a heavy weight to hold down the center. But place a thin piece of wood between the clamp and the screen frame.

Position the new piece of screening in place and staple one edge down securely. Then proceed to the opposite end and staple the edge down. Release the clamps and allow the screen to resume its normal shape. Then staple the sides down, making sure you start in the center and work toward the ends, pulling out any buckles that may form. Now, with the wire firmly stapled in place, retack the screen molding into place. Finally, using a sharp utility knife, cut away excess screening.

Installing screen wire on old wooden screens

1. With a large wood chisel, take off the screen molding along the edge of the old screen wire.

2. Gently pull the old screen wire up, pulling out tacks as you go. You may have to loosen some of the tacks with the chisel before removing the screen. In this case, slip the chisel under the screen wire next to the tack and pry up both wire and tack. With the old wire removed, cut a new section of screen, larger than the frame.

3. Place a couple of 2x4s on sawhorses or a flat surface, lay the screen down, then place a 1-inch strip under each end of the frame. Place C-clamps (with protective wood strips) over the center edges of the frame and under the 2X4s, and draw the frame down to bow it a bit. Now position the new screening in place and staple one edge.

4. Proceed to the opposite end and staple the edge down there.

5. Release the clamps and allow the screen to return to its usual shape. Now staple the sides, making sure that you start in the center and work toward the ends, pulling out any buckles that may have formed.

6. With the wire firmly stapled in place, retack the screen molding.

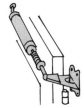

Pneumatic screen door closer.

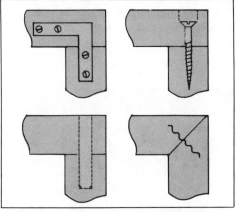

7. Using a sharp utility knife, cut away any screening that may be sticking out beyond the screen molding.

8. Corner bracing can save a screen. You can use a metal angle plate, a hardwood dowel, a long wood screw (countersink, fill with wood dough); or reinforce mitered joints with corrugated fastener.

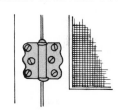

Spring hinges keep screen door tight.

Tight-locking screen door catch.

Screen door guard supports door and also acts as push bar.

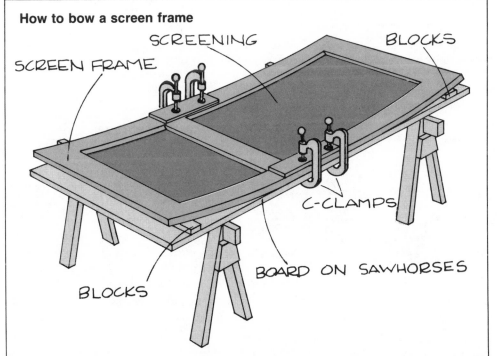

How to bow a screen frame

SCREENING — BLOCKS — SCREEN FRAME — C-CLAMPS — BOARD ON SAWHORSES — BLOCKS

Place screen on board with blocks at each end and draw center down with C-clamps.

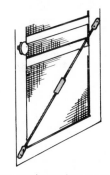

Brace on door takes up sag.

Installing storm windows

What it takes

Tools and materials: Hammer, screwdriver, chisel, Yankee push drill and bits, ruler or measuring tape, Phillips head screwdriver, 8-penny nail.

Probably the most simple job you can do to help combat high energy expenses in your home is to install storm windows. The easiest for the homeowner to put in, and the most practical as well, are aluminum combination windows. These come in all standard sizes to fit standard windows. Indeed, they can be ordered custom-made in case you have non-standard windows.

The really nifty thing about these windows is that once up, the job is done. No more does the homeowner have to take down the storms and lug them to the basement or attic and then put up screens, reversing the operation in the fall; he now benefits from year-round units that keep out insects or cold air as the case may be.

The combination storm window and screen units are available in both two-track and three-track, but for most uses the two-track unit is best. Moreover, some brands of storms tilt inward to facilitate cleaning the inside of the glass.

By pressing on the locking tabs on the sides of the windows you can raise or lower them to provide ventilation in summer or cold protection in winter.

A second advantage to these combination units is that they normally fit more tightly than the old-style storm units. Because they are in the window permanently, they can be caulked to provide even more protection from drafts and air leakage from a warm room.

Installing storm windows

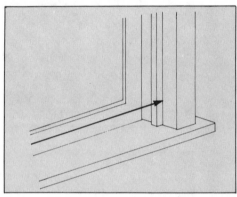

1. The most important thing in good installation of storm windows is to measure properly when ordering the units. There are basically two styles of window, each requiring a slightly different measurement, although the screens will be the same. The most common storm windows overlap the outside window casing and you merely measure the window frame opening in width and height. The width is between the side casings and the height is from sill to bottom of top casing.

2. A measurement for a window unit that fits against a blind stop is made in exactly the same manner, except the storm window fits back inside the window casing and against the blind stop. Naturally, storm windows to be used in this manner must be measured extra carefully.

TIP: If you notice window sweating on your storms check the seal. If the sweating is on the inside window, it means that your storm window is not properly sealed and is allowing cold air to seep in. If the sweating is on the inside of the storm window, it shows that the inside window is leaking warm air into the space between the two windows.

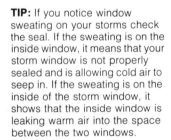

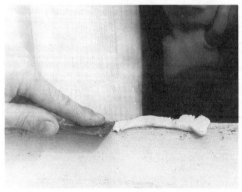

3. Examine the window to see if it needs recaulking and reglazing. It probably will if it hasn't been protected by storm units before. Reglaze and caulk any openings or cracks. This is also a good time to repaint the entire window.

4. Turn the window unit over on its front and slip the metal strip under the clips. This strip can be pulled down to adjust to any unevenness in the sill, giving an absolutely tight, weatherproof fit.

Your own do-it-yourself storm windows

You can create a pretty snappy looking storm window out of plastic sheets and trim. The plastic is clear and rigid and can be bought in standard window sizes. Wood trim or molding can be purchased according to measure. The sheets are placed in the window from the inside, and the molding tacked or screwed in, to hold it in place. This sort of storm window assembly can be purchased in kits or you can make up your own. One of the beauties of it is the fact that you don't have to be climbing up and down ladders outside the house.

The weather conversion
You can turn your window screens and screen doors into storm windows and doors simply by covering them with a clear plastic film. You'll need fiber strips for holding the film in the frame. You can either assemble these materials yourself, or buy a kit. While this system is not as good as a real storm window or storm door, it will save heat and energy.

TIP: Try putting a bit of caulking around the inside lip of the storm unit before screwing it in place, or you can apply a bead around the outside edge after you have finished. This gives even more protection from the winter winds.

5. Place the storm unit in place against the window and make sure it will slide easily in place. Do not force it, the soft aluminum bends quite easily and you'll end up with a distorted frame. If it doesn't go in, there may be a lump of paint or a bowed casing. Examine and carefully cut off what is needed to allow the unit to slip in place.

6. The screws furnished with these units are normally quite small Phillips head screws, so instead of using a drill to make the starting hole, just use an 8-penny nail, tapping it in about ¼ inch with your hammer. Then drive the screws in tight.

The great paint-out.
I didn't actually paint myself into a corner, but I did paint over the key numbers on some of my storm windows, and so I lost track of which sash they paired with. Next time I'll stick a piece of masking tape on the glass and write the number on it.

Practical Pete

Maintaining wood sash storm windows

While aluminum storms may be easier as far as maintenance goes, you could very likely have wood storm windows in your house. They are just as efficient, but there are certain points to watch for. See that they fit snugly in their frames. Put on weatherstripping so that the seal is even more tight. Periodic removal of the storms for repainting is necessary; this prevents swelling and distortion as a result of moisture absorption. Be sure to key the window and the frame with an identical number so that you'll know where it goes after painting. Also inspect every now and again for bent hooks or hangers, loose joints, loose screws, dried-out or missing putty.

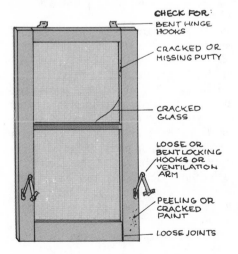

CHECK FOR:
BENT HINGE HOOKS

CRACKED OR MISSING PUTTY

CRACKED GLASS

LOOSE OR BENT LOCKING HOOKS OR VENTILATION ARM

PEELING OR CRACKED PAINT

LOOSE JOINTS

Painting professionally

What it takes:

Approximate time: About one hour each for painting.

Tools and materials:
3″ brush.
1½″ sash brush with the bristles cut at an angle.
Single-edged razor blade scraper.
Sandpaper and block.
Wire brush, putty knife, broad knife, and spackle for badly chipped paint.
Wood primer paint for new wood.
Metal primer paint for steel surfaces.
Safety glasses if you are chipping or scraping old paint.

Preparing surfaces

Chipped paint. After many coats have built up they may crack and begin to chip in spots. Slide the corner of a putty knife blade into the chip and force away as much loose paint as will come away. Sand the edges of the open area to feather them gradually into the old paint around them. Or, if the paint buildup is very thick, smooth premixed spackle into the hollows to even them up with the surrounding paint. Use your finger tip for filling chips in contoured moldings. After the spackle dries white (it looks gray when it's still wet), sand it smooth. Wear a kerchief over your nose, like a bandit, and cover your hair to keep the flying spackle dust out. Wipe the surface with a tack rag or dampened cloth.

Flaking paint. Usually this turns up on sills exposed to lots of sun or moisture. Perhaps the last painter did not clean off greasy soot first. A wire brush will remove the flakes, but don't dig grooves in plaster or old wood with the brush. Sand the area smooth and wipe off the dust. Put a primer coat on bare wood or metal.

Molding cracks. In old houses the molding strips sometimes warp or separate from the wall, leaving a crack that can't be closed. Fill it with spackling compound, draw a wet finger (or a rubber spatula) along it to make a smooth contour. Wipe off any excess, on either side of the crack, with a moist sponge.

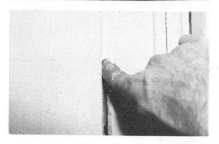

Planning hints:

Old surfaces with chipping, cracks, and many coats require a lot more preparation time (to scrape down, spackle, touch up, and sand smooth) than they do to paint.
Plan preparation and painting as two separate stages. Clean up after the preparation is done and start again with fresh newspapers, stamina, and patience.
If you are using a specially mixed color, get enough for all the windows, doors, and trim in that color. Figure at least a quart for one side of a door or two windows.
Check the rain forecast before starting to paint out-opening casement windows.
Plan to paint one whole side of a door, especially flush doors, without stopping. A line may show where you stopped because the fresh paint can't flow into the dried paint.
When painting doors, wedge them open and slip newspapers under them so you don't build up paint in the cracks and splatter on the frame or wall.

Painting sequence. The sequences given here for painting the parts of a door or window will produce a better result for two reasons: Most wooden doors and windows have vertical sides running top to bottom and horizontal pieces butted inside them. If you paint the horizontals before the verticals, the paint strokes will run with the grain of the wood in the same pattern as the door or window was constructed. These sequences also allow you to do the job in the shortest time without overlapping fresh paint on dried paint where it will be noticeable.

Paneled door: First do the panels, around the molding, then the flat part working from the edges of the panel toward its center; do the horizontal surfaces next, left to right; the vertical surfaces come last, top to bottom. If you are painting the panel moldings a darker, contrasting color, paint them first with a 1-inch angled trim brush and let that paint dry completely before painting the rest of the door.

Flush door: Use a 3-inch brush or roller. Paintbrush jobs should be done in foot-high strips across the width of the door. Start in the upper left corner and lay the paint on about halfway across the door, first with down-up strokes and then back-and-forth strokes; then do the same with the other half of that strip; smooth the full strip first up and down, then back and forth across the full width of the door. Repeat that procedure in foot-high strips until you reach the bottom of the door.

Frame and joint: Paint the edge of the door that opens toward you the same color as that side of the door. Also paint the door frame and jamb, including the section that has the lock striker plate in it, so that when you stand back into the room a little with the door open, everything you see on the frame and jamb is the same color.

New door: Take it off the hinges so you can paint the bottom and hinged edges to keep the wood from swelling (you won't have to paint them ever again). Lift out both hinge pins with pliers or drive them free with a spike nail set, bottom hinge first. Lift the door off both hinges simultaneously so one hinge never carries the full load and bends out of shape. If it is new wood, give it a primer coat first *all over*. If you paint only one side of a new wood door it will probably warp. Sand the primer lightly to smooth tiny bumps. And remember to wipe it off well.

Painting windows and screens

Double-hung windows. Push the inside sash almost all the way up and pull the outside sash almost all the way down. Paint all of the inside sash with a 1½-inch sash brush, cross pieces first, then vertical pieces, but don't paint the top edge of the sash yet. Then paint as much of the outside sash as you can reach. Don't paint the bottom edge of the lower sash (so you won't get paint on your fingers when you push it up), unless you can't reach it later.

Push the outside sash up almost to the top, and push the inside sash almost all the way down. Paint the parts of the sash you couldn't reach before, plus the frame, but not the inside and outside channels. Let the paint dry; then lower both windows all the way, paint the jamb and top halves of the inside channels lightly with a thin coat. After it dries, raise both windows and paint the bottom half of the inside channels. Lubricate the unpainted metal parts.

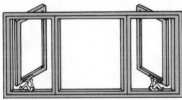

Casement windows. Swing the window out and lock it open. Paint the parts of the window in the following order: The strips surrounding the glass, horizontal first, then vertical; the sill; the frame, starting with the hinged side. If they are steel, rust will bleed through most interior paints. So after you have wirebrushed off loose paint or rust, touch up the bare spots with a metal primer paint. Sand the primer lightly before the finish paint job.

Painting metal screens. Tack a piece of short pile carpeting onto a small block of wood that you can hold comfortably in one hand. Dip it in the paint and wipe it across the screen. Then paint the frame. Use rust-preventive paint for protecting old steel mesh screens.

Painting doors

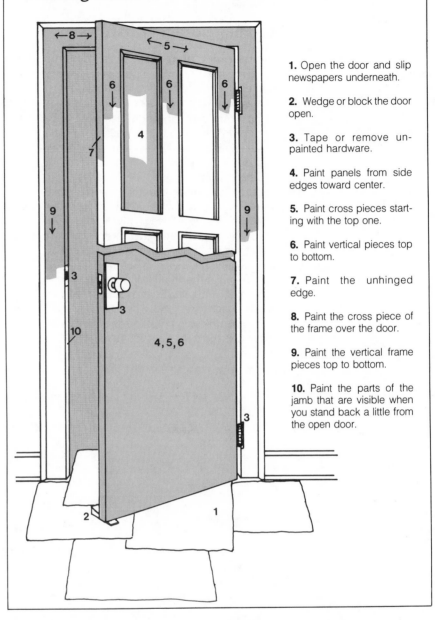

1. Open the door and slip newspapers underneath.

2. Wedge or block the door open.

3. Tape or remove unpainted hardware.

4. Paint panels from side edges toward center.

5. Paint cross pieces starting with the top one.

6. Paint vertical pieces top to bottom.

7. Paint the unhinged edge.

8. Paint the cross piece of the frame over the door.

9. Paint the vertical frame pieces top to bottom.

10. Paint the parts of the jamb that are visible when you stand back a little from the open door.

Cleaning paint off glass and hardware. Use a single-edge blade to scrape the paint off glass after it has dried a little. First, score along the edge where the glass meets the wood strip, then scrape the blade flat along the glass, and the unwanted paint will come off like a banana peel.

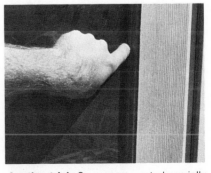

Another trick. Smear some petroleum jelly (Vaseline) on the glass with your fingers where the glass meets the wood. Also smear it on hardware. When the paint has dried, it scrapes off easily where the paint went over the jelly.

What goes with the window

Installing drapery hardware

What it takes

Approximate time: Under an hour.

Tools and materials: Hammer, screwdriver, 8-penny nail, Yankee drill, measuring tape or ruler, portable electric drill and bits, plastic wall anchors or expansion bolts, drapery or curtain rods, with fasteners provided by the manufacturer.

It is the easiest thing in the world to put up drapery rods that will be uneven. This is not only unsightly, it is perilous, for it can all fall when you open the drapes.

But this sad situation can easily be avoided. A bit of care in measuring and leveling, and a small amount of patience will do the trick.

The two main types of installation to consider are: concealed and exposed hardware. If the hardware is to be installed inside the window frames, merely measure, mark for position and then fasten in place either with screws or the small brads that are usually furnished when you buy the rod. Some of the smaller hardware, such as for small cafe rods, is furnished with tiny brads which you simply drive into place.

The simplest type of drapery rod is an extension rod with a spring inside it. Measure to allow for the contraction of the rod. Slip the drapery on the rod and squeeze the rod to fit in place. Regardless of what type of hardware is used, if it is to be placed on the window trim, measure, position, and screw in place. Incidentally, a small Yankee screwdriver can start screw holes, but don't bore too deep, or the screw won't hold.

Draperies that are designed to remain more or less stationary may be hung on poles or rods that are fixed; but if you require your draperies to open and close frequently, then a traverse rod is the best bet. This piece of hardware can be operated by hand or by an electric motor. The beauty of the traverse rod is that when your draperies are hung in this manner, no matter how wide the area that they cover, you can open both sides with a single motion, and just as easily close them.

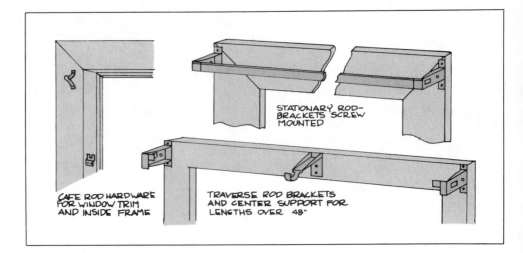

STATIONARY ROD-BRACKETS SCREW MOUNTED

CAFE ROD HARDWARE FOR WINDOW TRIM AND INSIDE FRAME

TRAVERSE ROD BRACKETS AND CENTER SUPPORT FOR LENGTHS OVER 48"

TIP: If any curtain rod is over 48 inches long make sure it has adequate support between the two ends.

1. In most cases the hardware won't be placed on the trim. The first step is to mark the location of the hardware. Drive an 8-penny nail at one of the screw hole locations to determine if the hardware will be located on a stud. If the hardware is located on a stud, predrill holes with a Yankee drill and fasten hardware in place.

2. If the nail goes through the wall, indicating the absence of a stud in the area, you'll have to use wall anchors. The first step is to bore a ¼-inch hole.

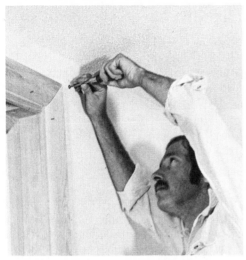

3. Next step is to position the wall anchor in the hole; then turn the screw in the anchor to pull it in place. Remove the screw.

4. Position the hardware over the anchor and replace the screw to hold the hardware securely. Remember that you will have to do this for two screws on each piece of hardware.

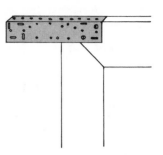

TIP: Should you want to hang draperies beyond the window frame to take full advantage of light you can use extender plates which are mounted directly on the window casing so that no wall mounting is required.

5. In many cases the rod will be supported by a center support. Fasten this in the same manner.

6. Do the end supports in the same way. Then snap the rod in place. Be careful that you have not pushed any of the hardware out of level.

More ain't better
I had no trouble at all putting up my new drapes; but the rod began to wobble after I had opened and closed them a few times. Luckily I figured out what the problem was before the whole shebang fell on top of me. I had drilled too deep and the screws didn't have enough to hold to. So I just got longer screws and the problem was solved. Next time I won't drill deeper than the length of the screw.
Practical Pete

7. Loosen the adjusting screw on the center support and move the support arm into the right position. Then snap the rod in place on the support, and tighten the adjusting screw.

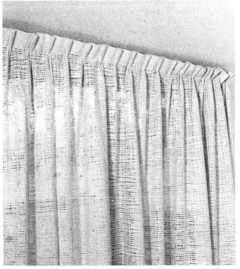

8. Your final step is to fasten the drapery material to the rod, using the hooks.

Installing and maintaining window shades

Standard inside bracket

Inside extension bracket

Sash-run bracket

Outside bracket

Combination bracket

Ceiling bracket

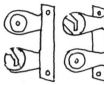

Double bracket

One of the most alarming—not to say noisiest—of those necessities of civilized living with which the homeowner must deal is the malfunctioning window shade. But what a deceptively simple mechanism it is. A plain-looking wooden roller, one end of which is hollow and holds a coil spring within. At either end of the roller is a pin. The one at the spring end is flat. It rotates, winding or unwinding the spring. When you pull down the shade the spring winds tight. The moment you stop pulling, a small lever, called a pawl, drops into place against a ratchet at the spring end of the roller. It is the pawl that prevents the spring from winding the shade back up.

When you want to raise the shade, you pull down slightly on it, thus moving the pawl away from the ratchet and so permitting the spring to take the shade back up.

The fasteners for installing shades are similar to those used for drapery hardware: brads and small screws in a wooden frame, and wall anchors when there is nothing in the wall to grip.

There are seven types of brackets.

Standard inside bracket. This is the most commonly used, and it is used any place that has enough depth inside the window frame to accommodate a roller.

Inside extension bracket. Also mounted inside a window frame, it requires less space than the standard inside bracket.

Sash-run bracket. A special bracket that is used with an all-wood, double-hung window. The bracket is mounted at the top of the sash rung.

Outside bracket. This type of bracket can be mounted on either the trim or the surrounding wall. It is commonly used where there is no space on the inside of the window frame. Shades wider than the window can be used with these brackets to block out the light.

Combination bracket. These dual purpose brackets hold both a window shade and a curtain rod.

Ceiling bracket. Useful on high windows, these brackets are mounted on the ceiling. They can also be used to give a standard window the illusion of extra height.

Double bracket. These are designed to utilize two shades at one time. As a rule, one is translucent, the other opaque.

While installation is fairly simple, it is the actual maintenance of the window shade that is one of the prime concerns of the homeowner.

If the shade does not want to stay down, it means that it is not catching. Check that the brackets are not interfering with the roller. A roller should have 1/16″ to ⅛″ clearance. Make sure that the flat projection of the roller is vertical in the slot in the bracket. Never, by the way, use oil in a shade mechanism.

If the shade pulls up too strongly, it means that the spring is too tight. Roll the shade up to the top and remove it from the brackets. Unroll two revolutions of cloth and replace on the brackets. Repeat until the spring has regained the proper position. Do not unroll more than half way.

If the shade refuses to return, this means that it lacks sufficient tension. In order to increase the tension, pull the shade down about two revolutions; then remove the flat pin from its bracket. Roll the shade back up by hand. When it is all the way up, put the pin back in its bracket and test for tension. If the shade still won't go up far enough, repeat the procedure until it does.

If the shade wobbles when it goes up or down, this probably indicates a bent roller pin. Straighten the pin with pliers, but with gentle pressure. If the pin is dirty or rusty you can clean it with sandpaper.

If the shade cloth is worn, on the bottom edge, the shade can be salvaged. Just trim off the damaged part; remove the cloth from the roller and remount it by tacking or stapling the cut bottom end of the cloth to the roller. Be careful that you keep the bottom of the shade absolutely straight.

The window shade

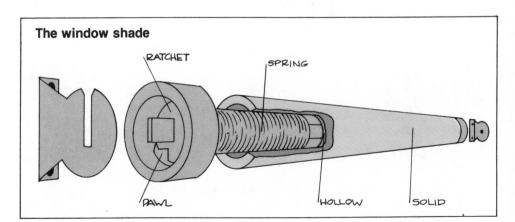

Venetian blinds—repair and maintenance

The two chief problems with any venetian blind are concerned with the webbing (the ladder tapes) and the cords. These can—and they do—become frayed or broken.

First of all you will see that there are two sets of cords. One set, known as the "lift cord system," raises and lowers the blinds. The other set is called the "tilt cord system," and it controls the amount of light by altering the angle of the blinds.

Some experts suggest that you make a drawing of your blinds so that you will more easily get the cords back to their right places. It's a good idea. After all, you simply need to replace the old with the new *in exactly the same way*.

Open the blinds. Starting with the lift cord, take a look at the knots under the tape at the base of the bottom rail. The tape might be held in place by a clamp, if the rail is metal, or if it is wood it may be stapled.

Untie the knot on the side that has the tilt cord and join the old cord to the new cord by butting the ends and wrapping them with transparent tape.

Now feed the new cord from the bottom up through the openings in the slats; and on through the entire route of the old cord until you reach the knot on the opposite end. You must make certain that the cord threads alternately back and forth on different sides of the ladder tapes—the webbing—as you feed it in.

You can change the tilt cord at the same time. Run it over the pulley and back down.

If you wish to replace the tapes, remove the blinds from the window and place them either on the floor or on a large table. Remove the cover from the bottom slat. Untie both ends of the cord and pull free. This releases the slats so that you can pull them out for washing and painting.

When you purchase new tapes be sure that they have the same number of ladders as the old tapes and that they are for the same width slats. Install them by securing them to top and bottom; now thread the lift cord through the tapes.

What else can you do in the way of maintenance? Check the gears and pulleys; these pick up lint, affecting their operation. Clean and lubricate with silicone spray.

What it takes.

Tools and materials: Scissors, pliers, replacement webbing, replacement cord, silicone spray.

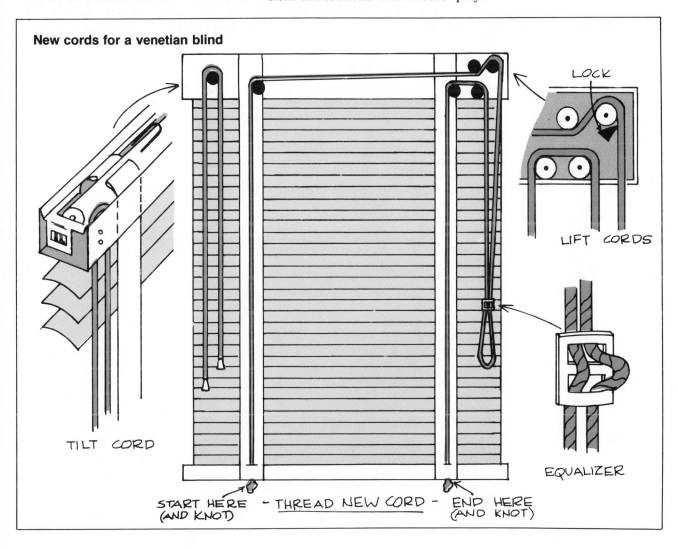

New cords for a venetian blind

LOCK

LIFT CORDS

EQUALIZER

TILT CORD

START HERE (AND KNOT) — THREAD NEW CORD — END HERE (AND KNOT)

4. DOORS

The door that binds or is loose

What it takes

Approximate time: Varies with the job from minutes to a couple of hours.

Tools and materials: Hammer, plane, screwdriver, carpenter's square, file, wooden toothpicks, glue, plastic wood, shirt cardboard, chalk, wooden wedges, and penetrating oil.

TIP: To keep the door upright while planing, anchor it with a C-clamp to a large wooden box.

The door is a basic part of any house. It is both entry and exit, it leads to other rooms, it leads to closets, basements and attics, hallways. Considering the simplicity of its shape, it is striking how many different kinds of doors there are. Yet, the point for us is the proper functioning of the door. Simply put: will it open and close without shoulders, tools, or a professional carpenter being brought to bear?

The principal door problems are binding and looseness. Why does a door stick? It could be because the hinges are loose or poorly mounted; possibly the wood has swollen, or the house may have settled, and so the door frame is out of shape.

Inspect the hinges and strike plate. If any screws are loose as a result of the holes being enlarged try longer screws, or you can fill the holes with wood plugs or plastic wood and reset the old screws. If the door still binds, try locating the places where it rubs by slipping some stiff but thin cardboard between the jamb and the edges of the closed door.

Suppose that the door is free near the bottom but is sticking near the top on the latch side. It means that the bottom hinge may have been mortised too deeply. The approach then is to open the door and place a wedge under it to make it secure. Remove

the screws from the bottom hinge leaf in the jamb, place a cardboard shim under the hinge leaf, and reset the screws. This will move the lower part of the door out from the jamb and will push it so that it is square in its frame, as it should be.

On the other hand, should the door be sticking near the bottom on the latch side, you can put a shim under the upper hinge in the jamb. If the door still binds, then sand or plane off some wood at the point where it rubs. You can do this without taking down the door. But remember that whenever you take off wood you must put finish on the raw wood to match the door and to prevent moisture which will cause swelling.

If the door is now binding at the top, wedge it open and sand or plane the wood. But should the binding be at the bottom you will need to remove the door; likewise if it is sticking along the whole of the latch side. Remove it and sand or plane down the *hinge* side. This method is recommended because it is easier to plane the hinge side since you don't need to remove the lock; also, the hinge side is not so noticeable as the latch side and may be easier to refinish.

What if the door is moving freely and the latch, though lined up does not reach the strike plate? You can put a shim under it to move it out far enough toward the door so it will hold. Should the door open by itself when it is not latched, then put a narrow cardboard shim under half the hinge leaf on the pin side of each hinge on the jamb.

The recommended way to remove a door—if it has loose pins—is to drive the pins up and out with a hammer and screwdriver or nail set. Take out the bottom (and middle) pin first and then the top hinge so the door won't fall while held with only one hinge. If the door is held by hinges that don't have loose pins, remove the screws from one leaf of each hinge on the door's jamb side. Do it with the door wide and with a wedge supporting its outer corner.

However, before you start this operation mark the place or places where it binds. Plane down to these marks. Be very careful.

If it is the hinge side you have planed, you may in certain cases need to deepen the hinge mortises so that the position of the door in the frame will remain as it was.

To plane the bottom of the door you will have to prop it so that the bottom is vertical to the floor. Plane from the top corner toward the center. Turn the door over so that it stands on the other long edge, and plane from the other corner toward the center. It is important when planing the side always to cut toward the edges. Remember that the latch side is slightly beveled to prevent the door edge from striking the frame when the door closes. And so if you do have to plane the latch side make sure that you don't lose the bevel.

A door will not stay closed if the latch tongue does not go into the strike plate opening. You can file the opening to make it larger. But if the strike plate is too much out of line you will have to move it. Remove the plate, cut the mortise to the new place, fill the exposed part with plastic wood, and plug the screw holes.

In some cases you can position wood shims under a threshold to bring it up into position and prevent door looseness.

In all cases doors should have at least ⅛-inch clearance on top and at each side to allow for shrinkage and expansion. In areas of high temperature and humidity changes, you may even wish to make this ¼ inch, and use weatherstripping around the opening.

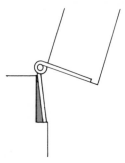

If the door is too tight, place a small piece of cardboard shim on the front side of the hinge.

If the door is too loose, then place a shim on the back side of the hinge.

1. In some cases you'll have to remove the door and so start by tapping out the hinge pin. Use a nail set or a screwdriver and hammer. After the door is down you can plane or sand it as needed. Remember, though, before taking the door down, to mark where it needs planing.

2. Use a jack plane and make sure the blade is in good condition. It's best to remove wood on the hinge side, but you may have to plane on the latch side; if so, make sure you leave a bevel edge.

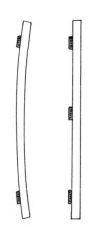

If a door becomes warped, one easy remedy is to install a third hinge centered between the other two.

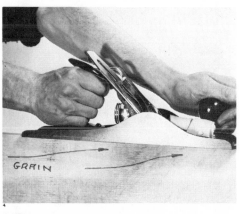

3. Plane with the grain, never against it. Also, make sure that the work is secure and won't wobble or move in any way while you are planing.

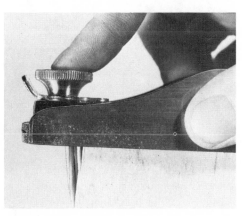

4. When planing across the edges of doors, work from the end toward the center in order to avoid splintering as shown here.

Cutting a new doorway

What it takes

Approximate time: One day.

Tools and materials: Hammer, saw, pry bar, level, square, large wood chisel, large utility knife, hacksaw (optional), plumb bob and chalk line, portable electric saw, and portable electric drill.

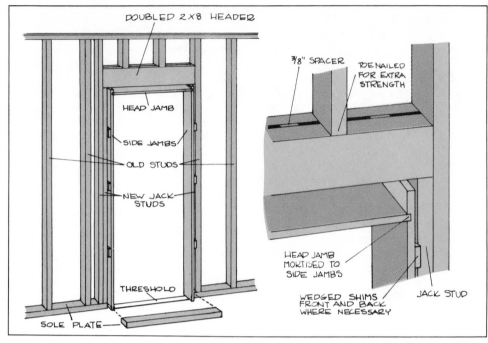

Decide the general position of the door opening. This will include the framing you will add. Tap the wall or drill small holes to locate the studs; use a ⅛-inch bit. Make sure that you aren't running into any heating ducts or pipes. You can check in the basement for this. Electrical wiring is easy enough to relocate.

Now mark the inside of the wall, using a straightedge or chalk line to make certain the lines are straight. Use a plumb bob or carpenter's level to make sure the sides of the opening are plumb.

Using a long bit on a portable electric drill, bore through the wall at the top corners of the marked opening. This should give a rough location of the opening on the outside wall. Now measure outside to make sure it is positioned properly, and drop a plumb bob chalk line down to mark the locations of the side cuts. The opening must be cut 5 inches wider on each side and 9 to 12 inches higher on top to allow for the new framing and door facings.

With both the inside and outside cut marked, the first step is to remove all nails from the cut lines on the outside, and then, using a general-purpose blade in a portable electric saw, saw out the outline on the outside. If you plan to install new siding, you can make the corner cuts larger. However, if you intend to save the siding, cut

1. After marking both the inside and outside cuts, remove all the nails from the cut lines on the outside; then, with a general-purpose blade in a portable power saw, saw along the outline from the outside. Here, a window is being removed so that a door can be installed in its place.

2. Remove all lath, plaster, or sheetrock from the inside of the opening lines. Make sure you remove all nails before making any cuts with your saw. Before removing the studs you should preassemble the framing so it can be placed in position quickly after the last stud is removed.

just barely past the corners, leaving enough so that the trim on the door will cover. Set the saw blade so it will go only through the siding and boxing and not into the 2x4 studs. Remove the siding from the opening.

With all the siding and boxing removed from the outside, go back inside the house and use a brick chisel or large wood chisel to score around the rough opening lines through the lath and plaster, if that is what's covering your wall. If the inside wall is covered with sheetrock, you can use a large utility knife. After scoring along the lines, remove all plaster or sheetrock from the inside of the lines. If the wall consists of lath and plaster, use a hacksaw or portable electric saw to cut the lath around the edges. Then pull the lath away.

You should now have only the studs left in the opening. Before removing them, assemble the framing. It can then be quickly placed in position after the last stud is cut away and removed.

The framing comprises two 2x4s on each side and a double header consisting of at least two 2x8s on end with a ⅜-inch spacer between to make the header the proper wall thickness. Make sure that the ⅜-inch spacer is right for your wall.

With the new frame completed, cut the 2x4s loose first at the bottom and then at the top. Leave the center 2x4 until last. Then cut it away at both bottom and top and quickly position your framing. Toenail it at the bottom, and toenail the existing studs into the header at the top.

Hanging a new door

The first decision is to pick the door that fits your requirements. The door will be either interior or exterior, either flush or sash, and there are also louver doors.

Be sure that your measurements are precise. Either you will have to cut an opening or the opening is already there; but in either case you will order the door from the lumber yard to fit your measurements.

First measure for height from the floor to the headpiece of the frame. Then measure for width. More than likely you will need a 6-foot-8-inch or a 7-foot door. But it will have to be cut to allow for the thickness of the saddle or threshold piece. As a rule the saddle will be ¾ inch, though this is variable. The point is to buy a door that will have ⅛-inch clearance at the top and on each side. But this is the maximum; more than that and the door will be too loose. It is important, especially for an exterior door, to see whether you need to paint the bottom and top edges to seal them against moisture and warping.

When you are ready to hang the new door, first saw off the two horns, the protective ends that are extensions of the vertical members or stiles. Measure the door and mark it for height and width. Cut it to size. With a plane, trim the edges of the hinge, latch stiles and bottom rail. Be careful not to lose the bevel on the latch side.

Place the door in the opening to try it for fit. Put wedges (wood shingles are good) under the bottom rail so that it is raised ¼ inch for clearance. If there is a rug or carpet over which the door is to open or close, then increase the clearance to ⅞ inch. To ensure the proper clearance around the door insert wedges; hammer

Diagram labels: CASING, STOP, HEAD JAMB, TOP RAIL, LATCH STILE, HINGE STILE, JAMB, PANEL, LOCK RAIL, THRESHOLD (OR SADDLE), BOTTOM RAIL, STILE EXTENSION (TO BE SAWED OFF), WEDGES

these in on all four sides to hold the door in its proper position.

Select your hinges. Depending on the size and weight of your door you will have either two or three hinges. Locate the top hinge 6 inches from the top of the door, and the bottom hinge 10 inches from the bottom. If you are using three hinges you can space these out a bit and locate the third hinge halfway between. Take the door away, and with a try square extend the hinge marks onto the jamb. Lay the hinge

What it takes

Approximate time: 4 hours.

Tools and materials: Saw, tape measure, plane, sandpaper, chisel, screwdriver, hammer, try square, level, plumb line, wedges, nails, hinges, cardboard shims, door.

The time I really got into a "jamb."
Sometimes it's the easiest thing in the world just to forget something. I forgot to bevel the latch edge of my new door when I planed it to size. And so it didn't clear the jamb as it was supposed to. Luckily it only splintered the edge a little and I was able to fix it. But next time I'll remember.

Some doors come with one edge beveled at the factory. In tha case you'll have to remember to hang the door with the bevel on the latch side.

Practical Pete

leaf down on the hinge edge of the door as a guide, and outline it with a pencil. The barrel of the hinge should lie beyond the inner face of the door. Mark the thickness of the hinge on the inside of the door face.

Use a chisel to score the outline of the hinge inside the pencil line. Hold the chisel vertically, keeping its beveled face toward the opening, and drive it to approximately the depth of the hinge. Make scoring marks inside the mortise outline and cut these out to the depth line. The chisel's beveled edge should be held downward. It is better to make several small cuts than a few large ones. You'll have a cleaner mortise. You can shave off your scored cuts by holding the chisel along the depth line and tapping it lightly against the grain of the mortise opening. The beveled side of the chisel should be facing up. Place the hinge to see how it fits. If it lies too deep in the mortise, shim it up with cardboard until it lies flush. Drill or punch holes for the screws; then drive the screws home. The hinge must be absolutely flush with the door edge.

You will have separated the hinge leaves to make it easier to attach them to the jamb and door. Now bring the door with the hinge leaves attached to the jamb. Engage the pairs of leaves, top hinge first, and insert the hinge pin. Repeat for the second pin, and for a third if there is one. Tighten all the screws. Now cut the doorstop to size and attach it with finishing nails (see diagram, page 135). The stop should contact the door on the latch side and at top, but there can be a slight clearance on the hinge side. Finally, check your door swing.

Mortising a hinge

1. Use the hinge leaf as a guide to outline the mortise. Let the hinge barrel extend beyond the edge of the door.

2. With a chisel, score the hinge outline inside the pencil mark. Keep the beveled face of the chisel toward the opening.

3. With beveled edge down, clean the mortise to the depth of the hinge leaf, using shallow feather cuts.

4. Holding the chisel on the depth line, tap across the mortise grain to shave off the cuts. Keep the bevel facing up.

5. Drill or punch holes for the screws, being sure to go straight down and not at an angle, nor too deep.

6. Drive the screws home. Check that the hinge leaf is flush with the edge of the door. Use a shim if cut is too deep.

Doorstop

Now is the moment to nail the doorstop in place. This essential door part consists of two vertical side pieces and one horizontal head piece (see illustration, page 135). Cut all the pieces of stop you need to their approximate length, with one end of each cut square. Hold the head piece in place at the top of the door, mark the other end at the edge of the jamb, and cut to length. With the door closed and latched, install the head piece, being careful not to force the stop against the door. Nail it with 1/16 inch of clearance between it and the door.

Now install the stop piece on the hinge side. Don't force it, make sure you have clearance, and try the door after you nail each piece in place. In this way if the door binds you will know right off which piece of the stop needs adjustment. Finally, nail the stop piece on the latch side.

Casing

The casing is the flat molding that goes around the door (see illustration, page 135). It's simple enough to nail up; chiefly it is a question of cutting accurate miter joints.

This takes care and it's a good idea to practice first on scraps. You will need a miter box so you can cut a 45-degree angle, and a backsaw with which to make a flat cut at the molding end.

The door casing consists of two legs and a head piece. Stand the leg that fits against the hinges in place. It should be the thickness of a hinge away from the edge of the jamb. Try to keep this distance all around the door as you install the casing. Casing is always installed with the wide part away from the door. Its bottom edge rests on the floor, not on the baseboard.

Start by cutting the miter in the leg, put it in place and tack it there temporarily. Cut a matching miter for the head. Tack this in place. If the joint doesn't fit perfectly you can work on it with a sharp block plane, or a sharp, fine-tooth saw (10 point), or sandpaper. Finally, cut the remaining leg to an exact fit.

When you have the fit, use 3-penny finishing nails through the thin side of the casing into the jamb, and 6-penny finishing nails through the thick side into the studs. Countersink the nails and fill the holes with wood filler.

Door accessories

Installing a mail slot

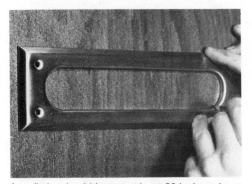

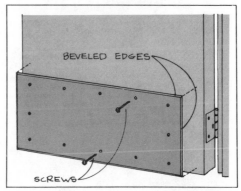

What it takes

Approximate time: Under an hour for all.

Tools and materials: Level, electric drill and bits, saber saw, screwdriver, pencil, and parts as illustrated.

A mail slot should be set at least 30 inches above the floor, and in the thicker part of the door. It should not be set in a panel, and if the door is hollow core, you will need a metal chute between the inside and outside plates. Place the inside plate (the one without a flap) on the *outside* of the door in correct position and outline its opening. Remove the plate and enlarge the outline by at least ½ inch to allow the flap door on the outside plate to open. Bore starting holes with a drill, and cut out the opening with a keyhole or saber saw. Finally, screw the plates to both the inside and outside of door.

Installing a drip cap

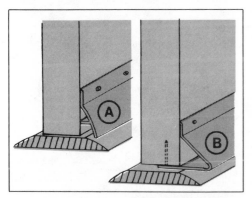

A drip cap keeps rainwater from draining or blowing under the door. It may be made of metal or wood and is easy to install, usually requiring only screws. One type is installed on the outside of the door over the threshold (A); another extends under the bottom of the door (B).

Installing a kick plate

BEVELED EDGES

SCREWS

A back door, or any door that is used a lot can benefit from a kick plate. Made of plastic or metal, it can be screwed to the bottom of any door to protect its surface. As a rule, the plate measures a couple of inches narrower than the door width; this allows clearance for the door stops.

Replacing a threshold

What it takes

Approximate time: One hour.

Tools and materials: Small wrecking bar, hammer, chisel (optional), awl or punch, screwdriver or electric drill and bit, hacksaw, backsaw (optional), square, portable electric saw or handsaw, and replacement saddle.

While the door itself is opened and closed with a frequency that you don't notice, it is actually the threshold that receives the most wear. There will come a time when you will want to replace the threshold, or saddle. Chances are your old saddle will be of wood; saddles are generally made of hardwood—oak as a rule—but you may wish to replace them with aluminum.

Swing the door wide; you may find it necessary to take it down. You may even have to remove the door stops from the jamb. Lift the old saddle with a pry bar or the claws of a hammer.

If the saddle is in bad shape it might be simpler to split the wood with a chisel and take out the pieces. The saddle may even extend under the jambs; if so, try first to remove it in one piece. But if you can't, cut it into three sections with a backsaw, take out the center piece and then the other two. Use the old saddle as a pattern for the new one. If you can't do that, take careful measurements. Cut the new saddle so the protruding ends fit neatly against the door casing. Drill holes and sink nails, or countersink screws to secure the new saddle to the floor. Fill holes with putty.

1. The first step is to remove the old saddle. You can use a pry bar. If this doesn't work, then try cutting the saddle out with a backsaw, or taking it out in pieces with hammer and chisel. **TIP:** When purchasing a new threshold, make sure you buy one at least as long as the opening. It can be cut to fit, but one that is too short will let in cold air and pests.

2. If you install an aluminum saddle (which we recommend), you will first have to remove the rubber sealing strip. Then, with the threshold held in position, mark for length and for any notches that might have to be cut out. Use a carpenter's square or straightedge to mark straight across the threshold. Cut the aluminum piece with a hacksaw. You can remove any burrs formed by using a small file on the corners and wherever else you made cuts. Position the saddle in place and use an awl to mark for screw holes; then bore with an electric drill.

TIP: If you bore too deeply, the screws will not hold the threshold down snugly. Wrap tape around the drill bit to let you know when you've reached the depth of your screw shanks.

3. Using the proper size screwdriver, screw the threshold down snugly. Many builders like to run a bead of caulk on the outside edge before installing the threshold, but this is optional.

4. After installing the metal portion of the threshold, replace the rubber grommet. Squeeze the edges together and slip them into the metal grooves. You may have to use a screwdriver with a thin blade to help push the rubber down properly.

Installing a prehung door unit

The prehung door is a great convenience for home handyman and professional alike. The unit comes with the door already hinged in a factory-assembled frame. All you do is order the right size, slip it into the door opening, square it up, and nail it into place. This not only saves a great deal of time but also eliminates much fuss, irritation, and uncertainty. Few tools are needed; just a bit of time, very little experience, and some plain common sense.

Position the door in the opening; be sure not to remove any diagonal packing strips or blocking. It is important that you have the door plumb as well as square. Shim it if you need to do so.

Fasten the door in place with 10-penny casing nails, but don't drive them all the way in. Remove the corner block from the upper corner. This holds the door square in the frame until you have installed it. Check for squareness again and if all is well then finish driving the nails into place. Last step is to install the knob.

What it takes

Approximate time: One hour.

Tools and materials: Hammer, 10-penny casing nails, level, square, screwdriver, and prehung door. Scrap cedar shingles make good shims. Doorknob, and lock hardware if desired, can usually be purchased with the door.

1. First position the door in the opening. Be sure not to remove any blocking or diagonal packing strips. The door shown will open onto a deck that is yet to be built.

2. Make certain that the door is square and plumb. Shim with pieces of wood shingle if necessary. Use both square and level on the top and both sides to make sure the door is in the correct position. Remember that there will be an opening at the bottom for a threshold, or saddle.

3. Fasten the door in place by driving 10-penny casing nails through the casing into the door framing. Do not drive the nails all the way in, but leave the heads protruding.

4. Remove the corner block from the upper corner. This holds the door square in the frame until it has been installed.

5. Again check to see if the door and frame are square. Realign if necessary and finish driving the nails.

6. Install the doorknob as per the instructions which are packed with the door.

Installing a sliding patio door

What it takes

Approximate time: A full day's work.

Tools and materials: Hammer, level, screwdriver, circular saw or handsaw, Yankee screwdriver, electric drill and bits, caulking gun and caulking compound, tape measure or folding rule, pencil, 2x4 for wedge, 10-penny casing nails, 8-penny finishing nails, Number 8 flathead screws (1 inch long), lumber for two 2x8 headers and for 2x4 studs, wood shims, and sliding door unit of your choice with accessories.

Here's a job that would seem a huge undertaking but can actually be quite simple. It all depends on the type of door you buy and how it is installed. The essential thing is to pay careful attention to leveling and plumbing the door to insure that it will work properly on the slide rails.

Basically, there are two steps: first the framing and then the actual installation of the door. For the first step follow the diagrams below and the accompanying instructions. The installation procedure is shown on the opposite page.

The framing sequence consists of measuring for the opening, constructing a header and jack studs, and sheathing the exterior. Installation involves several aspects of weatherproofing in addition to securing the door unit in place.

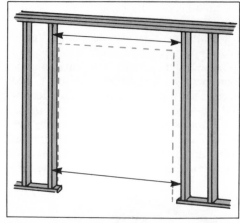

1. Lay out the door opening width between the regular studs to equal the width of the sliding door rough opening *plus* the thickness of the two regular studs, shown in dashed vertical lines. (Standard door widths conform to standard stud intervals.)

The corner you cut may be your own.
I read the instructions carefully about keeping everything level and square. Only I didn't realize that the square I was using was itself not square. I'd bought a cheap one thinking I could save. I know now that a good carpenter relies on good tools.

Practical Pete

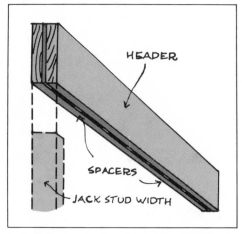

HEADER

SPACERS

JACK STUD WIDTH

2. Build the header (two 2x8s) to equal the rough opening width of the door plus the thickness of the two jack studs. Nail the header together with adequate spacers so that the header thickness will equal the width of the jack studs.

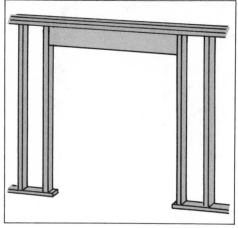

3. Position the header at the proper height and between the regular studs. Nail through the regular studs into the header in order to hold it in place until the next step.

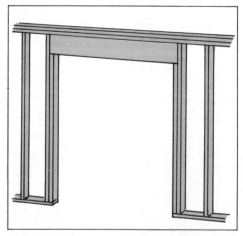

4. Cut the jack studs to fit under and support the header; then nail them to the regular studs.

EXTERIOR SHEATHING

5. Apply the outside sheathing flush with the header and jack stud framing members. It is important at this point to make sure that the rough opening is plumb and square and that the floor is level.

The installation

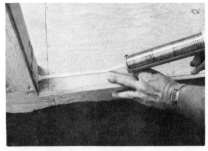

1. Run a bead of caulking compound across the bottom of the opening to provide a tight seal between the door sill and the floor.

2. Position the frame in the opening from the inside. Apply pressure to the sill to properly distribute the caulking compound. The door frame sill must be level. Shim if necessary.

3. Secure the sill to the floor by nailing along the inside edge with 8-penny finishing nails.

4. Temporarily secure the jamb in the opening with 10-penny casing nails through each side of the opening. Make sure the jamb is square and plumb by providing shims between the side jambs and the jack studs. Nail through the casing into the framing.

5. Position the flashing on the head casing and secure it by nailing through the vertical leg. The vertical center brace may now be removed but be sure to save the head and sill brackets for later use.

6. Apply the treated wood sill under the protruding metal sill facing. Fasten this tightly to the underside of the metal sill with 10-penny casing nails.

7. Position the stationary door panel in place in the outside run. Be sure the bottom rail is straight with the sill. Force the door into the run of the side jamb with a 2x4 wedge. Check the position by aligning the screw holes of the door bracket with the holes in the sill and the head jamb. If the door happens to be a triple door, repeat the procedure.

8. Note the mortise in the bottom rail for the bracket. Secure the bracket with Number 8 flathead screws, 1 inch long, through the predrilled holes. Position the head bracket in the top mortise; drill and secure in place. Align the bracket with the predrilled holes in the head jamb and secure with screws. Repeat the procedure for any other panels.

9. Install the security screws through the parting stop into the stationary door top rail.

10. Place the operating door on the rib of the metal sill facing and tip the door in at the top Then position the head stop and fasten in place with screws.

11. If the door sticks or binds, it is not square with the frame. Remove the caps from the two adjusting sockets on the outside of the bottom rail. Insert a screwdriver and turn to raise or lower the door.

12. Your final step is to install the hardware.

A new storm door is an easy job

What it takes

Approximate time: One hour.

Tools and materials: Hammer, screwdriver, electric drill and bits or Yankee push drill, caulking gun and cartridge, chisel, carpenter's square, and door unit plus accessories provided in kit.

TIP: If you're planning on repainting the door jamb and trim, now's the time for the job, before installing the new door unit.

One of the simplest jobs you can do is install a new storm door. This one task can save a tremendous amount of money on heating and cooling bills.

The most popular units are aluminum and combine both the glass for winter protection and screening for summer use. You can also purchase storm doors in wood, or even in fancy metal shapes that will complement any front entry way.

Simplest and fastest is to purchase a prehung door. These are available in all standard sizes at most building supply dealers. Before you shop, measure the inside of the door opening from casing to casing. A prehung door unit fits inside this measurement, while the outside aluminum flange fits over the outside of the casing. If your dealer doesn't have your size in stock, he can normally get it within ten days.

Remove the old storm door, or if you are making your installation on a door that does not already have a storm, then take off any fancy door trim.

See how the unit fits in the opening. It may be necessary to cut down the inside corners of the casing somewhat so the door rests flush on the sill. On the other hand you may find that the unit doesn't fit because the jamb is out of square, or there may be old paint in the way. In this event, a little chiseling will do the trick.

Try the unit again. If it fits this time remove it and run a bead of caulking compound along the inside edge of the outer flange; then push the unit into place permanently. Bear in mind that the unit has to fit the opening with the hinge side tight against the wooden jamb.

With the unit in proper position, bore pilot holes for the holding screws through the screw holes in the outside flange—but not too large, or the screws won't hold.

Fasten the flange in place securely with the screws that come with the unit; then remove the retainer clips. Install the catch, the automatic door closer, and the spring chain unit. Push down the bottom expander strip until the vinyl sweep touches the door sill; drive the screws in place to hold the strip.

Finally, you will need to adjust the closure and spring unit so the door will close tightly but without banging.

1. As soon as you have your new unit, remove the old storm door. If you are putting in your new storm door where there was no storm previously, then remove any fancy trim that might be in the way.

2. Try the new door in the opening. You may have to cut off some of the inside corners to allow the door to fit flush on the existing door sill. Or the opening itself may be out of square, or there may be old paint blocking a neat fit. In this case, try a bit of chiseling.

3. Once the unit is positioned well, bore pilot holes for the holding screws through the guide holes in the outside flange. Be careful to bore these to proper size.

4. Carefully read the instructions packaged with the door on how to install the catch, and follow them exactly. This is a simple job, but it must be precise.

5. Still following instructions, install the automatic door closer and the spring chain unit.

6. Adjust the closure and spring unit so the door won't bang shut, yet will close tightly each time. On many units this simply means turning the outside knob on the closure unit.

Maintaining a garage door

Nowadays, most garages are built with overhead doors; at the same time, a number of older structures still have hinged or folding doors. All require maintenance.

Hinge-mounted garage doors tend to sag, and so opening and closing can become difficult. The problem of loose screws or hinges can be dealt with by first tapping wood wedges under the corner that has dropped and raising the door until it is level. At this point tighten all the screws in the hinges. If this isn't possible, perhaps because the hole is too loose, use longer screws that will grip; or it may be necessary to reposition the hinges so that the screws can meet solid wood. Of course, if a hinge is damaged in any way it should be replaced. Hinges should be kept oiled.

Suppose the door sags, but its hinges are tight. It means that it is probably not square. To correct this problem, place wedges under the door until it is hanging straight. Reinforce the corners with right-angle metal mending plates, and attach a metal door brace with a turnbuckle. It is also possible to brace the door with a 1x4 piece of lumber, attaching it diagonally across the door face with flathead screws.

The most popular garage door, the overhead, comes in two basic types—the swing-up and the roll-up. Both use a heavy spring, or springs. The roll-up has a track; the swing-up may or may not.

Swing-up doors do not as a rule require much maintenance, except for their moving hardware. This should be kept lubricated with powdered graphite or oil. Lubricate the hinges and rollers when the door is in the down position. If there are tracks, check that they are clean because oil collects dirt. Any nicks that you notice in the tracks should be straightened out.

Most of the binding or dragging in the case of a roll-up garage door is the result of poor track alignment or the need for lubrication. The vertical tracks need to be plumb, and the two curved sections must be at the same height. When you inspect the track, make sure the overhead part slants slightly downward toward the rear of the garage so that when the door is raised it will stay up. Crimps in the track can very likely be straightened, but more serious damage of course means replacement.

When you have tried everything else as the possible source of trouble, you can check the spring. Perhaps you have the sort of roll-up door with a spring on either side. Try shortening the cable while the door is up. The cable is knotted to a hole in a plate above the door. Move the holding knot inward to shorten the cable.

The other type of roll-up door has a torsion spring in the center. This type really requires a professional, for the torsion is tremendously strong. You could get hurt.

But the springs on a swing-up door hook into holes or notches. These can be adjusted by moving the spring hook from one notch or hole to another.

Garage doors sometimes cause problems when they become too heavy. A wooden door for instance, can easily absorb a lot of moisture. You can prevent this situation by painting the door. Paint both sides, as well as the top, bottom, and side edges.

What it takes

Approximate time: Most check-ups and repairs take less than an hour.

Tools and materials: Hammer, screwdriver, carpenter's square, level, adjustable wrench, machine oil or powdered graphite, grease, paint, cleaning solvent, and wedges are among the items you may need, depending on the type of job you have to do.

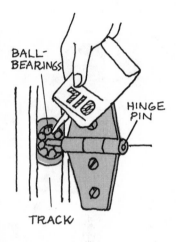

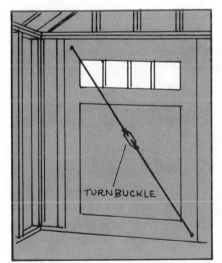

To eliminate sag in a swing-type door you can use a metal brace or wire with a turnbuckle. Install it diagonally from the top at the hinge side to the opposite corner.

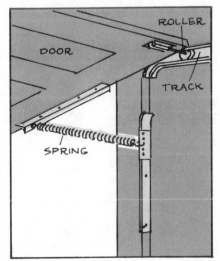

A swing-up garage door of this type has a track. It is important to check that all hardware is tight. (There is another type of swing-up door that does not have a track.)

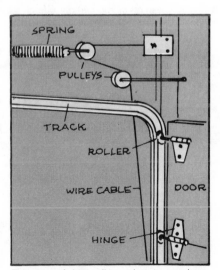

This type of door rolls up, has two springs, one at each side. The track, as well as the roller bearings, must be kept free of dirt and well oiled.

Safety glazing

What it takes

Approximate time: Half an hour.

Tools and materials: Screwdriver, hammer, acrylic cutting tool, ruler, straightedge, heavy gloves, and sheet acrylic to fit.

Glass can be a hazard around the house, especially where active children are present. The places to watch carefully are sliding glass doors, storm doors, and shower and bathtub enclosures. Many states have adopted safety glazing rules as part of their building codes. Even though these new codes may not be in effect where you live, you might wish to replace breakable glass in these particular locations with safety glazing materials.

Safety glazing materials include tempered glass, laminated glass, wire glass, and certain rigid plastics approved by the American National Standards Institute. There are drawbacks to some of these. Tempered glass cannot be cut to size after it leaves the factory. Laminated glass lacks impact resistance and is not available thinner than 1/16 inch. Wire glass lacks breakage resistance, is not optically clear, and is difficult to install.

The most effective and easiest safety glazing material for the homeowner to install is a rigid-plastic material such as acrylic sheet. In ¼-inch thickness this material is 17 times stronger than glass, and it does not break in the dangerous manner of ordinary glass; fragments are larger, have relatively dull edges, and seldom cause laceration injury.

Installing acrylic sheet in storm windows, doors, or even shower doors is a very simple operation that can be done quickly.

Storm doors

1. The first step in storm-door glass replacement is to take out the sash. Carefully remove the rubber retainer gasket and broken glass. Clean off all dirt and glass fragments. Wear leather gloves.

2. Before starting to cut be sure your measurements are exact. One method of cutting acrylic sheet is to use a straightedge as a guide and score with a sharp cutting tool.

3. After scoring, place scribed line on a wooden dowel and press down to snap off.

4. Remove protective masking paper and place in frame. Press rubber gasket in place.

5. Reinsert the repaired sash in the storm door frame.

6. Another method is to discard the sash frame. (This is your best option anyway if it's at all bent out of shape). Then measure the opening exactly.

7. After cutting acrylic sheet to an exact fit, place it directly into opening.

8. Rotate the frame clamps into place and tighten them. It's a good idea to caulk around the glass if you use this no-gasket method.

Shower doors

1. Remove the shower-stall door, usually by loosening screws in the hinges.

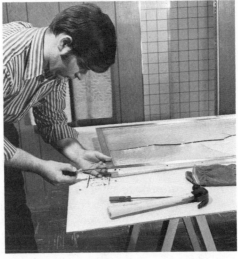

2. Remove the screws on all four corners of the shower door frame. Save the screws. Disassemble the entire frame. Take care that you don't produce burrs on the metal edges.

What it takes

Approximate time: One hour.

Tools and materials: Screwdriver, hammer, sheet acrylic cutting tool, straightedge, ruler, leather gloves, sandpaper, and plastic panel to fit (1/8-inch thickness usually works best).

3. Wearing leather gloves, carefully remove glass. Clean the rubber gasket and the frame. Measure the opening and cut plastic to fit. Cut 1/32″ per foot less than the measured dimensions to allow for thermal expansion of the material.

4. Fit the gasket around the plastic sheet. Gently sand the edges of the plastic smooth and carefully press the frame over the rubber gasket on all four sides. Replace the screws and rehang the door.

5.INSULATION

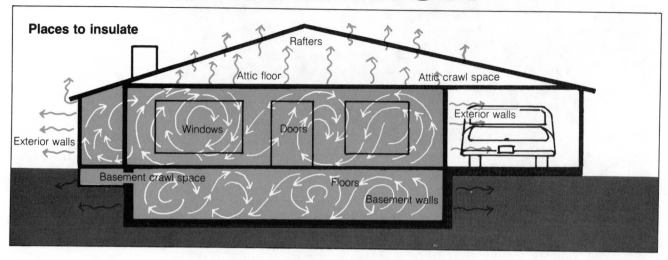

Places to insulate

Rafters

Attic floor

Attic crawl space

Windows

Doors

Exterior walls

Exterior walls

Basement crawl space

Floors

Basement walls

The best way to save money on your heating and cooling bills and to live comfortably in your home is to insulate the large, flat areas exposed to outside temperatures. With proper insulation, the average house (15% window area, two outside doors, and exposure to only light winds) can retain 75% of the heat that would pass out through uninsulated floors, walls, roof, and windows.

Heat enters or escapes not only through cracks but by radiation through the various materials your home is sheathed with. It travels through metal and glass quickly, through plaster and wood less quickly, and slowest of all through pockets of dead air sealed around with some other material. Commercial insulating material is like wool and feathers because it contains millions of these tiny air pockets.

The effectiveness of various insulation materials is rated in "R" values. The R value indicates the material's resistance to the flow of heat through it. The higher the R value the lower the loss of heat and the greater the saving on heating and cooling costs. The first inch of insulation has a much higher R value than the next inch, and so on.

Insulating the exposed areas of a house is a job anyone can do. It requires very little physical strength, simple tools, and no carpentry skills. Although the work area is awkward to reach sometimes, it is easier than painting. The one major exception is putting insulation in the spaces between interior finished walls and the outer skin of the house. It must be blown in by machine.

Insulation also absorbs sound, and many of the new materials will resist or retard fire. But a word of caution: read any safety warnings in the instructions for indications that gloves might be required, because the fibers can work into your skin; likewise, check to see if you'll need goggles or a mask.

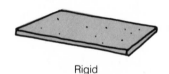

Rigid

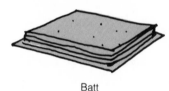

Batt

Blanket

Loose-fill

Where to check for heat loss

The attic is where a great deal of heat can be lost because hot air rises. Check between the floor joists in the attic to see if old insulation has settled. Be sure that you have insulation material between the rafters and/or on top of the attic ceiling. Insulating your attic can lower heat loss by as much as one-quarter in many cases.

The basement. Insulate interior walls between heated and unheated rooms. Where the basement is not heated, or in crawl spaces, insulate the underside of the overhead flooring. The place where the building meets the foundation walls and any outlet ducts should be sealed tight.

Exterior walls, especially on the windy side of the house, are extremely critical sources of heat loss because of their large area. Most houses have insulation blown between the interior and exterior walls when they are built. If you are in doubt about your house, check it by looking down between the wall studs from the attic, or bore a hole into the space between an interior and exterior wall. If you don't see insulation, then you can have it professionally blown into the walls.

Doors and windows often develop cracks, as the house settles, between the units and their framing, or between the framing and the interior or exterior walls. Glass conducts heat, so if you use double or triple pane windows, the air locks between the panes will provide good insulation. On the same principle, storm windows and doors can reduce heat loss by up to 15%. And you should also see that your house is caulked.

Types of insulation

There are four general categories of home insulating materials.

Blanket insulation comes in long rolls of different widths and thicknesses. You use it in the long spaces between floor joists and rafters or wall studs.

Batt insulation is almost the same as blanket except that it is cut or perforated into lengths of about 48 inches and 96 inches. Its outside covering can be of paper, or foil which will act as a vapor barrier.

Loose-fill insulation can be poured into walls and between floor joists. It is the least expensive form of insulation, but it does lose efficiency as it settles over the years and needs to be added to.

Rigid insulation comes in boards of various composition. It can be used either inside or outside the house. There are new forms of this type which look like decorative paneling. These are great if you're planning to turn your basement into living quarters.

	Insulation type	Packaging	Where to use	Installation	Pros and cons
BLANKETS	Mineral wool	Slag; rock; glass wool.	In ceilings; between studs in walls; between rafters.	Staple or tack between studs or rafters; bow in to form air space between wall and blanket.	**Plus:** Cheap; gives continuous vapor barrier. **Minus:** Can irritate eyes, skin, nose; must be cut to size.
	Cotton	Fireproof blanket.	In ceilings; between studs in walls; between rafters.	Staple or tack between studs or rafters; bow in to form air space between wall and blanket.	**Plus:** Clean; lightweight; efficient. **Minus:** Must be cut to size; can irritate eyes, skin, nose.
	Wood-fiber matt	Paper-enclosed rolls.	In ceilings; between studs in walls; between rafters.	Staple or tack between studs or rafters; bow in to form air space between wall and blanket.	**Plus:** Comes in many widths; efficient. **Minus:** Inconvenient for small jobs, as it must be cut to length.
	Fibrous blanket	Compressed roll.	In ceilings; between studs in walls; between rafters.	Expand by pulling to full length; then staple or tack between studs or rafters; bow in to form air space between wall and blanket.	**Plus:** Easy to handle; compact; does not irritate; can be cut to desired width. **Minus:** May require added vapor barrier.
BATTS	Mineral wool	Rock; slag; or glass.	In ceilings, walls, and roofs, where framing interval can accommodate standard batt width.	Lay between attic floor joists, or nail or staple to studs.	**Plus:** Inexpensive; handy size; built-in vapor barrier. **Minus:** Barrier is discontinuous; loose batts shed irritating particles.
LOOSE-FILL	Mineral wool	Sacks of rock, slag, or glass.	Spread on attic floor between joists; pack into areas around pipes and within walls.	Pour between joists, raking level.	**Plus:** Cheap; easy to install. **Minus:** No vapor barrier; irritates skin, eyes, sinuses.
	Vermiculite	Bags of shredded mica.	Spread on attic floor between joists; pack into areas around pipes and within walls.	Pour between joists, raking level.	**Plus:** Easy pouring; good for filling in masonry walls. **Minus:** No vapor barrier; on the costly side.
	Wood fiber	Bales.	Spread between attic floor joists.	Pack between joists; add vapor barrier if necessary.	**Plus:** Fills wall space; retards fire. **Minus:** Not widely sold; creates no vapor barrier.
RIGID	Compacted	Asphalt-impregnated fiber board; cellular glass.	Fasten to masonry walls; wedge against exterior foundation.	Cement to masonry or insert around foundation and then backfill.	**Plus:** Stiff; moisture-resistant; can be used in many places where other types can't. **Minus:** Expensive; limited insulating power.
	Board	Plank, board, or tile built into structure.	Additions; basements or attics to be converted to living space.	Fasten with staples, nails, or specially made clips.	**Plus:** Cheap. **Minus:** Insufficient in some climates.

The vapor barrier

A vapor barrier is actually a material that will neither absorb moisture nor allow moisture to pass through it. Thus it prevents the insulation from becoming wet or matted and losing its effectiveness.

Plastic, metal foil, and asphalt between layers of brown paper are commonly used as vapor barriers. While the main purpose of the barrier is to keep insulation from getting wet, it is also a way of retaining moisture in the air inside the house. Moist air is warmer than dry air. When the vapor barrier is made from a material with a shiny surface, such as foil (reflective insulation), it can reflect heat back toward its source.

The vapor barrier may completely enclose the insulation, as in blanket insulation, or it may be attached to one side of the batts and installed with the barrier toward the inside of the house. Another method is to place the insulation material where you want it and then cover the inside surfaces with a vapor barrier, perhaps polyethylene, before putting on the wall finish.

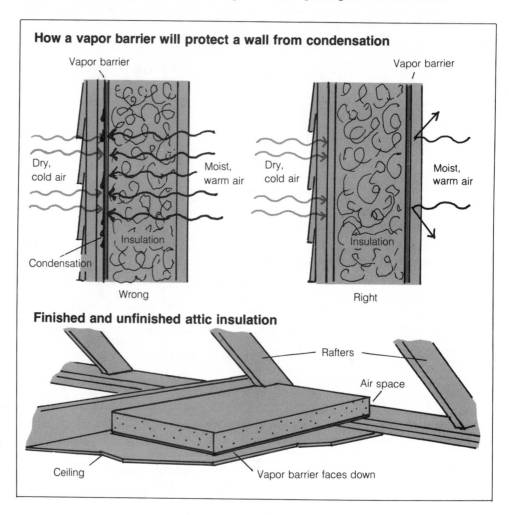

How a vapor barrier will protect a wall from condensation

Vapor barrier

Dry, cold air

Moist, warm air

Insulation

Condensation

Wrong

Vapor barrier

Dry, cold air

Moist, warm air

Insulation

Right

Finished and unfinished attic insulation

Rafters

Air space

Ceiling

Vapor barrier faces down

When you install a vapor barrier the rule is to place it as close as possible to the inside or warm surface of exposed ceilings, walls and floors. There is an exception to this in the case of insulation used with concrete floor slabs, where a barrier is put underneath the insulation in order to protect it from ground moisture that would otherwise rise.

When insulating a floor, place the insulation with the vapor barrier up except where you are using vapor-barrier paper in place of the building paper over the subfloor. In such a case, it may face down.

In reinsulating—your attic, for example— it is best to use unfaced insulation only. The facings are vapor barriers, and since they prevent moisture in warm air inside your house from rising to condense as it hits the cold air in the attic, you are creating a problem if you add one vapor barrier to another. If you find that you do have to add a faced batt to existing insulation then be sure that you slit the facing on the new material with long gashes.

In the case of insulating an unheated attic for the first time, you may dispense with a vapor barrier so long as you have proper ventilation. You can check with your local building supplier on what the adequate ratio of ventilation to attic area may be.

Insulating an unfinished attic

Your attic is a good place to start, first because heat normally rises and escapes through the roof and unfinished walls; second, because no carpentry or special skill is needed to lay or staple insulation between exposed floor joists, rafters and studs. Even if the area is partly finished with a floor and interior walls, but unused, you can attach blanket insulation right over them in a few hours. If the attic floor has insulation that has settled and matted down with age, destroying most of its effectiveness, simply lay new insulation right over it.

If there is no insulation, you must lay vapor barrier (polyethylene sheeting) material on the floor under the insulation. This will help prevent moist warm air from condensing into water when it hits the unheated attic air. Some types of batt and blanket insulation are sold with vapor barrier material on one or both sides. Face it down on the floor; out toward the room on the walls and overhead areas.

On the floor spread loose fill insulation to an even depth between the floor joists and on top of the vapor barrier material; or simply roll out blanket insulation between the joists without attaching it. It is sold as rolls in widths that fit between joists, beams and studs, so you need only cut them to the length you need. Cut scraps to fit irregular areas. To leave ducts, pipes and wiring accessible, cut the blanket at the obstacles and pour loose fill around them.

Rafters and walls. Blanket insulation can be fastened or batts stapled at 8-inch intervals between the rafters or studs on the walls, keeping the vapor barrier toward the inside of the house. Leave an inch or more of space for ventilation between insulation and roof sheathing when you staple the insulation to the rafters. Do not cover any vents, exhaust fan motors, wiring or lighting fixtures. Stuff the insulation between them and the exterior wall. Before you order insulation sold in rolls to fit between rafters, joists or studs, measure the distance between these wooden supports (usually 14 inches), as well as the total area you must cover in length.

If you wish to insulate under the floors of your home, go down to the basement or crawl space and staple insulation batts to the joists. If you can't staple the insulation, special gadgets are made for holding insulation in place. The most common are sheets of wire mesh, to be nailed to the bottoms of wood beams, or stiff wires precut to the right length to jam between rafters or joists, bowing upward to hold the insulation in its proper place.

Don't forget to attach insulation to the cold side of doors leading from unheated rooms into heated areas.

What it takes

Tools and materials: Staple gun and staples, or other support hardware, for blanket or batt insulation; knife or scissors, gloves, blanket, batts and/or loose-fill insulating material, wide boards (to walk on so you don't step through the ceiling of the room below); polyethylene sheeting if the insulation material does not have vapor barrier attached.

If there is no insulation on the attic floor, lay the insulation with the vapor barrier side downward. If you are using blanket insulation without a vapor barrier attached to it, or are spreading loose-fill insulation, lay polyethylene sheeting down first.

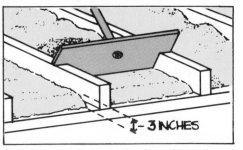

To make a rake for spreading loose-fill evenly, cut the blade out of ½-inch plywood about 4 inches wider than the distance between the floor joists. Notch the ends so that they will ride along the tops of the joists and cut the bottom of the blade flat so it will clear the floor below by the depth of fill you want.

Stapling batts to rafters or studs is one of the quickest methods of putting insulation on unfinished ceilings or walls. Batt insulation has flaps on each side to make stapling easy.

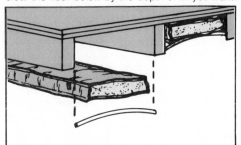

Wire fasteners can be used instead of staples on blanket insulation when it is used in attic, or in basement ceiling or crawl space. Simply jam the two ends between the wood beams at intervals that will keep the insulation firm. The tension will hold them in place and support the insulation.

To insulate and vent a crawl space

Attic and crawl space ventilation are mandatory both in summer and winter to keep condensation from collecting inside the house. In winter leave the louvers open; and always provide at least two vent openings. An exhaust fan is useful in areas that are difficult to ventilate. In an unheated crawl space, ground cover is required to keep down humidity and to protect the living area overhead from moisture.

How to calculate how much insulation to buy.

To determine the total floor area to be insulated, measure the distance between the joists as well as the length and width of the attic. You must account for space taken up by the joists, and so if your attic is built on 24-inch centers, multiply the area by 0.94. If it is on 16-inch centers multiply by .90. The insulation packages will have printed on them the amount of square feet of material, so it's easy to figure how many packages to buy.

Insulating around openings

Windows and doors

What it takes

Approximate time: Fifteen minutes for insulating an untrimmed window; two hours for removing and replacing trim, plus time for painting.

Tools and materials: Hammer, pliers, wide chisel or stiff putty knife, pry bar, flat piece of wood for paddle, insulating and vapor material, paint, spackle or putty, sandpaper.

Most old houses, and some new ones, lack insulation around windows and doors. Even if the rest of the house is thoroughly insulated, these areas can lose a good deal of heat, or cooling, through simple leakage.

If your house or addition is still in the process of being built you may consider putting in triple-pane windows, which lock air between the panes and provide good insulation. Glass is one of the areas through which heat escapes in winter and enters your house in summer. Another thing you can do is to make sure there is insulation around your door and window frames. You can also check for insulation around your attic windows, which may still not be trimmed even though your house is otherwise complete. Pack pieces of insulation into the cracks between the window and door frames and the rough framing. Remember that all insulated cracks should be covered with a vapor barrier.

1. Tear off pieces of insulation material and stuff them in between the window unit and framing. Wear gloves to protect your skin. Use a scrap of wood, as shown, to push the insulation in tight. The principle is the same for doors as for windows.

2. All areas that are insulated should be covered on the *inside,* or next to the living area, with a vapor barrier, as shown here. Staple it in place.

Removing trim

If you find that your windows and doors were installed and finished without adequate insulation, you will have to remove the trim to get at them. This isn't difficult, but it does take patience and care. If you are the type who likes to rush, then forget it and hire a professional. But if you wish to try for yourself, then allot a good amount of time for the job—at least a couple of hours. Try to work with patience.

Score and cut the paint line between the trim and the surface it joins. With a wide chisel or stiff-bladed putty knife, ease out the trim. Go very slowly, working from the corners toward the center of each strip. You can use a pry bar as a lever to reach under the trim. Be careful not to force the trim beyond its ability to bend, and also take

---

New wrinkles

In the effort to save energy, one of the most easily applicable devices is a transparent insulating window film. The film is actually a shield that reduces heat transmitted through windows, while maintaining a satisfactory level of visibility. An added advantage is that it turns ordinary glass windows into safety glass. Ask your hardware dealer about it. It's a simple procedure to attach the film.

The first step is to clean the window. Make a soapy mix with a teaspoon of liquid dishwashing detergent and one pint of water. Put it in a spray bottle and thoroughly spray the glass you wish to cover. Use a single-edge razor blade, if necessary, to clean off any debris that sticks. The important thing is to start with a window that is completely clean, dry, and free of lint.

Place the film on a clean, flat surface and cut it to ¼ inch larger all around, than the desired size. To separate the film from its backing, place a small piece of masking tape at one corner. Place a second piece of tape on the same corner, but on the opposite

side, without letting the two pieces touch each other. Pull the tapes apart and the backing will separate from the film.

Wet the side of the film that was next to the clear plastic backing. You can put it under the water faucet or spray it. The film must be completely wet, even the edges. Then wet the glass thoroughly; it should be soaking wet, right to the corners.

Lift the film by the corners and place the wet side on the glass. Move it until you have it positioned exactly. You will see now why it was necessary to use so much water. With the film positioned, spray the other side with water. Make sure it is completely wet.

Squeegee out all the excess water that has gathered under the film. Work from the center toward the edges of the glass. Use vertical and horizontal strokes only, but do not squeegee to the edges until you have trimmed the film. To trim, use a utility knife or single-edge razor blade and a straightedge. Leave a border of clear glass about 1/16 inch wide. Then squeegee to all the edges.

APPLY TAPE TO CORNERS TO SEPARATE FILM FROM BACKING.

LIFT FILM BY CORNERS AND LAY WET SIDE AGAINST GLASS.

care not to chip the wall. (This is why it was necessary to score and cut the paint line.)

When you have the trim partly raised, push it back in place so the nail heads protrude; then draw them all the way out. Use pliers, not a claw hammer or nail puller, to prevent scarring the wood. If you do have to use a hammer, be sure to place a piece of cardboard between the claw and

the wood for protection against scarring.

With the trim off, remove any nails that are left. Clean off chipped paint and sand away any hard bead of paint that may remain between trim and wall surface.

After installing the insulation, replace the trim exactly as it was. You may have to use slightly larger nails. Spackle or putty, sand, and paint.

Insulating the basement

The basement is sometimes a living area but more often simply a space for storage, laundry, carpentry, or painting. Whether or not you wish to convert your basement into a usable living quarter, you will still require proper insulation on the ceiling and in any crawl space, as well as around windows and vents. On the other hand, if you do intend to convert your basement into everyday space, you will have to insulate the walls as well; and they will very likely be of concrete block.

Masonry walls may be insulated either with blanket insulation material and a vapor barrier, or foil-backed gypsum board which requires no barrier. If you plan on gypsum board, 1x2 furring strips should be used. Rigid insulation also can be purchased in the form of paneling to serve double duty as finished wall.

Ceilings may be insulated with batt or blanket material placed between the joists. This can be stapled to the joists, or it can be set tightly against the floor above and supported with wire fasteners made for that purpose. Or you may use crossed wire which will allow the insulation to rest at the bottom edges of the joists. It makes for better insulation if the material is snug against the upper floor. If there is bridging or any other obstruction, insulation must go under it; the vapor barrier must be placed at the top, and the ends of individual pieces must overlap.

Another way to cut heat loss is to install an acoustical-tile ceiling. This not only

saves heat but insulates against undesirable noise as well.

The basement floor can of course be insulated if you are converting to living quarters, though this will probably require laying a whole new floor over the existing area. Insulation would be the same as for other floors in the house except if you have concrete floor slabs. In this case lay the vapor barrier under the insulation in order to protect against ground moisture.

Crawl space floors need as much insulation as the walls, plus a vapor barrier under the subfloor if the crawl space is unheated. There should be at least two inches of insulation around the walls of crawl spaces to reduce cold air from rising through the floors and walls.

Piping and ducts require insulation around, behind, or under them. It should be firmly secured, on the cold side of plumbing pipes, not in front on the warm side. Any pipe in an unheated basement or crawl space should be wrapped with insulation and then taped. Some companies sell special pipe and duct insulation which comes in various sizes, shapes, and styles. Insulation should be placed around electrical outlets but should not cover any outlet or hot-air vent.

Heaters and chimneys also need to be insulated; special covers can be purchased for heaters; a chimney needs insulation between the flue and any wood, such as rafters or floor joists or flooring. Make sure no paper backing is stuck to the pieces.

I almost got a real slow burn.
I insulated carefully throughout my house, and even stuffed pieces of insulation down around the edges of my fireplace flue where the rafters and floor joists meet the chimney. This would have been a good idea, except that I left some paper backing on a few of the pieces and almost had a fire. Next time I'll remember that when you light a fire the chimney gets hot, and placing paper next to it is risky business.
Practical Pete

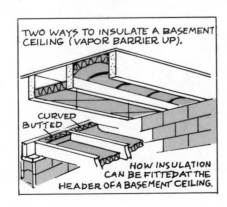

BLANKET INSULATION AND VAPOR BARRIER.

FOIL-BACKED GYPSUM BOARD REQUIRES NO ADDITIONAL BARRIER.

TWO WAYS TO INSULATE A BASEMENT CEILING (VAPOR BARRIER UP).

CURVED BUTTED

HOW INSULATION CAN BE FITTED AT THE HEADER OF A BASEMENT CEILING.

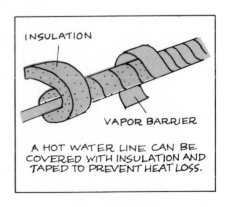

INSULATION

VAPOR BARRIER

A HOT WATER LINE CAN BE COVERED WITH INSULATION AND TAPED TO PREVENT HEAT LOSS.

Weather stripping

Approximate time: For an average door, one to two hours, depending on the material used; a window will take less time.

Tools and materials: Staple gun and staples, hammer, tinsnips, hacksaw, handsaw, weather-stripping material of your choice.

One of the essential energy savers is weather stripping. If you live in an old house, you should weather-strip the windows and doors so that cracks and openings are sealed against the escape of costly heat or the intrusion of wintry air. Weather stripping can be purchased by the yard, or in kits with rustproof tacks for installation.

The way to check whether your doors (or windows) need weather stripping is to direct a portable hair dryer against the areas where the door itself meets the frame. Move the stream of air along the door while a helper, on the other side of the door, holds his hand against the crack between the door and the frame and marks any place where he feels air coming through. If you have just a few leaky places, you can perhaps fix the present weather stripping, but it might be the moment for a complete replacement.

Doors

Felt stapled all around the inside edge of the stop is the quickest and easiest method of weather-stripping a door.

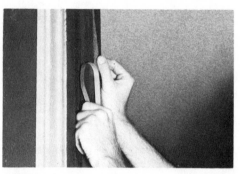

Adhesive-backed foam provides a somewhat tighter weather stripping. Just peel off the protective tape and adhere it to the inside of the door stop.

Foam-edged metal or plastic weather stripping can be purchased in kit form. It has two pieces for sides and one for the top. It is simply tacked in place on top of the stop and against the closed door.

Flexible metal weather stripping fits inside the door channel and behind the stop. The edge springs out and the door meets it to force it in place.

Foam-backed wood-molding weather stripping is also available in shapes similar to a doorstop. It can be applied over the door stop or instead of it. The same materials and methods of weather-stripping may be used on patio and roll-up garage doors.

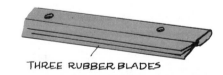

THREE RUBBER BLADES

Door sweep has triple blades of vinyl to close the gap that admits drafts under the door.

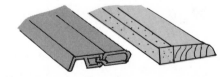

Aluminum strip with tubular vinyl (left) and **wood strip** with foam seal are both used for swing doors.

Windows

For double-hung windows the weather stripping is essentially the same as for doors: thin spring-metal strips, adhesive-backed foam, tubular vinyl as a covering over a sponge core. All of these attach to molding and fit neatly against sash. And the installation is simple.

Casement, jalousie, or awning-type windows which are metal-framed may be weather-stripped with a transparent vinyl tape which covers their edges, or with an adhesive-backed foam installed at the joints. Also available is an aluminum strip made especially for casements.

Stopgaps and copouts:

You don't necessarily have to mount a major campaign against that drafty door or window. Sometimes a fast application of a clay weather stripping will do the trick. It comes in rolls and looks like rope, but it acts like clay. Press it into place with your fingertips. It's self-adhering, yet comes off easily. And it can be used again.

Adhesive-backed foam strip is applied to exterior of upper sash bottom rail, exterior of parting strips, and bottom rail of lower sash.

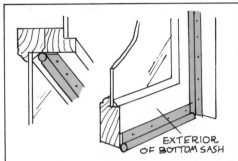

Vinyl weather stripping, either sponge or tubular kind, is nailed to exterior of upper sash bottom rail, and to exterior of parting strips and bottom rail on lower sash.

Another quickie is the door-stripping kit—two 7-foot lengths and one 3-foot length, plus nails. Cut the pieces to length and hammer home.

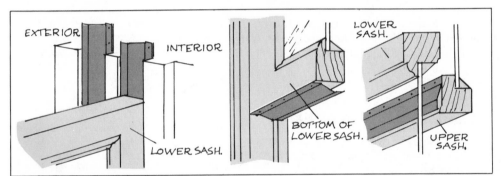

Spring-metal type is nailed to sash channels; be careful not to cover pulleys in upper channels. Nail a strip the full width of the sash to bottom of lower sash bottom rail; attach a strip to inside edge of upper sash bottom rail.

Getting Rid of Condensation

Condensation on windows is only mildly annoying when it simply interferes with vision. It can, however, be a source of serious damage when enough moisture is present to rot windowsills or stain walls.

Condensation takes place when moist, warm inside air comes into contact with any cooler surface. During fall and winter windows are likely to provide this cooler surface.

Little or no condensation will occur on well-insulated windows; anything that prevents heat loss through windows will also prevent or greatly reduce condensation. Exterior storm windows, or the inside do-it-yourself type (pages 124 and 125), or weather-stripping (also pages 124 and 125) will not only reduce heat loss but will reduce condensation as well.

Sometimes condensation occurs between the regular window and storm window. This is caused by heated inside air seeping into the space between the windows. With double-hung windows this seepage frequently occurs at the point where upper and lower sashes meet. A good way to eliminate this leakage is with an insulation lock. Insulation locks are similar to regular sash locks but have the added advantage of pulling the sashes together to prevent leakage between them. The secret in a good installation is to position the halves of the lock so they draw the windows tightly together, yet don't cause them to bind.

Insulation locks

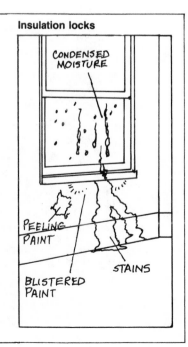

Caulking seams

What it takes

Approximate time: A few minutes for small patching jobs; a full day or so to completely caulk an average house. Professionals figure it takes 1¼ hours to cover 100 lineal feet.

Tools and materials: Wire brush or scraper; mat knife or single-edge razor blade; cartridge of caulking compound and gun, or a squeeze tube; cleaning solvent and a clean rag.

Planning hints: The best time to caulk is in the fall, in preparation for winter. Work in warm weather—above 50°F. If that is not possible, warm the caulking cartridge before you apply its contents. In extremely hot weather—above 90°F—the caulking can get too runny. Place the tube in a refrigerator for an hour or two to slow it down.

A cartridge of caulking compound will cover approximately 100 lineal feet if you spread an average bead—about ¼ inch.

TIP: Before you apply caulk, it's a good idea to try a practice run on a scrap of wood so that you get the feel of the gun.

Caulking compound is one of the most potent weapons in guarding your home against winter attack. It works two ways, serving not only as a barrier against cold drafts, insects, and moisture, but it also eliminates heat loss during winter and so contributes toward a lower fuel bill.

Caulking is a compound of a semisolid substance and a binder of natural and synthetic oils to keep it resilient and elastic. It comes in five basic types, and it can stick securely to wood, masonry, and metal. It is able to expand and contract along with the surrounding surfaces that will shrink or swell according to the weather.

Caulking comes in bulk form and in disposable cartridges which are used with an applicator gun. (It can also be purchased in squeeze tubes and in rope form.) The caulking gun forces compound out through a narrow nozzle. The nozzle is moved steadily along the joint being filled, overlapping it on each side. There are two basic types of caulking guns: the full-barrel type, designed for bulk filling, and the half-barrel (drop-in type) which is used with

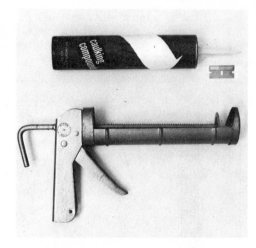

disposable cartridges; this is really handy.

Cartridges do cost a little more than bulk caulking, but they are more convenient. You just throw away the empty cartridge, which saves you a messy cleaning job on the gun each time you use it. Another advantage is that you can change color without cleaning or having to wait for the first cartridge to be finished.

Where should you caulk?

Caulk wherever two different parts (two different materials) come together with a crack in between. Here is a sample list of places to caulk:
1. Wherever wood meets masonry, for instance at the line where the house joins the foundation; 2. Around windows and doors where the framing and house siding join; 3. Where the chimney meets the roof; 4. At the place where porches or steps and the house itself come together; 5. Where plumbing vents come through the house;

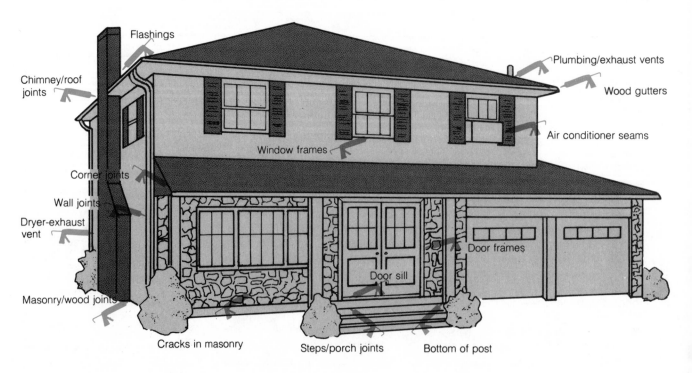

Flashings

Chimney/roof joints

Plumbing/exhaust vents

Wood gutters

Air conditioner seams

Window frames

Corner joints

Wall joints

Dryer-exhaust vent

Door frames

Door sill

Masonry/wood joints

Cracks in masonry

Steps/porch joints

Bottom of post

6. At corner seams where trim and siding meet; 7. In the space between an air conditioner unit and the window frame; 8. Between dormer cheeks and roof shingles; 9. Around the exhaust vent for a clothes dryer; 10. Around flashing and in the gap between flashing and shingles.

How to caulk

1. Clean out old caulking. This is important. Use a wire brush or scraper. Then clean the area with solvent so that it is quite free of dirt, oil, wax, or any dust. If it is not clean, the new compound will not hold.

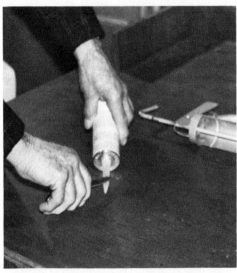

2. With a mat knife or single-edge razor blade, cut the tip off the nozzle at a 45-degree angle. Make your cut at the place where it will allow you the proper size bead for the work at hand. The bead should overlap onto both surfaces.

3. Load the half-barrel caulking gun by inserting the cartridge, rear first and with the nozzle opposite the trigger.
4. Break the plastic inner seal by pushing a nail or screwdriver back into the tip of the nozzle as far as the cartridge base.

It is best not to seal every seam in the house. A house needs to breathe and so you should allow some openings for moisture vapor to escape from inside the walls. Pick spots where strong drafts or water cannot enter, for instance where the bottoms of window sills and siding come together.

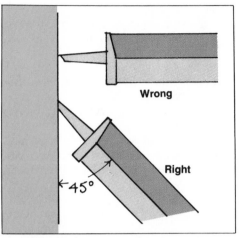

Wrong

Right

45°

5. To apply caulk to a seam, hold the gun at an angle of 45 degrees, tilted in the direction of movement. The slant on the tip will help guide this.
6. Squeeze the trigger with an even, gentle pressure and the caulk will flow out.

7. Move it slowly and steadily along the crack, pressing lightly with the tip of the gun as you go. On vertical seams work from top to bottom; on horizontals, move across from left to right, or the reverse, depending on which hand you work with.
8. When finished, quickly lift the gun from the joint and twist the plunger rod so that it disengages and so stops the caulk from coming out. You can clean with solvent, soap, and water.

If you have very wide cracks to fill, you can put in oakum, then apply one or more beads to cover.

The trick to a smooth bead is to try to finish a seam without having to stop in the middle of it.

Caulk won't grip? Made a mess?
I have found that just cleaning out the old caulking may not do the trick. Sometimes you have to scrub the area with solvent and clean up dirt, oil, and mildew as well. Caulking won't stick to damp surfaces either. If you make a mess, don't worry. I scrape it up with a putty knife first, trying not to spread the caulk any further in the process. Then I wipe off what's left with a clean rag soaked in solvent and start over. Take your time, keep your eye on the bead, and keep the pressure of your trigger finger steady.

Practical Pete

Humidity and temperature control

Good insulation includes more than prevention of simple heat loss in the winter and cooling loss in summertime. It is also a question of controlling the kind of air inside your home. Comfort in your home is only partially dependent on temperature. There is also the factor of moisture content in the air. At 70 degrees, moist air feels warmer than dry air at 75 degrees. The lack of moisture in the air can make you feel cold even though the thermostat registers a comfortable temperature. And so, if you take steps to keep the air in your house moist, you can operate it at a lower temperature and with less cost. Low humidity also causes physical discomfort, and it dries out the furniture, so you may invite permanent damage if you don't take corrective steps.

There are a number of things you can do to raise the moisture level in your home during the winter months. If you are heating your home with hot air, you can add to the moisture content of the air by installing an automatic humidifier in the heating system. If your home is heated by hot water, you can fill containers with water and hang them or place them behind the radiators.

But if your home is heated by steam, the air is probably already moist enough, because even a well-maintained air-release valve will leak a little steam.

It is sensible to turn down the thermostat for short periods, even for a few hours. There is no gain in leaving the thermostat at 70 degrees all day when the house is empty. It can be pushed up during breakfast time, lowered when everyone leaves for work or school, raised for an hour at lunch, if necessary, and set down again until supper and the evening hours.

While it is true that if the whole house cools down to 60 degrees, it's going to take a long time to heat it back up to 70, nevertheless, it will actually feel warmer in the house while the temperature is rising than when it has become stabilized. This is because radiators put out most of their heat while the furnace is working. When the temperature has reached its goal of 70, the radiators cool down and there isn't much radiated heat in the room. Actually, when you raise the temperature for just a short time you are doing the most good, because you are warming the people rather than the house.

Humidifiers

The type of humidifier you may add to your central heating system will depend upon the type of heating in your home. If your central heating system cannot accommodate a built-in humidifier unit you can purchase one or more freestanding humidifiers.

Maintenance of a humidifier is simply a matter of keeping it clean and maintaining the fan motor as you would any other. Your best guide for maintenance will be the owner's manual. The most common problems arise from the fact that the water leaves mineral deposits after it evaporates. These mineral deposits form a scale which can hamper the unit's operation. With some humidifiers a fungus forms, and an odor may even develop. (See opposite page.)

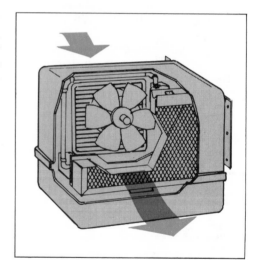

TIP: Winter colds are aggravated and prolonged by dry air. So keep an inexpensive, portable humidifier handy and, when illness occurs, run it continuously in the sickroom with doors closed.

Dehumidifiers

On the other hand, too much moisture in the air can make you feel uncomfortably hot during the summer. Most excesses of humidity are brought on by cooking, taking showers, doing laundry, running a dryer, washing floors. The way to handle high humidity levels in the home is to install an attic fan or one or more dehumidifiers.

A dehumidifier consists of a fan that pulls air into the unit and passes it over refrigerated coils, causing the air to condense on the coils. The condensation then drips into a tray and flows through a hose to a drain. It may be that you cannot hook up the dehumidifier conveniently to a drain, and in such an event it must be emptied by hand.

Maintenance of a dehumidifier involves simple cleaning, especially the coils. To clean the coils you can use a bristle brush or a vacuum cleaner with a brush attachment.

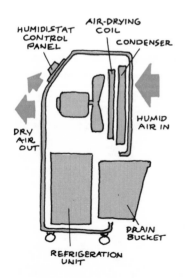

HUMIDISTAT CONTROL PANEL

AIR-DRYING COIL

CONDENSER

DRY AIR OUT

HUMID AIR IN

DRAIN BUCKET

REFRIGERATION UNIT

Hallmarks of a quality dehumidifier

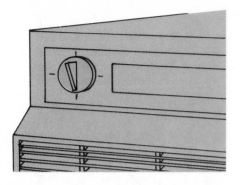

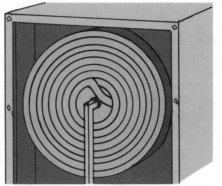

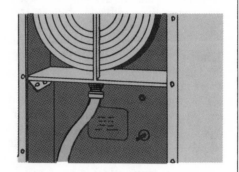

An adjustable humidistat automatically activates the unit as necessary to maintain desired humidity level.

Air-drying coils are exposed to simplify cleaning process.

A water catch bucket, holding up to 2½ gallons, can be easily removed and emptied.

A threaded connector for a garden hose alternatively allows direct removal to a nearby drain.

TIP: You can save fuel by keeping all doors in the house closed while leaving open the door at the head of the basement stairs. Closing the other doors reduces circulation of air and cooling, and leaving the basement door open allows heat to drift upstairs.

The mildew problem

Moisture in excess brings another problem in the form of mildew. Mildew is a fungus which feeds on moisture and dirt. Bathroom walls are one of the likeliest places for this household scourge. The soap dish at the sink is another.

The cure for mildew is to cover all the spots you see with household bleach. A plastic squeeze bottle is a good way to apply the bleach, for with it you can get into cracks, crevices, and grout lines between tiles. Be very sure that you follow all the caution notices on the label of the bleach bottle.

Most of the spots of mildew will disappear in a few minutes, but some will need more bleach and maybe a scrub. An old toothbrush is a handy tool for getting into corners and between tiles. When the mildew has gone, *rinse the area thoroughly with water. When you are satisfied that none of the bleach is left on the walls, wash the walls with household ammonia. This will kill the spores of the fungus and will prevent the swift return of the mildew. But it is very important that you do not mix bleach and ammonia. The two together release deadly chlorine gas.*

Unless you eliminate the conditions that encouraged the mildew in the first place, it will return. Find out what caused it. If mildew occurs in the kitchen, bathroom, or laundry, you know where the moisture came from. A dehumidifier or exhaust fan may be the best way to cope; or you may first want to try regular airing of the room. If the moisture comes from a leak under the house or faulty drainage, you will need to correct the problem to eliminate any return of mildew.

Mildew can also form outside your house. To get rid of fungus on exterior walls mix one quart household bleach, ⅓ cup of powdered detergent, and ⅔ cup of TSP—trisodium phosphate (get it at the paint store). Make a gallon of the solution by adding warm water. Scrub the area with a stiff brush; then hose it thoroughly.

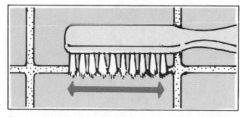

To get rid of mildew, scrub corners and between tiles with a stiff brush.

What it takes

Approximate time: Depends on the area involved; about 10 minutes per square foot.

Tools and materials: Old toothbrush, stiff hand brush or broom, garden hose, household bleach, household ammonia, plastic squeeze bottle, powdered detergent, and trisodium phosphate; for persistent problems, a dehumidifier or exhaust fan.

TIP: Trim back any foliage that prevents air and sunlight from reaching the problem areas.

When moisture accumulates

What it takes

Approximate time: Depends on the area involved and the extent of the problem. For cracks, figure about 15 minutes per square foot. For seepage, allow an hour per wall for waterproofing in an average-size basement; your outside work might involve a day or two. Condensation may be a matter of purchasing and plugging in a dehumidifier, a half hour, or installing an exhaust fan and/or louvers or vents, which can take up to a day or two for the average attic or basement.

Tools and materials: Among the items you may need are a hand mirror, hammer, stone chisel, garden hose, mason's trowel, stiff brush or broom, patching compound, waterproofing compound, louvers, dehumidifier and/or exhaust fan.

One of the more irritating household complaints is the damp basement. This usually results in a tremendous amount of wasted space in the house: a dry basement could be used for any number of purposes, whereas a basement that is damp becomes a liability.

The first thing to check out is where the moisture originates. Is it the house plumbing? If so, this may require professional attention. If the problem is not the plumbing, then the dampness must be due to leakage, seepage, or condensation.

Leakage is simply water that comes in from the outside through cracks. Seepage is also water from outside, but it travels through the pores in the concrete. Condensation is inside water which is actually humidity in the air until the moment it condenses on the cool masonry walls or cold water pipes.

It's simple enough to tell when the problem is leakage because you will see that the moisture is only present around cracks. But condensation and seepage are sometimes hard to differentiate. In order to find out which is present, attach a hand mirror to the wall in the center of a damp spot. Leave it overnight. If the mirror is fogged the following day, it means that there is condensation. If there is no fogging, then you have seepage.

Leakage can be dealt with by patching. You can buy hydraulic cement for this purpose. It sets quickly and in fact can actually set up while water is coming through the crack. Any crack that is more than a hairline should be undercut. You must make the crack wider beneath than it is on the surface. This is done best with a hammer and chisel. It will allow the cement to lock itself into place. Clean away all debris and wash out the opening. Use a hose

to force out loose material. Mix the patching compound, following the directions exactly. Work the mix into the crack, making certain it fills. Use a trowel. Finally, smooth the surface and let it cure as the instructions indicate.

Seepage may be dealt with further by coating the inside of your basement with waterproofing compound.

Waterproofing your basement walls is a simple job. Clean the walls. Wet them thoroughly. After mixing the compound as per directions, apply it with a stiff brush. Be sure to cover the walls thoroughly. If necessary put on a second coat. Of course, no matter how good the compound it will not reduce or eliminate your problem unless you handle the drainage situation outside the house.

The situation will simply recur, whether it is due to seepage or an outright leak. How did the water get to the crack in the first place? Check gutters and downspouts. They should be free of foreign materials and they should be pitched at an angle to carry the water off. The ground on which the downspouts spill should be sloped so that the water will flow away from the house. It's a good idea to put down concrete splash blocks.

Check the ground around the house to make sure it slopes away. If it doesn't, fill it until there is a proper run off. Roll and seed to prevent the soil from washing away. At the same time, be sure that walks and patios butting against the house also slope away. Check the joints to see that they are properly sealed and that they curve properly.

You may have a serious drainage problem outside the house which can be dealt with only by digging down around the foundation and laying drains. This may

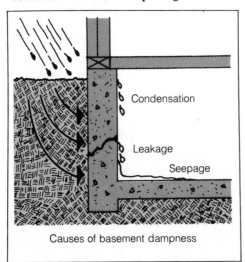

Causes of basement dampness

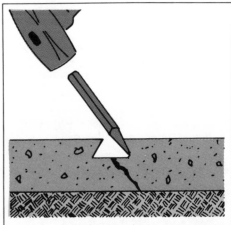

If a crack is more than a hairline, it should be undercut to let the cement lock itself in place.

require a professional hand, but it is possible to do it yourself if you are enterprising. Dig down below the basement floor, although not below the footing. Set a drain along each wall, and extend the drain out to carry the water away. The drain should consist of sections of clay tile pipe covered with about two feet of gravel. It's a good idea, while the outside wall is exposed, to coat it with waterproofing compound.

There are also companies that will pump a special sealing compound into the ground under pressure.

Condensation in your home simply means the transformation of water from vapor to liquid. This can be an all-too-familiar problem for the owner of even a well-insulated home. It is especially prevalent in the attic and in basement crawl spaces.

A house needs to breathe. In normal living, four people will produce 10½ pints of water vapor in a day. This will result from cooking, bathing, laundry, and breathing. This water needs to escape. When condensation shows on windows, it means the relative humidity is too high, and the moisture can't get out of the house. If you have water on your windows then you will know that there is water in your walls. Ice on the windows means ice in the walls. The first winter in a newly built home is the most troublesome as far as condensation

goes, for the building is still drying out. Condensation should not continue into the second heating season, however.

Attic condensation is best dealt with by louvers. Louvers should be placed at gable ends or under the eaves. The ratio of the louver area to the attic floor area should be about 1:300 to properly ventilate the attic, allowing humid air to escape but without losing a lot of heat. If your attic area is about 600 square feet, for example, the total louver area should be at least 2 square feet. (This figure should be doubled if you have screens on the louvers.)

Of course, if the attic is being used, then it should be insulated with a vapor barrier between all rafters, with adequate air space between vapor barrier and roof boards and venting at the eaves or ridge.

Crawl space condensation is equally a problem. Adding a ground moisture seal over the bare earth will help keep crawl space humidity at an acceptable level.

Attic and crawl space ventilation are as necessary in summer as in winter. Keep the louvers open in winter, and provide two vent openings as well. Try to face them so that air can flow in one and out the other, having traversed the insulated area or ground surface. If it is not possible to ventilate by natural means, then an exhaust fan can be the answer.

An attic fan

The attic fan's purpose is not to reduce temperature, but the air movement it causes will help cool the human body by evaporating perspiration. Because it replaces hot indoor air with cooler night air drawn in from outdoors, it will eventually reduce temperature and humidity.

There are two basic types of attic fan. One type is installed in the ceiling beneath the attic, and it draws air from the living area below into the unused attic space above. The air then moves outdoors through louvers, which are customarily in the gable ends. It is important that the louvers be big

enough to accommodate the volume of air that the fan will set in motion.

The other type of attic fan is installed in an opening that is cut in the gable end. The rest of the attic is sealed, with the exception of a louver through the ceiling to the living area downstairs. The indoor air moves into the attic as the fan draws out the attic air.

These fans come in a variety of sizes. It is the size of the blades and the speed of revolution that decide how many cubic feet of air can be moved per minute. Your building supplier can help you determine which size fan is best for your house.

Tips for keeping dry

- Turn off the humidifier.
- Ventilate wherever possible.
- Be sure the laundry dryer exhaust is vented to the outside.
- If you have a fireplace, open the draft.
- When cooking, turn on the exhaust fan; turn on the bathroom fan when bathing. Make sure that both of these exhaust outside.
- Remove inside screens in winter to allow more air circulation around windows. Open drapes and curtains.
- If you have a bow window and a condensation problem, make certain you have heavy insulation under the seat board as well as over the head board.
- Use one or more dehumidifiers.

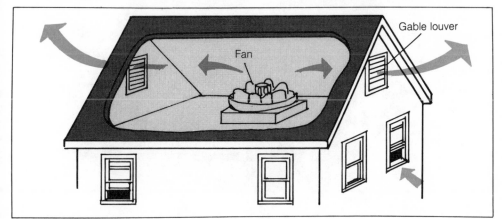

Fan

Gable louver

Air conditioners

Cooling it in the summer can be as important as heating it in winter. For this, of course the basic requirement is air-conditioning. There are two general air-conditioning systems: *central air-conditioning* which cools the whole house, and *individual room units* which cool only the room where they have been installed. With central air-conditioning, you will more than likely have a contractor do the installation. But the individual room or window unit you can put in yourself.

How the individual unit works. Whether it is mounted in a wall or in a window, the individual unit functions by venting hot air from both the fan motor and the condenser to the outside. Some air conditioners have more power than others and can cool more area than just the room in which they are installed. A couple of such powerful units could cool several rooms. The room air conditioner passes warm air from the room over the cooling coil; the cooled air is then circulated by a blower or fan. The heat from the warm room air causes the cold liquid refrigerant which is flowing through the evaporator to vaporize. The vaporized refrigerant carries the heat to the compressor, which in turn compresses the vapor and increases its temperature to a point higher than that of the outside air. In the condenser, the hot refrigerant vapor liquefies and gives up the heat from the room air to the air outside. The high-pressure liquid refrigerant then passes through a restrictor which reduces its pressure and temperature. The cold liquid refrigerant then re-enters the evaporator, and the cycle is repeated indefinitely.

Mounting a room unit is not a difficult procedure. Many window air conditioners come with a do-it-yourself installation kit. Instructions should be followed carefully to save time and trouble later. For installation of larger models you would probably need a professional. Check with your dealer.

The procedures of installation differ a good bit, because room units can be mounted a number of ways. It's best to take into consideration what mounting is most suitable to the conditions of your home and the local building codes. The most common methods of mounting are:

Inside flush: the interior face of the conditioner is approximately flush with the inside wall.

Outside flush: the outer face of the unit is either flush or just beyond the outside wall.

Upper sash: the air conditioner is mounted in the top of the window.

Balance: the unit is installed half inside and half outside the window.

Interior: the conditioner is completely inside the room, and so the window can be closed or opened at will.

There is also a special mounting designed for horizontal sliding and casement windows. Installation procedure is similar.

Location of the air conditioner. It is best to locate the unit as far as you can from exterior doors. This will help prevent drafts from interfering with the cooled air. Be sure there are no obstructions in front of the conditioner, especially draperies or furniture. See that the vents are directed upward so that the cool air will rise. Later it will drift to the floor.

Exterior windows and doors should be thoroughly weather-stripped; otherwise you'll overwork the unit.

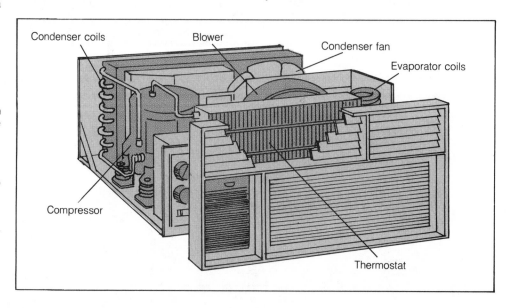

Condenser coils — Blower — Condenser fan — Evaporator coils — Compressor — Thermostat

Maintenance

Filter. Clean it often. Follow the directions in the service booklet. Vacuum, wash in warm water, dry, and replace.

Grille. Clean with warm water, soap, soft cloth. Do not use any cleaners. And do not allow any insect spray on it, for solvents may cause corrosion. Keep it well dusted.

Grille condensation. The grille may collect moisture when it is first turned on because of high humidity in the room. Close the doors and windows in the room to lower the humidity to let the moisture evaporate.

Installing a window unit

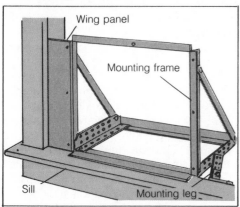

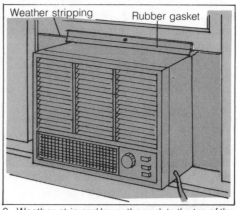

1. First assemble the mounting frame that comes with the unit. It must be centered in the window. Screw small mounting legs to the sill near the outer edge. A slight pitch to outdoors lets water run off.

2. Weather-strip and lower the sash to the top of the frame. Then slide the air conditioner into the frame until it is flush with the window. Tuck it in place with a heavy rubber gasket all around. This seals the space between the frame and the unit.

Installing a unit through the wall

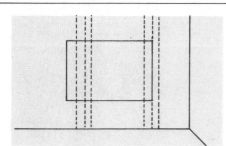

1. Mark an area and cut it out with a keyhole saw. Remove the outside wall and insulation.

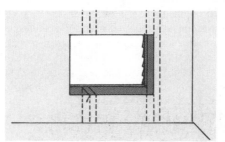

2. Saw out the center stud and take it away.

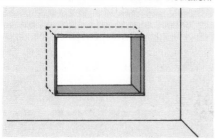

3. Insert a preassembled wooden frame. Its purpose is to act as buffer against vibration.

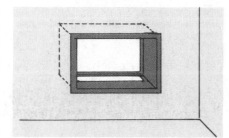

4. Insert metal sleeve that comes with unit.

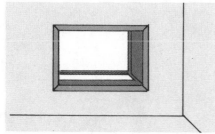

5. Put on molding, and caulk where needed.

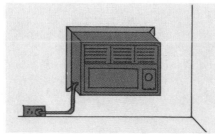

6. Place the air conditioner in the frame.

What it takes

Approximate time: Three hours.

Tools and materials: ¼" drill and bits with long shank to pierce wall, insulation, siding, keyhole saw, handsaw, hammer, wood chisel, screwdriver, caulking compound, weather stripping, and lumber for frame.

I was cool till I took a look at my electric bill.
I figured I'd beat the electric company by turning my thermostat way down at night and throwing open all the windows. Everyone knows it's cooler outside at night. Trouble was, this let moisture into the house because nighttime humidity can be high. As I learned later, this made my air conditioner run overtime during the day, just to reduce the humidity.

Practical Pete

Soundproofing your home

Two abbreviations you may run into when discussing soundproofing or soundproofing materials are STL and STC, followed by a two-digit number. STL means sound transmission loss, referring to the loss in sound level that occurs when sound moves through a surface or barrier. The amount of loss depends on the surface or barrier material and the type of construction. The higher the number, the greater the sound loss. STC means sound transmission class and is a method of rating soundproofing materials. The chart is a rough guide to the ratings most often applied to residential construction.

Soundproof Rating/ Approximate Meaning

35	Loud speech clearly audible
40	Loud speech audible but hard to understand
45	Loud speech audible as a murmur
50	Exceptionally loud speech barely audible
55	Strain required to hear exceptionally loud speech
60	Loud speech not audible at all

Noise is unquestionably one of the great problems of our time, especially for those who live in or close to urban areas. While there is little that the individual can do about environmental noise pollution, there are some steps that can be taken to eliminate a great deal of unwanted sound in and around the house.

Soundproofing a new home. If you are planning to build a new house, you might consider the following quite simple measures beforehand:

Specify double studs for walls instead of the usual single-stud construction. The studs are placed on two 2x4 sole plates instead of one (or on a single 2x8) and staggered. This permits weaving insulation between them to help deaden sound. See illustrations below.

Certain types of wallboard—and acoustical wall tile—are also available to reduce the passage of sound. Both are ideal for a rumpus room. Acoustical ceiling tile is also a good means of controlling sound, and it comes in attractive styles, is durable, and easy to install.

In planning your new home, try to place bedrooms toward the back of the house, away from street noises. Use solid-core doors throughout the house, and position closets as buffers between areas of noise and bedrooms. Use carpets wherever possible. It is also a good idea to avoid long, straight stairways and halls, because they act as channels for sound.

Soundproofing an existing house. Outside noise can be checked by the use of insulation, including storm doors and windows. See that all cracks are caulked and all doors and windows have weather stripping. Judicious planting of shrubs and trees will help check the invasion of your peace and quiet. High, solid wood fences, provided they do not conflict with zoning laws, will be a wise addition. The interior walls of your house which face the direction of the annoyance can be covered with heavy materials such as lined drapes. As a last resort, the wall itself can be furred out, and a

second, inner wall put up. This will create an air pocket to trap sound.

Plumbing noises. The roar and crash of household plumbing can frequently be lowered by such simple acts as wrapping pipes, replacing washers on faucets, securing loose pipes.

Ticking in pipes is caused by hot water flowing into a cold hot-water supply pipe. The pipe expands, and this produces a ticking sound. The cure is to make sure that the pipe has room to slide on its hangers.

Whistling comes when water which is under high pressure must flow past a restriction. The whistling toilet inlet valve is a sound familiar to countless homeowners. Some toilets are graced with an adjusting screw that allows you to reduce the flow to below the whistling level. If your toilet does not have this useful feature, you can turn the tank's shutoff valve to the point where the rate of flow decreases and the whistling stops. But this is an exception to the general rule: it is a good idea to check all the valves in the water-supply system to be certain that none of them are partially closed.

The gurgling drain, like the whistling toilet, not infrequently proves a major source of irritation. The customary causes are wrong drainage-pipe size and improper venting. The remedy might be an anti-siphon trap, an inexpensive hardware-store item that comes in a kit for easy installation.

Water hammer is a hard, knocking sound in the piping when a faucet or an automatic-washer solenoid valve turns off quickly. Water which has been moving quickly through the pipes while the valve is open will come to a dead stop as the valve is shut, with the result that heavy pressures are put on the whole water-supply system.

The problem in this case is improperly operating air chambers, or even a complete lack of them. Air chambers allow rushing water to bounce gently against a cushion of air when a valve closes, thus taking the strain off the pipes. Installing air chambers may be something you would pass on to your plumber.

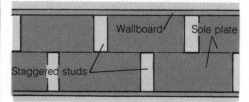

The view from above shows how studs can be staggered for the best effect.

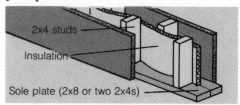

Soundproof a frame wall by placing staggered 2x4s on a single 2x8 sole plate, or on two 2x4 sole plates. Then weave insulation through the studs, leaving air locks to trap sound.

Acoustical ceiling tile

One of the easiest ways to dampen sound inside the house is to install an acoustical-tile ceiling. There are two ways to put up ceiling tiles: either with adhesive or with staples. It is important, right off, to gauge the condition of your existing ceiling. If it is a clean, firm surface of wallboard or plaster, then it should take adhesive or staples well. But if a plaster ceiling is not smooth, then you will have to put up furring strips and staple or adhere the tiles to these.

While there are a number of systems for joining tiles together, depending on the manufacturer, the principles of installation are essentially the same. First of all, find out how wide your border tiles should be. The borders at each end should be the same width. To do this, measure each wall, but in your calculation pay attention only to the leftover inches. For example, if a wall measures 9 feet 4 inches, then what counts is the number 4. Starting from this number, the rule is: Add 12 and divide by 2. This will give you 8, in the example given, which will be the width of the border tile on each end. If the other wall measures 13 feet 10 inches, the borders along the other sides will be 11 inches (10 plus 12 divided by 2).

Start at a corner, measure out the width of the border tiles, and snap a chalk line across the room in each direction.

Stapling. If you intend to staple the tiles, then cut the corner tile first with the staple tabs aimed toward the center of the room. For cutting, use a fine-toothed saw or sharp fiberboard knife, and always cut with the face of the tile up.

Place the corner tile carefully against the chalk line and staple it. The back edge of the tile can be nailed in place because it will be covered by molding later on. The exposed part of the staple will be covered by the interlock of the following tiles.

Staple a whole course of cut border tiles along one wall, nailing the back edges in place. Then run the border tiles along the other wall. And now work in rows with the full tiles, stapling them in place. At the other end, the border tiles will have no staple tabs. They will be held in place with nails and the interlocks.

Adhesive. You may wish to put up your ceiling tiles with adhesive rather than staples. Apply four dabs of adhesive to the back of a tile, about 1½ inches in from each corner. Don't put on too much—about the size of a silver dollar is good. Place the tile near the chalk line, and slide it into place. On later courses, slide each tile onto the tongues of tiles already in place.

Press each tile firmly with your hand to make sure that it holds well to the ceiling (but be sure that your hands are clean). If the tile seems not to be level, take it down and adjust the amount of adhesive to compensate. Don't forget to cut holes for light fixtures and other obstacles, and bear in mind that a fixture's outer rim will cover the opening. After all the tiles are up, finish off with molding along the edges.

What it takes

Approximate time: A good day's work, provided the original ceiling is in good condition.

Tools and materials: Measuring tape, chalk line, either adhesive and putty knife or staple gun and staples, fine-toothed saw or fiberboard knife, hammer and nails.

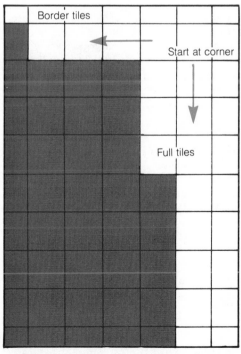

1. Start from a corner and install border tiles along two walls. Then work out into the room in both directions with full-size tiles.

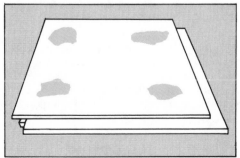

2A. Attach staples near the edge of the long inner tab on the two grooved sides of each tile. Then slip the tongue of the adjacent tile into the groove, covering the exposed staple. Use four staples per tile, one at each end of each tab.

2B. Alternate method: apply adhesive in four light dabs spaced 1 to 2 inches from each corner.

6. SECURITY

A burglary takes place every 15 seconds.

There is a fire every 58 seconds.

Protecting your home

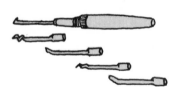

Lock pick set looks like a fountain pen. It is available only to locksmiths.

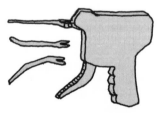

The pick gun, used by locksmith and burglar, vibrates pin into position within the cylinder. The tumbler core is then turned with a tension wrench.

It takes only one small match to start a four-alarm fire, one unlocked window to admit a burglar to your home. Carelessness is without question the principal contributor to accident, fire, and theft in the American home. Your carelessness, perhaps.

It is reported that in the United States a burglary is committed every 15 seconds. No target is beyond the range of today's thieves and vandals, and their numbers are rapidly multiplying along with their cunning and boldness.

The determined burglar can get into anything. The question is how much time and risk he wishes to take. For, though a tight house with strong locks may not stop every thief, it can stop a good many and will slow all of them down. Time is your ally in the battle with burglars. Your home's security should be geared to delay, foil, and discourage the intruder.

How a burglar operates

When the professional burglar really wishes, and has the time, he can defeat just about any lock or alarm system. Only there aren't a great many professionals about, and those who do merit top seeding are selective with their targets. They will only mount a strike after much casing and planning, and when assured of a brisk haul.

The pro does a lot of research. He will chat in neighborhood bars, with mailmen and repair and service personnel such as plumbers and carpenters, with shopkeepers and gas-station attendants. His effort is to learn who has bought valuable items, where they are kept, who is going on a trip and when, what sort of locks and security systems are popular in the area, who has dogs, and which dogs bark?

His target is not just your house, but you. He needs to know a great deal about you— your schedule of arrival and departure each day, for example. He will note such details as deliveries, how many people live in the house, and how many are at home during the day. The professional burglar notices if your lawn is well kept, if your house needs painting, whether the catch basin in your driveway is plugged up. Small things, but he needs to know who you are: a dilettante, or a generalissimo who double-locks even his toothbrush.

To really understand the burglar and your own vulnerability, why not try an exercise for yourself? Study your own home, and see how you would go about robbing it. Plan to burgle yourself! How would you enter your house as a burglar? When? How would you work without anyone noticing? And how would you make your getaway? In that game or exercise you might discover weaknesses in your home protection that you had no idea existed.

How the burglar enters

Burglary depends upon opportunity, and so a burglar will very often walk right into a house through an unlocked door or window. Failing that, he will resort to that marvelous tool, the jimmy, with which he can open almost any window or door. It is simply a common pinch bar with one end flattened sufficiently thin so that it can enter a very narrow space. In the hands of a pro it is a sophisticated tool.

Many burglars favor the use of the plastic credit card. This they slip between the door and the jamb to open ordinary beveled latches. To the trade, this operation is known as "loiding," from the time when the cards were made of celluloid.

A further talent is that of the lock picker. Yet the jimmy is faster, and so for the homeowner it is less important to have a lock that is pick-proof than to have a deadbolt latch, a heavy-duty door, and a tight and solid frame.

At the same time, the professionals are in the minority. Many thieves are amateurs, drug addicts, or kids looking for thrills. They are dangerous in the way that a dull knife is more to be feared than a sharp one, for they are usually quite ignorant in regard to sophisticated security equipment, and they frequently panic and resort to unnecessary violence.

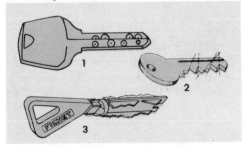

The unpickables. Each of these keys operates a cylinder which is supposedly pickproof. The Sargent Keso (1) has a radial pin arrangement. The Medeco (2) has V-shaped cuts crisscrossing the key, allowing millions of noninterchangeable key combinations. The Fichet cylinder (3), with each groove in the key cut to 10 possible depths, has 10 grooves, offering billions of combinations.

Preventing burglary

Without doubt the best way to secure your home is to protect its perimeter. This means sturdy doors, windows, locks, good outdoor lighting, and even fences and hedges. Above all, it is best to avoid confrontation with any hostiles, and so keeping them at a distance is only sensible.

Make it difficult to enter your house. Solid doors, strong locks, locked windows, lights, alarms, plus security habits such as locking up even when you go out for a short time all tend to discourage thieves. The burglar casing your house will appreciate the sort of person he is dealing with and will think again about invading your privacy.

Keep your life private. Do not attract burglars by letting neighbors or tradespeople know that you have a valuable coin collection, or that you are planning a trip. Don't let the contents of your house be seen through lighted windows. If you have an expensive hi-fi, keep it away from viewers who might be passing by. Also make your daily schedule erratic. Don't always arrive home from work at exactly the same time, if you can help it.

Let your house appear occupied at all times. Use timers to switch lights off and on and switch radios on when you're not at home. Have a neighbor pick up your mail and newspaper whenever you're away on a trip. Do not cancel your subscriptions with the announcement that you won't be at home for a month; but do notify the police. Keep garage doors closed and locked when cars are not there. Lock up even if you're just going next door for coffee.

Be suspicious, stay alert. Be careful about anyone posing as a salesman or pollster who wants to see the inside of your house. Watch out for strange cars parked near your home. It could be the burglar casing his next job. Never let anyone inside until you have checked them through your front door peephole and talked to them with the door on the chain, and you are fully satisfied. Be in touch with your neighbors whenever you see any suspicious-looking person hanging about the neighborhood.

About watchdogs

Any dog can be an excellent alarm system. A dog will almost always bark when a stranger approaches, or when it feels or smells something out of the ordinary. Even a very small dog can be effective in this regard. A large dog, such as a German shepherd, is an even greater help, for not only would its bark threaten the burglar, but so would its bite. In fact, when casing a neighborhood the sensible crook will pass up a home with a dog.

He didn't even leave me a drink! That security-system salesman seemed like one of the nicest fellows I ever met. I took him all through my house and showed him how my door alarm worked. He even said he'd come by and have a drink with me in a couple of weeks after I got back from vacation. Next time I won't let anyone into my house until I check out his credentials. *Practical Pete*

Doors and windows: first line of defense

Doors

How to share the wealth
I put my Christmas bonus into the best stereo I could get for the price. And it was great sitting in my picture window listening to music and watching the sunset. Trouble was, I didn't know that others were watching me—and my stereo. Next time I'll either keep my curtains drawn or put my valuables in another room where they can't be seen. At least they didn't steal the view.

Practical Pete

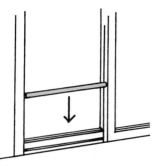

TIP: A good way to block entry through sliding glass doors is with a metal bar placed along the tracks.

Security isn't only a matter of locks and bolts. It is also doors and windows. And although a locked door will offer a psychological deterrent to certain amateurs, it will seldom put off a seasoned burglar. He knows very well that a lock, no matter how strong, is only as good as the door of which it is a part. A strong lock on a hollow-core door, a door with loose hinges, or a rotting frame is useless. A kick, a vigorous fist, and the intruder is within.

There are three types of doors: solid wood, hollow core, and paneled. Of these the solid wood is the most reliable. It is simply thick, hard wood. All exterior doors should be of this type, at least 1¾ to 2 inches thick.

A paneled door is only safe if the panels are of heavy wood and are well set. If the panels are glass, they should be replaced either with strong wood or with plastic panes. Otherwise the invitation to the burglar is irresistible. He will simply break the panel, reach inside, and open the door.

The hollow-core type should never be used as an exterior door. Hollow-core doors offer a measure of privacy, but they are no security for the homeowner. They are strictly for the interior of the house, blocking little more than other people's curiosity. A determined shoulder or boot is all that's needed to get through one of these.

Your first task in any home-protection program is to check what your burglar will be checking—the condition of your outside doors and windows.

A rotting door or frame. It's easy for any burglar to pry his way through rot. Your best action would be to replace either the rotted area or the entire door and/or frame with new, solid wood.

A poorly constructed door. It could be too thin, or it could have thin wood or glass

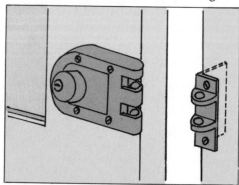

The best protection for a door with glass panes is a locking door bolt. Even if the glass is broken it prevents entry.

panels. All the thief has to do is make an opening with his elbow, knee or fist, reach in and open the door from the inside. Get a new door or fortify this one.

A door with loose hinges or with outside hinges. In either case you're in trouble. Even the callow apprentice would find it easy. Your remedy is to sink longer screws. But check that the wood isn't rotten. If it is, you'll need solid blocks or strips of wood so that the screws will hold. The screws should be nonretractable. Put glue on the threads before sinking; or you can purchase special screws which can be screwed in, but not out.

Many old houses have door hinges on the outside. All the thief has to do is knock out the hinge pin, and it's payday. The best approach here is to take down the door and reset the hinges inside, if possible; or put up a new door and frame.

A door with too much space between the door and its frame. This is a loud-and-clear invitation for the burglar to use his jimmy. Remember, the jimmy can get into very small crevices. If the thief can't jimmy the lock so that it pulls away from the frame and causes the bolt or latch to pop out of the receiver, he can make a large enough space to insert a hacksaw and cut through the bolt. To thwart him, allow no more than 1/64th of an inch space between the door and its frame.

Don't be fooled into thinking that modern construction techniques will see to it that you have sturdy door frames on your new house. Too often, modern construction is concerned with haste and there is a gap around your door frame which is simply filled in with small wedges and plaster. Time and frequent door slamming soon loosen this. It's a breeze then for the pro and his jimmy bar.

The clever thief will sometimes use a method that will bamboozle not only you but your insurance company as well. He can stretch the frame just above the lock with an automobile jack. As the jack expands, the frame stretches, and eventually the bolt can be pulled out of its place in the lock strike. The thief opens the door, loads up and departs without a trace. The frame returns to its original position and there will be no sign of forced entry. Try and collect on that one.

Reinforcing an outside door. You can easily do this yourself by attaching a panel of ¾-inch plywood or a piece of sheet metal to your door. It won't be necessary to take the door down. Be sure that the existing hinges will bear the added weight. If there is any question, get heavier hinges with longer screws.

If you live in a rented house and the landlord won't allow you to reinforce or change the door, then install a double cylinder lock which requires a key to open it from inside as well as outside. If a thief breaks through a panel and reaches in, he will find he has a lock to contend with rather than just a knob.

Sliding doors. The problem is that sliding doors have very narrow stiles and can be jimmied. Moreover, there is very little room in the door to mount the traditional horizontal latch or throw bolt.

There is a special lock, however, with a cylinder-operated deadbolt and tamper-proof screws; it is lightweight, inexpensive, and easy to install. Another lock has a pivoted latch which, when it is not in use, lies vertically in the housing, thus allowing for a long throw bolt within a small space.

Windows

The burglar will usually look for a window that has been left open. Failing that, he will try to defeat a window lock or, as a last resort, will take a chance on breaking or cutting glass. To protect your windows you will need one or more of these devices:

- A good window lock.
- Iron grilles or window gates.
- An alarm system on the window.
- Burglar-resistant glass.
- Windows with many small panes rather than a large area of glass.

The sash lock is actually not a lock at all but a latch made of a curved metal arm and a receptacle. The two pieces are supposed to draw the windows tightly together. Unfortunately, because of poor construction,

poor installation of the lock, or warping of the window, the device is often useless.

Some homeowners favor the wedge lock which has a rubber tip and is mounted on the upper part of the lower window frame. It holds the windows shut, but it does so by spreading them apart. All the burglar has to do then is slip a knife blade between the windows and cut off the rubber piece.

Your best protection is a window lock with a key. Even if the burglar breaks the window he must then cope with your lock.

Put window locks on all the windows in your house. It is wise to have all locks keyed alike and to give each member of the family a key; keep a key near the window, where children but not a burglar can reach it. (This is highly recommended as a fire-safety precaution.)

The window lock is customarily installed with self-tapping screws on the lower window frame. Drill a hole in the upper frame into which the bolt can slip. A second hole may be drilled a few inches higher in order to secure the window in a ventilation position when desired. Never leave the window opening wider than 6 inches when ventilating. Thin burglar arms and tools can pass through anything wider than that.

For the sake of economy, it is not necessary for every window in the house to have the same level of protection. Some windows are more accessible than others, and so their defense merits more time and money. Other windows, which can be reached only with difficulty, require less protection. Windows which you never use, basement windows for example, should be nailed shut. They are among the most vulnerable target areas in any case. Trees which are located near windows and from which a burglar may gain access, and shrubs around the house which can shield him from view as he attempts to break into your house, are major weaknesses in your line of defense.

TIP: After installing a window lock, drip some solder onto the screw heads. This will stop a burglar from unscrewing the lock after he cuts a small hole in the windowpane (a common means of entry).

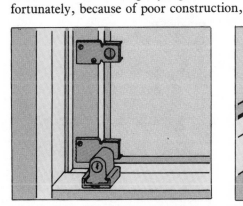

It's a good idea to put an auxiliary lock-pin on windows so that nobody can simply break the glass, reach in and open the window. At the same time, a steel pin can hold the window open for ventilation. Bore two holes for the pin—one in the closed position, and one so that the window can be open no more than 6 inches.

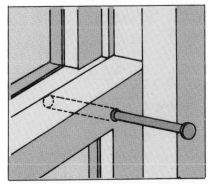

All downstairs windows should be securely locked so that even if the glass is broken they cannot be unlocked. Upstairs windows may not require prime security, but pins or bolts would not be amiss with these in any case.

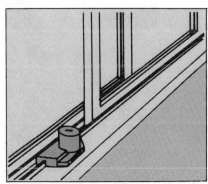

Sometimes it is a problem to lock an aluminum sliding window in a ventilating position. A locking, sliding window bolt allows you high security as it foils entry even if the glass is broken.

Lock options

Which lock to use

The locks which you can buy are almost without limit. To keep out the casual burglar you may use one or several. Much depends on what you wish to protect. If you have valuable paintings and jewels, for example, then you'll want a high-security system. The point is to decide how much you wish to invest in security. For basic security against the average thief, however, the cost is not high.

Spring-latch lock

Deadbolt lock

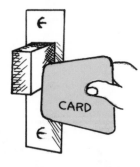

The spring-latch lock is highly convenient for the burglar who is adroit at "loiding"—slipping a plastic credit card against the latch tongue to depress it and unlock the door. The deadbolt, on the other hand, defies any attack. It is only vulnerable when the door has enough space from its frame so that the intruder can bring power tools or a hacksaw to bear. But that takes time, which is to his disadvantage.

Locks may be classified into two basic groups: surface locks, and locks which are installed within or through the door. Surface locks include sliding bolts, bars, safety chains—or any other locking device which is fixed to the surface of the door. The disadvantage of surface locks is that they can be ripped off. You can forestall this by fastening the surface lock in place with long, heavy screws coated in glue before driving them into the wood.

Door locks consist of three common types: key-in-knob, mortise, and rim lock. **Key-in-knob locks** (including tubular and cylindrical locks). These are quite common, and they range from the flimsy to the fairly secure. They are easy to install and come in standard sizes. There are certain disadvantages: the locking mechanism is in the knob, which puts it *outside* the house. A sledgehammer could dismantle the lock without much trouble. Also, these locks have a tapered latch which can be opened in a matter of seconds by an adroit "loid" user. Finally, the latches as a rule are pretty short and therefore easy to jimmy. To deal with these problems, some manufacturers have added longer latches or trigger bolts. **Tubular locks** are of the same type as key-in-knob locks. They are used on interior doors. Some have a push button in the knob or a small lever or button on the interior side. Tubular locks are most commonly used on bathroom doors. **Cylindrical locks** are similar to the tubular, only larger and stronger. They can be used on exterior doors. They are locked by a key in the outer knob or with a push button or

lever which is located in the inner knob. **Mortise locks** are installed in the edge of a door. They cannot be installed in a door that is less than 1⅜ inches thick. The mortise lock has a spring-loaded latch and a deadbolt. When the key is fully turned in the lock, the deadbolt will double-lock the door, thus offering top lock security. **Rim locks** are actually auxiliary locks. They add clout to the security you get from your key-in-knob or mortise lock. Rim locks are mounted on the inside face of the door. Some have deadbolts, while others have a spring-loaded latch that locks automatically when the door is closed.

Buying a lock

When you buy a lock, it comes already assembled. Bear in mind that the lock and the cylinder are two separate entities. You can take out the cylinder and replace it without replacing the entire lock. Some locks that are almost impregnable in the face of physical assault may have cylinders that are child's play to the experienced pickman. Yet there are cylinders that are nearly impossible to pick. On the other hand, the truly professional burglar is not without resource, and in answer to a difficult cylinder he will simply reach for his large, heavy set of pliers and yank the cylinder right out of the door. The cylinder puller needs only to get a grip on the cylinder. Protective cylinder plates are available which cover the cylinder and the surrounding area, leaving space only for the key, and so baffling the burglar.

A tubular lock has very few springs and working parts. Its basic action is contained in a small area, sometimes just in the latch itself. This type of lock often lacks the strength and smooth action you would find in a more sophisticated cylindrical lock. It is not for use as a keyed lock, but more for bathroom and passageway doors.

A cylindrical lock has a large chassis. It is strong, designed with precision, and highly serviceable. It may be used on exterior doors.

Primary locks

Key-in-knob locks and mortise locks are called primary locks because they are the locks that usually come with your house or apartment. These locks are really for keeping the door shut and do little to exclude the burglar.

If you are building your own home, or even if you are buying a home already built, it would be wise to put in a mortise lock. Get one that has a protective faceplate for the setscrew and an angling plate to cut down on the distance between the frame and the door. Unless you get these features you could be asking for trouble; mortise locks have a tendency to encourage the jimmy bar because the homeowner often forgets to deadlock the door and relies only on the regular latch. This makes him easy prey for a burglar who, posing as a fund raiser, will surreptitiously loosen the setscrew while your back is turned, and then return later to complete the job.

If your builder puts in a key-in-knob lock, make sure that it is made of pressed steel rather than zinc casting so as to be more resistant to physical attack. Also, make certain that it has a trigger bolt to prevent "loiding"; and get a latch that protrudes at least ½ inch.

Secondary locks

Though called "secondary" because they are added on, in terms of hard security they are the truly primary locks. Your heavier artillery may be anything from a vertical deadbolt to those locks which brace the door against the floor or deep into the door jamb. Don't forget that in deciding what lock you need you should first check the physical condition of both jamb and door.

A very strong wooden door or metal door can probably be protected best with the vertical deadbolt lock. With solid mounting this lock is usually as strong as the door itself. When buying, ask the salesperson for a jimmyproof deadlock.

Even if your wooden door is not in the best condition there are a number of locks which can help keep the burglar outside. With a wooden door that opens inward you can install a brace lock or police lock. It locks the door into the floor. A long steel bar fits into the lock mounting on the door and into a metal socket in your floor, so the would-be intruder will be pressing against the floor itself.

Another superb lock is the Fichet Vertibar. This bolts into the door frame in seven places. It is said to resist all physical attacks, while its ten-lever cylinder is considered pickproof. It's expensive.

Mortise locks are not as popular as they used to be, since the development of the cylindrical lock. Installation can be costly, and it is of course necessary to mortise out fairly large sections of the door and jamb.

Rim locks are usually installed above existing locks, and are therefore auxiliary. They are an additional security. Mounted on the inside of the door, some have deadbolts, and others have a spring-loaded latch that locks automatically when the door is shut.

A bored lock looks like this when you remove it from the door. Removal and replacement is a simple operation requiring little time and few tools.

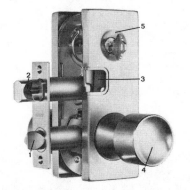

Double-locking security is what can thwart even the most determined burglar. 1 and 2: Combination of a ½-inch throw deadlocking latch and a 1-inch throw deadbolt in which is concealed a hardened-steel roller that resists sawing or just about any other attack. 3: Armor plate protects the lock mechanism from piercing, sawing, drilling. 4: When the door is locked, the outside knob is free-spinning, making it impossible to get any leverage on it to force or twist it. 5: Forceful entry is discouraged by the recessed cylinder. The lock is also panicproof for safety. Both the latch and the bolt retract simultaneously, permitting instant exit, with a simple turn of the inside knob or thumb turn.

About keys

Just as a lock without a key isn't much good, so a lock with a lot of keys is also of no use to your security. Be careful about the disposition of your keys, and change the cylinder on your lock from time to time, just in case someone has gotten hold of a key or has made a copy of a key you or a member of your family left lying around. If you lose your key, change the cylinder immediately.

Open sesame

The future of locking devices will very likely be determined in the field of electronics. Today, there is the "invisible keyhole" whose lock is operated by a hidden control. The "key" resembles a plastic credit card, and it is simply held near a sensor unit. Radio frequencies read it, and providing it is the correct key, the door is released. Furthermore, a door can be made to appear as part of a wall, adding even further security. Perhaps one day not very far from now, all that will be necessary will be for you to utter a special password and the door will open for you.

How to replace a broken or worn-out lock

It is an easy job to replace a lock, even if some door preparation is necessary. For the most part, no special tools are required. First of all, check the lock you are replacing. Make a list of the pertinent facts so that you can show them to your hardware dealer, and he will be able to help you.

• What type of lock are you replacing? Is it a bored or mortised lock, for instance.
• Name of manufacturer.
• What is the thickness of your door?
• Measure the lock hole diameter, latch-bolt hole diameter, latch unit faceplate, and the distance from the edge of the door to the center of the lock hole.

The parts of the lock that you will need to know are:

The strike. Located in the jamb, the strike can practically always be left where it is. Just check the hole that is mortised into the jamb to be sure it is deep enough to receive the new latch bolt. It should be in the correct position to depress the plunger on the deadlocking latch. If you find it necessary to lessen the gap between the frame and the door, you can shim the strike from behind with a small piece of cardboard.

The latch. Currently, there are two basic latch types in use. The standard, or traditional latch has a faceplate which is fastened to the door with two screws. The drive-in latch has a circular front about an inch in diameter in the edge of the door. It will either have spring clips that grip into the full length of the bore, or raised ribs that hold by friction. You can usually install a drive-in latch without additional mortising.

The lock mechanism. Using the template that comes with the new lock, you will be able to tell if the hole is of the right diameter to receive the new lock. If you need a larger hole, use a wood rasp to enlarge it to the necessary measurement. If you are replacing more than one lock, you will find a boring jig helpful. Ask your dealer about lending or renting you one.

Changing a bored lock

Full-lip strike   T strike

Proper installation of strike

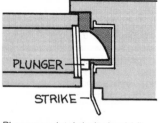

Plunger on latch bolt should fit exactly against strike so latch can't be forced when door is closed.

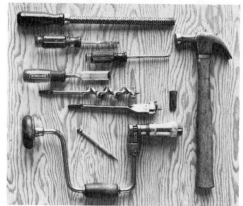

Replacing a bored lock—whether cylindrical or tubular—is a simple job if you have average mechanical ability and the usual home-shop tools.

1. Remove the worn out or broken lock.

2. Remove the latch. It should come out easily.

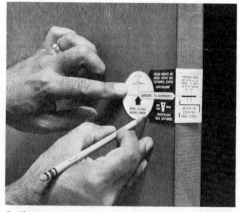

3. If necessary, use the symmetrical, reversible template to outline a new hole.

4. If you have the use of a jig, as shown here, use a hole saw to enlarge the area so it can accept the new lock mechanism.

5. . With a chisel, cut away excess wood in the edge of the door, if necessary, to accommodate the new latch plate.

6. Put in the new latch plate. It is important that your mortise and bored holes be precise. If you have mortised too deep, shim out with cardboard.

7. Insert the lock mechanism from the outside of the door. If you find that the hole requires only minor enlargement, you can use a wood rasp.

Deadlocking latch with standard faceplate.

Drive-in latch with circular front.

8. Attach the mounting plate on the inside of the door and finally put on the trim and knob. It is important to achieve precise alignment of the knob.

9. The completed installation looks as though a professional had done it. But the job isn't over. You must keep a maintenance check on all locks.

Replacing an old lock with a deadbolt

While the exchange of similar locks is a relatively simple affair, the replacement of an old lock by a new security lock equipped with a deadbolt is a little more time consuming, though still within the reach of the home handyman.

The old mortise lock in the photo sequence below had been on the door for a number of years and was loose. The door was also loose on its hinges and would not shut tightly. First, the hinges were repositioned so that the door fit snugly in its frame, and then the homeowner addressed himself to the door lock. His purpose in installing a deadbolt was to correct a serious weakness in the locking mechanism. The solid metal bolt spanning the gap between door and frame is called "dead" because it has no springs to operate it, and so cannot be loided (see page 168).

1. After removing the door so it will be easier to work, take out the old lock pieces; then cut a plug to fit into the mortise cut.

2. Using the installation template supplied with the lock, mark the locations of the various holes.

3. You can use a hole saw in an electric drill, or a saber saw to bore the large-diameter holes.

4. Bore the deadbolt hole, as well as the latch lock hole, with a drill and paddle bit.

5. Fit the new handle and latch in place.

6. Install the deadbolt, latch, and their respective plates, with the plates mortised in flush to the edge of the door; then fit the deadbolt key and escutcheon.

7. Now it is simply a matter of mating the pieces from each side and checking the lock and knob operation.

8. Fill any holes left from the old lock, and then paint or stain.

9. Mark the locations of both the deadbolt hole and the regular latch hole, and mark around the plates.

10. Bore the hole for the deadbolt, using a paddle bit.

11. Mortise for the deadbolt plate and fasten it securely in place.

12. Mortise and bore for the latch plate and fasten it in place.

13. Your final step is to install a new doorstop and paint it to match the rest of the door trim.

Invisible patching

In this and the following project, you may need to cover tracks left by old hardware. The best way to hide a cylinder hole is with diamond-shaped patches. Cut a patch from scrap wood for each side of the door. Pencil the outlines of the patches on the door; then chisel recesses. Bevel the sides of the recesses and the patches to ensure a snug fit. Glue the patches into the recesses and clamp for 24 hours. Fill any spaces, and when the filler is dry plane or sand the whole area smooth. Then give the entire door a coat of paint.

Installing a mortise lock

The heavy-duty mortise lock is one of the better security locks, chiefly because it is made of strong metal and rests within the actual door. Since it is fitted with a deadbolt and is not accessible from the outside, it is that much more effective. It is not difficult to install this type of lock. Just follow the manufacturer's instructions, which are basically similar to any other lock installation. The main concern will be cutting the mortise. For this operation it is best to take down the door.

Cutting a mortise

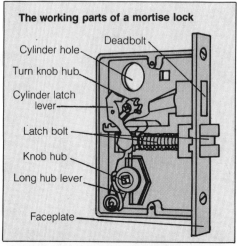

The working parts of a mortise lock

- Deadbolt
- Cylinder hole
- Turn knob hub
- Cylinder latch lever
- Latch bolt
- Knob hub
- Long hub lever
- Faceplate

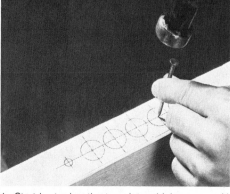

1. Start by taping the template which comes with the lock set to the edge of the door. With a sharp tool, such as an awl or nail, mark the centers of the areas to be drilled.

2. Drill on your center marks. The template will indicate how deep to go and what size bit to use.

3. When you have finished drilling, cut out the remainder of the mortise with a sharp chisel. Start by outlining the area to be removed with chisel cuts ⅛ inch deep. Then chisel out between the holes.

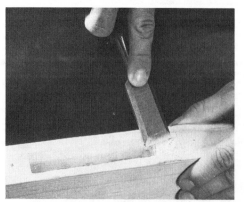

4. Chisel the ends and sides of the mortise so they agree precisely with the dimensions of the new lock. The cuts are for the ends of the faceplate, which will receive the screws to hold the lock to the door.

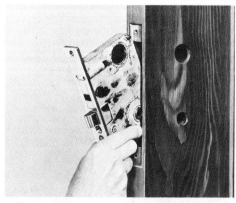

5. The mortise cut must be exactly centered, and the lock must fit snugly. Remove excess wood if necessary. Fasten the plate with screws and insert knobs and key cylinder.

Putting up a chain lock

One of the most popular extra security locks is the simple chain door guard. Although the chain door guard can be defeated by a knowledgeable burglar, it will offer pretty good protection against the more pedestrian crook.

Installation is simply a matter of positioning the device on the door and jamb in such a way that the door can open only slightly when the chain is latched, and the chain can be freed from the inside only.

Position the chain door guard with this in view; mark for screwholes. Predrill the holes with a hand drill; then insert screws.

There is also a new electronic door chain that can be put on when you *leave* your home. It has a battery-powered alarm.

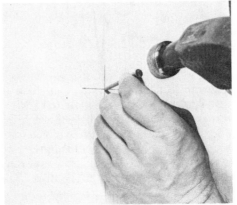

There are many styles of chain door guards, but the principle, as shown here, is simply to allow an opening for viewing and conversation, without permitting entry until the homeowner frees the chain.

What it takes

Approximate time: About twenty minutes.

Tools and materials: Screwdriver, hand drill, pencil, chain door guard, and screws.

A handy one-way viewer

A door peephole, or one-way viewer, is essential to the well-protected home. With this device you can observe any caller before you open the door.

Some peepholes are just a swinging cover over a hole in the door. A better version comes with lenses that give you a wide-angle view of what is outside. It is sensible to purchase the best-quality viewer even if it costs a little more. The difference between viewers is the range of vision they give you from the viewing side. Low-cost viewers have a limited range. One-way viewers are easy to install. All you do is drill a hole of the proper size, insert the viewer, and tighten it. Just make sure that the viewer is at the appropriate height.

1. Figuring the eye level of the shortest member of the household who is likely to be answering the door, mark a point on the door.

What it takes

Approximate time: About twenty minutes.

Tools and materials: Electric drill with ⅝-inch bit (for most viewers) or a keyhole saw; one-way peephole hardware.

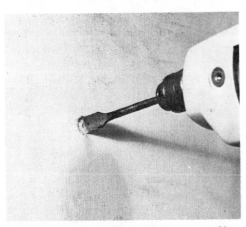

2. Depending on the type of viewer, you can either drill or saw a hole. If you drill, be sure to bore a small pilot hole and then drill from each side to prevent the door from splintering out. A better way is to clamp a piece of wood to each side of the door and bore through these.

3. Thread the two parts together, making certain that the proper viewing side is to the inside.

Installing a rim lock

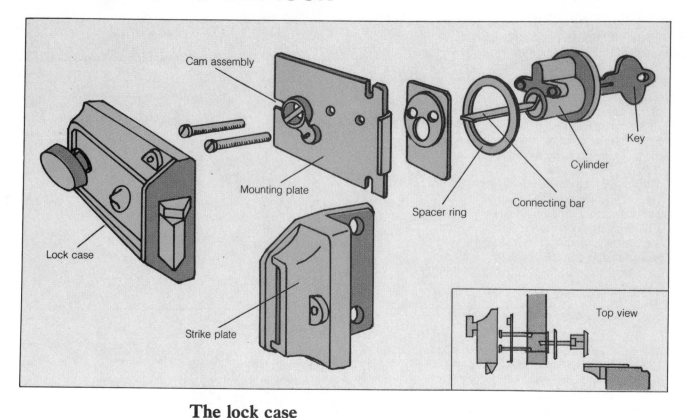

Cam assembly

Mounting plate

Lock case

Strike plate

Spacer ring

Connecting bar

Cylinder

Key

Top view

The lock case

The rim lock is the easiest door lock to install, since it is surface-mounted and requires drilling only one hole through the door. Make the hole at the height you want the lock to be. The manufacturer will specify the size of the hole and its correct distance from the edge of the door. The lock cylinder goes on the outside of the

door, and the connecting back-up plate on the inside. Secure the back-up plate with the bolts provided in the package, and fasten the lock in place with wood screws (also provided). This completes the installation of the larger portion of the lock; the strike plate is installed next on the door jamb opposite the lock.

The strike plate

With the door closed, mark the position that the strike plate must occupy to line up with the lock. Open the door. Position the strike plate in the marked area and trace its full outline with a pencil. Using a hammer and chisel, mortise (recess) the strike plate

so it falls flush with the inside of the door jamb and with the door trim. Secure the strike plate with the screws provided. Try the key to make certain there is no binding, and check to see that the strike plate is in exact relationship to the lock.

What it takes

Approximate time: A couple of hours.

Tools and materials: Electric drill and bits, hammer, screwdrivers (regular and Phillips head), wood chisel, combination square, and lock set.

TIP: Inexpensive locks have strike plates that need only to be mortised in the door jamb, while the more expensive locks need to be mortised in two places. If you're going to do this job at all, then pay a few dollars more and plan to spend a little longer on the installation. It's your security that's at stake.

Instant crime-stopper

A plain 2x4 with some sponge rubber or felt glued on one end and a metal T-bracket attached to the other end can prevent unwanted entry through a hall door.

Saw the 2x4 so it just reaches from the closed door to the wall facing it in the hallway. The felt on one end will prevent damage to the wall, while the metal T-bracket will prevent it slipping out from its purchase on the door. It's a good device for night-time when you're not so concerned about decor. Come the morning, stick it in the closet, out of sight.

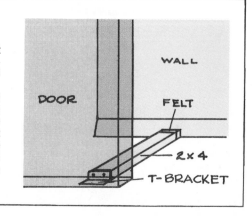

WALL

DOOR

FELT

2 x 4

T-BRACKET

Lock maintenance

One of the most important maintenance jobs with locks is to keep them properly lubricated—and too much lubrication is no better than too little. One of the best lubricants is powdered graphite. It is sold in tube form at most hardware stores. The tip is inserted into the lock and the tube squeezed a couple of times. Apply some graphite to the key while you're at it.

A light penetrating-oil lubricant can also be used. This type comes with a long, thin tube spout which can be placed in a keyhole for more exact servicing. Never use a heavy oil in the cylinder because it will gum up the tumblers. Lubricate the latch with light oil, wiping away the excess. If you wish to clean a mortise lock, wash it well in a grease solvent or paint thinner; then lubricate it.

Use a lock lubricant applicator with an insertable spout or tip. Go easy; be careful not to overlubricate.

When a key has broken off in the lock, try to retrieve the fragment first with tweezers, then with needle-nose pliers.

Lock problems

- **Broken key.** If the key has broken off in the lock, you may be able to take the broken piece out with tweezers or a pair of long, needle-nose pliers. Failing that, loosen the setscrew and unscrew the cylinder from the lock faceplate. Hold it face down and tap gently to dislodge the broken piece.
- **Stuck lock.** If the key fits into the lock but will not turn, use penetrating-oil lubricant around the key to try to loosen the lock, working the key gently to allow the oil to move around it. If this doesn't work, the cause of the problem may be that the cylinder has shifted in the lock faceplate, making it impossible for the cam to throw the bolt. Loosen the setscrew and turn the cylinder back to its correct position. A third possibility is that a wrong key has recently been used and has damaged the tumblers, in which case a new cylinder will be in order.
- **Stuck bolt.** When the key partially turns in the cylinder but the bolt does not move, check the door alignment to see if the bolt lines up with the strike plate. Depending on how far out of line it is, it may be necessary to realign the door on its hinges, change the location of the strike plate, or enlarge the bolt opening.
- **Frozen lock.** When the key will not enter the cylinder, chip away any ice that may be apparent, and then hold a heated key or lighted match to the cylinder entry. Turn the key gradually and with care to avoid damaging the tumblers.

Key control

It is essential that you maintain control of all the keys to your house. This means that you should know who has keys, and which ones they have. Moreover, other key holders should be instructed in key security. For instance, if a key is stolen, or simply lost, change the lock cylinder immediately. Keys left lying around offer too great a temptation; it takes only a moment to make an impression of a key and return it so that the owner will be none the wiser. For example, never keep your house key on the same ring with the key to your car; when left in a parking lot, it will offer a delightful opportunity to some unscrupulous person.

When you move into a new (or an older) house, there is always the possibility that extra keys are in the possession of others—the workmen, former owners, their relatives, or their friends. It is also not unlikely that master keys used by tradespeople and contractors are still around. It would be easy for any of these keys to fall into the hands of a burglar, professional or neophyte. So why encourage temptation?

It is a simple matter and a great convenience to have all your doors keyed alike. It is also possible to extend the range of the master key to include such areas as a hobby room, workshop, boat, or vacation cabin.

Automatic garage-door opener

Thanks to a push button inside your car, you will be able to open your overhead garage door as you approach your house and drive right into a lighted area. The lights will go on as the door opens. The door will also close automatically after you are inside. You will have avoided any prowlers who might have been lurking, and in the event of rain you'll keep dry. Installing an automatic garage-door opener is not generally considered a do-it-yourself project. Many retailers install the system for you. When shopping for your unit, check that it has an automatic return switch to reverse direction if the door encounters an obstacle, and a light-delay system which turns the lights off several minutes after you pull in. When you go away on a trip, remember to set the door so that it cannot be opened by remote control, but only by a switch inside the garage.

Changing locks

When it is possible, take off the lock which you want to replace and bring it to your hardware dealer or locksmith. If you don't wish to do that, take a photograph or make a sketch or two of the lock. At the same time collect the following information and give it to your locksmith or hardware dealer: door thickness, name of lock manufacturer, distance from edge of door to center line of lock, diameter of the lock mechanism hole, height and width of the faceplate.

Whenever you make changes in your security system, it is a good idea to check for any security provisions of the local building codes and ordinances. You should meet their requirements. It is also sensible to check with your insurance company's minimum standards for your home.

Lighting for security

Fence him out

Fences are very effective burglar deterrents. It isn't that a fence will stop the determined invader, but it will give him pause. He will note that you are telling him this is your place. He will see that you are not a careless homeowner. He will wonder whether the fence might impede his getaway. He will reason that if you take the trouble to put up a fence, then you will very likely take care of security inside your house, with good locks, alarms, and so forth. Yet, the fence must not be too high. Three feet is high enough. You want to make a difficulty for him, not offer him cover.

Another excellent homeowner ploy is a good hedge, especially if it includes thorn bushes.

What it takes

Approximate time: Under an hour per unit.

Tools and materials: Electric drill and bits, hammer, screwdriver, pliers, floodlight assembly, and a ladder.

A strong deterrent to burglars, prowlers, and undesirables in general is good exterior lighting. This may appear a rather droll statement in view of the fact that more than half of all burglaries take place in broad daylight. Yet thieves are naturally at an advantage in the dark. Moreover, lighting in and around your house can be helpful not only to your family's security but to their safety as well.

Outdoor illumination

The best lighting for a house that is centered on a lot and a bit removed from neighboring houses is a system which can cover the whole house with light. As a general rule, this type of lighting can be handled by a dozen or more floodlights mounted in clusters of two or three.

Floodlights are easy and also inexpensive to install. They are usually mounted on the eaves at the corners of the house. You can place additional lighting at ground level, and direct it toward the house if you wish. But it's a good idea to locate ground-level lights in planted areas where they are out of the way of general traffic.

If you cannot, or do not wish to illuminate the entire house, then at least make certain that the vulnerable areas are well lighted—for instance, the front and rear entrances, walks around the house, low windows, and the garage door.

It makes good sense to have most of your outdoor lighting controlled by one centrally located panel. This might be located in your bedroom as a matter of convenience. Entrance lighting—the one exception—can be handled by switches just inside the door. You can also have your exterior lights wired into any burglar alarm system so that when the alarm is tripped, lights suddenly flash on. The sudden wailing of the alarm plus the bright lights will rout even the most resolute marauder.

Plastic-covered cable makes underground wiring installations easier and less expensive than the older conduit wiring. It is also waterproof and will resist acids and alkali almost indefinitely.

Remember that all electrical installations must conform to local codes, so check before you start. If you should forget that, you also run the risk of voiding your insurance in the event of an electrically caused fire. Don't take a chance.

Eave lighting

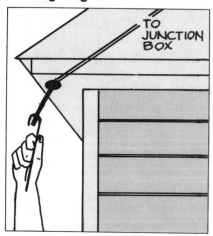

1. To install an eave light, drill a 1-inch hole in the soffit. Connect one end of the electrical cable to a grounded junction box inside the house; then pass the cable through the hole to the outside.

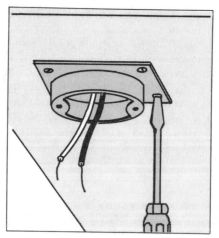

2. The outside end of the cable must now be secured with a locknut to a special outdoor box which is weatherproof. At least 4 inches of cable should be left hanging in order to connect the light fixtures.

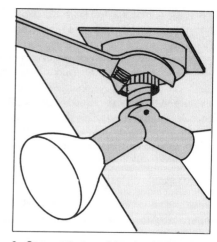

3. Connect the two white wires (cable wire to fixture wire) and the two black wires. Secure the fixture assembly with the hardware provided for that purpose.

Indoor lighting

The lights within your house can also be a line of defense against burglars. The point is to give the impression that your house is occupied, even when you are not there. One way you can do this is by setting an inexpensive timer to turn on certain lights and radios at times you have decided on. Experts say it pays to vary the routine of the lights you use and the hours of illumination. It will confuse possible intruders.

Burglar alarms

There are three basic types of electronic security systems in popular use: (1) self-contained alarms which cover a single door or window; (2) motion-sensing units that cover a single room; and (3) perimeter systems which have a central unit connected to each entry in the house.

Self-contained alarms are easy to install and inexpensive. They are generally battery operated and are attached to the inside of a window or door. Some types can be set when you lock up. The fly in the ointment is that they don't make very much noise. If you are at home, you will hear the alarm, but the next-door neighbors probably won't. The alarm might consist of a siren, horn, or bell, and it may well be enough to spook a nervous burglar. But because the alarm is right where the burglar is, he may figure out that you are not at home. All he has to do is execute an adroit snip with his pliers and the alarm will go off. Another problem with self-contained alarms: the larger your house, the more costly they will be, because each window and door requires a separate installation.

Motion-sensing units are usually set in a corner of the room and are plugged into the house current. The system works by sending ultrasonic waves across the room. If anything disturbs the waves, the unit senses it and triggers the alarm. The units are expensive and can only guard the room they are in; you may have to reconsider your financial involvement if you want total house protection. Moreover, nothing takes place until the burglar is actually within the premises. At the same time, pets or family members headed for a midnight snack can easily set off the alarm. This kind of alarm is generally best for a garage or outbuilding, though it is useful in the main house if you go away for days at a time.

The perimeter-alarm system is a sophisticated arrangement which not only announces unauthorized visits to your home, but it even can be connected via centralized control to sensors for smoke or fire (page 182). Most any homeowner will be capable of installing this system. Usually the units at each entry consist of two parts. One is attached to a fixed object, such as a door frame, and the other is on a movable object—in this case the door itself. When the door is shut, the two parts make contact. When it is opened, the circuit is broken. This will send a signal to the central control, and an alarm goes off.

An outside alarm is a useful addition to any system, for it will alert the neighbors to the situation at your house. Make sure the alarm is out of reach of the intruder.

A further deterrent is to show physical evidence that you have electronic security. Most manufacturers furnish stickers or decals, and these can be clearly posted.

A number of extra features can be worked in with your electronic system. You can add dialers that call the police or fire department and play a taped message. Or you can work out an arrangement with the neighbors so that an alarm will go off in their house when a burglar enters yours.

This is all very clever, yet your alarm system will never work unless you activate it when you want it on. Remember that if it uses batteries, you should check them and keep spares on hand.

Jimmy Valentine I was not!
I read that the best way to check my home security was to see how I would go about burglarizing the place myself. I found that the weak spot wasn't in my alarm system but in my neglecting to tell the police what I was up to.

Practical Pete

Installing your alarm system

The various components for alarm devices can be purchased from mail order houses, radio supply stores, and hardware stores. Some systems are available in complete kits. The units which are generally available include these components:

Panic buttons. Resembling regular doorbell buttons, they can be placed at strategic points such as front and back doors and in the master bedroom. When you press them the alarm is activated.

Magnetic contact switches. Installed on windows and doors, they sound an alarm when either is opened.

Sirens, bells, and screamers. These are the sound-shockers of the alarm system. Most experts go for the screamers, since the sirens tend to burn out, and bells don't have a great deal of effect.

Foil tape and foil block connectors. Apply these to windows to set off the alarm if a pane is broken.

Motion detectors. Monitoring the space in front of it with ultrasonic rays, the sensor in a small box sets off an alarm if anything in front of it moves.

Master control panel. The central unit around which an alarm system will be assembled, the master control can be hooked up with *heat sensors* (that trip the alarm when the temperature reaches 135 degrees Fahrenheit) and *smoke sensors*, both of which are excellent fire detectors.

Bear in mind that wherever you are, there will be a local electrical code with regulations that must be followed.

TIP: For the most effective system conceal all wiring. A burglar will be looking for any place where he can disconnect your security system.

Window burglar alarm

It's possible to run up a pretty stiff bill if you go all out for a sophisticated home-security system. This may include such items as ultrasonic motion detectors, window and door alarms, pressure-sensitive mats, and photoelectric beams. And unless you are an electronic whiz, you will need to engage the services of a professional to install it. Note: in some areas, it is possible to *rent* the more elaborate alarm systems.

In shopping for a system and in having it installed, you must exercise extreme care. Check out the company and the sales and service people before you commit yourself. It is no mere jest that today's salesman might be tomorrow's burglar. After all, who would know your security system better than the person who sold it to you?

Where to place the most protection

When designing your alarm system try to see where you need the most protection and where you need the least. Certainly, even the most simple alarm system would include the front door and any other exterior door. And of course ground floor windows should be protected, especially if they are concealed by shrubbery or are in the back.

Remember that no system offers absolute protection. The self-contained alarm is limited in not making a tremendous noise, but it is without question a discouraging factor in a good many cases. The master burglar, of course, will not be foiled by foil on your windows; he knows how that type of alarm works and he will cope accordingly. But how often is one visited by a master? More often than not it is the inept semipro, the crass amateur, the brute who seeks entry, and because of the lack of quality in his craft he will very often pass up anything that suggests a challenge and will move on to greener pastures. A simple burglar-alarm system like the one shown below is not difficult for the average do-it-yourselfer to install. In this system, a thin electrical wire is taped to a window in such a way that when the window is broken the tape breaks. An electrical circuit is thus broken, and this causes the alarm to sound.

Foil and wire devices

Burglarproofing a window begins by washing the interior glass with a solution of alcohol and water. The surface must be absolutely free of dirt, grease, and lint to insure proper adhesion of the foil. Do not use regular window-cleaner solutions; they leave a residue, and this will cause problems with your foil.

Use a straight-edged block of wood 3 inches wide as a guide for drawing lines around the border of the glass. Make the lines with tailor's chalk or a felt-tipped pen.

What it takes

Approximate time: About an hour for foiling and installing the foil connectors. The time for wiring the alarm circuit will vary with the job but will generally be less than an hour.

Tools and materials: Drill and bits, hammer, screwdriver, utility knife, block of wood or other straightedge, matchbook cover (for smoothing tape), foil tape, and connectors. (If you don't use connectors, then you will need a soldering gun and solder.)

1. Mark lines 3 inches in from the window edge on all four sides. Use a block of wood or other straightedge to guide your tailor's chalk or felt-tipped marker.

2. To make the right-angle turn, lift the tape up and then back down over itself, as shown in this sequence. Repeat for all 90-degree turns. To insure good contact at the turns, prick the foil with a pin four or five times.

3. It is important to bury the wiring—simply a matter of drilling holes so that it is out of sight and away from the hand of any burglar.

4. A finished window might look like this, with foil connectors on both upper and lower glass.

Run one edge of the wood block along the window frame as you scribe against the opposite edge with your marker. Make the marks on the outside of the glass, the side that will not have the foil. In that way you will be able to clean off the markings once you have completed your foiling.

The tape must be stretched as it is applied and must of course run in a continuous strip. You can smooth the tape as you go, using a matchbook cover. The corners should be right-angle turns. When you reach a corner, lay your tape back over itself at a 45-degree angle. Crease it at the bend with your fingernail, and fold again to complete the right-angle turn. The sticky side of the tape must of course face the glass at all times. Pierce the corner four or five times with a pin to insure proper contact.

Attach connector blocks to the window frame to join the taped portion of the circuit to the alarm wiring. The leads of the connector blocks can be attached to the foil by simply laying the contacts of the block beneath the foil. Alarms without connector blocks require a soldered connection.

Your final step will be to apply a coat of varnish to the tape. This not only protects the tape but is also an aid to severing it should the glass be broken.

Playing it safe

The best place for your valuables is of course the safe-deposit vault in your bank. Yet there are items you may want to keep at home—certain papers, for instance, which might clutter a small deposit box, or jewelry, which you don't want to have to withdraw from a bank each time you wear it to dinner. The best place for such things as these is in a safe at home.

Most heavy-duty safes will thwart the amateur burglar. They can be placed in any room in the house. You could even build your safe into a floor or wall. The bedroom is a good place to have a wall safe. There are many safes on the market, some of which resemble ordinary furniture such as bedside tables. Others look like light switches. When you buy a safe, make sure it is fireproof as well as burglarproof.

Outwitting the burglar

Though a good safe will stop most burglars, the real pros rejoice when they find a safe; it tells them where the valuables are, and they can usually break it open or haul it off with them. So if you have a safe, hide it just the same; and if you don't have a safe, you need a good hiding place all the more. Look around your house. Can you think of clever hiding places? Here are some:

A false closet ceiling is simple to make. Cut a piece of ¾-inch plywood the same size as the closet ceiling. Fasten containers for valuables to the tops of the walls. Then nail molding on two opposite walls a foot or two down from the actual ceiling. The plywood panel will rest on top of the molding but will slide out easily whenever you want to get at your valuables. Paint the panel so it matches the rest of the closet.

An acoustical-tile ceiling can provide a good hiding place. Remove a tile and restore it to place with a magnetic fastener or similar device which you can get at any hardware store. Be careful not to leave finger marks on the tile.

Hollow legs on a table or chair make good hiding places for small objects and are easy to create. Drill from the bottom and then cap *all* the legs with rubber tips.

Fireplace logs can also be hollowed out. This little trick is best done in a nonworking fireplace. Other good places might be the underside of a desk top, the linings of drapes, underneath insulation in the attic, inside a lamp, and so on. Avoid the obvious: mattresses, drawers, figurines on the mantelpiece, picture backs, and under carpets.

Money to burn
Last summer I figured a great hiding place for my extra cash was a drilled-out log in the fireplace. And it sure worked! Someone broke in while I was on vacation and didn't find my money. Trouble was, when it got to be cold weather again, I forgot and lighted a fire. Next time I hide something, I'll tell someone I can trust or write a note to myself for sure.
Practical Pete

Fire precautions

Fire exacts its greatest toll on the physically weak, the inexperienced, and those who become confused and panicky in a moment of crisis. The majority of fires happen between midnight and dawn, when most people are asleep, and so the danger is multiplied. Furthermore, there are more fires during cold weather than warm, which poses an added difficulty. It is estimated that once a fire actually breaks into flame a person will have about four minutes in which to escape before being overcome by noxious gases or superheated air. In many cases people who are sleeping do not awaken in time to escape smoke and gases—which reach them long before the flames.

Fire action plan. For greatest security, start this four-point program immediately:
1. Know the causes of fire.
2. Eliminate fire hazards.
3. Train your family how to react to fires.
4. Have an escape plan ready in case of fire.

Knowing and eliminating causes of fire

One of the major causes of fire is cooking. Grease fires can easily start while food is being fried, especially if the stove has not been kept clear. Pot holders, paper napkins and towels, curtains, and long hair worn loose can easily catch fire. Care of your clothing and the things you are handling—hot grease for instance—is essential when you are working in the kitchen, especially when alone.

Another prime cause of fire is heating appliances. Electric heaters in bedrooms and basement heating plants located near combustibles can be dangerous. If your furnace, for example, hasn't been properly serviced, it can give off sparks or flames which could catch on something and ignite.

Cigarette smoking is infamous as a fire hazard—especially smoking in bed. Fires frequently start, too, when someone empties an ashtray into a wastebasket just before going to bed. Electrical appliances are also a possible hazard. If you overload your circuit with appliances or if wiring is frayed, there is a risk of fire. Rags soaked with grease or paint can cause fire by spontaneous combustion. Flammable fluids, faulty chimneys, overloaded and unscreened fireplaces, and children playing with matches are other common causes.

Fire equipment

Fire-alarm systems can be tied into burglar-alarm systems or can operate on their own. It makes sense to get a two-in-one installation, but in any case, the fire alarm *must* sound differently than the alarm for burglary.

Detectors. The heat detector is a widely used sensor in fire-alarm systems today. It consists of a thermostat that trips an alarm when the temperature around it reaches about 135 degrees Fahrenheit. A heat detector is very useful but is best used in conjunction with a smoke detector, for smoke is usually detected sooner than heat.

The smoke detector is available in both electric and battery-operated models. An electric detector can of course operate only near an outlet, while a battery-operated detector can work anywhere, even during a power stoppage. Of course, you must always have fresh batteries on hand.

Some of the best detectors have an ionization chamber in which a current flow has been created. This flow is disrupted when

Security closet

Why not create a special closet for combustible materials, poisonous substances, and dangerous tools that you don't want children to play with? Put a good lock on the door and a heat detector inside to alert you to any danger of fire.

For maximum security, install a smoke detector outside each bedroom and at the top of stair wells, and heat detectors in other enclosed areas.

The guts of your alarm system—burglar and fire—will be your master panel. Label all wires clearly.

visible or invisible combustion particles enter the chamber. As a result, the alarm goes off.

The detector is battery operated and easy to install, requiring two screws, two mounting anchors, and less than 5 minutes work. With normal use, the battery will last over a year. Maintenance involves a monthly check and yearly vacuum cleaning.

If you mount the smoke detector on the ceiling, place it as close as possible to the center of the room. If your ceiling is sloped, gabled, or high peaked, the smoke detector must be mounted no more than 12 inches and no less than 6 inches from the highest point of the ceiling.

If the unit is wall mounted, it should be no closer than 6 inches and no farther than 12 inches from the ceiling. Check your local code, however, because in some areas wall mounting is not approved.

In any case, the detector must not be mounted in or near:
- The kitchen. Smoke from cooking might trigger the alarm inappropriately.
- The garage. When you start your car, combustion products are present and can set off the alarm.
- Bathrooms. Steam from a shower could set off an unwanted alarm.
- The very peak of an A-frame or gable type of ceiling.
- The front of forced-air ducts used for your house heating or air-conditioning.
- Unheated buildings. Smoke detectors are unreliable below 40 degrees Fahrenheit.

Extinguishers. It is wise to keep fire extinguishers at key points around your home. These are the weapons that will keep little fires from becoming conflagrations.

It is essential to know which type of extinguisher to use. Few people realize that extinguishers are rated according to the type of fire they can handle. According to the Underwriters' Laboratories (whose seal on an extinguisher guarantees that it meets certain minimum standards) there are four designations for fires:

A. Ordinary combustibles such as paper, cloth, wood.

B. Grease, oil, gasoline, and all other flammable chemicals.

C. Fires that involve electrical current.

D. Fires that involve combustible metals.

Although water can be used to put out a Class A fire, water may cause a Class B fire (grease) to explode. And if water is used on a Class C fire involving a live electrical line, it could prove fatal to the fire fighter. When you buy fire extinguishers look for the letter classification on them; the size will be indicated by number, with 2 being the smallest and 10 the largest. Fire extinguishers must be serviced at times stipulated by the manufacturer, usually twice a year, or they may lose their effectiveness.

Operation and deployment

Most fire extinguishers are easy to operate; usually it is only necessary to compress a squeeze valve. The commonest types of extinguishers are pressurized containers with carbon dioxide or dry powder charges. The former simply smother the fire by cutting off its supply of oxygen, while the latter work by spreading a powder which turns the heat into an inert gas. A third group, water extinguishers, are not recommended for the home because they are bulky, heavy, and for some people difficult to handle. Keep at least one Class B and one Class C extinguisher in or near the kitchen, and distribute others in other key areas throughout the house, such as bedrooms, the workshop, and the garage.

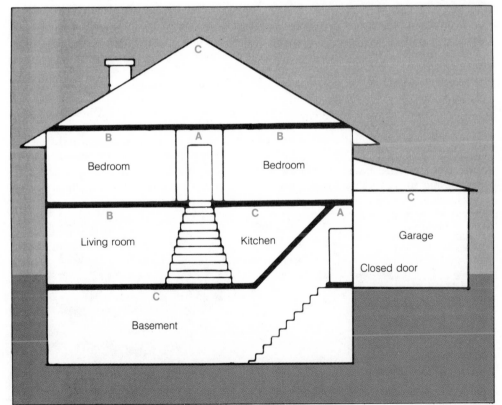

For basic protection at minimum expense, locate one detector in the hallway near each separate sleeping area. More complete protection calls for a detector on every level of your home. Shown here are locations in a typical two-story house. A: Smoke detectors for basic minimum protection. B: Smoke detectors for additional protection. C: Heat-activated detectors.

Lightning protection

Lightning is one of the most destructive forces in nature, and it poses a real threat to your home and family. It is an electric current with tremendous voltage and amperage. By way of comparison, ordinary house current is 110 to 240 volts, with 100 amperes available at the main service panel. One-tenth of an amp is enough to kill, should the current pass through the body, or to start a fire if there is a short in wiring. But a lightning bolt's amperage is 2,000 times greater than that of a typical house, and its voltage is in the millions.

Your house current consists of electric impulses which are continuous and which follow a controlled path of low-resistance wires. Lightning, on the other hand, is a tremendous, uncontrolled, instant surge of electric current that could lift a large ocean liner 6 feet in the air in a split second.

Lightning strikes trees, buildings or any other objects which consist of materials that are better electrical conductors than the air. Homes are among the most vulnerable targets because they usually stand out from the surrounding terrain, and their wiring and plumbing systems provide an ideal path to ground for an electrical charge. There are four ways lightning can strike:
1. By direct hit.
2. By following a power line or an ungrounded wire fence.
3. By flowing down the metal television attachments on a house after it has struck the antenna.
4. By leaping to a building after striking a tree to find a better path to the ground.

As a rule, lightning follows a metallic path to the ground, and sometimes even from the ground up. The bolt may leap from the metallic path to plumbing or wiring and so may cause fire or burn out electrical appliances.

A lightning-protection system should therefore offer an easy, direct path for the bolt to follow into the ground and thus prevent injury or damage while the bolt is traveling that path. Proper lightning protection should include the following:

Air terminals should be installed on the highest points of the roof and on all projections. These can be of copper or aluminum, at least 10 inches in height and no more than 20 feet apart. It is important that the terminals and their placement meet the requirements of the National Fire Protection Code and Underwriters' Laboratories. Chimneys should have separate terminals.

Main conductors are special cables made of heavy aluminum or copper that interconnect all the air terminals on the roof. In addition, there should be a minimum of two conductors on the ground.

Branch conductors connect into the main conductor system all antennas, gutters, plumbing stacks, water pipes, air conditioning, telephone grounds, and any other major metal units within 6 feet of the conductors. These lengths of cable are like those in main conductors, except smaller.

Lightning arresters are small devices mounted at the points of entry of overhead electrical service wires and also on television antennas. They connect to the system's grounding and provide protection against the smaller power surges produced by distant lightning strikes.

Grounding rods (at least two for small houses) should be placed at opposite corners of the house. Larger houses will need more than two grounds.

Special protection is also necessary for tall trees less than 10 feet from the house.

Lightning protection systems should be installed professionally; a faulty installation would be hazardous.

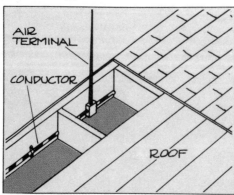

Air terminals are the only parts of a concealed lightning-protection system that are visible. They should be spaced a minimum of 20 feet apart along the ridges, and within 2 feet of the ridge ends.

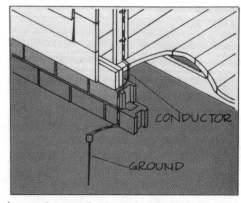

A ground connection is made through the base of the building wall. Your system should be inspected each year for loose or bent terminals, loose connecting clamps, and broken conductor cables.

Storm warnings

Whether you live in a high-wind area or just have to put up with an occasional hurricane or northeaster, you'll be wise to give some thought to storm problems before they arise. Glass may crack or shatter, shingles may blow off your roof, trees may fall dangerously. When the weather threatens, check storm warnings with your local weather bureau. If you are buying a house or planning to build in a high-wind area, inquire whether many trees have been blown down in earlier storms. Keep an eye on large trees—even healthy ones—that could damage the house if they ever fell. Cut them back as necessary.

Glass. In areas where wind is a chronic problem, local building codes set standards on the strength of glass that should be used. Depending on the prevailing wind velocity and also on the size of the window, plate glass, tempered glass, or double-strength glass will be designated. Storm doors and windows must also be glazed with either tempered glass or acrylic plastic. Be sure to check with your local code before you do any remodeling.

When a major storm is imminent, close shutters, board windows, or tape the inside of larger panes with an X along the full length of their diagonals. Even a light material like masking tape may give the glass the extra margin of strength it needs to resist cracking. Exception: When a tornado threatens, leave windows slightly ajar.

Shingles. To avoid having your shingles go like a deck of cards in the wind, check that they are adequately nailed or have proper adhesive. A lot of homeowners use self-sealing asphalt shingles in which short strips of adhesive are lined up to meet the underside of the shingle tabs in the strip above. The weight of the shingles together with the sun's heat, which softens the adhesive, produce a firm bond.

On a roof with shingles that are not the seal-down type, you can apply a little dab of roofing cement under each tab. This will give you good security in a storm. Again, check your local building code as to the best shingles for your area, how many nails should be used, and what sort of adhesive. The size and number of nails for each shingle strip are usually specified in the manufacturer's instructions. As a rule, this will be one nail on each end plus one above each slot. But in high-wind areas the Housing and Urban Development Department's minimum property standards specify six nails per strip. The nails should be large-headed roofing nails, a minimum of ¾

inch long, and galvanized. It is important to follow the requirements, not only to save your roof—but in the event of wind damage your insurance claim will be affected if you did not follow legal specifications.

Remember that structural damage can result from high winds which are less than the velocity of a tornado. Your house needs to be secured to its foundation by bolts or special steel anchors. The roof can be secured to the wall framing by special metal tie straps.

Tornadoes

A tornado is a violent, destructive windstorm of short duration. When a tornado hits a building, its winds rip and twist at the outside while the abrupt pressure reduction in the tornado's "eye" creates tremendous suction inside the structure, with the result that windows burst and walls crumble. When a tornado approaches, seek cover and stay low.

An ideal tornado shelter would be one that is constructed under the ground, outside your house yet near it. It must be far enough away so that if walls fall your shelter will not be affected. It's not a bad idea to dig your shelter into a small hill if there happens to be one; but the shelter should have no connection with the house gas or sewer pipes, drains, or cesspool. This is why the basement of the house isn't a good shelter.

The size of the shelter will of course depend on the number of people who would be using it. Figure on at least 10 square feet per person. Reinforced concrete is the best material, but split logs, hollow tile, brick, and cinder block can be used. The door must be hinged to open inward, and must be made of heavy material. The roof must of course be strongly reinforced and should slope so that water will drain off. The floor, too, should slope for drainage. And you will need a vertical ventilating shaft.

Equipment. Store a lantern, pick, shovel, crowbar, hammer, screwdriver, and pliers in the shelter; if your exit should get blocked you will have to dig your way out. Store canned food and bottled water.

Hurricanes

Though the force of hurricanes is not so concentrated as that of tornadoes, winds often exceed 100 miles an hour, and flooding is an added danger. In general, don't go out unless you have to, but seek high ground if flooding threatens, and follow instructions of civil defense personnel. Store drinking water, candles, and a radio.

I almost made it to the Land of Oz!
I figured I'd win first prize at my camera club contest if I could get a quick shot of that tornado before it really hit. But I forgot that you're supposed to get low and stay low. One minute the funnel was on the horizon, the next minute it passed right by me. The point is, you don't have as much time as you may imagine. Next thing I knew I was up a tree!

Practical Pete

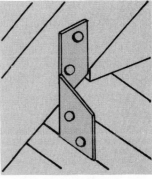

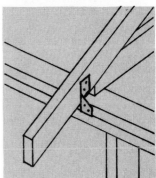

Metal tie straps for roof

7. PEST CONTROL

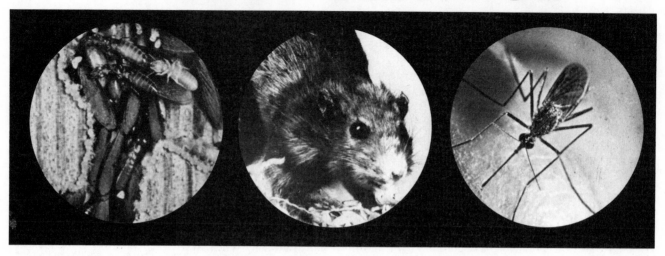

You are settled in your home, master or mistress of your castle, which is insulated, caulked, painted, weather-stripped, screened, storm-doored, locked and bolted, activated with temperature controls and alarms against fire or burglar; you feel secure in the knowledge that you can handle whatever exigency might arise.

But are you truly secure? What about those small, often hardly seen visitors who come singly or in armies wreaking damage, leaving fury in their wake; the ubiquitous cockroach, the insistent mosquito, the voracious termite, to mention but three of the more unpopular visitors? And let's not forget houseflies, squirrels, rats and mice, moths, snakes, birds, your neighbor's pets, lice and bedbugs, spiders, bats, and raccoons.

Some of these unwanted visitors are relatively harmless, but others, such as the termite, can be a severe annoyance, creating damage as well as anxiety.

Defense

Cockroach

Happily, the homeowner is not without recourse. At his disposal are means to cope with invaders from the animal world. The most useful step is to seal any potential point of entry. Put screening behind louvers, over roof ventilators, inside cupolas and other areas of ventilation where animals could enter, including crawl-space vents and flue liners on top of chimneys.

Check all screening on windows and doors. Seal any area that requires caulking, and fill in with mortar any openings in the foundation masonry. It goes without saying that all doors and windows in the house should fit snugly.

Moisture control is important in order to deter infestation by wood insects. These animals attack damp wood, especially around foundations and crawl spaces. Crawl spaces should be thoroughly vented, and you should position the vents to allow cross ventilation. Keep a check on dampness throughout the house (see pages 156-159), and keep all exposed wood painted.

Offense

Mosquito

Fly

There are over 86,000 varieties of insects in North America, and man's battle with these persistent creatures has been going on since the earliest days. Yet experts say that no insect is a pest in and of itself; it only becomes so when excess numbers get to be bothersome to their host. On the other hand, a single mosquito, carrying who-knows-what lethal payload in its warhead has more clout for the sleepless victim than an army of termites gorging on the house foundation. The damage may be less, but the emotional embroilment of the host still justifies the word "pest."

The solution to your insect problem lies at least partly in the correct choice of weapon. The insecticide you choose may do the job, or it may be the one from which a particular pest enjoys immunity. Your best bet is to call your county agricultural agent whenever you have any doubt about the potency of a given pesticide or what method would be most effective in a particular situation. The general guidelines that follow will solve most problems with any of the pesky pests.

Insecticides

The commonest pest killers are available as surface sprays, powders, and chemically treated strips. Surface, or residual sprays are applied by brush, aerosol bomb, or spray gun to surfaces where insects travel or breed. Surface spray liquid leaves a film that kills insects on contact up to several weeks after application.

Space sprays are dispensed in an aerosol bomb or spray can, and though they kill flying insects, they have little residual effect. Insecticide powders are dusted in feeding and breeding areas.

In handling any insecticide, it is most important to read the label for instructions on how often to use it, when to use it, in what strength to use it, and what to do if any of the compound should get in your eyes or mouth. Since the hazards of misuse are numerous and very real, look for special precautions on the label and keep the following general guidelines in mind:

1. Make sure that the product you are using is for the pest you are after.
2. Avoid contact with any pesticide, and do not inhale the fumes.
3. Keep the spray away from food, pets, dishes, cooking utensils, and children.
4. Do not smoke while using pesticides, and wash your hands before handling a cigarette afterwards.
5. Use only the amount required for the job. Overkill is dangerous.
6. Never spray near a flame, a furnace, lighted stove, or pilot light.
7. Do not reuse insecticide containers. Rinse and dispose of them. If there is leftover insecticide, leave it in the same container. Keep it well covered.
8. Never use residual insecticides where children will be playing.
9. Change your clothes after spraying, and store insecticides in a safe place.
10. As soon as you have used a space spray (bomb), leave the room; close the room tightly for at least a half hour, and then ventilate it.
11. Never hang a chemically treated strip in any room where people will be present for any length of time, especially sick or old people or infants.
12. When you dispose of insecticides make sure that they will not injure the environment. Never flush them down toilets, sewers, or drains.
13. If you should feel any ill effects after you have used an insecticide, contact your doctor immediately.

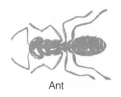

Ant

Wasp

Bedbug

The six least welcome visitors

The list of insect pests is long. The more notorious household invaders are described below, along with the key facts about their habits, habitat, appearance, and extermination methods.

The cockroach. He is tough, seasoned, and aggressive. Centuries of warfare have only honed his resistance to the onslaughts of determined householders. He is brown in color, ½ to 1 inch long, and nocturnal. He eats garbage, food, starch, and glue. He is immune to chlordane. Use a residual spray with malathion, ronnel, diazinon, lindane, or baygon. Spray wherever you think he and his fellows might hide. This means cracks, crevices, and areas around water pipes and the stove. Cleanliness is one of your major weapons. Get rid of any piles of newspapers and brown paper bags. Especially in apartment buildings, where cockroaches are free to hit and run, your attack must be relentless.

The ant. He lives in colonies. His trail is easy to follow. Interrupt it with residual dust (outdoors) or spray (indoors) containing lindane, malathion, diazinon, or baygon.

The bedbug. He feeds on blood—chiefly man's—and has an elongated beak which enables him to pierce the skin of his victim. He travels on clothing and luggage, on laundry, secondhand bedding, beds, and other furniture. The mature bedbug is brown and has no wings. His size depends upon the amount of food (blood) his body contains. A bedbug that has not fed is between ¼ and ⅜ inch long. Bedbugs feed mostly at night but will also eat during the day if the light is dim. They favor the hours when their victim is asleep. Bedbugs are found in seams, tufts, and folds of mattresses and crevices in the bedstead. Lindane, malathion, ronnel, and pyrethrum are effective against bedbugs. But many household sprays are not suitable for use on mattresses, so do not use any insecticide on a mattress unless the label states specifically that you may.

The mosquito. He is one of man's most redoubtable adversaries. Not only his bite but even his sound alone has driven generations of otherwise normal humans into massive retaliatory strikes with swatter, magazine, fist, and club. The mosquito grows from larvae deposited in stagnant water. His diet consists of animal and human blood. To cope indoors, spray in a closed room, keeping people and animals out for at least 30 minutes. Outdoors, see that all stagnant water is either drained or covered with a thin layer of oil. You can also spray your grounds with foggers, which are available at home centers and hardware stores.

The wasp. He is the B-29 of the flying insects. No one who has ever been stung by the wasp will ever forget it. Inside the house, squirt with a spray can which you can buy at any home center or hardware store. Act swiftly to level any nests. Use a freezing spray for this operation, and work at night when the inhabitants are not as lively as in the daytime.

The fly. He breeds in garbage, in food, in decaying organic matter, and he spreads a number of diseases injurious to man and animal. Screens are your initial line of defense. Kill flies indoors with spray or fumes from a chemically treated strip. Outdoors, make sure that you seal garbage in sanitary containers; spray inside the containers with residual pesticide.

Termite control

What it takes

Approximate time: Indeterminate. It depends on the extent of the job; but allow a minimum of one afternoon.

Tools and materials: Ice pick or other sharp instrument, shovel, power drill with masonry bit, garden hose, watering can or soil-injector tool, chlordane (liquid or cartridge), concrete patch mix, and caulking compound and gun.

Reproductive termite

Soldier termite

Worker termite

Tiny as he is, the termite is mighty enough to bring down a house. He is silent, virtually invisible, and does not advertise himself by biting people. Often his presence is realized only when the foundation of your house has reached a terminal stage.

Termites do about a half billion dollars in property damage every year. But because they work so unobtrusively, many people fail to acknowledge the need to cope with them. The only sensible approach is determined vigilance.

Extermination is not usually a project for the do-it-yourselfer; if you believe you have a problem, you'll be wise to consult a professional exterminator immediately. But whether you do your own exterminating or not, you should know what signs to look for, and what methods are best to stay ahead of the game.

There are dozens of different species of termites, but the most destructive is the subterranean termite. The termite is frequently called a white ant. But this is a misnomer; the termite's appearance differs considerably from that of the ant. The body of the termite is more or less equally thick along its entire length, unlike the ant's hourglass figure.

The termite lives on cellulose, which he obtains from rotting plant material, dead trees, and such wooden objects as furniture, house timbers, and fence posts. In colder areas, the subterranean termite can live for up to 10 months without cellulose.

Because the destruction caused by termites is not visible and takes place over a long period of time, it can be very thorough indeed. Termites believe in team work, large teams, and they eat just the inside portion of a piece of furniture or a timber, leaving a hollow shell. No opening ever appears on the surface, and nothing is known until the gutted member collapses.

Wherever the termite finds a source of wood in the soil he sets up a colony. The colony is comprised of three groups: reproductive termites, soldier termites, and worker termites. Each group has its function, as the names imply. The reproductive termites leave the nest to mate and start a new colony, the soldiers defend the colony against enemies, and the workers provide food for the colony. It is they who do the damage. Because the workers cannot tolerate exposure to light, they build tunnels from the ground up, to reach the new source of food. The width of one of these tunnels will be ¼ to ½ inch, while the length may be several feet.

What to look for

1. The termite mating season is spring through early summer. Look for large numbers of flying insects. They are seeking a place to start a new colony. Also watch for discarded wings. Look in crawl spaces, at basement window sills, and around the foundation of your house.
2. At any time of year, look for grayish mud tubes or tunnels that lead from the ground to wooden parts of your house. These are usually found on the foundation, on piers beneath the house, or on basement walls. Check around the openings where pipes enter the house. Seal the openings with caulking compound.

3. Wood trellises and fences that connect with the house are possible entries for termites, as are scrap lumber, firewood, and low wooden structures.
4. Check crawl spaces that have dirt floors, thresholds, wood stairs, paint that has blistered or peeled on a low wood structure.
5. Use a penknife, awl, ice pick, or other sharp-pointed instrument to probe any wood that may be suspicious to you. Try the underside of porches, window boxes, the lower steps in a basement. If the point of the instrument goes into the wood easily, with only hand pressure, to a depth of about ½ inch, it's a strong indication of trouble.

Preventive measures

The best way to deny termites access to your house is to install copper termite shields where the foundation meets the wood. The shields should extend 3 or 4 inches beyond each side of the masonry and should be anchored to the top of the foundation every 3 feet. These are best installed while a house is still under construction.

Another method of control (illustrated opposite) is to create a poisonous barrier around your home. The chemical chlordane is frequently used for this purpose. But chlordane must be used with great caution for it is also toxic to humans. It comes in concentrated form and must be diluted with water to produce the exact solution specified by the manufacturer's directions. Some states have certain restrictions in the use of chlordane, and so check with your county agricultural agent before you apply this chemical around the house.

You can use a watering can to pour the mixed chlordane. Remove the sprinkler head and pour the chemical into a shallow trench dug close to the foundation all the way around the building. Don't skip any areas, because termites are adept at finding gaps and so will still reach your house. The barrier will trap some of the colony; others will be unable to cross the barrier and so will look for other places to feed. Still others will carry the poison back to the colony.

You should also apply chlordane inside your house, around and into any visible cracks where a concrete floor joins a foundation wall, near the foundation wall of all crawl spaces, and in other areas that have a soil floor.

Remember that chlordane is poisonous, so ventilate when you use it indoors. After application leave the room right away, and close it off for several days.

Dig slanting trench outside and inside foundation walls. Pour chlordane solution carefully into trench.

Creating a termite barrier

Because chlordane can be harmful to humans if it is used carelessly, it is advisable that you follow these instructions as well as any others specified by the manufacturer.
1. Dig a slanting trench about 6 inches wide and 2 feet deep all the way around your house foundation. Do not dig below the footing.
2. Pour the diluted chlordane into the trench. Be sure you pour at the rate specified in the instructions.
3. Fill the trench and mix extra chlordane solution with the dirt.
4. Trench around all pillars that support any porch, and treat in the same way with the chlordane.
5. Treat the ground under all slabs such as patios, walks, garage floors, if they are near

foundation. The way to do this is to drill holes 6 inches out from the foundation and a foot apart. You'll need a power drill and masonry bit. Pour the chlordane into these holes at the suggested rate. Use a funnel. Then patch the holes with concrete.
6. Inside your house will be next. If your house is on a slab or the floor of the basement is concrete, then drill as you did for your garage floor or patio, and treat in the same way, using a funnel. Then patch the holes with concrete.
7. If you are working in a crawl space, trench inside along the foundation wall and, of course, around each pier.
Important: Any kitchen containers or utensils that you may use should be permanently retired from service.

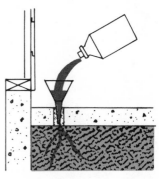

Pour chlordane into drilled holes in concrete slabs.

Soil injection

There is another method of exterminating termites that is much easier than the liquid chlordane method. You can shoot chlordane into the soil with an injector. No digging is necessary. The soil injector uses cartridges; it mixes the pesticide with water fed into it by a garden hose; the water forces the mixed chlordane into the soil. The injections are made inside the house as well as outside, in the same way as described above. The injector application costs more than the liquid method, but it is cleaner, easier, and less hazardous.

If you decide to call in a professional, be careful. Rates can vary widely. Do a lot of checking. Get several estimates on the job.

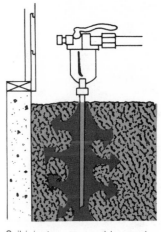

Soil injector, powered by garden hose, shoots chlordane into ground from surface.

Rodent control

When you hear "rodent" you immediately think rat or mouse, and it is these two rodents with which the homeowner is chiefly concerned. There are two ways to get rid of rats and mice in your house—with traps and with poisons.
Poisons are the most effective means. The problem is that they pose a danger to children and pets. (There is also a chance that a poisoned rodent could expire within the house and later produce an odor.) If it is possible, use poisons only where rats or mice can get them but children and pets cannot—for instance, under the house or in the attic. *Warfarin* and *red squill* will dispatch most rodents. But some rat com-

munities have developed defenses to certain poisons, so check with your county agricultural agent or local hardware dealer.
Traps can certainly catch rats and mice; but if you have a great many pests, there is the possibility that they will reproduce more quickly than you can catch them. Be sure that the traps you buy are for the particular type of rodent you are after.

Rat traps should be baited with strong-smelling cheese, raw or cooked meat, fish, or bread. Mouse traps should be baited with peanut butter, raw bacon, or cheese. At the same time, it is important to seal all cracks or openings where rodents may enter your house. Maintain a check.

8. SKYLIGHT

Strip skylight

Bubble skylight

For homeowners who are planning to convert attic space into living space, lighting is perhaps the single most vexing problem. For, unless major structural changes are envisioned that would provide additional windows, attic rooms tend to resemble dungeons. And yet, getting more light into the attic via a skylight is a task most homeowners can tackle by themselves. When it is realized that a skylight will brighten a room—even on a cloudy day— far more effectively than artificial lighting, the cost is surprisingly small. You can easily install a skylight by yourself—or, prefera-

bly, with a helper—in a day's work or less, even though it means cutting a hole in your roof. It is this last point that needlessly frightens a lot of people away. But that's foolish. Simply wait for a weather forecast of zero rain-probability—and have a tarp on hand just in case. Be sure to plan the entire project carefully in advance and have all the materials on hand when you begin. Of course, no two skylight installations will be exactly the same, but the following general procedures, along with your skylight manufacturer's detailed guidelines, should cover all the basic points.

General procedures

Planning hints:

The two simplest and commonest types of skylights are the plastic bubble and glass panels. The latter are often installed in series. Prefabricated bubbles may be set into a roof wherever a source of daylight is desired—work, play, or reading areas, or in a bathroom. The bubbles come preframed in a variety of shapes and sizes. Glass panels in series—also known as strip skylights—give even more daylight and create a studio effect. For best results, plan your skylight for the north or east slope of a roof. But make sure your attic is sufficiently ventilated, because a skylight can really heat up a room on a sunny day. Glass skylights are more apt to leak than plastic ones, so they must be especially well caulked at the joints. If they are not made from insulating glass, condensation can form on them and drip down a sloping ceiling. Double-plastic bubbles on the other hand, do not form condensation.

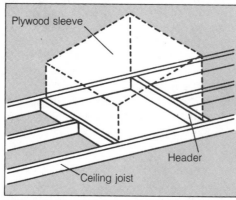

1. If your attic room has a finished ceiling with sealed space between ceiling joints and roof rafters, your first step will be to build a plywood sleeve to bridge the gap between the ceiling and the roof and to channel the light into the room. Most skylight panels span three rafters neatly, so you will have to cut a section from the center rafter and the center joist. The length of the section will be determined by the size of your skylight panel(s). Attach 2x4 headers at both ends of both cuts. Use ½-inch exterior plywood for sleeve, and slide into place as a unit.

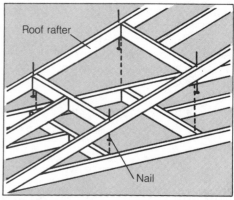

2. Whether or not you need to use a sleeve, as described in step 1, you will still have to position the skylight opening with reference to the rafters, and to install headers at opposite ends of any rafter cuts. In either case, plan your measurements carefully so the roof opening will be exactly the right size to receive the skylight panel. Then, still working from inside the attic, drive a long nail through the roof to mark each corner of the skylight.

3. Working on the roof, draw chalk lines connecting the protruding nail points to mark the size of the projected roof opening. But before cutting, double-check your measurements by setting the skylight panel in position to make sure it lines up properly with the chalk marks.

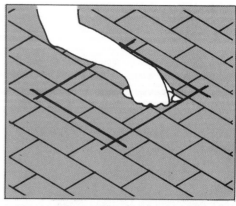

4. Use a linoleum knife or a roofing knife to cut the shingles along the chalk lines, and then remove all shingles within the rectangular area. The claw of a hammer can be used to tear up the shingles and roofing paper and to pull any roofing nails that lie on or near the cut line.

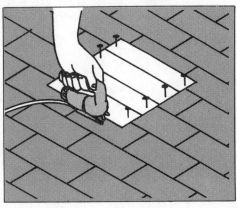

5. If your sheathing consists of a single piece of plywood, you'll have little trouble taking up the cutout as you complete the saw cut. But if you have board sheathing, drive a nail partway into both ends of each board you are about to remove. Then use the nail heads as handles to lift each cut piece and prevent it from falling into the house.

6. Cut through the sheathing boards or plywood with a saber saw. Assuming correct measurements, your saw blade will come out along the inside of the plywood sleeve (or rafter- and header-rimmed opening). But just to be sure, have a helper report to you on the progress of the saw blade within the attic.

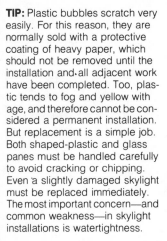

TIP: Plastic bubbles scratch very easily. For this reason, they are normally sold with a protective coating of heavy paper, which should not be removed until the installation and all adjacent work have been completed. Too, plastic tends to fog and yellow with age, and therefore cannot be considered a permanent installation. But replacement is a simple job. Both shaped-plastic and glass panes must be handled carefully to avoid cracking or chipping. Even a slightly damaged skylight must be replaced immediately. The most important concern—and common weakness—in skylight installations is watertightness.

7. Set the skylight panel in place over the opening. Note carefully the area of shingles that will have to be cut away at the top and sides to permit the base of the skylight panel to lie flat against the roof sheathing. But note also how much shingle matter must be left in place in order to overlap and seal off the flange on the bottom of the skylight.

8. After trimming away the excess, insert the skylight into place with the shingles resting above the flange along both sides and at the top. But for correct watersealing, the flange along the lower edge of the skylight must rest on top of the shingles.

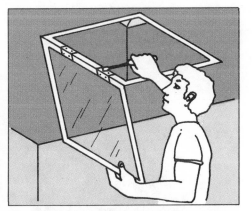

9. Seal the installation with a liberal coating of asphalt roofing cement, spreading it under the shingles at top and sides but under the flange at the bottom. Then secure the panel in place by nailing all around, through the shingles, flange, and sheathing. Finally, spread a second layer of cement all around the flange, taking particular care to cover the nail heads.

10. Many skylight installations are completed at the end of step 9. But with those that consist of both a roof and ceiling panel, install the ceiling panel last to forestall breakage due to falling debris. Clean both panels thoroughly and apply any finishing touches such as paint or trim to the area that will be enclosed. Then slip the ceiling panel inside the plywood sleeve or rafter opening, and fasten with screws or clips as provided by the manufacturer.

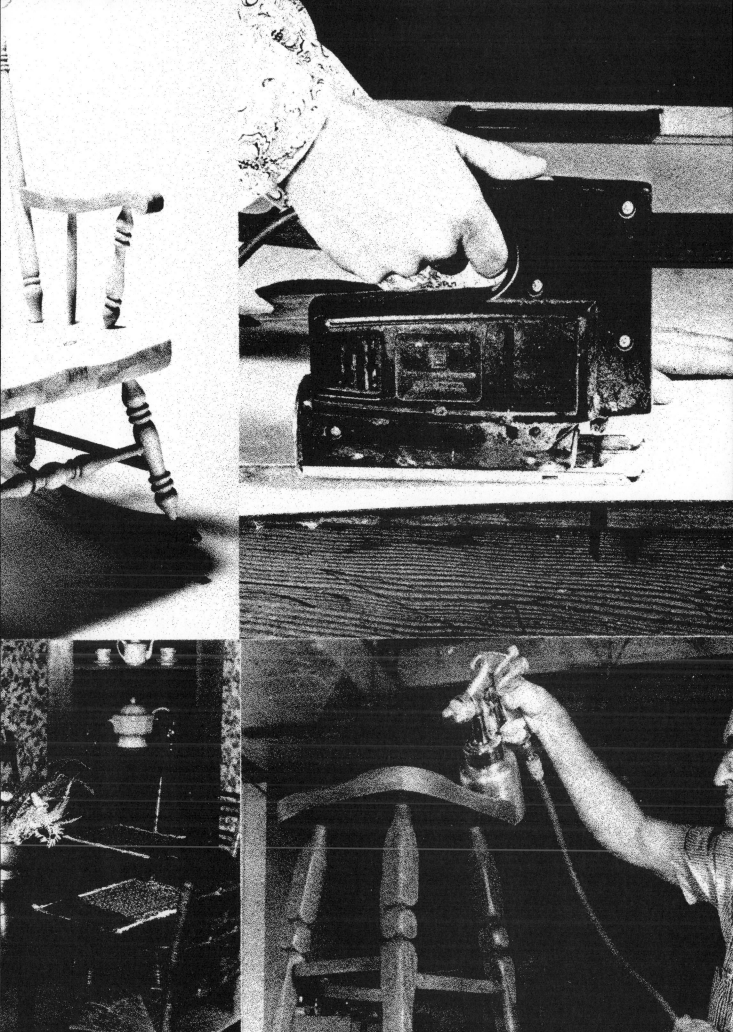

FURNITURE
CARE &
REFINISHING

Section Three

1. FURNITURE REPAIR 196
   Tooling up 197
   Clamps 198
   Tips on good clamping 199
   Chair repair 200
   Replacing dowels 200
   Tightening and regluing 201
   Broken legs 202
   Broken rungs 202
   Table repair 203
   Repairing curled or wrinkled veneer 204

   Casters and glides 205
   Drawer repair 206
   Replacing a drawer 207
   Slides and runners 207
   Screws and glues 208
   Pilot and clearance hole size for sinking screws 208
   Glues 209
   Concealing screw heads 210
   Making dowel plugs 211
   Patch repairing 212

   Replacing hardware 213
   Repairing appliance finishes 214
   Picture frame repair 215
   Repairing an ornate frame 216
   Gold leaf 217
   Installing plastic laminate 218
   Rushing 219
   Caning 220
   Hand caning step by step 220
   Replacing prewoven cane 221

2. SURFACE PREP 222
   Stripping 222
   Stripping procedures 223
   Cabinets and built-ins 224

   Windows 224
   Sanding 225
   Selecting the right abrasive 225
   Using sandpaper 227

   Sanding blocks 228
   Power sanding 228
   Final cleaning 229

3. BRUSHES 230
   Selecting a brush 230
   Cleaning 231

4. FIRST COATS 232
   A word about wood grain 232
   Planning hints 233
   Sealers 233

   How to cut shellac 233
   Spraying 234
   Wood filler 235
   Staining wood 236

   How to apply stains in general 237
   Particular types of stain 237

5. FINISHES 240
   Selecting the right finish 240
   A survey of common finishes 241
   Paste wax 242
   Shellac 242
   French polishing 244

   Penetrating resin 245
   Varnish 246
   Rubbed oil 248
   Lacquer 249
   Saving time with spray equipment 250
   Catalytics and polyurethane 252

   A synthetic substitute for varnish 252
   Paints and enamels 253
   Rubbing and polishing 254
   Tools and materials 255
   How to give your finish a good rubdown 255

6. SPECIALTY FINISHES 256
   A range of exotic effects 257
   Antiquing 258

   Gold drop 260
   Marbleizing 262

   Bleaching 264
   Rustproofing 266

7. CARE 268
   Identifying the finish 269
   Bad conditions and how to avoid them 270
   Dusting 270
   Cleaners and polishes 271
   Wax 272
   Quick reference chart for cleaning, polishing, and waxing care 272
   Filling scrapes and depressions 273
   Using wax sticks 274
   Using shellac sticks 274
   Filling cracks and gouges with wood dough 275
   How to make your own wood dough 275

   Repairing cigarette burn marks 275
   Removing stains 276
   New life for old finishes 278
   Using commercial refinishers 279
   Caring for upholstery 280
   Removing stains from upholstered fabrics 280
   Repairing the seat suspension 281

8. WOOD 282
   Storing wood 282
   Checkpoints for selecting the best stock 283

   How to order lumber 283
   Common furniture woods 284
   All about plywood 284

   Sources for furniture care and refinishing tools and materials 285

9. PICNIC TABLE 286

1. FURNITURE REPAIR

Fine furniture is something you can appreciate even more if you've ever found yourself repairing a broken chair, putting in a new drawer bottom, refinishing an antique dresser, or mending a broken picture frame. Furniture that has been well cared for, or restored to "like new" condition, really has an extra value, expecially to the person who has done the work.

The care and refinishing of furniture can be as simple as covering a scratch on your dining room table, or as extensive as stripping the finish off a bureau or rebuilding a chair. This section covers the basic areas of furniture care and refinishing. It is written for the beginner but deals with the same projects and problems that might be found in a professional furniture repair shop. You needn't be concerned if the piece you want to fix or refinish does not look exactly like the pieces of furniture pictured as examples for the how-to projects in this section. The important steps, materials, tools, and techniques covered on the pages ahead will help you solve just about any furniture problem you might encounter.

This chapter is on furniture repair. If you think of all the different kinds of furniture there are, from picture frames to refrigerators, it is easy to imagine the great number of repair jobs that might come up. Using different examples, this chapter covers the many general repair procedures you can use to restore your particular piece of furniture. Go slowly at first so you can enjoy the work. Good luck!

Tooling up

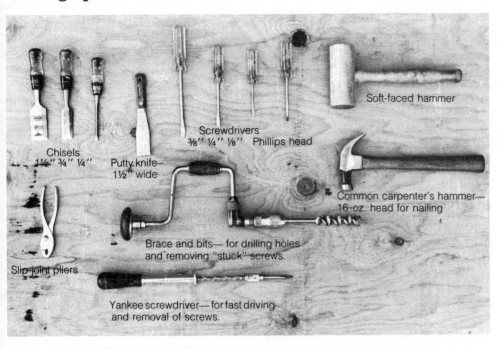

Chisels 1½'' ¾'' ¼''

Putty knife— 1½'' wide

Screwdrivers ⅜'' ¼'' ⅛'' Phillips head

Soft-faced hammer

Common carpenter's hammer— 16-oz. head for nailing

Brace and bits— for drilling holes and removing "stuck" screws.

Slip-joint pliers

Yankee screwdriver— for fast driving and removal of screws.

Any seasoned woodworker will tell you that there is no substitute for good tools, and if you are going to be doing many projects in furniture repair, you'll probably need most of the tools shown here. Special tools for particular jobs will be described in later chapters, as they are needed.

A good set of different-size screwdrivers is a real advantage, since it's important to match the head of the screwdriver to the screw slot when driving or removing screws. If the head is too large, you'll tear the wood around the screw; if too small, you won't have enough leverage and you'll probably end up damaging both screwdriver and screw head.

It is important to keep chisels, drill bits, and other cutting tools sharp, and store them so the cutting edges won't become nicked from banging into other tools. Dull tools are dangerous because of the extra force you must use to make them work.

An electric drill can be the most useful tool you own. With features like a reversing switch, variable speed control in the trigger, and sanding/grinding/buffing attachments, you can do much more than just drill holes. It's a worthwhile tool to have.

There are two different kinds of electric sanders. The belt sander is the more expensive type and is used mainly for rough work like removing finish and smoothing rough-cut lumber. For the finer sanding jobs more common to furniture repair, an orbital sander is your best bet. Both models use replaceable sandpaper which comes in a variety of coarseness grades.

Use your tools with care. Trying to force work with a tool that's not right for the job is just asking for trouble, so buy or borrow the proper equipment to avoid accidents and aggravation.

Power tools are a big help because they will usually do a job quicker, easier, and better than you could by hand, but they are far more dangerous than hand tools. If you are unfamiliar with the way your drill or sander works, read the operator's manual and get someone to instruct you. Take a scrap piece of material and practice before you try your tool out on a good piece of furniture. Make sure your power tool is grounded, and position the cord so it won't get in the way while you're working.

Unscheduled flights

My belt sander took off across the room when I plugged it in without checking the on-off switch. It didn't do any damage, but you might not be so lucky, so be sure to check those switches before you "turn on."

I also learned an easy way to keep track of the chuck key to my electric drill. I kept misplacing it until I attached it to the drill cord with some electrician's tape. It's a good idea to tape it down near the plug, so you *have* to pull it out of the socket before changing bits.

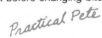

Orbital sander

Electric drill

Chuck key

Bits

Belt sander

Clamps

You can usually tell a professional cabinet or furniture maker by the number of clamps he owns. These tools come in an endless variety of sizes and shapes, and no craftsman ever really has a complete set, so don't be disturbed if your clamp collection seems small. A good basic set of clamps would include a band clamp, a pair of bar clamps (3 feet long), two 5-inch C-clamps, and two wooden hand screw clamps (12-inch jaw length). In general, though, it's a good idea to buy clamps as you need them. You'll be surprised how fast your collection will grow. For jobs that require many more clamps than you have, don't hesitate to borrow some from a friend. Clamping assignments are almost always short-term, and you can return them as soon as the glue dries. Clamps are indispensable tools that will last for years and years. Here are some of the main types and how they are used.

Wooden hand-screw clamps are the classics of woodworking clamps, and many of these fine tools have been around for several generations of woodworkers. The two jaws are smooth-grained hardwood, usually beech, with a finely threaded long metal screw through each end. A handle is fixed to one end of each screw, on opposite sides of the clamps. The clamps are loosened or tightened by turning these handles.

The quick way to open or close the jaws before attaching the clamp is to grasp one wooden handle in each hand and "flip-flop" them end over end. The jaws will remain parallel, which is important when clamping two flat pieces together. Otherwise you won't create an even clamping surface, and the material (usually called stock) may be damaged. The jaws can also be closed irregularly, to clamp tapered or oddly shaped pieces, by tightening or loosening one screw more than the other.

To maintain wooden screw clamps properly, wipe the wooden surfaces occasionally with linseed oil, and lubricate the metal screws with a light machine oil.

Bar and pipe clamps are the "long Toms" of the clamping line. They are available in lengths ranging from 2 to 6 feet and consist of a hardened-steel bar with two clamping feet attached. One of the feet moves up and down the bar and can be locked into position. The other foot is fixed at the end of the bar and has an additional, smaller screw-in foot for tighter adjusting. A similar set of clamping feet can be bought separately and attached to lengths of pipe, so you can buy your own pipe and make pipe clamps up to 20 feet long.

Bar or pipe clamps are most often used on large stock, such as chair bottoms and table tops. When doweling and gluing up wide pieces, always place at least two clamps on the bottom and two on the top. On sections longer than 4 or 5 feet, it's a good idea to use three clamps on each side. Watch carefully when tightening the clamps to make sure that all corners of the material ride down flat and secure against the clamps, so the surface will be flat with no warping or twisting. If the stock to be glued up is somewhat warped, you can often straighten it by clamping all four corners tightly against the bar of the bar clamp, using a number of small C-clamps.

Spring clamps work like large clothespins and are especially useful for quick clamping jobs where a great amount of pressure is not needed. They are available in different sizes, with maximum jaw openings ranging from 1 to 4 inches.

Stopgaps and copouts

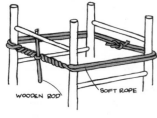

You can easily make your own band clamp (see opposite page) if you have a length of soft rope. Secure the rope so that it ties snugly around the item to be clamped; then simply slip a short stick or rod in the rope and turn like a tourniquet. It will exert a firm, even pull on the material.

Easy and inexpensive band clamps can also be made by cutting an old inner tube into strips. These large "rubber bands" can be stretched around the material to hold it securely.

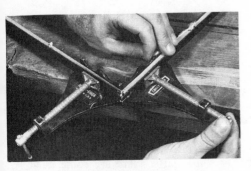

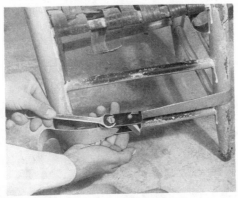

of clamps to operate, having only one screw with a clamping foot on its end. This screw is turned against a solid "anvil" foot on the opposite end of the C. Heavy-duty C-clamps are excellent for holding down large work, where extra pressure is needed, while tiny lightweight C-clamps are used for model-work and other delicate jobs.

Picture frame clamps are specialized clamps for bracing picture frames and similar rectangular constructions. There are several styles, but they all have adjustable clamps to accommodate different size frames, and a rigid form to brace the corners of the frame at 90 degrees.

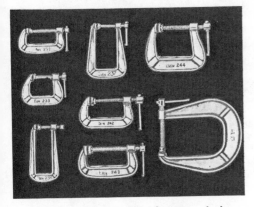

C-clamps come in many forms and sizes, but are all shaped like the C from which they get their name. They are the simplest

Band clamps are about the handiest types to have around. They can tackle many clamping jobs that would be impossible for any other kind of clamp. The clamp consists of a long band of nylon about 1½ inches wide and operates like a big belt, drawn tight around the material. Turning a rachet mechanism winds the band around a bolt, and tightens the loop to take up slack and provide the clamping force. Band clamps are great for clamping chair-leg/rung assemblies and bracing large boxes and oddly shaped containers.

Tips on good clamping

Regardless of what types of clamps you're using, there are several tips that make using them easier and more effective. Whenever possible:

Use small pieces of wood, leather, or hardboard between metal clamping feet and the material being clamped. These "clamping blocks" distribute pressure more evenly and cushion the stock from the abrasive metal parts.

Use a damp cloth to wipe excess glue off clamps and stock surfaces. Do this as soon as the material is clamped securely together, so that later sanding and smoothing will be easier, and clamps won't get clogged with glue. Always go slow when clamping materials and make sure you don't damage the pieces to be joined. Clamps are designed to exert tremendous pressure, and it can be extremely frustrating to break a delicate piece which took a great deal of time to fix or replace. When tightening clamps, don't distort the pieces by exerting excessive or uneven pressure.

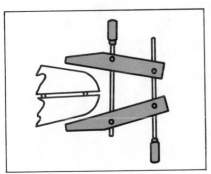

Wooden hand-screw clamps can be adjusted to fit irregularly shaped surfaces. Manipulate screws to open and shut jaws.

Keep the glue where it belongs—in the jar or in the joint. Use a damp cloth to wipe excess glue from stock and clamps as soon as clamps are secured.

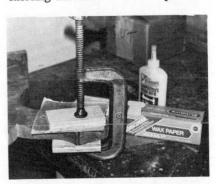

Use clamping blocks to distribute clamping pressure and protect the stock from metal clamping feet. Put wax paper between glue joints and clamps or clamping blocks so they don't become glued to the stock.

Chair repair

The most common repair job on a chair is tightening loose parts. Unlike dressers, chests, cabinets, and other furniture, a chair is a delicate system of rungs, legs, braces, and supports, all working together to support your weight, day after day. It's no wonder these parts gradually become loosened and require fixing. Chairs come in hundreds of sizes and styles, and chair repair may be as simple as replacing a glide on the bottom of a leg, or as complicated as total disassembly, regluing, and even replacing some parts. Here are some basic step-by-step guidelines.

Replacing dowels

1. Label each part before you start taking the chair apart. Remove all screws or bolts and keep them in a can or box. Then use a soft-face hammer to gently tap pieces apart. Be careful not to split the pieces, and note how they are joined together.

2. In this case a short length of dowel, used to fasten an arm to a leg, has splintered in two. The first step is to cut it off flush with the surface. Then scrape glue and old finish out of the joints. If the chair is to be refinished, now's the time to sand rough spots and mend or replace broken parts.

3. Dowels may be purchased in short lengths, with a spiral groove that allows the glue to seep down and bind it to the stock. You can also make your own dowels by cutting a length of solid dowel rod into custom-fitted pieces.

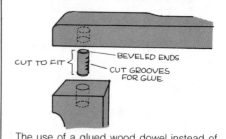

The use of a glued wood dowel instead of metal fasteners allows two pieces to be joined firmly, especially at a point of stress, without weakening either one by having to drill a hole completely through it or exposing the head of the fastener. The diameter of dowels used for this purpose is usually ⅜".

4. Sharpen the end of the dowel slightly, and shape it, if necessary, to allow a narrow space for glue. The fit should be firm, but not forced. Dowels can be shaped easily by hand, using a file or some sandpaper, and you can also use a length of solid dowel rod to replace a broken rung or spindle.

5. Use a sharp punch to mark the exact center of the old dowel in order to seat the drill bit correctly before you start to drill it out.

All the king's horses and all the king's men . . .

How about disassembling a chair and then not being able to figure out how it goes back together? I forgot to label the pieces before I took the thing apart, and ended up with a giant jigsaw puzzle. *Before* you begin disassembling the piece, just take a roll of masking tape and stick a number on each part, in some logical sequence, or write the name and location of each piece on the tape and stick it to that piece. It might also be a good idea to make a rough sketch of where everything goes.

Practical Pete

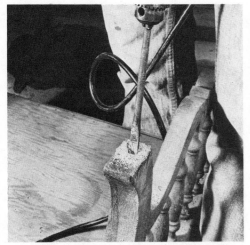

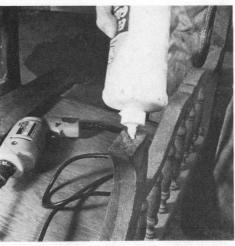

6. Drill out the old dowel, in both pieces if necessary, using a bit which is the same diameter as the old dowel. Go slowly and check frequently to be certain you are drilling exactly straight down.

7. Squeeze some glue into the dowel hole. "White" or "yellow" glue is the most commonly used glue among furniture repairmen, but refer to the chart on page 209 to determine which glue is best.

If you are going to be doing a lot of doweling jobs, or often have trouble drilling out holes that are exactly straight and centered, a doweling jig is a handy tool to have. You clamp it directly onto the stock over the point where you want to drill the hole, and it guides the bit in a straight and true line. Commercial doweling jigs can be adjusted for different diameter bits and different stock widths.

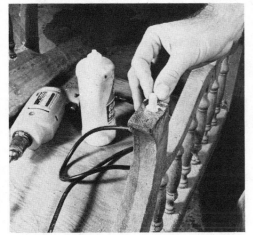

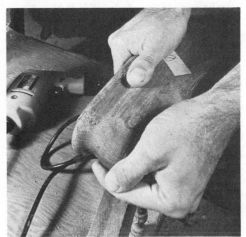

8. Insert the dowel into one piece, and smear a thin coat of glue on the surfaces around the holes, where the two pieces will join each other.

9. Fit the other piece on the dowel, press into place, and clamp the two pieces together, if possible, until the glue dries.

You can also make your own doweling jig in a few easy steps. Cut a thick piece of scrap wood into a square and locate the center on each face by drawing diagonals.

Tightening and regluing

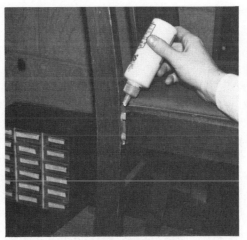

Check a chair for loose or missing screws before you decide to dismantle it. Sometimes a wobbly chair can be fixed simply by tightening these crucial screws, which are usually located under the seat, out of sight.

If joints are loose, but in good condition, and dowels are intact, you don't have to take the chair apart to cure unsteadiness. Pry pieces apart and smear surfaces of joint and dowel with glue. Press back together and clamp.

Then drill the guide hole straight through the middle, checking the reverse side to make sure the hole is centered. To use the jig, align the guide hole over the place you want to drill out and clamp the block firmly in place. The jig is only good for a bit the same size as the guide hole, but otherwise it should work just as well as a professional doweling jig.

Chisels

Wood chisels are specialized cutting tools used for shaping, carving, and trimming. They can be tapped with a hammer, or pushed by hand. In furniture repair work, chisels are used to shave away dried glue and to notch out an exact shape into which another piece or a hinge fits.

For fine shavings and extra control, work with the bevel of the chisel facing down. To remove large shavings, keep the bevel up, but be careful not to gouge the wood. Practice first on a scrap piece of hard or soft wood such as the furniture is made of.

Right

Cut with the grain running up and away from the chisel, so you shear off the tops of the fibers along the surface.

Wrong

If the grain is running back towards the chisel, the blade will follow the grain down into the wood uncontrollably, splitting off the fibers and leaving a rough, irregular surface.

Mortising a hinge

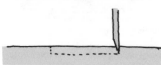

Use a sharp-pointed awl to trace the exact outline of the hinge.

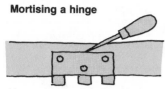

With the bevel facing in towards the mortise, chisel the outline of the hinge. Use a hammer to make the chisel cut straight down to a uniform depth, so the hinge will seat flush with the surface.

With the bevel facing down, remove the wood inside the mortise where the hinge will fit. Make sure the bottom of the slot is flat.

Broken legs

Chair legs stand up to plenty of strain, and sooner or later they are likely to become cracked or broken. If a chair leg breaks completely in two and cannot be glued along the break or joined with a length of dowel, you will have to take it to a professional cabinetmaker who can make a new one that is a perfect match of both the wood and pattern. However, if a piece has merely split off a sturdy block leg, you can glue on and shape a patch of the same wood to replace the lost piece. Here's how.

1. Use a chisel to smooth and flatten the surface of the leg where the piece has split off. Be sure the surface is flat so the glue bonds the patch piece securely to the leg.

2. Glue and clamp the patch in position. The piece is cut very roughly oversize to facilitate clamping. If the finished shape is at all intricate, or must match another leg, draw the exact shape on the patch block before gluing it. Use another leg as a template, if necessary.

3. After the glue has dried, saw off the excess material close to the line of the finished pattern.

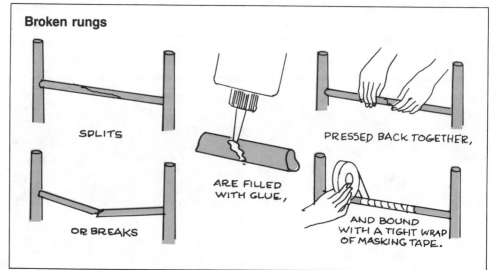

4. Do final shaping with a chisel, file, and sandpaper. Stain the new wood of the patch piece to match the color of the old wood. (Use a non-penetrating oil stain.)

Broken rungs

SPLITS

OR BREAKS

ARE FILLED WITH GLUE,

PRESSED BACK TOGETHER,

AND BOUND WITH A TIGHT WRAP OF MASKING TAPE.

Table repair

Although tables come in many different sizes and styles, they all share a few basic problems. Legs get wobbly, table tops become warped or cracked, and dowels holding drop leaves in place sometimes break or split. Tables which see a lot of use need to be refinished too (see pages 222-253). The structural repair procedures covered here apply to all tables. Be on the lookout for these trouble spots so you can fix them early. One wobbly leg can weaken the entire table by putting excess strain on other legs and joints. Hairline cracks can widen into splits, making major repairs or replacement of all or part of the top necessary, and small bows in the top can curl up into troublesome warps.

On most tables, the legs are not directly attached to the table top, but to a skirt which is screwed into the top. Remove the screws, glue the skirt together, glue it to the top, glue the legs in place and replace all the screws before the glue has dried.

Other tables have legs which screw into threaded metal hardware attached to the bottom of the table. Check the hardware to make sure it's screwed down tightly, then turn the legs to tighten them up.

The dowels which secure drop-in leaves to slide-out extension tables often splinter or break. Saw the dowel off flush with the surface and replace (as shown on page 200) with a dowel of the same diameter and length. Round off the protruding end so that it will mate smoothly with its matching hole.

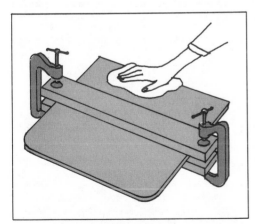

To fix a warped table top, wet the top thoroughly so you can bend it back straight again by clamping stiff boards to it. When it will clamp flat, glue and screw a brace underneath the table top, at right angles to the warp, and wait a week before removing clamps.

Use a mending plate to prevent cracks in table tops, dressers, or cabinets from widening. You can buy metal mending plates in different sizes at most hardware stores, or make your own from a piece of plywood. Glue and screw the plate across the crack at a 90-degree angle, on the unseen or unfinished side of the piece.

What it takes

Approximate time: Varies from several minutes to hours, depending on the job.

Tools and materials: Basic hand tools, glue, clamps, and hardware as needed.

Table types

Coffee tables are small, and often have shelves or drawers beneath their tops.

Drop-leaf tables have hinged leaves which can swing up for more table space. A hidden brace swings out to support the leaves from underneath.

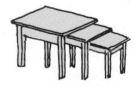

Nesting tables come in sets and can be stored neatly one under the other.

Extension tables can be made larger by sliding apart two permanent leaves and fitting one or more drop-in leaves between them.

Repairing curled or wrinkled veneer

Veneer

The hardwoods used in building fine antique furniture (oak, maple, cherry, walnut, rosewood, mahogany, and others) are today very expensive and difficult to obtain in great quantities. While the structural parts of furniture were usually made of solid hardwood, today plywood or softwoods can be covered by a layer of veneer to produce a less expensive table or dresser that appears to be solid hardwood. If you aren't sure a piece of furniture is veneer or not (it's easy to be fooled), look underneath the table, or behind the dresser, or inspect the inside edges of a drawer. If you spot the joints of thin layers of surface material, it's veneer.

Veneer comes in thicknesses ranging from 1/40-inch (the standard thickness of British veneers, which you can cut with a sharp knife) to 1/28-inch (which is the more common U.S. thickness, and sometimes requires a special veneer saw to cut a clean edge).

Veneers are usually not available at conventional lumber yards. They can be ordered by mail from the catalogs of specialty wood dealers (see list below). Veneers are stocked in a variety of lengths and widths, and are usually priced by the square foot, so be sure to specify the dimensions you want.

Sources

Minnesota Woodworker
Industrial Blvd.
Rogers, Minnesota 55374

Albert Constantine & Son Inc.
2050 Eastchester Road
Bronx, New York 10461

Craftsman Wood Service
2727 South Mary Street
Chicago, Illinois 60608

Homecraft Veneer
Box 3
Latrobe, Pennsylvania 15650

The surface veneer on old tables often comes loose and curls away from the solid top core. If they have been left out in the weather, for example, the wet veneer will separate from the solid core and dry curled, wrinkled, or blistered.

If the veneer is intact and otherwise unblemished it can be dampened to make it pliable and glued back into place. If pieces are missing and it is not worth replacing, you can remove the veneer entirely from the tabletop and refinish the surface of the solid core underneath it.

The old veneer can also be replaced with a new piece (this project is described in detail, page 218), but in a great many cases the simplest way to repair a curled veneer is to reglue it.

1. The veneer on old table tops sometimes curls away from the solid core around the edges and develops wrinkles or large blisters in the middle, but is otherwise unblemished.

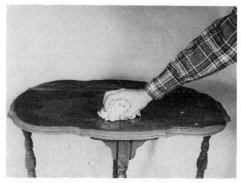

2. Wet down both sides of the exposed veneer thoroughly with water to soften it so it can bend easily without cracking or splitting apart.

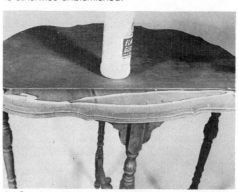

3. Carefully lift the curled portion away from the core as far as it will go without forcing it. Pour a generous amount of white glue onto the exposed core and spread it evenly, forcing it well back into the crack where the veneer is still joined to the core.

4. Make sure the veneer is flexible enough, wetting it again if necessary, and then clamp it down securely on the core. Use strips of wood as pressure blocks, and plenty of clamps. Use wax paper to protect the clamps from the glue that oozes out under pressure.

5. To flatten out a wrinkle or bubble in veneer, wet the raised section to make it flexible, then slit it down the middle with a sharp knife or razor blade.

Gluing veneer

When gluing one large flat surface to another, as is the case here, it's important to distribute clamping pressure as evenly as possible. Wood clamping strips can help to do this, along with as many clamps as you can muster. Glue spread over large surfaces also takes longer to set, so wait at least 24 hours before removing clamps.

Even with the most careful clamping techniques, you may end up with a bubble or two in the veneer, but if you have a glue injector, flattening these bubbles can be a simple job. This gadget is simply a hypodermic needle designed for "shooting" glue into tight places. White glue is too thick for the injector, so mix it with an equal amount of warm water before you load up.

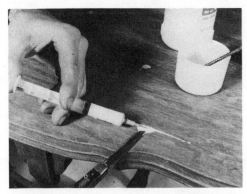

6. Pry up the flaps gently with the knife point and use the glue injector to shoot plenty of glue under the bubble.

7. Lay a piece of waxed paper over the glued area and clamp it flat. If it is a long wrinkle, you can lay a long piece of stiff, flat stock along the slit and clamp that down in three or four places.

8. When the glue has set, use a sharp chisel to scrape off any glue that has oozed out between the flaps and dried on the surface.

9. Lightly sand the repaired and scraped area. Apply a matching surface finish where you have sanded, feathering the new finish into the old.

Casters and glides

Casters and glides are used on furniture that must be moved around a lot, or on especially heavy furniture that is just plain hard to move. Glides are quite a bit less expensive than casters and are best suited for lighter furniture. You can also use glides on heavy pieces if the furniture will be in a room with wall-to-wall carpeting, since the glide will be able to slide easily on the carpet. Casters work better than glides on bare floors or on large furniture that you would rather roll than slide.

Rubber cushion glides are used on small furniture like chairs and coffee tables. They come in different sizes, with either a nail-in shaft as shown, or a socket shaft.

Hollow shaft glides are used mainly on more modern furniture with tapered legs and are available in different sizes and a variety of finishes.

Adjustable glides come in many styles but are all specially designed for use where leveling is a problem due to slanting floors or uneven legs.

Swivel casters are used on heavy furniture that must be moved around a lot. The wheel swivels on a plate that screws into the leg or base.

Socket casters are among the most commonly used casters and come in many sizes for use on all types of furniture.

Ball casters are available with a screw-in or socket mount and can be used in place of socket casters.

Fixing a loose socket caster
Socket casters often work loose because the hole in the table or chair leg becomes enlarged so that the stem of the caster no longer fits the socket snugly.

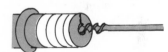

If the leg has split, force glue between the cracks and wrap masking tape tightly around the leg to force the split closed. Then drill out the socket.

Use a dowel the same size as the hole you have just drilled to plug the socket. Put plenty of glue on the dowel and in the hole.

When glue has dried, cut dowel flush and make a new socket hole. Match the size of the drill bit to the diameter of the caster stem so the fit is snug but not forced.

Drawer repair

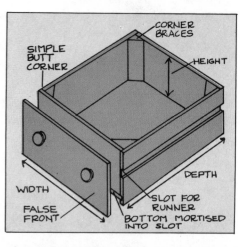

Anatomy of a drawer

The bottoms of wooden drawers usually fit into grooves cut in the sides. They shouldn't be nailed or glued but must float so the wood can expand or contract with changes in humidity, without warping the drawer out of its proper rectangular shape. Drawer bottoms are usually made of thin hardboard or plywood and are easy to replace.

Slides or runners are built into drawers to keep them in place and make it easy to pull them in and out. There are several different slide-and-runner assemblies (see page 207).

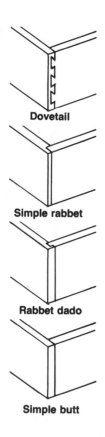

Dovetail

Simple rabbet

Rabbet dado

Simple butt

Corner joints are crucial points on most drawers. Strain from sides, back, and bottom meets at the corner. It is important for the joint to be strong so it remains perfectly square. The dovetail is the most complicated, and strongest, while the simple butt joint is the weakest.

Nothing is more irritating than a stuck drawer—or one whose bottom falls out or separates from the back so things fall through it—or one you have to fiddle with every time you close it because the joints have loosened and it keeps trying to be a trapezoid instead of a rectangle. It will be a lot easier to repair this type of problem if you tackle it the first time you notice it, rather than wait until something breaks or falls apart.

If a drawer snags or sticks when you slide it, some nails may have loosened and may be dragging against the sides or bottom. Remove the drawer and examine it for bulging sides or a bottom that has split, warped, or shrunk. Check the runners; they may simply be out of place. If they are broken or worn from use, they must be replaced. Corner joints on old drawers often pull apart, weakening the drawer and causing it to bind when you put stress on it by closing it. This can be corrected by regluing and clamping.

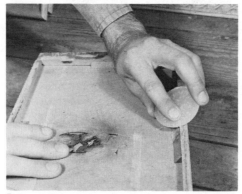

Rub paraffin or wax on the drawer runners to make them slide easily. This may be all that's needed to stop your drawer from sticking.

When the drawer has swollen or paint has built up on the front edges so it fits too tightly, trim down the edges with a plane where the wear-marks show. Unusually wet weather makes wood swell and can cause normally smooth drawers to stick. Dry weather shrinks the wood, so don't trim off more than you need to.

Brace weak corner joints with blocks of wood. Glue and clamp the blocks in place while fitting a try square into the inside corners to make sure they are perfectly square. The block used here is cut from a length of "quarter-round" stock. Since the exposed edge is rounded, you needn't worry about splinters to snag clothing.

Most bottoms fit into a groove cut in the sides and can be slid out and replaced easily. Drawer bottoms constructed in this way should not be nailed or glued in place and should not fit too tightly; there must be room for expansion and contraction due to changes in the weather.

Replacing a drawer

You don't have to be a master craftsman to replace a missing drawer. The tools you'll need are: a folding rule or tape measure, a crosscut saw, a small box of 1¼-inch finishing nails, a hammer, a try square, and some sandpaper. Plywood is your best bet for simple drawer construction, since it won't split, warp, shrink, or swell as easily as solid wood. A false front of the same thickness, style, and type of wood as the other fronts will hide the plywood construction from view.

1. Measure depth, height, and width of drawer. Then cut sides, front, and back to ⅛ inch less than dimensions for drawer opening and depth.

2. Make sure you've allowed for the width of the lumber when cutting pieces to size; then glue and nail back, front, and sides together.

3. As soon as pieces are nailed together, square up the box, using a try square and diagonal brace as shown. Nail down one side of the brace, hold corner true with try square, and nail down the other end of the brace. Measure and cut the bottom panel, and remove the brace after the glue has set.

4. Glue in triangular bottom braces for added strength at corners. These braces not only help keep the drawer square, but act as supports for the bottom panel as well. An option is to eliminate the braces and simply nail bottom in place, but be sure to seal the wood to minimize swelling and shrinking due to moisture and temperature changes.

5. With bottom in place, check the fit of the drawer and eliminate tight spots by sanding. Smooth down the wood in preparation for staining, sealing, or painting. The drawer is now ready for its false front. You can make your own, matching the thickness, style, and wood type to that of the original fronts, or have a cabinetmaker or millwork shop do it.

Slides and runners

No matter what type of slide assembly your drawer has, it's pretty easy to tell when something is wrong: the drawer sticks and doesn't work smoothly. If you find yourself forcing a drawer, take a minute to remove it and examine the slide and runner assembly. If it's an older desk or dresser with wooden runners, chances are one or more of the runners should be replaced. Check the sliding surfaces for smoothness and fit; most wood-to-wood slides will eventually wear down, but fortunately the three commonest types (shown at right) are simple in design and easy to fix or replace.

There are also a number of modern slide assemblies which work more smoothly than wooden slides and will last indefinitely with little or no maintenance. The ball bearings or plastic runners in these slides reduce friction to a minimum, so you might consider replacing the wooden slides and runners in your favorite drawer with some modern hardware, if you really want smooth sliding. These assemblies are available at most hardware stores, and come with installation instructions.

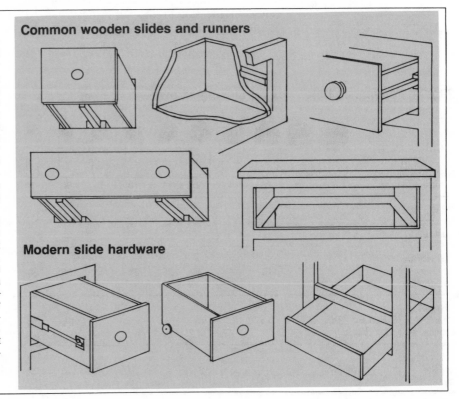

Common wooden slides and runners

Modern slide hardware

Screws and glues

Screws and glues are the basic fasteners in furniture construction and repair. While glue is used to make a permanent bond, screws can be removed easily, allowing for disassembly. Screws and glue are often used together because the screws can pull the stock together with great force, eliminating the need for clamps.

Before driving a screw, it's a good idea to predrill the screw hole, using one bit for the threaded section of the screw and a larger bit for the shank (diagram at right). This helps prevent splitting the stock and makes driving the screw much easier, especially in hardwoods. The pilot hole should go as deep as the length of the screw and should be just narrow enough to allow the threads of the screw to bite into the wood. (If the screw turns without any resistance at all, the pilot hole is too large.) The shank clearance hole should allow the unthreaded part of the screw an unforced fit and should go only as deep as the length of the shank. The chart below will help you select the right size bit for both pilot and shank clearance holes.

To determine what length of screw to use, remember that at least two-thirds of the total screw length should extend into the base material to which you are fastening. Driving screws into new holes can be made easier by waxing or oiling the threads. The blade or tip of the screwdriver should fit the slot in the screw head as exactly as possible.

Types of screw heads

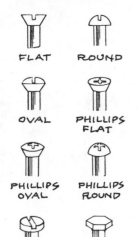

FLAT　ROUND

OVAL　PHILLIPS FLAT

PHILLIPS OVAL　PHILLIPS ROUND

PAN　LAG

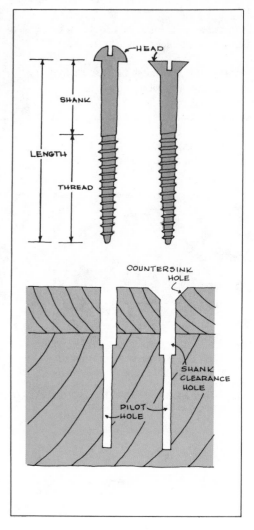

Pilot and clearance hole sizes for sinking screws

SHANK SIZES & DIAMETER NUMBERS (actual size)	20	18	16	14	12	11	10	9	8	7	6	5	4	3	2	1
PILOT HOLE Closest size twist drill	$7/32$	$13/64$	$3/16$	$3/16$	$5/32$	$1/8$	$1/8$	$7/64$	$3/32$	$3/32$	$3/32$	$5/64$	$1/16$	$1/16$	$1/32$	$1/32$
Drill number or letter designation	3	6	10	14	25	29	31	33	35	39	44	47	51	53	54	57
SHANK CLEARANCE HOLE Closest size twist drill	$21/64$	$5/16$	$5/16$	$1/4$	$7/32$	$13/64$	$3/16$	$3/16$	$11/64$	$5/32$	$9/64$	$1/8$	$7/64$	$7/64$	$3/32$	$5/64$
Drill number or letter designation	P	N	I	D	2	4	10	14	18	22	27	30	32	37	42	47

Glues

NAME & DESCRIPTION	ADVANTAGES & SUGGESTED USES	DISADVANTAGES	PREPARATION & APPLICATION	SETTING	CURING
				TIME IN HOURS	
Polyvinyl acetate (PVA). Familiar white glue; usually comes in a clear plastic squeeze bottle. Water soluble.	Inexpensive, easily obtainable, dries clear, sets quickly, ready for use; *for interior use on porous surfaces,* especially wood-to-wood joints.	Limited shelf life, poor moisture resistance, discolors metal; not for exterior use.	No mixing; apply generously to both surfaces and clamp firmly. Wipe away excess glue with a damp rag.	3-4	24
Aliphatic resin. Yellow glue similar to PVA glues. Comes in clear plastic squeeze bottles. Water soluble.	Same as PVA glues but especially made for *wood.* Makes a stronger joint on *furniture* glue jobs and is a little more water resistant.	Limited shelf life, poor moisture resistance, discolors metal, not for exterior use.	Same as PVA glues.	3-4	24
Plastic resin. A powder glue that comes in cans. Clean off with warm water before hardening.	High strength and water resistance, unlimited shelf life, less expensive than resorcinol and epoxy. Excellent for *furniture and cabinet-work* where joints are close fitting and no filling is required. The best glue to use on *oily woods like teak and rosewood.*	Requires mixing and long clamping periods. Joints must be tight.	Mix powder with water until glue has a thick, creamy consistency; spread on both surfaces and clamp well.	6-10	24
Hot melt glue. Comes in cartridges and is used with a glue gun. Must be heated to remove.	Excellent for *quick repairs and sealing jobs.* Sets very quickly and can bond a variety of materials. Good moisture resistance.	High initial cost, limited availability of glue cartridges. No bonding advantage over resorcinol glues.	Follow special instructions accompanying glue gun.	8 minutes	2
Contact cement. A specialized glue that comes in glass bottles or metal containers, usually with a brush applicator in the cap. Clean off with lacquer thinner.	Bonds on contact, reaching 50-75% of its adhesive strength immediately; flexible, high resistance. Used specifically for covering surfaces with *veneer linoleum, plastic, and other laminates.*	Expensive, extremely flammable, dangerous or irritating fumes; immediate adhesion makes it impossible to reset laminate once the materials touch. Not good for joints or as a filler.	Coat both surfaces with a brush or roller, allow to sit until tacky to touch, then align pieces and join them. No clamping necessary.	on contact	24-48
Resorcinol. A resin glue that comes in two cans, one liquid and one powder, which are mixed together to make the glue. Clean off with cool water before the glue hardens.	Completely waterproof, high strength glue for *exterior wood-to-wood joints.*	Expensive, complicated mixing, dark glue line.	Mix only amount needed, just before use. Heat hastens setting considerably.	6-10	24
Epoxy. A relatively new type of adhesive that comes in two parts: a resin and a hardener. Sold in cans or tubes, and is available in a variety of types. Clean with acetone. Very difficult to remove once it hardens.	Waterproof and oil-resistant, can be used on a wide variety of materials, both porous and nonporous. Very *good for bonding dissimilar materials:* glass and wood, metal and concrete, etc.; *can be used as a filler.* Interior or exterior use.	Expensive, complicated to mix, gives no advantage over aliphatic resin or resorcinol glues on wood-to-wood joints. Epoxies are best suited for small repairs, not large gluing jobs. Smells bad when mixing.	Combine hardener and resin together in homogeneous mix, using only as much as needed. Clamping is unnecessary. Use a discardable applicator.	¼-12	24

The main types of glue used to build and repair furniture are described in the chart above. *Setting time* is the time it takes the glue to dry and bond the materials together. After it sets, glue *cures*, and maximum bond strength is achieved. When choosing an adhesive, consider the conditions under which the particular piece of furniture will be used. Resistance to moisture is usually an important factor. Cost and ease of preparation, application, and cleanup will also determine your choice of glue.

Follow the directions on the glue container. Special instructions pertaining to mixing, application technique, proper setting temperature and time, clamping, and cleanup differ from brand to brand.

TIP: Here are two rules you can apply to all glue jobs:
1. Clean all surfaces to be glued; oil, dirt, grease and wax are all enemies of good adhesion.
2. Don't just bead glue onto the surface; work it in with a finger or improvise a spreading tool to make sure the entire glue joint is coated.

Concealing screw heads

Fine furniture is assembled with screws, rather than nails, to give it strength and durability. While screws are structurally important, the heads are usually hidden, either for aesthetic reasons or because they have sharp edges which can catch on fabrics and fingers. Therefore, screws must be set flush with, or recessed below, the exposed surface of the wood by countersinking (screwing the head into a shallow depression in the surface of the wood) or counterboring (drilling a cylindrical hole the same diameter as the head partway into the wood, then driving the screw down into the hole).

There are several methods of concealing screw heads. These include laying a sheet of veneer over the entire surface, covering screws and all; filling in screwholes with wood putty; or even covering heads with decorative metal caps and letting them show. But the most popular method among furniture craftsmen is to counterbore the screw hole and fill the area above the screw head with a furniture plug or a short piece of dowel.

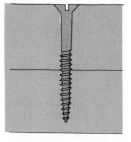

Counterbored screw

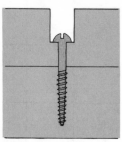

Countersunk screw

1. The most common method of concealing a screw is to counterbore the screw hole, drive the screw into the hole, and cover it with a dowel plug.

2. Match the width of the screwdriver tip to the head of the screw, and drive screw straight down so you don't mar the surface around the hole.

3. Smear some glue on the dowel, put some in the hole, and tap the dowel in place. The dowel should seat against the screw and protrude slightly above the surface.

4. When the glue has dried, cut off the protruding dowel with a coping saw just above the surface so you don't cut into the surrounding wood.

5. Sand the dowel plug down until it is level with the surface. Sanding strokes should be parallel with the grain of the surrounding surface.

6. The piece is now ready for finishing. The end grain of the dowel will absorb more stain or other tinted finish and show up as a darker spot.

Making dowel plugs

To conceal screw holes, you can either buy a length of dowel rod and cut off short pieces to fit the counterbore holes, or make your own plugs by boring them out of a solid piece of matching wood with a plug cutter. In both cases the plug must be exactly the same diameter as the counterbored hole.

Solid dowel rod is usually maple or birch, both light-colored woods which will contrast boldly with a darker wood surface such as walnut or mahogany, if you use a clear finish. But stain will seep into the end of a dowel plug more than it will into the surface of the surrounding wood—unless it too has been cut across the grain—so the plug will be darker in that case. If you want your dowel plug to blend in with the surrounding surface so it can't be seen, cut it from the same stock as the counterbored material, selecting a spot where the look of the grain is similar. Insert the plug so the lines of its grain run parallel with the grain of the parent stock.

If you are going to do a lot of countersinking or counterboring, you might invest in a combination countersink/counterbore bit, which fits onto the shaft of a regular twist metal drill. This allows you to drill the pilot and shank clearance holes at the same time.

If you don't have the special counterbore bit, you can still counterbore a screw by using a spade bit and some twist drills. Use the spade bit first to drill out the larger hole where the dowel plug will fit. Make sure that you have a dowel which is the same diameter as the bit, and that the hole is large enough to accommodate the screw head. Then use two twist drills to make pilot and shank clearance holes as shown on page 208-209.

Countersink bits are designed only to cut cone-shaped depressions in a surface, permitting the top of a flat-head screw to sit flush with the surface of the wood.

Plug cutters come in a range of sizes to cut dowels of different diameters.

1. To make matching wooden plugs, cut them out of a block of the same wood as the furniture is made of, using a plug-cutting bit in a drill press.

2. Pop the cut plugs out of the wooden block with a small screwdriver. Glue and insert them, beveled ends down.

3. After the glue has dried, use a sharp chisel to cut the plugs flush with the surface.

4. Sand the plugs smooth and apply the finish. The plug on the far left was cut and positioned so matching grain patterns make it almost invisible.

Combination countersink/counterbore bit

Countersink bit

Twist drill

Flat-bladed spade bit

Plug cutter

Stopgaps and copouts

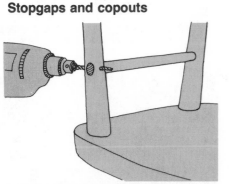

1. Dowels can also be used without screws to strengthen and secure joints in places like chair rungs, where a screw will not fit. Buy a length of dowel rod and drill out holes with a bit the same diameter as the dowel.

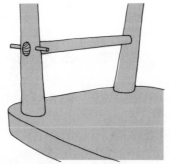

2. Cut spiral grooves in the dowel to hold glue, and use plenty of glue on the dowel and in the hole. The dowel should extend all the way through the joint, with the excess cut off and sanded flush after the glue has dried.

Patch repairing

A bad scratch, stain, gouge, or cigarette burn can ruin an otherwise perfect piece of furniture. Mild scratches or stains which are confined to the finish and do not extend into the wood can be easily repaired, and the procedures for this type of job are described on page 274. If the damaged area extends deep into the wood, however, a more drastic cosmetic repair is required. You will have to cut out the blemish much as a doctor removes a tumor, and replace it with a patch of veneer or solid wood whose grain and coloring matches the wood surrounding it. This is one of the best methods of repairing a deeply damaged area such as the charred wood of a cigarette burn, or even wood that has become rotted or mashed.

The plug or patch should be boat-shaped with tapered ends, or a trapezoid with the edges at a 45-degree angle to the grain of the parent piece. The borders of a rectangular patch will show up more. The biggest problem with this type of repair job is to fit the patch tightly within the grave or depression, and it requires starting with an accurate template. Keep matching the patch piece to the depression as you gradually chisel it out. Unless the fit is perfect, the open cracks will show up as dark lines when extra finishing compound or dirt collects in them.

1. Make a boat-shaped template for the patch, place it over the damaged area, and outline it with a sharp awl or scriber.

2. Cut a grave, or shallow depression, around the blemish following the outline of the template. Keep the bevel of the chisel facing into the grave.

3. Chisel out the material. The bottom of the grave should be clean and perfectly flat, and the sides should be vertical.

4. Place the template in the grave, and make sure the two match. This will require quite a bit of cutting and fitting.

5. Cut your patch from a piece of wood whose grain and color closely match the wood in the area being repaired, using the template as a pattern.

6. When the patch piece fits the grave exactly, smear waterproof glue on the back of the plug and in the grave, and clamp in place for 24 hours.

7. Next day, sand the plug down smooth with the surrounding wood, blending the two surfaces together until you can't feel any difference when you run your fingers across them.

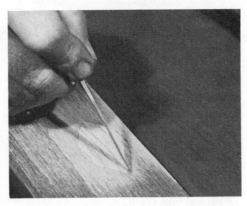

8. If the wood is an open-grained type such as oak, you can camouflage the repair further by scratching grain marks through the patch and into the surrounding wood. The stain will fill these and blend the two together.

9. Apply a stain, preferably a nonpenetrating oil stain, so you can control the color to match the surrounding stained wood.

10. Wipe with a soft cloth to remove excess stain and feather the stain into the surrounding wood. Without the arrow, perfect camouflage.

Replacing hardware

The techniques and tools required for replacing hardware are simple; the only problem is to find the exact style of hardware you're looking for. Often, especially on older pieces of furniture, it is impossible to find a single matching knob, hinge, latch, or handle. You may save a lot of time by purchasing all new hardware.

Almost all drawer pulls and knobs are held in place by a screw that goes through the drawer or door panel from the back and threads into the pull. Hardware stores, home centers, and lumber yards frequently stock simple wooden knobs that you can stain and finish to match the furniture.

The hardware for sliding drawer guides is sold in sets containing the parts for the drawer and the parts for the cabinet. Take the old hardware with you when you shop for replacements so you'll get the right size and style.

Repairing appliance finishes

Even a little scratch can be a problem on a kitchen appliance, mostly because it's irritating if you have to see it every day, and it's hard to get anyone to come to repair it.

The first and hardest step is finding a paint that matches your appliance color. If your stove or refrigerator is white or one of the new bright yellows or greens, you may be able to find the matching color with no trouble. The dealer who sold you the appliance might have small cans of touch-up paint. If your appliance is copper-colored, you could have problems. There are dozens of tones and shades of copper. The paint to use should be a fast-drying enamel in a spray can. Once you've located the right color, the rest is easy.

If the damage is only a small scratch or pinhole, the best repair method is to spray a bit of paint onto a piece of waxed paper, and pick up a bit of it on a small brush or sliver of wood. Dab this into the scratch to fill it up, taking care not to spread it out over the surrounding surface, or you'll end up with a rough and amateurish-looking job. Make sure the spray can has been thoroughly shaken and is spraying a full color onto the paper. This is especially important on copper colors.

If the damaged area is too wide or large to cover by this method, you'll have to spray the colors on. Using an extremely fine, silicon-carbide wet-or-dry sandpaper, gently roughen up the immediate area around the gouge or scratch. Mask off the area with newspaper and masking tape. Cover any cabinets or other appliances nearby with newspaper to prevent the fog droplets from getting on them.

Apply the paint in extremely light dusting coats. Overspraying causes runs, which require much time and trouble to remove. It will probably take at least 15 or 20 coats of paint to build up the patch enough to conceal it. The coating on most appliances is quite thick.

When the paint patch has built up to the proper thickness and color, remove the masking paper and give it a couple of hours to dry.

The sprayed patch will probably be somewhat rough in comparison to the surrounding finish and should be smoothed up and polished. Use a bit of automobile rubbing compound on a soft cloth wrapped around your finger to finish up the patch and blend it in with the surrounding finish. Give the entire appliance a good cleaning and wipe it down with a soft cloth.

Cures for the common clog
The nozzle on my almost-full spray can got clogged (because when I finished spraying last time I forgot to turn it upside down and push the spray button for a couple of seconds until it ran clear).

A pin wouldn't clear it. Just before chucking the whole thing I tried this:

Remove the nozzle by pulling it straight up; then soak the culprit in some alcohol or alcohol-based solvent, using a pin to open the hole while the thing is submerged. If that doesn't work, a last resort is to replace the clogged-up nozzle with one that works from another spray can. Whatever happens, don't get mad and bang the can against anything. Those pressurized containers are downright dangerous.

Practical Pete

To repair minor pinholes, spray some paint onto a piece of waxed paper, pick up a bit with a sliver of wood or a small brush, and dab a little into the spot.

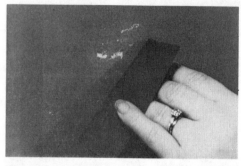
If the spot is too large for a dab touch-up, use a very fine wet-or-dry silicon-carbide sandpaper to lightly roughen the surrounding area.

Mask off the area surrounding the scratch with newspaper; then spray the paint on in light dusting coats. Don't apply the paint too thickly or you'll risk making drips or runs that are very difficult to repair.

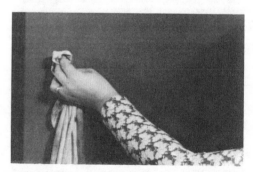
When enough coats are applied to blend the repair in with the rest of the appliance finish, use some automobile buffing compound to rub down the sprayed patch and give it a shine.

Picture frame repair

In spite of a bewildering range of sizes and styles, repairing picture frames is a pretty standardized procedure—mainly because there are only a few things that can go wrong and require your attention.

When corner joints separate, regluing them is easy if you have a picture-frame clamp. Scrape off all the old glue and clean the joint well before you reglue it.

Most picture frames, especially large ones, are hung by means of a twisted wire cable attached to screw eyes on either side of the frame. When these screw eyes work loose, the best thing to do is to remove them from their old holes and screw them into a new spot about ½ inch up or down.

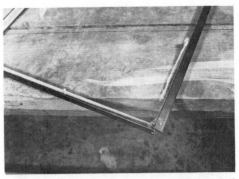

1. Picture frames are fragile and can easily split if the nails used to brace the corners are too thick. But glue will provide at least as strong a bond and will look better. Force glue into big splits and bind tightly before gluing the corners.

2. Remove nails, staples, or metal fasteners and scrape off old glue from corner joints. When the surfaces to be joined are clean, coat them liberally with glue.

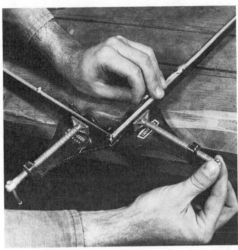

3. Use a picture frame clamp to secure the corner while the glue sets. This is a valuable tool because it clamps the corner at a perfect 90° angle while the glue dries, something you can't do by hand.

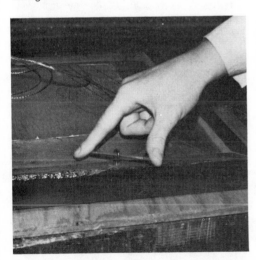

4. Use two screw eyes to hold the wire for hanging the picture frame. Position the screw eyes opposite each other, about four-fifths of the way up the sides. Use a nail as shown if you need more leverage when turning them in.

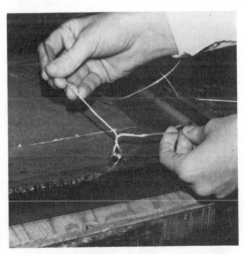

5. Loop twisted picture wire at least two times through the screw eye and then wind the loose end around as shown. The wire should be slack enough that it just misses showing above the top of the frame. To tighten it, twist it around the eyes.

What it takes to make a good corner joint

The sides of picture frames are jointed at 45° angles to make a square corner. These angles must be exact for a good corner joint, and professional craftsmen have special tools to make these precise cuts.

Miter boxes have slots in their sides which hold the saw straight up and down, and guide it for 45° and 90° angle cuts. The stock to be cut is clamped or held inside the box. A back saw is usually used for mitering, since it has fine teeth for cutting across the grain and a rigid blade for straight cuts. Metal miter boxes are more expensive than wooden or plastic ones, but they are more accurate, and can be adjusted for cuts at almost any angle.

Simple plastic miter box

Metal miter box with back saw in place

If you don't have a miter box, you can still make a 45° angle cut by using a combination square to mark the stock before you saw.

Hanging a picture

Attach screw eyes about 1/5 of the way down the sides. Leave enough slack in the cable so two hanger hooks can be used instead of just one. This will prevent the picture from leaning off to one side and will distribute the weight more evenly. The cable should be long enough so that it just misses showing above the top of the frame.

Repairing an ornate frame

Old ornate picture frames can be quite valuable if they are in good condition. Unfortunately, the intricate moldings which border these antique frames rarely survive without becoming cracked or broken. When a small piece of the decorative molding breaks off and is lost, it's a shame to have to discard the whole frame. You can replace a missing section of ornate molding by duplicating it yourself, which isn't as difficult as it sounds. The special tools or supplies you'll need to do this type of repair job are described in the margin at left. Don't expect to find this equipment at your local hardware store. Try a craft or art supply store; they should have everything you need.

A piece of the decorative molding on this ornate picture frame has broken off and can be replaced by making a mold of a matching section and casting a duplicate out of plaster of paris. The special supplies required are described at left.

1. Locate a section of the molding which is a duplicate of the section which needs to be replaced, and use a small (½-1 inch) brush which is clean and soft to paint on the liquid latex rubber.

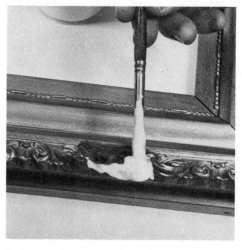

2. Patience is required here, because you must build up at least 6 layers, waiting from 30-45 minutes for each coat of latex to dry. The more elaborate the molding design, the more layers you should paint on.

3. When the final coat has dried, gently peel away the mold from the frame. Now you have an exact negative impression of the intricately contoured molding to use for making the casting.

4. Fill a small box with a mixture of plaster of paris and position the latex mold inside it with the hollow impression side facing up. Then brush some mold release on the inside of the mold.

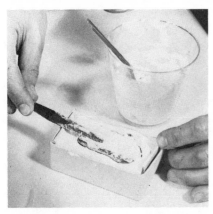

5. Mix up another small batch of plaster of paris and press some firmly into the mold, filling every contour of the impression. Use a small knife to flatten the top as shown.

6. When the plaster has set (wait at least 45 minutes), remove it from the latex mold. It will pop out easily if you coated the inside of the mold with commercial mold release or oil. If it doesn't, cut or peel off the latex mold.

7. Position the casting to determine where it must be trimmed to make a perfectly matching replacement section. If the missing section has an irregular edge, cut it off straight so the joint between the molding and the casting can be easily aligned.

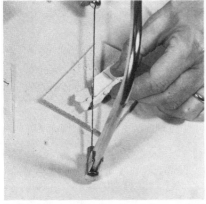

8. Cut the casting to fit, using a fine-toothed saw. Use fine-grade sandpaper or a sharp knife for final shaping to get the fit exact.

9. Clean the surfaces to be glued, especially the frame; then glue the replacement section in place with white glue.

10. When glue has dried, hide the joining edges by painting over them with some liquid gesso, which should dry for at least 30 minutes before refinishing.

Gold leaf

For a finish that looks better and lasts much longer than paint, you can apply gold leaf to your picture frame. Gold can be pressed into sheets which are thinner than tissue paper. These sheets are glued to the surface of the picture frame, pressed into place along every contour of the frame with a soft bristled brush.

You can buy different-sized sheets of gold leaf at most art supply stores. It is 3 to 4 times as expensive as gold enamel but gives a finish which is unique and truly authentic if applied correctly. Stores which sell gold leaf also sell a special type of contact cement designed for gluing the gold leaf to the surface. Apply a thin coat of this cement to the frame, using a regular paint brush or a brush applicator which usually comes with the glue. Then wait 15 or 20 minutes for the glue to become tacky before pressing the gold leaf into place with a clean soft brush. The bits and pieces of leaf that break off during application can be collected and glued down just like new gold leaf, or saved for another project.

Use special gold leaf contact cement to prepare the intricately contoured surface of the frame for the gold leaf.

A clean, dry, soft bristle brush is the best tool for working leaf into the contours of the picture frame.

Installing plastic laminate

What it takes

Approximate time: One or two hours for a medium-size table.

Tools and materials: Most lumber dealers sell sheets of plastic laminate in a variety of colors and patterns. You'll need some contact cement and three power tools: a router with an edge-trimming bit designed for plastic laminates; a saber or circular saw, with a fine-tooth carbide-tipped blade, for cutting the laminate roughly to size; and a belt sander, with medium-fine sandpaper belt.

Plastic laminates are used to cover surfaces that must take a lot of wear. They can withstand heat, water, oils, detergent, and exposure to many other conditions that would severely stain or ruin conventionally finished furniture.

To install a plastic laminate top on your table, workbench, or counter, you'll need the power tools listed at left. All three tools can be rented if you can't borrow them from a friend.

Prepare the surface by removing the old finish, filling any large holes or cracks, and smoothing it level with sandpaper. After the contact cement has been applied to both surfaces and allowed to dry, align the laminate perfectly before you press it into place. When gluing the laminate to the tabletop, separate the two with a paper slip-sheet until they are aligned; then slide out the paper. (Note that the procedure illustrated also applies to wood veneer, except that it can be cut and smoothed by hand.)

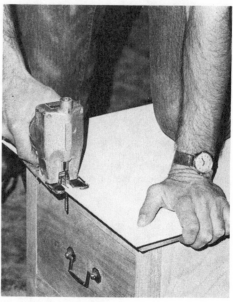

1. Support the plastic sheet near the cutting line and cut it slightly oversize. If you're using a saber saw, cut at slow speed to avoid chipping the plastic.

2. Apply the plastic to the edges before you cover the top. Coat the back of the plastic and the table edge with contact cement. Allow the glue to dry until it is no longer sticky to touch; then press the edge piece in place.

3. Use a belt sander with medium-fine grit sandpaper to sand the edge of the strip flush with the tabletop. Hand sanding will not do as good a job and will take too much time.

4. To apply the plastic to the top of the table, coat both surfaces with contact cement and let dry until barely tacky. Place a slip-sheet between the glued surfaces, align them exactly, and slide the paper out.

5. Press the plastic down evenly over the entire surface to force out air pockets and make a good bond. Use a rolling pin if you don't have the special roller pictured here.

6. Trim the edge flush with a router, using the edge-trimming bit specially designed for plastic laminates.

7. Round off the sharp edges slightly with a medium flat-file or a sanding block wrapped with fine-grit aluminum-oxide paper.

Rushing

Chairs designed for rush seats have a simple open rung construction without the grooves or holes typical of caned seat frames. The strands used for rushing have traditionally come from the long slender leaves of the cattail plant, which grows abundantly in shallow fresh water, swamps and wet lowlands. These leaves are twisted into the strands used for rushing. You can collect the leaves yourself, or buy them in bulk for making the rush strands.

An easier alternative, and one which is very popular, especially among professional furniture repairmen, is to use man-made *fiber rush* instead. Fiber rush is made from a strong paper which is twisted into strands and looks very much like natural rush. It is easier to work with than natural rush, inexpensive, and comes ready to use.

What it takes

Approximate time: Four to six hours for an average chair.

Tools: No special tools are needed, except for a wooden caul which is used for forcing the strands against each other.

Materials: Fiber rush is sold by the pound, and commercial outfits buy their rush in big 30-pound reels. You'll only need 2½-3 pounds for an average chair. Most craft supply houses sell rush in small 3-pound packets.

You'll also need some stiff cardboard for stuffing the pockets between courses.

A simple technique

Check the crosspieces of the seat to make sure they are securely joined to the frame and in good condition. Reglue them if they are loose. Smooth the crosspieces with some sandpaper and remove all tacks and nails that might catch on the rush.

Rush should be *dampened* to make it flexible and easy to work. *Don't soak* fiber rush or the paper will soften, unravel and break. Start the first bout (a bout is one trip around all four corners) by tacking one end of the strand to the sidepiece of the seat. If the chair is wider at the front than at the back, fill out the front corners first. Force the strands tightly against each other with a wooden caul. The completed seat can be left natural or finished with shellac or varnish.

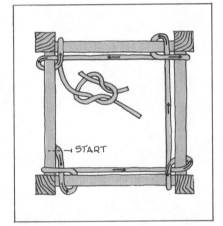

Use the simple under-over wrap shown above to rush your chair. Tack the end of the first strand to the crosspiece and tie on succeeding strands with a square knot. Make sure that all knots are hidden beneath the seat.

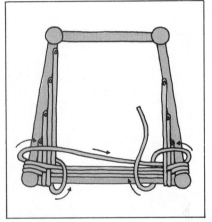

Most chairs are wider in front than in back. Compensate for this by rushing only the sides and front until you get a square or rectangle as shown, then begin rushing all four corners.

Use a wooden caul to force the strands together so you can keep the weave tight.

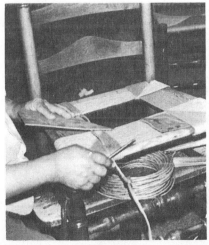

When corners fill out, stuff the pockets between courses with cardboard.

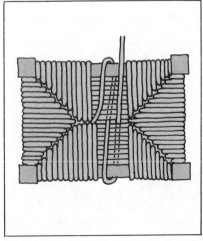

Rush extra-wide chairs by weaving the center section after sides are done. Tie off the last strand underneath the finished seat.

Caning

Approximate time: Six to eight hours for hand caning, or 45 minutes for prewoven cane.

Tools: No unusual tools are needed, except for some wax and three caning pins, if you are hand caning. These are small cone-shaped pegs which wedge into the holes around the seat and hold the cane in place. They are sold with the cane, or you can make them yourself. A wedge-shaped wooden caul is needed for installing prewoven cane. Both types of cane must be soaked before use, so you'll need a bucket or bathtub for this purpose.

Materials: Commercial caners purchase cane in 1000-foot hanks, but you may be able to buy it in 15-18-foot lengths from a craft supply house. It takes about 250 feet of cane to do a medium size seat. Cane comes in different widths. Choose the right width for your chair according to the chart below. *Binder cane* is one width wider than the cane you use for weaving the seat. You'll need about 5 feet of it. *Prewoven cane* comes in rolls or sections and is available through craft supply houses. *Splining* is usually sold with the cane. It comes in different widths so be sure it will fit snugly in the slot around your chair seat.

Cane size	Minimum hole size	Distance between holes
Carriage	1/8″	3/8″
Superfine	1/8″	3/8″
Fine fine	3/16″	1/2″
Fine	3/16″	5/8″
Medium	1/4″	3/4″
Common	5/16″	7/8″

There is no need to throw away an old chair simply because the cane seat is damaged or missing. In fact, the difference between a useless piece of furniture and a finely restored antique may be only a matter of recaning the seat. In general, once the cane in a seat has been damaged, it cannot be patched. Repairs are, at best, makeshift and neither look good nor give the seat the strength it needs.

There are two ways of replacing a cane seat. If the frame of your chair has a series of evenly spaced holes around the seat opening, then you'll be weaving individual strands of cane by hand to make the new cane seat. If the open seat frame has a groove cut all the way around it instead of holes, then the chair must be recaned with prewoven cane purchased in sheets.

Weaving or seating cane comes from the rattan tree, a species of palm tree which grows in the rich tropical forests of India, Ceylon and Malaysia. The thin strands of cane are stripped off the narrow stem of the tree in 10 to 20-foot lengths. Prewoven cane has been completely woven and is ready to be installed. Here are some important caning tips to go along with the step-by-step procedures on these two pages:

1. Cane has a good side which should face up. It is shiny and slightly rounded. The bad side is duller and flat.
2. Both types of cane must be soaked in water before they are used. Soaking gives the cane flexibility, reducing the chances of breakage or fraying. Wet cane shrinks slightly as it dries, pulling the weave tighter.
3. Waxing the cane makes weaving easier and protects the cane from friction wear.
4. When weaving cane, don't pull the strands tightly. Shrinkage and successive courses will pull the cane taut. Use just enough tension to keep the strands straight.
5. If the seat is not rectangular, skip holes or double up when weaving to keep the course as straight and parallel as possible. Remember to skip or double symmetrically, so both sides look the same.
6. Cane seats can be stained, shellacked, varnished, or left natural.

Weaving a cane seat takes time but is not as complicated as the pattern of the finished seat suggests at first sight.

Prewoven cane is held in place by a spline wedged into the groove which runs around the edge of the opening in the seat.

Hand caning step by step

1. Remove all old cane, clean out holes, and round off any sharp edges along the inside of the frame. Splits often develop along the hole line and should be repaired with screws and glue.

2. Find the middle of the front and back supports by counting holes and lay the first front-to-back course, working from center to sides. Use pegs to hold the cane in place, and keep cane slack but not sagging.

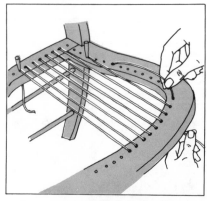

3. For seats which are wider at the front than at the back, skip holes as required to keep the course parallel. Make sure to skip the same holes on both sides of the frame.

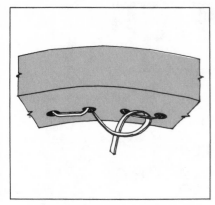

4. Tie off loose ends underneath the chair as shown. Prevent breaking and splitting by wetting the ends to make them more flexible.

5. Lay the first side-to-side course over the front-and-back course. Always keep an extra length of cane soaking so it will be ready when you need it.

6. Lay the second front-and-back course over the previous course. Don't worry about correct spacing between the paired lengths of cane; they will align when the fourth course is woven through.

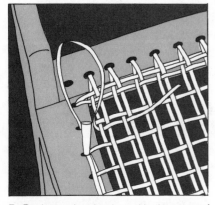

7. Real weaving begins with the second side-to-side course. Wax or moisten the cane to make it slide easier, and use an alternating under-over weave through the doubled front-and-back course.

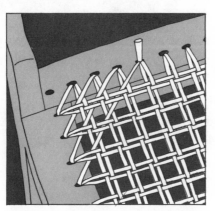

8. Start the first diagonal course in the back left-hand corner of the chair. Weave the cane over the front-and-back pairs and under the side-to-side pairs. Run the second diagonal course at right angles to the first beginning at the back right-hand corner. This time weave under the front-and-back pairs and over the side-to-side pairs.

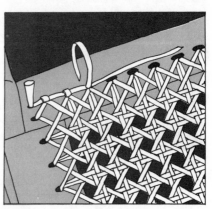

9. Fasten down binder cane with a long length of weaving cane. The weaving cane loops over the binder and pulls it down over the holes as shown. Use a separate length of binder cane for front, back and sides, with each piece running from corner hole to corner hole.

Replacing prewoven cane

The difference in appearance between prewoven and hand-caned furniture is a slight one. This is ironic because installing a prewoven cane seat requires about one-fifth of the time and effort it takes to hand-cane a chair. Chairs with prewoven cane seats all have a groove or trough around the seat frame instead of evenly spaced holes. A spline is forced into this depression to hold the caning in place.

To replace a prewoven cane seat, first remove the old spline and clean out the groove with a chisel. Cut the prewoven cane roughly to size and let it soak for at least 15 minutes. Soaking makes the sheet more flexible, and as it dries, the cane will shrink slightly and pull tight across the seat. Align the caning over the seat. Tamp down securely into the

groove using a narrow wooden caul. Remove the excess material with a sharp chisel, but leave enough caning

to cover the bottom of the groove. Pour glue into the groove and hammer the new spline into place.

After tamping the prewoven cane down into the groove, use a sharp chisel to remove the excess cane at the outside of the groove.

Pour glue liberally into the groove and tap the spline into place. Soak the spline in water beforehand if it has to bend around corners, and make sure it is forced well down into the groove against the cane.

Before

After

Stripping

What it takes

Approximate time: Will of course vary widely from item to item. The cupboard pictured above took about 4 hours.

Tools and materials: Rubber gloves, newspaper to protect floors, a soft-bristle paintbrush, paint remover in liquid or semipaste form, and a range of scraping tools which might include a putty knife, steel wool, wire brushes, tooth brushes, and a jackknife.

Stopgaps and copouts

Stripping furniture can really be a troublesome job, especially if the piece is large or intricately carved, with many layers of finish to come off. You can save a lot of messy work by taking your furniture to a professional stripper. He has special stripping equipment and large tubs of extra-strength finish remover in which entire tables or dressers can be submerged and stripped clean. Prices will vary according to the size and type of furniture. Professional strippers are listed in the phone book under furniture-finish removal or furniture strippers.

Sometimes there is nothing you can do to revive the old finish on a piece of furniture, or you might have a painted bureau or dresser that would look much nicer with a natural finish. In both cases, the solution is to remove the old finish and refinish the piece. Removing the finish to expose the bare wood underneath is called stripping.

There are three methods of stripping. The old finish can be sanded off. This is usually done with a belt sander, using coarse grade sandpaper, and is not a popular method of stripping quality furniture. The sander cannot maneuver to reach tight places and is likely to remove more wood than paint or varnish, leaving the bare wood in rough condition. Another method is to burn the finish off with a special electric heater or a blowtorch. The paint on exterior shingles or siding is often stripped off in this way. The best way to strip furniture, however, is to use a chemical paint remover which loosens the finish so that you can wash or scrape it off easily. Paint removers also remove varnish and other clear finishes.

Paint removers are sold in hardware and paint stores and come as a liquid or semipaste in several varieties. Stripping will be safer and easier if you buy a non-flammable, non-grain-raising remover that can be rinsed off with water (look for words like "waterwash," "washaway," or "water-rinse" on the label). Some inexpensive paint removers are extremely volatile and raise the wood grain or leave a residue on the stripped surface that is a problem to remove. **Note:** To prevent bubbles and wrinkles from forming, don't use a water-soluble remover to strip veneer furniture.

Use liquid paint remover for stripping jobs where you have flat surfaces and the remover can penetrate without running off. Use a semipaste paint remover for chair rungs, ornately carved moldings, legs, and vertical or slanting surfaces where runoff or penetration is a problem.

Stripping furniture can be a smooth operation if you take time to prepare well. The chemicals used to loosen paint and varnish are harsh, so a pair of rubber gloves is a good idea if you want to protect your hands. Work in a well-ventilated area too, since the fumes from paint remover can irritate your eyes and breathing passages. Work outside, if weather permits and if you plan to hose off the loosened paint and remover, but remember that the remover may kill the grass or vegetation on your lawn. A gravel driveway is an ideal place for rinse-off.

Buy plenty of paint remover. It should be applied very generously, and even reapplied for added loosening action if the first coat has dried out.

Allow the remover to penetrate. The most common stripping mistake is trying to scrape off the old finish before the full loosening action of the remover has taken effect. It may take from five to fifteen minutes to loosen the finish on a given piece of furniture, depending upon the type of finish and how many layers have to be removed. The important thing to remember is this: don't scrape too hard. Let the remover do the work. Make a test scrape with a screwdriver to see how easily the finish comes off. To strip off thick or multiple finish coats, you may have to scrape off one or two layers, reapply remover, then scrape off the remaining layers. If you leave the remover on too long, it will dry out and the loosened finish will harden and become difficult to scrape off. If this happens, another liberal coat of remover will rejuvenate the loosening action and make scraping easy again.

Stopwatch on stripping (liquid washaway on 3 layers of paint)

1 minute—Stripper has loosened first layer of paint and part of second.

5 minutes—Second layer has bubbled loose, but third layer of paint still can't be removed. Wait a little longer.

15 minutes—Bare wood revealed! A few swipes with a putty knife and all three layers are off.

Stripping procedures

1. When stripping a large piece of furniture, do one section at a time, so that the paint remover won't dry out and harden before you get to it. When the paint bubbles and flakes off easily, it's time to remove it.

2. Use a putty knife to remove paint from flat surfaces. Work quickly, but remember that the remover has softened the wood, so you can easily scratch or gouge the newly exposed surface. Let the paint remover do the work, and make a second application if necessary.

Striptips

Apply paint stripper using upward strokes. You can reduce the mess of removing the finish by placing table or chair legs inside cans or pie tins which will catch most of the stripped-off goop.

To determine if the finish has softened enough to begin removal, try scraping off a small section first.

3. Use steel wool to remove bits and pieces of paint that you couldn't get off by scraping, or to reach places the putty knife couldn't.

4. Remove drawers and strip them separately. Handles or pulls should be removed and cleaned separately. Soak hardware in liquid remover to take off caked-on paint.

Cabinets and built-ins

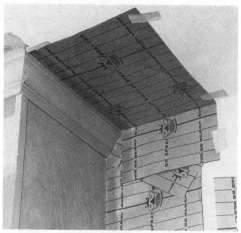

1. Unlike most other furniture, a cabinet or built-in can't be moved into a more convenient work space for stripping. Use masking tape and paper to protect surfaces that you don't want stripped. If possible, empty drawers or cabinets which you'll be working on, or cover their contents.

2. Use a semipaste paint remover on vertical surfaces like this one. Keep the can of remover close to the brush, as shown, and application will be quick and ample. Spilling or dripping will also be minimized by holding the can close to the work.

More striptips

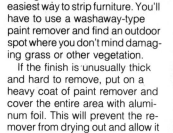

Hosing off the old finish is the easiest way to strip furniture. You'll have to use a washaway-type paint remover and find an outdoor spot where you don't mind damaging grass or other vegetation.

If the finish is unusually thick and hard to remove, put on a heavy coat of paint remover and cover the entire area with aluminum foil. This will prevent the remover from drying out and allow it to penetrate better.

Rolled-up steel wool or a piece of string or cord are excellent tools for removing finish from the narrow contours of table or chair legs. An old toothbrush also does a good job in hard-to-get spots.

3. Wait until the paint has softened; then use a putty knife to remove the finish. Keep a can or newspaper ready to hold scraped-off paint.

4. Use steel wool and a rag to remove the last of the old finish. Keep protective paper and tape in place if you're going to refinish.

Windows

Don't worry about getting paint remover on the glass. Semipaste is best because it will coat the cracks and crannies without running off. Put newspaper on painted sills or the floor to catch drips.

The paint on windows may be thick and difficult to remove. A wire brush will usually work better than a putty knife or steel wool, but brush lightly so as not to score the wood.

Sanding

Putting a beautiful finish on a piece of furniture begins with a good job of cleaning and smoothing the bare wood. The most important tools used to accomplish this are called *abrasives*, and the two types of abrasives used on furniture are sandpaper and steel wool. Sandpaper is commonly sold in sheets 9x11 inches, although it also comes in other circular or rectangular dimensions to fit different types of power sanders. Steel wool is available in one piece rolls or in packs of individual pads.

There are many different grades of sandpaper and steel wool, but they are all classified according to abrasive strength (see charts below). While steel wool is especially useful for removing stains or spots from metal and finished wood, or removing the loosened finish from furniture being stripped, sandpaper is better suited for use on bare wood. Sandpaper and steel wool are also used (in extra-fine grits) to remove the bubbles and ripples in hard finish coats, or to slightly roughen the underlying finish so the next coat will adhere better.

Selecting the right abrasive

Sandpaper

Grit	Classification	Common uses
600 500	super fine	wet or dry polishing
400 360 320	extra fine	
280 240 220	very fine	dry sanding between finish coats
180 150	fine	final sanding on bare wood before applying finish
120 100 80	medium	general wood sanding, preliminary sanding on rough wood
60 50 40	coarse	rough sanding, paint and finish removal

Steel wool

Grade	Common uses
0000 super fine	extra fine smoothing, final rubbing down after last coat of finish
000 extra fine	smoothing finished surfaces, removing spots from finished wood, cleaning metals
00 fine	rough smoothing, used to roughen the gloss between finish coats or to dull a high gloss finish
0 medium fine	most commonly used grade for general smoothing, removes stains and spots from metals, stripping
1 medium	coarsest grade for furniture work, removes shoe or furniture marks from floors
2 medium coarse	used on rough lumber
3 coarse	roughest grade, not used in furniture work

Use medium or medium-fine steel wool to remove the loosened finish when stripping furniture. Extra-fine or super-fine steel wool is used for smoothing and leveling between finish coats or for final smoothing before waxing or polishing.

Sandpaper is a general term used to describe flexible sheets of paper or cloth coated with abrasive particles. The size of the particles determines the grit designation (see chart) which can range from "super fine" (600 particles per square inch) to "coarse" (40).

The hardness and sharpness of the material the particles are made of, the strength of the backing, and whether the backing and adhesive are waterproof all determine how durable it is. Consider all these factors, as well as the grit, to select the best paper for the job you have to do.

Flint paper is light tan in color and is the commonest, least expensive grade of sandpaper. It is available in grits ranging from coarse to very fine. In the long run, flint paper is not the bargain it appears to be. It does not cut as well or as fast as the more expensive papers, is more prone to clogging, as shown above, and will wear out much faster.

Ripping off sandpaper
I ruined a couple of sheets of sandpaper before figuring out a reliable way of cutting those 9x11s into smaller pieces. With the sandy side facing out, make a fold along the line you want to cut. Place the sharpened side of a saw blade against the fold, holding it down against the paper, and pull away the smaller piece.

Practical Pete

True grit

After spending half an hour searching through my growing pile of sandpaper for some new sheets I'd just bought, I decided there must be a better way to store the stuff. I came up with a simple compartmentalized box that really makes finding the right grit paper a snap. It's easy to make too.

Label each shelf according to grit designation, and reserve at least one shelf for used sheets.

Practical Pete

Garnet paper is the most popular sandpaper for hand sanding on wood and is easy to recognize because of its reddish-brown color. It comes in grits from coarse to very fine and is considerably more durable than flint paper because the particles are hard crystals with sharp points rather than chips of stone. It is shown above, wrapped around a length of dowel rod to smooth a contoured molding.

Aluminum oxide abrasives can be used for hand or power sanding and come with a paper or cloth backing. The paper is available in coarse through very fine grits, while the cloth comes in grits ranging from coarse to fine. The durability of aluminum oxide abrasives more than makes up for their higher cost. They are suited for use on power sanding equipment.

Silicon carbide is a man-made abrasive like aluminum oxide but is much finer in consistency. It is black and easy to find at most hardware stores. Silicon carbide comes in fine, extra fine, and super fine

grits and is used almost exclusively for polishing smooth surfaces such as metal and finished wood. It comes on a waterproof paper and can be used wet or dry.

Emery cloth is a dull black, cloth-backed abrasive available in coarse to fine grits. It is used most commonly on nonplated metal for smoothing and cleaning off rust or scale. It can be used wet or dry.

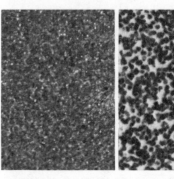

Open coat sandpaper has fewer abrasive particles per square inch than conventional sandpaper, as shown above. Because of the open spaces between particles, wood dust and other abraded materials are less likely to clog the paper.

Steel wool comes in different textures, like sandpaper, but is not used as widely for smoothing bare wood. On round, grooved, or contoured surfaces such as table legs (see above), steel wool does a better job than sandpaper because it can get into cracks and crevices that sandpaper can't. It is good to use when you can't work with the grain of the wood, as you must with sandpaper, since it can smooth the wood uniformly without leaving the severe cross-grain scratches that sandpaper does.

Using sandpaper

Abrasives are most often used in a sequence beginning with the coarser textures and ending with the finer ones. For example, you might start with an 80-grit sandpaper to smooth rough wood for finishing or to remove rough spots, round off sharp edges, and sand down scrapes or nicks on an otherwise smooth surface. Use coarse grits only to top off very rough spots; then switch to finer grits such as 150, 180, or 220. Otherwise, when you set out to smooth a small defect, you may cut a deeper impression than you need to or produce unnecessary scratches that you will only have to smooth again later with a finer grit.

The type of wood as well as the condition of the surface will determine the grit to be used. While softwoods such as pine or cedar can be prepared for finishing with a 150 or 180-grit abrasive, use finer grits on hardwoods like maple and oak to produce a satin-smooth surface. To achieve a similarly smooth surface on softwoods, apply a coat of sanding sealer to the wood after the piece has been sanded down as smooth as possible. Sanding sealer is a commercial preparation which you can duplicate by diluting 3-pound-cut shellac with three or four parts alcohol. It hardens the surface of the wood so that finer-grit sandpapers will be effective.

Always sand with the grain of the wood. If your abrasive cuts across the wood fibers instead of with them, scratches will show under the finish. At joints, corners, and other tight places try using a small strip of sandpaper under your thumb or finger to sand with the grain. Improvise your own sanding sticks (page 228) if you can't rely on finger work to do the job.

For most sanding jobs, it is difficult to use sandpaper in the 9x11-inch size it is sold in. (Some hardware stores sell sandpaper in special sizes to fit different makes of power sanding equipment.) Cut the sheets into smaller pieces as you need them, and fold them in half once or twice to make them stiffer and easy to work with.

All sandpaper eventually wears out and must be discarded, although some woodworkers use this "aged" sandpaper for finer smoothing and polishing, arguing that the softened edges of the abrasive particles are just right for this type of work. You can age new sandpaper by rubbing two sheets of identical grit against each other. This will remove the larger grains on each sheet and round off the cutting edges of the abrasive particles. To extend the life of your sandpaper, keep it unclogged, avoid sharp metal surfaces like screw or nail heads, and use sanding blocks wherever you can.

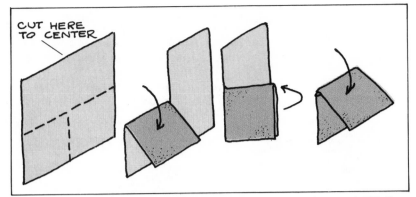

Fold sheets of sandpaper once or twice to make them stiffer and easier to work. **TIP:** Keep the abrasives from rubbing against each other and dulling prematurely by folding the sheet in on itself as shown.

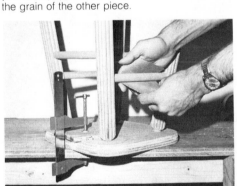

Always sand with the grain, being especially wary of places where two pieces of wood meet with their grains at right angles to each other. Try not to let your sandpaper cross the joint and scratch across the grain of the other piece.

Clamp smaller stock firmly in place before you start so you can concentrate on sanding instead of on holding the piece steady.

Use small strips of paper and finger or thumb pressure to reach tight spots or sand joints where the grains meet at an angle.

Sanding strips

For smoothing rungs, legs, or other round surfaces, cut sandpaper into strips and use it shoe-shine style, pulling the paper back and forth with both hands. Cover the bare side of the paper with lengths of cellophane tape to make the strip last longer.

Cures for clogging

Sandpaper can easily become clogged with abraded dust, and when this happens the cutting action of the paper is sharply reduced. Material trapped between the abrasive particles can usually be freed simply by using a fine bristle brush. (Brushes used for polishing shoes are ideal, but don't get shoe polish on the sandpaper.) A vacuum cleaner or compressed air are other effective means for unclogging sandpaper, and a little turpentine or solvent will help too.

If clogging is really a problem, as it will be when sanding such resin-rich woods as rosewood or ebony, try using an open-coat paper. On open-coat papers, the abrasive particles are spaced farther apart, so that wood dust is less likely to jam between them.

Sanding blocks

Sanding blocks make smoothing and shaping jobs easier by allowing you to use more pressure over a larger area than you could by hand. Using sanding blocks also extends the life of your sandpaper.

Hardware stores carry different types of refillable sanding blocks, but many craftsmen make their own. It's easy to do, and you'll often want to design one or more blocks to fit special sanding jobs. Some ideas are shown below. A narrow layer of felt or rubber between block and paper will cushion the abrasive action and further prolong the life of the sandpaper.

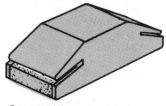

Commercial sanding blocks are easily loaded and unloaded; different types are available in most hardware stores.

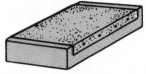

If you cut a full-size sheet of sandpaper in half, you'll have two (5½x9-inch) pieces that will fit a block of the size shown above. Use ⅝ or ¾-inch plywood for the block.

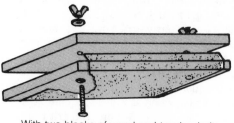

With two blocks of wood and two lag bolts with matching wing nuts and washers, you can make a sanding block that uses full-size 9x11-inch sandpaper sheet refills. Cut two 6½x12-inch blocks out of ⅝-inch plywood. The toughest part of the job is to mortise the lag-bolt heads into the board so that they are flush with the surface. Use epoxy to glue them in place if the fit isn't snug enough.

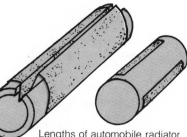

Lengths of automobile radiator hose or dowel rod make good sanding blocks for contoured surfaces. Make a slit down one side of the hose to hold the edges of the sandpaper as shown.

Make small sanding sticks "to order" for hard-to-reach areas. Cut and shape the stick to fit the problem surface; then glue the sandpaper in place with contact cement.

If you don't want to waste the edges of your sandpaper, cut a block the size of half a sheet (9x5½ inches) and glue the paper down with contact cement.

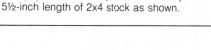

For small blocks, divide your 9x11-inch sandpaper sheet into quarters and shape a 5½-inch length of 2x4 stock as shown.

Power sanding

An electric sander will speed up your sanding jobs considerably. Orbital sanders are best for the medium to fine work common to furniture repair and refinishing. They depend on small, high-speed vibrations to accentuate abrasive action and are easy to operate. Belt sanders are designed for removing large amounts of material and are heavier, harder to operate, and usually more expensive than orbital sanders.

Observe the same rules you would for hand sanding. Move your sander with the grain of the wood and follow a sequence of coarse to fine grits for final smoothing. Hand-smooth the corners and crannies that you can't reach with your power sander. Clamp stock in place so you can use both hands, and work with moderate pressure. Forcing the sander against the wood will dampen abrasive action and actually slow down the job.

Clamp stock in place and use both hands to apply moderate pressure. Remember to hand-sand areas the power sander couldn't reach.

Final cleaning

Take a look at the instructions on any can of stain or finish and you are sure to see a special note on surface preparation that reads something like this: *surface should be clean and dry, free of dust, dirt, grease or oil before finish is applied.* In other words, sanding the wood down to an even smoothness is not the final step prior to applying the stain or finish. Just-sanded wood is full of sawdust that has been abraded and worked into the wood surface. It's difficult to detect this dust by eye, but a swipe across the surface with your hand or a dark cloth or glove will pick up some of these small wood particles. Each tiny speck of dust will grow to many times its original size when stain or finish is applied, due to the build-up of varnish or paint around it. Wood dust also gets worked into cracks or corners during sanding. If not removed before finishing, this dust absorbs the stain or varnish, leaving the wood underneath bare.

Wood dust and other particles can be removed from stock in several ways. The stock can be blown clean with compressed air, or you can use a vacuum to remove the dust. A paint brush whose bristles are dry and clean also does a good job of removing loose sawdust, but blowing or dry-brushing fills the air with fine particles which will contaminate the finish when they settle.

Using a tack rag is usually the simplest and most thorough way of cleaning the wood. This is simply a cotton cloth that has been impregnated with varnish to make it tacky. Wipe the rag across the surface of the wood and you can remove both loose and worked-in particles without throwing up a dust storm.

Grease or oil stains on bare wood present a special problem. Varnishes and other hard finishes will not adhere to grease-stained wood, and these types of stains will usually show through a paint or penetrating finish. To remove animal grease, rub the spot with a cloth soaked in benzene or some of the commercial cleaning fluid that is used on clothing stains. Use acetone to remove a vegetable grease stain. Apply the acetone with a small brush, working it into the stain, and then wipe the area with an absorbent paper towel. You may have to reapply the acetone several times to remove tough stains. For stains that go deep into the wood and can't be removed by rubbing, sand down the stained area until you can use the acetone or cleaning fluid to remove the rest of the spot. The stain-removing solvents may be incompatible with the finish you are going to apply, so wipe the surface well to remove the cleaning agent as well as the stain. Now you're ready for the finish.

The sawdust which is worked into the wood surface during sanding and smoothing shows up clearly on a dark glove wiped across the surface of the wood. It's important to remove this accumulation of dust before applying the finish.

Tiny particles of wood-dust covering the bare wood surface are not easily noticed until the finish is applied. Then these specks multiply to many times their own size because the finish builds up all around them.

A tack rag will remove the wood dust worked into the wood grain during sanding without spreading it around again.

Stains on bare wood should be rubbed off whenever possible with a suitable cleaning agent. If that fails, sand them off.

Make your own tack rag

Tack rags can be bought at most hardware or paint stores, but you can make one very easily if you have a dishcloth-size piece of fine cheesecloth (any cotton cloth will do, but cheesecloth is best), some turpentine and some varnish.

1. Wet the cloth in water; then wring it out to an even dampness.

2. Wad the cloth up and pour some turpentine on it. Work the turpentine through the cloth until it is evenly distributed. Open the cloth up and let it dry until damp.

3. Sprinkle some varnish on the cloth; wad it up and work the varnish through the wad until the cloth is uniformly yellow.

Tack rags should be just barely damp: tacky. Store them in a tightly closed glass container, reviving the tackiness with more water and turpentine when the rag dries out. The rag is too wet if it leaves a film on the surface of the wood. Hang it up to dry until it is still tacky but not moist.

3. BRUSHES

Selecting a brush

What it takes

Most furniture finishing and re-finishing is done with brushes between 1 and 3 inches wide; you should have at least two brushes to start with. A 3-inch brush and a 1½-inch brush make a good working combination.

Quality is the most important factor in selecting a brush, regardless of size or style. A good brush will hold a large amount of stain, paint, filler, or finish and will permit smooth, effortless application. Poorly made brushes can be used to apply paint remover, filler, or sealer coats, but using a low-quality brush with varnish, shellac, lacquer, or any finish coat is not worth the risk or the trouble involved.

The brushes you can buy today have either nylon or natural bristles. While many craftsmen prefer one over the other, the best way to choose a brush is not so much by bristle composition as by the following essential checkpoints:

Press the bristles against the back of your hand. They should feel resilient, springing back into place without undue stiffness. When pressed gently against a flat surface, the bristles should keep their shape and not fan out excessively. Shake the brush and fan the bristles vigorously to make sure they are set securely. Low-quality brushes have loosely set bristles which can fall out and ruin a good finishing job. The ferrule should be firmly fastened to the brush in at least two places, not just one, as is the case with inferior brushes. Good-quality brushes have aluminum or stainless-steel ferrules to resist corrosion.

Examine the ends of the bristles. Each bristle should be split several ways, forming a tiny fan. These tiny splits are called flagging, and this feature determines how well the brush will hold the finishing compound. Don't buy a brush if its bristles are blunt and unflagged.

In general, the bristles should be half again as long as the width of the brush. In other words, a brush 2 inches wide should have bristles about 3 inches long. This rule does not apply to very small brushes or brushes wider than 3 inches.

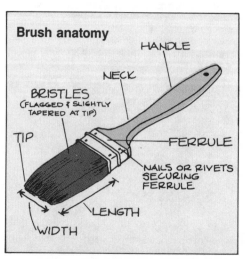

Brush anatomy

Examine the bristles carefully before you buy a brush. Make sure the tips are flagged and the bristles are resilient and firmly held in the brush.

Cleaning

If you take good care of your brushes, they will serve you well for many years. If properly treated, a quality brush will actually improve with use. Conversely, any brush that has been poorly cared for is little better than worthless.

Clean your brushes as soon as you're done using them. Except in working with latex paints or finishes, which can be cleaned from brushes with soap and warm water, wear rubber gloves when cleaning brushes in solvent or softener. Then work the solvent through the bristles with your fingers to remove all finish, filler, or stain.

When soaking brushes to soften stiff bristles, make sure that the bristles aren't resting against the bottom of the container and that there's enough solvent to cover the bristles right up to the ferrule.

Some of your old brushes might look like these two. The brush on the left has been well cleaned, but the bristles have fanned out because it wasn't wrapped before storage, or it was stored upright. The brush at right is not much good because of the dried-out paint extending up into the ferrule.

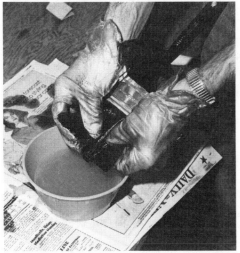

1. Always clean brushes as soon as you've finished using them. Check the label on the filler, stain, sealer, paint, or finish you've been using to determine what kind of solvent to use.

2. To soften hardened bristles or remove caked-on paint, soak the brush in a can of solvent or commercial brush softener. Drill a hole in the neck of the brush and suspend it from a rod as shown.

Avoiding a tacky problem

I know you're not supposed to leave a brush uncleaned, but sometimes it's impossible to do a thorough cleanup right after the job is done. Either that or you have to leave right in the middle of a refinishing job. If you must abandon a brush with the paint or varnish still on it, wrap it up in aluminum foil or plastic sheet before you go. I use those clear plastic sandwich bags. Just secure one around the neck of the brush with a rubber band, and you've got an airtight seal. This forestalls drying and stiffening, so you can run an errand or eat lunch without worrying about ruining the brush.

Practical Pete

3. Use a fork or metal comb to separate hardened bristles and remove paint. Be sure to work on inner bristles as well as outer ones. Resoak the brush if you find that it's necessary.

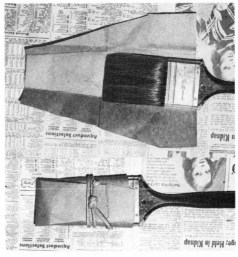

4. Wrap clean brushes in aluminum foil or heavy paper and store them flat or hang them up; never prop them on their bristles.

4. FIRST COATS

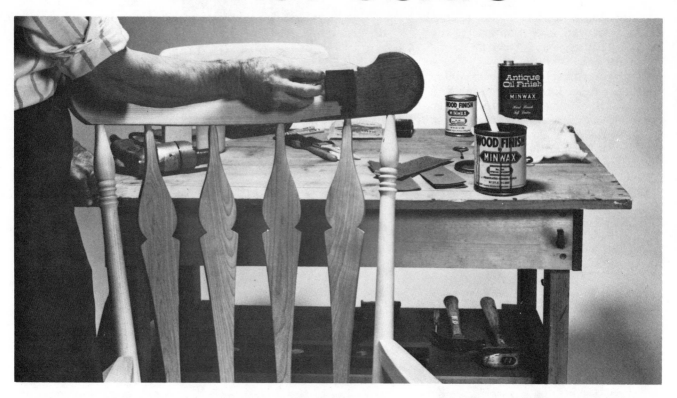

Wood is made up of millions of small cells or pores, held in a matrix of strong cellulose fibers—nature's way of providing great strength with a minimum of weight. However, it is easy for dirt, oil, grease, and other undesirable substances to get in between these pores and foul the surface of bare wood. Sealing, filling, staining, finishing, and polishing are ways of preserving, protecting, and accentuating the beauty of wood surfaces. This chapter will show you how to seal, fill, and stain your furniture.

A word about wood grain

The size of the pores in a piece of wood determines what kind of sealing, filling, and staining procedures you should follow when finishing the piece. Woods like oak, mahogany, and hickory are called *open-* or *coarse-grained* because their pores are so large and irregularly spaced that even the finely sanded surface of the wood has an uneven, coarse, or open texture (illustration at right). Applying any kind of stain or finish directly on coarse-grained wood usually results in a mottled or streaked appearance, so a wood filler should be used to fill the large and unevenly spaced pores and provide a more uniform surface.

Close-grained woods like maple, cherry, pine, and birch have very small and evenly spaced pores. These woods (especially maple) can be sanded to a very smooth texture, and no filler is needed prior to staining or finishing.

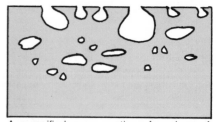

A magnified cross section of a piece of coarse-grained stock would look something like this. The pores are large and irregularly spaced.

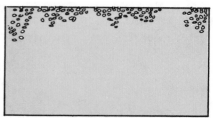

A similar view of close-grained stock would show a much finer and more regularly spaced pore structure.

Planning hints

Color. Most fillers, sealers, and finishes change the color of wood even if you also stain it. It is very difficult to predict exactly what color you will end up with as you apply one on top of the next. If you want the final finish to match a specific color you should run through the sequence as a test on a piece of scrap stock identical to the piece you want to finish or on an area that won't show. (The inside of drawer fronts, bottoms of table tops, and tips of chair legs are inconspicuous test spots.) Some paint and hardware stores have samples of stains on different kinds of woods.

Compatibility. Some finishes are chemically incompatible with some sealers. For example, a lacquer finish should never be applied over a varnish sealer. Read the directions on the cans of stain, filler, thinner, sealer, and finish you plan to use in sequence to check on their compatibility. Buying the same brand name of each preparation is safer than mixing brands.

Humidity. If possible, avoid applying sealer, filler, stain, or any kind of surface preparation under extremely humid conditions. Excessive humidity inhibits penetration and lengthens drying time. The moisture in the air saturates the surface pores of the wood and displaces the stain, sealer, or filler you're trying to apply. It pays to wait for a clear, dry day.

Work area. Find a well-ventilated place to work, away from children and free of dust, where you can leave unfinished work without its being disturbed. Most of the stains, fillers, and sealers are flammable as well as unpleasant or even harmful to breathe for long periods of time. Lay down some newspaper if spills or drips will hurt the floor, and keep an absorbent rag handy.

Sealers

Sealers do what their name suggests. They seal the wood by closing the surface pores, providing a uniform surface for later finish coats. Sealed wood can be sanded down far smoother than bare wood by using finer-grit abrasives, including steel wool. Wood stain, filler, and finish coats are absorbed more evenly (and with less penetration) by wood that has been sealed.

There are several different types of sealers, and the one you choose should depend on the type of finish to be applied over the sealer. If the finish is going to be lacquer, use shellac, commerical sanding sealer, or lacquer-sealer as the undercoat. Use shellac or varnish sealer under a varnish finish and polyurethane under polyurethane. Sealer coats should be thinned to *wash* consistency so they can penetrate fully. Refer to the shellac chart below and to instructions on varnish and polyurethane containers for thinning and sealing details.

Paint the sealer on generously, working it well into the wood with your brush. Pay special attention to end grains, which are extra absorbent. The dried sealer coat should not be shiny like a finish coat. For extra porous or dry wood you may have to apply two coats of sealer before applying finish coats.

How to cut shellac

Shellac is actually a granular substance which is dissolved in alcohol to make the sealing and finishing compound of the same name. The *cut* of the shellac is a measure of concentration in pounds of shellac granules per gallon of alcohol. Shellac is usually sold in 4-, 4½-, or 5-pound cuts, but a 1- or 2-pound cut is best for sealing. Refer to the chart for thinning down heavier cuts.

Original cut	Desired cut	Mixing Ratio Alcohol	Shellac
5-pound	4-pound	1 part	4 parts
5-pound	3-pound	1 part	2 parts
5-pound	2-pound	1 part	1 part
5-pound	1-pound	3 parts	1 part
4-pound	3-pound	1 part	4 parts
4-pound	2-pound	3 parts	4 parts
4-pound	1-pound	2 parts	1 part
3-pound	2-pound	2 parts	5 parts
3-pound	1-pound	4 parts	3 parts

Shellac can be used just as a sealer or applied in three or more coats as a final finish. Thinned to a 1- or 2-pound cut, it does an excellent job of penetrating and sealing. There are three different kinds of shellac: orange, dewaxed, and white (or

What it takes

Approximate drying times:

Shellac	1-2 hours
Sanding sealer	1 hour
Primer-sealer	1 hour or less
Varnish	24 hours
Polyurethane	3-5 hours
Lacquer-sealer	1 hour
Paste wood filler	24 hours
Water-base stain	24 hours
Oil-base stain	24 hours
NGR stain	45 min.

Tools and materials:

Rags. Use clean rags if possible. Burlap rags are excellent for removing excess wood filler. A fine-woven lint-free cotton cloth is best for wiping off stain. Rags can also be used to apply stain, although some finishers prefer using a brush or a sponge.
Cans. Have several empty, clean cans on hand for mixing and thinning wood filler, cleaning brushes, and holding small amounts of sealer or stain.
Thinner. Turpentine or paint thinner is used for varnish and most polyurethanes. Shellac and primer-sealer are thinned with alcohol. Thinners are inexpensive and are used for cleaning brushes and hands as well as for thinning, so keep a good supply on hand.
Brushes. Either natural or synthetic bristles are fine for sealing, filling, and staining.

bleached). White shellac is best for most furniture work, although orange can be used on dark woods. Allow one to two hours for the sealer to dry; then sand the surface lightly to level it and scuff it so the next coat will hold better.

easy sanding between coats without gumming up the sandpaper.

Primer-sealer paint is an alcohol-base primer designed specifically as an undercoat for painted finishes. It comes in white and can be used over any existing finish as well as on bare wood. This type of primer-sealer also covers stains and dries in less than an hour, so you can seal and apply the finish coat of paint in the same day.

Polyurethane can be used for both sealing and finishing. When you use it as an undercoat, apply the first finish coat as soon as the sealer coat dries (usually 3-5 hours) for best adhesion. If you wait longer, or if the sealer coat is uneven or bubbled, you'll have to fine-sand it. Thinners for polyurethane vary from mineral spirits to turpentine to synthetic, depending on what kind you buy. Some brands shouldn't be thinned down, so read the instructions on your can carefully before preparing the sealer coat.

Sanding sealer is a commercial sealer which is applied directly from the can without any thinning. These sealers come close to being ideal undercoaters, especially for shellac and all varnish finishes. They are ready to use without thinning, and easy to apply. Drying time is an hour or less, and most sanding sealers contain a special synthetic sanding agent that allows for quick,

Lacquer sealer is a special sealer used by many professional finishers as an undercoat for lacquer finishes. This preparation is usually sprayed on, and dries in an hour or less. You can make a similar quick-drying sealer by mixing a 2-pound cut of shellac with *mixing lacquer*. Spraying makes the job a snap, especially on contoured legs like these, but you can also apply this specialized sealer with a brush.

Varnish is thinned with turpentine or paint thinner. Although a varnish finish is much tougher than a shellac finish, varnish offers no advantage over shellac as a sealer. Shellac dries faster than varnish (varnish takes at least 24 hours) and is easier to sand between coats.

Spraying

Many hardware and paint stores carry varnish and shellac in aerosol spray cans. For small pieces like picture frames or contoured surfaces like table or chair legs, spraying is the fastest and easiest way to apply your sealer coat. Keep in mind that aerosol sealers and finishes have been thinned down considerably so they can be sprayed. You may have to apply a second coat to seal the wood effectively. Moreover,

shellac or varnish in spray cans is two to three times more expensive, so large projects may run into more money than you want to spend. If you decide to spray on your sealer coat, remember these two precautions as you work:

Work in a well-ventilated area, away from flame or intense heat.

Screen off your work area to protect nearby objects from overspray.

Wood filler

The best way to fill the large open pores on coarse-grained wood is to use a wood filler. You could simply apply five or six coats of varnish, shellac, or polyurethane until the irregular surface grain is level, but one application of wood filler is a faster and better way of doing the job. There are two basic kinds of wood fillers: liquid and paste.

Liquid fillers are essentially nothing more than thickened varnish or sanding sealer, and are poorly suited for use on coarse-grained woods because you usually need to put on more than one coat.

Paste fillers, which contain ground-up quartz crystals (silex) for thickness and filling power, are the real workhorses. They are used extensively by professionals but are often forgotten by the amateur.

Paste wood filler comes in different-sized cans just like paint and is sold at most paint stores. The natural color of paste wood filler is a grayish tan, but it's also available in different wood tones such as walnut or red mahogany. If you can't find the shade you want, add some wood stain to natural filler until you get the right color, but refer to the thinning and tinting instructions on the can beforehand. The instructions for most fillers recommend tinting with a penetrating or wiping oil stain. The shade of the filler should be darker than the wood being filled. Remember that the stain can also be applied separately after the surface has been filled with natural paste filler.

Wood filler works best when applied to stock that has already been sealed. Sealing the wood beforehand allows the filler to level the surface instead of penetrating it. You'll probably have to thin your paste wood filler before applying it. Most paste fillers are nearly as thick as peanut butter and will not work down deep enough into the pores at this consistency. Follow the thinning directions on your can of filler. Turpentine is most commonly used, but if you're blending stain into natural filler, the stain will act as the thinning agent. Aim for a thick creamy mixture, and stir up the filler thoroughly, so that no sediment is left on the bottom of the container. Mix only as much as you need.

Apply filler generously. Your object is to fill the pores of the wood, so work the paste in well with your brush. Coat the surface of the wood with a thick layer of paste. As soon as it begins to dull and thicken (anywhere from five to thirty minutes, depending on the dryness and porosity of the wood), wipe off the excess filler with a coarse, absorbent cloth such as burlap. Work carefully with even pressure so you can clean the surface of the wood without lifting the filler from the pores where it belongs. Don't stop until you have it all off. If the filler becomes too dry, it is difficult to remove and you'll have to soak a rag in benzene or turpentine to get the hardened residue off. Wipe only across the grain. This will force the filler into the pores and remove surface excess at the same time.

Woods that need filling

Ash
Chestnut
Elm
Hickory
Lauan
Mahogany
Locust
Oak
Rosewood
Teak

1. Thin filler to a thick, creamy consistency and apply it generously to the wood surface, using your brush to work the filler into the pores.

2. When the filler begins to dull over and dry out (in 5-30 minutes, depending on how dry and porous the wood is), use a coarse rag to remove excess. Always wipe across the grain.

3. Oil stain can be mixed with natural paste wood filler if you want to stain and fill in one step. Add stain until you get the right shade; then mix and apply.

4. With excess filler removed, the irregular surface of this open-grained oak board has been made even and level.

Staining wood

Before. The bare pine and maple wood in this rocker make it a good candidate for a darker stain.

After. With staining and finishing complete, the rocker appears to be made from the finest walnut.

Selecting the right stain

Wood stains are generally used for one of three reasons: to make one type of wood look like another, to give newer wood an aged appearance, or to make wood look more natural than it appears to be. For an example of the first use, consider a table with a walnut top and spruce legs. The dark walnut contrasts sharply with the pale spruce, but the legs can be stained so the table will appear to be walnut throughout. On the other hand, the wood in, say, a brand-new dresser could be stained to duplicate the warm, weathered look of antique furniture. Or stain might be used to give a more uniform appearance to the various parts of a chair or bookshelves, which sometimes appear dissimilar even though made from the same wood type.

You can use any type of stain on any kind of wood, but there are particular combinations which work out best. Pine, fir, and other softwoods will almost always take a penetrating or wiping-oil stain better than any other. These woods don't require filling and are porous enough to absorb just the right amount of the pigment that is suspended in the oil or mineral-spirit base. Penetrating and oil-base stains are usually the best stains to use for "transforming" pine or other light softwood furniture into cherry, walnut, or similar dark hardwoods.

Some woods, like mahogany, walnut, and cherry have such distinctive coloring that if they need to be stained at all, only the subtlest tone is required to achieve the desired highlights or to blend in with another piece of wood or furniture. Water-base or non-grain-raising stains are well suited for use on hardwoods, especially where lighter tones are needed.

The fastest way to stain wood is to spray on a non-grain-raising stain. These stains are made to be sprayed on, and applying/drying times are so short that the first coat of finish can be applied three to five hours after staining. With other types of stain, you have to wait at least 24 hours before applying finish coats.

When selecting a stain color or wood tone, don't rely on name or description. Stain colors are not standardized and will vary from brand to brand and even from can to can. (Tip: When using more than one can for a job, mix all the stain together first in a larger container to ensure uniformity.) Most stain manufacturers have sample displays showing various tones on different kinds of wood (examples: *special walnut* on pine; *special walnut* on birch; *colonial cherry* on maple; etc.). These displays will give you a fairly good idea of what final color to expect. Better, however, is to stain a scrap piece of wood of the same type as your furniture. Better still, turn chairs or tables over and do a test run on the unseen undersides. Methods for applying stain and advice on selecting the right product for your furniture begin opposite.

How to apply stains in general

Preparation. Before applying stain, be sure the wood has been sanded completely; in general, avoid sanding after the wood has taken a stain. Water-base stains are an exception because they will usually cause the grain of the wood to raise or swell, and you may have to do some fine smoothing with sandpaper or steel wool after the stain has dried.

Staining usually accentuates any scrapes, marks, or other imperfections in the wood surface, so bear in mind that scratches you can barely see on bare wood may show up loudly after stain goes on.

For staining close-grained woods, a preliminary sealer coat is often unnecessary. Because of the even grain and small pores, penetration is uniform and there is no streaking or mottled appearance. But you will have to use a sealer under stain if an irregular grain pattern and large pores indicate that the wood will absorb the coloring unevenly. Stain can be applied directly over wood that has been filled.

Mix stain thoroughly before you apply it. Pigment often settles in the bottom of the container, and unless this residue is blended in completely before application, the stain will darken as the job progresses, instead of being uniform throughout.

Technique. Although spraying equipment is used universally by commercial finishers to apply stain, most home craftsmen stain their furniture by hand. Brushes and rags are good tools for hand application, and it's equally important to have a rag handy for wiping off stain quickly. Since certain parts of the wood may be naturally darker than others, you can create a more uniform appearance by wiping the stain from these areas soon after it is applied.

Although techniques may vary from one product to another, there are only two essential steps in staining all wood: applying the stain and wiping off the residue. If you are concerned about controlling the depth and intensity of the color, use a cloth to apply the stain. With a cloth you can wipe the stain on carefully, instead of flooding the wood surface with stain as you would if you used a brush.

Wiping down the surface to remove excess stain is important. With the exception of nonpenetrating oil stains, the surface residue which has not been absorbed into the wood should be wiped off so the true beauty of the grain can show. A second coat can be applied for darker coloring. Refer to the instructions on your stain container for drying time between coats.

Particular types of stain

Water-base stains are used extensively in professional finishing shops but are not as popular among amateur craftsmen. In fact, very few hardware or paint stores stock this type of stain. (You can usually get them from specialty wood dealers.) Water stains are very inexpensive, but they require mixing, which is why they are not more widely used on the smaller projects most craftsmen do.

Water stains are blends of aniline dyes dissolved in a water base or *vehicle*. These stains are extremely brilliant and transparent, providing excellent coloring without hiding the grain of the wood. Unlike other stains, they will not lighten or bleach out when exposed to sunlight, and they can be mixed and thinned easily to nearly any tone or intensity.

The dyes for water-base stains come in powder form and are usually sold in one-ounce paper packets. Each packet makes a quart of stain, but you may want to add more or less water to lighten or darken the tone. (Keep track of your recipe for easy duplication.)

1. To mix stain, first pour powder into a clean container; then add a quart of nearly boiling water and stir until powder dissolves.

2. Apply stain generously, and keep the surface wet until the wood is saturated.

3. Remove the excess with a cloth dipped in stain. Wipe with the grain.

4. Water-base stains tend to raise the grain of the wood slightly, leaving an irregular surface that should be lightly smoothed with fine sandpaper or steel wool.

Nonpenetrating oil stains are also known as wiping stains. The latter name is more accurate, since the stain does actually penetrate into the wood pores. Unlike the penetrating stains, however, wiping stains have a linseed-oil base which makes them thicker and confines the pigment to the surface pores. Nonpenetrating oil stains are nearly opaque, like paint, and will cover and cloud the grain more than other kinds of stain. They are easy to apply because the intensity and uniformity of the color is determined simply by how vigorously you wipe the thick coating of pigment off the surface. Reapply stain to light areas. Nonpenetrating stain works equally well over bare, sealed, or filled wood, but remember that the wood grain will be clouded and camouflaged. Use nonpenetrating stains to darken pine or fir and change their appearance, or to cloud a bad-looking piece of stock whose grain is better off hidden than highlighted.

Avoiding stain strain
Even with my favorite paintbrush I couldn't work at more than a snail's pace, trying to stain this giant dresser with a penetrating oil stain. Penetrating oil stains are pretty thin, and you just can't carry much on a brush. Dripping is a problem too. I discovered that the quickest way to tackle large staining jobs is to use a sponge. Wear rubber gloves so you can dip right into the can and sponge on the stain without worrying about your hands. You'll still need a brush for some corners and tight spots, but a sponge can't be beat for doing those big flat areas.

Practical Pete

1. Apply wiping stain generously, using a brush to flow on an even coat.

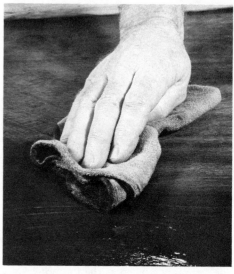

2. Wipe off the excess, using a cloth that has been dampened with stain.

Penetrating oil stains are among the most popular stains and can be found just about anywhere hardware or paints are sold. They are available, ready mixed, in many different wood tones (see list on opposite page). The mineral-spirit or turpentine base of these stains gives them a thin consistency which allows for deep penetration. You can use a penetrating oil stain on bare wood or on wood that has been filled or sealed. Sealing ensures uniform penetration on stock that normally would absorb stain unevenly. The color will be lighter than it would be on unsealed wood, and you may need a second application or a darker tone of stain to achieve the color you want.

The darkness or intensity of these stains is determined by how soon after application they are wiped off. For a very light tone, wipe off the stain as soon as it is applied; there will be little time for the stain to penetrate and fill the pores of the wood with pigment. Leave the stain on longer for deeper penetration and darker color. You can also apply a second coat of stain for darker, richer color, but wait at least four hours for the first coat to dry. When wiping down, use a rag that has been slightly dampened in the stain. Penetrating stain can be applied with a brush, sponge, or rag.

Walnut penetrating stain was applied to this piece of pine stock and partially wiped off after 30 seconds.

The same amount of walnut stain was applied to an identical piece of pine, but this time the stain was left on for 15 minutes before wiping. Deeper penetration has resulted in a darker color.

Non-grain-raising (NGR) stains are nearly identical to water-base stains in the brilliance and transparency of color they give to the grain of the wood. The main difference is that the NGR stains will not cause the surface wood fibers to swell and raise the grain like water stains do. Sanding or steel wooling after applying the stain is unnecessary. NGR stains are also fast drying. You can apply a second coat in 10 or 15 minutes, and apply finish in one to three hours.

NGR stains were developed for commercial use to replace water-base stains and are harder for the nonprofessional to find than oil stains. NGR stains are also sold under names like *non-fiber-raising, alcohol base,* and *fast drying;* they are available through some mail-order houses, if your hardware or paint store doesn't stock them. Most types of NGR stains are more expensive than water or oil stains and require a special thinner, which is sold with the stain.

NGR stains shouldn't be used on softwoods. They are best suited for hardwoods like maple, oak, or walnut which require a subtle shading to emphasize their already distinctive coloring.

Because of their quick-drying characteristics, the best way to apply NGR stains is to spray them on. Apply a moderate rather than wet coat. (See pages 250-251 for detailed spraying instructions.) There should be little or no excess to wipe off.

When brushing on NGR stain, do one section at a time so you can avoid brushing into areas that have already dried. Overlap marks will show up, and streaks or spots may result when staining large areas. You can prevent this by working very quickly with a full, wet brush or thinning down the stain and applying two or three weak coats instead of a single strong one.

Exterior stains are used on outdoor furniture or any other furniture that may be exposed to the weather. These stains contain special compounds which resist rot and mildew and repel termites and other wood-destructive insects. They are used not only on patio furniture but on exterior siding, fence posts, and wood shingles. Although sometimes referred to as wood stains, these compounds are more accurately called wood preservatives, since they are designed to protect wood from harsh outdoor conditions.

Some brands of preservative stain should not be covered with finish coats. Others, particularly if they contain creosote, have an unpleasant smell, so it's best to use conventional stain on indoor furniture.

Exterior stain can and should be applied at regular intervals to maintain maximum protection. Brush or spray the stain on generously and let residue soak in.

NGR stains are best for use on hardwoods like the maple stock shown here. Dark walnut stain has been partially wiped on in the top photo, while Salem maple was used on the bottom piece.

Use preservative stains to protect wood exposed to outdoor conditions. These stains contain special compounds which resist rot and repel termites.

Common wood stains
(in order of decreasing darkness)

Ebony
Jacobean
Dark walnut
Teak
Danish walnut
Red mahogany
Cherry
Early American
Ipswich pine
Fruitwood
Golden oak

Stopgaps and copouts

If you're operating on a low budget or if you want to cut down on refinishing costs, you can make your own stain so simply and inexpensively it's hard to believe. Use tea. That's right, tea. Penny-pinching finishing buffs have found that a strong mixture works best, and you don't have to add cream or sugar. A home-made tea stain wouldn't do much for darker woods like walnut or cherry, but if you'd like to darken maple or pine furniture, start saving those used teabags.

5.FINISHING

Selecting the right finish

Approximate time: Here's how long it should take, from first application to final drying, for each finish:
Paste wax (2 coats): 2 hours
Shellac (3 coats): 2 days
French polishing: 1 day
Penetrating resin (2 coats): 4 hours
Varnish: 3 days
Lacquer (3-4 coats): 1 day
Polyurethane (3 coats): 2 days
Rubbed oil (10 applications): 3 weeks
Catalytic: 1 day
Paint and enamel: 1-2 days, depending on drying time.

Tools and materials: Brushes and rags as required. Finishing materials, thinners, and special tools are described with each finish on pages that follow.

Choosing the right finish is not always easy. With the finishing options available today, any one of several choices might be the right one. Here are some important considerations, followed by a detailed description of each type of finish and how to apply it.
Beauty. Each finish has its own distinctive effect, and this effect depends largely on the type of wood and how it is prepared (sealed, stained, filled, or bare). If the texture of the wood is especially pleasing or unique, you might want to use an in-the-wood finish like oil or penetrating resin instead of covering the surface with a hard coat of varnish or lacquer. The best way to be sure of your finishing decision is to make a test run on a scrap of wood that matches your furniture.
Durability. Try to anticipate the conditions your furniture will be exposed to when selecting the finish. Resistance to water stains and damage from other liquids like alcohol and ammonia varies from finish to finish and even from brand to brand. Abrasion and temperature extremes are other wear factors. With the exception of shellac, wax, and French polish, most finishes offer excellent protection under normal conditions, even though each finish has particular wear characteristics (see chart opposite).

Application. Consider the time and techniques required for the finish you'd like to apply. Suppose you have a small end table that has been stained and sealed. A paste-wax finish (one coat) could be applied easily in less than 45 minutes. Finishing the same piece with two coats of varnish might take three days or longer, and you'd have to pay special attention to brush technique, dust control, and between-coat sanding. Penetrating resin and polyurethane finishes are popular among many craftsmen because of their easy application and short drying times. On the other hand, devoting the extra time and effort to a traditional finish like rubbed oil or French polish can be extremely rewarding.

Other important considerations are compatibility and surface preparation. Always check the instructions on your can of finish to make sure the wood surface has been prepared correctly. Most finishes are either incompatible with certain sealers, fillers, and stains, or should be used with recommended "first coats" for best results. For example, penetrating resin and catalytic finishes work best over bare wood, and polyurethane shouldn't be used over a shellac sealer coat.

A survey of common finishes

NAME AND DESCRIPTION	ADVANTAGES, SPECIAL QUALITIES	LIMITATIONS, DISADVANTAGES	RECOMMENDED USE
Paste wax is one of the oldest furniture finishes. It is made from a combination of durable natural waxes and is used over hard finishes for extra shine and protection.	Inexpensive; application is easy and can be repeated regularly to maintain shine and protection.	Dulls quickly under rough conditions; frequent buffing and reapplication are necessary to maintain beauty and durability.	Gives additional shine and protection to hard finishes; can also be used over stained wood; use on furniture that can be cared for regularly.
Shellac is made from a natural resin dissolved in an alcohol base. As a multiple-coat finish, *white* shellac highlights the grain with just a slight darkening effect. *Orange* shellac gives a darker tone.	Inexpensive and easy to apply; quick-drying (a multiple-coat finish can be applied in two days or less); easily sanded and waxed; thinning and cleanup are easy.	Low resistance to water and alcohol; stains easily; the least durable of the hard finishes; limited shelf life.	For furniture that will not be exposed to water, alcohol, or other liquids that might soften and stain the finish; use underneath a wax finish and when a more expensive finish isn't required.
French polishing is a traditional finishing technique used on fine "period" furniture. It requires a clean, lint-free cloth, shellac, and linseed oil.	Inexpensive; can be done in one day; durable; requires little care when applied correctly; will repair damaged shellac or lacquer finishes.	Applied over bare wood or water-base and NGR stains only; application is difficult and requires a lot of skill; finish must not be waxed.	For chairs, small tables and stands, quality furniture that will not see rough use; the traditional finish for fine antiques.
Penetrating resin is a relatively new finish which hardens and protects the wood without covering the wood surface. It is available in clear or various wood tones.	Simple application; excellent protection and beauty with little effort; filler and sealer coats not required; no sanding or polishing; simply reapply to rejuvenate.	Expensive; not to be used with any other sealer, stain, filler, or finish except for water-base and NGR stains.	Use anywhere good protection is important, but a hard, glossy surface finish isn't needed; to show off the grain without losing the texture and feel of the wood surface.
Varnish is a hard, clear finish made from natural or synthetic resins. It does not penetrate or highlight the grain as much as the other clear finishes; it comes in flat, glossy, and satin versions.	Extremely hard and durable; comes close to being indestructible when applied in multiple coats; can be rubbed and polished to a smooth, mirrorlike finish.	Must not be applied over an oil-base stain; extremely long drying and hardening time; prone to dust contamination; application requires careful brush technique.	Use on table or countertops, outdoor furniture, or anywhere weather or rough use threatens to harm the wood.
Lacquer is a surface finish with excellent hardness and durability. Available as a clear finish (flat, satin, or glossy) or in colors (colored lacquer is called lacquer enamel), it is usually sprayed on, although special *brushing lacquer* is also available.	Fast-drying; no danger of dust contamination; similar to varnish in appearance and wear characteristics but can be applied much more quickly and without the skilled brush technique.	Wood must be sealed with shellac or lacquer-sealer; only NGR or water-base stains can be used, requires thinning and special spraying equipment.	For a hard, durable finish where extra protection is important; preferable to varnish if you have spraying equipment.
Polyurethane is a clear surface finish nearly identical to varnish in appearance and durability but easier and quicker to apply. Made from synthetic resins, it is available in gloss or satin styles.	Quick-drying; gives excellent protection with simple brush application; a three- or four-coat finish can be applied in two days.	Incompatible with most sealers and fillers; bubbles easily; most brands cannot be thinned or require special synthetic thinners; costly.	Best for finishing bare wood or as a finish over water-base or NGR stain.
Rubbed-oil finishes penetrate into the pores and leave the wood exposed but offer good durability and resistance to water and staining. Rubbed-oil finishes give wood a clear, soft luster.	Inexpensive; application is easy but must be repeated at least 10 times for true hand-rubbed effect. Modern oil finishes require only two or three applications and less rubbing.	Cannot be used over sealers or fillers; multiple applications require more time and effort than other finishes; modern oil finishes are expensive.	Best on dark woods like walnut or cherry, or over a dark stain; for tables, desks, or chairs where a hard surface finish isn't desired
Catalytic finishes come in two parts which are mixed together and then solidify into a hard and extremely durable surface. Available in clear or colors.	Probably the toughest finishes you can apply.	Expensive; require mixing and careful application; suitable only for flat surfaces like tabletops; adhere poorly to most sealers, stains, and fillers; some types require heat curing.	Use on table, bar, and countertops that need extra protection.

Paste wax

Wax is one of the oldest finishing compounds known. It is the least expensive finish you can buy and is easy to apply, even though it does require more elbow grease than other finishes. Although there are many types of wax for different jobs like polishing cars and protecting floors, all wax comes in one of three forms: liquid, paste, and cream. Only paste wax is used for finishing furniture. You can put a wax finish on wood that has been stained, or wax can be applied over a final coat of shellac, varnish, polyurethane, enamel, or lacquer. A shellac finish should be waxed to protect it from water and alcohol damage, and a good wax finish makes a smart varnish, lacquer, or enamel job look even better.

Wax offers protection against scuffing and staining but will not stand up to heavy wear or water. The durability and beauty of a wax finish depend upon regular buffing and recoating, which is economical and enjoyable, provided you don't have too many waxed surfaces to look after.

Application

To apply a paste-wax finish, first make sure the wood surface is dry and free of dust. Sand any sealer or finish coats with fine or extra-fine sandpaper until they are uniformly smooth. The best way to get paste wax out of the container and onto the surface is with a piece of cheesecloth. Fold in some wax between two or more layers of cheesecloth and wipe a *thin* layer of wax over the surface, using a circular motion. A common mistake when applying a paste-wax finish is wiping on more wax than you need. Trying to buff a thick layer of wax is hard work, and it usually results in a dull, uneven, and gummy appearance. A thin film of wax over the surface is all you'll need for each coat. Durable wax finishes are built up in thin coats.

After about 10 minutes (the time may vary depending on what brand of wax you're using—read the label for instructions), the wax will dry out and lose its shiny look. Rub the surface with a clean, soft cloth. Use a circular motion at first; then change to a linear motion, working with the grain. Use a fresh cloth for the final rubbing down. There is no way around the hard work of buffing: the harder and longer you buff, the shinier the finish. You can use a lamb's-wool buffing attachment on an electric drill to speed up the work.

Wait at least an hour before applying another coat of wax, but remember that a high-luster finish depends not on multiple coats but on good buffing.

I rubbed my table the wrong way
Even if you're in good physical shape, buffing a paste-wax finish is tough work. An electric drill with a buffing attachment is the easiest way to get that mirrorlike shine, but if you don't have one, or have lent yours out at the wrong time like I did, there are still a couple of alternatives to muscling your way through a wax job:

Replace the sandpaper in your orbital sander with a buffing cloth cut to the proper size, and let the high-speed vibrations do the work. (Do not use a belt sander!) Or wrap your buffing cloth around a brick. Yes, a brick. You'd be surprised how much help that extra weight can be, especially over large areas like tabletops.

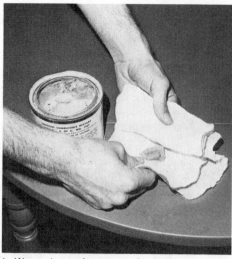

1. Wrap a lump of paste wax between two or more layers of cheesecloth and wipe a thin film over the surface with a circular motion.

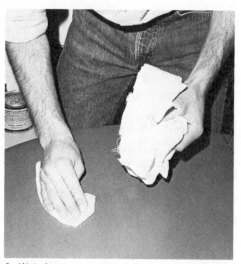

2. Wait for the wax to dull over; then wipe the surface with a clean, soft cloth. Buffing and removing excess wax are done at the same time.

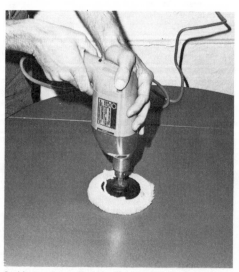

3. Use a clean cloth for final buffing, or an electric drill with a lamb's-wool buffing attachment, as shown above.

Shellac

Applying a shellac finish is one of the oldest and most traditional methods of finishing furniture. Despite the growing variety of modern finishing materials, shellac still offers many advantages in terms of economy, ease of application, and beauty. Shellac brings out the grain of the wood in deep, warm tones, and it can be used with equal success on dark or light woods. Although *white* shellac is used universally, some finishers prefer to use *orange* shellac on darker woods because of its light amber cast, which lends more warmth to the grain.

Shellac has a limited shelf life. Stale shellac loses its quick-drying characteristics and stays tacky for a long time. Most manufacturers date their containers—don't buy shellac more than four months old—and you can test the freshness of your shellac by applying a coat to a scrap of wood. If it dries in 45 minutes or less, go ahead and use it. Buy only as much shellac as you need, since what you don't use may have to be discarded. Remember also that shellac reacts chemically with ferrous metals; so store it in a glass or plastic container.

Compared to most other finishes, shellac has little durability. Water will leave stains on a shellac finish, and even the best shellac finish will dull over and soften when exposed to alcohol, ammonia, or other chemical solutions. A wax finish applied over two or three coats of shellac offers good protection against stains and softening, but in general, it's best not to shellac bar and tabletops or other furniture that might be exposed to wet glasses, hot objects, or alcoholic beverages.

Seven-step method

Shellac is never a single-coat finish. It must be built up in a series of three or more coats. Compared to other clear finishes like varnish, polyurethane, and lacquer, shellac can be applied quickly and without as much attention to technique or evenness or coverage. Its thin cut and nonbubbling characteristics make application easy. Shellac is also very easy to sand and level between coats. Follow this sequence or *schedule* for applying a shellac finish:

1. Fine-sand the bare wood and clean the surface in preparation for finishing.
2. Apply a sealer coat of 1-pound-cut shellac (see chart, page 233) by brush or spray.
3. Wait an hour for the shellac to dry; then sand the sealer coat lightly.
4. Remove any dust or powder from the surface with a tack rag and apply a coat of 2-pound-cut shellac.
5. Wait two hours for the second coat to dry; then sand as in step 3.
6. Clean the surface and apply a coat of 3-pound-cut shellac.
7. Allow the shellac to dry and harden for 24 hours; then smooth with extra-fine sandpaper or steel wool.

A few coats of shellac make an excellent base for a paste-wax finish. The final coat of shellac can be left as is, without any fine-sanding, but a buffed paste-wax finish always makes a good shellac job look even better. In addition, the wax protects the shellac from water and alcohol damage.

Later coats of shellac adhere well to previous coats, but it is nevertheless good practice to scuff-sand between coats. Use extra-fine sandpaper to level out uneven spots and remove any dust that may have settled into the finish. Shellac will sand easily, but it produces a fine white powder that is notorious for clogging up sandpaper. Use an open-coat paper or an inexpensive type that can be thrown away when it becomes badly clogged. Fine or extra-fine steel wool is also good for between-coat sanding, and it will not clog up like sandpaper. You can expect fine sanding to cloud the finish slightly, but subsequent finish coats (including paste wax) will clear up this condition.

Apply shellac with a wet, fully laden brush. Overlap each brush course slightly, but avoid excessive lapping and fast brushing to forestall bubbling.

Sand between coats to remove dust particles and smooth rough or uneven spots. Shellac dust is infamous for clogging up sandpaper. so use a cheap grade or an open-coat paper.

French polishing

Many fine antiques have a French-polish finish. This type of finish has been used for generations to give wood a clear, warm luster and provide more durability than shellac. If you have an antique desk or chair, you can actually increase its value by applying a French-polish finish. French polishing is a painstaking operation that requires patience, hard work, and a true feel for wood finishing. You'll need shellac, boiled linseed oil, a clean, lint-free cloth, and a lot of energy to do the job.

Prepare the wood by sanding it down as smooth as possible. French polishing will work best when done over bare wood or wood that has been stained with a water-base or NGR stain. Using filler or sealer under French polish is not recommended.

The finish should be applied on a dry day, with the work-area temperature at least 70 degrees Fahrenheit. Warmer temperatures will speed the operation. French polishing should be done quickly, but with careful attention to the proper technique. Here's how it's done:

1. Pour some 1-pound-cut shellac into a small bowl. Wad the cloth up into a ball, dip it into the shellac, and apply the shellac to the surface with straight, light, rapid strokes. Work with the grain of the wood.
2. When you have applied a full coat in this way, wait for it to dry; then sand it lightly with extra-fine sandpaper or steel wool. For even better results, rub each coat down with pumice and oil.
3. Apply additional coats in the same way until the finish begins to shine. Then add several drops of boiled linseed oil to the shellac and apply this mixture by dipping and rubbing. Switch to a rotary motion, instead of a linear one, and add a drop or two more linseed oil as the shine intensifies.

Stop when the finish has the look you want. Your arm will probably be ready to fall off from fatigue, but you will have built up a deep, virtually glowing finish that will last a lifetime with the proper care. If the finish ever dulls, you can revive it by rubbing down with rottenstone and oil, and then French polishing in the usual manner.

1. Apply the 1-pound-cut shellac with a lint-free cloth rolled up into a ball. Use a linear motion at first, rubbing with the grain.

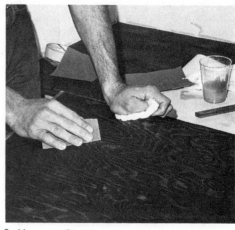

2. Use extra-fine abrasive paper to sand between coats. Wipe off abraded dust with a tack rag.

3. When the finish starts to build up to a light sheen, add a few drops of boiled linseed oil to the shellac and apply with a circular motion.

Stopgaps and copouts

Here's an alternative to French polishing that produces a similar finish but is much easier to apply:
1. Fill one bowl with 4-pound-cut shellac and another with a good grade of turpentine. Roll a clean, lint-free cloth into a ball.
2. Dip the cloth into the turpentine first, then into the shellac, and apply to the wood using a circular motion.
3. Sand between coats and keep applying until the finish builds to a soft gloss.
4. Wait for the final coat to dry; then rub the surface with a cloth dipped in linseed oil.

Penetrating resin

One of the newest and most unusual finishes available today is penetrating resin in liquid form. Unlike shellac, varnish, lacquer, and polyurethane, which are on-the-surface finishes, penetrating resin is an in-the-wood finish. It hardens and strengthens the wood without covering the surface. The synthetic resins which make up the finish penetrate deep into the wood and fill all the pores. When these resins harden, the wood becomes extremely strong and resistant to water, alcohol, heat, and abrasion. While it won't give you the smooth and glossy shine that varnish or lacquer does, a penetrating-resin finish lets you keep in touch with the texture and true feel of the wood.

Penetrating resin is its own sealer and filler; in fact, you shouldn't use other sealers or fillers before applying this type of finish. Open-grain woods like rosewood, oak, teak, and mahogany will take a penetrating-resin finish especially well, although you'll probably have to give these woods three applications to fill all the pores completely and evenly.

Clear penetrating resin will darken the wood slightly and highlight the grain considerably, making a drab-looking wood come alive. For darker woods, a penetrating-resin finish has more of a darkening effect than for lighter woods. Although most wood finishers prefer to use the clear type of penetrating resin, you can buy it in different wood tones. If the wood must be stained before applying a penetrating-resin finish, use only water-base or NGR stain. If the wood begins to dull or show signs of wear after initial finishing, simply reapply the penetrating resin. Don't try to use another type of finish in combination with penetrating resin. Even a light coat of wax seems to spoil the wood-grain highlights of this special finish.

Easy application

Penetrating resin is the easiest of all finishes to apply. Prepare the bare wood surface by sanding it smooth and cleaning any dust off with a vacuum or tack rag. The best way to apply this type of finish is to pour it on, so try to keep the wood surface horizontal. Spread the liquid and work it into the wood with fine steel wool. If pouring isn't possible, as with chair or table legs, brush or wipe the penetrating resin on as liberally as you can. The object is to totally saturate the wood. Keep applying the finish until the wood can't absorb any more. Keep the surface wet for at least 30 minutes (check manufacturer's suggested time). Then wipe the surface clean with a rag. It's important to remove all the resin that hasn't been absorbed into the wood, since this surface residue will harden and mask, rather than enhance, the wood grain. If the residue is difficult to remove, soften it first by applying more finish. For an even more durable finish, use the same technique to apply a second coat four or five hours later.

To apply penetrating resin, hold or clamp the work horizontal if possible, and pour the finish on directly out of the can. Spread it out and work it into the wood with steel wool.

When you've saturated the pores and no more finish can be absorbed, leave the surface wet at least 30 minutes before wiping off all excess.

Varnish

Finish styles

Varnish, lacquer, polyurethane, and enamel are usually sold in several styles, or degrees of shininess.
Glossy finishes have a very high sheen, and can be polished and rubbed to an even finer, mirrorlike shine. This type of finish is popular for bar and tabletops.
Satin and semigloss finishes contain chemical *deglossers* designed to tone down the shine slightly. This style of finish gives a moderate sheen without the sharp reflectivity of a glossy finish.
Flat finishes have no sheen.

Keeping the groove clean

No matter what kind of finish you're using, the groove around the lid of the container is a great place for material to collect and harden, making it difficult or impossible to close the lid correctly. You can avoid the task of prying this hardened material loose by punching seven or eight holes in the bottom of the groove after opening the can. Most of the finish will drain right back where it belongs, and reclosing the can will be a lot easier.

Varnishes have been popular among woodworkers for many years. They are made from tough natural or synthetic resins (sometimes a combination of the two) suspended in an oil-base vehicle along with drying agents and other chemical solvents. They are transparent and extremely durable. Wood that has been finished with several coats of varnish will endure impact and abrasion, heat, water, alcohol, and other chemicals without showing any wear.

Because of the great variety of resins used, it's difficult to choose what type of varnish to buy. First decide whether you want a flat, satin, or glossy finish on your furniture, and pay particular attention to drying and recoating times. The only disadvantage of varnish finishes is the unusually long time it takes each coat to dry completely. Applying several coats of varnish is a great way of protecting and beautifying your furniture, but it will take some careful work and at least several days, from start to finish.

Surface preparation. Bare wood must be sealed before you apply a varnish finish. Varnish can be thinned (refer to instructions on container for thinning agents and proportions) and used as a sealer, but you can also use shellac, which dries much faster. Never apply varnish directly over an oil-base stain. Some of the pigment in the stain will dissolve in the varnish and cloud the finish, so be sure to separate the varnish from the stain with a coat of shellac. When applying a varnish finish, it's important for the surface to be clean and dry.

Brushes. Use a new brush to apply varnish. Since each coat requires several courses of brushwork, any particles, pigments, or solvents in a used brush are bound to find their way into the finish and spoil the work. Even with a new brush, you should fan the bristles beforehand to remove any dust. More than any other kind of finish, varnishing requires a high-quality brush (see page 230). Some hardware stores carry brushes specially made for varnish.

Temperature and ventilation. Work in a warm and well-ventilated area. The lengthy drying and curing times can be shortened a little by using a portable heater or sunlamp to warm the furniture before and after application. Always respect the flammability of varnish or any other finish; keep heat sources at a safe distance.

Curing time. The main drawback of varnish is its lengthy curing time. While most varnishes dry to touch in 8-12 hours, they may not cure or harden for at least 24 hours, and each coat must be hard before the next one is applied. Some marine or *spar* varnishes take several days to a week to harden completely. The longer the drying and curing time, the more likelihood there is of dust and other particles accumulating in each coat. Find out how long you'll have to wait between coats before buying varnish.

To determine whether or not a coat of varnish has hardened, press your thumb against the surface in a spot that won't be seen. If you can't wipe away your thumbprint with a soft cloth, you'll have to wait longer before sanding or polishing.

Purity. Never mix one brand of varnish with another. Each manufacturer has a different varnish formula which shouldn't be altered by mixing. Never apply varnish straight from the can it is sold in. If you did, dust and other small contaminants would

It's best to use new varnish for finishing jobs, but you can remove the impurities in old varnish by straining it through a discarded pair of nylon panty hose.

Instead of applying varnish straight from the container it comes in, pour some into a smaller, shallower can. Make sure the can is perfectly clean and attach a strike wire across it as shown. Dip only the bottom third of the bristles into the varnish.

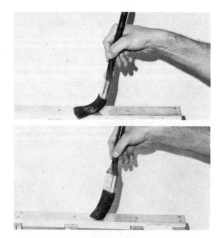

Never apply varnish by forcing the brush against the surface so the bristles bend as shown in the top picture. Spread the finish on with the tip of your brush, bending the bristles only slightly.

inevitably collect in the can, and leftover varnish wouldn't be pure for later finishing jobs. Pour the amount you think you'll need into a separate can. This can should be clean and shallow so you won't have to worry about dipping the bristles in more than one-third of their length.

Once you open a new can of varnish, the drying agents will start to evaporate, leaving old varnish too thick to apply correctly. When this happens, thin the finish with the appropriate solvent.

Bubbles. Few finishers can eliminate bubbles altogether, but you can minimize them. Shaking or fast stirring will create bubbles in the varnish even before you apply it. To mix varnish, stir it slowly and wait a few minutes for bubbles to disappear. Use a strike wire (a length of coat hanger) attached across the top of the can to remove excess varnish from the brush. Curving the bristles against the edge of the can tends to cause bubbles and waste varnish. To reduce bubbling when applying varnish, remember this: *Lay the finish on; don't work it in.* Stroking the brush back and forth over the same area causes bubbles; keep the brush in contact with the surface, moving it slowly and with light, even pressure. Each coat of varnish is laid on with two separate brush courses at right angles to each other (as shown in the first photograph below) and tipped off with a nearly dry brush to ensure uniformity. Any bubbles remaining after the varnish has dried must be removed by sanding or steel-wooling.

Technique. For large pieces of furniture, do one section at a time. If possible, turn the furniture so that you have a horizontal surface to make brushing easier and to forestall drips or sags. Divide large tabletops into sections with your mind's eye, and varnish one area at a time. Always brush from dry sections into wet sections, not the other way around.

Look what I did while closing the lid
Even with holes punched in the groove around the lid, there's bound to be enough paint or finish left down there to send splatters flying when you tap the lid shut. Place a rag or some newspaper over the lid before you tap it closed, and you'll avoid the speckling experience I had.

Practical Pete

How to apply a coat of varnish

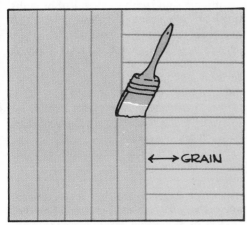

1. First apply varnish by brushing with the grain and overlapping slightly on each brush stroke. Then, keeping the brush wet, stroke across the grain, at right angles to the first brush course.

2. The final step in each coat is called tipping off. With an almost-dry brush, stroke very gently with the grain of the wood, using only the tip of the brush.

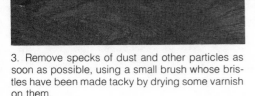

3. Remove specks of dust and other particles as soon as possible, using a small brush whose bristles have been made tacky by drying some varnish on them.

4. Use fine or extra-fine steel wool to level the surface between coats and remove bubbles and dust. Sanding or steel-wooling is also necessary before polishing the final coat.

Rubbed oil

While linseed oil has been used for many years to produce the traditional hand-rubbed finish, there are many modern oil finishes that give the same protection and beauty with less work.

The rubbed-oil finish has been popular in America since colonial times. It protects wood without covering it and gives a clear, warm luster that stands out even among modern synthetics. The old-fashioned oil finishes required little in the way of materials but quite a lot in the way of elbow grease. For that reason they have been more or less replaced by modern oil finishes that are far faster and easier to apply. Still, if you have a small piece of furniture and want to try your hand at tradition, you'll be rewarded with the satisfaction of fine craftsmanship. All oil finishes offer excellent protection against water, abrasion, and staining, and they will also stand up to hot serving plates.

You can put an oil finish on bare or stained wood but never over sealer or filler coats, since the strength and beauty of the finish depend on penetration. To apply an old-fashioned oil finish, you'll need some good-quality boiled linseed oil, turpentine, and a clean cloth. Thin the linseed oil with the turpentine—one part turpentine to three parts oil is a good mixture. For later coats, you can use the linseed oil at full strength. You'll get better results if you heat this solution and work in a warm room.

Caution: Oil and "turps" are flammable, so never expose them to direct flame. The safest method is to suspend the finish container in warm water over low heat.

Flood the oil onto the surface of the wood and let it soak in for 10 or 15 minutes. Then wipe off the surface residue and "buff" the oil into the wood with a cloth. Rubbing the finish in will produce a dull glow which grows deeper and more beautiful with each application. You should plan to apply at least 10 such coats of linseed oil for a true antique oil finish, although many old-timers apply up to 20 coats and keep their favorite furniture glowing with regular re-coating. It's best to allow a couple of days between applications.

Today there are many modern oil finishes that will produce the same deep, soft luster, but with much less effort. There are even special oil finishes for resin-rich woods like teak. No matter which brand of modern oil finish you use, only two or three applications are necessary, and you won't have to do much rubbing. They're quite a bit more expensive than linseed oil and turpentine, but the extra cost is worth it if you don't have the time or patience for the old-fashioned method.

1. Thin some boiled linseed oil with turpentine and flood the wood surface with this mixture. For best results, warm the finish before applying, and work in a warm room.

2. Let the oil penetrate into the wood for about 15 minutes; then wipe off the surface residue and rub the oil vigorously into the wood. Repeat application at least 10 times, waiting two days between coats.

Modern oil finishes will give the same beauty and protection as an old-fashioned hand-rubbed finish, but with much less effort and time. They are more expensive, though.

Lacquer

Lacquer is a surface finish very similar to varnish in hardness and durability, but more popular among professional finishers because it dries rapidly and sprays well. In fact, modern lacquer was originally developed for professional furniture makers who needed a fast, easy substitute for varnish. But lacquer is becoming more popular with the home craftsman, thanks to the development of low-cost spraying equipment, aerosol cans, and specially formulated brushing lacquers. (Note: The aerosol spray-can finishes are usually acrylics or imitation lacquers that aren't suitable for building the tough, multiple-coat finish achieved by brushing or using quality spray equipment.)

There are many kinds of lacquer, including a broad range of automotive and metal-work enamels—the main types used on furniture are listed at right—yet all modern lacquers consist of nitrocellulose or resin gums suspended in an acetone-base solvent. The acetone is what causes lacquer to dry so quickly—too quickly, in most cases, to be brushed on. Just about all lacquers are made to be sprayed on in thin coats and must be thinned down before spraying. (For detailed information on spraying equipment and techniques, see page 250.) Brushing lacquers, the exception to the rule, contain compounds in the solvent called retarders, which lengthen drying time.

Whether you brush or spray, the one catch in applying a lacquer finish is surface preparation. Good sealer coats are important under a lacquer finish. Only shellac, sanding sealer, or lacquer sealer should be used, so the lacquer doesn't penetrate. Surface preparation includes the usual compatibility precautions. If you apply lacquer directly over a penetrating or wiping oil stain, the strong solvents in the lacquer will loosen some of the pigment, producing clouds or streaks. Lacquer can be applied over water-base or NGR stains without bleeding, but it is good practice to sandwich a thin layer of shellac between stain and lacquer coats. If the wood has been treated with wood filler, it's also a good idea to apply a coat of shellac before the first coat of lacquer goes on.

Brushing lacquer usually comes ready to apply, so thinning is unnecessary. **TIP:** You can make brushing lacquer by adding slow-drying thinner to spray-on lacquer. Don't try to brush on spraying lacquer, though. Your brush will stick to the already-dry finish when overlapping courses, and the result will be uneven.

The technique for brushing on lacquer is simple: flow the finish on instead of working it in. Use only moderate pressure, so the bristles bend but slightly, and avoid lapping. Use as large a brush as possible, so you can carry more material. After the surface is covered, go over any areas that appear uneven, using only light pressure on the bristle tips.

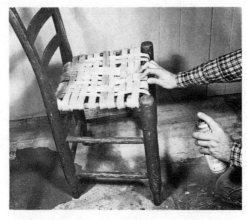

Lacquer is available in aerosol spray cans, but for quality furniture work, it is either brushed on or sprayed on with a refillable gun.

Dipping is often the best way to apply finish on small items like drawer pulls. If you turn the screw partway into the pull, you can use it as a holder for dipping, and later as a hanger for drying.

Spread brushing lacquer on in a generous but even coat, slightly overlapping previous brush strokes. Avoid excessive lapping and bristle bending.

Types of lacquer commonly used for finishing furniture

Clear gloss lacquer dries to a glossy finish and is thinned and sprayed on as a multiple-coat finish, with 1-2 hours allowed between coats. A longer drying time is required before sanding or rubbing.

Clear flat lacquer is a spray-on finish identical to clear gloss lacquer, except that it dries to a flat finish.

Lacquer enamels are colored lacquers which are usually sprayed from aerosol cans and are available in gloss, flat, or satin finish.

Brushing lacquer comes in different styles (gloss, flat, rubbing, enamel, etc.) and is slower drying than the spraying lacquers.

Buffing, rubbing, and polishing lacquers are usually sprayed on. They dry to an extremely hard finish and are ideal for polishing and rubbing to a mirrorlike sheen.

Bar-top lacquer is a tough, clear finish highly resistant to alcohol and other chemicals.

Saving time with spray equipment

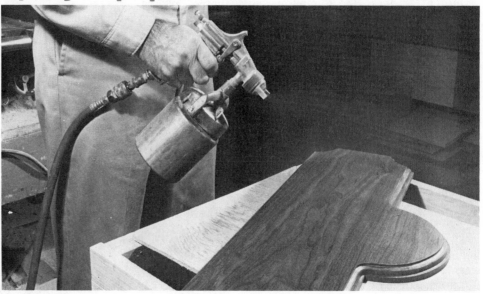

Nozzles

Round. For use with pressure-feed, internal-mix spray gun; good for small or irregularly shaped projects.

Fan. For use with pressure-feed, internal-mix spray gun; use for large, flat areas only.

External mix. For use with suction-feed, external-mix gun; use for spraying lacquer and other light-bodied, quick-drying compounds.

Spraying equipment for furniture finishing saves time and effort. When used with the quick-drying sealers, stains, and finishes, a spray gun can make many finishing jobs a snap, especially if you've got a large or complicated piece of furniture.

Equipment. There are two types of spray guns. On self-contained spray guns, the air compressor is built right into the handle/nozzle assembly. The second type of spray gun is connected to a separate air compressor by a rubber hose designed to carry air under pressure. Both types have plastic, metal, or glass reservoirs which screw into the bottom of the gun and hold the material being sprayed. Self-contained sprayers are generally less expensive than separate sprayer-compressor rigs, but they lack many of the features that the costlier equipment offers.

Air pressure is used in different ways to transform the liquid in the reservoir into a sprayed mist. *Siphon or suction-feed* spray guns are best suited for lacquer and other light-bodied compounds. For heavier liquids like paint and varnish, a *pressure-feed* gun is best, since greater force is needed to propel the thicker liquid. The heavier the liquid, the more pressure required from the compressor (see table opposite).

You'll also have to consider what nozzle (or nozzle adjustment) to use. Some sprayers have removable nozzles, while others can only be adjusted to different settings. *External mix* nozzles are designed for thin compounds like 2-pound-cut shellac, NGR stain, and lacquer. *Internal mix* nozzles are used for spraying heavier material (see illustrations at left).

Select your spray equipment in accordance with the materials you want to spray on. There are spray guns designed especially for applying lacquer or quick-drying stains, and there are guns made only for enamels, varnishes, and exterior house paints. On the other hand, you may want to invest in a multipurpose sprayer-

A self-contained spray gun has an air compressor that is built right into the handle/nozzle assembly. A graduated reservoir of plastic, glass, or metal screws into the bottom of the gun.

Independent spray-gun and compressor units are more versatile and more costly than self-contained sprayers. The separate compressor can drive a variety of spray guns as well as perform other jobs around the house and workshop.

compressor set which can switch from siphon to pressure feed, accept a variety of nozzles, and be used to spray insecticide, inflate tires, and do other jobs.

If you decide to buy a spray gun and separate air compressor, make sure the compressor has a pressure rating (pounds per square inch, or PSI) and volume rating (cubic feet per minute, or CFM) that are compatible with the gun.

Precautions. Most of the spray-on sealers, stains, or finishes and their thinners are not only flammable, but harmful to breathe as well. Spraying fills the air with these compounds in concentrations that can be very dangerous. Never operate spray equipment near a source of heat or flame. Even the pilot lights in your gas stove *must* be extinguished if you are spraying, especially with lacquer, which is extremely volatile. Always work in a well-ventilated area and wear a respirator-type mask for extra protection. Tape up newspapers or use dropcloths to protect the surrounding area from the inevitable overspray.

Preparation. Clean and smooth the surface to be sprayed just as you would prior to brushing or wiping on a sealer, stain, or finish. Lacquer and many other compounds must be thinned down before spraying. Follow the specific spraying instructions on the container and, for best results, use a thinner of the same brand as the stain or finish. Test the spray pattern on a large piece of cardboard. It should be round or oval, with paint or finish evenly distributed throughout and finely atomized at the edges. If you get an irregular, uneven pattern, the nozzle may be clogged, air pressure may be incorrect, or the material may be thinned to the wrong consistency.

Cleanup. Cleaning your spray gun is not only important, it's pretty easy—which is a good combination. Unscrew the reservoir, pour out all the unused finish, and rinse the reservoir clean with the solvent recommended by the manufacturer. Then fill the reservoir about halfway with solvent, screw it back into the gun, and spray out the solvent until all finish has been purged.

Recommended pressure
(in pounds per square inch)

NGR stain	25-30
Shellac (2-pound-cut)	30
Varnish	40
Lacquer	30-40
Polyurethane	40
Enamel	40

A successful finish

Successful spray-gun finishing takes practice. Whether you buy or rent your spray equipment, it should come with detailed instructions on how to use it. Follow these directions as closely as possible, and take the time to make a few test runs on scrap wood or cardboard until you gain familiarity with the equipment and confidence in your technique. Here are some important guidelines:

1. Thin the material according to the manufacturer's instructions and check to make sure you're using the correct nozzle and air pressure.

2. Hold the gun between 6 and 10 inches away from the surface, unless specific instructions say otherwise.

3. When you spray, keep the gun moving. Runs and sags occur when the gun is held too long over one spot.

4. Keep the gun pointing at right angles to the surface by moving it in parallel lines instead of arcs.

5. Pull the trigger just before you begin each stroke across the material and release it just after you end each stroke.

6. Spray edges and corners first, then do central portions.

7. Overlap each stroke by one-half.

8. Use a cardboard shield to catch overspray at the edges of the work and protect surrounding surfaces.

9. Always clean the sprayer thoroughly when you finish using it.

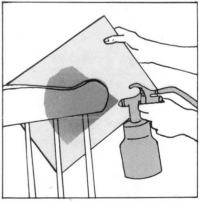

1. Work in a well-ventilated area and wear a respirator for extra protection against harmful fumes. Give yourself plenty of room to move around the piece. Spray corners and edges first.

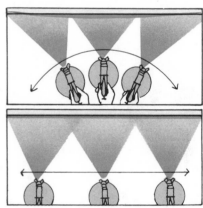

2. When spraying flat areas, always move the gun parallel to the surface by gradually flexing your wrist. Too stiff a wrist will cause your stroke to arc across the surface, producing an uneven coat.

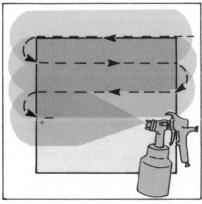

3. Keep the gun moving to avoid drips and runs. Overlap each stroke by one-half to make the coat uniform.

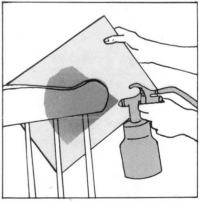

4. If overspray threatens surrounding surfaces, use a cardboard shield to catch it at edges and corners.

Catalytics and polyurethane

Although varnish and lacquer have been the standby clear finishes for many years, they are still far from perfect, especially where the home craftsman is concerned. The shortcoming of these finishes lies not in durability or beauty but in application time and technique. Most lacquers require spraying equipment and work space that many amateur woodworkers don't have access to. Applying a varnish finish in- volves special brushwork, dust-free condi- tions, and extended drying times. The de- mand for a finish similar to varnish and lacquer in durability and appearance but easier to apply has led to a new generation of man-made wood treatments. The most popular of these, catalytic and poly- urethane finishes, are rapidly displacing varnish and lacquer as the most widely used clear finishes.

Multiple-coat toughness in one application

Catalytic finishes—also called epoxies—are available in clear form or in a variety of col- ors. One of the unique features of catalyt- ics is that they come in two separate parts which are combined just prior to applica- tion. The paired parts may be labelled resin and hardener, base and catalyst, or simply part A and part B, but they are always sold as one unit. Like epoxy glue, the two components are useless if use separately. To make the working finish, you mix the two together in the ratio recommended by the manufacturer.

Most catalytics have a thick consistency, and a single application results in a finish that is equivalent to three or more coats of varnish or enamel. Although they offer exceptional durability and beauty with just a single coat, these finishes are expensive, and once you've combined the two parts, what isn't used immediately is wasted.

Many catalytics can only be applied over bare wood or wood that has been stained with water-base or NGR stain.

Go over the manufacturer's instructions carefully before applying a catalytic finish. Specifics for mixing, surface preparation, and application differ from brand to brand.

Catalytic finishes come in two parts that are mixed together prior to application.

A synthetic substitute for varnish

Polyurethane is a clear finish which can be brushed or sprayed on. Available in gloss or satin styles, it is very similar to varnish in durability and appearance. The important difference is that polyurethane is easier to apply and dries faster than varnish.

Polyurethane is slightly thinner in con- sistency than most varnishes, and two or three coats are normally required to achieve maximum protection and beauty. When finishing bare wood, use polyurethane as a sealer rather than shellac, varnish, or lac- quer. Some brands or polyurethane shouldn't be thinned at all; others require a special synthetic thinner, so consult the manufacturer's instructions before sealing the wood. Check the instructions also for compatibility with other finishes; some polyurethanes will not adhere well to oil- base stains, wood filler, or enamel. Never shake polyurethane—it bubbles easily and requires little if any stirring.

Apply finish coats generously; avoid bubbles by brushing as little as possible. If you have a flat surface, you can pour the finish on in little pools and spread it out from there. Most brands of polyurethane can be recoated in 3 to 5 hours; check the drying time stated on the container.

Apply polyurethane generously but lap the brush as little as possible to avoid bubbles.

Tacks tackle taxing task
The enamel finish on my bar stool turned out great—except for one small detail. The finish on the bot- tom of the legs stuck to the news- paper I had put down to protect the floor, and this left a ridge of caked enamel around the bottom of each leg. After a troublesome job of removing this unplanned-for platform, I thought up a way of avoiding the problem:

Hammer a tack or nail into the bottom of each leg to elevate it off the floor or workbench and thus keep the newspaper at a safe dis- tance.

Practical Pete

Paints and enamels

This sequence illustrates three important steps in applying an enamel finish: sanding and cleaning the surface (left), applying the undercoat (center), and painting on the enamel (right).

Paints and enamels differ from other kinds of finishes in that they hide the wood rather than show it off. Nevertheless, there are times when an opaque finish is the only one to use. Applying a paint or enamel finish is the easiest way to cover wood that has been marred by stains or wear. Many fine antiques have enamel as an original finish. Some of the Shaker furniture and most of the Windsor and Hitchcock chairs, for example, were enameled rather than finished with varnish, shellac, or oil. Paint or enamel is also the best finish for furniture made from such poor-quality wood that it can't be stained or clear-finished to advantage without emphasizing blemishes.

Enamel is much more popular than paint because it is very hard and durable and can be polished to a mirror shine just like varnish. In fact, most enamels are nothing more than varnish that has been tinted or colored. On the other hand, paints can't be polished or cleaned as easily either, and so are rarely used on good furniture.

Enamel is available in a wide range of colors. If your dealer doesn't have the exact color you want, he can probably custom-mix it for you with special tinting colors. You'll also have to decide if you want a gloss, semi-gloss, or flat finish (see page 246). Enamel comes ready to brush on, although you may want to thin the first coat of a multiple-coat finish (see manufacturer's instructions).

Preparation. The wood surface must be clean and smooth. Stripping off previous finish coats is generally unnecessary prior to enameling, so long as these coats are in good condition and there is no cracking or peeling. Exceptions are wax, rubbed oil, and polyurethane, which do not offer enough adhesion for an enamel finish. Shellac, lacquer, and other finishes should be scuff-sanded before applying enamel.

Bare wood that is to be enameled must be sealed first, and filled too, if it is coarse-grained. Shellac, sanding sealer, and primer-sealer are the best sealers to use because they are relatively inexpensive, easy to apply, and fast drying. Always use primer-sealer over badly stained wood or old paint. This compound is made specifically as an undercoat for paint or enamel finishes. It "kills" stains and covers dark wood with a uniformly neutral (off-white) surface that is an ideal base for enamel. Primer-sealer can be tinted to match the color of the enamel you're going to apply over it. This extra step in preparation often gives such bright and true results after the first coat that a second coat isn't required.

Application. Apply enamels the same way you would apply varnish. Use a high-quality brush. It's a good idea to install a strike wire (see page 246) across the top of your enamel container so you can press out excess finish and keep bristles straight. Confine the enamel to the bottom third of your bristles and avoid pressing the bristles hard against the surface. Flow the finish on in long, smooth strokes, working with the grain until the surface is covered. Then, keeping the bristles barely wet, brush lightly across the grain. Brush out excess enamel from thick spots and even out the finish with a nearly dry brush, using light pressure on the tips of your bristles.

If additional coats are required, consult the directions on the label for the correct drying time. Like varnish, enamels must be allowed to cure or harden completely before sanding, rubbing, or polishing.

Specialized enamels

Quick-drying enamels usually have a synthetic base and can be applied either by brush or spray. Many are designed to be baked on in an oven for increased gloss and hardness.

Latex enamels are similar to regular enamels except that they have a water base, so you can clean up with soap and water when the job is done. But some of the latex enamels are not as tough as the varnish-type enamels.

Lacquer enamels are simply tinted lacquers. They dry very quickly and are applied in thin coats with an external-mix spray gun.

Spray-can enamels usually have an acrylic base and are available in many colors. These aerosol enamels are good for touch-up work, but they don't provide the thick, tough, highly polishable finish required on good furniture.

Rubbing and polishing

Varnish, enamel, polyurethane, French polish, shellac, and lacquer finishes may be rubbed and polished to produce an even smoother and more beautiful appearance. Although it is tempting to call the finishing operation complete after the final coat has been applied, this is often not enough. Here are some reasons why you might want to rub and polish that last coat:

1. To make the finish more uniform. Sometimes the finish dries unevenly (this is particularly true of varnish and enamel), leaving some areas dull and others glossy. Rubbing is the best way to correct this.

2. To remove imperfections in the finish. Specks of dust and other foreign material may have dried into the final coat. Bubbles, scratches, brush marks, bristles, drips, and sags are other finish spoilers that must be removed. Rubbing and polishing can produce an incredibly smooth surface, removing any unevenness and making a good finish look even better.

3. To dull a high-gloss finish. The high shine of some glossy finishes is not always desirable on indoor furniture. The sharp reflectivity produces a glare which can obscure the beauty of the wood instead of emphasizing it. (Many clear finishes come in satin as well as glossy styles, so you can often get that soft, clear glow without having to rub down a high gloss.)

4. To increase the shine of your finish. This is easily done by rubbing it down with pumice followed by rottenstone and polish.

If you've decided your finish doesn't need rubbing down, congratulations—you're done, except for a coat of paste wax for additional shine and protection. Otherwise, read on; but don't start fine sanding or rubbing until your finish has cured completely. Always allow a little extra drying time to make sure your surface has achieved maximum hardness.

Before rubbing, wet-sand the surface with waterproof silicon-carbide paper (400 grit) to remove large imperfections and level off rough spots.

Begin rubbing by first sprinkling pumice (grade FF or FFF) over the surface and adding enough oil or water to make a thin paste. Then use a felt- or rubber-cushioned pad to rub the entire surface with firm, even pressure.

Tools and materials

Sandpaper and steel wool. Only super-fine grades should be used for the light smoothing and leveling that usually precede rubbing the finish down. Wet-sanding with waterproof silicon-carbide paper (400 grit) is usually the fastest way to get the job done. If you're working on a shellac finish, though, plan on dry-sanding or steel wooling.

Pumice. This abrasive powder made from volcanic rock comes in a range of grades: F is for leveling and coarse rubbing, while FF and FFF are the finer grades used for final rubbing. Before it is used, pumice should be sifted through a piece of cheese-cloth to remove lumps or foreign material.

Rottenstone. Similar to pumice but finer in consistency, rottenstone is made from decomposed limestone (thus the name) and comes in only one grade.

Rubbing felt. Used with pumice or rottenstone to cushion the cutting action of the abrasive powder against the finished surface. Solid felt rubbing pads (1x3x5 inches) are available in some paint and hardware stores, but you can also make your own from random pieces of felt. Dig up an old hat, or ask for spare felt at a fabric store. If the felt is thin, wrap several layers around a small block of wood, putting tacks or staples in the sides to hold the felt in place. Examine the felt rubbing surface to make sure it doesn't have any glazed spots, grit, or other imperfections that might scratch the finish.

Some finishing experts prefer to use a rubber-faced rubbing pad. You can make one by gluing a piece of rubber (sections from tire inner tubes are ideal) to a wooden block. A wad of cloth can also serve as a rubbing pad for pumice or rottenstone.

Rubbing oil. Used as a lubricant or vehicle for pumice or rottenstone during rubbing operations. A specially made finishing oil is ideal, but you can also use mineral oil, paraffin oil, or even a lightweight automotive or machine oil.

Polishing oil. For a high shine after final rubbing, use a good commercial furniture polish, or make your own by mixing equal parts of denatured alcohol and olive oil. Add a small amount of sifted rottenstone to this mixture for extra polishing power.

Benzene or naphtha. Removes the oil film that remains on the surface after an oil rubbing schedule is completed.

Use a sprinkler

The best way to apply pumice or rottenstone is to sprinkle it on. If you don't have an oversize saltshaker, you can make one from just about any can or container that has a plastic or screw-on metal lid. Simply perforate the lid with a thin nail or drill bit and you're all set—but make sure the container is clean before you fill it with abrasive powder.

How to give your finish a good rubdown

To remove large imperfections, wet-sand the surface with waterproof silicon-carbide paper before you begin rubbing with pumice. (Dry-sand shellac.) Soak the paper in a bowl of water to make it flexible, dipping back in to keep the work surface wet. You can sand by hand or use a felt- or rubber-padded sanding block.

Either water or oil can be used as a lubricant with pumice and rottenstone. Many craftsmen prefer water because oil leaves a film on the surface that is difficult to remove. For this reason, you should never use oil between coats—it provides poor adhesion for subsequent coats.

Start the rubbing operation by sprinkling some FF or FFF pumice onto the surface. Add water to the pumice until you get a thin paste, and begin working this mixture around the surface with your rubbing pad. Use firm, even pressure over the entire surface. You may need to add more water to maintain the consistency of your rubbing compound, but don't count on adding any more pumice. When you begin rubbing, sprinkle on enough pumice to last through the whole job. The abrasive particles grind finer and finer as rubbing progresses, so the addition of new, coarser material will disrupt this sequence and scratch the finish.

Keep rubbing until the surface is completely smooth and has a dull, flat appearance. You can spot-check your progress by rubbing a small area clean with your finger. Then clean the finish thoroughly with a moist cloth. Now you're ready for final rubbing. (You can stop right here if you prefer a flat finish, or don't want any more gloss than you already have. A coat of wax is a good idea, though.)

Sprinkle some rottenstone on the surface, add water or oil until you get a thin paste, and then rub as before. In general, rottenstone is most effective when used with a lightweight oil as a lubricant. It will not abrade into finer particles as pumice does, so you can add more as you need it. An alternative method is to put some rottenstone and oil into two separate bowls and dip your rubbing pad first into the oil, then into the powder, and apply. A wad of cloth is the best rubbing pad to use with this method.

Rottenstone will bring out a mellow, even gloss in your finish, but not without a good amount of rubbing. Work until you get the effect you want; then clean the surface thoroughly. Cleaning after oil rubbing is best done in two steps: first remove all the loose slush with a dry cloth; then wipe the surface down carefully, using a cloth dampened in benzene.

After final rubbing, you can bring out additional shine by polishing the finish. Apply the polish with a clean, soft cloth, using circular strokes. Polish needs vigorous rubbing to make it work; you can even use a lamb's-wool buffing attachment in your electric drill if you feel short on elbow grease. Remove the polish with a cloth dampened in benzene.

Lacquer finishes are harder to "cut" with pumice and rottenstone, but you can buy special *lacquer rubbing compound* to make the job easier. This preparation comes as a paste which can be thinned with naphtha or water, and is available in various abrasive grades. A medium or coarse grade will give a satin finish, and a fine grade a glossy finish.

6.SPECIALTY FINISHES

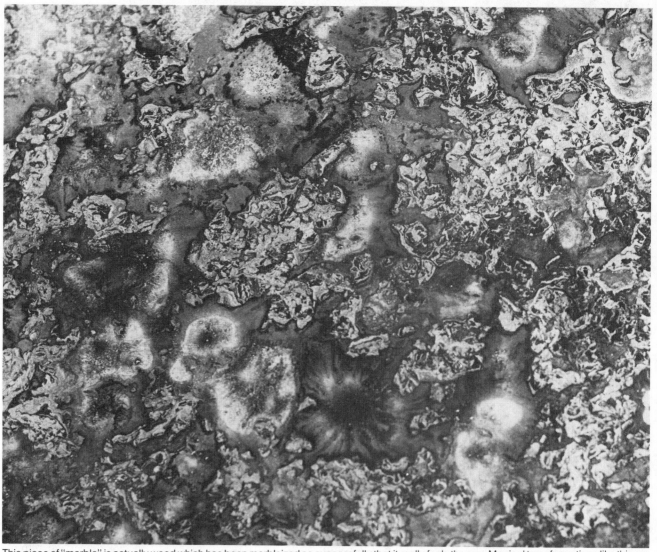

This piece of "marble" is actually wood which has been marbleized so successfully that it really fools the eye. Magical transformations like this are commonplace in the world of specialty finishes.

The virtue of specialty finishes is that they can transform an inexpensive piece of furniture into a real showpiece. No one will know whether the wood underneath your gold-drop or spatter finish is low-grade fir or the finest cherry. (The weight of the piece may give you away, though; fir and pine are much lighter than most hardwoods.) If you have a desk, chair, or dresser with a dull or dying finish, a specialty finish can give it a new and strikingly different life. An added bonus: most specialty finishes don't require the time-consuming stripping and sanding operations that are usually necessary for conventional refinishing.

These unusual finishes are a real challenge to even the most seasoned finishing buffs. The excitement of creating a marbleized or gold-drop finish is never lost,

since each effort will be totally unique. Specialty finishes are interesting because they don't adhere to plan or pattern. Each craftsman has his own special touches and variations in technique. In other words, there's plenty of room for experimentation. As far as final appearance goes, the end always justifies the means, so don't be afraid to try anything.

On the other side of the coin, specialty finishes can be a gamble, especially if you haven't tried one before. The results are truly unpredictable in some cases, but you'll gain control with each project. It's best to start on a small "practice" piece of furniture, or even do a complete test run on some scrap wood. Opposite is a brief rundown of the most popular specialty finishes. Those that involve special techniques are presented in project form on pages that follow.

A range of exotic effects

Antiquing is probably the best known of the specialty finishes. Many antiquing kits are now available which include everything you'll need for a high-quality finish. You can also buy the materials separately or make your own glaze, as shown, page 258. Either way, antiquing is fun, and often gives excellent results with little time or trouble. No wonder it's so popular.

To antique a piece of furniture, you apply a dark glaze over a stain or enamel undercoat, wait for it to dull over, and then wipe it off. With the right wiping technique, some of the glaze will be left on the undercoat in streaks, filling small cracks, contours, and depressions, and resembling the worn and well-rubbed surface of a true antique. Like many of the other specialty finishes, this one takes practice to perfect.

Gold drop, Venetian gold, and tortoise shell are specialty finishes that can transform an ordinary piece of wood into an expensive-looking object. They give an illusion of depth through the random and incomplete blending of different colors. Trays and the tops of small coffee tables, end tables, and nightstands are the best pieces for the special finishes. See page 260 for detailed information on how to apply a gold-drop finish.

Ebonizing. Ebony is an African wood that is unique, beautiful, and very expensive. It is the darkest of all woods, usually completely black with just a trace of grain pattern. Ebony is also extremely dense, resinous, and durable. By using a black or ebony stain, you can give many woods the look of real ebony. Maple is the best candidate for ebonizing because it is hard and has a straight grain pattern very similar to that of ebony. Several applications of stain are necessary to give lighter wood a deep and realistic ebony tone, and no sealer should be used prior to staining. When you've achieved the right color, apply a light coat of wax or a nonglossy (flat or satin) clear finish. Real ebony has a deep, warm glow that should never be glossed over.

Marbleizing. It may be hard to believe, but—as the illustration opposite suggests—it's possible to make a wooden tabletop look exactly like a fine piece of marble. Marbleizing is inexpensive and doesn't require any special tools, but don't expect to get a perfect marble look on your first try. It really takes practice. (See page 262 for successful techniques.)

Spatter finishes are fun and easy to apply. The first step is to finish your furniture with paint or enamel. When the final coat dries, spatter the surface with one or more different colors. The size of the specks depends on what spattering tool you use. For very small specks, use an old toothbrush. Wet only the tips of the bristles and simply drag your thumb or finger across the bristles to produce the spatters. For uniform size and density, hold the brush at a standard distance above the surface. It's a good idea to practice your technique ahead of time on a scrap piece of cardboard. For larger spatters, use a dry paintbrush. If you want a multi-colored spatter finish, it's best to wait for each color to dry before spattering on another. Complete the job by applying a coat of varnish or lacquer.

Bleaching. You can lighten the grain of most woods by bleaching them. The operation is similar to bleaching your laundry; in fact, the common laundry product can be used to bleach wood. For a more pronounced dark-to-light transformation, use the special wood-bleaching preparations available at most paint and hardware stores.

Texture effects. There's no limit to the number of texture effects you can create on a wood surface. Just about all texture effects consist of three steps: applying the undercoat, applying the glaze, and then treating the glaze to create the effect, using whatever method or implement you think is best for the job.

Usually the undercoat is lighter in color than the glaze, although it doesn't have to be. The undercoat can be enamel or stain, but stain should be followed by a clear coat of varnish before applying the glaze. Leave the glaze on just long enough for it to dull over (don't let it get tacky); then go over it to create your own personalized texture. How you do this is up to you. You may want to create a grain pattern by tipping across the glaze with the bristles of a dry paintbrush. Or crumple up a piece of newspaper and press it against the glaze. The crinkles in the paper will be transferred onto the furniture, resulting in a uniquely mottled effect. Fiberglass insulation, plastic wrap, and other materials can also be used in similar fashion. When the glaze dries, protect it by applying one or two coats of varnish or lacquer.

Liming. Ordinarily, open-grained woods are treated with a matching filler. But for a limed finish, a wood filler of contrasting color is used. The most common of all limed finishes is white filler on oak. Instead of blending in with the surrounding wood, the pores will be more noticeable, drawing attention to the interesting grain patterns typical of most coarse-grained woods. Many different combinations of tinted fillers and stains are possible, but it's best to test out your ideas on a scrap first.

Antiquing

An antique finish can make a dull or inexpensive piece of furniture look like a valuable heirloom. You can antique bare wood or work right over an existing finish—as long as the old finish is in good condition. In either case, the process isn't difficult. All you need are the materials listed at left, the general instructions given here, and the special techniques shown below. If you are working over an existing finish, give it a once-over with some fine-grit sandpaper. This will remove any chips or flakes and scuff the surface so the enamel undercoat will adhere well. You may have to apply two coats of enamel to completely cover the old finish and get the smooth surface you need.

When you antique bare wood, you can use either enamel or stain for the undercoat. In both cases, you can give the wood an authentic look by marking the surface with nicks and scratches—the battle scars often found on genuine old wood. This artificial aging technique is called distressing, and it can be accomplished with a number of different tools (see margin). **Tip:** It's easy to go overboard when distressing furniture. Make your marks in random spots, using an old piece of furniture as a guide.

When the undercoat is dry, apply the glaze. The success of an antique finish depends largely on your technique for wiping down the glaze. To make the furniture look well-worn or many times waxed and rubbed, leave extra glaze on corners, edges, and cracks. Various glazing techniques are shown here. Whichever one you use, be sure to let each coat dry thoroughly before you apply the next. When the glaze dries, apply a thin coat of paste wax or a coat of semigloss varnish for extra durability.

If you haven't tried antiquing before, it's a good idea to practice on a small panel of wood, like the one shown below, before you tackle a large desk or dresser.

What it takes

Approximate time: Two days, using an oil-base enamel and glaze. With a quick-drying latex enamel and glaze, you can finish the job (not including the protective coat of varnish) in one day.

Tools and materials: Antiquing kits are sold at many paint stores and home-decorating centers. They come in a variety of styles (undercoat-and-glaze combinations) and include everything needed for the job. To put together your own kit, you'll need some semigloss enamel for the base coat. Any color will do, so long as it's compatible with the glaze. Glaze can be made by darkening varnish with oil colors, or it can be bought premixed. Cheesecloth is the most popular material for wiping off the glaze.

Distressing

The art of aging wood before its time by marking up the surface is called distressing. There's plenty of room for innovation as far as tools and techniques go, and with a little practice, you can make a new piece of wood look like it has endured years of use. A set of keys will do a good job of making small nicks and scratches. Knock them against the surface. Swinging a small chain against the wood can also give good results. With a small V-shaped chisel, you can embellish the surface with narrow grooves that resemble the surface cracks and scratches found on old wood.

Transforming new into old

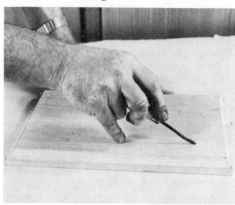

1. If you're putting an antique finish on bare wood, you can make the aged effect even more convincing by distressing the wood before you apply the undercoat. Since old wood has no sharp edges, sand all corners and distress marks smooth for an authentic look.

2. Apply an enamel undercoat to the wood and let it dry. To hide the grain and make the enamel stand out more, you can apply a coat of primer-sealer first, but this will tend to fill in and hide the distress marks.

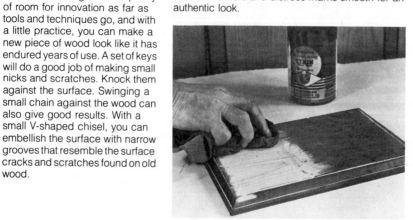

3. With bare wood, you can use stain instead of enamel for the undercoat. If this is the case, you'll have to apply a coat of varnish over the stain before the glaze can go on.

4. To make your own glaze, mix raw-umber and ivory-black oil colors with some interior varnish. Use enough varnish to cover the piece, and stir in the colors gradually until you get the right shade. You can also buy premixed, ready-to-use glaze.

5. Brush the glaze on the surface in a full, flowing coat. Make sure you fill all cracks, indentations, and other distress marks.

6. Wipe down the glaze immediately if you want only a little to remain on the surface; the longer you wait, the darker the effect will be. Dampen the cloth with some glaze before you begin wiping, and wipe with the grain of the wood.

Stopgaps and copouts

Here's an alternative method for creating the glazed look that ages furniture so convincingly. *Prepare the wood and give it an enamel undercoat, following the regular directions. But wipe the glaze on instead of wiping it off.* Instead of painting on an entire coat of glaze and then wiping it off, dip a pad of cheesecloth into the glaze and wipe on the dark antique tones. This is usually the best method for antiquing large projects, since it saves time and cuts down on the amount of glaze you need. It takes some skill to master this shortcut, though, and you might have to wipe over the same area several times to get the effect you want.

7. An enamel undercoat followed by a darker glaze coat gives wood a two-color antique effect, as shown above. This is one of the most popular methods of antiquing.

8. When you give bare wood a stain undercoat, the effect is totally different. On the piece shown above, nearly all glaze has been wiped off, leaving only the distress marks darkened.

Special touches

To create a texture that resembles wood grain, drag a dry brush across the glaze.

You can edge contours with gold or silver for additional antique effect. Wax-based pastes in these and other colors are available at craft-supply stores.

Once the glaze has dried, you can add a spatter finish to your new antique by using a toothbrush or paintbrush as shown.

Gold drop

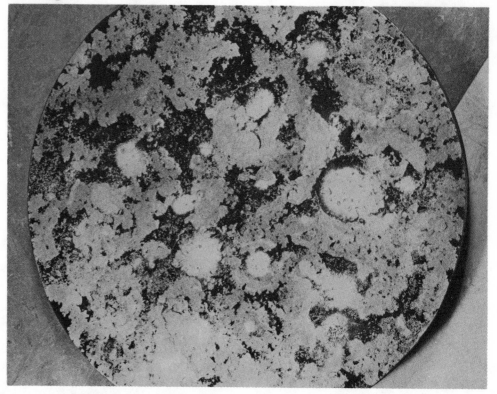

What it takes

Approximate time: Five hours, not including at least 24 hours' drying time before the clear finish is sprayed on. Both gesso and spray enamels require up to 45 minutes between coats.

Tools and materials:

Gesso. Used as a sealer, filler, and undercoat. Available at art-supply stores.

Spray enamel. Buy a quick-drying acrylic enamel in a satin or semi-gloss finish. You'll need a can of olive or forest green and a can of clear spray.

Pigment. Powdered, oil-soluble pigments are sold at art-supply stores. You'll need some gold and either burnt or raw umber.

Alcohol. Used in combination with the gold pigment to make the liquid gold that is dropped on the surface. Note: You can also make the liquid gold from the gold paste that comes in tubes (page 259). Simply thin it as recommended in the directions on the tube.

Gold drop is one of the most unusual and lavish finishes you can apply. It looks deceivingly three-dimensional, and the gold highlights give the finish a glowing, extravagant look. Tortoiseshell and Venetian-gold finishes are similar to gold drop in appearance and application technique. The distinctive appearance of these finishes makes them especially suitable for serving trays and small tabletops or dressers.

The first step in creating a gold-drop finish is to sand the wood smooth. Next, apply two or more coats of gesso to the surface. This seals the wood (or covers the old finish) and provides a level and smooth base for the first coat. The work surface should be completely level. When the coat of gesso has dried, fine-sand it to a uniform smoothness; then spray several coats of green enamel on the gesso. (Olive or forest green are the best shades.) Use one of the quick-drying acrylic sprays to save time and keep the surface smooth.

The secret of this finish is to let the colors mingle but not mix. When the green paint has dried, cover the surface with a thin layer of water. **Tip:** To reduce the surface tension of the water (increase its fluidity), add a small amount of laundry detergent. Then drop some of the powdered, raw- or burnt-umber pigment into the water and spread it over the surface with a clean brush. Let the green enamel show through here and there.

The pigment will remain suspended and uneven in appearance. That's just the way you want it.

The next step is to mix some gold pigment in alcohol and drop this solution onto the surface. (Use a teaspoon.) Because of the water on the surface, the drops will blossom out in random patterns. The green and umber undercolors will show in the spaces between the gold and, to some extent, be visible through it. It is this multicolored translucency that gives the finish such fascinating depth.

If you've applied too much umber or gold, remove it with an absorbent rag or paper towel. Otherwise, let the piece dry undisturbed, then spray on four or five coats of clear acrylic enamel to protect the delicate finish. Brushing on a clear varnish or lacquer might disturb the beautiful patterns you've created.

To make a Venetian-gold finish, follow the same procedure you would for gold drop, but make your first coat of paint red instead of green.

For a tortoiseshell finish, apply a heavy coat of dark glaze over an undercoat of brown enamel. Lightly tap the wet glaze with your fingertips. For a random look, hold your hand at different angles as you tap the finish. (If you wear rubber or plastic gloves, the finish will have a slightly different look.)

From bare wood to a beautiful finish

1. Sand the surface smooth and clean off all dust before you apply the undercoat. This tabletop is made from two disks of ¾-inch plywood that have been glued together.

2. Apply at least two coats of gesso. Sand the final coat as smooth as possible, using extra-fine-grit sandpaper.

3. Spray on a coat of green acrylic enamel. You may have to apply several coats to cover the gesso and build up a full, even color.

4. When the enamel is dry, paint a thin layer of water on the surface. Add a small amount of laundry detergent to the water to make it easier to work with.

Specialty combinations

A popular way of finishing a worn-looking table, desk, or dresser is to give the top a specialty finish like gold drop, and finish the rest of the piece conventionally, or by antiquing.

5. Sprinkle some powdered, burnt- or raw-umber pigment on the surface and spread it around with a clean brush. Don't worry if the appearance is uneven or you have spots of green showing through. That's the right look for this finish.

6. Mix some gold pigment with alcohol and drop small amounts onto the wet surface as shown. Spilling different amounts from varying distances creates a random effect. Allow the surface to dry completely; then spray on at least four coats of clear acrylic enamel. The final step is to fill and finish the sides to hide the plywood.

Marbleizing

Approximate time: One or two hours to marbleize a table like the one pictured below. This does not include applying the enamel base-coat. Drying time before the marble finish can be varnished is a week.

Tools and materials: You'll need a pale enamel for the base-coat, some linseed oil and turpentine, a few small brushes, and some artists' oil colors. The oil colors are available at any art-supply store. Choose compatible colors, like the ones you'd find in a piece of fine marble.

Putting a marble finish on a piece of wood is quite an adventure. Just as no two pieces of marble look the same, every marbleizing job turns out differently. This fact makes real fool-the-eye marbleizing difficult as well as exciting. Here's how it's done:

Preparation. Start by giving your table or bureau top a good enamel finish. A light color like cream or off-white is best. Use an oil-base enamel, and rub the last coat down until it's marble-smooth (see page 254). Marbleizing is a messy operation, so take some time to prepare your work area before you begin. **Tip:** Marbleize only the top surface of any given piece of furniture, and don't finish (or refinish) the rest of the piece until you're done with the marbleizing. The mixture used is bound to run off the top and drip onto furniture legs, front panels, and other surfaces. Make yourself a palette to hold the different oil colors you'll be using so you can apply them quickly and freely.

Technique. Real marble is formed at extremely high temperatures. The different compounds in the rock actually melt, flowing and curling around each other in a random pattern that "freezes" when the rock cools. By flooding the surface of your table with an oil-and-turpentine mixture, you create a fluid medium in which oil colors can be swirled about in much the same way. One good way to twist the colors together, once you have dabbed them on, is to drag a feather across the surface. Tilting the surface to create flow lines and painting in vein lines with a small brush are other effective techniques. Experiment with different tools or techniques and take a close look at some real marble before you choose your color and pattern.

Mastering the marble finish

1. Here's some of the equipment you'll need: several small brushes, some artists' oil colors, linseed oil, and turpentine. You can use oil-based enamels instead of oil colors—or in combination with them.

2. Combine equal parts of linseed oil and turpentine and brush a generous coat of this solution on the surface you're finishing. Then start dabbing on colors. It's best to work from an improvised palette, as shown, so all your colors are instantly accesible.

3. Work with several brushes to avoid blending darker and light colors. Instead of mixing the colors together on the surface, let them run into and over each other.

4. Tip the surface to let the colors flow together. This produces lines that simulate the veining in real marble. You can also add vein lines with a finely pointed brush or use a feather to run colors together.

5. Remove excess paint or linseed oil with a rag or absorbent paper. Notice how the oil colors have been turned in and around each other, mingling without mixing.

6. When you get the marble look you want, wipe the bottom edge of the tabletop to remove drips. At this point you can add veining to the edges with a small paintbrush.

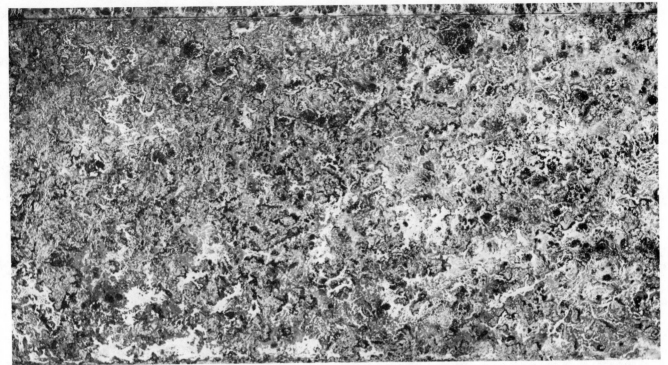

The final result looks a lot more like marble than wood. Allow at least a week for the finish to cure, then apply two or more coats of varnish. Rub and polish the final coat until you get a smooth, shiny surface.

Alternative methods and special techniques

There are several effective variations on the marbleizing technique shown opposite. Instead of waiting for the enamel base-coat to dry, you can flood the oil-and-turpentine mixture on while the paint is still tacky. This will cause some of the base coat to loosen and float on the surface with the other colors, which are applied as usual. Be prepared for unusually long drying times if you use this method, and don't try it in humid or rainy weather.

Another method of applying the colors is to flick them on with a dry, stiff-bristled brush. Load only the tip of the brush and tap it sharply against your free hand to deposit the colors on the surface. For a realistic look, flick large globs, rather than small splatters, of color on the surface. (You will have to thin down artists' oil colors for this technique, or use enamels, which are thinner in consistency.)

Here's another marbleizing technique that works quite well: Start by putting a smooth enamel finish on the surface. Then apply a liberal coat of high-gloss white enamel, covering the sides and edges as well as the top of the piece. After about five minutes, dip a stick or wooden paint stirrer into a can of gray enamel and dribble some across the surface in a random pattern. Apply some black enamel, or any other colors you want, in the same manner. Then wad up some newspaper and dab at the colors, moving them around to accentuate the marble pattern. Touch the newspaper gently to the wet surface so you don't remove too much enamel, and try to mingle rather than mix the different colors. When the newspaper becomes too wet, crumple up another piece. The dribble and wadded-newspaper techniques work well together, but can also be used with other marbleizing methods.

The *float technique* is a popular way of marbleizing small objects. You'll need some oil-base enamels and a container that is larger than the object to be finished. Prepare the wood surface by sealing it with varnish, lacquer, or primer-sealer. Add water to the container until it is three-quarters full. Then float the colors for your marble pattern on the water, forming a thin layer or "skin" on the surface. A good way of getting the enamel on the water is to dip a wooden paddle into the enamel container and then into the water. (Only oil-base enamels will float on the surface; don't substitute a latex or acrylic enamel.)

Once all the colors are on, swirl them around with a piece of wood until you get the marble look you want. Then, holding the object facedown, dip it in the water just slightly for an instant marble treatment. The paint floating on the water will stick to the sealed wood surface. You can dip the object as many times as you want, but you'll have to float more color on the water each time to replace the enamel that's been picked up. Once you've finished dipping, you can still add vein lines, dab on more color, or do other touchup work to make the marble finish even more realistic.

Bleaching

What it takes

Approximate time: One to two hours for a medium-size chair, (with two-part bleach made specifically for use on wood).

Tools and materials: See page 265 for different types of bleach you can use. You'll need some rubber gloves and a protective apron, if you don't want to risk bleaching out your clothes. Use a sponge or nylon-bristle brush to apply the bleach, and get some borax or white vinegar to neutralize the wood surface after the bleach has done its work.

Bleaching qualities of different woods

Easy

Ash

Beech

Mahogany

Maple

Oak

Teak

Walnut

Difficult

Cedar

Cherry

Chestnut

Redwood

Rosewood

Bleaching wood is just the opposite of staining it; instead of adding color, you take it away. There are two reasons for bleaching a piece of furniture. First, if you prefer light wood to dark, you might want to lighten an entire piece. A dark walnut chair, for example, might be a poor match for a roomful of light furniture. The second reason concerns stains found on bare wood. Bleaching is often the only way to save a badly stained wood surface. It does a good job of erasing most stains. If used over the entire piece, bleach will create a lighter but uniform tone as well as eliminate stains.

Bleaching can be done only on bare wood, and some woods are easier to bleach than others, as indicated in the list at left. (Pine and fir shouldn't be bleached except for stain removal). Once you have bleached the wood, you can put on whatever finish you want. Rubbed oil, penetrating resin, and polyurethane are the most popular finishes for bleached wood.

Caution: The chemicals in bleaching solutions are extremely harmful. Contact with skin or eyes can cause serious injury; even the fumes from these compounds are dangerous to breathe. Follow the precautions on the bleach container. Wear rubber gloves, work in a well ventilated area, and protect your eyes, skin, and clothing from contact with the solution.

Equipment: Oxalic acid comes in crystal form and is dissolved in water to make the bleaching solution. Two-part wood bleaches come ready to use and are best for tough bleaching jobs. Laundry bleach can also be used effectively on some woods. A sponge is the most popular application tool. Always wear rubber gloves when using any type of bleach.

Different kinds of bleach

Ammonia can be used for bleaching light woods, but is best for removing spots or stains. A common household product, it is economical and easy to use, but relatively weak when compared to other bleaches.

Laundry bleach can also be used for lightening wood. Like ammonia, it is inexpensive and easy to use, but don't expect a dramatic change from dark to light. You'll get a slight but even change in tone. If you are working with wood that is all the same type but varies in tone, use laundry bleach to achieve uniform color throughout.

Oxalic acid is a reliable bleaching agent that has been used on furniture for many years. You can buy it in crystal form at hardware, paint, and drugstores. It is sometimes used in combination with tartaric acid or hyposulfite, two other bleaching agents.

Using bleach

Preparation. Protect the floor and surrounding furniture and fabrics from damage due to contact with the bleach. Lightly sand the wood surface just prior to bleaching. This helps the bleach penetrate deeper into the wood and work more effectively.

Application. All bleaches should be applied generously. Use a nylon-bristle brush or a sponge. Ammonia and laundry bleach are used at full strength. Always read the maunufacturer's directions before using two-part wood bleaches.

If you're using oxalic acid to lighten your furniture, you can improve the bleaching action by flooding the wood with a hyposulfite mixture when the oxalic-acid solution begins to dry. Dissolve 3 ounces of *hypo* powder in warm water to make this "helper" bleach.

After about 15 or 20 minutes, most of the bleaching action will be complete. If the wood still isn't as light as you'd like it to be, rinse the surface with water and repeat the application procedure.

Neutralizing. Bleach leaves a residue on the wood surface that is sometimes difficult to see. Nevertheless, it must be neutralized before any stain, sealer, or finish can be applied. You can make a neutralizing solution by dissolving an ounce of borax in a quart of water. Or simply use white vinegar at full strength. When the bleaching is complete, rinse bleach from the wood surface with a sponge or rag dipped in water. Then wipe on some neutralizer, wait a few minutes, and wipe the wood clean.

Bleaching usually raises the grain of the wood, so plan on doing some sanding with extra-fine paper before you finish the wood. Allow at least 24 hours for the surface to dry before applying any stain, sealer, or finish.

To make the bleach solution, dissolve 3 ounces of oxalic-acid crystals in a quart of water (warm water will dissolve the crystals faster). You can add an ounce of tartaric-acid powder for extra strength.

Hydrogen peroxide is used in diluted form as an antiseptic. With a concentrated solution, you can lighten most of the darker woods. Available at most drugstores, it is considerably more expensive than oxalic acid, ammonia, or laundry bleach.

Two-part bleaches are made specifically for use on wood and will do a more thorough job of lightening than any of the other bleaches. These specialized preparations come in two parts that are either applied in succession or mixed together just prior to use. You'll find them in most paint and hardware stores.

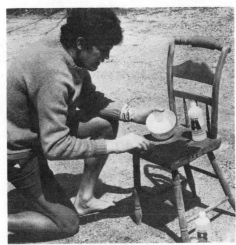

1. Most two-part wood bleaches are applied in sequence. (Techniques differ from brand to brand, so read the manufacturer's directions carefully.) Flow on solution generously, using a sponge or absorbent cloth. Be sure to saturate the wood.

2. Allow five to ten minutes for the first solution to work, then apply the second. The separate solutions combine, producing a chemical reaction that bleaches the surface wood fibers.

Spot bleaching
You can use bleach to lighten stains or spots without having to bleach the entire piece of furniture. Don't use the two-part bleaches for these small touchup jobs; they're too strong. Bleach out the spot bit by bit, with multiple applications of oxalic acid, ammonia, or laundry bleach. The gradual lightening effect worked by the weaker bleaches lets you achieve a tone that matches the surrounding unbleached wood.

Wise teaching on wood bleaching
The first time I used a two-part wood bleach, it really worked well—too well, in fact. I wanted to lighten some dark oak in an antique chair, but the bleach was so effective that I ended up with a much paler color than I'd anticipated. Later a friend told me I could have avoided the overbleach simply by flooding the surface with vinegar once the bleach had lightened the wood to my liking. If you have vinegar or borax handy while you're applying the bleach, you can stop the action as soon as you get the right tone.

Practical Pete

Rustproofing

What it takes

Approximate time: Four hours for a chair similar to the one pictured on page 267, including removing rust and applying three coats of antirust spray enamel.

Tools and materials: Get some naval jelly or other commercial rust remover. Even if you don't often use it on your furniture, it's one of those essential workshop items that always comes in handy. For scraping off rust and flakes of paint, you'll need a stiff wire brush and some medium or medium-coarse steel wool. (If you have an electric drill, using it with a wire-brush attachment can make rust removal a snap.)

There are many brands of anti-rust spray paint, and you should have no trouble finding the color you want. Check the label to make sure it says "rust stopping" or "rust preventive," and get a quick-drying paint so you won't have to wait long between coats.

All tools and materials described above are available at paint or hardware stores.

This wrought-iron chair is a good example of outdoor furniture that needs to be rustproofed.

With the many rustproof finishes available today (see photo opposite), there's no reason for furniture to become ruined because of severe rust buildup. Modern rustproof finishes are effective and easy to apply, as well. Rustproof finishes are available in paint-on and spray-on form. The spray-on finishes are far more popular, especially for furniture where narrow legs and contoured surfaces make brushing difficult. You can buy rustproof spray paints in just about any color you like and in a number of styles: flat, high gloss, heat resistant, fluorescent, and metal flake, among others. A fresh rustproof finish can restore old furniture to like-new condition. Here's how it's done:
Work area. If you plan to use naval jelly to remove extensive rust deposits, work outdoors. That way, you can simply hose off the jelly once it has loosened the rust. **Tip:** Rust removers will harm your lawn, so work in a driveway or similar area. It's a good idea to spray-paint outdoors too. You won't have to worry about overspray or poor ventilation. Avoid working in windy weather, though. It will make you waste a lot of paint and end up with a thin, irregular

coat on the furniture you're finishing.

If you must work inside, lay down plenty of newspaper or use a plastic sheet to protect the floor and catch rust, flaked-off finish, and rust remover. Protect the surrounding area from overspray (if you plan to spray-finish) and give yourself plenty of ventilation. Remove naval jelly with a damp sponge, then wipe down all metal parts with a dry towel.
Preparation. If you're painting over an existing finish that is free from rust and in good condition (no paint flaking off), preparation is simple; just clean the metal with soap and water or a commercial cleaner to remove dirt from the surface. Then scuff-sand the old finish with extra-fine sandpaper or steel wool to dull glossy areas and provide a good base for the new paint.

More often than not, the old finish on metal furniture will be in poor condition, with spots of rust showing through here and there. If this is the case, remove all loose flakes of paint with sandpaper or steel wool. Use fine to extra-fine grades, depending on how bad the old finish is. Work until all flakes are removed and you have a smooth,

There are many different rustproof finishes available. Take your time and select the right one for the furniture you'll be working on.

even surface. Small areas of rust can also be removed with sandpaper or steel wool.

If the piece is badly rusted, you'll have to use naval jelly or a similar rust-removing compound to clean the metal. Apply the compound generously, using an old paintbrush. Allow at least several minutes for the rust remover to work, then scrape the surface clean with a stiff wire brush. (If you have one, use a circular wire-brush attachment on your electric drill to speed up the operation, but make sure to wear eye protection when using this attachment.)

Tip: Use an old toothbrush for scraping corners, intricate curves, and other areas that you can't reach with the wire brush.

To finish cleaning the furniture, hose it down or wipe it off with a sponge, depending on where you're working. This will remove any remnants of the compound plus any loose rust or flakes that cling to the surface. When the piece dries completely (wipe it down with a clean, dry cloth to speed up the process), you're ready to paint. Use masking tape and newspaper to protect parts of the furniture that you don't want painted. Cover these parts thoroughly, since spray paint tends to find its way into imperfectly sealed areas.

Application. Spray-painting metal furniture is usually an easy job. Just shake the can vigorously and apply the paint. (Follow the manufacturer's instructions pertaining to surface preparation, primer coats, and drying time.) Work from top to bottom whenever possible and build up an even finish by applying at least three coats. Wait for each coat to dry thoroughly before applying the next. Move the can continuously so paint buildup doesn't cause drips and runs on the furniture. (For more information on spray-painting, see page 250.)

Be sure to paint the undersides of metal feet and chair seats and other unseen parts of your furniture. It's easy to forget these spots and expose them to rust conditions.

1. Use naval jelly or a similar rust remover to loosen rust on badly encrusted areas. Apply the jelly with an old paintbrush. Let it work for a few minutes, then rinse it off with water.

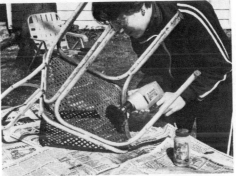

2. Use a wire-brush attachment with your electric drill to remove rust and loosen paint quickly and effectively. Remember to wear eye protection.

3. Build up an even finish by applying at least three coats of paint. Some rustproof finishes require a primer undercoat, so read the manufacturer's instructions before you apply the first coat.

Cleaning and protecting nonferrous metals

To remove surface oxidation from aluminum, use commercial aluminum jelly or rub the surface with extra-fine steel wool dipped in a solution of equal parts kerosene and automotive oil.

To clean oxidized brass, bronze, and copper, dissolve a teaspoon of salt in the juice from one lemon, and apply this mixutre to the surface with some extra-fine steel wool.

To protect nonferrous metal surfaces from oxidation, rinse them clean with water and apply a light coat of wax. You can also paint them with a rustproof finish, as long as you scuff-sand the surface beforehand.

7.CARE

Giving your furniture the proper care is as important as knowing how to repair or refinish it. Furniture care can mean anything from dusting to removing water stains or restoring small parts of the finish. You'll find a brief description of the three divisions of furniture care below, and step-by-step instructions on the pages ahead.

Prevention. It's important to use your furniture with care. Bad conditions can harm the toughest of finishes and give your furniture a worn appearance long before its time. While there's no way to change conditions like unfavorable weather or heavy wear, there are certain things you can do to avoid unnecessary damage (see page 270).

Protection. To preserve the distinctive look of a fine finish, you usually have to clean, wax, and polish it. (See the chart on page 272 for fuller information.) With the modern furniture-care products available, furniture upkeep is quick and easy, for the most part. There are only two rules of thumb for maintaining and protecting a good-looking finish. First, don't let dust, dirt, or grime get ahead of you; remove them as soon as you detect them clouding up the finish. Second, use the right product for the job. There are so many furniture-care preparations that choosing the right one can be difficult (see pages 269-272 for additional information).

Restoration. Furniture that becomes damaged in one way or another can often be restored by making spot repairs instead of refinishing the entire piece or replacing the damaged part. These touchup repairs can be real time-savers, if you have the right tools and materials and a little know-how (see pages 273-275).

Tuning in

There are some important things to know about your furniture before you try your hand at repairing scratches or removing stains—or even start waxing and polishing it. The first step in furniture care is tuning in on the many factors that determine the "health" of each piece of furniture in your home. It's important to know what type of finish you're dealing with and to have a good idea of what adverse or favorable conditions are affecting it. Take some time to consider this basic information before you get into the more involved elements of furniture care.

Identifying the finish

How you care for a particular piece of furniture depends largely upon what type of finish it has. Using the wrong technique or compound can do more harm than good, so it's important to know exactly what finish you're dealing with. Sometimes, especially with older furniture, it is difficult to distinguish between shellac, varnish, wax, and lacquer. Listed below are some tests you can run to find out what's what. (Do your testing in a spot that can't be seen.) Because some of the stronger solvents needed to dissolve varnish or polyurethane can also affect shellac and lacquer, make your test in the sequence outlined for reliable results.

Wax. Before you can test for other finishes, all wax must be removed. Old wax or multiple coats of wax will appear cloudy or yellow even though buffed to a dull shine. Dampen a cloth in some turpentine and rub the surface to remove wax buildup.

Penetrating resin and rubbed oil. You can tell a penetrating-resin or rubbed-oil finish simply by feel. The wood surface won't be coated, and you'll be able to feel and see the grain clearly.

Shellac. Dip a cloth in some denatured alcohol and rub the finish. If it dissolves, it's shellac. A shellac finish is easier to scratch or scrape than other clear finishes; it will also usually have white water stains in one or two places. The alcohol test is the only sure giveaway, though. This test can be used for a French polish finish as well.

Lacquer. If you can't dissolve the finish with denatured alcohol (also called shellac thinner), try using lacquer thinner. If the finish is lacquer, the area you rub will look worn or scuffed at first but will take on a glossy, smooth appearance as the thinner evaporates. Lacquer thinner affects some varnishes, but in a different way. The varnish will bubble or crinkle up without becoming smooth again.

Varnish. With a few exceptions, the only solvent that will dissolve varnish is commercial paint or varnish remover. If the other tests you've run have had negative results, you can be pretty sure you're working with a varnish finish. Turpentine can sometimes dissolve varnish, but only with soaking and hard rubbing.

Polyurethane and epoxies. These finishes are similar to varnish in their resistance to conventional solvents. The best way to check them out is by the process of elimination. If you really want to be sure, try softening some of the finish with a commercial stripper made for synthetic finishes.

Here's a basic tip on furniture care that applies to all finishes: Keep hot dishes or pots on protective pads to insulate the finish from excessive heat, and put coasters under "sweating" glasses to prevent water from damaging the finish.

Bad conditions and how to avoid them

Temperature and humidity. Regardless of how well a piece of wood has been weatherproofed, it will still respond to changes in temperature or humidity. Dry weather can cause wood to shrink, resulting in loose joints and small cracks where the end grain is exposed. High temperatures will soften some finishes. Damp weather makes wood swell, and prolonged exposure to high humidity can ruin a shellac or paste-wax finish. There's not much you can do about the weather, but you can make things a little easier for your furniture. Avoid extremes. If your workshop tends to be cool and damp, don't transfer a piece of furniture from shop to fireside without letting the wood adjust in a neutral area for a few days. The sudden swelling and shrinking caused by extreme changes in temperature or humidity can often be avoided by gradually introducing the wood to its new and different environment.

Hot dishes. Even the toughest finishes are prone to heat damage. Anything from a hot cup of tea to a casserole just out of the oven can spoil an otherwise perfect finish. Protect the finish from heat damage by using mats or coasters under hot objects.

Spills. Water, coffee, perfume, and alcohol are just a few of the many liquids often spilled on furniture. It's impossible to eliminate spills. But make it a policy to wipe them up immediately; the longer they are left standing, the more damage is done to the finish.

Dusting

It is surprising how a thin layer of dust can turn even the brightest finish dull. Regular dusting is one of the easiest ways of maintaining the beauty of your furniture.

Dust conditions may vary widely, not just from house to house, but from room to room. Consequently, you may have to dust some pieces more often than others. Most dust is easy to detect, especially on a clear, glossy finish. Simply rub your fingers across the surface. It may take anywhere from ten to thirty days for dust to build up on your furniture, but once you figure out how often you need to dust, stick to that schedule. Regular dusting actually saves work, since you prevent dirt and grime from building up to such an extent that major cleaning operations are required.

Never dust with a dry cloth; all that does is move the dust around on the surface or brush it off to settle somewhere else. Because dust particles sometimes act as abrasives, dry-dusting can eventually damage the finish. The best way to dust is to dampen a soft, lint-free cloth and go over your furniture gently from top to bottom.

Glasses and pitchers. Containers full of cold liquids are probably the single greatest cause of damage to furniture finishes. Condensation causes drops of water to form on the outside of the container, and they eventually collect in a small pool around the bottom of the glass or pitcher. The result, unless the pool is wiped dry promptly, is a white ring that is both unsightly and difficult to remove. Even the toughest varnish or polyurethane finish is susceptible to water rings, so make coasters under cold drinks a habit.

Scratches, gouges, and chips. This type of damage can usually be avoided simply by using common sense. Add a few children to a roomful of furniture, wait a few hours, and you're sure to find a crop of scrapes and gouges that need fixing. The same holds true for big parties, moving days, and room-repair days. Here are a few ways you can get your furniture through rough times without its suffering serious damage. Rearrange furniture so that delicate edges, legs, or other parts are not exposed to room traffic. Move your most valuable pieces into corners and other protected areas. Use tablecloths or pads where possible, and when you invite guests over or have a party, have plenty of napkins and ashtrays on hand.

Rough use isn't the only finish scratcher. Lamps, candlesticks, ashtrays, and other objects that rest on furniture will cause scratches unless they are padded with felt, leather, or some similar material.

There are so many commercial preparations (page 271) made for furniture care today that it's difficult to tell where dusting ends and cleaning, polishing, or waxing begins. Plain dusting doesn't require anything more elaborate than a cloth dampened with water or lemon oil. Lemon oil is best because it removes grime and cuts through grease film better than water.

Beware of wax-containing aerosol sprays when it comes to dusting. The labels on these products may say something like "cleans and waxes in one step," or "waxes while you dust." These sprays are fine if

Dust your furniture regularly, using a soft, lint-free cloth dampened with water or lemon oil.

False topping
I barely rescued my newly marbleized coffee table from the playful but destructive hands of my son and one of his new toys. Luckily, no damage was done, and I had time to figure out a way of protecting my creation. I came up with a false top that fits right over the real one. I made it from ½-inch plywood and stained it to match the other furniture in the room. It comes off in a jiffy and stores right under the living-room couch.
Practical Pete

you use them every fifth or sixth time you dust; but use them every time and you'll build up a thick layer of wax on the surface. It may shine at first, but before long you'll get a dull film that only obscures the beautiful finish underneath it. To save the piece you'd have to remove all the wax and expose the bare finish again. The same precaution applies to the spray polishes or any of the dust-polish-wax combinations. They're just not needed every time you dust, providing the finish is in top shape.

Cleaners and polishes

Choosing the right products for maintaining your furniture can be confusing. In the following sections, you'll find information on different products and how to use them.

Cleaning your furniture. Under normal conditions, dusting at regular intervals is all that is needed to keep furniture clean. There are times, however, when dusting isn't enough. A dresser that has been in storage for several years, a kitchen chair, a spice rack, a child's desk, or a dining-room table all need special cleaning attention at some time or other. To remove heavy accumulations of dirt, grease, soot, and other foreign material, you'll have to use a furniture cleaner.

Choose your cleaner according to the type of grime to be removed and the type of finish on the furniture. If the finish is waterproof, a sponge or rag dipped in a solution of warm water and soap will do a good job of removing most dirt, soot, or grime. Most of the commercial spray cleaners that come in cans or bottles are excellent, but always check the label to make sure the cleaner won't harm the finish. There are special cleaners for rubbed-oil finishes, or you can use a cloth dampened in a turpentine-linseed oil mixture (three parts turpentine to one part oil). Clean a wax finish with a cloth dampened in turpentine.
Tip: Don't use a combination cleaner-polish or cleaner-wax on a finish that's really grimy. These preparations are meant for light touchup cleaning.
Polishing. If you have to clean your furniture, chances are it needs a good polishing too. Polishes also act as cleaners, since their mild abrasive action tends to smooth the finish and loosen small particles that cling to it. An aerosol cleaner-polish is a good

investment if you have a lot of furniture to look after. These easy-to-use products are ideal for mild cleaning or shining up a dull finish. Furniture polish is also available in cream or liquid form. (You can make a good polish yourself by combining equal parts of denatured alcohol and olive oil.)

Regardless of what polish you use, apply it liberally to the surface, using a soft cloth, and rub it around with a circular motion. Work with firm pressure and go over dull areas again if necessary. Promptly remove any polish left on the surface, with a dry cloth. If you're polishing over one or more coats of wax, spend a few minutes buffing the wax once you've removed the excess polish. Don't apply any more wax to the surface if you can buff the existing finish to a good shine.

Restoring the shine to a finish is an easy job with many of the commercial spray polishes. These products are also good for mild cleaning. Spray on a generous amount and work it over the surface with a soft, clean cloth.

Wax

Wax comes in cream, paste, spray, and liquid form, but only paste wax is used as a furniture finish (page 242). Spray waxes or combination "cleans-as-it-waxes" sprays are not substitutes for the traditional paste-wax finish. They will, however, enhance the durability and beauty of most finishes including paste wax (see chart).

With the many different types of wax available today, it's important to make sure you're using the right product. Avoid waxes designed for automotive use, and never use a self-polishing floor wax on your furniture. A quick look at the label or instructions should tell you whether or not you've got the right type. Many spray waxes contain silicone, an ingredient that adds durability to the finished surface.

Caring for a wax finish calls for regular dusting, buffing, and cleaning. First wipe down the furniture with a damp cloth; then buff the surface with a soft, dry cloth to restore the shine. Dirt and surface stains can be removed with commercial cleaners or a cloth slightly dampened in turpentine. Areas that can't be buffed to a shine require more wax.

Wax buildup is a common problem on older furniture and furniture that has been waxed more frequently than necessary. Some common signs of wax buildup include: a finish that looks yellow or cloudy even after buffing; excessive buffing time required to produce shine; a gummy or sticky surface. Remove excess wax by rubbing the surface with a cloth dampened in benzene or turpentine. In cases where the buildup is severe, the best solution is to remove the old wax entirely and apply new wax to the exposed finish.

Most of the liquid, cream, or spray waxes recommended for furniture contain enough water, solvents, or lemon oil to qualify them as cleaners. They are easy to use and do a good job of light cleaning and touchup waxing. Don't use them too often, though. An application every four to six weeks should do.

One rule that applies, regardless of what wax you're using, is that durability and beauty depend on good buffing. Always try to buff a dull finish back to life before you decide to apply more wax. When you do apply wax, do so sparingly—a little makes a lot of shine. Heavy use and repeated cleaning with a nonwaxing cleaner will eventually wear down a wax finish. When this happens, apply a fresh coat of paste wax.

Sometimes only parts of a piece of furniture need waxing. Apply a thin coat of paste wax to areas that have been worn down by heavy use or repeated cleanings.

Quick reference chart for cleaning, polishing, and waxing care

Finish	Protection	Cleaner	Polish
Lacquer	Paste wax; additional coats as required; spray wax as a touchup and after polishing.	Commercial cleaners are preferable to soap and water.	Commercial polish.
Varnish enamel, polyurethane and catalytics		Soap and water; commercial cleaners.	Commercial polish or a one-to-one mixture of alcohol and olive oil.
Penetrating resin	Apply additional resin finish for more protection.	Soap and water; commercial cleaners.	Not polished.
Shellac and French polish	Paste wax; several coats are necessary for good protection; use a silicone spray wax for touchup waxing.	Commercial cleaners suitable for shellac (nonalcohol base).	Light spray polish (nonalcohol base).
Rubbed oil	Never wax; continue applying oil for increased protection.	Three parts turpentine to one part linseed oil, or special commercial cleaners.	Not polished.

Filling scrapes and depressions

No matter how carefully you protect your furniture, accidental scrapes, burns, and other minor "bruises" are bound to occur from time to time. This type of damage can range from barely visible scratches in the finish to large cracks and gouges that extend deeply into the wood. Many of these blemishes can be repaired quickly and easily; for others, a great deal of skill and experience is needed. Even spot-repair experts are sometimes unable to restore a badly scarred finish, so don't expect perfect results on your first few tries. It's often difficult to completely hide blemishes, but you can make them less noticeable.

Try to repair scrapes, nicks, or similar damage as soon as possible. Otherwise, they tend to collect dust and grime, leaving you with an extra chore: cleaning out the crevices before making the repairs.

The first step in any type of repair is to assess the damage. The size, depth, and location of the blemish will determine what tools and materials you'll need for making the repair. Spending a moment to figure out how the mark was made might prevent a similar accident from occuring.

Scrapes, gouges, and scratches come in all sizes and shapes, so there are no specific rules on what tools or materials to use where. In many cases, you'll have to depend on intuition or ingenuity to make the repair. Here are some general guidelines to work from:

Scratches in the finish. Use wax sticks or nail polish for superficial touchup work. Wax sticks work best on narrow scratches; they will not hold well if the scratch is wide or deep. Don't use nail polish on a penetrating-resin or rubbed-oil finish.
Wide scrapes. Refinishing is usually required—but on the damaged area only.

Determine what finishing materials (including filler and stain, if the scrape extends into the wood) were originally used. Then refinish the scraped area making it as identical to the rest of the piece as possible.
Deep scratches. Use shellac sticks to repair scratches that are too deep for wax sticks or nail polish.
Gouges, burn marks, and cracks. Large depressions like these are best filled with wood dough. (Bad burns must be dug out and filled.) Turn the page for step-by-step information on common spot repairs.

Clear nail polish can be used for filling in small scratches or chips in shellac, varnish, lacquer, polyurethane, or enamel finishes. Apply successive coats until the scratch has been filled. Nail polish dries in ten minutes or less, is available in many colors, and is ideal for fixing scratches in enamel.

Before doing major repair work protect the surrounding finish by masking off damaged area.

What it takes

Approximate time: Varies from ten minutes for hiding small scratches to several hours for filling large cracks or gouges.

Tools and materials: Many materials can be used for repairing scratches, cracks, and larger depressions on furniture surfaces. Here are some of the more helpful items you should have in your repair kit:
Wax sticks. Get sticks in various colors to match the furniture in your home.
Wood dough. Commonly known as plastic wood; available in several wood tones.
Steel wool and sandpaper. Extra-fine and super-fine grades.
Shellac sticks. Available in different colors. Note: Lacquer sticks have replaced shellac sticks to some extent. They are used the same way and work even better.

All of the above are sold at hardware and paint stores, but shellac sticks may be hard to find. If you have trouble locating them, try one of the specialty woodcraft-supply houses.

Tricks for storing sticks
Wax sticks are easy to use (see page 274), but very difficult to find when you need them. I spent about three-quarters of an hour rummaging through my workshop before I found a stick that matched the scratch in my coffee table. Ten minutes later the repair was complete, and I had also figured out a great place for storing the stick between repairs. I taped it to the underside of the table. No more chasing around to locate the right-colored wax stick—it's attached to the furniture.

Practical Pete

Repairing scratches

Wax sticks. You can easily repair minor scrapes in any type of finish with wax sticks. These are nothing more than specialized crayons, designed specifically for filling in shallow, narrow scratches in a finish. There are several types of wax sticks or pencils available. Ask for them at your hardware store. Each brand comes in a variety of colors to match different finishes and wood tones.

Prepare the blemish by going over it with a damp cloth or a cleaner compatible with the finish (page 272). This will remove any loose finish or foreign matter from the scrape, allowing the wax to adhere. Rub the stick across the scratch until you've filled the damaged area with wax. **Tip:** Most wax sticks work best at room temperature or warmer; cooler temperatures make the wax brittle and harder to use. Scrape off excess wax from the surrounding finish, using a stiff playing card or a piece of plastic as a scraping tool. (A metal scraper might make more scratches.) Then buff the repaired area with a soft cloth. The final step is to cover the patch with a thin coat of paste wax and buff the wax to a shine.

Shellac sticks. These touchup tools are easy to use and will work better than wax sticks on large scratches or scratches that extend into the wood. They are also preferred by professional woodworkers because they make a hard, durable patch that is difficult to detect. Shellac sticks come in a variety of colors and wood tones. Step-by-step illustrations for using them are given at right. In addition, the following tips will help you do a first-rate job:

If you can't find a shellac stick that matches the finish to be patched, select one that is lighter rather than darker than the finish. You can always darken the patch with a non-penetrating oil stain, but it's impossible to lighten shellac that's too dark.

Clean out the scratch thoroughly before you start filling it in with shellac. Using extra-fine sandpaper, scuff-sand the wood or finish where the shellac will go.

Shellac sticks must be melted to be used, but do this carefully. Using excessive heat or a smoky flame can char the stick and darken its color considerably.

Wax sticks and pencils are designed specifically for repairing minor scratches on finished surfaces. They are available in various colors and wood tones.

1. Rub over the scratch with the wax stick until the blemish is filled.

2. Remove excess wax from the surface surrounding the blemish, using a piece of plastic as a scraper.

3. Buff the patched surface with a soft cloth. Then finish the job by applying paste wax to the repair area.

1. Use a soldering iron or heated knife blade to melt the shellac stick into the crack, as shown. Fill deep depressions in stages.

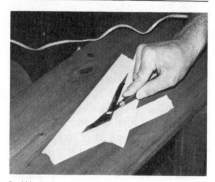

2. Work the shellac into the crack while it's still warm and pliable. Use a heated knife or leveling tool like the one shown above.

3. Let the shellac harden. If there is any excess, scrape it off with a sharp chisel or razor blade. Then use super-fine sandpaper or steel wool to smooth the patch flush with the surrounding finish.

4. Remove the masking tape and apply a coat of paste wax. Buff the area vigorously to protect the surface and restore the shine.

Cracks, burns, and gouges

The repair procedures for burns, large cracks, and gouges are all very much the same. This type of damage is too extensive to be handled with wax or shellac sticks. What some touchup experts do, however, is to partially fill a large depression with wood dough, and then complete the patch with stick shellac. This is an excellent way of restoring a severely scarred finish. **Tip:** Severe cracks may call for structural as well as cosmetic repairs (see right).

Wood dough, also known as plastic wood or wood putty, comes in cans or tubes. Don't confuse it with paste wood filler; the two products are used differently. If you're lucky, you'll be able to find wood dough in a color identical to that of the damaged finish. If not, you can stain the patch to match.

Prepare the damaged area by clean-ing it out completely. Remove all dust, loose wood splinters, and other foreign material. To repair a burn mark, scrape out the charred area with a sharp knife until you reach bare wood. Be prepared to dig down fairly deeply for bad cigarette burns—it's important to remove all the charred wood.

Apply the wood dough with a small scraper or spatula. Use more than you need because the dough may shrink slightly as it dries. Force it into the depression, using your fingers or a small knife blade, if necessary. Fill deep (¼-inch or more) gouges or cracks in stages, waiting for each layer of wood dough to dry before you apply the next. (Most plastic-based wood dough will dry in less than an hour.) When you apply the final layer, always overfill the depression so the patch can be sanded flush.

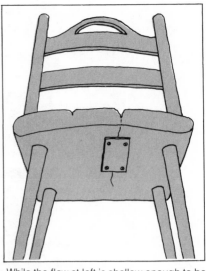

While the flaw at left is shallow enough to be repaired with a shellac stick, the one at right should be filled with wood dough. Deep cracks or gouges may weaken the furniture, so that mending plates or other structural repairs are necessary.

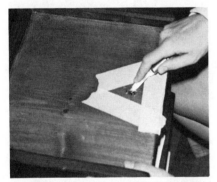

1. Cigarette burns aren't difficult to repair. Remove the charred wood with a sharp knife (a pocket knife is ideal). When you've dug out the burn so that only bare wood shows, remove all dust and loose splinters from the hole so the patch will adhere well.

2. Use a small spatula or scraper to apply the wood dough. Force it into the depression with your fingers, a small knife blade, or other suitable tool. Overfill the depression so that the patch is slightly higher than the surrounding surface.

3. When the wood dough has dried completely, sand it flush with extra-fine sandpaper. If necessary, stain the patch so it appears less conspicuous. Then apply two coats of paste wax to the patched area or spot-finish it to match the surrounding surface area.

How to make your own wood dough

You can make your own wood dough by adding sawdust to white or yellow glue (polyvinyl acetate or aliphatic resin). Use the sawdust that collects under an electric table saw or inside the dust bag of a belt sander. If you can't find such a sawdust stockpile, it's easy to make your own. In fact, you can use sawdust from a piece of wood identical to the stock you're patching. That way you're sure the patch will match.

Select a piece of wood and place it on a large sheet of waxed paper while you're sanding. Use fine or extra-fine sandpaper and keep brushing the sawdust off the wood surface and onto the paper. Pour some glue onto the waxed paper and gradually mix in the sawdust until you have a homogeneous, pasty dough.

To make wood dough, pour some white or yellow glue onto a sheet of waxed paper and mix in sawdust bit by bit until you have a wood-colored paste.

Wood dough can be sanded, stained, and even sawed, just like real wood. If your finished patch doesn't blend in well with the surrounding wood, touch it up with a small brush and some flat paint or nonpenetrating oil stain.

Removing stains

If the finish on your furniture is in good condition, it is unlikely that stains will really take hold and become a problem. What appears to be a stain in the finish is often actually nothing more than surface grime that you can remove with commercial or other cleaning agents. Only when you're sure the stain is *in* the finish instead of *on* it, should you proceed with the steps outlined below.

General procedures. If you can't remove a mark by cleaning, you'll have to rub out the stained finish with a suitable abrasive. It's a good idea to start with a mild abrasive like cigarette ashes or salt, and work up to stronger ones only if you have to. Once you have removed the stained finish, clean the surface and give it a good polishing to restore the smoothness and shine. A light coat of paste wax will give additional shine and protection to the repaired area.

White spots and rings. Stains of this type are commonly found on any finished surface that is flat enough to hold spilled fluids. The white stain is made when the standing liquid combines with the finish. This may happen in as little as half an hour on a shellac, wax, or French-polish finish. Lacquer, varnish, and polyurethane finishes can also be stained in this way, but the standing time is considerably longer.

Most watermarks can be removed easily, using any number of different abrasives. The type you use depends on how deep the mark extends into the finish.

To remove mild spots or rings, make a paste from cigar or cigarette ashes and water (use oil for a shellac or French-polish finish) and apply it to the stained area. Then rub the paste around with your finger or a cloth pad until the stain disappears. **Tip:** If you're a nonsmoker and don't relish the idea of making your own ashes, try using toothpaste instead. Most toothpastes are slightly abrasive and will rub out minor surface stains.

Always try to remove a furniture stain with a cleaner or polish before you resort to stronger abrasives.

For a tougher mark, sprinkle some table salt over the spot and use linseed oil as the rubbing lubricant. Salt is slightly more abrasive than ashes. If the stain still won't come out, you'll have to use pumice or super-fine steel wool to remove the damaged finish. Use linseed oil with the pumice to make a paste and to soften the cutting action of the steel wool. These stronger abrasives will remove even the worst watermarks, but they may scuff the finish so the repaired area stands out conspicuously. If this is the case, use a good-quality furniture polish to rub the area until it's as smooth as the surrounding finish. An alternative is to rub down the entire surface with pumice, and then use rottenstone and polish to give the piece a uniform shine. (For more information on rubbing and polishing, see pages 254-255.)

Once you have removed the white spot or ring, apply a thin coat of paste wax to the repaired area and buff it to a shine.

Blushing. This term applies to a clear finish that has become clouded or hazy. Blushing can be caused by continuous exposure to high humidity or low temperatures. To restore a blushed finish, give it a good rubdown with pumice or super-fine steel wool, using linseed oil as a lubricant. Keep rubbing until you have removed the clouded finish.

Black spots. Dark spots or rings on your furniture usually mean trouble. They may be burn marks caused by hot objects that have rested on the furniture or they may be caused by moisture that has worked through the finish and discolored the wood. Casserole dishes, coffee cups, and carelessly dropped matches or cigarettes frequently cause burns; flower pots, vases, and other stationary water holders can easily leave their mark in any finish.

Since these stains are *in* the wood, you'll have to remove the finish to get the mark out. Mask off the damaged area to protect the surrounding surface and sand the finish down until you reach bare wood. If the wood has been charred, scrape out the scorched wood and fill the depression with wood dough as shown on page 275. If not, apply bleach to the mark with an artist's paintbrush. Use ammonia, laundry bleach, or oxalic acid to bleach the stain (see pages 264-265). Lighten the mark gradually by repeated applications until it matches the surrounding wood. **Tip:** It's easy to overbleach, especially if the wood has been stained. If you've lightened the mark too much, touch it up with a suitable stain.

When you have finished bleaching, clean the repair area with a cloth dampened in vinegar and refinish it to match the surrounding surface.

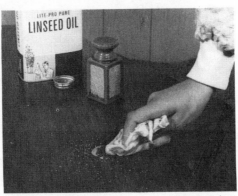
Use linseed oil and salt to rub out stubborn surface stains, then polish the finish.

Use pumice on stains that can't be rubbed out with milder abrasives. Make a rubbing paste by adding some oil to a small amount of pumice.

If the stain is really embedded in the finish, remove the damaged finish with some super-fine steel wool. Dip the steel wool in linseed oil to soften its cutting action.

To fix dark stains in the wood, remove all finish that covers the mark and bleach the darkened area to match the surrounding wood. Use a small brush to apply ammonia, oxalic acid, or laundry bleach.

New life for old finishes

Restoring an old piece of furniture doesn't have to involve stripping off the old finish. Unless the finish is peeling or severely cracked, you can probably recondition it with one of the techniques described below.

Wax. Old wax tends to darken. Even with regular care, it will collect impurities and eventually turn yellow or brown. At that stage, it becomes cloudy and difficult to buff to a shine. Old wax or thick accumulations of wax are also more prone to watermarks and other stains. A dull wax finish is not so well revived as it is replaced. Use a cloth dampened in turpentine to remove the old wax, then replace it with a thin layer of good-quality furniture wax.

Shellac and French polish. If you're not planning to use one of the special furniture-refinishing preparations (see opposite), the best way to save an ailing shellac or French-polish finish is to rub off the top layer of finish and apply one or two fresh coats. You'll need some double- or triple-F pumice, linseed oil, and a rubbing pad to remove the "tired" top layer of finish. (Note: Most shellac finishes are covered with several coats of paste wax for additional protection. Make sure you remove the wax with a turpentine-soaked cloth before you rub the finish down.) Make a generous amount of rubbing compound by combining pumice and linseed oil. Add extra oil as the paste thickens. Use firm pressure on the rubbing pad to work the finish down until the surface is smooth, clean, and uniform. On contoured pieces, use super-fine steel wool or work the paste around with a soft cloth. Don't worry if the newly exposed surface is clouded; it's due to the cutting action of the abrasive and clears up when you apply the new coat.

When you've removed the top layer of the finish, dampen a cloth with turpentine and clean the surface. Then refinish it with shellac or by French-polishing it. **Tip:** You may want to use lacquer, varnish, polyurethane, or enamel over a base coat of shellac. All are compatible with shellac—and considerably more durable. The "rubdown and recoat" technique described above can also be used to revive enamel, polyurethane, and catalytic finishes.

Lacquer. A lacquer finish that is full of minor cracks, scratches, and chips can often be restored by reamalgamation. With this technique the old finish is liquefied so that scratches, cracks, and other irregularities in the finish can melt into a smooth, uniform surface. Reamalgamation works best on a flat, level surface.

The first step is to give the old finish a thorough cleaning. Then paint on a thin coat of lacquer thinner, brushing it across the grain if possible. Lay the solvent on in long, slightly overlapping strokes, using very little pressure. As soon as you've covered the surface, brush over it again, this time stroking with the grain. Don't apply any more thinner, but keep your brush wet. This last brush course will distribute the liquefied finish evenly over the surface, but you may have to repeat the process several times to fill all cracks completely. Wait for the finish to harden before you reapply the lacquer thinner.

Varnish. Make a cleaning and reconditioning solution of turpentine and boiled linseed oil. (Use one part turpentine to three parts oil.) The turpentine cleans and softens the varnish; the linseed oil nourishes the wood and combines with the varnish, providing a richer, more durable surface. Heat the mixture by placing it in a large container of hot water. **Caution:** Never expose turpentine to direct flame; it's extremely flammable. Apply the solution to the surface with an absorbent cloth. Work on one section at a time, rubbing first in a circular motion and then parallel with the grain. When the cloth gets dirty, wring it out and moisten it with clean mixture.

If the finish is badly stained or rough and irregular in appearance, use more turpentine in the mixture (up to 50%) and apply it with a pad of super-fine steel wool. The extra turpentine and steel wool will dissolve bad marks in the finish and melt the varnish into cracks and scratches.

When the entire finish has been rubbed clean and all stains and scratches have been worked out, buff the surface with a soft cloth. To enhance the finish, polish it and then apply a thin coat of paste wax, buffing it to a shine.

Rubbed oil. Many fine antiques have a rubbed-oil finish. To revive this type of finish, use a mixture of linseed oil and turpentine. Remove all stains from the wood surface first, using turpentine or a commercial cleaner. Then combine one part turpentine with three parts boiled linseed oil. Apply this mixture to the wood in generous amounts, using a clean cloth. Wait for about 15 minutes to let the oil penetrate into the wood. Then wipe the surface clean and buff it with your hand or a soft cloth. Rubbing the oil into the wood is an important step in restoring the deep, warm glow that distinguishes this traditional finish.

Repeat this procedure once every two or three days until the wood surface regains its durability and beauty. Then keep it in shape by rubbing in pure boiled linseed oil whenever you get the chance. Unlike other finishes, linseed oil can be applied without limit. **Tip:** Heating the oil or oil-turpentine mixture will produce better results. But never expose the solution to direct heat; it is exceedingly flammable.

Using commercial refinishers

There are several commercial preparations designed specifically for reconditioning worn-out shellac, varnish, or lacquer finishes. These products do an excellent job, especially on finishes that appear to be ruined, but they may be difficult to find. *Gillespie's Old Furniture Refinisher* and *Formby's Furniture Refinisher* are two brand names to ask for. (The Gillespie refinisher can be bought in a kit that includes rubber gloves, metal pan, plastic dropcloth, steel wool, and tung oil in addition to the refinisher.) There's a real knack to using these relatively new products, so read the manufacturer's instructions carefully, and follow the technique explained below.

Commercial refinishers are actually no more than specially prepared *amalgamators* that liquefy the old finish, letting you remove the stains, dark spots, or discolorations that have accumulated over the years. Use super-fine steel wool to apply the liquid refinisher, filter out the impurities in the finish, and work the remaining clean finish back into the wood. When the steel wool gets gummy or starts to shed, replace it with a new pad. When the refinisher thickens or becomes too dirty to work with, wipe the surface off and apply a fresh batch. (Don't discard the used refinisher; once the grimy sediment settles out, the liquid can be poured off and used again.)

Tung oil is a wood preservative that has been used in China since at least the twelfth century. It is now a major ingredient in most high-quality varnishes. It can also be bought in pure form, although it is quite a bit more expensive than other finishes. Pure tung oil is recommended for reconditioning old finishes because it has excellent penetrating and protective qualities. It also dries faster than linseed oil, gives more luster to the finished surface, and does not need to be rubbed in as vigorously or reapplied as often.

1. Protect the floor in the work area with a plastic dropcloth or several layers of newspaper. Remove knobs, pulls, and other hardware covering the surfaces to be refinished.

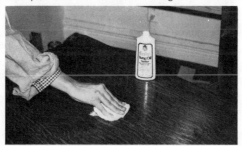

2. Pour about two cups of refinisher into a metal container and saturate a wad of super-fine steel wool with the solution.

3. Apply the refinisher with the steel wool. Work on one area at a time, rubbing in a circular motion. Rinse the steel wool frequently in the refinishing solution to remove the old finish.

4. When the refinisher thickens with the grime that's been filtered out of the old finish, pour it into another container. Use fresh refinisher and a clean steel-wool pad to continue reconditioning the finish.

5. When all the discolored or dirt-laden finish has been removed, use new steel wool and fresh refinisher to work the remaining finish into the wood. Rub with the grain, using moderate pressure.

6. Allow the piece to dry for 30 minutes, then rub it down lightly with a clean, dry pad of super-fine steel wool. Finally, rub in a light coat of tung-oil finish, using a clean cloth or your bare hand.

Caring for upholstery

What it takes

Approximate time: Varies from several minutes for removing stains to half an hour or more for retying a spring or replacing a strip of webbing.

Tools and materials: It's a good idea to have a commerical stain remover handy, as well as a commerical fabric cleaner. This way, you can remove most stains when they happen, preventing them from soaking in and taking hold.

Upholstery-repair equipment that you might need is described below.

Tack hammer. A lightweight hammer with two heads, one of which is magnetized. Use the magnetized head for holding and starting tacks, and the other head for driving them.

Upholstery tacks. Available in different styles and sizes, they all have large heads for extra fabric-holding power. Use No. 8 tacks for thick fabrics or webbing, and No. 4 tacks for fine materials.

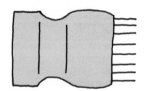

Web puller. A simple lever used to stretch webbing and hold it tight while it is tacked to the frame.

Upholsterer's needle. A curved, heavy-duty needle used for binding springs to webbing

There are many kinds of upholstered furniture. A dining-room chair with an upholstered seat panel is an example of simple upholstery. An overstuffed sofa on the other hand, is a complex system of padding, springs, webbing, tacks, and fabrics. Reupholstering furniture is usually far more difficult than refinishing it. You should bring badly damaged upholstery to a professional for repairs rather than undertaking the job yourself. With the proper care, however, there's no reason why your upholstered furniture shouldn't last for generations.

Basics. To understand the anatomy of a typical upholstered chair or sofa, consider the outer fabric of the furniture to be its skin. Like real skin, the fabric can easily be punctured, torn, or soiled without the right care and protection. Underneath the fabric there are protective tissues, padding and layers of burlap or other coarse cloth. These parts sometimes shift out of place and can be repositioned or replaced after the outer fabric has been removed. The skeleton of a piece of upholstered furniture is nothing more than a wooden frame to which all others parts are attached. This frame is prone to the same structural damage as conventional wood furniture, and can be repaired in the same way. On most types of upholstered furniture, a spring suspension system anchored to the frame provides the muscle to cushion your weight, making the seat soft and comfortable. With age and overflexing, parts of the suspension wear out or separate from the frame, and must be replaced or repaired.

Taking care of upholstered fabrics

Today, all upholstery fabrics carry a label. This label, usually found on the cushions, or the unseen side of the skirt that runs around the legs of the furniture, describes the fabric and gives instructions for taking care of it. Modern furniture fabrics are often treated to repel stains, or designed to be easily removed for cleaning. The fabric used on antique upholstery is usually wool, satin, or linen, and can't be removed unless a lot of tacks are pulled out first.

In any case, the best way to deal with stains and grime is to prevent them from getting on the fabric in the first place. Slipcovers are a good idea. They are inexpensive, provide excellent protection, and can be found in a great variety of colors and patterns. They can also be removed in an instant for guests or special occasions.

Remove dust and surface dirt from your upholstery with a vacuum cleaner. Most units have special attachments for cleaning fabrics. Follow the guidelines in the chart below to remove stains. A general rule for stains is to remove them as soon as possible; the longer they are left in the fabric, the tougher they are to get out.

Use a vacuum cleaner with a fabric attachment to remove dust and dirt from upholstered furniture.

TYPE OF STAIN	TREATMENT
Alcoholic beverages	Blot and rinse in cold water. For synthetics, sponge stain clean with solution of 1 part white vinegar to 8 parts water.
Blood, egg yolk	Blot immediately. For washables, rinse in cold water and launder, if needed. Add ammonia to water for white fabrics.
Fat	Dab or rub clean with commercial stain remover.
Glue	For washables, soak in hot water. Some glues will dissolve when sprayed with vinegar or liquid detergent.
Ink	Sponge with detergent suds. For linen or cotton fabrics, apply lemon juice and sprinkle salt over stained area; let stand at least ½ hour; then rinse clean. Ball-point-pen ink can usually be dabbed clean with alcohol.
Mildew	Saturate mildewed area with lemon juice and allow to dry, preferably in sunlight.
Milk, coffee, fruit juice, soft drinks	Blot and rub clean with commercial stain remover.
Oil, grease	Sponge clean with turpentine.
Paint	Blot immediately and dab clean with appropriate solvent. Don't use lacquer thinner on synthetics.

Keeping the spring in your seat

Over the years, furniture makers have developed several ways of giving upholstered furniture its traditional soft seat. Hidden underneath the fabric on your chair or sofa is a special suspension system, one that most people take for granted—until something goes wrong. While you'll probably want to take furniture with a severely damaged suspension system to a professional upholsterer, there are some important repairs you can readily make on your own. The first step is to turn your chair or sofa over and determine what kind of suspension the furniture has. You may have to remove a fabric cover tacked to the bottom of the seat frame to examine the suspension.

The most common suspension, especially on older upholstery, consists of webbing and coil springs. The webbing, made from a strong fiber called jute, is woven across the bottom of the seat frame. Each strip of webbing is stretched tight and tacked to opposite sides of the frame. The coil springs are fastened to the webbing at their bottom end and to each other at their top end. Note: There are some variations of this system. The coil springs may be attached to metal webbing or wooden slats.

As the suspension system wears, the webbing is likely to break, loosen, or separate from the frame; the coil springs tend to become detached at one or both ends. Neither one of these problems is difficult to correct, as long as you catch it early. Preventive care is the key word here, so take a troubleshooting look at seat suspensions at least once every season.

Replace broken or worn-out webbing with new material. Fold the new strip of webbing over on itself at one end and tack this double thickness to the frame. Then weave the webbing through the other strips and use a web stretcher to pull it taut while you tack it to the opposite side, as shown below. Cut the webbing off, but leave enough excess to fold it back over. Then tack this double thickness to the frame.

The coil springs in an upholstered seat hardly ever need to be replaced. They will eventually work loose, however, and should be attached as soon as possible. Otherwise, they may damage the fabric or get bent. Check the suspension to see how the springs are fastened to the webbing and to each other (strong cord is usually used). Then strengthen any weak points, using the same fastening method.

On most modern upholstered furniture, coil springs have been replaced by no-sag springs. The no-sag suspension system is simpler in design, less bulky, and easier to fix than its predecessor. No-sag springs are simply pieces of heavy wire bent in a zigzag pattern. They run from the front of the seat to the back and are attached to the frame with special holders. Neighboring springs are connected to each other at several points along their length with small coil springs (see illustration below). To keep a no-sag suspension system in top condition, make sure the spring holders are securely fastened to the seat frame. Replace weak coil springs, or add more to stiffen the suspension. If one of the no-sag springs breaks or twists out of shape, you can replace it yourself or have an upholsterer do it.

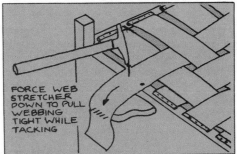

To replace webbing, fold one end over and tack this double thickness to one side of the frame. Weave the webbing through the other strips, stretch it tight with the web stretcher, and nail it to the frame. Cut off excess, leaving enough extra to tack down a double thickness, as on opposite side.

Stopgaps and copouts

If you have an upholstered chair or sofa with a ruined suspension system, you'll either have to junk the piece or take it to a professional upholsterer for extensive and expensive repairs. You can save some money, and a trip to the junkyard too, if you follow these instructions:

Remove the entire suspension system—webbing, springs, and all, leaving the frame open and free of any tacks or staples. Replace the webbing with a solid platform of ¾-inch plywood, cut to size (screw the plywood to the frame). Then order a pad of foam rubber than will fit in the space formerly occupied by the suspension. Now the furniture has a soft, though springless, seat.

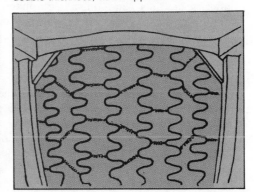

Use heavy cord to fasten springs to webbing. Also check the springs at their top ends to make sure they are all securely tied to each other.

No-sag springs are found on most modern upholstered furniture. Make sure the holders that secure the springs to the frame are firmly screwed in. Replace weak coil springs, or add more to stiffen the suspension.

8.WOOD

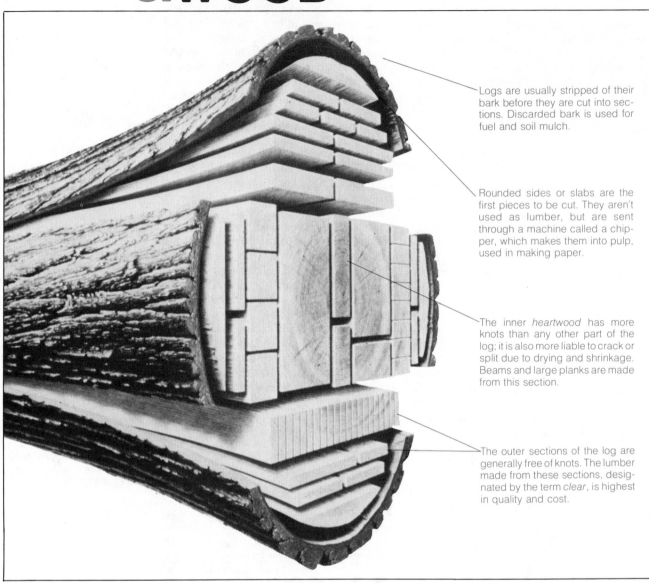

Logs are usually stripped of their bark before they are cut into sections. Discarded bark is used for fuel and soil mulch.

Rounded sides or slabs are the first pieces to be cut. They aren't used as lumber, but are sent through a machine called a chipper, which makes them into pulp, used in making paper.

The inner *heartwood* has more knots than any other part of the log; it is also more liable to crack or split due to drying and shrinkage. Beams and large planks are made from this section.

The outer sections of the log are generally free of knots. The lumber made from these sections, designated by the term *clear*, is highest in quality and cost.

It takes years of woodworking to really get to know wood: how to tell one type from another, separate good stock from bad, or choose a repair piece that will match even after stain, filler, and finish are applied. With each piece of furniture you repair or refinish, you'll learn more about different woods and their distinctive qualities. The information in this chapter will give you a head start.

Store your wood in a place where the humidity is low. Moisture may make the wood warp, and damp wood, on top of being difficult to glue, does not take stain, sealer, filler, or finish well. If possible, planks of wood more than three feet long should be stored flat.

Instead of throwing away the small pieces of wood that are left over when you cut stock to size, store them separately in a box or other container. Most of this so-called scrap wood isn't scrap at all. You can use it to make mending plates, patch pieces, corner blocks for reinforcing drawers, and for many other small repairs.

Store wood in a dry place, with planks laid flat and scrap wood kept separately in a cardboard box or other container.

Selecting the best wood

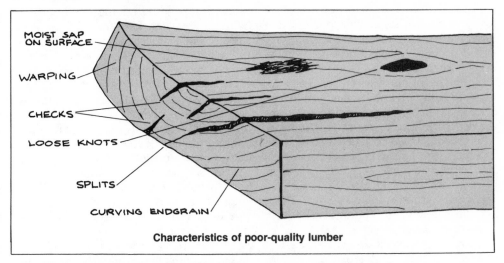

MOIST SAP ON SURFACE

WARPING

CHECKS

LOOSE KNOTS

SPLITS

CURVING ENDGRAIN

Characteristics of poor-quality lumber

All wood is not created equal. When you need new lumber for a repair job, it pays to look at each piece carefully before you buy it. If you're replacing a broken or missing part, bring the damaged section, or a piece similar in appearance, to the lumberyard. That way you can find a replacement piece of wood that will match the original.

Most lumberyards specialize in construction-grade lumber. This type of wood is fine for rough carpentry and building, but you'll probably want better quality for furniture work. Many lumber dealers don't stock hardwoods at all, so you may have to contact a specialty wood dealer (see page 285). In both cases, ask for cabinet or triple-A grade stock if you want to work with fine material. Below are some important tips you can use to single out the best pieces of wood.

Endgrain. The grain at the end of a piece of wood can tell you a lot about it. Cracks or splits that can't be seen running the length of the stock often show up clearly there. You're bound to find a few small cracks in just about any piece of stock. These are called checks, and are not a sign of low-quality lumber. Splits, large cracks, and excessive checking may, however, indicate weakness or poor-grade stock.

Take a look at the annual ring pattern in the endgrain. If you see a circular or long, curving pattern, the board is weaker and more likely to warp than it should be. As the wood dries, the circular "memory" locked in the rings often forces the board out of square, sometimes to the point of uselessness. In the strongest, straightest lumber, the growth rings are nearly straight, running parallel with the shorter edges of the stock. A special way of cutting the log, called *quartersawing*, produces this ring pattern. Maple, cherry, walnut, and other hardwoods are often quartersawn.
Tip: If you have trouble seeing the rings,

wet the endgrain to make them stand out.
Knots. The prevalence of knots varies from wood to wood and even from tree to tree. Knots often add a beautiful accent to the grain. Knotty-pine furniture is a good example of this. At other times, knots aren't desirable. Legs, rungs, and other structurally important parts should never be fashioned from knotty stock. If you decide to use a piece of lumber with a lot of knots in it, check each knot to make sure it isn't loose or broken. Avoid sawing into knots; they're tough to cut and often shatter or break off entirely.

Seasoning. Before lumber can be used, it must dry out. Green wood is full of sap and can't be glued or finished effectively. Seasoning, or drying, also tests the quality of the wood, since this is the time when warps and splits occur.

Wood that is naturally seasoned is simply stacked and dried in the open air. It is stacked with small skids separating each piece, allowing for free air circulation and even drying of all sides of the stock. Natural seasoning takes at least three months.

Kiln-drying is a much faster seasoning method. For this, the wood is dried in a large, oven-like structure called a kiln. Stock that is seasoned in this way usually has the words "kiln-dried" stamped on it somewhere.

Since all the sap has left the wood, leaving the pores empty and absorbent, seasoned wood is thirsty. To test for proper seasoning, rub a moistened finger across a smooth part of the wood. The moisture should be absorbed quickly, darkening the grain slightly as it penetrates into the pores.
Ordering lumber. Most lumber is sold by the board foot. To calculate the number of board feet in a given piece of stock, multiply its thickness (in inches), width (in inches), and length (in feet) together and divide the product by twelve.

Big deal
All I needed was a few small pieces of birch to make some corner blocks for an old drawer. Unfortunately, most lumber dealers will only sell wood in standard lengths. They'll cut it for you, but you pay for the whole piece. It seemed a shame to buy so much and use so little, and I was just about to return empty-handed to my wobbly drawer when the man behind the counter saved the day. He took me out to the warehouse where larger stock is cut to size for special orders. There we found a few birch scraps that fit my needs exactly—and cost but a few pennies apiece. If you ever need small "odds and ends," ask your lumber dealer if he has a scrap box you could look through. Chances are you'll find just what you need.

Practical Pete

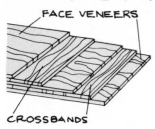

5-PLY FIR PLYWOOD
FACE VENEERS
CROSSBANDS

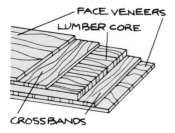

LUMBER CORE PLYWOOD
FACE VENEERS
LUMBER CORE
CROSSBANDS

All about plywood

Plywood is the most widely used product for woodframe building construction; it is increasingly used in furniture and home projects. It is relatively inexpensive for the coverage provided and its large sheet form makes many jobs quicker and easier to do. Plywood is strong, durable, and can be finished in a variety of ways. Its desirable characteristics are the result of the way it is made. Thin sheets of wood are glued together over a thicker core. The grain of alternate sheets is at right angles and sheets are added in pairs on each side of the core. This construction always results in an odd number of layers and accounts for the unusually high strength for size and weight.

Standard plywood sheets are 4 by 8 feet and are available in thicknesses of $1/4$, $3/8$, $1/2$, $5/8$, and $3/4$ inch. Special types as thin as $1/8$ inch and as thick as 1 inch or more can be obtained on special order.

The face veneers on fir plywood—the most common type—are given A, B, or C ratings, depending on the condition. A indicates a smooth knot-free surface; B is smooth, but with conspicuous patches and fill-in spots; C can have knotholes and splits. An A/C rating stamped on a sheet of plywood means one surface is good quality and the other is poor. Your dealer refers to this as "one side good" plywood. Only one side of a plywood sheet is usually visible on a finished project, so "one side good" is generally a satisfactory and economical buy.

There are basically three grades of plywood: interior, exterior, and marine. The difference in grades is due primarily to the type of glue used in laminating. Interior grade is suitable for most home projects, except where frequent wetness or humidity is present. Exterior grade should be used when the plywood will be exposed to moisture much of the time. Marine grade is suitable for direct contact with water; it is primarily intended for use below ground, on swimming pools, and boats.

Common furniture woods

Birch is a light-colored hardwood very similar to maple in appearance. It is often used in place of maple or cherry, as it is less expensive and can be stained to match either.

Cherry is a close-grained hardwood with a warm, reddish-brown color that grows deeper and more beautiful with age. Cherry is much harder to find than it once was; consequently, antique cherry furniture is very valuable. Never stained, this distinctively colored wood is usually finished with rubbed oil or varnish.

Mahogany, one of the softest hardwoods, varies in color from light brown to a dark reddish-brown and is found mainly in Honduras. Philippine mahogany, also called *lauan*, is lighter in color, less expensive, and of poorer quality than that from Honduras. Open-grained and large-pored, this wood always requires filling and is sometimes stained to a slightly darker tone. Mahogany is light, strong, and easier to work with than other hardwoods.

Maple is a traditional American wood that has been popular with furniture makers since early Colonial times. There are many species of maple trees, but the one used most in carpentry is called rock or hard maple. (Bird's-eye and curly maple are names given to hard maple with distinctive grain patterns.) As the name suggests, this wood is exceptionally hard, dense, and strong, making it ideal for use where strength and durability are important. Rock maple is light in color, with a grain pattern that can be exceedingly straight, curly, or anything in between. It is often hard to work.

Oak is a durable hardwood with an open and irregular grain that always needs filling. This wood is difficult to work, but its strength makes it popular for use in chairs, desks, and benches. It is best suited for furniture with simple lines, since its coarse grain makes carving and elaborate shaping very difficult. White and red oak are the two types most commonly used in making furniture.

Pine and fir are the least expensive and most readily available of all woods. Used extensively today for construction and rough carpentry, these softwoods have also been a favorite furniture wood since pioneer times. Pine furniture is traditionally simple and functional in design, reflecting the character of the early settlers. New pine or fir is light in color but will age to the golden or grayed tan that distinguishes valuable antiques. Modern pine furniture is usually stained to resemble aged or weathered pieces. Pine is a light, workable wood with a grain that is usually straight but may be knotty. Fir, also light and workable, can have a wavy, irregular grain, in addition to being knotty in places.

Poplar is a softwood similar to pine but with a grain that is even lighter and less noticeable. Very easy to work with, this wood is always stained, usually to resemble a walnut or mahogany finish.

Rosewood comes from Brazil or the East Indies and is one of the most expensive woods used for furniture. Rosewood veneers are often used on quality plywood furniture to give it a richer appearance. The grain of rosewood is straight or slightly wavy, with black and brown stripes. Rosewood is a very hard, heavy wood that is never stained, but always requires filling. It is also very rich in resin—so much so that all joints should be cleaned with benzene before they are glued.

Teak is an East Indian wood that is similar to rosewood. It is golden brown in color, however, and lacks the black highlights that rosewood has. Teak veneer is often used to cover less expensive wood.

Walnut is a dark hardwood with a beautiful black-and-brown grain pattern. It is strong and hard, but not as difficult to work with as maple or cherry. Walnut sometimes requires filling, but is seldom stained, since it is naturally dark to begin with. Penetrating resin and rubbed oil are the most popular finishes for enhancing the beauty of walnut furniture.

Plywood problems

Along with its many desirable qualities, there are two problems that plague do-it-yourselfers when using plywood. Because of the way it is constructed, plywood edges are unsightly. The alternate layers of end grain are rough and hard to finish. Also, the thin outer layers of plywood are highly susceptible to splintering when cut. This further complicates the edge-finishing job. Here are some tips on how to deal with these problems.

Sawing The trick in sawing plywood is to make the cut so that the cutting edge of the saw blade enters the wood on the side that will be exposed and exits in the side that will not show. Splintering occurs when the blade tooth exits. Mark your guide lines and make your cut with the sheet in the position shown below to keep splintering to a minimum.

    Hand saw—good side up
    Portable circular or sabre saw—good side down
    Table saw—good side up

The same general rule can be applied to drilling holes. Drill so that the bit enters on the good side.

If you have a situation where both sides of the sheet will show when the job is done, drilling and cutting must be done with a backing piece clamped to the side on which splintering would ordinarily occur.

Finishing edges There are four ways to solve the edge problem. The choice of method depends largely on how the piece is to be finished.

If the piece is to be painted—

—glue a wood strip or wood molding along the exposed edge. You can use small brads to keep the strip in place until the glue dries.

—premixed spackling compound can be worked into the rough edge. Smooth the compound with a knife edge and sand it when dry.

If the piece is to have a natural finish—

—flexible strips of natural wood can be glued to the edges. These strips are available in a variety of wood types and lengths in lumber yards and hardware stores. The strips are 1 or 1½ inch wide. After gluing to a thinner piece of wood, the projecting part can be trimmed off. These edges will take stain or any other finish to match the plywood.

Another product for edge treatment is plastic tee molding. While this material cannot, of course, be finished to match the plywood, it is available in a variety of colors that will blend with most finishes. The molding is held in place by forcing a ridged flange on the back into a precut slot. You will need a power saw to cut the slot. The molding is available in two widths: ¾ inch and 13/16 inch. The larger size will match ¾-inch plywood after a plastic sheet finish (such as Formica) has been glued to the surface.

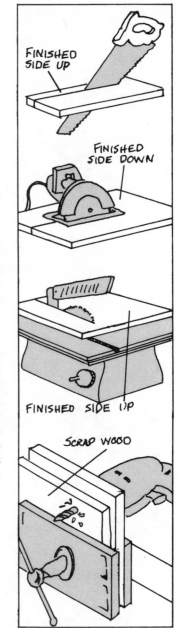

FINISHED SIDE UP

FINISHED SIDE DOWN

FINISHED SIDE UP

SCRAP WOOD

Sources for tools and materials

A good number of the tools and supplies described in this book may not be available in your hardware or paint store. The mail-order suppliers listed below specialize in woodworking tools and materials. They are the most reliable sources for hard-to-find items. For the most part, they offer good prices and are constantly updating their stock with new equipment and supplies. When you write for a catalog, briefly describe the project you are working on or one which you'd like to undertake.

Barap Woodworkers and Hobbyists Catalog* Barap Specialties 835 Bellows Frankfort, Michigan 49635	Woodworking tools and wood-finishing supplies.	Morgan Veneer Catalog Morgan Veneers 915 East Kentucky Street Louisville, Kentucky 40204	Complete selection of veneers from all over the world, plus valuable instructions for veneering.
Brookstone Hard-to-Find Tools* Brookstone Company Peterborough, New Hampshire 03458	A quality selection of unique and helpful tools for the home craftsman.	Silvo Tool Catalog* Silvo Hardware Company 107 Walnut Street Philadelphia, Pennsylvania 19106	Hand and power tools for the home workshop.
Constantine Woodworker's Catalog* Constantine's 2059 Eastchester Road Bronx, New York 10461	Woodworking tools and supplies, including cabinet-grade lumber and an extensive selection of veneers and veneering equipment.	U.S. General Tool and Hardware Catalog* U.S. General Supply Corporation 100 General Place Jericho, New York 11753	Good prices on brand-name hand and power tools.
Craftsman Woodcraft Supply Catalog Craftsman Wood Service Company 2727 South Mary Street Chicago, Illinois 60608	Hand and power tools for the home workshop, plus a wide selection of cabinet-grade lumber.	Woodcraft Tool Catalog Woodcraft 313 Montvale Avenue Woburn, Massachusetts 01801	Woodworking tools, including many hard-to-find items.
Minnesota Woodworkers Catalog Minnesota Woodworkers Supply Company Industrial Boulevard Rogers, Minnesota 55374	Veneer and woodworking tools and supplies.	Yankee Wood Craftsman Catalog Garrett Wade Company 302 Fifth Avenue New York, New York 10001	Fine hand tools for woodworking.

9.PICNIC TABLE

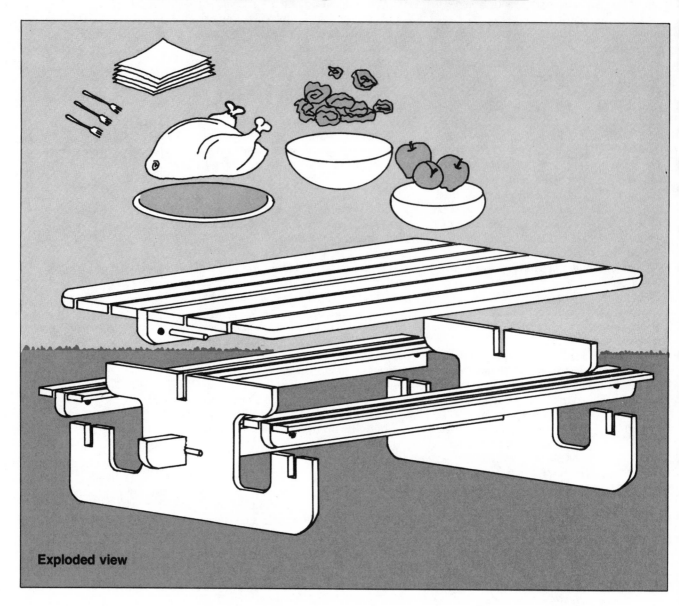

Exploded view

Perfect for casual outdoor dining, this one-piece picnic table will make an attractive addition to your patio or garden. More attractive still, the materials are relatively inexpensive, the construction is simple, and you can expect to enjoy the finished product for years to come.

First step is to draw the pattern for the end panels on the sheets of 4x8-foot plywood, two panels per sheet. Use a table saw or portable circular saw for the outside cuts and a saber saw for the inside and corner cuts. Cut as indicated in the pattern shown opposite, except for the notches and slots, which will be cut later.

Next, pair the four end panels so that their smooth surfaces face outward. Laminate each pair using a waterproof glue applied evenly to both surfaces. Fasten the

two pieces together with 1-inch wood screws, around 20 for each end-panel pair. Then cut and sand smooth the notches and slots that will accommodate the 2x8-inch cross members. Fill holes with wood putty.

Make your corner cuts on the cross members and drill ¾-inch holes in each, as indicated. Assemble the cross members and the end panels, then drive ¾-inch-by-3½-inch cut dowels into the predrilled holes.

For the table and bench tops, first make the necessary end cuts on the 2x6-inch boards; then nail the boards into place on the end panels using 3-inch galvanized nails. Leave ¼ inch between each board.

As a final step, the completed picnic table may be painted, stained or oiled to give it a weathered finish.

To make the picnic table, cut plywood and 2-inch lumber to the dimensions shown.

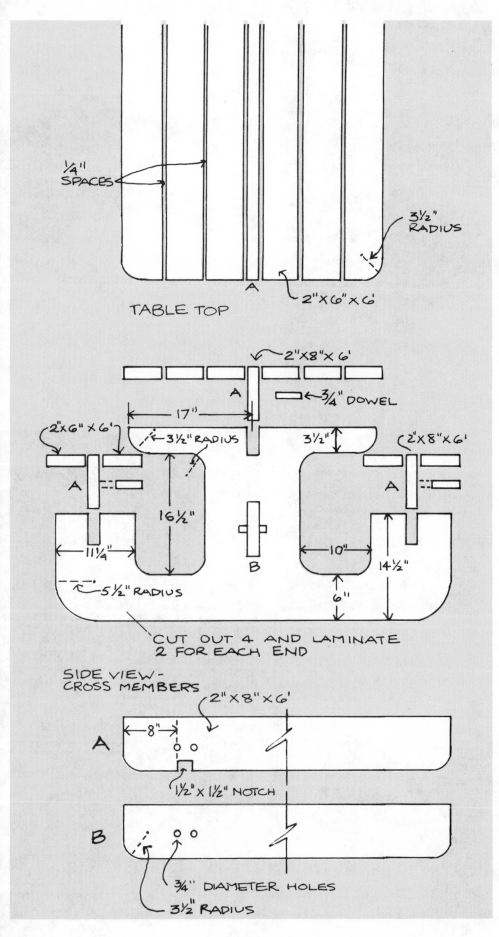

¼" SPACES

3½" RADIUS

A

2"×6"×6'

TABLE TOP

2"×8"× 6'

A

¾" DOWEL

2"×6"×6'

3½" RADIUS

17"

3½"

(2"×8"×6'

A

A

16½"

10"

11¼"

B

14½"

5½" RADIUS

6"

CUT OUT 4 AND LAMINATE
2 FOR EACH END

SIDE VIEW -
CROSS MEMBERS

2"×8"×6'

8"

A

1½" × 1½" NOTCH

B

¾" DIAMETER HOLES

3½" RADIUS

What it takes

Approximate time: A full day or less, and thus an ideal Saturday project.

Tools and materials: Table saw for the outside cuts, saber saw for insides and corners. You can use a portable circular saw but it should have a minimum rating of 1½ horsepower and at least a 7¼-inch blade. You'll need two 4x8-foot sheets of ¾-inch exterior plywood, smooth on one side; four pieces 2x8-inch by 6-foot lumber; 10 pieces 2x6-inch by 6-foot lumber; 16 hardwood dowels ¾ inch by 3½ inches; 40 1-inch wood screws; 3-inch galvanized nails; waterproof glue; wood putty.

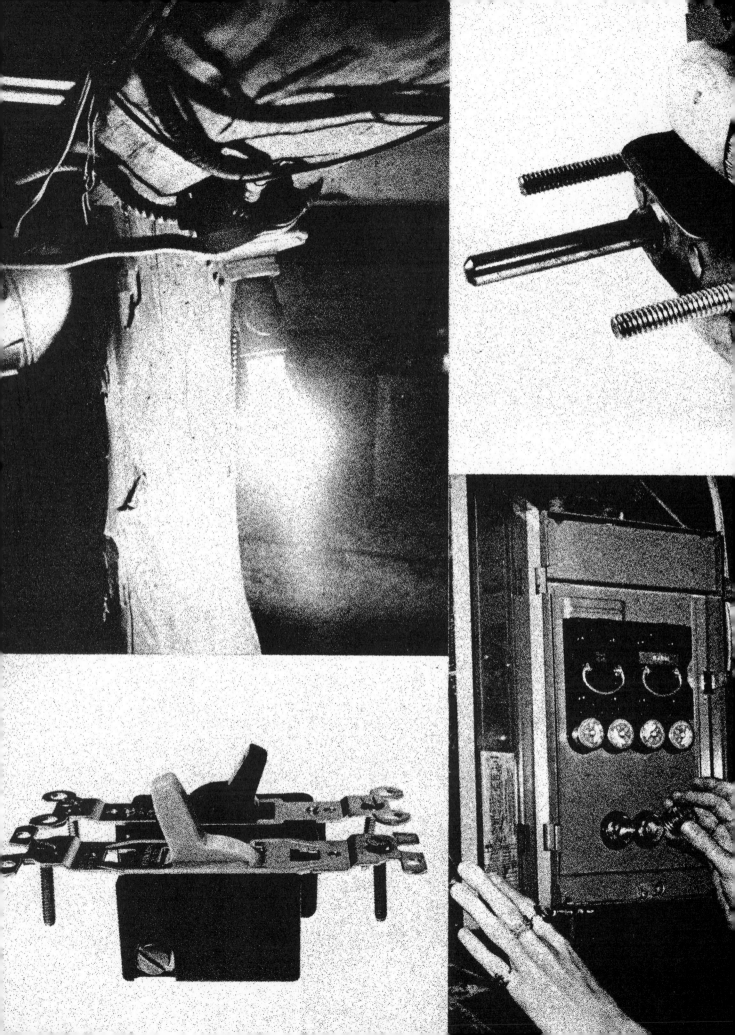

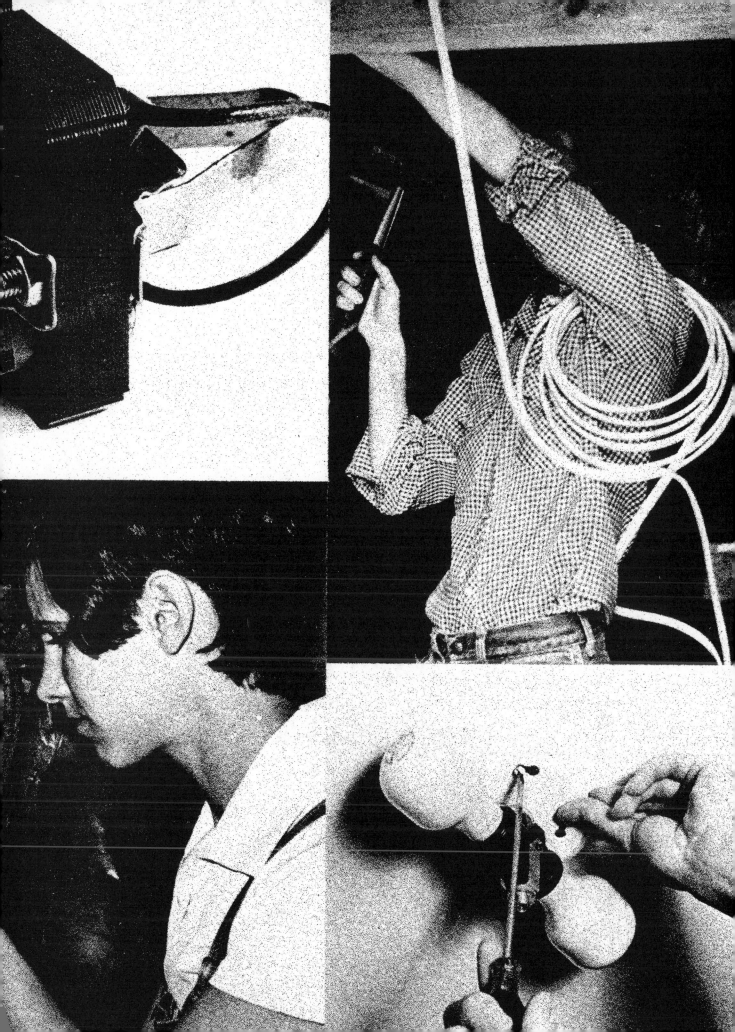

ELECTRICAL FIXTURES, WIRING & APPLIANCES

1. BASICS   292
   Basic safety   293
   Additional precautions   293
   Shock   293
   System grounding   294
   Ground fault interrupters   294
   Not all appliances should be
      grounded   295
   Why breakers trip or fuses blow
      when nothing's wrong   295
   Safeguards against fire   295
   When should a licensed electrician
      do the job?   295
   How electricity works   296
   Definition of electrical terms   297
   What is an electric circuit?   298
   What do AC and DC mean?   299
   Tools and supplies   300
   Power to your house   302
   How to read your meter   303
   Consuming watts   303
   Power ratings for typical home
      appliances   303
   Service panel   304
   Household circuits   304
   Circuit breakers and fuses   305
   Safety rules for fuse panel work   306
   Why did the fuse blow?   306
   How to map your circuits   307

2. TECHNIQUES   308
   Sheathed cable   308
   Removing plastic sheathing   308
   Removing steel armor   309
   Choosing the correct wire   310
   Common wire sizes and uses   310
   Aluminum wire   311
   Removing insulation   311
   Joining wires in electrical boxes   312
   Basic types of boxes   312
   Inserting and securing cable   313
   To secure separate clamps   313
   Mounting electrical boxes   314
   Joining wires together   315
   Solderless connectors   315
   Wiring lamp, appliance plugs   315
   Splicing wires   316
   Soldering   317
   Conduit   318
   Cutting and bending   318
   Supporting and coupling   319
   Connecting to boxes   319
   Threading wires through conduit   319

3. SIMPLE REPAIRS   320
   Rewiring a lamp   320
   Testing the parts of a lamp   322
   Wiring multiple-socket lamps   323
   Three-socket lamps   323
   Replacing a switch   324
   Replacing a wall receptacle   325
   Replacing small ceiling fixtures   326
   Replacing chandeliers   327
   Troubleshooting fluorescents   328
   Troubleshooting doorbells and
      chimes   330
   How doorbells are wired   331
   Troubleshooting branch circuits   332
   Junction box   333
   Middle-of-run ceiling box   333
   Middle-of-run wall outlet   333

4. NEW WIRING   334
   Which circuit to add onto?   334
   Evaluating available power   335
   Where to join into a circuit   336
   How to distinguish typical wiring
      functions   336
   Planning where to run new cable   338
   How to identify wires in electrical
      boxes   339
   Connecting new cable   340

5. SWITCHES   342
   What switches do electrically   342
   Standard toggle switches   342
   Special-function switches   343
   Wiring switched receptacles   345
   Pilot-light switches   345
   Incandescent dimmer switches   346
   Wiring multiple-switch circuits   347
   Connecting new source cable   348
   Grounding cable   348

6. CEILING FIXTURES   350
   How to install a ceiling box   350
   When ceiling is accessible from
      above   351
   When ceiling is between finished
      floors   352
   With plaster-and-lath ceiling   353
   Wiring a ceiling box to a wall
      switch   353
   Running cable to ceiling box   354
   Between finished floors   354
   Ceiling box cable run in attic or
      crawl space   356
   Mounting a ceiling fixture   357

7. FLUORESCENTS   358
   Fluorescent characteristics   359
   Installation in halls, kitchens, large
      areas   360
   Installation in bathrooms   361
   Fluorescent dimmers   362
   Joining fixtures   364
   Two-circuit wiring   366
   Luminous ceilings   367
   Unfinished areas   367
   Installing ceiling support hardware
      and plastic panels   368
   Finished ceiling areas   369

8. TRACK LIGHTING   370
   Components   371
   Electrical rating   372

9. SURFACE WIRING   372
   Metal and plastic   373
   Baseboard wiring   374

10. TROUBLESHOOTING
    APPLIANCES   374
    Troubleshooting checklist   376
    Small motors   378
    Large motors   378
    Motor parts: function and
       malfunction   379
    Heating elements   380
    Temperature control in appliances
       that heat   380
    Room air conditioners   381
    Wiring   381
    Seasonal maintenance   381

11. PROJECT   382

1.BASICS

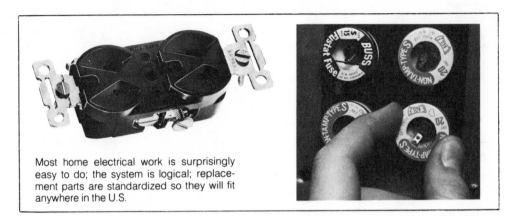

Most home electrical work is surprisingly easy to do; the system is logical; replacement parts are standardized so they will fit anywhere in the U.S.

This section provides step-by-step words and pictures—including safety precautions—for doing a wide variety of home electrical repairs and modifications.

A section starting on page 296 describes how electricity works and what electrical terms mean. If electrical work is new to you, read that section first.

From time to time you will notice hints from Practical Pete. Everybody makes mistakes sometimes—Practical Pete will help you avoid the more common ones and will give you tips on quicker or easier ways to get a job done.

The sizes, shapes, and characteristics of electrical materials are standardized, and the materials are relatively inexpensive. You can therefore buy what you need at modest cost and with complete confidence that—with the help of this book—you can do a safe, professional-type job that will increase the convenience, beauty, value, or safety of your home.

Most electrical work can be done by the homeowner without a permit and without conflict with local codes. However, requirements do vary. Contact your city or village building department for a copy of local regulations. Read the section in this book on the *National Electrical Code*.

Electrical work by the homeowner does not affect fire insurance coverage. However, if a fire loss claim results from wiring you installed, the company may classify you in a higher risk category.

Adequate precautions and instructions on checking your work are included in this section, beginning opposite.

The UL seal. Underwriters' Laboratories Inc. is a nonprofit organization that performs tests on electrical products. If an item meets minimum safety standards for avoidance of fire and shock, it is listed with the Underwriters' Laboratories. Listed items display the UL seal on the item itself or on its package. Note that the UL seal indicates minimum compliance with safety standards. Products having a wide range of prices may all have the UL seal. Higher-priced items will generally have additional features for convenience or longer life.

National Electrical Code Book. This book provides thorough, very detailed instructions for determining the adequacy of your wiring system and guides you in the safe repair and modification of your appliances, lighting, and wiring.

The chances are your house wiring was safe and adequate when your house was built. It is probable, too, that your house wiring was originally done in accordance with the National Electrical Code. This code was developed by the National Fire Protection Association and is periodically revised. The code itself has legal status only insofar as it has been adopted by cities, towns, counties, and other governmental units as part of local building codes and ordinances. The status of the code in your locality can be determined by contacting the building inspection department of your local government.

The National Electrical Code does not provide step-by-step instructions as this book does. Rather, the code specifies the preferred method of performing electrical wiring tasks and the proper materials to use in various applications. The instructions in this guide conform to the recommendations of the National Electrical Code. Incidentally, the code does *not* limit or prohibit electrical work by a homeowner.

Copies of the code are probably available at your local library. Copies are often on sale in electrical supply stores and in some book stores. You can obtain a copy directly from the National Fire Protection Association by sending a prepaid order to the association at Batterymarch Park, Quincy, MA 02269. The complete code is currently priced at $10.25. A somewhat simplified version of the code, known as the "One- and Two-Family Residential Occupancy Electrical Code," is priced at $8.25. The simplified edition covers the most popular and widely used wiring methods and is limited to materials and methods related to the buildings mentioned in the title.

Safety rules

1. Always turn power off before working on an electrical circuit. (Page 304, Service panel, tells you how.)

Rule 1 applies to all jobs described in this guide. There are no exceptions to this rule.

2. Always test before you touch. (The device you need to make the test is described on page 301. The step-by-step instructions tell when to make the test.)

Rule 2 is necessary because it double-checks rule 1. Defects in house and appliance wiring can cause power to be present at times and places when it should not be.

Additional precautions

1. Always wear rubber-soled shoes.
2. When in your circuit breaker or fuse panel area, wear rubber gloves and avoid contact with damp floor by standing on a dry board or rubber mat.
3. Plan your job carefully in advance. Inspect the areas in your home in which you will be working. Note safety hazards and decide how to avoid them. Safety precautions for particular jobs are included in the detailed instructions in this book.
4. Plan to work as much as possible during daylight hours. Power will be off most of the time you are working. You may still need a flashlight for dark areas, but generally daylight will make your work easier and a great deal safer.
5. Don't hurry and don't work when you are tired. Haste and fatigue lead to carelessness. Carelessness leads to trouble.
6. Periodically test the circuit tester. Make sure the voltage tester (described under Basic tools) is working properly by checking it in a "live" receptacle.
7. Don't work alone. Have someone around for assistance if you need it.

Who tests the tester?
A voltage tester is a handy little device to have around. It's just two wires with a little bulb between them that lights up when there is power in a circuit. Before I start working on an electrical fixture I poke the tips of the tester's wires into the slots of a wall plug, for example, or touch one end to the live wire on a switch and the other to the side of the metal box to make **sure** I flipped off the right switches and pulled the right fuses to turn off the power.

But what if the tester doesn't work? Have you checked your voltage tester in a **live** outlet recently?

Shock

What is electric shock? Electric shock occurs when a human body becomes a path along which electric energy can flow. When electric energy can flow along two or more paths, the bulk of the flow will occur along the path that offers the least resistance to the flow. The human body is generally a low-resistance path, and if it accidentally becomes part of an electrical circuit, it will experience the heaviest flow of electrical energy in that circuit.

How can it be avoided? The way to avoid shock, then, is to avoid becoming a path for the flow of electrical energy. The standard methods of avoiding shock are by insulation and grounding.

Insulation is the containment of electrical energy in wires, lamps, electrical outlets, appliances, etc., by enclosing the energy carrier in some material through which electrical energy cannot flow. The rubber or plastic covering on electric wire is insulation in this sense.

Grounding means simply providing a better (that is, lower resistance) path to ground for electric energy than the human body. (For a description of electrical grounding, refer to How electricity works, page 296.)

If shock occurs, the victim may not be able to release his grip on the "hot" lead. If main power can be turned off immediately, do it. If not, use a nonconductor such as dry wood or cloth to break the victim's grip on the hot lead. Don't touch him yourself.

When the victim is free of contact with power, call a physician or rescue squad. Keep the victim warm and give artificial respiration by any approved method until help arrives.

System grounding

Proper grounding of electrical circuits and appliances is the most important single safety feature in your home. If you are a bit rusty on what grounding means electrically, the section on How electricity works, beginning on page 296, will help refresh your memory in short order.

Codes and standard wiring practices require that all the metal boxes used for switches, outlets, and fixtures in your home must be grounded. A simple test to assure that this ground is not faulty is described on page 301.

The complete home electrical system or particular parts of it—especially outdoor wiring—can be protected by devices known as ground fault interrupters (GFIs). These devices turn off power to a circuit if current leakage develops in that circuit. Individual appliances can be grounded by connecting the outer metal enclosure of the appliance to any portion of the plumbing system—preferably the cold water line. Appliances that have three-pronged plugs are automatically grounded when plugged into a mating receptacle in a circuit with a properly wired grounding system. A three-pronged plug may be used with a grounding adapter that fits a two-slot outlet. This should be thought of as a temporary device until a grounding receptacle can be installed.

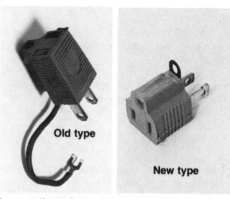

A grounding adapter is for temporary use until the receptacle can be permanently wired into the grounding system.

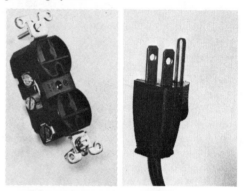

Permanently grounded receptacles have sockets that accept appliances wired with a three-pronged plug like this one.

Ground fault interrupters

GFIs are supersensitive circuit breakers that monitor the current flowing in the black and white wires of a circuit. If no faults exist, the current in the two wires will be the same. If more current flows in one wire than the other, it means there is current leakage to ground. The GFI will sense this current difference and cut off power to the circuit within 1/50 of a second. This could save your life because a continuous flow through your body, even of one-third ampere for one-third of a heartbeat, can be lethal. The most recent electrical code requires GFIs in outdoor and bathroom circuits because current leakage can easily pass through a wet human body to the ground, and these are likely areas for such a mishap.

Three types are available: one for permanent installation, one that can be added to existing circuits by merely plugging it into an outlet, and a unit that combines the functions of circuit breaker and GFI in one package. The combined unit is designed for mounting in the circuit-breaker panel on the main service center.

Portable GFI receptacle plugs into three-prong grounding outlets. First test the grounding in your wall outlet (see page 301).

Permanent GFI receptacle installed in place of a standard receptacle. It will work only if the separate grounding system in that circuit has been correctly wired.

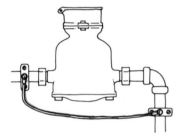

Make certain your water meter has a jumper wire. If any ground circuit is broken—even for a short time—the danger of shock is greatly increased. Many home electrical devices are grounded directly or indirectly to cold water pipes. Removal of the water meter may break this ground circuit. Check your meter to make certain a jumper is installed. If it is not, you can purchase the necessary clamps and cable in an electrical or plumbing-supply store. Install the jumper as shown. At the point where the cable touches the water pipe, scrape the pipe surfaces clean with a file or knife. Tighten clamps securely.

Not all appliances should be grounded

In particular, this is true of appliances containing a heating element that can be touched by the user. This includes toasters, broilers, and electric heaters with exposed coils. The reason for not grounding these appliances is that the heating element is connected across the power lines when the unit is turned on. Grounding the outer shell or case of these appliances would provide a path for electric energy from the heating element to the outer shell. A user then touching the heating element and the outer shell—with a fork, for example—would be subject to severe shock.

Why breakers trip or fuses blow when nothing's wrong

It may appear that circuit breakers go OFF or fuses blow in a haphazard manner. The reason for the overload is often a matter of timing. For the first few seconds after electric motors are started, they use four to six times as much power as they require when they are running. If a room air conditioner, large fan, or even a vacuum cleaner is on the same circuit with a TV set, electric heater, clothes dryer, etc., the temporary starting load of the motor in the air conditioner, fan, or cleaner added to the load already on the circuit from the other appliances will cause the breaker to go OFF or the fuse to blow. If you map your house circuits as shown on page 307 of this guide, you will be able to decide if you can avoid overloads by better use of your house circuits or if you need higher-capacity electric service installed.

Safeguards against fire

Electrical fires are caused by overloaded circuits or "short" circuits. The basic protection against overload and the danger of fire is provided by your house circuit breakers or fuse box. These devices are designed to turn off automatically part or all of the electricity if a serious overload and consequent overheating occurs anywhere in your home. As you will see later on, you will learn how these devices work, what to do when they turn off your electric power, and how to deal with them safely.

To protect your house from electrical fire, the circuit breaker or fuse panel must be able to work as it was designed to work. Never restrict the action of circuit breakers, insert coins in fuse holders, or use oversized fuses. The safety provided by proper overload protection is more important than the temporary inconvenience of resetting circuit breakers or replacing fuses. This point cannot be overstressed.

How to toast a toaster
When I was a little kid, my mother nearly killed me when she caught me trying to fish stuck toast out of an electric toaster with a fork. I was lucky the toaster didn't do the job for her. Technically, if the heating elements are not grounded to the metal case, **and** you are not touching anything that is grounded (most things in a kitchen are), and you are lucky in a lot of other ways—you won't get electrocuted when you poke a metal object into a live toaster. But it's like trying to cross a busy highway with your eyes closed. Did you know, for example, that it is possible for old matted crumbs in a toaster to conduct electricity from the heating wires to the metal case?

Practical Pete

When should a licensed electrician do the job?

If a review of your home electrical system —as described in this book—shows the need for higher-capacity electric service, your utility company and a licensed electrician must do the work.

In some instances your local electrical code may require some types of work to be done only by a licensed electrician. In other cases the inspection requirements of your local code may make it desirable to have a licensed electrician do the job. Or, you may decide the particular job is too complicated or time-consuming for you to do. Even if you decide you would rather have a licensed electrician do the job, this book can be helpful. Read the sections of the book that cover the type of work you will have done. You will then be familiar enough with materials and work involved to discuss the job you want done and to judge the time and cost estimate. You may even get a lower price if you appear knowledgeable.

How electricity works

Working safely and efficiently with your home wiring and appliances is easier if you understand what electricity is and how it works. Basic electrical terms are briefly defined on the opposite page. If you want more than a definition, read the next few pages. They describe some of the how and why of electricity.

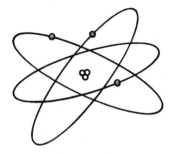

This diagrammatic model of an atom shows electrons (color) orbiting around the nucleus at the center. Electrical energy is made by making free electrons move in the same direction so they jump from one atom to the next.

Electricity is energy

Electric utility generating stations convert either fossil fuel (coal, oil), hydroelectric energy (flowing water), or atomic energy (nuclear reactors) to electrical energy. The electric energy so generated is transported by wires to the factories, offices, schools, and homes that use it.

The basic building blocks of all matter are atoms. Electrons are one of the tiny particles that form atoms. Electrons are the stuff that electrical energy is made of. Some electrons can move from one atom to another. These are called "free" electrons. Metals such as copper, steel, and aluminum are called conductors because their atoms have many free electrons and so can conduct electricity efficiently. Wires made of copper, steel, or aluminum provide an ideal way to transport electrical energy with little loss of power.

The atoms that make up materials such as rubber, plastic, paper, and wood have almost no free electrons. These materials are called insulators because they cannot conduct electricity. A safe and efficient way to move electric energy, then, is to enclose a wire made of copper, steel, or aluminum in some insulating material and then use the wires to carry electricity from the generating plant to the final user.

A free electron leaves the orbit of one atom, is temporarily "captured" into the orbit of the next, leaves that for a third, and so on. Metals with atoms having lots of free electrons, like copper, make good conductors.

Why are two wires needed to operate electrical devices?

Electricity is generated by causing all the free electrons in a conductor to move in the same direction. This creates a surplus of electrons in the atoms of one wire at the output of a generator and a shortage of electrons in the atoms of a second output wire from the generator. When an electrical device is connected to these two wires, electrons will move along an electrical path through the device in order to restore the natural balance. As long as the generating station at the source continues to operate, the shortage and surplus in the two wires will be maintained and electron movement will continue. The phrase "current flow" is used to describe this electron movement. The rate of the current flow (that is, the number of electrons that pass a point in one second) is measured in units called amperes, or more commonly, amps. The device that measures this current flow is called an ammeter.

The pressure that exists to restore the electron balance depends upon how large the difference is between the surplus and the shortage. The greater the difference, the higher the pressure. This pressure is called voltage and the units in which it is measured are called volts. The device for measuring voltage is called a voltmeter.

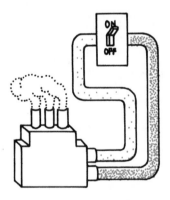

A generator creates a surplus of free electrons in the atoms of one wire and a shortage in another. When the two wires are connected (when you flip a switch to ON, for example) the excess electrons rush through toward the atoms where there is a shortage, creating electrical current.

Why are some wires called *grounding, neutral* or *hot*?

Ground means simply Mother Earth or something connected to earth, such as a cold water pipe in your home or a copper rod driven onto the ground outside your house near where electric power enters.

The earth is such a huge volume of matter that a measurable surplus or shortage of electrons never exists. Earth or ground, therefore, is always electrically neutral. Ground, and wires connected to ground, can accept electrons or give them up as necessary to cause current to flow between ground and a point at which a shortage or surplus exists.

While both grounding wires and neutral wires are connected to ground, there is a difference in the job each performs in electric wiring. The job of the ground wire is to provide a path to ground for electric energy when faults occur in the primary power wiring or in electrical devices. Throughout this guide the term *grounding wire* refers to these safety wires. Grounding wires may have green insulation or be bare (no insulation). Throughout this guide the term *neutral wire* always means the primary power wire with white insulation. The job of the white wire is to provide the normal path for return current flow to the source when no wiring faults exist. Throughout this guide the term *hot wire* refers to the wire with black or red insulation. This is the wire that causes current to flow between it and the neutral wire (or grounding wire if a fault occurs).

Normally the hot wire is more dangerous because it can cause current to flow between it and *any* path to ground. In some cases in home wiring, wires with black, red, or white insulation are used for some other-than-normal function all or part of the time. When this is done, the wire should be marked at each end and at any terminal point with the color of its "live" function; that is, either black or red. As this marking may be forgotten or may wear off or flake off with time, NEVER rely on color of insulation alone to tell you a wire's function. *Always test before you touch.*

Definition of electrical terms

Alternating current (AC). The form of electric power used in almost all home utility systems. In this form of electric energy the voltage and current are constantly changing in amount and periodically changing in direction of flow.

Amps (amperage). The amount of current that flows in a circuit as a result of the voltage applied and the resistance of the load (appliance, light bulb, etc.).

Ballast. Part of a fluorescent fixture that controls voltage.

Branch circuit. Each circuit wired from the service panel to various parts of your house. Each branch circuit has its own circuit breaker or fuse for overload protection.

Circuit. A combination of source, conductor, load, and switching that enables electric power to do some useful work.

Circuit breaker. An automatic switch that cuts off power to a circuit when the current flow exceeds the rating of the circuit breaker. Circuit breakers can also be operated by hand to turn off power when desired (such as while making a repair).

Conductor. Any wire, bar, or strip of metal that offers little resistance to electric current and is therefore used for carrying it.

Direct current (DC). This is the form of electric energy available from batteries. If the battery source remains charged, the voltage in a DC circuit remains constant.

Electron. One of the tiny particles that make up atoms. Some electrons are called "free" because they can move from atom to atom and produce an electrical current.

Fuse. A safety device that breaks the flow of current when the amperage in the circuit exceeds the rating of the fuse.

Grounding wire. This is a safety wire. It is usually a bare wire but may have green or green and yellow insulation. This wire provides a safe path to ground for hot wire current, in the event of a circuit fault.

Hertz (Hz). A term that is replacing the older cycles-per-second. Hertz applies to AC power only. The number of Hertz of an AC source is the number of times per second the electric power goes through a complete change in amount in each direction. Most home power systems are 60 cycles-per-second or 60 Hertz.

Hot wire. The electric wire in your home usually having black or red insulation. This wire can cause current to flow through any path to ground. Though any wire can give a shock, a hot wire is most dangerous.

Kilowatt hours (KWH). The unit to measure power consumed in your home. One KWH equals 1,000 watts used for one hour. Your electric bill is calculated in kilowatt hours.

Load. The operating device in an electric circuit that converts electric energy to some other form; light in a bulb, mechanical movement in a fan, heat in a toaster, etc.

Neutral wire. The electric wire in your home having white insulation. This wire provides the normal return path for current flow to the power source.

Ohm. Unit of measurement for resistance to current flow.

Overload. A condition that results from too many devices on one circuit or from a circuit fault. Overloads can cause overheating in wires and tripped circuit breakers or blown fuses.

Power, electrical. The product of voltage and current that provides energy to do work. The unit of measurement of power is the watt.

Resistance. The characteristic of some materials and devices that restricts the flow of current. Unit of measurement is the ohm.

Service panel. The unit that distributes power to the various circuits in your home. Either circuit breakers or fuses are located on this panel.

Source. The point at which power originates. In your home, the service panel may be considered the source.

Starter. An automatic switch that controls current flow in a fluorescent fixture.

Switch. A device that can interrupt and restore current flow in a circuit.

Transformer. In AC power systems, transformers are used to raise or lower voltage.

Volts (voltage). The pressure that causes current to flow between a hot wire and a neutral or ground wire. In home electrical systems the voltage is either 120 volts or 240 volts, depending on type of wiring.

Watts (wattage). A unit of measure of the power consumed by a load. The wattage is calculated by multiplying the voltage by the amperage. For example, if a current of two amperes flows in a 120-volt circuit, the load is consuming 240 watts.

Current is measured in amperes. An amp is a measure of the number of free electrons moving past a point. (If dust particles being sucked through a hose into a vacuum cleaner were electrons, you would have to count 6.28 billion billion per second to equal one amp.)

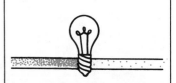

Voltage is the amount of pressure pulling the electrons through the conductor (like the suction power in the hose). The resistance to current flow caused by the load uses up the pressure (volts) but doesn't change the number of electrons (amps) flowing through the load and back into the circuit. Most houses are wired to supply two voltages—about 120 volts for most outlets, and about 240 for loads that require a lot of power.

Volts (pressure) X AMPS (current) = Watts X 1000 per hour = Your electric bill

Watts are simply the current in amps multiplied by the pressure in volts. Watts indicate the rate at which the load is consuming the power you pay for on your electric bill. A radio uses about 10 watts, an electric frying pan about 1,000, a clothes dryer about 5,500. (This is one reason why modern appliances make us use so much more power per capita than we used to—and why we face the shortages in energy needed to generate it.)

What is an electric circuit?

A closed path of electron movement is required to put electric energy to use. This closed path is called a circuit. Every circuit has four parts:

1. Source

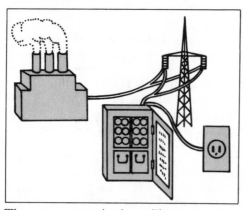

The true source is the utility generator. However, for practical purposes, the source may be thought of as the circuit breaker panel or fuse box from which power is distributed throughout your home. Junction boxes and wall outlets may be thought of as secondary sources.

2. Conductors

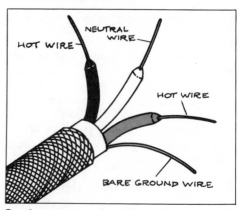

Conductors are the wires that carry the electric energy to the point at which it will be used. Conductors offer little (but not zero) resistance to current flow because the atoms in the metals they are made of have lots of free electrons and therefore can transport it efficiently.

3. Load

The load is any device (a light bulb, your toaster or your washing machine, for example) that uses electric energy to perform some work. The load (unlike the conductors) offers resistance to current flow. This resistance makes it possible for the device to convert electric energy to another form (heat, light, mechanical movement, etc.). The load resistance determines how much current will flow in a circuit. Increase the resistance in the load and you automatically decrease the current flowing in the circuit. If the voltage applied to a circuit is multiplied by the current in amperes, the result is in units called watts. The watt is a unit of power and indicates the rate at which the load is consuming power.

4. Switches

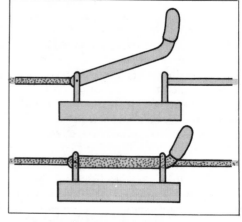

The fourth element in a circuit is a means of controlling the energy. This is a device that can interrupt and restore current flow as desired by the user. Switches used in home electric systems control current flow by inserting a very high resistance (air gap) in the circuit to stop the current flow and by removing the resistance (closing the air gap) to start current flowing again. A basic principle of electrical wiring is that switches should always be wired into the hot (black or red) line leading directly to a device or outlet. When switches in the hot line are turned off, no hot line power is present in the load device. This greatly reduces the possibility of injury or damage resulting from accidental grounding.

Important: Turn off power at main panel before working on switches or outlets. Even when a hot line switch is off, one terminal on the switch is still connected to the power source. Before doing any work on the switch, the power source must be turned off by setting a circuit breaker to OFF or removing a fuse.

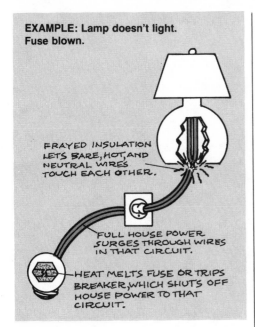

EXAMPLE: Lamp doesn't light. Fuse blown.

FRAYED INSULATION LETS BARE, HOT, AND NEUTRAL WIRES TOUCH EACH OTHER.

FULL HOUSE POWER SURGES THROUGH WIRES IN THAT CIRCUIT.

HEAT MELTS FUSE OR TRIPS BREAKER, WHICH SHUTS OFF HOUSE POWER TO THAT CIRCUIT.

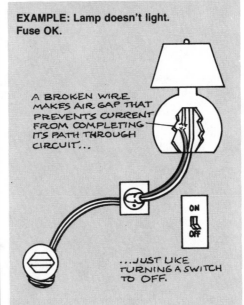

EXAMPLE: Lamp doesn't light. Fuse OK.

A BROKEN WIRE MAKES AIR GAP THAT PREVENTS CURRENT FROM COMPLETING ITS PATH THROUGH CIRCUIT...

ON
OFF

...JUST LIKE TURNING A SWITCH TO OFF.

Short circuit

A short circuit is a fault that occurs when a low resistance path exists between the hot lead and some grounded points. When this happens heavy current will flow in the circuit for as long as it takes for the circuit breaker to trip to OFF or for the fuse to blow. Because the circuit breaker or fuse cuts off the current flow quickly, the circuit wiring will not have time to overheat to the point where fire may occur.

Open Circuit

An open circuit is a fault that cuts off current flow in a circuit. The break that causes the open circuit may be in the hot line, the neutral line, or the load. An open circuit appears to be off. The break that causes an open circuit may be quite small. Vibration or even changes in temperature may suddenly turn the circuit on again. When looking for the cause of an open circuit, be sure power is off at the source.

What do AC and DC mean?

The electrical energy that flows in circuits and operates loads can be generated in either of two quite different forms. One form is called alternating current (AC); the other form is called direct current (DC).

Alternating current is almost universally used for home electric power and is, therefore, the kind this book is primarily concerned with. In an AC circuit, the amount of voltage applied to the circuit is constantly changing from zero to a maximum and back to zero in one direction and then from zero to maximum and back to zero in the other direction. The maximum voltage is set by the generating plant. Because voltage is the pressure that causes current to flow, the current will also change from zero to maximum to zero and will reverse direction and repeat. The maximum amount of current, however, is determined by the load resistance and can vary as the load resistance varies. Each complete change from zero to maximum to zero in one direction and then zero to maximum to zero in the opposite direction is called one hertz (formerly cycle). The term hertz implies

"per second." So, 60 hertz means the same as 60 cycles per second. Hertz is abbreviated Hz. Cycles-per-second, which you will still see marked in some electrical devices, is abbreviated cps.

Direct current is most commonly found in homes in the form of electrical energy stored in batteries. In a DC circuit, the amount of voltage and the direction of application are constant. The amount of voltage is determined by the type and size of battery. The direction of current flow is also constant and, as in AC circuits, the amount of current flow is determined by the load resistance. Batteries convert chemical energy to electrical energy. The chemical energy can be in wet form, as in your car battery, or in dry form as in flashlight and transistor-radio batteries. Some batteries are designed to be recharged from an AC source. The voltage from all batteries, unless recharged, will gradually decrease. AC power can be converted to DC power for some uses in the home. The conversion is performed by a device called a rectifier or current converter.

To review the main points:

- Electricity is energy.
- Electricity consists of voltage (pressure) and amperage (electron flow).
- Electricity can be generated at a distant point and carried by wires to where it will be used.
- Electricity is used by applying it to a circuit. The circuit consists of wires connected to a source, a load connected between the wires, and one or more switches to turn the circuit on and off.
- Resistance determines the amount of current flow in a circuit. Conductors offer little resistance to current flow, loads offer moderate resistance, open switches are an extremely high resistance, and closed switches almost zero resistance to the flow.

Tools and supplies

With a few exceptions, you probably have the tools you need for most electrical repairs. All you need are common hand tools, some power tools, electrical supplies, and the special items described on the opposite page.

Basic tools

Long-nose pliers
Linemen's pliers
Screwdriver set (small and medium sizes will do the job)
Phillips-head screwdriver set (needed for appliance work)
Folding rule or steel tape
Utility knife or pocketknife
Hammer
Keyhole saw
Hacksaw
Flashlight

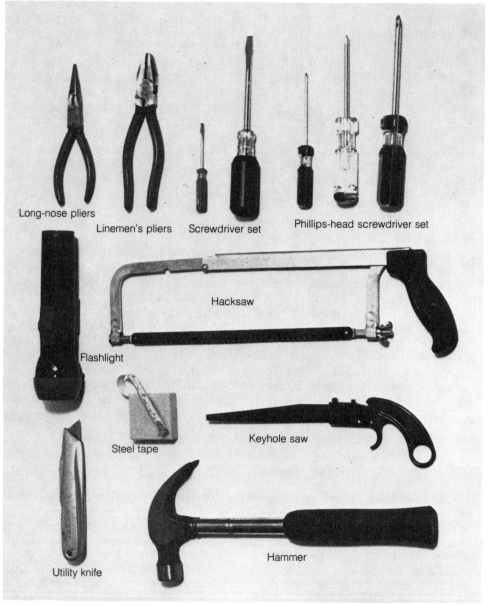

Long-nose pliers   Linemen's pliers   Screwdriver set   Phillips-head screwdriver set

Hacksaw

Flashlight

Steel tape   Keyhole saw

Utility knife   Hammer

Supplies

Solderless connectors (get a variety of sizes and types)
Plastic electrical tape
Cable staples
Rosin-core solder (marked as suitable for electrical work)
Noncorrosive flux

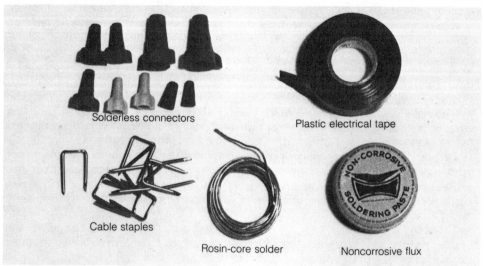

Solderless connectors   Plastic electrical tape

Cable staples   Rosin-core solder   Noncorrosive flux

Specialized tools

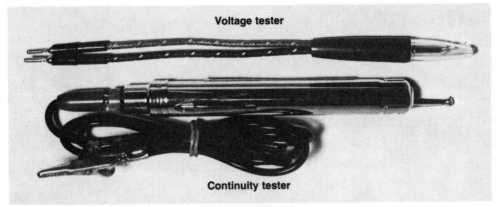

Voltage tester

Continuity tester

Testers
Two simple and inexpensive testers are absolutely essential to electrical work. If you own a handitester or similar volt-ohm meter, that will do the same job.

Voltage tester. This tester consists of a holder containing a neon bulb. Two probes are attached to the holder. The neon bulb will light when the probes touch the hot and neutral power lines or anything connected to those lines when power is present on the wires. For the procedures in this book, the tester is primarily used to make certain NO voltage is present before you touch any wiring or device. When no voltage is present the bulb does not light. Since the bulb will also not light if the tester is defective in any way, it is especially important that you test the tester from time-to-time. Simply place the test probes in a live receptacle. If the bulb lights the tester is OK. Make sure the tester you buy can be used on both 120 and 240 volt lines.

Continuity tester. This is a pen-like probe with an alligator clip lead attached. The probe contains a battery and bulb. When current flows from the alligator clip to the tip of the probe, the bulb lights. The continuity tester is always used with power off. The low battery voltage can be used to check switches, lamps, fuses and wiring. This is an excellent device to use to check your work before applying power for the first time. The continuity tester is easily checked before use by touching the alligator clip to the tip of the the probe. If the light goes on, the battery is OK and the tester is ready for use.

Testing correct grounding with a voltage tester

3-slot receptacle. Touch one probe inside the ground slot and the other probe to each of the prong slots in turn. The bulb should light in one of them.

2-slot receptacle. Touch one probe to the screw on the outside of the cover plate and the other probe in each slot in turn. The bulb should light in one of them.

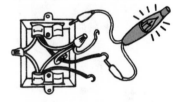

Switch. Unscrew the cover plate and remove the switch without touching any wires. Touch one probe to the metal box (or white ground wires on a plastic box). Touch the other probe to the bare end of the "hot" black wires in turn. The bulb should light when the probe is touched to the one which leads back to the main service panel, not to the other one.

Testing for dead circuit

Receptacles and switches. To be sure power is off, insert the probes into the two slots of an outlet. For switches, follow the procedure above for testing correct ground. If power is off, the bulb will *not* light. The procedure for testing wall or ceiling fixtures and outlets is described on page 325.

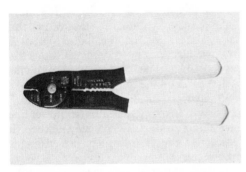

Wire stripper. Many types of tools are available for stripping insulation from wire. All consist of a pliers-like tool with cutouts on the jaws corresponding to various wire sizes. The cutouts allow the stripper to cut through the insulation without cutting or nicking the conductor. Some strippers also have provision for cutting wires and small bolts.

Fuse puller. If there are cartridge fuses on your service panel, you will need a fuse puller for safe removal of fuses. Check the sizes of the fuses you will have to remove before you purchase a fuse puller. Make certain the puller you buy is the right size for your use.

Fish tape. This is a flexible tape available in various lengths. It is used to "fish" wire through walls and floors when installing new wiring. The tape has a hook at the end to which the wire can be attached after the tape is worked through the opening. The tape is then withdrawn pulling the wire through.

Soldering gun. If your work involves wire splicing, it is desirable to solder the splice to assure good electrical contact. A high heat electric iron, or gun, or a pencil flame propane torch, will heat the joint faster and assure a good flow of solder.

Power to your house

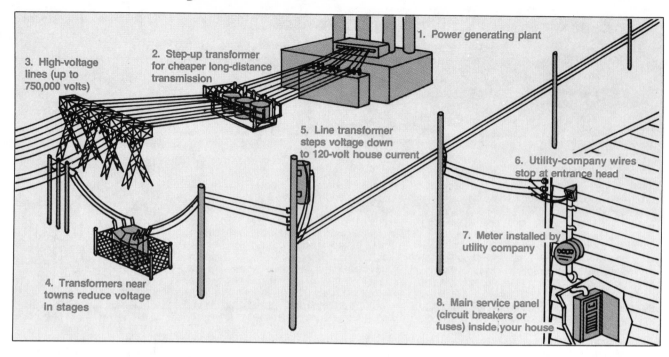

1. Power generating plant

2. Step-up transformer for cheaper long-distance transmission

3. High-voltage lines (up to 750,000 volts)

4. Transformers near towns reduce voltage in stages

5. Line transformer steps voltage down to 120-volt house current

6. Utility-company wires stop at entrance head

7. Meter installed by utility company

8. Main service panel (circuit breakers or fuses) inside your house

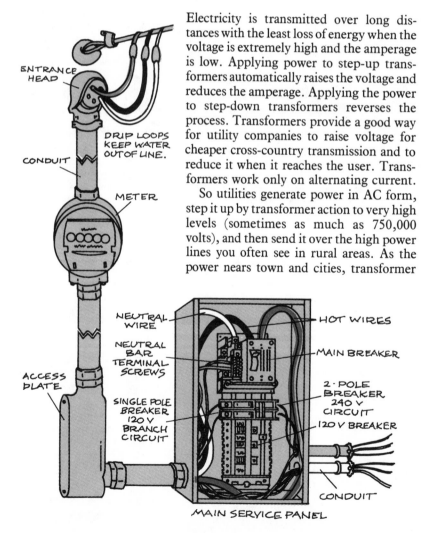

ENTRANCE HEAD

DRIP LOOPS KEEP WATER OUT OF LINE.

CONDUIT

METER

ACCESS PLATE

NEUTRAL WIRE

NEUTRAL BAR TERMINAL SCREWS

SINGLE POLE BREAKER 120 V BRANCH CIRCUIT

HOT WIRES

MAIN BREAKER

2-POLE BREAKER 240 V CIRCUIT

120 V BREAKER

CONDUIT

MAIN SERVICE PANEL

Electricity is transmitted over long distances with the least loss of energy when the voltage is extremely high and the amperage is low. Applying power to step-up transformers automatically raises the voltage and reduces the amperage. Applying the power to step-down transformers reverses the process. Transformers provide a good way for utility companies to raise voltage for cheaper cross-country transmission and to reduce it when it reaches the user. Transformers work only on alternating current.

So utilities generate power in AC form, step it up by transformer action to very high levels (sometimes as much as 750,000 volts), and then send it over the high power lines you often see in rural areas. As the power nears town and cities, transformer action is again used to reduce the voltage. The reduction is done in steps rather than all at once, so that the highest practical voltage level can be maintained for as long as possible. The final voltage reduction takes place on the line transformers you see mounted on utility poles in your neighborhood. In many communities power lines are underground. Of course, neither the lines nor the transformers are visible in these areas.

Unless your house was built before World War II, the chances are that power enters your house on three lines. Two of these are hot lines and the third is a neutral line. This combination provides two voltage levels for use in your home: 120 volts and 240 volts.

Various devices are used by utility companies to secure the power lines to the house. Power lines must be able to withstand heavy winds, ice loads, etc. In many cases the neutral wire is made to do double duty for this purpose. The wire is made of braided steel strands for strength and is thicker and stronger than the hot wires. The three wires are then held together by twisting or enclosing them in an outer sheath so that the anchoring of the neutral wire to the house provides support for the other two lines as well. The incoming power lines—heavily insulated or enclosed in a metal conduit—are then routed to your meter. Meters are almost always mounted on the outside of the house.

How to read your meter

If you know how to read your meter, you can check the reading against the amount on your bill from time to time and make certain the meter was read or estimated accurately.

Meters record the power used in your home in units called kilowatt hours. Watts, you will recall, are units of power equal to the voltage times the current. The prefix kilo means 1000, and a kilowatt hour therefore represents your use of one thousand watts for one hour. For example, a washing machine and a refrigerator running for one hour would consume about one kilowatt of electricity together.

Your meter reading is determined by the positions of pointers on five dials. Each dial has ten markings, from zero to nine. But the markings on different dials represent different amounts: units, tens, hundreds, and so on. The pointer always moves from 0 to 1 to 2 to 3, etc., and back to zero. However, the dials are marked in different directions. That is, the numbering of the 10,000 unit dial increases in a clockwise direction, the 1000 unit dial counterclockwise, etc.

Determine the direction of a dial rotation by the way the dials are numbered. All meters are not the same. As long as any electricity is being used in your home all the dials will be moving. The amount of movement will be ten times slower on each dial from right to left. Unless power consumption is unusually heavy, movement will be noticeable only on the right-hand dial. To read the meter, note the number the pointer has just passed—keeping in mind the direction of rotation—on each dial, starting from the left.

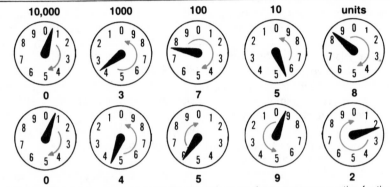

10,000	1000	100	10	units
0	3	7	5	8
0	4	5	9	2

For example: At left is a reading of 03758 or 3758 KWH. Meter dials are not precisely marked. A pointer on any dial may appear to be exactly on a number, but actually be above or below it. To decide which it is, note the pointer on the dial to the right of it. If the pointer to the right has not reached zero, the preceding dial has not reached the nearest number. If the pointer to the right has passed zero, use the next higher number for the preceding dial.

In the example at left, the middle dial appears to be on 6, but because the next dial to the right is below zero, 5 is the correct reading for the middle dial. Full reading 04592, or 4592 KWH.

If the readings above were taken about a month apart, the power consumption for that month would be the difference between the two readings—or 834 kilowatts.

Consuming watts

This list of appliance wattage ratings can be used to estimate the total power load in your home. You can also use it along with your circuit map to figure out how to distribute your appliance load more evenly over available circuits. The wattages given here are typical and should be satisfactory for estimating purposes. You can determine the exact wattage of your appliances from information on the manufacturer's nameplate. If the nameplate lists amperage only, multiply by the listed operating voltage (either 120 or 240 volts) to get the approximate wattage. If motor horsepower (HP) is listed, figure about 1,000 watts for one horsepower and gauge other sizes proportionately. For example, ½ or 0.5 HP = 500 watts. But for motors larger than 1½ HP, power consumption should be obtained from the manufacturer's published data. In addition to the wattages listed here, be sure to include all your lighting fixtures. Wattages are marked on bulbs.

Power ratings for typical home appliances

Appliance	Wattage	Appliance	Wattage	Appliance	Wattage
Air conditioner (room size)	800-1500	Fan, attic	400	Radio (solid state, plug-in)	10
Air conditioner (central, 240 v.)	5000	Fan, kitchen	70	Range (240 v., one unit)	8000-16,000
Blanket (single)	150	Fan, large pedestal type	500	Range (surface burners)	5000
Blanket (dual)	450	Fan, small table type	80	Range (oven)	4500
Blender	250-450	Floor polisher	300	Refrigerator	300
Broiler	1500	Freezer	600	Rotisserie	1400
Can opener	100	Frying pan	1000	Saw, radial	1500
Clothes iron (large unit)	1800-3000	Furnace (gas)	800	Saw, table	600
Clothes dryer (120 v.)	1400	Furnace (oil)	600-1200	Soldering iron	150
Clothes dryer (240 v.)	5500	Garbage disposal	900	Stereo hi-fi	300-500
Coffeemaker/percolator	600-750	Hair dryer	400	Sun lamp	250-400
Crock pot (2-quart)	75-150	Heater, portable	1300	TV, color (25″, solid state)	250
Deep fryer	1350	Heater, built-in	2000	TV, b & w (12″, solid state)	50
Dehumidifier	400-600	Hot water heater (240 v.)	2500	Toaster	1200
Dishwasher (with water heater)	1800	Iron	1000	Vacuum cleaner	600
Drill, portable	200-400	Microwave oven	650	Waffle iron	1100
Drill press	500	Mixer	150	Washing machine	900

Service panel

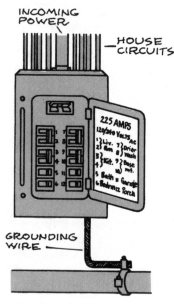

Fuse panel

Circuit-breaker panel

From the meter, the three power lines enter your home and are connected to a service panel that divides the incoming power into branches or circuits. The service panel also provides overload protection by means of circuit breakers or fuses, which shut off the power when an overload is imminent.

Both types of service panel contain a means of shutting off all incoming power. On circuit-breaker panels, two main circuit breakers are provided. Fuse panels may either contain a main fuse block that can be removed or will have a separate box with a main power switch that must be turned off before the box can be opened. The box contains the cartridge fuses that protect the main line. In addition to providing a shut-off point, the main fuse or circuit breaker sets the maximum power available to your home. You should become familiar with the main shut-off on your service panel. In an emergency it is the best means of making certain that all power is off.

Both circuit breakers and fuses are rated for various loads, such as 15, 20, 30 amperes and higher. The rating of each circuit breaker or fuse is marked on your service panel, or on the breakers and fuses, or both. You can read the rating without touching the panel or turning off power.

If your home has three-wire service, you can easily determine the total power available. Note the rating of the circuit breaker or fuse on each side of the main input line. Add these two numbers. Multiply by 240. The result will be the total watts available in your home at any one time. For example, two 50-ampere breakers or fuses will allow 24,000 watts to be used.

By referring to the list of typical wattages for home appliances (page 303), you can determine the total wattage used in your home. If the total wattage used is 80 percent or more of the total available, a bit of additional calculation should be made. Keep in mind that the total wattage on your list would occur only if all appliances were on at the same time. Make a separate list of those appliances that are used only during one season of the year. (Air conditioners will not be used with the furnace or heaters, for example.) Include in your grand total only the appliance with the higher wattage rating. If this still does not give you a margin of safety greater than 20 percent, you should consider increasing your basic service. Changes in your basic power service must be done by your utility company. The 20 percent safety margin is a rough guide rather than an exact number. It is based on three considerations:

1. Electrical systems and devices age the same as other parts of the house. It's unwise to push them to the limit.

2. Even after the seasonal adjustment is made, the appliances in use at any one time are not uniform in their power needs. Appliances containing motors consume from four to six times as much current during the first few seconds of operation as they do when running at normal speed. The heavy starting current is caused by the need to overcome the inertia of the load the motor is driving. A reasonable margin of safety will prevent the starting current surge from tripping circuit breakers or blowing fuses.

3. Even with careful use and conservation of power, family electric needs tend to increase over the years. Be sure to allow for this increase when deciding on the service you require. Incidentally, the cost of increasing your electric service can prove to be a good investment even if you intend to sell your house. Appraisers give considerable weight to adequate electric service.

Household circuits

The service panel—whether circuit breakers or fuses are used—is the point at which the main power into your home is divided into individual circuits. Each circuit is separately protected by its own circuit breaker or fuse. Modern service installations have anywhere from 12 to 32 individual circuits. Four types of individual circuits are used in home power systems:

1. General purpose circuits. These circuits provide basic lighting and wall-outlet power. They are usually protected by a 15-ampere circuit breaker or fuse.

2. Appliance circuits. Kitchen and laundry areas generally have greater power needs, so these circuits are protected by 20-ampere circuit breakers or fuses.

3. Special-purpose circuits. These circuits serve a single large appliance—such as a furnace or washing machine—through a single, three-wire wall outlet. They are protected for a 20- or 25-ampere load.

4. 240-volt circuits. Heavy-load appliances—such as central air conditioners, ranges, and clothes dryers—are more efficiently operated at 240 volts than at 120. These are three-wire circuits on paired circuit breakers or fuses.

Circuit breakers

Circuit breakers are special-purpose toggle or push-type switches. These switches are triggered automatically but can also be operated manually. Circuit breakers are available in ratings of 15 to 150 amperes. The load rating is determined by the internal switch mechanism and is marked on the outside of the circuit breaker. Circuit breakers will remain in the ON position indefinitely if the load remains at or below the rating. If the load exceeds the rated amperage, the circuit breaker will automatically switch to the OFF or TRIPPED position before any damage can occur.

Push-button circuit breakers have an indicator to show whether the circuit is ON or OFF. To reset a push-button type, simply depress and release it. The indicator will change from OFF to ON. Toggle-type circuit breakers have either two or three positions. The condition of the circuit breaker is shown by the position of the toggle: up for ON and down for OFF. Three-position toggles have a center position marked TRIP. Toggle-type circuit breakers are reset by moving the toggle back to the ON position. Some three-position types must be moved from the center TRIP position to the down OFF position and then back to ON.

Circuit breakers normally are reliable devices and have a long life span. However, they can, and sometimes do, become defective. Replacing circuit breakers can be hazardous. It is recommended that you have a licensed electrician do the job.

If you want to replace your screw-in fuses with circuit breakers, you can buy individual screw-in circuit breakers and substitute them for the fuses yourself. Replacing an entire fuse panel with a breaker panel should be done by a licensed electrician. Be sure you match the voltage and amperage ratings of the new breakers to the existing fuses.

Fuses

All fuses contain a special piece of metal designed to melt when more than a specified amount of current flows through it. The type of metal chosen and the thickness of it determine how much current it can carry. The metal is enclosed in insulating material. All except cartridge types can be removed by hand.

Plug-type fuses have screw-in bases like light bulbs and can be screwed into the fuse panel in a similar way. The metal strip that protects the circuit is visible through a plastic window. When a short circuit blows a fuse, the plastic window is clouded by the flash. A blown fuse with a clear window usually means the circuit is overloaded.

Time-delay fuses are similar in appearance to the ordinary plug type, but these fuses are designed to carry more than the rated current for a short period of time. These fuses are particularly useful in circuits in which the load consists of a motor-driven appliance. The normal high starting current of the motor will not blow these fuses.

Type-S fuses (also called non-tamperable fuses) are time-delay fuses with a special, separate base that is inserted into the fuse panel socket. The special base allows only one size fuse to be screwed into a particular socket. A 20-ampere fuse will not fit a 15-ampere socket. This prevents using a higher-rated fuse than the circuit allows.

When darkness falls
Suddenly everything goes black. Did the electric company go out of business? Did a tree fall on a power line? Did a fuse blow? I need a flashlight to see the fuse panel in the dark, but the kids lost mine on the last Boy Scout hike. Tomorrow morning I'll buy an inexpensive pencil flashlight and clip it to the handle of the fuse box.

Practical Pete

Cartridge fuses are used in heavy-load circuits or in main circuits that carry heavy loads. Both types make electrical connection by snapping into clips.

Ferrule-type cartridges (from 10 to 60 amperes) have round ends that make electrical contact.

Knife-blade-type cartridges (above 60 amperes) have flat ends for electrical contact.

Safety rules for fuse-panel work

All the general safety rules mentioned at the beginning of this chapter should be observed when changing fuses. In addition, special care must be taken because hot terminals are exposed on fuse panels.

1. Wear rubber-soled shoes. Stand on a dry board or rubber mat. Never stand on a bare, damp floor.

2. Use only one hand to insert or remove fuses. Keep the other hand in your pocket, or make certain you are not touching any surface that may be grounded.

3. Never place your finger or a hand tool in a fuse socket.

4. Never use a hand tool to bend or straighten a cartridge fuse clip.

5. Always use a fuse puller to remove cartridge fuses.

If an appliance fails on a circuit protected by a cartridge-type fuse, there is no way to tell whether the fuse is blown or is good just by looking at it. If you think it may have blown, throw the main cutoff lever to OFF and remove the fuse with a fuse puller. If the bulb in the continuity tester lights up when you simultaneously touch the caps at each end of the fuse, it is still good, the appliance may be faulty.

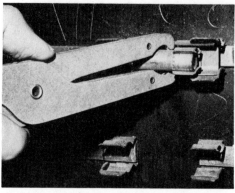

You must use a fuse puller to remove cartridge fuses because the two exposed clips that hold them tightly at either end carry a live voltage charge. In addition to the danger of severe shock if you touch them without having turned off the safety switch (the door of most cartridge-type fuse boxes won't open unless you first throw the switch), the cartridge is likely to be hot to the touch.

Why did the fuse blow?

Blown fuses

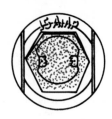

Short circuit usually causes discoloration of the plastic window.

Circuit overload melts strip slowly, so the plastic window usually stays clear.

Before resetting a circuit breaker or replacing a fuse, find out what caused the breaker to trip or the fuse to blow. In many cases you will know the cause of the overload because the circuit went off just as some appliance was plugged in or turned on. The section on mapping your house circuits, opposite, gives you some hints on how to make best use of the power you have available so that this can be prevented.

You can uncover other clues to the cause of an overload by touch and smell. If a defective lamp or appliance caused the overload, the cord and plug will be hot to the touch, and frequently a somewhat acrid odor can be detected from hot or burned insulation. But if there is no apparent sign of what caused the breaker to trip or the fuse to blow, the following procedure should solve the problem.

1. Turn off all the lights and disconnect all plug-in devices on the circuit. If you have a circuit map, this will be easy. If you do not have a circuit map and are not sure whether a device is on the overloaded circuit, assume it is on the bad circuit and turn it off or unplug it.

2. Remember: even after you have turned off and disconnected all the items on the circuit, the short that caused the overload may still exist in the wiring.

3. With a flashlight and a replacement fuse handy, turn off all power by removing the main fuse block, or turning off the main power breaker.

4. Reset the breaker or insert the new fuse.

5. Turn on main power again.

If the breaker trips or the replaced fuse blows immediately, there is probably a defect in the house wiring. Once again, turn off main power. Leave the breaker in the OFF position or remove the blown fuse and leave that socket empty. Turn on main power to the remaining circuits. Troubleshoot the defective circuit as described on page 332.

But if the breaker stays on or the new fuse does not blow, one of the devices that you turned off or unplugged was the cause of the overload. Turn on whatever lights are on the circuit one-by-one. If the breaker trips or the fuse blows, the last light turned on was faulty. Turn off all power to the circuit and troubleshoot as described on page 322. If lights are OK, troubleshoot other appliances on that circuit.

How to map your circuits

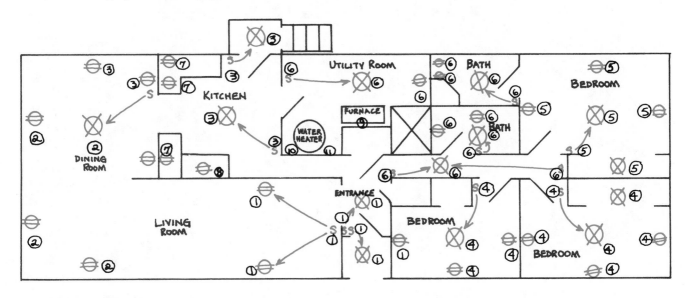

Each circuit breaker or fuse on your service panel should be identified in some way to show the general part of the house it protects. This can be done by putting adhesive-backed paper or plastic stickers next to each circuit breaker or fuse. Or you can make a sketch of the panel layout with circuits identified, and attach it to or keep it near the service panel. In addition to this, however, a map of your house showing exactly which lights, outlets, appliances, etc., are on each circuit can be a great help in planning electrical work and in tracking down troubles. If yours is a new home, the builder or electrical contractor may be able to supply you with a copy of his wiring diagram. The symbols shown above will help you to understand the diagram and enable you to mark it up so that it is more useful to you. If you cannot get a circuit map ready-made, you can make your own. The map you make will probably provide a few surprises. Circuits are often split between rooms—and outlets within a room are split between circuits—in ways you could never have guessed.

To start with, draw a floor plan of your house. Make it floor-by-floor or room-by-room, whichever is more convenient, but be sure to include every area that has electric service. Include porches, garages, outbuildings, etc. Use some system of symbols (the ones on the example are commonly used) to identify every fixture, wall outlet, and switch. Don't forget outside outlets, entrance lights, outdoor floodlights, etc.

Then number each circuit breaker or fuse on your service panel. Next, turn on all the ceiling and wall fixtures and lamps in your house. It is not necessary to turn on major appliances at this time. The procedure is to turn off each circuit breaker or remove each fuse individually. Then determine which lights are off. Mark the number of the circuit breaker or fuse just turned off or removed next to the fixture and switch symbol on your diagram. Next check all the wall outlets in the rooms in which lights went out. Plug a small lamp or work light in each outlet. If the lamp does not light, mark the number of the circuit breaker or fuse next to the outlet symbol on your diagram.

Repeat the procedure for each circuit breaker or fuse on your panel. When you finish, every symbol on your floor plan should have a circuit number next to it. If any symbol has been missed, recheck the area by turning on the light or plugging your work light into the outlet. Next, turn off, one at a time, each circuit that your diagram shows on nearby fixtures and outlets until you find the one that applies.

You will find that some of the circuit breakers you have turned off or fuses you have removed have had no effect on lights or outlets. These are circuit breakers or fuses that protect large appliance circuits. Turn off these remaining circuit breakers or remove these fuses one at a time and check your appliances to find out which one does not work. Remember that furnaces and air conditioners may appear to be off because of temperature-control settings.

Be sure to note on your diagram any circuit uses that are not covered by symbols and may be useful to you. For example, two circuit breakers or fuses are used in electric range circuits. Note on your diagrams which device protects the oven and which the surface burners. When you finish your diagram, store it near your service panel in a protective envelope.

Play it by ear

I ran upstairs and back down to the cellar until my tongue hung out trying to find out which lights and wall plugs went dead when I pulled out each of the fuses in turn. You can save some sweat by using a small plug-in radio (instead of a work light) to check wall outlets. Plug the radio into the outlet you want to check. Tune to a strong station and turn the volume up. Back at the service panel, turn off the circuit breakers or remove fuses one-by-one. When the sound goes off, you have found the circuit.

Practical Pete

2.TECHNIQUES

 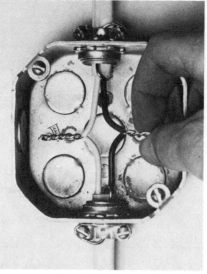 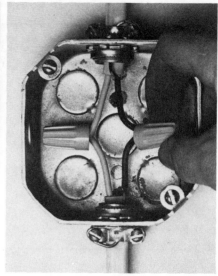

The next few pages show you how to work with the kinds of cables and wire commonly used in home electrical systems. Included are basic techniques and routine tasks that are necessary for any wiring job. These tasks are really easy to do, but practice always helps. Before actually working with a type of wire or cable that is new to you, cut off a short piece and try stripping, joining, etc. Experiment a bit to find out which of the tools you have available are easiest for you to use and which do the best job. A little time spent in trial and error will make the job go faster.

Sheathed cable

Permanent indoor installations are made by running lengths of wire between outlets and switches along or inside walls, floors, and ceilings. An electrical circuit always needs a hot and a neutral conductor plus a ground for safety. When these individually insulated wires (black for hot, white or gray for neutral) are held together inside plastic or metal sheathing, the unit is called cable.

The most commonly used cable for indoor wiring is the flat, white plastic type sometimes called by one trade name, Romex. There are three kinds. Code letters are printed on the plastic. Type NM is designed for normal indoor use; type NMC is insulated well enough to use above ground or in damp areas indoors; type UF can be buried outdoors.

Another kind of cable, usually called BX, is wrapped with a spiral of flexible, galvanized steel armor. This is more expensive and cannot be used outdoors.

Removing plastic sheathing

 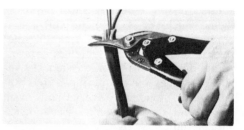

Place cable on a solid flat surface. Use a utility knife to cut the sheathing along the flat side. Try to make the cut straight and as nearly as possible in the center of the sheathing. The cut should be six to eight inches long. Use enough pressure to penetrate the sheathing but not so much that you cut the insulation on the inner wires.

Peel back the plastic sheathing to the beginning of the cut. Trim off the plastic with wire cutters or large shears. Remove and cut off the paper that is wrapped around the inner conductors. If you accidentally nick the conductors or the ground wire, simply trim off the section and try again.

Removing steel armor

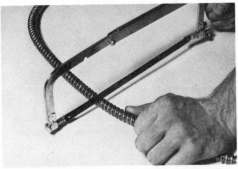

Hacksaw method. If you use a hacksaw, a fine-toothed blade will work best. Cut diagonally across one of the metal ribs. Cut carefully and stop as soon as you have cut through the metal to avoid cutting into the wire insulation.

Next grasp the cable on each side of the cut. Bend the cable back and forth until the armor snaps. Slide the armor off the cable. Unwrap the paper from the inner conductors and cut it away.

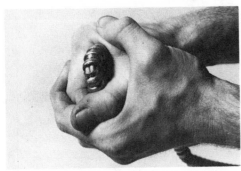

Cutting-tool method. First, bend the cable sharply until the armor buckles.

Twist the cable in the direction that will unwind the armor spiral. This causes a section of the armor to spring out at the point of the bend.

Slip the cutting tool through the armor where it has buckled. Trim away sharp edges. Slide off the end of the armor.

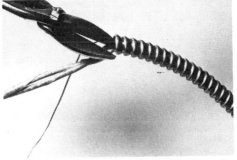

Use the shaping grip in the jaws to reform the buckled cable-end after stripping the paper from the inner conductors and trimming it off.

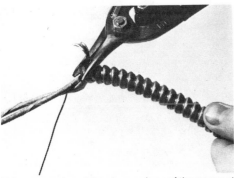

Trim away or bend the sharp edges of the armor at the point of the cut. Make sure no edges are in position to cut into the insulation in the inner conductors. This is important.

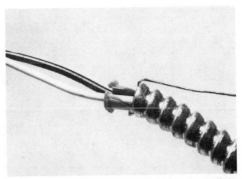

To eliminate the possibility of sharp edges of the armor cutting into the conductor insulation, a fiber bushing should be inserted under the armor, at the point where the conductors emerge.

Choosing the correct wire

The wire to use for a particular job will often be specified by your local electrical code. A good source of information on this is the store where you buy your electrical supplies. They know local codes and will be glad to advise.

The table below gives the physical and electrical characteristics of the most common types of wire. Many of them you will already be familiar with.

The wire codes listed in the table below are National Electrical Code designations.

These wire designations are essential to the electrical industry but can be confusing to the "do-it-yourselfer." For example, the wire codes in the table apply to the complete wire or cable as described. But, in addition to these wire codes, there are codes for the individual conductors in the cable. The simplest solution is to check the table to get an idea of what is available. If you have any question about the particular job you are planning, check with your local building department or electrical supplier.

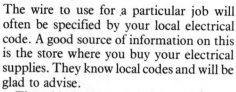

Common wire sizes and uses					
Code designation	Common name	Conductor size	Number of conductors	Outer covering	Use (See load guide at left.)
UF	—	12	3 plus ground	Heavy plastic	Underground*
UF	—	12	2 plus ground		
UF	—	14	3 plus ground		
UF	—	14	2 plus ground		
NMC	—	12	3 plus ground	Waterproof plastic	Damp indoor location
NMC	—	12	2 plus ground		
NMC	—	14	3 plus ground		
NMC	—	14	2 plus ground		
AC	BX	12	3 plus ground	Steel armor	Dry indoor location
AC	BX	12	2 plus ground		
AC	BX	14	3 plus ground		
AC	BX	14	2 plus ground		
NM	Romex	12	3 plus ground	Nonmetallic reinforced fabric	Dry indoor location
NM	Romex	12	2 plus ground		
NM	Romex	14	3 plus ground		
NM	Romex	14	2 plus ground		
SO	Heavy-duty cord	16	2 plus ground	Rubber or plastic	Power tools, mowers, etc. Oil resistant
HPD	Heater cord	16/18	2	Plastic, asbestos, fabric	Heaters, toasters, irons
SPT	Lamp cord	16/18	2	Rubber or plastic	Lamps, small appliances, extension cords, etc.

The uses shown in this table apply only to copper wire. Special precautions must be taken if you work with aluminum wire. See page 311 for details.

*Must be protected at the source by circuit breakers or fuses.

Aluminum wire

Aluminum is a less satisfactory conductor than copper. Copper-clad aluminum (aluminum wire with a thin coating of copper) is a reasonable compromise, but copper still has the edge. If your house has copper or copper-clad aluminum wiring, stick with it. Safely adding aluminum wiring to a copper wire system is a tricky business. Avoid it.

If aluminum wire is used in your present electrical system, and the correct switches, receptacles, etc., are used, the system is perfectly safe and efficient. Changes and additions to the system can be safely made using aluminum wire.

The *only* switches and receptacles that are safe to use with aluminum wire are those marked CO/ALR or CU/AL by the manufacturer. Both markings mean that the de-vice is designed for use with either copper or aluminum wire. The CO/ALR marking is used on devices rated up to 20 amperes. The CU/AL marking is used on devices rated at more than 20 amperes. Aluminum wire must never be used with any device having push-in type wire connections. Push-in type connections can be used only with copper or copper-clad aluminum.

If you use aluminum wire, remember that most recommended wire sizes on appliances or in manufacturers' data are based on copper wire. Unless other data is given for aluminum wire, a good rule is to use aluminum wire two sizes larger than the size specified for copper. For example, if number 14 copper wire is recommended, use number 12 aluminum wire.

Aluminum wiring is potentially dangerous. Check and tighten all connections on switches and outlets periodically. Make sure all switches and receptacles are marked CO-ALR or CU-AL. Replace any that are not.

Removing insulation

Before you can make a connection to a switch or fixture or before you can join two wires, you must remove the conductor insulation or sheathing.

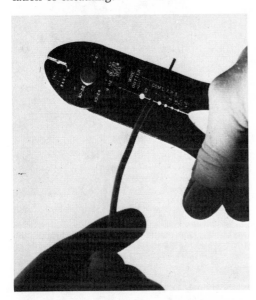

Using a wire stripper is the best method of removing insulation. Place the wire in the proper size hole on the stripper. Close the stripper jaws to cut through the insulation. Rotate the stripper back and forth a quarter turn or so until you can pull the insulation off the wire.

If you are not sure of the wire size, cut off a bit and make a few test cuts. If you can't spare any cable for testing, try one of the larger stripper openings first. Remember, the smaller the wire number, the larger the wire diameter. If you can't pull the insulation free after rotating the stripper, try the next smaller hole, until you get a clean strip and a bare, undamaged wire end.

If a wire stripper isn't available, a knife can be used to remove insulation. To avoid nicking the conductor, cut through the insulation at an angle. Check the conductor closely after removing insulation to make certain the knife has not gouged the metal. If the conductor is nicked even slightly, it will almost surely break before the job is finished. Best to start over now.

Connecting wires to screw type terminals

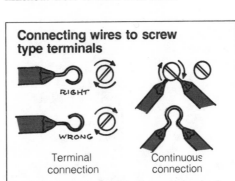

Terminal connection — Continuous connection

Conductor wire should be formed into a hook for connection to screw type terminals on switches and receptacles. Long nosed pliers are best for the job. The hook should be placed on the screw so that tightening the screw tends to close the hook. The screw turns clockwise, toward the opening in the hook. This type of connection keeps the conductor securely under the screw head. Remember—only black wires (or wires coded black) should be connected to brass terminals.

Don't bet on long shots

It got real cold last winter in the garage, where my workbench is, so I brought an electric heater out there and plugged it into the house wiring via a long extension cord. When I turned it on, the lights dimmed and the heater gave off such a feeble glow that I thought it was broken. I didn't realize that wire itself puts up resistance, and thin wire in a long extension cord drains a lot of power from the system on its way to the appliance. It makes a big difference with an electric heater that uses a lot of watts, but even my power tools won't spin up to their full rpms if the extension cord is very long. Guess I better read chapter 4 and put an outlet out there.

Practical Pete

Joining wires in electrical boxes

For permanent home wiring to switches, outlets or fixtures, wires should be joined only in a wiring box. Three representative types of metal boxes are shown below. There are many variations. Plastic boxes are also available. Your dealer can tell you if your local code allows them to be used in your area.

The general procedure for joining wires in a box is to remove two or more knockout holes in the box, mount the box securely at a point where you wish to make the joint, insert the cables through the opening in the box, secure them with cable clamps, make the electrical connections with solderless connectors, press the wires back into the box, secure a cover on the box. Boxes are available in a wide variety of sizes and shapes. The box to use in a particular location depends on the number of cables to be joined, the kind of mounting available, and whether the box must also provide a mounting for a switch, outlet, or fixture. Check the table below each illustration to determine the box best suited to your installation. As a general rule, unless space is limited, select a box larger than the minimum size. It will be easier to work in and can accommodate additional wiring, if need be, at a later date.

Basic types of boxes

Ceiling box

Typical size (inches)	Max. Number of Wires	
	No. 14	No. 12
4 x 1¼	6	5
4 x 1½	7	6
4 x 2⅛	10	9

Junction box

Typical size (inches)	Max. Number of Wires	
	No. 14	No. 12
4 x 1¼	9	8
4 x 2⅛	15	13

Rules for counting the number of conductors in a box

1. The count refers to each individual conductor, not each cable.
2. Do not count ground wires or jumper wires.
3. Do not count wires from a fixture into the box.
4. *Internal* cable clamps or fixture mounting studs count as one conductor no matter how many clamps or studs there are. External cable clamps do not affect the count.

Wall box

Typical size (inches)	Max. Number of Wires	
	No. 14	No. 12
3 x 2 x 2½	6	5
3 x 2 x 2¾	7	6
3 x 2 x 3½	9	8

Ganging. Wall boxes are designed to be combined into two or more units when more conductor space is needed or when several switches or receptacles must be mounted in one location. Loosen the screw in the flange at the bottom of one box and remove the left side. Loosen the screw in the flange at the top of another box to remove the right side. The two open sides can now be joined by mating the notches with the flanges and tightening the screws at the top and bottom.

Inserting and securing cable

All boxes have knockout holes through which the cables enter the box. Before mounting the box, decide which knockout holes you want to use.

Cables entering the box must be secured with cable clamps. Some boxes have internal cable clamps that will hold either armored or plastic cable. Others don't come with clamps installed, so you must buy and attach separate two-piece clamps.

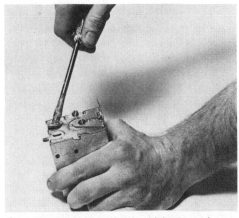

Some knockouts have slots in which you can insert a screwdriver and twist out the knockout.

Other knockouts are solid and must be removed with a hammer and punch.

Preinstalled clamps with steel armor cable. Slide the cable through the knockout hole and under the clamp. Feed the conductors through the upper ring. Tighten the screw in the center of the clamp to secure the clamp against the steel armor.

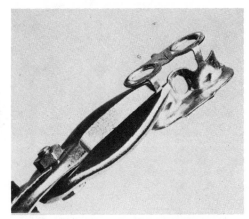

Preinstalled clamps with plastic sheathed cable. Bend and break off the upper ring section. Screw it loosely inside the box next to the knockout hole. Insert the cable through the knockout and secure it by tightening the clamp screw.

Securing clamps to boxes

1. First remove the nut with the pointed "ears" from the threaded end of the clamp. Slide the clamp on the cable and secure to the end of the sheathed portion of the cable by tightening the screw at the side of the clamp. With two-wire cable wrap a separate ground wire around the screw; then tighten.

2. Insert the conductors through the knockout opening and draw the conductors through until the threaded end of the clamp projects into the box. Slip the clamp nut over the conductors so that the ears on the nut will press against the wall of the box when the nut is tightened.

3. After tightening the nut as much as possible by hand, place a screwdriver or punch against one of the ears and tap the screwdriver or punch with a hammer to tighten the nut. Make certain the ears make solid contact with the wall of the box.

Mounting electrical boxes

Mounting in new construction is simple and straightforward. Studs and joists are readily accessible and a wide variety of mounting brackets are available. On new construction, wall and ceiling boxes should be installed so that the open front edge of the box will be flush with the finished surface. This means that the front of the box must project into the room beyond the front edge of the stud by an amount equal to the thickness of the wallboard, paneling or plaster that will be fastened to the bare studs as the finished interior surface.

Mounting in existing walls and ceilings requires some ingenuity to keep damage to walls or ceilings to a minimum. Different types of wall boxes are available, some designed to be attached directly to a stud and some that attach to the finished wall material between studs. Either way, position the new box at the same height as other outlets or switches in the room. Make a cardboard template the same shape as the open face of the box. Trace it onto the wall and drill holes in the wall at diagonal corners of the tracing to start the saw cuts.

Wall box, direct mounting.
Metal boxes for outlets or switches can be nailed beside studs through holes in the box or flange on the side. All such boxes must jut out from the stud by the thickness of the finish wall or ceiling material to be applied later, so the box ends up flush with the wall.

Wall box, flange mounted. Some wall boxes have flanges attached to them that can be nailed to the front of the stud. The flange is offset so the face of the box will be flush with the finish wall. Armored ("BX") cable can be looped through the hole in the flange.

Junction box, direct mounting. Junction boxes that can be nailed or screwed to the sides of studs have knockout holes on three sides and the back so cables can be fed into them from all sides.

Between-stud mounting. When a box must be positioned between two studs, joists or beams (as frequently happens in ceilings) adjustable straps or hangers can be attached to the back of the box and fastened to the structural wooden supports at both ends.

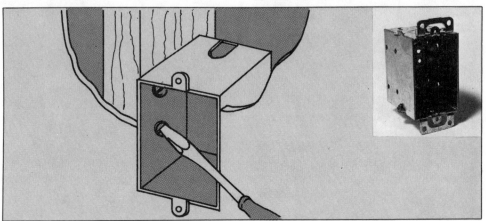

If you can locate a stud in the wall, outlet boxes can be mounted with wood screws. Cut the wall opening even with one side of the stud. Hold the box in position in the opening. Make a pencil mark on the stud to correspond with two mounting holes in the box. Pick one hole near the top of the box and one near the bottom. Remove the box. Use a power or hand drill with a long bit to drill two pilot holes at an angle into the stud. The drill bit should be of smaller diameter than the screws you plan to use. About one-half inch depth should be enough. After cables have been installed in the box, reposition it in the opening. Secure it with wood screws through the box mounting holes and into the pilot holes in the stud. Ceiling boxes with mounting flanges can be similarly mounted on joists.

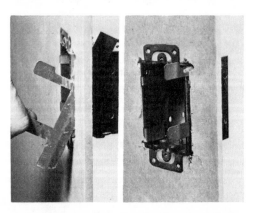

For appearance or convenience, electrical boxes must often be mounted between studs and joists. The devices shown above make the task fairly simple. Expansion brackets located on the box spread when the screw is tightened. When the box is ready for final installation, push the box into the wall so that the ears at the top and bottom hold the front edge flush with the wall surface. If necessary, adjust the ears. Secure the box by tightening the screws on both sides. Tightening the screws spreads the bracket and holds the box in place.

Push the box into the wall so that the ears at the top and bottom hold the box flush with the wall surface. If necessary, adjust the ears. Slide a bracket between the edge of the box and the wall opening. Hold the bracket by the arms and pull it tight against the wall. Bend the arms toward the inside of the box. Install another bracket on the other side of the box in the same way. Use pliers to bend the arms tight and flat against the sides of the box.

Joining wires together

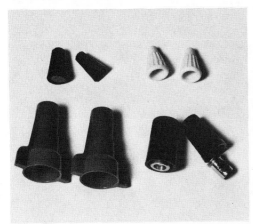

Solderless connectors

Solderless connectors are used to make electrical connections between the conductors within the metal box. Plastic screw-on connectors, sometimes called "wire nuts," are the most common type and are satisfactory for most uses. They come in a variety of sizes to accommodate different combinations of wire thicknesses and number of conductors to be joined. They are so inexpensive you can keep a variety of sizes on hand to be sure you have one that will make a good electrical contact and not work loose. (If there is any vibration, wrap tape around the wires and the base of the nut. If you ever need to rewire, unscrew the nut and screw it back on the new wires.)

Plastic screw-on connectors contain a tapered metal insert with spiral grooves that grip the ends of the wires when you screw on the connector. The bare conductors do not have to be twisted together first, but they must be trimmed in length so that when the connector is screwed down tight over them, no bare wire is exposed.

Hold the conductors together and approximately parallel. Twist the connector onto the wires clockwise by hand. Check each conductor to make certain it cannot be pulled free.

Ceramic screw-on connectors are used in high temperature locations, such as heaters and irons.

Metal set-screw type. Wires are inserted under the set screw. The set screw is tightened and the plastic cap is screwed on the connector afterwards.

Heavier connectors for larger size wire are tightened with a wrench to clamp the wires together. These connectors must be insulated by wrapping with tape.

Wiring lamp, appliance plugs

Use the Underwriters' knot to attach lamp cord to plugs with screw terminals.

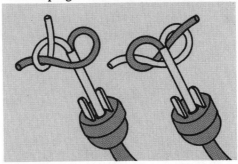

1. Feed the end of the cord through the plug. Separate the conductors for about three inches. Tie the knot as shown.

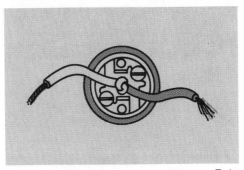

2. Strip insulation from each conductor. Twist stranded wire tightly.

3. Pull the knot securely back into the plug. Route each conductor around a prong.

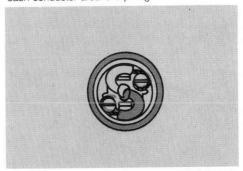

4. Loosen the screw terminals and wrap one bare conductor around each. Be sure the direction you wrap the conductor around the screw is the same direction you turn the screw to tighten it securely.

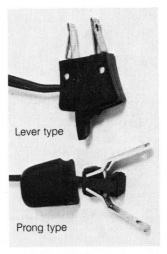

Lever type

Prong type

Crimping-type plugs for flat wire
Several kinds of plugs are available that accept flat wire and make connections automatically without your having to take them apart and strip the insulation off the ends of the wires. Most of them grip the wires when you either close a lever or squeeze two prongs together.

To use these plugs, cut the lamp cord squarely at the end. Some designs also require that you make a short slit between the two insulated wires to divide them. Do *not* remove insulation. Insert the wire into the opening on the plug as far as it will go. Fully depress the lever on the plug, or squeeze the prongs together and insert them into the housing of the plug. The lever or prongs make the electrical connection in the plug by forcing sharp metal points through the insulation to make contact with the conductors. The lever or prong action also crimps the wire to provide some mechanical strength.

If the cord is likely to be plugged and unplugged frequently, a screw type plug with a molded grip, wired with the Underwriters' knot, is stronger and will last longer than automatic crimping plugs.

Splicing wires

Cabling to wall outlets, switches, and large appliances should never be spliced. All connections should be made within metal or plastic boxes, as previously described.

Occasionally, it may be necessary to splice wires when repairing or modifying appliances or for emergency repairs. The proper way of making safe, secure splices is to make a good mechanical and electrical joint—that is, strong enough not to pull apart and tight enough so there is no loss of voltage. As this is tricky work, a continuous run of new wire is always better than any splice.

Taping wire splices

Spliced and soldered joints should always be taped. The right amount of tape to use on a joint is the amount that will provide insulation about as thick as the original insulation on the wire. A good brand of plastic electrical tape is best for wire joints.

Apply the tape by wrapping it diagonally along the joint starting on the insulation at one end.

Plastic tape sticks best if it is kept taut while wrapping. Continue the tape for an inch or so on the insulation at the other end.

Make as many wraps as necessary to build the tape to the proper thickness. Cut or tear the tape at the end of the last wrap and press it smooth around itself.

The twist splice

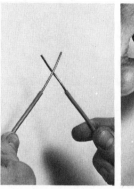

For light wire, when two wires are joined, cross about two inches of each end of prepared wire. Bend the ends of the wires over each other at right angles and twist them around each other.

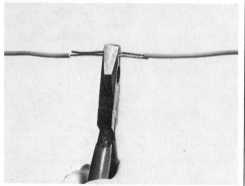

For heavy-gauge wire, two pairs of pliers are needed to make sure the connection is tight. Use one pair of pliers to hold the wires at the beginning of the twist.

Use the other pair of pliers to twist the wires. Use wire cutters to trim off the excess wire so that no sharp ends can penetrate the tape. Solder the wires at the twist and tape them.

The pigtail splice

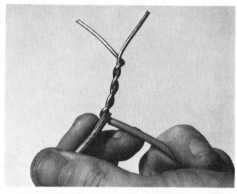

1. Strip off at least 1½ inches of insulation from the end of each wire. Twist the wires together tightly starting at or near the first bit of exposed wire.

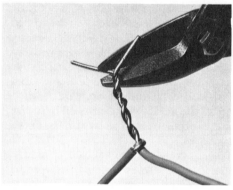

2. Trim off sharp points protruding from the end of the twist. Solder the twisted wires at the point where the twist began.

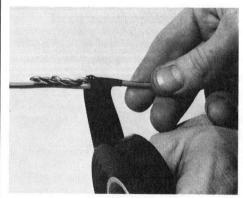

3. Bend them parallel to one of the conductors and tape the bare splice from the end of the insulation on one side to the beginning of the insulation on the other side.

Splicing three or more wires

The pigtail type of splice is best when joining three or more wires. The thing to guard against when more than two wires are involved in the twist is the tendency for one or more of the wires to remain fairly straight while the others are wrapped around it. When this happens the straight conductors can be pulled free of the splice fairly readily. The way to prevent this is to make certain the twist is started with all the wires bent at approximately a right angle. Then if the bent wires are interlocked and held with pliers, the twist will continue as started. Solder and tape the splice.

Starting a three-wire pigtail splice. To interlock all three wires bend each one at a right angle when you make the first twist. A straight wire will pull out under relatively little stress.

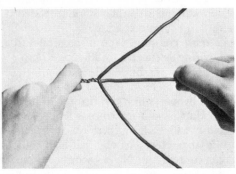

Finishing a three-wire pigtail splice. Before soldering and taping the exposed wire, pull on each of the three wires to be sure they are firmly interlocked.

Don't get caught in a lousy joint

Personally I think wire nuts are just as good as splicing, soldering, and taping—and a heck of a lot less work. But my granddaddy said, "Solder," so I soldered. Trouble was, I touched the hot iron to the solder and tried to drip it onto the wire. Even when the drop didn't miss altogether, it hardened so fast on the cold copper that it didn't run into the little crevices between the twisted wires, and they pulled apart. "Heat the *wires*, sonny boy," he said, "and hold the solder on *them* so it melts into them." It works fine that way, but it's a little hard to take that kind of talk when you're going on 37 years old.

Practical Pete

Tap splice

Sometimes it is desirable to join one wire to another at some midpoint without cutting the second conductor. The tap splice can be used in this case. Remove insulation from about two inches of the continuous run wire. Wrap the joining wire tightly around the continuous wire. Solder and tape.

If the joining wire is stranded, the strands may be separated into two bunches and then wrapped in opposite directions along the continuous wire.

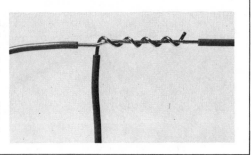

Soldering

For a good solder joint in house wiring you need a high heat soldering tool and rosin core solder. The solder should be marked as suitable for electrical use. A high heat electric soldering gun or iron can be used, but pencil-flame propane soldering torches work faster. Of course considerable care must be taken with the open flame to avoid injury or damage from fire. The trick with house wire is to heat the joint as rapidly as possible.

The large diameter wires are good heat conductors, as well as electrical conductors. They tend to carry heat away from the joint. This causes scorched insulation and can cause a poor solder joint.

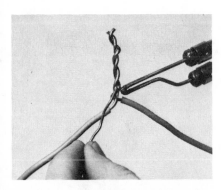

Hold the wires to be soldered tightly against the tip of the iron. Unwind a few inches of solder from the spool and hold the end of the solder against the wire, not against the iron. To make a good joint the wire must become hot enough to melt the solder on contact.

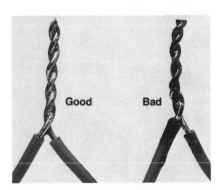

Inspect the solder closely in a good light after soldering. The solder should look smooth and a bit shiny. If the solder looks dull and "grainy," the chances are a good joint has not been made. Reheat the joint until the solder flows again. Recheck the joint for strength after it has cooled.

The soldering procedure using a propane torch is essentially the same. Make certain the flame is adjusted and positioned for electrical work in accordance with the manufacturer's instructions; its intense heat can melt the wires. Use a soldering tip that pinpoints the flame.

Conduit

Conduit is often used to hold and protect house wiring. In some localities conduit is required by the local code. Conduit protects house wiring from damage better than steel armor or plastic sheathing. However, it is more difficult to install.

There are three types of conduit available: thin-wall metal conduit, rigid threaded conduit, and plastic conduit.

The most common type of conduit for house wiring is the thin-wall type. Thin-wall conduit is too thin for threaded joints. It is joined to other lengths of conduit and to boxes by pressure-type fittings. Thin-wall conduit is sold in ten-foot lengths in either one-half inch or three-quarter inch (outside) diameter. The one-half inch conduit can contain four No. 14 wires or three No. 12 wires. Three-quarter inch conduit accommodates four No. 10 or five No. 12 wires. These capacities are for individual wires, not pairs. The wires used in conduit are the same as the individual conductors found in steel armor cable and plastic sheathed cable. Wires in conduit must follow standard coding. In a two-wire conduit circuit you need one black wire, one white wire, and one ground wire. A three-wire circuit requires one black wire, one white wire, one red wire, and one ground wire.

The general procedure for using thin-wall conduit is similar to the use of steel armor cable. The big difference is that conduit cannot be "snaked" through openings in ceilings and walls. You must have full access to joists and studs to install conduit. So you probably won't want to use it unless your local code requires it.

The tools you need and the procedures for using conduit are shown on these pages.

Cutting

Thin-wall conduit can be cut with a special cutter. To use the cutter, clamp it around the conduit. To cut the conduit, tighten the knurled nut in the handle. As you tighten, force the cutter around the conduit. The sharp cutting blade cuts a groove that deepens with each revolution, making a smooth, quick cut. After cutting through the conduit, file off any burrs around the edge of the cut.

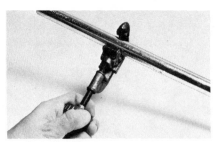

1. Turn knurled nut to open jaws of cutting tool and tighten them again onto conduit.

2. Rotate cutter around conduit as you tighten until blade scores through.

Bending

Thin-wall conduit can be readily bent by using a special tool designed to make a smooth, even bend with little effort. The more bends in a run of conduit, the more difficult it is to "fish" the wires through. Plan the conduit run carefully to avoid sharp bends and to make as few bends as possible. Never have more than four right angle bends between openings. Follow the manufacturer's instructions for the type of bender you use.

How a conduit bender works

Screw a 30-inch length of threaded pipe into the bender head (sometimes called an "electrician's hickey"

Insert the conduit into the bender through the hook at the top of the head. The hook marks where the bend will start.

Put one foot on the conduit near the head and lever the pipe handle backward, checking the angle of the bend as you go.

HICKEY

LENGTH OF PIPE

CONDUIT

CONDUIT

Supporting and coupling

Support lengths of conduit with a pipe strap every 6 feet for inside runs; 10 feet on exposed runs. Mount empty conduit in place and make all couplings and connections to boxes *before* threading the insulated indoor wire through it.

Join two lengths of unthreaded conduit with couplings. One type has three nuts in a row. Force the ends of the thin-wall conduit into each end of the coupling and tighten the center hex nut. The other type has two set screws.

Connecting to boxes

To attach conduit to a junction box, use a ring-nut connector. Insert the conduit in the connector and tighten the hex nut on the connector to squeeze a compression ring inside the nut. This secures the connector on the conduit

Next, insert the connector through the knockout on the box. Thread the ring nut on the end of the connector projecting into the box. Tighten the ring nut by placing a screwdriver against one of the "ears" on the ring nut. Tap the screwdriver with a small hammer to tighten the ring nut.

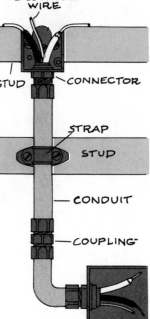

Typical conduit installation

Threading wires through conduit

A fish tape is a thin, flexible metal tape with a hook on one end. The tape is usually packaged on some type of reel. The tape is used to pull wires through conduit or through openings in walls. For conduit use, the tape is inserted in one conduit opening and worked through to the next opening. The wires to be drawn through the conduit are bent around the hook on the fish tape.

If the run is long and has a few bends it is a good idea to wrap some electrical tape around the wires to hold them on the hook.

The tape is then reeled in to draw the wires through the conduit. A slow, steady pull is less likely to kink the tape or jam the wires than is a series of sharp tugs.

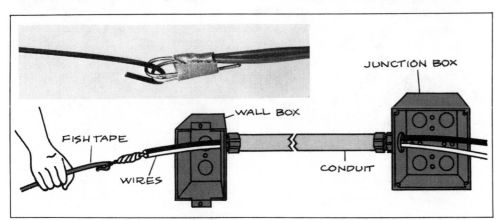

3. SIMPLE REPAIRS

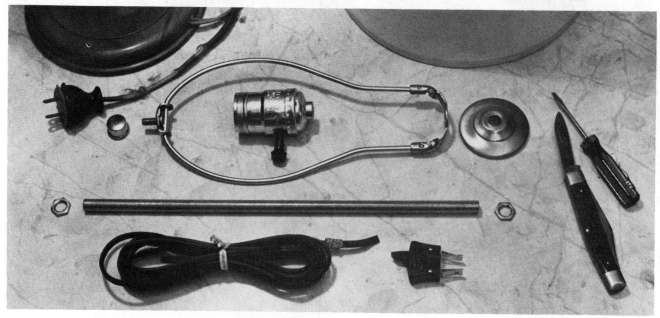

Rewiring a lamp

What it takes

Approximate time: Half an hour.

Materials: If you purchase the items separately, you will need:

Line cord. Buy type SPT, No. 16 or 18, grooved ripcord. This is available in brown or ivory and is sold by the foot or in 30-, 50-, and 100-foot spools. Buy enough cord to reach from the lamp location to a wall outlet without an extension.

Line plug. Plugs of many types are available in colors to match the cord. The "automatic" connection types are the easiest to connect. If the lamp is frequently unplugged, a screw-terminal plug with a grip is stronger than a clamp-on plug.

Socket. You will probably be able to obtain an exact duplicate of the original socket. Sockets are available in either brass or chrome finish, with either push-type or turn-type switches. Any lamp with one socket can take either a standard socket for a single-wattage bulb, or a three-way bulb socket. The wiring is the same.

Perhaps the most common household electrical problem is the table or floor lamp that will not light, flickers on and off, or sometimes works and sometimes does not.

Fortunately this common problem is easily corrected. The possible sources of trouble are the same in all lamps. The first thing to check, of course, is the bulb. Make sure it is fully screwed into the socket. If that doesn't do it, switch bulbs with a lamp that you know is working. If the first lamp now works and the second one doesn't, the bulb has burned out. Or, if you have a continuity tester, you can check the bulb by placing the tip of the probe on the center of the base of the bulb and touching the alligator clip to

the threaded part of its base. If the light in the tester goes on, the bulb is good.

If bulb life seems unusually short in a lamp, the lamp may be faulty. (The average life of a 100-watt bulb is 750 hours of operation.) Try the bulb in another lamp or fixture, as suggested above, before discarding it. If the bulb is not at fault, the cause of the trouble is either the lamp socket and switch or the lamp cord. You can check these with continuity testers (page 322) and replace only the defective item. You can also purchase lamp rewiring kits with various socket-and-switch combinations. The wiring for three-way sockets is the same as for single-wattage sockets.

Single-socket lamp

1. Unplug the lamp from the wall outlet. If the lamp has a harp (shade support bracket), remove it by lifting up the ferrules at each side of the base of the harp, compressing the bracket slightly, and lifting it free so you can get at the socket more easily.

2. Press in the side of the socket near the base (where the word PRESS is sometimes marked). Twist slightly and pull up to remove the metal shell. Then remove the cardboard insulator under the metal shell to expose the socket terminals.

3. Push the line cord in at the base of the lamp and pull up on the socket to inspect the line cord and to gain some slack to work with. Loosen the screw terminals and disconnect the line cord conductors from the socket.

4. Check the insulated portion of the line cord near where it is connected to the socket. If the insulation is brittle and cracks when bent, either the cord is quite old or the socket is getting too hot. In either case, both socket and cord should be replaced. If the cord looks OK and tests OK, it can be reused.

5. The opening in the bottom of the lamp base is often covered with a felt pad. It will be easier to remove the old cord and to thread the new cord through the lamp if you peel off the pad. Peel carefully to avoid tearing the felt. The pad can be glued back on the base when you have finished wiring and testing.

6. To remove the power cord, simply pull the old cord out of the base after disconnecting it from the socket. If the cord does not pull out readily, check for strain knots at the top where the cord enters the base and at the bottom where the cord leaves the base.

7. Remove the old socket base (loosen the set screw on the side if there is one) by unscrewing it from the threaded pipe in the lamp. Feed the new cord through the base, tie a simple strain (overhand) knot in the cord inside the base opening, and then feed the cord up through the threaded pipe.

8. Slip the new socket base over the line cord, thread it onto the pipe, and secure it by tightening the set screw. The set screw should keep the cord from slipping back through when you pull on the plug end. If it slips, separate the two halves of insulated cord and tie Underwriters' knot (page 315).

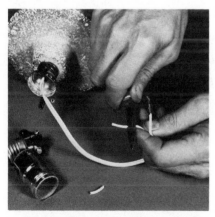

9. To separate the two line cord conductors at the socket end of the line, grip each conductor half with your fingers or with pliers and gently separate them along the groove. Make the tear about 2 inches long. Strip about 1 inch of insulation from each conductor. Clean the bare wires by scraping lightly with a knife or razor blade. If the conductor is braided, twist it tightly.

10. Wrap each conductor around one of the screw terminals on the socket. Wrap the wire so the insulation is close to the terminal, and wrap in the direction in which you will turn the screw to tighten it. One turn around the screw is enough. After you have tightened the screw, trim off the excess exposed conductor as close to the terminal as possible. Before assembling the socket, check and retighten each screw terminal.

11. Slip the insulator over the socket and slip the outer metal shell over the insulator. Push the excess line cord down through the socket base and snap the metal socket shell onto the base. Replace the felt pad on the base. If the lamp does not operate properly, unplug it immediately and recheck your work, testing if necessary to locate the trouble. Replace the harp. Connect a plug to the line cord (page 315).

Testing the parts of a lamp

What it takes

Approximate time: A few minutes for testing; up to half an hour for replacing switches.

Tools and materials: Continuity tester (page 301) for testing: screwdriver, pliers, knife, and new switch for replacing.

The electrical parts of any lamp can be tested with a continuity tester. In the majority of cases, testing will identify the defective part. You then have to purchase and replace only one item. This makes the job quicker and more economical. Keep in mind, however, that the small flashlight battery in the tester does not duplicate the relatively high voltage in the line and resultant heat of actual operation. If the low-voltage tests do not reveal the source of the problem, check the cord and the plug; then replace all the electrical parts because some may be defective under high voltage.

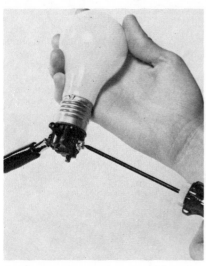

Socket. Put a bulb you know to be good in the socket. Connect the alligator clip to one terminal. Hold the probe against the other terminal. Turn the switch on and off. The tester should light steadily when the switch is on. Jiggle the switch a bit. If the tester flickers, the switch is defective and should be replaced.

Three-way bulb socket. Connect the alligator clip to the brass-colored terminal. Touch the probe to the small tab near the edge inside the socket. The tester should light when the switch is turned to the first ON position. Move the probe to the metal tab in the center of the socket. It should light with the switch in the second ON position. In the third ON position, the tester should light when touched to both tabs in turn.

Plug. Connect the alligator clip to one of the bare conductors. Touch the probe to each of the plug prongs. The tester should light when one—and only one—prong is touched. Hold the tester in place on the prong and jiggle the cord. If the tester flickers, the cord is defective and should be replaced. Connect the alligator clip to the other conductor and repeat the test.

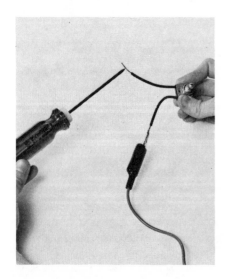

On-off switch. Connect the alligator clip to one of the switch leads. Hold the other switch lead against the probe. Turn the switch off and on several times. The tester should light steadily when the switch is on and should not light up when the switch is off. Replace the switch if the tester flickers in either position or does not light at all.

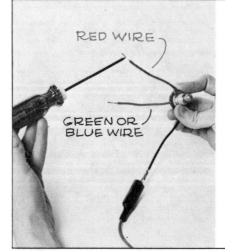

Combination switch. Connect the alligator clip to the black lead. Move the switch through all four positions. At each position, touch the probe to each of the other two leads. If the switch is OK, the tester will light or not light as indicated in the chart above. Although the color of the three leads may

Switch position	Touch probe to wire listed	Tester light
1	Red	OFF
	Green or Blue	OFF
2	Red	ON
	Green or Blue	OFF
3	Red	OFF
	Green or Blue	ON
4	Red	ON
	Green or Blue	ON

vary, the on-off pattern for any three-bulb lamp switch will be the same. If the tester flickers when it should be on, does not light when it should, or lights when it should not, the switch is defective. Repeat the test to be certain the results are correct.

Wiring multiple-socket lamps

Two-socket lamps

There are two basic types of two-socket lamps. In one type, the two sockets are contained in one molded plastic or metal package. In this type the sockets are connected internally, and only two wires—one black, one

white—must be connected to wire both sockets. The switch is separate from the socket. The other type of two-socket lamp has two separate sockets. The sockets may have built-in switches—as in the single-socket lamp—or they may be wired to a common switch.

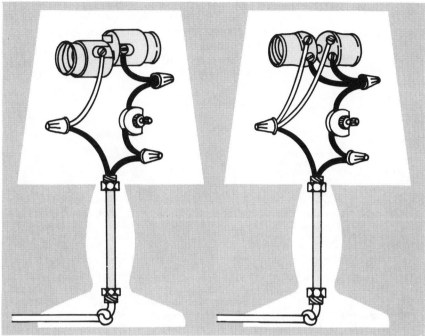

Two-socket lamp with prewired two-socket unit and separate on-off switch (both bulbs on or both bulbs off).

Two-socket lamp with separate sockets and rotary switch (both bulbs on or both bulbs off). If sockets have screw terminals, install black and white jumpers as shown. Connect black jumpers to brass terminals and white jumpers to chrome terminals.

Three-socket lamps

Three-socket lamps—such as pole lamps and swag lamps—usually have switches that allow one, two, or three bulbs to be turned on as desired. This

makes the wiring a bit more complicated, but it can be easily done with the help of the diagram. Sockets in these lamps are prewired with black and white leads.

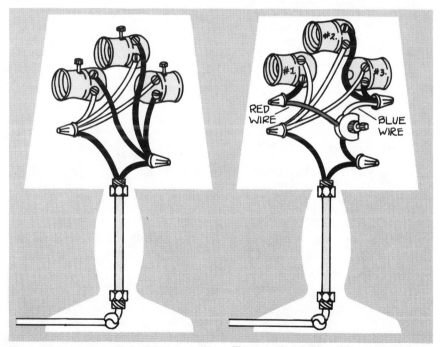

Three-socket lamp with individual on-off switch in each socket. If sockets have screw terminals, install black and white jumpers as shown—black jumpers to brass terminals, white jumpers to chrome terminals.

Three-socket lamp with separate four-position rotary switch. The switch positions are: off, only bulb #1 on, only bulbs #2 and #3 on, all bulbs on. Switch wires are usually black, red, and blue. Black connects to the line, red connects to one socket, blue to the two other sockets.

Replacing a switch

Wall-mounted toggle switches usually give a warning before they fail completely. When you snap on a light and there is a brief delay before the lamp lights, or if the lamp flickers a bit when turned on, the switch is approaching the end of its useful life.

Switches that are used the most fail first. When a frequently used switch shows signs of failing, it is probable that other much-used switches of the same age will also need replacement soon. It may save time and trouble to purchase and install several switches at once, rather than wait for unexpected failure.

When switches need replacement, take the opportunity to consider changing to other types of switches. See pages 342 through 349 for a rundown of your options.

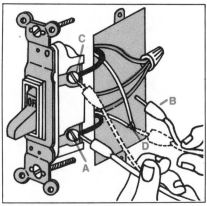

Testing for power in the circuit. Turn off power to the switch at the circuit-breaker or fuse panel. Touch one probe of voltage tester to one of the switch terminals (A). Touch the other probe to the wall box (B). (If the switch has a green-tinted terminal at the bottom, touch the probe to that.) The tester should not light. Touch one probe to the other switch terminal (C) while holding the second probe on the box or green-tinted terminal (B). Again the voltage tester should not light. If there is a white wire in the box, carefully remove the plastic solderless connector joining the white wire. Do not touch the bare wire. Touch one probe to the bare white wire (D) and the other probe to each of the terminals. The tester should not light.

Removing the old switch. Dismantle the switch by removing the wall plate, then the mounting screws at the top and bottom. Pull the switch out of the box. Loosen the screw terminals and remove the electrical connections. If the switch has push-in type connections, insert a small screwdriver in the slot next to the hole where the conductor enters the switch. Press in on the screwdriver and pull the conductor out. Notice carefully which wires connect to which terminals so you can replace them the same way on the new switch. A white wire may be painted black or wrapped with black tape to show it is hot. Plain ON-OFF switches do not need neutral conductors. They break the flow of current through hot conductors only.

Testing the old switch. Use a continuity tester to check whether a switch is good or not. Connect the alligator clip to one of the brass-colored terminals and touch the probe to the other brass-colored terminal. Flip the switch on and off several times and jiggle the toggle. If the switch is good, the tester light will respond clearly to the ON and OFF positions of the toggle without flickering. Move the alligator clip to the switch mounting bracket (or green-tinted grounding terminal if it has one). Touch the probe to each of the brass-colored terminals in turn and flip the switch from off to on several times. If the switch is good, the tester will not light at any time during the test.

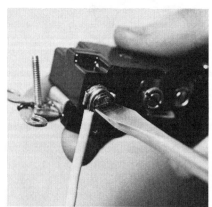

Installing the new switch. The replacement switch should have—in addition to the two brass-colored terminals—one green-tinted grounding terminal (a recent requirement of the electrical code for new installations). If the old switch had a green-tinted terminal, simply connect the green wire to the green terminal on the new switch.

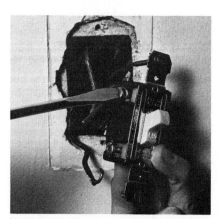

Next, connect the black wires (one may be a black-coded wire) to the brass-colored terminals on the switch. Remount the switch in the wall box. (If a grounding jumper wire must be added, see the box at right.) Replace the cover plate, turn on the power, and test the switch.

Connecting jumper wires

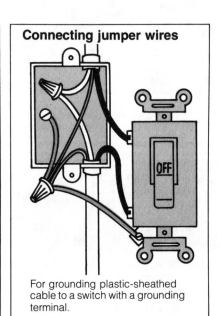

For grounding plastic-sheathed cable to a switch with a grounding terminal.

Replacing a wall receptacle

Unlike switches, wall receptacles have no moving parts, so they generally last for many years. They can, however, develop trouble. Plastic parts can become dry and brittle and can chip or crack when plugs are inserted or removed. Metal electrical parts can become loose and make poor contact with plugs. The present electrical code requires that all wall receptacles be the three-prong type with a green-coded grounding screw. Be sure the replacement you purchase is this type. Before touching any part of the receptacle, turn off power. Then follow the testing procedure shown below.

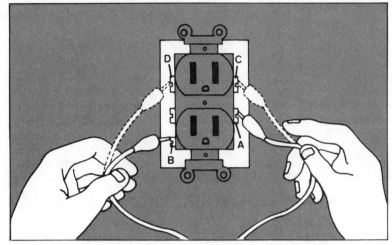

Testing for power in the circuit. Turn off power to the circuit at the main service panel. Take off the faceplate. Touch one probe of a voltage tester to one of the brass-colored terminals (A); touch the other probe to the wall box. If the outlet has a green-tinted terminal at the bottom, touch the probe to that (B). The tester should not light.

Next, touch one probe to the other brass-colored terminal (C) while holding the other probe on the box or green-tinted terminal. Again the voltage tester should not light. Touch one tester probe to one of the chrome-colored terminals (D); touch the other probe to each of the brass-colored terminals, as in A and C. The tester should not light

Removing the old receptacle. After taking off the faceplate and testing, remove the mounting screws at the top and bottom. Pull the receptacle out of the box.

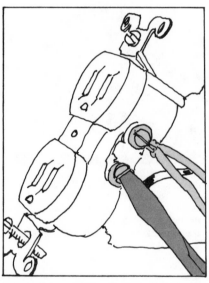

Loosen the screw terminals and undo the electrical connections. If the receptacle has push-in type connections, insert a small screwdriver in the slot next to the hole where the conductor enters the outlet. Press on the screwdriver and pull out conductor.

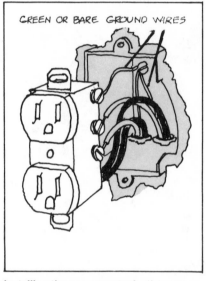

Installing the new receptacle. If the receptacle you removed had a green-tinted terminal, connect the existing green-insulated wire to the green terminal on the new receptacle. Connect the black wire or wires to the brass-colored terminals, and connect the white wire or wires to the chrome-colored terminals. Remount the receptacle in the wall box. If a grounding jumper must be added, see box.

Connecting jumper wires

The procedure for adding a grounding jumper to a wall box depends upon the type of cable in the box.

If the power cables to the wall box are the steel-armored type, simply connect a jumper of green-insulated or bare wire to a grounding screw in the wall box. Connect the other end of the jumper to the green-tinted screw on the switch or receptacle.

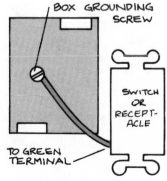

If plastic-sheathed cable is connected to the box, the bare grounding wires from the cables, including any already connected to the box, and two bare or green-insulated jumpers should be joined with solderless connectors. Connect one of the jumpers to a box grounding screw. Connect the other jumper to the green-tinted screw on the switch or receptacle.

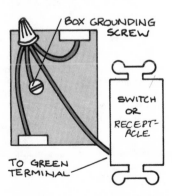

Replacing small ceiling fixtures

What it takes:

Approximate time: Forty minutes if the new hardware fits the old—more if mechanical adapters are necessary. Allow an extra half hour for chandeliers.

Tools and materials: Voltage tester, screwdriver, locking pliers or wrench, wire stripper or knife, solderless connectors (if you can't reuse the old ones), and a wire coat hanger bent into an S-hook.

When redecorating a room, it is often helpful to temporarily remove fixtures. The first step is to turn off power to the fixture at the circuit-breaker or fuse panel. Do not depend on the wall switch to remove power. Use a voltage tester to check wires before you touch them. The procedure for checking wires in a ceiling box to make sure power is off is basically the same as that used for wall outlets (page 325). Carefully remove all solderless connectors and check between all wires and ground. (The ceiling box should be grounded.) Next, check between all black (or black-coded) wires and all white wires. If the tester lights at any time, voltage is present in the box. Do not continue until the source of the power has been discovered and turned off.

The electrical connections for small ceiling fixtures are quite simple. The box may contain other wiring, but you need only disconnect the two wires that lead to the fixture. To reinstall the fixture, or to replace it with a new one, connect the fixture wires to the same two power wires. If the fixture wires are color coded, connect the black fixture wire to the black power wire. Connect the white fixture wire to the white power wire. Some fixtures have wires of the same color. In this case either fixture wire can be connected to either power wire by using solderless connectors.

Screw-mounted fixtures

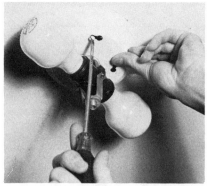

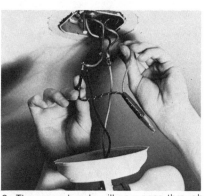

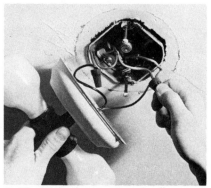

1. This type of fixture is held in place by two long screws inserted through slots in the canopy and threaded into ears on the ceiling box. To remove the fixture, loosen the screws (you need not remove them). Turn the canopy slightly so that the screw heads line up with the larger end of the mounting slot.

2. The screw heads will now pass through the larger opening and the canopy can be lowered. With the glass or plastic globe removed, small fixtures are light enough to hang by the power wires briefly while you make a voltage check to be sure power is off in the ceiling box.

3. When you are sure power is off, support the canopy with one hand. Remove the solderless connectors that attach the fixture wires to the power wires. Check them with a voltage tester. Touch a probe to each. The tester should not light. Untwist the wires and remove the fixture.

Strap adapter

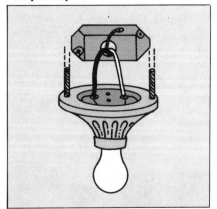

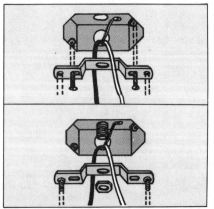

Center-mounted fixtures

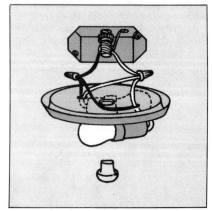

1. The mounting slots in the canopy of a replacement fixture may be too widely spaced for the mounting screws to be threaded into the box ears. In this case, a strap can be mounted on the box. The strap provides threaded holes at each end. Measure the distance between the mounting slots in the canopy, and purchase a strap that matches the spacing.

2. The strap can be attached to the ceiling box in two ways. The strap at top is attached with screws put through the strap slots and into the threaded ears on the box.
3. If the box has a threaded nipple (bottom), the strap can be placed over the nipple and secured with a locknut.

Some ceiling fixtures—particularly those having two sockets—are center mounted. The ceiling box contains a threaded nipple. For mounting, the canopy is placed over the nipple. An end cap is then threaded on the nipple to secure the fixture. To install this type of fixture on a box without a center stud, put a strap-and-nipple combination on the box first.

Replacing chandeliers

Chandeliers differ from small ceiling fixtures in the way they are suspended from the ceiling box and in how they are wired internally. Chandeliers frequently weigh 10 pounds or more, in which case they must be attached to a ceiling box containing a threaded metal stud, or nipple. If you are replacing a small chandelier with a large one, and the ceiling box does not contain a stud, you may be able to add one; otherwise, the box must be replaced with one that can accommodate a stud (pages 350-357). **A chandelier weighing less than 10 pounds** can be mounted with a strap and nipple. The nipple is attached to the strap with locknuts. The strap is then attached to the box with screws put through the strap and into the threaded ears on the box, as shown at

the bottom of the opposite page. **Mount fixtures weighing more than 10 pounds** by threading a hickey (which resembles a C-shaped bracket with threaded holes at top and bottom) on the box stud and threading a nipple into the hickey. Thread them so that the nipple will project through the canopy enough to allow the collar to be securely threaded onto the nipple.

Chandeliers are fully wired when you purchase them. Only two wires from the chandelier need be connected to the two power wires in the ceiling box. If the chandelier wires are color coded, wire the black chandelier wire to the black power wire. Wire the white chandelier wire to the white power wire. If both chandelier wires are the same color, use either.

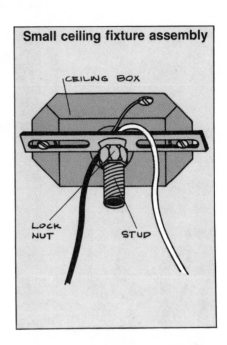

Small ceiling fixture assembly

Replacing sockets

Occasionally one or two sockets on a chandelier may become defective. This is sometimes the case when a bulb flickers or does not light. First thing is to check the bulb in another socket or fixture. If the bulb is OK, the problem is in the socket or wiring. **Turn off the power to the chandelier.** Then loosen the collar so that the canopy can be dropped to expose the

box wiring. Do not allow the chandelier to hang by the power wires. Support it by making a hook of heavy wire (a wire clothes hanger works well). Attach the hook to the chandelier and the hickey. Take care that the hook does not come in contact with any exposed conductors.

Make certain the power is off (page 326) before you disconnect the wires.

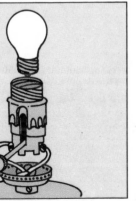

To replace a screw-terminal socket, loosen the terminal screws and disconnect the wires. Tag or mark the wire that was connected to the brass terminal. Remove the socket by unscrewing it from its threaded mount or by loosening the setscrew in the base. Lift the socket from its mounting base. You can probably obtain an exact replacement socket from your electrical dealer or from a lighting-fixture store. Install the new socket on the mounting base. Connect the wire you tagged or marked to the brass terminal. Connect the other wire to the chrome terminal. Replace the outer shell.

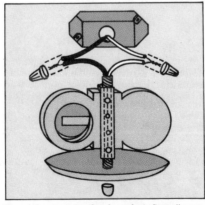

To replace a prewired socket, first disconnect the wires in the center section of the chandelier in order to remove the socket. Remove the lower cap nut and canopy to expose the socket wiring. Then take off the solderless connector joining the socket wires to the other fixture wires. If the wires aren't color coded, tag or mark the wire connected to the black socket wire. Free the socket wires. Unscrew the socket from its threaded mount or loosen the setscrew in the base. Remove the socket and its wires. Install the new socket by routing the socket wires to the center section. Mount the socket. Connect the socket wires to the other fixture wires.

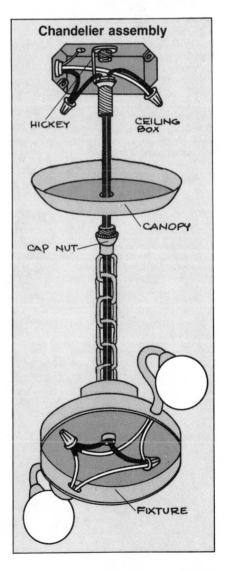

Chandelier assembly

Troubleshooting fluorescents

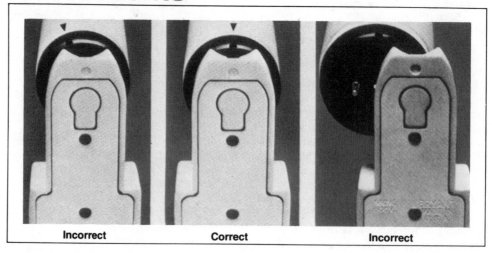

| Incorrect | Correct | Incorrect |

The bee in the ballast
We decided to put fluorescents in the family room to save electricity. Our teenager's super-sophisticated stereo equipment is set up there too. The lights looked great, but I didn't think to find out the noise level of the ballast beforehand. The buzz was so bad, at first our teenager thought his amp or speakers had blown. Guess which had to go?

Practical Pete

Correct installation

The most common cause of fluorescent lamp trouble is incorrect installation of the lamps in the holders. Fluorescent lamps have marks on each end to indicate proper positioning in the fixture.

The lamp on the left in the photographs above was inserted into the holder correctly but was not rotated enough. The center lamp was correctly installed. The lamp on the right is hanging by one pin.

Noise level

All fluorescent ballasts generate a hum. It can range from barely audible to an annoyingly high level. Ballasts have a sound rating ranging from A (low) to F (high). If the hum level is an important consideration, ask about the sound rating when buying the fixture. The chart, right, recommends rating levels for some living and working areas.

Application	Sound rating
Residence, TV-broadcast studio, church	A
Library, classroom	B
Commercial buildings, stockrooms	C
Retail stores, noisy offices	D
Light industry, outdoor lighting	E
Street lighting, factory	F

Discoloration

Various patterns of light and dark gray appear in the ends of most fluorescent tubes. Although discoloration generally increases with age, it does not affect the operation of the lamp. You can ignore it if the lamp is concealed by a plastic cover or is located behind a cornice or valance. But if the lamp is exposed and discoloration is objectionable, the lamp ends should be concealed in some way or the tube replaced.

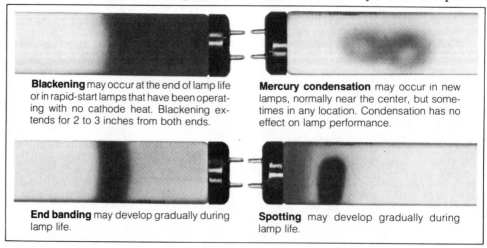

Blackening may occur at the end of lamp life or in rapid-start lamps that have been operating with no cathode heat. Blackening extends for 2 to 3 inches from both ends.

Mercury condensation may occur in new lamps, normally near the center, but sometimes in any location. Condensation has no effect on lamp performance.

End banding may develop gradually during lamp life.

Spotting may develop gradually during lamp life.

Troubleshooting checklist for fluorescents

The troubleshooting chart below lists some of the more common problems that develop in fluorescent lighting and tells how they may be corrected. Unless otherwise indicated, the cause and correction apply to all types of residential fixtures.

Problem	Cause	Correction
Lamp will not light.	Fuse blown or circuit breaker tripped.	Replace fuse or reset circuit breaker.
	Lamp defective or burned out.	Replace lamp.
	Lamp not properly installed in holders.	Check and install lamp correctly (see page 328).
	Starter defective or wrong size.	Replace starter.
	If fixture is on a dimmer circuit, dimmer is defective or improperly adjusted.	Replace or adjust dimmer (see pages 362-363).
	Ballast defective.	Replace ballast as last resort and only if there is clear evidence of failure (smoke from fixture, acrid odor, fixture too hot).
Lamp flickers or blinks on and off.	Newness (normal for a short period with some new lamps).	None required.
	Low line voltage.	Check with local utility company if low line voltage is suspected.
	Temperature below 50 degrees Fahrenheit in lamp location, or cold draft on lamp.	If condition is permanent, shield lamp from draft or install low-temperature ballast.
	Starter defective.	Replace starter.
	Lamp-ballast mismatch.	Make sure lamp is type specified by fixture manufacturer.
	Lamp not properly seated in holders, or lamp pins bent.	Remove lamp. Check pins. If necessary, straighten pins with pliers. Clean pins with steel wool. Make sure lamp is properly seated in holders.
Short lamp life.	Specified lamp life is average. Some lamps will fail early.	None required (some lamps will burn longer than average).
	Lamp turned off and on frequently.	Avoid turning lamp off and on for short periods.
	If lamp fails within a few hours, ballast is wrong for fixture or is incorrectly wired.	Correct wiring or replace ballast.
	In some rapid-start and instant-start two-lamp fixtures, when one lamp burns out, the other lamp will dim or fail.	Replace burned-out lamps immediately. Substitute a good lamp for each lamp in the fixture, one at a time. When burned-out lamp is replaced, both lamps will light.
Tube ends discolored.	Normal near end of lamp life (see page 328).	Replace lamp.
	If lamp life is short, poor contact between pins and socket.	Clean and straighten lamp pins. Clean or replace lamp holder.
	Discoloration consisting of brownish rings at one or both ends may occur during normal operation.	None required.
Dark lengthwise streaks on lamp.	Condensed mercury on the lower part of the lamp; occurs when lower part is cooler than upper part.	Reposition lamp so that dark streaks are at top.
Excessive hum from the fixture.	Ballast causes hum. Some hum is normal. Hum will increase if ballast is loose or is overheating.	Turn off power. Open fixture. Check that ballast is securely mounted. Check that all connections are tight. Check that ballast is marked as correct for that fixture. Make sure ballast is properly ventilated. See page 328 for more on noise level.
Color variations in lamps of same type.	Some variation in color is normal.	None required.
	Significant age difference in lamps.	Substitute new lamps.
	Lamps operating at different temperatures.	Check for drafts. Equalize temperature as much as possible.
Radio interference (audible buzz).	Lamp radiation being picked up by radio antenna.	Separate radio and fixture as much as possible. Radio and antenna lead should be at least 8 feet from 40-watt fluorescent lighting and 20 feet from high-wattage tubes. Place metal screening (decorative screening may be used) around the fixture. Ground the screening to the fixture ground. Starter or ballast may be defective. Replace starter or ballast.
	Fixture radiation being transmitted through 120-volt power line.	Install a radio-interference filter between the fixture and the 120-volt power source. Both wired and plug-in type filters are available.

Doorbells and chimes

Doorbells and chimes operate on a much lower voltage than other home electrical devices. The operating voltages range from 10 to 20 volts; 16 volts is the most common. This low voltage is obtained by reducing the normal 120-volt power to the required 10- to 20-volt level. The device that provides the drop in voltage is a transformer. The transformer used for doorbell and chime circuits is a small apparatus—roughly the size of a softball. It has four electrical connections: two wires and two screw terminals. The wires are black and white and connect to a 120-volt power source. The screw terminals are the low-voltage output.

Normally, the transformer is located in the basement, close to a power source. The rest of the circuit—connected to the screw terminals on the transformer—is low voltage. Low-voltage wiring may be done with lightweight wire. No. 18 or 20 insulated wire, known as bell wire, is commonly used. There is no danger of serious shock or fire from low-voltage wiring.

In addition to the transformer, the doorbell or chime circuit consists of one or more push buttons at doors and, of course, the bell, buzzer, or chime unit. The low-voltage wiring may be routed through walls and behind baseboards and moldings with no special covering or protection. All the techniques shown elsewhere in this book for routing cable between floors and through walls may be used to route bell wire.

The diagrams opposite show the most frequently used installation circuits. Use these diagrams to make new installations or repair old circuits.

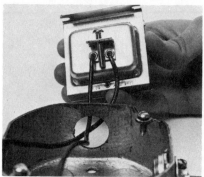

Installing the transformer. The connection of the transformer to the 120-volt power source is the only part of doorbell-circuit wiring covered by most electrical codes.

Turn off power at the service panel. Select a convenient wall or ceiling box for power tie-in near the planned transformer location. Connect the new transformer power cable to a 120-volt source cable in the wall or ceiling box. Terminate the new cable at a junction box. Remove a second knockout from the junction box and mount the box at the point where the transformer will be mounted. In basement areas the box and transformer are usually mounted on a joist.

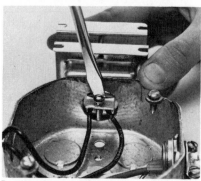

Put the threaded projection of the transformer (on the high-voltage side where the black and white wires are) through the knockout in the box. Secure the transformer to the box with a locknut. Connect the transformer wires to the power wires. Connect black to black and white to white. Be sure to connect the source-cable grounding wire to the junction box.

Connect the low-voltage wires to the screw terminals on the transformer. It will be easier to wire the rest of the circuit if the low-voltage bell wires are different colors. One color wire can be routed directly to the doorbell unit or units. The other color can be used to wire the push button or buttons to the doorbell unit.

Mounting the button and bell. Doorbell push buttons are mounted with two wood screws. You need only route the bell wire to the door, drill a ⅝-inch hole at the unobstructed button location, and fish the bell wire out through the opening. The wires are connected to screw terminals on the button. The button is secured to the door frame with wood screws. Whenever possible, situate the button under an overhang and out of the rain so the metal contacts on the button won't corrode. Route the bell wire through the wall to come out directly behind the bell, buzzer, or chime unit, following the manufacturer's instructions.

Troubleshooting doorbells and chimes

Bell does not sound.

Cause: Defective push button.
Correction: Remove push-button mounting screws. Loosen one screw terminal and remove wire. Touch wire to other terminal. If bell sounds, replace push button. If bell does not sound, check transformer and bell unit.

Cause: No power to transformer, or defective transformer.
Correction: Use voltage tester to check for 120-volt power at transformer wires. If OK, check for voltage at transformer low-voltage terminals. Use a low-voltage tester or voltmeter. If voltage does not register, replace transformer.

Cause: Defective bell unit.
Correction: If transformer is OK, connect two wires directly from transformer to bell unit. If bell does not sound, replace bell unit. If chime units do not sound, check for free movement of plunger. If plunger sticks, it can be cleaned with a small brush dipped in lighter fluid or silicone spray. Do not oil plunger.

Cause: Defective wiring.
Correction: If push button, transformer, and bell unit check OK, defective wiring is probable. Rewire the circuit. Use old wires to pull new ones through floor and wall openings.

Bell not loud enough.

Cause: Wrong combination of transformer and bell unit.
Correction: Check voltage required for bell unit. It is marked on unit near the screw terminals. Check voltage output marked on transformer. Replace either transformer or bell to get proper match.

Cause: Loose wire or corroded terminal.
Correction: Check terminals on transformer, push button, and bell unit. Clean, tighten, or replace as necessary.

Bell sounds continuously.

Cause: Shorted push button.
Correction: Check push-button contacts. Clean contacts or replace push button.

How doorbells are wired

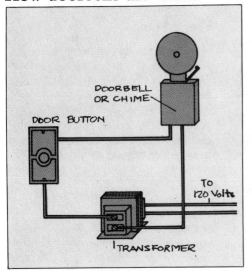

Two-terminal doorbell, chime, or buzzer wired for control from a single button.

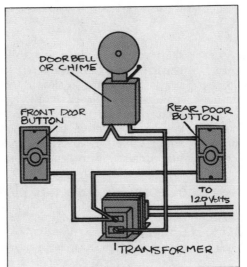

Two-terminal doorbell or chime wired to allow two buttons to ring one bell.

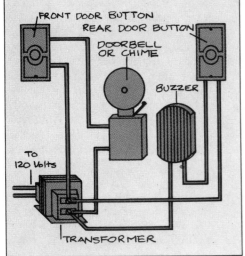

Two-terminal doorbell or chime and two-terminal buzzer wired for separate control.

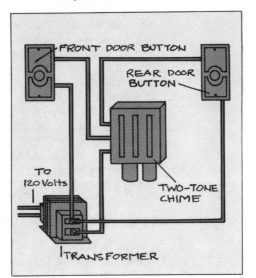

Two-tone chime wired for front- and rear-door control—two tones for front door, one tone for rear.

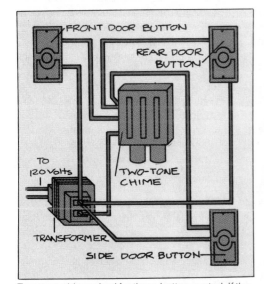

Two-tone chime wired for three-button control. If the chime has three terminals, the two-tone terminal can be wired to the front door and the single-tone terminal to the other doors.

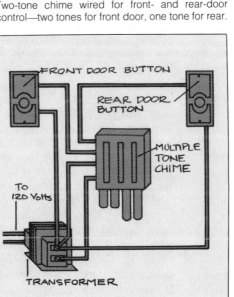

Multiple-tone chime wired for a two-button control—multiple tones for front door, single tone for rear door. Connect wires as marked on terminals.

What it takes

Approximate time: 1 to 2 hours.

Tools and materials: Bell, buzzer or chimes, one or more door buttons, bell transformer, junction box, cable clamps, cable, screwdriver, wire stripper or knife, solderless connectors.

Bats in the belfry

I bought a set of chimes that gave off a lovely, loud sound when I tested them at the hardware store. But when I wired them into the transformer on my old doorbell system, they gave off a dull, feeble "bonk" you could hardly hear. After I made a couple of trips to the store and back, the dealer asked what kind of transformer I had. It turned out that the old transformer could handle the doorbell but was the wrong match for the new chimes. Copy the specs from the old transformer and bring them with you when you go to buy new chimes, or be prepared to make a second trip for a new matching transformer.

Practical Pete

How to check the sound level of a new doorbell location.

After the transformer has been installed, temporarily connect two long lengths of bell wire to the transformer low-voltage terminals. Connect one of the wires to one terminal on the bell, buzzer, or chime. Turn on power to the transformer circuit. Then hold the doorbell at or close to the planned location. Briefly touch the other wire from the transformer to the other terminal of the doorbell. This will cause the bell or chime to ring. Have a helper go around the house to check that the bell is audible. A change in location of only a few feet can often make a big difference in the sound level.

Troubleshooting branch circuits

If trouble develops in part of your home electrical system, you can usually determine the cause and, in most cases, correct the trouble by making a series of inspections and tests.

Two types of branch-circuit failure can occur: no power in one or more circuits or a short in one circuit. The short will cause a circuit breaker to trip to OFF as soon as you reset it, or it will cause a fuse to blow as soon as main power is turned on. Either condition may occur due to failure in your house power cables. Failure within cables, however, is extremely rare. Breaks in wires and even shorts between conductors may occur in *new* wiring. But they seldom appear in wiring that has been satisfactory for a period of time *unless a cable is damaged*. When power failures or shorts occur, make an especially careful check of all wiring and circuit boxes near recent repairs or renovation.

No power—circuit breaker not tripped, fuse not blown

Complete power failure in your home is probably due to failure in utility power lines. Report this type of problem to your utility company.

There are three types of *partial* power failure:

Loss of power on several circuits—like full power failure—is most likely to be a problem that must be corrected by your utility company. If your house has three-wire service (most homes do), failure can occur in half of the utility-supplied power. Report this type of failure to your utility company.

Loss of power on only one circuit appears to be the same as a tripped circuit breaker or blown fuse. If a check reveals that the circuit breaker is not tripped, or the fuse is not blown, the power loss must have occurred between the service panel and the first outlet, junction box, or ceiling box that's on the circuit. Set the circuit breaker to OFF, or remove the fuse, and make the circuit inspection described below. If there are no loose or broken wires, the trouble is probably in the service panel. The circuit breaker may be defective or the fuse contacts broken. Working inside a service panel can be dangerous. Your best bet is to let a licensed electrician find and correct the trouble.

Partial loss of power on one circuit can almost always be traced to a defective switch or outlet or an open connection in a box. With circuit power turned on, use your voltage tester to determine exactly which parts of the circuit have power and which do not. Next, turn off power to the circuit. Make a careful inspection of the wiring in each electrical box that appears to have no power. Look for loose connections on switches and outlets. Check that solderless connectors are in place and are tight. Check for broken wires at or near connections. Conductors can be nicked when insulation is removed. Additional strain is put on the conductor when it is bent around a screw terminal. Breaks can occur at these points.

Short circuit—breaker trips or fuse blows immediately

Follow the procedure described on page 306. If plug-in appliances and lamps on the failed circuit have been checked and found to be OK, the short circuit must then be in the circuit wiring.

Visual check. With the circuit breaker off, or the fuse removed, take off faceplates and check wiring in all switch and outlet boxes. Keep your voltage tester handy and remember to test before you touch any bare wires. *When a circuit is defective, power may be present where it normally would not be.*

In each box, look for broken or exposed conductors or missing solderless connectors. If wiring appears OK, disconnect and check switches. Use your continuity tester and follow procedures on page 324. If the tester lights when it should not, the switch has an internal short and should be replaced. Shorts in outlets are rare but can happen. Remove the outlet. Connect the alligator clip on the continuity tester to a brass terminal. Insert the probe in all slots. Touch the probe to the mounting bracket and, if the outlet has one, to the green-tinted grounding screw. The tester should light only in one top slot and one bottom slot. If the connecting metal tab between the brass terminals has been removed, repeat the test with the alligator clip connected to the other brass terminal. In this case the tester should light in only *one* slot during the test of each brass terminal.

Ceiling boxes and junction boxes are harder to get at than wall outlets, so leave them until last. Make the same inspection described above for wall boxes. The canopy on a ceiling fixture must be loosened and the fixture lowered for you to check the wiring inside a ceiling box (see pages 326-327). Do not allow fixtures to hang by their electrical connections.

Electrical check. If the cause of the short circuit cannot be determined by the visual check, electrical tests should be made to locate the trouble. The general procedure for the electrical check consists of disconnecting portions of the circuit and then turning on power to the remaining portions. At the point where the circuit breaker no longer trips—or the fuse does not blow—when power is again turned on, the disconnected portion of the circuit contains the short.

Once you have isolated the trouble to a small part of the circuit, the job of locating the defect becomes easier. Detailed continuity checks can be made for every device on the defective portion of the circuit. Check cabling with your continuity tester. Connect the alligator clip to a black wire. Touch the probe to all white wires and to ground wires in the box. The tester should not light. (Remove all light bulbs from fixtures on the defective portion of the circuit when checking cabling.) The procedure for making electrical checks at the main test points in a branch circuit is described opposite. Adapt it as necessary to fit test points available in your particular circuit.

Junction box

The junction box serves as a tie point for two sections of the circuit. Be sure power is off at the service panel and test all wires before you touch them. Remove solderless connectors and separate all wires. No wires should touch each other or any metal.

Turn on power at the service panel. If the circuit breaker trips to OFF or the fuse blows, the short must be in the service panel or in the wiring between the service panel and the junction box.

If the circuit breaker stays on or the fuse does not blow, the wiring from the service panel to the junction box is OK. At the junction box, use your voltage tester to determine which black and white wires are connected to the service panel. Touch the tester probes to each pair of wires until the tester lights. Do not touch bare wires.

Turn off power at the service panel. Connect the black and white wires from the service panel to one of the other pairs of wires, using solderless connectors. Turn the power back on at the service panel. If power stays on, the portion of the circuit connected to the service-panel line is OK. In the diagram at right, for example, if pair A is connected to pair B, and pair C is left unconnected, the short would have to be in the portion of the circuit powered by cable C.

Middle-of-run ceiling box

Turn off power to the circuit. At a middle-of-run ceiling box, disconnect and separate all cables. Disconnect the fixture. At the junction box, connect source-cable A to source-cable B. Turn on power. If power stays on, either the fixture or one of the cables connected to source-cable B contains the short.

Turn off power. Connect one cable to the source cable. Turn on power. If, for example, cable D is connected to source-cable B and power stays on, the short is either in the fixture or in the loop switch.

Turn off power. Connect the black-coded white wire from the loop switch to the power cable. Turn power on again. If power stays on, the short is in the ceiling fixture. Check it with your continuity tester as described under "Testing the parts of a lamp" (page 322).

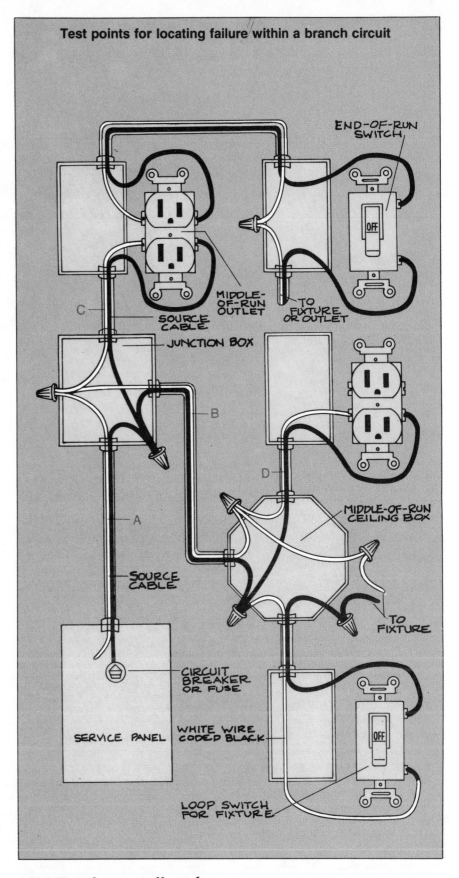

Test points for locating failure within a branch circuit

Middle-of-run wall outlet

A middle-of-run wall outlet is a good point at which to disconnect a portion of the circuit. With power off, disconnect and separate all wires. Turn on power. If power stays on, the short is in the portion of the circuit past the end-of-run outlet, as shown in the diagram above.

4. NEW WIRING

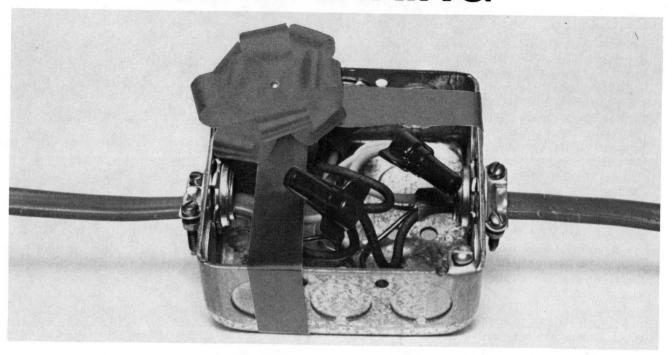

This chapter tells you:
- How to plan your new wiring to make the best use of the electric power available (page 335).
- How to select the best place to connect your new circuit to your present wiring (page 336).
- How to route cables to keep the carpentry work as simple as possible (page 338).
- How to make the electrical connection (page 340).

As your family grows and matures and as your life-style changes, your home wiring system should change too. When receptacles become crowded with plugs and a tangle of extension cords is concealed behind a sofa or chair—or when you want to make an attic livable—you can make your system safer and more convenient yourself by adding new wiring, outlets, and fixtures to the circuits in your existing wiring.

Advance planning. When you install a circuit extension, two important points must be considered: First, the additional electrical load that will be carried by the new wiring must be added to your present circuits in a way that will avoid overloads. Second, the outlets, switches, and cables you will install must be planned to fit the construction of your house. Advance planning in this area will make it possible to do a neat, professional job with minimum effort and a maximum of satisfaction.

Which circuit to add onto?

Check the circuits that are available in the area of your house in which the circuit extension is needed. Usually you will find that more than one circuit can be used. Your main service panel shows the voltage and amperage rating of the circuit breaker or fuse that protects each available circuit. Multiply the amperage rating of the circuit breaker or fuse by the voltage of the line (120 or 240) to determine the maximum wattage that the circuit can carry.

For example, a 15-amp circuit breaker or fuse on a 120-volt line can carry 1800 watts; a 20-amp circuit breaker or fuse on a 120-volt line can carry 2400 watts.

Next, calculate the present load on the circuits. To do this, add up the wattage of all lights on the circuit and all appliances that are plugged into receptacles on the circuit. The difference between the present circuit load and the maximum circuit wattage is, in principle, the amount that can be added. But it is wise to leave a margin of safety in this calculation in case you later want to add a new appliance or replace an existing one with another that consumes more watts. On a 120-volt line, for example, try to limit the 15-amp circuit to 1500 watts and the 20-amp circuit to 2000 watts. Remember, too, that appliances containing motors of one-quarter horsepower or more (humidifiers, fans, small air conditioners) always draw heavy current when starting. The margins of safety noted above will

allow for this. The motors in phono turntables and tape players are quite small and need not be given special consideration. Use the wattage rating on the manufacturer's nameplate.

If you wish to add a larger appliance (large air conditioners, room heaters, stoves, dryers), a new 240-volt circuit, or even an increase in the service provided by your utility company, may be required. In either case, these changes should be made by a licensed electrician.

If a new circuit is needed, you can keep the cost to a minimum by having an electrician wire the new circuit from your circuit-breaker or fuse panel to a convenient junction box. You can do the wiring from there to the outlets you need.

Evaluating available power

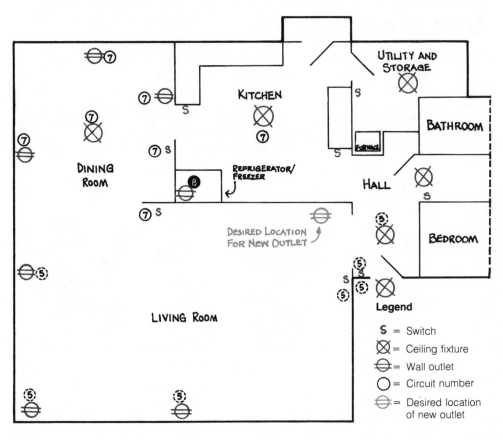

The best source of information for planning circuit extensions is a circuit map. The procedure for preparing a circuit map of your home is explained on page 307. The map shown here is a typical example. It is referred to in the text and in the circuit-analysis chart below.

Legend

S = Switch

⊗ = Ceiling fixture

⊖ = Wall outlet

○ = Circuit number

⊖ = Desired location of new outlet

In this example, let's assume the new outlet you are planning is to be used for a console-type color-television set. The manufacturer's nameplate on the TV indicates that the power rating of the set is 280 watts.

All three circuits appear to have sufficient capacity available for this extra load. It would be unwise, however, to connect the new outlet to circuit number eight. At first glance it would appear that there is sufficient capacity (1250 watts for a 280-watt load) and a convenient location on the opposite side of an interior wall.

The difficulty in this case would arise from the heavy surge of current that occurs each time a large motor, such as that used in the refrigerator/ freezer, is started. This surge would cause an annoying shrinkage of the TV picture and loss of synchronization for several seconds. A momentary circuit overload would also occur. The choice then is between circuits five and seven. Since circuit five has greater capacity available, it should be the first choice, but either circuit could handle the additional load. The next step in planning the circuit extension is to check the electrical boxes on circuits five and seven to find the easiest place to connect the new power cable. The decision on where to make the connection should also take into account the possible ways of routing the new cable. The next few pages give you the information you need to complete the plan.

How to calculate unused capacity in circuits potentially available for extensions			
Circuit available	**No. ⑤ circuit (15 amps)**	**No. ⑦ circuit (15 amps)**	**No. ⑧ circuit (20 amps)**
Total power available	1800 watts	1800 watts	2400 watts
Less safety margin	300 watts	300 watts	400 watts
Less present load*	650 watts	1050 watts	750 watts
Capacity available	**850 watts**	**450 watts**	**1250 watts**

*Analysis of present load	Outside
	  light ———— 100 watts
	Entrance
	  light ———— 100 watts
	Living-room
	  lamps (3) ——— 450 watts
	
	Total ———— 650 watts
		Dining-room
		  ceiling fixture ——600 watts
		Kitchen
		  ceiling fixture ——150 watts
		Dining-room
		  stereo outlets ——300 watts
		
		Total ———— 1050 watts
			Refrigerator/
			  freezer ——— 750 watts

Where to join into a circuit

To decide where to connect into an existing circuit, you must be able to identify the job each wire is doing inside each box on the circuit. Various kinds of wall and ceiling boxes are used on general-purpose circuits. All of the types that you are likely to be using are shown on page 312. To deter-mine the function of a box and where it is connected electrically in the present circuit wiring, compare the connections in the box with the descriptions on these pages. On page 312, you will find the recommended maximum number of wires for each box. (See page 310 for additional information.)

To open ceiling boxes

1. Turn the fixture on by setting the wall switch that controls the light to the ON position.
2. Turn off power at the service panel. The fixture should now be off. Leave the wall switch in the ON position.
3. Remove the screws or nuts that hold the fixture to the ceiling. Pull the fixture out of the box to expose the wires to view.

4. Support the weight of the fixture with one hand while you unscrew the wire nuts (page 315). The weight of the fixture should now separate the wires; if not, grasping them by the insulation, pull each set apart.
5. Set the fixture aside and loosely reassemble the hardware so you won't forget how it goes together.

The receptacle diagrams show three-prong-type outlets with ground-ing wires attached. On page 339, for the sake of simplicity, grounding wires are not shown. Grounding wires must be connected when the new cable is installed. Illustrations on pages 340 and 341 show how to connect ground-ing wires.

To open wall boxes

1. Before you start taking any electrical box or fixture apart, turn off the circuit breaker or remove the fuse that protects the circuit to be checked.
2. Remove the cover plates from the wall boxes that are most convenient for con-necting the circuit extension you wish to add. Remember to *test before you touch* any exposed wires or terminals.
3. To see how the box is wired, you may have to loosen the screws that secure switches and receptacles to the boxes, and pull the switch or receptacle all the way out.

How to distinguish typical wiring functions

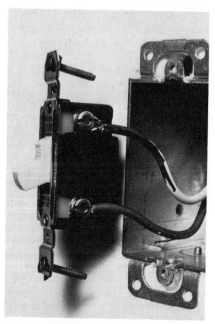 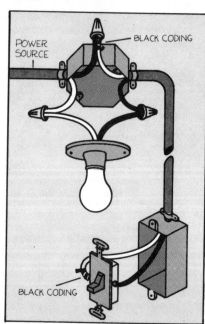

Loop switch. The wall switch shown here is called a loop switch because it completes the hot-wire circuit to a fixture. It can be identified by the black coding added to the white wire (paint or tape put on the ends of the white neutral wire when it was used as a hot wire). Loop-switch receptacles contain no true neutral wire, so you cannot make a connection to the circuit at that point.

Case number 1: End-of-run ceiling fixture with loop-switch control. This ceiling fix-ture is the last device on the circuit (end-of-run) and is controlled by a wall loop switch. You can connect into the line only at the ceil-ing box. This is easy if the box is accessi-ble from an attic or crawl space. If a larger box is required, you can install it from the attic or crawl-space side without damaging the finished ceiling.

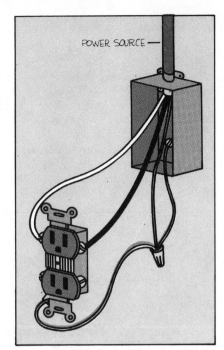

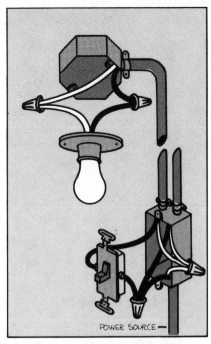

Case number 2: Middle-of-run ceiling fixture with loop-switch control. This is similar to case number 1, except that circuit power continues beyond the fixture. Because of the extra cable to the rest of the run, the middle-of-run ceiling box is likely to become overcrowded if an additional cable is added. As in the case of the end-of-run ceiling box, the ease or difficulty of box replacement depends on box location.

Case number 3: End-of-run receptacle. If the receptacle is *not* controlled by a switch this is the ideal point at which to tie in new wiring. The box is uncrowded. Only one cable is in the existing box. The new cable can easily be brought into the box and connected to the spare receptacle terminals.

Case number 4: Middle-of-run switch. As in case number 2, overcrowding of the box is likely, and enlarging the box will require considerable wall repair. Unless you are planning to install paneling or paper the walls, this is not a good choice for tie-in.

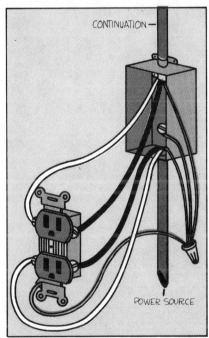

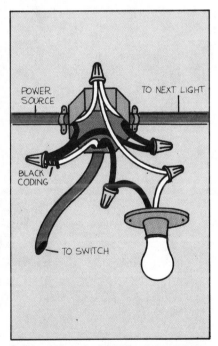

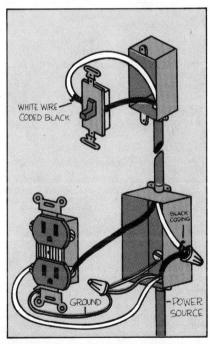

Case number 5: Middle-of-run receptacle. If the box is large enough and the receptacle has no switch, tie in at this point. You should not connect more than one wire to screw-type terminals, and jumpers might overcrowd the box. Substitution of a larger box or ganging the existing box with another can be a problem, as noted in case number 4. If so, look for another tie-in point.

Case number 6: Junction box. Junction boxes are good tie-in points if they are reasonably accessible. CAUTION: Junction boxes may be used for more than one circuit. Don't assume all power is off because one circuit breaker is off or one fuse has been removed. TEST BEFORE YOU TOUCH.

Case number 7: Switched end-of-run receptacle. Electrically, a switched receptacle is similar to a switched ceiling fixture. Since a switched receptacle is wall mounted, cable routing is usually easier. But you must take special care when making connection to a switched receptacle. Page 341 shows the difference in connection, depending on whether the added circuit is, or is not, to be controlled by the switch. Check box size. Overcrowding of the box may be a problem.

Planning where to run new cable

At this point you have checked the electrical boxes available for the circuit extension, and you have decided which box is the best place to make the connection to your existing system. If possible, at this stage in the plan, have more than one tie-in box in mind. The best way to route the new cable depends mostly on the purpose of the extension. Cable-routing ideas for specific installations are included in the detailed instructions in the balance of this chapter. There are, however, certain points that you should keep in mind when planning the best way to route cables for any installation. These points are related to common structural factors found in most houses built within the last thirty years. The illustration below shows a typical frame construction.

Places to run electric cable

A. Interior walls and ceilings are easiest to work with. The space between wall surfaces is usually empty—except for existing wiring—and clear of obstructions.

B. In multifloor homes with basements, it is usually best to make first-floor runs along floor joists, accessible from the basement.

C. Second floor runs are best made along second-floor ceiling joists, accessible from the attic or crawl space.

D. Exterior walls are difficult to work with. They may be solid masonry (or concrete block), with no hollow spaces for routing wires and sinking boxes. Even if they are made of wood and framed like interior partitions, the spaces between studs are likely to be insulated, are almost certain to be interrupted by fire-stops (horizontal wood pieces inserted between studs to block the spread of flame). They may also have diagonal braces running across them. If you must extend wiring across an exterior wall, consider surface wiring. See page 372.

E. To make a run between basement and attic or crawl space, check the plumbing-vent-pipe area. This pipe runs from the basement sewer line up through the house to the roof. The space provided for the pipe is usually clear, fairly large, and unobstructed from the basement to the attic. It is much easier to drop a cable through this area than to penetrate walls and floors.

Instructions for carpentry required to run cable in various locations begin on page 350.

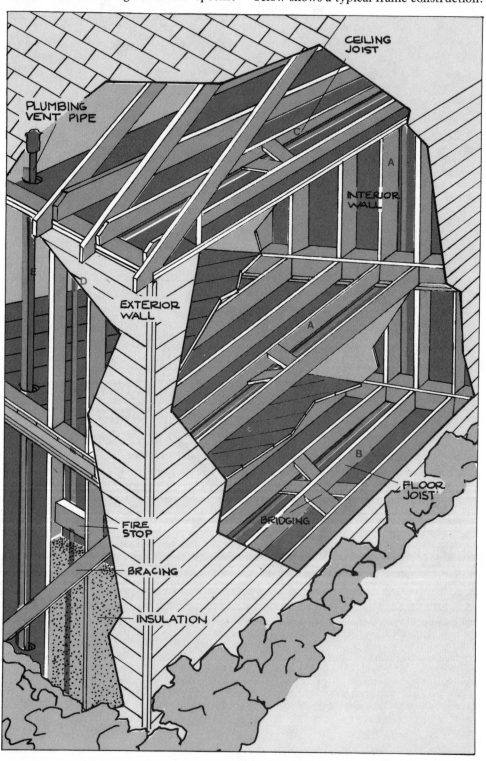

How to identify wires in electrical boxes

When you have decided which box you will use to connect your new cable to the existing wiring, you have to identify and tag the wires in the box. You need to know which wires go to the power source. Your new cable will be connected to the source cable. To avoid wiring errors, it is necessary to know which wires go to the rest of the run (if the box is middle-of-the-run) and which are switch wires. The continuity tester is helpful in checking switch wiring.

Check the testers before using them. The voltage-tester bulb should light when the probes are inserted in the slots of a "live" receptacle. The continuity-tester bulb should light when the probe and alligator clip are touching.

When you have identified the source cable and, if present, the switch cable, you know all you need to know about the wires in the box. Cables in the box other than source cable and switch cable are cables to receptacles, outlets, switches, or ceiling or junction boxes on the same circuit.

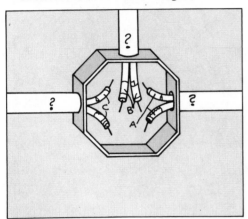

Source cable

1. Turn off all power to the box.
2. Separate all conductors that were joined by wire nuts. To simplify reconnecting the wires, tag wires to show which were joined. Use colored plastic tape or tape that can be marked with ball-point pen. Code all wires joined by one wire nut with one letter. Code the first group "A," the next group "B," and so forth.
3. After tagging, spread out all the wires in the box so that the bare conductors do not touch each other, the box itself, or any nearby metal surface. It is important to do this carefully to avoid a short circuit between black and white conductors or between a black conductor and ground.

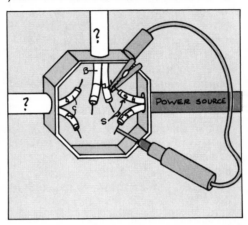

4. Use alligator clips to connect your voltage tester to a black and a white wire entering the box from a single cable, as shown above.
5. Turn on power at the service panel. If the tester bulb lights, the cable the tester is connected to is the source cable. If the bulb does not light, turn off power at the service panel. Remove the tester from the first pair of wires and connect it to the wires of another cable entering the box. Repeat the procedure. Continue until you locate the source cable.
6. When you have identified the source cable, turn off power and mark the tags on the source-cable wires with an "S" or other code letter. You will connect your circuit extension to these two wires, either directly or by means of jumpers, as shown.

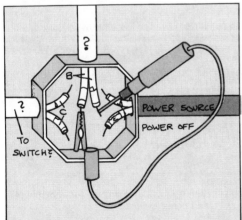

Switch wires

If the box you are working with has a switch connection, the loop cable to the switch can be easily identified with the continuity tester.

1. Turn off all power to the box.
2. The wires in the box should be disconnected and spread, as in step 2 above.
3. Set the wall switch to ON.

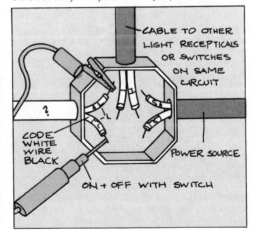

4. Touch the continuity-tester probe and alligator clip in turn to each pair of black and white wires.
5. When the tester lights, have an assistant flip the wall switch on and off a few times.
6. If the tester light goes on and off as the switch is moved, mark those wires "L" for loop.
7. If the tester light remains on, regardless of the switch position, continue checking other pairs of wires until you find the pair controlled by the switch.

Connecting
new cable

Remember, if you are working with a junction box containing cables on more than one circuit, you will have to turn off two circuit breakers—or remove two fuses—to turn off all power in the box. In this case there will be two source cables. You can identify both by following the procedure given on page 339. When the voltage tester is connected to the wires in the box, turn on power to one circuit at a time. In this way you will know which source cable is connected to which circuit breaker or fuse.

Also, grounding wires of all cables entering a box should be joined. If plastic-sheathed cable is used, a jumper should be connected from the (usually uninsulated) grounding-wire connection to the metal box. If steel-armored cable is used, the box is grounded automatically when the cable ground wire, the cable clamp, and the clamp mounting are installed.

What it takes

Approximate time: 1 to 2 hours.

Tools and materials: Plastic-sheathed, or armor-covered cable, cable clamps, screwdriver, wire stripper or knife, solderless connectors.

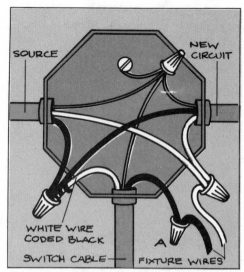

Connecting new cable to end-of-run ceiling fixture with loop-switch control. When the new circuit is added, two of the connections will join three wires, rather than two. Be sure to use large-size solderless connections (wire nuts). As shown, the new circuit will not be controlled by the loop switch. If control by the switch is desired, connect the new-circuit black wire with the switch cable and fixture wire at point A.

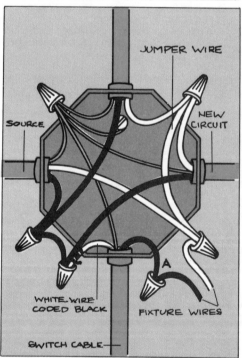

Connecting new cable to middle-of-run ceiling fixture with loop-switch control. Note that jumper wires are required to assure a good conductor connection with wire nuts. Bare grounding wires may be joined as shown. As with the end-of-run ceiling fixture with loop-switch control, if you want to control the new circuit from the present ceiling light switch, connect the new-circuit black wire at point A. Assuming that the box shown also contains a mounting stud for the ceiling fixture, the box would have to be at least 2⅛ inches deep to accommodate the additional connections.

Connecting new cable to end-of-run receptacle. This is the easiest connection to make. The outlet shown is a three-prong grounded type, not under switch control. The new circuit is connected to the spare screw terminals at the outlet. Be certain both black wires are connected to the brass-colored terminals on the receptacle.

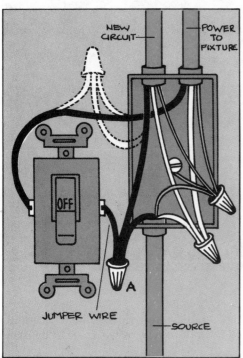

Connecting new cable to middle-of-run switch.
To provide switch control of the new circuit in this instance, connect the new-circuit black wire, the black wire to the fixture, and a jumper to the switch, as shown by the dotted lines. In this case the connections at point A would not have to be made. The black wire from the source would remain directly connected to the switch.

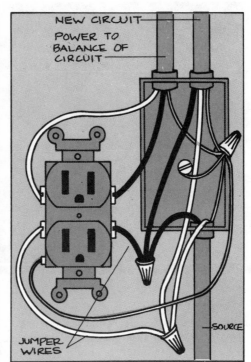

Connecting new cable to middle-of-run receptacle. Screw-type terminals should never be used to join wires. Only one wire should be connected to each terminal. Make additional connections with jumper wires, as shown, or by using spare terminals.

Population explosion
Have you ever tried to carry two mean dogs, a strange alley cat, and a bantam rooster in the back of your station wagon?

I picked the perfect wall box to run my new wiring out of. Opened it up and it was already pretty full. Well, trying to connect the new wiring onto that mess of connectors and jam it all back in the box was only slightly easier and quicker than performing dentistry on a diamondback rattler in a gunnysack full of his relatives.

Practical Pete

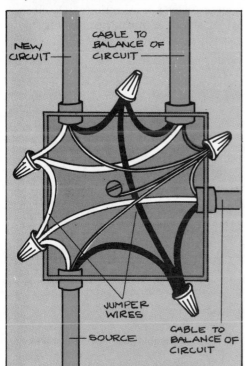

Connecting new cable to junction box. This junction box contains wiring for only one circuit. Remember, junction boxes may contain wiring for more than one circuit. Test before you touch.

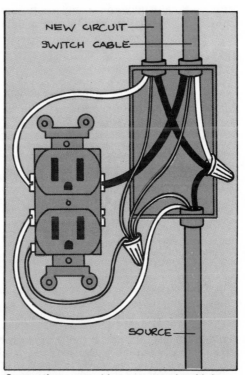

Connecting new cable to receptacle with loop-switch control. If the new-circuit black wire were connected to the spare brass-colored terminal on the outlet, the new circuit would be controlled by the same switch that controls the outlet.

5.SWITCHES

What switches do electrically

The simplest and most common switch used in home wiring is the Single-Pole, Single-Throw (SPST) type. This switch completes or interrupts the hot-wire circuit. Electrically, it acts just like the old-fashioned knife switch (drawing, page 343). SPST switches have two terminals.

Another type of switch is used in circuits that allow lights or outlets to be controlled from two locations. This type is the Single-Pole, Double-Throw (SPDT) switch. This switch allows a conductor connected to the center (or common) terminal to be connected to either of two wires. SPDT switches have three terminals and are sometimes known as three-way switches. Don't let this name confuse you. Remember, these switches can be used only to control a light or outlet from *two* locations, and the switches have only *two* positions.

When you want to control lights or outlets from three or more locations, a third type of switch must be used. This is referred to as a special type of Double-Pole, Double-Throw (DPDT) switch. This switch has four terminals. Current can flow through the switch in both switch positions. The difference is that one position provides straight-through connections and the other position provides crossover connections. Connected pairs of terminals need no OFF.

Standard toggle switches

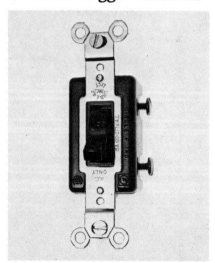

Single-pole, single-throw toggle switch. This is the type of switch most often encountered in house wiring. It has two brass-colored terminals. The switch positions are marked OFF and ON. Terminals may be located on the side, top or front of the switch.

Single-pole, double-throw toggle switch. Two things are special about this switch; it has three terminals, and it does *not* have OFF and ON markings. The three terminals usually consist of two brass-colored terminals and one copper-colored terminal. In all cases, one terminal (the common terminal) is darker than the other two.

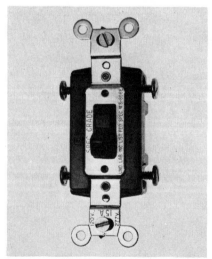

Special double-pole, double-throw toggle switch. This switch can be distinguished from the SPDT switch only by the number and color of terminals. The DPDT switch has four terminals all the same color. It, too, has no OFF or ON markings. There is always an electrical connection between pairs of terminals, and so the switch is never "off."

Special-function switches

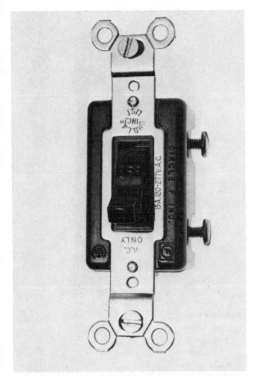

Quiet switch. This switch is mechanically designed to move from one position to the other with almost no noise. It is available in all electrical types. A quiet switch is slightly more expensive than a snap-action switch. In any installation where switch noise is objectionable, a quiet switch should be considered.

Locking switch. This switch must be unlocked with a key before power can be turned on. It is especially useful when you want to prevent unauthorized use of power tools or outside outlets. Locking switches with the UL symbol are designed so that metal objects inserted into the keyhole cannot come in contact with electrical parts.

Old-fashioned knife switches

Three common types are shown, below, to demonstrate how switches act to complete the electrical circuit. Because of their exposed terminals, knife switches should *never* be used in home power wiring.

SPST
Single-Pole, Single-Throw

SPDT
Single-Pole, Double-Throw

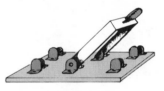

DPDT
Double-Pole, Double-Throw

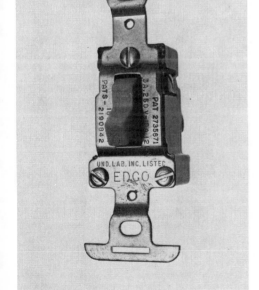

Time-delay switch. This switch contains a short-term timer (about 45 seconds). When the switch is turned off, the timer is started, and the light will remain on for about 45 seconds. This gives you enough time to get into the house or to another lighted area before the switch turns the light off.

Time-clock switch. This switch provides the same control as a plug-in timer, but it can be mounted in wall switch boxes. It can be used to control lights, air conditioners or other devices over a 24-hour period.

A toggle switch with four terminals *and* OFF and ON markings is sometimes used to control each 120-volt half of the 240-volt power to large appliances. This type of DPDT switch *cannot* be used for multiple-control installations.

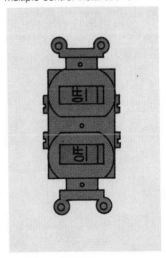

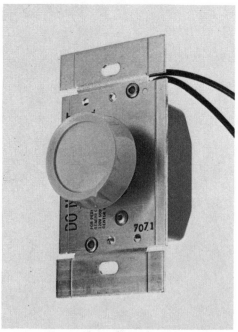

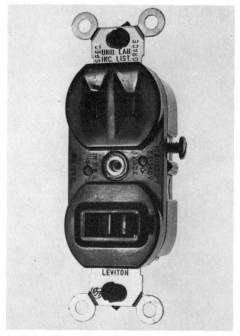

Dimmer switch. A dimmer switch combines switch control and brightness control in one package. A dimmer switch is slightly larger than a standard switch but can be installed in the same switch box. In addition to the usual switch markings, a dimmer switch has maximum-control wattage ratings. A common rating is 600 watts. This means that the total wattage of bulbs in the fixture controlled by the dimmer must not be greater than 600 watts.

Switch-receptacle combination. This device combines a standard SPST switch and one wall outlet in a single package. It provides an easy way to add a receptacle at any middle-of-run or end-of-run switch location. Loop switches contain no neutral wire conductor, and therefore a receptacle cannot be installed at that location. (For switch-receptacle wiring, see page 345.)

Who needs static?
Don't take it out on your TV set when interference is caused by a lighting-fixture dimmer switch on the same circuit. Dimmer switches are for lighting control only and can disrupt reception on TVs and radios. It's better to plug these appliances into another circuit. If you must use the same circuit, various kinds of interference suppressors, which may be added to the TV or radio power cord, are available. See page 346 and 347 for dimmer-switch installation guidelines.
Practical Pete

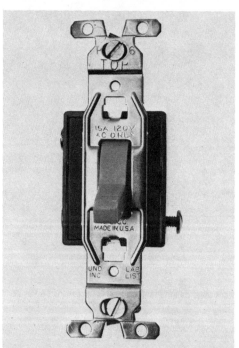

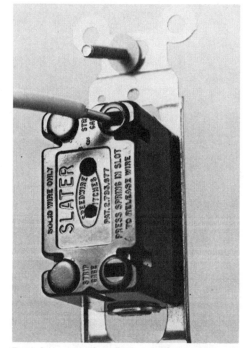

Silent (mercury) switch. This type of switch makes electrical contact by tilting a sealed container of mercury. When the mercury flows to one end of the container, it completes the circuit between two switch contacts. When tilted the other way, the mercury flows away from the contacts, and the switch is off. This action is completely silent and almost wear-free. A mercury switch is more expensive than a snap-action or quiet type but will last indefinitely. Because gravity controls the flow of mercury, this switch is marked TOP at one end and must be mounted vertically with that end up.

Push-in connection. Both switches and receptacles are available with push-in type connections. The back of the body of these switches or receptacles has a molded indentation called a strip gauge. This shows how much bare wire is needed to make good electrical contact. After you strip insulation from the wire, cut the bare conductor to the length of the strip. To connect the wire, simply push it into the terminal hole. To disconnect the wire, insert a small screwdriver into the adjacent release slot and pull the wire out of the terminal hole. These devices should only be used with copper wire.

Wiring switched receptacles

To gain an extra outlet quickly and easily, replace a standard toggle switch with a switch-receptacle combination. The switch to be replaced must be a middle-of-run or end-of-run switch. Refer to pages 336-337 for a description of how to identify the switch's position on the circuit. The switch-receptacle combination can be wired so that the new switch operates the same as the old one and the receptacle is always "live," or the new switch can operate the same as the old one and also control the receptacle, as shown in the two diagrams below.

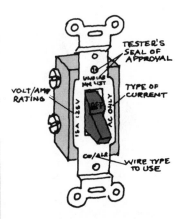

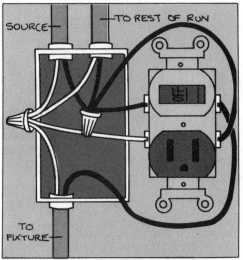

Switch-receptacle combination wired so receptacle is always "live."

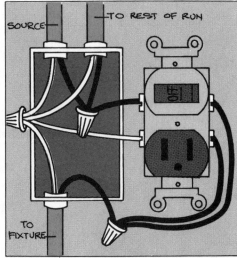

Switch-receptacle combination wired so receptacle is switch controlled.

What the markings mean: Both switches and receptacles are marked to indicate how the device should be used. These markings are stamped into the metal mounting strap or are molded into the plastic body. The markings tell you the maximum voltage and amperage at which the device can be used. A typical marking is "15A-120V." This means that the total power that can be controlled by the switch or plugged into the receptacle is 15 amperes at 120 volts, or 1800 watts.

Pilot-light switches

Two types of pilot-light switches are available. One type is designed to glow in the dark so it will be easy to find at night or in dark locations. The other type has an indicator light to call attention to the fact that the switch is on. This is particularly useful when the light or appliance controlled by the switch is in a remote location, such as with outdoor lights or garage lights. Its energy-saving potential is significant.

Acceptable wire types are indicated by abbreviations, as follows: "CU" or "CU-CLAD only" means either copper or copper-clad wire may be used (solid, uncoated aluminum may *not* be used). "CO-ALR," "CU-AL," or "AL-CU" means that solid aluminum, copper-clad aluminum or solid copper may be used. Listing by Underwriters' Laboratories, Inc. is shown by the UL symbol.

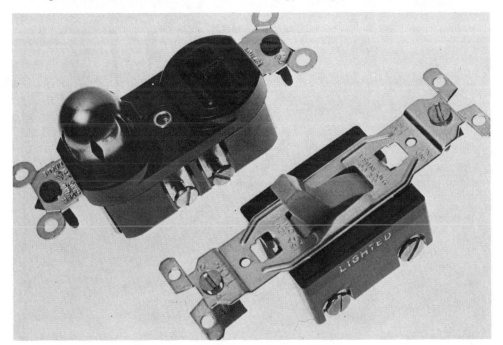

Incandescent dimmer switches

Dim, dimmer, dimmest
My wife wanted me to replace the old toggle switch in the dining room with a dimmer switch. But I didn't realize that the big housing on the back of the dimmer would fill up almost all of the space in the wall box. In addition, I had to allow space for at least two wire nuts. Now, since my wall box was nailed to the studs, the nail heads stuck out so much that the housing wouldn't fit all the way inside the box and the faceplate wouldn't screw flat against the wall.

Measure the available space inside the wall box *before* you buy the switch. *Practical Pete*

Dimmer switches are connected by wires rather than screw-type terminals. Standard (single-pole, single-throw) dimmer switches have two black leads. These are connected to the two black (or black-coded) switch leads in the box by means of solderless connectors (wire nuts).

Single-pole, double-throw dimmer switches have three leads. Markings on the switch and the package indicate which is the common terminal. Wire the dimmer the same as the single-pole, double-throw switch that it replaced. If the dimmer is used in a new two-switch installation, wire the dimmer the same as the switches shown on the diagrams on pages 347 through 349.

Dimmer switches provide continuously variable levels of light to suit the mood or use of an area or a room. When adjusted for less than full brightness, they also have the practical advantages of reducing power consumption and therefore cost, and of prolonging the life of the bulbs.

Any standard toggle switch that controls incandescent lights can be replaced with a dimmer switch. Dimmer control of fluorescent lights is a bit more complicated. (See page 362.)

The most common incandescent-light dimmer switch has a push-pull, on-off switch and a rotating brightness control.

Dimmer switches should be used only to control brightness of illumination. Any attempt to control appliances by means of a dimmer switch will result in severe damage to the appliance.

Dimmer switches are available in various wattage ratings. The rating applies to the total wattage of all lights controlled by the dimmer. A common rating is 600 watts, which would be more than adequate, for example, for control of a dining-room fixture containing six 75-watt bulbs.

Single-pole, double-throw dimmer switches are available for use on lights under two-switch control. Only one switch, however, can contain a dimmer. The level of illumination is controlled by the dimmer, but the light may be turned off or on from either switch.

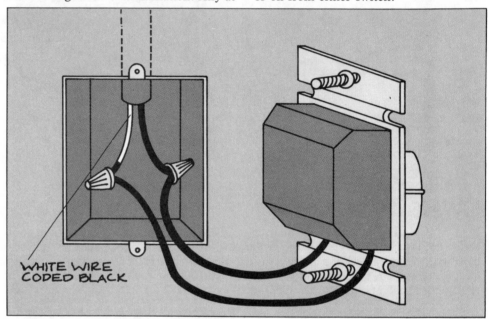

WHITE WIRE CODED BLACK

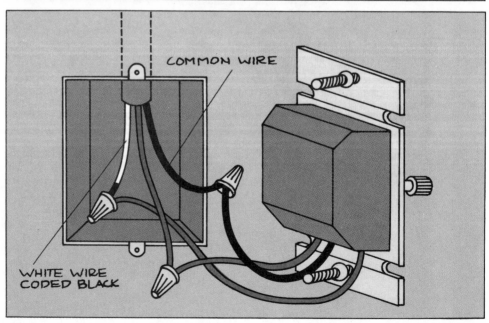

COMMON WIRE

WHITE WIRE CODED BLACK

Wiring multiple-switch circuits

The diagrams on the next three pages show how to wire Single-Pole, Double-Throw (SPDT) switches and special Double-Pole, Double-Throw (DPDT) switches. Both types enable you to turn fixtures on and off from two or more locations. DPDT switches are sometimes called four-way switches because they have four terminals. They can be combined with SPDT switches to control a light or outlet from *three or more* locations. The switches have only two positions however.

Controlling fixtures from more than one location is desirable in many situations. For example, stairways and long hallways should have light control at both ends. Control of garage lights from several locations is often useful. Outlets that can be turned on and off from several places are also handy for TV sets and music systems.

The following diagrams can help you add switches to an existing fixture or outlet (perhaps already having single-switch control) or plan entirely new installations.

To pick the diagram best suited to your project, decide first where the power-source cable will be in the circuit. If you are modifying an existing outlet or fixture, check the fixture, outlet, or switch boxes to find the source cable. Page 339 tells you how to identify the cables in the boxes.

Page 339 tells you how to identify the cables in the boxes.

> **NOTE:**
>
> SPDT—denotes a single-pole double-throw switch
>
> DPDT—denotes a double-pole double-throw switch
>
> A white wire coded black is represented as follows:

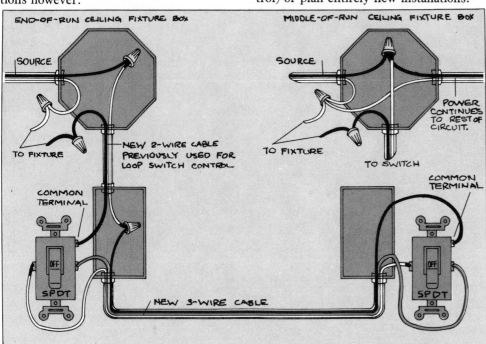

Two-switch control of ceiling fixture (Source power available at fixture box)

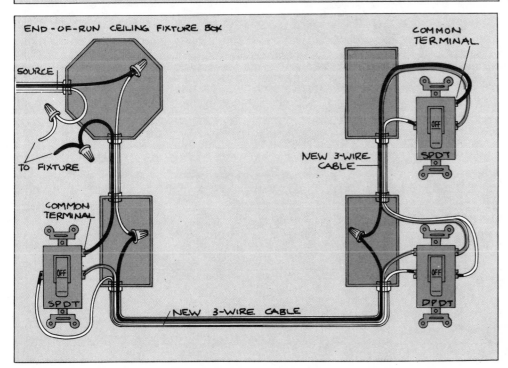

Three-switch control of ceiling fixture (Source power available at switch box)

What it takes

Time: 2 to 4 hours.

Tools and materials: Two single-pole, double-throw (3-way) switches; one or more double-pole, double-throw switches (4-way); two-wire and three-wire cable; screwdriver; wire stripper or knife; solderless connectors.

NOTE:

SPDT—denotes a single-pole double-throw switch

DPDT—denotes a double-pole double-throw switch

A white wire coded black is represented as follows:

═══════════

Connecting new source cable

If the complete circuit is new, the source cable, shown entering one of the boxes, must be connected to another source. By using the appropriate diagram, you can join the power-source cable to this circuit at the fixture, outlet or switch box, whichever is most convenient. See pages 340-341 for diagrams showing how to connect new-circuit source cables to existing wiring at various points.

Grounding cable

The diagrams below apply for either steel-armored or plastic-sheathed cable. For simplicity, ground wires are not shown. However, ground wires must be connected. If plastic-sheathed cable is used, the ground wires should be joined and connected to the boxes, as shown on pages 340-341. If steel-armored cable is used, the ground wires should be connected to the cable where the cable enters a box.

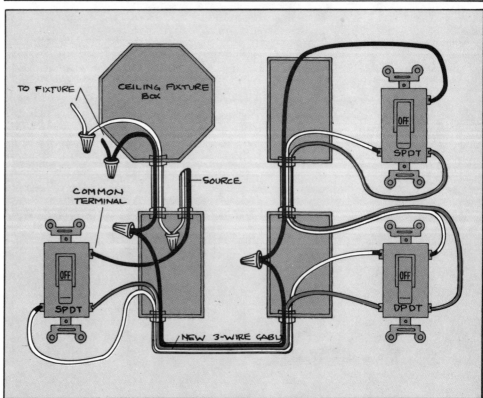

Two-switch control of ceiling fixture (Source power available at switch box)

Three-switch control of ceiling fixture (Source power available at fixture box)

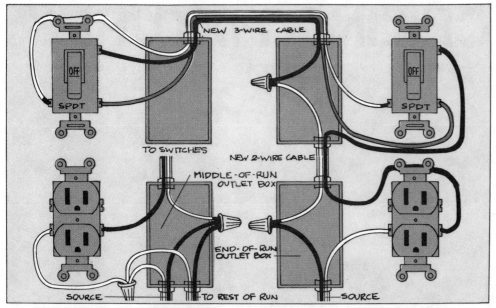

Two-switch control of wall outlet (Source power available at outlet box)

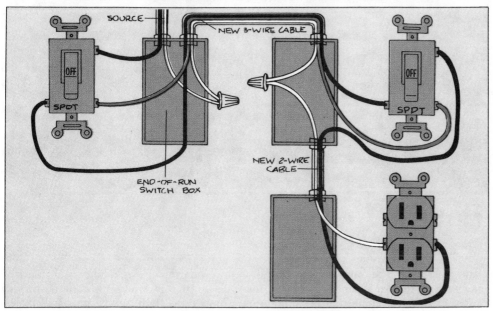

Two-switch control of wall outlet (Source power available at end-of-run switch box)

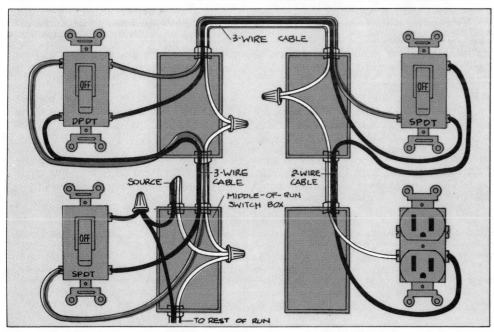

Three-switch control of wall outlet (Source power available at middle-of-run switch box)

6.CEILING FIXTURES

How to install a ceiling box

What it takes

Approximate time: 2-4 hours.

Tools and materials: Power drill; ⅛-inch bit; keyhole saw; carpenter's square; patching plaster; ceiling box and hanging hardware (for plaster-and-lath ceiling, a hammer and chisel); screwdriver; steel rule; 12- to 16-inch piece of stiff wire; masking tape.

The procedure to be followed when installing a ceiling fixture depends, first of all, on whether or not the ceiling is accessible from an attic or crawl space above it.

If the ceiling is accessible from above, the procedure is fairly simple and can be done with little or no visible damage to the ceiling. Cable routing is also easier.

When the ceiling is not accessible from above (that is, when it is between finished floors), the fixture must be installed from below. This requires cutting into the ceiling and patching the opening when the job is complete. Routing the new cable to the ceiling fixture is also more difficult when working between floors.

Planning a switch?

A key factor in your choice of location for a ceiling fixture will be the type of switch to be used and its location. The tips on switch wiring below include how to connect a ceiling fixture with a built-in switch. For how to wire a wall switch to a ceiling fixture see diagrams on page 353. For details on cable routing see pages 354-356.

- Whenever practical, select a ceiling fixture with a built-in switch. This eliminates the wiring, cable routing, and carpentry involved in adding a wall switch.
- Switched fixtures are available in a wide variety of styles, ranging from simple porcelain pull-chain fixtures suitable for a garage or utility room to elaborate, counterweighted chandeliers suitable for living and recreation areas.
- To install switched fixtures, you need only connect the ceiling box to a power source. If the area above the ceiling is not finished, it is often possible to obtain power for the new fixture from an existing ceiling box in the same area. Check the section on ceiling-box wiring to determine the right way to make the connection.
- Once you have found a power source for the new ceiling box and have completed the box and wiring installation, you need only connect the black and white power wires to the black and white fixture wires. Use solderless connectors and connect black to black and white to white. If the fixture has screw-type terminals, connect the black wire to the brass screw and the white wire to the chrome screw.
- There are many situations, of course, when single or multiple wall-switch control of a ceiling fixture is desirable for appearance, convenience, or safety. For these installations some additional planning is necessary.
- First check existing wiring to find the most convenient place to connect your new fixture-and-switch circuit to a power source. Be sure to consider various switch positions. Sometimes routing the new cable can be made much easier if you investigate all possible switch locations.

When ceiling is accessible from above

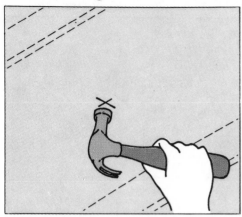

1. Check the area above the ceiling to determine the direction in which the joists run. Working from below, test the area where the fixture is to be located to be sure it is clear of joists and bridging. See detailed instructions at right. Locate the fixture at least 4 inches from a joist.

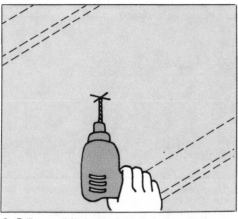

2. Drill a small (⅛-inch) pilot hole in the ceiling at the point you marked. This hole will locate the center of the opening you will make in the ceiling. If the area over the ceiling has flooring, you will need an extension bit so that the pilot hole will be visible from the room above.

Checking for clearance:

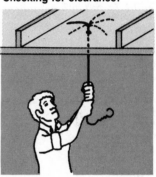

To be sure the area above the fixture site is between joists and clear of bridging, make a small (⅜-inch) test hole in the ceiling. Bend a piece of stiff wire into a right angle 4 inches from the end and insert this end into the hole. Rotate the wire to feel for obstructions. If there is not sufficent clearance, drill another hole several inches away and test again.

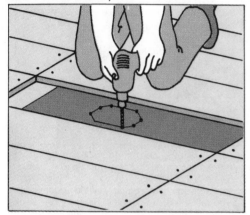

3. In the area above the ceiling, find the pilot hole. If necessary, remove a floorboard. Use the new ceiling box as a template. Center it over the pilot hole and trace the outline. Drill a ⅜-inch hole at each corner of the outline.

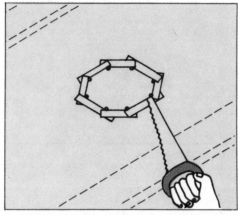

4. Again working from below, use a keyhole saw to cut through each each section between the holes. If the ceiling is plaster and lath, use tape around the outline of the box to prevent cracking and chipping the adjacent plaster. Saw carefully and slowly. Protective goggles should be worn.

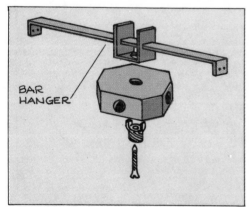

BAR HANGER

5. When the box cutout is finished, work from above again. Loosely connect the ceiling box to the bar hanger. Bend back or break off the tabs at the ends of the hanger so that the hanger will fit flush against the joists. If the best location for the ceiling fixture should turn out to be within an inch of a joist, a side-mounting ceiling box can be used. Hold the box against the joist and mark the mounting-hole locations. Prepare the cable and attach it to the box as described at right. Drill pilot holes in the joist at the points marked. Use wood screws to mount the box to the joist.

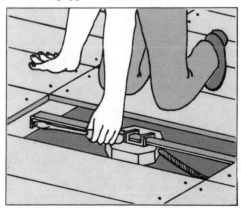

6. Prepare the end of the fixture cable and install it in the box. Secure it with a clamp. (See pages 308-313.) Hold the hanger and box so the edge of the box is even with the lower surface of the ceiling. Spread the hanger to fit the space between the joists. Tighten the stud screw to secure the box on the hanger. Holding the box and hanger in place, mark the joist with the positions of the screw holes at the ends of the bar hanger. Drill the pilot holes in joists. Mount the box and bar hanger.

When ceiling is between finished floors
With plasterboard ceiling

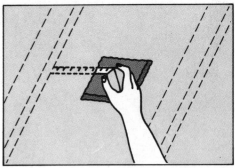

1. Make certain the area above where you plan to install the fixture is between joists and clear of bridging. You will need at least 4 inches of clearance in all directions around the fixture installation point. See detailed instructions on page 351.

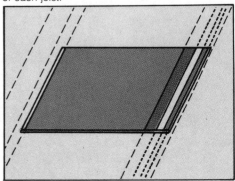

2. Cut a hole around the test hole, large enough for your hand to go through comfortably. Hold a steel rule in the space above the hole and measure the distance from the edge of the hole to each joist. Draw a line on the ceiling corresponding to the edge of each joist.

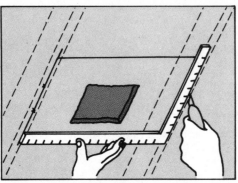

3. Use a steel square to mark two lines at right angles to the joist lines. The space between these lines should be sufficient (8–12 inches) to allow you to mount the ceiling box and hanger between the joists when you have cut out the rectangle of plasterboard. Drill a ⅜-inch hole at each corner of the rectangle. Use a keyhole saw to cut out the rectangle of plasterboard. A saber saw with a slow speed-setting can also be used, but be prepared for considerable plaster dust.

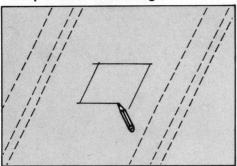

4. Cut two 1- by 2-inch furring strips slightly longer than the sides of the opening parallel to the joists. Secure the furring strips to the joists with wood screws. Position each strip so that the bottom edge is even with the bottom edge of the joist. The piece of plasterboard that will close the opening will be nailed to these strips. Cut a section of plasterboard to the dimensions of the opening. Locate the ceiling-box position on this piece of plasterboard. Draw the outline of the ceiling box, using the box as a template.

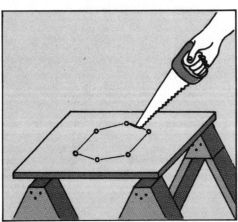

5. Drill a ⅜-inch hole at each corner of the outline and cut out the box opening with a keyhole saw. Loosely connect the ceiling box to the hanger. Bend back or break off the tabs at the ends of the hanger so that it will fit flush against the joists. Prepare the end of the fixture cable by removing the outer covering and conductor insulation (page 308). Remove one of the box knockouts and install the cable in the box. Secure the cable with a clamp suitable for the type of cable you are using. (See pages 312-313).

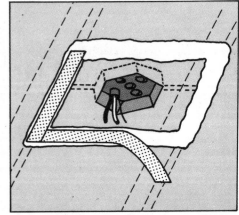

6. Hold the hanger and box in place so that the edge of the ceiling box is even with the surface of the ceiling. Spread the hanger to fit the space between the joists. Tighten the stud screw to secure the box. Again hold the box and hanger in place and check the position. Mark the joists with the positions of the screw holes, and drill pilot holes in the joists. Use wood screws to mount the box and bar hanger. Nail the plasterboard square to the furring strips to close the opening. Fill the cracks around the square with patching material and sand it smooth.

There's my way and the easy way

It seemed logical to run the new cable straight up the wall from the wall box to the ceiling, then directly across to the center of the ceiling for my overhead fixture. It was logical, but it was also dumb. I didn't realize that the second-floor joists my ceiling was attached to ran *at right angles* to the route of my cable. I would have had to cut a channel through the ceiling plaster and notch every dang one of the joists to fit that new cable flush.

Moral: Don't try to run cable across the ceiling from east to west, if your joists run north and south.

Practical Pete

With plaster-and-lath ceiling

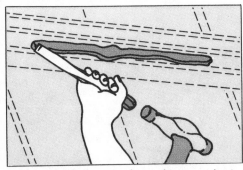

1. Make certain the area above where you plan to install the fixture is between joists and clear of bridging (page 351). When a suitable location has been found, cut a hole around the test hole large enough for your hand to go through comfortably. Hold a steel rule in the space above the hole and measure the distance from the edge of the hole to each joist. Put a mark on the ceiling corresponding to the edge of each joist. Use a hammer and chisel to chip out a channel in the plaster between the joists. The channel should be wide enough and long enough to accommodate the offset hanger. Widen the channel at the point where the box will be mounted. Use the box as a template to mark the plaster so that the box opening will be large enough.

2. Assemble the ceiling box to the offset hanger. Prepare the end of the fixture cable by removing the outer covering and conductor insulation (see page 308). Remove one of the knockouts, and install the cable in the box. Secure the cable with a clamp suitable for the type of cable you are using. (See page 312.) Secure the offset hanger to the joists with wood screws. Fill the channel with patching plaster, but leave room for a finishing coat of spackling compound or plasterboard joint cement. Allow the patching plaster to dry thoroughly before applying the finishing coat. Sand the finish coat smooth when the plaster has dried.

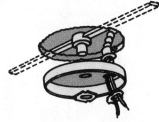

A special hanger is available for mounting ceiling boxes between finished floors. This mount requires only a small ceiling hole. The bar rests on the plasterboard or plaster-and-lath ceiling material. A shallow box mounts on the bar. The space available in the box is limited but adequate for connecting power-cable conductors to a fixture. Because the bar rests on the ceiling material and is not fastened to the joists, this hanger should be used only for fixtures under 5 pounds.

Wiring a ceiling box to a wall switch

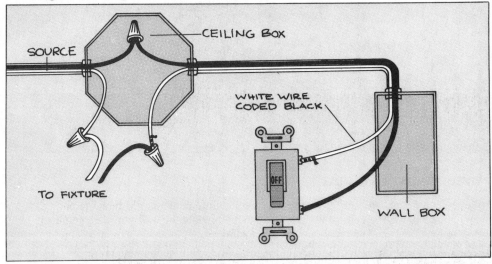

Source power connected at ceiling box

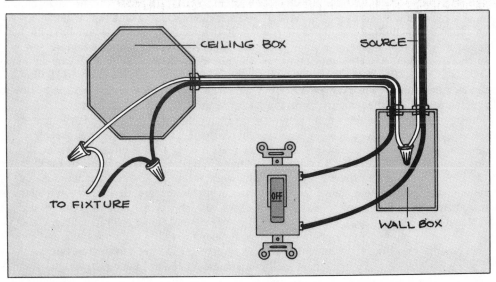

Source power connected at wall box

Running cable to ceiling box

If the wall and ceiling material is plasterboard or conventional plaster and lath, the wall material is not thick enough to cover the cable at the wall-ceiling opening. The top plate must be notched to recess the cable. Use a saber saw to make vertical cuts in the top plate, about 1 inch apart and ½ inch deep. Use a chisel to chip out the wood between the cuts. Push the cable into the notch and secure it with a cable staple.

What it takes

Approximate time: This involves carpentry and planning. Allow more time than you think you will need and remember that the power must stay off on all the circuits you are working with until you are done, so work in the day-time. Plan on a good eight hours for each between-floor run.

Tools: Hammer, utility knife, nail set, keyhole or saber saw with fine-toothed blade, electric hand drill, 1/16-inch twist-metal bit and ¾-inch spade bit with 18-inch drill-extender attachment, fish tape, electrician's tape, screw-driver, chisel (to loosen baseboards or notch studs), multipurpose tool for stripping insulation off conductors, voltage tester, safety goggles (if you must install a box in a plaster ceiling).

Materials: Solderless connectors, nails, cable, fixtures, junction boxes, wall boxes, receptacles, switches, and accessory hardware required in your wiring plan.

Between finished floors

It takes a bit of work to run cables from walls to ceiling when the ceiling is below a finished floor.

Access holes must be cut in the wall and at the point where wall and ceiling meet. (These are patched when the job is done.) Top plates and sometimes studs must be notched to accept the cable.

In this example the power connection is being made at a wall receptacle. As shown, the cable runs laterally across two studs, up through the wall to the switch, from the switch to the ceiling, and between joists to the ceiling-box opening.

To start, you would cut access holes where the wall and ceiling meet and at each stud. Through the access holes, notch the studs so you can run the cable laterally across them. Use a saber saw to make two horizontal cuts, about 1 inch apart, in each stud. The cuts should be ½ inch deep. Chisel out the wood between the cuts.

The access hole at the point where wall and ceiling meet should be large enough to extend below the wall top-plate and into the ceiling itself.

The best way to make the holes in the wall and ceiling depends on the material. For plasterboard, the hole can be cut with a utility knife, or a pilot hole can be drilled and the material cut out with a keyhole saw. Plaster walls with wood lath can be similarly cut. If the plaster is over metal lath, a saber saw with a fine-toothed cutting blade can be used.

When you have cut the top-plate hole and the corresponding lower access hole, you can select a spot for mounting the switch. The switch box can be mounted on a stud or between studs. The various methods for mounting boxes are described on pages 351-3. Whichever method you choose, use the switch box as a template. Mark the outline on the wall. Drill a pilot hole and cut the opening. Do not mount the box until the cable has been "fished" through.

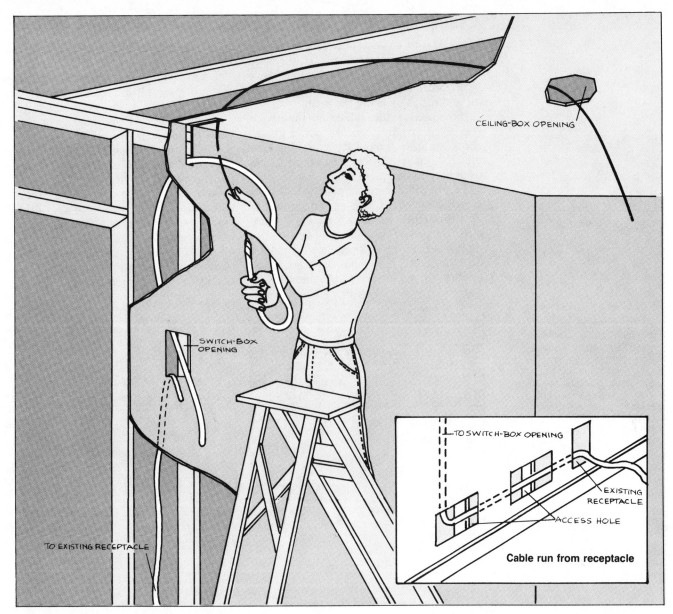

CEILING-BOX OPENING

SWITCH-BOX OPENING

TO EXISTING RECEPTACLE

TO SWITCH-BOX OPENING

EXISTING RECEPTACLE

ACCESS HOLE

Cable run from receptacle

Starting at the ceiling-box opening, feed the cable into the hole in the direction of the ceiling hole at the top plate. Use a fish tape or a piece of wire to locate and pull the wire down through the ceiling hole. Next, feed the cable into the wall through the hole below the top plate. Use the fish tape or wire again to pull the cable out through the switch-box opening.

Continue to pull the cable through the switch-box opening, while a helper feeds it into the ceiling-box opening, until there is about a foot of cable extending through the ceiling box.

Cut the cable extending through the switch-box opening. Again, leave a foot or so of cable hanging out. Power must be turned off at the circuit-breaker or fuse panel so there is no power at the receptacle box before you do the next step. *Test before you touch.* At the receptacle box where the power connection is to be made, remove one of the box knockouts and feed a length of cable through the knockout hole in the direction of the first stud-access hole. Use a fish tape or a piece of wire to pull the cable through the wall and around the first stud. Repeat this procedure until the cable is routed around each stud.

At the end of the lateral run, feed the fish tape down from the switch-box opening to the bottom access hole. Connect the fish tape to the cable that has just been run laterally from the receptacle box. Pull the cable up and out of the switch box.

Tag or mark the two cable ends at the switch opening so you know which is the source cable and which end goes to the ceiling fixture. Feed the cables through knockouts in the new wall box. Mount the box on the stud or on the wallboard. (See pages 351-3.) Use the internal cable clamp in the box to secure the cables.

Make the electrical connections for this type of installation as shown (page 353) ("Source power connected at the wall box").

How to scare a cat
Go easy with the hammer when you use staples to attach plastic-sheathed cable to studs. Drive the staple into the wood only far enough to hold the cable firmly. If you drive it in too far, the staple can damage the sheathing—even short the conductors. Even if all the damage you do is to scare eight lives out of your cat, you'll still have to splice or rerun the cable.

Practical Pete

Ceiling-box cable run in attic or crawl space

In an attic or crawl space, cable runs are simple and straightforward. If the area contains flooring, you will have to remove some boards temporarily and route the cable through or along the joists.

If you need to run a cable from the attic to the basement, perhaps for power tie-in, check the space around the plumbing vent pipe. It usually provides a clear, open area from attic to basement.

To run cable from the attic to walls for switch connections, it is only necessary to drill through the wall top plate. The top plate consists of two 2-by-4s, sometimes topped with a 1-by-4. This means you must drill through approximately 4 inches of lumber. A long bit or a paddle bit must be used. If you are using a light-duty drill, stop occasionally to allow the drill to cool.

When making measurements in an attic or crawl space, always use a reference point that is visible on the floor below. For example, measure from the edge of a stairway opening or the access-hole opening to the point on the wall where you plan to mount the switch. If necessary, measure in two directions at right angles. The idea is to make measurements that can be repeated with reasonable accuracy in the attic or crawl space. Remember, it's easy to misjudge locations when you are working in an unfamiliar area. Careful measurement and checking will save unnecessary work and perhaps an unexpected patch job.

Short tempered

It is tough on the temper to discover that the cable you just fished through the wall is almost—but not quite—long enough. The way to avoid this is simple—cut long.

A good rule is to add about 20% to your straight line measurement. Cable does not bend sharply, lie perfectly flat, or even hang straight. You may also find you have to go around an unexpected obstruction.

Practical Pete

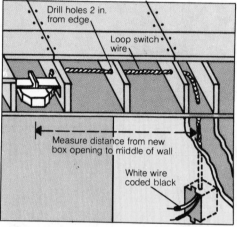

Remove one or more floorboards and drill joists as shown to run cable from top plate to ceiling box in a floored area.

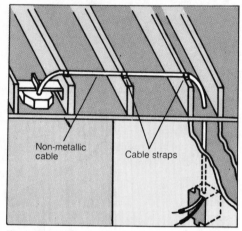

If area has no flooring, simply run cable across joists and secure with cable straps.

To route new cable to existing wall box

1. Drill a hole in the top plate just above the box.
2. Then remove a knockout from the top of the box.
3. Have a helper drop a weighted string through the top-plate opening.
4. Use a fish tape or a piece of wire to hook the string and pull it through the box opening. Use a weight that will pass through the box opening (for example, a medium-size bolt). If you cannot locate a suitable weight, use any disposable piece of metal and simply cut the string after you have fished a loop through the hole.
5. Attach the cable securely to the string.
6. Have your helper pull the string up slowly while you feed the string and cable through the box opening and top-plate opening. The cable will go through openings more readily if you smooth the connection between cable and string by wrapping it with tape.

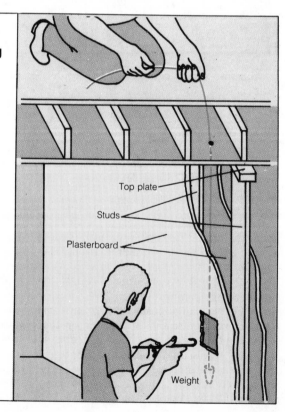

Mounting a ceiling fixture

What it takes

Approximate time: Half an hour. More if you must wire and install a wall or ceiling box for the fixture.

Tools and materials: Screwdriver, utility knife, pliers, crescent wrench to loosen stuck nuts on old, large fixtures (use pliers to tighten nuts on new fixtures, not a wrench), tape, solderless connectors, wire coat hanger bent in S-shape, voltage tester.

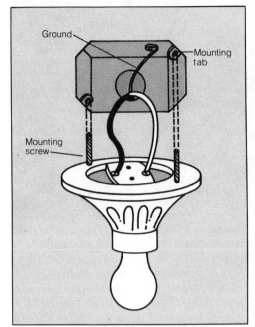

Directly to the ceiling box. A simple, porcelain single-bulb fixture can be mounted directly to the ceiling box with two screws. These fixtures have screw-type electrical connections. Attach the black wire to the brass-colored terminal and attach the white wire to the silver-colored terminal.

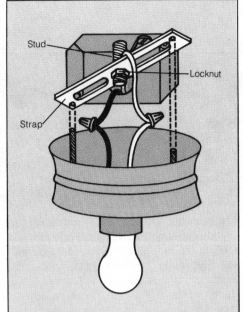

Stud mounting. If the box has a fixture stud, the strap can be secured to the stud with a locknut. The fixture is then mounted on the strap with screws.

Electrical connections are made by means of solderless connectors. Connect the black power wire to the black fixture wire and connect the white power wire to the white fixture wire.

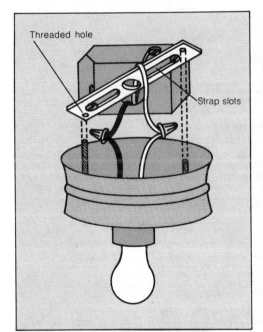

Strap mounting. Mounting a strap on a ceiling box is done by putting two screws through the strap slots and screwing them to the threaded ears in the outlet box. The fixture is screw-mounted to the holes in the ends of the strap. The slots in the strap allow you to shift the fixture position so that it need not be directly centered under the box.

Electrical connections are made by means of solderless connectors. Connect the black power wire to the black fixture wire and connect the white power wire to the white fixture wire.

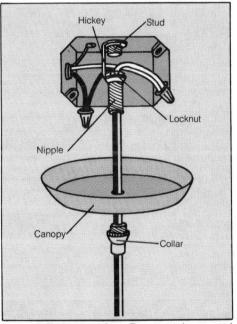

Large fixture mounting. To mount larger and heavier fixtures, first thread a hickey onto the fixture stud and then secure a nipple to the hickey with a locknut. The nipple extends through the base of the fixture. Thread the collar on the fixture onto the nipple to hold the fixture canopy snugly to the ceiling above it.

Electrical connections are made by means of solderless connectors. Connect the black power wire to the black fixture wire and connect the white power wire to the white fixture wire.

7.FLUORESCENTS

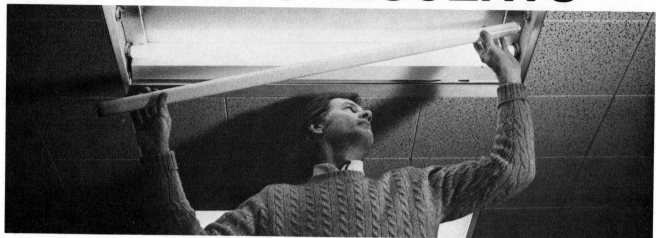

Fluorescent lighting provides a bright, even illumination that is desirable in many areas of the home. It is more complex and, initially, more costly than incandescent lighting. Fluorescent lamps, however, produce more light per watt of power used, and they last four or five times longer than incandescent lamps. The long-range cost of fluorescent lights, then, is significantly lower than the cost of incandescents.

The life of fluorescent lamps is determined primarily by how often they are turned on and off; the less this occurs, the longer they last. Since fluorescents use little power, it is better to leave them on than to turn them on and off for short periods.

The three most common types of fluorescent fixtures in homes

Rapid start. This is currently the most widely used type of fixture. It lights almost immediately when switched on. Rapid-start fixtures also have the advantage of being readily adapted for use with fluorescent dimmer switches. Lamps for rapid-start fixtures have two pin-type connectors at each end.

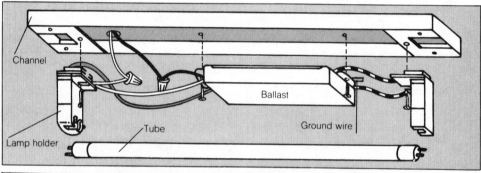

Instant start. This type of fluorescent fixture lights a second or two after it is switched on. It requires a higher initial voltage surge than other types. Lamps for instant-start fixtures may have one or two pin-type connectors at each end. On this type of fixture, the lamp holder contains a built-in switch that allows high voltage to be applied only when the fixture contains a lamp.

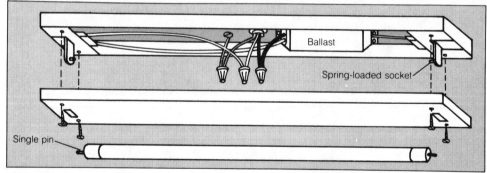

Starter type. This type of fixture has a separate starter. It uses lamps that have two pin-type connectors at each end. The starter, like the lamps, has a specified life, but is replaceable. It is located in a socket near one of the lamp holders. For replacement, power to the fixture is turned off, and the lamp is removed. Then the starter is twisted and pulled out of its socket. Replacement starters must match the wattage of the lamp.

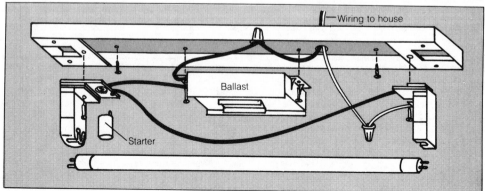

Fluorescent characteristics

Fluorescent light and incandescent light have different characters, and, generally, the two do not blend well. Some recently developed fluorescent lamps, however, produce illumination that is compatible with incandescent lighting. These include the warm-white types and those that have the word *deluxe* in the type name. Warm-white and deluxe-type lamps can be effectively combined with incandescent lights. It is also possible to add dimmers to fluorescent fixtures to control the light intensity. This, too, is a help in blending fluorescent and incandescent light. When blending, never use more than one type of fluorescent lamp, as different types often do not blend well and create a poor mix of lighting.

For areas where maximum light is important—workbenches, kitchen work surfaces, and desks, for example—use cool-white and daylight-white lamps. They produce the maximum light per watt of power. For decorative use in living areas, warm-white and deluxe types are better, as they produce a softer light. Warm-white and deluxe-type lamps put out about 30 percent less light per watt of power than do cool-white lamps.

This chart summarizes the most commonly used fluorescent lamps.

Color characteristics of commonly used fluorescent lamps

Lamp description	Atmosphere	Effect on colors	Compatibility with incandescent light
Cool white (standard)	Cool	Intensifies cool colors; dulls warm ones. Light output high.	Poor
Cool white (deluxe)	Cool	Improves appearance of all colors. Light output medium.	Poor
White	Warm	Little effect on cool colors; dulls warm colors slightly. Light output high.	Fair
Warm white	Warm	Distorts all colors slightly. Light output high.	Good
Warm white (deluxe)	Warm	Leaves colors true. Flattering to human complexions. Light output medium.	Very good
Living white (natural)	Cool	Especially designed to flatter human complexions. Leaves all colors reasonably true. Light output medium.	Very good
Cool green	Cool	Intensifies cool colors. Light output high.	Poor

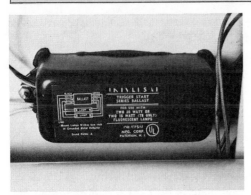

The ballast is a special type of transformer that produces the high-voltage surge necessary to start current flowing in the fluorescent tube. Once the current flow has been established, the ballast limits the flow through the tube to the rated value. The limiting action is required because, once current is flowing in a fluorescent lamp, the lamp's internal resistance drops to a low value. If not limited, the current would destroy the lamp in a short time. The ballast prevents this.

The starter found in some older fluorescent fixtures is a small metal canister that fits in a socket on the fixture. The starter does the switching needed to turn the filaments on and off, apply the high-voltage surge to start the lamp, and switch in the ballast to limit the current.

How fluorescent lights operate

Fluorescent lights and incandescent lights operate on entirely different principles. All fluorescent lamps contain a small filament (similar to the filament of an incandescent lamp) at each end. The glass tube is filled with a gas (mercury vapor) and the inner surface of the tube is coated with a phosphorescent substance.

When the current is turned on, power is applied to the filaments, causing them to heat up. The hot filaments vaporize the gas in the tube, making it a good conductor of electricity. The filaments are then turned off and a high-voltage surge of power is momentarily applied to the tube. The surge starts current flowing through the tube. Once the current flow is established, it continues with only normal line-voltage applied. In fact, current flows so easily in the vaporized gas that it must be limited by a device called a ballast.

The flow of current through the gas produces ultraviolet light. Although it is barely visible to human eyes, the ultraviolet light causes the phosphorescent coating on the tube to emit strong and visible light.

Installation in halls, kitchens, large areas

What it takes

Approximate time: If you need no carpentry or plastering work, you can mount a new fluorescent fixture onto an existing outlet or ceiling box wired for an old incandescent fixture in about an hour.

Tools and materials: Hammer, screwdriver, pliers, voltage tester, solderless connectors.

It is practical to replace incandescent fixtures in your home with fluorescent ones anywhere that they will not be turned on and off frequently. The channels of fluorescent fixtures are provided with a number of knockouts, any one of which can be used for mounting.

Remove the channel cover, tap the knockout with a hammer to break a section free, then grip the knockout with pliers and twist it off.

Next, turn off the power to the incandescent fixture and remove it. Mount the fluorescent fixture by placing the knockout over a threaded nipple and securing the fixture with a washer and locknut.

(You can add a strap-mounted nipple to wall outlets or a hickey and nipple to ceiling boxes that do not contain nipples.)

Feed the black and white fluorescent power-wires through the nipple and join them to the source-cable conductors with solderless connectors. Connections are black-to-black and white-to-white.

Large fixtures have a mounting cutout. To mount these fixtures, place a metal strap inside the channel, across the cutout. Then place the fixture and strap over the nipple. Use a locknut to hold the strap and fixture against the ceiling.

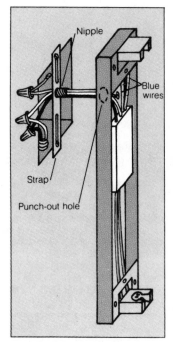

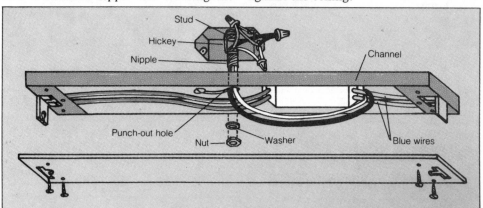

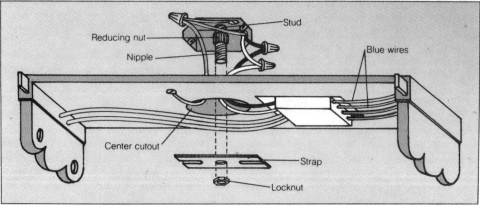

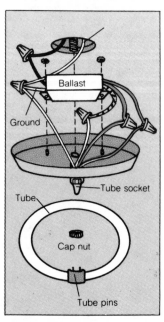

Circular fluorescent fixtures make good replacements for kitchen-ceiling fixtures. To make the substitution, first turn off power to the kitchen-ceiling box. Remove the cap nut or mounting screws and lower the incandescent fixture. Support the fixture so it does not hang by the electrical connections. Remove the solderless connectors that join the black and white fixture wires to the power wires. *Test before you touch.* Untwist the black and white fixture wires and set the incandescent fixture aside. Using solderless connectors, connect the fluorescent fixture wires to the power wires in the box (black-to-black and white-to-white is the invariable rule).

If necessary, use a hickey or reducing nut to install a nipple long enough to project through the fixture. Fold the wires into the fixture canopy and secure to the ceiling by tightening the cap nut on the nipple.

The simplest installation of all can be used for workbench lighting. Purchase a complete fixture. Twin-lamp, 48-inch fixtures, complete with reflector and switch, are widely available. Hooks and chains are supplied with the fixture. Attach the hooks to the ceiling and hang the fixture from the chain. To make the electrical connection, permanently wire the fixture to a nearby ceiling or wall box. If a spare grounded outlet is available, plug the fixture in.

Installation in bathrooms

Fluorescent illumination is well suited to bathroom use—applying makeup, shaving, and so forth. The fixtures can be mounted on either side of, or above, bathroom cabinets; cabinets with built-in fixtures are also available.

Bathroom cabinets are generally recessed into walls and secured to studs with wood screws. To remove a cabinet, simply remove the screws on each side and lift the cabinet from the wall opening. The opening provides easy access to electrical connections on the interior wall. If an incandescent fixture was mounted near the cabinet, and is to be removed, the fluorescent fixture can be wired to the same box.

Turn off power to the wall box by removing the fuse or turning off the circuit breaker for that circuit. Connect the fluorescent-fixture wires to the same wires that were connected to the old fixture (black-to-black and white-to-white).

If the incandescent fixture was controlled by a wall switch, the fluorescent fixture will now be controlled by the same switch.

If you wish to retain the incandescent fixture with switch control and have separate control over the fluorescent light, two wiring schemes are possible. Switch and fixture wiring in bathrooms is the same as switch and ceiling-fixture wiring (page 340).

Inspect the wall-box wiring and compare it with the switch and ceiling-fixture diagrams on page 340 to determine if source power is available at the wall box. If it is, you can wire the fluorescent fixture to the source-power cable and turn it on and off by means of an individual fixture switch.

If a new circuit is required for the fluorescent lights, install a junction box in the wall stud behind the cabinet.

Power for a junction box is obtained by running a cable to an existing wall or ceiling box. Connect the leads from the fluorescent fixtures to the power cable in the junction box with solderless connectors. **A word of caution:** Many local codes now require that GFIs (ground fault interrupters) be installed on bathroom circuits. If there is one on the bathroom circuit in your home, be sure you make the power connection for the junction box to a wall or ceiling box on the GFI-protected circuit. You must, of course, turn off power to the existing wall or ceiling box before you connect the new cable. Make sure that when the bathroom-circuit GFI is turned off, power is off in the box you are using for the new circuit.

Color me green
My wife wanted fluorescents on each side of the bathroom mirror so she would have plenty of light to make up her face. So I put them in (she needs all the help she can get). The lamps I picked out had high light output and a refreshing, cool color. They were called "cool green." They made her look like the victim in a Dracula movie. Heck, anyone can make a mistake. If you don't want to make that one, see the chart on fluorescent lamp colors on page 71.

Practical Pete

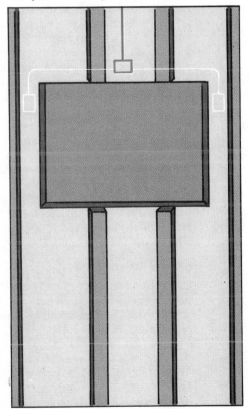

Remove bathroom medicine cabinet for easy access to the inside of the surrounding wall when you want to add new, or replace old, wiring.

Rear view of wall with cabinet removed showing location of original wiring for incandescent fixture (red), and new wiring for vertically mounted fluorescent fixtures (white).

Fluorescent dimmers

With fluorescent dimmers, you can have full-range intensity control over fluorescent fixtures. This provides variety in lighting and is a help in blending fluorescent and incandescent light for more pleasing effects.

Fluorescent-dimmer circuits are really special lighting systems—that is, all the devices involved must be matched. The dimmer control, the fluorescent fixture, the fixture ballast, the lamps, and the wiring must be selected according to the number of lamps to be controlled.

For applications (such as cornice and valance lighting) where a maximum of eight 40-watt, single-lamp fixtures will be used, a two-wire dimmer system can be installed. For this, the existing wiring is sufficient.

For larger applications—such as luminous ceilings and walls—where more than eight single-lamp fixtures are required, a three-wire dimmer system is needed. For example, a luminous ceiling in a 12-by-15-foot room would require fifteen to eighteen 40-watt fluorescent lamps and, therefore, a three-wire system would be needed. The three-wire system can handle as many as forty 40-watt fluorescent lamps in either single or double fixtures.

For both the three-wire and two-wire dimmer systems, special ballasts must be installed in each fixture to be controlled. Rapid-start fixtures and lamps should be used in both types of dimmer systems.

What it takes

Approximate time: Half an hour.

Tools and materials: Voltage tester, small and medium screwdrivers, pliers, solderless connectors, utility knife, special dimmer ballast that matches dimmer control, fixture(s), and lamps.

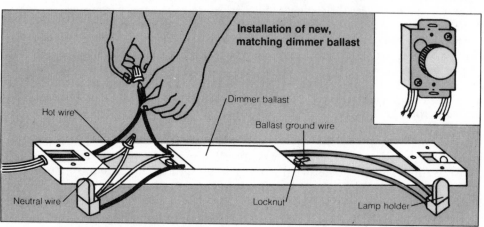

Installation of new, matching dimmer ballast

Hot wire — Dimmer ballast — Ballast ground wire — Neutral wire — Locknut — Lamp holder

Installing a two-wire-system dimmer ballast. To replace the ballast, disconnect the fixture from the power source wires for that circuit.

Remove the lamp, the screws that hold the channel cover, and then remove the cover. Next, remove the solderless connectors from the black and white wires. Untwist the wires. Remove the screws securing the lamp holders and those that hold the old ballast in place. Take out the ballast and lamp holders. Disconnect the lamp holders from the ballast wires. Some lamp holders are attached to the ballast wires by push-in type connectors. To release these connections, insert a small screwdriver in the slot next to the wire entry hole. Press in on the screwdriver and pull on the wire to release it. The short white wire in one lamp holder will be reused as is and need not be removed. Connect the dimmer ballast to the lamp holders at either end of the fixture as shown in the drawing.

The new connections will be the same as the original ones: two wires from each end of the ballast to each lamp holder. Mount the dimmer ballast and the lamp holders in the chan-nel. Make sure the bare ground wire from the ballast is wrapped securely around one of the mounting screws. Use the old solderless connectors to join the black power wire to the black ballast wire and the white power wire to the short white wire you will find on the lamp holder at one end.

The installation of a three-wire dimmer system for single-lamp fixtures is similar to the installation of the two-wire ballast, but two additional connections are required.

As shown in the three-wire system diagram, opposite, the ballast-control lead must be connected to the black wire in the three-wire cable.

Fixtures used on the three-wire system must have one circuit-interrupting lamp holder. This lamp holder has a built-in switch that is actuated by the pins on the fluorescent lamp.

If the fixture does not already have this type of holder, the holder wired to the blue and white ballast leads must be replaced with a circuit-interrupting type. Remove all three wires from the standard holder and connect the short white wire, as well as the blue and white ballast wires, to the circuit-interrupting holder, as shown opposite.

Dimmer controls are designed to fit in standard toggle-switch wall boxes. Boxes, however, may be mounted in various ways. So, if an existing box is to be used, check the amount of space in it against the dimmer-manufacturer's data. For new installations, use a box large enough to handle the dimmer and its connections conveniently. (You will have to make four connections, plus ground, in the wall box.)

If they are to operate properly, all elements of the dimmer circuit must be matched. All fixtures should be rapid start and of the same size and type. Four-foot, 40-watt, single- or double-lamp fixtures are usually specified, as are the recommended ballasts. All fixtures controlled by one dimmer must have the same type dimmer ballast. Nothing other than fluorescent fixtures should be on the dimmer circuit.

To get the most uniform illumination at all brightness settings, use only new lamps on a dimmer circuit. The new lamps should be operated at full brightness for the first 100 hours.

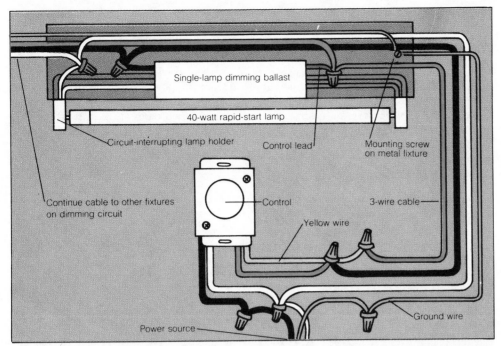

Single-lamp dimming ballast

40-watt rapid-start lamp

Circuit-interrupting lamp holder

Control lead

Mounting screw on metal fixture

Continue cable to other fixtures on dimming circuit

Control

3-wire cable

Yellow wire

Power source

Ground wire

Wiring diagram for rapid-start single-lamp dimmer ballast

The diagram at left shows how one fluorescent-dimmer system is wired. The system is intended for use with single-lamp fixtures. The number of single-lamp fixtures that can be added to the circuit is limited only by the rating of the control. Additional fixtures should be wired like the one shown. The ballast ground wire (not shown) must be attached to the fixture. To do this, wrap it around one of the mounting screws.

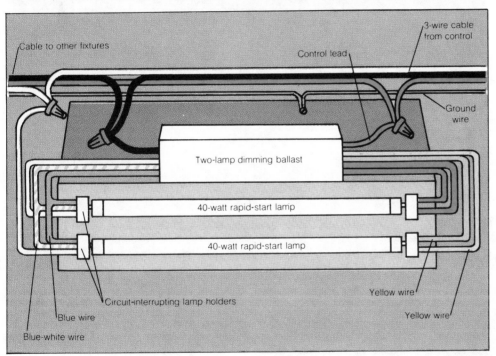

Cable to other fixtures

Control lead

3-wire cable from control

Ground wire

Two-lamp dimming ballast

40-watt rapid-start lamp

40-watt rapid-start lamp

Circuit-interrupting lamp holders

Blue wire

Blue-white wire

Yellow wire

Yellow wire

Wiring diagram for rapid-start, two-lamp dimmer ballast

This diagram shows how a two-lamp dimmer ballast is wired in a three-wire dimming system. The cable ground wire (not shown) must be attached to the fixture channel, and the ballast ground wire must be wrapped around one of the ballast mounting screws.

How to adjust fluorescent dimmers is described on the switch package or in a separate instruction sheet. For the most common types, the adjustment is made by means of an adjustment screw or a knurled collar on the switch-control shaft. Set the control shaft to the extreme counterclockwise position. Turn on circuit power. Turn the shaft to the extreme clockwise (brightest) position. With the shaft in this position, use a screwdriver to turn the adjustment screw (or pliers to turn the collar) clockwise as far as it will go. Now turn the control shaft to the lowest setting at which the fluorescents still light. Rotate the adjustment screw or collar counterclockwise until the lamps begin to flicker, then turn it back (clockwise) just enough to eliminate the flicker. With this adjustment, the lamp will provide light until the power is off.

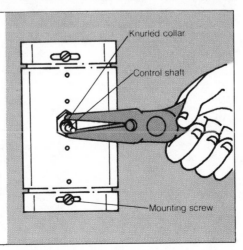

Knurled collar

Control shaft

Mounting screw

Joining fixtures

In many decorative fluorescent installations—such as valance and cornice lighting or luminous walls and ceilings—it is necessary to wire several fixtures from a single power source and to control them with a single switch. Run jumper wires from the power connections in one fixture through the channel to the next fixture, and so on. Two types of fixtures offer different ways of connecting channels.

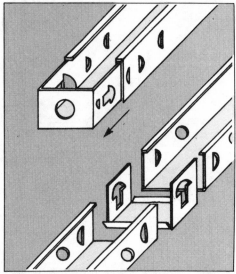

In fixtures like this one, the end sections are removable. After they are removed from adjacent ends, one of the end pieces can be used to join the channels together.

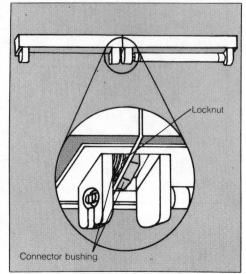

In this type of fixture, a knockout is removed from adjacent ends of the fixtures and a connector-bushing fitting, secured with locknuts, is installed to join the channels.

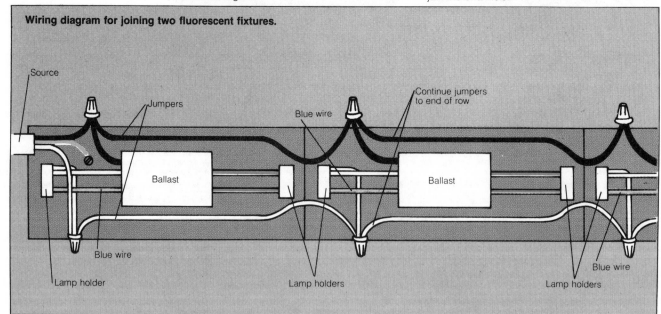

Wiring diagram for joining two fluorescent fixtures.

To wire one fixture to another you will need type TW No. 14 wire for jumpers. If you are joining 4-foot fluorescent fixtures (the longest available fixture is usually the easiest to use), figure on using 5 feet each of black and white wire per fixture. Use plastic-sheathed or armor-covered cable to connect one row of fixtures to another and to connect the fixtures to the source box. Type TW wire should be used only inside the fluorescent channels. Be sure to purchase wire with black and white insulation. The conductors in the wires are the same; but, if you maintain the black-to-black and white-to-white connection col-

ors all the way, you will be less likely to make a wiring mistake. Further, coded wires make future changes, additions, or maintenance easier. In the first fixture, join the black power wire, the black ballast wire, and a black jumper wire with a solderless connector. Join the white power wire, the short white wire from one lamp holder, and the white jumper wire with a solderless connector. Connect the bare ground wire from the power cable to any convenient channel screw. Lay the jumpers in the channel. Run one on each side of the ballast. Feed the jumpers through the connector bushing between channels, or

simply run them along the channel to the next fixture, according to the method used to connect the fixtures. Make similar black and white wire connections at the next fixture. Continue until all the fixtures are joined. The bare-wire ground connection made at the first fixture will ground all fixtures joined together metal-to-metal. If another row of fixtures is to be installed, run a ground jumper from the power-cable ground connection in the first row to the first fixture in the second row. Wrap the ground jumper around a ballast mounting screw Use green-insulated wire for the ground jumpers.

For multiple-row installations, such as those used to create luminous ceilings, connect ground jumpers to the power-cable ground wire at the source box. Connect as many jumpers as necessary to provide one direct ground connection for each row of fixtures. This assures you of a good ground for each row. Rapid-start fixture channels must be grounded to ensure proper operation. Where luminous ceilings are being installed, a ceiling box previously used for an incandescent fixture is often available. If the ceiling box contains a source cable, the rows of fluorescent fixtures can be wired to the box, as shown. If a loop circuit to a wall switch is also available at the ceiling box, the same switch circuit can be used to control the fluorescent fixtures.

Since the old ceiling material will be concealed by the new luminous-ceiling panels, you can simply cut away ceiling material around the box, as necessary; remove knockouts from the box; and install

cable clamps for the new wiring.

Another method of connecting the new cables is to add an extender to the ceiling box. The extender is simply another box with the back cut out. Use screws to attach the extender to the existing box. Remove knockouts from the extender, and install cable clamps for the new wiring. Whichever method you use, be sure to install a cover plate on the box or extender when the wiring has been completed.

When a ceiling box with source cable is not available, power for the luminous ceiling must be brought from another source—such as a wall outlet. In this case, the fixture rows can be wired as shown. The cable from the wall box to the ceiling need not go through the wall top plate if the new ceiling is to be below that level. The power cable can be brought through the wall at any convenient point. It is easiest to start wiring from an end row. Route the cable to the nearest corner and then wire as shown.

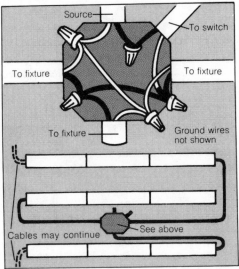

Wiring diagram for ceiling-box power source and cable run from box to rows of fluorescent fixtures.

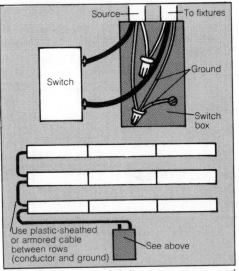

Wiring diagram for switch-box power source and cable run from box to rows of fluorescent fixtures.

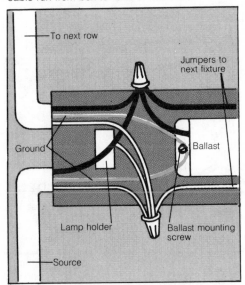

Wiring diagram for cable into fixture between rows of fixtures.

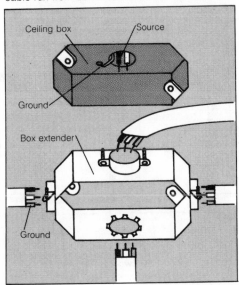

Wiring cables into a ceiling box extender.

Black and white and red all over
Sure, you *can* buy TW wire with conductors the same color, but don't. Make sure the insulation on the two wires is of different colors. When I started connecting all those wires inside the fixture, and running from one to the next, I went plumb batty trying to keep track of which was the "white" wire and which "black" so I wouldn't hook a neutral wire to a hot one and blow the whole shebang. Wiring diagrams are hard enough to follow without complicating the job even more.

Practical Pete

Two-circuit wiring

Luminous ceilings and walls can be wired so that some of the fixtures are on one switch circuit and the rest are on another circuit. This provides two levels of illumination without the work and expense of installing dimmer systems.

In a recreation room, for example, you may want low-level lighting for watching television and full illumination for card playing and similar activities. You can use the same scheme for valance, soffit, and cornice lighting. You can wire any number of fixtures, and fixtures of different sizes, on each circuit to provide whatever light levels you want.

In an unfinished room where you have easy access to wall studs you can use plastic sheathed, three-conductor cable. Buy TW No. 14 wire with red, black, and white insulation for wiring within the fixtures.

Wire one group of fixtures on the red wire and the other group on the black wire, and maintain the same coding throughout the room. The wiring within and between fixtures is the same as single-circuit wiring, except that you alternate fixtures on the black and red circuit. Otherwise, join fixtures and route cables as described on pages 364 and 365.

In a finished room you must add another two-conductor cable to a power source, install a switch, and route the cable through walls and ceilings, as shown on pages 352 and 353. Use cable containing one red and one white conductor. Maintain red as the "hot" line throughout the second circuit. If red-and-white conductor cable is not readily available, color code the black wire in one circuit by coloring the insulation red at each connection.

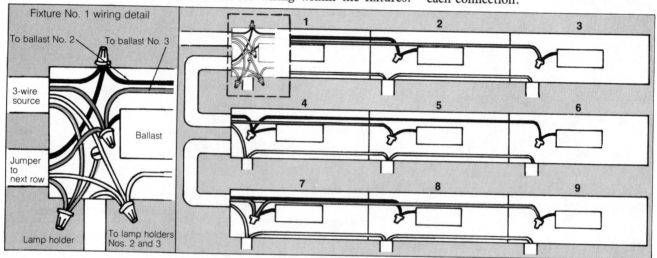

Wiring diagram for running three-wire power cable between rows of fluorescent fixtures so that half of them (Fixtures 2, 4, 6, and 8 on the black circuit) will be controlled by one wall switch and the other half (Fixtures 1, 3, 5, 7, and 9 on the red circuit) will be controlled by another wall switch. Insert shows detail of wiring for the first fixture.

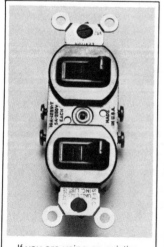

If you are using an existing switch box, use a double switch. Wiring is the same as for separate switches shown at right.

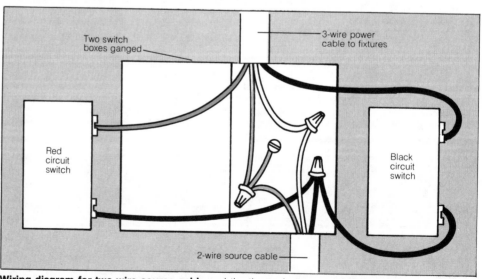

Wiring diagram for two-wire source cable and the three-wire power cable that leads to the fixtures, connected to two switches in two, gauged switch boxes. Connect the black wire from the source cable to two switches. Connect the black wire from the three-conductor cable to one switch, and connect the red wire in the three-conductor cable to the other switch. Wire the white wire and ground wire as shown.

Luminous ceilings

A luminous ceiling is the easiest type of ceiling to install in an unfinished area. The first step consists of mounting fluorescent fixtures, end-to-end, in evenly-spaced rows. Next, fasten hooks to the ceiling or to joists, and use wires to suspend metal runners from the hooks. Insert crosspieces between the runners to make equally square (2-by-2-foot) or rectangular (2-by-4-foot) openings. Finally, slip precut plastic panels—slightly larger than the square

or rectangular openings—in place. They will be supported by the runners and crosspieces. These steps are shown in detail on the next two pages.

The various combinations of fluorescent-lamp types and plastic materials make it possible to achieve a wide variety of light levels and tints.

Pages 364 and 365 describe how to join fluorescent fixtures in rows and how to wire multiple rows.

Unfinished areas

When you want to maintain maximum overhead clearance, as in a finished basement for example, you can mount the fluorescent fixtures between floor joists and attach the plastic panels, runners, and crosspieces to the bottom edge of the joists. Forty-watt, single-lamp, rapid-start fixtures are best for this type of installation.

The ballasts in fluorescent fixtures consume power and, therefore, give off heat. Take this into consideration when you plan how you will mount the fixtures. Make a mark on the outside of each fluorescent fixture to show the location of the ballast. Allow at least an inch or two of airspace above the ballast for heat dissipation.

What it takes

Approximate time: About two hours to install a luminous ceiling in a small area such as an entrance way or bathroom.

Tools and materials: You will need a pencil and ruler for marking old surfaces as you plan your ceiling layout. Hammer, bit and brace, and pliers will be needed for removing parts of old surfaces and fixtures. Materials you will be using are precut plastic panels, metal plastic-panel runners, 1-by-2-inch wood for side-support strips, round-head stove bolts (or wooden screws), and finishing nails.

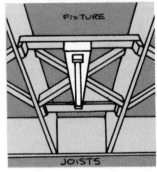

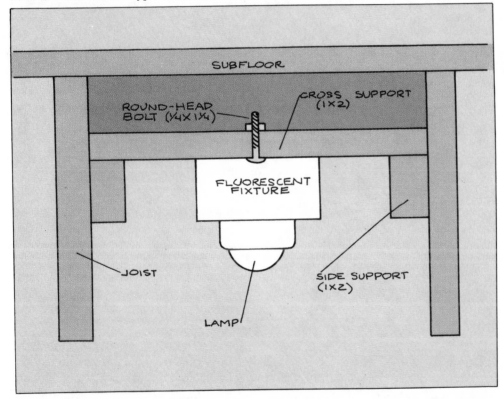

Measure the distance from the bottom edge of the floor joist to the subfloor above. A typical distance is 7¼ inches. Fluorescent lamps should be about 1½ inches above the plastic panels. The fixture (from the bottom edge of the lamp to the top surface of the fixture) measures about 3¾ inches. Mount 1-by-2-inch side-support strips along each joist between the bridging, as shown. (Do not remove the bridging.) Measure the exact distance between each of the joists (about 14½ inches) and cut the crosspieces to fit. Remove the lamps and cover from the fixtures. Then, use wood screws or round-head stove bolts to mount the crosspieces on the fluorescent channels. Hang the fixtures between the joists by tilting the fixtures and resting the crosspieces on the side-support strips. Do not fasten the crosspieces at this time. It will be easier to wire the fixtures if you can move them slightly. Wire the fixture for either one-circuit or two-circuit operation (pages 364-66). After the fixtures have been wired and tested, secure the crosspieces by driving finishing nails through the supports and into the joists at about a 45-degree angle. Once the fixtures are nailed in place, insert the lamps.

Installing ceiling support hardware and plastic panels

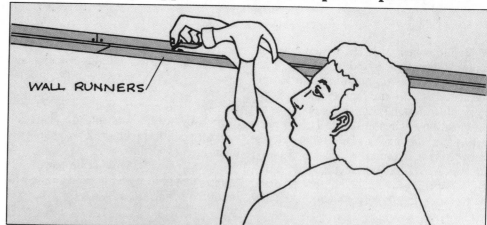

Wall runners are L-shaped pieces that are nailed directly to all four walls. Measure carefully, use a carpenter's level, and mark guidelines on the walls before you mount the runners.

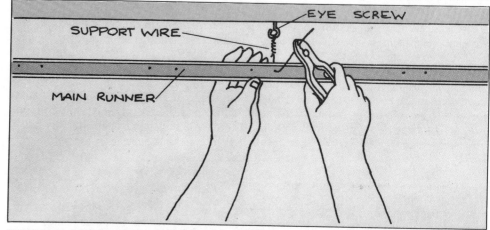

Install the main ceiling-panel support runners (T-shaped pieces) at right angles to the floor joists. Use support wires for this, as shown. Check the main runners with a carpenter's level and adjust the support wires as necessary. There may be a significant difference in the level of various floor joists.

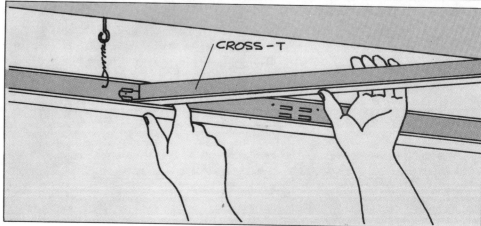

Install the cross-T pieces between the main runners and insert the panels. Open-mesh paneling or paneling with small perforations is best for between-joist installation. It allows for freer air flow. If you prefer solid paneling, install small sections of perforated or open-mesh paneling at each end of a joist run.

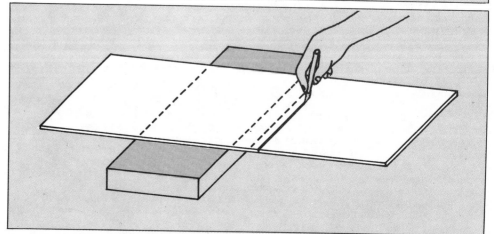

To finish areas that require panels of less than standard size, you will need an inexpensive plastic-cutting tool. Use this tool to score the smooth side of the plastic; then place a support under the panel along the scored line and break off the excess material.

Finished ceiling areas

When you install a luminous ceiling below a finished ceiling, determine the direction in which the ceiling joists run, and plan to mount the fixtures at right angles to them.

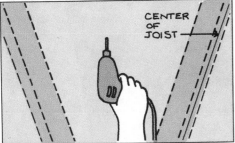

Locate each joist by drilling test holes or breaking away ceiling material (the existing ceiling will be concealed when you finish). Draw lines on the ceiling corresponding to the center of each joist. Take measurements and make a sketch of the ceiling, including the location of joists. If the space between the new, luminous ceiling and the original ceiling will be 1 foot or more, simply hang standard rapid-start fixtures on chains. These fixtures are available in 48-inch lengths with one or two lamps. The fixtures have built-in reflectors and come with hooks and chains for mounting. Use your ceiling sketch to plan locations, so you can screw the hooks into the joists.

Since standard center-to-center joist spacing is 16 inches, you will have at least three points to mount each 48-inch fixture through the ceiling to a stud.

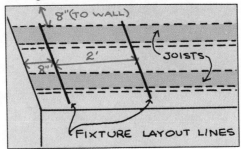

If there isn't enough room for hanging fixtures, use the following guidelines to plan your layout.
1. Unless an unusually high level of illumination is required, use 40-watt, rapid-start, single-lamp fixtures throughout.
2. Make a mark on the outside of each fixture to indicate the location of the ballast. Mount the fixtures so that there is at least 1 or 2 inches of airspace above the ballast.
3. Space the fixtures 8 to 12 inches from each wall.
4. Approximately 2 feet between rows of lights will provide good illumination.

Ruling the waves
You have to cut all those wires for suspending the main runners from the ceiling joists, right? Naturally, your suspended ceiling is lower by the length of the wires. Seems sensible, doesn't it, to cut all the wires the same length and attach them to the same spot on each joist? Don't you believe it. I get seasick every time I look up at my nice wavy ceiling. The darn floor joists were slightly different heights. So lay a level on the runners and adjust the wires *before* you attach the rest of the hardware and put in the panels.

Practical Pete

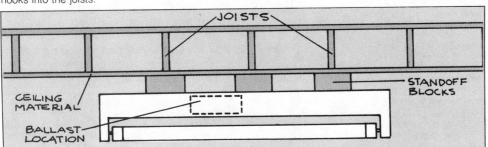

Cut pieces of 2-by-3-inch or 2-by-4-inch lumber, each about 4 inches long. Working on the 2-inch surface, drill a hole through the center of each piece. Use these blocks of wood as standoff mountings for the fixtures. Use 3-inch wood screws to attach the fixtures to the blocks. Insert a screw through a hole in the channel, then place a standoff block over the screw. Secure the fixture to the ceiling by putting the screw through the ceiling material and into a ceiling joist. Mount the L-shaped runners on the walls. Check these carefully with a carpenter's level. Secure the T-shaped main runners with hooks and wires. Check the runners with a carpenter's level at several points to ensure a level ceiling. You can easily make minor changes in runner height by adjusting the wire hanger. Snap crosspieces in place between runners, and insert plastic panels. Cut the panels as necessary.

Complete two-lamp and four-lamp fixtures are available for installation in suspended ceilings. There are sizes for 2-by-2-foot and 2-by-4-foot panels. Make a ceiling layout and decide upon the fixture locations. Install cabling first. Route cabling to the location of each fixture. Secure cables to the ceiling with cable staples. Remove sheathing and

wire insulation at each location and let the cables hang. Install main runners and crosspieces as previously described. Mount and wire the fixtures in position, following the manufacturer's instructions. You can wire these fixtures for one-circuit or two-circuit control by following the wiring diagrams provided for ceiling-mounted fixtures.

8. TRACK LIGHTING

Track lighting is sophisticated and highly versatile. Originally, it was developed for use in museums and department stores. But in recent years, several manufacturers have adapted it for use in homes. Track lighting provides what decorators call accent light. It can be used to focus a narrow pinpoint of light on a single object or to flood large areas with light. In short, it can be used to create and to change the mood of a room.

Track lighting consists of an electrified track and matching fixtures—usually in-stalled on the ceiling, 2 to 3 feet from the wall. Eight-foot sections can be mounted and joined at angles to follow the shape of a room. The track consists of continuous lengths of electrical conductors, mounted in plastic and enclosed in a metal channel. When specially designed fixtures are in-serted in the track at any point, electrical connections are automatically made.

To make power connections, you can wire the track directly to a ceiling box, or attach a cord-and-plug adapter to the track and plug it into a wall outlet.

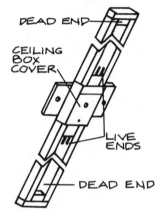

Center-feed components
These variations of live-end con-nectors accept track connections at both ends. You can use an existing ceiling box that happens to be in the middle of the run and install them like live-end connec-tors.

Cord-plug connection
Simply connect the end-piece adapter to the end of the track, plug the cord into a nearby outlet, and staple it to the ceiling and walls or conceal it behind drapes. The maximum electrical load on the track must not exceed 1000 watts.

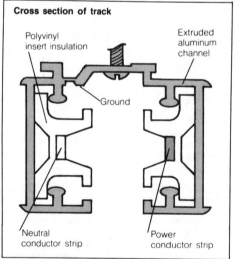

Cross section of track

Polyvinyl insert insulation

Extruded aluminum channel

Ground

Neutral conductor strip

Power conductor strip

Electrified track consists of an extruded aluminum channel that contains molded polyvinyl inserts. Three strips of metal are held in place by the polyvinyl. The strips of metal are connected to the power source. One strip (connected to the black power wire) is the "hot" line; another (connected to the white wire) is the neutral line; the third strip is connected to the ground wire. The polyvinyl insulates the aluminum channel from the conduc-tors. When track sections are connected, the connectors make contact with the conductor strips in each section. In this way power is continued from section to section. The aluminum channel and the polyvinyl insert are designed to make accidental contact with the conductors almost impossible. Still, don't go poking around in there.

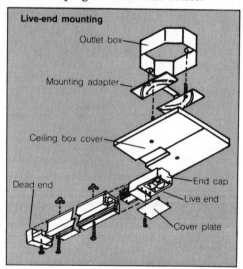

Live-end mounting

Outlet box

Mounting adapter

Ceiling box cover

Dead end

End cap

Live end

Cover plate

Connecting electrified track to a power source is easiest if you make the connection at a ceiling box. The fittings consist of a ceiling-box cover, an adapter that connects the cover to the ceiling box, and a "live" end piece that connects power to the track. To make the connection, first turn off source power to the ceiling box. Attach the cover to the box by means of the adapter. Feed the black, white, and ground power wires through the openings in the adapter and the cover. Then connect the power wires to coded, screw-type terminals in the live end piece. Attach the live end to its cover plate. When you connect the track to the live end, power will be applied to the metal track strips. Use end caps to close off the track. This will protect you from contact with the conductor strips at the end of the track.

Electrical rating

When connected directly to a ceiling or wall box, a track is rated at 20 amperes (2400 watts on a 120-volt line). The actual safe load, however, depends on the rating of the circuit to which the connection is made. If the circuit available at the ceiling or wall box is protected by a 15-ampere circuit breaker or fuse, then the track load on that circuit must not exceed 1800 watts.

If the circuit to which the track is connected also powers other lamps or appliances, the track load must be correspondingly reduced. For example, if the 15-ampere circuit mentioned above also supplied power to two wall outlets in which 150-watt lamps were plugged, the track load would have to be limited to 1500 watts. Different sections of the track can, of course, be connected to different circuits.

When track is connected with a cord-and-plug fitting, the maximum load is about 1000 watts. Make certain the circuit you plan to use can handle the additional load, however.

What it takes

Approximate time: Allow half an hour for each circuit wiring connection; 45 minutes for mounting and connecting each length of track; half an hour for positioning and mounting each lighting fixture.

Tools and materials: Track hardware, as described on pages 370 and 371 to fit your layout. solderless connectors, pliers, screwdriver, and voltage tester for circuit wiring; electric drill for mounting track. Most mounts include fasteners.

Track is made in 2-, 4-, and 8-foot lengths. Cut it to any length with a fine-toothed hacksaw. Remove burrs from the channel and conductors with a fine-toothed file; then brush any particles out of the track. Mount it directly onto joists with wood screws through holes or knockouts spaced along the track, or onto ceilings with toggle bolts.

There are many types of special mounts for use with track systems: clips for mounting track on uneven surfaces; extenders for lowering track; wall brackets; special fittings for attaching track to suspended ceilings.

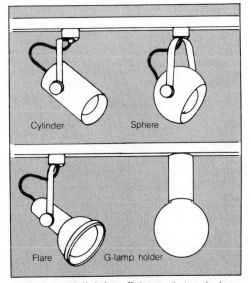

The variety of connectors allows track runs of almost any shape. In addition to straight connectors, right and left elbows provide right-angle, L-shaped track connections; T-connectors join three sections of track; X-connectors make four-way runs possible.

Typical track-lighting fixtures that swivel are cylindrical, spherical, and flare-end types. Lamps for the fixtures are available in 30- to 300-watt sizes. Standard general-service lamps, reflector lamps, and PAR (parabolic-aluminum-reflector) lamps can be used. G-lamp globes can be fitted to fixed holders that attach to track.

Planning hints:
While all track-lighting systems are essentially the same electrically, parts made by different manufactuers cannot be combined. Check the hardware available for track installation, the styles and types of fixtures available, and of course the cost.

9. SURFACE WIRING

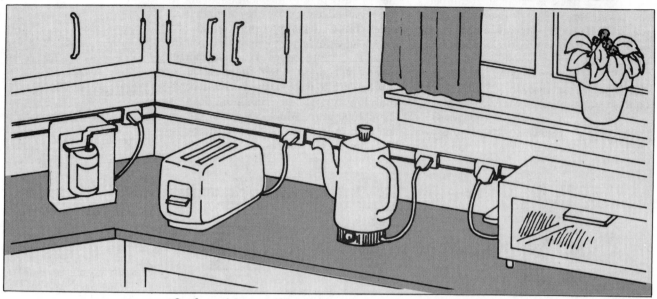

Approximate time: Surface wiring goes faster than adding outlets by fishing cable inside walls and installing new outlet boxes. Allow about two hours for running plastic strip wiring over a kitchen counter or workbench. Double the time for installing the same amount of baseboard surface wiring.

Tools and materials: There is little or no carpentry, plastering or painting required. To cut metal strip housing use a 40-tooth hacksaw blade. Plastic strip can be scored and broken with flat-end pliers (or a special trimming tool that cuts the housing and strips insulation off wires in one motion). Screwdriver, drill and bits, pliers, solderless connectors, the necessary lengths of track and associated hardware.

Surface wiring provides a safe, easy way to add outlets where you need them. As the name indicates, it is a way of adding outlets and fixtures to circuits without penetrating walls, ceilings, or floors. The wiring itself and the outlets and fixtures are all installed on wall or ceiling surfaces. There are two basic kinds of surface-wiring systems. One type consists of metal fittings and raceways (the channels that enclose the wiring); the other type is made of plastic. Metal raceways and fittings are grounded the same way armored cable is. Plastic raceways and fittings need a grounding conductor.

Surface wiring has some important limitations. It can be used only in protected, dry locations. Electrical codes in many areas limit surface wiring to one room; that is, a given surface circuit must begin and end in the same room. You can, of course, install another circuit in another room. The intent of this restriction is to keep surface-wiring raceways from penetrating walls or ceilings. Surface wiring is too conspicuous to be used in some areas. However, raceways and fittings are available in many finishes that blend well with surrounding surfaces. You can also help make surface wiring inconspicuous by keeping raceway runs low and horizontal. Vertical runs—unless concealed by drapes—are quite noticeable because the raceways cast shadows. Make vertical runs in or near corners or along door frames.

Metal and plastic raceway channels come in different sizes that hold various numbers of wires. The smallest size will easily accommodate three type-TW No. 14 or No. 12 wires. This should be large enough for most installations used for ordinary household appliances.

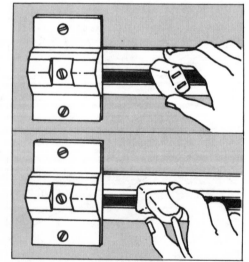

A plastic-surface wiring system has conductors embedded in a strip that is molded to accept specially designed outlets. The outlets are inserted in the strip at an angle and then twisted to a straight up-and-down position. This action makes an electrical connection between projections on the back of the outlet and the conductors in the strip.

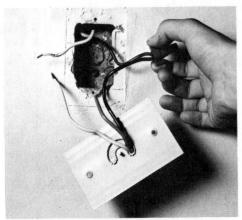

Power is connected to the plastic strips from an existing wall-outlet box. A special cover plate is provided to make electrical connections. The plate has two wires at the back and a fitting on the front. To install the plate, turn off power to the outlet. Remove the existing outlet faceplate, and disconnect and remove the receptacle.

Connect the wires on the cover plate to the power wires in the outlet box by means of solderless connectors. Then attach the cover plate to the box.

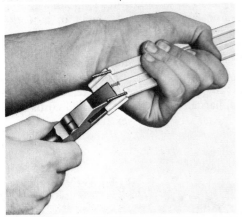

Trim the plastic strip at the ends to expose the conductors. To connect power to the strip, simply insert it in the fitting on the cover plate.

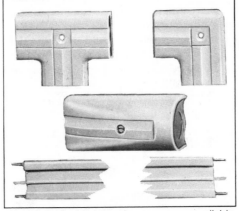

Elbows, Ts and right-angle corners are available, so you can route the strip wherever you want it. A special fitting is available to start the run from armored cable, if an outlet box cannot be used.

Metal raceways

Raceways are attached to walls in several ways. In one method, a two-piece channel is installed. The base piece is attached to the wall with nails or screws. Wires are routed along the base and then concealed by a cover that snaps into the base. In another, mounting clips are attached to the wall. Wires are fed through a rectangular tube held in place by the clips. An existing wall outlet usually provides power for the surface circuit. With power off, remove the faceplate and receptacle from the box. Then take the electrical connections from the receptacle. Mount an extension frame on the wall box. The extension frame has removable twist-out sections. Remove one and insert the raceway in the frame. Reattach the original electrical connections to the receptacle. Attach the wires for the surface circuit, routed through the channel, to the spare-receptacle terminals. Remember to connect black wires to brass colored terminals and white wires to chrome terminals. Be sure to maintain the wire color coding throughout the surface circuit.

Mount the receptacle on the extension frame, then mount the faceplate.

Baseboard wiring

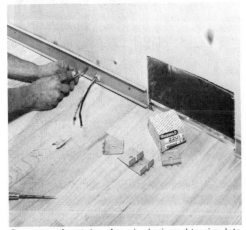

One type of metal surface is designed to simulate and replace baseboard. Outlets are installed directly in the raceway, eliminating the need for projecting boxes.

The metal channel has two sections. The rear section is attached to the wall in place of the original baseboard. Knockouts in the rear section can be removed, the power cable inserted, and secured to the raceway with a cable clamp. Use solderless connectors to join the power wires to the raceway. The front section of the channel has openings for receptacles. The outlets are held in place by spring clips. Spacing of outlets can be varied to suit your needs. In some models an additional snap-on strip can be put on top of the power channel to conceal low-voltage wiring (hi-fi or intercom) or TV/FM antenna wires.

10. TROUBLESHOOTING APPLIANCES

Most of us have come to depend on appliances to do dozens of jobs around the house. And with proper use, they will perform for many years. The typical life span of a toaster, for example, is ten years. A refrigerator will last for 15 years; an electric range may last for 20 or more.

Appliances do break down, however. The next few pages will tell you how to prevent early breakdown and how to correct the majority of troubles that may arise in the life of an appliance.

When appliances suddenly stop

1. **Check the power.** Most kitchens have an appliance circuit with outlets near the work areas. When small appliances fail to work, check the circuit breaker or fuse for the appliance circuit. If several appliances—especially those that heat—are being used simultaneously and all stop working, a simple overload is probably the cause. A toaster and an electric frying pan on the same circuit can easily cause an overload, even on a 20-amp circuit.

When an appliance will not start, or if it stops working during operation, turn the switch off and unplug the cord as soon as possible. Plug in another appliance or use a voltage tester to check for power at the outlet. If power is OK, check the appliance cord and plug for damage.

For large appliances, plug in a work light or voltage tester to check for power at the outlet. If the appliance is wired directly to the service panel and the circuit breaker is not tripped or the fuse not blown, assume that power is reaching the appliance. If power circuits and cords are OK, go on to the next step.

Testing appliance cords

Small appliances. Remove the cord from the appliance. Using a continuity tester, connect the alligator clip to one prong of the cord plug. Insert the probe in each receptacle at the end of the cord that attaches to the appliance. The tester should light when the probe touches one—and only one—receptacle. Repeat the test with the alligator clip connected to the other plug prong. The continuity tester should light once on both tests. If it fails to do so on either test, there is a break in the cord. If, in either part of the test, the tester lights up when the probe is touched to *both* receptacles, the cord is shorted. In both cases, replace the cord.

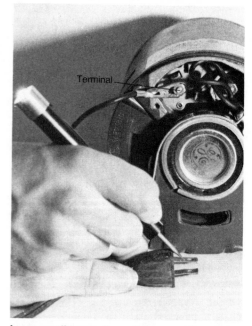

Terminal

Large appliances. Turn off power at the service panel. Unplug the appliance; then find and remove the access plate to the power source. (This will be located near the point where the power cord enters the appliance.) Behind the access plate, you will find two threaded terminals to which conductors in power cable are attached. Use your continuity tester to check from each plug prong to each terminal. The procedure and results should be the same as described for small-appliance cords.

2. Disassemble and inspect. The objective in fixing appliances is to inspect the workings with the least amount of disassembly. The procedure varies with different appliances, and may involve some detective work since main housing screws are often hidden. Typical methods of concealing screws are shown below.

The charts on page 378 will help you identify the type of motor generally used in the appliance you are troubleshooting. The motor characteristics column of the chart will help you locate trouble spots. **TIP:** For small appliances, first turn the appliance over and gently shake it. Loose parts will rattle or fall out.

Tips on locating screws

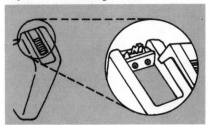

Snap-on parts. Check for removable plastic parts on the main housing. Mounting screws are often concealed underneath.

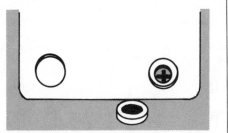

Felt, rubber, or plastic feet. Projections attached to the main housing to protect work surfaces may be glued over screws.

Deeply recessed screws. Don't pass up an opening in the housing because no screw is visible. Look in carefully with a flashlight. Screw heads are sometimes recessed an inch or more.

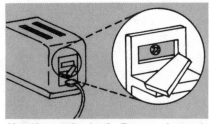

Metal inserts in plastic. The manufacturer's metal nameplate may actually conceal assembly screws. If you can, slip a knife blade between the edge of the metal insert and the plastic, and pry out the insert.

NOW you read the instructions
She said something about the sewing machine not working right. So big-deal, fix-anything Pete does his macho bit and tears into the thing to find what's wrong. Kinda fun until—you guessed it—he finds he has a couple of strange-looking parts left over when he's got it back together. Big bill and no sympathy from the repairman. Turned out that the bobbin had not been inserted correctly and thread tension was turned a little high. Reading the manufacturer's instruction manual doesn't do much for the ego, but that's how repairmen make a lot of their money. *Practical Pete*

Disassembly techniques

Small motor-driven appliances. Housings usually support all internal parts—motor field, armature, bearings, gears, and so on. If you must take the unit completely apart, support the housing as you remove the main screws. Separate the housing parts slowly and carefully. This will reduce the chance of breakage and will also give you a chance to see how parts are positioned in the housing before they fall free.

Small heating appliances. These have no gears or bearings and generally have few small parts. Here, the trouble will most likely be due to a break in the heating circuit—the power cord, the heat control, or the heating element itself. You can locate the break by (1) disassembling the unit and testing the cord, as described on page 374; (2) checking the heat control (page 380); and (3) inspecting the heating element for breaks.

Large appliances. Remove front, side, or rear panels to expose the key parts. Rear panels are usually secured with accessible sheet-metal screws. For front and side panels, remove the screws or snap-out spring clips at the bottom edge. Bring the panel 2 or 3 inches from the appliance and push it up. This will free the panel at the top. Try removing the front panel first to expose the side-panel mounting screws.

Troubleshooting checklist

Many defects that appear electrical are not. You can save a lot of time and money by making sure you are following the operating instructions for the appliance. Manufacturers provide detailed instruction manuals for most appliances, especially those requiring delicate adjustments, like sewing machines. Since these vary from model to model, write to the manufacturer for the correct manual if you don't have one. Take the time to read the instructions for your model. It's tedious, but better than paying a repairman to "fix" your appliance by telling you how to operate it correctly. An iron that "spits" water, for example, is possibly doing so because of a faulty thermostat. More likely, though, the iron is at the wrong setting or the reservoir is too full. Before you decide to repair an item, make sure you're using it correctly.

Problem	Cause	Correction
Food Mixers and Blenders		
Will not run	Speed control dirty or defective	Clean or replace speed control.
Lacks power on all settings	Control switch defective	Replace switch.
Excessive noise and vibration	Brushes worn or chipped	Reshape or replace brushes (page 377).
Mixer heats up excessively	Gears misaligned or damaged	Realign or replace gears (page 377).
	Bearings worn or binding	Replace or lubricate bearings.
Can Opener		
Slow running	Cutting edge dull or chipped	Inspect. Sharpen or replace cutting edge.
Noisy	Gears defective	Disassemble and inspect gearbox. Lubricate if necessary. Replace broken gears.
Portable Fan		
Fan erratic or slow	Motor armature binding	Clean and lubricate motor bearings (page 379).
	If oscillating fan, oscillator gears broken or jammed	Check oscillator gearbox. Lubricate or replace broken gears.
Fan vibrates or "walks"	Blade unbalanced	Check blade for dirt accumulation. Clean as necessary. If blades are bent, realignment is difficult but worth a try.
Vacuum Cleaner		
Motor slow, little suction	Brushes worn or chipped	Reshape or replace brushes (page 377).
	Motor bearings worn or misaligned	Align, lubricate, or replace motor bearings.
	If cleaner has belt-driven brush, belt off drive pulley	Check belt. Reposition belt on drive pulley. If belt seems loose, it will jump out of pulley. Replace belt.
Motor sounds normal, poor suction	Vacuum leak	Check hose for clogging or breaks. Check attachments for tight fit at joints. Hose may be temporarily patched with plastic tape. Worn attachments should be replaced.
	Exhaust outlet blocked	Check exhaust filter. Clean or replace.
Sewing Machine		
Machine slow and noisy	Lubrication required	Check instructions and lubricate as indicated.
Waffle Iron		
Too little or too much heat	Defective thermostat	Check thermostat. Clean if necessary. If temperature is still off, replace thermostat.
Waffles stick to grill	Grill not seasoned	Heat for 30 minutes after brushing grids with cooking oil.

Problem	Cause	Correction
Toaster		
Toasts one side only	One heating element open	Repair or replace broken element.
Toast does not pop up	Bread caught in carriage wires	Unplug toaster. Remove bread. Shake out crumbs.
	Pop-up spring broken	Check spring. Replace if broken.
	Hold-down latch caught or binding	Check latch mechanism. Clean, straighten, or replace.
Toast too light or too dark	Linkage from color control to release mechanism broken or loose	Check linkage. Make sure sliding parts are properly engaged. Replace if broken.
Coffee Maker		
Water gets warm, but doesn't perk	Defective thermostat	Replace thermostat—the circular unit located in base.
Steam Iron		
No steam	Steam ports clogged by mineral deposits	Clean with small brush dipped in vinegar.
Iron too hot or not hot enough	Thermostat incorrectly set or defective	Check and correct thermostat setting. If temperature is still wrong, disassemble and check thermostat. Have repair shop replace if defective.
Automatic Washer		
Tub does not fill	Water hoses disconnected or blocked	Connect hoses. Check for kinks or pinching.
	Shutoff valve closed somewhere in water-supply line	Disconnect hose at supply. Check water flow. Open valves as necessary.
Tub does not drain	Drain hose blocked	Check drain hose for kinks or pinching. Remove kinks and reroute hose as needed.
No spin cycle	Drive belt loose or broken	If belt is loose, tighten; if stretched or broken, replace.
Washer vibrates and "walks"	Small or uneven load distribution	Load must be large enough for even distribution.
Electric Clothes Dryer		
Does not start	Defective door interlock switch	Replace door interlock switch.
Does not heat	Defective heating element	Disassemble dryer and check heating element. Repair or replace as indicated.
Drum does not rotate	Drum binding or drive belt broken	Check drum for free movement. Small items of clothing can work between drum and housing. Disassemble and clear. Replace belt if broken.
Automatic Dishwasher		
Does not fill	Supply line turned off or blocked	Check supply line.
Dishes not clean	Water not hot enough	Check domestic water temperature. If heating system is *instantaneous*, be sure no other hot water is used during fill and rinse cycles.
Does not drain	Drain hose blocked	Clear or unkink as needed.
Refrigerator		
Interior temperature not cold enough	Control setting too low or control defective	Adjust control. If still not cold enough, check other items below. Have control replaced if defective.
	Door seal worn out	Replace door gasket if brittle, split, or worn.
	Inadequate ventilation around vents	Check for and remove obstructions.
	Defrost cycle on continuously	Timer defective. Have timer replaced.

Small motors

Appliance	Motor type	Characteristics
Food mixers Blenders Vacuum cleaners Sewing machines	Universal	High power. AC or DC. Wide range of speeds. Has commutator and brushes. Current flow is from one power line through one of the flat-wound, stationary field coils to one brush, through rotating armature, through other brush to second flat field coil to other side of power line.
Fans Can openers Hair dryers	Shaded pole	Light-duty motor. AC only. No commutator or brushes. Current is supplied to stationary field coil only. Small and compact.
Rotating cordless devices	Permanent magnet	Similar to universal motor except field coil is permanent-magnet type and requires no power. Brushes and commutator apply power to rotating armature. Low power output and consumption. Usually designed to run from rechargeable batteries.
Clocks Turntables Tape decks	Synchronous	Constant speed linked to 60 Hertz AC. Power is applied to stationary field. No brushes. Little maintenance required. Suited to any light-load application requiring constant speed.

Large motors

Appliance	Motor type	Characteristics
Washing machines Grinders Saws Lathes	Split phase (⅓ hp or less)	Operates on 60 Hertz AC. No commutator or brushes. Two sets of windings—one for starting; one for running. Centrifugal switch cuts out power to the start-winding when motor reaches running speed. Motor enclosed in own housing.
Large fans Water pumps Heavy shop tools	Capacitor start (up to 10 hp)	Operates on 60 Hertz AC. Capacitor provides power "kick" to start heavy loads. Centrifugal switch cuts out capacitor circuit when motor reaches running speed. Motor enclosed in own housing; capacitor mounted on top.

Universal motor

Shaded-pole motor

Permanent-magnet motor

Synchronous motor

Split-phase motor

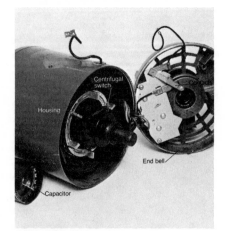

Capacitor-start motor

Motor parts: function and malfunction

Commutator and brushes supply power to the rotating part (armature) of a motor. The commutator is a segmented metal cylinder separated by insulating material. Brushes are small blocks of carbon that remain stationary and press against the commutator as it rotates. This causes current to flow between them.

If an appliance is sluggish, check brush contact by running the appliance in a dimly lighted area. Sparking will be visible through the ventilation openings in the appliance.

Small bluish sparks where commutator and brush meet are normal. Light bright sparks or bright and dim sparking indicate uneven contact and loss of power. You can shape new or chipped brushes to make good contact in two easy steps. First, wrap a piece of fine-grit sandpaper (rough side out) around the commutator. Then insert the brushes in the holder so they press against the sandpaper. Rotate the commutator back and forth by hand until the brush ends are shaped to fit.

Centrifugal switches are used on split-phase and capacitor-start motors that have one circuit to start the motor and another to keep it running. The part that switches it from one circuit to the other is a spring-loaded centrifugal switch.

Centrifugal-switch contacts are normally closed when the motor is at rest. As the motor starts to turn and build up speed, centrifugal force moves the flyweights outward. This causes the arm to turn on the pivot, removing pressure from the switch and allowing the contacts to open.

Tip: If switch contacts become clogged or dirty, the switch mechanism will stick and the *motor will not start.* To clean, remove the motor end bell and run a fine-toothed file between switch contacts to clean them. Clean mechanical parts of switch with small brush dipped in any household solvent. Dab light oil on sliding surfaces and pivot points. Hand operate parts to ensure free movement. Badly bent or broken switch parts will have to be replaced.

Gears convert motion from the motor to the part which is being driven and may be made of either metal or plastic. Metal gears are usually heavily lubricated; plastic gears are not. If an appliance motor hums but the appliance runs slowly, noisily, or doesn't run at all, the gears may be faulty. Gears can jam if they suffer mechanical shock (as by dropping or by severe overloading). Jammed gears can be repaired; broken or worn gears cannot. To repair faulty gears, separate them with a wooden or plastic stick. Rotate gears by hand to check for free movement. If they don't move freely, the gearing or the appliance must be replaced.

Motor bearings reduce friction between a fixed and moving part. If worn, dry, or misaligned they can cause poor performance and motor burnout. If the motor is permanently lubricated, make no attempt to add more. If oil is required, check for clogged wicks at lubrication points. Pull wick out of holder with tweezers and clean it in dry-cleaning solvent. Replace it when dry and add specified amount and type of lubricant.

When motors overheat
Heat can be destructive to any motor. Small appliances often have fan blades attached to one end of the motor armature to force air through the housing. Make sure ventilation openings are not blocked.

Most appliances are not intended for continuous use. Motor bearings will overheat and may bind or sieze, causing severe motor damage. Units should be turned off and allowed to cool any time the housing becomes too hot.

Heating elements

Heating coil

Sheathed heating coil

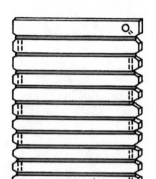

Flatwire heating element

Element	Appliance	Characteristics
Heating coil	Waffle iron	Spiral coil of heat-producing wire mounted on ceramic standoffs. Used in appliances where coil heats a surface that in turn cooks food. Breaks in wire are easy to spot by inspection.
Sheathed heating coil	Broiler	Heating coil enclosed in a ceramic-lined, steel tube that protects coil from grease. Heats food directly. Breaks not visible. Continuity check must be made.
Flatwire heating element	Toaster	Resistance wire wound on flat mica insulator. Spacing of windings can be varied to produce even heat. Breaks can be found by careful visual inspection.

Temperature control in appliances that heat

The basic element in controlling heat is a bimetallic unit that consists of two different metals fused together. Both expand when heated. But one expands faster than the other, causing the bimetallic unit to warp or bend. This, in turn, opens and closes electrical contacts, turning current on and off.

Electrical heating appliances are always either on or off. The heat level is controlled by varying the time between the on and off stages. If the current is on more than off, a relatively high temperature is maintained. If it is off more than on, a lower average temperature results.

There are two types of heat controls in general use:

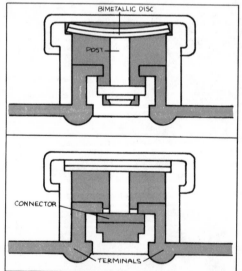

Fixed heat controls, like those on coffee makers, have a factory-set temperature. They are often operated by a circular bimetallic unit. When the desired temperature is reached, the bimetallic disc bends, pushing a plunger that opens the switch contacts. As temperature drops, the disc

straightens, closing the contacts. Thus, an average temperature is maintained.

Repair work on this type control is limited. If the unit is faulty, all you can do is clean the switch contacts. To do this, press contacts together with a piece of soft cloth or a dollar bill between them gently sliding cloth back and forth.

(Note: On many fixed-heat appliances, the heat-control housing is sealed. In this case, when something goes wrong, the complete heat-control unit must be replaced.)

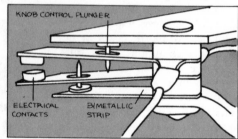

Adjustable heat controls are found on units like toasters and electric frying pans. On these units, a temperature-control knob activates a plunger that applies pressure to one of the electrical contact arms. When heated, the bimetallic unit—usually in strip form—applies pressure to the other arm. The less pressure applied by the control knob, the more pressure required by the bimetallic strip to separate the contact arms and switch off current.

Adjustable temperature appliances are fairly easy to repair, as the control-knob unit is accessible with some disassembly. The most common problem is uneven operation, caused by bits of food lodged between the contact arms and the knob or plunger. To fix, brush or scrape out food particles, and lightly rub the contact points with cloth or paper.

Room air conditioners

Wiring

Before buying a unit, know the amperage of the outlet it will be plugged into. Be sure installation will not overload existing circuits. Most home and apartment circuits are wired for a minimum of 115 volts/15 amps, although utility rooms (laundries and kitchens) may be wired for 20 amps to handle the load of large appliances.

Units rated at 12,000 BTUs or more are designed to operate on 208 or 230 volts and, like electric dryers, require special circuits. However, if circuit capacity is not overtaxed, you may be able to accommodate a unit of a maximum of 14,000 BTUs on a 120-volt circuit. Check with your local utility company for precise information on adequate circuitry.

Never remove the third prong from your unit's plug. Two-hole adapters known as "cheaters" are not recommended because they may not provide adequate grounding for the electrical charge. If your home has only two-prong outlets, install one that accepts a three-prong air-conditioner plug.

15 Amps 125 Volts

20 Amps 125 Volts

15 Amps 250 Volts

20 Amps 250 Volts

30 Amps 250 Volts

Seasonal maintenance

Wash air filters—located behind removable front panel—in warm, sudsy water, dry thoroughly, and replace. Some units require complete filter replacement when dirty; others are made of a metal mesh which can be cleaned and coated with a special dirt-catching aerosol. Check owner's manual on filter care. Wash every two to four weeks, depending on air quality of your area.

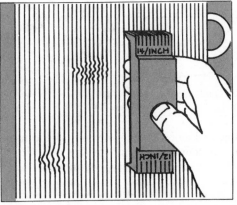

Vacuum coil fins with radiator attachment to clear away dirt, or clean with a soft brush. Straighten bent coil fins with fin comb available at refrigerator-parts stores. Spacing of teeth should match coils on unit. Coil fins are aluminum and bend out of shape from vibration and severe temperature changes due to ice forming on coils.

Tip: Exterior metal housing, though usually treated with rust- and corrosion-resistant materials, can become unsightly from severe exposure to the elements. You can touch up and further protect by wire-brushing rusted areas down to the metal finish and smoothing the surface with medium-grade sandpaper, feathering the edges as you go. A coat of metal primer and a finish coat of metal paint will protect it for years to come.

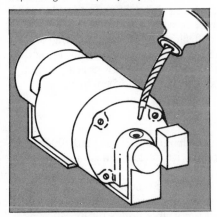

Oil fan bearings and condenser motor with SAE #10 or #20 nondetergent motor oil or type specified by manufacturer. Three drops on each spot will do it. Straighten bent fan blades. Check for refrigerant leaks—oily looking deposits around copper tubing. Check evaporator and condenser fan and motor belts for slippage. Replace or adjust by tightening.

Check mounting screws, nuts, and bolts which may have worked loose from vibration Periodically tighten those on mounting frame. Also check screw mountings on mechanical moving parts inside unit. Some will need slight adjustments, others, like the compressor, should float in their mountings, and overtightening hold-down bolts causes noisy operation. Check owner's manual.

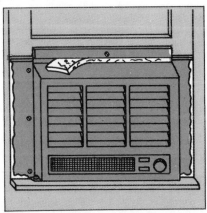

Replace loose or brittle window seals (weather stripping). Check for defective caulking on through-wall units. Air leaks reduce efficiency. Trim outside shrubbery to allow sufficient air flow.

11.OUTDOOR LIGHTING

The components of a complete outdoor lighting system include lamp post, entryway lights, garden lights, walkway lights, eave floodlights, and step lights. You can install the entire system or select only the items that suit your needs.

More and more, homeowners are including the outdoors in the indoor life and vice versa. Gardens are now appearing in living rooms, as are miniature fountains and pools, while the barbecue and the patio have greatly extended the dining habits of the family. And without outdoor lighting, much of the new indoor-outdoor life of the home would be quite impractical.

Family gatherings and entertainment, however, are not the only good reasons for outdoor lighting. Safe, well-lighted walkways and steps, and security against unwanted intruders are of prime importance.

The plan

It's a good idea to make a sketch or plan of your house and property so that you can lay out on paper where you will need lighting, for what purpose, and of what kind. You'll need to know where receptacles and fixtures will go, and what tools you'll require. You must also plan the best route to the indoor connection. As soon as you have reached a decision on what you require, contact the local authorities to see how your requirements fit the electrical code. At the same time, it will be wise to check your electrical dealer to see what wiring and other needed materials are available, and whether or not there are new developments and products that would benefit you.

Temporary wiring

Outdoor wiring must be placed under the ground if it is to have any permanency. On the other hand, you may wish to plan for temporary wiring only. For instance, you might be giving a party and will need a certain kind of lighting, which you might simply string up just for that one occasion; or you may wish to experiment with various kinds of lighting before you come to a final decision on a permanent installation.

It is necessary in temporary outdoor wiring to use at least No. 16 wire heavy extension cords of rubber. These can be purchased in lengths of 25, 50, and 100 feet. They come with sockets and plugs set in weatherproof rubber.

First step is to connect the cord into the nearest house (or garage) outlet. You will also need a portable outlet fixture such as shown in the sketch at right. Cords and outlets come in 2-conductor and 3-conductor grounded types; the latter are recommended. Be careful that you do not put too heavy a load on any circuit, since you will be hooking into the regular house circuits already in use.

Permanent wiring

If you have had some experience with installing wiring, then you might wish to undertake your own permanent outdoor wiring. If not, call in an electrician.

The cable (type UF) is buried in trenches which will go to the various areas you wish to light. Cable should be buried at least 18 inches below the ground so that it is protected from gardening tools. It can be buried only 6 inches if it is properly protected, either in a galvanized conduit or with a piece of metal over it.

The cable will be connected to underground junction boxes to which you can install fixtures permanently, or to weatherproof outdoor outlets. Be sure to check your electrical code because most codes require that metal conduit or sheathing be installed where cable comes out of the ground. Underground-type cable, if grounded, can also be used in certain areas.

It is easy enough to locate new outlet boxes on the side of the house, or on a fence, a tree, or any number of other places. Be sure to separate circuits for outdoor lighting on the house service panel; and for convenience, have a one-for-all switch installed inside the house.

For security purposes, you can install an electric-eye or timer that will control certain lighting units in order to light your grounds after nightfall whether or not you are home.

Try to plan your outlets and permanent lighting fixtures carefully so that you won't have to use extension cords. Measure the distance between the house and the planned outlet and fixture, and then add another 20 feet. This should give you enough slack for burying the wire. For permanent installations, it is recommended that you use No. 14 wire, or heavier.

Drill or cut any holes in the side of your house close to the circuit breaker or fuse box. Cut between studs if your house is wood. Always plug around the holes with caulking compound after the cable wiring has been run in.

It goes without saying that all your outdoor wiring must be complete, including the connection of terminals, before you connect it to the fuse or circuit-breaker box.

Additional wiring precautions

- Never work when the ground is not dry.
- Turn off the current while you are working.
- Elevate temporary wiring or any fixture, using string or tape, so that it cannot fall into a pool of water.
- Use only equipment—plugs, cords, sockets, connections—that was manufactured for the outdoors and that is waterproof.

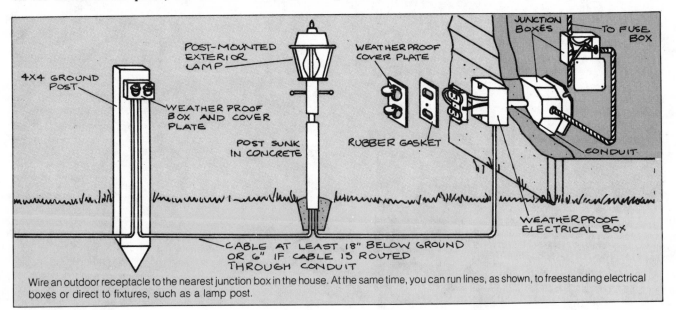

Wire an outdoor receptacle to the nearest junction box in the house. At the same time, you can run lines, as shown, to freestanding electrical boxes or direct to fixtures, such as a lamp post.

Ground fault interrupter

The ground fault interrupter (GFI) is a supplementary circuit breaker which the National Electrical Code requires in any new outdoor circuits. A GFI can detect even a slight current leak and will shut off a circuit so fast that it prevents serious shocks from happening. This receptacle with a GFI will fit an outdoor box. Except for a push button labeled R (which resets the interrupter after it trips), and another labeled T (which simulates a leakage when you want to test the device) it looks just like an ordinary receptacle. Check with your local electrical code, and electrician before installing.

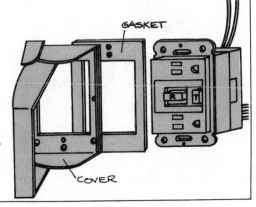

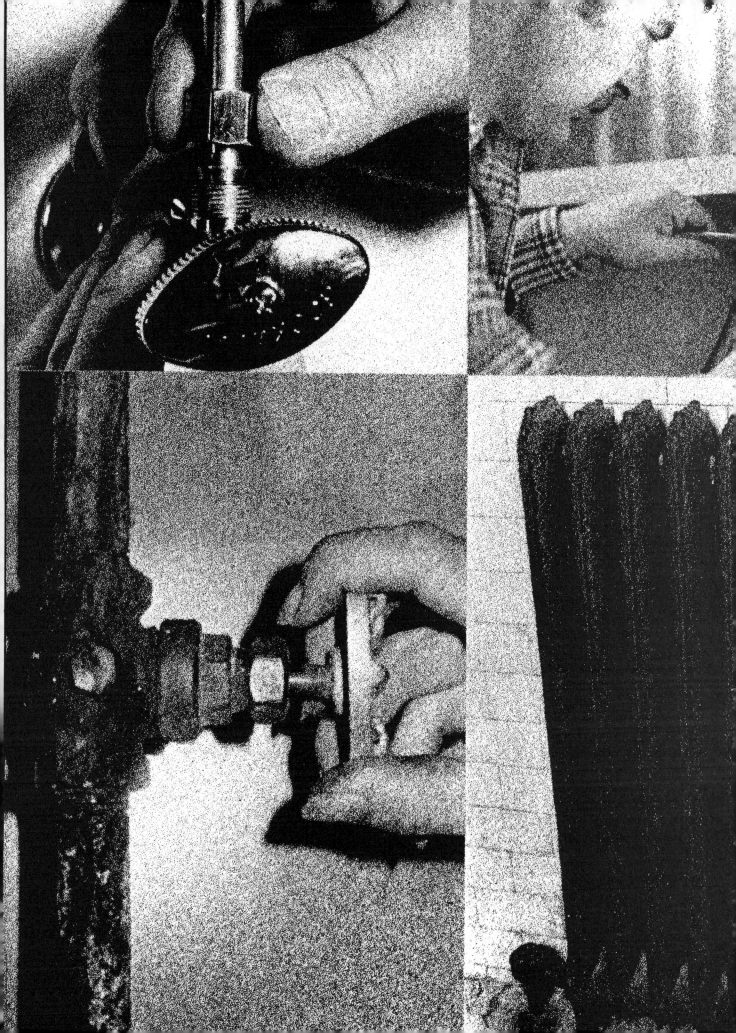

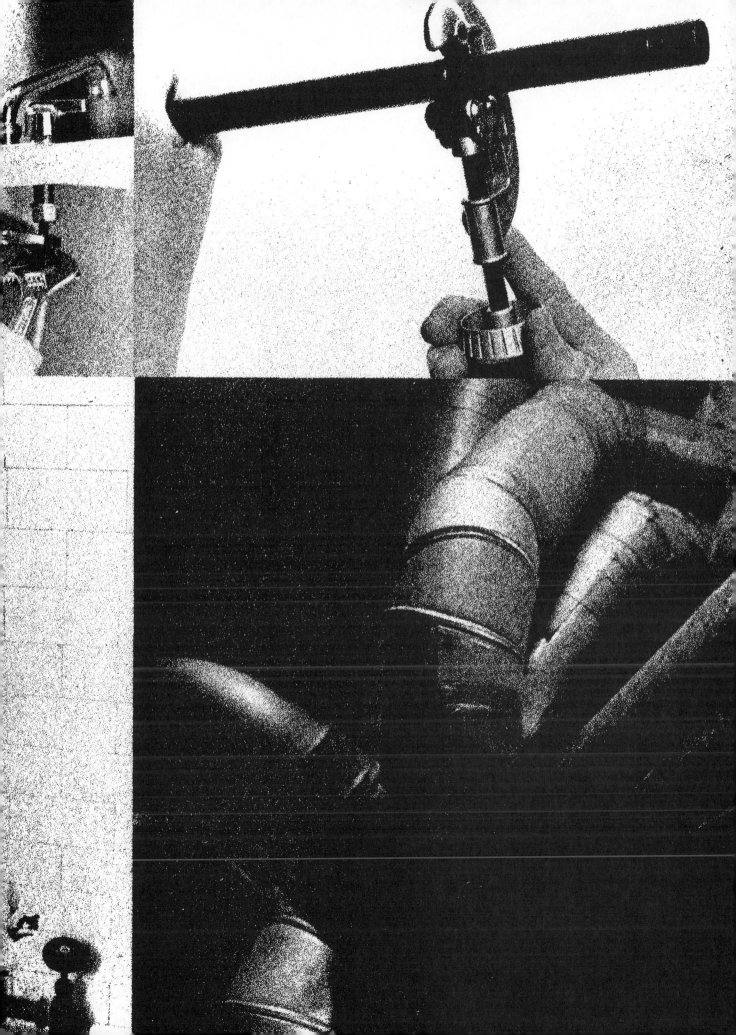

PLUMBING
& HEATING

1.	BASICS	388	How an air chamber works	391	Plumbing tools	396
	Getting started	388	Drain-waste-vent system	392	How to use basic tools	396
	Home-buyer's checklist	389	Parts of the system	392	Tips for general plumbing tools	398
	Water-supply system	390	Drain-waste-vent pipe sizes	393	Tools for plastic pipe	399
	Parts of the system	390	Fixture and appliance hookup	394		
2.	FAUCETS	400	Disc faucet repair	403	Lever-type washerless faucets	405
	Faucet repairs	400	Lever faucet repair	403	About valves	406
	Washer-type faucets	400	Washerless faucets	403	Cross connections and	
	Replacing a washer	401	Troubleshooting faucet leaks	404	vacuum-breaker valves	407
	Fixing valve seats	402	Fixing aerators	404		
3.	SINKS AND BATHS	408	Replacing faucets	409	Upgrading a shower head	411
	Installing faucets	408	Installing traps	410	Installing fixture shutoffs	412
	Modernizing fixtures	408	Replacing a sink sprayer	411	Caulking	413
4.	TOILETS	414	Flush valve parts	417	Replacing a toilet	418
	Unveiled: the mystery of the flush toilet	414	Tankless flush valves	417	Removing the old toilet	418
			Troubleshooting tankless flush		Installing the new toilet	419
	Troubleshooting toilet tanks	415	valves	417		
5.	PROBLEM SOLVING	420	Freeing toilet drains	422	Curing condensation	426
	Unclogging drains	420	Freeing branch and main drains	422	Preventing freezing	426
	Freeing sink or lavatory drains	420	Solving frequent clogging	423	Thawing pipes	426
	Freeing tub drains	421	Fixing leaks	424	Curing water hammer	427
	Freeing floor drains	421	Troubleshooting leaks	425		
6.	PIPING	428	Cast-iron DWV piping	433	Sizing DWV runs	438
	Vinyl water-supply piping	428	Plastic DWV piping	434	Sewer pipe is different	439
	Threaded water-supply piping	430	Solvent welding	435	Comparison of popular sewer	
	Joining sweat-soldered copper		Running a vent stack	435	pipes	439
	tubing	431	Sweat-soldered copper DWV	436	Adapting pipes	440
	Running water-supply pipes	432	Running DWV pipes	437	Problems with low flow	441
7.	APPLIANCE REPAIR	442	Sump pumps	444	How a water softener works	448
	Clothes washers	442	Replacing a sump pump	445	Water-softener connections	448
	Troubleshooting an automatic		Dehumidifiers	446	Arrangement of water-treatment	
	clothes washer	442	Caring for your water heater	447	units	449
	Dishwasher repairs	443	Troubleshooting water heaters	447		
	Troubleshooting a dishwasher	443	Water treatment	448		
8.	PRIVATE SYSTEMS	450	Troubleshooting well pumps	452	Percolation table	455
	The hydrologic cycle	450	Hand-dug well	453	Tank-size table	455
	Water supply	450	Comparison of well types	453	Building a seepage field	456
	Drilling a well	451	Sewage treatment	454	Single-family sewage-treatment	
	Connecting a pump	451	Parts of a septic system	454	plant	457
	How a pressure tank works	451	Building a sewer	455		
	Lowering a submersible pump	452	Installing a tank	455		
9.	HEATING	458	Electric heating	463	Adjusting blower speed	467
	Heat moves in three ways	458	Heat exchangers, distributors,		Pulley alignment	467
	Elements of a heating system	459	and conduits	464	Steam-heating systems	468
	Humidity	459	Routine maintenance	465	Routine maintenance	468
	Heat producers	460	Draining the system	465	Fireplaces	469
	Oil burners	460	Draining the expansion tank	465	Solar heating	470
	How to maintain an oil burner	461	Flushing and refilling	465	Heat pumps	472
	How to restart an oil burner	461	Bleeding the line	465	Where heat pumps are most	
	Draft control	461	Forced hot-air systems	466	efficient	473
	Gas burners	462	Maintenance and adjustment	466	How a heat pump works	473
10.	PROJECTS	474	Shutdown checklist	474	A garden pool and waterfall	476
	Cold-weather house shutdown	474	Building a dry well	475	•INDEX	478

1.BASICS

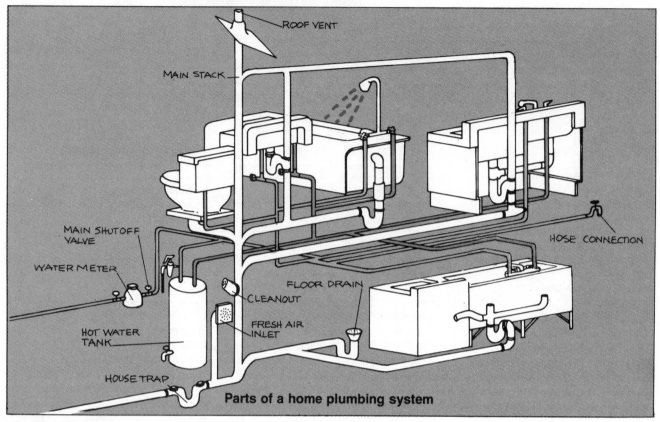

ROOF VENT

MAIN STACK

MAIN SHUTOFF VALVE

WATER METER

HOSE CONNECTION

CLEANOUT

FLOOR DRAIN

FRESH AIR INLET

HOT WATER TANK

HOUSE TRAP

Parts of a home plumbing system

Getting started

If you know that water flows downhill and that a large-diameter pipe can carry more water than a small-diameter one, you're a long way toward becoming a do-it-yourself plumber, and saving some money.

In the old days, when leaded joints were the standard, house plumbing was limited to skilled journeymen. Today, with the introduction of plastics to plumbing, it is very much a do-it-yourself project. Even though your present plumbing system uses materials other than plastics, today's fittings provide a better, easier means of connection than the old leaded ones did. In short, you can do your own plumbing and carry the job as far as you wish. You can merely handle emergencies, such as a stopped-up drain or a pipe leak. Or you can go the whole route and install new piping, even putting in the plumbing for an added bathroom or a vacation cabin. It is not our purpose, or intent, to turn you into a professional plumber. However, after reading it, and with some practice, you will be able to do quality household plumbing.

Every home-plumbing system features three parts: the water-supply

system, the fixtures and appliances that use water, and the drain-waste-vent (or DWV) system. The water-supply system brings water into the house and distributes it to all the fixtures and appliances. These include hose attachments called bibbs, as well as fixtures like toilets, sinks, bathtubs, showers, and laundry tubs. Appliances consist of the water heater, water-treatment unit, dishwasher, clothes washer, furnace, humidifier, drinking fountain, garbage disposer, and boiler.

The drain-waste-vent system collects wastes from the fixtures and appliances and runs them out of the house into the sewer. It also is responsible for venting gases to the outside air, and is designed to provide access to the drain system, a necessity for clearing clogs.

For your purposes, the water-supply system begins at the point where water enters the house. This system consists of small pipes because the water in them is under pressure. The drain-waste-vent system ends 5 feet outside the house foundation, where the sewer begins. DWV operates on the principle of gravity flow.

The pipes in this system are large since they must pass solids along with the liquid wastes. Fixtures and appliances are joined to one or both systems, depending on their use of water and their function.

To do your own plumbing, all you need is to learn the parts of the plumbing system, and accumulate a few simple tools. You probably already have some of them. If you plan to install any pipes, you'll need to know how they are joined, the different fittings that are available, and the limitations of the kind of pipe you will be using.

This section will give you all the know-how you need to do your own plumbing. Beyond that, the best teacher you can have is the job you do yourself. If you should run into problems, you can always ask questions of your local plumbing-supply dealer, hardware dealer, or home-center plumbing clerk. After reading this section, however, you may find that you know more than they do.

Another source of free advice—your plumbing inspector—will even make house calls. He will make the trip only to enforce local building codes, however, not to get on the end of a pipe wrench. All new plumbing you do will probably have to be inspected. Interior plumbing, whether on the water-supply or DWV system, comes under the jurisdiction of your city or county building-inspection department. Outside sewer building involves the local public-health department. These agencies will want to examine the finished work—before it is hidden from view—to see that approved methods have been used. Method and material requirements are both spelled out in your local plumbing code. Ask for a copy. A code is nothing to fear. It's for your protection and the protection of anyone who might buy your house later.

Many local codes adopt the provisions of the National Plumbing Code. Illustrations and descriptions given here are based on the current code, which is probably available in your local library. If no local requirements exist, follow the provisions of the National Plumbing Code. Study it before you tackle a major job.

If your local code contains overly restrictive provisions that prevent you from using easy-does-it methods or materials—like flexible water-supply pipes—ask the plumbing inspector for what's called a *variance* or *experimental permit*. It's *your* house. If you want to use a simpler system than the local code allows, there's no good reason why you should not be granted a variance permit—as long as your system meets the standards of the National Plumbing Code. Although it is sometimes possible to avoid an inspection, much of what the inspector checks is what you would want to check anyway. Leak-testing is an example. If you work with your local inspector, you should find him more help than hindrance.

Some communities require you to apply for a permit to do even minor plumbing. In other communities, whether or not you need a permit often depends on what you call your project (see table below). If you term it *new work*, you'll need a permit. But if you can see your way clear to calling it maintenance, you don't need a permit. This can eliminate more than red tape. Your tax assessor looks at permits with an eye to increasing your property value, and thus your taxes. So, if you don't need a permit, don't get one. If in doubt, ask at your local buildings department.

What's the single most important thing to know about house plumbing? Where the main shutoff valve is located. That valve shuts off all water flow to the house. It's often in the utility room or crawl space, next to the water meter (if you have one). You may need to find it in a hurry someday. So all family members should be familiar with its location and be able to get to it on short notice.

Home-buyer's checklist:

When you buy a house, your investigation should include the plumbing system. You want to know the quality of materials used and whether the system works as it should.

1. Throw a cigarette butt or crumpled piece of toilet paper into the toilet bowl and flush it down. If it doesn't disappear, the system may be sluggish and prone to stopping up.

2. Run a bathtubful of hot water and throw in some dimes. The water should be clean enough for you to tell whether they're showing heads or tails.

3. Thump on the bathtub. A loud, tinny sound indicates stamped metal—cheap. Likely the whole system is cheap. A more muffled, ringing sound points to cast iron—much better.

4. Turn on the hot- and cold-water faucets in all sinks and listen. The flow should be vigorous and there should be no piping sounds—rattling, creaking, groaning, and so on. If you hear them, it indicates restricted water flow.

5. Turn the faucets off rapidly and listen for "water hammer" (banging) in the piping. If you hear it, the system was probably built without protective air chambers. This points to poor design.

6. Look in the basement, crawl space, or attic to see what kinds of water-supply and DWV pipes were used. Compare them with the pipe charts (pages 428 and 433). From the standpoint of longevity, the best pipes are copper or brass for water-supply systems and copper or cast iron for DWV. Nothing wrong with the other types, though.

7. Note any evidence of water leaks on walls, floors, and ceilings.

Before a home water-supply system is approved, it usually needs a pressure test. For this, all system openings are capped or valved off and a pressure gauge is attached at one outlet. The water is turned on and then off at the main valve. If there are no leaks, pressure should hold steady overnight.

When a drain-waste-vent system is tested for leaks, all trap and fixture openings are sealed off. Then the system is filled with water at a roof vent-stack. The water level should hold in the stack overnight to prove out the system.

Is a permit needed?

Type of project	Typical jobs	Permit required?
Maintenance	Repairs, emergencies, replacing damaged or worn-out fixtures, replacing old piping.	No.
Remodeling	Replacing outmoded fixtures, modernizations, re-arranging new or existing fixtures, adding fixtures.	Sometimes. Term it "maintenance" if possible.
Additional or new plumbing	Adding a bathroom, installing plumbing in a new garage, house, or vacation cabin.	Yes.

Water-supply system

House-service entrance pipe. Brings water underground into the house.

Water meter. Measures the gallons of water used between readings so that the user may be billed for it.

Main shutoff valve. Cuts off water flow to the entire house.

Cold-water main. Routes cold water close to the fixtures and appliances that use it.

Hot-water main. Routes hot water close to fixtures and appliances that use it. Runs parallel to the cold-water main, about 6 inches away from it.

Branches. Fittings attached to the mains, that deliver hot or cold water to fixtures. The pipes are normally one size smaller than the main.

Fixture shutoff valves. Used in both hot and cold fixture-supply lines at the wall or floor behind the fixture. Permits selective shutoff of water to that fixture.

Air chamber. Used in both the hot- and cold-water lines behind fixtures and fast-shutoff appliances. Cushions water turnoff, preventing water hammer. A must for every system. Not needed on slow-shutoff fixtures such as toilets.

Temperature-and-pressure relief valve. Also called T&P valve. Used on the water-heater tank to release excessive steam pressure and heat. Prevents explosion. A must in all systems.

A house water-supply system is supposed to bring an adequate flow of clear, pure water to each fixture without much piping sound. And it should continue to do this job for a long time. The life of a water-supply system depends in great part on the pipe used. Some types resist corrosion and internal scaling better than others, and thus last longer.

Water for the supply system comes from a water utility—usually the city—or from a private water source such as a well. The quality of the water can vary from clear and delicious to murky and foul-tasting. In any case, the water *must* be potable—drinkable. If there is ever a doubt about potability, local health officials will test water free of charge. City water is tested for purity daily at the water-treatment plant. Private water sources should be tested at regular intervals, especially during wet times of the year, when contamination is most likely.

For full flow and pipe silence there must be pipes of adequate size throughout the water-supply system. A pipe that's too small, or one that has become scaled up on its inside surface, makes water speed up as it passes. This creates a disconcerting "water-running" sound. Using the right size pipe (see "Water-supply pipe sizes" table) ensures a quiet, efficient system.

In a piping system, lengths of straight pipe are joined by fittings. With fittings, you can have pipes to branch off, go around bends, and generally fit your plumbing plan. Since water flows through straight pipe much more easily than through angled fittings, the fewer fittings used in a system the better. Of course, a certain number of fittings are necessary just to make the installation.

The water in a house-supply system is under pressure—city water pressure runs about 50 psi (pounds of pressure per square inch; a standard measure). It is because of this pressure that the water-supply system can utilize much smaller pipes than a DWV system, and the water can flow up, down, or around as needed to reach fixtures. Gravity flow is important, however, should you need to drain the system, if, for example, the house is to be

Water-supply pipe sizes

Purpose	Pipe diameter
Fixtures	½ inch
Branches to fixtures	½ inch
Outdoor spigot	½ to ¾ inch
Cold, hot main	¾ inch
Service entrance	¾ or 1 inch

Some older houses use ⅜-inch supply tubing to toilets and sinks.

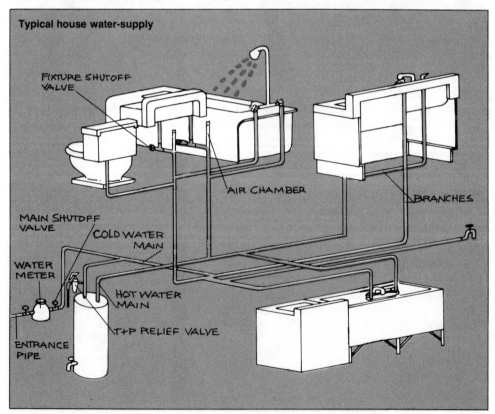

Typical house water-supply

FIXTURE SHUTOFF VALVE

AIR CHAMBER

BRANCHES

MAIN SHUTOFF VALVE

COLD WATER MAIN

WATER METER

HOT WATER MAIN

T+P RELIEF VALVE

ENTRANCE PIPE

Main shutoff valve

unheated during below-freezing weather. Therefore, a well-designed water-supply system slopes slightly toward one or more low points. Drain or stop-and-drain valves located at those points are used to empty the system of water. Lacking these, other methods are available for cold-weather shutdown (see page 474).

When a water-supply system is built, direct pipe routings are chosen where possible. This is especially true of pipe runs that are hidden behind walls or in the attic. These are routed as directly as possible to reach their destination—across ceilings, through walls, and so on. With hot-water pipes, short direct runs are especially important. Shorter distances mean less heat loss—and saved energy. Where piping is exposed to view, however, as in a basement, most people want it to look neat and orderly. For this reason, visible pipes—even flexible-pipe installations—run with neat, square 90-degree turns.

The information above refers to the water system in general. With a detailed look, the system breaks down into three major types of pipes. The entry pipe, which supplies water to the house; the hot- and cold-water mains; and the branches that lead from the mains to the fixtures and appliances requiring water.

There are several types of branches. Parallel branches lead from the hot and cold mains to all fixtures that need both types of water. Hot water enters on the left side of these fixtures, cold on the right. Cold-only branches lead to the toilet and furnace humidifier. A dishwasher gets a hot-only branch. Sometimes a branch pipe serves more than one fixture. For example, single hot and cold branches may lead to a distant bathroom where they branch again to the various bath fixtures. This saves you the trouble of running mains to that room. In addition, smaller branch pipes have the advantage of delivering hot water more quickly, and with less heat loss, than main pipes can.

Some older water-supply systems have double piping between the water heater and bathroom fixtures. This maintains continuous circulation of hot water through the pipes and permits immediate hot-water flow from fixtures connected to them. Double piping is no longer installed because of its wasteful use of energy. The modern method is to insulate hot-water piping, and thus help it retain heat between water uses and in transit between the water heater and fixture. Page 426 shows the procedure for insulating a cold-water pipe to prevent condensation. The process is the same for a hot-water pipe, though the purpose is different.

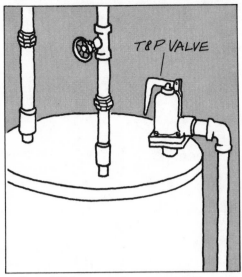

T&P VALVE

In addition to the water-delivering pipes, the water-supply system has a variety of other components. A temperature-and-pressure relief valve (T&P valve) on top of the water heater harmlessly bleeds away explosive pressures and temperatures.

To prevent annoying, potentially damaging water hammer, air chambers are placed in the wall behind each fast-shutoff fixture. These chambers usually consist of capped, 12-inch vertical lengths of pipe, of the same diameter as the water-supply pipe. As water flows toward an open valve, inertia prevents it from stopping immediately after the valve is closed. Instead, the water can "bounce around" violently for a moment inside the pipe, causing the hammering sound. Severe hammering can build up enough force to split fittings, particularly in plastic-pipe systems. Air chambers harmlessly absorb the inertia and prevent both water hammer and damage. Fixtures, like toilets, that are not subject to quick shutoffs, don't need air chambers at all.

The last component of the water-supply system is the riser tube. One reaches from the shutoff valve (or adapter fitting) on each fixture to the faucet tailpiece. These tubes are often flexible, and they are used chiefly to simplify water-supply connections to fixtures.

All pipes of a water-supply system must be installed in such a manner as to be safe from freezing. When running pipes in exterior walls cannot be avoided, the pipes must be placed on the warm side of the wall's insulation. To protect pipes in unheated crawl spaces, either heat the crawl space slightly or wrap the pipes with electric heating cables. Pipe insulation is of little help in preventing freeze-up because, after a time, all heat escapes through even the thickest insulation. And insulation makes it more difficult to thaw out pipes that have already frozen.

How an air chamber works
When the faucet is turned off, water stops abruptly, compressing air in the chamber and cushioning the shutoff.

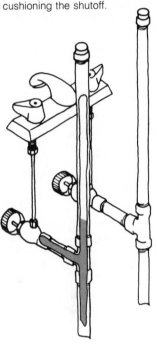

Fixture shutoff valve

Drain-waste-vent system

Parts of the system

Stack. A vertical pipe that collects wastes from fixtures. It vents up through the roof and is open at the upper end.

Vent. The upper portion of a stack that releases gases to the atmosphere.

Main stack. A stack that serves fixture drain and vent lines. Also called a soil stack.

Fixture waste pipe. Combination drain-vent pipe that connects a fixture or appliance with the rest of the DWV system. Sometimes called a branch drain.

Trap. Simple water-seal device between a fixture drain and the DWV system. Keeps sewer gases out of the house.

Revent. A vent-only run attached to a fixture to prevent trap siphonage. Rises from fixture and elbows into a stack above the highest fixture-waste connection.

Building drain. Drainpipe that collects all house wastes and leads them into the house sewer outside the foundation.

Cleanouts. Access openings in horizontal drainpipes, necessary for removing clogs.

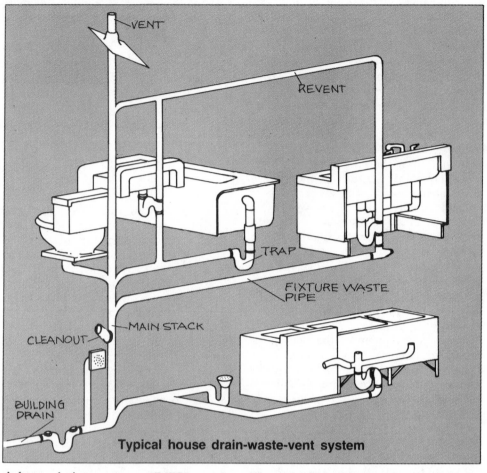

Typical house drain-waste-vent system

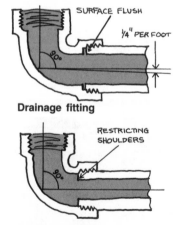

Drainage fitting

Water-supply fitting

A house drain-waste-vent (DWV) system carries fixture and appliance wastes away by gravity flow. Like a water-supply system, it should operate quietly, efficiently, and with proper flow. Some portions of the system, called vents, carry gases only. Others, called drains, carry wastes only. And some portions, called wet vents, carry both gases and wastes. Working together, these three components of the DWV system handle the remainder of the plumbing chores, picking up where the water-supply system leaves off.

Because DWV pipes and fittings are expensive, this system takes precedence in both the planning and installation stages. The rest of the plumbing system is planned around it. As many fixtures as possible are drained into a single main-drainage pipe, which is large enough to carry the entire flow. The idea is to plan your DWV system to use as little material as possible, yet not underpower it. Too big a system, besides being dollar wasteful, can be as troublesome as one too small.

DWV systems using lightweight pipes, such as copper and plastic, are likely to be noisier than those made of heavy cast iron. The additional noise usually doesn't amount to much. However, if there are sucking sounds as a fixture drains, there are problems with the DWV system's design or construction. Sluggish draining, or gurgling in one fixture trap as another fixture drains, likewise indicates troubles.

Used water coming from house fixtures contains solids. These tend to build up as greasy deposits on the insides of pipes and fittings. Build-ups are not serious in vertical drainpipes because the fast downflow of wastes scours them clean. But horizontal drain sections—that is, those sections that are only slightly sloped—can eventually get clogged. For this reason, every horizontal pipe must be accessible for cleaning. If the pipe is accessible through a fixture's drain, it may be cleaned from there. If not, an access point, called a cleanout, must be provided. Cleanouts are usually located at the higher ends of horizontal drainpipes, and they are usually covered with screw-on plugs. All cleanouts must be within easy reach, so when they're located in walls or ceilings, access doors should be provided. Sometimes access is through a toe-plug in the floor.

Drain-waste-vent pipe sizes

Purpose	Pipe diameter
Fixture waste pipes	1½ or 2 inches
Toilet waste	3 or 4 inches
Fixture vents	1½ inches
Toilet vent	2 to 4 inches
Vent increaser	4 to 6 inches
Building drain	3 or 4 inches
House sewer	4 inches

Some systems use 1¼-inch waste pipes for lavatories.

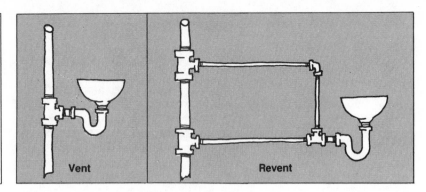

Vent   **Revent**

No cleanout should be located less than 18 inches from a wall or obstruction behind it. If this cannot be worked out, then the pipe is extended through the wall or obstruction and a cleanout fitting placed on the other side. Without the 18-inch clearance, getting a snake or auger into the fitting to clear a blockage may prove an impossible task.

Proper slope of the drainpipes is important. Too steep a slope lets liquids run ahead of solid wastes, leaving solids stranded in the pipe to form clogs. Too shallow a slope causes sluggish drainage and is also apt to clog. Properly sloped pipes drain quietly and efficiently and operate for long periods without clogs. A ¼-inch-per-foot slope is optimum.

Drain-waste-vent fittings are built differently from water-supply fittings, which need not work by gravity flow. DWV fittings are made with gently curving passages rather than sharp turns. The absence of shoulders in the fitting leaves no catch-points for the solids as they flow through. Scaled-down DWV fittings would work well in a water-supply system, but water-supply fittings, with their inner shoulders and obstructions, would soon short-circuit a DWV system. For this reason, even though water-supply fittings are less expensive, they should not be used for the DWV system. Of course, the pipe and fitting sizes are different for the two systems, and mixing them would be tough, in any case.

Drainage fittings may be used throughout a DWV system. But in portions where no waste water is present—the vent portions—it is better to use vent-type fittings. These fittings do the same job as drainage fitting, but cost less.

Every fixture must have a trap (see drawing opposite). The one in the space under your kitchen or bathroom sink is probably the most familiar. These traps are usually the same size as the waste pipe—often 1½ inches—but can be scaled down to 1¼ inches. Avoid using a trap with a larger diameter than the waste pipe, as it may cause clogs. The best traps are those with built-in cleanout plugs.

Though you can't see the traps on most other fixtures, they all have them. Bathtub, shower, and automatic-washer traps are underneath the fixture, below floor level. Dishwashers and garbage disposers share the kitchen-sink trap, while every toilet has a built-in trap.

If it weren't for these traps, another part of the DWV system, the vents, would not be needed. Vents provide an outlet for gases, and keep air pressure from building up. This pressure could siphon fixture traps dry, making them useless. Thus every fixture must be vented. Venting extends the DWV system upward through the house and opens it to the atmosphere, 12 inches above the roof.

Some fixtures perform both draining and venting tasks through their waste pipes. These pipes are known as wet vents. If wet vents have to travel too far (between the fixture's trap and the vent stack), extremely rapid waste flow, and siphonage, can occur. To avoid this, revents are used. These are simply vents that extend upward from a fixture and join the vent stack higher up. Fixtures with small waste pipes are especially subject to wet-vent siphonage and should be placed close to the vent stacks that serve them. Otherwise, revents must be installed. Reventing a toilet, with its large drain pipe, should be avoided. If the toilet is within 24 inches of a main vent, no reventing is needed. If this placement is impossible, a specialized treatment for a toilet revent is necessary. With a Y-fitting, the toilet waste pipe is extended "upstream" from the toilet. There it is connected with a secondary stack that is the same size as the waste pipe, usually 3 inches. This is hardly reventing at all, since an entire new stack must be extended through the roofline. So, try to design toilet locations near main vent-stacks. In fact, reventing in general, because of the additional pipe, fittings, and time it requires, should be avoided if possible. Do so by placing fixtures close to vent-stacks. A few very restrictive local codes, however, still prohibit wet vents and make it necessary to revent all fixtures.

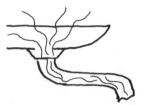

Usealed drain would let gases into room.

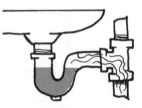

Gases sealed off by drain-trap water.

Unvented trap would be sucked dry by siphon action.

Vented trap is not siphoned so water seal stays in place.

Fixture and appliance hookup

Using riser tubes

Flexible metal riser tubes can be cut to size and bent by hand to fit between fixture and its water-supply shutoff valve, eliminating the need to line up the two pipes perfectly. Tube with bullet-nosed end inserts into sink or lavatory faucet tailpiece; tube with flat end connects to toilet tank inlet pipe.

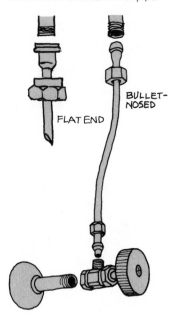

FLAT END

BULLET-NOSED

Using trap adapters

Slipjoint trap adapter connects fixture trap to waste pipe quickly. Adapter slips over trap arm which can be slid in or out as needed to reach fixture drain. Then trap slip-nut, with O-ring washer inside, screws onto adapter's outer threads to form gas-tight, water-tight joint.

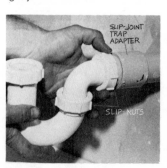

SLIP-JOINT TRAP ADAPTER

SLIP-NUTS

If you add a bathroom or a new appliance, you'll be working with fixture plumbing. The following paragraphs will give you a general introduction to installing fixtures and appliances. The various jobs have much in common. The table of contents for this section shows the page numbers where instructions for each type of installation will be found.

Bathtubs and showers drain below the floor, either through a P-trap or a drum trap. The P-trap may be cleaned through the tub's drain. A drum trap has a removable cover. This must be accessible below the floor or through a floor plate.

For a shower, the piping is installed first. Then the shower floor pan is laid over it and the drain caulked. For bathtub installations, you need access from below the tub once it is in place. Where bathtub access must be from above, as in a concrete-floor house, it's provided through a wall-access panel at the head end of the tub. Trap connections are made in a 12-inch-wide, 14-inch-long galley in the floor below the tub's drain. A toilet connects to its closet flange without underneath access (see page 419).

Water-supply connections to tubs and showers cannot use the flexible riser tubes shown at left because of the greater (5-gallon-a-minute) flow required. (Most fixtures need only about 3 gpm.)

Most tub and shower mixing controls are designed to take ½-inch threaded pipes or adapters. Some contain ½-inch sweat-solder fittings for a direct copper-tube hookup. A giant-sized escutcheon, or shield, covers the hookup hardware.

In framing for fixtures, be sure to provide headers—horizontal 1-by-4-inch boards nailed into the framing. They are necessary supports for lavatory sinks and also hold the lavatory water-supply outlets. They're needed for tubs, too, where they secure the faucet and control, the shower arm, and the tub-rim supports. See the drawing on the next page.

Lavatories and sinks drain through separate P- or S-traps. Use P-traps for wall waste pipes, S-traps for floor waste. A wall-waste setup is preferable.

Water-supply hookups to sinks and lavatories are made with fixture shutoff valves and riser tubes. Use angle-stops from walls, straight-stops from floors.

A water heater needs an energy connection and, if it's a fuel-fired heater, a vent. Plumbing connections consist of a valved cold-water inlet and a hot-water outlet. A heater also requires a T&P valve with a ¾-inch relief pipe, which leads to a floor drain or other convenient emergency-disposal spot, as shown at right.

A water softener is connected in series with the cold-water main. Easiest to use are flexible connectors designed for that purpose.

Garbage disposers are mounted in kitchen-sink drains between the sink and the fixture trap. Besides the plumbing hookup, a disposer requires an electrical connection. Be sure to follow the manufacturer's instructions for this.

A dishwasher—if not a portable—gets a hot-water-supply pipe all its own. The simplest connection is made with flexible tubing and a flare fitting at the dishwasher inlet valve. Be sure to provide a shutoff valve in the line. Dishwasher wastes are pumped out through a flexible rubber tube into a side tapping on the sink drain.

An automatic washer often utilizes an existing laundry tub with its hose bibbs and drain features. It can also be installed with separate hot and cold hose bibbs of its own. Drainage then is into a 1½-inch standpipe that reaches 36 inches above the floor. This standpipe should have a below-floor trap.

New wrinkles

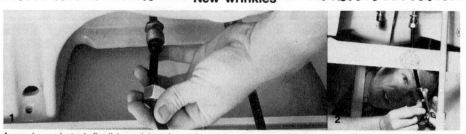

A newly marketed, flexible polybutylene riser tube bends easily to reach between the wall or floor fixture-shutoff-valve and the faucet tailpiece. It withstands hot and cold water; bends without kinking. The new riser fits standard ⅜-inch fixture shutoff valves. To install it, (1) cut the riser to size with a knife and slip the compression nut and brass ferrule on the riser, (2) install the riser in the shutoff valve and tighten the compression nut.

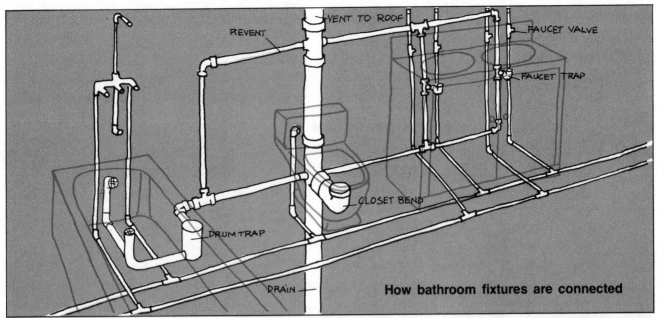

VENT TO ROOF
REVENT
FAUCET VALVE
FAUCET TRAP
CLOSET BEND
DRUM TRAP
DRAIN

How bathroom fixtures are connected

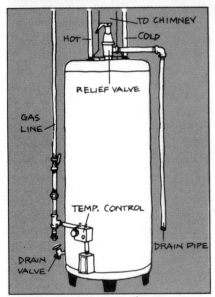

TO CHIMNEY
HOT
COLD
RELIEF VALVE
GAS LINE
TEMP. CONTROL
DRAIN VALVE
DRAIN PIPE

Water heater and connections

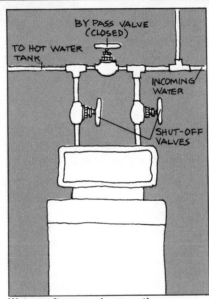

BY PASS VALVE (CLOSED)
TO HOT WATER TANK
INCOMING WATER
SHUT-OFF VALVES

Water softener and connections

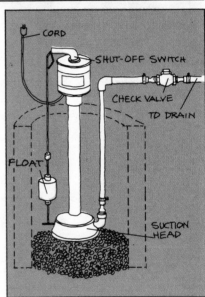

CORD
SHUT-OFF SWITCH
CHECK VALVE
TO DRAIN
FLOAT
SUCTION HEAD

Sump-pump connections

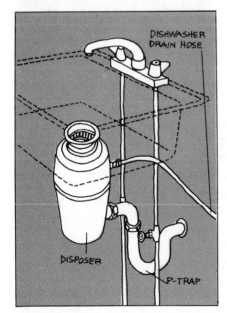

DISHWASHER DRAIN HOSE
DISPOSER
P-TRAP

Garbage disposer

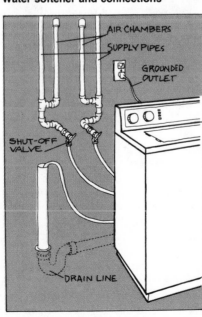

AIR CHAMBERS
SUPPLY PIPES
GROUNDED OUTLET
SHUT-OFF VALVE
DRAIN LINE

Automatic-washer hookup

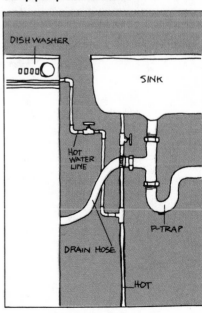

DISH WASHER
SINK
HOT WATER LINE
P-TRAP
DRAIN HOSE
HOT

Dishwasher connections

Plumbing tools

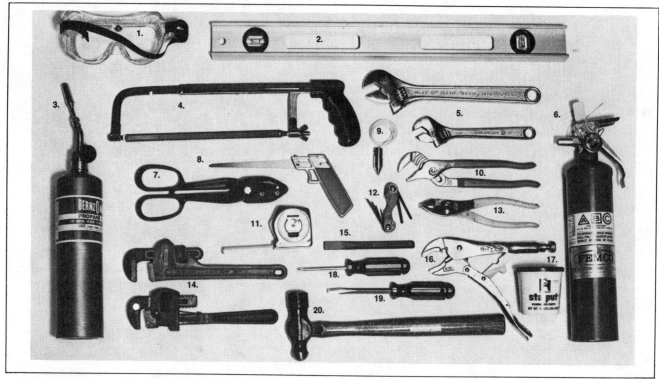

(**1.**) Goggles or safety glasses $2–$6. (**2.**) Level $6–$10. (**3.**) Propane torch $8–$18. (**4.**) Hacksaw $4–$7. (**5.**) 6- and 12-inch open-end adjustable wrenches $5–$10. (**6.**) Fire extinguisher (ABC rated, with gauge) $13–$30. (**7.**) Metal or aircraft snips $4–$7. (**8.**) Keyhole saw $2–$4. (**9.**) Plumb line $1–$2. (**10.**) 10-inch channel-pliers $5–$9. (**11.**) Retractable measuring tape $5–$12. (**12.**) Allen-wrench set (for setscrews) $3–$5. (**13.**) 8-inch slip-joint pliers $5–$7. (**14.**) Two pipe wrenches $7–$11 each. (**15.**) ¾-inch cold chisel $3–$4. (**16.**) 10-inch locking plier/wrench $4.50–$7. (**17.**) Plumber's putty $1–$2. (**18.**) Phillips screwdriver $2.50–$4. (**19.**) 10-inch screwdriver $3–$5. (**20.**) Ball-peen hammer $7–$12.

Get sharp

It didn't take me long to get the point. Now I believe in keeping tools sharp. You not only work faster, you work safer. Properly sharpened tools cut well without being forced. It's when you have to force a tool to do its job that you get bruised knuckles, scraped hands, and worse. So keep a proper edge on chisels, screwdrivers, knives, and saws. And if the gripper jaws on a pipe wrench get rounded off after long use, get a new wrench. It will pay off in saved knuckles.

Practical Pete

Basic tools used for plumbing (see above) may include many you already own. They belong in every home workshop. If the list includes any tools you don't have, consider acquiring them. It's a lifetime investment.

In order to do any actual work with plumbing pipes and fittings, you also need most of the tools in the general-plumbing category. Here you can be selective. Choose tools according to the type of pipe you'll be installing. Only for systems using No-Hub drain pipes, for instance, would you need to buy the No-Hub torque wrench.

Maintenance tools are often acquired only when a problem arises. Basic to plumbing maintenance, and the first tool to reach for when a clog occurs, is the plumber's force cup (see page 422). When the clog is tougher, maintenance tools with a bit more clearing power can be bought. But these tough-clog clearers and other tools are often too costly to warrant ownership for just occasional use. Most can be rented on an hourly or daily basis.

How to use basic tools

A **claw hammer** and a **ball-peen hammer** are not interchangeable. Use a claw hammer only for driving and pulling nails. If you pound on a cold chisel with a claw hammer, you risk chipping its face and ruining it. A ball-peen machinist's hammer has a harder face and is designed for this use. Grip a hammer close to the end of the handle. Don't "choke" it. This improves your leverage; it also helps to keep the face of the hammer flat to the work.

There's a right and a wrong way with other tools, too. A **screwdriver** should fit snugly into the screw slot, with little or no play. Keep the shaft of the tool vertical to the head of the screw. The 10-inch screwdriver is for driving or removing standard slotted screws; the other is for Phillips-head screws. (No. 2 is the most common Phillips screwdriver size. It will also handle the small No. 1 Phillips-head screws found on some faucet handles.)

Pliers are among the most often misused tools. They were never intended to take the place of a wrench. The hardened jaws of a pair of pliers, when used on a soft brass or plastic nut, will chew it up. Pliers can also round off the corners of harder nuts, sometimes making them unremovable. Pliers are great when you need more leverage than your own hands can supply. But a good rule to follow is to never use pliers if another tool can do the job as well. Most standard pliers are of the slip-joint type. These can be set at two widths for gripping narrow or wide objects.

Similar to the slip-joint pliers, but with a greater range of width settings, are **channel-joint pliers.** A good pair may be substituted for a pipe wrench if the turning isn't too hard.

Completing the common plier types are **locking pliers.** These feature adjustable jaws. Properly adjusted, and with the handles squeezed together, locking pliers form a portable vise. As such, they can be used for holding pipes when you need to saw them, or for temporarily securing a part before it is permanently attached. Use locking pliers with care, however, because they have enough leverage to deform copper tubing and fittings. The best locking pliers have an easy-release lever that lets you remove them without pulling on the handles, which would otherwise be hard to open.

Longer and longer lengths have become the trend in **measuring tapes.** The 25-footers are now commonly used, meaning that very long measurements can be taken directly. Adding up shorter lengths isn't necessary. Handiest of all the measuring tapes are those with a spring-loaded, self-return mechanism. For plumbing jobs where long measurements aren't often needed, a less expensive yardstick will do.

The **carpenter's handsaw** is used for notching framing members to make way for pipes. It can also be used—in conjunction with a miter box—to cut plastic pipe. (The miter box is necessary for getting a square edge.)

If you have an old saw that's ready to be thrown out, save it for cutting pitch-fiber sewer-septic pipes. These will leave black stains on any saw used to cut them. If you don't have an old handsaw, remove the stains from your good saw with solvent. Then oil it to protect from rust.

Metal pipe should be cut with a **hacksaw.** Slice through thin-walled copper tubing with a fine (32-teeth-per-inch) blade. For other cutting, use a regular 24-tooth blade. A hacksaw works just as well as a carpenter's handsaw on plastic pipe.

Where holes are needed in tight quarters, as for a pipe run, a **keyhole saw** does the job. Its narrow, pointed blade allows you to start a cut in a drilled hole. The handiest type has removable, reversible blades in different sizes. Put in backwards, the blade can saw right up to a flat surface, letting you cut through a pipe that runs along a wall.

Open-end **adjustable wrenches** are used for turning nuts up to 1¼ inches in width. Use the 6-incher for small nuts, like those found on faucets, and the 12-incher for larger ones, as on valve bonnets. Always position adjustable wrenches so that you are working the handle toward—not away from—the movable jaw. This keeps the stress on the strong cast housing, rather than on the weaker lower jaw. An old-fashioned **monkey wrench,** which has the opening on the side instead of the end, can be substituted for either or both of the open-end wrenches.

Allen wrenches are used for setscrews which are sometimes found on faucets and their escutcheons, or shields. These wrenches have closed, hexagonal heads that can be inserted into the recess of a setscrew to turn it. Allen wrenches usually come in sets. One handy version includes most of the smaller sizes in a single tool, with the wrenches hinged like the blades of a pocketknife.

Most **propane torches** come in kit form, complete with various tips that give small or large flames. You'll want a large tip for sweat-soldering copper pipes. When you turn off the torch between uses, be sure that the flame goes out. Unscrew the torch from the canister between jobs, and follow the storage cautions on the container. You'll find that a flint striker is much handier than matches for torch lighting.

The **cold chisel** made completely of metal, has many uses in plumbing. It's used for severing cast-iron pipes (see page 433), and chewing through stubborn nuts that won't come off. Any time you need real power for cutting through metal, a cold chisel can provide it. Pound on this chisel only with a ball-peen hammer, and always wear goggles when you use it. A chisel whose head is badly "mushroomed" from long use should be ground flat, with a slightly beveled edge. Otherwise, flakes of metal may dislodge. The tip may occasionally have to be restored too. When you do this, be careful not to change its original angle. For both jobs (known as redressing) use a grinding wheel and wear eye protection.

You'll need a **level** for most plumbing jobs. The 2-footer recommended in the tools list is best. Look for one with three bubble tubes. These are opposed to one another, enabling you to check for level horizontally and for plumb vertically.

Whenever you work with hand tools, minimize all possibilities for injury. A pair of **work gloves** can save splinters and blisters, and **goggles** or safety glasses are a must whenever loose particles or hazardous liquids that may enter your eyes are present. A **fire extinguisher**—the dry-chemical type—should be a part of every tool kit. One is especially vital when you are working with a propane torch.

TRAP/SPUD WRENCH

SOCKET WRENCH SET

MONKEY WRENCH

PIPE WRENCH

STRAP WRENCH

TUBE CUTTER

BASIN WRENCH

Tips for general plumbing tools

Having **pipe wrenches** in two sizes, as noted in the tool list on page 396, is helpful in many plumbing jobs. Either may be used singly for turning threaded pipes and fittings when the opposite end is well anchored. They can also be used as a pair when one end is not anchored (see illustration below). A small wrench is best unless you need greater leverage than it provides. Where this added leverage is needed, go to a larger wrench. Never put anything over the handle of a tool to increase its leverage. Pipe wrenches will bite in only one direction and only when the handle is pulled toward the movable jaw. Pushing the other way removes the wrench, or lets it alternately bite and release for a kind of ratchet action.

On exposed pipes, where you want to avoid making teeth marks, use a **strap wrench.** This has a heavy nylon strap instead of jaws. To use one, start with the strap coming out the convex side of the wrench, as shown in the illustration below. Wrap the strap around the pipe. Then feed it back into the slot in the wrench. If properly installed, the strap will tighten as you pull on the handle.

Use flame with care
What's the worst possible time for a house fire to start? When the water supply is turned off! Remember that fact whenever you are soldering. A torch flame can easily start a house fire. If it gets sawdust smoldering, a fire can break out later. Carry a small dry-chemical fire extinguisher with you wherever you solder. And when you solder a fitting that's close to wood, always put a sheet of asbestos behind the fitting to stop the flame. Soaking the wood behind the fitting with water helps, too. Be careful where you direct the torch's flame while you're concentrating on feeding solder into a fitting. And, of course, don't use a flame around combustible liquids or gases.

Practical Pete

Tighten fittings with two pipe wrenches, one to hold and one to turn. Apply force toward the jaw openings.

Use a strap wrench to avoid leaving teeth marks on soft pipes such as brass.

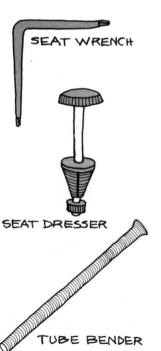

SEAT WRENCH

SEAT DRESSER

TUBE BENDER

Water-supply pipes, whether steel, copper, or plastic, can be cut with **pipe or tubing cutters.** These have sharp wheels that neatly slice through pipes. To use a cutter, open it wide and place it over the pipe. Position the cutting wheel over your mark. Tighten the wheel securely, then revolve the cutter around the pipe until it cuts through the wall. After each full revolution, you'll have to retighten the clamp. Many tubing cutters contain a built-in **pipe reamer,** making separate purchase of that tool unnecessary.

Flaring tools are used in conjunction with flare nuts to make flared joints in soft-tempered copper tubing. These tools are of two types: drive-in and clamp-in. A drive-in flarer is simply a cone-shaped device that is driven into the end of the pipe until the desired flare is created. Clamp-in flarers have two parts, a vise bar that holds the pipe and a clamp with cone-shaped die that makes the flare. The farther the pipe protrudes from the vise, the bigger the flare. Whichever type you use, always put the flare nut on the pipe before shaping.

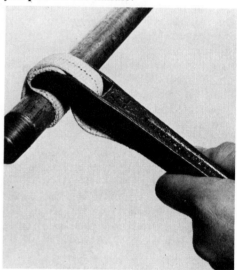

Cutting wheels in pipe and tube cutters slice into pipe or tubing as cutter is rotated. After each circular cut is made, cutter is tightened slightly.

To flare a tube end, slip flare nut on tubing, insert tube end in opening the same size in die, tighten wing nuts, insert flaring tool tip in center of tube, and tighten by turning clockwise.

For working in tight quarters underneath and behind fixtures, you'll need a **basin wrench**. It has a long arm that can reach behind a lavatory to loosen or tighten fixture nuts on the water-supply tubes. An **adjustable trap** or **spud wrench** is for use on large nuts such as those on sink strainers, traps, and toilets. Another fixture tool, used for installing or removing faucets, is the **faucet spanner**. One usually comes with a new-faucet installation kit.

Most well-stocked rental centers carry **drain augers**, **rotary root cutters**, and **pipe-threading equipment**. These relatively high-cost items should be rented unless steady use is anticipated.

Pipe threaders are used only for metal water-supply pipe, not plastic. Most come with an assortment of dies, as well as the pipe stock (handle) and vise. The important thing to remember is to use plenty of thread-cutting oil to keep from chipping the newly-formed threads and to prolong die life (see page 430).

Usage of specialized tools not described here will be covered in later sections.

DRAIN/TRAP AUGER

TOILET/CLOSET AUGER

PLUMBERS FORCE CUP

A basin wrench gets into snug quarters underneath sinks and lavatories.

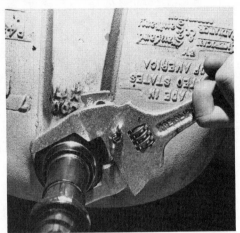

Adjustable spud or trap wrenches fit large slip nuts such as those on toilet tank connections.

A faucet spanner, provided with new faucets or repair kits, is used to tighten or loosen faucet adjusting ring to prevent stem leaks. Get one that matches your model faucet.

Tools for plastic pipe

Working with easy-does-it plastic pipe takes very few tools beyond those shown in the illustration on page 396. The only additional items you'll need are: a 1½-inch paintbrush; 9/16- and ¾-inch hexagonal Allen wrenches (for tightening transition unions); penknife and sandpaper (for smoothing pipes). One of the tools shown—the tubing cutter—is optional. If you use one, get one with a plastic-cutting wheel. But, you can substitute a handsaw. It works as well as the cutter.

Not much of a tool kit. But it's about all you'll ever need for plastic pipe.

A chip off the old block
A few years ago, I used to laugh at the idea of wearing goggles. "Not me," I'd say. Then, one time when I was sharpening a chisel on a grinder, a chip of metal nearly flew into my eye. That taught me a lesson. Now I wear safety glasses or goggles whenever there's any chance for eye injury. Be smart. Protect your eyes whenever you are grinding, drilling, chipping, soldering, using a chisel—for any job where a particle or liquid could get into your eye. Believe me, it can happen.

Practical Pete

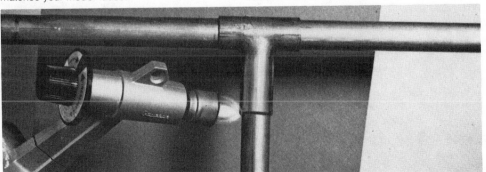

When soldering or thawing pipes always place an asbestos sheet between the flame and nearby beams or wall surfaces. To solder a joint, heat the fitting and pipe until tip of solder, touched to opposite side of joint, melts and flows into the joint. Don't heat solder.

2.FAUCETS

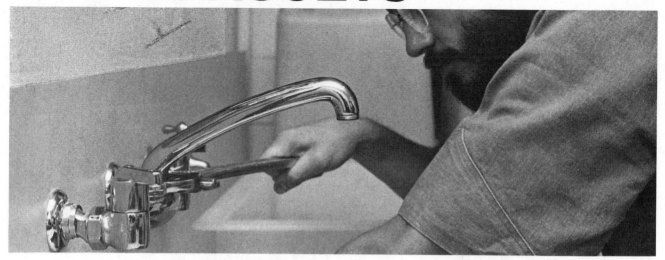

Faucets are valves attached to the ends of pipes. Fixing them can vary from simple washer replacements to installing new spindle assemblies. Replacement parts are available separately or in kits.

Buy parts that match your type of faucet. There are several types. Simplest of all, and the original one, is the washer-type faucet.

Washer-type faucets

Despite the increasing popularity of washerless faucets, many washer faucets are still around. And although they require more frequent repairs, they are usually the simplest to fix. These faucets work by means of a rubber washer attached to the faucet spindle. When the handle is turned to the *off* position, the spindle is lowered, and the washer is clamped tightly onto a metal seat. This closes off water flow through the faucet body. The clamping is done by fast-acting threads on the spindle.

This is the type found in most old plumbing systems, and is the least expensive faucet to buy. In more modern systems, you are likely to find washerless faucets—units that use diaphragms, discs, valves, balls, or cartridges in place of washers. More costly but less troublesome than washer-type faucets, these are becoming standard.

It's a beautifully simple system, but rapid wear results from the closing action because the washer is twisted as it is pressed onto the seat. In time, especially on the hot-water side where the washer is softened by heat, you must turn harder to stop all flow. This causes still more wear, and ultimately, when the faucet no longer can be shut off completely, you must repair it. As soon as you have to force the handle to stop the flow, get set to make the repair.

(*continued on page 402*)

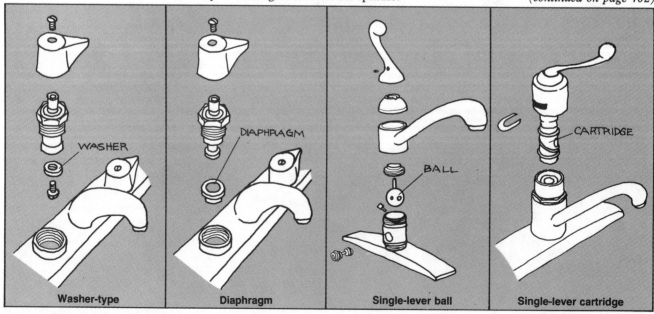

Washer-type | Diaphragm | Single-lever ball | Single-lever cartridge

Replacing a washer

1. To replace a leaking faucet washer, first turn off the water at the fixture shutoff. Remove the handle, escutcheon, if any, and other parts to expose the packing nut.

2. Unscrew the packing nut by turning it counterclockwise with a wrench. Some nuts seal around the faucet spindle with packing. More modern ones use rubber O-ring seals.

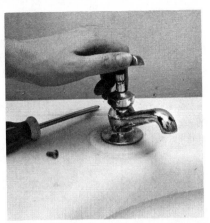

3. By reinstalling the handle temporarily and turning it in the *on* direction, you can thread the spindle out of the faucet body and lift it free. Examine it for damage to O-rings, packing, and washer. Replace damaged parts, including the washer.

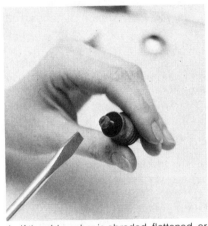

4. If the old washer is abraded, flattened, or has become hard, replace it with a new one of the same size. To take it out, remove the brass central screw and pry it loose. Your dealer can probably match it up with a new washer and sell you a new brass screw, if replacement is necessary.

5. Install the new washer on the spindle, flat face in. In a pinch, you can install the old washer backward as a temporary repair. Inspect the faucet seat for nicks, scratches, abrasion. Some worn seats can be threaded out for replacement. Others must be dressed smooth with seat-dressing tool (see page 402).

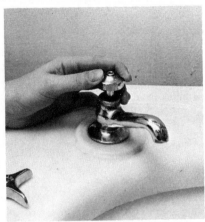

6. Once you have replaced or repaired worn parts, reassemble the faucet in the reverse order in which you took it apart.

If faucet packing needs to be replaced, use Teflon packing. With the packing nut removed, wrap the new material tightly around the faucet stem, winding clockwise, until it is thick enough to be compressed. Then replace the nut. This draws the packing against the stem.

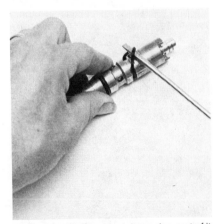

To replace O-ring, pinch it to raise part of it, insert knife or screwdriver blade under raised part and roll the ring off. Roll on new ring. New ring must match old one in size, so take old ring or spindle along when buying.

A swiveling faucet washer is available as a direct replacement for the original screw-on one. Its expanded prongs hold it in the empty screw opening. As the faucet is turned off and the swiveling washer contacts the faucet seat, it turns freely instead of wearing on the seat. File off the spindle's shoulder before installing the washer.

That beats waiting until the faucet seat is damaged. It's a good idea to fix *both* sides of a washer-type faucet even though only one side requires it.

When you replace a washer, you may see that the brass screw that holds it in place is worn or corroded and in need of replacement. Renew it with another brass screw, never with one of a different material. The right size screws, along with other faucet-repair parts, are available at your plumbing-supply store. The surest way to obtain the correct replacements is to get the manufacturer's name from the faucet body—(new parts are designated by faucet make and model)—and then take the old part in with you.

Washer-type faucets come in two forms: the packed-stem type and the more modern O-ring-sealed type. The names refer to the method used to keep the faucet from dribbling around the handle stem when the faucet is turned on. Packing is graphite-impregnated cord, a material that looks like fine black spaghetti. O-rings do a more effective job of sealing than packing does. They also create less friction on the valve stem and are more easily replaced. An O-ring-sealed stem can actually be loose in the faucet body, yet remain leak-free. You can get new O-rings or a complete spindle assembly with the washer installed.

A good many washer-type faucets have removable seats. It's often easier to remove and install a new seat than it is to repair a worn one. Once you get the faucet's spindle out, it's easy to tell whether or not the seat is removable. If it is, it will have a square or hexagonal hole through its center. If the seat is an integral part of the faucet body, it will have a round hole. Insert a seat-removal tool—sometimes a large setscrew wrench will do—into the hole, and turn it counterclockwise to thread the seat out of the faucet. Turn the new seat clockwise to install it. If you lack the proper seat-removal tool, an alternative is to find a screwdriver blade that will fit tightly across two corners of the hole. Tap it in, then grasp the screwdriver handle with both hands, and turn it hard to loosen the seat. If that won't work, break a tool-use rule and try turning the screwdriver with pliers. If you install a new seat with the somewhat brutal screwdriver method, be sure not to jam up its threads or damage its seating surface in the process.

To install a new seat in a faucet that doesn't have removable seats, get a seat-replacement kit. This method, cheaper than replacing the entire faucet, creates a space in the old seat where a new stainless-steel seat can be glued. It works on laundry, tub, and shower faucets as well as deck-style (counter- or sink-top mounted) faucets. In fact, the repair methods and parts described in this section apply to all household faucets.

With all the talk about faucet seats, something more on faucet washers is in order. Washers come in many sizes, from ¼ inch up. They're made of fiber or medium-hard neoprene rubber. Those for faucets should state on the package that they're *faucet* washers, meaning that they are made to withstand hot water as well as cold. Valve washers, though they look much the same, may not be able to take heat. One side of the faucet washer is flat; the other side is flat, tapered, or rounded. Flat washers are used with crowned and ridged seats, usually replaceable ones. Always install the washer with a flat side against the spindle. In time, all washers become hardened and compressed. The seat forms a groove in them. That's when

Fixing valve seats

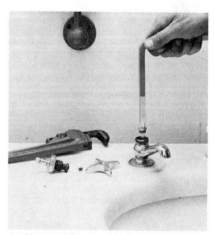

1. With the spindle out, most valve seats can be removed with a seat wrench or screwdriver. Smooth slightly worn seats with a seat dresser; replace badly worn seats.

2. Fit seat dresser into faucet body and turn to dress the old valve seat smooth.

3. Get a matching replacement seat, coat its threads with pipe joint compound, fix it to seat wrench tip, and screw it into the faucet body. Then reassemble the faucet.

Disc faucet repair

1. To fix a leaking disc-type faucet, remove the spindle assembly from the faucet and replace it. Sometimes it takes quite a pull to get the cartridge out (if it isn't threaded in). For added leverage, reinstall the handle.

2. Some disc-type faucets with ceramic cartridges are held together with screws. Remove cap and handle, and the two screws. You can repair this kind by installing new O-rings around the inlet and outlet and spout holes in the bottom. Remove the screws and lift out the parts to get at the O-rings.

Lever faucet repair

1. Single-lever faucets are easily repaired with kits. To repair a dripping faucet, all you need is a basic seat-and-spring kit. Also available are complete parts kits that can be used to stop dripping and leaking around the control handle. Directions are included with the kits.

2. You can stop most handle leaks simply by screwing down the adjusting ring with a spanner wrench that's part of the repair kit. Tighten until you feel a slight drag as the stem is moved back and forth.

3. To repair a dripping faucet, replace the seats. First take faucet apart and discard the old seats and springs. Install new ones, springs down. Reassemble. Be sure to reset the adusting ring tension properly.

4. To stop a leak coming from beneath the bonnet cap, replace its seal (from the kit). Cut the old O-ring seal to remove it, stretch a new one, and snap it into the groove. Reassemble the faucet. If your faucet is built differently, write the manufacturer for an instruction sheet.

they're likely to leak. If it happens to a new washer in a short time, a roughened seat is probably scoring the washer.

A faucet that vibrates or chatters as water flows may have a loose washer or worn threads on the spindle. Tightening the washer or replacing a worn spindle can stop the noise in most cases.

If a faucet handle is lost or broken, it can be replaced. If you cannot find a duplicate of the original handle, try replacing both handles with a matched pair that has the right kind of splines or strips to fit your faucet's spindle. When you reinstall a handle, first put it on the shaft loosely, without using the hold-down screw. With the water

supply on, turn the faucet on and off a few times. This will establish the *off* position, enabling you to remove the handle and replace it on its splined shaft in neat alignment. Install the hold-down screw and cap and you're done. Should the *off* position change as the washer wears, simply take the handle off again and replace it in proper alignment. You may find that alignment on the hot side changes faster than on the cold side.

Though they are simple and their workings are easy to understand, washer-type faucets are more prone to problems than washerless because they have more parts that can wear out.

Washerless faucets

Washerless faucets are of many types. The main visible difference between the types is that some have a single handle and others have dual handles. All washer-type faucets have a pair of handles, one controlling the hot-water flow and the other the cold. But some washerless faucets also have dual handles and, externally, they closely resemble the washer type. The handles of a washer-type faucet move up and down, if only slightly, when they're opened

and closed. This happens as the spindle, with attached washer, threads in and out. With a washerless-faucet handle, there is no visible up-and-down movement. This distinction is important because repair parts for the two faucet types are completely different from one another.

Discovering that a dual-handled faucet is the washerless type is good news, for the most part. Washerless faucets rarely need replacement parts. The bad news is that

Hidden handle tricks

Faucet manufacturers are experts at hiding just how faucet handles are held to their shafts. For appearances, the screws are often secreted beneath trim caps on the faucet handle. Common is the snap cap. To remove this type, work a knife blade under the cap and pry it up gently. Don't use one of your best knives. It's likely to get bent. Other caps are threaded in. You can try unscrewing this type simply by turning it counterclockwise with your fingers. If that won't budge it, tape around the cap and turn it with pliers. Be careful not to break, bend, or mar the cap. Once you get it off, the rest is easy. Simply remove the screw and lift the handle off its shaft. Whatever you do on a faucet, don't force anything.

Parts of a kitchen faucet with sprayer

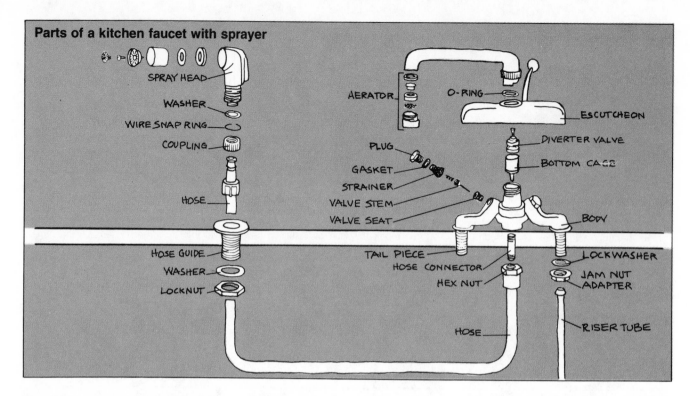

SPRAY HEAD
WASHER
WIRE SNAP RING
COUPLING
HOSE
HOSE GUIDE
WASHER
LOCKNUT

AERATOR
O-RING
ESCUTCHEON
PLUG
GASKET
STRAINER
VALVE STEM
VALVE SEAT
DIVERTER VALVE
BOTTOM CASE
BODY
TAIL PIECE
HOSE CONNECTOR
HEX NUT
LOCKWASHER
JAM NUT
ADAPTER
RISER TUBE
HOSE

Troubleshooting faucet leaks

Problem	Solution	What it takes
Faucet drips from spout, or forced turnoff is required to prevent dripping.	Replace washer or install basic repair kit or cartridge in washerless faucet. (See pages 401 and 403.)	Household tools, repair parts
Washer-type faucet still drips after above repair.	Dress seat or replace it if worn beyond repair.	Household tools, seat-dressing tool, seat-removal tool, seat-replacement kit
Washer-type faucet drips from around handle.	Repack or install new spindle O-ring. (See page 401.)	Household tools, O-ring or packing
Washerless faucet leaks at handle.	Adjust tension ring, if any. Remove cartridge and repair or replace. (See page 403.)	Household tools, faucet spanner wrench
Kitchen faucet leaks at base of swing spout.	Remove spout-retaining nut, spout and old O-ring. Install new O-ring and replace spout.	Household tools, O-ring

Fixing aerators

After a long period of use, faucet aerators clog up with scale and debris. Instead of replacing the aerator with a new one, try cleaning the old one. Wrap the aerator with tape and thread it out with a pair of pliers moving counterclockwise. If there was any leakage, replace the old washer with a new one. Turn the aerator upside down and run water through it to clean it. Take the screens out, remembering how they go so you can put them back in the same order. Scrape off any scale with a knife and poke out any blockages with a toothpick. Reassemble and reinstall the aerator.

washerless-faucet parts, when needed, cost more than washer-type ones. These replacements often come in kit form. A complete rebuilding kit contains all wearing parts. Once the new parts are installed, a washerless faucet is ready to begin its new lifetime. It should go far longer than a washer-type before it needs additional repair.

It's a good idea, when repairing washerless faucets, to have a copy of the manufacturer's instruction sheet in front of you. This shows how the faucet is built, and often gives step-by-step instructions for taking the faucet apart and putting it back together. Sometimes the sheet also lists part numbers for replacement parts. Since the directions apply to *that* faucet, they're the ones that should be followed in fixing it. The instructions given here can only apply generally to most kinds of faucets.

If you don't have an instruction sheet for your faucet, you can get one through your plumbing supplier or by writing to the manufacturer. The address, if not available from your dealer, can be looked up in a library. Look in the *A-to-Z Thomas Register*—which is a basic products reference—or in Standard & Poor's *Directory of Corporations*. When you write the company, either give a faucet model number or describe it as completely as possible. This helps the manufacturer send you the correct instruction sheet.

One washerless faucet, of the dual-handled style, is the diaphragm type. A spindle that moves up and down compresses or releases a neoprene diaphragm. The spindle has a swivel end to avoid the twisting friction of a washer and seat. Thus a diaphragm will outlast many washers. The faucet's spindle is kept dry, without packing or an O-ring, by the diaphragm. And so it may be lubricated—and should be—whenever the faucet is taken apart. Use white grease on the spindle's threads to make for smoother on-off action. Diaphragm faucet disassembly is similar to that of washer-type. And repair is usually simple. Replacing the diaphragm with a new one cures most problems. In other words, a single part usually does the trick.

Some newer faucets use metal-to-metal disc construction. While metal-to-metal wear in an automobile engine is avoided through oil lubrication, a disc faucet works well with just water lubrication. The special metal alloys used in the discs are made to resist corrosion as well as abrasion. Some such faucets are guaranteed dripless for ten

Lever-type washerless faucets

Washerless faucets sometimes have only a single control handle, a swinging lever that's attached to the top or rear of the faucet body. A variation is a single, cap-like handle in place of the lever. The lever or cap, when slid or turned from side to side, varies the water temperature. It controls the flow through up-and-down movement. Lever and cap faucets are both valve-type faucets. Both have hot and cold valves inside the body that are actuated by the control handle. Each valve is accessible through hex-head pipe plugs, one on each side of the body. To get at the plugs, remove the faucet trim cover to expose the body. On a kitchen faucet, this comes off after the spout is removed. On a bathroom model, it comes off after handle removal.

Turn off the fixture shutoff or main water supply. Remove the plugs with a wrench—not pliers—and lift out the valve parts. One part is a small strainer screen that keeps debris out of the sensitive valve. If this is clogged, it makes faucet flow sluggish. Clean it, and that may be the total of needed repairs. Screens should be checked periodically for clogging. New valve stems, springs, and strainer screens come with repair kits, but are rarely needed. Install the parts in the same order—and facing in the same direction—as they came out. While you've got the faucet torn down, adjust the handle tightly enough to prevent drift of the temperature setting. A screw may be provided for this.

Taking some cartridge faucets apart can be a baffling task. These function with a washerless cartridge that can be replaced as a unit with a new cartridge if the faucet fails. Their secret is a horseshoe-shaped retaining clip located outside the faucet or inside the handle. To remove the cartridge, you must first get at the clip and remove it.

shaft seals instead of packing. The cap nut is often round rather than hex-shaped. In that case, finger-tight is tight enough. If the nut resists removal, wrap it with tape and try turning it gently with pliers. Counterclockwise removes, clockwise tightens. Spindle-nut removal exposes a knurled, threaded ring beneath, which is also removed by finger power. The valve can then be pulled out past its O-rings. Sometimes a good hard pull is required. Replace the worn discs with a new disc assembly, pushing it in tightly, with the O-rings installed. Screw the ring and spindle-nut back on.

Some disc-type faucets have three rubber seals between their discs. To repair leaks in this type, take the disc assembly apart and replace the seals.

If there's a cap on the handle, look under that. If there's a gap between the handle and spout, look there. And if there's a removable faucet trim panel, take it off to expose the faucet body. Once the retaining clip is off, the cartridge should lift right out of the faucet.

An on-the-blink sink spray-hose can usually be repaired. The spray-hose receives water from a diverter valve in the faucet body. Some sprayers are designed to allow a slight flow of water from the faucet spout even when the spray-hose bottom is depressed. Diverter-valve action will be affected if the aerator and spray-hose head aren't clean and open. Both may be replaced if they cannot be cleaned. Check to see that the hose is free from kinks and sharp bends. If there's any doubt about the hose, remove it (see page 411).

Trouble with the diverter valve is rare, but if the hose isn't the cause, it's most likely the valve. To get at it, remove the faucet spout via its compression nut. The diverter valve rests immediately beneath, inside the center of the faucet body. Lift or screw out the diverter assembly. If it's clogged with foreign matter, it may need replacement. You can probably obtain the parts from your dealer.

One bit of advice when removing faucet trim with pliers: Always protect it by wrapping two layers of masking, adhesive, or plastic electrical tape around it. (If you have a small strap wrench, you can use that instead.) Finished surfaces of faucets, including their escutcheons, may scratch easily. These scratches don't only look bad; they can make the faucet rust and corrode.

Any faucet that cannot be repaired, or is so badly deteriorated that it is not worth repairing, can be replaced. See pages 408 and 409 for replacement instructions.

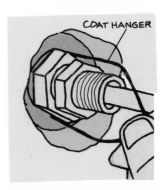

When a faucet in the wall drove me up it
I know tub and shower faucets operate pretty much like sink and lavatory faucets. So when the shower head began to leak—no problem. Just take the valve apart and replace the washer or dress the seat like any other washer-type faucet. The hooker was that none of my wrenches could get at the valve bonnet nut to turn it—it was recessed too deep in the wall. Talk about frustration!

Getting mad won't help. Beg, borrow or steal a plumber's socket wrench (see page 397) to remove a washer-type spindle recessed in a wall. To find the wrench size needed, bend a pipe cleaner in two so that its tips touch opposing faces of the nut, and measure the distance between tips. Or, if the cleaner's too short, cut a length of coat-hanger wire and bend it so that its tips can gauge the nut's size. Use a plumber's socket wrench which fits that size snugly.

Practical Pete

Cleaning a diverter valve

About valves

Valve problems

Globe valves can have all the problems that beset washer-type faucets. But, most often they suffer from leaking around the shafts due to deterioration of the packing, freezing, and scale.

Any inner scale deposits render globe valves (and gate valves, as well) incapable of being securely turned off. Complete disassembly and cleaning is called for.

If a pipe that contains a valve freezes, it will damage the valve—either by cracking the body or ruining the washer and spindle. Replacement spindles can sometimes be found, but there's no cure for a cracked valve body other than a new valve.

Ground-key valves, after much use, may suffer from metal-to-metal wear between the key and valve body. There is no cure short of replacement.

Parts you can get

Replacement parts for valves are not widely available. You *can* get replacement washers, however, as well as packing for leaking spindles. (Installation parallels that for a faucet.) Worn-out gate valves can be rebuilt, but that's a shop job.

Valves are merely mid-pipe faucets. The best ones are made of brass. Others are made of steel or plastic. All come ready for attachment to the kind of pipe they are designed for. Some can be adapted to use with other pipes also.

A **globe valve** is built very much like a washer-type faucet. It has washer, spindle, packing, and seat. With this type of valve, water flow is somewhat restricted due to the path it must take (see illustration below). If this drawback didn't exist, no other kind of water valve would be needed.

Highly useful for some systems is the **stop-and-waste valve.** Also called a stop-and-drain valve, it's a globe valve with an added feature: an auxiliary valve that opens into the closed end of the main valve. With the main valve off, the auxiliary valve can be opened to release water in the line beyond the valve. This lets you easily drain the pipes when the house is to be vacant and unheated in below-freezing weather (see page 474). Some types have a side drain-screw rather than a valve.

All globe valves should be installed with water-flow direction in mind. Many globe valves have directional arrows on the valve body. If you are using one that doesn't, install the valve so that water flows in *below* the valve seat, through it, and then out around the valve spindle. If one is installed backward, water pressure would be on the spindle, which might tend to leak, even with the valve turned off. Directional alignment applies only to water flow, not to the angle of the valve handle. This may be pointed in any direction: up, down, or sideways. Position it for convenience.

Where full water flow is needed, a **gate valve** is used. A gate valve features a wedge-shaped gate or stopper that presses firmly into a reciprocal chamber when the valve is closed (see illustration below). The two surfaces meet tightly, sealing off flow. When the valve is opened, the gate lifts completely out of the chamber, permitting full water flow through the valve. Moreover, flow through a gate valve is straight. The water does not have to go around a corner, as it does inside a globe valve. This, too, works for full flow. The careful parts fitting and large size of a gate valve make it costly—considerably more so than a globe valve. Therefore, gate valves are not used unless full flow is required. They're normally used in the service entrance only.

Another kind of valve—the **ground key**—is used for water, gasoline, and solvent liquids. It is also used for a buried, outdoor service-entrance line. A cone-shaped key is held tightly in a cone-shaped body. The mating surfaces are machined smooth so that no leakage can take place between them. A handle attached to the key is used to turn it within the body. Both key and body have a round hole through them.

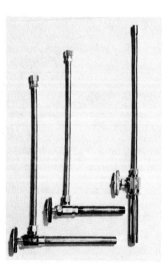

Water supply should be controlled with fixture shut-off valves below each fixture, with one for hot-pipe line and one for cold-pipe line below sinks or lavatories.

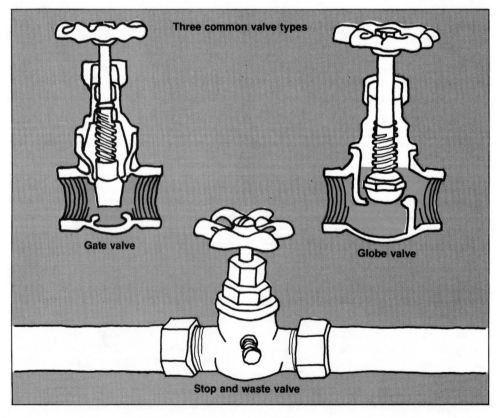

Three common valve types

Gate valve

Globe valve

Stop and waste valve

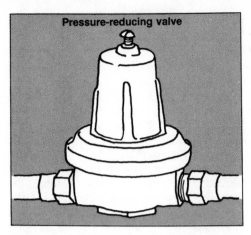

Pressure-reducing valve

Vacuum-breaker valve

A vacuum-breaker valve in the underground sprinkler system protects the house water supply in case of back-siphonage.

How vacuum breaker works

If the water starts to flow backward, suction pulls the disc down, closing off the opening.

When the handle is turned and the holes line up, flow occurs; when they are only partially aligned, partial flow occurs. When they don't line up, no flow occurs. They are sometimes built with a tab or recessed key so that a wrench or special tool must be used to operate them. In this way, the water utility uses them in underground service pipes to homes to turn off water to customers who don't pay their water bills.

Houses built in low areas may suffer from excessively high water pressure. When the pressure reaches more than 80 psi, it puts a strain on faucets and valves, including the toilet-tank float valve. High pressure also wastes water because it makes too much flow out of the taps. Finally, it makes for noisy plumbing. There's an easy cure: installation of a **pressure-reducing valve**. Even if the water company will not install one in its water main, you can put one in your house. It not only lowers house water-pressure levels; it evens out any fluctuations in pressure.

Vacuum-breaker valves serve a special purpose (see margin at right). They are used with underground sprinklers and tankless flush-valve toilets. The best quality tank-type toilets—recognizable by an air vent reaching above the tank's water line—also have vacuum-breaker valves. Under normal conditions, a vacuum-breaker valve is inactive. But should a vacuum occur in the water-supply system, a spring-loaded valve inside the vacuum breaker opens up. This lets air into the valve, creating an air gap. Since a supply-line vacuum cannot back-siphon water through the air gap, your water system is protected from contamination by any polluted water source beyond the valve.

Other useful valves include **fixture shutoffs**. These are usually located immediately beneath a fixture, either on the wall or floor. Usually a fixture's water comes to it from the wall. Then **angle-stop shutoffs** are used. When a fixture's water supply comes through the floor, **straight-stop shutoffs** are used. Whatever the type,

in case of emergency, both shutoffs should be accessible from the room in which the fixture is located. Those in a branch supply-line below the floor are less handy. Adding accessible shutoffs to a fixture without them is a worthwhile one-day plumbing project. For fixture hookup with riser tubes and shutoffs, refer to pages 394, 409, and 412.

Valve placement in a water-supply system begins at the buried service-entrance line out front. Between the water main and the house there may be a ground-key valve. This is where the water company usually controls your service from. Another valve—a gate valve or a large stop-and-waste valve—should be installed next to the meter, which is located close to the point where the water service enters the house—usually indoors in freezing climates, outdoors in mild climates. This becomes your emergency shutoff valve, stopping all water flow to the house.

Other gate valves are placed below both inlet and outlet connections to a water softener. A third valve is placed between the tees to allow water to flow with the softener disconnected. Next in the system is the cold-water inlet valve for the water heater. If the inlet has a ¾-inch diameter, a globe valve may be used. If the diameter is ½ inch, a gate valve is necessary.

Sometimes intermediate valves are used—for example, a stop-and-waste valve on the basement or crawl-space end of a supply pipe leading underground to a garage, or on hot or cold branches leading to a distant bathroom.

Finally come the valves for branches to fixtures. Individual hot and cold shutoffs for each sink or lavatory fixture are best.

For homes with hot-water heat, one more valve should be installed. This is a backflow-preventer valve, which goes between the water supply and the hot-water boiler. Filling the boiler is its main job, but this valve doubles as prevention against back-siphonage. Without it, boiler water could enter the potable water system.

Cross connections and vacuum-breaker valves

A cross connection between a possibly polluted water source and your potable house water can cause sickness and even death. Any submerged water outlet is a cross connection. A garden hose with its end left in a wading pool is a cross connection. If an upstairs faucet is turned on, water from the pool can flow backwards through the open hose bibb and into the potable water system. Backflow of bacteria can even occur through a closed faucet or valve. A broken fire hydrant down the block can create back-siphonage in all houses on the street, including yours. As shown, an underground sprinkler head is a potential cross connection. All underground sprinkling systems should have vacuum-breaker valves. These, in the event of back-siphonage, create an internal air gap that keeps polluted water out of potable water. A toilet tank should have a vacuum-breaker or anti-siphon intake valve. No fixture faucets should discharge below the rim of the basin. If any do, replace them with higher faucets. Don't leave the ends of hoses resting below the flood rims of pools, pails, sinks, or ponds.

3. SINKS AND BATHS

Installing faucets

What it takes

Approximate time: Replacing a faucet is a one-morning or afternoon project. Changing a lavatory or sink fixture takes most of a day.

Tools and materials: A pair of adjustable open-end wrenches and a basin wrench will handle the faucet change. For fixture modernization, you'll need most of the tools listed on page 410, the new parts for installation, plumber's putty and putty knife, and new riser tubes.

Fittings

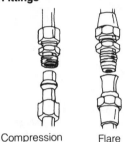

Compression   Flare

Standard two-handle mixing faucet

Single-handle mixing faucet

Single-handle kitchen faucet with spray attachment

If you have repaired a leaking faucet too many times—or if it has gotten unattractive with age—you may want to replace it with a modern one. The steps at the right show how it's done.

If you are not planning to replace the riser tubes beneath the faucet, the job goes best if the new faucet has exactly the same tailpiece as the old one. This governs how you connect the fixture's water supply to the faucet. The handiest faucets are the "do it yourself" type. They come with ½-inch threaded tailpiece adapters that accept the bullet-nosed ends of riser tubes. A ⅜-inch fixture flange nut (sometimes called a jam nut or supply nut) holds things together. This type of faucet will also fit a ½-inch pipe coupling or take a ½-inch flare adapter. Making faucet water-supply connections with riser tubes is recommended. It saves a great deal of extra effort.

Faucets with other kinds of tailpieces can be adapted to risers, but not quite as easily. Some lavatory faucets end in plain-ended, ¼-inch O.D. (outside dimension) copper tubes, which you have to connect to the water supply. A riser-tube hookup still is best. Cut off the upper end of the riser tube, flare it and the faucet tailpiece, and connect the two with a ⅜x¼-inch reducing flare coupling and two flare nuts.

Still other faucets end in tailpieces with ¼-inch pipe threads. These are about 3 inches long and are held to the faucet with fixture flange nuts. They are most common on kitchen-sink faucets. Discard both tailpieces and make the connections with bullet-nosed riser tubes, using the same fixture flange nuts.

Some kitchen faucets merely end in a threaded opening, but not tapered pipe threads; these accept fixture nuts. If the opening is too large to accommodate a standard riser tube, get a rubber bullet-nosed fixture washer to put between them. Then a larger fixture nut can be used to secure the connection.

If you're in doubt as to how to adapt a new faucet to the water supply, tell your dealer what your fixture's water-supply setup is. Ask him to sell you the parts needed to make the new hookup—with riser tubes. (In nearly every case, a pair of riser tubes does it best.) At the lower end, these tubes must fit into a compression nut at the wall or floor, and if one is not already there, you'll have to provide it. A new pair of fixture shutoffs provide compression. Next best but lower in cost would be a pair of compression adapters for fixture supply. Use *straight* for a floor installation, *angled* for a wall installation. The lower end of the riser tube slips into the compression fitting and tightens to form a watertight, yet removable, coupling. Compression couplings use a brass ferrule and compression nut that squeezes the ferrule onto the riser tube for a snug, watertight connection.

Modernizing fixtures

You can change a bathroom or kitchen sink at the same time you change faucets. Or you can change the fixture and retain the old faucet. How you do the job, as well as the existing parts you'll want to save, depends on what you have now and what you're replacing. For example, an in-the-counter sink or lavatory bowl can be reused in a new counter-top installation. Merely remove it from the old counter and mount it in the new one. Or you can discard it altogether. A wall-hung lavatory or sink most likely would be junked and replaced with a cabinet or counter-top unit. You can make the cabinet yourself or buy one. You can have cabinets made to order or purchase component units combining them to fit your space. You can also buy prebuilt units, completely finished and ready for bowl installation. Standard single-bowl lavatory units are 17 inches deep, 30 inches high, and available in lengths ranging from 30 inches to 4 feet. Kitchen-sink cabinets are single or double-bowl and vary in length from 3½ to 8 feet. Most have 2-foot-deep counters and stand 3 feet high. In all cabinets, space is provided for water-supply and waste hookups. The selection is enormous; your dealer will be glad to show you what's available.

Counter sink and lavatory bowls are held from underneath by levers and bolts arranged around the perimeter of the bowl. A stainless-steel flange, contoured to fit the bowl, surrounds it. T-shaped in cross-section, the flange is forced down tightly against the counter top at the same time the bowl is pressed tightly up against the flange. Levers placed in the flange and adjusted with bolts do both jobs as the clamps are tightened from below. Plumber's putty placed between the bowl and flange and counter top and flange prevents leaks. Don't use ordinary putty. It stains and becomes brittle. Use only plumber's putty made for this purpose.

The stainless-steel flange and clamps to go with it come with the bowl. Mount the faucet in the fixture before you put the fixture in place. It wouldn't hurt to have the upper riser connections completed; that will save you from making the connection while lying on your back under the fixture. Slide the new fixture to the wall and fasten it. Then, make the lower riser-tube connections, hook up the trap as explained on pages 410 and 411, and turn on the water. Your new faucet is ready to go.

Replacing faucets

1. To install a new lavatory or sink faucet, turn off cold- and hot-water supply valves and turn faucet on to drain the pipe. Loosen hold-down nuts, using a basin wrench, if needed, to get at them.

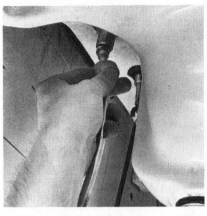

2. To remove the old faucet, take off the hold-down nuts and washers and remove piping attached to the faucet tailpieces. If riser tubes have been used, remove them from their compression fittings.

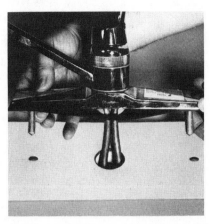

3. The new faucet should match the old faucet's hole spacing, with two holes 4 inches apart for lavatories, or 8 inches apart for sinks. There may also be a center hole for mixing faucets, and a fourth hole for a sink spray attachment.

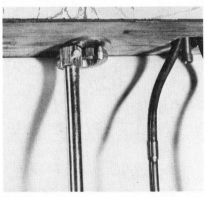

4. If faucet has no gasket, seat it with plumber's putty between it and the sink top. Attach washers and hold-down nuts firmly (but not tight enough to crack a china fixture, if that's what sink is).

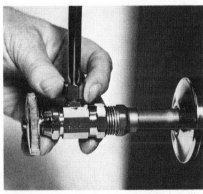

5. Connect the riser tubes or pipes from the water supply to the faucet tailpieces. After finger-tightening, use two wrenches—one to hold and one to turn—to keep from twisting the tailpieces.

6. With water lines securely connected, remove aerator if faucet has one. Then turn on both hot and cold water at full pressure for one minute to clear pipe scale or other debris from system. Shut off water and reinstall the aerator on the faucet.

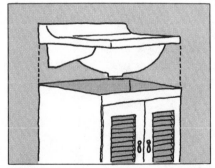

Old pedestal-type lavatories can be replaced with modern units that come complete with cabinet to match almost any decor. Or you can build a cabinet to go under a wall-hung lavatory basin.

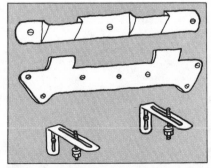

Various types of brackets are available for hanging wall-mounted lavatories, using either toggle bolts or, better still, a wall backing board. Front support legs are available on some models.

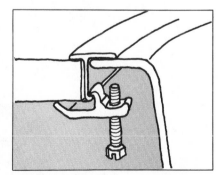

Levers placed in the sink flange hold counter-top units in place. Tightening the bolts draws the flange tightly against the putty seal between the flange and sink or counter top. The flange, levers, and bolts are supplied with the fixture.

Installing traps

What it takes

Approximate time: Under an hour per trap.

Tools and materials: Monkey wrench or trap-and-fixture wrench. Possibly a hacksaw. A new trap to fit. Use P-traps for waste pipes coming from walls; S-traps for pipes from floors. Double-bowl kitchen sinks may require other new parts if the two bowl drains are to be connected to a single trap. The trap may go on the right, left, or be centered between the two bowls. (Note: A centered trap calls for centered drain fittings.) You'll also need an additional slip nut to connect the trap to the adapter. If you're joining a 1¼-inch lavatory trap to a 1½-inch trap adapter, use a 1¼-by-1½-inch reducing slip nut.

Planning hints: Choose a time when the fixture will be unused for an hour or so.

Drain traps for sinks, lavatories, tubs, or showers are usually either the P-type or the S-type shown below. On some models, known as fixed traps, the J-bend and trap arm are one piece. More common are traps with a removable J-bend that can be swiveled to one side to remove tailpiece connections. Cleanout plugs make unclogging easier; some traps don't have them.

Replacing rotted O-ring washers or corroded metal slip nuts or pipe sections calls for disassembly. Shut off water supply pipes, place a pail or plastic wastebasket under the trap, and remove cleanout plug to drain water from the trap. Loosen slip nuts with wrenches, one to hold and one to turn with, so that you don't twist the fixture or waste pipe parts the trap is attached to. If a slip nut won't budge, saw through it gently with a hacksaw until it expands enough to come off easily. But don't saw deeply enough to cut into the threads of the trap arm or fixture tailpiece.

Lavatories usually use 1¼-inch traps;

sinks and laundry tubs, 1½-inch traps. It's wise to replace an S-trap with an S-trap, or a P-trap with a P-trap the same size. The drum traps for tubs (page 421) found under some old bathroom floors may need to be replaced with a P-trap if no drum trap replacements are available where you live. Consult your plumbing supplier on this.

To install the new trap (or the old trap with its new washers and slip nuts), attach the washer and one end of the J-bend to the tailpiece with a slip nut, threading it on just enough to hold these pieces together. Slide two slip nuts onto the trap arm, with their threads facing toward the pipes to which they will attach at each end. Slide washers onto both ends of the trap arm. Push the trap arm into the drain stub-out (or trap adapter, if there is one), sliding it to line up the J-bend and trap-arm connection. When everything lines up without straining, connect the washer and slip nuts and tighten all the slip nuts with wrenches. But don't tighten so hard that you bend the trap.

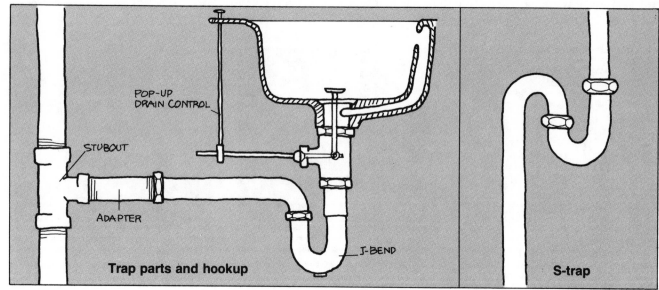

Trap parts and hookup

POP-UP DRAIN CONTROL

STUBOUT

ADAPTER

J-BEND

S-trap

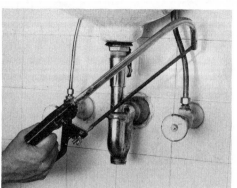

1. To replace a corroded trap, remove the old one without damaging the fixture or trap adapter at the wall or floor. To make the job easier, put penetrating oil on the thread slip nut the night before. You can even saw through a trap, if necessary, to get it out.

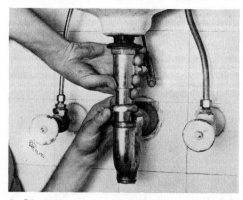

2. Slip the new trap arm into the adapter and put the J-bend up onto the fixture's drain tailpiece. Use new slip nuts and washers installing the nuts facing the threads they attach to. Before tightening with a wrench, tape slip nut to protect it.

3. The last step is to tighten all the slip nuts to secure the trap in place and make it free of leaks. To further guard against leaks, you can precoat the three trap connections with silicone-rubber sealant on metal, PVC, and polypropylene-plastic traps. Don't use it on black ABS plastic.

Replacing a sink sprayer

If you can't repair a sink sprayer, you can easily replace it. Loosen the coupling nut holding the hose end to the faucet underneath the sink. (If connection is made with tapered pipe threads, simply twist the hose counterclockwise to free it.) Stand aside as you disconnect as some water in hose may drain out. Pull the hose out through the sink top and take it to your plumbing supplier. Have him match it with an equally long replacement; if it doesn't match your faucet tailpiece connection, he can provide an adapter.

Upgrading a shower head

If your old shower is a tired performer with a shabby look, you can update it with one of the new shower heads shown at right. Most simply thread onto the old shower arm. Remove the old shower head by turning it counterclockwise with a wrench. Put pipe thread dope on the shower arm threads—or else wrap threads with TFE Teflon tape and thread on the new head and tighten with a wrench.

If you want to save water—and the cost of heating it—get a shower head cutoff valve or a flow-restricting device from your supplier. Either attaches onto the shower arm before the shower head is attached (see drawing below). The flow-restricting water saver cuts all water flow to 2 gallons per minute (versus the 5 gpm many showers now use). The cutoff valve is controlled by the user manually.

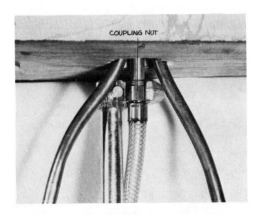

COUPLING NUT

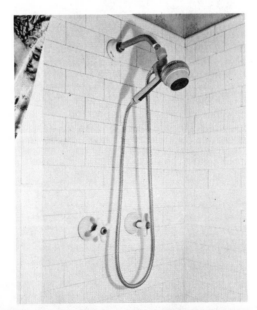

The mark of an amateur

Boy, have I got trouble. I just installed a beautiful new chrome shower arm. At least it *was* beautiful. Trouble is I scarred it up so badly with the wrench that it looks worse than the old one did. A professional plumber told me that when he needs to tighten exposed plumbing pipes he gives them a double wrap of plastic electrical tape to protect them from wrench teeth. Afterward, the chewed-up tape strips off, leaving the pipe undamaged. I'm going to try that next time. I may even buy a strap wrench for tightening exposed pipes. It sure beats scarring a smooth finish with a pipe wrench.

Practical Pete

Fixing shower heads

Water holes in a shower head's faceplate or around its rim may clog. Remove screws or knob holding faceplate, soak overnight in vinegar and scrub with a brush. Poke out any blockages remaining with a toothpick. If shower head drips or pivots stiffly, unscrew head and collar connected to shower arm, replace washer, and smear petroleum jelly on swivel ball before reassembling.

FLOW ADJUSTER

Installing fixture shutoffs

Today's houses are usually built with fixture shutoff valves beneath every sink, lavatory, and toilet. The valves let you change a faucet washer, repair a fixture, or stop a flooding toilet without shutting off the water supply for the entire house. If your house doesn't have fixture shutoffs, you may want to add them.

All piping between the water-supply pipe coming through the wall or floor and the fixture tailpiece can be removed and replaced with a fixture shutoff valve and a riser tube. Follow the sequence of steps shown in the pictures below. Get the angle shutoff valve shown for water-supply pipes coming through the wall, or a straight shutoff valve for supply pipes coming through the floor.

Modern shutoff valves end in 3/8-inch or 1/2-inch compression couplings that fit 3/8- or 1/2-inch riser tubes. The end of the valve that will be connected to the wall or floor water-supply pipe may be made to fit threaded pipe, sweat-soldered copper tube, or plastic tube. Take the old pipe you have removed from the water-supply pipe to your plumbing supplier so that he can provide a valve that will fit it, or an adapter that will let you connect the shutoff valve to the water-supply pipe.

What it takes

Approximate time: Give yourself an hour and a half for each valve. If riser tubes are already in place, the job will go more quickly.

Tools and materials: Monkey or open-end wrenches, pipe dope or TFE tape; propane torch, soldering flux, and 50/50 wire solder for copper water-supply pipes. Possibly a pair of pipe wrenches for removing threaded piping.

Planning hints: In most cases, much of the house will be without water when you make valve installations. So tackle this work when others are not going to be using water. Know beforehand what adapters and fittings you'll need and have them on hand. At a minimum, this includes the necessary fixture shutoff valves (angle-type for wall supplies, straight-type for floor supplies). Sinks and lavatories take two valves—one for hot water, one for cold. Toilets take one. If you use new riser tubes, get the bullet-nosed type for sinks and lavatories and the flat-ended type for toilets. All risers must be long enough to reach from the valve to the fixture's tailpiece. If they aren't already present, you'll need enough fixture flange nuts to connect all riser tubes to the faucet tailpieces or toilet valve.

1. To install fixture shutoff valves, turn off water supply, unscrew nuts connecting old pipes to fixture tailpieces, and remove piping connected to the water supply stub-outs. If there isn't enough give to remove the old pipes, hacksaw a small section of the old pipe just above the joint that connects to the stub-out.

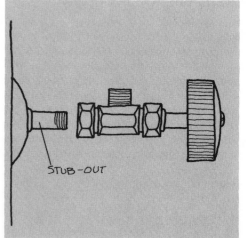

2. Unscrew elbow or other piping connected to the stub-out (or melt apart soldered connections) and get a fixture shutoff valve that will attach to your stub-out. Put Teflon tape or pipe dope (joint compound) on the threads and attach valve to stub-out so that its compression nut lines up vertically with the faucet tailpiece.

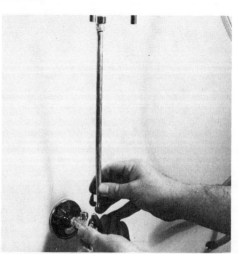

3. Cut a riser tube to fit between the new shutoff valve and faucet tailpiece with its lower end inside the compression nut on the valve but not quite touching the shoulder. Allow for some bending if needed to get a lineup between valve and tailpiece.

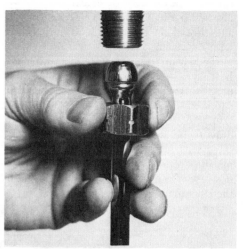

4. Fit lower end of riser tube into compression nut on valve and tighten the nut. Fit the upper end to the faucet tailpiece, bending as needed, and tighten this connection. When all nuts are secure, remove aerator (if faucet has one), turn on water, and test as described on page 409.

Caulking

A tub-to-wall crack looks ugly and lets water leak against the wall, damaging it. The remedy is to rake out all the old caulk and reseal the joint with silicone tub caulk, which lasts more than 20 years outdoors and even longer indoors.

For the patch to work, the gap between the tub and wall must be wide enough for a decent-sized bead of caulk, and its depth should be roughly the same as its width. If your tub-wall joint is deeper, fill it in with rope oakum (jute fibers coated with preservative) or closed-cell plastic foam to a depth of about ¼ inch before you caulk.

If the wall has been damaged by water, you may have to replace it with one of the waterproof materials made for bathroom walls. If you do, leave a ¼-inch gap between the tub and wall material, even if it's tile.

Silicone tub caulk tends to bulge in spots and dip in others as you apply it. Apply masking tape above and below the tub/wall gap and have dampened cloths handy to wipe off hands and spills. Hold spout at a 45-degree angle and parallel to the joint and move it forward as you squeeze the bead in the joint.

A bathtub has two ends and two long edges, including the one at the floor. Do the end away from the faucet first, because it is looked at least. Apply caulk to the entire end joint. Try for neatness but not perfection. Fill the joint with caulk, then immediately tool it down—before any skin-over, or surface-hardening, can occur. Use a finger, the curved handle of a spoon, an ice-cream stick, or a tongue depressor to put a concave surface on the bead of caulk. Wetting the tool will keep fresh caulk from sticking to it.

When you have the first tub/wall section tooled into shape, go on to the next section. If the bead gets worse instead of better as you tool, stop. The more you try to smooth skinning-over silicone caulk, the rougher it is likely to get.

The use of toxic silicone caulk solvents is not recommended, especially in an unventilated bathroom or bathtub enclosure. If the smell of caulk seems strong, open a bathroom window for ventilation. Also, if you have a skin allergy, better not touch the caulk. Use rubber gloves.

A day later, you can repair any serious roughness by slicing excess caulk with a single-edged razor blade. At the same time, you can scrape off any unwiped caulk spills. Since the silicone bead cures clear through, this is like cutting soft rubber, which is what the bead is. Do not try to paint silicone tube caulking, however. It comes in colors so you won't need to.

Don't mess around
Have trouble caulking without getting all messed up? I did too until I tried using masking tape. Lines of tape laid along both sides of the tub-wall crack lets the bead of caulk go only where you want it. The bead can be tooled after applying, still without messing you up. Finally, when the caulk has gotten a little "tack" to it, you can pull off both strips of tape, leaving a nice, neat bead. Hey, and no mess.

Practical Pete

1. Apply masking tape above and below gap between tub and wall. Lay a bead of caulk in the gap, pushing tube forward as you go so that spout forces caulk into the gap.

2. If the caulk won't hold or you think it is unsightly, you can cover the gap with a quarter-round ceramic tile, which is available in kits from plumbing supply houses.

What tub caulk to use in the bathroom

Caulk type	How sold	Advantages/disadvantages	Solvent	Colors	Relative cost
PVA tub-and-tile	Tubes, cartridges	Easy to use. Excellent adhesion, but shrinks. Should be painted. Short-lived.	Water	White	Lowest
Acrylic latex tub-and-tile	Tubes, cartridges	Low cost, easy to use. Excellent adhesion. Cheapest type recommended. Should be painted.	Water	White	Low
Silicone rubber tub-and-tile	Tubes	The best. Lasts and lasts. Accepts great joint movement. Never becomes brittle. Needs no painting, but hard to use neatly.	Paint thinner, naphtha, toluol, xylol	White, blue, pink, green yellow, beige, gold	Highest

4.TOILETS

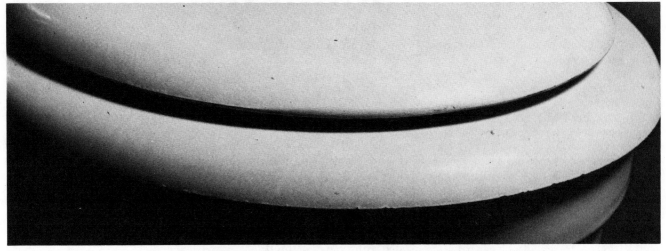

Unveiled: the mystery of the flush toilet

The flush toilet was invented more than 300 years ago but many people are still baffled by its inner workings. When a toilet won't flush, doesn't fill or won't stop running, they jiggle the handle and then call a plumber. If they understood how a toilet mechanism works, they could repair it themselves.

What happens is this. Like the "hand-bone-connected-to-the-wrist-bone" song, the handle connects to the trip lever which in turn connects to the tank ball, as shown below. Pressing the handle raises the tank ball from its seat, letting water rush from the tank into the toilet bowl (as shown at left, top illustration).

As water level drops, the float lowers, opening the intake valve to let water enter the tank (left, center). Releasing the handle lets the tank ball drop into its seat, closing off the tank and allowing it to fill.

As the tank fills, the float rises until it closes the intake valve when the water reaches its fill-level (left, bottom). Meanwhile, the emptied toilet bowl is partially filled by water flowing from the refill tube into the overflow tube as the tank is filling.

What to do when a toilet mechanism misbehaves, uses too much water, or needs replacement is explained on pages 415-19. For the special problems of unclogging blocked toilet drains, see page 422.

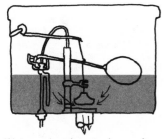

Water rushes from tank, causing

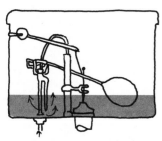

float to drop and open intake valve,

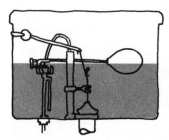

filling tank with fresh water and closing valve.

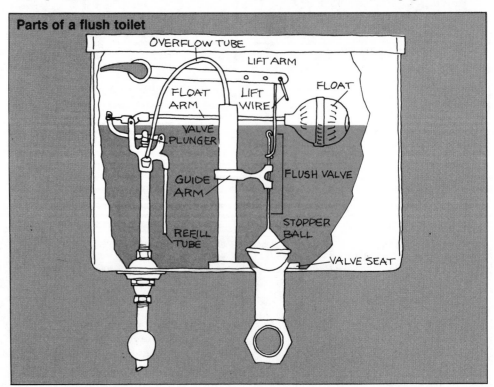

Parts of a flush toilet

OVERFLOW TUBE
LIFT ARM
FLOAT ARM
LIFT WIRE
FLOAT
VALVE PLUNGER
GUIDE ARM
FLUSH VALVE
REFILL TUBE
STOPPER BALL
VALVE SEAT

Troubleshooting toilet tanks

Problem	Solutions	What it takes
A. Tank fills but water keeps flowing. See steps 1–6 below.	Bend float rod to lower ball. Replace leaking float ball. Replace washer and seat in intake valve, or install a new valve.	One minute to an hour using inexpensive replacement parts and household tools.
B. Tank doesn't fill but water keeps flowing. See page 32.	Make sure lift wires and guide arm are not binding so tank ball can't seat firmly in flush valve seat. Check trip lever and trip handle for binding. Bend or replace parts and rotate guide arm on overflow tube as needed.	Less than an hour using household tools and inexpensive replacement parts.
C. Water level is too low or too high. See page 32.	Bend float rod up or down to raise or lower water level.	A minute or so.
D. Tank doesn't flush completely. See page 32.	Rehook upper lift wire through alternate hole or holes in trip lever. If that doesn't work, shorten wire and then rehook.	A few minutes. Tin snips and needle-nose pliers may be needed.
E. Splashing noise from tank during filling. See page 32.	Make sure refill tube feeds directly into overflow tube, bending if needed. If that doesn't solve it, replace seal and washer in intake valve, or install a new valve.	Less than a minute to a half hour if needed parts can be obtained readily.
F. Air condenses on tank, making it sweat. See page 32.	Line tank with plastic foam sheets.	Less than half an hour if material is readily available.

Problem A: Tank fills, but water keeps flowing.

1. If water shuts off when you lift the float rod, gently bend the rod down until the float rests about ½ inch lower in the water. Water should now shut off when its level is about ½ inch below the top of the overflow pipe.

2. If pulling float rod up did not shut off the water, turn off the shutoff valve below the tank and flush the toilet to empty it. If there's no shutoff valve below the tank, look for a stop valve on supply line feeding the toilet, or shut off main valve.

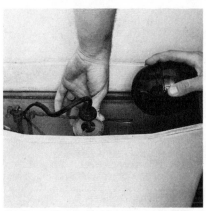

3. If more than half of float is under water, it may have a leak. Unscrew it from the float rod and shake it to see if there's water inside. If there is, replace it. If there isn't, reinstall it.

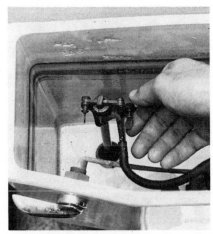

4. If toilet still runs on after filling, remove the screws that hold the float rod and its attached linkage to the intake valve. These screws are usually thumbscrews or have L-shaped heads you can hand-turn.

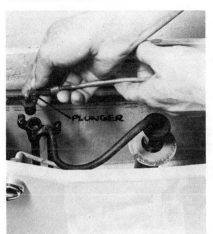

5. Remove float rod and its attached linkage from the intake valve and pull the valve plunger up out of its seat. You may need to pry it up gently to get it started moving out.

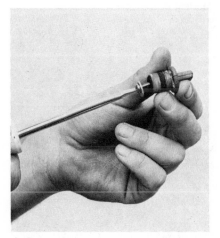

6. Replace the washer at the base of the plunger and the second washer or packing that fits in a groove partway up the plunger's body. If toilet still runs on after filling, install a new fluid-level control valve (page 417).

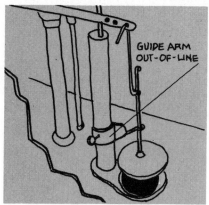

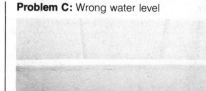

1. A bent lift wire or an out-of-line guide arm may keep tank ball from dropping into its seat to close the tank. Straighten lift wires and rotate guide arm on overflow tube until tank ball slides down easily and snugly into its seat. Tighten clamp on guide arm to prevent slippage. If ball is worn, replace it.

2. If trip lever stays up after flushing, try bending and oiling it, and then tightening the screw that fixes the trip lever to the toilet handle. If the trip lever still won't release, replace it.

1. The tank water level should be no higher than the level line marked inside the tank—or ½ inch below the top of the overflow tube. To save water, you can lower the level as far as it will go and still flush adequately. To lower water level, gently bend float rod down. To raise level, bend it up. Flush and test after each adjustment.

Problem D: Incomplete flushing

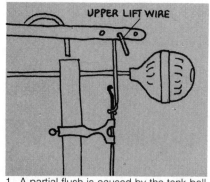

Problem E: Splashing

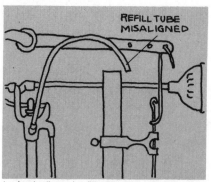

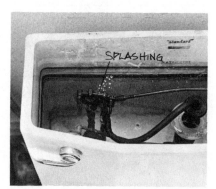

1. A partial flush is caused by the tank ball not being lifted high enough when the lever is tripped. To correct this, first make sure that the lower lift wire is screwed all the way into the tank ball. If it is, unhook the upper lift wire from the trip lever and hook it in a hole position closer to the valve. If that doesn't solve the problem, bend the hook again, making the trip wire shorter.

1. A misaligned refill tube that spouts water directly into the tank will cause splashing, often accompanied by a lack of trap-sealing water in the toilet bowl. Reposition refill tube so that it spouts into the top of the overflow tube. Do not let the tube's end reach below the tank water level. That would make it siphon tank water away, causing constant slow running of water.

2. A faulty toilet inlet valve is rare, but can cause splashing. If the valve is at fault, you will be able to see it leaking during tank refill. Either replace the entire valve assembly or repair the valve as shown on page 415. For either job, water supply to the toilet must be turned off.

Problem F: Tank sweats

1. In a humid climate when house water is cold, the toilet tank may sweat. Installing a tempering valve that mixes hot and cold water to refill the tank might stop sweating, but that uses scarce fuel to heat water. Try insulating the inside of the tank. Kits are available. Start by turning off the water and completely drying the inside of the tank. Use a sponge and paper towels, or a hair dryer.

2. Cut a piece of foam-board to fit the inside of your toilet tank. Bottom, sides, front, and back should be protected up to the highest water level. Some of the pieces may have to be sectioned to fit around tank hardware. Try not to leave any gaps.

3. Using the cement furnished with the kit, glue each piece into place. Scraps and cement can be used to fill any openings. The insulation's thickness reduces the volume inside the tank, also reducing the amount of water used for each flush. When the cement has set, the tank's ready for use.

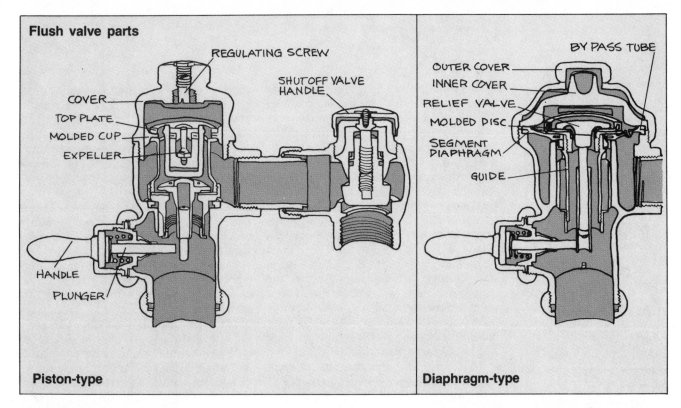

Flush valve parts

REGULATING SCREW
SHUTOFF VALVE HANDLE
COVER
TOP PLATE
MOLDED CUP
EXPELLER
HANDLE
PLUNGER

Piston-type

BY PASS TUBE
OUTER COVER
INNER COVER
RELIEF VALVE
MOLDED DISC
SEGMENT DIAPHRAGM
GUIDE

Diaphragm-type

Tankless flush valves

Tankless toilets with pressure valves—like public toilets—seldom act up. When they do, repairs are easy. How you go about it depends on whether your toilet has a diaphragm-type valve or a piston-type. If there's an adjusting screw and nut on the valve's cover, it's a piston type. A diaphragm type has no cover adjusting screw, and its inner cover is much wider than the pipe leading to it. Either type has a shutoff valve located in the pipe that comes from the wall. It may be controlled by a knurled handle or a screw you can reach after a cover nut is removed (see above). To shut off water when making repairs described in the chart below, turn handle or screw clockwise. When repairs are complete, open shutoff valve only one or two turns on a diaphragm type. Open valve fully on a piston type, whose flow is then controlled by adjusting the regulating screw and nut on the pressure valve cover.

Troubleshooting tankless flush valves

Problem	Solution	What it takes
Incomplete flush	Turn regulating screw beneath cover to the left to increase flush duration (piston-type only). In diaphragm-type, molded disc and diaphragm not assembled tight. Take valve apart and tighten disc by hand.	Strap wrench or pipe wrench and tape, screwdriver.
Too much water during a flush	As above for piston-type unit, but turn screw to the right. No regulation required on diaphragm-type unit.	Strap wrench or pipe wrench and tape, screwdriver.
Water runs after flush	Relief valve or piston not seated properly, or foreign material clogging bypass tube. Disassemble working parts of valve, rinse off, and replace.	Strap wrench or pipe wrench and tape, screwdriver.
Short-flushing	On piston-type only: (1) Water bypassing molded cup. Flare out or replace cup to fit tighter in valve cover. (2) Loose piston assembly. Tighten screws on top plate. Screw guide hand-tight. (3) Bypass in top plate enlarged from corrosive water. Replace top plate and expeller.	Strap wrench or pipe wrench and tape, screwdriver.

Replacing a toilet

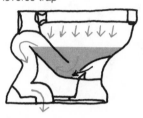

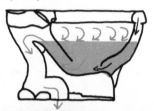

Toilets come in three basic types, according to how they flush. The *washdown* toilet (left, above) costs less, but it is noisier, uses more water and provides less trap-sealing protection. It usually has a rounded bowl. A *reverse-trap* toilet (left, center) costs more but flushes quietly and has a deeper trap seal and larger water area. Its elongated bowl shape is more comfortable. Reverse-trap toilets with front-of-the-bowl traps usually flush better. A *siphon-jet* toilet (left, below) is like a reverse trap but has a built-in orifice through which water jets to start flushing action rapidly. It uses the least water per flush and has the most positive flushing action. A siphon-vortex toilet is like a reverse trap with water entry holes set at an angle to make water swirl into and out of the bowl.

Toilets are also mounted in different ways, as shown below. Older styles have a wall-hung tank that feeds flush water through a chromed metal elbow into a floor-mounted bowl. On newer models, the tank mounts on a ledge at the rear of the

bowl. In these popular close-coupled models, all water passages are internal and a gasket between tank and bowl prevents leaks during flushes.

Even more modern is the one-piece integral tank/bowl toilet. Since its tank is not much higher than its bowl, flushing action tends to be more sluggish but quieter than a close-coupled model's. A one-piece unit is also less likely to overflow, since the tank's overflow outlet is at a slightly lower level than the bowl's rim.

Quite modern is the wall-mounted toilet whose tank hides behind a removable access panel in the wall. Its bowl bolts to a metal hanger mounted to wall framing behind the toilet. It's easy to clean under since the bowl doesn't touch the floor. But to get at the tank, you have to remove the panel and work in the confines of the wall.

You can replace one type of toilet with another—a washdown model with a siphon-jet, for example. But avoid replacing a floor-mounted toilet with a wall-mounted one. It requires extensive replumbing.

Wall mounted

Close coupled

One-piece, integral model

Removing the old toilet

Replacing a toilet takes half a day if you have the new toilet on hand before you begin. Most toilets are built to what is called a 12-inch rough-in. This means that the toilet will mount over a waste pipe centered—as most are—a foot away from the wall behind the toilet. The center of the two porcelain caps on the base of the bowl (or of the rear pair, if there are four) should also be 12 inches from the wall. If it isn't, ask your supplier for a toilet that fits your dimensions. Plan to clean up or paint the wall behind the toilet, once the old toilet is removed. If the new bowl's base is smaller, you may also want to redo the floor where the old bowl was.

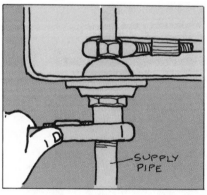

1. Shut off water supply to old toilet and hold down handle to flush it completely. Sponge out water remaining in the tank and bowl. Disconnect water supply pipe from the base of the intake valve.

2. Apply penetrating oil to hold-down bolts connecting the tank and bowl of a close-coupled unit; remove them and lift tank off the bowl. If tank is wall mounted, remove the elbow connecting it to the bowl and lift the tank from its wall bracket.

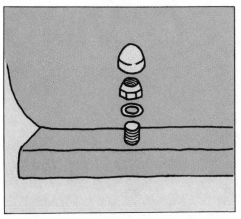

3. Unscrew or pry off the porcelain caps on the two or four nuts around the base of the bowl, chip off any plumber's putty from the nuts, and unscrew the exposed nuts.

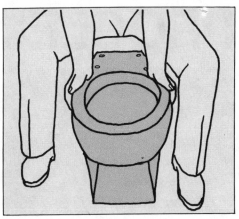

4. Straddle the bowl and rock, twist, and pull up on it until its seal with the floor flange breaks and you can lift it free. Keep it level while lifting so no trap water spills out. Clean old putty or wax out of the recess in the floor flange.

Installing the new toilet

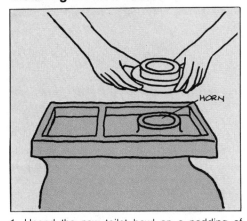

1. Upend the new toilet bowl on a padding of newspapers and slip a new wax toilet gasket, tapered side up, over the waste-water outlet, which is called the horn.

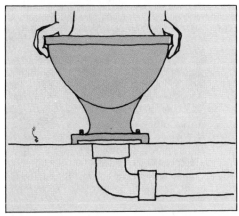

3. Twist and rock bowl gently as you press it down firmly. As excess wax squeezes out, the bowl will settle into position with its base against the floor. Install washers and nuts on the hold-down bolts and get them snug but not tight enough to crack the bowl. Cover the nuts with porcelain caps filled with plumber's putty.

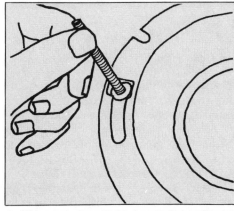

2. Slide a pair of new hold-down bolts into the slots in the floor flange, packing them with putty if needed to hold them upright. Lay a rim of plumber's putty around the bowl's flange. Pick up the new bowl, turn it right-side up, and lower it gently over the upright bolts in the floor flange. The wax gasket should meet the flange squarely.

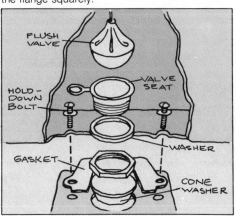

4. On a close-coupled model, position the big gasket around the bowl's flush-water inlet and set the tank on it. Install tank hold-down bolts and washers and snug them down. Connect water supply pipe to base of intake valve. Turn on water and test flush. If the new tank is wall mounted, install its bracket and hang it. Install elbow between tank and bowl and complete connections and testing.

Need for a cover-up

Nothing attracts small tools like a hole in the floor. That's what I found when I put in a new toilet. Getting the old bowl up was no sweat but I didn't cover the hole in the floor until the new bowl could be put in place. Somehow one of my small wrenches "fell" into the hole. Lucky it was large enough to get stuck in the waste pipe where I could fish it out.

Fellow next door said to cover the hole with a small pie plate until you're ready to install the new bowl. Good idea. And, he added it might be smart not to leave tools in pockets they can fall out of, or on floors where they can be stumbled over or kicked into holes.

Practical Pete

Replacing toilet seats

The trick to replacing an old toilet seat is getting off the corroded bolts that hold the old one. Dose them overnight with penetrating oil. Fit a deep-throated socket wrench to the nuts under the bowl and try to turn counterclockwise. If the nuts won't budge, saw off the bolt heads with a hacksaw, being careful not to scratch the bowl.

Trace the bowl outline on stiff paper or cardboard so your supplier can provide the right shape replacement seat. Those with plastic hinges and mounts won't corrode. If you buy one with metal bolts, taping the bolts with Teflon tape before installing will make later removal easier.

5.PROBLEM SOLVING

Unclogging drains

If only one fixture is clogged, clearing its trap and waste connection should free the drain. If several fixtures are clogged, the blockage is in the branch drain serving them, or in the main house drain or its connections to the sewer. Unclogging these is explained on pages 422 and 423.

To clear a drain, you can use a force cup plunger or a drain auger (page 399), or pour in a chemical drain cleaner. Sometimes even a coat hanger or garden hose will do the trick. Using drain cleaners sounds easy, but some are so caustic that they should not touch skin, eyes, or clothing. Don't use them on a completely blocked drain. If they fail to clear it, you will have to handle and dispose of the caustic mixture when you clear the trap mechanically. But a once-a-month dose of drain cleaner in a cleared drain may keep it from clogging up as often as it otherwise would.

Whenever you clear a blockage with a plunger, auger, or other tool, flush the drain with hot water and detergent.

Freeing sink or lavatory drains

1. To clean out hair and grease caught in the stopper, lift out the stopper. Some must be rotated before they will lift out. If the stopper won't budge, it's held by a pivot rod and retaining nut under the sink. Put a pail under the sink drain. Then loosen the nut as above and pull the pivot rod back to release the stopper. If the stopper is clean and the drain is still blocked, try a force cup plunger, as in step 2.

2. Spread papers around the sink. Remove strainer or back pivot rod holding a pop-up stopper out of waste pipe. Close any overflow opening with wet rags. Leave enough water in the basin to cover the cup. Smear petroleum jelly around cup's rim and seat cup firmly over center of drain hole. Without lifting the cup, pump up and down with short, rhythmic strokes eight times, and then jerk it up off the bowl sharply. If blockage persists, repeat twice more before trying an auger.

3. Insert the boring head of a drain auger into the pipe and use thumbscrew to set the handle three or four inches from the drain opening. Rotate the handle slowly as you push the auger in. As the handle nears the opening, loosen it, move it back, and retighten. If you hook onto the clog, move auger back and forth slowly while continuing to rotate it in the same direction, then withdraw it. If this doesn't pull out the clog, crank the auger back into the clog until it breaks through. Then work it back and forth several times.

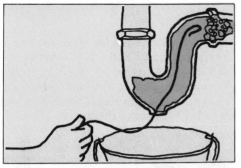

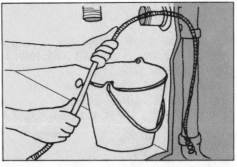

4. If the first go with the auger doesn't do the trick, put a pail under the trap's cleanout plug and unscrew the plug. Straighten a wire coat hanger and form a small hook on one end. Use this to probe up toward the basin drain hole and back toward the wall stub-out. If you can't hook onto the clog and draw it out, work the drain auger up into the openings as you did the coat hanger. If this doesn't do it, you'll have to remove the trap. You would have to do this anyway if the trap had no cleanout plug.

5. Loosen the trap slipnuts and take off the trap (page 410). Clean it out with rags wrapped around a stiff wire, a bottle brush, and water and detergent. Replace any that are worn out or corroded. If the blockage wasn't in the trap, run the drain auger into the open end of the drain pipe that goes into the wall or floor. If the auger moves in freely until it has gone far enough to meet the vertical soil stack, the blockage is probably in the main drain system (page 422).

(page 410) ... (page 422)

New wrinkles

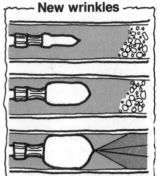

Plumbing suppliers now carry a low-cost rubber hose nozzle for clearing drains. Feed it into the drain and, when water is turned on, the nozzle expands to seal the drain more tightly than rags or a makeshift cover can do. Meanwhile a stream of water is directed toward the clog from the front of the nozzle, and the resulting pressure usually clears the clog.

Freeing tub drains

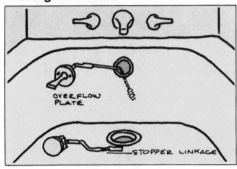

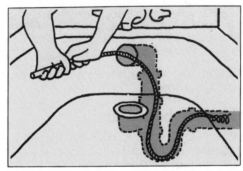

1. To clear blocked tub drains, you must first remove the strainer over the drain opening, and the pop-up or trip lever and stopper linkages from the drain and overflow pipes. Unscrew the strainer or lift out the metal stopper and its linkage. Unscrew the overflow plate and draw out the lift linkage of the trip lever or pop-up drain. Clean off any hair and other debris from the strainer, stopper, or linkage parts.

2. If the stopper or its parts weren't clogged enough to cause blockage, close the overflow hole with rags or masking tape, and try the force cup plunger. If that fails, feed an auger through the overflow opening rather than the tub drain. It has a better chance of working its way through the P-trap below the floor.

Stopgaps and copouts

Apartment dwellers faced with frequent sink backups and a landlord who won't listen can now install a small plastic check valve. It fits between the sink drain and its waste pipe, opening to let water drain out but closing to block off waste water backing up into the sink.

Freeing floor drains

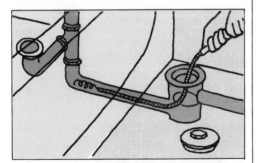

3. Some tubs in older houses have cylindrically shaped drum traps located at floor level beside the bathtubs. Their metal covers can be unscrewed and lifted off to expose a lower opening going to the tub, and a higher one going to the main drain. Feed an auger through the lower opening first, then back through the higher one. If the trap's gasket is worn, replace it while you have the cover off.

Force cups and augers can be tried on floor drains but a garden hose may be more effective if the blockage is beyond the trap. Remove the strainer and screw a garden hose to the nearest faucet. (Get a threaded adapter for a lavatory or sink faucet.) Feed the hose into the drain as far as it will go and pack rags tightly around it at the drain opening. Or, slit a sturdy plastic kitchen bowl cover and fit it around the hose to seal the drain opening (above). While you hold down the rags or plastic cover firmly, have someone turn the water full on and full off repeatedly. The short bursts of water should clear the clog.

Caution: Always remove and clean a hose used to clear drains. Leaving the hose in can result in hazardous back-siphonage (page 407).

(page 407)

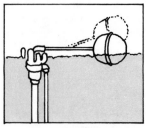
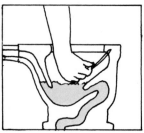
Freeing toilet drains

Clogged toilets are cleared with force cup plungers or augers that are specially designed for the task. The plunger has an extended lower cone that more nearly fits into a toilet's built-in trap opening. The auger—called a closet auger—has a long tube with a curved tip that is placed close to the trap opening. Cranking and pushing the handle feeds auger wire from the tube into the opening. Pulling the handle back retracts the wire into the tube. Follow the steps below in using these tools.

1. The toilet bowl should contain just enough water to cover the plunger cup. Don rubber gloves and fit the cup over the large opening near the bottom of the bowl. Without lifting the cup from the bowl, pump up and down 8 or 9 times with quick, rhythmic strokes, then jerk the cup up sharply. If the bowl water disappears, you have probably freed the drain. Pour in some water as a test. If the drain is still clogged, plunge away a few more times before using the auger.

2. With the bowl half full of water, place the curved tip of the closet auger tube so it faces into the drain opening, push in and turn the handle to feed the auger's boring head into the drain. Use the same pushing and withdrawing motions used for clearing sink or lavatory clogs with a drain auger.

If the blockage is obviously in the built-in toilet trap and the auger won't clear it, you'll have to remove the bowl (pages 418-19) to get it out.

Freeing house drains

When a clog occurs in the main drain or its branches, every fixture drain above the clog will be affected. Turn on a faucet or flush a toilet and waste water may suddenly appear in the bathtub or shower, which have lower drains. Or a clothes washer in the basement may flood. You'll have to clear the clog from the branch or main drain.

If drain water is still flowing out—but sluggishly—try running water after a long time of not running it. If the drain backs up again quickly, the clog may be close enough to reach with an auger through the nearest fixture drain. If it takes a long time for the water to back up, the clog is probably far down in the waste system. Or, if you've noticed unpleasant odors in the house, the vent system that connects to the waste system may be blocked. Blocked vents also create a sluggish flow.

To clear the vent and the main soil stack to which it attaches, rent a 50-foot long electrically powered auger from a local tool rental firm or plumbing supplier. Feed this down through the stack vent on the roof, as at right. Alternately push and withdraw it if you meet resistance, until the auger breaks through the clog. When it does, flush the stack with a garden hose.

The rented auger should reach down to the main, Y-shaped cleanout from the roof. If you encountered no blockage, the clog is somewhere beyond the main cleanout plug. Try step 1, opposite.

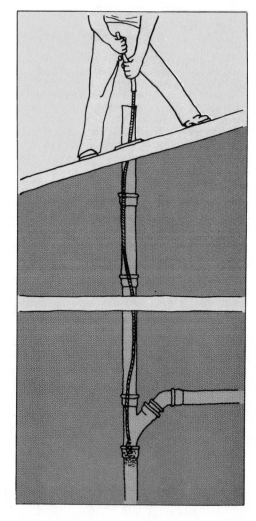

1. Spread several layers of newspapers around the main cleanout plug and station a pail under it. Loosen and remove the plug as above. But keep it handy to help slow down any flow of water that might come out. When the flow has subsided, go to step 2. (If you can't loosen a plug with a wrench, nick its edge with a chisel, hold the blade in the nick and drive the plug counterclockwise with a hammer.)

3. Spread layers of newspapers round the trap and slowly loosen the plug nearest the outside sewer line as above. If no water seeps out as you loosen, the clog is in the main house trap. If you see the clog, poke a small hole in it with a stiff wire and let water drain through gradually. When the flow subsides, open the adjacent plug and clean trap thoroughly with an auger, a stiff brush and a hosing.

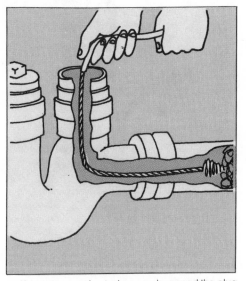

2. Feed an auger through the opening toward the main house trap, as above. If this clears the clog, flush line with a garden hose and recap the opening after coating the plug's threads with pipe dope. If you still have blockage, the clog is in the U- or Y-shaped main house trap with its adjacent cleanout plugs. Or it's between the main trap and the town sewer connection. Try step 3.

4. If water seeped out when you loosened the plug nearest the sewer, remove the plug and quickly feed an auger, or better yet, a sewer rod or tape into the drain leading to the sewer, as above. If this doesn't remove the blockage, recap the trap and consult with town officials, or with a professional plumber if you have a septic system.

Rescuing valuables

Valuables dropped into a drain may not be lost forever. Shut off all water immediately and make sure no one flushes a toilet until the prize is recovered. On a sink or lavatory, lift out stopper gingerly; the valuable may be caught in it. If not, shine a flashlight down the opening; if you see the valuable, you may be able to fish it out with needlenose pliers.

If it's not there, place a dishpan under the trap cleanout and remove the plug. Form a hook on an end of coat-hanger wire. Work this up toward the drain opening and pull it down gently. Then remove the trap and probe through it. For a toilet, wrap your arm in a plastic bag and work coat-hanger probe through top of trap and back toward you along the bottom of the trap to either hook or roll the object to you.

Tap horizontal drainpipes between the fixture and the main house trap with a soft-faced hammer or mallet while listening for a rattle inside. If the valuable is metal and the pipes are not, you may be able to rent or borrow a metal detector to help locate it.

As a final step, remove a main house trap-cleanout plug and cut a circular piece of wire screening whose mesh is small enough to catch the valuable. The screen diameter should be larger than the pipe's so it can be fitted tightly in the pipe. Turn on water and run either the sink faucets or the toilet the valuable fell in. The flow of water may move the valuable to your trap. Whether it does or not, remember to remove the wire screen and recap the drain.

Solving frequent clogging

A house sewer that clogs ever more frequently may be filling with tree roots. You can rent an electrically powered root auger that will clean them out, but if you do, get careful directions on its use and follow them. Misused, this cutting tool can chew right through some of the softer kinds of sewer pipe.

Throughly wash and dry any equipment used for drain cleaning before storing. Oiling will keep it from rusting.

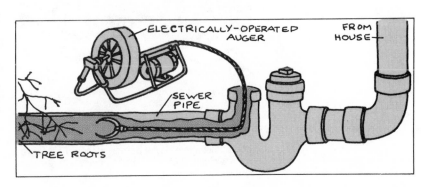

Fixing leaks

Tip: Sometimes it's hard to tell whether a toilet tank is leaking or just dripping condensation. Add some vegetable dye to the tank water, wait an hour, and touch the bolt tips and nuts under the tank and on the elbow connecting the tank to the bowl with white tissue. Where dye color shows, there's a leak. Shut off water, flush tank and mop out with a sponge. If a hold-down bolt leaked, tighten and re-test. If leak persists, remove bolt and replace washers. If leak is at base of intake valve, install new fluid-level control valve (page 417). Loosen leaking elbow slipnuts, replace washers, coat threads with silicone rubber sealant or self-forming packing and re-tighten.

If leak is around flush-valve seat (page 419), remove hold-down bolts and disconnect water supply and intake valve. Lift tank from bowl, lay it down and remove lock nut on valve seat. Replace round and cone-shaped washers and remount the tank.

Loose or poorly fitted joints and corroded pipes and fittings all cause leaks. Some joint leaks can be stopped by replacing washers, if any, and tightening or resoldering. On others, corroded fittings must be replaced. Where pipes or storage tanks leak from corrosion or mechanical damage, the leaks can sometimes be stopped with commercial patching devices. If pipe or tank has corroded from inside enough to leak, it's best to replace it.

Burst supply pipes are scary but shutting off the nearest stop valve will stop the flow. If it's a hot-water pipe, close the stop valve above the hot-water heater. If you can't locate a nearby stop valve, close the main shutoff valve (page 390).

Water dripping from or staining a ceiling usually means a leak in the water system above. Check all fixtures for visible leaks. If you find any, replace gaskets, washers or worn parts, retighten or resolder faulty connections and test for further leakage.

If no fixtures were leaking, the leak may be behind the wall. With the water on, listen upstairs along the wall where you know water pipes run for a hissing, gurgling or muffled dripping sound. It should be loudest when you're closest to it, with no signs of leakage above it. Some plumbing supply stores sell simple sound-amplifying devices that help pinpoint leaks.

Don't try to patch a pipe leaking behind the wall or one that has burst. Replace it.

1. Small, pinpoint leaks in pipes can be sealed with tightly wrapped plastic tape but fix small joint leaks with epoxy paste. Shut off water, drain pipes and clean and then dry the outside of the pipe with a hair dryer before applying the epoxy. Let it cure overnight before turning on the water.

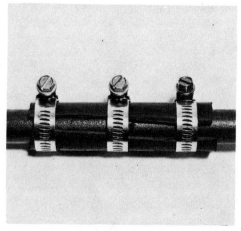

2. Larger cracks can be sealed temporarily by binding a section of hose tightly around the crack with twisted picture wire or, better yet, worm-drive hose clamps, as above. Use enough wire or clamps to keep pressure uniform all along the clamp.

3. As soon as you can, replace a homemade hose clamp with a rubber-lined pipe leak clamp or sleeve of a diameter that fits the damaged pipe. The sleeve can be cinched tight around the cracked area with screws and nuts.

4. Small leaks in tanks can be temporarily plugged with self-tapping repair plugs (see Table, opposite). These are screwed into the rusted-out hole until the plug's gasket seals the leak. But don't count on this fix lasting indefinitely.

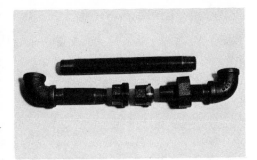

5. Leaks may be visible on exposed piping or they may show up as stains on walls or ceilings. If the sweep hand or one-cubic-foot dial pointer on your water meter moves when all fixtures are shut off, the leak is from your plumbing and not a hole in the roof or wall.

6. To replace a leaking section of galvanized threaded pipe, get two shorter sections of matching pipe and a union which, when put together, are the same length as the pipe being replaced. Hacksaw a section out of the old pipe and remove its pieces. Then fit the new pipes and union in position as shown. Remember to tape threads and tighten nut with two opposing wrenches.

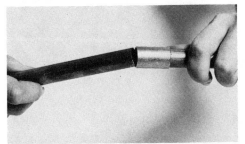

7. To repair a small leak in copper pipe, cut through pipe where leak is, coat the inside of a clean copper slip coupling with flux, and spread cut pipe ends enough to slip coupling onto one end of pipe. Clean and flux pipe ends, center slip coupling over cut, and sweat solder each end of the coupling to the pipe. Wrap wet rags around first coupling end soldered to keep it from melting as second end is soldered.

8. Leaks in cast-iron waste pipes can often be stopped by wrapping pipe in a rag soaked in silicone sealant. If a lead-caulked waste joint leaks, tamping it down with a hammer and chisel or sealing it, after drying, with epoxy paste should stop the leak.

Troubleshooting leaks

Problem	Solution	What it takes
Water spurts from pipe.	Install clamp-type patch until pipe can be replaced.	Patch and wrench or screwdriver.
Water leaks from joint.	Tighten threaded pipe joint. Drain and resolder sweat-copper joint. Cut out and replace solvent-welded plastic joint.	Pipe wrenches, hacksaw, pipe cutter, knife.
Water leaks from tank of hot-water heater.	Remove insulation jacketing and install repair plug, until heater can be replaced.	Tin snips, drill, bit, wrench.
Water drips from a ceiling or along foundation.	Locate hidden leak and remove wall or ceiling material to expose it for repair. Replace pipe or fitting.	Carpentry and pipe tools.
Continually wet spot in ground above service entrance pipe.	Have ground-key valve turned off, dig hole above leak and replace leaking pipe or fitting.	Shovel and pipe tools.
Water leaks at water heater's T&P relief valve pipe.	Check house pressure. If too high, install pressure-reducing valve. Valve off some water to clear sediment: If that doesn't stop leak, replace valve with one rated according to local code.	Plumbing tools, O-100 psi pressure gauge, pipe wrenches.
DWV system leaks at cleanout fitting.	Tighten fitting.	Wrench.
DWV system leaks at pipe or joint.	Make permanent pipe repair. Lead-and-oakum caulked joints may be repaired by repounding lead with caulking tool.	DWV piping tools, joint caulking.
Trap leaks at slipnut.	Tighten slipnut. Remove trap and install new O-rings. Or, as a temporary repair, coat with silicone rubber sealant and wrap with electrical tape.	Trap wrench, O-rings or silicone sealant and tape.

Curing condensation

Water condenses on cold metal pipes when humid air flowing over them is cooled below its dew point. If you don't want to solve the problem with a dehumidifier, you can keep the pipes from dripping by wrapping them with insulation. Several types are available: fiberglass, aluminum-and-vinyl and other plastic-tape wraps, or preformed plastic sheathing. Tapes are wrapped around pipes and fittings like a tight bandage. If they are not self-adhering, fasten the ends with string, tape or household cement. Preformed sheathing is slit on one side to snap around pipe and then tape tight. Both types eliminate condensation and provide some insulation. But some are meant primarily to stop condensation and should not be used on hot-water pipes. Ask your plumbing supplier to provide the type you need.

Torch song

Boy, did I get burned the first time I tried to thaw a frozen pipe. Fellow who knows the ropes told me I didn't know how lucky I was just to get burned—and not have a pipe burst in my face.

The right way, he said, is to use a flame spreader nozzle and never to let the pipe get too hot to touch with your bare hand. Always start near an open valve or faucet and work away from it until water begins to flow. This lets any steam pressure from heating escape harmlessly through the faucet. Otherwise it could form a pocket blocked by ice and burst the pipe.

Some other cautions: Always keep a sheet of asbestos between the flame and any nearby framing or walls; and it won't hurt to have a fire extinguisher handy just in case.

Practical Pete

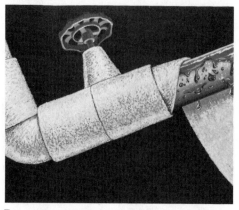
Tape wrap prevents condensation and dripping.

Slit sheathing snapped around pipe stops the drip.

Preventing freezing

The best cure for freezing pipes is prevention. A wrapping of electric heat tape should keep pipes from freezing. To make the heat tape work better and last longer, wind a plastic-tape wrap over it.

The water supply to hose bibbs and other outside piping should be cut off and the pipes drained in winter to prevent freeze-up. If a power failure and subfreezing weather catch you with uninsulated pipes, turn faucets on to a trickle and wrap pipes with several layers of newspapers tied with string. If the power failure and cold snap continue for some time, drain the house system and pour antifreeze into the fixture traps as explained on page 474.

Thawing pipes

When unusually cold weather or a power failure freezes up pipes you never expected to freeze, what to do? If you have power, placing an electric hair dryer on the pipe near an open faucet or drain valve, or wrapping an electric heating pad around it will thaw the pipe (see opposite page, above left). Or you can tie towels or rags around the frozen pipe and pour boiling water over them until the ice melts (opposite, above center). If you have the time and think the pipes may freeze again, buy electric tape and use that to thaw the pipes and keep them from refreezing.

A quicker method that requires caution but works even when power fails is to use a propane torch. Fit it with a flame spreader nozzle and play it along the pipe (opposite, above right). But be sure to observe all safety precautions (see Torch song at left).

Frozen pipes behind walls or ceiling can often be thawed by aiming a heat lamp at them. Keep it about 8 inches away to avoid marring or scorching the wall or ceiling.

For buried pipe that has frozen, call local arc welding shops and ask whether they have any experience in thawing pipes by sending electrical current through them. This is tricky work that should only be done by experienced operators.

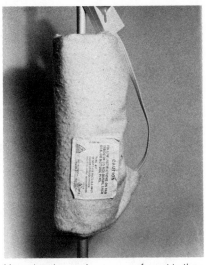

Use a heating pad near open faucet to thaw frozen pipe.

Pour boiling water over pipe wrapped with towels or rags.

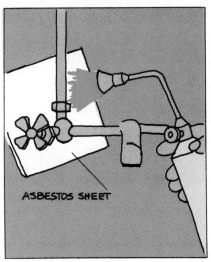

Torch with flame spreader nozzle.

Curing water hammer

When fast shutoff valves—like those on faucets or clothes washers—stop incoming water abruptly, it may make pipes vibrate noisily. This is known as water hammer. It is annoying and it can damage the water supply system.

The cure is to have air chambers (page 391) attached to the water-supply lines of every fast shutoff fixture. Most newer homes have them. Adding them to behind-the-wall fixture piping in older homes is tedious and costly. Owners of older homes will probably wait to do it until some remodeling gives them an excuse to get behind the wall. In the meantime, installing the add-on chamber shown below will provide some noise protection in older homes.

Sometimes water hammer occurs when existing air chambers become waterlogged. The first step is to turn off all faucets slowly to stop the hammer. A longer lasting cure is to drain the water supply system and refill it. This replenishes the air cushions in the chambers. Shut off the main supply valve and open all water faucets. Draw air into the system through the faucets by opening the drain valves at the bottom of the water heater and the outdoor hose spigots. Then close all faucets and valves and refill the system. If water hammer has disappeared, its cause was waterlogging. Whenever it reappears, another draining will stop it.

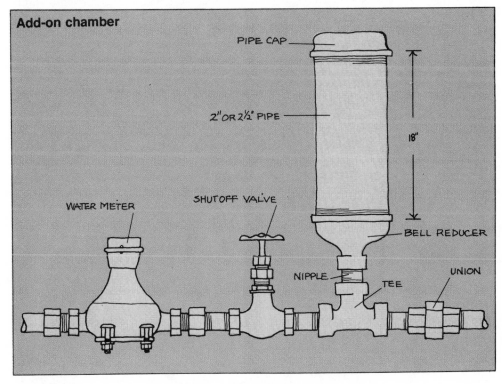

Add-on chamber

PIPE CAP

2" OR 2½" PIPE

18"

WATER METER

SHUTOFF VALVE

BELL REDUCER

NIPPLE

TEE

UNION

6.PIPING

Pipe fittings

Typical fittings used in water supply piping include: **1, 2,** and **3.** Sweat-solder copper tees; **4.** Standard copper coupling and, below it, copper slip coupling; **5.** Threaded steel union; **6.** Steel coupling; **7.** All-thread close nipple; **8.** CPVC tee; **9.** CPVC 45-degree elbow; **10.** CPVC cap; **11** and **12.** ¾- and ½-inch 45-degree copper elbows; **13.** Thread-to-sweat solder adapter; **14.** Threaded nipples; **15.** CPVC coupling; **16.** CPVC 90-degree street elbow; **17.** CPVC 90-degree elbow; **18.** CPVC adapter to threads; **19.** Left to right, flexible pipe tee, adapter and 90-degree elbows; **20.** Brass flare fittings: (a) elbow; (b) tapped elbow; (c) adapter; (d) tee; **21.** Brass hose adapter; **22.** Threaded brass 90-degree elbow and pipe section; **23.** CPVC pipe with brass adapter attached.

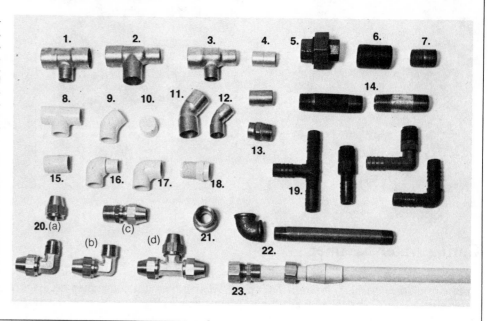

Joining CPVC solvent-welded pipes

CPVC plastic pipe may be cut with a hand saw, hacksaw, or a tubing cutter with special wheel.

Remove the burr from the inside and outside of pipe. Do the inside with a knife, the outside with sandpaper.

First apply cleaner to both mating surfaces; then brush solvent liberally onto the pipe end and fitting socket.

Immediately join the pipe and fitting with a slight twist and hold for a few seconds.

Vinyl water-supply piping

Hot/cold vinyl tubing is ideal for homeowner installation. It's low in cost, lightweight, easy to use, and it lasts and lasts without corrosion or scale buildup. It comes as rigid ½- and ¾-inch inside diameter tube in 10-foot lengths. Outside diameters are about ⅝ and ⅞ inch. You can cut CPVC tube with any saw and join it to a wide variety of CPVC fittings by easy, almost foolproof solvent-welding (see photos at left). Adapters permit connection to threaded and sweated pipes and fittings. CPVC water-supply tubing is rated to withstand 100 psi pressure at 180 degrees Fahrenheit. Do not confuse CPVC with PVC cold-water pipe. The latter is similarly rigid, but is not heat-resistant. Used for hot-water supply, PVC would soften and eventually fail.

If, for some reason, you must buy tube and fittings made by different manufacturers—and even if you don't—it's a good idea to test-check a fitting on the tube before solvent-welding. Solvent cement used to join CPVC tubes and fittings is different from PVC cement.

Perhaps the biggest drawback to CPVC tubing is its one-way joining process. Solvent-welding is so simple, that, unless you are careful, you can get into trouble. Once you join the tube and fitting, you're committed. A wrongly installed fitting must be sawed off and replaced.

Leaks are rare. If you do the job right, using lots of solvent on both tube and fitting, you need not worry about them. The chief cause of leaks is too little solvent. CPVC joints can be handled in minutes and are ready for water pressure in an hour.

Vinyl water-supply tubes expand and contract more with changes in temperature than do metal pipes. For this reason, all hot water adaptations to metal pipes and fittings should be made with what are called *transition fittings*.

A 10-foot length of CPVC hot-water tube will expand and contract about ½ inch with temperature changes. Be sure that the ends of pipe runs aren't installed tightly against framing. Leave the tube room to move. Likewise, the tube should be fastened to framing with its own special hangers that permit endwise movement without cutting or abrading. Use one support every 32 inches. Also, vertical lengths of CPVC tube taking off from mains and up through a floor or down through a ceiling need room to bend as the main moves with tempera-

Vinyl water-supply pipe sizes			
Nominal size	Outside dia.	Inside dia.	Wall thickness
½″	0.625″	0.489″	0.068″
¾″	0.875″	0.715″	0.080″

ture changes. Either slot out the holes for them or make sure they have at least 8 inches to flex before being bound into a hole in floor or ceiling.

Both plastic and threaded pipe fittings come in a type called *street*. Not the road in front of your house, street means simply pipe-sized. Fittings normally accept pipes in all sockets. On the other hand, a street fitting contains one socket that fits into another fitting.

CPVC water-supply tubing may be used to plumb an entire house or you can use it for extending a present system made of metal. In that case, the correct adapters will get the project started. At sinks, lavatories, and toilets, CPVC now can be adapted directly to riser tubes via fittings or fixture-shutoff valves. At bathtubs and showers, connections are made by adapting CPVC to the faucets by making use of transition fittings.

CPVC fittings

Special hangers for CPVC water-supply pipe are designed to hold the pipe to the framing, yet not bind or cut it. Be sure to use this kind of hanger.

Runs of CPVC pipe longer than 35 feet should be dog-legged by installing a 12-inch offset with two elbows. This allows for thermal expansion and contraction.

Caution: Vinyl solvent-welding cements contain volatile chemicals that should only be used in a ventilated room. Do not smoke while doping joints, and do not solvent-weld near an open flame. Also, don't spill solvent on plastic materials, such as some toilet seats. It dissolves the plastic.

CPVC pipes can be reduced from one size to another by the use of bushings. The bushing is solvent-welded into the fitting; the smaller pipe solvent-welds into it.

New wrinkles

Polybutylene

Now you can get a flexible plastic tube for water-supply lines made of a new high-temperature thermoplastic polybutylene (PB). Use PB where soft-copper water-supply tubing is now used, such as for burial beneath concrete slabs where a single length averts having buried joints that might leak. PB also is fine for remodeling where pipes have to be snaked through walls, floors, and ceilings. Joints in PB tubing are made with adapters and CPVC or acetyl copolymer fittings: solvent-welding is not possible. Don't confuse PB pipe with polyethylene pipe. Polyethylene is flexible but can't carry hot water.

1. The tube is cut with ordinary garden shears. Tube cutter, saw with miter box, or even a sharp knife may also be used. 2. A metal insert or stiffener which comes with fittings is pushed into the tube end. 3. After the fitting nut is loosened by hand, the tube is pushed in and the fitting is tightened.

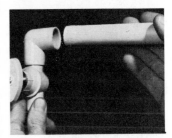

One type of CPVC line stop is called *street*, which takes either a ½-inch pipe in it or a ¾-inch fitting over it. It can thus serve as a reducing valve.

Comparison of plastic water-supply piping

Type of pipe	Type of use				Joins with	Form	Cost	Where to install
	Under-ground	Cold water	Hot water	Inside house				
Polyethylene (PE)	Yes	Yes	No	No	Slip-on clamped fittings	Flexible coils	Very low	Underground sprinkler systems, irrigation systems; generally for cold water, out-of-doors, and underground.
Polyvinyl chloride (PVC)	Yes	Yes	No	No	Solvent-welded fittings	Rigid lengths	Low	Same as for polyethylene.
Chlorinated polyvinyl chloride (CPVC)	Yes	Yes	Yes	Yes	Solvent-welded fittings	Rigid lengths	Moderate	For inside the house water-supply systems, cold or hot water. Ideal for exposed use in basements, utility rooms rooms where neat corners count.
Polybutylene (PB)	Yes	Yes	Yes	Yes	Mechanical O-ring fittings	Flexible coils	Moderate	For inside the house hot/cold water-supply systems. Best suited for hidden use, where appearance won't matter. For uses, see New wrinkle above.

Threaded water-supply piping

Joining threaded pipes

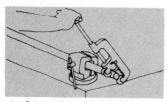

1. Cut steel and brass pipes with a pipe cutter, tightening a little each turn until the pipe severs. Remove resulting burr with a pipe reamer.

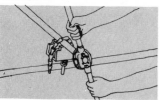

2. Use a pipe die inside a stock to cut threads. Start the die, guide first, and push and turn clockwise until the threads are established. Use lots of cutting oil on the pipe end and back up a quarter-turn every half-turn to clear the cuttings. Continue until one thread shows beyond the die.

3. To install a fitting, apply pipe dope or tape to the male threads and start the fitting by hand. When it starts getting tight, turn with a pipe wrench, the wrench's jaws faced to turn clockwise, and tighten.

Threaded galvanized-steel and brass water-supply pipes make the strongest, most damage-resistant systems which can be put in. Brass, while costly, gets around the corrosion and scale-buildup drawbacks of galvanized-steel pipe. Threaded pipes join to their fittings by tapered pipe threads. The farther the pipe screws into the fitting, the tighter the joint becomes. New pipes come threaded on both ends. In cut lengths of pipe, threads are made with a die—a thread-cutting tool—held in a stock.

Threaded pipes are sized nominally by their inside diameter. Because of their thick walls, outside diameters are much greater. The accompanying table shows how to judge threaded-pipe size by measuring a pipe's circumference. Popular house-water-supply pipe sizes are ¾ and ½ inch, with 1, ⅜, and ¼ inch used occasionally.

Pipe nipples of various lengths up to 12 inches long are widely sold. These are cut to length and come already threaded. Nipples short enough to leave almost no distance between fittings joined by them are called *close* nipples. So-called *short* nipples leave about ½ inch between fittings. Others come even-numbered, up to 12 inches.

Since most faucets and valves are already set up for threaded pipes, fewer adapters are required than with plastic or copper pipes. Galvanized pipes and fittings are

Neatest way to lubricate and seal pipe threads is with a wrapping of TFE white tape. Apply to male pipe threads before screwing them into a pipe fitting. Direction of wrap is important. Hold the pipe in your right hand and turn it away from you to pull the tape over the top. Give one full wrap plus some overlap and tear off. Use enough tension so the threads show through the TFE tape.

worked with toothed-jaw pipe wrenches. Cutting may be with a hacksaw, or more professionally, with a pipe cutter.

Each male thread should be coated with a good pipe dope or wrapped with TFE tape (see photo). When joining threaded pipes and fittings, it is possible to tighten them too much and crack the fitting. With new threads, tighten the joint until about three pipe threads still show beyond the fitting. Never tighten more than one turn after the last thread has disappeared into the fitting. You can gauge tightness by feel.

Judging galvanized pipe size

Approx. circum.	Nominal inside dia.	Actual inside dia.	Outside dia.
1¹¹⁄₁₆″	¼″	0.36″	0.540″
2⅛″	⅜″	0.49″	0.675″
2⅝″	½″	0.62″	0.840″
3⁵⁄₁₆″	¾″	0.82″	1.050″
4⅛″	1″	1.04″	1.315″

Fixture requirements

Fixture	Gpm flow
Bathtub	5–8
Tank toilet	2–3
Flush-valve	30–40
Laundry tub/ Sink	5
Lavatory/ Shower	5
Shower-water conserving	2
Garden hose	5–10

Comparison of Pipe Types

Pipe	Advantages and Disadvantages	Relative cost (CPVC/PB=1)	Sizes available
CPVC/PB	Very lightweight, smooth flow, nonconducting, resists corrosion and scaling, self-insulating, easy to use. Sensitive to over-temperatures, over-pressures, and hard blows. CPVC joints cannot be undone. Comes rigid or flexible. Cannot be used for electrical grounding.	1.0	½″ ¾″
Copper water tube	Lightweight, smooth flow, resists corrosion and scaling. Sensitive to over-pressures and hard blows. Offers rigid and flexible alternatives, choice of weights. Requires flame-soldering.	1.2*	⅜″ ½″ ¾″ 1″
Threaded galvanized steel, brass	Super strong, larger internal diameters for fast flow. Resists nails and most drilling, connects easily to threaded tub/shower faucets but requires threading. Brass is noncorroding, nonscaling, longest-lasting system. Requires more tools, skill.	1.7**	¼″ ⅜″ ½″ ¾″ 1″

*Type M tube. **Galvanized steel. Brass is many times as costly.

Joining copper tubing

Copper water-supply tubing is the easiest-working metal piping for house water-supply systems. Copper tube comes in three weights in nominal sizes according to inside diameter. Common house supply sizes are ½ and ¾ inch. Diameters of ⅜ and 1 inch are also used occasionally. No factory-made nipples are available. Instead, they are cut from tubing as required.

Type K tubing, the heaviest-walled, is too costly for most residential uses. Type L is the normal choice for buried service entrance lines and other below-ground purposes. Type M, thinnest-walled, is for aboveground house plumbing and for hydronic heating systems. Types K and L come in hard-temper straight lengths 20 feet long (sometimes sold cut to 10-foot lengths), and in 30- and 60-foot soft-temper coils. Type M tubing comes in hard-temper, straight lengths only. One difference between temper types is that while hard-temper tube cracks on freezing, soft-temper can take several freezings and thawings. Color-coding is: Type K—green; Type L—blue; and Type M—red.

Rigid tubes make a neater installation; flexible ones are best for underground uses and for unexposed remodeling work where they may be snaked into framing. Flexible tubes can be run long distances without fittings. Sweat-soldering may be used to join both hard- and soft-temper tubes by heating to about 400 degrees Fahrenheit and applying 50/50 lead-tin solder (see below). Soft-temper tube may also be joined by flaring (see page 398).

Joints in copper tubing can be made in any one of three ways: by compression fittings, by flare fittings, or by sweat-soldering. Compression and flare fittings are often used to join tubing to faucets (page 408). Some appliances, such as dishwashers, also use flare or compression fittings. Only sweat-soldering should be used for lines that will be cast into concrete or buried. For these uses, be sure to coat the tubing with asphalt and make a careful leak check before covering the tubing.

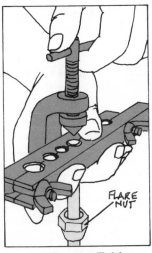

Flaring Copper Tubing
If a flare fitting is to be used, slip a flare nut on the end of the tubing, then clamp the tubing into a flaring tool. Put a drop or two of oil on the tubing and tighten the flaring head firmly. Remove the flaring tool. The flared end can now be joined to a flare fitting.

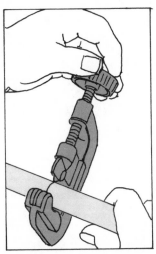

Cutting Copper Tubing
Tubing can be cut with a fine-tooth hacksaw, but a tubing cutter makes a cleaner cut. Adjust the cutter for a shallow first cut. Rotate the cutter, tightening it after each turn, until tubing is cut through.

Most tube cutters have a built-in reaming device to remove burrs after cutting.

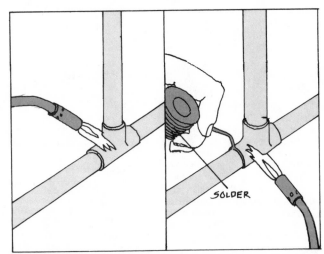

Sweat-soldering Copper Tubing
Cleanliness is the secret of a good sweat-solder joint. Use a wire brush, fine sandpaper, emery cloth, or steel wool to make both surfaces bright and shiny. Apply a thin coat of soldering flux to the end of the tubing and insert it into the fitting. Twist the parts a bit to spread the flux. Set your torch for a large flame and heat the overall joint first. Next, set your torch for a pencil-size flame and apply it to the joint. When solder will flow, remove the flame and feed 50/50 wire solder into the joint until a bright fillet forms all around.

Sizing of copper water-tube supply

Nominal size	Outside dia.			Inside dia.			Wall thickness			Water flow (Type M copper tube)	
	Type K	Type L	Type M	Type K	Type L	Type M	Type K	Type L	Type M	Tube size	Gals / min
⅜″	0.500″	0.500″	0.500″	0.402″	0.4030″	0.450″	0.049″	0.035″	0.025″	⅜″	2
½″	0.625″	0.625″	0.625″	0.527″	0.545″	0.569″	0.049″	0.040″	0.028″	½″	5½
¾″	0.875″	0.875″	0.875″	0.745″	0.785″	0.811″	0.049″	0.045″	0.032″	¾″	12

Running water-supply pipes

Probably the hardest thing about running pipes is remembering to allow for makeup. This is the distance taken up by a fitting minus the distance the pipe screws or slips into the coupling, tee, or whatever. Suppose you are running a supply pipe from a main line along the joists, and that it must come out of the wall centered 16 inches above the floor. You could take measurements and calculate exactly how long the pipe should be cut using the makeup table below. Subtract for distance taken up by fittings and add for socket makeup.

An easier way is to position the actual fittings at each end of the pipe where they will connect and measure what is called face-to-face between fittings. Then simply add for the socket makeup at each end—distance X for that pipe size times two. For example, if the face-to-face measurement is 23½ inches, then ½-inch threaded water-supply pipe joining the two ½-inch fittings would need to be 24½ inches long (23½ + ½ + ½). Threaded up, the fittings should position perfectly. But write down all the pluses and minuses to keep them straight in your mind.

Or, you can sketch out the pipe runs on paper, showing the measured distances the piping must traverse. Then, using the table and a pocket calculator, below, figure how long each pipe must be. The first time through, you'll make errors and have to recut some pipes. Don't worry. Order enough extra pipe to permit a few slip-ups.

The balance of water-supply piping work is merely a matter of drilling or sawing access for pipes and installing them with the proper fittings. Proceed in the direction of water flow, especially when working with threaded pipes where one end has to be free for tightening.

Drilling and notching

It's better to drill holes for pipes than cut out notches in joists or studs. Joists may be drilled anywhere along the span but the hole diameter should be no more than one-fourth the joist depth. Keep holes as small as possible and at least 2 inches away from edges. Joists should be notched in the end quarters only, never in the middle half. Notch should not exceed one-fourth the joist's depth. Studs may be notched up to 2¼-inches round or square, if strap steel is nailed over the notch opening to reinforce it. Notches up to 1¼ inch don't need the straps. Stud drilling rules are the same as those for notching.

Take great care to avoid boring into pipes or electrical cables hidden within the walls. Don't stand in water. When standing on concrete, lay down a block of wood to help keep you from being grounded. Use either a double-insulated electric drill or one that is grounded with a three-pronged grounding plug and grouding extension cord. Never defeat an electric drill's safety features by adapting a three-pronged grouding plug to a non-grounding outlet. Don't take chances with electricity.

Calculating pipe length between two fittings

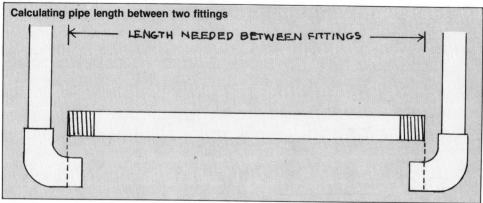

LENGTH NEEDED BETWEEN FITTINGS

Makeup table for threaded fittings

Add distance		Subtract distances				
Pipe size	Pipe screws into fitting	A	B	C	D	E
½″	½″	1⅛″	⅞″	1⅝″	1⁵/₆″	1¼″
¾″	½″	1⁵/₁₆″	1″	1⅞″	1½″	1⁷/₁₆″
1″	⁹/₁₆″	1½″	1⅛″	2⅛″	1¹¹/₁₆″	1¹¹/₁₆″

Makeup table for Genova CPVC fittings

Pipe Size	Pipe slips into socket	A	B	C	D	F
½″	½″	1⁵/₁₆″	¹¹/₁₆″	1″	1³/₁₆″	—
¾″	¾″	1¼″	1″	1⁵/₁₆″	1⁹/₁₆″	3″

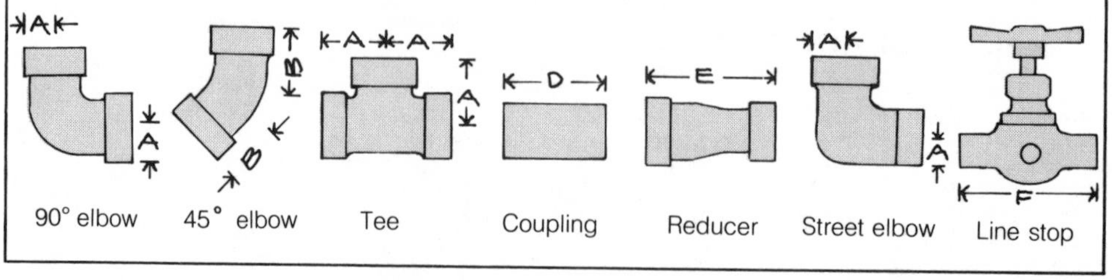

90° elbow   45° elbow   Tee   Coupling   Reducer   Street elbow   Line stop

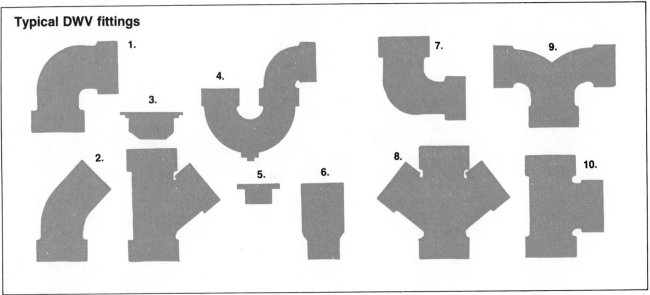

Typical DWV fittings

1. 90-degree sanitary elbow (hub and hub); **2.** 45-degree street elbow (hub and spigot); **3.** Cleanout wye with plug; **4.** P-trap; **5.** Closet flange; **6.** Reducing coupling; **7.** Closet bend (hub and hub); **8.** Double wye (all hub); **9.** Reducing double elbow; **10.** Sanitary tee.

Cast-iron DWV piping

Ask any plumber what is the best drain-waste-vent plumbing system, and he will likely say cast iron. Once installed, it cannot be surpassed. And installation is not difficult, except for cutting pipes to length, which is plain hard work unless you rent a lever-type cutting tool. The joining labor once connected with cast iron pipe disappeared with the introduction of the No-Hub system. It comprises simple hubless fittings and plain hubless pipes. Joining of pipes and fittings is by neoprene rubber gaskets (sleeves) and ribbed stainless steel shields held by worm-driven clamps. Pipes fit together so closely that no allowance need be made for makeup.

Another thing, a No-Hub joint, once made up, may be taken apart again to correct an error. A drawback, house walls containing 3-inch or larger No-Hub piping, such as behind toilets, must be furred out or built thicker than the standard 3½ inches to accommodate any fittings. However, this also is true of most other DWV fittings.

Hubless cast iron pipe comes in 5- and 10-foot lengths and 2-, 3-, and 4-inch inside diameters. No-Hub may be used vertically or horizontally, above or below ground. It is supported with a special clamp every 12 feet on vertical runs; every 4 feet on horizontal runs. Branch drains smaller than 2 inches are made with galvanized threaded steel, using galvanized drainage-type fittings. These are joined to 2-inch No-Hub via adapters. Traps and adapters are made in the 1½- and 1¼-inch galvanized pipe size. Pipe is standard; you can rent 1¼- and 1½-inch threading equipment.

No-Hub is particularly useful for connecting new DWV lines to older lead-and-oakum-caulked cast iron piping systems. Simply cut out enough of the old pipe to fit in a No-Hub wye, installing it with two No-Hub joints. Avoid caulking cast iron.

Joining No-Hub DWV

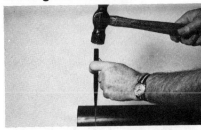

1. Groove pipe ⅛ inch deep all the way around with a hacksaw. Then, wearing safety goggles, work around the groove with a chisel until the pipe parts on the line. Hub-type cast-iron pipe is cut the same way.

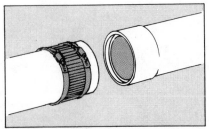

2. To join a No-Hub pipe and fittings, put the parts together with a neoprene gasket on one piece and a stainless steel sleeve on the other. Slide the gasket over and center it on the joint. Then, slide the stainless steel sleeve over the gasket.

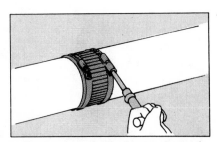

3. Finally, tighten the clamps alternately, bringing each a little tighter than the previous one until you reach a torque of 60 inch pounds (about what you'd tighten a small wood screw).

Plastic DWV piping

Plastic drain-waste-vent pipe is made in two materials: polyvinyl chloride (PVC) and acrylonitrile-butadiene-styrene (aren't you glad it's called ABS?). PVC is usually beige-colored, while ABS pipe and its fittings are black. Both kinds are joined by solvent-welding to fittings with solvent cement designed for that material. Both can be worked with ordinary tools like CPVC water-supply pipe. The chief difference in handling DWV plastic piping is its larger sizes. These call for use of a wider dauber or brush for joining.

Both ABS and PVC are safe for all the usual household wastes. They're also resistant to fungi, bacterial action, and adverse soil conditions. The simplicity and ease of installation of a plastic drain-waste-vent system make it the perfect choice for do-it-yourself plumbers.

Plastic DWV pipes should be supported every 48 inches—from every third joist. Stacks can rest on a wooden block at the bottom, as well as on the horizontal pipes that enter along their length. Pipes and fittings should be protected from subsequent damage by installing steel straps in locations where nails could penetrate. Plastic DWV pipe may be used above or below ground.

Ordinary roof flashings have trouble sealing around plastic DWV stacks. Thermal pipe movements tend to crack any sealant buttered around the flashing. Specially designed flashings that grip tightly to the vent pipe are best. These need no sealant to provide raintightness (photo, opposite).

Both PVC and ABS pipes and fittings come in 1½-, 2-, 3-, and 4-inch diameters and 10-foot lengths. Fittings for use with them should be labeled "DWV," signifying that they're designed for drain-waste-vent use. Schedule 40 fittings in the 3-inch size need 4½ inches of wall clearance to install. Lighter, smaller Schedule 30 3-inch DWV pipe and fittings will fit inside an ordinary 2x4-inch stud wall. Fittings for it mate with 2- and 1½-inch Schedule 40 pipes. Thus no adapters are needed between 3-inch Schedule 30 and smaller sizes of Schedule 40 pipe. The in-the-wall size of Schedule 30 is a great advantage in add-on plumbing, where the walls are already framed.

To ensure that fittings and pipes share the correct tolerances to fit together, do not use pipes by one manufacturer and fittings by another. And always test-fit the fitting on the pipe.

To get square pipe ends, saw pipes in a miter box. Before joining, examine pipe ends and fittings for deep scratches, abrasions, and hairline cracks caused by heavy impacts. If need be, cut off a damaged pipe end and discard it. Before applying solvent cement, chamfer the pipe end all around at a 45-degree angle with a file or sandpaper to help it enter the fitting cleanly. Don't use solvents around flames or cigarettes while you solvent-weld. Also, have the room well ventilated and keep solvent containers closed when not in use.

To tighten PVC or ABS threaded fittings, use a strap wrench. Pipe wrenches chew up plastic fittings. Use TFE tape or non-hardening pipe dope on the male threads before assembling. Don't put silicone rubber onto ABS piping.

For caulking shower drains around plastic DWV pipe, use special plastic lead seal compound instead of molten lead. If you must use hot lead, get a special high-temp adapter intended for a lead-caulked joint.

Stopgaps and copouts

Instead of sawing into a stack and installing a tee or wye to tap into it, you can get a solvent-welding saddle tee that lets you achieve the effect more easily. Simply weld the saddle tee onto the vent pipe in the desired location. After an hour, drill out the pipe inside the tee. A 1½-inch run takes off by solvent-welding into the saddle tee. (See below.)

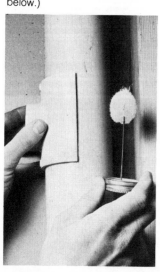

Schedule 30, 3-inch PVC pipe (right) will fit in a 2x4 stud wall. Schedule 40 PVC pipe (left) needs 4½-inches of wall clearance. See Wall thickness chart, page 438.

Solvent welding

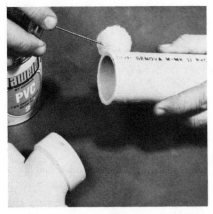

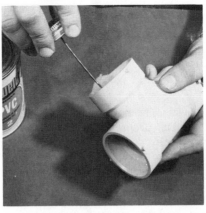

1. After cutting, deburring, and test-fitting the pipe and fitting, same as for a CPVC water-supply pipe (see page 428), apply the proper solvent cement to the pipe end. Brush width should be half the diameter of the pipe.

2. Apply solvent to the fitting socket, also. Be generous and don't miss any spots. Be quick, too.

3. Without waiting, join the fitting and pipe full depth with a slight twist and align fitting. Hold for a few seconds. Wipe up any excess solvent cement with a cloth.

Running a vent stack

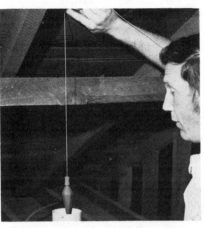

1. Drill holes in the floor and ceiling plumb over one another to pass the vent stack piping. Large holes can be made by drilling a circle of smaller ones, then sawing out the remaining block of wood.

2. As you raise the stack through the attic, it's easy to clear framing members by off-setting it slightly, using a pair of 45-degree elbows. Use plumb line to fix vent location from offset.

3. A flashing at the roof keeps rain water from entering the house between the vent stack and roofing. This one is two-piece plastic. It snaps together, holding tightly around plastic DWV vent-stack piping.

⸻ New wrinkles ⸻

A new product you'll appreciate is the special waste-and-vent fitting. It takes the place of a sanitary tee under the floor behind the toilet. A pair of reduced side tappings allow 2- or 1½-inch waste pipes from lavatory, tub, or shower to drain and be vented at the same time. If you don't need the side tappings, solvent-welding plugs are available. The special waste-and-vent fitting also comes with caps that accept the vent stack at full bore. One also has an extra 1½-inch side tapping for another drain or vent. The fitting is available in single- or double-configuration for use with one toilet or two toilets back-to-back. It simplifies your early steps in building a DWV system.

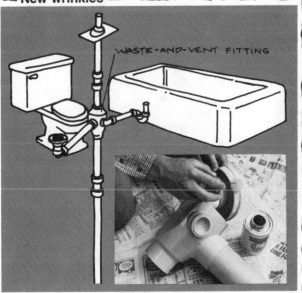

WASTE-AND-VENT FITTING

PVC or ABS?

Your local code and what is available may determine whether you use light-colored PVC pipe or black ABS pipe for your drain-waste-vent system. The two materials may even be joined to each other if you use ABS solvent. PVC solvent softens ABS pipe excessively, because ABS has less solvent-resistance. For joining PVC pipes and fittings, use PVC cement; for ABS pipes and fittings, use ABS cement.

Sweat-soldered copper DWV

Copper drainage tubing comes in drain-waste-vent sizes. It weighs about one-fourth what cast iron does. Tube/fitting sizes are: 1¼-, 1½-, 2-, 3-, and 4-inch diameters. Available length is usually 20 feet, though many dealers offer less than full lengths, if desired.

Copper drainage tube is suitable for above or below-ground plumbing. To prevent in-ground damage, however, it is better to use Type L copper tube in below-ground runs, since drainage tube has thinner walls. Otherwise copper drainage tube is like smaller-sized hard-temper copper water-supply tube (page 431). Its outside diameter is always ⅛ inch larger than its nominal size. Fittings, though, are different, being drainage-type rather than water-supply fittings. Either copper or cast-bronze DWV fittings, which are made to mate with copper tubing, may be used. Copper drainage tube, which is color-coded yellow, is designed for nonpressure DWV application. But it may be used for pressurized piping if pressures are controlled. With soldered joints, about 55 psi is the maximum allowable safe working pressure.

Copper drainage tubing may be cut with a pipe cutter or with a hacksaw and miter box. Deburr the tube both inside and outside with a pipe/tube deburrer. Then test-fit the fitting onto the tube. Best clearance for proper soldering is a uniform 0.002″ to 0.005″ space.

Prepare a copper joint, as always, by scrubbing it shiny with steel wool. To facilitate solder entry, go an inch beyond where the tube will be covered by the fitting. And don't neglect to clean up the inside of the joint, too. Joint preparation should not be done with a coarse sandpaper or other harsh abrasive.

Copper drainage-tube joints are sweat-soldered much the same way as copper water-supply tubing (see page 431). But the extra-large sizes usually call for a larger propane torch, or for two torches. A pair of torches at opposite sides of the joint often works best. Heat up the entire joint before applying any solder, then fill it up all at the same time. Retorch the joint while solder is being applied, but always keep the torch or torches moving to maintain a constant temperature. Overheating will burn the solder. Less expensive 40/60 tin/lead solder will work for sweat-soldering. But 50/50 wire solder is recommended because it is easier to work with.

Don't forget the flux when sweat-soldering. Its purpose is to remove traces of oxides left after brightening, and to protect the surfaces from additional oxidation while they are being heated to soldering temperature. Fluxes are not meant to take the place of cleaning. So avoid types labeled "self-cleaning." Apply a light coat of a good paste flux to both surfaces to be joined. Since the best fluxes are mildly corrosive, don't apply with your fingers. Use a rag or small brush.

Fasten copper-drainage piping to joists at 40-foot intervals using perforated metal "plumber's tape." Vertical vent runs can be supported by the horizontal drain-and-vent pipes entering them. Copper flashings may be soldered to vent stacks at the roof. Generous application of roofing cement between flashing and vent pipes works, too.

How to avoid reheating a fitting

If you prepare all the pipes leading into a single fitting, you can sweat-solder them in one heating. This avoids having to heat the fitting again, which risks losing the solder in a part of the fitting that has already been completed. Be careful that you don't overheat the fitting. This burns the flux and oxidizes the copper so it will no longer accept solder. Do not clean too many fittings at one time, for they will oxidize if left more than three hours without soldering.

Joining copper DWV

1. As with copper water supply tubing, start sweat soldering DWV piping by cleaning mating surfaces with emery cloth or 00 steel wool. Clean 1 inch more of pipe than will fit into fitting. Wipe off dry and apply even coat of flux to all mating areas. Join pieces with a slight twist to spread flux evenly.

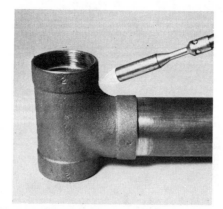

2. Apply flame all around first the heavier fitting and then the pipe. Heat both until tip of 50/50 wire solder touched to heated joint starts to flow. On large 3-inch DWV joints you may need big flame tip or two torches to heat joint adequately.

3. Melting solder is drawn into joint by capillary action. Make sure it flows into the joint all around to provide an even seal. Don't apply flame to solder. When joint is evenly filled, smooth solder and wipe off any excess with soft cloth before it cools completely.

Running DWV pipes

Here is the installation sequence for DWV: (1) underground drains and sewer; (2) building drain (from toilet tee); (3) main stack, secondary stack(s); (4) branch drains; and (5) fixture-waste and revent runs. Keep drainage runs with as few turns as possible. Long-turn elbows are preferable to short-turn ones, and two 45-degree elbows beat one 90-degree elbow. Wherever possible, use wyes instead of tees. Never change from vertical to horizontal flow with a tee. Use a wye instead. Be sure to include a cleanout, in an accessible location, for each horizontal drain run that cannot be augered through a nearby trap opening. This includes the house sewer.

Here are some rules for the installation of a DWV system: Always use drainage-type fittings for waste runs. Vent runs may be made with regular fittings or else with more expensive drainage fittings installed upside-down. In freezing climates, use vent-increasers on 1½- and 2-inch roof vents to protect against ice closure. Fixture waste pipes should enter a stack above a toilet. Entry in the same fitting as a toilet is okay, too. A fixture that is revented may be drained into the 90-degree elbow below the toilet (if it has a tapping).

Fixtures whose waste pipes enter below a toilet drain must be revented. Revent runs go directly out the roof or are connected into another vent stack at least 6 inches above the flood rim of the highest fixture emptying into that stack. A lavatory, which often drains into the waste line below the toilet, is normally revented into the main stack above the toilet.

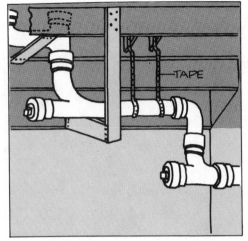

Drain-waste-vent piping should be well supported by the framing. Horizontal runs are hung from joists as shown, with supports 48 inches apart. Use perforated metal plumber's "tape" and wood bracing. Vertical vent runs can rest on wood blocks installed at the lower end.

A good place to begin DWV plumbing is at the floor beneath the toilet. When a sanitary tee—in this case, a special waste-and-vent fitting—is held in position, DWV piping may take off from it in three directions: toward the toilet, up and out the roof for the vent stack, and toward the building drain.

Haste makes waste

I learned that it pays to dry-assemble your plastic DWV system. It can save lots of headaches if things don't fit up the way you planned. This lets you make corrections and get everything right before welding the parts. Wherever a fitting-up problem is anticipated, dry-assembly is a good idea.

Practical Pete

Tapping into a drain run

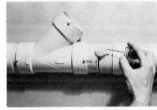

1. Using shoulderless slip-couplings, tap into an old plastic run. Cut out the old pipe to make room for the made-up wye assembly with pipe extensions.

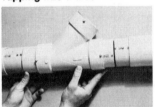

2. With the wye assembly held in place of the cut-out pipe, all four pipe ends are liberally buttered with solvent cement.

3. Then quickly slide the slip couplings over the joints until centered on them. Align the wye.

Comparison of DWV pipe types

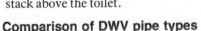

Pipe	Advantages and disadvantages	Relative cost (Plastics =1)	Sizes available
PVC/ABS plastic	Very lightweight, smooth bore for full flow, resistant to corroding, easiest to install. Solvent-welded joints cannot be parted. Won't conduct electricity and may not be used for electrical grounding. Few tools needed. Resists all household wastes but affected by a few potent, flammable solvents. Needs protection from nailing. Easy to add onto. Widest selection of fittings. Use above or below ground.	1.0	1½" 2" 3" 4"
No-Hub cast iron	Strongest, quietest, most indestructible system available. No makeup allowances to bother with. Requires threaded galvanized piping for sizes smaller than 2 inches. Joints may be taken apart at will and replaced as often as desired. Easy to add onto. Use above or below ground. Difficult to buy, except from a plumber. Heavy to work with. Easily the best system, but also toughest to install.	2.3	2" 3" 4"
Copper drainage tube	Lightweight, smooth insides for good flow, resistant to corroding, not difficult to use. Is dented by hard blows. Not best for underground. Flame-soldering can be risky. Not melted except by intense heat. Few tools needed. The 3-inch size and smaller fit in a standard 2x4 stud wall. Needs protection from nailing.	3.2	1¼" 1½" 2" 3" 4"

Sizing DWV runs

In most single-family houses, drain-waste-vent runs may be sized according to the Rule-of-Thumb table below. But if two bathrooms are plumbed together, or a

DWV pipe sizes—Rule-of-thumb (check local code)

Purpose	Pipe size	Purpose	Pipe size
Main stack	3″ or 4″	Bathtub waste	1½″
Secondary stack	1½″ or 2″	Shower waste	1½″ or 2″
House drain	Matches stack	Tub/shower vent	1½″
House sewer	3″ or 4″	Sink waste/vent	1½″
Toilet waste	Matches stack	Laundry waste	1½″
Toilet vent-only	2″	Laundry vent	1½″
Lavatory waste	1½″	Basement drain	2″
Lavatory vent	1½″	Other drains	2″–4″

Pipe capacity

Pipe size	Fixture units permissible	
	Horizontal pipe	Vertical pipe
1½″	3	8
2″	6*	16
3″	20**	30***
4″	160	240

*waste only
**not more than two toilets on horizontal line
***not more than six toilets on one stack

Importance of pipe-sizing

Oversized drain pipes become "lazy," not being sufficiently charged with water to carry wastes away. So wastes accumulate until the pipe clogs. Drain pipes that are too small are easily clogged by waste build-ups, too. Size pipes correctly—neither too small nor too large—according to the criteria at the right.

What's horizontal? What's vertical?

The terms horizontal and vertical have different meanings to a DWV plumber than to a carpenter. No DWV pipe is strictly horizontal. Drainage lines should always pitch downward about ¼ inch per foot in order to drain. And vent lines that are "horizontal" run upward toward the vent stack at the same ¼-inch slope. So neither is strictly horizontal, even though they are called that.

Vertical vent or drain-vent pipes—stacks—are often truly vertical. But they needn't be. Offsets may be placed in them to clear obstructions, such as roof rafters. And there's nothing wrong with installing them slightly off vertical if necessary to accomplish some other purpose. Vertical simply means that they run in a general up-and-down direction.

Nominal sizes for fixture drains and vents

Fixture	Pipe diameter
Toilet	3 inches
Shower	2 inches
Bathtub, sink, lavatory, laundry tub, clothes washer, dishwasher, garbage disposal	1½ inches

bathroom, kitchen, and laundry all use the same drainage pipe, then the flow produced by all the fixtures should be checked using the Fixture Units table. Then use the Pipe Capacity table to figure how large the drain piping must be to carry the calculated flow.

A fixture unit is a National Plumbing

Fixture units

Fixture	Fixture units
Toilet	4
Bathtub/shower	2
Shower only	2
Sink	2
Lavatory	1
Laundry tub	2
Floor drain	1
One 3-piece bathroom group (toilet, bathtub, lavatory)	6

Code term used as the basis for figuring DWV pipe sizes. It represents a waste flow of one cubic foot a minute (about 7½ gal.).

After checking on drain pipe diameter, size the main stack. If only one or two toilets will empty into its base, a 3-inch stack is plenty large. Add up the fixture units for all house fixtures to see how large the main building drain must be to handle

the load. Again, in most single-family residential uses, a horizontal 3-inch drain will do. Pipe sizes given in the Rule-of-Thumb table are minimums.

Fixture vent pipes should be the same size as their drain pipes. An exception is toilets, for which some codes permit 2-inch venting if it serves no other fixtures. Check your code. This important provision can get you around the need for thickening a wall behind the toilet to handle a 3-inch stack. However, if a 2-inch toilet vent is used, be sure to vent the other bathroom fixtures into another stack, perhaps a 1½-inch secondary stack installed just for them.

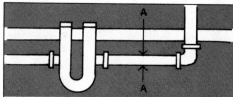

How large does the horizontal drain pipe at A-A need to be? First, since it handles wastes for a toilet, it must be at least 3 inches in diameter. Is that enough to handle everything else, too? To find out, calculate how many fixture units it handles. From the Fixture Units table, you'll find that the toilet gives 4, the bathtub/shower gives 2, and the lavatory gives 1 for a total of 7 fixture units. However, the table also shows that a single bathroom group actually contributes only 6 fixture units, so the actual total is 6. Next look in the Pipe Capacity table to see whether the required 3-inch pipe will carry 6 fixture units when running horizontally. The table shows it capable of up to 20 fixture units. Thus, 3-inch pipe is easily able to handle the load.

Wall thickness to accommodate vertical DWV pipes and fittings

Pipe size	Plastic		Copper	Cast iron	Galv. steel
	Sched. 30	Sched. 40			
1½″	—	3″	2″	—	3″
2″	—	3½″	3″	4″	3½″
3″	3½″	4½″	3½″	5¼″	—
4″	—	5½″	4½″	6¼″	—

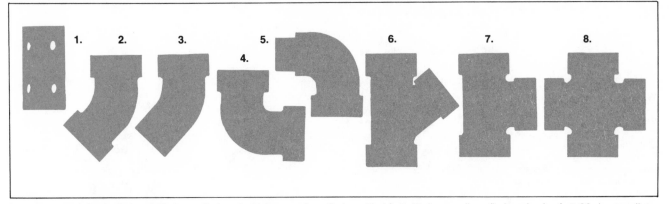

Typical sewer piping includes: **1.** Perforated pipe; **2.** 45-degree elbow (hub and hub); **3.** 45-degree elbow (hub and spigot); **4.** 90-degree elbow (hub and hub); **5.** 90-degree street elbow (hub and spigot); **6.** Wye (all hub); **7.** Sanitary tee (all hub); **8.** Cross (all hub).

Sewer pipe is different

Solid-walled sewer pipe is used for sewer lines between the house and the town sewer or septic tank. Loose-jointed or perforated seepage pipe is used in seepage fields and to dispose of roof runoff. It lets effluent, or runoff, percolate into the ground.

Plastic sewer pipe comes in two weights: heavy duty, and a lighter duty called "sewer and drain" pipe. Both are considered "soft" pipes that can be damaged by loads from above. Pitch-fiber sewer pipe is soft, too. Soft sewer pipes should be buried deeply enough under driveways so that car or truck weights won't affect them. Put them in a trench with a uniformly shaped bottom of unexcavated earth that is free of lumps or rocks that might cut or pinch the pipes. Dig out underneath couplings so that both pipe and couplings are supported.

Hard pipes—cast iron and clay—may go under driveways if there's enough earth over them to prevent crushing or bending from above. Cast-iron pipe may be suspended on concrete blocks placed in a trench beneath pipe joints. Uniform ground support is better, though.

A 4-inch sewer should handle all wastes from a single-family residence. A 3-inch line might do if it satisfies the total fixture flow estimated from table, opposite.

Joining sewer pipes

PVC, ABS, and rubber-styrene sewer pipes are joined by solvent-welding. The process is the same as that for plastic DWV piping. Use perforated pipes for septic seepage lines.

Pitch-fiber pipes are joined by tapered ends that fit tapered couplings. Tapping with a heavy hammer sets the joint. Use perforated pitch-fiber pipes for septic seepage lines.

Comparison of popular sewer pipes			
Pipe	**Advantages and disadvantages**	**Relative cost** (PVC/ABS/RS=1)	**Sizes available**
PVC/ABS/RS plastic	Lightweight, good flow, resists corrosion, easiest to install. Joints cannot be undone in case of error. Few tools needed. Needs rock-free sub-base and fill, plus uniform support for its entire length. Wide selection of fittings. Adapts to other pipes. Resists root infiltration.	1.0	3″, 4″, 6″ in 10′ lengths
Pitch-fiber	Not heavy, will not corrode. Joints can be taken apart, but require tooling to use cutoffs. Easy to install. Comes in long lengths.	1.8	3″, 4″, 6″ in 5′, 8′, 10′ lengths
Clay tile	Hard, rigid, durable. Difficult to work with, cut, and join, without special self-sealing joints. Prone to root infiltration. Joints permit offsetting in trench without fittings. Few fittings available. Few tools required. Heavy, breakable, short lengths. Builds into municipal-quality system.	2.2	4″, 6″ in 1′, 2′, 5′ lengths
Cast iron No-Hub	Strongest, most indestructible. Resists corrosion and rock damage. Adapts to other pipes. Joints may be taken apart at will. Easy to add onto. Difficult to buy, except from a plumber. Heavy to work with. Easy to install. Flexibility of joints allows offsetting without fittings. No root infiltration.	5.1	3″, 4″ in 5′, 10′ lengths

Adapting pipes

What can be adapted

Water supply
Female threads to copper sweat
Male threads to copper sweat
Female threads to flared copper
Male threads to flared copper
Female threads to garden hose
  bibb
Male threads to garden hose bibb
Female threads to rubber hose
Female threads to CPVC plastic
Male threads to CPVC plastic
Female threads to compression
Male threads to compression
Female threads to polyethylene
Male threads to polyethylene
Brass threads to galvanized
  threads (dielectric)
Copper sweat to galvanized
  threads (dielectric)
Copper sweat to CPVC plastic
CPVC plastic to PB plastic
Copper to PB plastic
CPVC plastic to faucet supply
Chromed brass to faucet supply

Drain-waste-vent
ABS/PVC DWV to caulk cast iron
ABS/PVC DWV to clay tile sewer
ABS/PVC DWV to pitch-fiber DWV
ABS/PVC DWV to ABS/PVC/RS
  sewer pipe
ABS/PVC DWV to copper DWV
ABS/PVC DWV to threaded DWV
ABS/PVC DWV to trap
Downspout to PVC DWV
Hub cast iron to No-Hub cast iron
Copper DWV to caulked cast iron
Copper DWV to threaded DWV
Copper DWV to trap
Threaded steel DWV to trap
Threaded steel DWV to caulked
  cast iron
DWV of all types to cleanout

Special
Dishwasher to fixture trap
Sump pump to discharge pipe

What cannot be adapted
Water supply to DWV piping
Water supply to sewer piping
Water supply to lawn sprinkler
  piping (except through a
  vacuum breaker)
Water supply to hydronic heating
  piping
DWV pipe to buried "drain" pipe
Sewer pipe to buried "drain" pipe

1. When joining steel to copper in a hard water area, use a special transition fitting with rubber washer to prevent dielectric action. Solder the copper adapter to its pipe, and tighten the threaded portion to its pipe, before joining the union. 2. In soft water areas this copper sweat-to-threads adapter will work, but make the soldered connection first. 3. CPVC adapter screws directly into threaded fitting. 4. Plastic fitting for adapting flexible polyethylene tubing to steel has stainless steel clamp to hold tubing.

Pipe adapters are not only the most useful of fittings, but they are frequently essential, and they come in just about any form you could want. They allow one type of pipe to be connected to another. Many come in straight form, but others come in the form of elbows, tees, wing elbows, reducers, and valves. Some are intended to prevent dielectric action between pipes made of dissimilar metals. In hard water areas, dielectric action can cause electrolytic corrosion, as when steel and copper are combined in a water-supply system. The same goes for a DWV system.

Installing an adapter requires that you make up two different kinds of pipe fitting. One end of the adapter installs like fittings for one type of pipe; the other end installs like fittings for the other. Thus, to connect an adapter you may have to use a pipe wrench on one end and a soldering torch on

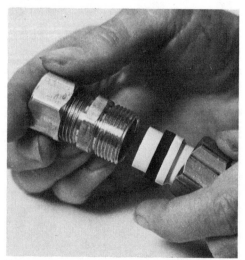

Adapters join different kinds of pipe, each pipe requiring its own joining method. Rubber washer on this transition adapter relieves stresses between the dissimilar materials—plastic and brass.

the other. Or, one end may be solvent-welded and one lead-and-oakum caulked.

All CPVC-to-copper-sweat transition fittings should be taken apart before you heat the solder side. Otherwise, the heat may destroy the plastic side and rubber mating gasket. For a male-threads transition, on which the collar cannot be removed for soldering, slide the collar 18 inches back along the copper tube. If this much tubing is not freely available, the collar and tube next to it should be wrapped in wet rags to protect them from heat.

A CPVC-to-male-threads transition fitting has insufficient space to tighten the male-threads portion into a threaded female fitting with a pipe wrench. A pair of channel-locking pliers—which have narrower jaws than a pipe wrench—will do the trick. Or, you can use a giant-sized Allen wrench on the broached inner hex nut.

Threads-to-sweat-copper adapters should be tightened at their threaded ends fully before soldering. Once soldered, they can no longer be threaded. Removal of them, if needed, requires heating the copper side to melt the solder and unthreading while still hot. Reinstallation will require heating and simultaneous threading. Apply more solder before leaving the joint.

Cleanout fittings, used in all drain-waste-vent systems, are wye adapters with a threaded cleanout plug. One type of PVC DWV piping uses an O-ring seal cleanout fitting hub. Every fitting thus becomes a cleanout adapter. The O-ring is first coated with petroleum jelly to ease installation.

A No-Hub joint becomes its own adapter in joining hubless cast-iron pipes to same-sized plastic, copper, clay and pitch-fiber pipes. Where sizes vary, a similar Calder coupling performs the same job.

Problems with low flow

Scale on the inside walls of galvanized steel pipes can sharply reduce water flow. Flow may be so feeble that it's hard to rinse dishes, and bathtubs take a long time to fill. Water running through the restricted pipe may make a loud running sound. The cure is new water-supply piping. Use flexible copper or polybutyline tubing which resists scale buildup and can be snaked around and through walls readily. If the low flow is caused by a combination of scaled-up pipes and low house water pressure (less than 40 psi), replacing the piping and installing a booster pump (see below) should cure the condition.

The only cure for scaled-up piping is to replace it. That's a big job, so tackle it in stages, perhaps doing the most affected runs first. Old pipes need not be removed first. Polybutylene pipes can be fished through holes, to save tearing out walls.

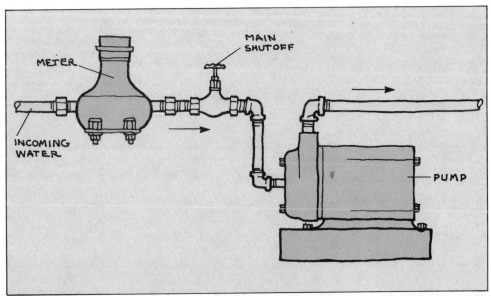

Pressure booster pump has an automatic switch that kicks on whenever a water tap is opened. It's expensive, but it will solve the problem of low flow from low house pressure if the water-supply pipes have unrestricted flow.

7.APPLIANCE REPAIR

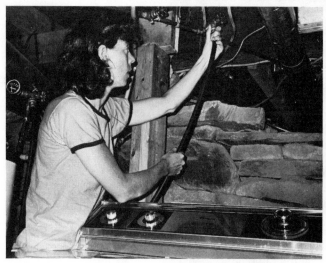

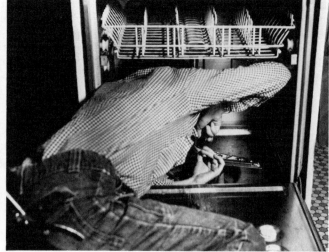

Clothes washers

What it takes

Approximate time: From a few seconds to several weekends. Set your own time limit. When you reach it, if you haven't corrected the trouble, call in a professional.

Tools and materials: Electrical test-light or volt-ohm-milliammeter (VOM), screwdriver, wrenches, pliers.

Planning hints: Repairs to automatic washers are often electrical or mechanical. If you have only a shaky knowledge of electricity, call a professional.

A modern clothes washer consists of electric motor, drive belt, transmission, water pump, tub, frame, and enclosure. It also has electrically operated hot/cold mixing valves. Controlling all of a washer's electrical functions—filling, shifting, agitating, pumping out, spinning—is a timer.

It helps to have a copy of the owner's sheet before you dig into a washer's innards. Areas you can probably tackle are water-inlet valve disassembly and cleaning, belt adjustments, pump cleaning, and checking for loose electrical connections. Do not try to tackle timer repairs or replacements, transmission or clutch work,

or shifter repairs. As with all appliance repairs, pull the wall plug before touching any electrical parts. **Caution:** Electricity can be deadly. Never remove the access panel of a *plugged-in* washer. And don't ever poke anything, including your hands, into one that's connected. A professional, when making electrical tests, will plug the cord in, then, using one hand, cautiously touch the leads of a test light across portions of the washer's circuit. The other hand will be held behind to keep from creating a grounded path through the body. Electrical testing finished, the machine is unplugged again.

Troubleshooting an automatic clothes washer

Problem	Solution	What it takes
Washer won't run.	Make sure plug is in, fuse or circuit breaker is not out, both faucets are turned on, timer control knob is "on," load is balanced and washer door is closed. If it still won't run, call pro.	No tools required.
Will not fill.	Water valve off—turn on. Mixing valves not opening—check for loose lead, repair or replace valve. Pinched hose—unkink it. Sediment in hose inlet screen—clean. Bad timer—call pro.	Electrical test light.
Water won't shut off.	Valve stuck open from sediment or defect—clean or replace. Defective timer—call for service.	Test light.
Wash cycle not working.	Loose or broken drive belt—adjust tension or replace. Motor won't run—lighten load, reduce suds, check for loose leads, call for service. Thermal protection needs resetting—push red button in until it clicks. Defective timer—call for service. Also check for broken or loose wires.	Test light, wrenches.
Will not spin dry.	Uneven load—reposition. Broken or loose belt, defective timer, broken wire or loose connection—see same problems above. Broken transmission spring, brakes not releasing, defective bearings, motor not reversing if it should—call for service. Tub not drained—repeat drain cycle, unclog stopped drain, or check belt tension and pump (see below).	Test light, wrenches.
Will not pump out tub.	Broken or loose belt—tighten or replace. Clogged or locked up pump—clean or replace. Clogged or kinked drain lines—clean and straighten out. Timer or motor problems—call for service. Also, look for loose electrical leads or broken wires.	Test light, wrenches.

Dishwasher repairs

A dishwasher consists of tub, rack, motor with pump and impeller or spray arm, inlet valve, and Calrod heating element. A timer controls all electrical functions.

In the normal cycle, water enters tub, streams of water shoot against dishes, rinse water is pumped out and wash water enters. Sudsy water jets onto dishes and pumps out. This is followed by three rinses and the drying cycle.

Serious dishwasher repairs are best left to a professional. But you may try replacing a leaking drain hose or a worn-out door switch yourself.

What it takes

Approximate time: Three to four hours should be enough to troubleshoot most problems.

Tools and materials: Electrical test-light, pliers, screwdriver, Phillips screwdriver, wrenches.

Planning hints: While repairs often can be made with the dishwasher in place, you may want to work with the tub out on the floor.

Water flow during wash cycle

TUB

DRAIN PORT

When dishes are not cleaned satisfactorily, the spray arm may be blocked. Make sure nothing is keeping it from rotating, and lift it out and clean out the holes in it. On some models, the nut holding it must be loosened before the arm will lift out.

If condensation forms and runs down behind the door, install a vapor barrier. Using metallic tape, fasten it at the top. Tape the lower part to the door panel as shown.

Troubleshooting a dishwasher

Problem	Solution	What it takes
Washer won't run.	Make sure machine has power, door is latched, and cycle button is fully activated. If machine is between functions, wait for change. If utensil is blocking pump or impeller, remove. Thermal protection device may have tripped—push red button until it clicks. If none of the above work, call a professional.	Electrical test light.
Water will not enter.	Solenoid inlet valve defective—check for loose terminal or broken wire, remove and clean valve. Door interlock switch not working—adjust or replace switch. Overflow switch defective—test, replace if necessary. Filter screen completely clogged—remove and clean.	Test light, screwdriver, pliers.
Water won't shut off.	Sediment in solenoid inlet valve—take apart and clean. Replace needle, spring, and diaphragm if worn or damaged. Inlet solenoid problems—replace valve if defective. Faulty timer—call for service.	Test light, screwdriver, pliers.
Water stays in tub.	Motor won't reverse—call for service. Outlet strainer clogged—take apart and clean. Check discharge tube for blockage, kinking. Impeller problems—if jammed or sheared, repair or replace (may be a pro job). Timer or motor problems—call a pro.	Test light, screwdriver, wrenches.
Timer does not advance.	Call in a professional.	No tools required.
Incomplete drying.	Cool water—check water temperature. Should be 160 degrees Fahrenheit. Increase temperature setting, insulate piping to dishwasher. Calrod heating element defective—check at terminals (carefully) for current, replace if open-circuited. Call for repairs if timer is defective.	Test light, wrenches, thermometer.
Leaks from tub.	Door not closing on gasket—adjust, if possible. Hoses faulty—tighten clamps, unkink hose. At water inlet—tighten inlet fitting. Hole in tub—seal with silicone rubber or epoxy glue. Broken spray arm—replace. Gasket problems—install new gasket, or repair old one.	Screwdriver, pliers, glue, gasket.

Sump pumps

What it takes

Approximate time: The time to troubleshoot a dead-in-the-water sump pump and get it pumping again can vary from half a minute to a good part of a day.

Tools and materials: A screwdriver, a pair of pipe wrenches, possibly a mechanic's wrench set for pump repair rather than replacement. A new float switch can be installed with a wrench and perhaps a screwdriver.

Planning hints: Don't tear into a working sump pump when rain is forecast. But if the pump does not work, you'd best get it going again before a storm comes. While a sump that is connected to footing drains will take lots of water before it overflows onto the basement floor, a good rain can provide that amount of water in minutes. Don't buy a new pump until you've determined that the old one cannot be rejuvenated with a switch repair or replacement.

Caution: A fatal shock can be suffered while working on a pump with an ungrounded internal short. Always unplug the pump (and the switch lead, if the unit has separate cords) before touching the pump or its metal piping. Also, make sure that the pump is grounded through a three-prong grounding plug used with a three-hole grounding receptacle.

A sump pump consists of a motor, a pump unit with impeller and volute-shaped housing, and a shaft connecting the two. In an upright sump pump, a long shaft is required to reach from the motor above the sump to the impeller at the bottom of the sump pit. A costlier, submersible pump has a very short shaft which is connected almost directly to the impeller.

Most sump-pump problems are electrical—chiefly corrosion of the switching mechanism. These can be corrected by repairing or replacing the switch. Other no-run problems come from mechanical switch failure, waterlogged floats, sticking actuation rods, and float supports hung up on internal pump or discharge piping parts. Another common sump-pump problem is plain wear-out of the pump impeller or, less often, a shot motor.

In some uses, sump pumps move significant amounts of sand and other gritty materials, causing rapid impeller wear. Furthermore, impeller bearings are water-lubricated, and when a pump runs dry and does not shut off, the bearing wears quickly.

Sump-pump maintenance consists of a regular cleaning of the sump pit—a not-so-pleasant job. With a tin can on a stick, scoop out debris that collects in the sump. Then spray the pit vigorously with a garden hose to stir up remaining debris while the pump runs to pump it out.

If the pump does not turn on when the water reaches its high level in the pit, or does not shut off before the level drops to the pump's intake screen, the problem is likely in the switch. Unplug the pump before investigating switch troubles. Pump-parts lists include new floats and new mi-

croswitch units. Installation of one of these may be the cure. But if the pump makes lots of noise when it runs, the bearings have probably worn out. While new bearings can be installed, replacement of the entire pump is usually more economical in the long run. The photo series on the next page illustrates this procedure. It is also possible to replace just the pump portion of most sump pumps. One type simply twists out, leaving the pump and motor separated.

Whether to replace with an upright or a submersible sump pump is a hard choice. The submersible costs more, but it will not be damaged by basement flooding and can safely pump it dry once power is restored.

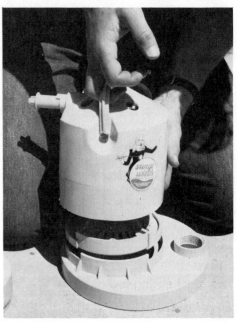

Removing sump-pump motor from the base for replacement.

New wrinkles

A new switch is available as original equipment or as a replacement for a worn-out sump-pump switch. The microswitch heart of the unit cannot become corroded because it is hermetically sealed inside a noncorroding vinyl float chamber. (Photos at right show float chamber cutaway to illustrate how it works.) The pump plugs into a piggy-back switch receptacle that itself is plugged into the wall outlet. In this way pump operation can be checked manually by plugging the motor lead directly into the wall outlet, bypassing the switch.

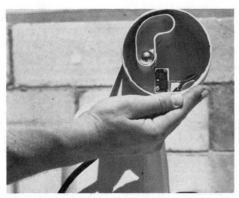

The new sump-pump starts running when its rolling steel ball drops into contact with the internal microswitch arm. Then, as the water level pumps down

and the sealed floating switch chamber follows, the rolling ball moves out of contact with the microswitch arm, turning off the pump motor.

Replacing a sump pump

1. After removing the worn-out pump and any defective piping discharge, lower the new pump into its floor crock. It should rest level in the crock with the switch farthest from the sump wall. Properly positioned, the discharge pipe comes up in the center of the crock.

2. If you convert from a submersible to an upright model, you'll have to make a new crock cover. This one is ready-made of plastic with preformed cut-outs that need only to be sliced through.

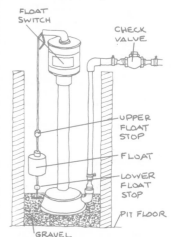

How a sump pump works

Water rising in pit pushes float up to the upper float stop which turns on the pump motor. As water is pumped out, float drops down to lower float stop which turns off the motor.

3. The sump pump's cover can be split and installed around the pump. If you use a plywood cover, make it of ¾-inch exterior-type plywood and cut in half to fit around the pump.

4. Every sump-pump installation should have a check-valve to prevent drain-back of discharge water with resultant short-cycling of the pump and waste of electricity. This check-valve is designed especially for sump-pump use and allows connection to vari-sized pipes.

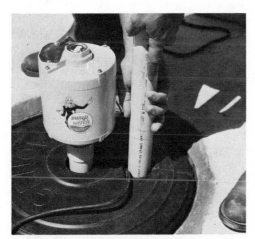

5. Run the discharge piping to a convenient location where sump water can be drained. Although harder to install, rigid pipe is preferred because it won't bend and interfere with the pump's float switch. Use 1¼-inch or 1½-inch pipe.

6. The last step is plugging the pump into a nearby electrical outlet. Be sure that it's a three-pronged grounding-type outlet. The pump features separate motor and switch leads. The motor plugs into a piggy-back receptacle on the switch lead.

Dehumidifiers

CONDENSER
DEHUMIDIFIER COILS
HUMID AIR IN
AIR CIRCULATING FAN
DRY AIR OUT
DRAIN BUCKET
SEALED REFRIGERATION UNIT

What it takes

Approximate time: It takes only minutes to unpack and set up a dehumidifier for action. Maintenance is a pittance (see text).

Tools and materials: Unless your unit comes knocked-down, you won't need any tools to get it going. Mounting a humidistat on the wall will require a screwdriver.

Planning hints: A dehumidifier must be used in an enclosed space. So little as an open window nullifies its effectiveness, because vapor pressure from the more humid outdoor air will move humidity like steam into the drier room. Vapor can even move through walls. Walls, floors, and ceilings of rooms to be dehumidified should be protected with vapor barriers. Ordinary insulation batts and blankets contain vapor barriers. Paint or prefinished wall paneling and floor tile are also effective. Wallpaper, unpainted wallboard, plasterboard and the like are poor barriers, though they help. The surest vapor barrier is a layer of plastic sheeting placed over the studs before installing the wall material.

Rooms that are troubled with dampness and mildew make good prospects for dehumidification. A basement office or rec room, an upstairs den, a workshop where tools tend to rust because of high humidity during the off-season—all these can be dried out with a dehumidifier.

A dehumidifier works like a small air conditioner. However, while an air conditioner carries heat out of a room and deposits it outdoors, a dehumidifier puts the heat right back into room air. At the front of the machine is an evaporator, which is cold while the dehumidifier runs. In the center is a motor, fan, and refrigeration compressor unit. At the rear is a condenser. All three are plumbed together.

As air flows in through the finned coils of the cold evaporator, it cools rapidly, giving up much of its moisture. The effect is the same as when damp air meets a cold water pipe. Condensate drips off the evaporator into a collection container below. Cooled air then is blown out through the fins of the warm condenser to be recirculated. With its moisture thus wrung out, the air is more comfortable. An average dehumidifier can suck from the air up to 25 pints of water a day. However, air temperature, because of the unit's 500-watt-or-so power draw, may be several degrees higher than without the dehumidifier. But if the old maxim can be believed—that it's not the heat, it's the humidity—then the slightly higher mercury won't be noticed.

The cost of a unit varies according to how automatic it is. Top of the line is a unit that comes with a *humidistat*. This electric control has strands of horsehair that shrink and stretch along with changes in relative humidity. The action opens and closes a pair of electrical contacts. Wired through the contacts, the dehumidifier switches on or off. A reasonable setting for a humidistat, which is adjustable, is 50 percent relative humidity. If you set one too dry, the dehumidifier will run constantly trying to catch up.

Another method of humidity control is by means of a timer, but it has the drawback that as outdoor humidity changes, indoor relative humidity will change too, unless the timer setting is corrected.

One dehumidifier will handle one or two enclosed rooms. For a whole house you would need two or three large units. Units are rated by their water-removing capacity in pints per day at 80 degrees Fahrenheit and 60 percent relative humidity.

Dehumidification is needed in a non-air-conditioned house only during the heating off-season when indoor relative humidity climbs to about 60 percent. During the heating season you can pack the unit up and store it away.

Maintaining a dehumidifier

Costlier dehumidifiers turn themselves off when their drain containers fill. Otherwise collected water would begin overflowing onto the floor. Thus a dehumidifying unit that is not direct-draining needs daily emptying of its container. The iron-free water is excellent for steam irons and topping off the cells of auto batteries. The only other care a unit needs is once-a-month cleaning of the evaporator coils. To do it, the front panel of the unit is removed to expose the fins. A stiff shop brush or a vacuum-cleaner-brush attachment will remove built-up dust and dirt. After about a year of use, the unit's condenser coils may need cleaning, too. Any other problems—rare with a dehumidifier—require the service of a trained refrigeration technician.

Caring for your water heater

A booklet that comes with every water heater tells what steps are necessary to maintain it. Care is standard among the different makes of heaters.

Every modern water heater has what is called an energy-cutoff device. This is a nonadjustable temperature-limit switch that stops all energy flow to the heater should its temperature reach that limit. It prevents boiling of tank water. If the heater's temperature selector fails, the energy cutoff switch opens, stopping the heating process. Even though the cutoff closes again upon cooling, the pilot of a gas-fired burner goes out. It and the burner stay out. Continued pilot light outages preceded by higher-than-normal water temperatures indicate heater thermostat failure. A dealer correction is called for.

Some gas water heaters have air adjustments to obtain a blue flame. To adjust one, loosen the shutter locknut, raise the temperature setting to operate the burner, and rotate the air shutter to get a blue flame. Flame adjustment of oil-fired water heaters should be made by a service technician with combustion-checking equipment.

Every few months, drain a pail of water from your water heater. This gets rid of heat-insulating sediment at the bottom of the tank. Stop draining when the water runs clear.

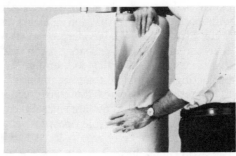

An additional layer of insulation installed around the outside of your water heater's storage tank will pay for itself rapidly at the present high cost of energy.

Stopgaps and copouts

You can save on your energy bill simply by setting back the heater's temperature selector one mark (20 degrees). If you overdo it, the last shower of the day may end up cold.

Check that relief valve!

For the safety of your household, the relief valve atop your water heater should be checked once a month for proper operation. If this valve gets stuck, its vital relief functions could fail. You'd be unprotected against explosion of a runaway water heater. Lift the pressure-test handle on the valve and run a few pints of water down the relief tube to be certain that the valve is working. It is a second line of defense against tank explosion.

Troubleshooting water heaters

Problem	Solution	What it takes
Insufficient hot water or water too cool.	Undersized heater—get a larger one. Too low a temperature setting—increase it. Defective thermostat—replace it. Bare piping—insulate it (see page 426). Heating element faulty—replace.*	Plumbing tools, pipe insulation, test light.
Water too hot.	Thermostat set too high—lower it. Thermostat defective—replace it.*	Test-light, screwdriver.
Boiling sound from tank.	Droplets of water beneath sediment turning to steam—flush out tank. Electric heater with scaled-up element—remove element and clean off scale or replace it.	Screwdriver, garden hose.
Rusty hot water.	Silt or mud in tank—turn off heater and water, turn on hot water and drain tank. Refill and flush. Turn everything on again.	Garden hose.
Popping relief valve.	Large water flow—check for too-high temperature setting or a failed relief valve.	No tools required.
High fuel consumption.	Scale in tank or around heating element. Improper air intake to oil or gas burner. Gas pilot too high—turn adjustment screw clockwise while watching flame. Uninsulated piping.	Screwdriver for pilot light.
Rapid tank corrosion.	Screw out the magnesium anode inside the heater tank every few years and inspect it. Install a new anode if it has been eaten away.	Screwdriver, wrenches.
Gas pilot snuffs out.	Install draft diverter if missing. Replace pilot thermocouple. Also, see text above.	Screwdriver.
Electric shocks.	Shorted element or thermostat—replace. Broken grounding wire—replace it. Defective insulation on lead wire—install new lead.	Test-light, screwdriver.

*Unless you're at home with electrical testing and wiring, troubleshooting of electric heater wiring problems should be left to competent service personnel. Do not take chances. Electricity can kill.

Water treatment

What it takes

Approximate time: Hooking up a water softener is a pleasant one-day project if everything goes well. Count as pluses: basement, garage, or utility-room water entrance. Count as potential problems: crawl space water entrance and attic water-supply mains. Copper and plastic water supply tubes make for the simplest softener installation; threaded pipes are harder.

Tools and materials: You'll need a full set of joining tools for your house piping. Or else plan on using short-cut adapter fittings that are available for galvanized steel piping and copper tubing. Materials include the necessary teeing-off fittings, piping to and from the softener, and connections to the treatment unit. One more thing you'll need is a drain hose leading to a place where you can dump regeneration water. In most cases this goes to a nearby floor drain or sink trap with a side connection for the hose. The hose may be rubber garden hose or polyethylene pipe with the necessary attachments.

Planning hints: A valid water test should precede your selection of a water treatment unit. If you use municipal or utility water, the water company will furnish an analysis of it. Beyond that, local treatment unit dealers probably know what's required in your area. If you draw water from a private water source, you'll need to make a water test to tell exactly what kind of treatment your water needs and how much treatment capacity is required. Capacity also depends on how much water you use. This can be estimated from the size of your family, the number of animals you have, and what other uses of treated water you will make. Plan on doing the installation at a time when the whole house water supply can be turned off for a few hours.

When the subject of water treatment comes up, most people think of a water softener. Yet softeners are only one form of water treatment. You can get a treatment unit to cure almost any water defect. The problem is that water on or under the ground contains many of the impurities of the ground: minerals, acids, and bases. These create hardness, stain fixtures, and smell and look badly. Treatment removes these unwanted products, making water more usable.

The primary problem is hardness, in which ground-rock transfers calcium and magnesium ions (electrically charged atoms) to the water. These ions react poorly with soaps and detergents, and so the water is considered hard. The modern water softener contains an ion-exchange resin bed that trades its good-acting sodium ions for bad-acting calcium and magnesium ions in the water. So, dissolved minerals are not actually removed, they are merely exchanged for more desirable ones.

When the resin bed becomes loaded with bad-acting ions and gives up most of its sodium ions, the process must be reversed, or else softening would come to a halt. Reverse processing is called regeneration. During regeneration, the resin is first given a rapid backflow—backwashed—to lift out collected solids. Then, switched to forward flow again, the unit resin bed is inundated with very salty water created by dissolving softener-salt in water and flowing it slowly past the bed. Sodium ions from the salt drop off into the bed and take the place of the more loosely attached magnesium and calcium ions. These go back into the water and are carried away to drain. Regeneration is, unfortunately, somewhat wasteful of water. This process—a required one for water softening—is one of the main drawbacks of home water softeners.

The simplest water-softener installation is to tap into the cold water main and connect it as shown at right. A good location is along the cold-water line between the last tap-off to an outdoor hose outlet and the first to a fixture other than the toilet. If just hot water is to be softened, connect only into the cold-water line going into the heater (see opposite).

Turn off the main shutoff valve and locate the mineral tank under the pipe it will connect to. Measure perpendicularly from the tank inlet and outlet openings up to the pipe and mark the pipe. Then, allowing for the makeup space required for the two adapters and elbows shown, cut out a section of the pipe and attach the adapters

How a water softener works

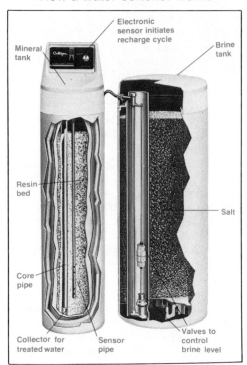

Running water through the resin bed converts calcium and magnesium ions—which react badly with detergents—into good-acting sodium ions. Resin is periodically backwashed with brine to regenerate its ion-exchange ability.

Water-softener connections

and elbows to the pipe ends. Then connect flexible riser pipes from the tank's inlet and outlet connections to the elbows.

For an installation that lets you bypass or remove the softener when you want to, install the two shutoff valves and the bypass

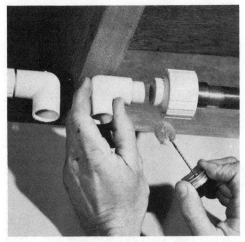

valve shown below. Softener installation kits come with many of the pipes and fittings needed. Fill with softener salt and you're in business.

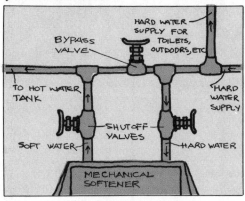

To soften water, both tee-off valves should be fully open and the main valve between them should be closed. This makes water pass from the main through the softener and back to the main again. Modern softeners also contain built-in

bypasses that conduct hard water around the softener during regeneration. If, for any reason, the softener must be taken out, the manual bypass you have created with your three valves will provide hard water to the whole house.

If other types of treatment units are required, all should be located ahead of the water softener. All, that is, except a small activated-carbon filter placed in the cold water line and connected to a fixture where your drinking water is drawn. These filters remove scum and suspended solids and

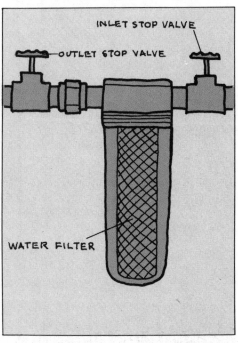

counteract bad taste in the water you drink. They're good at removing chlorine, too.

Many water treatment units are said to "purify" water. Do not make the mistake of thinking that they remove harmful bacteria. Only a chlorinator can do this by killing it with small amounts of chlorine. If your drinking water won't pass a health department purity test, then it needs germ purification before it can be safely drunk.

Arrangement of water-treatment units

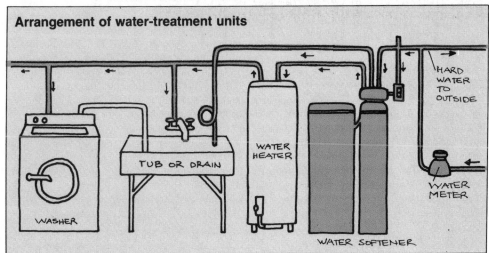

The hydrologic cycle

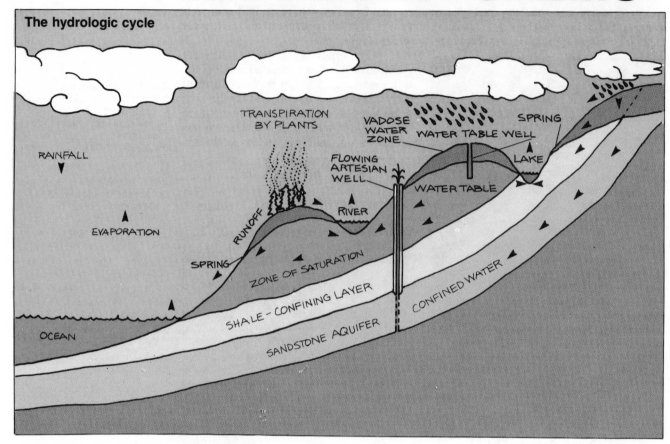

Water supply

What it takes

Approximate time: It takes a professional well-driller about one week to drill an average water well. Hand-digging a shallow well could take months, but developing a nearby spring to produce household water could be done in a long weekend.

Tools and materials: Drilling your own deep water well is not recommended. To install a pump in a well, you'll need steel or polyethylene pipe and fittings, wrenches, screwdriver, pliers, the pump, electrical controls, well seal or pitless adapter, an electrical switch box and cable, and a pipe dog to keep the pipes from slipping into the well while you make connections.

Planning hints: If you don't fully understand the electrical side of pump hookup, hire an electrician to handle it, and if your well is much more than 150 feet deep, you may prefer to have the well-drilling crew handle the lowering of piping into it.

The water can come from several sources: rain or melting snow; a surface supply, such as a lake or river; and in-the-ground water. This last source—ground water—is the typical water source for a private supply system. Water-table ground water closest to the surface results from water saturating the ground. A water-table source is likely to be contaminated, and its depth tends to vary seasonally, depending on past rainfall. In most areas, water-table wells are second rate, if not altogether unusable, for drinking water.

Deep water trapped in what's called an *aquifer* beneath layers of rock is usually pure, though sometimes heavily mineralized. To get at it, a deep well must be drilled through the rock layer into porous strata beneath. (Be sure you own the water rights.)

A third kind of ground water is the spring or seep. It brings ground water from a higher elevation, sometimes moving it many miles, then flows it out onto the ground.

Vertical well systems. These consist of

motor, pump, pressure tank, and the piping between them. An automatic pressure switch turns the pump on when pressure falls below a preset level. It turns the pump off when it has pumped back to the desired maximum pressure.

In some ways, a private water system is better than a public one. Water from a private source is chlorine-free. And there's no water bill to pay. But the higher electric bill for pumping may make up for the free water supply, and you must maintain the pumping equipment yourself.

Before you drink well water, it should be tested either by public health authorities or a private testing laboratory. This is required in many areas, and in some areas, a permit must be obtained to drill a private well.

Pumps for residential wells. There are four types: centrifugal, piston, jet, and submersible (see page 452). They may be shallow-well—where water level is within 25 feet of the pump—or deep-well. Centrifugal pumps are shallow-well only. The others may be used in shallow or deep wells.

Drilling a well

The most practical way to drill for water is to hire a professional. With modern equipment it takes only a few days to bore down under hundreds of feet through solid rock. Lining the hole with well-casing pipe prevents it from collapsing. Wells are usually cased down to solid rock, sometimes all the way from top to bottom.

Installing casing and piping

Lowering 12-gauge culvert pipe that will form the casing for a well 30=inches wide that was drilled with a 36-inch auger.

Grout cement is worked around the culvert pipe casing along its entire length to strengthen the well installation.

For drilling wells in soft rock such as limestone, you can buy a do-it-yourself well-drilling outfit at a price less than you might have to pay for a single professionally-drilled well. The driller comes with power unit, drill pipe, and hardened drill bit. You supply water from a garden hose to flush out drillings. About 100 feet is a comfortable do-it-yourself drilling depth. Where the unit really pays off is in drilling multiple wells for yourself and your neighbors.

Submersible pump is attached to a length of discharge pipe and then lowered into the well casing. If the well is not too deep, the pipe may be polyethylene plastic. Installations over 220=feet deep should be made with galvanized-steel pipe.

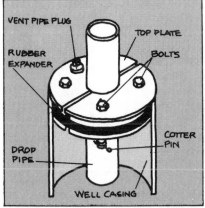

VENT PIPE PLUG
TOP PLATE
RUBBER EXPANDER
BOLTS
COTTER PIN
DROP PIPE
WELL CASING

The well seal at the top of the casing prevents infiltration of surface water and other contaminants. Two pipes going into a well indicate a deep-well jet. A single pipe indicates that either a shallow-well jet or a submersible pump is in use.

How a pressure tank works

Well-pump pros and cons

Jet pump: High volume, low energy consumption, few moving parts, simple to repair. Sediment or scale in water may lodge in jet and plug it. Can be tough to cure if there is much pipe to pull out of well. Flow rate drops drastically at greater depths.

Submersible well pump: Requires larger well. Deep-pumping models available with low pumping rates. Trouble-free pumping, except in sandy wells where they're not suited. Vulnerable to lightning strikes and to pumping well dry. The best, but the costliest residential-type well pump.

Shallow-well centrifugal pump: Simplest pump for low-pressure, low-lift applications. Low cost and practically trouble-free.

Piston pump: Can develop extremely high pressures. Most practical as a low-volume, shallow-well pump. Has more wearing parts than other pumps.

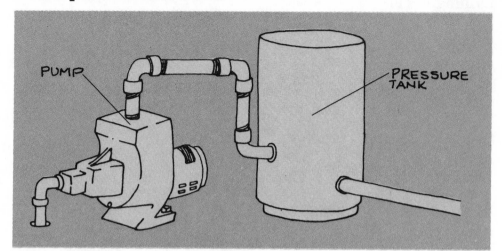

Well pipes lead to the pressure tank, which keeps water stored under pressure for use whenever a tap is opened. The pump motor will cycle on and off automatically at preset pressures.

Pumping depth vs. gallons per minute

Jet pump	Pumping depth in feet, to yield given gpm at 40 psi													
Pump horsepower	40	60	70	80	100	120	140	160	180	200	210	240	260	280
¾	8.4	5.8	4.7	4.3	3.7	2.7								
1	11.7	11.1	10.2	9.2	6.4	5.1	4.5	4.0	3.2	2.9	2.1			
1½	12.2	12.2	11.7	11.3	9.9	8.3	5.0	4.9	4.9	4.7	4.3	3.7	3.0	2.3

Submersible pump	Pumping depth in feet, to yield given gpm at 40 psi										
Pump horsepower	20	60	100	140	180	220	260	300	340	380	450
½	12.3	10.8	9.1								
¾		12.8	11.4	10.4	8.8						
1				12.1	11.1	10.2	9.4	8.0			
1½						12.1	11.6	11.0	10.3	9.3	7.4

Troubleshooting well pumps

Problem	Solution	What it takes
Pump will not run.	Check power, fuse, circuit breaker, switch, pressure switch, wires leading to motor, flow-cutoff switch (if used). If current reaches pump but unit doesn't run, call for service.	Test-light, VOM.
Pump draws power but doesn't pump.	Jet pump: debris in jet—remove and clean. Submersible pump: locked rotor—check amperage draw and compare with locked-rotor specifications in manual. Also, check water level below intake pipe, lost prime, or stuck check-valve.	Ammeter, pipe tools, pipe dog.
Pump runs briefly, then stops.	Pressure tank is waterlogged—recharge tank. Pressure switch differential set too close—adjust switch to increase differential to about 20 psi. Pressure switch installed too far from pressure tank—locate switch next to tank.	No tools required.
Pump delivers water too slowly.	Well-water level has receded—lower pipes deeper into well. Pump too small—check for valve sticking. Inadequate voltage to pump—check voltage with pump running and compare with manufacturer's minimum requirements; use heavier wires to increase voltage. Jet pump: partially plugged jet—remove and clean.	Pipe tools, well tools, new wires, VOM.
Pump starts when no water is being used.	Leaking check-valve—remove and replace. Other leaks: listen at well casing for a spraying sound—pull out pipes and repair leak.	Pipe tools, well tools, check-valve.
Pressure low or variable.	Adjust setting of pressure switch to correct. See the pump manufacturer's manual for recommended pressure settings. Switch has two settings, one for level of pressure, another for differential between lowest and highest pressure.	Screwdriver, pliers.
Noisy pump.	Motor bearing worn out—replace bearing.	Shop tools.
Leaks around pump shaft.	Seal worn out—replace.	Pipe tools.

Jet pumps are the most common for both shallow and deep wells. The pump's impeller spins water from center to outside. Discharge water flows into a pressure pipe leading to a 180-degree turn, through an orifice called a *jet*. The jet leads up to a larger suction pipe, and is open to well water at the bottom. The powerful jet of water streaming up the suction pipe carries some well water along with it. At the pump, water is forced back down through the jet. The excess flows off to the pressure tank for home use.

On a shallow-well jet pump, the jet is mounted on the pump and only a single suction pipe from the backside of the jet reaches into the well. Motor, pressure tank, and controls mount with the pump. For deep-well use, the jet is placed down in the well within 25 feet of the lowest water level.

Piston pumps use a piston in a cylinder, working like a syringe, to suck water up out of the well. For deep-well use, the piston is placed down in the well and worked by a motor-driven rod. The mass of moving parts makes it less desirable than a deep-well jet pump, unless wind-driven.

Centrifugal, jet, and piston pumps must be primed before they will pump. This is done by pouring water into a priming opening, then closing it and operating the pump. Normally, no further priming is necessary.

Submersible pumps have a long, narrow motor directly driving a long turbine pump with multiple impellers. Supported below the lowest well-water level by the discharge pipe, it may also have a safety cord to prevent pump loss down the well if the discharge pipe becomes detached. A waterproof cable goes down the well with the pump to bring it electricity. Controls and pressure tank are above ground.

In any well, it is important that the intake opening be low enough to always be under water. Air entry makes a pump lose its prime. In a submersible type, lack of water can even destroy the pump. An intake should not be at the very bottom of the well, however, where it could draw in debris. An experienced well-driller can usually tell you what is the best depth to place your pump parts and can accurately estimate what the pumping capacity will be.

The gallons per minute rate of a pump depend on the type of pump, pumping depth, friction pipe losses, and the pressure required at the farthest faucet. Well pumps come in a number of models (see table on opposite page) and well and pipe size should be integrated with the pump used.

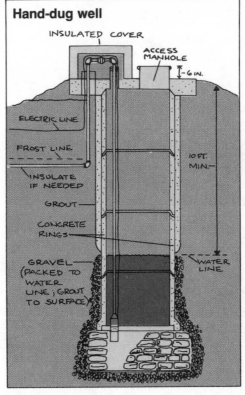

Hand-dug well

INSULATED COVER
ACCESS MANHOLE
6 IN.
ELECTRIC LINE
FROST LINE
INSULATE IF NEEDED
GROUT
CONCRETE RINGS
GRAVEL (PACKED TO WATER LINE; GROUT TO SURFACE)
10 FT. MIN
WATER LINE

Wire sizes for pumps

To be certain submersible-pump motors have adequate voltage, the size (gauge) of cable serving them must be right. Figure the distance from switchbox to well, plus that from wellhead to submersible pump. Then consult the table below. Wire sizes are AWG copper.

Cable length	Cable gauge
½–hp motor (115-volt)	
To 35'	No. 14
55'	No. 12
85'	No. 10
140'	No. 8
220'	No. 6
½–hp motor (230-volt)	
To 140'	No. 14
220'	No. 12
340'	No. 10
560'	No. 8
875'	No. 6
1–hp motor (230-volt)	
To 85'	No. 14
140'	No. 12
200'	No. 10
340'	No. 8
525'	No. 6

Lightning bug
I didn't believe it when they advised me to install a lightning arrester on my submersible-pump control box. One night, lightning struck the wiring and grounded itself through my submersible pump. It was burned out, and I was burned up. It cost me a lot to replace the pump. I installed a low-cost lightning arrester which fits on the pump's control box. Now my pump is protected.

Practical Pete

Comparison of well types

Type of well	Advantages/disadvantages	Cost ranking
Professionally drilled (to 1000' deep, 4"-24" diameter).	Most trouble-free. Can be any size, any depth, depending on ground factors. Best chance of getting bacteria-free water, but water may have high mineral content. Least dependent on ground water table. Can choose solid or perforated casing, as strata permit. May not need to be cased beyond first rock strata.	Highest.
Hand-dug (to 50' deep, 3"-20" diameter).	Hardest to make. Not workable where water table is far down. Best in porous soils away from sources of pollution and near a lake or stream for recharge. Greatly affected by seasonal water table. Flow may be low. Risk of collapse.	Low.
Hand-driven (to 50' deep, 1¼"-2" diameter).	Excellent where potable water exists above rock strata and ground is not rocky. Numerous wells can be driven vertically or horizontally to tap more water than one well can produce. May be hard work. Flow not as great as in a drilled well.	Lowest.

Sewage treatment

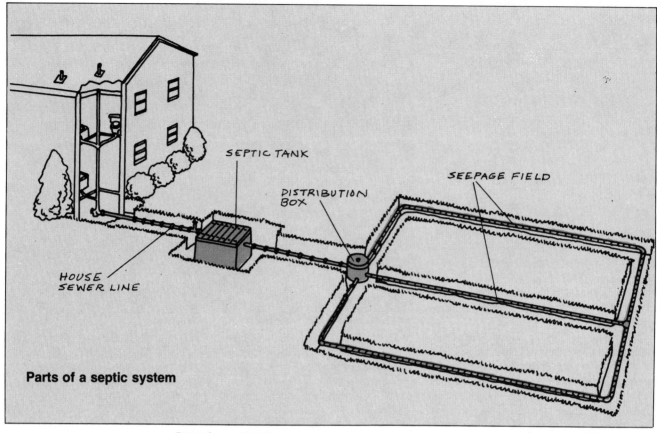

Parts of a septic system

Septic systems

Living in an area not served by a municipal sewage disposal plant requires that an alternate method be found for getting rid of sewage. The most commonly used is a private sewage-disposal facility called a septic system.

Once household wastes travel from the house sewer, they enter a large tank where the septic system takes over. In this tank, decomposition takes place by bacterial action. Solid wastes settle to the bottom and are pumped out every two or three years. The remaining liquid, called *effluent*, flows out of the tank through another sewer pipe into a distribution box which distributes effluent among seepage lines, where it seeps out through perforated pipes or loose-jointed tiles into the surrounding soil.

Septic tank sizes vary from about 500 gallons capacity to 1250 gallons or more. The larger the tank, the less frequently it needs to be maintained. Use the table on the next page to help estimate how large a septic tank you'll need.

To determine the rate at which your soil will absorb effluent, run a percolation test. Dig half a dozen or so holes, spaced evenly throughout the area where you plan to install the lines. Go about 36 inches deep; then put 2 inches of a porous material, such as gravel or coarse sand, into the bottom of each hole. For a minimum 4-hour period—better yet, 12 hours—saturate each hole by keeping it full of water. Now you're ready to make the test.

Refill each hole to a depth of 6 inches above the porous fill. After 30 minutes, measure the distance that the water level has dropped. Then refill the holes to 6 inches above the fill. Do this for eight 30-minute periods—a total of four hours. During the last period, measure the time it takes for the water level to drop 1 inch. Using this time as your key, refer to the Percolation Table, opposite, for the minimum amount of seepage area you should have for each bedroom in the house. Percolation rates shouldn't vary much from one test hole to another, but if they do, average the results.

For extremely porous soil that soaks up water in less than 30 minutes, use a somewhat different testing procedure: Allow only 10 minutes between refillings, and run your test for just one hour rather than four. The percolation rate then would be the time the soil needs, in the last 10-minute period, to pull down the water level 1 inch.

Building a sewer

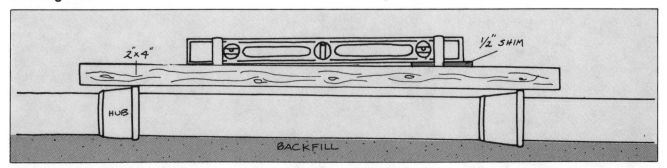

1. A sewer line should slope evenly away from a house at ¼ inch per foot. A 2-foot carpenter's level with a ½-inch plywood scrap under one end and taped to a long, straight 2x4 will help achieve slope. Sewer may slope steeper, but the last 10 feet should conform to the mentioned ratio.

2. Sewer pipes, except clay tile and cast iron pipe, need uniform support in the trench bottom. Dig out for pipe hubs so that pipes are supported along their full length. Trench bottom should be unexcavated earth, sand, or pea-gravel fill.

3. All rocks in contact with the pipes on trench bottom and in backfill should be removed. Earth backfill is okay, provided that it is fine and rock-free. Final fill above the pipes may be rocky.

Installing a tank

The easiest septic tank to buy is a precast concrete one. The dealer will tell you what size hole to dig. Be sure it's large enough, and that the bottom is perfectly level. Tank suppliers are equipped to deliver tanks in place. An A-frame on the rear of the truck lowers a tank into the hole facing in the direction you want it. When tank is in place, racks are removed.

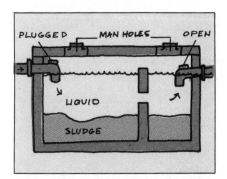

The typical two-compartment septic tank lets solids settle out at the bottom while sewage decomposes by bacterial action. Sewage enters through a plugged tee, leaves tank through a lower, open-topped tee.

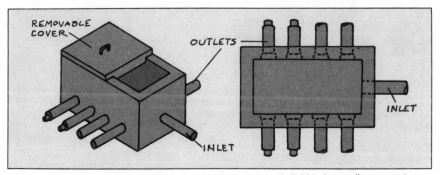

A distribution box accepts effluent from the septic tank and divides it equally among two or more seepage lines. Its outlets, which are all at the same elevation, sit slightly lower than the inlet. The distribution box itself must be level.

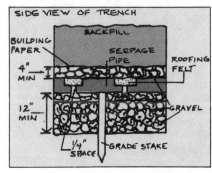

A typical seepage trench—12 to 36 inches wide, 3 feet deep—either slopes slightly away from tank or is level. The bottom 12 inches of trench are filled with coarse stones. Perforated pipes are laid and topped with more stones.

Percolation table											Tank-size table				
Percolation rate: minutes required for water level to drop 1 inch after initial saturation.	2 or less	3	4	5	10	15	30	45	60	Over 60	**Number of bedrooms**	1–2	3	4	5
Minimum seepage area: in square feet of trench bottom per bedroom.	85	100	115	125	165	190	250	300	350	Soil not suitable	**Minimum tank capacity**	750 gal.	900 gal.	1000 gal.	1250 gal.

Building a seepage field

1. Position grade stakes in seepage trenches to get the proper pipe slope. For one of 2 to 4 inches per 100 feet, tape a 1/16-inch shim under one end of a 2-foot level. Position the shim at the lower stake, then tap down until bubble is centered.

2. Dump the initial stone fill into the trench bottom and level it off even with the tops of the grade stakes. Both the trench bottom and the fill should have the same slope.

3. Lay the seepage pipes on the gravel. Perforated pipes should be placed perforations down. Instead of solvent-welding the joints, use loose couplings. Cover joints of open-jointed clay tiles with strips of asphalt felt or shingles.

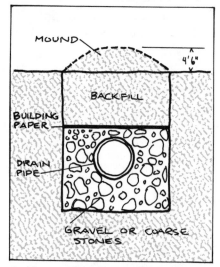

4. After covering the seepage lines with 4 inches of coarse stones, roll untreated building paper out over the stones. A layer of straw will do, also. Then back-fill with loose earth, mounded up above grade.

5. Ends of seepage runs need to be blocked off so effluent doesn't run out and erode the trench. Do it by placing a large rock against the pipe end. Or use a cap.

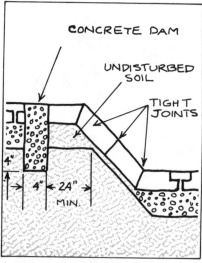

6. Changes in trench elevations call for cast concrete dams. Properly constructed, effluent in the higher trench cannot overflow into the lower trench without going through the pipe. Pipes between trenches are tight, not perforated.

Layouts for seepage fields

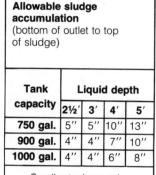

Allowable sludge accumulation (bottom of outlet to top of sludge)

Tank capacity	Liquid depth			
	2½'	3'	4'	5'
750 gal.	5"	5"	10"	13"
900 gal.	4"	4"	7"	10"
1000 gal.	4"	4"	6"	8"

Smaller tanks require more frequent cleaning.

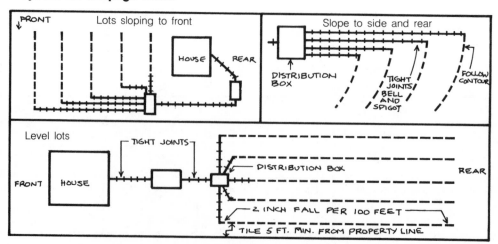

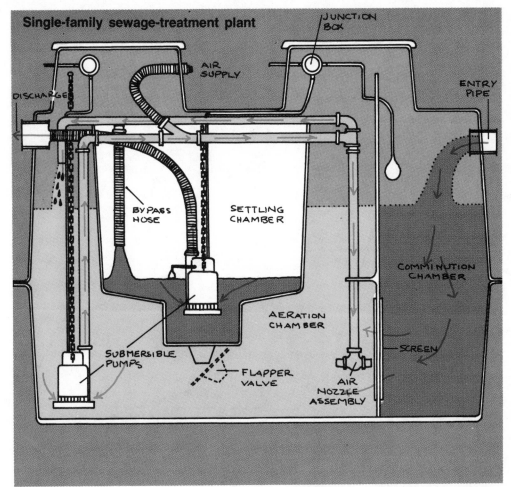

Single-family sewage-treatment plant

JUNCTION BOX

AIR SUPPLY

ENTRY PIPE

DISCHARGE

BYPASS HOSE

SETTLING CHAMBER

COMMINUTION CHAMBER

SUBMERSIBLE PUMPS

AERATION CHAMBER

FLAPPER VALVE

AIR NOZZLE ASSEMBLY

SCREEN

This aerobic sewage treatment unit for homes can process up to 480 gallons of waste in 16 hours. Sewage flows through entry pipe into comminution chamber. As it flows from there through screen into aeration chamber, air from nozzle, drawn in through air-supply hose, breaks up and mixes the waste materials. Floating materials flow into the settling chamber and are aerated by air from the bypass hose. Treated effluent is then pumped out through the discharge pipe. Any settled solids are voided back into the aeration chamber through the flapper valve. Process is noiseless and odorless.

Sewage-treatment plants

A step above the septic system for handling household sewage is the private sewage-treatment plant, a number of types of which are available. Select a system that is locally approved or one for which you can secure an experimental installation permit.

The sewage-treatment plant eliminates some of the drawbacks of the anaerobic (without air) septic system, chiefly the quality of effluent. Liquid left over after a septic system's 70-day bacterial-action process is finished is unhealthy and smells bad. Septic effluent cannot be discharged onto the ground, or into a stream or lake. It is so high in biological-oxygen demand that it would kill plant and animal life.

Fully treated 4-hour effluent from a private aerobic (with air) treatment plant is the next thing to being pure enough to drink. After chlorination, some health departments will permit its discharge into a flowing stream. Thus, if you're saddled

with soil that is poorly suited for a septic-tank seepage field, the private treatment plant could be your answer. Even when used with a seepage field for disposing of effluent, a sewage-treatment system beats a septic tank. Septic effluent may, in time, fill soil pores with suspended solids—especially if the tank is not regularly maintained. This clogs up the field, making it necessary to extend it into a new seepage area.

Treatment-plant effluent is free of suspended solids. It will not harm a seepage field any more than plain water would. Also, if a seepage field should become waterlogged, treatment-plant effluent is not as objectionable to neighbors or passersby.

The cost of a private sewage-treatment plant is about twice that of a simpler septic system. Some units come ready to bury or to install aboveground in a shed; others need cast-in-place concrete tanks.

What it takes

Approximate time: A little longer than a septic system, so you may prefer to hire a contractor. Additional time is needed for the electrical wiring that serves the pumps. Digging and seepage field work (unless discharge is into a stream) will take about the same time as a septic system.

Tools and materials: Calls for the same tools as required for a septic system. If you do the wiring part of the job yourself, you'll need wire-working tools, too.

Planning hints: Work closely with both the dealer who sells the unit and local health officials. If you can, get the two parties together to advise you.

Stopgaps and copouts

If your ground is unfit for a conventional seepage field, a dug-out seepage pit with walls of loose-jointed concrete blocks can be put in. No bottom is installed other than a foot-thick layer of gravel to allow effluent to percolate into the soil.

A seepage pit is usually called for when an impermeable surface layer of soil sits atop a permeable layer, or when the available ground is too hilly to accommodate seepage lines.

In some areas, a precast concrete seepage pit, substituting for the home-built block one, can be purchased. If a single pit won't handle the load, a series of them, served by a distribution box, may be used. Not all codes okay seepage pits, so be sure to check before you start digging.

A pit should be located at least 100 feet from any water supply source, 10 feet from property lines, and 20 feet from buildings. In multiple-pit installations, the distance between them should be at least three times the diameter of the largest one. Pit diameter should be 4 feet or more and dug into at least 4 feet of porous soil.

If you build the pit with special loose-laid seepage-pit blocks, lay them with their small openings facing into the pit and their large openings facing out. Back the wall materials with at least a 3-inch thickness of coarse, crushed stones up to the level of the inlet. Above the inlet, lay the masonry with solid mortar joints.

9.HEATING

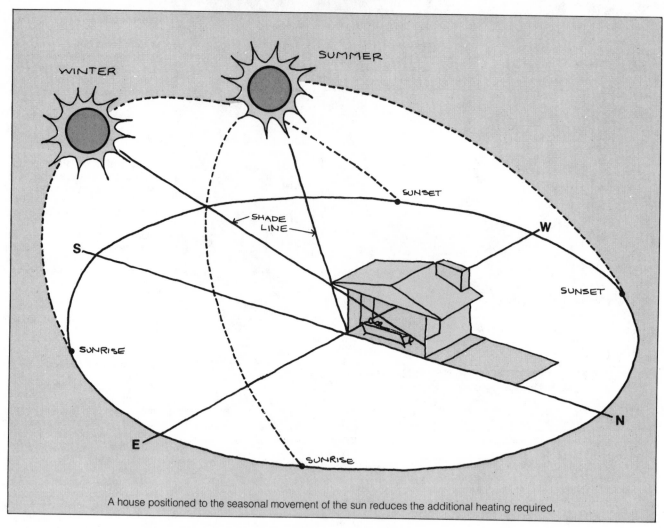

WINTER

SUMMER

SUNSET

SHADE LINE

W

S

SUNSET

SUNRISE

N

E

SUNRISE

A house positioned to the seasonal movement of the sun reduces the additional heating required.

Energy shortages and increasingly higher fuel costs have prompted homeowners to take a closer look at home-heating systems.

This chapter will help you understand how various heating systems work and how to get the most heat with the least fuel consumption. Each section includes tips on how to maintain and service your heating system.

Hot and cold, warm and chilly, are relative terms. An electric heater may be hotter than a radiator, but colder than a furnace. In most parts of the country, an outside temperature of 50 degrees is warm for January, but cool for July. Differences in temperature cause heating systems to work. Heat always moves toward a cooler area. This movement of heat makes it possible to generate heat in one part of the house and then move it to cooler areas.

Heat moves in three ways

All forms of heat movement can, and usually do, occur at the same time. The various types of heating systems are designed to cause one kind of movement to predominate.

The purpose of a home-heating system is, of course, to maintain a comfortable temperature in the house. But comfort is dependent on humidity as well as temperature. Humidity is moisture content in air.

In warm weather, when the humidity is high, the air is holding as much, or almost as much, moisture as it can. Our body's cooling system depends on water evaporation (perspiration) to lower body temperature. The body's cooling system doesn't work well in a humid area. The moisture stays with us and we feel "sticky." In cool weather, the reverse occurs. The chilliness we feel when humidity is low (air is dry) is caused by rapid evaporation. So, both humidity control and temperature control are important in maintaining a comfortable home temperature (see opposite page).

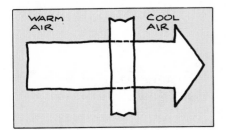

Conduction: In winter, heat is conducted through the walls toward cooler outside air, and the house loses heat. In summer, the reverse happens. Storm windows, insulation, reflective surfaces all slow down the heat conduction loss.

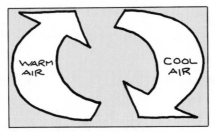

Convection: Warm air is lighter and less dense than cool air. This makes warm air rise and cool air descend, a movement called convection. It can cause annoying drafts, or help to keep temperatures even, if controlled.

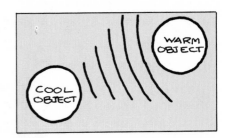

Radiation: Warm objects radiate heat toward cooler objects, as the sun warms the earth or as a radiator warms the people in a room.

Heating system

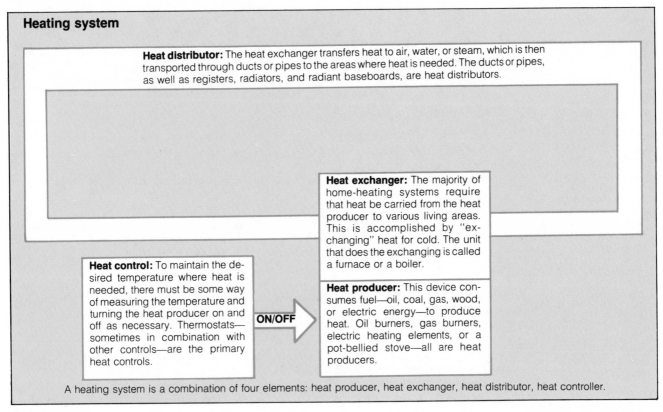

Heat distributor: The heat exchanger transfers heat to air, water, or steam, which is then transported through ducts or pipes to the areas where heat is needed. The ducts or pipes, as well as registers, radiators, and radiant baseboards, are heat distributors.

Heat exchanger: The majority of home-heating systems require that heat be carried from the heat producer to various living areas. This is accomplished by "exchanging" heat for cold. The unit that does the exchanging is called a furnace or a boiler.

Heat control: To maintain the desired temperature where heat is needed, there must be some way of measuring the temperature and turning the heat producer on and off as necessary. Thermostats—sometimes in combination with other controls—are the primary heat controls.

ON/OFF

Heat producer: This device consumes fuel—oil, coal, gas, wood, or electric energy—to produce heat. Oil burners, gas burners, electric heating elements, or a pot-bellied stove—all are heat producers.

A heating system is a combination of four elements: heat producer, heat exchanger, heat distributor, heat controller.

Humidity

Correct level: What is the correct level of humidity? The most practical indoor humidity level is between 30 and 35%. If the humidity is too high (40% or more), a significant amount of condensation can form, possibly even resulting in serious damage.

Control: Normal household activities such as washing, showering, and cooking add humidity to the air. Normally this provides 10 to 15% relative humidity. To reach and maintain the desired level, a humidifier must be installed in the house.

Humidifiers can be readily added to hot-air heating systems. The humidifier can be installed in the air ducts, close to the place where heated air leaves the furnace. A humidistat, built into the unit, controls the humidity level. A plumbing connection is required to supply water to the humidifier.

With any other type of heating system, a separate humidifier is required. These units require both electrical and plumbing connections. For best results, humidifiers should be centrally located in your home. For proper operation, doors should be left open as much as possible throughout the house.

Before purchasing a humidifier, you need to know the volume of living space and lowest expected outdoor temperature. To calculate the volume (in cubic feet), multiply the floor area of each room by the height of the ceiling. Add up the volume of all the rooms, hallways, and entrance ways to get the total volume. Include the basement and attic unless they are separated from the living area by insulation with a vapor barrier.

Calculated trouble
When I bought a new humidifier, I did not calculate *both* the volume of living space *and* the lowest expected outdoor temperature. Now that my new wallpaper has started to peel off, I know what I did wrong. Next time, I'll be sure to double-check all my calculations with the data supplied by the manufacturer.
Practical Pete

Heat producers

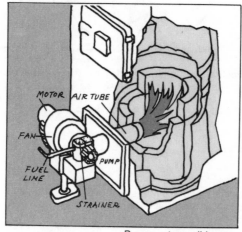

Pressure-type oil burner

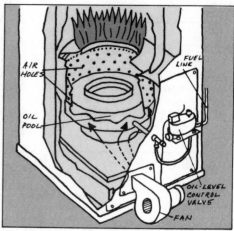

Pot-type oil burner

Oil burners

Oil burners have been widely used in home-heating systems for more than fifty years. Oil-fired heat producers work well with either hot-water, steam, or hot-air systems.

There are two types of oil burners in general use: the pressure type and the pot type. Both of these burners are located outside of the furnace or boiler fire box and so are relatively easy to service.

A third type of burner—called a rotary burner—has just about disappeared from use for home heating but is still used in some large building installations. The entire rotary burner unit is located within the fire box. This makes even routine service and adjustment rather complicated.

Pressure-type burners: Pressure-type burners pump oil, under pressure, through a small nozzle to form an oil spray. Air is mixed with the oil spray to form a combustible mixture. High voltage is applied to two electrodes and a spark jumps between them to ignite the mixture.

When operating properly, the oil and air mixture will continue to burn until the burner is turned off. Vanes mounted at the tip of the burner deflect the flame into a swirling form which allows more complete combustion of the mixture. As the combustion process becomes more complete, more heat is extracted from the fuel and less soot remains.

The operating parts of a pressure burner are an electric motor and a transformer. The motor drives a pump which creates the oil pressure and a fan which draws air into the burner. The transformer steps up the 120-volt house power to a high enough voltage to ignite the flame. Pressure-type burners can be turned on and off as needed, by means of a manual switch.

Pot-type burners: In this type of burner, a quantity of oil flows into a container (pot) in the fire box. The oil is ignited by a pilot flame. Once ignited, the heat causes the oil to vaporize. Air from a small blower mixes with the oil vapor and causes it to ignite. Heat level is controlled by regulating the flow of oil to the pot. When the oil flow is changed, the air flow must also be changed to maintain good combustion.

Pot-type burners are simple in operation and easy to maintain. Initial adjustment, however, is tricky and should be left to an experienced serviceman.

Stack relay

In either type of burner, if ignition fails and oil continues to be pumped into the fire box, the fire box and surrounding area are soon flooded. To prevent this, all burners have a device to turn off the oil flow if ignition fails. The most common device is the stack relay, which consists of a heat-sensitive switch, a relay circuit, and a restart button. The relay circuit and the restart button are enclosed in a metal box.

The stack relay is mounted on the sheet-metal stack that runs from the top of the furnace to the chimney flue. A hole is cut in the stack so that the heat-sensitive switch can project into the stack. When the burner is on and working properly, heat from the fire box keeps the heat-sensitive switch closed. This, in turn, keeps the relay circuit energized and maintains electric power to burner motor. If the flame goes out, the heat-sensitive switch opens and shuts off power to the burner fan and oil pump.

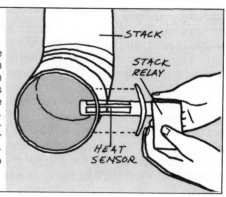

How to maintain an oil burner

Oil burners should be adjusted, inspected, and cleaned by burner-service personnel at the beginning of each heating season. Once adjusted, there are a number of things the homeowner can do to maintain efficiency and correct minor defects.

The following items should be serviced once about the middle of each heating season. If you have a burner-service book, read and follow the detailed instructions given for each of these items. If you need additional help, ask your serviceman to show you what needs to be done.

Turn off the burner master switch and clean the blower fan blades. The blades can be reached through the air-intake opening next to the fan. If you must remove a plate partially covering the air-intake opening, mark the exact position of the plate beforehand so it can be correctly replaced. Brush dust and dirt from the fan blades.

Turn off the burner master switch and take out the stack relay by removing the two mounting screws. Clean the heat-sensitive switch element. Use a small brush dipped in detergent and warm water. Hold the stack relay with the heat-sensitive switch pointed down so water does not run into the relay box. Shake off excess water before replacing the stack relay.

With the burner turned on and operating, check the position of the draft vane (see box, below).

Once or twice each heating season, step outside and take a look at the chimney. Do this at a time when you know the burner is on. If smoke or soot can be seen coming out of the chimney, the oil-spray-and-air mixture is not burning properly. Notify your burner service company.

How to restart an oil burner

If your burner does not start automatically as it should, make a few quick checks before you call your service company.

Check that the burner master switch has not accidently been turned off.

Check the circuit breaker or fuse that protects the oil burner circuit. If the circuit breaker is tripped to OFF or the fuse is blown, you may have an electrical short in the burner circuit. Notify your burner service company. Do not reset the circuit breaker or replace the fuse until the cause of the turn-off is known.

Check the oil level in your tank. If the tank is empty, the burner should not operate. If the float gauge indicates oil, check it by tapping lightly to be sure it is not sticking.

Check the thermostat setting against the indicated temperature. If the setting is five degrees or more higher than the indicated temperature, the burner should start. Remove the thermostat cover and check whether inside electrical contacts are exposed or sealed in glass. If the contacts are exposed, you can clean them by rubbing a crisp dollar bill between them. Do not use a file or any abrasive to clean contacts. If contacts are sealed in glass, no maintenance can be done. If the thermostat is defective, it must be replaced.

If the thermostat seems okay, if there is oil in the tank, and if the circuit breaker or fuse is okay, press the restart button on the stack relay once. If the burner starts, fine. For the next hour or so, check the burner every 10 to 15 minutes. If you see any evidence of oil leakage or if the smell of oil is unusually strong, turn off the master switch and notify your service company.

If pressing the restart button does not start the burner, the ignition system may be at fault. Notify your burner service company.

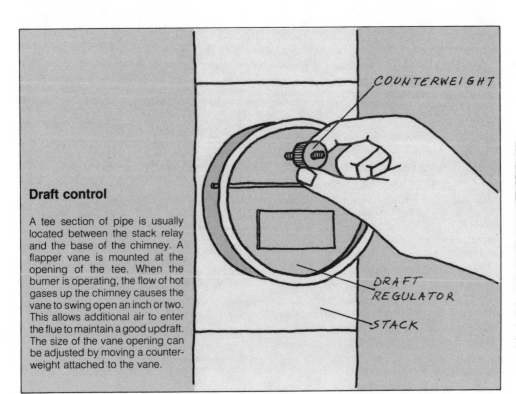

Draft control

A tee section of pipe is usually located between the stack relay and the base of the chimney. A flapper vane is mounted at the opening of the tee. When the burner is operating, the flow of hot gases up the chimney causes the vane to swing open an inch or two. This allows additional air to enter the flue to maintain a good updraft. The size of the vane opening can be adjusted by moving a counterweight attached to the vane.

COUNTERWEIGHT

DRAFT REGULATOR

STACK

Add a few drops of light oil to each burner motor-bearing cup. A few drops are all that should be added, since over-oiling can lead to serious motor trouble.

Gas burners

Approximate time: One hour to clean pilot jet and relight and adjust pilot flame.

Tools and materials: Piece of soft copper wire, matches.

1. Put thermostat on lowest setting, usually marked OFF.

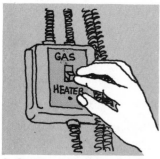

2. Switch off current to furnace.

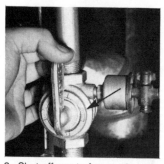

3. Shut off gas to furnace but not to pilot light.

4. Light pilot, start current, open main valve, set thermostat.

A gas-fired heat producer operates much like a gas range. The gas-fired furnace is larger and, because it is out of sight, contains safety features not required on cooking ranges.

The gas is ignited by a pilot light. An automatic system turns off the gas supply if the pilot light goes out.

A gas furnace or boiler may be used with an air, water, or steam-heating system. Gas heating has the advantages of clean, low-pollution burning and no home storage of fuel. In cities served by gas utility companies, mains carry gas to the home. Where bottled gas is used, containers of gas are delivered by truck. In most parts of the country, gas is more expensive than oil or coal.

Gas-fired furnaces require less service than other types of heat producers. It is customary in most localities for servicing to be done by the utility company which supplies the gas. The customer is charged for replacement of defective or broken parts, but not for routine service.

The home owner's maintenance of the gas furnace itself consists of relighting and adjusting the pilot light and cleaning the pilot jet.

Gas-fired furnaces are vented to the outside through stack connections from furnace to chimney, as are other furnaces. The only difference is the addition of a draft hood on the vent pipe. The draft hood is designed to prevent chimney downdrafts from blowing out the pilot light. The draft hood is effective most of the time, but strong, sudden downdrafts can still occasionally blow out the pilot.

A device called a thermocouple is located near the pilot flame. The thermocouple generates a small amount of electric current when heated by the pilot flame. This current is used to energize a solenoid valve that keeps the main gas supply line open. If the pilot flame goes out, the thermocouple cools and no longer generates electric current. The solenoid valve closes and turns off gas to the main and pilot jets.

The detailed procedure for cleaning the pilot jet and relighting and adjusting the pilot flame varies for each make and model of gas burner. The step-by-step procedure, together with the names and locations of controls, is given on a metal plate attached to the burner unit. The general procedure for all units is as follows:

1. Set the room thermostat to the lowest temperature, or to the OFF setting if it has one marked on it.
2. Turn off electric power to the furnace. This can be done by turning off a master switch or by setting a circuit breaker to OFF or removing a fuse.
3. Set the gas supply valve to the position that turns off both the main gas supply *and* the pilot supply.
4. Pull off the metal deflector attached to the top of the pilot jet.
5. Clean the jet by inserting a piece of soft copper wire in the pilot hole. Replace the deflector.
6. Set the gas supply valve to the position that keeps the main gas supply shut off, but turns on gas to the pilot jet.
7. Light the pilot. Adjust the pilot control valve for a flame about 1¼ inches high.
8. Set the gas valve to the full open position and turn on electric power.
9. Set the thermostat to the normal house temperature.

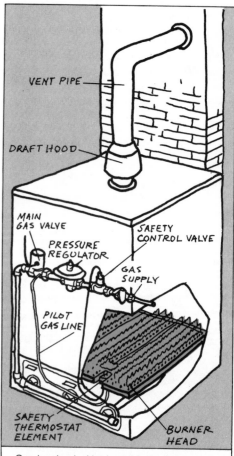

Gas is mixed with air and fed to a burner in the furnace. The burner may have a single large flame, a pattern of small jets, or a ribbon flame.

Electric heating

Electric heating is easy to control, requires little or no maintenance, and is clean and quiet. The only disadvantage of electric heating is the high cost in most areas. To be economically practical, electric heating requires an exceptionally well-insulated house. It is best used in areas having moderate winter temperatures.

Electricity can be used as the heat producer in hot-water or hot-air systems. Conventional hot-water baseboard systems using gas or oil can be readily converted to electric heating. No change is required in the system of pipes and convectors. The oil or gas boiler is replaced by an electric water-heating unit. The electric unit requires much less space and needs no flue connection. The unit can be mounted on a wall or installed in an attic or basement area.

Electric hot-water systems are controlled by a thermostat and an aquastat (see page 464) in the same manner as an oil or gas-fired system. Control of the individual convectors will depend upon the arrangement of the circulating loop (see page 464 for more on circulating loops).

Similarly, the hot-air and return-air ducts of a conventional hot-air system can be used with an electric heat producer. The circulating fan draws in cool air and passes it through a network of resistance wiring. When power is on, the wiring is hot and it heats the air as it passes through. The heated air is then carried by ducts to the living areas of the house, as it is in an oil- or gas-fired system.

Self-contained electric baseboard-heating units can be used for special areas or as auxiliary heaters. In a mild climate, these units can be used as the main heat source. Several types are available.

One type of baseboard unit uses a single heating element much like an electric furnace. The heating element runs through a ceramic-lined metal tube. The tube is surrounded by metal fins. The heating unit is enclosed in a metal housing designed to resemble conventional baseboard. Openings at the bottom and top allow air to flow through to heat the room. Units are made to operate on either 120- or 240-volt power. The 240-volt unit, of course, produces more heat. Each unit has its own switch, thermostat, and over-temperature control to prevent burn-out if air flow is blocked.

Another baseboard unit, similar in appearance to the heating-element type, contains a liquid in a sealed tube. The sealed tube is surrounded by fins. The liquid is electrically heated. The fluid, in turn, heats the fins and the air that passes through. Because the fluid retains heat for a time after power is turned off, this unit offers a somewhat more even heat flow.

In areas where extra heat is required for short periods of time (bathrooms, for example), self-contained wall units can be installed. These units use an electric heating element similar to the baseboard unit. In place of fins, the heating element is formed into a grid. A fan is used to move air through the unit. The units are designed to fit between wall studs. They, too, are equipped with manual on-off and temperature controls.

Electric radiant heating uses resistance wiring to produce heat. Resistance wire heats up when current passes through it. In principle, it is the same as the heating element in your electric toaster.

The heating wires are embedded in some insulating material—such as plaster—in walls or ceilings. When power is turned on, the wire heats up and radiates heat to the people and objects in the room.

At left, heat exchanger, expansion tank, and controls for electrically heated system. Above, radiant heating elements.

Electric baseboard heater

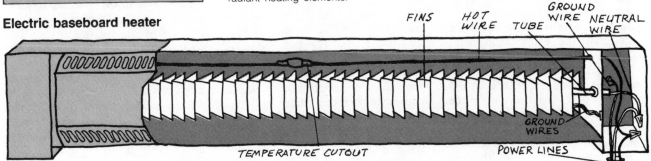

FINS HOT WIRE TUBE GROUND WIRE NEUTRAL WIRE

TEMPERATURE CUTOUT

GROUND WIRES

POWER LINES

Heat exchangers, distributors, and conduits

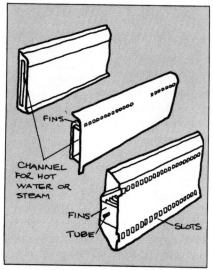

Baseboard convectors are generally used in series loops. The convectors transfer heat from the water circulating through them to the air in the room.

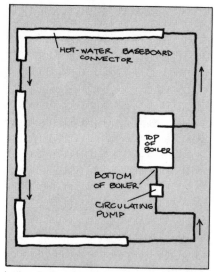

In a series loop, each baseboard unit is part of the loop. There is no way to turn off individual convectors. Thus, heat control is limited in this system.

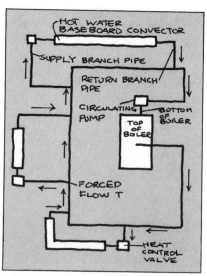

In the two-pipe system, one pipe supplies hot water to convectors and one returns cooled water to the boiler.

Forced hot-water systems. These systems work by heating water as high as 240 degrees and circulating this water through pipes, radiators, and convectors.

Any heat producer—oil, gas, coal, or electricity—can be used with a hot-water system. Each is economical, efficient, and heats domestic hot water in the same boiler. However, hot water has the disadvantage of higher initial cost than hot air, and the difficulties associated with a piped-water system.

Hot-water heating is a closed-loop system. The loop—consisting of heat exchanger, piping, and radiators—is filled with water. Water is pumped through the loop by a circulator pump. An expansion tank is included to allow for expansion of water and to maintain it under pressure.

The tank contains trapped air and water. As heated water expands, it compresses the air. Air resists compression and maintains the water under pressure. Because water in the system is under pressure, it can be heated above the normal boiling point and not become steam.

The heat producer is located in the base of the hot-water boiler. Heat and gases flow over closed sections in the heat exchanger. Water for the heating system flows through the closed sections and absorbs heat. The heat exchanger also contains coils through which cold water flows to be heated for household use.

It is important to remember that domestic hot water and heating hot water are independent systems, sharing only boiler heat.

The simplest system for distributing hot-water heat is the series loop. However, heat control is limited in this system, since there is no way of turning off individual baseboard convectors. The two-pipe system allows heat to be controlled as desired, because one convector can be adjusted without affecting the others.

A variation of the series-loop and two-pipe systems uses convectors in parallel with the circulating pipe. When a convector is turned off, hot water is diverted to the main line and continues to the next one.

Zoned heating. This is a combination of two systems operating from one boiler. The systems may be independent, each having a circulator, thermostat, and flow controls. A variation uses one circulator for both zones, created by dividing the main supply into two loops. The two loops are joined back to the boiler when they have completed their run. Flow is controlled by electric zone valves with separate thermostats.

Hot-water-system gauge. A pressure and temperature gauge is mounted on the side of the boiler. High and low heating-system water-temperature

readings should be within 5 or 10 degrees Fahrenheit of the aquastat settings.

The altitude scale is a reference scale and has two pointers. One is set during installation or major servicing, and, once set, does not move during operation of the system. The other, movable pointer indicates water pressure. The correct readings and limits for this scale vary with sizes and types of systems. When your system is serviced, determine your normal readings. Then make a sketch of the gauge on a small card and mount it nearby for future reference.

An aquastat senses water temperature in the boiler and turns the heat producer on when the temperature falls below a preset limit and off when it reaches a preset high. Two types of aquastats are in general use. The newer model has two dials under a removable front cover, one setting the high limit, one the low. Dials can be adjusted to suit heating requirements. A high setting of 160 degrees and a low of 120 degrees provide adequate heat in moderate weather; for colder weather a high of 180 degrees and a low of 150 degrees provide more heat. These levels are not the same for all systems. Your service company can advise on correct limits. Older aquastats have one high setting indicated by a dial and pointer. The low limit is preset.

Routine maintenance

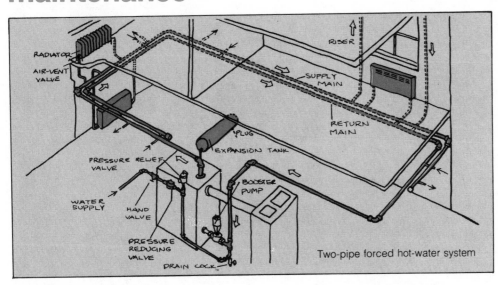

Two-pipe forced hot-water system

Bleeding the line

Some or all of the radiators or convectors in a hot-water system have small valves at one end. These allow trapped air to be released. Have a cup handy. Use a screwdriver (or vent key) to open the valve. Escaping air will cause a hissing sound. Water will spurt out when air has been released. Catch the water in the cup. Turn off the valve when a solid stream of water is coming out.

Circulator lubrication

At the beginning of each heating season, add a few drops of oil to the oil cups at each end of the motor. SAE grade 20 oil is usually specified somewhere on the motor housing. The circulator may also contain an oil cup. If so, add a few drops of SAE grade 20 oil to it as well.

Draining the system

Any time there is danger of freezing temperatures within the house—when electric power fails, for example—the system should be drained to keep pipes from bursting.
1. Turn off the heating system by turning off the master switch. Also set the heating-system circuit breaker to OFF or remove the heating system fuse. This should be done, even though electric power is off. The heating boiler could be seriously damaged if power was restored while the system was drained.
2. Allow the water in the system to cool down to a lukewarm or cool temperature.
3. Turn off the valve from the household's cold-water supply.
4. If practical, attach a hose to the drain at the lowest level in the system. This drain is located below the circulator, near the base of the boiler.
5. Run the other end of the hose to a basement floor drain. If no floor drain is available, the system can be drained into a pail. You will have to empty the pail several times.
6. Open the drain and open the air vents on the highest radiators.
7. If the system is being drained because of the danger of freezing, leave all drains open.

Flushing and refilling

1. With a hose attached to the boiler drain (or a pail beneath it), turn on the valve from the household's cold-water supply.
2. This will flush clean water through the boiler. Continue flushing until the water coming out of the boiler is clean.
3. To fill the system, close the boiler drain valve. Also, close the air vents you opened to drain the system.
4. Restore power to the system. Adjust the thermostat to start the burner. (You may also have to press the restart button on the stack relay.)
5. After the system has operated for several hours, bleed the radiators or convectors to free trapped air.

Draining the expansion tank

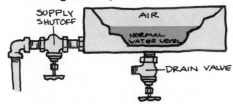

The expansion tank should be about half full of water for proper system operation. Over a period of time, the water level tends to rise because the system water absorbs small quantities of air. When too much air is absorbed, the water pressure may become high enough to open the pressure-relief valve, allowing hot water to flow out of the valve. If this should happen, turn off the heat producer immediately. Allow the system to cool. The pressure-relief valve will close automatically when the pressure drops.

The following procedures will prevent pressure build-up:
1. Attach a hose to the drain valve at the bottom of the expansion tank. Run the hose to a pail or drain.
2. Turn off the expansion-tank inlet valve.
3. Open the drain valve and allow the tank to drain completely. Disconnect the hose and close the drain valve. Open the tank inlet valve. Water will flow into the tank and compress the air in the tank to establish normal system pressure. The pressure reading on the boiler gauge should agree with the normal reading marked on your card.

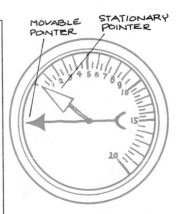

Boiler gauge showing pressure reading. If movable pointer drops below stationary pointer, as it has here, system needs more water.

Forced hot-air systems

What it takes

Approximate time: Two hours.

Tools and materials: Flashlight or utility light, mirror, screwdriver, T-square or carpenter's level.

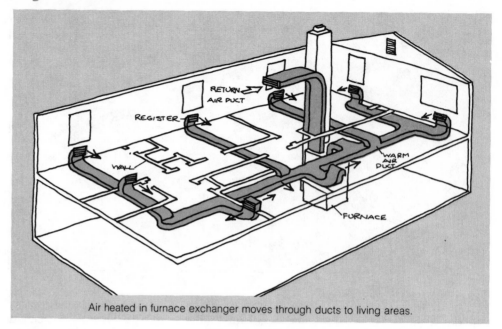

Air heated in furnace exchanger moves through ducts to living areas.

One of the simplest and most widely used heating systems in the United States is forced hot air. Forced air systems usually have oil or gas burners as the heat producers. A squirrel cage or centrifugal fan, driven by an electric motor, is the heat distributor.

In a typical basement hot-air furnace, heat from the burner passes through metal pipes in a heat-exchanger section. Hot gases from the burner heat the pipes to temperatures of several thousand degrees. The hot gases are ducted to the flue and vented to outside the house. Air is heated as it passes over the hot pipes of the heat exchanger.

The heated air is then carried by ducts to the living areas of the house. In some systems, the heated air first goes to a large sheet metal enclosure called a *plenum*. Ducts to various parts of the house are connected to the plenum.

When the furnace is on the same level as the living area—as in homes built on a poured concrete slab—the air flows through the furnace from top to bottom. The fan draws air in at the top. The air is forced through the heat exchanger and then into the ducts that are embedded in the concrete slab. Forced-air systems are controlled by a room thermostat. When heat is called for, the thermostat completes an electrical circuit to turn on the oil or gas burner.

An additional device is needed in hot air systems to control the blower. If the blower were to start immediately before the heat exchanger reached operating temperature, cool air would be blown into the living areas. A device called a fan-and-limit switch senses the temperature in the heat exchanger and turns on the blower only after the exchanger reaches a preset temperature. The fan-and-limit switch also turns off the burner when the temperature in the heat exchanger reaches the high limit. The switch allows the blower to continue operating as long as heat remains in the exchanger.

Maintenance and adjustment

The most common problem with forced hot-air systems is insufficient or uneven heat. In correcting this condition, see if air flow is blocked. If not, adjust flow controls to get the desired heat, as follows:

1. Remove and clean or replace the air filter at the furnace air inlet. A dirty filter restricts air flow and causes both a reduced air volume and slower flow.

2. Check for blockage in ducts. This can be caused by damage or by an accumulation of dirt and lint. Remove registers. Have someone hold a light at one register. Aim the light toward the next register on that duct line. At the next register, look back toward the light. This will show up significant blockage, even with a bend in the duct.

3. Damper function. Heat flow can be adjusted if the filter is clean and the ducts are clear. Dampers are metal vanes in the air ducts. A control handle on the outside of the duct allows you to adjust for more or less air through the duct. The angle of the control handle is the same as that for the vane. When the control handle is horizontal, the damper is fully open; when vertical, the duct is closed.

4. Adjusting dampers to suit your individual needs is a matter of trial and error. Two guidelines may be helpful. First, reducing air flow in one duct increases the air flow in another duct, if the same volume of air is coming into the system. Second, dampers are installed in ducts near the furnace or main plenum. Reducing the air flow in a duct reduces the heat coming from registers farthest from the furnace more than from those nearest.

Adjusting blower speed

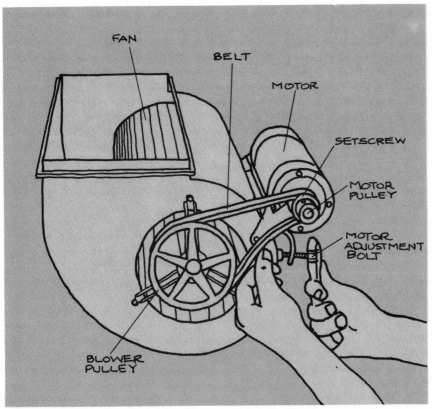

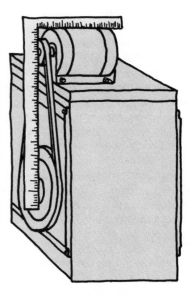

Belt tension. If blower speed is too low, air flow is reduced and rooms will not heat as fully or as rapidly as they should. If blower speed is too high, the blower will be noisy. The high speed will not improve heating.

Blowers are driven by electric motors. A small pulley is attached to the motor shaft and a larger pulley is on the fan shaft. The fan is driven by a belt between the pulleys. If the belt is too loose, it will slip and fan speed will be reduced. With the fan turned off, midway between the pulleys you should be able to depress the belt no more than ¾ inch to one inch. More slack than this means slippage is likely. Less slack usually means noise and rapid wear.

Belt tension is adjusted by turning an adjustment bolt located on the motor-mounting frame, which moves the motor toward or away from the fan.

Pulley alignment

For the least noise and bearing wear, the motor and fan pulley should be aligned. Use a straight-edge, T-square, or carpenter's level to check alignment. To adjust, loosen the set-screw on the inner section of the motor pulley. Move the pulley in or out as necessary. Tighten the set-screw.

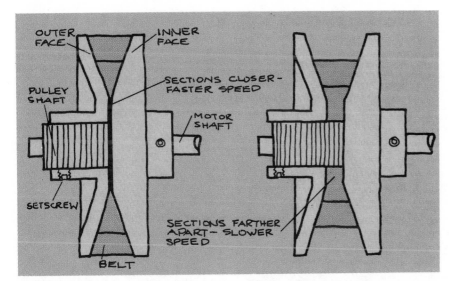

Blower speed. On some blower units, the motor pulley may be adjusted to change the fan speed. The pulley consists of two sections mounted on a threaded stud. Both sections have collars with setscrews. When the setscrew in the outer collar is loosened, the outer section can be turned while the inner section is held stationary. In this way, the space between the sections can be changed. When the sections are brought closer together, the belt rides higher on the pulley. This increases the speed of the fan. If the space between the sections is made larger, belt rides lower; speed is decreased.

Steam-heating systems

Steam-heating systems, once widely used, have largely been replaced in recent years by less costly hot-air or hot-water systems. However, steam heat is durable and efficient.

The system works by heating water in a boiler until steam forms. The steam, being lighter than air, rises naturally through the pipes to the radiators. Vents on the radiators allow air to escape as the steam rises. The steam gives up heat to the radiators. The radiators, in turn, heat the surrounding area. As the steam cools, it condenses back into water. The water flows back through the same pipes to the boiler where it is reheated, and the cycle is repeated.

The entire steam system—boiler, piping, and radiators—must be solidly constructed to withstand steam pressure and temperature changes. In addition, for maximum efficiency, steam pipes must be insulated to prevent excessive heat loss before the steam reaches the radiators.

To monitor and control the system, the steam boiler contains a water-level gauge and a pressure-relief valve. The water-level gauge is a glass tube containing water. The level in the tube represents the level in the boiler. When the water in the gauge is

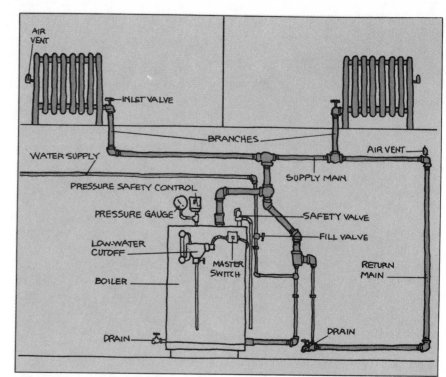

about midway between the top and bottom, the correct amount of water is in the boiler.

The pressure gauge registers the steam pressure within the boiler. When the system is operating properly, the gauge should indicate 10 to 12 psi (pounds per square inch). If the pressure exceeds a predetermined level, the relief valve opens to allow steam to escape. When the pressure falls to a safe level, the relief valve closes automatically. Many steam boilers also contain a float valve to cut off the system if the water level in the boiler is too low.

Radiators

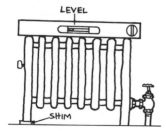

Radiators can be checked with a carpenter's level. The radiator should slope toward the shutoff valve and pipe end. It can be shimmed with pieces of wood or metal to get the proper slope. Also, make sure the shutoff valve is either fully open or fully closed.

Hammering can also be caused by sagging pipes. The noise will localize the trouble to some extent. Check the piping in the vicinity of the noise. Pipes should slope toward the boiler. Sagging can generally be corrected by adding additional pipe-strap hangers.

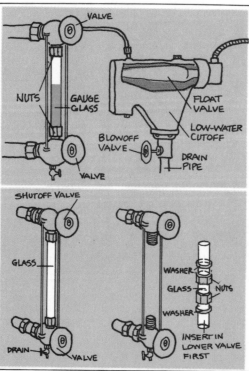

Routine maintenance

At least once a week, check the water-level gauge. If the water is below the midpoint of the tube, open the boiler-inlet valve and fill to the proper level. While some boilers have an automatic fill valve, a weekly check is still advisable to guard against failure of the automatic valve. If, at any time, no water is visible in the gauge, turn off the heat producer *immediately*. Allow the boiler to cool before adding water.

After a time, the water gauge may become so dirty that it is difficult to read. When this happens, turn off the valves at the top and bottom of the gauge and loosen the collar nuts. You can then lift the glass tube out. Use a bottle brush to clean sediment out of the tube. Replace the tube, tighten the collar nuts, and open the valves.

Sediment will also collect in the float valve, which can be cleaned by flushing. Open the blow-off valve and allow water to flow out until no sediment is visible.

The most common problem with steam systems is noise (hammering). The noise is usually caused by poor drainage which allows water to collect in radiators or pipes.

Fireplaces

In modern homes, fireplaces are generally more decorative than functional. However, as fuel costs become an increasingly greater economic burden, all forms of auxiliary heating must be considered.

Most building codes require that masonry fireplaces be completely self-supporting. The fireplace must have its own masonry footing. This means that adding a fireplace to a home that does not have one represents a major expenditure.

If a fireplace is to be more than decorative, it must be well designed. There is a definite relationship between the front opening and the flue opening. The former should be about ten times larger than the latter. If the cross-sectional area of the flue opening is 100 square inches (10 by 10 inches, for example), the front opening should be approximately 1000 square inches and should be wider than it is high (10 inches wide by 25 inches high, for example).

For safety and good operation, fireplaces should have a damper and a smoke shelf. When the fireplace is in use, the damper can be adjusted to control the updraft and so control fire. When the fireplace is not in use, the damper should be fully closed to prevent loss of room heat through the flue. The smoke shelf is a projection running horizontally across the smoke chamber. It deflects downdrafts to prevent smoke and sparks from being blown into the room.

Cleaning chimneys. The first step in chimney cleaning is to seal the fireplace opening with paper and tape to prevent dirt from getting into the room. Leave the damper open. Fill a burlap bag with old rags and a couple of bricks so that it blocks the chimney opening. Tie a rope on the bag and lower it down the chimney from the roof. Pull the bag up and lower it again several times to loosen soot and dirt on the sides of the flue.

Allow time for dust and dirt to settle, then remove the paper from the opening. Brush dirt and soot off the smoke shelf and damper. Brush all dirt into the ash pit opening. Empty the ash pit.

Soot and smoke stains around the fireplace opening can generally be removed with a strong solution of detergent and hot water.

Tip on lighting a fire. In cold weather, the flue is filled with heavy, cold air. Unless quickly heated, this cold air prevents a natural updraft from starting and causes the fire to die out.

A large, hot, initial flame will heat enough air to push out the cold-air column and get a natural draft going. Use plenty of light kindling or several wads of newspaper to get a large, hot flame going quickly.

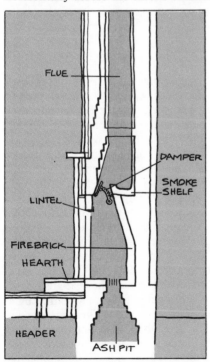

A ground-floor fireplace should have a damper and a smoke shelf for best operation. An ash pit, with a clean-out in the basement, is a great convenience but not essential.

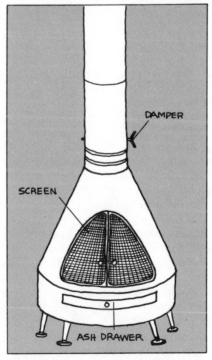

Freestanding fireplaces are essentially small, metal stoves. They are a less costly substitute for masonry construction and much easier to install. They are adequate for supplementary heat, hence suitable for vacation homes.

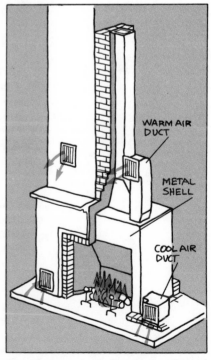

Fireplaces can be built around preformed double-walled sheet-metal forms which establish proper proportions for the fireplace and improve heating efficiency by providing for air flow through the double-walled area.

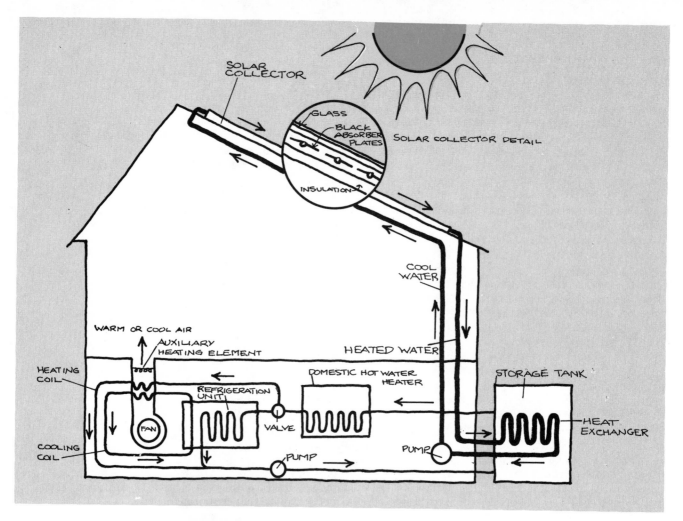

SOLAR COLLECTOR

GLASS

BLACK ABSORBER PLATES

SOLAR COLLECTOR DETAIL

INSULATION

COOL WATER

HEATED WATER

WARM OR COOL AIR

AUXILIARY HEATING ELEMENT

HEATING COIL

REFRIGERATION UNIT

FAN

VALVE

DOMESTIC HOT WATER HEATER

STORAGE TANK

HEAT EXCHANGER

COOLING COIL

PUMP

PUMP

Solar heating

Using solar energy for everyday heating has been talked of for many years. It is now—at least partially—a reality.

More than 200 companies are currently marketing solar-heating systems of various capacities, starting with those designed only to heat some of the water required for domestic use. Cost savings from solar heating vary according to geographical location. The more days of sunshine you can expect in a year, the more effective your solar-heating unit will be. Many solar-heating units are sold in kit form for installation by the home owner. The installation is fairly easy, and the savings are substantial.

The most widely used solar water-heating system operates as a simple preheating unit. A liquid is pumped to the roof, heated by the sun, and returned to a heat exchanger. In the heat exchanger, the heated liquid transfers heat to the domestic water supply. Water is then piped to a conventional water heater. The water heater raises the temperature of the water as necessary and stores it for use as needed.

The cost saving results from the preheating of the water before it reaches the water heater. The water heater has to raise the temperature of the water only a few degrees when the solar unit is working at peak efficiency. The conventional water heater also maintains the water temperature during evening hours or periods of little sun.

The unique element in the solar-heating system is the collector panel installed on the roof. A typical collector panel measures about eleven feet long by three feet wide. The collector panel consists of a heat-absorbing surface covering a continuous length of coiled tubing. The heat-absorbing surface is protected from the weather by a curved plastic shield. The shield also creates a "greenhouse" effect that retains heat in the collector. Each collector panel weighs about 75 pounds. The number of collectors used in a system varies according to the space available and the heating capacity desired. Two collectors of the size indicated above are recommended for an average house.

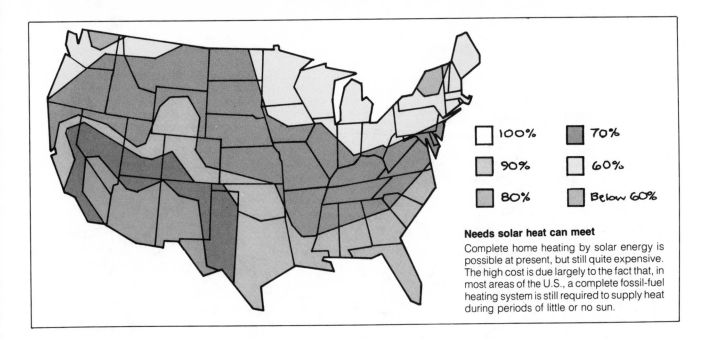

100%   70%

90%   60%

80%   Below 60%

Needs solar heat can meet

Complete home heating by solar energy is possible at present, but still quite expensive. The high cost is due largely to the fact that, in most areas of the U.S., a complete fossil-fuel heating system is still required to supply heat during periods of little or no sun.

The collectors should face south and should be mounted at an angle of 30 to 50 degrees above horizontal. If a flat roof is used or a roof with a shallow pitch, the collectors can be mounted on wooden frames to get the best angle. It is not essential that the collectors face directly south. However, deviations of more than 30 degrees from due south will cause a significant reduction in efficiency.

In addition to the two collector panels, a typical solar water-heating kit includes a storage tank with heat exchanger, circulating pump, thermostatic control, expansion tank, check valve, and antifreeze solution. The antifreeze circulates in the collector and heat-exchanger line. The use of antifreeze solution protects the system against unseasonable temperature drops. Kits do not normally include the piping to run from the collectors to the heat exchanger, or lumber for mounting the collectors on frames attached to the roof.

Solar-heating units designed to heat swimming-pool water are also available. These units are similar to domestic water-heating units. The principal difference is that swimming-pool water flows through the collectors and is returned to the pool. Heat exchangers and storage tanks are not required. However, all collector tubing and system piping must be fabricated of material that can withstand the corrosive effects of chlorinated water. Collectors for domestic hot water and swimming-pool use cannot be interchanged.

Schematic of typical water-heater installation for solar collector

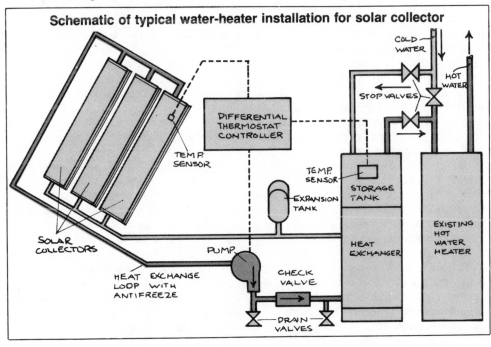

Heat
pumps

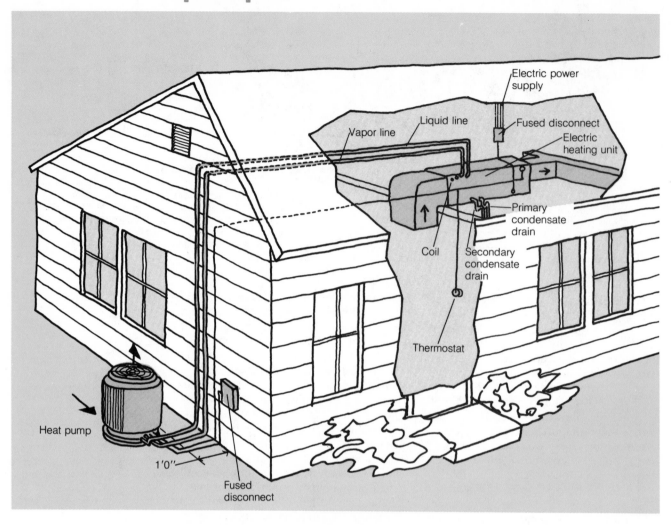

Labels in diagram: Electric power supply, Vapor line, Liquid line, Fused disconnect, Electric heating unit, Primary condensate drain, Coil, Secondary condensate drain, Thermostat, Heat pump, 1'0", Fused disconnect

Heat from the outside air

The drawing above shows typical piping and wiring for a heat-pump system installed with a supplementary electric heating system. Most heat pumps of this type have the coil unit inside and the heat exchanger outside the house. Some pumps, used extensively in mobil homes, have both contained in one unit.

Heat pumps, originally developed from air-conditioning technology, were first used for cooling air inside the home. They are now used for heating as well, since they can automatically change direction. During hot weather they can extract heat from the inside air and pump it outside; and in cold weather, take the warmth from the sun in the outside air and pump it into the house. Some heat pumps are designed to exchange heat with natural bodies of water.

Heat pumps differ from conventional heating systems because they use existing heat; moving some of the natural warmth of the outside air into the house. More conventional systems produce their own heat by burning oil or gas, or by using electricity to heat wires.

Although there is always *some* natural heat from the sun in the outside air most heat pumps operate efficiently (that is, produce more heat energy than they use up electrical energy to run) only when the

outside temperature is over 30 degrees Fahrenheit. For this reason, heat pumps are used in tandem with other home heating systems in most parts of the country.

Heat pumps are considerably more expensive to buy and install than traditional room air conditioners. Like central air conditioning, they are best installed as part of the basic temperature control system when the house is built. Their plumbing, electrical, carpentry and duct systems make them too complex for do-it-yourself homeowners to install. The components of a representative heat-pump system, coupled with an electrical-heating system, are shown in the diagram at the top of this page. To determine the practicality of using a heat pump, you should balance the purchase prices, installation costs and operational expenses of the heat pump and a supplementary heating system against the cost of purchasing, installing and operating alternative heating and cooling systems.

When are heat pumps most efficient?

The map below shows the approximate percentage of time (expressed in decimal portions of a year) that a heat pump, piggy-backed on a conventional heating system, will be in operation to heat or cool your home to keep it at a comfortable temperature. The percentage of time the heat pump is in operation depends on the percentage of time the outdoor temperature is above 30 degrees Fahrenheit. When the temperature drops below that, the heat pump shuts off automatically and signals the conventional heating system to begin normal operation.

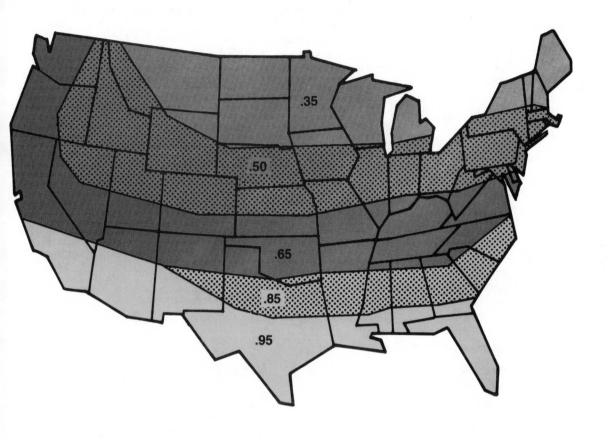

How a heat pump works

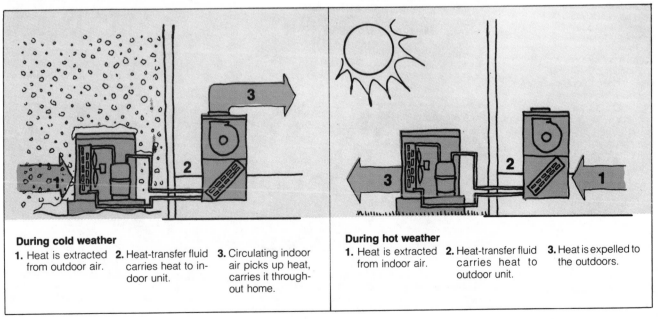

During cold weather

1. Heat is extracted from outdoor air.
2. Heat-transfer fluid carries heat to indoor unit.
3. Circulating indoor air picks up heat, carries it throughout home.

During hot weather

1. Heat is extracted from indoor air.
2. Heat-transfer fluid carries heat to outdoor unit.
3. Heat is expelled to the outdoors.

10.PROJECTS

Cold-weather house shutdown

What it takes

Approximate time: Complete house shutdown for a wintertime absence may take about two hours.

Tools and materials: You'll need a pair of pliers, some trap antifreeze (see text), a length of garden hose, and perhaps pipe tools.

Planning hints: Be sure that you are through using water before you start the shutdown. Posting a checklist of what was done may be a good idea, so that you can quickly get the house reopened when you return.

Getting out from under
Let me clue you in on a fast way to clear your house water pipes of water. A plumber who owns a vacation cabin in Michigan showed it to me. After the water heater has been drained in the normal way and everything else is empty, there may be water left in some of the low spots in horizontal mains. To get it out fast, just stick the end of a running air-compressor hose into an opened outdoor hose faucet. The air pressure will shoot the water out wherever there is an opening. When only air comes out, you're done. This method sure beats crawling under the house to drain your pipes. Neat trick, I've found!

Practical Pete

The checklist at right gives step-by-step procedures for closing your house during a winter absence. Obviously, all fixture traps must contain some liquid other than water to keep them from venting sewer gases into the house while you're away, and the liquid must not evaporate in the time you're gone. Consider the following options:

Remove all trap water by draining or blowing out sink and lavatory traps. Refill all with kerosene (hard on rubber trap gaskets) or glycerine (more costly). Here's an alternative: fill traps with a mixture of a little kerosene and a lot of denatured alcohol. The kerosene will keep the alcohol from evaporating. Another alternative is to leave water in the traps and pour a cupful of auto antifreeze in each. Also, pour at least one quart in each toilet and basement drain. During reopening, be sure to fill the water-heater tank and hydronic heating-system boiler before you fire them up again.

Shutdown checklist

1. Turn off house water supply at underground street valve.
2. Open all faucets and outdoor hose spigots to drain.
3. Turn off the fuel to the water heater, connect a garden hose to its drain and drain the tank.
4. Flush toilet and sponge out remaining water from tank.
5. After all draining ceases, open stop-and-waste valve(s) in crawl space or basement.
6. Drain or blow water out of fixture traps, including toilet.
7. If there are any low spots in horizontal piping, take joints apart and drain by hand (or see Practical Pete's idea at left).
8. Drain hydronic heating system, including boiler. Turn off fuel first. Be sure that the boiler's water-supply valve is open to drain its piping. Open radiator air valves.
9. Drain appliances: washer, dishwasher, furnace humidifier.

Preparing a toilet

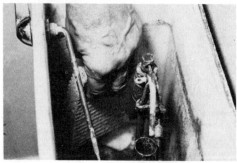

1. Don't leave any water in the toilet tank that might cause it to freeze and crack. Flushing will remove most water. Then sop out the rest with sponge.

2. Pour permanent-type auto antifreeze coolant into the toilet bowl to protect it. One-third gallon—a 33% mixture—should protect the bowl down to about zero degrees Fahrenheit.

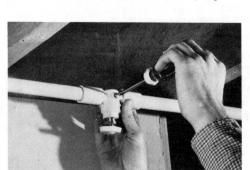

3. Drain all house piping in crawl space, basement, and attic. Low point of water-supply piping system should have a stop-and-waste valve where it can be drained. This one contains a drain screw.

4. Finally, pour about 4 ounces of auto antifreeze coolant into each fixture trap. Remember that a 1:2 antifreeze-water mixture protects to zero degrees Fahrenheit; a 1:1 mixture protects to 34 below zero.

Building a dry well

A dry well is a rock-filled underground pit into which non-effluent surface water can be drained. It works something like a seepage field. Water filters through the well's porous fill, then eventually soaks into the surrounding soil.

Although other applications are practical, the most common usage for dry wells is the disposal of roof runoff via the gutter and downspout system. If, for aesthetic reasons, you don't want downspouts to drain directly onto your yard, or if rainfall in your area can be extremely heavy and erosion becomes a problem, then a dry well may be the answer. A dry well also may be used to dispose of water from a floor drain, or backwash/recharge from a water softener.

Dry wells can be simple or complex. The simpler ones involve little more than a hole dug into the ground, then filled with rock, gravel, or old bricks and concrete blocks. Almost anything that will not absorb water, yet will leave air pockets through which water can filter, will work as dry-well fill. Fancier wells can be fashioned by chiseling holes through a steel drum, then filling the drum with rock or masonry rubble.

Where the volume of water is so great that a single dry well just won't handle it, a whole series of wells is possible. Provide an outlet near the top of one well and, when the level in it reaches that outlet, water will flow out into another dry well. A series of wells has the effect of spreading the water absorption over a large area and minimizes the possibility of any water resurfacing.

Dig a hole in the ground to form as large a

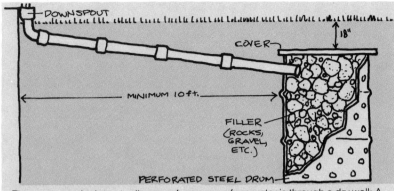

The most practical way to dispose of excess surface water is through a dry well: A steel drum or just a rubble-filled hole in the ground. Use a solid cover to force water to percolate downward and outward, not upward.

dry well as you need. Of course, if you're using a steel drum, the hole needs to be only large enough for it. Regardless of the type of dry well you install, it should be no less than 10 feet from your house foundation wall. This prevents seepage into your basement. And keep the top of the well at least 18 inches below grade.

Downspouts can be connected directly to the dry-well inlet, using 4-inch sewer pipe for underground portions. (See page 439 for how to work with various types of sewer pipe.) Be sure that the water dumps into the top part of the well, so that it can filter downward through the fill. Inlets should slope about ¼ inch per foot away from the bottom of the downspout, and should be placed below frostline if you want them to work year-round. Where the frostline is deep, a dry well may have to be installed more than 18 inches below grade.

What it takes

Approximate time: Digging for the dry well and digging a trench for its inlet take the most time and are the most work. From there, you're limited only by the time it takes to chunk in the fill, make the necessary pipe connections, and backfill with soil.

Tools and materials: No huge collection of tools is needed for this job. You'll need a sharp-bladed shovel, of course. Breaking up excessively large rocks or blocks for the fill material may be done with a sledge hammer, but be sure to wear eye protection. The use of PVC drain pipes is recommended, and they require PVC solvent-welding cement and an applicator brush. Other drain pipes, using a different connection method, may require other special jointing methods (see page 435).

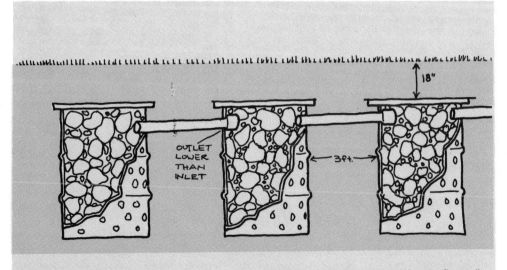

Hooked in tandem, a series of dry wells can dispose of large amounts of water. What the first well can't handle passes to the next, and so on until all the water is absorbed. Outlets should be lower than inlets to prevent back-up.

A garden pool and waterfall

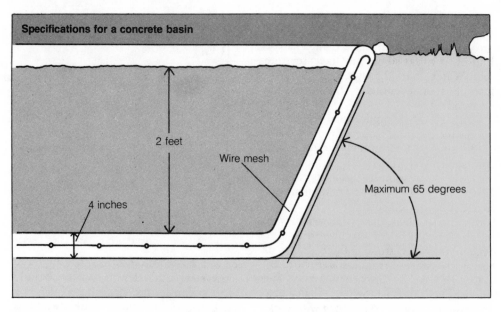

Specifications for a concrete basin

2 feet

Wire mesh

Maximum 65 degrees

4 inches

What it takes

Approximate time: One day, but add extra time for planting.

Tools and materials: Shovel, plastic liner or materials for concrete (see page 538), level, pump with tubing, gravel (sand or peat moss), driftwood, rocks, electrical wiring.

Building your own backyard Shangri-La, including a pool and waterfall, is a simple and satisfying project. The pool can be either a concrete basin or a plastic-lined pit.

Concrete pool. Pouring concrete to form a bowl is easier than pouring it for a slab (see page 542), and you can create all kinds of decorative effects out of it, such as a wading pool sunk in your lawn or garden, or a pool for fish or with statuary; add a recirculating pump and you can have a waterfall.

Such pools can be built without wood forms. In general, the concrete can be poured right onto tamped earth and you will not need a gravel bed. The sides and base need only be 4 inches thick because the bowl will not bear a great deal of weight.

However, because the concrete is poured without forms, the sides of the hole should slope at an angle of not more than 65 degrees; if they are steeper the concrete will run before it has a chance to set. Wire mesh will be needed to reinforce the concrete. If your pond is for fish, you'll also need to incorporate a runoff channel in the rim so that excess water can flow out.

Plastic-lined pool. This is a great deal simpler and less costly to install. It can be removed with a minimum of effort should you wish to change your landscaping. You can purchase the plastic liner with a pump (if waterfall is desired), or separately.

The first step is to pick your location. Use a shovel to outline the pool area, which can be any shape from square, to kidney, to free form. Then dig the hole for the pool. If the pool is to be used for plants, it must be at least 2 feet deep. If you plan also to build a waterfall, then pile the excavated dirt where the waterfall will eventually be. Level the bottom of the pool, making sure it is free of sharp rocks, roots, and any other encumbrances. Spread a thin layer of sand, fine gravel, or peat moss, sufficient to cover well, over the bottom of the pool excavation. Cover the entire pool and waterfall area with the plastic liner. Secure it where necessary with rock. If you plan to introduce fish to the pool, make sure that the plastic is of a kind that won't harm them.

Installing the pump. In most cases, simply place the pump on the bottom of the pool and run a length of plastic tubing (which comes with it) up to the top of the waterfall. Cover any exposed tubing with dirt.

The waterfall. Make an uneven stairway out of the dirt you dug from the pool. Cover with the plastic liner. Then place flat rocks as steps so that the water can cascade down. Decorate the area of both waterfall and pool with driftwood, rocks, moss, and other natural materials. Cut slits in the plastic liner to accommodate poolside plants such as ground cover and cattails. Fill the pool with water and connect the pump to an electrical outlet.

Wiring for the pool. Check local codes for wiring regulations regarding pools. All electrical outlets must be grounded, and they must be weatherproof. Install a ground fault interrupter in the line as an extra precaution against shocks. Wiring of types USE or UF are best, and either of these can be run underground without enclosing them in conduit. Either type should be buried 18 inches deep as protection against accidental breakage or someone severing them with a gardening tool.

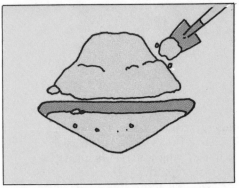

1. With a sharp instrument, or the blade of a shovel, outline on the ground the area of your pool. Let it take any shape you want.

2. Dig the hole. Pile the dirt at one end of the pool, where it will eventually be formed in shelves for a series of falls. It's a good idea to first pour a slab of concrete for the dirt to rest on.

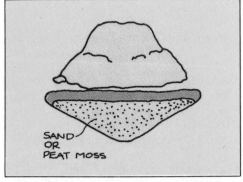

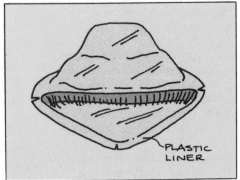

3. Make certain that the bottom of the pool is level and free of sharp rocks and other debris. It's best to spread a thin layer of sand or peat moss over the bottom—enough to cover.

4. Cover the whole pool and falls area with a plastic liner. Excess liner may be trimmed back.

Wiring

Wiring is essential for operation of your pool and waterfall, and for lights. Either bury the electric cable, or, if this is not possible, you can fasten it with cable straps to the underside of a 1x4-inch redwood board, or lay metal over it. This will protect it from garden tools.

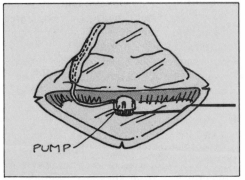

5. Install the pump in the bottom of the pool, and run the tubing up to the top of the waterfall structure. You may cover the tubing with sand so it won't show.

6. Line the edges of the plastic liner with stone, rock, and driftwood, which will help keep the liner in place and add to its attractiveness.

7. Place flat rocks as steps in the dirt you have piled for the waterfall. Wash the rocks so that muddy water won't get into your pool.

8. Add more rocks, driftwood, and plants around the pool and waterfall to finish the natural setting.

Glossary

Air chamber. Prevents water-hammer in a supply system by providing an air cushion for fast-flowing water to bounce off when flow is stopped.

Appliance. General term applied to any water-using device that is somewhat mechanical in nature.

Aquastat. Device in a hot-water heating system that turns the heat producer on and off to maintain circulating water at a preset temperature.

Bleeding. As applied to heating systems, refers to opening small valves on convectors or radiators to release air trapped in water or steam lines.

Branch drain. Extends from fixtures and appliances to the main building drain.

Check-valve. A valve that allows fluid or gas to flow in one direction only.

Circulator. A pump driven by an electric motor. In forced-hot-water heating systems, the circulator pumps water from the boiler to the radiators.

Cold-water main. Brings cold water to the vicinity of the fixtures and appliances using it.

Collector. A roof-mounted device in solar heating systems. The collector traps heat from the sun and transfers it to a circulating liquid.

Condensation. Water released by warm air when it comes in contact with a cooler surface.

Conduction. Method of heat transfer in which heat moves through solid material toward cooler air or liquid.

Convection. Heat movement characterized by rising warm air and falling cold air.

Cross-connection. A link between the potable water system and a nonpotable, possibly contaminated, water source.

Damper. Device for controlling the flow of air through a duct or flue.

Dielectric coupling. Used to connect pipes of unlike metal types, such as copper to galvanized steel. Prevents electrolytic corrosion between the two metals.

Draft control. A flapper vane that controls air flow in an oil-burner stack.

Drain tailpiece. Section of drain pipe extending below a fixture. Connects to the fixture at the top and the fixture trap at the bottom.

Drain-waste-vent system. The final portion of a plumbing system. Collects wastes, routes them to the sewer, and vents gases to the outside. Often abbreviated "DWV."

Effluent. As applied to plumbing, this is the liquid waste material discharged into sewer system.

Expansion tank. A tank in a closed-loop hot-water system that allows for the expansion of water when heated.

Fan-and-limit switch. A device that controls blower operation in a hot-air system.

Faucet tailpiece. Lengths of pipe extending below a faucet used to connect it to the water-supply system.

Fixture. General term applied to water-using devices such as sinks, lavatories, and toilets.

Fixture-shutoff valve. Allows selective shutoff of individual fixtures and appliances without affecting the rest of the water-supply system.

Hammering. Characteristic noise in water and steam systems caused by rising water or steam meeting cool air or water trapped in pipes or radiators.

Heat control. That portion of a heating system that controls the heat producer to maintain a desired temperature. Includes thermostats and aquastats.

Heat distributor. The air, water, or steam that carries heat from the heat exchanger to the living areas of the home.

Heat exchanger. Part of the heating system where heat from the heat producer is transferred to air, water, or steam.

Heat producer. The device that consumes fuel (oil, gas, coal, wood) to produce heat.

Hot-water main. Begins at the water heater and carries hot water to the vicinity of the fixtures and appliances.

Humidifier. A device for adding moisture to the air.

Humidity. The moisture content of air. The warmer the air, the more moisture it can hold.

Hydronic. Applied to any heating system using water as a heat distributor. Frequently used to describe electric hot-water systems.

House sewer. Connects with the main building drain to carry wastes to a municipal sewer or private septic system.

Leach field. See *seepage field*.

Local code. Set of construction regulations administered by a local government agency.

Main building drain. Carries house wastes outside the house foundation, where it connects to the house sewer.

Main shutoff valve. Valve that cuts off the entire house water supply.

Main stack. One or more vent stacks that can serve more than one fixture or appliance, including a toilet.

National plumbing code. Nationally recognized code that forms the basis for many local plumbing codes.

P-trap. A type of fixture trap designed for a waste pipe located in the wall.

Pilot jet. Small flame in a gas furnace (or gas range) that ignites the main burner.

Plenum. A large air chamber to which individual air ducts are connected in hot-air heating systems.

Plumbing. The pipes, fixtures, and appliances comprising a building's water-supply and drain-waste-vent systems.

Radiation. The direct transfer of heat from a warm object to a cooler one.

Revent. A pipe installed to carry gases only. It connects to a main vent above waste-water lines.

Riser tube. Small, flexible piping that eases the connection between the water-supply system and a water-using device. Eliminates the need to line up a faucet tailpiece exactly with its water-supply pipe.

S-trap. A type of fixture trap designed for a waste pipe located beneath the floor.

Secondary stack. A vent stack, usually of smaller diameter than a main stack, that serves fixtures other than toilets.

Seepage field. An area where liquid effluent from a septic tank is allowed to percolate into the soil.

Septic tank. A tank, often concrete, that uses organic action to break down wastes. Called for where a public sewer system is not available.

Service entrance. Supply pipe bringing water into a building. Usually located with water meter and main shutoff valve.

Sewage-treatment plant. A more effective private or public sewage-disposal system than a septic tank.

Soil stack. Another name for a main stack serving a toilet.

Stack relay. A safety device used on oil burners to turn off the flow of oil if ignition does not occur.

Stop-and-drain valve. Allows water to be drained from the water-supply system to prevent freeze-ups. Also called "stop-and-waste."

Temperature-and-pressure-relief valve. The safety valve on top of a water heater that bleeds off potentially explosive temperatures and pressures in case of runaway heater operation. Abbreviated to "T&P valve."

Thermocouple. A device that generates an electric current when heated.

Thermostat. A device that controls heating to maintain a nearly constant temperature.

Trap. The P- or S-shaped device in a fixture drain that holds a small amount of drain water, preventing the entry of sewer gases and vermin into the building.

Vapor barrier. A reflective surface on insulation which faces the warmer (inside) air. The barrier prevents condensation from occurring inside building walls.

Vent stack. Piping that reaches up through the roof of a building to vent sewer gases to the outside. Can be either a main stack or a secondary stack.

Water-supply system. The first part of a plumbing system. Brings both hot and cold water into the house and distributes it to the fixtures and appliances.

Well. An underground, private water source that usually uses a pump to extract water for use.

Wet vent. A pipe that serves as both a drain and a vent. Practical when the distance between the trap and vent is short and local codes permit.

Zoned heating. Heating systems (usually hot water) having two (or more) independent circulating systems.

EXTERIOR MAINTENANCE & IMPROVEMENTS

Section Six

THE PROUD HOUSE	484	Top-to-bottom inspection	485		

THE TOOLS	486	Heavy maintenance tools	486	Ladder use and safety	487
Light maintenance tools	486	Specialized tools	486		

ROOF REPAIRS	488	Preventing ice dams	496	Digging a dry well	504
Finding leaks	488	Gable vents	497	Reshingling a roof	505
Fixing leaks in asphalt shingles	489	Roof vents	497	When, how to remove shingles	505
Fixing leaks in wood shingles	490	Gutters and downspouts	498	Calculating your shingle needs	506
Fixing leaks in slate shingles	490	General maintenance	498	Selecting shingles	506
Fixing leaks in flat roofs	491	Fall/spring maintenance	498	Preparing old surfaces	507
Repairing flashing	492	Maintaining gutters	499	Applying shingles	508
Preventing leaks around chimney	492	Maintaining downspouts	500	Shingling hips and ridges	508
Preventing leaks around vents	492	Repairing gutters, downspouts	501	Flashing valleys	509
Replacing flashing	493	New gutters and downspouts	502	Flashing and shingling dormers	509
Valley flashing	494	Pitching gutters	503	Flashing a vertical wall	509
Chimney repairs	495	Creating underground drainage	504		

SIDING	510	Patching vertical siding	513	Caulking your house	516
Maintaining wood siding	510	Repairing aluminum	513	Types of caulking and uses	516
Repairing wood siding	511	Repairing stucco	514	Caulking roundup	516
Replacing wood siding	512	Replacing asbestos siding	515	How to caulk	516
Patching clapboard	512	Replacing vinyl siding	515		

EXTERIOR PAINTING	518	Removing paint	521	Estimating paint needs	524
Sequence to follow when painting	518	Stripping paint	522	Buying brushes	525
Avoiding common paint problems	519	Knots and resins	522	Caring for brushes	525
Preparing the surfaces	520	Preparing metal surfaces	522	Applying paint	526
Washing a house	520	Selecting and buying paint	523	Mixing paint	526
Identifying and preventing mildew	520	What paint to use and where	523	Scaffolding	526
Preparing wood surfaces	521	Choosing the colors	524	Practical points and procedures	527

INSULATION	528	Checking your home for insulation	529	Ventilation	533
The R system	528	Adding insulation	530	Point of diminishing returns	533
R values of insulation types	528	R values for unfinished attic floors	530		
Types of insulation	529	In addition to insulation	532		

FOUNDATIONS & MASONRY	534	You-haul	538	Concrete block	546
Treating concrete cracks	534	Mix-it-yourself	538	Building with brick	550
Waterproofing	535	The materials	539	How to estimate materials	550
Splash blocks	535	Mixing	539	Laying a brick patio in sand	551
Drainage	536	Concrete formulas	539	How to lay brick	551
Drains	536	The concrete form	540	Building a stone retaining wall	552
Termite protection	537	Reinforcing the pour	540	How to buy stones	552
Where and what to look for	537	Choosing and using steel mesh	541	Construction techniques	552
Preventive measures	537	Using reinforcing rod	541	A country dry wall	554
Putting down a termite barrier	537	Pouring small slabs	542	A flagstone walk or patio	556
Concrete	538	Pouring concrete steps	543	Patching asphalt	557
Transit-mix	538	Step-by-step steps	544	Filling holes	557

FENCES	558	Old-fashioned		Hanging a gate	561
Setting posts	559	post-and-rail fence	560		

IMPROVEMENTS	562	Structural elements	562	Laying the decking	565
Decks	562	Laying out the deck	564	Special situations	565

1.THE PROUD HOUSE

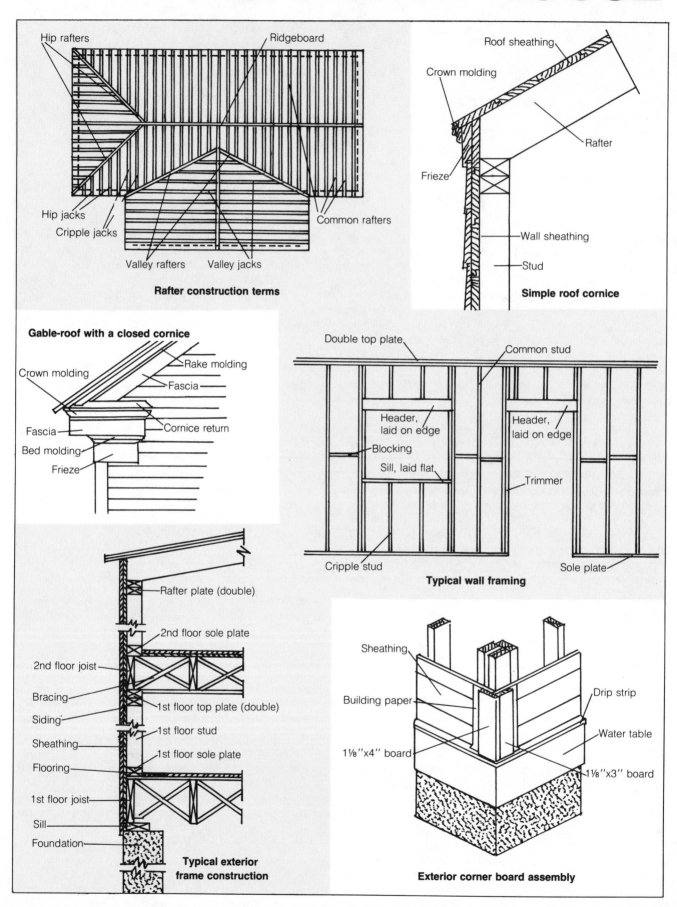

Rafter construction terms

Hip rafters
Ridgeboard
Hip jacks
Cripple jacks
Valley rafters
Valley jacks
Common rafters

Simple roof cornice

Roof sheathing
Crown molding
Rafter
Frieze
Wall sheathing
Stud

Gable-roof with a closed cornice

Crown molding
Rake molding
Fascia
Fascia
Cornice return
Bed molding
Frieze

Typical wall framing

Double top plate
Common stud
Header, laid on edge
Header, laid on edge
Blocking
Sill, laid flat
Trimmer
Cripple stud
Sole plate

Typical exterior frame construction

Rafter plate (double)
2nd floor sole plate
2nd floor joist
Bracing
1st floor top plate (double)
Siding
1st floor stud
Sheathing
1st floor sole plate
Flooring
1st floor joist
Sill
Foundation

Exterior corner board assembly

Sheathing
Building paper
Drip strip
Water table
1⅛″x4″ board
1⅛″x3″ board

Preventive maintenance

The checklist below encompasses inspections you need to complete a top-to-bottom examination of your home's exterior. In addition to helping you to spot problems, present or potential, the chart refers you to directions you can follow to remove the cause.

As you will see, some of the inspections should be made at a stated frequency; others can be made only when nature cooperates, for example, by raining. To insure that you make the periodic inspections, pencil them in on your calendar or incorporate them in a list of things you want to do each fall and spring.

You may be able to make additional use of this checklist: Take the book along when you are going to look at a house you might buy. By inspecting it systematically, you might detect defects you otherwise could have missed. The list also suggests some questions to ask the present owner.

Top-to-bottom inspection

Chimney
Install chimney cover to keep out birds and rain. (Page 495)
Inspect concrete cap for cracks. Patch if necessary. (Page 495)
Inspect joints for missing or crumbling mortar, and loose bricks. Tuck-point. (Page 495)
Inspect flashing for cracks or gaps where it has pulled away from mortar. (Page 493)
Clean every three or four years—every year if you have a fireplace or wood-burning stove. (Page 495)

Roof
Check attic and attic crawl space during rain for signs of leaks. (Page 488)
Check for loose or broken shingles. Replace. (Page 489)
Observe asphalt shingles in high wind to see if tabs are blowing up. Cement down. This prevents lost shingles. (Page 489)
Check attic vents and repair any holes in the screening. (Page 497)
Inspect flashing in valleys and around dormers for holes and tears. Patch. (Page 494)
After snow, look for fast-melting areas, revealing excessive heat loss. Add insulation. (Page 528)
When temperatures just below freezing follow heavy snow, look for ice dams on uninsulated overhang. If observed, correct by melting or removing causes. (Page 496)

Gutters
Inspect during rain for water pouring over sides. Correct. (Page 499)
Inspect after rain for pools of water. Correct. (Page 499)
Look for damp spots on the ground below or for erosion of top soil. Correct. (Page 500)
Check for blistered paint. Treat and repaint. (Page 499)
Every fall and spring remove leaves, twigs, balls and other obstructions. (Page 499)

Downspouts
Observe during heavy rain for water pouring out at connection with gutter and between joints of downspouts. Correct. (Page 500)
Observe movement of water to make sure it is not flowing into basement or washing away soil. Correct. (Page 500)
Make sure metal cage covers top and is not clogged. (Page 500)

Walls and siding
Test to determine need for repainting. Sides exposed to sun go first. (Page 510)
Probe for rotten wood. (Page 510)
Look for blistered or peeling paint, revealing that moisture is getting into wood. (Page 510)
Inspect bricks for white, dusty discoloration, revealing moisture inside wall.
Remove sources of moisture causing rot or discoloration. (Page 510)
Look for mildew. Remove and prevent. Shady sides are susceptible. (Page 520)
Probe for shriveled or brittle caulking in seams around windows, doors, air conditioners, and other openings. Recaulk. (Page 516)
Inspect joints in brick wall for missing or crumbling mortar. Tuck-point. (Page 550)
Inspect stucco for holes and hairline cracks. Patch. (Page 514)
Look for strips of siding that have pulled loose, shingles that have curled up at edges or slipped out of place. Correct. (Page 514)
Cut shrubs back 18 inches from wall and pull down ivy, wisteria, and other creeping vines. In northern climes shut off and drain outside faucets each fall or install nonfreeze type.

Windows
Replace missing or peeling putty.
Replace cracked glass.
Oil hinges and crank handles of casement windows annually.

Storm windows
Make sure vents in frame carry off condensed water that collects on sill. (Page 532)

Basement windows
Check areaway during or right after rain to see if water has collected. Remove leaves and other debris in areaway and/or drain.

Doors, locks, and hinges
Inspect sticking doors for sources of moisture causing expansion. Correct.
Adjust threshold weather strip.
Inspect top and bottom surfaces to see if they are protected from moisture.
Tighten drip cap.
Look for glued joints that have opened up.
Clean channels of sliding doors with steel wool.
Lubricate locks.
Lubricate pins and tighten hinge screws.
Lubricate hinges, rollers, and tracks on garage doors.

Porches, decks, and stoops
Inspect undersides for signs of wood rot, termites, and carpenter ants. (Page 562)
Check paint to make sure it's in good condition. (Page 562)
Make sure cracks between boards are filled. (Page 562)
Install drains in floors where water can collect.

Driveways and walks
Inspect concrete for cracks.
Patch cracks in concrete. (Page 538)
Inspect concrete for rough surfaces caused by chemical ice melters. Smooth. (Page 538)
Reseal blacktop every other year. (Page 556)
Inspect blacktop for holes and cracks. Patch. (Page 556)

Grounds
Inspect fences for needed repair and repainting after the shrubs have died back each fall. (Page 558)
Check galvanized steel fencing for rust. (Page 558)
Inspect trees to make sure no limbs touch house or overhang power lines.

Termite detection/prevention
Look under porches, wood steps, and near crawl spaces for mud tunnels. (Page 536)
Check plumbing access hole on concrete-slab houses. (Page 536)
Remove any accumulations of wood near the house. (Page 536)

Septic tank
Make sure downspouts do not run into septic tank system.
Remove shrubs or trees near tank or in drainage field.
Have tank inspected annually and cleaned every two or three years.
Take steps to prevent heavy vehicles from running over the drainage field.

Lawn and garden equipment
Fall
Store garden tools, preparing motors on all powered equipment for storage.
Drain and store hoses.
Disconnect sprinkler timer.

Winter/Spring
Sharpen cutting tools.
Clean, adjust, and/or overhaul motors on powered equipment.
Repaint lawn furniture as needed.
Replace missing or burst webbing on lawn chairs and lounges.

2.THE TOOLS

Light maintenance tools:

1. Electric hand drill: ¼″ chuck, variable speed, reversing
2. Drill bits: 1/64″ to ¼″
3. Brace and screwdriver bit: 5/16″
4. Center punch and nail set
5. Electric saber saw with carbide-tipped blade
6. Pliers: slip joint, 8″
7. Pliers: locking grip, 10″
8. Wrenches: open end
9. Utility knife
10. Hacksaw blade and frame
11. Hammer: 16 oz., curved claw
12. Screwdrivers: flat tipped, 4″, 6″, and 10″
13. Surform planing tool
14. Wrench: adjustable, 8″
15. Screwdrivers: Phillips, sizes 1 and 2
16. Wood chisels: ⅜″ to ¾″
17. Files: round, half round, rasp
18. Rule: wooden, 6′ with slide extension
19. Carpenter's square

Heavy maintenance tools:

20. Crosscut saw
21. Combination square
22. Drop cord with light: 20′
23. Extension cord: grounded, 20′
24. C-clamp: 4″
25. Smoothing plane: 8″ to 10″
26. Safety goggles
27. Metal shears: straight cutting
28. Tape measure: 16′, ¾″ wide
29. Hammer: ball peen, 20 oz.
30. Caulking gun: cartridge
31. Cold chisel
32. Carpenter's level: 24″
33. Step ladder: 5′ or 6′
34. Extension ladder: 24′

Specialized tools:

35. Wrecking bar: 24″
36. Paint scraper: hook type
37. Utility bar
38. Putty knife: 1½″ wide
39. Mason's trowel
40. Sanding block: rubber
41. Circular saw: 7¼″ blade, minimum 1½ horsepower
42. Mini-hacksaw
43. Mortar joiner (for smoothing fresh mortar in pointing between bricks, blocks, etc.)
44. Offset screwdriver
45. Square-shank screwdriver
46. Whetstone: combination, 7″
47. Staple gun: heavy duty
48. Pipe-bar clamps
49. Pop rivet tool

Ladder use and safety

In maintaining and improving the exterior of your house, sooner or later you'll find yourself on a ladder, perhaps even an extension ladder. As even a short fall can be—and often is—disastrous, special precautions are in order. Consider the following for your future safety:

When purchasing an extension ladder, select one with safety treads. Before extending a ladder to the height you want, get it in position. If you are going to shift its position any distance, lower it first. It's dangerous to yourself, others, and your windows to try to waltz an extended ladder around your lawn. The best way for a lone worker to raise a ladder is to pin its feet against the base of the house and push the ladder up from the other end, hand over hand, until it is upright.

Before you climb a ladder, jump on its bottom rung a few times to make sure it is solidly footed. If the ground slopes, put a broad board or beam—never bricks—under the lower foot until it is level with the other one. If the ground is soft or muddy, place both of the ladder's feet on a wide board. If you are planning to work on a ladder extended to its full length, you can gain stability by lashing the bottom rung to a stake driven into the ground under the ladder. If yours is an aluminum ladder, watch out for power lines. Electricity flows readily through aluminum. Make sure the ladder has firm support at the top. Never place it against a window sash or so close to an edge that a slight shift would send it and you sailing. For comfort, don't wear soft-soled shoes if you are going to work on a ladder for a long spell. The rungs will be hard on your arches.

Don't knock it
The front stoop seemed just the spot to place the ladder when I was cleaning out a clogged gutter. Wasn't it firm and level? I had reached the top and begun to scoop away when my teenage son decided to come out of the house. He pushed open the door, knocking the ladder clean off the stoop. That's me clinging to the gutter until he could get the ladder back up, and thinking "never again put up a ladder in front of an unlocked door."

Practical Pete

Position your ladder so that the distance of its feet from the base of the house is about one-quarter its length. Measure the distance between rungs so you can estimate the ladder's extended length.

Keep your hips within the ladder's rails. Extend the ladder two rungs higher than the place you are working on.

Here's a way to free both hands when you need them. Note how the heel is locked against the rung. Have somebody else brace the ladder when you use it this way.

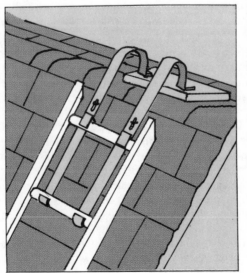

A ladder makes it safer for you to work on a pitched roof—also easier on the shingles. You can buy brackets that hook over the ridge, holding your ladder in place.

TIP: This ladder stabilizer comes in handy when you're painting or working on gutters.

Finding leaks

Repairing roofs usually involves fixing leaks. To fix a leak you first have to find it, and this can be the most time-consuming part of the job, especially when the leak is in a sloping roof. Often it is not located directly over the damage that it produced in the ceiling. What happens is this: the water flows in through the hole, runs diagonally down the sheathing or a rafter until it meets something—say, a knot or the end of a nail—and only then drops straight down. This can happen three or four feet from the hole and be very misleading.

The common causes of leaks are loose, torn, cracked, or missing shingles, and defective flashing around a chimney or vent, or in a valley between gables. Shingles along the ridge or hip of a roof tend to get cracked or blown away because the wind lifts them, causing the nails to pop.

To find a leak, go up to the attic or crawl space during a rainstorm. Take along a flashlight, felt-tip pen, and several pieces of wire about a foot long. **TIP:** Paint the wire a bright color; it will be easier for you to spot when you are looking for it later on the roof. Once in the area of the leak, shine your flashlight along the sheathing and rafters. Work in the dark. It will be easier for you to spot the gleam of the water when your flashlight illuminates it. When you locate the hole, push a wire up through it and draw a circle around the hole as a permanent record. On the next day, locate the

wire from the outside and make the repair as shown on the following pages.

If your roof is insulated and you have reason to suspect a leak, take off the batts one by one until you find one that is damp or discolored. Then start looking above it for the hole.

If you can't examine your roof from below, you'll have to wait for a dry day and examine it from the outside. Crawl over the suspected area, examining it for loose or missing shingles, cracks in flashing, and popped or missing nails.

If dripping water is not localized but appears over a wide area, check the flashing around the chimney. This can pull away from the mortar. Instead of deflecting water, it collects it. Water then flows down *under* the shingles and spreads out before getting into rooms below.

If you live in a northern region, your house may develop mysterious water spots and dripping in winter. When ice dams form in gutters, melting water can back up the roof and under the shingles, then seep through the sheathing into your house.

If you have a flat roof, finding a leak is simplified by the fact that water from a hole tends to fall directly below. Leaks generally develop in low spots where water collects, around a chimney or vent pipe, or in the flashing where the roof joins a vertical wall. Also check for popped nails, especially along the seams.

The solvent solution
I was pleased with the job I did patching cracked shingles along the ridge of my house. I was sure the leak was stopped. But when I climbed down to admire my work from the ground, I saw that I had left smears of black roofing cement on my beautiful, silvery shingles. I quickly called the lumber yard where I bought the stuff. A clerk told me to soak a rough rag or brush in kerosene and scrub the stains off right away. It beats having to paint the whole roof black.
Practical Pete

Fixing leaks
in asphalt shingles

What it takes

Approximate time: Once the leak is located and you have all your materials assembled on the roof, allow 5 to 10 minutes per shingle. The preliminaries are what take time, and they cannot be predicted.

Tools and materials: Hammer, putty knife, pry bar, hacksaw blade or nail ripper, caulking gun, roof cement or asphalt paint, 1½-inch galvanized or aluminum roofing nails, and replacement shingles.

1. If the leak comes from a cracked, loose, or raised shingle, your task is usually simple. A small crack can be filled with asphalt roof paint. To repair a badly torn shingle or one with curled edges, first lift its bottom portion. On "stick-down" shingles, you may need a putty knife to pry the edge up. But be careful not to push the knife through the shingle.

2. Smear roof cement on the exposed underside of the shingle as well as the area on which the shingle will rest. You can use a caulking gun for this step. Then push the shingle back into position. On cold days place a flat board over the repair and press down until the shingle is firmly in place. If you have to nail into the exposed portion of the shingle, do so sparingly; cover nailheads with cement.

To remove a badly damaged shingle, lift the surrounding shingles to expose the nails in the flawed one. Pull the nails out (gently!) with a pry bar or chisel. After extracting the shingle, scrape away any old roofing cement. Round off the corners of the new shingle before inserting it so it will slip into place more easily. Fold back the next higher shingle with one hand and hammer with the other. Nail only into that portion of shingle to be overlapped.

Replacing a course. A big wind can rip several shingles off your roof. Replacing them is no more complicated a job than putting in a single shingle. When you are replacing more than one row or "course" of shingles, be sure before you nail the first one in the bottom course that its lower edge is properly aligned with the other shingles in the same course and that its joints are staggered with the joints in the courses above and below it. Then nail succeeding shingles in place.

Planning hints:
- Wait for a sunny day if you can. Shingles will be easier to work with. A wet roof is dangerously slippery.
- Wear sneakers or soft-soled shoes.
- Buy a tool holster in which to carry your hammer, putty knife, and other tools.
- A carpenter's or roofer's apron is handy for keeping nails, small cans, and tools.
- If you're new to a house, search the attic, basement, and garage for leftover shingles before buying a new bundle. It may be hard to match the old color.

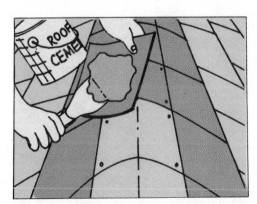

Ridge shingles. Shingles along the ridge of your house are whipped by the wind and are most prone to cracking or blowing away. To replace one, first nail down the corners of the ones below it. Apply a coat of roof cement to the underside of the new shingle. Space it so its overlap is proportionate to the others on the ridge; then nail it in place and cover nailheads with dabs of roof cement.

Stopgaps and copouts

Sheet-metal shingle. For an emergency repair, until you can get a permanent replacement shingle, you can make a patch from a piece of sheet metal. Cut it to fit over the damaged area and slip it well under the shingle above it. Apply a coat of roof cement to the bottom of the patch, smoothing down any beads with your putty knife. Tack in place. Be sure to cover the heads of the tacks with cement. When you get the proper size and type of shingle, pry up the patch.

Fixing leaks
in wood shingles

The most common causes of leaks in a wood-shingle roof is that one or more shingles have become warped or split. If so, they can let in a lot of water. Some houses roofed with wood shingles have no attic sheathing underneath the shingles. You may even see cracks between the shingles, but these will not admit water if the roof has been well laid and the shingles are solid.

Leaky wood shingles usually have to be replaced. They can't often be repaired or patched. Replacing one isn't a particularly hard job, but it does require care so you don't split or damage surrounding shingles. The job will look better and go faster if you can replace it with one of exactly the same size and shape. The raw wood color will weather and blend in after about a year. If you are new to the house, explore the attic, cellar, and garage. The builder or previous owner may have left a supply to be used as replacements when needed.

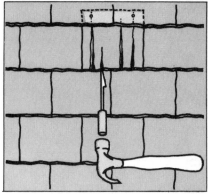

1. To replace a wood shingle, remove the defective shingle (without pulling out the nails that hold it) by splitting it into strips with a sharp wood chisel and a hammer. When the shingle splits at the nail holes, you can dislodge it from beneath the shingle above. Measure the opening left by the removed shingle and trim a new shingle about ⅜ inch narrower so it won't buckle when it swells in the rain.

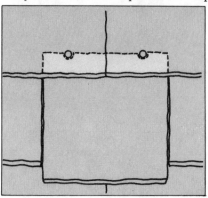

2. Push the new shingle gently into the opening and under the shingle above until it meets the nails left by the old one. Force the shingle up against these nails hard enough to mark their positions in the end. Withdraw the shingle and inspect it to make sure you can see the indentations made by the nails.

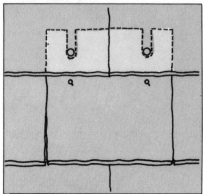

3. Measure the depth of the nail holes in the original shingle. Put the new shingle in a vise and cut slots to these depths with gentle strokes of a coping saw so it doesn't split. Push the new shingle up under the ones above it so the bottom lines up with the adjacent shingles. Tap in a couple of roofing nails, but since they will be in the exposed portion of the shingle, set the nails and cover the heads with caulking compound.

Fixing leaks
in slate shingles

Because slate shingles crack so easily, major repairs on a slate roof should be made only by an experienced roofer. But you can repair a loose or slightly cracked shingle yourself. Lift off the damaged piece and coat its underside with roof cement. Then fit it exactly back into position. If you have a cracked shingle, cover the crack with cement and smooth the bead down with a putty knife.

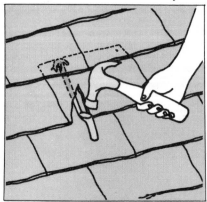

1. To replace a slate shingle, first remove nails with a nail ripper. Hook the ripper over the nail and hammer on it until the nail comes out. Starting the nail from inside the house will shorten this step.

2. Position and nail two metal strips as shown. Strike the nail sharply and it will go through the slate without splitting it. Cover the nail heads with cement and leave the excess on.

3. Slide the new slate into position and fold back the metal strips so that each fits snugly to the slate. (If you don't have a supply of slates, have them cut to size for you.)

Fixing leaks in flat roofs

Most flat roofs are covered with layers of felt paper saturated with asphalt. (The surface of some older roofs is covered with gravel or stone chips to protect the roof from the sun.) If the leak comes from a small hole or crack, the remedy is to seal it with roof cement. If the roof is in bad shape with many leaks, cover it with a coat of roof paint. This will do the job and costs less than roof cement. If the roof has pebbles, brush them off; no need to replace them. Apply the paint in sections measuring about 25 feet square. Since even flat roofs have some slope, work from highest point.

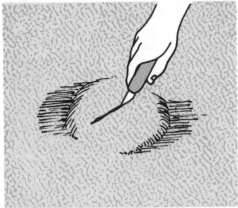

1. If you have a cracked blister, slice it down the middle, being careful not to cut into the layer below. Raise the flaps to allow the area to dry. Then force roof cement under both edges with a putty knife or caulking gun.

2. Nail down the edges with roofing nails and place a tar-paper or shingle patch over the blistered area. Nail the patch down with roofing nails every ½ inch. Cover entire patch with roof cement.

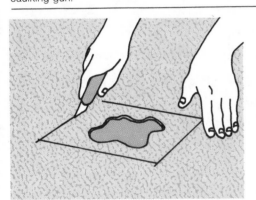

1. If you have a long rip or extensively damaged area, cut away the top layer of the entire area. Measure this to the nearest full inch so it will be easier to cut a patch that fits exactly.

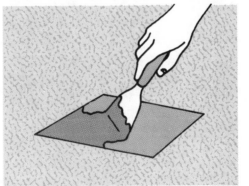

2. Fit patch of 15-pound roofing felt into cutaway section. Coat this with roof cement. No need to nail.

3. Cut patch to overlap inset patch about 2 inches on all sides. Nail, and cover nail heads with roof cement to prevent new leaks.

Patching a deep hole

Flat roofs are more vulnerable to damage than pitched roofs because they absorb rather than deflect the blow of falling objects. If your flat roof suffers a deep puncture, repair it this way:

1. Cut away all materials down to the sheathing. Replace the broken sheathing if necessary.
2. Cover sheathing with building paper and lay a piece of 15-pound roofing felt over the paper. Coat with roof cement.
3. Repeat this until felt is level with roof.
4. Patch with overlapping piece as shown above and at left.

Repairing flashing

One of the main causes of leaks on older roofs is faulty or damaged flashing. It can also be the source of leaks in new homes. If a flashing is not properly installed, gallons of water can pour in from an otherwise perfect roof. Flashing is used to provide a watertight joint wherever shingles won't do the job: around chimneys and vent pipes, in valleys where two planes of the roof meet or where a dormer meets the roof, along the peak of the roof, and where a flat roof meets a vertical wall. You will also find flashing around window and door jambs.

Flashing is now made from a number of different materials: roll roofing, roofing felt, galvanized steel, aluminum, and rubber. If your home is an older one, the flashing may be copper, which is the best —and worth salvaging. You'll find it especially around the chimney and in the valleys. Boots of other metals are used for flashing around vent pipes. Whichever flashing material you use, you will often be sealing joints with roofing cement or tar.

It is worth the effort to inspect your flashing once a year, especially around the chimney, a common place for leaks to develop. It won't be hard to spot large cracks in your flashing or gaps between it and other elements of your roof, such as bricks in the chimney. But a flashing can also develop pinhole leaks or cracks which can admit quantities of water. If the flashing looks old, give it a coat of roofing cement or roof paint. Fill any large holes with roofing felt and coat with cement.

Preventing leaks around chimneys

Flashing around chimneys is commonly embedded in mortar. But the mortar can age or the flashing pull away. In either case the old mortar must be cleaned out and replaced. Chisel out the old mortar, reposition the flashing, and embed it in new patching mortar. This will create a tight, waterproof joint.

When the flashing material is roofing felt or paper, fill holes and cracks by smearing roof cement over them with a putty knife.

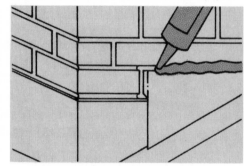

If your flashing is metal, use a caulking gun loaded with roof cement to refill the joint between the cap of the flashing and mortar.

Preventing leaks around vents

Vents may be flashed with a metal boot or tightly fitted shingles. On some new homes, the vent flashing is a plastic boot cemented or nailed to the sheathing. In any event, the flashing must be closely fitted and tightly sealed, or water is sure to enter.

Water can run down the vent pipe and into the house if the lead flashing around the pipe's neck becomes loose. Tamp it with a cold chisel or screwdriver so that the boot grips the pipe tightly all around its circumference.

Caulk vent flashing with roof cement, covering partway up the pipe. Pick up the covering shingles where you can and apply roof cement underneath them. Then press them back in place.

Replacing flashing

Metal chimney flashing should usually be replaced outright as soon as it begins to leak. Holes tend to develop in the corners of metal flashing and in rust areas. Flashing made of asphalted felt or roll-roofing paper begins to melt after a while. When you see tarry streaks running down the chimney inside the house, you know it's time to replace felt or paper flashing, even if it isn't leaking. If you are laying a new roof you should install new flashing because this job is much easier to do when the new shingles are being applied. Metal flashing is so much more durable, leak-resistant, and easier to maintain than the felt-and-paper types that it is worth the investment.

What it takes

Approximate time: Varies with the job. Allow a full day to replace flashing around chimney, half a day around vent pipe. Fitting the new flashing is often time consuming and trying.
Tools and materials: Flat chisel, pry bar, putty knife, hammer, mason's trowel, pointer, wire brush, 1½-inch roofing nails, sheet metal, roof cement, patching mortar, shingles, sheet-metal shears, and boot-type vent flashing.

Repairs around chimneys

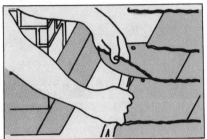

1. Remove the shingles covering the flashing. Get under the nail heads with a wide, thin chisel; then lift them out with a pry bar. Chip away the mortar and caulking that secure the flashing to the chimney.

2. Remove the nails that fasten the flashing to the sheathing. Then pull the flashing away from the chimney. But keep the old flashing intact; you will use it as a pattern for cutting out a replacement.

3. If the old flashing was of soft material, cut a pattern out of heavy cardboard. You will need separate patterns for base flashing and cap flashing. Try your patterns for size on the chimney. Adjust until they fit.

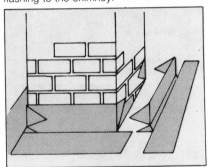

4. Cut the new flashings with sheet metal shears and adjust each section of base flashing to the chimney for a snug fit. Trim as necessary. Then assemble, cementing mating surfaces and undersides. Nail bottom flange to sheathing.

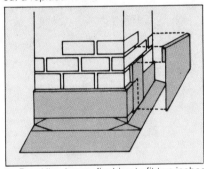

5. Bend lips in cap flashing to fit two inches into horizontal space between bricks; bend flaps around sides of bricks. Cut bottom of cap flashing to match roof's pitch.

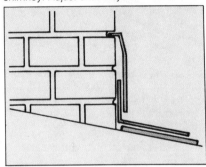

6. Fasten cap in place by filling space between bricks with patching mortar. After mortar has cured, caulk space with roof cement. Replace shingles, coating nail heads.

Repairs around vents

1. Remove shingles around pipe. Chip off cement holding boot to roof. Lift off boot. Wire-brush cement off pipe. If you tore roofing paper, patch with 15-pound roofing felt.

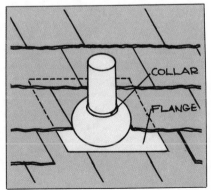

2. Slide new boot down pipe. Adjust flange until it is flush with roof; then cement. Do not nail. Slip collar down pipe and push into tight union with boot. Replace shingles, coating nail heads with cement.

New wrinkles

Plastic boots are now available for flashing vent pipes. They are easier to install than metal ones. Leaks around electrical service masts can also be stopped with boot flashing.

Valley flashing

What it takes

Approximate time: Will vary from an hour (roll-roofing an open valley) to several hours, depending on material and extent of damage.

Tools and materials: Hammer, putty knife, pry bar, metal shears, roofing cement, 1½-inch roofing nails, sheet metal, 15-pound roofing felt, and roll roofing.

Two different methods are used to waterproof the valleys formed where two slopes of a roof meet. When the shingles border the valley but do not enter it, the flashing is called open valley. But when the shingles cover the flashing entirely, it is called a closed valley.

The flashing used in valleys may be roll roofing or sheet metal. Either material may develop cracks or holes from age, damage,

or decomposition. Open-valley flashing is of course easier to work with than closed valley. Replacing the latter is a big job because the covering shingles must be replaced with new ones. However, leaks in closed-valley flashing can be patched (without any need to tear and replace the shingles) by forcing overlapping squares of sheet metal under the shingles as shown in the second sequence below.

Open valley

 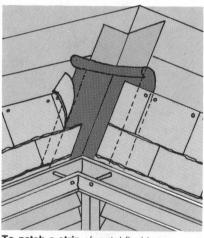 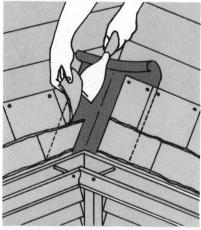

To patch a hole in a valley flashed with metal, cut a piece from the same kind of metal. Make it big enough to overlap the hole at least an inch. Coat the area with roofing cement. Press the patch in place and hold it down for several minutes. To patch a hole in roll roofing, cut the patch from 15-pound roofing felt and apply as above.

To patch a strip of metal flashing, remove the holding nails from adjacent shingles. Do not remove the old metal flashing. Cut a strip of roll roofing to cover the flashing and extend at least 4 inches under the shingles on either side of the valley. Nail the shingles back in place, and seal the nail heads with roofing cement.

To replace roll-roofing flashing, pry out the holding nails. The flashing will be cemented to the shingles, so separate them carefully with a broad-bladed putty knife, and pull out the old flashing. Cut a strip of roll roofing the same size as the old flashing. Slip it back under the shingles and nail it in place along each side so the nail heads are covered by the overlapping shingles. Cement the nail heads and shingle tabs to the new flashing.

Closed valley

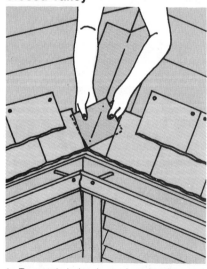 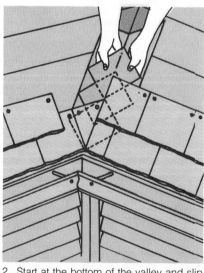 

1. To patch holes in a closed valley, cut squares of metal large enough to extend at least 2 inches under the second shingle on each side. Bend squares to fit the angle of the valley.

2. Start at the bottom of the valley and slip the squares under the shingles and over the old flashing until all the leaky areas have been covered. Insert roofing cement with a caulking gun between the metal squares and the shingles.

3. Lift out any nails that prevent you from pushing a square into place. Use a pry bar. Replace the nails and seal nail heads with roofing cement.

Chimney repairs

Chimneys should be inspected each year just before the cold season. Inspection reduces chances of fire and increases chimney efficiency. You will see more if you inspect the chimney from the top. If it's a bright day, reflect sunlight down it with a mirror. Or use a flashlight. If you can't look down a chimney, inspect it with a strong flashlight and a mirror from a fireplace, from the cleanout door at the base, or through a flue opening for a stove pipe.

Look for obstructions such as birds' nests and for thick deposits of soot and tar. A hot fire can ignite these, turning your chimney into a torch.

To clean a chimney, weight a burlap bag with a chain and stuff it with paper or old clothes. Seal off the fireplace with wrapping paper and masking tape. Tie a strong rope around the neck of the bag and lower it all the way down the chimney. Extract the bag by giving the rope short, vigorous tugs. Lowering the bag should knock down any obstructions. Tugging it up will loosen tar and soot. When you are finished, dispose of the wrapping paper carefully so as not to track soot through the house.

If rain or drafts come down your chimney, you can install a deflector. This item is available in a variety of styles and material: concrete, wire, and conical caps in sizes to fit standard-size flues. In addition to keeping out wind and rain, a chimney deflector can end a bird's-nest problem and trap flying sparks.

If you see smoke oozing out from between your chimney bricks, you may have a cracked flue. Don't use the chimney until the flue is checked and fixed by a pro.

Sooner or later the mortar between the bricks in chimneys begins to bake dry or weather away. If cracks are allowed to form, water can get in and cause serious leaks. And if the mortar deteriorates beyond a certain point, a strong wind could topple a section of the chimney.

Tuck-pointing

1. Check your chimney for crumbling mortar. If you need to repair it, go easy as you chip away cracked, loose mortar in preparation for tuck-pointing, or remortaring. A chimney in bad shape could topple over at any time.

2. Wear safety goggles to protect your eyes against flying chips when you chip out old mortar with a hammer and cape chisel. Brush joints to remove dust and mortar fragments, then hose down the chimney to prevent the fresh mortar from drying out too quickly.

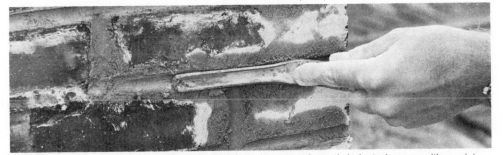

3. Trowel smooth but not soupy mortar into the joints; then smooth neatly indented seams with a pointer. Let the mortar harden overnight; then, wearing rubber gloves, wash the bricks down with a solution of 1 part muriatic acid and 10 parts water to clean cement stains from the brick. Flush down chinmey exterior with fresh water.

Electrical heating tapes

After a heavy snow, ice dams can easily form on roof overhangs, causing trapped water to back up under shingles and enter the house. You can forestall this by cleaning gutters and drains in late fall and providing soffit ventilation (page 496) and extra insulation so roof snow melts evenly. Another method is to install electrical heating tapes that keep the overhang warm enough to prevent ice from forming. These usually come in pairs, one for the overhang and the other for the gutter and downspout.

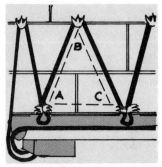

To determine how much tape you will need for your overhang, measure off the length of line **a-b-c** on your roof. Point **b** lies at the upper limit of the overhang; points **a** and **c** are a shingle's width apart. Then divide line **a-c** into the length of the gutter. Multiplying line **a-b-c** by this factor will give you the length you need for the overhang cable. The length of the gutter-downspout cable can be determined by direct measurement.

Lay one tape along the gutter and down the full length of the downspout. Zigzag the other across the overhang Hold it in place by affixing clips to the asphalt shingles. If your shingles are slate or wood, use epoxy cement.

What it takes

Approximate time: Three hours.

Tools and materials: Goggles, ⅜-inch cape chisel, 2½-pound mason's hammer, trowel, pointer, rubber gloves, stiff brush, old broom, premixed mortar or your own mix (1 part portland cement, 1 part hydrated lime, 6 parts sand), and muriatic acid solution (10 parts water, 1 part acid).

Preventing ice dams

Approximate time: Inserting insulation—2 hours; installing strip vent—4 hours; installing vented soffit—3 hours; installing single vent—1 hour.

Tools and materials: Depending on the job, a hammer, wood chisel, saber or keyhole saw, chalk line, 10-penny nails, soffit vents or fully vented soffit, and insulation with vapor barrier.

Heating tapes keep ice dams from forming, but they have several disadvantages. They consume electricity; somebody has to remember to turn them on when it starts to snow—and off when the roof is bare; and if you have to install an electrical box, you will incur additional expense (page 495).

You can avoid these problems by removing the conditions that cause ice dams to form in the first place. This can be done by adding insulation and by providing ventilation for the attic through the soffit, the wooden panel beneath the roof overhang.

There are three types of soffit ventilation: single vent units that fit into openings cut in the soffit; vented strips that fit into channels cut the full length of the soffit; and soffits that come with vent holes in them.

An additional benefit of vented soffits is that air flowing through them will keep the attic cooler in hot, sunny weather and allow it to cool more quickly at night. Vents in the gables or roof are essential for proper attic ventilation throughout the year.

Install insulation between rafters in the attic. Use insulation with a vapor barrier and leave air space between the vapor barrier and roof boards under an overhang. Insulation should be 6 inches deep.

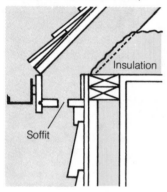

Fitting a full-length vent

1. Mark cutting lines in the soffit for the channel into which you will fit the vent. The channel should be the width of the vent and begin 3 inches from the overhang. Snapping chalk lines is a quick, professional step.

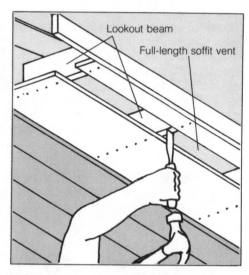

2. Cut the strip out of the soffit with a saber or keyhole saw. Chisel out the lookout beams so the vent will seat properly. When vent is in place, nail it to the lookouts.

Single vent units

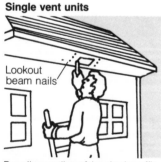

Pencil an outline of the single soffit vent in the soffit where you will place it. Be sure to position it between lookout beams; you can locate them by nail heads in the soffit. Cut the hole with a saber saw or keyhole saw. Screw the vent in position.

Installing a vented soffit

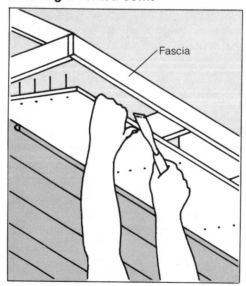

1. Pull the nails holding the present soffit to the lookouts and remove any molding; then remove the soffit with a pry bar.

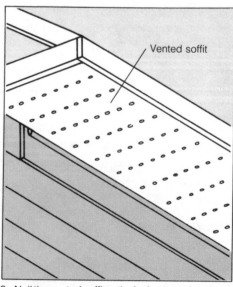

2. Nail the vented soffit to the lookouts and put back any molding. **TIP:** Paint the new soffit before you put it in place.

Gable vents

For adequate under-roof ventilation, air flowing in through soffit or eave vents must be able to get back out. Therefore vents are needed in the gables or roof. Proper air flow will not only forestall ice dams, but by allowing the escape of warm, moist air rising from living areas, it will also prevent rafters and roof sheathing from rotting. Good air circulation helps in another way, too. During the summer, an unvented attic can get as hot as 150 degrees Fahrenheit. This hot blanket radiates heat after the sun has set, keeping the house uncomfortable and putting an extra strain on the air conditioning downstairs.

Adequate circulation of attic air requires louvers in the gables or vents in the roof. If the pitch of your roof is shallow, you may need to install an electrically powered fan. As a rule of thumb, every 300 square feet of attic floor area requires a square foot of louver. (Add 50 percent more louver area, if you plan to screen them.) Two louvers in opposite gables are more efficient than one large one: You can purchase either rectangular or triangular louvers at lumber yards. The triangular type is more efficient and less evident, being fitted up under the roof. Get one with the same pitch as your roof. (See page 506 for measuring pitch.) Adjustable types are available. Installing a triangular louver is more difficult, but because it is more desirable, directions are given for installing this type. They can easily be adapted to the less difficult task of installing a rectangular louver.

What it takes

Approximate time: Six hours.

Tools and materials: Carpenter's rule, pencil, drill with 1-inch bit, saber or keyhole saw, hammer, 3-inch common nails, 2x4s, louvered vent unit, and roofing cement.

1. Draw a triangle on the inside wall to mark the opening. Its top should be as close to the bottom of the ridge beam as you can saw. At the three corners, drill starter holes.

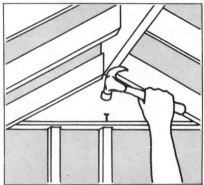

2. Cut out the opening with a saber or keyhole saw. Saw enough off the tops of any studs to fit in a 2x4 header as the base of the triangle. Nail two more 2x4s to the rafters to complete the frame.

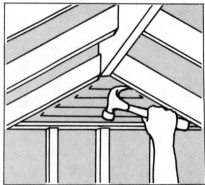

3. Slide the vent in place to ensure a snug fit. If necessary, adjust the 2x4s. Then apply roofing cement to the flange or lip on the outside of the vent. Insert in place and nail. Caulk the outside edges of the vent with roofing cement.

Roof vents

Another way to get adequate attic ventilation is to install a roof vent. Being on the roof, such a vent allows more air to escape than a comparable vent in the gables. Attics of any size require two roof vents, unless you use a unit with an electric fan. One such vent will suffice for areas as large as 2,000 square feet. The directions here apply to either type of unit, except that a fan will of course require electrical power.

Approximate time: Eight hours.

Tools and materials: Carpenter's rule, compass, pencil, drill with ½-inch bit, roofer's knife, hammer, 1½-inch roofing nails, and roof vent unit.

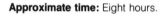

1. Lay the vent in position on the roof, as close to the ridge line as possible. If installing only one vent, position it as close to the center of the roof as possible. When the fan is in position, measure from the ridge line to the center of the fan.

2. Measure down from the ridge line inside the attic. Drill a hole on center between two rafters. Back on top of the roof, scribe a circle equal to the diameter of the vent housing. Remove shingles and roofing paper within this circle.

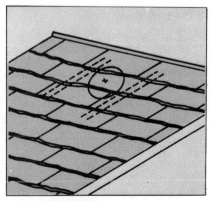

3. Cut away sheathing with a keyhole or saber saw. Do not cut rafters. Nail headers between rafters on either side of the hole. After caulking the base, slide the vent up under the loosened shingles. Fasten base to sheathing with roofing nails. Caulk the edges and restore the shingles around the vent.

Gutters and downspouts

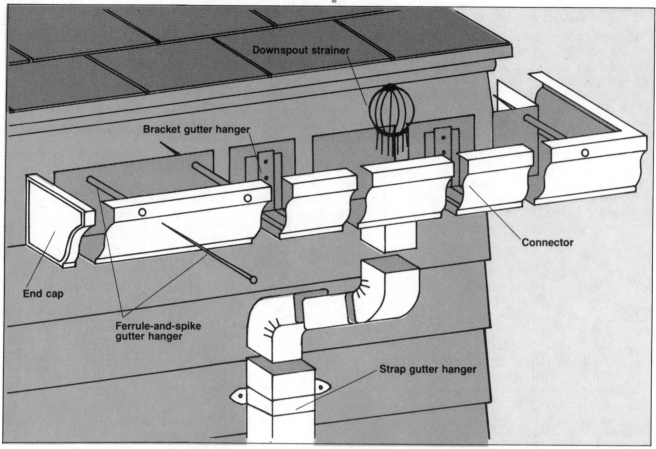

Downspout strainer

Bracket gutter hanger

Connector

End cap

Ferrule-and-spike gutter hanger

Strap gutter hanger

The case of the mysterious sags
I couldn't keep my gutters from sagging. Every time it rained, pools of water would collect in the low spots. Up the ladder I would go to bend them back into shape and hammer the spikes back into the rafters. But the problem persisted. One day a neighbor came by to see why I was spending so much of my spare time on a ladder. "You're the problem," he announced. That's when I learned not to rest a ladder on a gutter. It bends the gutter out of shape.

Practical Pete

Gutters and downspouts, also called leaders, have an important job to do in maintaining your house—its solidity as well as its exterior appearance. If your gutter/downspout system doesn't do its job of collecting and carrying water away, runoff can wash the topsoil away from the foundation below, cause basement flooding, and rot siding and fascia boards. Moreover, gutters and downspouts that are not properly maintained will have to be prematurely repaired or replaced. You can forestall these time-consuming and costly problems by adopting the following measures:

General maintenance

1. Insert strainers at the tops of all downspouts.
2. Cover gutters with leaf guards.
3. Correct overflowing and drips as soon as they are observed.
4. Paint galvanized steel gutters and downspouts; treat the exterior of wooden gutters with preservative.
5. Be sure that no downspout feeds onto a lower roof; connect it directly to a gutter.
6. Install splash blocks beneath open-ended downspouts.
7. Seal joints at connectors and end caps with caulking compound.

Fall / Spring maintenance

1. Remove debris from all gutters.
2. Clean strainers.
3. Rod out downspouts.
4. Look for evidences of gutter sags and improper pitch; test with a pail of water or a garden hose at full blast.
5. Check all hangers for loose nails and bent straps.
6. Inspect gutter alignment with fascia.
7. Tighten elbows from gutters to downspouts.
8. Inspect straps holding downspouts to the siding; hammer down any loose or popped nails.
9. Tighten elbows at the tops and the ends of downspouts.
10. Inspect topsoil under gutters and downspouts for erosion.

Maintaining gutters

Some of the leaves, twigs, and other debris that land on your roof make their way into your gutters. Most of the light material is carried to the downspouts. But even swiftly flowing water does not carry everything along. Leaves rot, seeds sprout, balls and rocks impede. After a while, a neglected gutter along your roof can resemble a gutter in a neglected city street.

Gutters should be cleaned at least twice a year: in the autumn after most of the leaves have fallen, and again in the spring after seed pods and leaf buds have dropped. If a number of large trees are nearby, it may be necessary to clean your gutter more frequently. There is another reason for semi-annual cleaning: it gives you a chance to inspect your gutters. They are subject to considerable force in a heavy rain. And if you live in a cold climate, ice can form in gutters and as it expands, push them out of alignment or loosen joints.

Cleaning gutters

1. Muck out gutters by hand. Wear a rubber glove or old work glove for protection. Remember, do not rest the rails of the ladder on the gutter; this can push the gutter out of alignment and strain hangers. Keep an eye open for water or discolored spots that reveal sags or inadequate gutter pitch.

2. Hose down the gutter after you have removed most of the debris. This will flush out the last remnants while giving you an opportunity to observe the flow of water and look for low spots or improper pitch. Check for leaks at the joints and end caps. Be alert also for leaks caused by rust holes.

Inspect each hanger as you work your way along the gutter. You may spot bent straps and popped nails. If your house has fascia or board trim, check the gutter's alignment with it. The gutter should rest firmly against it for maximum support.

Keeping out debris

1. Install leaf guards in gutters under trees. The type shown comes in 3-foot sections. It is made of semirigid hardware cloth. You fit it into the gutter by compressing it. Once in the gutter, the screen snaps into place.

2. Fit rolled leaf guard by cutting sections of expanded metal screening to fit. One edge goes up under the shingles and the other down under the front lip of the gutter. This type is lighter than the snap-in type and can thus bend and crush more readily.

Paint galvanized steel gutters and downspouts, but only after they have been up for a year. Paint will blister on galvanized steel unless you first apply a special primer. Painting extends the life of galvanized steel greatly. If paint has begun to peel, wire-brush, prime, and paint the spots.

Maintaining downspouts

Being enclosed and vertical, downspouts are not subject to the same stress and wear that gutters are. But downspouts require regular maintenance and inspection. They become clogged; they develop leaks; they pull away from the house; they come apart; water from a heavy rain gushing out can force an elbow off.

Water from a defective gutter usually cascades over a fairly wide stretch. That's bad enough, but water from a defective downspout pours in a concentrated stream. In a very short period it can carry off topsoil, flood a window well, or put several inches of water in a cellar. It is no fun to have to clean up one of these messes; likewise to have to go out in a heavy rain and try to put a downspout back together again. A stitch in time saves nine. Here are five key aspects of preventive maintenance.

What it takes

Approximate time: One hour or less.

Tools and materials: Leaf strainer, hammer, caulking compound and gun, splash block, and downspout sleeve are among the items that may be useful.

1. Put strainers into the mouths of all downspouts. But don't force them deep into the neck; set them just far enough in so they remain in place. Because so much debris flows to downspouts, strainers should be inspected and cleaned more frequently than gutters.

2. Rod out the upper elbows of downspouts with a bent coat hanger. Use a plumber's snake if you have one. Even with strainers, debris can get into downspouts and build up in the bends.

Vulnerable parts of a downspout

Downspout fitting

Elbow

End elbow

3. Grasp the elbow linking the gutter to the downspout. Make sure it is secure. When you are hosing down the gutters, look for leaks in the downspout, particularly in the joints of elbows. If you spot any leaks, seal them with caulking compound.

4. Check the nails or screws in the straps holding the downspout to the house. These can work themselves loose when a downspout has been used as a ladder support, or as a result of use and age.

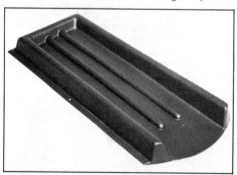

5. Control the direction in which water flows out of downspouts—unless it goes directly into a storm sewer, dry well, or underground drainage system. A splash block like the one shown will divert water in the desired direction. The open end of the downspout should be only a few inches above the splash block.

New wrinkle

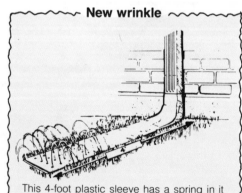

This 4-foot plastic sleeve has a spring in it that will coil it up and out of the way when rainwater stops flowing out the downspout. Water seeps from holes in the sleeve rather than streaming out from the downspout. An 8-foot model is available without the spring.

Repairing gutters and downspouts

Water from a leaky gutter can drip onto the cornice and down the siding. Over a period of years the resultant dampness can blister paint and cause the siding to rot. One response to a leaky gutter is to pull it off. But this is not a remedy. The fact that your house has gutters probably means that it needs them.

Often the water that leaks from gutters and downspouts comes from cracked seams or holes that have rusted through. In repairing gutters and downspouts, remember to use nails, screws, and sheet metal of the same material as the existing system—galvanized steel with galvanized steel, alu-minum with aluminum, and copper with copper. If you mix metals, galvanic corrosion will take place where the two metals meet. This will eat new holes in your gutter or downspout.

Occasionally a gutter will leak even though it is free of holes and cracks. It leaks at its joints because the sections were not assembled correctly. Upper sections must overlap lower sections, not vice versa. The solution to this problem is to take the run down and lap the sections correctly: the open joint facing the direction the water will flow. The wrong and right ways are illustrated below:

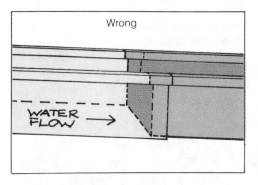

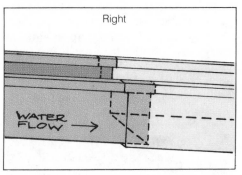

What it takes

Approximate Time: One hour.

Tools and materials: Wire brush, putty knife, sheet-metal shears, pliers, 100-grit sandpaper, roof cement, and sheet metal to match existing gutter.

Sealing holes

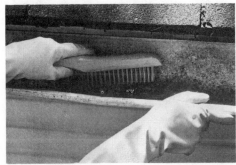

1. Wire-brush or sandpaper around the hole after first sweeping away the debris adjacent to the area. Clean the spot with paint thinner or other solvent.

2. Spread roof cement around the hole and in it with a putty knife. Be sure to keep the surface smooth; globs of cement in a gutter can catch twigs and leaves, damming water.

Patching holes

1. If a hole or crack is too large to be filled with roof cement, cut a matching pattern out of heavy paper to serve as a template for a patch. The patch must completely line the gutter and have a lip that fits over the gutter's outer edge.

2. Lay down a layer of roof cement before you fit in the patch, then crimp the lip of the patch over the gutter, and coat the patch with roof cement. Be sure to fill the joints between the patch and the gutter.

New wrinkles

A mixture of fiberglass and epoxy provides a quick, effective way to stop leaks in gutters and downspouts. It comes in a repair kit with mixing instructions. Application is similar to that used for roofing cement.

New gutters and downspouts

- A gutter section for every 10 feet of run.
- A hanger for every 3 feet of run; if you use the ferrule-spike type, one spike for every other rafter.
- Downspouts for both ends of runs 30 feet or longer. (Shorter runs can feed into a single downspout.)
- A connector for each joint between sections of the gutter.
- A drop outlet or downspout fitting for each downspout.
- An elbow for the top of each downspout.
- An elbow for the bottom of each downspout.
- An end cap for gutters next to downspouts.
- An outside corner wherever a gutter wraps around the house.
- One downspout strap for every 10 feet of run.

TIP: Get a helper. Lifting long gutter sections into place requires four hands.

Some gutters become so rusty and damaged that they should be replaced. Often it makes sense to put up an entire gutter run rather than fit in a single section or two. The finished run will look better and will eliminate repair work you would otherwise have to do later. If your house is an older one, you may want to install a complete new gutter-downspout system. This will give you an opportunity to select the material you want.

If you are replacing only a section or two, take a cross-sectional piece of the old gutter along when you buy the new one. You need an exact match of shape and metal. The standard length of a gutter section is 10 feet, but some gutters also come in longer lengths.

Should you decide to put up an entirely new system, consider the various materials in which gutters and downspouts are available, and select the best one for your needs. **Plastic** is simple to install and easy to maintain. The joints are sealed by a special mastic. Plastic gutters and downspouts expand on hot days and will buckle unless room is allowed at the joints.

Aluminum can be cut with a hacksaw, and its lightness makes it easier to lift into place. Because aluminum gutters and downspouts lack structural strength, they are easily dented. However, they resist corrosion well. In addition to their natural finish, they also come in white enamel.

Galvanized steel gutters and downspouts require priming and painting after a year, as detailed on page 18. You can avoid painting by buying enameled units, but these are more costly.

Copper leaders and gutters should be put up by a professional because the joints must be soldered. Copper is the most expensive material but the most durable and, when aged, the most handsome. Leaks in the seams, however, have to be resoldered occasionally.

Assembling the parts

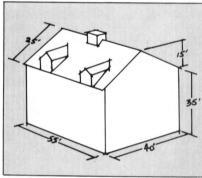

1. Make a sketch of the roof, if you plan to put up a new run or a complete system. To determine what and how much to buy, consult the requirements list above. Don't simply replace old elements; they may have been incorrect in the first place.

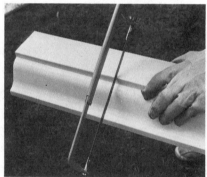

2. Cut a gutter section to length with a hacksaw. Support aluminum or plastic gutters from the inside with wood blocks. If the gutter is metal, remove the burrs with a file.

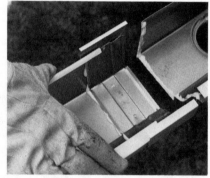

3. Assemble the gutter on a workbench. An important part of the job is fitting the connectors so that the joints don't leak. Apply caulking to gutter and connector before joining.

4. Tap the two sections together; then crimp the connector down over both sections. If you lap sections of the gutter instead of using connectors, put a ½-inch sheet-metal screw through each joint to keep the parts linked. Remember, the opening in the joint must face downstream.

5. Fasten the downspout fitting to the gutter after first applying caulking compound. Install this fitting on the *outside* of the gutter, rather than on the inside.

6. Crimp the end cap to the gutter, then secure with sheet-metal screws and caulking compound. The screws go through each side of the cap and into the gutter at the top. The gutter is now ready to be hung in place.

Pitching gutters

The water in gutters should flow swiftly enough to carry along leaves and other light debris to the downspouts. When it does not, a soggy mass builds up in the bottom of the gutter; if this is not cleaned out frequently, it promotes rust and corrosion; it can also cause damaging overflows.

For water to flow fast enough, gutters must have the proper pitch. The following instructions show how to repitch existing gutters and hang new ones correctly. Neither project calls for special skill.

Adjusting old gutters

1. Snap an absolutely level line on the trim board a few inches below the gutter from end to end. Use a carpenter's level to ensure accurate measurement.

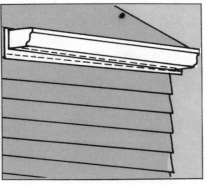

2. Snap another line along the bottom of the gutter from end to end. **TIP:** If the gutter slopes below the trim, mark the lines on the ends of the rafters or along the eaves.

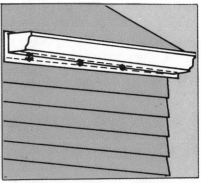

3. Measure the distance at intervals between the level line and the one marking the gutter's pitch. The gutter should slope ¼ inch toward the downspout for every 5 feet of run. Where it does not, adjust the gutter until it conforms to the proper pitch.

Hanging new gutters

1. Install the high end of the gutter in its permanent position. It should just touch the shingles. Support the downspout end in a sling of twine or wire wrapped around a nail.

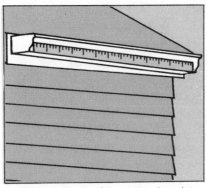

2. Measure the run of the gutter; then determine what the total drop should be. The standard slope is ¼ inch per 5 feet of run.

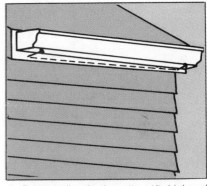

3. Drive a nail under the gutter at its high end and another at the downspout end where the bottom of the downspout must be to produce the required slope. Snap a chalk line between the two nails.

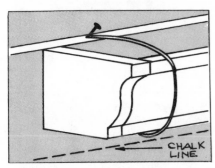

4. Loosen the sling so that you can adjust the slope of the gutter. Beginning at the high end, you will secure the gutter at 30-inch intervals or fasten it to every other rafter. As you work your way across, be sure the bottom of the gutter stays even with the sloping chalk line.

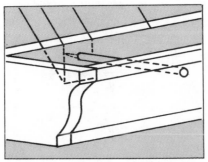

5. When the gutter is in position, pierce holes for the spikes—if you use ferrule-and-spike hangers. Drive the spikes into the ends of the rafters, rather than into the trim board or fascia.

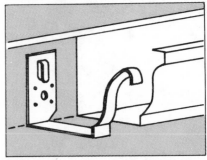

6. Screw the brackets into the fascia, if you are use to this type of hanger. To fasten the brackets, you will have to take down the gutter temporarily. The lower lip of the bracket goes on the chalk line.

Creating underground drainage

What it takes

Approximate time: Up to four hours per 10-foot length of tubing, depending on soil type. A full day for a dry well.

Tools and materials: Shovel, rule, string, stakes, 4-inch-diameter flexible plastic tubing (perforated and non-perforated), downspout adapter, and pea gravel or 6A stone. For a dry well, you'll also need a trowel, plastic or terra cotta tile, a 55-gallon drum, gravel, rubble, planks or a concrete slab, and cement mix.

Over several rainy days, thousands of gallons of water can pour out of a downspout. If the ground slopes away from your house, splash blocks or downspout sleeves will usually distribute the water so that it does no damage. But if your house rests on level ground or in a slight basin, a heavy rain can flood your basement; light rains will keep it dank and mildewy. Strangely enough, an absolutely waterproof foundation poses an even greater problem. What can happen is this: As water seeps down and collects around the foundation, pressure builds up. This can become intense; one cubic foot of water weighs about 63 pounds. The force can reach the point where it will crack a concrete foundation or floor. Then the water floods in.

To prevent damp or flooded basements, it is necessary to have a means of carrying the water off underground. If your house is on a street that has a storm sewer, investigate the cost of linking up with it. This is often the simplest and least expensive solution. But if it is not feasible, you can create your own underground dispersal system in either of two ways. One is by digging a dry well. The other is by laying perforated plastic tubing under the ground. Water seeps from the perforations over a wide area, feeding the lawn as well as any nearby plants, shrubs, and trees. **CAUTION:** Building codes and health-department rules often control the use of storm sewers and the digging of dry wells. Check with the authorities before you dig. Keep dry wells and perforated tubing out of septic-tank fields. Do not run perforated tubing near trees, as this can attract roots. Hooking up with a sanitary system is not recommended.

Laying tubing or drainage tile

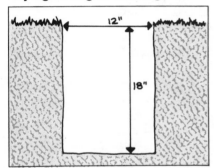

1. Dig a ditch from the downspout leading directly away from your house, following the dimensions shown above. A slope of 2 inches per 10 feet will promote rapid drainage. Make the slope continuous over the entire line, with no reversals in grade.

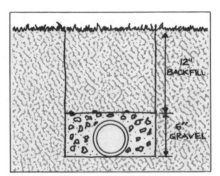

2. Bed the tubing or tile in a gravel or stone envelope as shown. You can also bed with backfill, but use only small, loose particles of earth that will flow around the tubing, and remove stones and clods to avoid excessive settling. Link tubing firmly to downspout with an adapter.

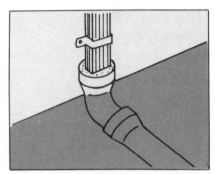

3. Make the first 10-foot section of tubing solid, not perforated, to divert water from the house. Use all solid tubing if you are connecting with a dry well or storm sewer. You can feed several downspouts into a single line to a dry well or storm sewer.

Digging a dry well

1. Chisel the top and bottom out of a 55-gallon drum, and make an opening in its side for 4-inch tubing. Then punch about three dozen holes around the sides of the drum for adequate drainage.

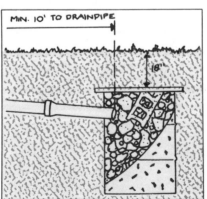

2. Place the drum in a hole dug to the depth shown and fill it with rubble: stones, bricks, broken cinder blocks. Insert the tubing into the drum; then cover the top with a slab or planks. Replace earth and sod.

Alternative method: Use cinder blocks alone instead of a steel drum. Dig a hole about 3 feet by 6 feet and line it with the blocks, leaving gaps of several inches and an opening for the tubing. Fill the hollow space with rubble, cover with planks, and replace earth and sod.

Reshingling a roof

Sometimes it becomes necessary or desirable to reshingle a roof. The old shingles may have become brittle or curled. With asphalt shingles, loss of the mineral granules speeds deterioration. Reshingling a roof is a project that demands careful planning and execution. It also involves hard work. On a multistory house, it is *hazardous* work. But putting asphalt shingles on a roof is within the capabilities of the homeowner who is willing to plan, take pains, and move cautiously when on the roof or ladder. The reward is saving 50 percent or more of what a roofing contractor would charge for the job.

A package of asphalt shingles usually contains a set of step-by-step directions for laying that particular type of shingle. While such directions were prepared by the manufacturer for professional roofers, you will be able to follow them once you have grasped the procedures and techniques explained on this and the following pages.

Several factors affect your choice of shingles and method of application: slope of the roof, wind velocity, and direction. The priority consideration, however, is your physical safety and that of anybody helping you. If yours is a two-story house, you would do well to obtain special scaffolding from a rental outlet, or construct or buy the ladder hooks shown on page 7.

ladder hooks shown on page 7.

Planning hints:
Before starting to reshingle:
- Inspect the chimney and tuckpoint if necessary.
- Realign the gutters, replacing defective ones.
- Repair or replace any rotting wooden trim.
- Check for signs of moisture condensing on the sheathing caused by inadequate ventilation in the attic or crawl space.
- Obtain scaffolding, ladder hooks, etc., needed to make reroofing less risky.
- Obtain tarp or other cover for roofs overnight.
- Wait for a weather prediction of zero percent rain probability over the next 48 to 72 hours.

When and how to remove old shingles

New asphalt shingles can be put down over old asphalt shingles, wood shingles, and roll roofing. Cedar shakes, however, must be taken off as must slate shingles. Here are the general tests for whether or not you have to remove the old shingles:

1. Are the roof supports strong enough to carry the added weight of the new shingles, plus that of yours and any helpers who will be on the roof with you? Usually, yes.

2. Is the deck solid enough to provide anchorage for the nails? (Nails should go into sheathing at least ¾ of an inch and go completely through ⅝-inch plywood.)

3. Does the decking provide a continuous nailing surface, with solid sheathing?

If you can't answer yes to all three of these questions, the old shingles must go.

1. Remove old shingles with a wide, flat shovel. **TIP:** You can take the old felts off the same way. If the deck under the old shingles is spaced sheathing, begin at the ridge so that debris does not fall through the spaces into the house.

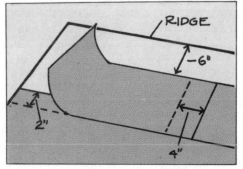

2. Use a pry bar to remove the soil stack and the vent flashings. The old shingles, flashings, and felt create a large volume of debris. Sweep the deck clean periodically and remove debris from the gutters. Loose material underfoot is especially hazardous on a pitched roof.

3. Inspect the deck for holes, rotted or broken sheathing, and loose or protruding nails. Patch over the holes with sheet metal. Hammer down the nails. Replace defective sheathing. If the old deck was spaced sheathing, cover it with ⅝-inch plywood.

4. Apply No.15 asphalt-saturated felts to the deck. Lay the felts horizontally, lapping each course 2 inches over the lower one; where ends join, lap them 4 inches. Lap the felt 6 inches from both sides of hips and ridges. Nail every 2 inches along the outside edges. Note: This underlayment is for roofs having a pitch of 4 inches per foot or greater.

What it takes

Approximate time: The time it will take you to tear off shingles from a roof depends on the roof size and whether your house has one or two stories. A good worker can rip up 200-300 shingles an hour.

Tools and materials: Claw hammer, pry bar, shovel, No. 15 asphalt-saturated felt, 1-inch roofing nails, ladder, and scaffolding.

Calculating your shingle needs

What it takes

Approximate time: Under an hour.

Tools and materials: Carpenter's rule, pencil, and pad of grid paper, or house plans if available.

Shingle requirements are estimated in *squares*. A square of roofing covers 100 square feet of roof. The number of packages of shingles making up a square varies according to the type of shingle, as does the number of shingles in a package. To find out the number of squares you need, you have to compute the area of the roof in square feet, divide by 100, and then add 10 percent for waste and cutting.

To compute the area of your roof, you need to know the dimensions of its sloping plane. This can involve you in dangerous scampering, unless you have a copy of the plans. A much safer, simpler way is to determine the horizontal area your roof covers by taking direct measurements on the ground, and calculate its pitch, as shown below. Then take these figures to your roofing supplier, who will convert them into slope area and then into squares.

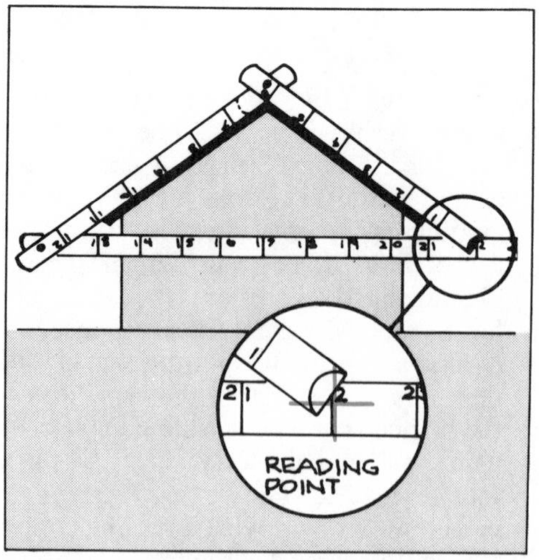

1. Step back from your house until you can frame it within a triangle formed by a carpenter's rule, as shown. Keeping the base of the triangle horizontal, adjust its sides until they align with the roof. Read the base of the rule at the reading point.

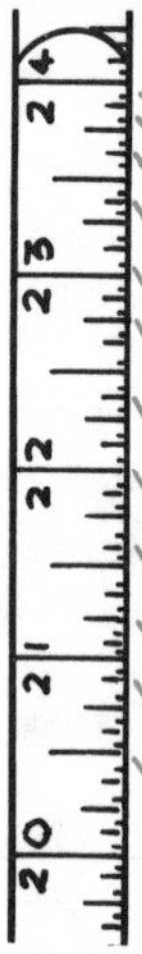

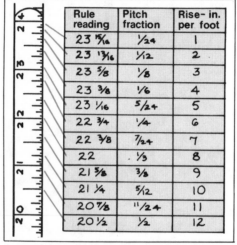

Rule reading	Pitch fraction	Rise- in. per foot
23 15/16	1/24	1
23 13/16	1/12	2
23 5/8	1/8	3
23 3/8	1/6	4
23 1/16	5/24	5
22 3/4	1/4	6
22 3/8	7/24	7
22	1/3	8
21 5/8	3/8	9
21 1/4	5/12	10
20 7/8	11/24	11
20 1/2	1/2	12

2. Locate the reading on the line marked Rule Reading in this chart. In the example, the reading on the rule is 22; this represents a 1/3 pitch with 8 inches of rise per horizontal foot. For any given horizontal area and pitch, a roof has the same slope area, regardless of its design or type.

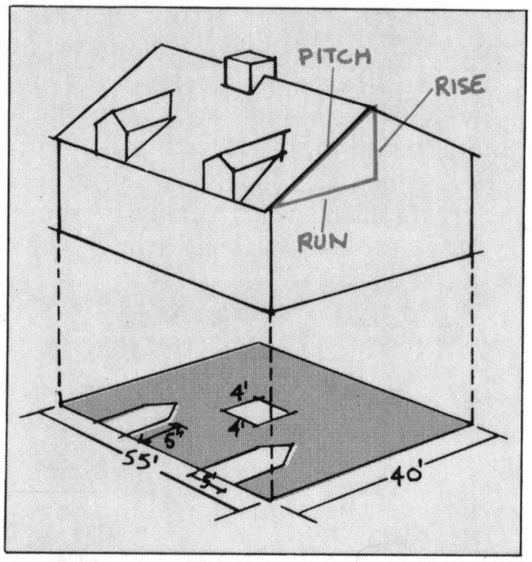

Map the horizontal area covered by your roof, leaving out areas occupied by a chimney and where one element of the roof projects over another. Be sure to figure the pitch over dormers separately.

Selecting shingles

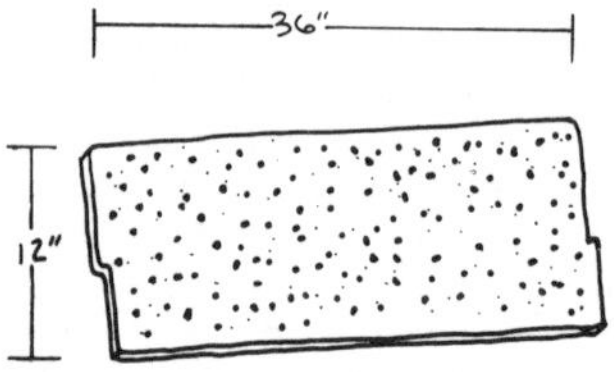

One-tab shingle (no cutout)

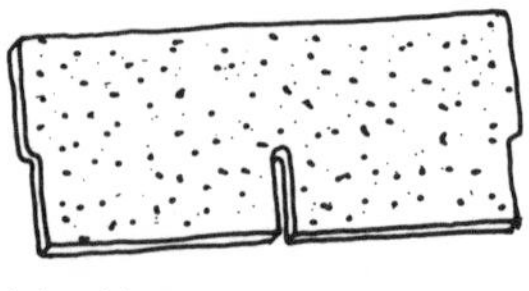

Two-tab shingle

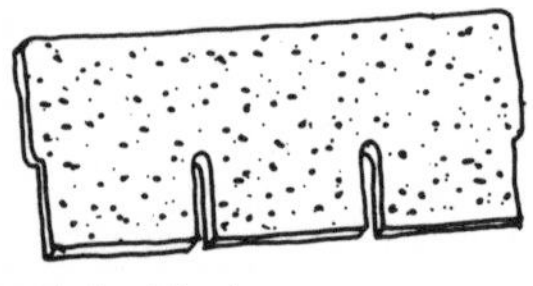

Three-tab shingle

Shingles are a simple product that have several difficult and essential jobs to do. They have to shed water. They must not blow off and away. They should resist fire from chimney sparks. They ought to look nice and last long. In recent years many shingle manufacturers have devoted large sums to research; as a result, you now have a variety of improved asphalt shingles to select from. For example, white asphalt shingles often turned a gray-green from algae and fungi. Several manufacturers now use granules on white shingles that repel mildew-forming organisms.

A local building code may specify the rating of the shingles you put on. Chances are it will be an Underwriters' Laboratory Class C. Even if you are not covered by a building code, you should purchase nothing less fire resistant than a Class C shingle. If your roof is exposed to high winds, consider buying a self-sealing shingle whose flaps won't raise even in a 60-knot gale. You can, however, seal down shingles yourself with a technique shown opposite.

Maintaining proper alignment is difficult, particularly when putting new shingles down over old. If the latter is the case, try to find shingles that have the same dimensions as the old. Fitting and applying shingles will be simplest for you if you select one of the square-butt types.

Preparing old surfaces

When you are planning to put asphalt shingles down over old wood shingles, you have to prepare the surface to receive the new roofing. Here are the things you should do beforehand:

1. Replace missing shingles with new ones.
2. Nail down all loose shingles.
3. Remove all loose or protruding nails; drive new nails but not into the old nail holes, as this will cause them to pop.
4. Split badly warped or curled shingles and nail down the segments.

When the shingles along the eaves and up the rakes—the outside edges of the roof—are badly weathered, prepare the surface according to the steps below. Feathering strips nailed as shown will produce a more professional job.

Cut the shingles back far enough so that wood strips can be fitted in. Nail these strips in place with the outside edges projecting beyond the deck the same distance the wood shingles did.

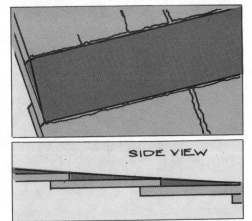

Build a smooth deck for asphalt shingles by nailing beveled feathering strips along the butt of each course of the old shingles. This will give the new roof a more even appearance and anchor the nails better.

What it takes

Approximate time: Maximum times are likely to be 2 hours to prepare surface, 8 hours to cut and fit edges, 4 hours to put down feathering strips, 4 hours to install drip edge, and 3 hours to apply eave flashing.

Tools and materials: Claw hammer, wood chisel, metal shears, ladder, broom, 1x4 or 1x6 boards, feathering strips, noncorrosive metal, 1½-inch roofing nails of same material, and 8-penny wire nails.

The preparation procedure is simpler when you are reshingling over asphalt shingles. Nail down or cut away all loose, curled, or lifted shingles. Remove all loose and protruding nails. Replace all badly worn edges with new edging. Just before you apply the new shingles, sweep the surface clean of all debris.

One advantage of tearing off shingles is that you can install a drip edge along the eaves and the rakes. But you can also install a drip edge on the wood strips you fit when preparing to cover wood shingles. A drip edge provides a neater, more watertight corner. Water drips from it more readily than from wood.

Another advantage of applying roofing to a clean deck is that you can apply flashing at the eaves if you live in a region where ice dams are a problem. (See pages 496-97.)

Cut a strip of corrosion-resistant metal wide enough to cover the edge and extend 3 inches back on the roof. Apply it over the No. 15 asphalt-saturated felt used as underlayment. Bend the strip down over the edges. Secure with roofing nails of the same metal as the strip. Drive a nail every 10 inches along the strip.

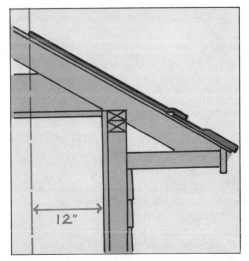

Lay a strip of roll roofing, smooth or mineral surface, over the roofing felt and drip edge. The flashing should be wide enough to extend up the roof at least 12 inches inside the interior wall line.

Applying shingles

A smooth, well-patterned, asphalt-shingle roof is within the reach of anybody who can carefully follow the directions below. They are written for the application of three-tab shingles but could easily be adapted for other types as well.

It didn't take me long to catch on
There I was working from a ladder, trying to get a shingle in place in the very first course. I forgot myself and reached out to the side. The ladder started to slide, and I grabbed for the gutter. I didn't fall, but my hammer did. As soon as my wife got the ladder back in place, I climbed right down and bought a ladder stabilizer like the one you can see back on page 487.

Practical Pete

What it takes

Approximate time: Two hours to apply a square (100 square feet); roof area will determine total time.

Tools and materials: Hammer, carpenter's rule, chalk line, ladder, scaffolding, special tab cement, and galvanized steel or aluminum roofing nails with ⅜-inch heads. Nail length will vary from 1½ inches on a clean deck, to 1¾ inches over old asphalt shingles, to 2 inches over wood shingles.

TIPS:
Do not store asphalt shingles directly on the ground or on the roof overnight.
Cover shingles with a tarp, not with plastic (moisture can condense underneath plastic).
Stack shingles no higher than 4 feet.

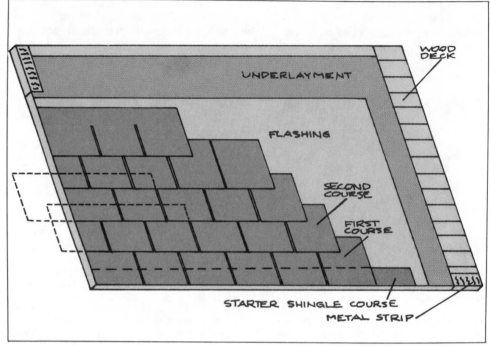

1. Remove the tabs from shingles needed for a starter course, which should be placed under the first visible course. Cut 3 inches off the side of the first shingle so that cutouts of shingles in this course will not coincide with those of the first course. Place starter-course shingles so they overhang eaves and rakes ¼ inch.
2. Start the first course with a full-length shingle. Its top edge should line up with the butt edge of the old shingle in the next higher course. If it doesn't, make it fit by cutting along its top edge. Trim the remaining shingles in the course to make the same fit.
3. Cut 4 inches (or half a tab) from the first shingle in the second course and 8 inches (or a full tab) from the first shingle in the third course. On the fourth course, begin to repeat the process that you started with the first course. Continue it for the rest of the roof. Varying the length of starting shingles over three courses ensures that joints and cutouts in one course are not aligned with those in the next.
4. Apply shingles across and up, rather than completely laying one course before starting the next one up. This method will make less noticeable any package-to-package color variation by spreading shingles from one package fanlike over several courses rather than stringing them out in a few rows.
5. Align each shingle carefully. Make sure that cutouts and end joints are no closer than 2 inches from any nail in the underlying course. Follow the manufacturer's specifications for exposure. Lay the butt edge of the tabs even with the top of the cutouts in the course below.
6. Start nailing from the end of the shingle that adjoins the shingle you just laid, and move across the shingle from there, using four nails per shingle. Drive nails straight so the edge of the nail head does not cut into the shingle. Hammer nail heads flush, not into the asphalt surface. Replace immediately any shingle you cut into or rip.
7. Begin to shingle at the rake that is most visible and work toward the other one. Where a roof is interrupted by a valley or dormer, begin at the rake and lay shingles toward the break.
8. If your roof is exposed to high winds and the shingles you bought don't have factory-applied adhesive, put a spot of special tab cement about the size of a 50-cent piece under each tab. Use a putty knife or caulking gun. Don't bend shingles back more than is neccessary. Press the tab down. Cement should not come out beyond edge of tab.

Shingling hips and ridges

Before applying new shingles at a ridge, remove the old ridge cap. Do the same for hips. Replace any badly deteriorated shingles with new shingles to provide a good nailing surface. Do not use metal material on hips or ridges. Corrosion may discolor and ruin the appearance of the roof.

To cover hips and ridges, you can buy shingles made specially for that purpose, or you can cut rectangular pieces not less than 9x12 inches from the shingles you are applying to the main roof. Here is the fitting and nailing procedure.

1. Bend a shingle lengthwise along the center so that it will have equal coverage on each side of the hip or ridge. In cold weather, warm the shingles inside the house before bending them.
2. Begin at the lower end of a hip, or at either end of a ridge, and lay the shingles over the edge, securing each side with a nail 5½ inches from the exposed end and 1 inch up from the edge. Lay the succeeding shingles to obtain a 5-inch exposure. On ridges, apply laps away from the direction of the prevailing wind.

Flashing valleys

If you are covering old shingles, it is not necessary to replace the valley flashing unless it leaks or is deteriorating badly. But in working on a roof, do not step in the valleys. When you put down new flashing in valleys, the following procedure, known as open-valley flashing, is recommended. It works equally well on a roof whose shingles you have just torn off, on one where you are covering old shingles, or on a new roof.

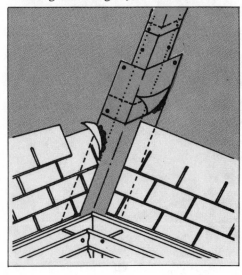

1. Lay an 18-inch-wide strip of mineral-surface roll roofing, surfaced side down, along the full length of the valley. Cut the lower edge flush with the eave flashing. Secure with two rows of nails, 1 inch in from the sides. Nail one entire row before you begin the second. As you proceed along the second row, press the roofing firmly in place in the valley.
2. Place a 36-inch-wide strip of the roll roofing, surfaced side up, centered in the valley. Secure it the same way you did in the first strip. On both strips use only enough nails to hold the paper in place. If you have to splice a strip, make the ends of the upper segment overlap the lower segment by 12 inches and secure with asphalt cement.
3. Snap two chalk lines the full length of the valley. The lines should be 6 inches apart at the ridge and diverge at the rate of 1/8 inch per foot. Thus a valley 8 feet long, for example, will be 7 inches wide at the eaves. Trim the shingles to the chalk line. Cut off the upper outside corner of each shingle to deflect water into the valley. Secure the shingles with asphalt cement. Do not nail within the chalk lines.

Flashing and shingling dormers

Open-valley flashing is a good way to obtain waterproof, water-shedding roofing in the joint between a dormer and the main roof. Follow the procedure described above for flashing the valley between two roofs, but note the following special techniques that apply to flashing a dormer valley:

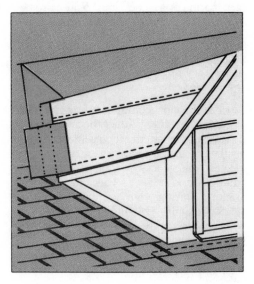

1. Continue the courses of main-roof shingles to a point just above the lower end of the valley. Then lay the 18-inch strip of roll roofing. Extend its bottom end 1/4 inch below the edge of the dormer deck.
2. Fit the second strip of roll roofing, cutting the dormer side to match the lower end of the underlying strip. Cut the side that lies on the main deck to overlap the course of shingles. Make this overlap the same as the shingle-to-shingle overlap.
3. Snap vertical and horizontal lines to ensure proper alignment of courses above the dormer. You want the edges of shingles to be in line and any cutouts to be vertical.

Flashing a vertical wall

When reshingling a roof that abuts a vertical wall, you face a special flashing problem. But you can handle it with the simple technique described below.

1. Lay a strip of smooth roll roofing 8 inches wide over the old shingles next to the wall. Nail this strip down with a row of nails along each edge, spaced about 4 inches apart.
2. Cover the strip with asphalt cement just before you apply a shingle over it. The end of each new course is secured by bedding the shingle in asphalt cement. No nails are used in the finish course. When you have completed the roof, lay a bead of asphalt cement in the joint with a caulking gun. It will tighten the joint and improve its appearance.

What it takes

Approximate time: To flash a valley, 2 hours; to flash and shingle a dormer, 3 hours; to flash a joint between a vertical wall and roof, 1½ hours.

Tools and materials: Hammer, caulking gun, carpenter's rule, chalk lines, mineral-surface roll roofing, smooth-surface roll roofing, asphalt cement, and galvanized or aluminum roofing nails.

4.SIDING

Unlike roofing, siding can and should last as long as the house itself. But regardless of the material it consists of—even aluminum or vinyl—siding requires maintenance.

It pays to inspect siding once a year. The early spring is a good time. You can spot any winter damage; shrubs around the foundation will not yet have leafed, so you can see more. Look for peeling paint, blisters, loose or warped boards, cracks, shrunk caulking, and evidence of termites. While you're at it, prune back shrubs that have grown closer than two feet to the house, and pull down all climbing vines.

Maintaining wood siding

Wood is the most common siding and has a number of advantages over the newer materials: ease of repair and replacement, higher insulation and soundproofing value, and greater resistance to dents. On the other hand wood is subject to decay and deterioration. During your annual inspection, check for signs of rotting in your siding. If you spot the decay early enough, you can often prevent real damage. Look also for peeling or blistered paint. Water is usually the culprit. Often it is not water from the outside but from the inside. Warm, moist vapor from the house flows through the walls and, reaching the cold sheathing, condenses. Even a few drops of water between the siding and the film of paint will cause paint to blister and peel. Moisture doesn't reveal itself on unpainted wood siding, but if present will start wood rotting. The answer to such a problem is to install vents in the siding. There are several different types available. The two below are the most popular.

What it takes

Approximate time: Two or three hours for preventive maintenance of an average house.

Tools and materials: Brace and bit, hammer, scraper, paintbrush, vents, latex caulk, and latex paint.

Venting wood siding

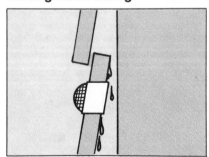

Drill holes in the siding the same diameter as the vent you are installing. Locate the holes between the studs and 6 inches below the ceiling level. Line the holes with latex caulk. Insert the vent. Plug-type vents can be used on flat siding as well.

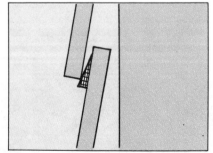

Push a wedge-shaped vent under the lower edge of clapboard siding. This type of vent is made of plastic or aluminum. It is permanent, being held in place by pressure from the clapboard. The vents should be 2 feet apart in the problem area.

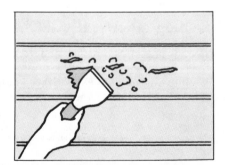

Allow a month for moisture to escape and the siding to dry. Then scrape off the blistered and peeling area, and repaint with latex exterior paint.

Repairing wood siding

One of the advantages of wood siding is that it's easy to repair or splice a replacement piece into any gaps. A wood shingle in a siding is repaired or replaced in the same way as a wood shingle on a roof. See the directions on page 490. In addition to shingles, wood siding comes in a variety of boards. The siding type will govern how the repair or replacement is made.

The most common wood siding is clapboard. There are two types. One has a tapered profile, thicker at the bottom and gradually narrowing toward the top. This is called beveled siding. The other type has a uniform thickness.

A course of clapboard overlaps the one below it. Nails in the bottom of the upper course go through the top of the clapboard below. Despite the overlapping, it is easy to replace a piece of defective clapboard.

Your house, or portions of it, may also have vertical board-and-batten siding. This is the easiest type of siding to replace.

Holes occasionally occur in wood siding. Regardless of the type of siding, they are patched the same way.

What it takes

Approximate time: One-half hour per defective board.

Tools and materials: Hammer, chisel, putty knife, wooden wedges, electric drill with 1/8-inch bit, finishing nails, waterproof glue, wood putty, and oil-based caulking and gun.

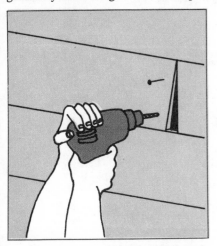

Straighten warped or buckled clapboards by first removing nails. Then sandpaper any joints that were too tight. The board will now need new nails to hold it in place. But to avoid splitting the wood, drill pilot holes for the nails. Set the nails and fill holes with wood putty or caulking.

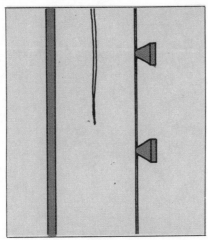

Repair splits in board-and-batten siding by forcing waterproof glue into cracks. To close a large split, remove the strip of batten and force one or more wooden wedges into the exposed joint along the length of the split.

Clean all dust and debris from a hole in wood siding. Deepen the hole around the edges if it is too shallow there to retain a filling. Fill the hole with several layers of wood putty, allowing each layer to dry for several hours. This will prevent the center from sinking as it dries. Sand and paint the next day.

Closing splits in clapboard

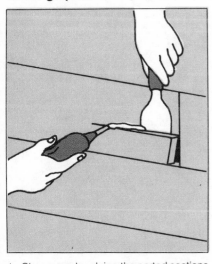

1. Close gaps by gluing the parted sections together. Remove the nails in the lower section, then pry it out, being careful not to split the board more. Coat exposed edges of both sections with waterproof glue and work some into the crack.

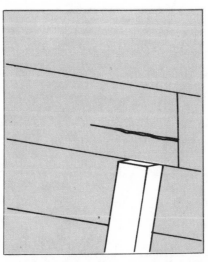

2. Wedge a 2x4 between the ground and the clapboard to hold it tight until the glue sets. Wipe off excess glue. If wedging is impractical, nail a board under the split to clamp the crack tightly.

Stopgaps and copouts

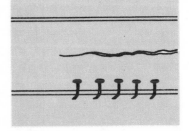

Cracked, warped, or loose siding should be repaired as soon as you notice it. Water works its way through such defects into the interior wall, where rotting can take place undetected. If you don't have time for a thorough repair, seal the splits with oil-based caulking compound and clamp them together by driving nails and clinching them over the boards. This method is recommended as a temporary expedient only.

Replacing wood siding

Some wood siding becomes so badly split, warped, or rotted that the boards can no longer be made weatherproof by repairing them. Such boards should be replaced. Because of their overlapping pattern, clapboards must be replaced differently from board-and-batten siding. Replacing the lat-

ter is simpler, but neither job is difficult.

The ideal time to replace siding is just before you are going to paint the house. This is because the spliced-in piece will have to be painted or treated, and if you cover only it, the contrast with the rest of the siding will be of the sore-thumb variety.

Patching clapboard

1. Cut the board at each end of the deteriorated section. If a joint is nearby, use it to save a saw cut even though the section contains some good wood. Start the cutting with a backsaw and finish it with a large, flat chisel.

2. Split out strips of the deteriorated section with the chisel, being careful not to damage the building paper and sheathing underneath. Pull out the nails in the overlapping board and chisel out the remains of the damaged board beneath it.

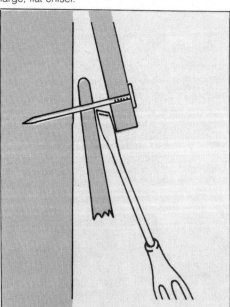

3. Trim the hidden edges of the cut-out section with a small chisel so that they are even with the exposed edges. You can push a screwdriver up under the overlapping board so you have room to work and to see what you are doing. Replace any building paper you cut into.

4. Measure the new board so that it makes a tight patch. Drive it into place so that its butt edges line up with those of the boards on either side. Drive nails and set. Fill the nail holes with wood putty. When putty is dry, paint or stain the board.

Patching vertical siding

Most vertical siding is either board or strips of plywood, and batten. The boards are generally 1x12 feet in size. Except for removing the batten strips, the same procedure can be used for patching any defective piece of vertical siding. **TIP:** If your siding is plywood, be sure to make the patch out of exterior grade plywood.

What it takes

Approximate time: One hour per patch.

Tools and materials: Claw hammer, small pry bar, saber saw, 1¼-inch galvanized or aluminum finishing nails, and wood putty.

1. Remove the battens on both sides of the board, using a small pry bar. Then pull out the nails that hold the board to the studs. Be careful when pulling the nails not to scar the exposed surface, nor enlarge any holes you are not going to reuse. Then lift out the board or plywood section.

2. Trim off the defective portion and place it over the new board or plywood. Using the old piece as a pattern, mark cutting lines on the new one. Cut the patch with a saber saw. Nail the patch and remaining section of the old wood in place. Fill the joint between the two pieces with wood putty. Replace the battens.

Repairing aluminum

Aluminum is one of the most popular materials for nonwood siding. Aluminum siding does not need repainting and lasts indefinitely. But it is susceptible to denting; a baseball, even a heavy hailstorm can mar it. Fortunately such dents are usually easy to remove. A more serious but less common problem with aluminum siding is that if not correctly applied, sections may buckle from the heat of the summer sun. Then it is necessary to remove the siding and install it correctly, straightening or replacing the buckled section. This process is simple if the correct sequence is followed.

What it takes

Approximate time: One-half hour for a dent; two hours to replace a section.

Tools and materials: Screwdriver, pair of pliers, file, small self-tapping screw with rubber ferrule, tube of plastic aluminum material, aluminum paint, and brush.

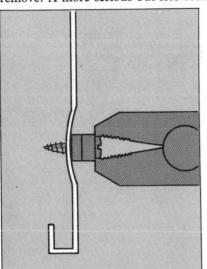

1. Twist a small self-tapping screw into the center of the dent. Place a rubber ferrule or a few washers around the screw's shank as a spacer. Grasp the end of the screw with a pair of pliers and pull until the dent has popped or flattened out.

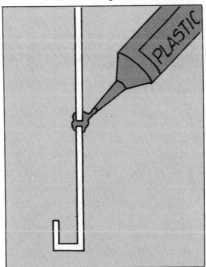

2. Squeeze plastic aluminum, a hardware-store item, into the hole made by the screw. Allow this to harden, then file and sand smooth. Touch up with matching paint. The same technique can of course be used to patch small holes in aluminum.

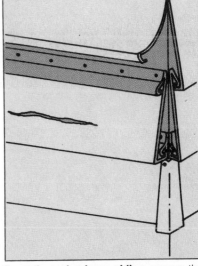

To replace aluminum siding remove the corner caps and pry up the overlapping piece. Pull out the nails in the top flange and both end flanges. Lift out the piece. With some siding you may have to start at the top piece and remove each succeeding piece.

Repairing stucco

Repairing a stucco wall usually means filling a crack or patching a hole. The nature of the defect determines the treatment required. You can deal with a hairline crack by painting over it with a cement water paint. A somewhat larger crack must be caulked first, then painted. But large holes must be filled with mortar in stages over several days.

Any crack or cavity in stucco should be repaired as soon as you notice it. Otherwise water will seep in. If your house has a wooden frame, the dampness will rot the wood. If you live in a cold climate, water in the crack will freeze in the winter and enlarge the opening. If your house walls are masonry block, the moisture will keep them damp.

There is little you can do to prevent cracks in stucco. They result from a number of irremediable causes. The original mortar may have been incorrectly mixed, may have lacked the proper ingredients, or dried too rapidly; or walls may have settled due to poor foundations. Stucco over brick or stone can crack because different materials expand and contract differently.

What it takes

Approximate time: One half hour to prepare a hole, and half-hour sessions over three days to patch it.

Tools and materials: Dull knife, wire brush or whisk broom, trowel, bucket, striker board, wire cutters, wire, lath, white silica sand, and white portland cement.

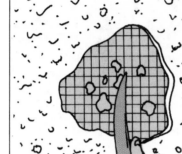

1. Scrape away all loose materials in large cracks and holes. A dull knife works well. Then undercut the edges so that the patch will be wider inside than at the surface, securing it better to the old stucco. Clip out and replace any wire lath that has rusted through. Brush out all dust and particles.

2. Mix a mortar using the same ingredients and proportions as the existing stucco. If this is unknown, use one part white portland cement to four parts white silica sand, adding just enough water for a puttylike consistency. The mortar should stand on its own when pulled up with a trowel.

New wrinkles

This adjustable rubber pad fits on a ladder. By distributing the force, it reduces the marring of surfaces and the damaging of vinyl and metal siding.

3. Spray the damaged section with water, then force mortar in and around the wire lath. Fill the hole less than halfway, blending the mortar into the surrounding stucco with a wire brush. Scratch up the surface with the tip of the trowel and allow to set up, but not dry out completely.

4. Apply a second layer the next day, almost filling the hole. Allow the mortar to set overnight. On the third day, apply the final coat, using a small wooden striker board to smooth it off flush with the surrounding surface. Texture the surface to match the old stucco surrounding it. After allowing it to dry for a couple of days, paint the patch to match the old stucco's appearance.

Replacing asbestos siding

Because of their rigidity, asbestos shingles tend to pop nails. Since they are brittle, they crack easily. When hammering a nail back into place, exercise care. It's safer to use a nailset to drive it home. Do not try to start a nail through an asbestos shingle; they come with nail holes in them. If you need a new hole, drill it; locate it at least an inch from an existing hole to avoid cracking the shingle.

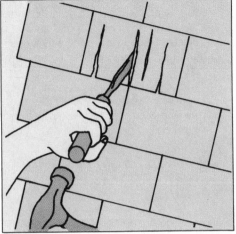

1. Break up a shingle that needs to be replaced. Being brittle, it will fragment readily and you can extract it piece by piece. Then pull out the exposed nails with a pair of pliers. If there are nails in the overlapping shingle, cut them off from behind with a hacksaw blade.

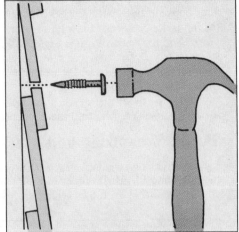

2. Slide the new shingle into place until its bottom edge is aligned with those of the others in its course. Its nail holes may or may not line up with the ones in the shingles above and below. If you can't line them up with minor readjustments, drill new holes.

Replacing vinyl siding

Vinyl siding—polyvinyl chloride—needs little maintenance or repair. Unlike aluminum siding, it does not dent. But like aluminum, it will buckle during hot weather if any pieces were not correctly measured and fitted together. In addition to expanding from heat, vinyl siding contracts markedly from the cold, and can become brittle enough to be cracked by a sharp blow. The limb of a tree crashing into vinyl siding can do extensive damage in any season. People in vinyl-sided houses should be prepared to replace pieces. Here is a simple method.

1. Pull off the blocks at the corners. A piece of vinyl siding interlocks with the one above and below it. Being brittle, it can't be pried like aluminum siding. So start at the top, removing the nails and lifting off each piece. Work your way down to the damaged piece, numbering the pieces you remove so that you can replace them in the same order.

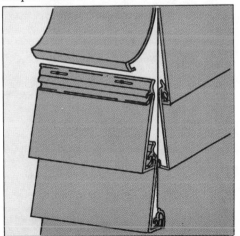

2. Remove the damaged piece or pieces and replace with new ones, then reassemble the rest of the siding, being careful to interlock the pieces and nail them so there's no gap between courses. The color of the replacement may differ from that of the others at first but will gradually blend in.

Caulking your house

Caulking is one of the simplest jobs a homeowner can undertake. It requires no special skills or expensive tools. And it does not consume much time. Working a few hours a day, you can recaulk all the seams in your house in two or three weekends. Once the job is done, it should last for four or five years. And the rewards are many. Caulking keeps water, drafts, dirt, and insects such as termites out of your house. It also keeps heat from escaping in cold weather.

Cracks and holes that need caulking exist in every house. You will find them wherever two parts of your house come together or different materials meet. Common trouble spots are: areas around door and window frames; areas between siding and chimney; where the house foundation and siding meet; where a wing or garage intersects the main part of the house; around a water pipe or electrical conduit that penetrates the foundation or siding; around vents set in the siding; at all points where the siding meets the trim. Caulking is also necessary in repairing roof leaks (pages 489 and 492). It is one of the homeowner's greatest allies.

(pages 489 and 492)

What it takes

Approximate time: A few minutes for small patching jobs; 30 minutes to prepare and recaulk the seams around one door or window frame.

Tools and materials: Wire brush, old screwdriver, putty knife, squeeze tube of the caulking compound (or cartridge and cartridge gun), recommended cleaner/ solvent (see chart), a clean rag.

Types of caulking and uses

Caulking is now available in a variety of materials and forms. It comes in bulk form and in disposable cartridges which are used with an applicator gun. Use the chart below to select the type best suited to the job you have to do.

TYPE	USED FOR	SPECIAL REQUIREMENTS	SOLVENT CLEANER	COMMENTS
Oil-based	Routine caulking and glazing	Needs priming and painting	Turpentine or paint thinner	Shrinks; maximum life: five years. Least expensive.
Oakum	Very wide or deep cracks	Must be pounded in	None needed	Needs to be covered with additional compound.
Polybutane cord	Wide or deep cracks	Does not adhere, must be pressed in	None needed	Can't be painted.
Butyl rubber	Metal-to-wood or metal-to-masonry joints	None.	Paint thinner	Hard to use. Can be painted over immediately.
Neoprene	Cracks in concrete	Requirements vary from brand to brand	Toluene	Fumes are toxic.
Silicone	Joints that must be waterproof	Follow manufacturer's instructions	Paint thinner	Does not stick well to painted surfaces; costly. Lasts 15-20 years.

Caulking roundup

Most of the compounds listed above are available in three forms: bulk (one- or five-gallon cans); disposable cartridges for use in cartridge guns; and squeeze tubes. The latter are meant for special applications, so the choice is usually between the first two. Bulk form is the least expensive—but also the least convenient. The barrel of the caulking gun must be loaded and cleaned with each use. With cartridges, loading and cleaning the gun means merely slipping the cartridge in and out of it.

How to caulk

Caulking is not difficult if you take a few preparatory steps and follow the application techniques on the next page. To begin, work with clean seams. Using a scraper or screwdriver, chip off the exposed caulk- ing. If it has not dried completely, try pulling it out in strips. After you have removed the caulking, wire-brush the seams to remove dust and chips. Then wipe them with a rag dipped in the indicated solvent or cleaner. **TIP:** Digging dried caulking out of deep seams takes time. In such cases, your best choice may be to leave the old caulking in place and apply oil-based caulking over it. While the oil-based material has a limited life (five years or less), it is inexpensive, will stick well to the caulking beneath it, and is relatively easy to apply. It's a good idea to check your house's caulking periodically.

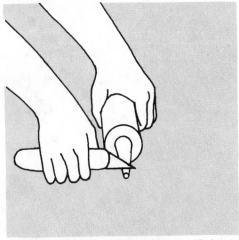

To caulk, cut the end of a cartridge at a 45-degree angle, using a sharp knife. Push a nail down the nozzle to break the inner seal. Leave the nail in place until you are ready to begin working.

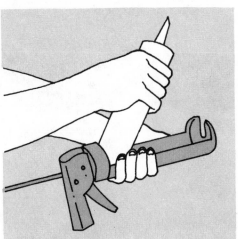

Place the cartridge in the gun, and twist the plunger until the ratchet side is down. Pulling the gun's trigger forces the ratchet forward, squeezing compound out the nozzle.

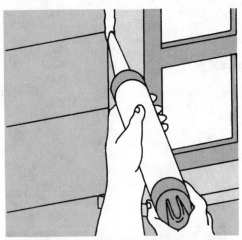

Work from top to bottom on vertical seams and in the direction of your stronger arm on horizontal ones. Slant the gun at a 45-degree angle, with the base pointing toward the direction you're working in. This keeps the nozzle level with the seam and creates an even bead of caulking.

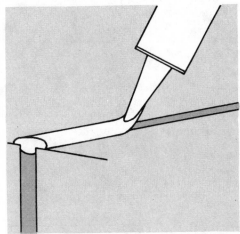

Draw the gun along slowly, so the caulking fills the crack and the bead overlaps both sides. The trick is to keep even pressure on the trigger. If you have to stop before you complete a seam, quickly release the trigger. **TIP:** To keep the caulking soft, plug the nozzle of the cartridge with a nail when done.

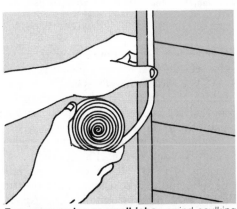

For emergencies or small jobs unwind caulking rope as shown, and force it into the crack with your fingers. You can unroll more than one strand at a time if the crack is large.

Planning hints

Caulk in warm weather, never when the temperature is below 50 degrees Fahrenheit. For an emergency job in cold weather, use polybutane cord.

On hot summer days, caulking gets runny. Chill the tube or cartridge in the refrigerator for an hour or so to firm it up.

A cartridge will cover about 100 feet of seam with a ¼-inch bead.

The best time to caulk is when you are painting your house. Apply primer to the seams first; then caulk. (The primer helps the caulking stick.) Let the caulking cure for several days. Then apply the finish coat. Remember to use a compound that will take paint without bleeding.

Runaway caulk?
I remembered too late that on a warm day, caulk should be placed in the refrigerator for an hour or two before using, or it will get runny. (Change to a fresh tube each time you go in for a beer.)
Practical Pete

5. EXTERIOR PAINTING

Sequence to follow when painting your house

1. Wash the siding and trim with warm water and detergent. **2.** Scrape off loose and peeling paint. Sand the wood. **3.** Prime bare wood; set exposed nails. **4.** Sand glossy surfaces under the eaves and other protected places. **5.** Wire-brush loose paint from gutters and downspouts. **6.** Remove loose caulking from around windows, doors, and other joints. Replace. **7.** Remove loose putty from windows. Reglaze. **8.** Cover exposed roofs, steps, and shrubs with drop cloths. **9.** Paint the trim, gutters, and downspouts first, beginning at the top. **10.** Paint the siding, working across the house from left to right. Always end at a door, window, or edge.

Planning hints:

- Spring and fall are good times to paint a house.
- Don't paint until all gutters, downspouts, and siding have been repaired and all joints have been caulked.
- Preparing the surface is the essential first step.
- Buy your paint and brushes from a store with an experienced sales clerk.

Painting the outside of a house is not for the lazy or slapdash. Pushing a brush back and forth is hard on the forearm. Climbing up and down a ladder is hard on the feet. The job requires planning and patience, too. There are many small jobs to complete before you pick up a brush. BUT . . .

On the plus side, it is not a job that requires technical skill or the use of complicated equipment. And painting your house can save you quite a bit of money. When painting is done by a professional contractor, labor represents about 75 percent of the cost. These days, it can cost $750 or $1,000

to have even a small house painted. As you can see, the savings are substantial.

If you prefer not to spend time on a ladder, have a professional paint the gables and other upper parts of your house; then paint the lower sections yourself.

Paint is designed to preserve as well as beautify your house. Physically, it is a coating of film. What is underneath must be solid and in good shape. Thus painting can't be done until gutters, downspouts, and siding are repaired, and joints and cracks are caulked. It will also be necessary to sand and even wash the surface.

Avoiding common paint problems

Shown below are six common paint problems, along with information that will help you avoid them—or deal with them correctly should one confront you.

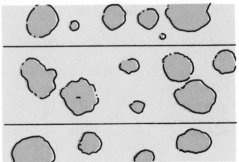

Blistering. This is caused by gas or liquid pressure under the paint. Most blisters are caused by moisture resulting from poor household ventilation; to correct this, install vents in the siding (page 30). Blisters that appear a few hours after the paint is applied arise from unevaporated solvent. The surface of the paint dried too rapidly, trapping the solvent. This can happen when you paint on a surface exposed to direct sunlight or on a very hot day. Dark paints are especially susceptible to blistering because they absorb more heat than light paints do.

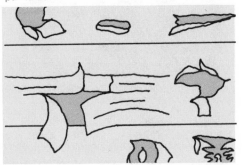

Peeling. Peeling occurs because the paint did not bond with the underlying surface. This can happen when the surface is wet, dirty, oily, or glossy. Paint will not bond with a surface that is wet from morning dew or with a prime coat that was not given time to dry thoroughly.

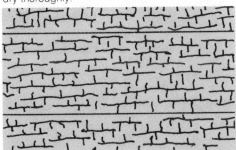

Alligatoring. This somewhat fanciful term refers to paint that has separated into rectangular segments. The result is a surface that resembles the hide of an alligator. Alligatoring results from surface paint and underlying paint that fail to expand and contract at the same rate. This condition arises when paint is applied over an incompatible surface, and when it has been thinned with an incompatible solvent. It can also occur if the paint is applied before the prime coat has dried.

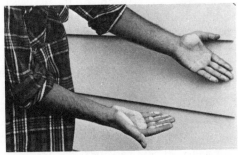

Chalking. If you've ever brushed up against dry paint and gotten covered with powder, you know what chalking is. The powder is pigment that is shed by the paint. Some chalking is desirable, especially in white paint, and is formulated into the mixture. One benefit of chalking is that it cleans the surface, making the paint look fresh for a long time. Another is that by gradually wearing away, it eliminates the need to sand. When it's time to paint again, the coat is thin enough to take new paint without buildup.

Excessive chalking, however, is bad. The pigment washes away too quickly, exposing the siding it should protect. This has three possible causes: The paint was of poor quality and lacked sufficient binder; the undersurface was not sufficiently primed and was so dry it soaked up all the binder; or the paint was applied in cold weather.

Chalking is undesirable on siding above bricks, as the pigment will streak the bricks. (To remove streaks, wash the bricks with a strong solution of hot water and dish detergent.)

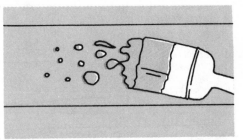

Crawling. With this problem, the paint fails to form a continuous coat. Instead it gathers in globules, like water on an oily surface. Crawling occurs when latex is applied over a high-gloss surface that has not been sanded. An oily or dirty surface will also make paint crawl. Such surfaces are apt to be found under eaves and in other sheltered places.

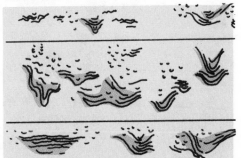

Wrinkling. This occurs when too much paint is applied or when the paint itself is too thick. It is especially likely to take place in cold weather. Wrinkles develop soon, and you can quickly correct them. Sand the surface and brush on paint of a lighter consistency.

House pox
A week after I'd finished painting my house, it began to look sick. A month later, it *was* sick. The paint was blotched and peeling. I had bought "one-coat-covers-all" bargain paint and hurried it on. Well, I had to sand it off and begin the job from scratch. But then I got smart. I bought the best paint I could find and applied it right.

Practical Pete

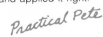

Preparing the surfaces

What it takes

Approximate time: Three hours to wash an average one-story house; eight hours for a two-story house.

Tools and materials: Push broom, garden hose, aspirator, dish detergent, trisodium phosphate (a paint-store item).

Not all painting errors reveal themselves in problems like those shown on the previous page. A common and expensive problem is that the whole coat of paint deteriorates rapidly—and soon you're back on the ladder, repainting the entire house. The most common causes for this general deterioration are: inadequate preparation of the surfaces to be painted; use of poor-quality paint; and errors in applying the paint. The following pages deal with each, starting with how to prepare surfaces.

Washing a house

All surfaces to be painted must be scrupulously clean. The first step is washing down the house. (There's an unexpected bonus in this first step, by the way. You may find that your house doesn't need repainting at all. It may only have needed a thorough cleaning to rid it of dust, soil, and mildew that made the paint appear dingy.) You will need a high-pressure spray cleaner to wash the house. You can rent one from a paint store, hardware store, or equipment-rental company. You can also make your own, as shown in step 1, below. It will do the necessary job of removing both dirt and loose, peeling paint. In performing this operation, keep the work area clean.

What it takes

Approximate time: Two hours to clean a wall 6 feet high and 15 feet long.

Tools and materials: Heavy rubber gloves, thick rubber apron, goggles, muriatic acid, wire or other stiff brush.

Identifying and preventing mildew

Blotches of what appears to be dirt on siding may actually be mildew. It grows on the north side of houses and on other shaded surfaces, especially damp ones. Washing will remove the mildew stains but not its spores. These are embedded in the surface of the paint. To determine if a stain is mildew, dab chlorine laundry bleach on it. If the stain disappears in a few minutes, it is mildew. Ordinary soil will not come off.

To remove mildew, scrub the surface with a bleach-and-water solution (1 cup of bleach to a gallon of warm water). Flush the area with clear water, and allow it to dry well before painting. **TIP:** If you are using an oil-based paint, add a mildew inhibitor to it when you are painting the area. This is not necessary with water-based paints because they don't have the oil that the fungus feeds on.

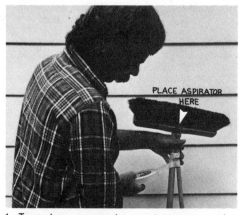

1. To make a spray cleaner, tape your garden hose to a stiff-bristled push broom. Fill an aspirator/sprayer with a concentrated solution of dish detergent and TSP (trisodium phosphate), and place it between the hose and the nozzle. Attach the hose to a hot-water faucet, and brush vigorously.

Acid tips

- When mixing acid and water, always add the acid to the water, never vice versa.
- For heavy deposits, double the strength of the solution and the length of time left on.
- Put on the gloves, goggles, and apron before you mix the solution; leave them on until after you rinse it off.

2. Flush off the detergent solution before it dries. Whether or not you remove the hose from the broom for better control, hold the nozzle about 6 inches from the wall, and at a sharp angle to it, so the jet can knock off loose paint and soil. Use clear water; it does not have to be hot. Let the wall dry.

3. To remove white, powdery deposits on brick or concrete surfaces, go over them with a stiff, dry brush, Then wet the surface with a weak (5 percent) solution of muriatic acid and water After the solution has been on five minutes, brush the wall and immediately rinse with clear water. Work 4-foot-square sections.

Preparing wood surfaces

Most siding and trim is made of wood. It presents a fine surface for paint, provided it is in good shape. Cracked boards should be repaired (page 511) or replaced (page 512), and loose boards nailed tight. Popped nails should be hammered home. It is building practice to use nonrusting flathead nails on exterior siding and trim. If these nails were used on your house, caulking is not necessary. But if you see signs of rust, correct the problem as soon as possible and as it is described below.

Dealing with rust

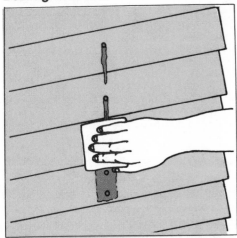

1. Sand the rust stains around the nail and the nail itself until it shines. Then set the nail about ⅛ inch below the surface. Prime the nailhead with a rust-inhibiting paint. When this has dried, caulk the hole. When the caulking has dried, prime it.

2. Paint over rust stains that are too deep to be sanded off. **TIP:** Using an opaque stain will help obscure the rust and may keep it from bleeding through the paint. Do not try to set flathead nails.

What it takes

Approximate time: About 10 minutes per nail.

Tools and materials: Sanding block, medium-grit sandpaper, wire brush, nail set, putty knife, 2-inch paintbrush, rust-inhibiting metal primer, caulking compound, opaque stain.

Removing paint

For painting, the surface must be smooth and firm. To start, scrape off all loose and peeling paint that the hosing did not remove. Generally, all you'll need for this is a wire brush, scraper, or putty knife. However, where a deeper paint problem exists—blisters, alligatoring, or cracking, for example—you may have to remove large areas of paint down to the bare wood. This calls for specialized tools and materials. What you use will depend on the thickness of the paint, its extent, and your own schedule. A sanding block will do for small areas. For larger ones, use a power sander, an electrical paint remover, or a chemical paint remover.

What it takes

Approximate time: About two hours for a section 4 feet wide by 8 feet long.

Tools and materials: Hook-shaped scraper, putty knife, and either an orbital power sander, sanding block, electrical paint remover, or semipaste chemical paint remover. Also needed: solvent, steel wool, open-coat—60- or 80-grit—sandpaper (for the sander), brush, and clean rag.

Rent a vibrating sander if you need to remove large areas of blistered and peeling paint. Get one with legs that prevent gouging. Maintain even pressure on the device so that the entire sanding surface is flat against the siding. Never hold it motionless over one spot. **TIP:** Don't use a sander with a revolving disc. It will gouge the surface.

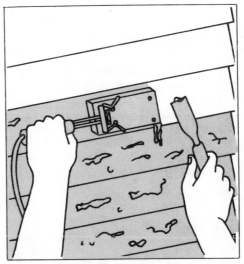

Remove wrinkles and other thick, rough paint with an electrical paint remover. The higher its wattage, the faster the unit will work. While the unit scrapes as well as softens paint, you will have to scrape off paint remnants and sand the surface smooth before you paint it. **TIP:** Don't use a flame to soften paint; you may ignite the siding.

Where there's flame . . .
It happened this way: I had a huge patch of alligatored paint on my house. It would have taken a week to sand. I'd seen painters use a blowtorch to soften old paint. So I rented a propane torch. It took off the paint fine. But a fire took off the siding. Firemen told me that the flame probably shot into a crack and ignited the sheathing.

Practical Pete

Stripping paint

Use chemical paint remover for cleaning off large areas of paint. Apply it in 2-foot sections. Use a semipaste type on vertical surfaces. Lay it on in thick, short strokes, all going in the same direction. Wait about 20 minutes before you scrape it off. When you have finished, use the indicated solvent—water or benzene—to remove all traces of the chemical. Then sand the wood smooth with fine-grit paper.

Feather the edges of paint that border an area you have cleaned down to bare wood. Rub the edges first with coarse sandpaper, then with fine. This will enable you to smoothly blend the new paint with the old. Paint stripping is only necessary on especially problematic areas, where ordinary scraping leaves an irregular surface.

Knots and resins

You can locate knots under old paint. The paint just over the knot will be discolored. This is caused by resin bleeding through the paint. Resin will discolor the new paint, too, unless you take steps to prevent it. This is easily done, as is dealing with knots on new wood. It's a good point not to just order lumber, but if you can, to select it.

To prepare new wood, scrape off soft resin with a knife blade or putty knife. If the resin has hardened, chip it off with a chisel or sharp knife. Once you have removed all resin, clean the area with alcohol and seal it with thinned shellac or a sealer designed for resinous wood. The sealer is not a primer; limit it to the affected area.

To prepare old wood for paint, simply seal all knots with thinned shellac, and sand when dry. (It is not necessary to remove the old paint.) If the knot is loose, do not remove it. Tighten it with wood caulking. After the caulking has dried, shellac the area, let dry, and then sand it smooth.

Preparing metal surfaces

Remove loose paint and rust from metal surfaces. You don't have to remove paint to the bare metal, but the surfaces must be free of dirt and oil. Application of a rust-inhibiting primer is advisable. Of course, the most useful thing is to keep up your maintenance. Checking periodically can save you a lot of time and effort.

Use a wire brush to remove loose and peeling paint from curved metal surfaces. A scraper or putty knife will take such paint off flat surfaces. Use steel wool on rust spots. Inspect under surfaces with a mirror.

Prepare large areas like those on gutters and downspouts with an electric drill fitted with a wire brush. If they are made of aluminum, wash the surface with a specially formulated aluminum cleaner available at hardware stores. While aluminum is not subject to rust, it does oxidize and will pit if left exposed.

Selecting and buying paint

Paints are formulated to adhere to specific surfaces and to possess certain performance characteristics. Thus, there are surfaces to which a paint will not adhere and performance characteristics which it will lack. The chart below summarizes the qualities of various exterior paints. Use it to select the type best suited for your house and job.

There are three different types of paint you can apply to trim and siding: oil-based, alkyd-based, and latex. Oil-based paint was the standard paint for many years. It has been made less popular by developments in paint chemistry. Its big handicap is that it is difficult to apply and lacks durability. Nowadays, it is used primarily for painting trim when a high gloss is desired.

There are two widely used types of latex paint. One has a polyvinyl-acetate binder; the other has an acrylic-latex binder. The latter is more durable and is used in expensive paints. Latex paint of both types has many advantages. It can be applied to damp surfaces, goes on easily and usually dries within an hour. Since it is thinned with water, you can clean the brushes in water. It is especially well adapted to siding that has blistered, as it lets trapped moisture escape. The major drawback of latex paint is that it does not adhere well to surfaces already coated with a different type of paint.

Alkyd-based paint contains a resin-and-oil binder. It spreads easily and covers better than latex paint, especially on chalky surfaces. It must, however, be applied to dry surfaces and thinned with paint thinner or turpentine. Brush cleaning is a chore.

Exterior siding paint in all types is available in flat and semigloss styles; paint for trim in semigloss and gloss.

TIP: When you buy paint, open the cans first. If there is a cake of pigment on the bottom or the paint is lumpy, reject it. The paint is not fresh, and it will be hard to apply. Have every can of paint you buy mixed in the store's agitator. This will save you time. Get a supply of free mixing sticks, painting hats, and hooks for hanging paint cans from the ladder.

What paint to use and where

A dot indicates that a primer or sealer is necessary before the finish coat (unless surface has been previously finished).

	House paint (oil)	Transparent sealer	Cement-based paint	Exterior clear finish	Aluminum paint	Wood stain	Roof coating	Roof cement	Asphalt emulsion	Trim and trellis paint	Awning paint	Spar varnish	Porch and deck paint	Primer or undercoat	Metal primer	Latex types	Water-repellant preservatives
Clapboard siding	✓•				✓									✓		✓•	
Brick	✓•	✓	✓		✓									✓		✓	
Cement & cinder block	✓•	✓	✓		✓									✓		✓	
Asbestos cement	✓•													✓		✓	
Stucco	✓•	✓	✓		✓									✓		✓	
Natural wood siding & trim				✓		✓						✓					
Metal siding	✓•				✓•					✓•					✓	✓•	
Wood-framed windows	✓•				✓					✓•				✓		✓•	
Steel windows	✓•				✓•					✓•					✓	✓•	
Aluminum windows	✓•				✓					✓•					✓	✓•	
Shutters & other trim	✓•									✓•				✓		✓•	
Canvas awnings											✓						✓
Wood-shingle roof						✓											
Metal roof	✓•														✓	✓•	
Coal-tar felt roof							✓	✓	✓								
Wood porch floor													✓				
Cement porch floor													✓			✓	
Copper surfaces												✓					
Galvanized surfaces	✓•				✓•					✓•	✓				✓	✓•	
Iron surfaces	✓•				✓•					✓•					✓	✓•	

Choosing the colors

Deciding on the color—or colors—to paint your house is a process directed by personal taste. There are, however, some practical matters to consider. If the house is now a dark color and you are thinking about painting it white, you may be converting a one-coat job into a two-coat process. You may have to apply two coats anyway, but using white paint over dark will make a second coat more likely.

The following tips can help you make color serve your purposes:

• If you want your house to appear larger, choose a light color. A dark color will reduce its apparent size.

• Painting the trim and window and door frames in a contrasting color will add interest to the house. But if there are a number of different materials on the outside of the house—clapboard, shingles, bricks, and stucco, for example—using a single color will unify the house and reduce the clash between textures.

• When you select a color, you may be working from color swatches. When using them, remember that printing inks can only approximate the color of the paint. There will be further variations due to the surface of the house, the method of application, and the lighting. The color of the paint, seen in its container, is not a reliable guide either. Here are some facts to remember when you select a color from paint in a container:

1. Paint always appears darker in the container than it will on a surface.
2. Artificial light darkens color; the paint will look lighter in daylight. If in doubt, take the container outside.
3. All paint dries to a lighter shade than the one you see when it is first applied.
4. A color can saturate your eyes. To insure accuracy when you are mixing paints, look away from the mix for several minutes to let your eyes readjust.
5. When you are seeking a particular shade, it is a good idea to paint a test patch about 2 feet by 2 feet, and let it dry. What appeared to be the lemon yellow you want may dry to a washed-out tint.

Estimating how much paint you need

It is better to buy too much paint than too little. Running out of paint in the middle of a job is no joke. Any leftover paint (in unopened cans) can probably be returned to the store for a refund or credit. Be sure to have an understanding on this before you buy; have it written on the sales slip.

It is better still to estimate your needs accurately. Using this formula, you'll be able to come close:

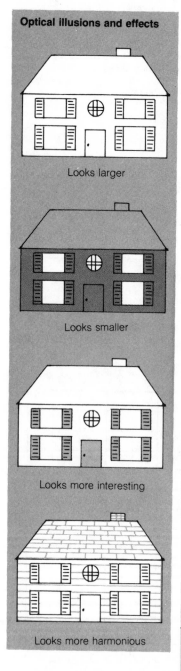

Optical illusions and effects

Looks larger

Looks smaller

Looks more interesting

Looks more harmonious

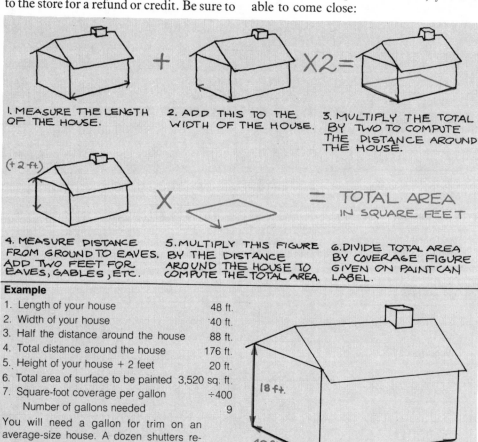

1. MEASURE THE LENGTH OF THE HOUSE.

2. ADD THIS TO THE WIDTH OF THE HOUSE.

3. MULTIPLY THE TOTAL BY TWO TO COMPUTE THE DISTANCE AROUND THE HOUSE.

(+2 ft.)

= TOTAL AREA IN SQUARE FEET

4. MEASURE DISTANCE FROM GROUND TO EAVES. ADD TWO FEET FOR EAVES, GABLES, ETC.

5. MULTIPLY THIS FIGURE BY THE DISTANCE AROUND THE HOUSE TO COMPUTE THE TOTAL AREA.

6. DIVIDE TOTAL AREA BY COVERAGE FIGURE GIVEN ON PAINT CAN LABEL.

Example

1. Length of your house	48 ft.
2. Width of your house	40 ft.
3. Half the distance around the house	88 ft.
4. Total distance around the house	176 ft.
5. Height of your house + 2 feet	20 ft.
6. Total area of surface to be painted	3,520 sq. ft.
7. Square-foot coverage per gallon	÷400
Number of gallons needed	9

You will need a gallon for trim on an average-size house. A dozen shutters require about half a gallon of paint.

18 ft.

40 ft.

48 ft.

Buying brushes

The type of paint you are to apply will determine the type of brush you need. Do not use natural-bristle brushes for applying latex or water-based paint. The bristles will absorb the water and swell. These brushes are better for oil- and alkyd-based paints, epoxies, varnish, shellac, and lacquer. Use brushes with nylon bristles for applying latex and water-based paint. Do not use them with shellac, lacquer, or varnish; all will make the bristles soften or dissolve.

If you are buying a natural-bristle brush, look for one made of imported hog bristles. These are superior because the end of each bristle is split into many tiny branches. This "flagging" enables the brush to carry a great deal of paint and leave very fine brush marks that flow together to create a smooth finish. The bristles of good nylon brushes are artificially flagged. Horsehair bristles are used in poor-quality brushes. The bristles hold little paint, do not spread it well, and soon become limp.

Before you buy a brush, apply the following tests: 1. Press it against a flat surface; the bristles should not fan out. 2. Squeeze the bristles; they should feel full and spongy. 3. Poke your fingers into the brush to determine fullness of the bristles. 4. Look at the bristle ends; they should be split into a number of fine branches. 5. Inspect the length of the bristles; they should be varied. This permits the brush to carry larger paint loads and increases the life of the brush. As the tip wears, new bristle ends replace worn ones. 6. Squeeze and jar the brush; few loose bristles should fall out. 7. Examine the metal band, or ferrule around the bristles. It should be made of aluminum or stainless steel.

For painting siding, you will need a 4- or 5-inch brush; for window frames, sashes, and other narrow boards, a 2-inch trim brush. A 1½-inch trim brush with a beveled end is excellent for painting narrow strips like the muntins in windows. If you will be painting stucco or masonry, get a brush designed for those surfaces. Choose one with nylon bristles because they can resist abrasive surfaces.

Caring for brushes

Brushes with nylon and other synthetic bristles are ready for use when you buy them. But you will lengthen the life and improve the performance of the brush if you soak it in thinner before first using it. This removes loose bristles and tightens the others. **TIP:** Do not soak any brush in water. That can split the handle and may rust the ferrule.

Before you use a natural-bristle brush for the first time, soak it in linseed oil for 48 hours. In addition to tightening the bristles, the oil makes them more flexible. It also removes the loose bristles.

When you are done painting for the day, clean all brushes thoroughly—even if you intend to resume painting the first thing in the morning. Any paint left on the brush will thicken, stiffening the bristles and making it difficult to draw the brush over the surface. When you clean brushes, be sure to use the solvent appropriate for the type of paint used:

Paint	Solvent
Oil-based or alkyd	Turpentine followed by benzene or paint thinner
Latex or water-based	Warm water and detergent

What it takes

Approximate time: An average of 10 minutes to clean a 4-inch siding brush.

Tools and materials: Clean can, appropriate solvent, metal paint-brush comb, clean rags.

1. Lower the brush into the solvent up to the ferrule. Withdraw it and let the bristles drip. Repeat several times; then place the brush on newspapers, and squeeze the paint out by dragging a mixing stick down the bristles, from ferrule to tip. Turn the brush over and squeeze the other side.

2. Spin the brush in the solvent, ferrule-deep, rinsing it thoroughly. Remove and run a paintbrush comb through the bristles. Spin the brush in the solvent a second time, and comb it out again. Repeat until the brush is free of paint.

3. Suspend the brush overnight in a clean can filled with the solvent. For this, drill a 1/16-inch hole in the handle of the brush and run a stiff wire through it. The can must be tall enough to keep the bristles from resting on the bottom. (This is also a good way to soften dried paint on old brushes.)

Applying paint

Before you begin painting, be sure you have all the necessary materials at hand. Check that all surfaces have been properly prepared. If possible, also enlist a helper. This does more than cut your working time in half. It provides a safety factor and takes a lot of the chore out of the job. For bigger jobs, you may need more than one helper.

Mixing paint

Even though you have bought fresh paint and have had the cans agitated, you will have to mix the paint throughout the project. As you work, stir the paint frequently to keep the pigment from settling to the bottom. Lower a mixing stick to the bottom and move it in a figure-eight pattern. Paint will thicken in a can as the thinner evaporates. If necessary, add the appropriate thinner and stir as above. When you open a can of paint, fix it as described below. Pour the paint into a clean can, the larger the better. Pour the paint back and forth from one can to the other. Professionals call this *boxing* the paint. Continue this procedure until the color and consistency are uniform. If there is pigment caked at the bottom, break it with a mixing stick and pour in a little paint at a time. And of course, keep stirring.

What it takes

Approximate time: Figure on eight days—four weekends—to paint an average-size house.

Tools and materials: Drop cloths, ladders, scaffolding (planks plus an extension ladder and ladder jack, or planks plus two A-ladders), mixing bucket, mixing sticks, 4- to 5-inch siding brush, 2-inch trim brush, 1½-inch trim brush with taper tip, paint-can hooks, siding paint, trim paint, primer paint, appropriate solvent, clean rags.

Planning hints:

Take down screens and storm windows.
Fold newspaper over the tops of doors and shut them.
Having a helper will more than halve the time required.
Protect walks and driveways with weighted-down newspapers.
Don't paint in direct sunlight.
Wait for a no-rain forecast before you paint.
Prime new wood and all surfaces you have taken down to bare wood.

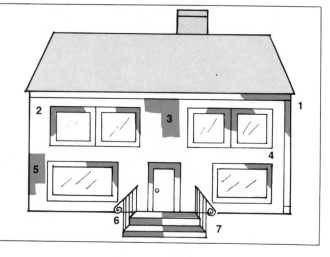

Follow this sequence when painting your house:
1. Gutters—use appropriate paint on the outside (see page 523); asphalt paint on the inside. **2.** Top trim; eaves, window frames, and any other edges. **3.** Upper siding. **4.** Lower trim. **5.** Lower siding. **6.** Ornamental iron railings. **7.** Steps.
By painting trim first, you avoid ladder marks on freshly painted siding. Top-to-bottom painting covers drips.

Scaffolding

If your house has two stories or more, you will need an extension ladder. Follow the procedures for ladder safety given on page 7. If the house is large, you can paint it more quickly from a scaffold. Scaffolding enables you to paint large areas at one time, and planking is easier on your feet than are ladder rungs. For safety, do not raise scaffolds above 10 feet. And be sure always to work with a helper.

To make a scaffold, separate an extension ladder into its two segments. Fit each with ladder jacks, which you can rent from a paint store or equipment-rental firm. Despite the length of the planks, keep the ladders within 10 feet of each other.

A better scaffold consists of two A-ladders with a plank resting on the rungs. To adjust the height, just move the plank to different rungs, a much faster process than adjusting ladder jacks. Keep the ladders positioned so that the working length of planking is not longer than 10 feet.

Practical pointers and procedures

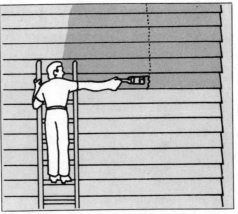

Dip the brush into the paint at least one-third the length of the bristles but not more than one-half. This loads the brush so the paint flows on easily. Remove excess paint by tapping the brush against the lip of the can. **TIP:** Don't wipe the brush against the lip. It will soon fill up and the paint will run down the side and drip off.

Work across the siding in a horizontal band, from left to right if you are right-handed; from right to left if you are left-handed. Progress by painting squares. If you are on a ladder, the size of the squares will be determined by how far you can safely reach. If you are on the ground or a scaffold, paint squares roughly 2 feet high and 3 feet wide.

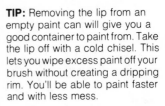

TIP: Removing the lip from an empty paint can will give you a good container to paint from. Take the lip off with a cold chisel. This lets you wipe excess paint off your brush without creating a dripping rim. You'll be able to paint faster and with less mess.

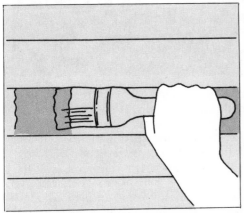

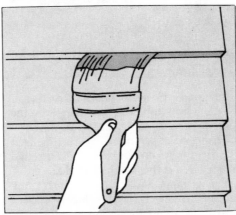

Apply the paint in brush-wide strokes, about 20 inches long. Then, starting about a foot from the wet edge, paint back toward it. Painting dry into wet saves you the work of rebrushing an area you've already painted. Blend the paint evenly into the wet area with a light stroke, lifting the brush as you end. Smooth off excess paint with a long, even stroke.

Paint clapboard with a brush as wide as the face of the board, if possible. First cover the undersides of four or five boards. Then paint the face of each one, working one board at a time. Follow the procedure of painting into the wet. Brush pads are good for painting clapboard, especially for the hard-to-reach undersides.

No more holidays
From the ladder, I seemed to be covering the surface thoroughly. But when I got down and looked up, I saw that I had skipped the lower edges of clapboards. Professional painters call skipped spots *holidays*. It sure was no holiday for me, having to put the ladder back up. Now I inspect my work *as* I work.
Practical Pete

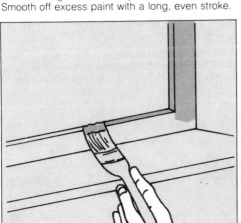

Paint window frameworks from an angle that allows you to see the tip of the bristles meeting the wood. Use a tapered trim brush. Work from the inside of the frame out toward its edges. If you get paint on the glass, wipe it off with a rag wrapped around your finger. **TIP:** Drive nails in the bottoms of the upper and lower sash so that you can move the windows without marring the wet paint.

Keep stairs in use by painting every other tread. When the paint on the first set has dried, paint the treads you skipped. Paint the risers and other elements when you paint the first half of the treads. Instead of painting every other tread, you can paint half of each step and when this has dried, paint the the other half.

6.INSULATION

Insulation is the most functional and cost-effective way to conserve energy in the home to date. It cuts heat loss in winter—and heat gain in summer—by creating dead air spaces between temperature-controlled indoor air and the weather outside.

Yet, as important a role as it plays, many homes, particularly those built before 1960, have little or no insulation. While most older homes have some attic insulation, the majority of homes built before 1960 have nothing in the walls. Homes built between 1960 and 1970 often have only a thin 1½-inch layer of insulation in the walls. Those built later generally have 2½ to 3½ inches.

One contractor's rule of thumb is: If the home is more than 10 years old, you can assume it needs some insulation. How much varies from house to house and from locality to locality.

The R system

Insulation materials are evaluated in terms of *R values*. The R value of a material is a measure of how effectively it can hold heat in—or out. R values are given in terms of numbers; the higher the number, the more effective the insulation. For example, glass fiber, in sheet or blanket form, has an R value of 3.2 per inch, whereas glass fiber in loose-fill form has an R value of 2.2 per inch. As indicated in the chart below, R values vary by material as well as form. When you purchase insulation, specify what R value you need to install, not the number of inches of thickness.

R VALUES OF DIFFERENT INSULATION TYPES					
TYPE	**Batts or blankets**		**Loose fill (poured in)**		
R VALUE	Glass fiber	Rock wool	Glass fiber	Rock wool	Cellulosic fiber
R-11	3½''-4''	3''	5''	4''	3''
R-19	6''-6½''	5¼''	8''-9''	6''-7''	5''
R-22	6½''	6''	10''	7''-8''	6''
R-30	9½''-10½''*	9''*	13''-14''	10''-11''	8''
R-38	12''-13''*	10½''*	17''-18''	13''-14''	10''-11''

*Two batts or blankets required

Types of insulation

Batts or blankets. Thick sheets of insulation are known as *batts*. Like blanket insulation, batts are usually made of glass fiber or rock wool. Both fit between joists, studs, or rafters with standard spacing. Batts come in 4- and 8-foot lengths. Blanket insulation is cut to the desired length. Both are available with or without a vapor barrier on one side. Batts and blankets are commonly used for insulating attic floors and ceilings, sidewalls, basement walls, and crawl-space ceilings.

Loose fill. Generally made of glass fiber, rock wool, cellulosic fiber, vermiculite, or perlite, this insulating material is either poured in by hand or pneumatically blown into closed spaces. It is used in finished and unfinished attic floors and finished walls.

Rigid board. Rigid-board insulation is made of extruded polystyrene, urethane, glass fiber, or expanded polystyrene beads. It is available in thicknesses ranging from ¾ inch to 4 inches and offers a high insulation value for a relatively thin material. Rigid-board insulation can be applied to finished interior walls, basement walls, and crawl spaces. If used inside the home, it should be covered with gypsum board for fire safety. On outside walls, extruded-polystyrene board can be applied to the foundation wall all the way to the footer.

Foam insulation. Urea-formaldehyde insulation can be pumped in place through holes drilled in finished walls and finished attic floors. This is usually done by contractors because the equipment is expensive. Be sure to use a qualified contractor who will guarantee his work.

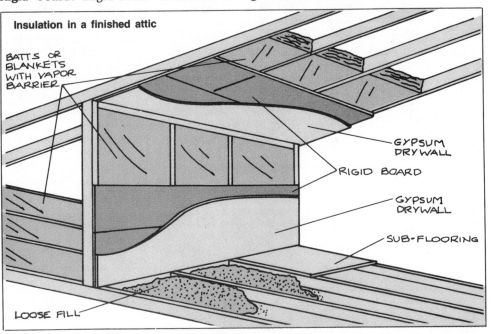

Insulation in a finished attic

BATTS OR BLANKETS WITH VAPOR BARRIER

GYPSUM DRYWALL

RIGID BOARD

GYPSUM DRYWALL

SUB-FLOORING

LOOSE FILL

RIGID

BATT

BLANKET

LOOSE FILL

Checking your home for insulation

Once you know how much insulation you need (page 528), find out how much you have. This can be tricky in areas, such as finished sidewalls that are not readily accessible. There, you'll have to take a guess or have a professional look into the matter. But for the most part, you can check insulation yourself. Here's what to look for:

Attic floor and roof. Insulation material will generally lie between joists or trusses. You may want to add more insulation yourself (see chart on page 530). If so, the kind of insulation that is already there will determine what kind you add. If the attic floor is finished, pry up a board and look under it.

Sidewalls. A tough place to inspect if the house is already finished. Your best bet is to locate the contractor who built the house and check his specifications. If that isn't possible, you can have an energy audit made. In this process, called thermography, a heat-sensitive camera is used to determine if areas of your house are losing too much heat. To locate a firm offering this service, check your hardware dealer.

Another way to check is to feel the inside wall of a finished room on a cold day. It should be room temperature. If it's cold, insulation is in order.

Crawl spaces. These are easy to assess because the insulation is often exposed. Be sure to check all crawl-space ceilings, even if they may already be insulated.

Basement walls. Finished or unfinished, it's an easy matter to insulate a basement against heat loss. If your basement is finished, remove a ceiling or wall panel so you can check for insulating material.

Adding insulation

What it takes

Approximate time: Depending upon the kind of insulation material used and the size of the area of work, anywhere from a few hours to a full day.

Tools and materials: Linoleum knife or heavy-duty shears, wooden rake or board (to level loose fill if you use it), heavy-duty staple gun and staples, gloves, breathing mask (when using mineral-wool or glass-fiber materials), hammer, nails, ruler, insulation material of your choice, vapor-barrier material, wire holders (if necessary).

Starting at the top of the house, the following material will show you how to add insulation to your home and how to get the most value for it.

Attic floor. Use fibrous batts, blankets, or loose fill, referring to the chart below for ideal R values. If you are using a batt or blanket with a vapor barrier, place the material so the vapor barrier faces the floor below. Otherwise, lay polyethylene sheeting over the flooring before you install the insulation. You can staple it. For more on vapor barriers, see pages 532-33.

If you already have batt or blanket insulation, you can add more by laying batts or blankets—without vapor barriers—over the existing material, or simply pour loose fill over it. Make sure you don't cover ventilation louvers in the eaves, and remember that insulation must be 3 inches away from recessed light fixtures.

Attic walls. Place batts or blankets between rafters, and staple them in place. You can also secure them by attaching wire fasteners between the rafters.

Sidewalls. For new construction, use batts, blankets, or rigid-board insulation. On finished walls, have a contractor pump loose fill or foamed-in-place material into the walls. (The contractor makes and repairs the holes.) Another option is to install extruded-polystyrene rigid board on inside surfaces and cover it with gypsum board. If you are installing new siding, you can also use rigid-board insulation underneath it.

Crawl spaces. When it comes to crawl spaces, you can insulate either the ceiling or walls; it is not necessary to do both. For ceilings, place batts or blankets between joists and support them with wire fasteners, available at hardware stores. For walls, use 1-by-1½-inch nailers (strips of wood) to secure insulation to the header. Make sure the batts fit snugly. Allow the material to hang down the wall. For even better protection let the insulation come out at least 2 feet across the floor from the wall. The size and height of your crawl space will determine whether it's easier to do ceilings or walls. Whichever you choose to do, place a polyethylene vapor barrier across the earth before you install floor insulation.

R VALUES FOR UNFINISHED ATTIC FLOORS				
Thickness of existing insulation	0″	0″-2″	2″-4″	4″-6″
How much to add	R-22	R-11	R-11	none
How much to add if you have electric heat or if you have oil heat and live in a cold climate	R-30	R-22	R-19	R-11
How much to add if you have electric heat and live in a cold climate	R-38	R-30	R-22	R-19

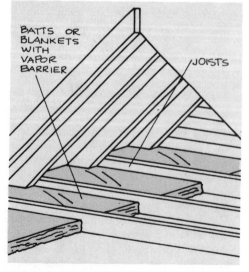

Unfinished attic insulation

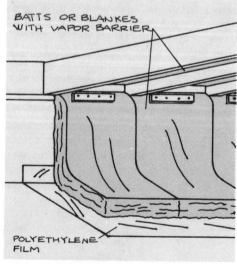

Crawl-space insulation

Basement walls. The easiest way to insulate basement walls is with extruded-polystyrene boards. You can apply them directly to masonry walls, using mastic, and then cover them with gypsum dry wall. An alternative is to have the walls framed out, place batt or blanket insulation between the studs, and cover it with extruded-polystyrene board and gypsum dry wall.

Basement floors. To insulate concrete floors, apply extruded-polystyrene boards directly to the floor with mastic paste. Then regular flooring must be installed over the insulation to finish the job.

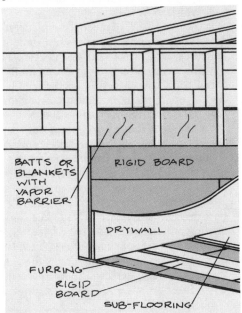

Basement insulation

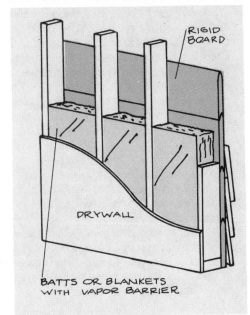

Insulation in new construction

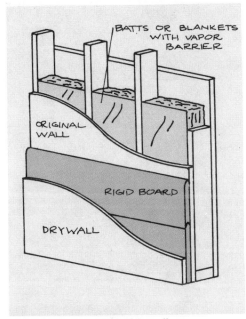

Insulation in existing inside walls

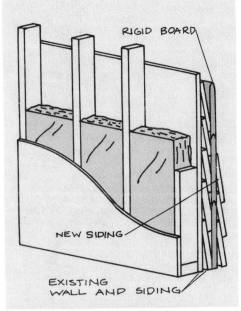

Insulation in existing outside walls

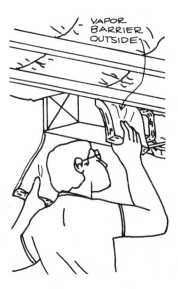

Ducts. If you have ducts for either air conditioning or heating running through your attic, garage, or any other space that is not heated or cooled, and they are exposed, then you should insulate them.

Generally, duct insulation comes in blankets 1 or 2 inches thick. It's sensible to get the thicker kind, especially if the ducts are rectangular. The important thing is to do the job thoroughly; after all, it's energy and money that you will be saving—or losing, as the case may be.

For air conditioning ducts, you should have the kind of insulation that has a vapor barrier. The vapor barrier goes on the outside. Seal the joints of the insulation tightly with tape to avoid condensation. Also, it is important to check before you start, to see if there are any leaks in the duct. If there are, tape them tightly.

In addition to insulation

While insulation plays a very important part in conserving energy in the home, it is not the only answer. There are a number of supplementary steps the homeowner can take, some of which are:

Storm windows and doors can save a lot of energy. If you have a choice between wood and aluminum frames, choose wood. It transfers heat more slowly than metal. An alternative step is to place plastic sheeting over windows. This is an inexpensive and effective way to block cold air.

You can also install combination storms. That is, storm doors and screens, and storm windows and screens. These are becoming more and more popular and they do save all that taking down and storing, and then putting up again every spring and fall.

Weather stripping placed around windows and doors is another heat saver. It comes in a variety of materials and there are numerous application techniques. Weather stripping is excellent for blocking drafts through joinings; where the floor and door meet or at the center of a double window where the two frames join, for example.

There are several types of weather stripping for doors and windows. You can buy it by the running foot or in kit form. Foam rubber with adhesive backing, spring metal, rolled vinyl, and foam rubber with wood backing are some of the materials that you will find available.

You won't need many tools, and installation is quite simple. For doors, installation is similar for the two sides and the top. The threshold may offer a variety of methods of installation; a vinyl tubing threshold, a sweep, an interlocking threshold are some.

Caulking, in tubes or cords, can be used around outside window frames and door frames to close gaps that let drafts into your living area. Caulking can be applied at any opening where two different materials meet. (See page 516 for caulking details.)

Efficient use of energy in the home will in part determine the size of your heating or cooling bill. There are dozens of small ways to cut down on your energy costs: Closing off unused rooms, turning down the thermostat at night, closing the fireplace flue when it is not in use are simple examples.

FOAM-EDGED WOOD

ADHESIVE-BACKED FOAM

METAL-BACKED VINYL

FOAM-FILLED GASKET

CASEMENT STRIPPING

TUBULAR GASKET

FELT

SPRING METAL

Weather stripping is available in many forms, both flexible and rigid, for either doors or windows.

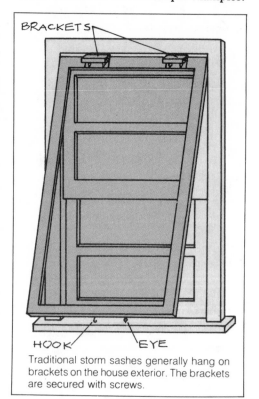

BRACKETS

HOOK   EYE

Traditional storm sashes generally hang on brackets on the house exterior. The brackets are secured with screws.

Vapor barriers

Since heat is lost more easily through water than through air, insulation that is damp loses its effectiveness. Vapor barriers prevent water from condensing in the insulation material and in the wooden frame of your house.

Always use vapor barriers in sidewalls. Proper alignment is shown on page 531.

You may not need a barrier in your attic, however, provided there is adequate ventilation. Batt and blanket insulation can be purchased with the vapor barrier already attached to one side. Always install a vapor barrier *toward* the living space so the insulation is between it and the *cold* wall or area. Use 2-mil or thicker polyethylene as a vapor barrier for any insulation material, such as loose fill, that is not supplied with one. Extruded-polystyrene board serves as its own vapor barrier, but some other rigid boards require one.

Caution: Never use vapor barriers between layers of insulation. If, for example, you plan to add fibrous batts over existing batts in your attic floor, get them *without* a vapor barrier. Otherwise, moisture will gather in the existing insulation, causing wood rot and substantial loss of heat.

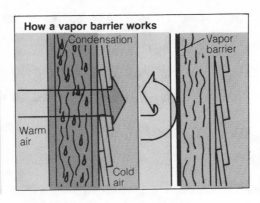

How a vapor barrier works

Condensation

Vapor barrier

Warm air

Cold air

Street scene
My roof vent cools the attic just fine but I should have had a helper down on the ground when I positioned it. I got the dern thing so far up front that it can be seen from the street. A few feet back and it would have done the job just as well but out of sight.

Practical Pete

Ventilation

Whenever you add insulation you may also need to add ventilation. Adequate ventilation, especially in the attic, removes water vapor before it gets a chance to condense into drops of water, which mat down insulation and also rot beams and rafters.

A ventilated attic will also keep your house cooler in summer. If you live in the cold northern part of the country, your attic ventilation area should equal 1/300th of your attic floor area if you do not have a vapor barrier and if you notice any condensation. In the warmer south, you should have both ventilation and vapor barrier. If your house is air-conditioned, however, you'll only need half as much ventilation area to be effective. For how to install vents, see pages 496 and 497.

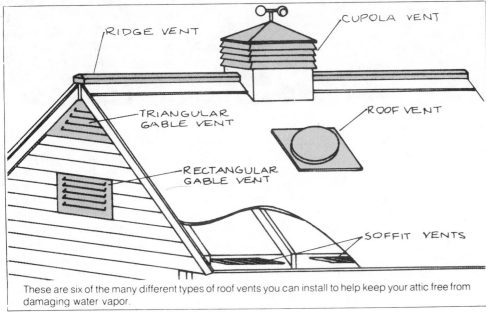

RIDGE VENT

CUPOLA VENT

TRIANGULAR GABLE VENT

ROOF VENT

RECTANGULAR GABLE VENT

SOFFIT VENTS

These are six of the many different types of roof vents you can install to help keep your attic free from damaging water vapor.

How much is enough?

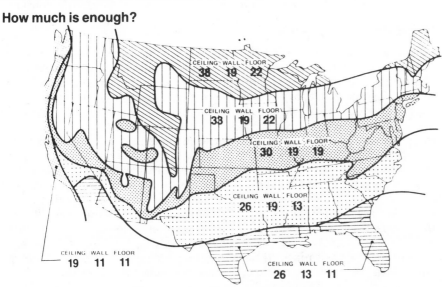

CEILING WALL FLOOR
38 19 22

CEILING WALL FLOOR
38 19 22

CEILING WALL FLOOR
30 19 19

CEILING WALL FLOOR
26 19 13

CEILING WALL FLOOR
19 11 11

CEILING WALL FLOOR
26 13 11

Recommended R-value for ceilings, walls, and floors by climatic zone.

Point of diminishing returns

There comes a point at which you have the perfect kind and amount of insulation for your home and for the geographic location you live in. After this, additional insulation will not save you any money on fuel bills. Your local or regional Federal Energy Administration office can give you the maximum recommendations for your area. It's a good idea to check with them *before* you purchase and install insulation because geographical areas do have different insulation requirements.

You can get the names of reputable local insulation contractors from the local FEA, FHA office, or Better Business Bureau.

For detailed information and reliable instructions on step-by-step installation of all kinds of insulation, write for *In the Bank or up the Chimney?*, a book prepared under contract H-2179R for the Office of Policy Development and Research; Division of Energy, Building Technology, and Standards; U.S. Department of Housing and Urban Development; Washington D.C.

In Canada, write for: *Keeping the Heat In,* published by the Office of Energy Conservation, Department of Energy, Mines and Resources, Ottawa, Canada.

7. FOUNDATIONS AND MASONRY

The foundation is the support for your house; without proper care and maintenance it can cause some drastic and expensive problems.

Taking worst things first, a foundation can crack. This can be caused by several things, but the most common factors are water pressure on the foundation or having the building located on unstable ground. If your home has been built on ground that is not reasonably solid, it may settle and shift to such an extent that the foundation cracks badly no matter how it is repaired. In this case, there isn't really anything you can do except call in a professional firm.

On the other hand, if water is the problem, you can correct it. Excessive water pressure is caused by large amounts of water seeping into the ground. Like any fluid, water will flow downhill, taking the path of least resistance. If there is a foundation in its path, you can count on trouble. The pressure of the water may be great enough to actually lift the house out of the ground like a giant boat, or it may crack the foundation wall and flood the basement. Of course, in a situation that extreme you would call in professional help.

Treating concrete cracks

Concrete cannot be used to repair concrete. It will not bond properly. Grout, mortar, premixed cement, latex compounds, and cement-sand-epoxy compounds are all good repair materials. Which you use depends on the job at hand. Of course, you could do a whole section of wall over with concrete (see page 535).

For small jobs, you can use a masonry-paste patcher. These come in handy cartridges, ready for use. (For cartridge-gun how-tos, see page 516.) On larger jobs, one of the premixed cements is best.

For any job, first clear out all loose material to a depth of at least 1 inch. If the crack is more than the width of a hairline, it should be undercut. As shown at left, this results in a cut that is wider at the bottom than on the surface, and helps lock the cement or patching compound in place.

It is essential that the cut be thoroughly clean. Hose it out with water. Then press the compound into the area with a trowel, making sure to fill each crevice. (If you're using the cartridge and gun, press down with the tip of the nozzle.) Be sure not to leave any air bubbles. Smooth the compound with a putty knife, and allow it to cure according to the manufacturer's directions. It's a good idea to wear gloves when working with concrete, and goggles when breaking up the surface.

What it takes

Approximate time: Depends on the extent of the damage, but allow at least 30 minutes.

Tools and materials: Hammer, cold chisel, old screwdriver and wire brush (for cleaning crack), garden hose, trowel, putty knife, gloves, goggles, and patching material.

UNDERCUTTING

Waterproofing

No repair, no matter how professionally executed, will stop water from leaking into your house if there is excessive water pressure on the foundation. In order to avoid this kind of problem, have the soil around your house graded so that water flows away from the house. You should also waterproof the foundation.

Waterproofing interior basement walls is a relatively simple matter. Exterior waterproofing, however, requires digging. You will need to expose at least some of the foundation; how much depends on the extent of the leak.

To waterproof the top of the foundation, have a trench, 4 feet wide and 2 feet deep, dug all around the house. Make sure the trench slopes downward, away from the house. Using a trowel, apply asphalt foundation coating to the wall, from the bottom of the trench up to grade level. Smooth the asphalt and press a sheet of polyethylene plastic against it. At the same time, extend the sheeting to line the bottom of the ditch. Fill in the trench with a 1½-foot layer of rocks; cover with topsoil.

If the leak is lower on the foundation, it is necessary to excavate right down to the footing. This is the time to call in a professional. He will do the excavating and waterproof the entire wall with concrete. At that point, either you or your contractor can lay drain tile to carry underground water away from the house.

What it takes

Approximate time: Indeterminate, depending on the extent of the area. From minutes to days.

Tools and materials: Pick and shovel (if you do the digging yourself), trowel, stiff brush, asphalt foundation coating, heavy hammer, polyethylene plastic, rocks.

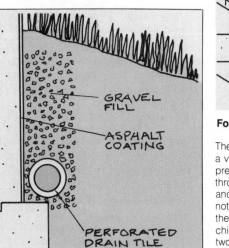

Waterproofing options

WATERPROOF CAULKING
EXPANSION JOINT
GRAVEL FILL
ASPHALT COATING
PERFORATED DRAIN TILE

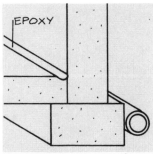

EPOXY

Foundation seam

The seam of the foundation is a vulnerable area. Under pressure, water may be forced up through the joint where the wall and floor meet. This condition is not difficult to remedy. Undercut the surface of the joint with a cold chisel, and fill the cavity with a two-part epoxy mix that will seal the joint. Check with your hardware dealer on the most desirable epoxy. Do this job during a dry spell, and allow at least 24 hours for the epoxy to cure.

Splash blocks

In a heavy rainstorm, the water running off your house and down the guttering can become a torrent. When it comes out of the downspout, it can both damage your lawns and can act as an environmental pollutant, by washing sediment from your yard into city storm drains. It can also soak the area beneath the pipe and create enough water pressure to weaken the foundation. By placing splash blocks under the downspout, you can slow the water and control it as well. There are basically two kinds of splash blocks. Both are described below.

But how do you keep it repaired?
I followed all the instructions on the sealing-compound package, but I forgot that for any crack in the foundation wall that's bigger than a hairline, you've got to make an undercut. Otherwise the compound will just fall out.

Practical Pete

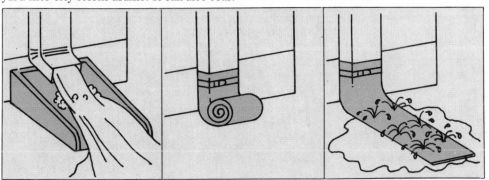

The type of splash block shown at left is simply a concrete or plastic trough with one end open. Placed under the downspout, it directs water away from the house foundation and takes some of the force from the water as it spreads. A better type of diverter is similar to a loaded hose. During dry weather, the hose automatically rolls up against the end of the downspout, out of the way, as shown in the center illustration. As water comes down the downspout, it forces the hose out, which then spreads the water evenly and without force over a wider portion of the yard, as shown at right.

Drainage

What it takes

Approximate time: Figure your time in days, depending on the size of the job.

Tools and materials: Pick and shovel (if you plan to do your own digging), gravel, drain tiles.

If waterproofing and patching don't solve the problem, the entire drainage system may be at fault. Proper drainage is essential to problem-free foundations. Indeed, the only sensible approach lies in intelligent preparation during house construction. But you may not have built your own home, in which case you could be the inheritor of certain problems in this area. Here are a few points to consider:

1. Make sure that the grade around your house slopes *away* from the foundation.
2. There will very likely be some natural drainage around your house, small channels which were created when the property was first graded or which formed by themselves. These should not be filled in, nor should they be dammed.
3. Check flower beds next to the house to make sure that they slope away from it. Also check that the edge of the bed does not act as a trap for water.
4. Water lawns and flower beds equally so that the moisture content around the house will be uniform.
5. Do not plant shrubs or trees right next to the house. They take moisture out of the soil, and you can have a foundation problem from too little moisture as well as from too much. Moreover, tree roots can crack a foundation wall.
6. Check gutters and downspouts to be sure they are working effectively and that the water is being routed far enough away from the foundation.
7. Check that any water outlets in the foundation are in good shape, and in case of a problem, deal with it immediately.

You can tell if there is unequal settling of the house or upheaval by noticing if there are spaces developing between the doors and walls and windows, if there are cracks in the inside walls, doors that all at once don't fit properly in their frames, and certainly if there are cracks in the foundation itself. Many of these you can handle.

Drains

Drainpipe, known as tile, is similar to storm-sewer pipe, but is perforated. It is available in many lengths and has various types of connectors, including elbow fittings for corners. The easiest kinds of tiles to use are those made of rigid plastic or the asphalt-impregnated type.

If your house is on level land, you will need to create a slope so the water drains away. Put a 4-inch layer of gravel in the trench, alongside the foundation footing (see page 535). Arrange the gravel so it slopes from the foundation; then set the tiles on top of it, letting them slope slightly with the gravel. Connect the tiles to a dry well (see page 504 for digging instructions).

On the other hand, if your house is on land that slopes, you can probably lay out the tiles without connecting them to a dry well. Lay the tiles around the three sides of the house that are uphill, and let the open ends extend 12 feet beyond the foundation on the lower side. This will cause the water to flow away from the house. You will need a dry well only if the soil has especially poor drainage or your house is in a crowded area.

To finish the job, in either type of installation, bury the tile in gravel, fill the trench with soil and gravel, and replace the sod carefully.

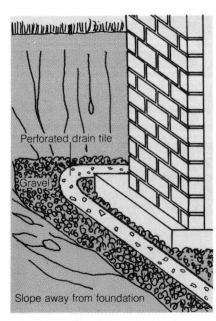

Perforated drain tile

Gravel

Slope away from foundation

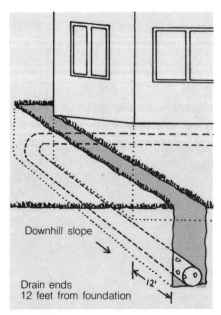

Downhill slope

Drain ends 12 feet from foundation

12'

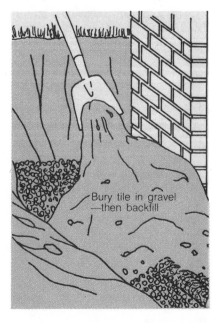

Bury tile in gravel —then backfill

Termite protection

So respected has the termite become, and so feared, that in the current vocabulary, his name is a synonym for silent, invisible destruction. More than 40 species can be found in the United States and Canada. The most destructive type is the subterranean termite, a tiny animal that requires mois- ture for its survival. The termite is highly social, living in colonies that are composed of three groups: reproductive termites, soldiers, and workers. It is the workers—wingless, blind, and white—who are the providers for the community; and they can and do eat one out of house and home.

Where and what to look for

1. Foundation walls, inside as well as outside the house, should be checked periodically. Notice cracks or any looseness in the areas around basement windows and doors. Look for wings, rotted wood. Check floor-wall joinings closely.
2. Check crawl spaces in the basement. Remove any scrap lumber stored in such areas, and any old boxes.
3. During spring and early summer look for shed wings at any of these sites. They are a sure sign of termites.
4. Look for earthen tunnels or tubes that connect the colony in the moist soil with the wood that the workers convert into food for themselves and their fellows. The tunnels are half-round in shape and about ½ inch wide. They may be found on foundation walls, basement walls, porches, and openings where pipes enter the house through the foundation. Seal such openings with caulking compound.
5. Check suspect wood by poking it with a sharp instrument such as an awl, pocketknife, or ice pick. If the instrument sinks into the wood to about ½ inch with just gentle hand pressure, you can be fairly sure that termites or dry rot have been at work.

Preventive measures

The best defense against termites is to have copper termite shields where the foundation meets the wood. These shields deny access to all those tasty joists and sills. Since the shields must extend about 3 inches beyond each side of the masonry and be anchored to the top of the foundation every 3 feet, they must be installed while the house is being built. If your home was not provided with these shields, there are other measures you can take.

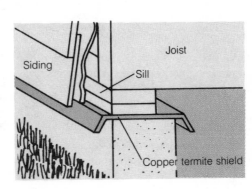
Siding / Joist / Sill / Copper termite shield

Putting down a termite barrier

You can control termites with a chemical known as chlordane. It is toxic to humans, however, and so must be used with extreme care. It comes in concentrated form and must be diluted with water to create the exact solution specified by the manufacturer. Certain states have restrictions concerning the use of chlordane. Check with your county agricultural agent before you use this chemical around your house. Be careful about children and pets in the area.

If you use chlordane, follow this procedure: Dig a shallow trench all around your house, placing it close to the foundation. Mix the chlordane with water, following the package instructions—and any local regulations that may exist. Use a watering can (with the sprinkler head removed), and carefully pour the chlordane into the trench. Wear gloves for protection.

Also apply chlordane inside the house, putting it in and around any cracks where the foundation wall meets a concrete floor, near the foundation wall of all crawl spaces, and in any area that has a soil floor.

Don't ever forget that chlordane is poisonous; when you use it indoors be sure to have adequate ventilation. Leave the room after you use the chlordane, and close it off for several days.

Soil injection. A much easier way of exterminating termites is by soil injection. Chlordane is simply shot into the ground. No digging is required. For this, a soil injector is fitted with chlordane cartridges. This costs more than the liquid method, but it is cleaner, easier, and less dangerous. It's easy enough to do yourself.

Eaten out of house and home!
I figured I was all set when I accepted that "free" termite inspection from the door-to-door salesman. He really scared me with his report, so I went ahead and had his company do the job. But now I've learned that termites don't work all that fast, and there's time to check with at least three companies and the County Agent so as to get a quality job without paying a small fortune.

Practical Pete

What it takes

Approximate time: Indeterminate, but you should inspect periodically.

Tools and materials: Ice pick, awl, or other sharp instrument; shovel, power drill and masonry bit, garden hose, soil-injector tube or watering can, chlordane (or liquid cartridge), concrete-patch mix, caulking compound and gun.

Caution

Since chlordane can be harmful to humans, it is a good idea to follow these instructions as well as those specified by the manufacturer:
1. Dig a trench 2 feet deep and about 6 inches wide all around your house foundation. Do not go below the footing and make sure that the trench slants well away from the house.
2. Pour the diluted chlordane into the trench, at the rate specified in the instructions. Fill the trench and mix extra chlordane solution with the dirt.
3. Make a trench around each pillar that supports a porch or any other structure, and treat it with chlordane in the same way.
4. Treat ground beneath slabs, such as garage floors, patios, and walks, if they are near the foundation. With a power drill and masonry bit, drill holes in the slabs, 6 inches out from the foundation and a foot apart. Using a funnel, pour the chlordane into the holes at the required rate. Then fill in the holes with concrete.

Concrete

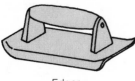

Edger

Mason's trowel

Wood float

Steel trowel

Mortar hoe

TIP: The best kind of hoe for mixing is one with holes in the blade.

TIP: Use a square-bladed shovel for mixing concrete ingredients.

Unquestionably, concrete is one of man's most useful inventions. It is also the one material you are bound to find in any house. There is good reason for its popularity: Beyond being inexpensive and relatively easy to work with, concrete is strong, fireproof, and can be formed in many shapes.

Most homeowners who are do-it-yourselfers get their hands into concrete at one point or another, either to repair existing work or to install a patio, pool, or the like. Since large repairs call for tearing the old structure apart and starting from scratch, this chapter treats all concrete installations as new projects. (For minor repairs, see page 534.)

Whether you are planning a repair or a new installation, you have to know how to buy concrete. There are two ways to purchase it: already mixed or in raw materials that you mix yourself.

Transit-mix

You can purchase concrete in this form from a concrete-manufacturing plant and have it delivered to your house ready to pour. Transported in large trucks, the concrete is held inside mixers that prevent it from hardening. The advantage of this method is apparent on large jobs such as foundations, patios, walks, and steps. Not only do you save a great deal of time and work; the resulting work will be smoother and better in all ways because the concrete was poured at one time.

The disadvantage of transit-mix is that you must have everything ready for the truck's arrival, including extra help to man shovels and wheelbarrows if the truck can't get close enough to the work site.

Here are a few points to consider when you use transit-mix concrete.
1. Get the ground ready well ahead of time. Level the work-site area and tamp it to compact the soil. If the soil is hardpan or clay, or if it has poor drainage, add a few inches of cinders or gravel as fill.
2. Build forms that are level and strong (page 542). Remember that you will be dumping tons of concrete in a few minutes, and once the work begins, you won't have time to do any adjusting. Brace the forms from the outside. If they look as if they might fall inwards, brace them internally as well, with blocks of wood you can remove as the mix flows in.
3. Prepare the route that the truck will take to your work site. You'll have perhaps 25 tons moving in there, and you'll have to allow for clearance as well as weight.

4. Be sure of your tools and the help you might require. Let the family pitch in, and ask your friends for help.
5. Estimate the amount of concrete as well as you can and place your order early.
6. Prepare some extra forms in case there is excess concrete. You may find that you have ordered more than you needed, and this way you won't waste it. Build the forms with future projects—steps, slab paths, and so on—in mind. If nothing is planned, forms 4 inches deep and 2 feet square are the most practical because that size slab is most versatile. (If you have ordered too little concrete on the other hand, you might be able to make up for it by putting small rocks into the mix. Have them handy.)

You-haul

One of the most convenient ways of getting concrete is via the you-haul system. You simply purchase the concrete in a rented trailer or pickup-size truck and haul it yourself. When done, you return the vehicle. This method is best for middle-size jobs—those calling for something between a quarter of a yard and a yard of concrete.

As with transit-mix, be sure to have everything ready before you start pouring. And remember to hose the trailer or mixer clean before you return it to the dealer. The last type of premixed concrete is known as dry-mix. It is sold ready for use with the addition of water. For very small jobs, dry-mix is an excellent choice. For anything else, its cost makes it prohibitive.

Mix-it-yourself

With all the premixed concrete available, in many cases your most practical choice is to buy the raw materials and mix the concrete yourself. The reasons are several: Many jobs are too small for transit-mix and you-haul (most companies will not deliver under a specified amount). The same jobs are frequently too large for dry-mix. Add to this the fact that many areas do not offer you-haul concrete, and you can see why you may have to mix your own. This should be a last resort, however. Never mix your own concrete when you can use transit-mix or you-haul. Not only is it unnecessary, it's impractical. The first part of the concrete may set before you can fill the form.

There are two methods for mixing your own concrete: in a wheelbarrow, or in a concrete mixer. For the first, merely shovel the specified amount of sand, gravel, and cement into a wheelbarrow, and mix thoroughly with a garden hoe. Make a hole in the center, add a little water, and mix. Continue adding small amounts of water and mixing thoroughly until the concrete is a good consistency (see "Mixing" below). Then wheel the mix over to the job.

A good alternative is to rent a portable concrete mixer from your dealer. Shovel the ingredients into the mixer, then let it do the work. The result will be a mix made in much less time, with less effort, and one that is more thoroughly blended.

Caution: If the mixer is powered by electricity, make sure that all electrical connections are correct and in good condition and that the extension cord is grounded. If possible, plug into an outside ground-fault-interrupter circuit.

The materials

Portland cement is the material used in making concrete. This is a type of material, not a brand name, and it is manufactured by several different companies. It comes in paper bags weighing 94 pounds.

Cement must be stored in a dry place; never place it on a damp floor or in a damp room. It will take up moisture and become hardened, lumpy, and useless. Once the bag is open, concrete takes up moisture more readily. Always seal the bag tightly.

The sand used in concrete should be well washed to remove any salt or organic matter. It may run from fine beach sand to coarse particles; the crucial thing is that it must be free of impurities such as soil, clay, plant life, and other foreign materials. To test it, rub some of the dry sand through your hands. If they become soiled, the sand is not suitable.

The larger particles or aggregates used in concrete range in size from ¼ inch to stones as large as 3 inches. A good rule to follow is that none of the aggregate should be larger than one-third the thickness of the concrete being poured.

The water used in mixing concrete must not have alkalies or oils in it; if it does, it won't mix properly. To be safe, use only potable water—and measure it out from a clean container.

Mixing

The secret in mixing concrete lies in using the proper materials, mixing them thoroughly, and being sure you have used them in the correct proportions. This is especially so with respect to water, which determines the strength of the concrete.

	Cement	Sand	Gravel
Walks, driveways, floors, curbs, steps, basements, etc.	1 part	2 parts	3 parts
Footings, foundations, porous walls	1 part	3 parts	4 parts

Concrete formulas

It's a good idea to mix only one sack of cement at one time; that makes it easier to figure the amounts and keep the proportions correct.

The first step is to measure out the concrete. If you're mixing only small quantities, use a shovel and count the shovelfuls to get the proper total. Then add the sand and gravel in the correct proportions. Lastly, add the water, a little at a time. For most work, you'll need about 6 gallons of water to each sack of cement.

Estimating quantities

One of the most puzzling parts of concrete work is figuring out just how much you will need. Normally slabs such as terraces and walks should be 3½ to 4½ inches thick. Driveways are usually 6 inches thick. The first step in estimating is to multiply the width times the length of the project to determine the square footage. Then multiply this by the thickness of the project. The following chart gives a rough estimate of how much of each material you will need for 100 square feet to a depth of 3, 4, and 6 inches.

Depth	3 inches	4 inches	6 inches
Cement	6 cu. ft.*	7.8 cu. ft.*	12 cu. ft.*
Sand	15 cu. ft.	19.5 cu. ft.	30 cu. ft.
Gravel	21 cu. ft.	27.3 cu. ft.	42 cu. ft.

Regardless of whether you're purchasing ready-mix concrete or making it up yourself, you can use the above formulas for purchasing materials.

*One bag of dry cement contains one cubic foot of the material.

Yards and feet

People who work around concrete often speak in terms of "yards." This standard measurement confuses some people, for in this case a "yard" is definitely *not* 3 feet. Rather, it is short talk for a cubic yard, and that's 27 cubic feet not 3, or 9 either.

The concrete form

What it takes

Approximate time: At least a day for an average, home-handyman job.

Tools and materials: Hammer, saw, nails (regular and double-headed), 2-by-4, 2-by-6, or 2-by-8-inch wood for forms, ¾-inch plywood sheet (as needed), level.

Next in importance to the concrete mix is the form. Your project will look only as good as the form it takes, and this depends on how the moist concrete is held until it sets. Forms must be sturdy enough to hold the concrete without breaking or bulging. Of course, there should be no leakage, and the concrete must be uniformly level.

There are dozens of different kinds of forms, depending on the specific job. Drawing A shows a form that would hold a slab pouring for a patio, walk, or something similar. Drawing B shows the form used for pouring a foundation wall.

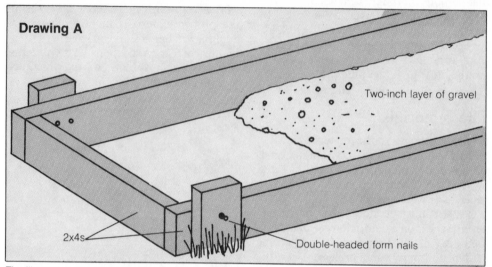

Drawing A

Two-inch layer of gravel

2x4s

Double-headed form nails

The illustration above shows the wooden form for a typical slab pouring. The drawing below pictures the form for a foundation wall. All form lumber should be straight-grained and solid. Brush it with old crankcase oil to keep the concrete from sticking to it. However, if the lumber is to remain in the concrete, use a wood preservative instead of oil.

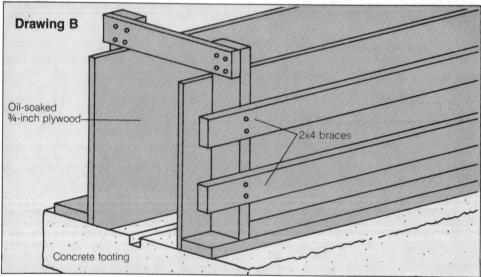

Drawing B

Oil-soaked ¾-inch plywood

2x4 braces

Concrete footing

Reinforcing the pour

With a good concrete mix and well-made form, your concrete pour is bound to give you good results. For the results to last, however, one more step is necessary—reinforcing the concrete. There are a few exceptions to the rule. A small slab that rests on solid ground does not require reinforcement. Nor does a slab broken into short segments, as in the steps shown on pages 544-45. But all vertical pours and long, unbroken slabs must be reinforced. Otherwise, chances are good that the concrete will buckle or crack in a few years.

The reinforcing material used for concrete is steel. It is available in two forms: a wire fabric, known as steel mesh, and steel rods. In general, steel mesh is used for ground-supported slabs; steel rod for elevated slabs and vertical pours, such as foundation walls.

Both materials are sold at lumberyards and building-supply stores. Mesh wire is available in widths of 5 and 6 feet and is sold cut to the length you specify. Steel rod is sold in a variety of lengths and diameters. For most household work, ½-inch-diam- eter rod is used. **Caution:** Most areas have building codes that specify the minimum rod spacing and rod diameter for freestanding structures. Check these codes before you make your purchase. Suppliers are generally knowledgeable.

Choosing and using steel mesh

Reinforcing mesh is available in many strengths. The two factors that determine this variable are the amount of space between the wires and the gauge of the wire itself. For flat areas like sidewalks and patios, 10-gauge wire spaced to create 6-inch squares is adequate. For stairwells, driveways, and other structures requiring more support, 6-gauge wire is a better choice. These figures are, of course, general. Where the subsoil offers exceptionally poor drainage, you will want to use stronger wire. Check with your dealer for the best wire for your locale and project.

There are several ways of positioning the mesh in the concrete. Since in most cases, it should be placed midway between the top and bottom of the concrete, the easiest method is to pour half the thickness of the concrete, put the precut wire on top of it, and then pour the remaining half, as shown below, left.

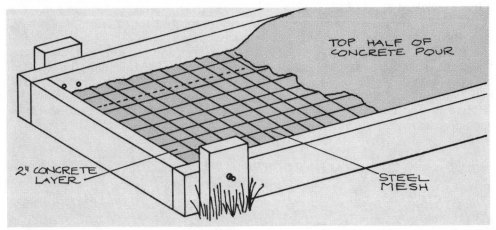

Pour concrete in the form to half the desired thickness. Lay the wire mesh on top; then pour the remaining half. Be sure to keep the mesh at least 1 inch below the surface of the concrete, and make sure that cut wire ends don't poke up through the surface. If any do, push them back in place before the concrete sets.

Using reinforcing rod

Reinforcing rod is placed in the wet concrete in much the same way as mesh wire. However, most projects in concrete that the do-it-yourselfer would engage in will not require reinforcing.

If, however, you do take on an ambitious job requiring rod, then check your local code on specifications. You can tie the rod in with wire to stone or brick. If there is overlapping, it should be about 18 inches, and tied with wire. Rod comes in 20-foot lengths and can be cut with a hacksaw.

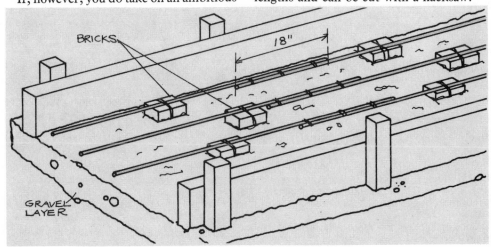

Pouring small slabs

From plain to fancy

There are dozens of ways to liven up concrete. It can be painted with specially formulated coatings, textured, or embedded with exposed aggregate. To paint concrete, clean it with trisodium phosphate and water (1 pound to a gallon), rinse well, and scrub with a solution of 1 gallon of muriatic acid and 3 gallons of water. **Caution:** Handle acid with extreme care, and use a long-handled shop broom for the scrubbing. Rinse well, then apply the paint according to the manufacturer's directions.

To texture concrete, go over it with a stiff-bristled broom before it sets. Cover with burlap bags until it cures.

To create exposed-aggregate concrete, mix and pour the concrete just like any other slab. After the initial smoothing, scatter washed pebbles over the surface. Using a wooden board, pound them flush with the surface. Let the surface of the concrete harden slightly. Then flush away the surrounding concrete with a soft stream of water.

Nine out of ten concrete projects involve pouring ground-supported slabs. Small slabs serve as paths, barbecue-pit supports, and like objects. Extend the length of the form and you have a sidewalk or driveway. Enlarge it all around and you have a porch or patio. The basic techniques for all slab pouring are the same.

For most slab work, figure on pouring a 4-inch layer of concrete, and thus on using 2x4s for your forms. Start by grading the work-site ground. If the slab is to join the house, grade the land so it slopes away from the house at a rate of ½ inch for every foot. Otherwise, the ground should be level.

Excavate the area to a depth of 4 inches. **TIP:** If your land has poor drainage, excavate to 6 inches and fill in with a 2-inch layer of tamped gravel or medium-coarse rock.

Lay the 2x4s in place, wedging them into the ground slightly to prevent leakage. If the slab is to be level side-to-side and back-to-front, check for level all around. If the land was graded to slope, check that opposite sides of the form are level (step 4, page 544). In both cases, check that opposite sides are parallel, and make sure the form doesn't get distorted in the following steps.

With double-headed nails, nail the form together. Reinforce it with 2-by-4-inch stakes all around. Drive the stakes at least 1 foot into the ground and make sure they rest flat against the form. Saw the stakes so they are level with the top of the form. Nail the form lumber to the stakes from inside the form, using common nails.

If you need reinforcing steel (page 541), have it cut and ready to be placed.

With the form ready and everything needed at hand, either mix or purchase the concrete. Pour the concrete into the form and settle it thoroughly, using an iron rake. Be sure you push the mix firmly against the sides of the form.

To finish the surface, follow the steps shown below. Then, to allow the concrete to cure properly, keep the surface moist for three days. You can do this either by sprinkling it with water or covering it with burlap or polyethylene plastic.

1. To remove excess concrete, use a long 2x4. Resting it on either side of the form and starting at the top, run the 2x4 down the form in short back-and-forth strokes. Have a helper man one end of the 2x4 while you hold the other.

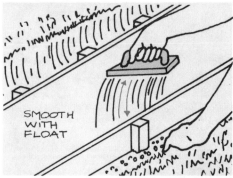

2. Use a wood float to smooth and level the surface. This also removes excess water on the surface. Work the float back and forth until you are thoroughly satisfied with the job.

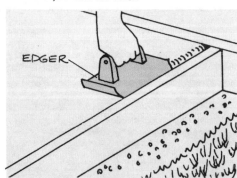

3. With an edger, round off the concrete where it meets the form. This keeps edges from chipping or getting broken. If you are pouring a long run, such as a walk, use the edger to divide the walk into sections. This will not only improve the appearance of the walk, but will help prevent it from cracking.

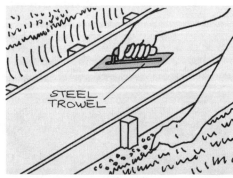

4. Finally, use a steel trowel on the surface to clear it of all water and smooth it down to a finish. Be sure to allow the concrete to cure properly before walking on it. Moisten the surface each day for three days with a fine spray of water.

Pouring concrete steps

One major home-repair job that may seem a bit difficult until you try it is pouring concrete steps. There are dozens of different kinds of concrete steps and all sorts of places where they can be put. You may want steps off the front or back porch, to connect with a walk, or to run from a patio to a swimming pool. No matter what kind of steps you have in mind, the method of pouring is the same; although with a larger job you will need reinforcing mesh. Check your local building code.

There are two things to remember when you pour concrete steps: The steps must be safe to use, and the forms you use must be sturdy enough to hold the weight of the concrete until it sets or cures.

On most entrance steps, the risers—the vertical portions of the steps—should be about 7½ inches high. The step tread or depth varies, but is usually 10 to 11 inches. On most main walks and steps, the width of the steps should be about 4 feet. When you pour entrance steps for a door, make sure that the top step is actually a small platform at least 3 feet in depth. This prevents the possibility of someone walking out the door and having a nasty fall.

Although most homemade steps have straight up-and-down risers, the professional job will angle in about 15 degrees at the bottom. For this, the bottom edges of the risers are beveled to a 15-degree angle, so the trowel can be pushed under them.

Drawing A shows the proper method of constructing an entrance platform and steps to a front or back door. Note that the stakes are held securely in place by cross braces. This prevents the forms from bulging out at the top. Most step forms are made from 2x8s. These provide the proper strength and support, as well as the most commonly used riser height.

Drawing B shows the form used if you pour steps down a basement stairwell, and the walls are already poured.

What it takes

Approximate time: A day for the average home-handyman job.

Tools and materials: Hammer, nails, level, shovels, iron rake, hoe, cement, aggregate, water (or mix, as desired).

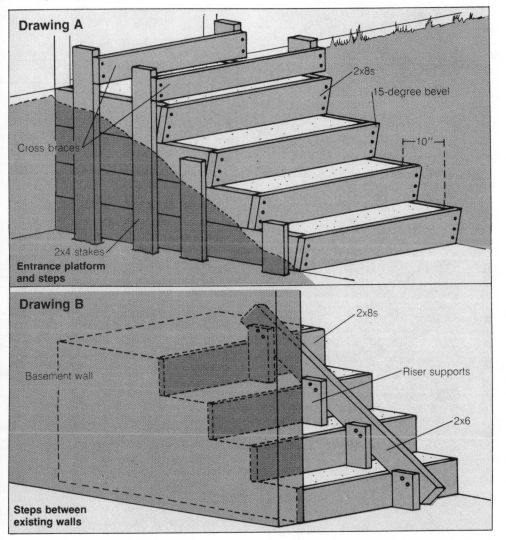

Drawing A

2x8s

15-degree bevel

10"

Cross braces

2x4 stakes

Entrance platform and steps

Drawing B

2x8s

Riser supports

2x6

Basement wall

Steps between existing walls

Step-by-step steps

1. First determine the size of the steps needed, and build individual forms for each step. On entrance steps, the norm is to build the form for the bottom step first, then the succeeding forms, so you finish at the top. Stack these forms on top of each other and put them in place. Drive 2-by-4 inch stakes at least a foot into the ground every 3 feet around the forms.

2. Make sure the stakes are driven in true and square with the form. They should not lean in or out, nor should they be twisted in relation to the side of the form. If you are pouring steps over 3 feet wide, or more than two steps high, let the stakes extend at least a foot above the forms so you can nail braces to them. Check that the form is level from all sides.

3. After you have leveled the forms, fasten them to the stakes with nails. Drive the nails from inside the form so they go through the boards, then into the stakes. All nail heads should be flush with the wood.

4. Using a long straightedge to hold the level, check across the ends of the form, which must also be square. The form for each step must fit tightly on the one below it. If there is any opening, the concrete will flow through it, creating an ugly line in the finished steps when it dries.

5. You may find, as we did, that your terrain requires special considerations. Because of the slope of the ground, this form was constructed backwards. Here the form for the bottom step is being installed under that for the top step.

6. The form is again leveled and nailed to stakes driven squarely against the sides and end of the form. If your steps are wide or high, nail cross braces to the stakes. This prevents the forms from bulging in the middle.

7. If the steps are to cross a small ditch, insert a culvert in the form to allow for water runoff. The pipe may be purchased at building-supply dealers in any length needed and in a range of diameters.

8. Once the culvert is in place, secure it to the ground with a U-shaped piece of ½-inch reinforcing rod. Any hollow object buried in concrete has a tendency to float up out of the concrete regardless of its weight.

9. With the form completed, rocks and chunks of old concrete rubble are used for fill, cutting down the amount of concrete needed. If you use this tactic, remember to keep fill away from the outer edges of the form. Otherwise, it may show when the form boards are removed.

10. You can mix the concrete yourself in a rented electric mixer. We used a formula of 1 part cement, 3 parts clean sand, and 4 parts gravel. Mix the three thoroughly, then add water until the mixture is fairly thick, but thin enough to flow. The proportion of water in the mix determines the strength of the finished project. The best method is to add water slowly until the right consistency is reached.

11. While the concrete is being poured into the form, jab a heavy rake into the concrete to help settle it. Do this especially around the edges of the form; otherwise you'll end up with air bubbles at the edges of the concrete. After using the rake to settle the concrete, you'll need to level or screed it off.

12. With a long, straight 2x4 and a helper, screed the concrete surface. Allow the edge of the 2x4 to rest on the forms, and using short back-and-forth strokes, drag off the excess concrete as you push toward the end of the form. This produces a level, fairly smooth surface, but it takes muscle and you may have to go over it a few times. This action drives the aggregates down in the mix.

13. With the surface screeded off, work the surface until it is the way you want it. Be careful when working in this position not to lock knees. This will help you maintain a free and even stroke.

14. Unless you round the edges of the steps with an edger, they will be flat and sharp and may break off. Gently drag the edger between the form boards and the concrete to round the edges and provide a nosing for the steps. After edging, trowel the concrete to smooth out any rough spots left by the edger.

15. On outdoor steps, a smooth surface is a hazard. After the concrete has set up fairly hard, but is still workable, gently drag a stiff broom across the steps to create a roughened surface. If the concrete is poured in hot weather, cover it with plastic for several days. The longer it cures, the harder and more waterproof it will be.

16. The final step is to remove the form boards and clean up any excess concrete dropped around the edges. (Wait several days for this.) Rake the area smooth and landscape as desired.

17. The actual pouring of these steps took a day, with the previous day spent in building the forms. With experience, a day would be adequate for the entire operation.

I really got horse collared!
It looked easy enough, but I should have asked my neighbor how he poured his steps. Then I would have known that any hollow object buried in concrete has a tendency to float to the surface. (Secure it with reinforcing rod.)

Practical Pete

Concrete block

This house has a concrete block foundation and a carport made of decorative blocks.

What it takes

Approximate time: Depends on the size of the job, but allow a day as a starter for even a small project.

Tools and materials: Wheelbarrow or mixer, 3-foot level, string line, string level, string holders, trowel, tape measure, brick chisel, hammer, jointer. (See step #2 at right.) For block and mortar needs, see pages 67 and 68.

When many of us think of cinder or concrete blocks, we think of ugly commercial buildings or institutions of some sort or other. But today's concrete blocks can be decorative as well as functional. What is more, with a little practice, even the unhandy handyperson can learn to lay blocks. And although the work is physically taxing, the results can be highly rewarding when you see what you can do.

Concrete blocks come in many different shapes and sizes for a wide variety of jobs. In addition to the basic H blocks, there are a half dozen or more other types for special purposes, for instance, corner blocks which have their ends shaped flush, or jamb or joist blocks for use around door and window jambs, thin half blocks for building interiors consisting of non-load-bearing walls. There is also a great variety of decorative blocks available that can be used for anything from a carport wall to an interior divider wall.

As in any masonry work, strict attention must be paid to using the right type of mortar and to good, safe building techniques. The following sequence shows basic procedures for all block-work projects.

1. One of the most common uses of concrete blocks is in house foundations. The first step in most block work is to excavate for the footing and pour it. Normally it should be 18 inches deep, or below the frost line, and 12 to 18 inches wide.

2. You'll need something to mix the mortar in (the model shown can be rented inexpensively), a 3-foot level, string line and level, string holders, tape measure, brick chisel, hammer, trowel and jointer.

3. Position batter boards on each side of the corner wall. These can be 1x4s or 2x4s nailed to stakes 2 feet apart.

4. Determine the exact location of the wall and tie string to nails driven into the boards. Dry-lay the block in place to determine how it will lay. Drop a plumb bob down to the outside corner of the end-corner block and find its exact location.

Mixing mortar

Mortar is the basic material that holds bricks, blocks, and stones together. It also serves as a grout for repairing brick, and as a patching compound. There are basically two methods of mixing mortar. You can purchase premix mortar which is already dry mixed, or you can mix your own, using:

    1 part portland cement
    6 parts sand
    1 part hydrated lime
    Just enough water to give a puttylike consistency.

Mix the mortar in a wheelbarrow, or, if you have quite a lot of block to lay, in a concrete mixer; in this case you'll need a helper to keep the mortar mixed and hand you blocks.

Mix all the ingredients together except the water; then gradually add water until the mortar is well mixed but not soupy. It should stand up on its own when pulled up with a trowel or hoe. But it should not be dry or crumbly.

One sack of portland cement, one sack of hydrated lime, and 600 pounds of sand will lay approximately 100 regular-size blocks.

5. Spread mortar on the location of the first corner block. It is important to have your block ready before you start.

6. Position the block in place, and settle it in so that it is well seated.

7. Check with the plumb bob to make sure that the block is positioned correctly.

8. Fasten a string holder to the corner of the block. This is a wooden block which clips to the cinder block corners and holds a string taut along the outside edge of the block. Lay the two end blocks first; then position the string and lay line blocks against it.

9. Level the block and tap it into position. Of course, this must all be done before the mortar begins to set.

10. The line of blocks must follow the taut string exactly. Check with a string level every so often to see that the tops are level also.

Block options

The most common size of concrete blocks is, nominally, 16 inches long by 8 inches high by 8 inches wide. (The blocks are actually 3/8 inch shorter and lower than that, to allow for the mortar joints on two faces.) But there are also blocks that measure only 4 inches high, and their adobelike look is preferred by many designers and builders. Solid cinder blocks are available in exactly the same size as standard brick. Thinner, flatter blocks are ideal for paving jobs on patios and paths. Textured thin blocks are used on walls to give a stonelike appearance.

11. Before laying a block, prepare a bed of mortar along each side of the block position and across the end and center.

12. Stand the block up and "butter" one end. The amount of mortar shown in the illustration is about right. Apply a little pressure with the trowel, so the mortar clings to the block.

13. Then in one smooth, quick motion pick up the block and lower it onto the mortar bed and against the next block. The mortar joints should be approximately 3/8 inch wide and kept even.

14. Tap the block into position against the string line and make sure it is level with the adjoining block, as well as in every other direction.

Painting blocks

For vivid color on concrete block, use one of the paints developed especially for masonry. The old standby for outdoor use is portland-cement paint. It comes in powder form and must be mixed with water and then applied only to a *dampened* wall.

15. The second course is also started at the corner, positioned with the string line, and of course leveled. Note that the positioning of the corner block in the second course is perpendicular to the block below it.

16. As each block is laid, the excess mortar is squeezed out of the joints and caught so that it can be used for the next block.

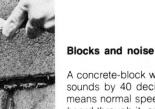

Blocks and noise

A concrete-block wall reduces sounds by 40 decibels. This means normal speech cannot be heard through it, and loud speech can be faintly heard but not understood. Within a room, fully two thirds of the noise that strikes a block wall is absorbed and does not bounce back. Few other building materials even approach these standards.

17. After the row or course of blocks is laid, a jointer is used to smooth out and round up the joints for a more even bond.

18. Then a quick downward swipe with the flat of the trowel knocks off any excess mortar that may be sticking to the joints.

19. To cut a block, as will sometimes be necessary, score it by tapping on a wide brick chisel with a mason's hammer or other metal-striking hammer. Don't try to break through on the first side; score across the block.

20. Then turn the block over and score the opposite side until it cracks on the scored line.

Building with brick

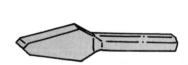

Trowel

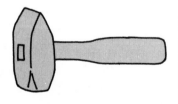

Bricklayer's hammer

Wide chisel

Brick jointer

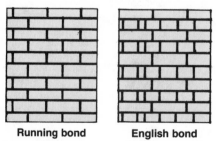

Cape chisel

Heavy-duty hammer

For centuries brick has been the most popular masonry material for all kinds of structures: house walls, patios, fireplaces, steps. It is attractive to begin with and becomes more so with age; it is easy to handle and is solid and long lasting. Brick has been used for at least 5,000 years, and while today's bricks are made in literally thousands of combinations of size and shape, color and texture, most fit into three kinds: *building, face,* and *paving bricks.*

Building bricks. These are the standard bricks, all-purpose, reasonably priced, and they can be used for any outdoor structure. As a rule, they are red in color, and about 8 inches long by 3¾ inches wide by 2¼ inches deep. This can vary.

Face bricks. These come in many sizes, and in colors that range from purplish-black to near-white, and also in textures from very smooth to rough. Face bricks make handsome walls, steps, and bar-becues, but generally they are too expensive and too highly textured for walks and patios.

Paving bricks. These are best for patios and walks, for they have a smooth surface and are often shallow—as thin as ½ inch—so that they can be laid like tiles in a mortar bed. Paving bricks come in a variety of colors, though generally in shades of red, and they also come in many shapes and sizes, including squares and hexagons.

The chief consideration when you choose bricks for an outdoor project is the question of weather resistance. The three types mentioned above will have specifications indicated by the manufacturer. The code will read SW, MW, or NW. Bricks with an SW rating can withstand severe weathering, MW moderate weathering, and NW no weathering. SW bricks are the only kind that are fit for direct contact with the ground, so you should only do paving or patio work with bricks of this type.

How to estimate materials

To estimate your brick needs, first calculate in square feet the total area that needs to be covered. Should the area be irregular, then a good way is to divide it into squares, circles, or rectangles for easier arithmetical handling. That is to say, you can use a standard formula for each section and then add the sections together. The area of a rectangle is equal to the length times the width. The area of a circle can be computed by multiplying the radius by itself and then multiplying the product by 3.14.

Then figure the number of bricks needed to cover a square foot, as follows: For mortared paving, brick steps, and walls, add ⅜ inch to each face dimension. That is, for a brick that measures 8x2¼x3¾ inches deep, your figures would be 8⅜ and 2⅝. Then multiply these figures, and divide the result into 144 to compute the number of bricks to a square foot. For the standard brick mentioned above, the answer would be 6.55 bricks per square foot. (In the case of paving that is not mortared, do the same except for adding the ⅜-inch allowance to the brick dimensions.)

You can figure the quantity of brick needed by multiplying the number of square feet to be covered in the work area by the number of bricks to a square foot. Then add on an additional 5 percent to allow for breakage and cutting.

To estimate your mortar needs, figure as follows: For a thick (double) wall, figure 20 cubic feet of mortar for each 100 square feet of bricks. For paving, figure 8 cubic feet of mortar for each 100 square feet of bricks. Then add a little extra for waste.

Types of bonds

The pattern formed by the courses in a brick wall is called the bond. The bricks are always laid in such a way that vertical joints in two courses never fall together but are staggered. Yet, in most bonds the vertical joints of *alternate* courses should be in line. There are many kinds of bonds and you can simply take your pick. A few are shown below.

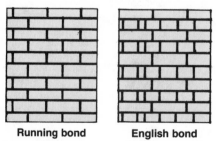

Running bond   **English bond**   **American bond**   **Flemish bond**

How to lay brick

The techniques for laying brick are much the same as for block (pages 546-49), except for the fact that in a wall brick is normally laid in double thickness for extra strength. Another difference in handling brick is that all brick should be well moistened before laying. (Blocks, on the other hand, must be kept dry during the laying process.)

Joints. The proper mortar mix is crucial. Refer to page 547 for the basic recipe. But for brickwork, prepare a slightly moister mix, say, to about the consistency of heavy cream. The form of the joint ranks next in importance. Joints should be about ⅜ inch thick. If a joint is too thin, too wide, or just plain sloppy, it will not only spoil the appearance of the block or brick, but will weaken the wall as well.

The secret to laying bricks really lies in handling the trowel. It is essential that mortar be properly spread before the bricks are placed, and proficiency with the trowel is therefore mandatory. The techniques are the same as those shown on pages 546-49. But since you'll be working "in miniature," speed becomes more of a factor, and good work habits can only be acquired on the job. You might want to find a site where a professional bricklayer is at work and spend some time watching him.

Cutting bricks. Before cutting a brick, test it by striking it against another brick or tapping it with a hammer. If you hear a clear ring, then you'll know the brick is a good one. If the sound is dull, the brick will very likely crumble when it is cut. Before you start to work, determine how many half-bricks you will need. In this way they can be cut in batches. Use the chisel and a heavy hammer. Wear safety glasses. Place the chisel on the cutting point of the brick, tilt the handle a little toward the waste end, and strike sharply.

Line and level. To lay a course of bricks you will need a line to keep it straight, that is, level and plumb. The usual way to proceed is to build up the corners and ends first, and then attach your line, using plastic or wooden line blocks. Then lay the intermediate bricks flush with the line. (It is necessary to determine spacing by setting a course in place without mortar.)

Use a 4-foot spirit level to check your brickwork before the mortar sets. The vertical and horizontal bubbles in the level will tell you if your work is true. When necessary, you can tap the bricks into line against the level. But always keep the bottom of the level clean; even a small bit of mortar will create inaccuracies.

Tuck-pointing (brick repair)

A badly cracked wall should be repaired immediately or it may cause even more damage. First determine what caused the cracking. With a star chisel or a round-nosed cape chisel, remove all flaking debris and deepen the crack or mortar joint to about ⅝ to ¾ inch. Refill the joint with mortar and smooth it with a jointer. An alternative, if the crack persistently reopens, is to use latex patching cement.

Replacing a damaged brick

If the brick is loose in the wall and can be removed, simply chip away the loosened mortar and take it out. On the other hand, if it is in solid, you may have a good deal of trouble. If so, you may have to patch the area with mortar or patching cement rather than try to extract and replace the brick.
TIP: If you dampen a brick, it will sometimes loosen up. After the brick is out, it's a simple matter to mortar in the opening and place a new brick.

Fasten line blocks to corner bricks, and lay intermediate bricks flush with line.

Laying a brick patio in sand

One of the simplest and easiest patios you can build is the loose-laid brick-in-sand variety. There's no problem of mortar setting, or the work being spoiled if it is interrupted. You work when you wish.

The area should be smoothed and leveled as much as possible. If you like, excavate the area so that the finished patio will be flush with the surface of the yard.

Although it isn't always necessary, it's a good idea to outline the patio with redwood 2x4s. These can be fastened together with screws or nails to act as little retaining walls.

After you have secured your 2x4s, shovel a two-inch layer of sand between them and smooth it level. Then lay in the bricks in the pattern you wish, such as basket weave, or perhaps herringbone. When the bricks are in, sprinkle dry sand in the cracks and sweep away any excess.

Paving brick patterns

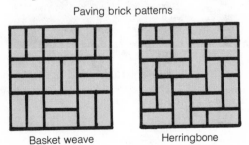

Basket weave   Herringbone

What it takes

Approximate time: Depending on size, from a couple of hours to a day or so.

Tools and materials: Hammer, nails or screws, shovel, rake, a long level, redwood 2x4s, bricks, sand.

Building a stone retaining wall

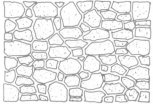

In random-rubble masonry, the crudest of all stonework, little attention is paid to laying the stone in even courses.

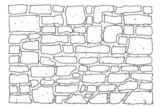

In coursed-rubble masonry, roughly squared stones are assembled in such a way as to produce roughly continuous horizontal layers.

Handling brick, and even cinder block, is one thing, but heavy stone is something else. Being your own stonemason is both one of the hardest and one of the simplest jobs. The techniques in stone masonry are actually quite easy to learn, but the work can be physically taxing. Let's face it: stone is heavy. Yet, few tools are needed —the same as for concrete or block work.

Take care in selecting the proper stones, and try to keep all the rocks in a project the same type, although not necessarily the same size or shape.

Basically, there are three categories of stonework construction: rubble, ashlar, and trimmings.

Rubble stonework is uncut stone, or stones that have not been cut to a specific shape. This type of masonry is used for rough work such as retaining walls or foundations. The stones can be laid in courses or at random; that is, without continuity of the joints.

Ashlar stone is cut on four sides so that it resembles, albeit roughly, brick. The surfaces can be smooth (that is, dressed), or left as they are.

Trimmings are cut on all sides, and used for moldings, sills, lintels, and ornament.

For do-it-yourself work, six kinds of natural stone are generally used: granite, limestone, slate, marble, bluestone, and sandstone, the most porous.

Natural stone can be purchased in three finishes: Dressed, the most expensive, is cut to your requirements; semidressed stones are cut to approximate sizes (you'll have to do some trimming yourself); undressed stone, the cheapest finish, is raw stone right out of the quarry.

How to buy stones

You can purchase stone from a stonemason, a quarry, or even from some lawn and garden-supply centers in the larger communities. Or, if you know a farmer, you might get all the rocks you can haul just for picking them up out of his fields.

Stones are sold by the cubic yard (except flagstone which is sold by the square foot). To determine just how much stone ycu will need, multiply the height of the project times the width times the length in feet. This gives the number of cubic feet. Then divide this by 27. The resulting number is the approximate cubic yardage of stone required.

In laying a wet, rubble stone wall, such as the one shown on these pages, first assemble the stones you will need to begin. Then pour the base or footing.

It is best to place the larger stones on the lower courses, so that the size of the stones will gradually grow smaller as the wall gains height.

Lay each stone on its broadest face.

Wet any porous stones before placing them in mortar so that the stone will not absorb water from the mortar and weaken the bond between stone and mortar.

Be sure that the spaces between adjoining stones are as small as practicable and that these spaces are completely filled with smaller stones and mortar.

Construction techniques

1. Pour a concrete footing for the wall. It should be at least 18 inches wide and below the frost line in your particular area. After the footing has set up, mix mortar and spread a heavy layer on the footing.

2. Now position the first inside layer of rocks, mortaring in between as you go.

3. Set the outside rocks in place; then fill in around them with rubble and mortar.

4. A string and level are essential if you want the top of the wall to be flat and even.

5. The top of the wall will tie everything together. These are the cap stones. Note the prop stick holding an unstable rock in place until the mortar sets up. Note the mortar and rubble running throughout the wall.

It wasn't just the grass that came up that spring!
I was real proud of my new wall; and it didn't take long to build. Thing is, I should've taken longer. When I do it over now, I'll know to dig below the frost line for my footing.

Practical Pete

6. A retaining wall should have pieces of pipe set in it to allow water behind the wall to drain away.

7. After the mortar has set a bit, scrub it out of the joints between the rocks with a bristle brush, and clean out any debris with a whisk broom.

8. Wash down the wall with a solution of muriatic acid and water.

9. Plantings on the upper level absorb moisture and reduce pressure against the wall.

A country dry wall

One of the most challenging, satisfying, and yet not very difficult projects a homeowner can undertake is the building of an old-fashioned dry stone wall. Moreover, if you live in a part of the country, such as New England, where fieldstone abounds, the expense is negligible.

A dry wall does not need mortar or a concrete footing because the weight and interlocking placement of the stones hold everything together. For a start, try building a wall no more than 3 feet high and a couple of feet thick. As you gain in proficiency, you can move to larger structures. Of course, you can build the wall as long as you like.

Basically, you can use stones that you find lying in fields; but these may need cutting so that they join better. Otherwise, you can buy quarried rubble. Try sandstone, bluestone, or limestone, which have fairly regular faces.

You can build your dry wall right on the ground, or in a bed of sand, which will allow for better drainage. The wall's joints will overlap. The important stone is the bonding stone, which is the first stone of the first course. Its length should equal the wall's thickness because it is set crosswise as an anchor. It ties the course on the front to the course on the back. However, if you

cannot find a stone large enough, use two stones. The space between the front and back courses must be filled with small pieces of stone, while gaps on the outside are filled with chinking; that is, little stones are hammered into crevices. The idea is that the large course stones and the smaller ones balance each other.

At the same time, the ends and faces of the wall slope slightly inward from a wide base; each successive course being set a little in from the one underneath it. This slope can be judged by eye, or you can make a simple device called a slope gauge (see step 3, opposite).

As you build, remember to let the stones tilt toward the center so that the gravitational pull against the stones will tighten the wall and help hold it together. The entire wall ties in and down toward the center.

Do not make mitered joints when you turn a corner. Always overlap joints, never stack one right above the other.

Finally, while a dry wall contains no mortar, many builders do spread mortar beneath a top surface of broad flat stones, because this cap will keep out water that may freeze and dislodge the stones. Whether you plan to mortar the top layer or not, be sure to save enough broad, flat stones for the final course.

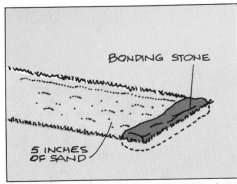

1. Your first step is to dig a trench 6 inches deep, the length and width of the wall. Fill it with 5 inches of sand. (Alternately, you can build the wall right on the ground, but a sand bed will be better for drainage.) Find a stone that is as long as the wall is thick, preferably with even faces. Place it at the end. It is your bonding stone, and it helps hold the wall together.

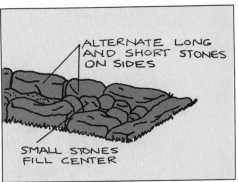

2. Start your first course by laying stones along one side, then the other. Alternate large and small stones, thin and thick. Place the long ones lengthwise, and lay each stone flat. Set each stone so that any angle in the top surface will slope toward the center of the wall. For the first course use the largest stones, then as you go up the wall use smaller stones; and on top place flat stones. After you have laid about 8 feet of stone on the first course (both sides) fill the center with small stones until the first stage is more or less level.

3. For the next course start at the bonding stone and lay a long stone at right angles to it so that it overlaps the joint of the stone on the course below. The top surface of this stone should tilt down slightly toward the center while its outer edges should be set in a little from the first course. Here is where you check with the slope gauge and level. Lay the second course along one side, then the other. Be sure the stones are long enough to overlap the joints in the course below. Work down each side, checking with the level and slope gauge as you go. Fill the center.

4. Because the stones will not always seat solidly, you will need to shim them with small pieces under the edges. Check each stone by trying to rock it. After you have laid a couple of courses, fill the openings between the stones with chinking—narrow stones which you can drive in with a hammer. This will lock the wall and will help it tighten toward the center. Keep checking with the slope gauge. The horizontal level does not have to be exact, but you can check it by eye as you go.

5. To turn a corner, lay the stones in the same way you would for a wall. However, for the last stone in the first course of the outer face, use a large stone to overlap the first outer course at the turn. But in the second course, set the last stone of the outer face short of the corner. This will cause its end to meet the side of the first stone on the turn. The principle is to overlap for a secure bond.

6. If you want a mortared cap as protection against water, cover the next-to-last course with a layer of mortar, 1 inch thick. A mix of 1 part cement to 3 parts sand should do it. You have been saving flat stones for the top. Set these now, filling in the gaps with mortar if you wish, and building up the center of the joint so that there will be no pockets to collect water. Finally, trowel-trim excess mortar.

A flagstone walk or patio

What it takes

Approximate time: Depends on the size of the project, but at least half a day as a start.

Tools and materials: Stonemason's hammer, chisel, goggles, rubber mallet, trowel, mortar, sand, shovel and pick, level.

Planning hints: Flagstone is sold by the square foot. Measure the space you wish to pave, and allow about 10 percent for waste.

One of the simplest do-it-yourself projects with stone is the flagstone patio or walk. Flagstone can be laid dry or wet (mortared). Dry-laid flagstone may be laid over a bed of sand with sand, not mortar, forced between the stones. Or, set the stones far enough apart to place soil between them, allowing grass or other plantings to come up for an unusual and natural-looking patio.

Dry-laid flagstone. The first thing is to stake out the area you intend to cover with flagstone. Excavate to a depth of 3 inches, and put down 2 inches of sand. Use 1½ to 2-inch-thick flagstones. Put down three or four at a time, lining up the straight edges with your outside lines, and keeping the irregular edges toward each other. Be sure to wear goggles if you do any trimming with a stonemason's hammer and chisel.

Work from one corner and tap each stone down with a rubber mallet. After you have put down a couple of rows, check with a mason's level to see if the surface is even. Put more sand under low stones, and remove sand from beneath high ones.

Shovel more sand over the flags, and sweep it across the stones so that the joints are filled. Water the surface and allow it to dry. Repeat this until the joints are compacted and completely filled.

Wet-laid flagstone. This is started in the same way as dry. After the sand has been leveled and the stones placed, a fairly dry mortar is forced down between the stones. Allow it to dry more, then sweep away the excess with a stiff-bristle broom.

Another method is to cover a level area with sand, arrange the stones on it, sweep over them with a mixture of cement and sand, and then sprinkle with a hose. The sand should be at least 2 inches deep, so that you can push the flags down into it.

If you are covering a fairly large area, then it will be necessary to allow a pitch for drainage. This is also sensible if you live in a part of the country where severe freezing occurs. Freezing and thawing of standing water can crack the cement bond.

You can put down a bed of cinders several inches deep before you put down the sand, or as an alternative, you can make the sand a good 6 inches deep.

Repair. Repairing or replacing a stone is quite simple. If dry laid, merely lift the stone up out of the sand, clean out the excess sand, and set a new stone, filling in around it with sand. If the flagstone was wet laid, chip away the surrounding mortar, replace the stone, and remortar it.

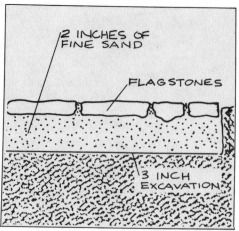

Dry-laid flagstone is a simple matter—just stone and sand. You can work at your own speed, stopping at any point for as long as you wish.

The beauty of this kind of walk is that its roughness is part of its charm. Leveling is necessary, but not difficult. You should be careful that there are no high or low points where a person can trip, or which will hold water.

Wet-laid flagstone on the other hand should not be left unfinished. It's almost as easy as putting down dry laid. All you need is mortar and a trowel, and of course, a little muscle.

Patching asphalt

Cracks and holes in your asphalt or blacktop driveway can easily be patched, and the sooner done, the better. Not only is it an annoyance when you run over a large crack or pothole with your car, but the hole can soon widen and deepen to the point where you have a major driveway problem to tackle.

The asphalt that is used on driveways is really a kind of concrete. But while ordinary concrete is a mixture of gravel with a binder of cement, asphalt is held together with a crude-oil extract.

For best protection, asphalt should be coated every four or five years with a waterproof sealer, which is also chemical resistant. You simply pour the sealer from the can onto the driveway, and spread it evenly with a push broom. It is important first, however, to make sure that the driveway is swept clean of all dirt. Most sealers come ready mixed in 5-gallon cans, and will coat from 200 to 300 square feet. This depends of course on the porousness of the driveway surface.

This coating procedure will also fill any cracks that are not over ⅛ inch wide. For larger cracks, you can thicken the sealer with sand and push it into the crack with a putty knife or trowel; then seal over it.

What it takes:

Approximate time: For most repairs allow a few hours. Extensive work could take days.

Tools and materials: Shovel, stonemason's hammer and chisel, trowel or putty knife, 2x4 tamper, sealer, asphalt mix, sand, stiff push broom.

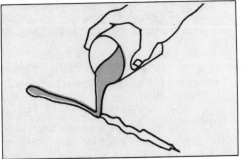

1. For small cracks, use liquid sealer; for cracks that are more than ⅛ inch wide, mix sealer with sand. It's best to do this work in warm weather.

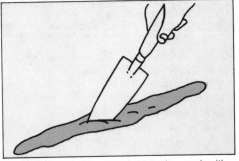

2. Press the sealer and sand into the crack with a putty knife or trowel. Then seal over it if necessary to bring it up to driveway level.

I shouldn't have brought my work home with me!
I did a real neat job patching my asphalt driveway. But I just didn't notice where I'd been standing— till I saw my wife's face when I walked into the kitchen. Next time I'll know to spread sand on that sealer so it won't stick to my shoes.

Practical Pete

Filling holes

To repair a hole, use cold-mix asphalt. Cold-mix asphalt comes in two varieties: cut-back asphalt and emulsion mix. For dry holes you may use either type, but for damp holes you should use emulsion mix only, which is made with water. The mix comes in 66-pound bags. It should be loose in the bag for best application. If it is hard, then you must warm it. Asphalt should be worked on during warm weather—never if the temperature is below 40 degrees Fahrenheit or it will be difficult to work with.

First, clean the hole thoroughly. Make certain that the sides are cut all the way back to solid asphalt and are vertical. If the hole is deep, fill it partially with coarse gravel. Then use a push broom to fill the hole with mix to within an inch of the top.

To eliminate any air pockets, slice the mix with the blade of a shovel and then tamp it with the end of a 4x4. Finish filling the hole, bringing the mix to a mound. Level the mound to the rest of the driveway surface with a roller or a 4x4 tamper. The mix must be pressed firmly against the sides of the hole. You can also drive your car over the patch to compact it. Spread sand over the new asphalt so that it won't stick to your shoes. Sweep off the sand when the asphalt dries.

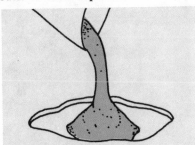

1. Pour blacktop mix into the hole, mounding it above the edges, and making sure that it fills.

2. Alternately spread the mix with a push broom and compact it with the tip of a shovel.

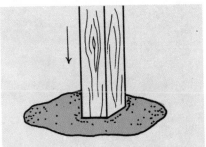

3. Then tamp it down with a 4x4 (you could also use a roller). Keep adding and tamping until it is even with the rest of the driveway.

8.FENCES

There are innumerable kinds of fences of varying designs and materials, as well as purpose. Some fences are for privacy, some for protection, and some are for looks. Many are for all three.

The first thing to take into account when you decide to put up a fence is the local building code. There may be certain restrictions as to height, materials, style, and location in relation to your property boundary lines.

Your fence can be metal, stone, wood, or, if you happen to run cattle or sheep, barbed wire. For the average homeowner, the wood fence seems to be the most popular as well as the simplest to install.

Of this type there are a great many; from the old-fashioned split rail and the picket fence, to the closed-screen type. But no matter what sort of fence you decide on, the most important thing is the durability of the posts.

Chain link

Post and rail

Old-fashioned hurdle

Screen

Salem picket

Basket weave screen

Setting posts

A wood post should be set with one-third of its length in the ground. It should first be treated with a preservative; creosote and pentachlorophenol ("penta") are the most popular.

You can dig the hole with a shovel and crowbar, or a posthole digger. Try not to disturb the ground surrounding the hole, and make the hole as narrow as possible, flaring it slightly at the bottom but keeping it small at the top.

When the hole is dug, place a flat rock or some gravel in the bottom and rest the post on top of it. Use a level to get the post plumb, and then secure it with braces. Fill around the post with concrete: 1 part portland cement, 2 parts sand, 3 parts medium gravel. (A wheelbarrow is ideal for mixing small quantities of concrete.)

When you shovel in the concrete, poke the mixture now and then to eliminate any air bubbles. Add extra concrete above ground level so that the footing slopes away from the post for drainage. Now go on to your next post. Let the concrete cure fully on all the posts before putting up your horizontals. Allow a full week if you can.

Steel posts can be set the same way, except that the lower end should be coated with asphalt paint to avoid rusting. Concrete should be set below the frost line to prevent the posts from heaving.

A simpler but less permanent way of setting a post is to dig the hole, line the bottom with gravel, or a flat rock, place the post erect and fill in with gravel and earth, tamping with a shovel handle or a piece of lumber as you go.

What it takes

Approximate time: An hour per post, if the digging is not too difficult. In rocky soil, good luck.

Tools and materials: Measuring tape, string, short sticks, level, wheelbarrow, braces, shovel, posthole digger, paint brushes, fence posts, wood (or metal) preservative, flat rocks, gravel, portland cement, sand.

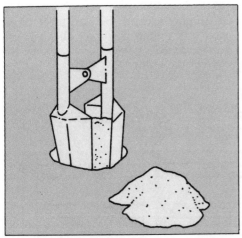

1. To dig holes with a posthole digger, drive the digger's paired shovels into the ground with the handles close together. Then force the handles apart to compress the loosened earth between shovel blades. Finally, lift with the handles still spread, and trapped earth will rise.

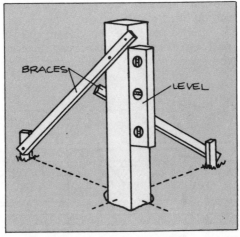

2. After positioning the post in the hole, use a level to get it plumb. Then brace the post in two directions, and stake the braces to the ground. Double-check for plumb and make final adjustments in the braces if necessary.

It turned out to be a rotten deal!

I set my fence posts good and solid. But before long the posts began to rot and my fence weakened. Then I realized that you have to slope the concrete footing so that water can drain away, and not into the posthole.

Practical Pete

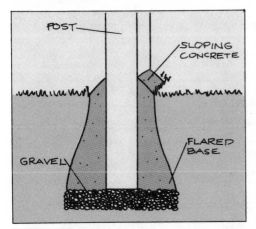

3. Fill the hole to ground level with concrete, and then add a small mound of concrete on top, sloping away from the post for good drainage.

Removable post

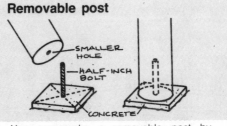

You can make a removable post by inserting a half-inch bolt into concrete before it has set. Drill a hole in the bottom of the post, slightly undersize. Then screw the post onto the bolt until it is firm. This type of post can of course be set on top of the ground and is less subject to weathering; digging is necessary only for the base. Be sure your bolt and your bolt hole are perfectly vertical.

An old-fashioned post-and-rail fence

The charm of a really rustic fence is something many homeowners wish to see on their property. You can buy such fences ready built, and all you have to do is dig the postholes, set the posts, and assemble the fence. The steps are as follows:

1. Drive stakes into the ground at each end of your proposed fence.
2. Stretch a string tightly between them, about 6 inches above the ground. This will be your guide for setting your posts in a straight line.
3. Dig your first posthole at one end of the line. For a fence that has two horizontal rails, the hole should be about 2 feet deep. For three or four rails, 30 inches is good.
4. Stand your first post in the hole so that it just touches the line you have stretched. In most kits, there will be holes in the posts to receive the cross pieces; so make sure that they face along the fence line. Then finish setting the post.
5. Insert a rail in the bottom hole of the post, and using the rail as a measure, locate the second posthole. Remove the rail and

dig the second hole as detailed in step 3.
6. Reinsert the rail in the first post and in the corresponding hole in the second post. If a rail is not straight, turn it so that the bow is up.
7. If your rails are cedar, they may be slightly tapered. In this case, alternate them so that the thicker end of one is over the thin end of another. You should also place them so that the thick end of one meets the thin end of the next in the holes in the posts.
8. Plumb the second post. Make sure it is the correct height and that it touches the string. Then fill the hole and tamp it. Continue setting succeeding posts and inserting rails in like manner.

If ground is not even, make sure that you account for differences so that your fence is even. It doesn't have to be absolutely level, but it should be built up and cut back so as not to give a choppy appearance.

On sloping ground, be sure to erect the posts in a plumb position. The rails can then be tilted as necessary to follow the slope of the ground.

I was plumb dumb!
My neighbor sure got a laugh when he took a look at my new fence. I'd set it straight and even, and when I got to the point where the ground began to slope, I just followed it downhill. But that's where I went wrong. So he helped me do it over, and this time I set the posts plumb no matter what the ground did.

Practical Pete

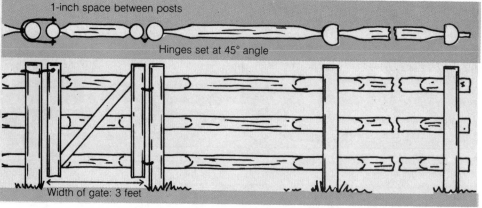

1-inch space between posts

Hinges set at 45° angle

Width of gate: 3 feet

Illustrated above is the standard configuration for a three-rail fence. Two- and four-rail styles are similar. Aerial view is shown at top. The gate is built just like the fence, but smaller; it has a diagonal brace and hook-over catch. The drawings below show the right and wrong ways to deal with uneven ground. A choppy look can be avoided by setting some posts deeper than others and then filling in or cutting back under the completed fence.

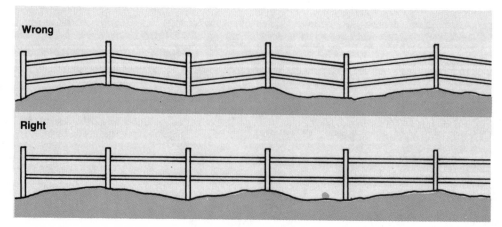

Wrong

Right

Hanging a gate

No matter what kind of fence you build, a most important aspect of the overall project—and one that is all too easy to muff after everything else has gone well—is the gate. Not every fence requires a gate, but if you elect to incorporate one into your project, follow these five steps carefully. The style of fence and gate shown here may not be at all similar to the one you are building. But if you get the basic principles right, the details (such as latch style, shape and girth of gate posts, and so on) will be of lesser importance and are simply a matter of taste and circumstances.

The essential thing, as with a door, is to hang the gate so that it opens and closes well. This means that it will have to adjust to the gate posts, even if not exactly plumb.

1. The essential thing is that the gate, like any door, should hang well. The fence posts must, therefore, be plumb.

What it takes

Approximate time: One hour.

Tools and materials: Hammer, screwdriver, pencil and measuring tape, block of wood, level, drill, hardware, gate.

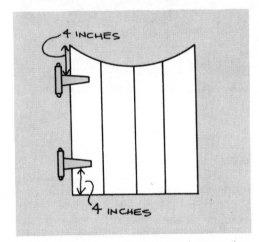

2. Place the gate on a flat surface—the ground or two sawhorses—while you apply the hinges. The straps should be about 4 inches from the top and bottom of the gate on the side that is to be hinged. Mark the location for the screws and drill the pilot holes. Then screw the straps into position.

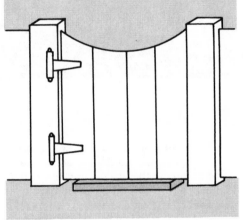

3. Place the gate in the opening, allowing the right amount of space between the bottom of the gate and the ground. You can use a wooden block under the gate to assure the correct amount of clearance. The block will act like extra hands while you work.

Common latch styles

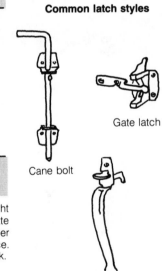

Gate latch

Cane bolt

Ornamental thumb latch

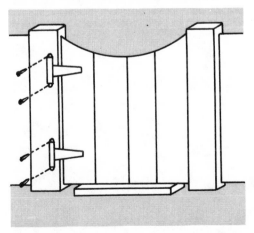

4. When you have the gate properly aligned with the adjacent posts, mark the locations of the hinge holes on the fence post. Drill pilot holes, and secure the gate with screws.

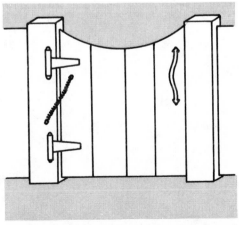

5. You may wish to add a spring to the gate and post, so that it will close by itself. Notice that the spring is always inclined to the right. You should place the spring as close to the vertical as conditions allow.

9.IMPROVEMENTS

Decks

Planning hints

The first step in planning a deck is to survey the landscaping situation and decide which problems the deck should solve. Determine a rough location for the deck and then check local building regulations to see what provisions, restrictions, or guidelines are placed on a deck of the type you want.

Building regulations may include foundation requirements, railings, load limits, height and protection limits, and other requirements. Knowing the specifics of the local code will permit more precise planning, prevent construction delays, and provide greater assurance of approval by the planning or building commission.

If the construction problem is a difficult one, if the deck area is to be extensive, or if the deck is to be more than a few feet above the ground, a building professional such as a structural engineer, architect, or contractor should be consulted.

A deck is simply a handsome platform on or above the ground. But it's a platform that can add much to the livability, beauty, and value of a house. A well-designed deck can turn a hilly site into a useful, enjoyable outdoor living area at a fraction of the cost of adding an inside room. And there's no substitute for the style of living it can provide as an area for sunbathing, entertaining, dining, conversation, container gardening, children's play and parties.

Good deck design eases the transition from deck to garden—and is part of each. Where the land slopes down and away from the foundation of a house, the deck extends the floor level of the building out into otherwise wasted space. And where paving of a flat area may be a practical expedient, a ground-level deck is often preferred for its resilient comfort and drainage advantages.

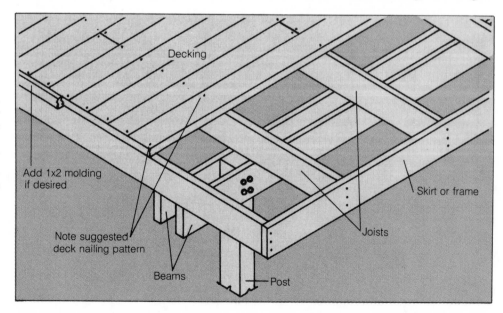

Decking

Add 1x2 molding
if desired

Note suggested
deck nailing pattern

Beams

Post

Skirt or frame

Joists

Structural elements

The deck structure gathers the weight and load of the deck and transmits it downward to the ground. The top layer is the *decking* itself, often decorative in pattern, but always designed to support a stated load with a minimum of deflection. The decking rests on *joists*, which are the primary structural element of the floor. The joists rest upon *beams*, which gather the load and transmit it to *posts* or other vertical supports. The posts rest on *footings* which bear the concentrated load of the deck and structure. In extremely low decks beams rest directly on footings.

Decking. The deck surface is the most visible part of the entire deck structure, and its size, grade, and placement determine the arrangement and size of the framing. Two-inch nominal redwood is recommended for most decking situations. The most common sizes are 2x4 and 2x6. Nominal 1-inch-thick material may be used where joists are placed within 16 inches of each other. Where a pattern of narrow lines is desired, 2x4s may be used on edge, with longer spans than are possible when the decking is laid flat. The decking spans possible with the common sizes and general-purpose grades of redwood are given in the table below.

Suggested decking spans

Size	Grades that may be used	Span
1x4	Clear only	16''
2x4	All grades	24''
2x6	All grades	36''

Joists. The joists (usually 2-inch dimension lumber) bear the load of the decking and whatever loads are placed upon the deck. The joist span is determined by the joist spacing and the grade of lumber. Typical joist spans for redwood general-purpose grades are given in the table below.

The joists usually rest upon a beam or header and are anchored to it. The joist can overhang slightly beyond the beam for appearance or added space if desired. Overhang depends upon joist thickness and shouldn't exceed one-fourth of length.

Suggested joist spans

Joist size		Clear	Select	Construction
		Grade		
2x6	16"o.c.	10'0''	8'0''	6'0''
	24"o.c.	9'0''	7'0''	5'0''
	36"o.c.	6'6''	5'6''	4'0''
2x8	16"o.c.	13'0''	12'0''	9'0''
	24"o.c.	12'0''	10'0''	7'6''
	36"o.c.	9'0''	8'0''	6'0''
2x10	16"o.c.	17'0''	16'0''	13'0''
	24"o.c.	15'0''	12'6''	11'0''
	36"o.c.	11'0''	10'0''	9'0''

o.c. means "on center"

Beams. Beams rest upon the posts and support the joists. Size of beam required depends upon the spacing and span of the beams. However, a general rule is to utilize as large a beam as necessary in order to minimize the number of posts and footings. Beams of 4-inch thickness and greater are often used. The beams can be bolted to the tops of posts. Typical beam spans are given in the table below.

Suggested beam spans

Beam size	Grade	Width of deck			
		6'	**8'**	**10'**	**12'**
4x6	Clear	6'6''	6'0''	5'0''	4'0''
	Construction	4'6''	4'0''	3'6''	3'0''
4x8	Clear	9'0''	8'0''	7'0''	6'0''
	Construction	6'0''	5'0''	4'6''	4'0''
4x10	Clear	11'6''	10'0''	8'6''	7'6''
	Construction	7'6''	6'6''	6'0''	5'6''

Ledgers. Where one side of the deck meets a house or other building, joists can be supported by a ledger attached to the house. Usually a ledger 2 inches thick is sufficient. But better bearing and easier toe-nailing is obtained if a thicker ledger is used. To prevent rain or snow from wetting interior floors, the ledger should be located so that the surface of the deck is at least an inch below the floor surface of the house.

Posts. The posts bear the weight of the deck, transmitting it through the footings to the ground. For most low decks, the 4x4 is an adequate post. While supporting the deck, the post can continue upward to support railing, seat, and overhead structure.

Cross bracing may be necessary to prevent lateral movement of the deck, particularly if it is elevated high above the ground.

Footings. The footing anchors the entire structure to the ground as well as transmitting the weight of the deck to the ground. Building codes are usually very specific on the subject of footings. Generally they must extend to undisturbed soil or rock, and in cold climates usually must extend below the frost line. For low-level decks, concrete blocks or precast footings may be used, by seating them firmly in the soil. If concrete footings are site-poured, metal post anchors or steel straps may be set in the wet concrete. Drift pins offer a concealed method of connecting the post to the footing when the underside of the deck is to be in view.

Location and placement of footings are determined by the design of the deck's structural members so that weight is properly transmitted to the ground. Once the perimeter of the deck has been established, refer to the table of suggested beam spans to determine the spacing of footings, based on the size of the beam to be used.

Note well:
The tables on this page are based on nonstress-graded redwood used in a single span. They assume a live load of 40 pounds per square foot (that is, normal use). Abnormal loading such as planter boxes or heavy barbecue grills will require shorter spans or larger beams and joists.

Alternative footings

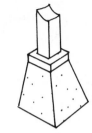

Concrete block or precast footing

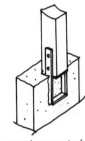

Site-poured concrete footing with metal post anchor or steel strap

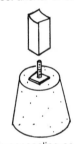

Drift pin concealing connection between post and footing

Alternative ledger placements

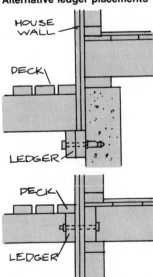

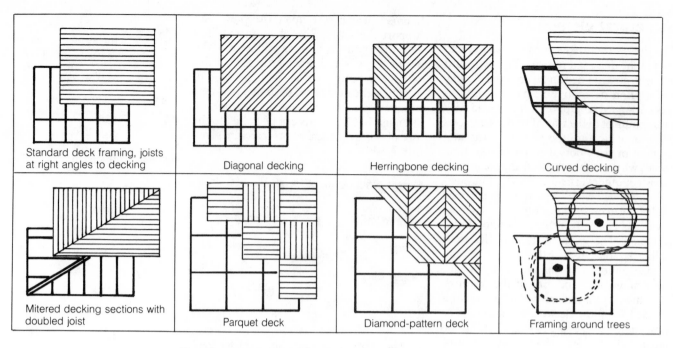

Standard deck framing, joists at right angles to decking

Diagonal decking

Herringbone decking

Curved decking

Mitered decking sections with doubled joist

Parquet deck

Diamond-pattern deck

Framing around trees

Laying out the deck

The size and pattern of the decking affects the framing plan of the deck. So determine the decking pattern first. The most common pattern is to have decking in one direction with joists at right angles to the decking. The beams are at right angles to the joists. This arrangement is referred to as *standard* framing. In standard framing, layout is simply a matter of determining decking spans, choosing joist size and span, and locating posts or other supports for beams.

But there are many other variations in surface patterns, and some require modification of the standard framing pattern.

Diagonal patterns. Decking may be laid on a diagonal to the joists at any angle greater than 45 degrees. Diagonals are often used to give visual relief to very regular deck shapes, or to give a distinctive shape to the deck. If decking is laid in a herringbone or zigzag pattern, it should be remembered that too much repetition may have a dizzying effect. Standard framing may be used for the diagonal patterns. But note that diagonal decking spans are greater, and joists may have to be set closer together than would be necessary with standard pattern decking. Where one side of the deck follows the diagonal, a header should join the joist ends to support the decking.

Laying the decking

In all situations, the decking is laid on joists and may be installed in basically the same manner regardless of pattern or shape.

First make an estimate of the lengths needed, and lay out the decking on the joists, so that any butt joints which may occur can be planned to occur at random

Geometric shapes and free forms. These are variations of standard or diagonal decking patterns, including triangles, hexagons, circles, curves, etc. Almost any form or shape can be achieved so long as a joist or joist-header lies near enough to the edge of the deck to support it properly.

Changing directions. Wherever there is a major change in the direction of the decking, a single beam or double joist must continue under the miter joining line, with joists at an angle to it and perpendicular to the decking.

Parquet and diamond pattern decks. These sectional decks require a grid pattern of support, which is achieved by blocking between the joists at a distance equal to the joist spacing. If the joists used are of 2-inch material, it may be necessary to nail a 2x2 nailer strip to the joists for better bearing and nailing.

Framing around trees. In the planning of both low and high-level decks, a friendly tree is sometimes encountered which can pierce the deck to bring its shade to the platform. Plan framing so that it permits adequate clearance for the tree. Leave room for the tree to sway in the wind and for tree growth. The higher the deck, the more room the tree needs to sway.

intervals and over joists. Joints should never occur on adjacent pieces of decking unless the pattern indicates it. It is usually better to trim the decking as it is used, rather than trimming first, in order to fit any variations caused by installation of the framing or other decking.

If the decking is laid parallel to the house, make sure the first piece is properly aligned both to the house and at the proper angle to the joists.

Vertical or flat grain. Vertical-grain redwood is recommended for decking; but if flat-grain lumber is used, make sure that the "bark side" of each piece is up (the side that was outermost on the tree). This minimizes raising of grain in flat-grain pieces. Either side of a vertical-grain piece may be up.

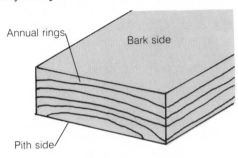

Annual rings
Bark side
Pith side

Nails and fastenings. Use only noncorroding nails and fastenings on your deck to prevent staining; these include stainless steel, aluminum alloy, and top-quality, hot-dipped galvanized materials. Nails and fastenings galvanized by the electroplating method should not be used. For 2-inch decking, use 16-penny nails. Use 8-penny nails for 1-inch decking.

Nailing. Predrill holes for nails at the end of decking pieces to avoid splitting and to achieve secure fastening. For most decks, seasoned decking materials should be spaced about ⅛ inch apart. This will be sufficient to allow drainage of water. At ends of deck plank, nail through predrilled holes. Use only one nail per bearing, alternating from one side of the piece to the other. This method is sufficient for retaining kiln-dried redwood, which does not require heavy nailing because of its stability. The nailing of alternate sides forestalls any tendency to pull or cup.

When decking rests on only two supports and each piece only completes a single span, as in herringbone and parquet decking, nail two nails at each end.

Use any handy measuring template to make sure spacing is uniform between boards. One common method is to use a nail as a spacer, pulling it out when the decking has been secured.

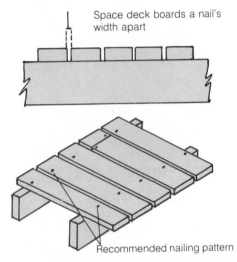

Space deck boards a nail's width apart

Recommended nailing pattern

Special situations

Decks on ground. On level ground it is often desirable to use decking as paving. The deck on the ground may serve either as a complete patio paving, or alternating with concrete, brick, grass, or plantings. This provides a quick-draining terrace at ground level and is possible only with a decay-and insect-resistant wood such as heartwood redwood.

Preparation of ground. First, a 3-inch bed of tamped sand should be laid below the planned surface of the deck to promote drainage and to help control weeds. If the soil is poorly drained, 3 inches of coarse gravel under the sand will improve drainage of a deck on the ground.

The decking should be nailed to all-heartwood 2x4 cleats, laid flat in the sand. If the decking is laid in the standard parallel pattern, the cleats should be at 2-foot intervals to allow use of random-length wood.

If the decking is laid in a parquet pattern, the squares can be fabricated separately, then laid down as large paving squares. Regular parquet or diamond design can be handled this way. Careful leveling is necessary to lay the parquet deck. When plantings or other materials are to be alternated with the parquet decking, a border strip of 2x4 heartwood on edge will suffice to contain the planting and may serve as formwork for concrete or other paving.

Downhill slopes. If the deck is begun on grade and then extends out over a slope, the transition from nailing-strip framing to joist-and-beam framing can be achieved without any interruption of the surface decking.

Decking over concrete. A deck can be laid directly over a concrete patio, and it will provide a better insulated and faster draining surface than the concrete alone. If the deck lies directly on the concrete, the same basic framing can be used as when the deck is laid directly on the ground. One modification will be required: Although the ground can be leveled, the slab probably has a slight slope, so the deck framing may have to be shimmed. If the deck is to be elevated above the slab, as in the case of a floor-level deck with a 12- to 18-inch air space below, standard framing should be used.

Plantings. Plantings are an important part of the garden picture and can be combined with the deck in a number of ways: If the deck is above ground, a planter box can be dropped in at deck level or raised above the level of the decking to provide relief in a broad expanse of deck. Portable planters can provide a changing splash of color and can be moved to the side for entertaining. **Caution:** Planters and other containers are likely to increase the load upon the deck considerably and the framing should be strengthened if such loads are planned.

Rooftop decks. The areas above first-floor rooms, carports, garages, and other flat-roofed areas offer attractive possibilities for outdoor living areas adjacent to second-floor rooms. If a rooftop deck is planned with the original construction of the building, allowance can be made for the added weight of the deck, its occupants, and planters, furniture, etc. If the deck is added in remodeling, additional bracing of the roof may be required.

For most normal, light use, decking is usually nailed into flat cleats, but one has to make sure that the nails don't penetrate the roofing beneath. The decking should maintain the previous drainage pattern of the roof. Two-inch decking will permit greater spans, and minimize nailing-cleats. One-inch decking is lighter in weight but requires supports at about 16-inch intervals.

STAFF FOR THIS VOLUME

Editor-in-chief	Allen D. Bragdon
Art Director	John B. Miller
Art Director (Revised Edition)	Lucinda Schaefer
Designer	Lillian Nahmias
Art Associate	Clara Rosenbaum
Production Editor	Jayne Lathrop
Section Editors	Allen D. Bragdon, Michael Donner, Donal Dinwiddie, Tim Snyder, James Wyckoff

CONTRIBUTORS

Consulting Authors   Monte Burch, Doug Day, Joe Foley, Dutch Meyers

Contributing Editors   Michael Eastman, Joe Fernandez, Charles Johnson, Jill Munves, Hannah Selby

Contributing Artists   Pat Lee, Chuck Pitaro, Clara Rosenbaum, Jerry Zimmerman

Contributing Photographers   Jack Abraham, Monte Burch, Norma Chacona, Ken Clare, Donal Dinwiddie, Chérie Francis, Jay Hedden, Jayne Lathrop, Michael Mertz, Dutch Meyers, John B. Miller, Tim Snyder

ACKNOWLEDGEMENTS

The editors wish to thank the following individuals and firms for their help in the preparation of this book:

INTERIOR REPAIRS & DECORATION

Armstrong Cork Co.; Art Commercial Studios; Azrock Floor Products; Benjamin Moore; Bilco; Decro-Wall; Georgia-Pacific Corp.; Johns-Manville; Jim Walter Corp., Celotex Division; Marlite Paneling; Masonite Corp.; Minwax Corp.; National Gypsum Co.; Nicholson, The Cooper Group; Ola M. Pfeifer; Plexiglas; Power Tool Institute; Rockwell International, Tool Div.; Simpson Timber Co.; The Birge Co.; The Molly Company, USM Corporation; Stanley Tools, Division of the Stanley Works; U.S. Department of Housing and Urban Development; U.S. Plywood, Division of U.S. Plywood-Champion Papers, Inc.; Urefoam Corporation of America, Subdivision of My-Toy, Inc.; Wallcovering Industry Bureau; Western Wood Moulding and Millwork Producers; Western Wood Products Assn.; Window Shade Mfrs. Assn.

ELECTRICAL FIXTURES, WIRING & APPLIANCES

Anaheim Manufacturing, a Tappan division; Borger's Television; Circle F Industries; Fedders Corporation; General Electric Company; Gould, Inc., Electrical Products Group, Special Markets Department; Harvey Hubbell, Inc., Wiring Device Division; William C. Huber, Pass & Seymour, Inc.; Illuminating Engineering Society; Lightcraft, NuTone Division; Sperry Remington, Division of Sperry Rand Corporation; William M. Teed, Slater Electric Inc.; Westinghouse Electric Corporation, Lamp Division; The Wiremold Company; Whirlpool Corporation.

WINDOWS, DOORS, SECURITY & INSULATION

Abloy, Inc.; Adams Rite Manufacturing Co.; American Plywood Assn.; Andersen Windowalls; Armstrong Cork Co.; Biltbest Windows; BRK Electronics; Caldwell Manufacturing Company; Consolidated Edison of N.Y., Inc.; Fedders Corp.; Federal Chemical Co., Inc.; Fichet, Inc.; General Aluminum Products, Inc.; Home Center Institute, National Retail Hardware Association; Honeywell Inc.; Johns-Manville; K-S-H, Inc.; Kwikset Sales and Service Company; Lafayette Radio Electronics Corp.; Madico; Medeco Security Locks, Inc.; Mortell Company; NuTone Division, Scovill Manufacturing Co.; Owens-Corning Fiberglas Corp.; Plaskolite, Inc.; Quaker Window Channels; Radio Shack; Reynolds Metals Company; Schlage Lock Company; Stanley Tools, Division of the Stanley Works; United Press International; U.S. Department of Agriculture; U.S. Department of Housing and Urban Development; United States Gypsum Company; Westinghouse Security Systems.

PLUMBING & HEATING

American Iron and Steel Institute; American Standard, Inc.; Bernzomatic Corp.; Bituminous Pipe Institute; Black and Decker Mfg. Co.; Carrier Corporation; Cast Iron Soil Pipe Institute; Chicago Pneumatic Tool Company; Cinch-Pipe System; Clow, Waste Treatment Division; Committee of Steel Pipe Producers; Copper Development Association, Inc.; Cromaglass Corp.; Culligan, Inc.; Deeprock Manufacturing Company; Delta Faucet Company; General Electric Company; Genova, Inc.; Lennox Industries, Inc.; Montgomery Ward and Co.; Mortell Company; Peerless Faucet Company; Ridge Tool Co.; Sears, Roebuck and Co.; the Stanley Works; Sunstream, a division of Grumman Houston Corporation; U.S. Department of Agriculture; Water Pollution Control Federation; Water Well Journal, Anita Stanley; Westinghouse Electric Corp.

FURNITURE CARE & REFINISHING

Borden Chemical, Krylon Division; the Darworth Co.; Janovic Plaza; 3M Co.; Minwax Co.; St. Regis Paper Co.; the Stanley Works; Thomas Industries, Inc.; W.M. Barr and Co.; W. R. Brown Corp.; Richard Wilson; Yorkville Caning Co.

EXTERIOR MAINTENANCE & IMPROVEMENTS

Asphalt Roofing Manufacturers Association; California Redwood Association; Dow Chemical USA, Functional Products and Systems Dept.; Georgia-Pacific Corp.; Johns-Manville; Little Giant Pump Company; National Paint & Coatings Association, Inc.; Rockwell International, Tool Div.; Stanley Tools, Division of the Stanley Works; U.S. Department of Agriculture; U.S. Department of Housing and Urban Development; Walpole Woodworkers, Inc.; R.D. Werner Co. Inc.; Westinghouse Electric Corporation, Lamp Division.

Index

Acoustical-tile ceilings, installing, 48-49, 163
  security and, 181
  soundproofing and, 48, 163
aerators, fixing, 404
air chamber, water-supply system and, 390, 391
air conditioners
  installation and maintenance, 160-61
  troubleshooting, 381
  wiring, 381
alarms
  burglar alarms, 179
    window system, 180-81
  fire alarms, 182
alligatoring, avoiding, painting exterior and, 519
alternating current (AC), 297, 299
aluminum
  screening, replacing, 119-20
  siding, repairing, 513
  wire, 311
aluminum oxide, as abrasive, 226
amps (amperage), 297
angle-stop shutoff valve, 407
ant control, 187
antiquing furniture, 257, 258-59
  distressing, 258
  special touches, 259
appliances
  finishes on, repairing, 214
  grounding, reasons not to, 295
  power ratings for (table), 303
  troubleshooting, 374-81
    causes and corrections of problems (charts), 376-77
    heating elements (chart), 380
    motors (chart), 378
    stopped appliances, 374-75
  water-using appliances
    hookups to water system, 394-95
    repairing and troubleshooting, 442-49
  See also names of appliances
asbestos siding, replacing, 515
asphalt
  filling holes in, 557
  patching, 577
  shingles, fixing leaks in, 489
  tile flooring, 83
    laying, 84-86
attics
  framing walls in, 35
  insulation for, 35, 529, 530
    adding insulation, 530
    checking insulation, 529
    fan in, moisture accumulation and, 159
    heat loss and, 146
    R values for unfinished floor, 530
    unfinished attics and, 149, 530
  subfloor in, 83

Ballast, 297, 359
basements
  drains in, freeing, 421
  framing walls in, 35
  inspection of house structure and, 6-7
  insulation for, 35, 151, 529, 531
    adding insulation, 531
    checking insulation, 529
    heat loss and, 146
    moisture accumulation in, 158-59

bathrooms
  ceramic tile renovation of, 91
  fluorescent lighting installation in, 361
  See also plumbing; *names of fixtures*
baths, bathtubs. *See* sinks, baths, lavatories
batt insulation, 147, 529
beams
  in decking structure, 563
  in house structure, 5
bedbug control, 187
bells
  alarm bells, 179
  doorbells, troubleshooting, 330-31
benzene, 255
birch, 284
black spots, removal of, 277
blanket insulation, 147, 529
bleaching wood, 257, 264-65
  kinds of bleach, 265
  using bleach, 265
bleeding heating-system line, 465
blenders, food, troubleshooting, 376
blistering, avoiding, painting exterior and, 519
blown fuse, 306
  troubleshooting, 332
blushing, cause and restoration of, 277
boxes, electrical
  inserting and securing cables in, 313
  joining wires in, 312-13
  mounting, 314
  types of, 312
  See also ceiling boxes
branch circuits, 297
  troubleshooting, 332-33
branch plumbing, 390
  drains in, freeing, 422-23
bricks, building with, 550-51
  estimating materials, 550
  laying brick patio in sand, 551
brushes
  for exterior painting, 525
    buying, 525
    caring for, 525
  for furniture finishing, 230-31
    cleaning, 231
    selecting, 230
    varnish application, 246
  for interior painting, 54, 55, 57, 58, 59, 61
  See also painting; rollers; wallpapering
building codes, renovation and, 31, 292, 389
building drain, in DWV system, 392
built-ins and cabinets
  inspection of house structure and, 8
  stripping, 224
burglars, protecting home against, 164-65
  hiding places, 181
  See also alarms
burns, scratches, etc.
  filling, 273
  repairing, 212-13, 275

Cabinets. *See* built-ins
cables, electrical
  connecting new source and ground, 348-49
  sheathed cable installation, 308-309
    plastic sheathing, removing, 308

  steel armor, removing, 309
  See also wiring
caning, 220-21
  prewoven cane, replacing, 221
can opener, troubleshooting, 376
care, furniture, 268-79
  cleaners and polishes, 271, 272
  cracks, burns, gouges, 275
  dusting, 270
  filling scrapes and depressions, 273
  identifying finish, 269
  prevention, 268, 270
  protection, 268, 270
  repairing scratches, 274
  restoration, 268, 278-79
  stain removal, 176-77
  upholstery, 280-81
  wax, 272
  See also finishes and finishing; repairs; surface preparation
carpeting, wall-to-wall shag, installing, 92-93
  roll, 93
  tiles, 92
cartridge fuses, 307
casement windows, painting, 127
casters, types of, 205
  fixing loose socket caster, 205
cast-iron DWV piping, 433
catalytic finishes, 241, 252
caulking
  exterior, 516-17
    how to caulk, 516-17
    as supplement to insulation, 154, 532
    seams, where and how to caulk, 154-55
    types and uses of caulking, 516
  interior, sink or bath, 413
    replacing tiles, 25
ceiling boxes, electrical
  installing, 350-53
    accessible from above, 351
    between finished floors, 352-53
    switches and, 350
    wiring to wall switch, 353
  opening, 336
  running cable to, 354-56
    between finished floors, 354-55
    in attic or crawl space, 356
ceiling fixtures
  installing ceiling box, 350-53
  mounting ceiling fixtures, 357
  replacing ceiling fixtures, 326-27
    chandeliers, 327
    small fixtures, 326
  running cable to ceiling box, 354-56
  See also fluorescent lighting; track lighting
ceilings
  inspection of house structure and, 7
  installing new ceiling, 46-51
    repairs instead of, 46
    suspended ceilings, 50-51
    tile ceilings, 48-49, 163
    wallboard ceilings, 46
  insulating basement and, 151
  wallpapering, 69
ceramic tile
  applying, 43-45
  bathroom renovation with, 91
  flooring with, 90
    installing, 90
    replacing tiles, 90

replacing broken tiles, 25, 90
chain lock, putting up, 175
chairs, repairing, 200-202
    broken legs, 202
    caning, 220-21
    dowel replacement, 200-201
    prewoven cane, 221
    rush seat, 219
    seat suspension, 281
    tightening and regluing, 201
chalking, avoiding, painting exterior and, 519
chandeliers, replacing, 327
cherry wood, 284
children's room, redecorating, 94-95
    furniture, easy-to-build, 95
    supergraphics, 94
chimes, troubleshooting, 330-31
chimneys
    insulation for, 151
    preventing leaks around, 492
    repairing, 495
    replacing flashing around, 493
chipped paint, painting preparation and, 126
chips in furniture, care and, 270
chisels, 15-16, 397
    correct use of, 202
circuit breaker, 297, 305
    tripped, nothing wrong, 295
    tripped, troubleshooting, 332
circuits, electrical, 297, 298-99
    branch circuit, troubleshooting, 332-33
    dead circuit, testing for, 301
    mapping, 307
    multiple-switch wiring, 347
    See also wiring
circular saw, 17
clamps and clamping, 198-99
cleaners and cleaning, furniture, 271, 272
cleanouts, in DWV system, 392
climate, maintenance calendar (chart), 101
clogging. See drains
clothes washers
    hookup, 394, 395
    troubleshooting, 377, 442
cockroach control, 187
coffee maker, troubleshooting, 377
cold-water main, in water-supply system, 390
cold-weather house shutdown, 474
color, selecting, painting and
    for exteriors, 524
    for interiors, 53
        chart, 54
concrete, 538-49
    block concrete, 546-47
    cracks in, treating, 534
    decking over, 565
    form of, 540-41
        reinforcing pour, 540
        reinforcing rod, using, 540
        steel mesh, choosing and using, 541
    formulas, 539
    materials, 539
    mixes, 538-39
        mix-it-yourself, 538-39
        transit-mix, 538
        you-haul, 538
    mixing, 539
    pouring, 542-45
        small slabs, 542
        steps, 543-45

condensation, 159
    air conditioners and, 161
    on plumbing pipes, curing, 426
conductor, 297, 298
    lightning, 184
conduits
    electrical, 318-19
        bending, 318
        connecting to boxes, 319
        cutting, 318
        threading wires through, 319
    in heating system, 464
continuity tester, 301
contractors and consulting firms, inspection of house structure and, 8
cooling. See air conditioners; insulation
copper, sweat-soldered
    in DWV system, 436
    joining tubing, 431
cords, appliance, testing, 374
cork, wall renovation and, 45
corners, finishing, 39, 69
cracks
    in concrete, testing, 534
    in furniture, filling or repairing, 273, 274
crank handles, 111
crawling, avoiding, painting exterior and, 519
crawl spaces, insulation for, 151, 529, 530
    adding insulation, 530
    checking insulation, 529
cutting, tools for, 102, 104
cylindrical locks, 168

Deadbolt, replacing old lock with, 172-73
dead circuit, testing for, 301
decks, building, 562-65
    laying decking, 565
    laying out deck, 564
    special situations, 565
    structural elements, 562-63
dehumidifiers, 156-57, 446
    maintaining, 156, 446
depressions, filling, 273
detectors, fire, 182-83
dimmer switches, installing, 344
    for fluorescent lighting, 362-63
    for incandescent lighting, 346
direct current (DC), 297, 299
disc faucet, repairing, 402
discoloration, fluorescents, 329
dishwashers
    connections, 394, 395
    troubleshooting, 377, 443
distressing wood, 258
distributors, heating system and, 464
diverter valve, cleaning, 405
doorbells, troubleshooting, 330-31
doors
    accessories for, installing, 137
        drip cap, 137
        kick plate, 137
        mail slot, 137
    closing in doorway, 125
    cutting new doorway, 134-35
    framing, 34
    garage door, maintaining, 143
    hanging new door, 135-37
        casing, 137
        doorstop, 136
        mortising hinge, 136
    heat loss and, 146

installations
    accessories, 137
    prehung door unit, 139
    sliding patio door, 140-41
    storm door, 142
insulation, 150
maintenance
    calendar (chart), 101
    garage door, 143
new doorway
    cutting, 134-35
    hanging door, 135-37
painting, 60, 127
panels, stained-glass, 117
patio door, sliding, installing, 140-41
prehung door unit, installation, 139
safety glazing, 144-45
    shower doors, 145
    storm doors, 144-45
security and, 166-67
shower doors, safety glazing for, 145
stained-glass door panel, 117
storm doors
    installation, 142
    safety glazing, 144-45
    as supplement to insulation, 532
threshold, replacing, 138
tight or loose door, 132-33
weather stripping, 152
doorstop, installing, 136
doorway, closing in, 115
dormers, flashing and shingling, 509
double-hung sash windows
    painting, 127
    replacing, 112
dowels, replacing, chair repair and, 200-201
downspouts. See gutters and downspouts
draft control, oil burners and, 461
drainage
    creating underground, 504
    foundations and, 536
draining heating system, 465
drains
    foundation drainage and, 536
    unclogging, 420-23
        branch and main drains, 422-23
        floor drains, 421
        frequent clogging, solving, 423
        sink and lavatory drains, 420-21
        toilet drains, 422
        tools for, 399
        tub drains, 421
drain-waste-vent (DWV) system, 388, 389, 392-93
    piping for
        cast iron, 433
        copper, sweat-soldered, 436
        plastic, 434-35
        running pipes, 437-39
drapery, installing hardware for, 128-29
drawers
    repairing, 206
    replacing, 207
    slides and runners, 207
drills and drilling, 16, 17, 102, 105, 197
    bits for concealed screw heads, 211
drip cap, installing, 137
dryer, clothes, troubleshooting, 377
dry-laid flagstone, 556
dry well, construction, 475, 504
ducts, adding insulation for, 531
dusting, furniture care and, 270

Ebonizing, 257
electrical systems
  glossary, 297
  inspection of house structure and, 8
  techniques for working with, 308-19
    choosing correct wire, 310-11
    conduit, 318-19
    joining wires in electrical boxes, 312-13
    joining wires together, 315
    mounting electrical boxes, 314
    sheathed cable, 308-309
    soldering, 317
    splicing wires, 316-17
    See also lighting; wiring; *names of electrical fixtures*
electric heating, 463
electrician, licensed, when to call, 295
electricity, 296-97
electrons, 296, 297
emery cloth, 226
enamel finishes, 241, 253
endgrain, wood selection and, 283
energy
  efficiency, as supplement to insulation, 532
  electrical, 296
  epoxies. *See* catalytic finishes
expansion anchors, installing, 29
expansion tank, draining, 465
exterior of house
  preventive maintenance, 101, 485
  walls, heat loss and, 146
  See also names of parts of house exterior (e.g., foundation; roof; siding); *names of structures associated with house exterior (e.g.,* decks; fences); *names of tasks (e.g.,* painting)
extinguishers, fire, 183

Fan, portable, troubleshooting, 376
fasteners and fastening, 26-29
  for decks, 565
  installing fasteners, 28-29
  tools for, 102, 105
  types, purpose (chart), 26-27
faucets, 400-407
  installing, 408
  lever-type washerless faucets, 405
  repairing, 400
  replacing, 409
  valves for, 406-407
  washerless faucets, 403-405
  washer-type faucets, 400, 402-403
faucet spanner, 399
felt, rubbing, 255
fences, building, 558-61
  gate, hanging, 561
  post-and-rail fence, 560
  setting posts for, 559
fiberglass screening, 121
fieldstone wall, building, 554-55
fillers, wood floor refinishing and, 79
filling
  tools for, 102, 105
  wood, 235
  See also care, furniture
film insulation, 150
finishes and finishing
  and finishing floors, 80-81
    shellac, 80
    varnishes, 80
    wax, 80
  furniture finishes, 256-67

antiquing, 257, 258-59
bleaching, 257, 264-65
ebonizing, 257
gold drop, Venetian gold, tortoise shell, 257, 260-61
identifying, furniture care and, 269
liming, 257
marbleizing, 257, 262-63
rustproofing, 266-67
scratches in, touching up, 273
selection of, 240
spatter, 257
survey of common, 241
texture effects, 257
furniture finishing, 240-55
  catalytics, 252
  French polishing, 244
  lacquer, 249
  paints and enamels, 253
  paste wax, 242
  penetrating resin, 245
  polyurethane, 252
  rubbed oil, 248
  rubbing and polishing, 254-55
  shellac, 243
  spray equipment for, 250-51
  varnish, 246-47
    painting and, 60
  See also care; repairs; surface preparation
fir, 284
fire extinguisher, 397
fireplaces, 469
fires, precautions against, 182-83
  causes of fire, knowing and eliminating, 182
  electrical, 295
  equipment, 182-83, 397
fish tape, 301
fixtures, plumbing
  hookup, 394-95
  modernizing, 408-409
  See also appliances; faucets; sinks, baths, lavatories; toilets; *for electrical fixtures, see* ceiling fixtures; lamps, etc.
fixture-shutoff valves, 390, 391, 406, 407
  installing, 412
fixture waste pipe, in DWV system, 392
flagstone walk or patio, building, 556
flaking paint, painting preparation and, 126
flaring tools, 398
flashing
  dormers, 509
  repairing, 492
    valley, open or closed, 494
  replacing, 493
  valleys,
    repairing, 494
    shingling, 509
  vertical wall, 509
flint paper, 225
floors and flooring
  inspection of house structure and, 7-8
  installing new flooring, 82-93
    attic subfloor, 82
    carpet installation, 92-93
    ceramic-tile flooring installation, 90-91
    hardwood strip flooring installation, 88-89
    subfloor preparation, 82
    tile floor installation, 84-85
    types of flooring (chart), 83
    underlayment, 82
    vinyl sheet installation, 86-87
  repairing floors, 72-81

finishing floors, 80-81
maintenance, routine, 72-73
moldings and other trim, 81
refinishing floors, 78-79
resilient floors, 74, 77
sectional floorboard damage, 76, 89
spot and stain removal, 74
squeaky floors, 75
threshold removal, 81
fluorescent lighting, 358-69
  bathroom installation, 361
  characteristics, 359
  dimmers, 362-63
  halls, kitchens, large area installation, 360
  joining fixtures, 364-66
  luminous ceiling installation, 367-69
  troubleshooting, 328-29
    checklist, 329
    correct installation, 328
    discoloration, 328
    noise level, 328
flushing and refilling heating system, 465
flush toilets, 414-16
  mechanisms, 414
  troubleshooting, 415-16
  See also tankless flush toilets
fly control, 187
foam insulation, 529
foil and wire alarm devices, 180-81
footings, in decking structure, 563
forced hot-air heating system, 466-67
  adjustment and maintenance, 466
  blower speed adjustment, 467
  pulley alignment, 467
foundations, 4-5
  cracks in concrete, treating, 534
  drainage, 536
  splash blocks, 535
  termite protection, 537
  waterproofing, 535
  See also masonry
frame, house, 5
frames, picture, repairing, 215
  gold leaf, 217
  ornate, 216-17
framing walls, 32-35
  attic walls, 35
  basement walls, 35
  doors, 34
  layout and assembly, 33
  lumber sizes, 32
  openings, 34
French-polish finish, 241, 244
  restoration for, 278
frosted glass, making, 116
furniture
  easy-to-build, children's room renovation and, 95
  picnic table, building, 286-87
  See also care; finishes and finishing; repair, wood furring, ceiling tile installation and, 49
fuse panel, 306
  safety rules, 306
fuse puller, 301
fuses, 297, 305
  blown, nothing wrong, 295
  types of, 305

Gable vents, preventing ice dams and, 497
ganging boxes, 312
garage doors, maintaining, 143
garbage disposer connections, 394, 395

garnet paper, 226
gas burners, 462
gate, hanging, building fence and, 561
glass
  cleaning paint off, 127
  cutting, for windows, 108-109
  frosted, making, 116
  safety glazing for doors, 144-45
  stained, making, 117
  storm precautions, 185
  See also windows
glides, types of, 205
globe valve, 406
gloves, work, 397
glues and gluing
  regluing chair, 201
  types of, 209
  veneer and, 204
goggles, 397, 399
gold-drop finish, 257, 260-61
gold-leaf finish, picture frame,
    repairing, 217
gouges, furniture care and, 270
  filling, 273
  repairing, 275
grain, wood, 232
  endgrain, wood selection and, 194
grease stains, surface preparation and,
    279
ground, types of, deck construction and,
    565
ground fault interrupters (GFIs), 294
  outdoor lighting, system and, 383
grounding, 294-95
  appliances, 295
  GFIs, 294, 883
  rods, 184
  testing, 301
  wires, 296, 297
ground-key valve, 406-407
grouting, 44. See also caulking
gurgling drain, 162
gutters and downspouts, 498-503
  maintenance, 499-500
    fall/spring, 498
    general, 498
  new, 503
  repairing, 501
gypsum wallboard. See wallboard

Halls, fluorescent lighting installation
    in, 360
hammers and hammering, 13, 396
hand-dug well, 453
hand saws, 14
hanging wallpaper. See wallpapering
hardboard, wall renovation with, 45
hardware
  cleaning paint off, 127
  crank handles, 111
  drapery, installing, 128-29
  replacing, on furniture, 213
  for windows, 111
  for window shades, 130
  See also fasteners; nails, etc.; tools
hardwood strip flooring, installing,
    88-89
  application, 89
  damaged boards, repairing, 89
  nailing, 89
  types of wood, 88-89
heat detectors, 182
heating, 458-73
  cold-weather house shutdown and, 474
  electric heating, 463

elements of system, 459
exchangers, distributors, and conduits,
    464
fireplaces, 469
forced hot-air systems, 466-47
gas burners, 462
glossary, 480-81
heat producers, 460-61
heat pumps, 472-73
  efficiency, 473
  functioning, 473
hertz (hz), 297
hinge, mortising, 136
hips, roof, shingling, 508
hollow-door anchors, installing, 28
hot dishes, furniture care and, 270
hot-water main, water-supply system and,
    390
hot wires, 296, 297
household circuits, 304
house-service entrance pipe, water-supply
    system and, 390
humidifiers, 156
humidity, 156-57, 459
  furniture care and, 270
hurricanes, 185

Ice dams, roof, preventing, 496-97
illumination, outdoor, 178, 282-83
insects and insecticides, 187
  See also termite control
inspection of house
  exterior (chart), 485
  interior, 6-9
insulation, 146-63, 528-33
  adding insulation, 530-33
    supplements to, 532-33
  air conditioners and, 160-61
    maintenance, 161
    wall unit, 161
    window unit, 161
  attic, unfinished, 149
  basement, 35, 151
  caulking seams as, 154-55
    how to caulk, 155
    where to caulk, 154-55
  checking home for, 529
    heat loss, 146
  humidity and temperature control, 156-57
    dehumidifiers, 156-57
    humidifiers, 156
    mildew problem, 157
  moisture accumulation, 158-59
    around openings, 150-51
    attic fan, 159
    damp basement, 158-59
    windows and doors, 150
  on pipes, 151, 426
  places to insulate, 146
  R value system, 528
  types of, 147, 529
  vapor barrier, 148
  weather stripping, 152-53
    doors, 152
    windows, 153
  on wires, removing, 311
iron, steam, troubleshooting, 377

Jet pumps, 453
joint knife, 15
joints, taping, 38
joists, in decking structure, 563
junction box, troubleshooting, 377

Keys
  broken, 177
  -in-knob locks, 168
  See also locks
kick plate, installing, 137
kilowatt hours (KWH), 297
kitchens, fluorescent lighting installation in,
    360. See also aspects of renovation
    (e.g., painting; wallpapering; etc.)
knives
  putty and joint knives, 15
  utility knife, 15
knots
  surface preparation for painting
    exterior and, 522
  wood selection and, 194

Lacquer finish, 241, 249
  identifying, furniture care and, 269
  restoration of, 278
  as sealer, 234
ladders, using and safety, 487
laminates, plastic, installing, 218
lamps
  rewiring, 320-21
  testing parts of, 322
  wiring multiple-socket lamps, 323
  wiring plugs, 325
  See also ceiling fixtures
lathes, wall construction and, 18
lavatories. See sinks, baths, lavatories
leaks
  foundation leakage, 158, 534, 535
  plumbing system
    faucet leaks, 404
    fixing, 424
    in pipes, fixing, 424
    troubleshooting, 425
  roof, finding, 488
  roof, fixing
    in asphalt shingles, 489
    in flat roofs, 491
    in slate shingles, 490
    in wood shingles, 490
  roof, preventing
    around chimneys, 492
    around vents, 492
ledgers, in decking structure, 563
levels and leveling, 16, 103, 397
lever-type faucets
  repairing, 402
  washerless, 405
lighting, outdoor, installing, 382-83
  ground fault interrupter, 383
  permanent wiring, 383
  plan for, 382
  temporary wiring, 383
  for security, 178
  See also fluorescent lighting; aspects of
    lighting and electricity; names of
    fixtures for lighting
liming, 257
linoleum removal, 79
liquid fillers, 235
load, electrical, 297, 298
locking switch, 343
locks
  bored lock, changing, 170-71
  broken lock, replacing, 170
  buying, 168
  chain lock, putting up, 175
  maintenance, 177
  mortise lock, installing, 174
  old lock, replacing with deadbolt,
    172-73

locks (continued)
  options for security, 168-69
  primary locks, 169
  rim lock, installing, 176
  secondary locks, 169
  unpickable locks, 165
  worn-out lock, replacing, 170
loose door, 132-33
loose-fill insulation, 147, 529
loose window, securing, 111
  window channels and, 113
low flow, problems with, 441
lumber
  for decks, 565
  standard sizes, 30
  See also wood
luminous ceilings, installing, 367-69

Magnetic contact switches, 179
mahogany, 284
mail slot, installing, 137
main drains, freeing, 422-23
main floor, inspection of house structure
    and, 7
main shutoff valve, water-supply system
    and, 390
main stack, in DWV system, 392
maintenance. See names of objects and
    systems to be maintained; names of
    maintenance processes or tasks
maple, 284
marbleizing, 256, 257, 262-63
  special techniques, 263
  variations, 263
masonry
  brick, 550-51
  concrete, 538-39
  country dry wall, 554-55
  flagstone walk or patio, 556-57
  imitation, wall renovation and, 45
  patching asphalt, 557
  stone retaining wall, 552-53
  walls, insulation for, 151
  master-control panel, alarm system 179
measuring, 103
  instruments and tools for, 14-15, 102,
    103, 397
mercury switch, 344
mesh, steel, concrete reinforcing and
    541
metal
  casement and sliding windows, replac-
    ing panes in, 108
  furniture, rustproofing, 266-67
  surfaces, preparation of, for painting,
    522
    See also names of metals e.g., alumi-
    num; cast iron
meter, electrical, how to read, 303
middle-of-run ceiling boxes, troubleshoot-
    ing, 333
mildew, identifying and preventing, 157,
    520
mirror tiles, wall renovation and, 45
miter boxes, 215
mixers, food, troubleshooting, 376
mixing concrete, 539
mix-it-yourself concrete, 538-39
moldings
  cracks in, preparation for painting and,
    126
  ornate, repairing, 216
  repairing floor and, 81
  working with, 42
mortise locks, 168
  installation, 174

mortising hinges, 136
mosquito control, 187
motion-sensing burglar alarms, 179
motors, troubleshooting, 378-79
  large motors, 378
  overheating, 379
  parts function and malfunction, 379
  small motors, 378
mountings
  ceiling fixtures, 357
  electrical boxes, 314
multiple-socket lamps, wiring, 323
multiple-switch circuits, wiring, 347

Nails and nailing, 13, 17
  deck construction and, 565
  floor installation and, 89
National Electrical Code Book, 292
National Plumbing Code, 388
neighborhood, shopping for house and,
    6
neutral wires, 296, 297
noises
  concrete blocks and, 549
  fluorescents and level of, 328
  plumbing noises, 162, 427
  See also soundproofing
non-grain-raising stains, 239
nonpenetrating-oil stains, 238

Oak, 284
ohm, 297
oil burners, 460-61
  draft control, 461
  maintaining, 461
  restarting, 461
  stack relay, 460
oil finish, 241, 248. See also rubbed oil
oil staining, penetrating and nonpenetrat-
    ing, 238
oil stains, surface preparation and, 229
one-way viewer, installing, 175
open circuit, 299
open-coat sandpaper, 226
openings, framing, 34. See also doors;
    windows
outlets, wall, replacing, 325. See also
    switches
overload, 297

Paint
  finishes, 241, 253
  selecting and buying paints
    color selection, 53, 54, 523-24
    kinds of paint, 52, 53
    quantity estimation, 524
  surface preparation and
    removal of paint, 521
    stripping paint, 522
painting concrete blocks, 549
  doors, 126-27
  exteriors, 518-27
    applying paint, 526-27
    buying brushes, 525
    problems, avoiding, 519
    selecting and buying paint, 523-24
    sequence, 518
    surface preparation, 520-22
  interiors, 52-61
    brushwork, 58
    cleanup, 61
    color selection, 53, 54
    finishes, 60
    kinds of paint, selecting, 52, 53
    preparation for, 56
    special problems, 60

superqraphics for children's room, 94
    systematic approach, 57
    time estimation, 55
    tools for, 54-55
  windows and screens, 126-27
paneling, wood
  inspection of house structure and, 8
  putting up, 41-42
    moldings, working with, 42
  repairing, 25
panic buttons, 179
paste fillers, 235
paste-wax finish, 241, 242
  application, 242
patch repairing
  asphalt, 477
  ceramic tiles, 25
  furniture and finishes, 212-13
  paneling, wood, 25
  plaster walls, 19-21
    materials, 19
    special problems, 21
  wallboard, 22-24
  wallpaper, 63
patios
  brick patio, laying, in sand, 551
  flagstone patio, building, 556
  sliding patio door, installing, 140-41
peeling, avoiding, painting exterior and,
    519
peephole, door, 175
percolation table, 455
perimeter-alarm system, 179
penetrating-oil stains, 238
penetrating-resin finish, 241, 245
  application, 245
  identifying, furniture care and, 269
permits, codes and, 31, 292, 389
pest control, 186-89
  defense, 186
  offense, 186
    insecticides, 187
    insect invaders, 187
  rodent control, 189
  termite control, 188-89, 537
    barriers, 189, 537
    preventive measures, 188-89, 537
    soil injection, 189, 537
    what to look for, 188, 537
picnic table, building, 286-87
picture frame repair, 215
  gold leaf, 217
  ornate frames, 216-17
pigtail splice, 316
pilot-light switches, 345
pine, 284
pin fasteners, installing, 28
piping, 428-41
  adapting plumbing-system pipes,
    440-41
  cast-iron DWV piping, 433
  cutters for, 398
  freezing, preventing, 426
  insulation for, 151, 426
  joining sweat-soldered copper tubing,
    431
  leaks in, fixing, 424
  low flow in, problems with, 441
  plastic DWV piping, 434-35
  running pipes
    DWV pipes, 437-39
    water-supply pipes, 436
  thawing pipes, 426
  threaded water-supply piping, 430
  vinyl water-supply piping, 428-29
planing, 104

plank flooring, 85
plaster
  ceiling repairs, 47
  patch repairing, 19-21
plastic
  laminates, installing, 218
  piping, 434-35
    tools for, 399
  sheathing, removing, 308
  wall materials, wall renovation and, 45
plantings, deck construction and, 565
pitching gutters, 503
pliers, 13-14, 396-97
plugs, wiring, 315
plug-type fuses, 305
plumbing system
  basic features, 388-89
  cold-weather house shutdown and, 474
  fixture and appliance hookup, 394-95
  glossary, 480-81
  home-buyers checklist, 389
    inspection of house structure and, 8
  noises, 162
    water hammer, curing, 162, 427
  problem solving, 420-27
    condensation, curing, 426
    drains, unclogging, 420-23
    freezing, preventing, 426
    leaks, fixing, 424-25
    thawing pipes, 426
    water hammer, curing, 162, 427
    tools for, 396-97
  See also drain-waste-vent (DWV)
    system; water-supply system; water
    systems, private; names of
    appliances and fixtures (e.g.,
    dishwashers; faucets; toilets)
plywood, 284
pockets, cutting, in wallboard, 38
poisons, rodent control and, 189
polishes and polishing, furniture, 271
  272
  finishes, 254, 255
polyurethane finish, 241, 252
  identifying, furniture care and, 269
  as sealer, 234
pool and waterfall, garden, building,
  478-79
poplar, 284
post-and-rail fence, building, 560
  hanging gate for, 561
posts
  in decking structure, 563
  fence posts, setting, 559
pot-type oil burner, 460
power, electrical, 297
  failure, troubleshooting, 332
  flow to house, 302-307
    appliance ratings, 303
    meter reading, 303
    service panel, 304-307
    watt consumption, 303
prepasted wallpaper, 71
pressure-reducing valve, 407
pressure tanks, 451
pressure-type oil burner, 460
primer-sealer, 234
propane torches, 397
pumice, finishing furniture and, 255
pumps, plumbing system
  connecting pump, 451
  for garden pool and waterfall, installing,
    478
  jet pumps, 453
  lowering submersible pump, 452
  for residential wells, 450

  troubleshooting well pumps, 452
  See also heat pumps
push-in connection switches, 343

Quiet switch, 343

Radiators, baseboard, painting, 60
  See also steam-heating system
refinishers, commercial, 279
refinishing. See care, furniture;
    finishes and finishing,
    furniture; wood, floors
refrigerator, troubleshooting, 377
reinforcing concrete, 540-41
repairs
  electrical, simple, 320-33
    branch circuits, troubleshooting,
      332-33
    ceiling fixtures, replacing, 326
    chandeliers, replacing, 327
    doorbells and chimes, 330-31
    fluorescents, troubleshooting, 328-29
    lamps, 320-23
    outlets, wall, replacing, 325
    switch, replacing, 324
  furniture, 196-225
    appliance finishes, 214
    caning, 220-21
    casters and glides, 205
    chairs, 200-202
    clamps and clamping, 198-99
    concealing screw heads, 210-11
    drawers, 206-207
    hardware replacement, 213
    ornate picture frame, 215
    patch repairs, 212-13
    picture frames, 215
    plastic laminate installation, 218
    rushing, 219
    screws and glues, 208-209
    tables, 203
    tools for, 197
    veneer, curled or wrinkled, 204-205
  roof, repairs on, 488-509
    chimney repairs, 495
    downspouts, 498, 500, 501, 502
    drainage, creating underground, 492
    flashing, 492-94
    gutters, 498-99, 501-503
    ice dams, preventing, 496-97
    leaks, 488-91
  See also appliances; care, furniture;
    surface preparation; names of
    appliances, fixtures, processes,
    etc.
reshingling roof, 505-509
  applying shingles, 508
  calculating quantity, 506
  dormers, flashing and shingling, 509
  hips and ridges, shingling, 508
  old shingle removal, when and how, 505
  selecting shingles, 506
  surface preparation, 507
  valleys, flashing, 509
  vertical wall, flashing, 509
residential wells, pumps for, 450
resilient floors
  linoleum removal, 79
  repairing damaged section, 77
  spot and stain removal, 74
resistance, 297
restoration, furniture, 268, 278-79
  commercial refinishers, 279
  See also finishes, furniture
retaining wall, stone, building, 552-53
revent, in DWV system, 392

rewiring lamps, 320-21
ridges, shingling, 508
rigid insulation, 147, 529
rim locks, 168
rings (stains), removal of, 276
rod reinforcement, concrete and, 541
rodent control, 189
rollers, painting with, 55, 59, 61
roof, repairs on, 488-509
  chimney repairs, 495
  downspouts
    maintaining, 498, 500
    new, 502
    repairing, 501
  drainage, creating underground, 492
  flashing
    repairing, 492
    replacing, 493
    valley, 494
  gutters
    maintaining, 498, 499
    new, 502
    pitching, 503
    repairing, 501
  ice dams, preventing, 496-97
  leaks
    finding, 488
    in asphalt shingles, fixing, 489
    in flat roofs, fixing, 491
    in slate shingles, fixing, 490
    in wood shingles, fixing, 490
    reshingling, 505-509
    See also caulking
rooftop decks, 565
room air conditioners, See air
    conditioners
rosewood, 284
rottenstone, finishing and, 255
rubbed-oil finish, 241, 248
  identifying, furniture care and 269
  restoring, 278
rubbing, finishing and, 254-55
rungs, broken, repairing, 202
rushing, 219
rust, surface preparation for painting
    exterior and, 521
rustproofing finishes, 266-67
R values, insulation and, 528
  for different types of insulation, 528
  for unfinished attic floors, 530

Saber saw, 17
safes, 181
safety, 293
  fuse panel work, 306
sanders, electric, 17, 197
  using, 228
sanding and sandpaper, 225-29
  clogging, cures for, 227
  final cleaning, 229
  finishing and, 255
  grits and grades, 225-26
  power sanding, 228
  sanding blocks, 228
  sealers, 234
  using sandpaper, 227
  wood floor refinishing by, 78
sash repairs and hardware, 110-14
  crank handles and other hardware, 111
  replacing cord with chain, 114
  replacing double-hung sash windows,
    112-13
  replacing sash cord, 114
  securing loose window, 111
  unsticking windows, 110
  window channels, 113

saws and sawing, 104, 397
  circular saw, 17
  hand saws, 14
  how to saw board, 15
  saber saw, 17
scaffolding, for painting exterior, 526
scrapes, filling, 273
scratches, furniture care and, 270
  filling, 273
  repairing, 212-13, 274
screamers, alarm, 179
screens, installing, replacing, maintaining,
      118-23
  fiberglass, 121
  installing screen wire on old wooden
        screens, 122-23
  painting, 127
  replacing aluminum-storm screening,
        119-29
  replacing wood-frame screen, 122
screw anchors, installing, 28
screwdrivers, 13, 396
screws, 15
  concealed heads, 210
  dowel plugs for, 211
    pilot and clearance hole size, 208
sealers, 233-34
  cutting shellac, 233
  polyurethane, 234
  primer-sealer, 234
  sanding sealer, 234
  shellac, 233-34
  spraying and, 234
  varnish, 234
  wood floor refinishing and, 79
seasoning, wood selection and, 273
security, 164-84
  broken or worn-out lock replacement,
        170
  burglar alarms, 179
  chain lock, putting up, 175
  changing bored lock, 170-71
  doors and windows, 166-67
  fire precautions, 182-83
  home protection, 164-65
    how burglar enters, 165
    how burglar operates, 164-65
    preventing burglary, 165
    watch dogs, 165
  lighting, indoor and outdoor, 178
  lightning protection, 184
  lock maintenance, 177
  lock options, 168-69
  mortise lock, installing, 174
  old lock with deadbolt, replacing, 172-73
  one-way viewer, 175
  rim lock, installing, 176
  storm warnings, 185
  window burglar alarms, 180-81
seepage, 158
seepage field, building, 456
self-contained burglar alarms, 179
septic system, 454
  installing septic tank, 455
  tank-size table, 455
service panel, electric system, 297,
      304-307
  blown fuses, 306
  circuit breakers, 305
  fuses, 305
  household circuits, 304
  mapping circuits, 307
  safety rules, 306
sewage treatment, private, 454-57
  building seepage field, 456
  building sewer, 455

installing septic tank, 455
septic system, 454
sewage-treatment plants, 457
  for single family, 457
sewer, building, 455
sewer pipe, 439
sewing machines, troubleshooting, 376
shades, window, installing and maintaining,
      130
shag carpeting, wall-to-wall, installing,
      92-93
  rolled carpet, 93
  tile carpet, 92
sheathed cable, installing, 308-309
sheet metal shingles, fixing leaks in, 489
sheet-vinyl flooring, installing, 86-87
  seams, 87
shellac finishes, 241, 243
  floor, 80
  identifying, furniture care and, 269
  restoration techniques, 278
  seven-step method for, 243
shellac sticks, 274
shingles
  fixing leaks in
    asphalt, 489
    sheet metal, 489
    slate, 490
    wood, 490
  storm precautions for, 185
  See also reshingling roof
shock, electric, 293
short circuit, 299
  troubleshooting, 332
showers
  doors, safety glazing for, 145
  freeing drains, 421
  upgrading shower head, 411
shutdown, of house in cold weather, 474
sidewalls, insulation for
  adding insulation, 530
  checking insulation, 529
siding, 510-17
  aluminum, repairing, 513
  asbestos, replacing, 515
  caulking and, 516-17
  maintaining, 510
  repairing, 511
  replacing, 512
  stucco, repairing, 514
  vinyl, replacing, 515
  wood, 510-12
  wood, 510-12
  See also painting
silent (mercury) switch, 344
silicon carbide, as abrasive, 226
sinks, baths, lavatories, 408-13
  caulking, 413
  freeing drains, 420-21
  installing faucets, 408
  installing traps, 410-11
  modernizing fixtures, 408-409
  replacing sink sprayer, 411
  upgrading shower head, 411
  See also bathrooms
sirens, alarm, 179
skylight, installation of, 190-91
slabs, concrete, pouring, 542
slate, shingles, fixing leaks in, 490
slide assembly, drawer repair and, 207
slopes, downhill, decking over, 565
smoke detectors, 182-93
smoothing, tools for, 102, 105
soffits, vented, ice dam prevention and,
      496
soil injection, termite control and, 189

solar heating, 470-71
soldering, 317
  pipes, 399
soldering gun, 301
solderless connectors, 314
solvent welding, 51
soundproofing, 162-63
source, power, 297, 298
spatter finishes, 257
spills, furniture care and, 207
splash blocks, foundations and, 535
splicing wires, 316-17
spots and stains, removing
  resilient floors, 74
  wood floors, 74
  See also stains
spray equipment, finishing and, 250-51
sprayer, sink, replacing, 411
spray sealers, 234
stack, in DWV system, 392
stack relay, oil burner, 460
staining wood, 236-39
  application, 237
  refinished floors, 79
  selecting stains, 236
  types of stains, 237-39
stains, removal of, 276-77
  surface preparation and, 229
  from upholstery fabric, 280
starter, fluorescent, 297, 359
steam-heating systems, 468
steel armor, removing, 309
steel mesh, reinforcing concrete with,
      541
steel wool, 226
  finishing and, 255
  grades and uses, 225
steps, concrete, pouring, 543-45
stone
  fieldstone dry wall, building, 554-55
  retaining wall, building, 552-53
  buying stones, 552
  construction techniques, 552
stop-and-waste valve, 406
storage, tool, 12
storm doors
  installing, 142
  safety glazing, 144-45
  as supplement to insulation, 532
storm warnings and precautions, 185
storm windows
  installing, 124-25
    do-it-yourself substitute, 125
    wood sash, maintaining, 125
  replacing panes, 108
  as supplement to insulation, 532
straight-stop shutoff valve, 407
strip flooring, 88. See also hardwood
stripping
  paint, surface preparation for painting
        exterior and, 522
  wood, 222-24
    cabinets and built-ins, 224
    procedures, 223
    windows, 224
structure, house inspection and, 4-9
stucco, repairing, 34
stuck door, unsticking, 132-33
stuck window, unsticking, 110
  window channels and, 113
subfloors, preparation for flooring, 82
  attic subfloor, 82
submersible pump, lowering, 452
sump pumps, 444-45
  connections, 395
  replacing, 445

supergraphics, children's room redecoration with, 94
supplies. *See* tools
surface preparation
  furniture, 222-29
    sanding, 225-29
    stain application and, 237
    stripping, 222-24
    varnishes and, 246
  for painting exterior, 520-22
    knots and resins, 522
    metal surfaces, 522
    paint removal, 521
    for reshingling roof, 507
    stripping paint, 522
    washing house, 520
    wood surfaces, 521
  for painting interior, 56
surface wiring, 372-73
suspended ceilings, installing, 50-51
sweat-soldered copper
  DWV, 436
  joining tubing, 431
switches, 297, 298, 342-49
  ceiling fixture installation and, 350
  connecting new source cable, 348
  function and types, 342-44
  grounding cable, 348-49
  incandescent dimmer switch, 346
  multiple-switch circuits, wiring, 347
  pilot-light switches, 324
  See also wiring
switch plate, wallpapering, 70
switch-receptacle combination, 344
  wiring, 345

Tables
  picnic, building, 286-87
  types of, repairing and, 203
tack rags, making own, 229
tankless flush toilets, 417
  troubleshooting, 417
  valves, types and parts, 417
teak, 284
temperature
  control, 156-57
    heating appliances and, 380
  furniture care and, 270
temperature-and-pressure relief valve, 390
termite control, 188-89, 537
  barriers, 189, 537
  preventive measures, 188-89, 537
  soil injection, 189, 537
  what to look for, 188, 537
testers, electrical, 301
  testing parts of lamp, 322
texture effects, finishing and, 257
thawing pipes, 399
threaded water-supply piping, 430
threshold
  removal, floor repair and, 81
  replacing, 138
tightening, chair repair and, 201
tiles
  carpet tiles, wall-to-wall shag, installing, 92-93
  ceiling tile, installing, 49, 163
  floor tiles, laying, 84-85
    border tiles, 85
    size calculations, 85
  See also ceramic tile
time-clock switch, 343
time-delay fuses, 305
time-delay swtich, 343

toasters, troubleshooting, 295, 377
toggle anchors, installing, 29
toggle bolts, installing, 29
toggle switches, 342
toilets, 414-19
  cold-weather house shutdown and, 474
  flush toilet mechanisms, 414
  freeing drains, 422
  replacing toilets, 418-19
  tankless flush valves, 416
  tanks, troubleshooting, 415-16
tools
  basic, 102-105
    selection and use, 101-103
  buying tools, 13
  chisels, 15-16
  circular saws, 17
  cutting, 102, 104
  drilling, 102, 105
  electrical, and electrical supplies, 300-301
    basic tools, 300
    specialized tools, 301
    supplies, 300
    testers, 300
  fastening, 102, 105
  filling, 102, 105
  for furniture repair, 196
    clamps, 198-99
    sources for, 285
  hammers, 13
  hand drills, 17
  hand saw, 14
  how to saw board, 15
  ladders, 487
  levels, 16
  for maintenance, exterior, 486
  measuring, 14-15, 102, 103
  painting, 54-55
    cleanup, 61
  pliers, 13-14
  power drills, 16
  plumbing, 396-99
    how to use, 396-97
    for plastic pipe, 399
    tips for, 398-99
  putty and joint knives, 15
  for rubbing and polishing finishes, 255
  saber saw, 17
  sander, 17
  screwdrivers, 13
  smoothing, 102, 105
  specialized for exteriors, 6
  storage of, 12
  utility knife, 15
  wallpapering, 64
  workbench, 12
  workshop, 12-13
  wrenches, 16
  See also brushes; *names of tools and tooling*
tornadoes, 185
tortoise-shell finish, 257, 260
track lighting, 370-71
  electrical rating, 371
transformer, 297
transit-mix concrete, 538
traps
  plumbing
    adapters, using, 394
    in DWV system, 392
    installing, 410-11
  rodent control and, 189
trim. *See* moldings
tubes, tubing. *See* piping

tubs. *See* sinks, baths, lavatories
tubular locks, 168
tuck-pointing, chimney repair and, 495
tung oil, 279
twist splice, 316

UL (Underwriters' Laboratories) seal, 292
underground drainage, creating, 504
underlayment, installing flooring and, 82
upholstery, care of, 280-81
  seat suspension repair, 281
  stain removal, 280
utility knife, 15

Vacuum-breaker valves, 407
vacuum cleaner, troubleshooting, 377
valleys, roof, flashing
  repairing, open and closed, 494
  reshingling roof and, 509
valves, plumbing, 406-407. *See also names of valves (e.g.,* fixture shutoff valve)
valve seats, fixing, 402
vapor barriers, 148
  as supplement to insulation, 532-33
varnish finish, 241, 246
  application, 246-47
    for floors, 80
  identifying, furniture care and, 269
  restoration of, 278
  synthetic substitute for, 252
veneer, curled or wrinkled, repairing, 204-205
  gluing, 204
venetian blinds, repair and maintenance, 131
Venetian-gold finish, 257, 258
ventilation, as supplement to insulation, 533
vents
  in DWV system, 392
  ice dams prevention and, 496-97
  leaks around, preventing, 492
  replacing flashing around, 493
vent stack, running, 435
vertical well systems, 450
vinyl sheet flooring, installing, 86-87
  seams, 87
vinyl siding, replacing, 515
vinyl water-supply piping, 428-29
volts (voltage), 297
  testing, 293, 301

Waffle iron, troubleshooting, 377
walk, flagstone, building, 556
wallboard (gypsum)
  for ceiling, installing, 46-47
    repairing, 47
  patch repairing, 22-24
    defects, correcting, 24
    materials, 19
    screen method, 22
    sectional damage, replacement, 24
    triangular patch method, 22
    using plastic slips, 23
  for walls, installation, 36-40
    corners, finishing, 39
    cutting, 36-37
    pockets, cutting, 38
    taping joints, 38-39
wall boxes, opening, 336
wall outlets, replacing, 325

wallpapering, 62-71
    ceilings, 69
    choosing wallpaper, 62
    double cutting, 71
    hanging wallpaper, 66-68
    preparation of walls, 65
    prepasted papers, 71
    quantity estimation, 63
    repairing wallpaper instead of, 63
    starting point, 65
    switch plate, papering, 70
    tools for, 64
walls
    building or renovating, 30-45
        attic walls, framing, 35
        basement walls, framing, 35
        building codes and, 31
        ceramic tile, applying, 43-45
        doors, framing, 34
        framing walls, 32-33
        gypsum-wallboard installation, 36-40
        materials for walls, 45
        openings, framing, 34
        paneling, putting up, 41-42
        planning hints, 30-31
    country dry wall (fieldstone), 554-55
    inspection of house structure and, 7
    preparation of wall surface
        for painting, 56
        for wallpapering, 65
    repairing walls, 18-25
        ceramic tile, 25
        lathes and wall construction, 18
        panels, 25
        patching materials, 19
        plaster walls, 19-21
        wallboard, 22-24
    stone retaining wall, 552-53
    vertical wall, flashing, 29
    See also attic; basement; fasteners
wall-to-wall carpeting, shag,
        installing, 92-93
    rolled, 93
    tiles, 92
washerless faucets, 403-405
    lever-type, 405
washers. See clothes washers; dishwashers
washing exterior of house, surface prepa-
        ration for painting exterior and, 520
    and, 520
washer-type faucets, 400, 402-403
    replacing washers, 410
wasp control, 187
watch dogs, 165
water-base stains, 237
waterfall and pool, garden, building,
        478-79
water hammer, curing, 389, 427
water heaters
    caring for, 447
    connections, 394, 395
water meter, jumper wire for, 294
waterproofing, foundations and, 535
water softeners, connections, 394, 395,
        448
water-supply system, 388, 390-91
    piping
        running, 432
        threaded, 430
        vinyl, 428-29
    private system, 450-53
water systems, private, 450-57
    sewage treatment, 454-57
    water supply, 450-53

water-treatment appliances, repairing,
    448-449. See also water softeners
watts (wattage), 297
    consumption, 303
wax and waxing
    floor finish, 80
    furniture, 272, 278
    removal, to identify finish, 269
    See also paste-wax finish
wax sticks, 274
weather stripping, 152-53
    as supplement to insulation, 532
welding, solvent, 435
wells
    building dry well, 475, 504
    drilling well, 451
    hand-dug well, 453
    pumps for residential wells, 450
    types of wells compared, 453
    vertical-well systems, 450
    See also pumps
wet-laid flagstone, 556
whistling noises, 162
white spots on furniture, removing,
    276
windows
    accessories for, 125-31
        drapery hardware, installing, 125-26
        venetian blinds, repair and mainte-
            nance, 131
        window shades, installing and maintain-
            ing, 130
    air conditioner installation through,
        161
    burglar alarms for, 180-81
    closing in window, 115
    heat loss and, 146
    inspection of house structure and, 7
    insulating, 150
    maintenance calendar (chart), 101
    painting, 60, 126-27
        screens, 127
    replacing panes, 106-109
        glass cutting, 108-109
        metal casement windows, 108
        metal sliding and storm windows,
            108
        wood sash windows, 107
    sash repairs and hardware, 110-14
        crank handles and other harware, 111
        replacing double-hung sash windows,
            112-13
        replacing sash cord, 114
        replacing sash cord with chain, 114
        securing loose window sash, 111
        unsticking windows, 110
        window channels, 113
    screens, installing, replacing, maintain-
        ing, 118-23
        fiberglass screening, 121
        installing screen wire on old wooden
            screens, 122-23
        replacing aluminum-storm screening,
            119-20
        replacing wood-frame screen, 122
    security and, 167
    skylight, installing, 190-91
    special treatments for, 116-17
        frosted glass, 116
        stained glass, 117
        window box, 116
    storm windows, installing, 124-25
        do-it-yourself substitute, 125
        maintaining wood-sash storm windows,

    125
        as supplement to insulation, 532
    stripping, 224
    weather stripping, 153
wires
    choosing correct, 310-11
        aluminum wire, 311
    common sizes and uses, 310
        removing insulation, 311
    connecting to screw-type terminals,
        311
    joining wires in electrical boxes,
        312-13
        inserting and securing cables, 313
        types of boxes, 312
    joining wires together, 315
        lamps and appliance plugs, 315
        solderless connectors, 315
    splicing wires, 316-17
wire stripper, 301
wiring, new
    air conditioners and, 381
    connecting new cable, 340-41
    for garden pool, 478
    how to distinguish functions, 336-37
    for outdoor-lighting system, 382-83
        ground fault interrupter, 383
        permanent wiring, 383
        temporary wiring, 382
    planning cable run, 338-39
    surface wiring, 372-73
    where to join into circuit, 336-37
    which circuit to add onto, 334-38
wood
    floors
        damaged floorboard section repair, 76
        finishing, 80-81
        hardwood strip floor installation,
            88-89
        maintenance routine, 72-73
        refinishing, 78-79
        separated floorboard repair, 74-75
        spot and stain removal, 74
        surface flaw repair, 74
    for furniture, 282-85
        common kinds, 284
        grains, 232
        ordering lumber, 283
        plywood, 284
        sealers, 233-34
        selecting, 283
        staining, 236-39
        storing, 282
    shingles, fixing leaks in, 490
    siding
        maintaining, 510
        repairing, 511
        replacing, 512-13
    surface preparation, painting exterior
        and, 521
wood dough, making and using, 275
wood fillers, 235
wood paneling. See paneling
workbench, 12
workshop, 12-13
wrenches, 16, 397, 398, 399
wrinkling, avoiding, painting exterior
    and, 519
wrought-iron furniture, rustproofing,
    266-67

You-haul concrete, 538